Michigan Manual 2019-2020

100th Legislature

**Published Biennially
Pursuant to §24.24 of the
Michigan Compiled Laws**

**Compiled and Published by
THE LEGISLATIVE SERVICE BUREAU**

**Under the Direction of
THE LEGISLATIVE COUNCIL**

Michigan Manual (ISBN 1-878210-06-8, ISSN 0091-1933). Published biennially by the Legislative Service Bureau, 124 W. Allegan, Lansing, MI 48913, under the direction of the Michigan Legislative Council, pursuant to §24.24 of the Michigan Compiled Laws.

Loanna E. Ammerman, Editor; **Neil Weinberg,** Assistant Editor.

Photo Credits: *apple blossom, white pine,* and *American lotus blossom* – Michigan Department of Transportation Photography Unit; *robin* – Sujit Kumar; *Petoskey stone* – Sandra Debnar, Legislative Service Bureau; *chlorastrolite* – A. E. Seaman Mineral Museum, Michigan Technological University; *brook trout* – Eric Engbretson, U.S. Fish and Wildlife Service; *painted turtle* – André Karwath; *white-tailed deer* – Joe Kosack/PGC Photo; *dwarf lake iris* – Dr. Thomas G. Barnes, U.S. Fish and Wildlife Service; *mastodon* – University of Michigan Exhibit Museum of Natural History. Photos on the Profile of Michigan title page are courtesy of the Michigan Department of Transportation Photography Unit with the exception of the Comerica Park image, which was supplied by the Michigan Economic Development Corporation, and both Hart Plaza images, which are credited to Bill Bowen.

100th Legislature Logo Credit: Joshua Risner, Artist in Residence, Michigan State Capitol Commission.

PREFACE

The *Michigan Manual* is published biennially by the Legislative Service Bureau, under the direction of the Legislative Council, pursuant to Public Act 44 of 1899, as amended. As the State's official manual, it includes fundamental reference information about Michigan, its history, constitutional development, government organization, and institutions. The contents of the *Manual* are divided into the following chapters: Michigan History, Constitutions, The Legislative Branch, The Executive Branch, The Judicial Branch, Michigan's Congressional Delegation, Institutions of Higher Education, Local Government, Elections, and General Information.

The 2019-2020 edition of the *Manual* includes a wealth of updated material, including the biographies of legislators and other public officials, descriptions of the agencies of the executive branch and the courts, and a summary of primary and general election results.

In recognition of the 100th Michigan Legislature, this manual includes a listing of all individuals who have served in the House or Senate over the last 184 years. We thank the Library of Michigan for making available their legislator database which was our starting point in compiling this extensive list.

The *Michigan Manual* is again presented in two versions: print and an online pdf. The online pdf version is available from the "*Michigan Manuals*" link at the website of the Michigan Legislature at legislature.mi.gov. The complete text of the *Michigan Manuals* published since 1999 can be searched online using keywords, legislators' names, or full text capabilities. In addition, we have uploaded the legislative information from older *Manuals*, dated 1961 to 1997, to the website. The information from the older *Manuals* can be searched similarly as the more current publications. If you have comments or suggestions for improvements, please use the email address below to communicate them.

Loanna Ammerman, Editor
Research Services Division
Legislative Service Bureau
MIManual@legislature.mi.gov

ACKNOWLEDGMENTS

Any project of the size and scope of the *Michigan Manual* can be brought to completion only as a result of the cooperation and hard work of many people.

Staff from each of the executive departments and all of the state's public universities contributed essential information. Of particular note was the work of *Lynn Seaks* of the State Court Administrative Office coordinating the information for the Judicial Branch chapter.

Karley Abramson, Michael Campana, Tammye Cannon, Amanda Gallaher, Jacob Ignatoski, Chelsea Kazlauskas, Brandon Lever, Alex Stegbauer and *Neil Weinberg* of the Legislative Service Bureau's Research Services Division provided assistance in gathering information presented in the Legislative Branch, Local Government, Elections, Institutions of Higher Education, and General Information chapters. Also notable, special thanks to our editor, *Loanna Ammerman*, for her continued dedication and hard work compiling and organizing this publication.

The Print Production Manager of the Bureau's Legislative Printing Division, *Suzanne Mendel*, coordinated and oversaw the integral work on composition and production. *Patti Romain-Denney* lead the typographical and proofreading operations; *Carol Morrison* and *Rhonda Patterson* served as typesetters; *Sandra Debnar* and *Rhonda Patterson* as proofreaders; *Randy Miller* and *Mary Kennedy* as compositors; *Sandra Debnar* designed the Profile of Michigan section; *Carol Morrison* created, and *Jennifer Quinn* maintains, the electronic files for the web version; *Brian Rennaker* lead the print and bindery operations; *Derek Dancer* and *John Marshall* worked as pressmen; *Nic Violante, Stephen Graham*, and *Derrick Pline* as bookbinders; and *David Ferrigan* as courier.

Jennifer Dettloff
Legislative Council Administrator

HISTORICAL NOTE

Compiling information on government, public institutions, elections, and officials in the *Michigan Manual* is a tradition as old as Michigan itself, dating back to the Michigan Territory's organization as a state and the formation of the first constitution in 1835. First published in 1836 as a manual entitled *Legislative Manual of the Senate and House of Representatives of the State of Michigan*, the *Michigan Manual* has evolved, over the last 180 years, into one of the most important sources of information on this state and its historical, political, and cultural background.

Originally developed as an information handbook for members of the Michigan Legislature, the early manuals included such legislative data as the rules of the Senate and House of Representatives, joint rules, membership lists, and orders of business. The first manual to provide information not strictly related to the conduct of legislative business was published in 1839. That book included data on banking associations and bank returns, judicial circuits, miscellaneous incorporations, the state militia, and tolls on the Central Railroad. With each subsequent edition, the amount of nonlegislative information increased, reflecting the needs of the legislature and the new state government for readily available data.

Public Act 263 of 1879 first specified the contents of the *Michigan Manual*. It required that legislative material and other information which had previously been published only sporadically be included in the publication. Since that time, the basic contents of the manual have remained relatively unchanged.

Commonly called the "Red Book", which has been the color of its cover since the 1836 publication, the manual has undergone several changes in both its title and publisher. From 1836 through 1883, the title retained, in one form or another, its reference as a manual for the use of the Michigan Legislature. Public Act 263 of 1879, the first legislation to mandate publication of the handbook, specifically authorized the Secretary of State to prepare and publish a biennial legislative manual. Recognition in its title of the manual's value and scope as a reference work came in 1885, with the title's change to *Official Directory and Legislative Manual of the State of Michigan*. The Law, Documents and Reports Act, Public Act 44 of 1899, made that title, which was retained through the 1957 edition, official. Public Act 161 of 1958 renamed the handbook the *Michigan Manual*. Printed yearly from 1836 to 1851, the manual has been published on a biennial basis since the adoption of the Constitution of 1850. The Michigan Legislature, by authority or resolution, published the document from 1836 to 1879. Public Act 263 of 1879 transferred publication authority to the Secretary of State, where it remained from 1881 to 1967. The Department of Administration and its successor agency, the Department of Management and Budget, maintained responsibility for compiling and publishing the manual from 1969 to 1987.

On June 22, 1988, the legislature enacted, and the governor approved, legislation (Public Act 185 of 1988) that returned responsibility for producing the *Michigan Manual* to the legislature. Since that time, the Legislative Service Bureau, under the direction of the Legislative Council, has published the book. From 1989 until 2004, Roger W. Peters served as editor. From 2005 to 2012, Christopher Carl served as editor. Beginning with the 1999/2000 edition, the *Manual* is available on-line at www.legislature.mi.gov.

— L.E.A.

TABLE OF CONTENTS

State legislators who only appear in the manual on the list of all current and former legislators (pp. 261 to 349) are not included in this index. Legislators who appear on that list and appear in other sections of the manual are included in this index.

PROFILE OF MICHIGAN

KEY FACTS OF MICHIGAN

AREA
58,110 square miles of land, 1,305 square miles of inland water, and 38,575 square miles of Great Lakes water area; there are 10,083 inland lakes of more than 5 acres in surface area and 3,288 miles of Great Lakes shoreline. Combined water and land area makes it the 10th largest state in the Union.

ELEVATION
Highest point in the state is Mt. Arvon in Baraga County, 1,981 feet above sea level; lowest point is along the Lake Erie shoreline, 572 feet above sea level.

HISTORY
First permanent French settlement by Father Jacques Marquette at Sault Ste. Marie, 1668; French forces surrendered Detroit to British at close of French and Indian War, 1760; became part of the Northwest Territory, 1787; became Michigan Territory, 1805; admitted into the Union as the twenty-sixth state, 1837.

NICKNAME
The Wolverine State.

POPULATION
9,883,640 — ranks eighth among the 50 states.

STATE CAPITAL
Detroit served as the state capital until 1847, when it was permanently moved by the Legislature to Lansing.

STATE MOTTO
Si quaeris peninsulam amoenam circumspice
(If you seek a pleasant peninsula, look about you.)

STATE SEAL
The Great Seal of the State of Michigan was adopted at the Constitutional Convention of 1835.

DELEGATION TO U.S. CONGRESS
Two (2) U.S. Senators (2 Democrats)
Fourteen (14) U.S. Representatives (7 Republicans, 7 Democrats)

SALARIES OF ELECTED STATE OFFICERS

	2019–2020
Governor	$159,300
Lieutenant Governor	111,510
Secretary of State	112,410
Attorney General	112,410
State Legislators	71,685
Justices of the Supreme Court	164,610
Court of Appeals Judges	151,441

POPULATION	Michigan	United States
2000 Total	9,938,444	281,421,906
2010 Census	9,883,640	308,745,538
2000-2010 % Increase	–.06	9.7

MICHIGAN'S STATE SEAL

First adopted in 1835, Michigan's Great Seal was designed by Lewis Cass. The seal evokes strong national images, with *E Pluribus Unum* on a scroll across the top and the American Eagle prominently displayed. Below these are an elk and a moose on either side of a shield bearing the Latin word *Tuebor*, which means "I will defend," and reflects Michigan's position as a border state. Below this, an image of a man stands with one hand raised in peace and another holding a rifle, symbolic of his willingness to protect our state and nation. The state's motto, *"Si Quaeris Peninsulam Amoenam Circumspice,"* which means "If you seek a pleasant peninsula, look about you," is at the base of the shield. The Great Seal may not be used for commercial purposes.

MICHIGAN'S STATE FLAG

Michigan's present state flag was adopted by the Legislature in 1911 with a simple phrase, "The State Flag shall be blue charged with the arms of the State." This is Michigan's third flag. The state coat of arms appears on both sides. The first flag, bearing the State Seal, a soldier, a lady on one side and a portrait of the first governor, Stevens T. Mason, on the other, was first flown in 1837 — the year Michigan became a state. In 1865, the second flag carried the state coat of arms on a field of blue on one side and, on the reverse side, the coat of arms of the United States. The state flag flies over the Capitol on the main flagstaff, just below the flag of the United States.

MICHIGAN'S STATE SYMBOLS

Flower

APPLE BLOSSOM

The apple blossom, the symbol of spring-time beauty and the bounty of Michigan's orchards and agricultural lands, has been the official State Flower since its adoption by the Legislature on April 28, 1897. The resolution stated "a refined sentiment seems to call for the adoption of a State Flower." It continued, "Our blossoming apple trees add much to the beauty of our landscape, and Michigan apples have gained a world-wide reputation...one of the most fragrant and beautiful species of apple, the *Pyrus coronaria*, is native to our state." Michigan has been one of the leading producers of apples and apple products since those early days.

(Joint Resolution 10 of 1897)

Bird

ROBIN

The robin redbreast became the official State Bird on May 21, 1931, when the Legislature, by resolution, made the selection as the result of an election conducted by the Michigan Audubon Society. Nearly 200,000 votes were cast, of which robin redbreast "received many more votes than any other bird as the most popular bird in Michigan." The resolution added that the robin redbreast is "the best known and best loved of all the birds in the state of Michigan."

(House Concurrent Resolution 30 of 1931)

Tree

WHITE PINE

The towering white pine (*Pinus strobus*) of Michigan's lush forests of the pioneering days was adopted as the official State Tree on March 4, 1955. The white pine was the focal point of one of Michigan's greatest industries, lumbering. It is the largest coni-fer of the eastern and upper Midwest forests, reaching 150 feet in height and up to 40 inches in diameter. On Arbor Day in 1955, lawmakers attended special ceremo-nies during which small white pine trees were planted on the Capitol lawn.

(Public Act 7 of 1955)

PETOSKEY STONE

The Petoskey stone is Michigan's official State Stone. Petoskeys are fossilized fragments of ancient corals. The corals were found in the northern counties of Michigan's lower peninsula about 350 million years ago. The living corals died and were transformed into large fossil reefs. Fragments from the fossil reefs were scattered by glaciers about 1.8 million years ago. These fossil fragments are found on beaches as pebbles and cobbles, rounded by the action of the waves. Petoskey stones are most often found along the shorelines of Lake Michigan, Lake Huron, and inland lakes.

(Public Act 89 of 1965)

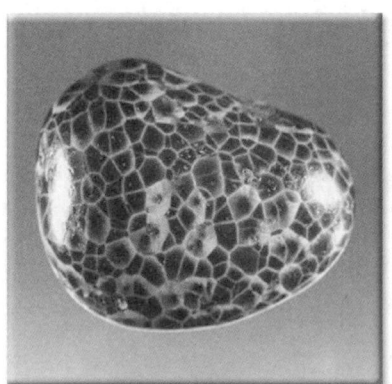

CHLORASTROLITE

Chlorastrolite, the official State Gem, is a mineral that is formed in association with lava flows. Its common name, "greenstone," comes from its green color. Typical gems have a pattern of overlapping edges, ranging from yellow-green to almost black. Chlorastrolite is derived from three Latin words: *"chloros,"* meaning green; *"aster,"* meaning star; and *"lithos,"* meaning stone. In Michigan, chlorastrolite pebbles can be found on rocky beaches in Northern Michigan's "copper country," particularly on Isle Royale.

(Public Act 56 of 1972)

BROOK TROUT

Michigan lawmakers chose the trout as the official State Fish in 1965. Since four trout species are found in Michigan — brook, brown, rainbow, and lake — many felt that clarification was needed. Legislation enacted in 1988 designated the Brook Trout as Michigan's official State Fish. The trout lives in many of Michigan's lakes, rivers, and streams. Sportspersons love it for its gameness, good flavor, rich flesh, and pretty colors. Most trout live year-round in fresh water.

(Public Act 5 of 1988)

MICHIGAN'S STATE SYMBOLS

KALKASKA SOIL SERIES

Michigan has about 400 different kinds of soils. Each soil has its own unique set of properties and supports different types of vegetation or activities. Michigan's official State Soil, the Kalkaska Soil Series, was formed from the chemical and physical activities of vegetation in sandy glacial deposits. As one of the most extensive soil series in Michigan, it is found in both peninsulas. It is typically several feet thick and made up of many distinct layers. The soil is easily identified and conducive to varied uses, including forests, wildlife, cultivation, recreation, and business.

(Public Act 302 of 1990)

PAINTED TURTLE

In 1995, the Michigan Legislature formally adopted the *Chrysemys picta*, or "painted turtle," as Michigan's State Reptile. The painted turtle is found throughout the entire state of Michigan. It ranges in size from four to ten inches in length. It has distinctive yellow and red markings on its head, limbs, and shell. It lives in shallow water and eats pond vegetation, insects, crayfish, and mollusks, including the zebra mussel. During the cold winter months, it buries itself in the mud and hibernates.

(Public Act 281 of 1995)

WHITE-TAILED DEER

The white-tailed deer, Michigan's official State Game Mammal, is found in much of the United States and Canada. Abundant throughout our state, these herbivores can run up to 35 miles per hour. Photographers, tourists, hunters, and nature enthusiasts are drawn to Michigan for this beautiful animal. The deer's distinctive tail, when raised, is like a flag that provides a flash of white, signaling other deer when there is danger.

(Public Act 15 of 1997)

DWARF LAKE IRIS

On December 30, 1998, the Dwarf Lake Iris became the State Wildflower by act of the Legislature. This wildflower is found on rocky shorelines in the Great Lakes region, with 90 percent of the species found in Michigan. The Dwarf Lake Iris is most likely to be found on the Lake Huron shoreline along the northern part of Michigan's Lower Peninsula.

(Public Act 454 of 1998)

MASTODON

The elephant-like Mastodons roamed virtually all of Michigan's Ice Age landscape from 20,000 years ago until approximately 10,000 years ago, when they became extinct. Dining on leaves, pines, and acorns, these creatures grew nine feet tall and stretched 15 feet from tusk to tail. They may have weighed as much as six tons. More than 250 Mastodon remains have been discovered; and, near Saline, scientists found the only set of Mastodon footprints known to exist in the world. In recognition of the importance of gaining knowledge of this ancient mammal, the Legislature designated the Mastodon (*Mammut americanum*) as the official State Fossil of Michigan.

(Public Act 162 of 2002)

AMERICAN LOTUS BLOSSOM

The country's largest aquatic plant, the American Lotus Blossom (*Nelumbo lutea*), is the official Symbol of Clean Water in Michigan. The lotus blossom helps to clean the waters it lives in, and its selection as a state symbol highlights Michigan's unique and abundant fresh water resources.

(Public Act 78 of 2004)

MICHIGAN LEGISLATURE
ONLINE INFORMATION
www.legislature.mi.gov

▶ Track recent bill activity, including daily introduced bills, bills passed by chamber, and enrolled bills.

▶ Follow current issues and legislative sessions; the committee schedules include the time and place for meetings and the bills on the agenda for each meeting.

▶ Search the Michigan Compiled Laws and the Michigan Constitution, by section or keyword.

▶ Access electronic legislative publications including Public Act tables, Michigan Manuals, Official Journals, Michigan Compiled Laws, and more than 20 general interest booklets available for download.

▶ The Notification System allows a person to select items of interest and receive email notice of changes to the items.

Chapter I

MICHIGAN HISTORY

2019–2020

CHRONOLOGY OF MICHIGAN HISTORY

1618-1701

1618 Etienne Brulé passes through North Channel at the neck of Lake Huron; that same year (or during two following years) he lands at Sault Ste. Marie, probably the first European to look upon the Sault. The Michigan Native American population is approximately 15,000.

1621 Brulé returns, explores the Lake Superior coast, and notes copper deposits.

1634 Jean Nicolet passes through the Straits of Mackinac and travels along Lake Michigan's northern shore, seeking a route to the Orient.

1641 Fathers Isaac Jogues and Charles Raymbault conduct religious services at the Sault.

1660 Father René Mesnard establishes the first regular mission, held throughout winter at Keweenaw Bay.

1668 **Father Jacques Marquette** takes over the Sault mission and founds the first permanent settlement on Michigan soil at Sault Ste. Marie.

1669 Louis Jolliet is guided east by way of the Detroit River, Lake Erie, and Lake Ontario.

1671 Simon François, Sieur de St. Lusson, lands at the Sault, claims vast Great Lakes region, comprising most of western America, for Louis XIV.

St. Ignace is founded when Father Marquette builds a mission chapel.

First of the military outposts, Fort de Buade (later known as Fort Michilimackinac), is established at St. Ignace.

1675 Father Marquette dies at Ludington.

1679 The ***Griffon***, the first sailing vessel on the Great Lakes, is built by René Robert Cavelier, Sieur de La Salle, and lost in a storm on Lake Michigan. ➤

La Salle erects Fort Miami at the mouth of the St. Joseph River.

1680 La Salle, with a small group, marches across the Lower Peninsula, reaching the Detroit River in ten days, the first Europeans to penetrate this territory.

1681 Earliest known use of "Michigan" on a map.

1686 French build Fort St. Joseph at Port Huron.

1690 Father Claude Aveneau explores the upper reaches of the St. Joseph River; establishes mission on the present site of Niles.

1694 Antoine de la Mothe **Cadillac** is appointed commandant of the Michilimackinac (St. Ignace) post; remains until 1697.

1697 Fort St. Joseph is built at mission on the St. Joseph River (Niles).

1701 Detroit is founded as Fort Pontchartrain by Cadillac as a permanent settlement to protect and secure the fur trade.

Ste. Anne's Church, a log structure, is erected by Cadillac's men and dedicated two days after the founding of Detroit. Ste. Anne's is the second oldest continuously maintained Roman Catholic parish in the United States.

In the fall, Madame Cadillac and Madam Tonty arrive at the fort as the first European women in the region.

1712   British-inspired Indian raids begin, including the siege of Fort Pontchartrain.

1715   **Fort Michilimackinac** is reestablished on the southern shore of the Straits of Mackinac.

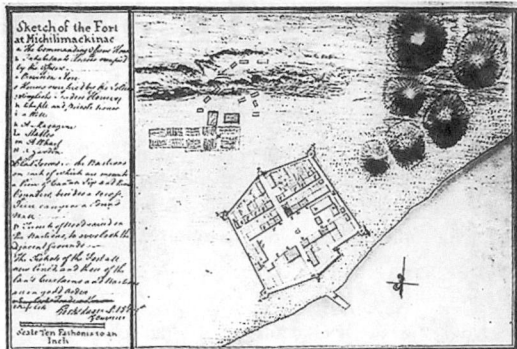

1756   France and England begin the Seven Years' War (also known as the French and Indian War).

1759   The French surrender to the English at Montreal; this marks the decline of French power in Michigan.

1760   British Major Robert Rogers receives the surrender of Detroit, after taking Great Lakes fortifications. About 2,000 people are within the stockade; warehouses found to contain furs worth $500,000.

1761   The British occupy Fort Michilimackinac.

1762   Pontiac, an Ottawa chief, plans a conspiracy against British; calls for a council near Detroit in the spring.
The English take possession of the Sault.

1763   With the ratification of the Treaty of Versailles, France loses North American mainland possessions.
Pontiac and followers enter the fort at Detroit in an abortive effort to capture it from Major Henry Gladwin by surprise attack. Detroit endures a siege of several weeks.

1765   **Chief Pontiac** signs a treaty with the British at Detroit, nearly a year after other tribes have made peace. ➤

1775   Henry Hamilton takes command at Detroit.

1777   British conduct raids from Detroit into Kentucky.

1778   Construction begins on Fort Lernoult, Detroit.
Daniel Boone brought to Detroit as a prisoner.

1779   Nearly 3,000 persons living in the Detroit area.

1781   Spanish forces from St. Louis take Fort St. Joseph (Niles); all residents are taken prisoner; the Spanish flag is raised. Raiders depart the next day and the fort reverts to British possession.
The British transfer garrison from Michilimackinac to a new fort on Mackinac Island.

1783   The Treaty of Paris is signed, ending the Revolutionary War and including Michigan in the United States. The British control the Michigan area, however, for 13 more years.

1784   First ordinance passed by Congress governing the Northwest Territory.

1785-1810

1785   Congress passes first act relative to the disposal of western lands.

Michigan appears for the first time on a map as a land division of the United States.

Sloop *Otter* becomes the first vessel to navigate Lake Superior.

1787   Congress enacts the Ordinance of 1787 (second Northwest Ordinance), outlining the government of the "Territory northwest of the Ohio River."

1788   The first stage of American territorial government is established under the Northwest Ordinance, except in British-occupied Michigan.

1791   The Americans under Arthur St. Clair suffer a major defeat at the hands of British-allied Indians in Ohio.

1792   Detroit, including settlements on both sides of the river, holds its first election, sending three representatives to the Parliament of Upper Canada.

1794   General **Anthony Wayne** decisively defeats Indians and allied British troops at the Battle of Fallen Timbers, near Toledo.

1795   The Jay Treaty is ratified by Congress. The British finally agree to relinquish all Northwest Territory lands.

The Treaty of Greenville (Ohio) is signed. The first major Indian land treaty involving Michigan, it included land on the Detroit River, the Straits of Mackinac, and Mackinac Island.

1796   The British withdraw their garrison from Detroit. The Stars and Stripes are raised for the first time on Michigan soil by Wayne's advance guard.

1798   Father Gabriel Richard comes to assist at Ste. Anne's in Detroit.

1799   The Territorial Assembly convenes at Cincinnati, Ohio. The county of Wayne (embracing all of the Michigan Territory) sends one representative, elected in the first local (Michigan) election held under United States rule.

1800   Wayne County circuit court created by act passed December 9.

1801   First post road established in Michigan.

1802   Detroit holds its first election following incorporation under an act passed January 18 by the Legislative Council at Chillicothe, Ohio.

1803   Ohio is admitted to the Union, excluding the strip of land that 30 years later will be known as the "**Toledo strip**." Michigan becomes part of the Territory of Indiana.

1804   United States land office established at Detroit.

1805   The Territory of Michigan is created, with Detroit as the capital.

Detroit is completely destroyed by fire.

General William Hull becomes the first territorial governor.

Important commercial timbering begins, when sawmills are built on the St. Clair River to aid in rebuilding Detroit.

1806   Governor and judges authorized to lay out new town of Detroit after fire had destroyed the settlement.

Bank of Detroit chartered by the governor and judges; Congress disapproves the act on March 3, 1807.

1807   The Treaty of Detroit is signed by Chippewa, Ottawa, Wyandot, and Potawatomi tribes meeting with General Hull.

Duties paid to the United States on furs at Mackinac exceed $40,000.

1808   American Fur Company founded by John Jacob Astor.

1809   The *Michigan Essay and Impartial Observer,* the state's first newspaper, is printed by James M. Miller on a press imported by Father Richard.

1810   The Michigan Territory's population is 4,762 and includes 32 slaves, most of whom are Native Americans.

1811-1820

1811   A memorial to Congress stresses the defenseless position of Michigan and begs for military aid against the Indians.

1812   The United States declares war against England. Father Richard urges the population to support the American cause.

Fort Mackinac falls to the British, who know of the declaration of war earlier than the frontier post.

Hull surrenders Detroit to General Isaac Brock without firing a shot. Hull later is court-martialed.

1813   At the Battle of River Raisin at Monroe, the main body of Americans is forced to surrender and promised protection from Indian allies of British.

The massacre of the River Raisin occurs. This proves to be a powerful factor in uniting American sentiment for expulsion of the British from the west.

Commander Oliver Perry's victory on Lake Erie and William Henry Harrison's defeat of Proctor's army in Canada end hostilities on northwestern American border.

Harrison, departing for Washington, leaves Colonel (later General) Lewis Cass as the military governor at Detroit. Cass continues, under presidential appointment, as the governor of the Michigan Territory for 18 years. ▶

1814   The Americans make an unsuccessful attempt to recapture Mackinac Island.

The Treaty of Ghent ends the War of 1812; the British leave Mackinac Island.

1815   Governor Cass and judges adopt legislation reincorporating Detroit (city) and restoring a restricted municipal government.

1816   Part of Michigan Territory given to the state of Indiana.

First recorded shipwreck on Lake Superior occurs at Whitefish Point with the schooner *Invincible.*

Due to unfavorable reports on Lower Peninsula lands by the Surveyor General, Congress decides not to place military bounty lands in Michigan.

1817   The Catholepistemiad, or **University of Michigania**, is incorporated. ▶

John Jacob Astor establishes a trading post at Mackinac Island, centering his fur-trading activities there.

1818   Public land sales begin at Detroit; immigration from the East is under way.

Michigan's first Protestant church, the Methodist Episcopal, is erected along the banks of the River Rouge.

Walk-in-the-Water, the first steamboat on the Upper Great Lakes, arrives at Detroit on its maiden voyage. ▶

1819   William Woodbridge is elected as the first delegate to Congress from the Michigan Territory.

With the Treaty of Saginaw, Governor Cass obtains for the United States about 6,000,000 acres of Michigan land, marking the beginning of the Indian exodus from the territory.

1820   The population of the territory is 8,096; Detroit, Mackinac, and Sault Ste. Marie are its largest towns.

The Treaty at Sault Ste. Marie is negotiated by Cass; Indians cede a 16-square-mile tract on the St. Mary's River for a fort site, but reserve fishing rights.

1821 Cass negotiates a treaty at Chicago, gaining from the Chippewa, Ottawa, and Potawatomi virtually all Michigan territory south of the Grand River that had not previously been ceded.

1822 Public stagecoaches begin running from Detroit.

Fort Brady established at Sault Ste. Marie.

Dr. William Beaumont at Mackinac begins study of human digestive processes by observing through a hole in the stomach of Alexis St. Martin.

1823 General Hugh Brady and soldiers construct Fort Brady at the Sault, ending domination of the region by the British.

Congress advances the Territory of Michigan to the second governmental grade, authorizing the Legislative Council of 9 members presidentially appointed and 18 locally elected. Enacted laws are subject to congressional approval. The first capitol, in Detroit, is built.

Father Gabriel Richard takes office as the territorial delegate to Congress (1823-1825), the only priest to serve in Congress until 1971.

United States government opens second land office in Michigan at Monroe.

1824 On motion of Father Richard, Congress appropriates $10,000 for a survey of the Great Sauk Trail (now U.S. 12) between Detroit and Chicago and makes an additional appropriation in 1825.

1825 The opening of the Erie Canal in New York facilitates settlement of Michigan and shipping of farm products to the East.

1827 Fort Shelby, Detroit, is demolished.

1828 **First capitol** occupied in Detroit on May 5. ➤

State Library is established.

State Historical Society organized (now Historical Society of Michigan).

1829 "Cabinet Counties" are established, named after members of President Jackson's administration (Barry, Berrien, Branch, Calhoun, Eaton, Ingham, Jackson, and Van Buren).

1830 Michigan's population is 31,639.

Fur trade reaches its peak. Its subsequent decline leaves some regions without commercial activity.

Michigan issues a railway charter to the Detroit & Pontiac Railway, the first incorporated railway in the limits of old Northwest Territory.

1831 General Lewis Cass, appointed secretary of war by President Jackson in July, resigns the governorship.

Stevens T. Mason, at age 19, becomes the acting governor of the Michigan Territory. ➤

Federal government opens third land office in Michigan at White Pigeon.

1832 A seven-week cholera epidemic devastates Detroit; Belle Isle is used for quarantine.

Father Richard, priest, legislator, and educator, dies of cholera, contracted while nursing the sick.

1833 Steamboat *Michigan* launched at Detroit.

1834 The Territorial Legislature petitions Congress for permission to form a state government. Southern states protest the admission of another free state; Ohio protests the boundary Michigan claims. Congress refuses to grant its permission.

The second cholera epidemic at Detroit begins with the death of Governor George B. Porter. It wipes out one-seventh of the population.

1835 Pioneers in Macomb and adjoining counties discover oil.

The Ohio Legislature passes an act asserting claims to the "Toledo strip" along its northern boundary.

Governor Mason calls out the militia as the "Toledo War" begins with more anger than gunfire. Border incidents continue into September, and jurisdictional wrangling goes on through all of 1836.

A convention at Detroit drafts a state constitution in preparation for statehood.

Stevens T. Mason, who had been removed from office by President Jackson because of Mason's action on the Toledo question, is elected as the first governor of the state of Michigan at 23 years of age.

1836 Congress accepts Michigan's constitution. It agrees to admit the state upon condition that Michigan accept Ohio's boundary in return for four-fifths of the Upper Peninsula.

At the first convention of assent held at Ann Arbor in September, the conditions set by Congress are rejected.

The horse-powered Erie & Kalamazoo Railroad chartered in 1833 reaches Adrian from Toledo. The **first steam locomotive** in the state is put in operation on this line the following year, as the railroad is the first west of New York State to operate. ➤

Democrats call a convention on their own initiative and assent to entry into the Union. Whig opponents take no part in this "frost-bitten" convention held in Ann Arbor in December.

Daily stages from Detroit begin carrying mail and passengers to Sandusky, Chicago, and central Michigan; a railroad between Detroit and Jackson is under construction; shipbuilding becomes important along nearby rivers and lakeshores. During seven months of navigation, 200,000 people pass through Detroit's port.

Bituminous coal mining begins in Michigan.

A Quaker preacher employs an **underground railroad** to bring slaves into Cass County, and movement of fugitive and freed slaves into the state begins.

1837 Detroit's population is almost 10,000.

Michigan is admitted to the Union as a free state as Arkansas is admitted as a slave state.

The Panic of 1837 strikes Michigan.

Michigan experiences its first strike as journeymen carpenters parade through Detroit streets.

1838 Detroit elects Michigan's first school board under state law.

The Grand Rapids furniture industry has its beginning.

1839 Effects of the Panic of 1837 help break Democratic monopoly, and Whigs carry state election.

Michigan State Prison located at Jackson.

1841 **Dr. Douglass Houghton**, the first state geologist, reports on rich copper deposits of the Lake Superior region and makes cautious mention of the possibility of iron ore in the Marquette district. ➤

The University of Michigan, reorganized and offering college curriculum, opens at Ann Arbor.

1842 Indians cede Keweenaw Peninsula and Isle Royale, the last Indian holdings in the state.

1843   Former Governor Stevens T. Mason dies in New York City.

       U.S.S. *Michigan*, first iron ship in the U.S. Navy, is launched.

       Celebrated Ontonagon copper boulder arrives in Detroit from Lake Superior for exhibition.

1844   Surveyor William A. Burt (inventor of the solar compass and other important items) accidentally makes the first iron ore discovery at Negaunee.

       General Lewis Cass, former governor, former secretary of war, and ambassador to France, is elected U.S. senator from Michigan.

       The first major copper operations begin in the Keweenaw district.

1845   Dr. Douglass Houghton drowns near Eagle River on October 14.

1846   Dr. A. C. Van Raalte, Dutch secessionist pastor, sails from Rotterdam with 53 Hollanders; they form the nucleus of western Michigan's large Dutch settlements begun the following winter.

       The Jackson Mining Company begins operations on the site of Burt's 1844 discovery, first iron ore mining in the state.

       Michigan becomes the first English-speaking jurisdiction in the world to abolish capital punishment.

1847   The old capitol in Detroit is used for the last time by the state legislature, which makes Lansing the new, permanent capital of the state.

1848   **King James J. Strang**, a Mormon leader, builds a tabernacle and lays out the town of St. James on Big Beaver Island. ➤

       The state legislature meets for the first session in the new capitol at Lansing.

1849   The first annual statewide fair is held at Detroit.

       The Cliff Mine pays a dividend of $60,000, the first sum of this magnitude distributed in North America on copper investment.

       Michigan's manufactured goods are valued at more than $11,000,000. There are 558 sawmills operating in the state.

1850   Michigan's population is 397,654.

       The second state constitution is approved.

1851   Lumber mill output of Saginaw amounts to 92,000,000 board feet.

       Elizabeth D. Camp receives first academic degree conferred upon a woman in Michigan.

1852   The Michigan State Normal School is dedicated at Ypsilanti. It is the first teacher-training institute west of the Alleghenies.

       First teacher's association in Michigan is organized.

1853   Construction begins on the Soo Canal.

1854   The Republican party is formed and named at meetings held in Jackson.

       Michigan School for the Deaf created at Flint.

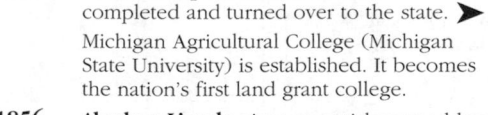

1855   The **Soo Ship Canal and Locks** are completed and turned over to the state. ➤

       Michigan Agricultural College (Michigan State University) is established. It becomes the nation's first land grant college.

1856   **Abraham Lincoln** gives an antislavery address in Kalamazoo.

1857 General Lewis Cass is appointed U.S. Secretary of State and is succeeded in the U.S. Senate by Zachariah Chandler.

The Christian Reformed Church in North America is founded by Michigan's Dutch settlers, following secession from the Reformed Church.

1858 The Detroit & Milwaukee Railroad completes its line connecting Detroit and Grand Haven.

First elevated iron ore dock constructed at Marquette.

Grand Trunk Railroad opens line from Detroit to Port Huron.

Michigan Asylum for the Insane opens at Kalamazoo on August 24.

Classes begin at Adrian College.

1860 Michigan's population is 749,113.

Successful well drilling of salt begins in Saginaw County.

1861 Thomas A. Edison erects his first electrical battery and begins experiments at Fort Gratiot (Port Huron).

The **First Michigan Regiment** leaves Fort Wayne. It is the first western regiment to reach Washington during the Civil War, in which 90,000 Michigan soldiers see service. ➤

1862 Passes to Canada required to prevent Michigan citizens from fleeing military service.

1863 Brotherhood of Locomotive Engineers (the oldest railroad labor union in the Western Hemisphere) founded in Michigan.

1864 First Michigan Colored Infantry is mustered in. Michigan's black troops number 1,673.

Bessemer steel is first manufactured in any appreciable amount in America, at Wyandotte.

The copper lode at Calumet is discovered. Michigan's production of copper has for 17 years exceeded that of any other state (holds first place until 1887).

1865 **Jefferson Davis** captured by members of the Fourth Michigan Cavalry.

1866 Michigan statesman Lewis Cass dies on June 17.

1867 Constitutional convention convened in Lansing, voters reject proposed revision.

1869 Memorial Day first observed in Michigan.

Nation's first "university hospital" established at the University of Michigan.

1870 Michigan's population is 1,054,670.

The value of agricultural produce for the year is estimated at $88,000,000.

Annual lumber production for the state averages 3 million board feet, and is the highest in the country for a period of 20 years.

1871 Forest fires ravage the state, destroying towns and leveling thousands of acres of valuable pine, causing losses in the millions of dollars.

Calumet & Hecla Mining Company consolidates local (Calumet) mining interests, controlling one of world's richest copper districts. Calumet becomes a company town typical of the copper country.

Negaunee's average annual iron ore production reaches 135,000 tons.

1872 **Republic Mine** opens; the 88 percent pure iron deposits permit continuous high-level production for 55 years.

Construction begins on present state capitol building. ➤

The Michigan Grange is organized to help Michigan farmers.

1873 Financial panic begins early in the year.

Michigan Department of Public Health created, fifth in the nation.

The *Detroit News* begins publication.

1874 Pioneer Society of the State of Michigan organized.

The Portage Lake canal is opened across the Keweenaw Peninsula.

1875 **Mackinac Island** becomes the second national park in the United States, preceded only by Yellowstone.

1876 At the Centennial Exposition (Philadelphia), Detroit is given first place among world's stove-manufacturing centers and receives prizes for shoes. The best display of furniture from the United States is credited to Grand Rapids. Michigan has the finest exhibit in forestry products and fruit.

An Ontonagon mine operator, after seeing Alexander Graham Bell's invention at the Philadelphia exposition, builds the first telephone system (20 miles) in Michigan.

1877 Active operations begin in the mines of the Menominee iron district.

1878 Eastern Michigan Asylum for the Insane opens at Pontiac on August 1.

1879 Six years after the cornerstone was laid, the new state capitol at Lansing is dedicated and occupied, several months after completion at a cost of more than $1,500,000.

1880 Michigan's population is 1,636,937.

Iron ore is discovered in large quantities at Bessemer in the Gogebic Range.

Detroit Baseball Company is organized.

Michigan School for the Blind opens in Lansing.

1881 The Soo Ship Canal and Locks are taken over by the federal government.

Railroad ferry service connects Upper and Lower Peninsulas, making the Upper Peninsula readily accessible for the first time.

A permanent hydroelectric plant is erected at Grand Rapids — one of the earliest anywhere.

Another devastating series of fires scorch the state, with the newly established American Red Cross sending help in its first disaster relief.

1882 **Josiah Williams Begole** elected governor on the Fusion ticket, interrupting an almost unbroken Republican rule that began in 1854. ➤

1883 A compulsory school attendance law is enacted.

Half of copper mined in United States since 1847 has come from Michigan.

Cherry orchards in the upper fruit belt first begin to bear.

1884 Working of iron ore deposits of the Gogebic Range begins, when transportation facilities are acquired.

John and Thomas Clegg build Michigan's first self-propelled vehicle, a four-wheeled steamer auto.

Ferris Institute is established in Big Rapids.

1885 A series of lumber strikes occur in Saginaw Valley, and the militia is called out.

The ten-hour workday law is passed.

Michigan Soldiers' Home established in Grand Rapids.

1886 Prospecting for oil and gas and first commercial production in St. Clair and Saginaw Counties begin.

Michigan Mining School is opened at Houghton.

1887 Ransom E. Olds' first auto steamer appears.

Iron ore shipments from the Menominee Range begin; at the end of the year, total shipments amount to 6,000,000 tons.

The Grand Hotel is completed on Mackinac Island.

1888 Michigan's lumber boom peaks with the production of 4,292,000,000 board feet. ➤ Shipments of iron ore from Escanaba alone reach 1,107,129 tons.

1890 Michigan's population is 2,093,889.

1891 Port Huron, Michigan, and Sarnia, Ontario, are joined by the Grand Trunk R.R. tunnel under the St. Clair River, first subaqueous railroad tunnel linking foreign countries.

1892 First railroad car ferry begins operating on the Great Lakes between Frankfort, Michigan, and Kewaunee, Wisconsin.

William Webb Ferguson becomes first African-American elected to the Legislature (House). ➤

1893 Michigan Home for the Feeble Minded and Epileptic established at Lapeer.

Michigan Naval Militia is first organized.

1894 Hazen S. Pingree, mayor of Detroit, attracts national attention with his city-lot potato patches for feeding 1893 depression sufferers.

Fort on Mackinac Island is given to the state for a public park.

1895 Central Michigan University, founded as a private school, becomes a state normal school.

Mackinac Island becomes the first state park in Michigan.

1896 **Ransom E. Olds** brings out a practical four-wheeled, gasoline-powered auto in Lansing.

Henry Ford's "quadricycle" is tested in Detroit.

Rural Free Delivery mail service begins in Michigan at the town of Climax.

1897 Olds Motor Vehicle Company is organized by Ransom E. Olds in Lansing.

1898 Michigan activates 5 regiments plus its naval reserves for the Spanish-American War.

1899 Olds Motor Works in Detroit erects the first factory built in America for the manufacture of automobiles.

Northern Michigan University is founded.

1900 Michigan's population is 2,420,982.

1901 Detroit celebrates its 200th birthday.

1902 Packard Motor Car Company and Cadillac Motor Car Company are organized.

1903 The House of David (a sect founded in 1792) is established in Benton Harbor by **"King" Benjamin and "Queen" Mary Purnell**. ➤

The Ford Motor Company is incorporated in Detroit.

1904 The organization of Buick Motor Company marks the beginning of auto manufacturing in Flint on a large scale.

Western State Normal School (Western Michigan University) opens in Kalamazoo.

1905 State Highway Department organized.

Railroad depots in Michigan reach an all-time maximum of 1,776 buildings.

Michigan begins registering motor vehicles.

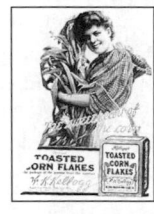

1906 Timbering of second-growth forests begins in the Upper Peninsula.

W.K. Kellogg Cereal Company is organized in Battle Creek. ➤

1907 Michigan's third constitution is drafted (approved by electorate in 1908).

The Detroit Tigers, led by Ty Cobb, win the first of three consecutive pennants.

President Theodore Roosevelt addresses joint session of legislature and visits State Agricultural College (now Michigan State University).

1908 **William C. Durant** organizes General Motors Company as Ford introduces the most famous of the early cars, the Model T.

Fisher Body Corporation is founded.

1909 Department of Labor created.

World's first mile of poured concrete road built in Detroit on Woodward Avenue.

Railroad mileage in Michigan reaches its highest point with 9,059 road miles in operation.

1910 Michigan's population is 2,810,173.

1911 Durant organizes the Chevrolet Motor Car Company, when the Chevrolet brothers complete experiments on a new auto.

Wayne County Road Commission invents the white center line for dividing two-way traffic.

Chase S. Osborn becomes first and only Governor from the Upper Peninsula.

Harriet Quimby, born near Arcadia in 1875, becomes America's first licensed female pilot. ➤

1912 Grand Rapids Board of Education establishes the state's first junior high school.

1913 The Western Federation of Miners calls a strike among 13,514 Upper Peninsula copper miners. Violence and bloodshed result from demands for an 8-hour day, a minimum daily wage of $3.50, and abolition of the "widow-maker," a one-man drill.

The legislature passes a bill providing for ten trunkline highways. There are 60,000 autos registered in Michigan.

Michigan Historical Commission is organized.

1914 **Henry Ford** announces the adoption of a $5 minimum wage for an 8-hour day.

A congressional committee arrives to investigate the copper miners strike, which terminates shortly afterward, each side claiming victory. The union fails to gain recognition.

The first Dodge auto is produced.

Following the 1913 strike, Finns initiate cooperative stores in the copper country.

1915 *Michigan Manual of Freedmen's Progress,* showing the professional, political, religious, and educational achievements of African-American citizens of the state, is published by Freedmen's Progress Commission.

Michigan issues its first stamped metal license plate.

1916 Many Michigan men join Canadian units leaving for France to fight in World War I.

Annual copper production reaches a peak of 270,000,000 pounds of refined copper, while iron ore production from the Marquette Range is 5,500,000 tons.

1917 The country's first War Preparedness Board is organized in Michigan. In the first year of war, Detroit builds 120 ships, spends $10,000,000 improving plants for the making of munitions. Auto manufacturers contract to deliver 19,000 engines.

Camp Custer is built near Battle Creek.

Selfridge Field is constructed near Mount Clemens.

1918 Michigan men in World War I service reaches a total of 135,485.

Snow removal inaugurated on Michigan roads.

War contracts let in Detroit now total $705,000,000.

1919   Commercial airplanes are placed on sale for the first time.

The influenza epidemic strikes the country and much of the world, killing 3,814 in Detroit.

Michigan issues its first driver's license on July 1.

1920   Michigan's population is 3,668,412.

Radio station WWJ in Detroit opens as a pioneer station in the broadcasting of regular daily programs.

World's first four-way traffic signal with red, yellow and green lights appears in Detroit.

Eva Hamilton becomes first woman elected to the Michigan Senate. ➤

1921   Edwin Denby, who had enlisted at Detroit as a private in the Marine Corps in 1917, becomes secretary of the navy.

Important administrative reforms in state government are legislated. The superintendent of public instruction is given supervision of all schools, private, denominational, and public, and the departments of conservation, labor, public safety, welfare, and agriculture are created.

1922   Airline service is instituted between Detroit and Cleveland.

First practical highway snow plow developed in Munising.

1923   State ferries begin operating at the Straits of Mackinac on July 31.

1924   Cora Anderson becomes first woman elected to the Michigan House.

Michigan High School Athletic Association is organized.

1925   Chrysler Motor Corporation organized.

The Michigan gasoline tax is adopted.

1926   The worst disaster in Michigan iron mining occurs at the Barnes-Hecker Mine, when quicksand breaks through the walls, entombing 52 men 1,000 feet below the surface. The mine is sealed and abandoned.

1928   The first all-metal dirigible, constructed for the Navy by Detroit manufacturers, is successfully flown at Grosse Ile Airport.

Michigan develops the yellow line to indicate no-passing zones on highways.

Upper Peninsula State Fair begins.

Interlochen National Music Camp is opened near Traverse City.

1929   Some large copper mines of the Keweenaw Peninsula close; 85 percent of the Keweenaw County population goes on relief.

First Tulip Festival is held in Holland, Michigan.

Henry Ford Museum and Greenfield Village are dedicated.

Ambassador Bridge is opened between Detroit and Windsor.

Stock market crash begins the Great Depression. Thousands of unemployed stand in **soup lines in Detroit**. ➤

1930   Michigan's population is 4,842,325, an increase of more than 1,170,000 since 1920. Urban centers account for 68.2 percent of the population, almost an exact reversal of the situation in 1880.

The vehicle tunnel between Detroit and Windsor, Ontario, is opened.

1932   The "Ford Hunger March" riot occurs at the Ford plant in Dearborn.

1933   Governor William A. Comstock calls a statewide "banking holiday" to avoid bank runs, after disclosure of the condition of the Union Guardian Trust Company, Detroit.

Michigan votes to end national prohibition.

First Michigan sales tax inaugurated.

1934   Wayne University is organized in Detroit.

1935-1947

1935 Michigan celebrates its centennial of statehood.

One-fifth of Michigan's employables are without work; the state population has dropped 28 percent since the 1930 census.

The United Automobile Workers (UAW) is organized.

Nation's first travel information lodge opened on US-12 at New Buffalo.

The Detroit Tigers win the World Series. With championships in this era from the Lions in professional football, the Red Wings in hockey, and Joe Louis in boxing, Detroit is known as the "City of Champions."

1936 Mass organization of labor under the CIO is strengthened by the affiliation of International Union, United Automobile Workers of America, with the CIO.

With the Flint sit-down strike leading the way, General Motors shuts down, affecting 150,000 workers and closing more than 60 plants in 14 states.

1937 **Joe Louis**, who moved to Detroit at age 12, becomes world's heavyweight champion in boxing. ➤

The UAW strike reaches a peaceful conclusion as collective bargaining agreements are signed by General Motors and most other automotive and parts manufacturers, except the Ford Motor Company, which fought unionization until 1941.

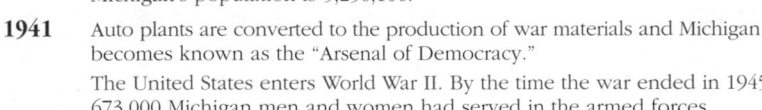

Keweenaw Peninsula copper mining again turns upward, with production reaching 75,000 pounds.

Civil Service merit system introduced to Michigan government.

A wave of sit-down strikes in various industries eventually leads to a breakdown of the open-shop tradition in the state.

1938 International "Blue Water Bridge," connecting Port Huron and Sarnia, Ontario, is dedicated.

1939 Frank Murphy, former governor, takes office as Attorney General of the United States. Governor Frank D. Fitzgerald dies.

1940 Luren D. Dickinson, acting governor of Michigan, appoints Matilda R. Wilson as lieutenant governor, the first woman to serve in that capacity.

Attorney General **Frank Murphy** is appointed to the United States Supreme Court to succeed the late Associate Justice Pierce Butler. ➤

Michigan's population is 5,256,106.

1941 Auto plants are converted to the production of war materials and Michigan becomes known as the "Arsenal of Democracy."

The United States enters World War II. By the time the war ended in 1945, 673,000 Michigan men and women had served in the armed forces.

1942 Sidewheeler *Seeandbee* converted to the aircraft carrier U.S. *Wolverine* for training naval air pilots on Lake Michigan.

1943 Interracial riots strike Detroit, leaving 34 dead and hundreds injured.

1944 Governor Thomas E. Dewey of New York, a native of Michigan, nominated by the Republicans for President.

1945 Senator **Arthur H. Vandenberg** of Grand Rapids helps frame the United Nations Charter. ➤

Michigan Tourist Council created.

The Detroit Tigers win the World Series.

1946 Lake Superior State College is opened at Sault Ste. Marie.

1947 Walter Reuther assumes the presidency of the U.A.W.

WWJ-TV, Detroit, begins commercial television broadcasting in Michigan.

1948-1962

1948   G. Mennen Williams elected Governor, serves six terms.

1950   Michigan's population is 6,371,766.

The Detroit Red Wings win the Stanley Cup.

1951   Fire destroys much of the State Office Building in Lansing.

1952   The Detroit Lions win the first of three world championships in professional football in the decade (also 1953 and 1957).

1953   About 250,000 Michigan men and women see military service during the Korean War (1950-1953).

1954   American Motors Corporation is formed by the merger of Hudson Motor Car Company and Nash-Kelvinator Corporation.

The first slogan — Water Wonderland — appears on Michigan license plates.

Construction begins on the Mackinac Bridge.

1955   During its centennial year, Michigan State College becomes a university.

1956   Wayne University in Detroit becomes a state university.

The Interstate Highway Act is passed. It provided for federal-state cooperation in highway construction.

1957   Oakland University founded.

After ages of dreams and efforts in the 1930s halted by the war, the five-mile-long **Mackinac Bridge is completed**, finally uniting Michigan's two peninsulas.

Professional basketball comes to Michigan when the Fort Wayne Pistons move to Detroit.

1958   G. Mennen Williams, a native of Detroit, is elected to an unprecedented sixth term as governor.

Computers are first used by state government.

1959   Detroit and the entire Great Lakes region gain access to world markets with the opening of the St. Lawrence Seaway.

First annual Labor Day Mackinac Bridge walk is held.

1960   Cobo Hall is built as the Detroit Civic Center.

Michigan becomes the first state to complete a border-to-border interstate highway (I-94).

Michigan's population is 7,823,194.

1961   Constitutional convention meets in Lansing.

Otis Smith becomes first African-American to serve on the Michigan Supreme Court.

G. Mennen Williams named Assistant Secretary of State for African Affairs by President John F. Kennedy. ➤

1962   The International Bridge at the Soo is opened, connecting the U.S. and Canada.

1963-1984

1963   Grand Valley State College is opened.

Michigan's fourth state constitution, drafted in 1961-1962, is approved by the voters.

1964   James McDivitt of Jackson commands the Gemini IV mission and becomes Michigan's first astronaut.

1965   State Executive Organization Act passed.

Saginaw Valley State College is chartered as a state institution.

Michigan begins putting photos on driver's licenses.

1966   Last operating mine on the Gogebic Iron Range closes.

1967   The urban unrest that has been evident in several U.S. cities strikes Detroit with a riot that leaves 45 dead.

The state income tax act is enacted.

1968   The Detroit Tigers win the World Series.

1969   Governor **George Romney** resigns to become the U.S. Secretary of Housing and Urban Development in the Nixon administration. ➤

1970   Michigan's population is 8,881,826.

1971   Privately operated, nonrecreational railroad passenger service ends in Michigan as Amtrak is formed.

1,000-foot-long vessels appear on the Great Lakes.

1972   The Michigan Lottery Bureau is created.

1973   **Mary Stallings Coleman** becomes the first woman to serve on the Michigan Supreme Court. ➤

American military involvement in Vietnam ends; over 400,000 Michigan men and women serve.

An accident in which a fire retardant containing polybrominated biphenyl (PBB) is mixed with livestock feed sets off a crisis that threatens Michigan's agriculture and public health.

1974   **Gerald R. Ford**, former congressman from Grand Rapids, becomes the 38th President of the United States and first Michiganian to serve in that office. ➤

1976   Throwaway bottles are banned as the result of an initiative requiring deposits on beer and soft drink containers.

1977   The Detroit Renaissance Center is completed.

1979   The Michigan State University Basketball Team wins the NCAA championship.

1980   Michigan's population is 9,262,078.

A presidential convention (Republican) is held in Detroit for the first time, with Ronald Reagan becoming the nominee.

1981   **William G. Milliken** becomes the state's longest-serving governor. He serves a total of 14 years. ➤

1982   The movement to renovate Michigan's 103-year-old capitol begins with the organization of Friends of the Capitol.

1983   Martha Wright Griffiths becomes first elected woman lieutenant governor.

1984   The Detroit Tigers win the World Series.

"Big Three" American automakers — General Motors, Ford, and Chrysler — report total profits for year of $9.8 billion, a new high.

Detroit holds its first Grand Prix automobile race.

1985-1998

1985   Michigan begins celebrating its sesquicentennial.

Michigan's mandatory seat belt law goes into effect (third state in nation to enact such a law).

1986   Republican William Lucas is the first black candidate to represent a major party in a gubernatorial election in Michigan.

1987   Michigan celebrates its sesquicentennial of statehood.

1989   The **Michigan Library and Historical Center** is dedicated in Lansing. ➤

The University of Michigan Men's Basketball Team wins the NCAA championship and the Detroit Pistons win the first of two consecutive National Basketball Association crowns.

1990   The restored chambers of the Senate and of the House are reopened and the lawmakers return to their traditional home after holding sessions elsewhere. The Senate becomes the first state legislative body in the nation to include microcomputers on the chamber floor.

Michigan begins the Adopt-a-Highway program.

Michigan's population is 9,295,297.

1992   The U.S. Congress passes the Michigan Scenic Rivers Act protecting over 500 miles on 14 rivers from development.

The Twenty-Seventh Amendment to the U.S. Constitution is ratified by the vote of Michigan. The text of the amendment, which provides that no law varying the compensation of Senators and Representatives shall take effect until an election of Representatives has intervened, was originally submitted to the states as part of the Bill of Rights in 1789.

The restored Michigan State Capitol is rededicated. ➤

1993   The Michigan House of Representatives operates throughout the Eighty-Seventh Legislature under a shared power agreement that reflects the 55-55 Democratic-Republican split, with co-speakers and co-chairs of committees rotating responsibilities each month.

1994   Governor **John M. Engler** is reelected to a second term; coupled with state legislative victories, Republicans control both houses of the legislature and the governor's office for the first time in 26 years.

Michigan State Parks celebrate 75th anniversary. ➤

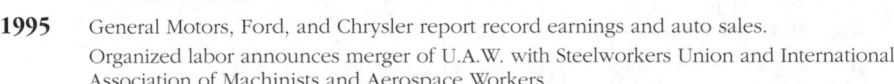

Michigan accounts for 32.6% of all U.S. car production, building 2.1 million passenger cars; Lansing reclaims title as "Car Capital of North America."

1995   General Motors, Ford, and Chrysler report record earnings and auto sales.

Organized labor announces merger of U.A.W. with Steelworkers Union and International Association of Machinists and Aerospace Workers.

1996   Voters approve Proposal E, an initiative to permit casino gaming in qualified cities.

1997   President Bill Clinton addresses joint session of Michigan Legislature, the first U.S. President to do so since President Theodore Roosevelt visited the state capital in 1907.

Lansing celebrates its sesquicentennial as Michigan's state capital.

1998   **Frank J. Kelley** retires as the longest-serving (1962-1998) attorney general in the nation.

1999 Casinos open in Detroit.
State welfare caseloads reach their lowest level since 1970.

2000 Michigan's resident population is 9,938,444, up 6.9% from 1990.
Michigan's unemployment rate drops below 3% for the first time since records kept.

2001 Detroit celebrates its tricentennial. Events include a parade of tall ships on the
Detroit River, a reenactment of Antoine de la Mothe Cadillac's founding of
"D'etroit" in 1701, and the dedication of the Underground
Railroad Monument.

2003 **Jennifer M. Granholm** is inaugurated as the first woman governor
of the state of Michigan. ➤

2004 The Detroit Pistons win their third National Basketball
Championship.

2006 Michigan's **Gerald R. Ford**, our nation's 38th president, dies at the age of 93.

2008 The Detroit Red Wings win their fourth Stanley Cup since 1997, their eleventh overall.

2009 A credit crisis that begins in the late summer and fall of the previous year triggers a
severe economic downturn that results in the bankruptcy of General Motors and
Chrysler and significant government ownership of both corporations.

2010 Michigan's resident population declines between 2000 and 2010, the only state in the
nation to lose population since the last census. Michigan's population of 9,888,635
results in the loss of one Congressional seat in the U.S. House of Representatives.

2011 The Oakland University William Beaumont School of Medicine admits its first class of
students and becomes the first Michigan public university to establish a medical school
in over 40 years. Central Michigan University formed the CMU Medical Education
Partners Alliance on its path to admit its first class to the new College of Medicine in
2013. Western Michigan University names the founding dean for their new School of
Medicine with plans to admit their first class in 2014.

2013 Representative John D. Dingell, Jr. is honored as the longest serving member in the
history of the U.S. Congress. Representative Dingell first took office on December 13,
1955 at the age of 29. He represents Michigan's 12th Congressional District.
The city of Detroit files for bankruptcy protection in U.S. District Court. It is the largest
municipality in U.S. history to file for bankruptcy.

2014 Four senior members of Congress from Michigan — Senator Carl Levin and
Representatives John D. Dingell, Jr., Mike Rogers and Dave Camp — retired at the end
of 2014 after a collective 134 years of Congressional service.
The city of Detroit formally emerged from court protection on December 11, 2014,
bringing to a close the largest municipal bankruptcy in American history after about
17 months.

2015 Great Lakes ice coverage peaked at 92.5% in the winter of 2014 and just over 88% in
the winter of 2015, making it the first time since 1977 that the ice coverage exceeded
80% two winters in a row.

2016 A drinking water crisis in the city of Flint due to high lead levels leads to a declaration
of emergency, resignation of state officials, and criminal charges against several
government employees.

CONVENTIONS OF ASSENT

FIRST CONVENTION OF ASSENT
OF THE TERRITORY OF MICHIGAN

Convened at Ann Arbor, September 26, and adjourned September 30, 1836

OFFICERS

WILLIAM DRAPER, *President*
CHARLES A. JEFFERIES, *Secretary*
SAMUEL YORKE AT LEE, *Vice President*
MARTIN DAVIS, *Sergeant-at-Arms*

Delegate	County	Delegate	County
Allen, Ethan	Jackson	McDonell, John	Wayne
Axford, John S.	Macomb	McKinstry, David C.	Wayne
Beaufait, Louis	Wayne	Newton, James.	Cass
Bradshaw, Elias	Wayne	Noble, Elnathan	{ Washtenaw
Brown, Ammon	Wayne		Livingston
Brownell, John L.	Oakland	Noyes, Horace A.	Wayne
Butts, Mason.	Lapeer	O'Dell, James.	Cass
Clark, Robert	Monroe	Peck, Edward W.	Oakland
Collamer, Lorenzo B.	Calhoun	Richardson, Origen D.	Oakland
Comstock, Darius	Lenawee		{ Ottawa
Conklin, Ebenezer H.	{ Washtenaw	Richmond, William A.	{ Kent
	Livingston		Ionia
Dort, Titus	Wayne		Clinton
	{ Saginaw	Rickey, Joseph.	Lenawee
Drake, Thomas J.	{ Genesee	Satterlee, Samuel	Oakland
	Shiawassee	Smith, Joseph.	Kalamazoo
Draper, William	Oakland	Stubbs, Michael P.	{ Washtenaw
Ellis, Edward D.	Monroe		Livingston
Gilbert, Linus S.	Macomb	Sumner, Watson	St. Joseph
Glover, George W.	{ Washtenaw	Tucker, John	Macomb
	Livingston	Van Duser, Zachariah	Hillsdale
Hutchins, John	Lenawee	Warner, Harvey	Branch
Jefferies, George P.	{ Washtenaw	Warner, S. A. L.	Oakland
	Livingston	Weare, Richard.	{ Allegan
Kercheval, Benjamin B.	Wayne		Barry
Kimball, Charles T.	St. Clair	Welch, William H.	Kalamazoo
Lancaster, Columbia	St. Joseph	Wilkins, Ross	Lenawee
Lane, Marcus	{ Washtenaw	Willard, Titus B.	Berrien
	Livingston	Wing, Austin E.	Monroe
Lawrence, Wolcott	Monroe	Wood, Stephen R.	Chippewa
Markham, Seth	{ Washtenaw		
	Livingston		

NOTE: The First and Second Conventions of Assent of the Territory of Michigan occurred as a result of the Act of June 15, 1836, 5 Stat. 49, of the United States Congress establishing a northern boundary for the State of Ohio and providing for admission of the State of Michigan to the Union upon acceptance of certain conditions. The purpose of the act was to resolve the long-standing dispute between Michigan and Ohio over 400 square miles of territory known as the "Toledo strip." Congress required Michigan's assent to the establishment of the northern Ohio border to include that area before Congress would vote to admit Michigan to the Union. In compensation, Congress offered 9,000 square miles of territory in what is now Michigan's Upper Peninsula.

In response to that requirement, the Legislature approved an act on July 25, 1836, calling for the election of delegates to a convention to consider the issue. Fifty delegates elected September 12, 1836, convened in Ann Arbor on September 26. The delegates rejected a proposed compromise by a vote of 28-21. In the resolution rejecting the conditions of admission, the delegates stated that Congress had exceeded its authority by imposing conditions contrary to the provisions of the Ordinance of 1787. The resolution also criticized the state legislature for adopting a congressional act as the basis for its action in calling for a convention.

Later in 1836, the Committee of the Democratic Convention of Wayne County recommended another convention to reverse the earlier decision, citing sentiment to comply with the conditions of Congress. At the committee's urging, new delegates were elected on December 5 and 6, 1836. The "Frost-Bitten Convention" convened in Ann Arbor on December 14 and 15, immediately and unanimously approving a resolution of assent to the conditions specified in the congressional act of June 15, 1836.

Although some question existed in Congress as to the legality of this second convention, both houses voted to approve the December convention results and Michigan's admission to the Union. President Andrew Jackson signed the bill making Michigan the nation's 26th state on January 26, 1837.

SECOND CONVENTION OF ASSENT
OF THE TERRITORY OF MICHIGAN

Convened at Ann Arbor, December 14, and adjourned December 15, 1836

OFFICERS

JOHN R. WILLIAMS, *President*
KINTZING PRITCHETTE, *Secretary*
J. E. FIELDS, *Secretary*
JOHN HUSTON, *Sergeant-at-Arms*

Delegate	County	Delegate	County
Adam, John J.	Lenawee	Morey, Peter	Lenawee
Adams, William.	St. Joseph	Morris, Benjamin B.	Oakland
Avery, Charles B.	Van Buren	Morse, Elihu	Wayne
Babcock, Henry S.	Oakland	Murray, Archibald Y.	Wayne
Bacon, Marshal J.	Wayne	Noble, Nathaniel	Washtenaw
Barritt, Hiram	Oakland	Noyes, Horace A.	Wayne
Bradley, Samuel B.	Washtenaw	Packard, Benjamin H.	Jackson
Bradshaw, Elias	Wayne	Page, Joab	Jackson
Bridges, Edward N.	Cass	Percival, Samuel.	Kalamazoo
Bucklin, James	Wayne	Pray, Esek	Washtenaw
Champion, Salmon, Jr.	Washtenaw	Rickey, Joseph	Lenawee
Chase, David	Oakland	Schwartz, John E.	Wayne
Coates, Joseph	Oakland	Searle, Ambrose	Kalamazoo
Comstock, Addison J.	Lenawee	Silver, Abiel	Cass
Congdon, Elisha	Washtenaw	Silver, Jacob.	Cass
Crooks, William	Oakland	Smith, Joseph.	Cass
Davidson, Norman	Lapeer	Southerland, Solomon	Washtenaw
Denton, Samuel	Washtenaw	Stewart, Hart L.	Berrien
Dexter, Samuel	Kent	Thompson, Jeremiah D.	Lenawee
Downes, Lyman	Washtenaw	Tisdale, Peris A.	Branch
Eaton, Orasamus.	Allegan	Toll, Philip R.	St. Joseph
Gates, Parley W. C.	Oakland	Tompkins, James B.	Branch
Gillett, Reynold.	Wayne	Truesdell, Stephen W.	St. Joseph
Goodwin, Daniel	Wayne	Tucker, Joel	St. Clair
Goodwin, Justus	Calhoun	Tuttle, Warren	Wayne
Grant, Charles A.	Oakland	Twitchell, Stodard W.	Washtenaw
Gray, Harvey	Lapeer	Van Duser, Zachariah	Hillsdale
Hart, James B.	Oakland	Wadhams, Ralph	St. Clair
Hoffman, George W.	Berrien	Walker, Charles J.	Kent
Huston, James	Washtenaw	Warner, Jesse	Washtenaw
Hutchins, John	Lenawee	Watkins, Aaron B.	St. Joseph
Irwin, Charles F.	Wayne	Watson, Samuel G.	Saginaw
Jackson, Darius C.	Lenawee	White, Samuel	Oakland
Jewett, George W.	Washtenaw	Whittemore, Gideon O.	Oakland
Keeler, H. H.	Van Buren	Wilkins, Ross	Wayne
Littlejohn, Silas F.	Allegan	Willard, Isaac W.	Kalamazoo
Livermore, John S.	Oakland	Williams, Gardner D.	Saginaw
Lyon, Ira.	Kalamazoo	Williams, John R.	Wayne
Manning, Rockwell	Hillsdale	Wing, Nelson H.	Washtenaw
Mason, Josiah.	Wayne	Witherell, Benjamin F. H.	Wayne
Miller, Oliver	Lenawee	Wright, Benjamin	Calhoun
Moran, Charles	Wayne		

NOTE: The First and Second Conventions of Assent of the Territory of Michigan occurred as a result of the Act of June 15, 1836, 5 Stat. 49, of the United States Congress establishing a northern boundary for the State of Ohio and providing for admission of the State of Michigan to the Union upon acceptance of certain conditions. The purpose of the act was to resolve the long-standing dispute between Michigan and Ohio over 400 square miles of territory known as the "Toledo strip." Congress required Michigan's assent to the establishment of the northern Ohio border to include that area before Congress would vote to admit Michigan to the Union. In compensation, Congress offered 9,000 square miles of territory in what is now Michigan's Upper Peninsula.

In response to that requirement, the Legislature approved an act on July 25, 1836, calling for the election of delegates to a convention to consider the issue. Fifty delegates elected September 12, 1836, convened in Ann Arbor on September 26. The delegates rejected a proposed compromise by a vote of 28-21. In the resolution rejecting the conditions of admission, the delegates stated that Congress had exceeded its authority by imposing conditions contrary to the provisions of the Ordinance of 1787. The resolution also criticized the state legislature for adopting a congressional act as the basis for its action in calling for a convention.

Later in 1836, the Committee of the Democratic Convention of Wayne County recommended another convention to reverse the earlier decision, citing sentiment to comply with the conditions of Congress. At the committee's urging, new delegates were elected on December 5 and 6, 1836. The "Frost-Bitten Convention" convened in Ann Arbor on December 14 and 15, immediately and unanimously approving a resolution of assent to the conditions specified in the congressional act of June 15, 1836.

Although some question existed in Congress as to the legality of this second convention, both houses voted to approve the December convention results and Michigan's admission to the Union. President Andrew Jackson signed the bill making Michigan the nation's 26th state on January 26, 1837.

ACT ADMITTING MICHIGAN TO THE UNION

[5 U.S. Statutes at Large 144]

AN ACT to admit the State of Michigan into the Union, upon an equal footing with the original states.

WHEREAS, In pursuance of the act of congress of June fifteenth, eighteen hundred and thirty-six, entitled, "An act to establish the northern boundary of the State of Ohio, and to provide for the admission of the State of Michigan into the Union, upon the conditions therein expressed," a convention of delegates, elected by the people of the said State of Michigan, for the sole purpose of giving their assent to the boundaries of the said State of Michigan, as described, declared and established in and by the said act, did, on the fifteenth of December, eighteen hundred and thirty-six, assent to the provisions of said act, therefore:

Section 1. *Be it enacted by the Senate and House of Representatives of the United States of America, in Congress assembled,* That the State of Michigan shall be one, and is hereby declared to be one, of the United States of America, and admitted into the Union on an equal footing with the original states, in all respects whatever.

Section 2. *And be it further enacted,* That the secretary of the treasury, in carrying into effect the thirteenth and fourteenth sections of the act of the twenty-third of June, eighteen hundred and thirty-six, entitled, "An act to regulate the deposits of the public money," shall consider the said State of Michigan as being one of the United States.

Approved Jan. 26, 1837.

NOTE: The admission of Michigan into the Union on equal footing with the original states concluded a long and bitter battle over approximately 400 square miles of territory known as the "Toledo strip." The dispute, which eventually entangled the government of Michigan (both as a territory and a state), the government of Ohio, and the federal government, ended only with Michigan's accession to the demands of the United States Congress as specified in the Act of 1836, 5 Stat. 49.

Ohio, in its first constitution written in 1802, defined its boundaries to include that territory. Michigan, relying on the Ordinance of 1787 and the Act of 1805, 2 Stat. 309, claimed the same territory in defining its boundaries in its first constitution in 1835. Congress, which had debated the issue for several years, elected to award the territory to Ohio, making Michigan's ratification of that boundary preliminary to her acceptance into the Union. Lacking full-fledged representation in the U.S. Congress and, perhaps, recognizing that admission to the Union offered more than would have been gained by withholding acceptance, delegates, on December 15, 1836, at the second of two conventions, convened to discuss the issue and assented to the conditions Congress had established. Although some in Congress questioned the validity of the action, Congress approved Michigan's admission on January 26, 1837, 5 Stat. 144. See Ordinance of 1787; Act of Congress, 2 Stat. 309; Journal of the Proceedings of the Convention to Form a Constitution for the State of Michigan in Pursuance of an Act of Congress of June 15, 1836; Act of the Legislature of Said State on July 25, 1836, for the Purpose of Taking into Consideration the Proposition of Congress Relative to the Admission of the State of Michigan into the Union, 1836; First and Second Conventions of Assent, Territory of Michigan, September 26-30, 1836, and December 14-15, 1836, 1894 Reprint, Secretary of State; Early Michigan History (Pamphlets), vol. I, 1873; "The Quest for Statehood," Roger L. Rosentreter, Michigan History, January/February 1987; Congressional Globe, 23rd Congress, 1st and 2nd Sessions, vols. I and II, 1835; Congressional Globe, 24th Congress, 1st and 2nd Sessions, vols. II, III, and IV, 1836 and 1837.

Chapter II

CONSTITUTIONS

2019–2020

MICHIGAN'S CONSTITUTIONS

Introduction

The people of Michigan have adopted four constitutions, those of 1835, 1850, 1908, and 1963. Each document was the product of a convention composed of delegates elected to draft a proposed constitution for submission to the voters.

The 1835 Constitution

During the period 1824 to 1835, the legislative power of the Territory of Michigan was vested in a unicameral territorial council; it was by an act of this council, approved January 26, 1835, that the first constitutional convention was called. Ninety-one delegates convened on the second Monday of May 1835 at the Territorial Capitol in Detroit to draft a constitution, a key step in the process for achieving **statehood** established by the Ordinance of 1787. Convention sessions lasted until June 24, when the various provisions were adopted by the delegates. The question of adopting the constitution was submitted to the people at an election held on the first Monday in October 1835. The electorate voted to adopt the new constitution by a 5-1 margin, 15 months before Michigan was admitted to the Union.

Several characteristics of this first constitution are notable. It included a **bill of rights**, though voting privileges were restricted to white males over the age of 21 years, and it divided the powers of government into three dis-

The Constitution of Michigan of 1835.

tinct departments: legislative, executive, and judicial. The governor, lieutenant governor, and legislators were to be elected, while the attorney general, secretary of state, auditor general, and supreme court judges were to be appointed by the governor with the advice and consent of the senate. To promote settlement and commerce, it authorized the government to encourage a program of **internal improvements** in relation to roads, canals, and navigable waters. Perhaps most significant, however, was the education article, which provided for a superintendent of public instruction and established a perpetual fund, consisting of federal land grants, for the support of schools.

Although the 1835 document is generally regarded as Michigan's best constitution, it proved unsatisfactory. Financial difficulties associated with the state's new internal improvements program and changing political attitudes favoring **elected rather than appointed officials** soon led to a demand for constitutional revision.

The 1850 Constitution

On June 3, 1850, a constitutional convention met at Lansing and completed its revision on August 15 of that year. The proposed Constitution of 1850 was presented to the voters at the election of November 5, 1850, and was adopted by a vote of 36,169 to 9,433. More than twice as long as its predecessor, the 1850 document restricted the legislative power regarding state fiscal matters, including involvement in internal improvements. It circumscribed the gubernatorial appointment power by making elective the offices of secretary of state, attorney general, auditor general, and judge of the supreme court, as well as various local offices. It directed the legislature to establish an agricultural school, and added articles on county and township government, finance and taxation, and corporations. The 1850 constitution also provided that the question of a general revision of the constitution be submitted to the electors in 1866 and every sixteenth year thereafter.

Convention of 1867

At the general election in 1866, voters approved the calling of a constitutional convention, and, on the first Monday in April 1867, the people elected 100 delegates. The delegation met in Lansing on the third Wednesday in May 1867 and adjourned on August 22. Their proposed revision was rejected by the people at the election of April 1868, by a vote of 71,733 for and 110,582 against. It is believed the principal barriers to voter approval were the proposed salary increases for state officers and circuit judges and the establishment of equal suffrage for white and black. The latter feature was subsequently adopted as an amendment both to the Federal and Michigan constitutions.

Constitutional Commission of 1873

By a joint resolution approved April 24, 1873, the legislature provided for the appointment by the governor of a commission to report to the legislature at its next session "such amendments, or such revision to the Constitution, as in their judgment may be necessary for the best interests of the State and the people." The commission convened in the senate chamber at Lansing, on Wednesday, August 27, 1873, and remained in session until October 16; on December 1, 1873, it submitted its formal report for a revised constitution to the governor. In the spring of 1874, the revised constitution was submitted by the legislature to the voters and rejected by a vote of 39,285 for and 124,034 against.

The 1908 Constitution

It was not until October 22, 1907, that a new constitutional convention assembled at Lansing. Ninety-six delegates met at the Capitol until they completed a revision of the constitution on March 3, 1908. The Constitution of 1908, much like its predecessor in tone, length, and extent of detail, was adopted on November 3, 1908, by a vote of 244,705 to 130,783.

The 1963 Constitution

Four attempts were made to call a constitutional convention to revise the Constitution of 1908 before April 3, 1961. A primary election for the purpose of electing delegates was held on July 25, 1961, and, on September 12, 1961, 144 delegates were elected. The delegates met at Convention Hall in the Civic Center, Lansing, on October 3, 1961, and adopted the proposed constitution on August 1, 1962. This constitution was submitted at the election of April 1, 1963, and adopted. A recount established the vote as 810,860 to 803,436.

In 1978, 1994, and 2010, the voters of Michigan rejected opportunities to approve a convention for revision of the Constitution of 1963.

Since it became effective on January 1, 1964, the 1963 document has been amended 32 times.

CONSTITUTIONAL CONVENTIONS
CONVENTION OF 1835
Convened at Detroit, May 11, and adjourned June 24, 1835

OFFICERS
JOHN BIDDLE, *President*
CHARLES W. WHIPPLE, *Secretary*
MARSHAL J. BACON, *Secretary*
OLMSTEAD HOUGH, *Sergeant-at-Arms*

Delegate	District	County	Delegate	District	County
Adam, John J.	3	Lenawee	Manning, Randolph	5	Oakland
Axford, J. S.	6	Macomb	McClelland, Robert	2	Monroe
Axford, Samuel	6	Macomb	McDonell, John	1	Wayne
Barry, John S.	13	St. Joseph	Miller, Lewis T.	9	{ Hillsdale / Branch }
Beaufait, Louis	1	Wayne			
Biddle, John	1	Wayne	Moore, William	4	Washtenaw
Boughton, Seleck C.	3	Lenawee	Morris, Benjamin B.	5	Oakland
Brewer, John	4	Washtenaw	Mundy, Edward	4	Washtenaw
Briggs, Russell	4	Washtenaw	Newberry, Seneca	5	Oakland
Brower, Richard	4	Washtenaw	Newton, James	12	Cass
Brown, Ammon	1	Wayne	Noble, Nathaniel	4	Washtenaw
Calkin, Ephraim	6	Macomb	Norvell, John	1	Wayne
Case, Emanuel	4	Washtenaw	O'Dell, James	12	Cass
Chapman, Bela	16	Chippewa	Otis, Asa H.	1	Wayne
Chase, Jonathan	5	Oakland	Patrick, William	5	Oakland
Clark, Eliphalet	2	Monroe	Patterson, Joseph H.	3	Lenawee
Clark, John	7	St. Clair	Porter, Henry	6	Macomb
Colbath, Lemuel	2	Monroe	Porter, Solomon	6	Macomb
Collins, Alpheus	4	Washtenaw	Purdy, Robert	4	Washtenaw
Comstock, Darius	3	Lenawee	Raynale, Ebenezer	5	Oakland
Convis, Ezra	10	Calhoun	Rexford, Roswell B.[1]	8	Jackson
Cook, Elijah F.	5	Oakland	Riggs, Jeremiah	5	Oakland
Crary, Isaac E.	10	Calhoun	Shattuck, Gilbert	4	Washtenaw
Crossman, Rufus	4	Washtenaw	Shellhouse, Martin G.	13	St. Joseph
Curtis, Thomas	5	Oakland	Stevens, Amos	1	Wayne
Davis, J. D.	1	Wayne	Stubbs, Michael P.	4	Washtenaw
Davis, Rosevelt[1]	8	Jackson	Sutphen, Josephus V. D.	2	Monroe
Davison, Norman	5	Oakland	Tallman, Theophilus E.	1	Wayne
Dousman, Michael	15	Mackinac	Taylor, Joshua B.	5	Oakland
Ellenwood, John	5	Oakland	Ten Eyck, Conrad	1	Wayne
Ellis, Edward D.	2	Monroe	Tiffany, Alexander R.[2]	3	Lenawee
Ferrington, George W.	1	Wayne	Tucker, Jacob	6	Macomb
Ferry, Peter P.	2	Monroe	VanEvery, Peter	1	Wayne
Gidley, Townsend E.	8	Jackson	Voorheis, Isaac I.	5	Oakland
Godard, Abel	4	Washtenaw	Wadhams, Ralph	7	St. Clair
Godfroy, James F.	2	Monroe	Welch, William H.	11	Kalamazoo
Herrington, Caleb	1	Wayne	Wells, Hezekiah G.	11	Kalamazoo
Howe, Orrin	4	Washtenaw	White, Alpheus	1	Wayne
Howell, Joseph	3	Lenawee	White, David	2	Monroe
Hutchins, Allen	3	Lenawee	White, Orrin	4	Washtenaw
Ingersoll, Samuel	2	Monroe	White, Samuel	5	Oakland
Irwin, Charles F.	1	Wayne	Whitney, John[2]	3	Lenawee
Jenkins, Baldwin	12	Cass	Wilkins, Ross	3	Lenawee
Lacy, Elijah	14	Berrien	Willard, Titus B.	14	Berrien
Loomis, Hubbell	13	St. Joseph	Williams, John R.	1	Wayne
Lyon, Lucius	11	Kalamazoo	Woodbridge, William	1	Wayne

NOTE: It was this convention that formed Michigan's first constitution.
Relying on provisions of the Ordinance of 1787 and the Act of January 11, 1805, 2 Stat. 309, creating the Territory of Michigan, the Legislative Council of the Territory of Michigan enacted legislation providing for the election of delegates to a convention to form a constitution and state government. The act, passed January 26, 1835, defined the time and manner of the election, the number of delegates from each district, and the time and place of the convention. As the Northwest Ordinance had provided that "whenever any of the said states shall have sixty thousand free inhabitants therein . . . [it] shall be at liberty to form a permanent Constitution and State government," the act also declared Michigan's population to be 87,273, the result of a census the council had authorized September 6, 1834.
Delegates to this convention were elected April 4, 1835, and convened in Detroit, then the capital of the territory, on May 11, 1835. The delegates adopted the constitution on June 24, 1835, for submission to a vote of the people. On October 5 and 6 of that year, the people approved the constitution by a vote of 6,299 to 1,359. This vote total, which was printed in the Journal of the Senate (November 3, 1836), did not include vote totals from Kalamazoo County. That vote, 453 in favor and 15 against, appears in the Record of Elections 1835-1845, Office of the Secretary of State.

[1] The vote for Davis and Rexford was a tie. The convention passed a resolution sending the matter back to the district for a special election, which was held on May 25, 1835. Both delegates were permitted to hold seats with the privilege of debating but not voting issues until the election returns were received. Rexford won the election and was seated by the convention on June 3, 1835.
[2] A credentials check led to the seating of Tiffany on May 16, 1835. Whitney served until that date.

CONVENTION OF 1850

Convened at Lansing, June 3, and adjourned August 15, 1850

OFFICERS

DANIEL GOODWIN, *President*
JOHN SWEGLES, JR., *Secretary*
HORACE S. ROBERTS, *Assistant Secretary*
CHARLES HASCALL, *Assistant Secretary*
DAVID HUBBARD, JR., *Sergeant-at-Arms*

Delegate	County	Delegate	County
Adam, Wales.	Branch	Hascall, Volney	Kalamazoo
Adams, Peter R.	Lenawee	Hathaway, Hiram.	Macomb
Alvord, Henry J.	Wayne	Hixon, Daniel	Washtenaw
Anderson, Robert H.	Jackson	Kingsley, James	Washtenaw
Arzeno, Alexander M.	Monroe	Kinne, Daniel.	Hillsdale
Axford, William T.	Oakland	Leach, DeWitt C.	Genesee
Backus, Henry	Wayne	Lee, Daniel S.	Livingston
Bagg, Joseph H.	Wayne	Lovell, Cyrus	Ionia
Barnard, Ely	Livingston	Marvin, Henry B.	Monroe
Bartow, Henry	Ionia	Mason, Lorenzo	St. Clair
Bartow, John	Genesee	McClelland, Robert.	Monroe
Beardsley, Charles E.	Eaton	McLeod, William Norman.	Mackinac
Beeson, Jacob.	Berrien	Moore, Edward S.	St. Joseph
Britain, Calvin.	Berrien	Morrison, William V.	Calhoun
Brown, Alvarado.	Branch	Mosher, John	Hillsdale
Brown, Ammon	Wayne	Mowry, Zebina M.	Oakland
Brown, Asahel	Branch	Newberry, Seneca	Oakland
Burns, John D.	Eaton	O'Brien, Morgan	Washtenaw
Bush, Charles P.	Ingham	Orr, Joseph W. T.	Barry
Butterfield, John L.	Jackson	Pierce, John D.	Calhoun
Carr, William S.	Washtenaw	Pierce, Nathan	Calhoun
Chandler, Charles	Lenawee	Prevost, F. J.	Shiawassee
Chapel, Charles W.	Macomb	Raynale, Ebenezer	Oakland
Choate, Emerson	Monroe	Redfield, George	Cass
Church, Thomas B. . . . . { Kent		Roberts, Elijah J.	Chippewa
	Ottawa	Robertson, Andrew S.	Macomb
Clark, John.	St. Clair	Robinson, Elisha S.	Jackson
Clark, Samuel	Kalamazoo	Robinson, Mitchel	Cass
Comstock, Addison J.	Lenawee	Robinson, Rix . . . . { Kent
Connor, William	St. Joseph		Ottawa
Cook, John P.	Hillsdale	Skinner, Elias M.	Washtenaw
Cornell, Jerry G.	Jackson	Soule, Milo	Calhoun
Crary, Isaac E.	Calhoun	Storey, Wilbur F.	Jackson
Crouse, Robert	Livingston	Sturgis, David	Clinton
Danforth, Ephraim B.	Ingham	Sullivan, James.	Cass
Daniels, Ebenezer.	Lenawee	Sutherland, Jabez G.	Saginaw
Desnoyer, Peter	Wayne	Tiffany, Alexander R.	Lenawee
Dimond, Reuben B.	St. Clair	Town, Oka	Allegan
Eastman, Timothy . . . . { Kent		Van Valkenburgh, Jacob	Oakland
	Ottawa	Waite, Benjamin W.	Washtenaw
Eaton, Ebenezer C.	Wayne	Walker, Dewitt C.	Macomb
Edmunds, James M.	Washtenaw	Warden, Robert, Jr.	Livingston
Fralick, Henry.	Wayne	Webster, James.	Oakland
Gale, Elbridge.	Genesee	Wells, Hezekiah G.	Kalamazoo
Gardiner, Earle P.	Washtenaw	Whipple, Charles W.	Berrien
Gibson, John	Wayne	White, Jonathan R.	Lapeer
Goodwin, Daniel	Wayne	Whittemore, Gideon O.	Oakland
Graham, Jonathan B.	Hillsdale	Willard, Isaac W.	Van Buren
Green, Nelson	Lenawee	Williams, Joseph R.	St. Joseph
Hanscom, Alfred H.	Oakland	Witherell, Benjamin F. H.	Wayne
Hart, Noah H.	Lapeer	Woodman, Elias S.	Oakland
Harvey, George C.	Lenawee		

NOTE: This convention occurred as a result of Joint Resolution No. 21, approved by the legislature on March 12, 1849, asking electors to approve a constitutional convention to revise the Constitution of 1835.

One hundred delegates, elected May 6, 1850, in accordance with Act 78 of 1850, convened in Lansing on June 3 and adjourned August 15, 1850, after adopting a revised constitution. The proposed revision was submitted to, and adopted by, the people at the general election held November 5, 1850, by a vote of 36,169 to 9,433.

CONVENTION OF 1867

Convened at Lansing, May 15, and adjourned August 22, 1867

OFFICERS

CHARLES M. CROSWELL, *President*
THOMAS H. GLENN, *Secretary*
G. X. M. COLLIER, *Assistant Secretary*
T. P. MILES, *Assistant Secretary*
D. B. PURINTON, *Sergeant-at-Arms*
SEYMOUR FOSTER, *Postmaster*

Delegate	County	Delegate	County
Aldrich, Levi	Cass	Longyear, John W.	Ingham
Alexander, Lorenzo P.	Berrien	Lothrop, G. V. N.	Wayne
Andrus, William W.	Macomb	Lovell, Henry R.	Genesee
Barber, Julius S.	Branch	Luce, Cyrus G.	Branch
Bills, Perley	Lenawee	McClelland, Robert	Wayne
Birney, James	Bay	McConnell, Willard M.	Oakland
Blackman, Samuel H.	Van Buren	McKernan, John Q.	Houghton
Bradley, Milton	Kalamazoo	Miles, Marcus H.	St. Clair
Brown, Asahel	Branch	Miller, Hiram L.	Saginaw
Burtch, Milton P.	Eaton	Morton, Edward G.	Monroe
Burtenshaw, James	Ontonagon	Murray, Lyman	Kent
Case, George F.	Montcalm	Musgrave, Joseph	Eaton
Chapin, DeWitt C.	Gratiot	Mussey, Dexter	Macomb
Chapman, Bela	Mackinac	Ninde, Thomas	Washtenaw
Conger, Omar D.	St. Clair	Norris, Lyman D.	Washtenaw
Coolidge, Henry H.	Berrien	Parsons, S. Titus	Shiawassee
Corbin, William	Monroe	Pratt, Daniel L.	Hillsdale
Crocker, Thomas M.	Macomb	Pringle, Eugene	Jackson
Croswell, Charles M.	Lenawee	Purcell, William	Wayne
Daniells, Nathaniel I.	Clinton	Rafter, William A.	Monroe
Desnoyer, Peter	Wayne	Richmond, Charles H.	Washtenaw
Divine, John	Sanilac	Root, Simeon P.	Hillsdale
Duncan, Delamore	Kalamazoo	Sawyer, Jacob C.	Lenawee
Duncombe, Charles	Van Buren	Shearer, Jonathan	Wayne
Elliott, Adam	Barry	Sheldon, Horace J.	Lenawee
Estee, Perry H.	Midland	Smith, Thaddeus G.	Genesee
Farmer, William S.	Berrien	Smith, William A.	Wayne
Ferris, Jacob	Kent	Stockwell, Martin P.	Lenawee
Giddings, Marsh	Kalamazoo	Stoughton, William L.	St. Joseph
Goodwin, Daniel	Wayne	Sutherland, Jabez G.	Saginaw
Goodwin, William F.	Jackson	Thompson, Lewis J.	Hillsdale
Gulick, Robert F.	Keweenaw	Turner, Josiah	Shiawassee
Haire, John	Ottawa	Tyler, Comfort	St. Joseph
Harris, Edward P.	Oakland	Utley, William S.	Newaygo
Hazen, Ezra	St. Clair	Van Riper, Jacob J.	Cass
Henderson, Eden F.	Calhoun	Van Valkenburgh, Jacob	Oakland
Henkel, Peter	Wayne	Walker, Alvah H.	Clinton
Hixon, Daniel	Washtenaw	Warner, P. Dean	Oakland
Holmes, Charles D.	Calhoun	Warner, William E.	Wayne
Holt, Henry H.	Muskegon	Watkins, Freeman C.	Jackson
Howard, Sumner	Genesee	Watkins, Milton C.	Kent
Huston, Benjamin W., Jr.	Tuscola	White, William E.	Allegan
Hull, Levi T.	St. Joseph	Willard, George	Calhoun
Ingalls, Eleazer S.	Menominee	Williams, William B.	Allegan
Jennison, Hiram	Ottawa	Winans, Edwin B.	Livingston
Jermain, George W.	Ionia	Winsor, Richard	Huron
Kenney, Myron C.	Lapeer	Withey, Solomon L.	Kent
Lamb, John M.	Lapeer	Woodhouse, Lemuel	Ingham
Lawrence, Benjamin W.	Livingston	Wright, Harvey	Barry
Leach, DeWitt C.	Grand Traverse	Yeomans, Sanford A.	Ionia

NOTE: The 100 delegates elected on April 1, 1867, under the provisions of Act 41 of 1867, convened in Lansing on May 15 and adopted a revised constitution on August 21, 1867. The people rejected the proposed revision at the April 6, 1868, election by a vote of 71,733 for and 110,582 against.

CONSTITUTIONAL COMMISSION OF 1873

Convened at Lansing, August 27, and adjourned October 16, 1873

OFFICERS

SULLIVAN M. CUTCHEON, *Chairman*
HENRY S. CLUBB, *Clerk*
STEPHEN B. MCCRACKEN, *Assistant Clerk*
WILLIAM BURNHAM, *Doorkeeper*

Delegate	Congressional District	County
Crane, Isaac M.	3	Eaton
Crouse, Ira D.	6	Livingston
Cutcheon, Sullivan M.	2	Washtenaw
Devereaux, James R.	9	Houghton
Divine, John	7	Sanilac
Ferry, William M.[1]	5	Ottawa
Giddings, Edwin W.[2]	7	Macomb
Hatch, Herschel H.	8	Bay
Jerome, David H.	8	Saginaw
Mason, Lyman G.[3]	5	Muskegon
Meddaugh, Elijah W.	1	Wayne
Moffatt, Seth C.	9	Leelanau
Pond, Ashley.	1	Wayne
Riley, Henry H.	4	St. Joseph
Upson, Charles	3	Branch
Wells, Hezekiah G.	4	Kalamazoo
Willits, Edwin	2	Monroe
Withey, Solomon L.	5	Kent
Woodward, Lysander.	6	Oakland

NOTE: Arguing that the 1850 constitution "is defective in many respects, and needs to be amended to conform to the growth and development of the State," the legislature approved Joint Resolution No. 19, on April 24, 1873, providing for the governor to appoint a commission to report "such amendments and revision of the constitution . . . [as] may be necessary for the best interests of the State and the people."

Under the terms of the resolution, the governor appointed an 18-member commission, 2 members from each of the state's 9 congressional districts, to consider amending or revising the Constitution of 1850. The commission convened at Lansing on August 27, 1873, adjourned on October 16 after completing its work, and reported to the governor on December 1 that the "work of the commission . . . has been equivalent to a revision, although it is technically recognized in the official records of the commission as the amended constitution . . . ."

Calling a special session of the legislature in 1874, the governor submitted the commission's report and suggested amendments to the legislature as required by Joint Resolution No. 19. After studying the most advisable method of submitting the proposed amendments to the constitution to a vote, the legislature further amended the commission's proposals. On March 26, 1874, it approved Joint Resolution No. 4, proposing amendments to the Constitution of 1850.

At the election of November 3, 1874, the people rejected the proposed constitution by a vote of 39,285 for to 124,034 against.

---

[1] Appointed October 2, 1873.
[2] Granted an indefinite leave of absence September 23, 1873; resigned October 8, 1873.
[3] Granted an indefinite leave of absence September 10, 1873.

CONVENTION OF 1907-1908

Convened at Lansing, October 22, 1907, and adjourned March 3, 1908

OFFICERS

JOHN J. CARTON, Flint, *President*
CHARLES H. WATSON, Crystal Falls, *President Pro Tem*
PAUL H. KING, Lansing, *Secretary*
ANDREW J. SCOTT, Saginaw, *Sergeant-at-Arms*

Delegate	Senatorial District	Post Office
Acker, William H.	12	Richmond
Adams, Edgar J.	16	Grand Rapids
Atwood, Theron W.	21	Caro
Babcock, Robert S.	26	Manistee
Baird, John	22	Zilwaukee
Baldwin, Clarke E.	5	Adrian
Baldwin, Frederick J.	18	Coral
Barbour, Levi L.	2	Detroit
Barnaby, Horace T., Jr.	17	Grand Rapids
Barnett, James F.	16	Grand Rapids
Bishop, Roswell P.[1]	26	Ludington
Black, Charles M.	23	Muskegon
Boynton, Nathan S.	11	Port Huron
Broomfield, Archibald	25	Big Rapids
Brown, Jefferson G.	11	Avoca
Brown, Thomas H.	1	Highland Park
Brown, William E.	21	Lapeer
Burt, Wellington R.	22	Saginaw
Burton, Clarence M.	2	Detroit
Calverly, William D.	32	Houghton
Campbell, Gordon R.	32	Calumet
Campbell, Henry M.	1	Detroit
Carton, John J.	13	Flint
Cavanaugh, Martin J.	10	Ann Arbor
Chandler, Merritt	29	Onaway
Cook, Albert B.	14	Owosso
Coomer, George W.	4	Wyandotte
Cranor, Ozro N.[2]	26	Ludington
Dawson, William	20	Sandusky
DeLand, Charles J.	10	Jackson
Deuel, Andrew L.	29	Harbor Springs
Fairlie, John Archibald	10	Ann Arbor
Fall, Delos	9	Albion
Flannigan, Richard C.	31	Norway
Fleischhauer, Alfred M.	25	Reed City
Foster, Eugene	28	Gladwin
Freeman, Herbert L.	13	Flushing
Fyfe, Lawrence C.	7	St. Joseph
Gore, Victor M.	7	Benton Harbor
Hall, James H.	20	Port Austin
Hally, Patrick J. M.	3	Detroit
Hawkins, Victor	6	Jonesville
Heald, Henry T.	16	Grand Rapids
Heckert, Benjamin Franklin	8	Paw Paw
Hemans, Lawton T.	14	Mason
Holmes, John W.	19	Alma
Horton, George B.	5	Fruit Ridge
Houk, Calvin E.	32	Ironwood
Ingram, Frederick F.	3	Detroit
Jones, Walter C.	7	Marcellus
Kilpatrick, William M.	14	Owosso
Knowles, Leonard F.	27	Boyne City
Lillie, Colon C.	23	Coopersville
Louisell, Medor E.	27	Frankfort
Manchester, William C.	4	Detroit
Mead, Frank D.	30	Escanaba
Merrell, Joseph	3	Detroit
Milnes, Alfred	6	Coldwater
Monfort, Frank R.	19	Ithaca

Delegate	Senatorial District	Post Office
Moore, Andrew L.	12	Pontiac
Moore, George W.	11	Port Huron
Morgan, David T.	31	Republic
Nichols, Edwin C.	9	Battle Creek
Oberdorffer, William J.	30	Stephenson
Osmun, William E.	23	Montague
Post, Floyd L.	24	Midland
Powell, Herbert E.	18	Ionia
Pratt, Frank S.	24	Bay City
Robertson, Leslie B.	5	Adrian
Rockwell, Kleber P.	12	Pontiac
Rowe, George E.	17	Grand Rapids
Russell, Frederick J.	26	Hart
Salliotte, Ignatius J.	4	Ecorse
Sawyer, Eugene F.	27	Cadillac
Sharpe, Albert E.	30	Sault Ste. Marie
Shaw, Edwin O.	25	Newaygo
Simons, Charles C.	2	Detroit
Smith, John M. C.	15	Charlotte
Smith, Osmond H.	28	Harrisville
Snow, Ernest A.	22	Saginaw
Stewart, Hugh P.	6	Centreville
Sutherland, Justin L.	18	Portland
Taylor, Walter Ross	9	Kalamazoo
Thew, Charles N.	8	Allegan
Thomas, Charles H.	15	Hastings
Thompson, Charles D.	20	Bad Axe
Tossy, Louis E.	1	Detroit
Townsend, Willis L.	29	Gaylord
Turnbull, Edward A.	15	Grand Ledge
Van Kleeck, James.	24	Bay City
Walbridge, Henry E.	19	St. Johns
Walton, Jay C.	13	Howell
Watson, Charles H.	31	Crystal Falls
Wicksall, Guy J.	8	South Haven
Wixson, Walter S.	21	Caro
Woodruff, Henry H.	28	Roscommon
Wykes, Roger I.	17	Grand Rapids

NOTE: Under the provisions of Constitution of 1850, art. XX, sec. 2, 96 delegates, 3 from each of the 32 senatorial districts established by Public Act 264 of 1895 and elected according to the provisions of Act 272 of 1907, convened in Lansing on October 22, 1907. The convention adopted the proposed revision of the constitution February 21, 1908, and adjourned March 3, 1908.

By Public Act 272 of 1907, the legislature had required the revised constitution be submitted to the people for a vote at the April 1908 election. The convention, however, due to the length of its deliberations (they did not end until February 21), voted to submit the constitution to a vote at the November general election. The secretary of state, doubting the power of the convention to fix a date other than that provided by the legislature, refused to comply with the order of the convention.

In *Carton* v *Secretary of State*, 151 Mich. 337; 115 N.W. 429 (1908), the Michigan Supreme Court held that in the absence of an express grant of power to the legislature and by the implications drawn from Constitution of 1850, art. XX, secs. 1 and 2, the convention did have the power to set the date for submission of the constitution to a vote. Therefore, by order of the Supreme Court, the people voted on November 3, 1908; the revised constitution was adopted by a vote of 244,705 for to 130,783 against.

---

[1] Resigned November 15, 1907.
[2] Appointed November 27, 1907, to replace Roswell P. Bishop.

CONVENTION OF 1961-1962

Convened at Lansing, October 3, 1961, and adjourned August 1, 1962

OFFICERS

STEPHEN S. NISBET, Fremont, *President*
TOM DOWNS, Detroit, *Vice President*
EDWARD HUTCHINSON, Fennville, *Vice President*
GEORGE ROMNEY, Bloomfield Hills, *Vice President*
FRED I. CHASE, Lansing, *Secretary*

Delegate	Politics	Post Office	District
Allen, Glenn S., Jr.	Rep.	Kalamazoo	Kalamazoo Co., 1st Dist.
Andrus, Vera.	Rep.	Port Huron	St. Clair Dist.
Anspach, Charles L.	Rep.	Mt. Pleasant.	Isabella Dist.
Austin, Richard H.	Dem.	Detroit.	Wayne Co., 6th Dist.
Baginski, Martin W.	Dem.	Detroit.	Wayne Co., 5th Dist.
Balcer, Frank A., Jr.	Dem.	Detroit.	Wayne Co., 8th Dist.
Barthwell, Sidney	Dem.	Detroit.	Wayne Co., 2nd Dist.
Batchelor, Don G.	Rep.	Grand Blanc.	Genesee Co., 2nd Dist.
Beaman, Berry N.	Rep.	Parma	10th Senatorial Dist.
Bentley, Alvin M.	Rep.	Owosso.	15th Senatorial Dist.
Binkowski, Don	Dem.	Detroit.	2nd Senatorial Dist.
Blandford, Robert H.	Rep.	Grand Rapids.	Kent Co., 1st Dist.
Bledsoe, Harold E.	Dem.	Detroit.	Wayne Co., 11th Dist.
Bonisteel, Roscoe O., Sr.	Rep.	Ann Arbor.	33rd Senatorial Dist.
Boothby, Lee	Rep.	Niles	7th Senatorial Dist.
Bowens, Robert[1]	Dem.	Pontiac	Oakland Co., 2nd Dist.
Bradley, Russell W.[2]	Dem.	Menominee	30th Senatorial Dist.
Brake, D. Hale	Rep.	Stanton	25th Senatorial Dist.
Brown, Garry E.	Rep.	Schoolcraft.	6th Senatorial Dist.
Brown, Theodore S.	Dem.	Garden City.	Wayne Co., 20th Dist.
Buback, Peter L.	Dem.	Detroit.	Wayne Co., 3rd Dist.
Butler, Ruth G.	Rep.	Houghton	Houghton Dist.
Conklin, Anna M.	Rep.	Livonia	Wayne Co., 21st Dist.
Cudlip, William B.	Rep.	Grosse Pointe Shores	Wayne Co., 13th Dist.
Cushman, Katherine Moore	Dem.	Dearborn.	Wayne Co., 16th Dist.
Dade, Malcolm Gray	Dem.	Detroit.	Wayne Co., 4th Dist.
Danhof, Robert J.	Rep.	Muskegon	23rd Senatorial Dist.
Davis, Charles J.[3]	Rep.	Onondaga	Ingham Co., 2nd Dist.
Dehnke, Herman	Rep.	Harrisville	Alpena Dist.
Dell, Clarence B.	Rep.	St. Ignace	Chippewa Dist.
DeVries, Walter D.	Rep.	Grand Rapids.	Kent Co., 1st Dist.
Donnelly, Ann E.	Rep.	Highland Park	Wayne Co., 15th Dist.
Doty, Dean.	Rep.	Grand Ledge	Eaton Dist.
Doty, Donald D.	Rep.	Monroe	Monroe Co.
Douglas, Edward L.	Dem.	Detroit.	Wayne Co., 8th Dist.
Downs, Tom.	Dem.	Detroit.	Wayne Co., 4th Dist.
Durst, Clyne W., Jr.	Rep.	Adrian.	Lenawee Co.
Elliott, Arthur G., Jr.	Rep.	Pleasant Ridge	Oakland Co., 5th Dist.
Elliott, Daisy L.	Dem.	Detroit.	Wayne Co., 4th Dist.
Erickson, Claud R.	Rep.	Lansing.	Ingham Co., 1st Dist.
Everett, Stanley.	Rep.	Battle Creek.	Calhoun Co., 2nd Dist.
Farnsworth, James S.	Rep.	Allegan	Allegan Co.
Faxon, Jack	Dem.	Detroit.	5th Senatorial Dist.
Figy, Charles.	Rep.	Morenci.	19th Senatorial Dist.
Finch, Francis	Rep.	Mattawan.	Van Buren Co.
Follo, Charles L.	Dem.	Escanaba.	Delta Co.
Ford, William D.	Dem.	Taylor.	Wayne Co., 19th Dist.
Gadola, Paul V., Sr.	Rep.	Flint	13th Senatorial Dist.
Garvin, Wynne C.	Dem.	Detroit.	Wayne Co., 3rd Dist.
Goebel, Paul G.	Rep.	Grand Rapids.	16th Senatorial Dist.
Gover, William G.	Rep.	Sheridan	Montcalm Dist.
Greene, William O.	Dem.	Detroit.	3rd Senatorial Dist.
Gust, Rockwell T., Jr.	Rep.	Grosse Pointe Farms	1st Senatorial Dist.
Habermehl, Donald M.	Rep.	Alpena	29th Senatorial Dist.
Hanna, William F.	Rep.	Muskegon	Muskegon Co., 2nd Dist.
Hannah, John A.	Rep.	East Lansing.	14th Senatorial Dist.
Hart, Adelaide J.	Dem.	Detroit.	Wayne Co., 10th Dist.
Haskill, Ervin J.	Rep.	Lapeer.	Lapeer Co.
Hatch, H. V.	Rep.	Marshall.	Calhoun Co., 1st Dist.

Delegate	Politics	Post Office	District
Hatcher, Lillian	Dem.	Detroit	4th Senatorial Dist.
Heideman, Bert M.	Rep.	Hancock	32nd Senatorial Dist.
Higgs, Milton E.	Rep.	Bay City	Bay Co.
Hodges, Robert G.	Dem.	Detroit	Wayne Co., 1st Dist.
Hood, Morris W., Sr.	Dem.	Detroit	Wayne Co., 2nd Dist.
Howes, Roy	Rep.	Copemish	Wexford Dist.
Hoxie, T. Jefferson	Rep.	St. Louis	Gratiot Co.
Hubbs, Lewis T.	Rep.	Gladwin	28th Senatorial Dist.
Hutchinson, Edward	Rep.	Fennville	8th Senatorial Dist.
Iverson, Arthur T.	Rep.	Detroit	Wayne Co., 10th Dist.
Jones, Howard L.[4]	Dem.	Webberville	Ingham Co., 2nd Dist.
Judd, Dorothy Leonard	Rep.	Grand Rapids	Kent Co., 3rd Dist.
Karn, Dan E.	Rep.	Jackson	Jackson Co., 1st Dist.
Kelsey, John T.	Dem.	Warren	Macomb Co., 1st Dist.
King, Raymond L.[5]	Rep.	Pontiac	Oakland Co., 2nd Dist.
Kirk, Shuford	Rep.	Caro	Tuscola Co.
Knirk, Blaque	Rep.	Quincy	9th Senatorial Dist.
Koeze, Ella D.	Rep.	Grand Rapids	Kent Co., 2nd Dist.
Krolikowski, Ray	Dem.	Hamtramck	Wayne Co., 14th Dist.
Kuhn, Richard D.	Rep.	Pontiac	Oakland Co., 1st Dist.
Lawrence, J. Don	Rep.	Ypsilanti	Washtenaw Co., 2nd Dist.
Leibrand, Karl K.	Rep.	Bay City	24th Senatorial Dist.
Leppien, William J.	Rep.	Saginaw	22nd Senatorial Dist.
Lesinski, Edmond	Dem.	Detroit	Wayne Co., 5th Dist.
Liberato, Ralph A.	Dem.	Warren	11th Senatorial Dist.
Lundgren, Kent T.[6]	Rep.	Menominee	30th Senatorial Dist.
Madar, Arthur J.	Dem.	Detroit	Wayne Co., 1st Dist.
Mahinske, Paul R.	Dem.	Detroit	Wayne Co., 7th Dist.
Marshall, William C.	Dem.	Taylor	21st Senatorial Dist.
Martin, John B., Jr.	Rep.	Grand Rapids	17th Senatorial Dist.
McAllister, Thomas R.	Rep.	Bad Axe	Huron Co.
McCauley, John E.	Dem.	Wyandotte	Wayne Co., 18th Dist.
McGowan, Marjorie	Dem.	Detroit	Wayne Co., 5th Dist.
McLogan, Edward A.	Rep.	Flint	Genesee Co., 1st Dist.
Millard, Frank G.	Rep.	Flint	Genesee Co., 1st Dist.
Mosier, Carl D.	Rep.	Dowagiac	St. Joseph Dist.
Murphy, Raymond M.	Dem.	Detroit	Wayne Co., 11th Dist.
Nisbet, Stephen S.	Rep.	Fremont	26th Senatorial Dist.
Nord, Melvin	Dem.	Detroit	Wayne Co., 6th Dist.
Norris, Harold	Dem.	Detroit	Wayne Co., 6th Dist.
Ostrow, Samuel B.	Dem.	Detroit	Wayne Co., 2nd Dist.
Page, G. Keyes	Dem.	Flint	Genesee Co., 1st Dist.
Pellow, William P.	Dem.	Bessemer	31st Senatorial Dist.
Perlich, Frank T.	Dem.	Bessemer	Gogebic Dist.
Perras, Clifford E.	Rep.	Nadeau	Menominee Dist.
Plank, Raymond A.	Rep.	Ludington	Mason Dist.
Pollock, James K.	Rep.	Ann Arbor	Washtenaw Co., 1st Dist.
Powell, Stanley M.	Rep.	Ionia	Ionia Co.
Prettie, Kenneth G.	Rep.	Hillsdale	Hillsdale Dist.
Pugsley, Earl C.	Rep.	Hart	Newaygo Dist.
Radka, Elmer L.	Rep.	Rogers City	Presque Isle Dist.
Rajkovich, Nick J.	Rep.	Traverse City	Grand Traverse Dist.
Richards, J. Burton	Rep.	Eau Claire	Berrien Co., 2nd Dist.
Richards, Leslie W.	Rep.	Negaunee	Marquette Co.
Romney, George	Rep.	Bloomfield Hills	12th Senatorial Dist.
Rood, James R.	Rep.	Midland	Midland Co.
Rush, Allen F.	Rep.	Lake Orion	Macomb Co., 3rd Dist.
Sablich, Joseph F.	Dem.	Caspian	Iron Dist.
Seyferth, Don F.	Rep.	Muskegon	Muskegon Co., 1st Dist.
Shackleton, James M.	Rep.	Saginaw	Saginaw Co., 1st Dist.
Shaffer, John C.	Rep.	Gladwin	Arenac Dist.
Shanahan, Edward K.	Rep.	Charlevoix	Charlevoix Dist.
Sharpe, Thomas G.	Rep.	Howell	Shiawassee Dist.
Sleder, Julius C.	Rep.	Traverse City	27th Senatorial Dist.
Snyder, Joseph M.	Dem.	St. Clair Shores	Macomb Co., 2nd Dist.
Spitler, H. Carl	Rep.	Petoskey	Emmet Dist.
Stafseth, Henrik E.	Rep.	Grand Haven	Ottawa Co.
Staiger, Frank O., Jr.	Rep.	Port Huron	34th Senatorial Dist.
Stamm, Anthony	Rep.	Kalamazoo	Kalamazoo Co., 2nd Dist.

Delegate	Politics	Post Office	District
Sterrett, James H.	Rep.	Detroit	Wayne Co., 12th Dist.
Stevens, J. Harold	Rep.	Detroit	Wayne Co., 12th Dist.
Stopczynski, Stephen	Dem.	Detroit	Wayne Co., 7th Dist.
Suzore, William G.	Dem.	Lincoln Park	Wayne Co., 17th Dist.
Thomson, James F.	Rep.	Jackson	Jackson Co., 2nd Dist.
Tubbs, Robert S.	Rep.	Grand Rapids	Kent Co., 1st Dist.
Turner, Herbert M.	Rep.	Saginaw	Saginaw Co., 2nd Dist.
Tweedie, S. Martin, III.	Rep.	Port Huron	St. Clair Dist.
Upton, David F.	Rep.	St. Joseph	Berrien Co., 1st Dist.
VanDusen, Richard C.	Rep.	Birmingham	Oakland Co., 4th Dist.
Walker, Lee.	Dem.	Madison Heights	Oakland Co., 6th Dist.
Wanger, Eugene G.	Rep.	Lansing	Ingham Co., 1st Dist.
White, Ink	Rep.	St. Johns	Eaton Dist.
Wilkowski, Anthony J.	Dem.	Detroit	Wayne Co., 9th Dist.
Wood, Claude L.	Rep.	Brown City	20th Senatorial Dist.
Woolfenden, Henry L.	Rep.	Bloomfield Hills	Oakland Co., 3rd Dist.
Yeager, Weldon O.	Rep.	Detroit	18th Senatorial Dist.
Young, Coleman Alexander.	Dem.	Detroit	Wayne Co., 9th Dist.
Youngblood, Charles N., Jr.	Dem.	Detroit	Wayne Co., 3rd Dist.

NOTE: Under the provisions of Constitution of 1908, art. XVII, sec. 4, the call for a constitutional convention was submitted to a vote at the general election held November 4, 1958. The proposal was defeated, as it did not earn a majority of the total vote cast.

On November 8, 1960, voters approved an initiative proposal to amend Constitution of 1908, art. XVII, sec. 4, to permit the submission of the question of a general revision of the constitution at the spring election of 1961 and in every sixteenth year thereafter. At the election held on April 3, 1961, voters approved a constitutional convention to revise the Constitution of 1908.

One hundred forty-four delegates were elected under the provisions of Public Act 125 of 1960, as amended by Public Act 8 of 1961 and Public Act 230 of 1961. The delegates represented each of the 110 house of representatives districts and the 32 senate districts. The members convened in Lansing on October 3, 1961, and adopted the proposed constitution on August 1, 1962, by a vote of 98-43. Ninety-three Republicans and five Democrats voted for adoption, and 40 Democrats, joined by three Republicans, voted against the revision. Voters adopted the constitution on April 1, 1963, by a vote of 810,860 for to 803,436 against.

[1] Appointed July 11, 1962, to replace Raymond L. King.
[2] Appointed April 11, 1962, to replace Kent T. Lundgren.
[3] Resigned March 16, 1962.
[4] Appointed March 20, 1962, to replace Charles J. Davis.
[5] Resigned May 17, 1962.
[6] Resigned March 31, 1962.

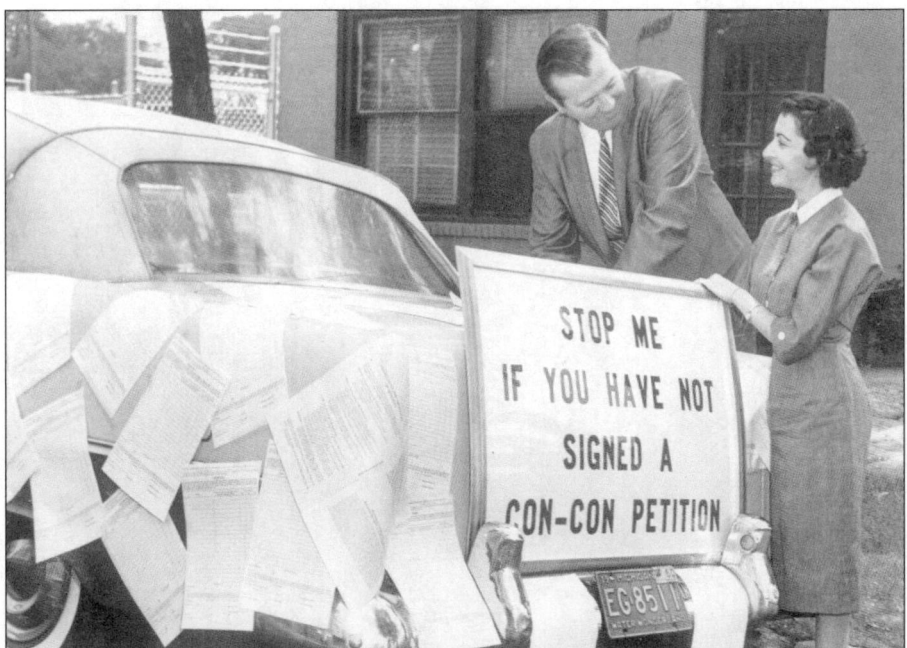

League of Women Voters, 1960.

CONSTITUTION
OF THE
STATE OF MICHIGAN
OF 1963

CONSTITUTION OF
THE STATE OF MICHIGAN OF 1963

TABLE OF CONTENTS

CONSTITUTION OF THE STATE OF MICHIGAN OF 1963
TABLE OF CONTENTS

ARTICLE V
EXECUTIVE BRANCH

CONSTITUTION OF THE STATE OF MICHIGAN OF 1963
TABLE OF CONTENTS

CONSTITUTION OF THE STATE OF MICHIGAN OF 1963
TABLE OF CONTENTS

CONSTITUTION OF THE STATE OF MICHIGAN OF 1963
TABLE OF CONTENTS

CONSTITUTION OF THE STATE OF MICHIGAN OF 1963
TABLE OF CONTENTS

CONSTITUTION OF
THE STATE OF MICHIGAN OF 1963

PREAMBLE

We, the people of the State of Michigan, grateful to Almighty God for the blessings of freedom, and earnestly desiring to secure these blessings undiminished to ourselves and our posterity, do ordain and establish this constitution.

ARTICLE I
DECLARATION OF RIGHTS

Political power.

Sec. 1. All political power is inherent in the people. Government is instituted for their equal benefit, security and protection.

History: Const. 1963, Art. I, §1, Eff. Jan. 1, 1964.
Former constitution: See Const. 1908, Art. II, §1.

Equal protection; discrimination.

Sec. 2. No person shall be denied the equal protection of the laws; nor shall any person be denied the enjoyment of his civil or political rights or be discriminated against in the exercise thereof because of religion, race, color or national origin. The legislature shall implement this section by appropriate legislation.

History: Const. 1963, Art. I, §2, Eff. Jan. 1, 1964.

Assembly, consultation, instruction, petition.

Sec. 3. The people have the right peaceably to assemble, to consult for the common good, to instruct their representatives and to petition the government for redress of grievances.

History: Const. 1963, Art. I, §3, Eff. Jan. 1, 1964.
Former constitution: See Const. 1908, Art. II, §2.

Freedom of worship and religious belief; appropriations.

Sec. 4. Every person shall be at liberty to worship God according to the dictates of his own conscience. No person shall be compelled to attend, or, against his consent, to contribute to the erection or support of any place of religious worship, or to pay tithes, taxes or other rates for the support of any minister of the gospel or teacher of religion. No money shall be appropriated or drawn from the treasury for the benefit of any religious sect or society, theological or religious seminary; nor shall property belonging to the state be appropriated for any such purpose. The civil and political rights, privileges and capacities of no person shall be diminished or enlarged on account of his religious belief.

History: Const. 1963, Art. I, §4, Eff. Jan. 1, 1964.
Former constitution: See Const. 1908, Art. II, §3.

Freedom of speech and of press.

Sec. 5. Every person may freely speak, write, express and publish his views on all subjects, being responsible for the abuse of such right; and no law shall be enacted to restrain or abridge the liberty of speech or of the press.

History: Const. 1963, Art. I, §5, Eff. Jan. 1, 1964.
Former constitution: See Const. 1908, Art. II, §4.

Bearing of arms.

Sec. 6. Every person has a right to keep and bear arms for the defense of himself and the state.

History: Const. 1963, Art. I, §6, Eff. Jan. 1, 1964.
Former constitution: See Const. 1908, Art. II, §5.

Military power subordinate to civil power.

Sec. 7. The military shall in all cases and at all times be in strict subordination to the civil power.

History: Const. 1963, Art. I, §7, Eff. Jan. 1, 1964.
Former constitution: See Const. 1908, Art. II, §6.

Quartering of soldiers.

Sec. 8. No soldier shall, in time of peace, be quartered in any house without the consent of the owner or occupant, nor in time of war, except in a manner prescribed by law.

History: Const. 1963, Art. I, §8, Eff. Jan. 1, 1964.
Former constitution: See Const. 1908, Art. II, §7.

Slavery and involuntary servitude.

Sec. 9. Neither slavery, nor involuntary servitude unless for the punishment of crime, shall ever be tolerated in this state.

History: Const. 1963, Art. I, §9, Eff. Jan. 1, 1964.
Former constitution: See Const. 1908, Art. II, §8.

Attainder; ex post facto laws; impairment of contracts.

Sec. 10. No bill of attainder, ex post facto law or law impairing the obligation of contract shall be enacted.

History: Const. 1963, Art. I, §10, Eff. Jan. 1, 1964.
Former constitution: See Const. 1908, Art. II, §9.

Searches and seizures.

Sec. 11. The person, houses, papers and possessions of every person shall be secure from unreasonable searches and seizures. No warrant to search any place or to seize any person or things shall issue without describing them, nor without probable cause, supported by oath or affirmation. The provisions of this section shall not be construed to bar from evidence in any criminal proceeding any narcotic drug, firearm, bomb, explosive or any other dangerous weapon, seized by a peace officer outside the curtilage of any dwelling house in this state.

History: Const. 1963, Art. I, §11, Eff. Jan. 1, 1964.
Constitutionality: The last sentence of this section was held invalid as in conflict with U.S. Const., Amend. IV. Lucas v. People, 420 F.2d 259 (C.A. Mich. 1970); Caver v. Kropp, 306 F.Supp. 1329 (D.C. Mich. 1969); People v. Pennington, 383 Mich. 611, 178 N.W. 2d 460 (1970); People v. Andrews, 21 Mich. App. 731, 176 N.W. 2d 460 (1970).
Former constitution: See Const. 1908, Art. II, §10.

Habeas corpus.

Sec. 12. The privilege of the writ of habeas corpus shall not be suspended unless in case of rebellion or invasion the public safety may require it.

History: Const. 1963, Art. I, §12, Eff. Jan. 1, 1964.
Former constitution: See Const. 1908, Art. II, §11.

Conduct of suits in person or by counsel.

Sec. 13. A suitor in any court of this state has the right to prosecute or defend his suit, either in his own proper person or by an attorney.

History: Const. 1963, Art. I, §13, Eff. Jan. 1, 1964.
Former constitution: See Const. 1908, Art. II, §12.

Jury trials.

Sec. 14. The right of trial by jury shall remain, but shall be waived in all civil cases unless demanded by one of the parties in the manner prescribed by law. In all civil cases tried by 12 jurors a verdict shall be received when 10 jurors agree.

History: Const. 1963, Art. I, §14, Eff. Jan. 1, 1964.
Former constitution: See Const. 1908, Art. II, §13.

Double jeopardy; bailable offenses; commencement of trial if bail denied; bail hearing; effective date.

Sec. 15. No person shall be subject for the same offense to be twice put in jeopardy. All persons shall, before conviction, be bailable by sufficient sureties, except that bail may be denied for the following persons when the proof is evident or the presumption great:

(a) A person who, within the 15 years immediately preceding a motion for bail pending the disposition of an indictment for a violent felony or of an arraignment on a warrant charging a violent felony, has been convicted of 2 or more violent felonies under the laws of this state or under substantially similar laws of the United States or another state, or a combination thereof, only if the prior felony convictions arose out of at least 2 separate incidents, events, or transactions.

(b) A person who is indicted for, or arraigned on a warrant charging, murder or treason.

(c) A person who is indicted for, or arraigned on a warrant charging, criminal sexual conduct in the first degree, armed robbery, or kidnapping with intent to extort money or other valuable thing thereby, unless the court finds by clear and convincing evidence that the defendant is not likely to flee or present a danger to any other person.

(d) A person who is indicted for, or arraigned on a warrant charging, a violent felony which is alleged to have been committed while the person was on bail, pending the disposition of a prior violent felony charge or while the person was on probation or parole as a result of a prior conviction for a violent felony.

If a person is denied admission to bail under this section, the trial of the person shall be commenced not more than 90 days after the date on which admission to bail is denied. If the trial is not commenced within 90 days after the date on which admission to bail is denied and the delay is not attributable to the defense, the court shall immediately schedule a bail hearing and shall set the amount of bail for the person.

As used in this section, "violent felony" means a felony, an element of which involves a violent act or threat of a violent act against any other person.

This section, as amended, shall not take effect until May 1, 1979.

History: Const. 1963, Art. I, §15, Eff. Jan. 1, 1964;—Am. H.J.R. Q, approved Nov. 7, 1978, Eff. May 1, 1979.

Effective date: The language certified by the Board of Canvassers was identical to House Joint Resolution Q of 1978, except for the deletion of the last sentence which contained the proposed May 1, 1979, effective date.

The May 1, 1979, effective date provision of House Joint Resolution Q was not stated in the text of ballot Proposal K or in any of the material circulated by the Secretary of State, and was neither considered nor voted upon by the electors in the November 7, 1978, general election.

Therefore, the effective date of Proposal K is December 23, 1978, which was the date 45 days after the election as provided by Const. 1963, Art. XII, §1. Op. Atty. Gen., No. 5533 (1979).

Former constitution: See Const. 1908, Art. II, §14.

Bail; fines; punishments; detention of witnesses.

Sec. 16. Excessive bail shall not be required; excessive fines shall not be imposed; cruel or unusual punishment shall not be inflicted; nor shall witnesses be unreasonably detained.

History: Const. 1963, Art. I, §16, Eff. Jan. 1, 1964.
Former constitution: See Const. 1908, Art. II, §15.

Self-incrimination; due process of law; fair treatment at investigations.

Sec. 17. No person shall be compelled in any criminal case to be a witness against himself, nor be deprived of life, liberty or property, without due process of law. The right of all individuals, firms, corporations and voluntary associations to fair and just treatment in the course of legislative and executive investigations and hearings shall not be infringed.

History: Const. 1963, Art. I, §17, Eff. Jan. 1, 1964.
Former constitution: See Const. 1908, Art. II, §16.

Witnesses; competency, religious beliefs.

Sec. 18. No person shall be rendered incompetent to be a witness on account of his opinions on matters of religious belief.

History: Const. 1963, Art. I, §18, Eff. Jan. 1, 1964.
Former constitution: See Const. 1908, Art. II, §17.

Libels, truth as defense.

Sec. 19. In all prosecutions for libels the truth may be given in evidence to the jury; and, if it appears to the jury that the matter charged as libelous is true and was published with good motives and for justifiable ends, the accused shall be acquitted.

History: Const. 1963, Art. I, §19, Eff. Jan 1. 1964.
Former constitution: See Const. 1908, Art. II, §18.

Rights of accused in criminal prosecutions.

Sec. 20. In every criminal prosecution, the accused shall have the right to a speedy and public trial by an impartial jury, which may consist of less than 12 jurors in prosecutions for misdemeanors punishable by imprisonment for not more than 1 year; to be informed of the nature of the accusation; to be confronted with the witnesses against him or her; to have compulsory process for obtaining witnesses in his or her favor; to have the assistance of counsel for his or her defense; to have an appeal as a matter of right, except as provided by law an appeal by an accused who pleads guilty or nolo contendere shall be by leave of the court; and as provided by law, when the trial court so orders, to have such reasonable assistance as may be necessary to perfect and prosecute an appeal.

History: Const. 1963, Art. I, §20, Eff. Jan. 1, 1964;—Am. H.J.R. M, approved Aug. 8, 1972, Eff. Sept. 23, 1972;—Am. S.J.R. D, approved Nov. 8, 1994, Eff. Dec. 24, 1994.

Former constitution: See Const. 1908, Art. II, §19.

Imprisonment for debt.

Sec. 21. No person shall be imprisoned for debt arising out of or founded on contract, express or implied, except in cases of fraud or breach of trust.

History: Const. 1963, Art. I, §21, Eff. Jan. 1, 1964.
Former constitution: See Const. 1908, Art. II, §20.

Treason; definition, evidence.

Sec. 22. Treason against the state shall consist only in levying war against it or in adhering to its enemies, giving them aid and comfort. No person shall be convicted of treason unless upon the testimony of two witnesses to the same overt act or on confession in open court.

History: Const. 1963, Art. I, §22, Eff. Jan. 1, 1964.
Former constitution: See Const. 1908, Art. II, §21.

Enumeration of rights not to deny others.

Sec. 23. The enumeration in this constitution of certain rights shall not be construed to deny or disparage others retained by the people.

History: Const. 1963, Art. I, §23, Eff. Jan. 1, 1964.

Rights of crime victims; enforcement; assessment against convicted defendants.

Sec. 24. (1) Crime victims, as defined by law, shall have the following rights, as provided by law:

The right to be treated with fairness and respect for their dignity and privacy throughout the criminal justice process.

The right to timely disposition of the case following arrest of the accused.

The right to be reasonably protected from the accused throughout the criminal justice process.

The right to notification of court proceedings.

The right to attend trial and all other court proceedings the accused has the right to attend.

The right to confer with the prosecution.

The right to make a statement to the court at sentencing.

The right to restitution.

The right to information about the conviction, sentence, imprisonment, and release of the accused.

(2) The legislature may provide by law for the enforcement of this section.

(3) The legislature may provide for an assessment against convicted defendants to pay for crime victims' rights.

History: Add. H.J.R. P, approved Nov. 8, 1988, Eff. Dec. 24, 1988.

Marriage.

Sec. 25. To secure and preserve the benefits of marriage for our society and for future generations of children, the union of one man and one woman in marriage shall be the only agreement recognized as a marriage or similar union for any purpose.

History: Add. Init., approved Nov. 2, 2004, Eff. Dec. 18, 2004.
Constitutionality: In Obergefell v Hodges, 576 U.S. __(2015), the United States Supreme Court held that the Fourteenth Amendment requires a state to license a marriage between two people of the same sex and to recognize a marriage between two people of the same sex when their marriage was lawfully licensed and performed out-of-state.

Affirmative action programs.

Sec. 26. (1) The University of Michigan, Michigan State University, Wayne State University, and any other public college or university, community college, or school district shall not discriminate against, or grant preferential treatment to, any individual or group on the basis of race, sex, color, ethnicity, or national origin in the operation of public employment, public education, or public contracting.

(2) The state shall not discriminate against, or grant preferential treatment to, any individual or group on the basis of race, sex, color, ethnicity, or national origin in the operation of public employment, public education, or public contracting.

(3) For the purposes of this section "state" includes, but is not necessarily limited to, the state itself, any city, county, any public college, university, or community college, school district, or other political subdivision or governmental instrumentality of or within the State of Michigan not included in subsection 1.

(4) This section does not prohibit action that must be taken to establish or maintain eligibility for any federal program, if ineligibility would result in a loss of federal funds to the state.

(5) Nothing in this section shall be interpreted as prohibiting bona fide qualifications based on sex that are reasonably necessary to the normal operation of public employment, public education, or public contracting.

(6) The remedies available for violations of this section shall be the same, regardless of the injured party's race, sex, color, ethnicity, or national origin, as are otherwise available for violations of Michigan anti-discrimination law.

(7) This section shall be self-executing. If any part or parts of this section are found to be in conflict with the United States Constitution or federal law, the section shall be implemented to the maximum extent that the United States Constitution and federal law permit. Any provision held invalid shall be severable from the remaining portions of this section.

(8) This section applies only to action taken after the effective date of this section.

(9) This section does not invalidate any court order or consent decree that is in force as of the effective date of this section.

History: Add. Init., approved Nov. 7, 2006, Eff. Dec. 23, 2006.

Human embryo and embryonic stem cell research.

Sec. 27. (1) Nothing in this section shall alter Michigan's current prohibition on human cloning.

(2) To ensure that Michigan citizens have access to stem cell therapies and cures, and to ensure that physicians and researchers can conduct the most promising forms of medical research in this state, and that all such research is conducted safely and ethically, any research permitted under federal law on human embryos may be conducted in Michigan, subject to the requirements of federal law and only the following additional limitations and requirements:

(a) No stem cells may be taken from a human embryo more than fourteen days after cell division begins; provided, however, that time during which an embryo is frozen does not count against this fourteen day limit.

(b) The human embryos were created for the purpose of fertility treatment and, with voluntary and informed consent, documented in writing, the person seeking fertility treatment chose to donate the embryos for research; and

(i) the embryos were in excess of the clinical need of the person seeking the fertility treatment and would otherwise be discarded unless they are used for research; or

(ii) the embryos were not suitable for implantation and would otherwise be discarded unless they are used for research.

(c) No person may, for valuable consideration, purchase or sell human embryos for stem cell research or stem cell therapies and cures.

(d) All stem cell research and all stem cell therapies and cures must be conducted and provided in accordance with state and local laws of general applicability, including but not limited to laws concerning scientific and medical practices and patient safety and privacy, to the extent that any such laws do not:

(i) prevent, restrict, obstruct, or discourage any stem cell research or stem cell therapies and cures that are permitted by the provisions of this section; or

(ii) create disincentives for any person to engage in or otherwise associate with such research or therapies or cures.

(3) Any provision of this section held unconstitutional shall be severable from the remaining portions of this section.

History: Add. Init., approved Nov. 4, 2008, Eff. Dec. 19, 2008.

ARTICLE II
ELECTIONS

Qualifications of electors; residence.

Sec. 1. Every citizen of the United States who has attained the age of 21 years, who has resided in this state six months, and who meets the requirements of local residence provided by law, shall be an elector and qualified to vote in any election except as otherwise provided in this constitution. The legislature shall define residence for voting purposes.

History: Const. 1963, Art. II, §1, Eff. Jan. 1, 1964.
Compiler's note: U.S. Const., Amendment XXVI, §1, provides: "The right of citizens of the United States, who are eighteen years of age or older, to vote shall not be denied or abridged by the United States or by any State on account of age."
Former constitution: See Const. 1908, Art. III, §§1-3.

Mental incompetence; imprisonment.

Sec. 2. The legislature may by law exclude persons from voting because of mental incompetence or commitment to a jail or penal institution.

History: Const. 1963, Art. II, §2, Eff. Jan. 1, 1964.

Presidential electors; residence.

Sec. 3. For purposes of voting in the election for president and vice-president of the United States only, the legislature may by law establish lesser residence requirements for citizens who have resided in this state for less than six months and may waive residence requirements for former citizens of this state who have removed herefrom. The legislature shall not permit voting by any person who meets the voting residence requirements of the state to which he has removed.

History: Const. 1963, Art. II, §3, Eff. Jan. 1, 1964.

Place and manner of elections.

Sec. 4. (1) Every citizen of the United States who is an elector qualified to vote in Michigan shall have the following rights:

(a) The right, once registered, to vote a secret ballot in all elections.

(b) The right, if serving in the military or living overseas, to have an absent voter ballot sent to them at least forty-five (45) days before an election upon application.

(c) The right, once registered, to a "straight party" vote option on partisan general election ballots. In partisan elections, the ballot shall include a position at the top of the ballot by which the voter may, by a single selection, record a straight party ticket vote for all the candidates of one (1) party. The voter may vote a split or mixed ticket.

(d) The right to be automatically registered to vote as a result of conducting business with the secretary of state regarding a driver's license or personal identification card, unless the person declines such registration.

(e) The right to register to vote for an election by mailing a completed voter registration application on or before the fifteenth (15th) day before that election to an election official authorized to receive voter registration applications.

(f) The right to register to vote for an election by (1) appearing in person and submitting a completed voter registration application registration application on or before the fifteenth (15th) day before that election to an election official authorized to receive voter registration applications, or (2) beginning on the fourteenth (14th) day before that election and continuing through the day of that election, appearing in person, submitting a completed voter registration application and providing proof of residency to an election official responsible for maintaining custody of the registration file where the person resides, or their deputies. Persons registered in accordance with subsection (1)(f) shall be immediately eligible to receive a regular or absent voter ballot.

(g) The right, once registered, to vote an absent voter ballot without giving a reason, during the forty (40) days before an election, and the right to choose whether the absent voter ballot is applied for, received and submitted in person or by mail. During that time, election officials authorized to issue absent voter ballots shall be available in at least one (1) location to issue and receive absent voter ballots during the election officials' regularly scheduled business hours and for at least eight (8) hours during the Saturday and/or Sunday immediately prior to the election. Those election officials shall have the authority to make absent voter ballots available for voting in person at additional times and places beyond what is required herein.

(h) The right to have the results of statewide elections audited, in such a manner as prescribed by law, to ensure the accuracy and integrity of elections.

All rights set forth in this subsection shall be self-executing. This subsection shall be liberally construed in favor of voters' rights in order to effectuate its purposes. Nothing contained in this subsection shall prevent the legislature from expanding voters' rights beyond what is provided herein. This subsection and any portion hereof shall be severable. If any portion of this subsection is held invalid or unenforceable as to any person or circumstance, that invalidity or unenforceability shall not affect the validity, enforceability, or application of any other portion of this subsection.

(2) Except as otherwise provided in this constitution or in the constitution or laws of the United States the legislature shall enact laws to regulate the time, place and manner of all nominations and elections, to preserve the purity of elections, to preserve the secrecy of the ballot, to guard against abuses of the elective franchise, and to provide for a system of voter registration and absentee voting. No law shall be enacted which permits a candidate in any partisan primary or partisan election to have a ballot designation except when required for identification of candidates for the same office who have the same or similar surnames.

History: Const. 1963, Art. II, §4, Eff. Jan. 1, 1964;—Am. Init., approved Nov. 6, 2018, Eff. Dec. 22, 2018.
Former constitution: See Const. 1908, Art. III, §§1, 8.

Time of elections.

Sec. 5. Except for special elections to fill vacancies, or as otherwise provided in this constitution, all elections for national, state, county and township offices shall be held on the first Tuesday after the first Monday in November in each even-numbered year or on such other date as members of the congress of the United States are regularly elected.

History: Const. 1963, Art. II, §5, Eff. Jan. 1, 1964.

Voters on tax limit increases or bond issues.

Sec. 6. Whenever any question is required to be submitted by a political subdivision to the electors for the increase of the ad valorem tax rate limitation imposed by Section 6 of Article IX for a period of more than five years, or for the issue of bonds, only electors in, and who have property assessed for any ad valorem taxes in, any part of the district or territory to be affected by the result of such election or electors who are the lawful husbands or wives of such persons shall be entitled to vote thereon. All electors in the district or territory affected may vote on all other questions.

History: Const. 1963, Art. II, §6, Eff. Jan. 1, 1964.
Former constitution: See Const. 1908, Art. III, §4.

Boards of canvassers.

Sec. 7. A board of state canvassers of four members shall be established by law. No candidate for an office to be canvassed nor any inspector of elections shall be eligible to serve as a member of a board of canvassers. A majority of any board of canvassers shall not be composed of members of the same political party.

History: Const. 1963, Art. II, §7, Eff. Jan. 1, 1964.
Former constitution: See Const. 1908, Art. III, §9.
Transfer of powers: See §16.128.

Recalls.

Sec. 8. Laws shall be enacted to provide for the recall of all elective officers except judges of courts of record upon petition of electors equal in number to 25 percent of the number of persons voting in the last preceding election for the office of governor in the electoral district of the officer sought to be recalled. The sufficiency of any statement of reasons or grounds procedurally required shall be a political rather than a judicial question.

History: Const. 1963, Art. II, §8, Eff. Jan. 1, 1964.
Former constitution: See Const. 1908, Art. III, §8.

Initiative and referendum; limitations; appropriations; petitions.

Sec. 9. The people reserve to themselves the power to propose laws and to enact and reject laws, called the initiative, and the power to approve or reject laws enacted by the legislature, called the referendum. The power of initiative extends only to laws which the legislature may enact under this constitution. The power of referendum does not extend to acts making appropriations for state institutions or to meet deficiencies in state funds and must be invoked in the manner prescribed by law within 90 days following the final adjournment of the legislative session at which the law was enacted. To invoke the initiative or referendum, petitions signed by a number of registered electors, not less than eight percent for initiative and five percent for referendum of the total vote cast for all candidates for governor at the last preceding general election at which a governor was elected shall be required.

Referendum, approval.

No law as to which the power of referendum properly has been invoked shall be effective thereafter unless approved by a majority of the electors voting thereon at the next general election.

Initiative; duty of legislature, referendum.

Any law proposed by initiative petition shall be either enacted or rejected by the legislature without change or amendment within 40 session days from the time such petition is received by the legislature. If any law proposed by such petition shall be enacted by the legislature it shall be subject to referendum, as hereinafter provided.

Legislative rejection of initiated measure; different measure; submission to people.

If the law so proposed is not enacted by the legislature within the 40 days, the state officer authorized by law shall submit such proposed law to the people for approval or rejection at the next general election. The legislature may reject any measure so proposed by initiative petition and propose a different measure upon the same subject by a yea and nay vote upon separate roll calls, and in such event both measures shall be submitted by such state officer to the electors for approval or rejection at the next general election.

Initiative or referendum law; effective date, veto, amendment and repeal.

Any law submitted to the people by either initiative or referendum petition and approved by a majority of the votes cast thereon at any election shall take effect 10 days after the date of the official declaration of the vote. No law initiated or adopted by the people shall be subject to the veto power of the governor, and no law adopted by the people at the polls under the initiative provisions of this section shall be amended or repealed, except by a vote of the electors unless otherwise provided in the initiative measure or by three-fourths of the members elected to and serving in each house of the legislature. Laws approved by the people under the referendum provision of this section may be amended by the legislature at any subsequent session thereof. If two or more measures approved by the electors at the same election conflict, that receiving the highest affirmative vote shall prevail.

Legislative implementation.

The legislature shall implement the provisions of this section.

History: Const. 1963, Art. II, §9, Eff. Jan. 1, 1964.
Constitutionality: A law proposed by initiative petition which is enacted by the Legislature without change or amendment within forty days of its reception takes effect ninety days after the end of the session in which it was enacted unless two-thirds of the members of each house of the Legislature vote to give it immediate effect. Frey v. Department of Management and Budget, 429 Mich. 315, 414 N.W.2d 873 (1987).
Former constitution: See Const. 1908, Art. V, §1.

Limitations on terms of office of members of the United States House of Representatives and United States Senate from Michigan.

Sec. 10. No person shall be elected to office as representative in the United States House of Representatives more than three times during any twelve year period. No person shall be elected to office as senator in the United States Senate more than two times during any twenty-four year period. Any person appointed or elected to fill a vacancy in the United States House of Representatives or the United States Senate for a period greater than one half of a term of such office, shall be considered to have been elected to serve one time in that office for purposes of this section. This limitation on the number of times a person shall be elected to office shall apply to terms of office beginning on or after January 1, 1993.

The people of Michigan hereby state their support for the aforementioned term limits for members of the United States House of Representatives and United States Senate and instruct their public officials to use their best efforts to attain such a limit nationwide.

The people of Michigan declare that the provisions of this section shall be deemed severable from the remainder of this amendment and that their intention is that federal officials elected from Michigan will continue voluntarily to observe the wishes of the people as stated in this section, in the event any provision of this section is held invalid.

This section shall be self-executing. Legislation may be enacted to facilitate operation of this section, but no law shall limit or restrict the application of this section. If any part of this section is held to be invalid or unconstitutional, the remaining parts of this section shall not be affected but will remain in full force and effect.

History: Add. Init. approved Nov. 3, 1992, Eff. Dec. 19, 1992.

ARTICLE III
GENERAL GOVERNMENT

Seat of government.

Sec. 1. The seat of government shall be at Lansing.

History: Const. 1963, Art. III, §1, Eff. Jan. 1, 1964.
Former constitution: See Const. 1908, Art. I, §2.

Separation of powers of government.

Sec. 2. The powers of government are divided into three branches: legislative, executive and judicial. No person exercising powers of one branch shall exercise powers properly belonging to another branch except as expressly provided in this constitution.

History: Const. 1963, Art. III, §2, Eff. Jan. 1, 1964.
Former constitution: See Const. 1908, Art. IV, §2.

Great seal.

Sec. 3. There shall be a great seal of the State of Michigan and its use shall be provided by law.

History: Const. 1963, Art. III, §3, Eff. Jan. 1, 1964.
Former constitution: See Const. 1908, Art. VI, §§11, 12.

Militia.

Sec. 4. The militia shall be organized, equipped and disciplined as provided by law.

History: Const. 1963, Art. III, §4, Eff. Jan. 1, 1964.
Former constitution: See Const. 1908, Art. XV, §§1-3.

Intergovernmental agreements; service by public officers and employees.

Sec. 5. Subject to provisions of general law, this state or any political subdivision thereof, any governmental authority or any combination thereof may enter into agreements for the performance, financing or execution of their respective functions, with any one or more of the other states, the United States, the Dominion of Canada, or any political subdivision thereof unless otherwise provided in this constitution. Any other provision of this constitution notwithstanding, an officer or employee of the state or of any such unit of government or subdivision or agency thereof may serve on or with any governmental body established for the purposes set forth in this section and shall not be required to relinquish his office or employment by reason of such service. The legislature may impose such restrictions, limitations or conditions on such service as it may deem appropriate.

History: Const. 1963, Art. III, §5, Eff. Jan. 1, 1964.

Internal improvements.

Sec. 6. The state shall not be a party to, nor be financially interested in, any work of internal improvement, nor engage in carrying on any such work, except for public internal improvements provided by law.

History: Const. 1963, Art. III, §6, Eff. Jan. 1, 1964.
Former constitution: See Const. 1908, Art. X, §14.

Common law and statutes, continuance.

Sec. 7. The common law and the statute laws now in force, not repugnant to this constitution, shall remain in force until they expire by their own limitations, or are changed, amended or repealed.

History: Const. 1963, Art. III, §7, Eff. Jan. 1, 1964.
Former constitution: See Const. 1908, Schedule, §1.

Opinions on constitutionality by supreme court.

Sec. 8. Either house of the legislature or the governor may request the opinion of the supreme court on important questions of law upon solemn occasions as to the constitutionality of legislation after it has been enacted into law but before its effective date.

History: Const. 1963, Art. III, §8, Eff. Jan. 1, 1964.

ARTICLE IV
LEGISLATIVE BRANCH

Legislative power.

Sec. 1. Except to the extent limited or abrogated by article IV, section 6 or article V, section 2, the legislative power of the State of Michigan is vested in a senate and a house of representatives.

History: Const. 1963, Art. IV, §1, Eff. Jan. 1, 1964;—Am. Init., approved Nov. 6, 2018, Eff. Dec. 22, 2018.
Former constitution: See Const. 1908, Art. V, §1.

Senators, number, term.

Sec. 2. The senate shall consist of 38 members to be elected from single member districts at the same election as the governor for four-year terms concurrent with the term of office of the governor.

History: Const. 1963, Art. IV, §2, Eff. Jan. 1, 1964;—Am. Init., approved Nov. 6, 2018, Eff. Dec. 22, 2018.
Former constitution: See Const. 1908, Art. V, §2.

Representatives, number, term; contiguity of districts.

Sec. 3. The house of representatives shall consist of 110 members elected for two-year terms from single member districts apportioned on a basis of population as provided in this article.

History: Const. 1963, Art. IV, §3, Eff. Jan. 1, 1964;—Am. Init., approved Nov. 6, 2018, Eff. Dec. 22, 2018.
Former constitution: See Const. 1908, Art. V, §3.

Annexation or merger with a city.

History: Const. 1963, Art. IV, §4, Eff. Jan. 1, 1964. Abrogated. Init., approved Nov. 6, 2018, Eff. Dec. 22, 2018.

Island areas, contiguity.

History: Const. 1963, Art. IV, §5, Eff. Jan. 1, 1964. Abrogated. Init., approved Nov. 6, 2018, Eff. Dec. 22, 2018.

Independent citizens redistricting commission for state legislative and congressional districts.

Sec. 6. (1) An independent citizens redistricting commission for state legislative and congressional districts (hereinafter, the "commission") is hereby established as a permanent commission in the legislative branch. The commission shall consist of 13 commissioners. The commission shall adopt a redistricting plan for each of the following types of districts: state senate districts, state house of representative districts, and congressional districts. Each commissioner shall:

(a) Be registered and eligible to vote in the State of Michigan;

(b) Not currently be or in the past 6 years have been any of the following:

(i) A declared candidate for partisan federal, state, or local office;

(ii) An elected official to partisan federal, state, or local office;

(iii) An officer or member of the governing body of a national, state, or local political party;

(iv) A paid consultant or employee of a federal, state, or local elected official or political candidate, of a federal, state, or local political candidate's campaign, or of a political action committee;

(v) An employee of the legislature;

(vi) Any person who is registered as a lobbyist agent with the Michigan bureau of elections, or any employee of such person; or

(vii) An unclassified state employee who is exempt from classification in state civil service pursuant to article XI, section 5, except for employees of courts of record, employees of the state institutions of higher education, and persons in the armed forces of the state;

(c) Not be a parent, stepparent, child, stepchild, or spouse of any individual disqualified under part (1)(b) of this section; or

(d) Not be otherwise disqualified for appointed or elected office by this constitution.

(e) For five years after the date of appointment, a commissioner is ineligible to hold a partisan elective office at the state, county, city, village, or township level in Michigan.

(2) Commissioners shall be selected through the following process:

(a) The secretary of state shall do all of the following:

(i) Make applications for commissioner available to the general public not later than January 1 of the year of the federal decennial census. The secretary of state shall circulate the applications in a manner that invites wide public participation from different regions of the state. The secretary of state shall also mail applications for commissioner to ten thousand Michigan registered voters, selected at random, by January 1 of the year of the federal decennial census.

(ii) Require applicants to provide a completed application.

(iii) Require applicants to attest under oath that they meet the qualifications set forth in this section; and either that they affiliate with one of the two political parties with the largest representation in the legislature (hereinafter, "major parties"), and if so, identify the party with which they affiliate, or that they do not affiliate with either of the major parties.

(b) Subject to part (2)(c) of this section, the secretary of state shall mail additional applications for commissioner to Michigan registered voters selected at random until 30 qualifying applicants that affiliate with one of the two major parties have submitted applications, 30 qualifying applicants that identify that they affiliate with the other of the two major parties have submitted applications, and 40 qualifying applicants that identify that they do not affiliate with either of the two major parties have submitted applications, each in response to the mailings.

(c) The secretary of state shall accept applications for commissioner until June 1 of the year of the federal decennial census.

(d) By July 1 of the year of the federal decennial census, from all of the applications submitted, the secretary of state shall:

(i) Eliminate incomplete applications and applications of applicants who do not meet the qualifications in parts (1)(a) through (1)(d) of this section based solely on the information contained in the applications;

(ii) Randomly select 60 applicants from each pool of affiliating applicants and 80 applicants from the pool of non-affiliating applicants. 50% of each pool shall be populated from the qualifying applicants to such pool who returned an application mailed pursuant to part 2(a) or 2(b) of this section, provided, that if fewer than 30 qualifying applicants affiliated with a major party or fewer than 40 qualifying non-affiliating applicants have applied to serve on the commission in response to the random mailing, the balance of the pool shall be populated from the balance of qualifying applicants to that pool. The random selection process used by the secretary of state to fill the selection pools shall use accepted statistical weighting methods to ensure that the pools, as closely as possible, mirror the geographic and demographic makeup of the state; and

(iii) Submit the randomly-selected applications to the majority leader and the minority leader of the senate, and the speaker of the house of representatives and the minority leader of the house of representatives.

(e) By August 1 of the year of the federal decennial census, the majority leader of the senate, the minority leader of the senate, the speaker of the house of representatives, and the minority leader of the house of representatives may each strike five applicants from any pool or pools, up to a maximum of 20 total strikes by the four legislative leaders.

(f) By September 1 of the year of the federal decennial census, the secretary of state shall randomly draw the names of four commissioners from each of the two pools of remaining applicants affiliating with a major party, and five commissioners from the pool of remaining non-affiliating applicants.

(3) Except as provided below, commissioners shall hold office for the term set forth in part (18) of this section. If a commissioner's seat becomes vacant for any reason, the secretary of state shall fill the vacancy by randomly drawing a name from the remaining qualifying applicants in the selection pool from which the original commissioner was selected. A commissioner's office shall become vacant upon the occurrence of any of the following:

(a) Death or mental incapacity of the commissioner;

(b) The secretary of state's receipt of the commissioner's written resignation;

(c) The commissioner's disqualification for election or appointment or employment pursuant to article XI, section 8;

(d) The commissioner ceases to be qualified to serve as a commissioner under part (1) of this section; or

(e) After written notice and an opportunity for the commissioner to respond, a vote of 10 of the commissioners finding substantial neglect of duty, gross misconduct in office, or inability to discharge the duties of office.

(4) The secretary of state shall be secretary of the commission without vote, and in that capacity shall furnish, under the direction of the commission, all technical services that the commission deems necessary. The commission shall elect its own chairperson. The commission has the sole power to make its own rules of procedure. The commission shall have procurement and contracting authority and may hire staff and consultants for the purposes of this section, including legal representation.

(5) Beginning no later than December 1 of the year preceding the federal decennial census, and continuing each year in which the commission operates, the legislature shall appropriate funds sufficient to compensate the commissioners and to enable the commission to carry out its functions, operations and activities, which activities include retaining independent, nonpartisan subject-matter experts and legal counsel, conducting hearings, publishing notices and maintaining a record of the commission's proceedings, and any other activity necessary for the commission to conduct its business, at an amount equal to not less than 25 percent of the general fund/general purpose budget for the secretary of state for that fiscal year. Within six months after the conclusion of each fiscal year, the commission shall return to the state treasury all moneys unexpended for that fiscal year. The commission shall furnish reports of expenditures, at least annually, to the governor and the legislature and shall be subject to annual audit as provided by law. Each commissioner shall receive compensation at least equal to 25 percent of the governor's salary. The State of Michigan shall indemnify commissioners for costs incurred if the legislature does not appropriate sufficient funds to cover such costs.

(6) The commission shall have legal standing to prosecute an action regarding the adequacy of resources provided for the operation of the commission, and to defend any action regarding an adopted plan. The commission shall inform the legislature if the commission determines that funds or other resources provided for operation of the commission are not adequate. The legislature shall provide adequate funding to allow the commission to defend any action regarding an adopted plan.

(7) The secretary of state shall issue a call convening the commission by October 15 in the year of the federal decennial census. Not later than November 1 in the year immediately following the federal decennial census, the commission shall adopt a redistricting plan under this section for each of the following types of districts: state senate districts, state house of representative districts, and congressional districts.

(8) Before commissioners draft any plan, the commission shall hold at least ten public hearings throughout the state for the purpose of informing the public about the redistricting process and the purpose and responsibilities of the commission and soliciting information from the public about potential plans. The commission shall receive for consideration written submissions of proposed redistricting plans and any supporting materials, including underlying data, from any member of the public. These written submissions are public records.

(9) After developing at least one proposed redistricting plan for each type of district, the commission shall publish the proposed redistricting plans and any data and supporting materials used to develop the plans. Each commissioner may only propose one redistricting plan for each type of district. The commission shall hold at least five public hearings throughout the state for the purpose of soliciting comment from the public about the proposed plans. Each of the proposed plans shall include such census data as is necessary to accurately describe the plan and verify the population of each district, and a map and legal description that include the political subdivisions, such as counties, cities, and townships; man-made features, such as streets, roads, highways, and railroads; and natural features, such as waterways, which form the boundaries of the districts.

(10) Each commissioner shall perform his or her duties in a manner that is impartial and reinforces public confidence in the integrity of the redistricting process. The commission shall conduct all of its business at open meetings. Nine commissioners, including at least one commissioner from each selection pool shall constitute a quorum, and all meetings shall require a quorum. The commission shall provide advance public notice of its meetings and hearings. The commission shall conduct its hearings in a manner that invites wide public participation throughout the state. The commission shall use technology to provide contemporaneous public observation and meaningful public participation in the redistricting process during all meetings and hearings.

(11) The commission, its members, staff, attorneys, and consultants shall not discuss redistricting matters with members of the public outside of an open meeting of the commission, except that a commissioner may communicate about redistricting matters with members of the public to gain information relevant to the performance of his or her duties if such communication occurs (a) in writing or (b) at a previously publicly noticed forum or town hall open to the general public.

The commission, its members, staff, attorneys, experts, and consultants may not directly or indirectly solicit or accept any gift or loan of money, goods, services, or other thing of value greater than $20 for the benefit of any person or organization, which may influence the manner in which the commissioner, staff, attorney, expert, or consultant performs his or her duties.

(12) Except as provided in part (14) of this section, a final decision of the commission requires the concurrence of a majority of the commissioners. A decision on the dismissal or retention of paid staff or consultants requires the vote of at least one commissioner affiliating with each of the major parties and one non-affiliating commissioner. All decisions of the commission shall be recorded, and the record of its decisions shall be readily available to any member of the public without charge.

(13) The commission shall abide by the following criteria in proposing and adopting each plan, in order of priority:

(a) Districts shall be of equal population as mandated by the United States constitution, and shall comply with the voting rights act and other federal laws.

(b) Districts shall be geographically contiguous. Island areas are considered to be contiguous by land to the county of which they are a part.

(c) Districts shall reflect the state's diverse population and communities of interest. Communities of interest may include, but shall not be limited to, populations that share cultural or historical characteristics or economic interests. Communities of interest do not include relationships with political parties, incumbents, or political candidates.

(d) Districts shall not provide a disproportionate advantage to any political party. A disproportionate advantage to a political party shall be determined using accepted measures of partisan fairness.

(e) Districts shall not favor or disfavor an incumbent elected official or a candidate.

(f) Districts shall reflect consideration of county, city, and township boundaries.

(g) Districts shall be reasonably compact.

(14) The commission shall follow the following procedure in adopting a plan:

(a) Before voting to adopt a plan, the commission shall ensure that the plan is tested, using appropriate technology, for compliance with the criteria described above.

(b) Before voting to adopt a plan, the commission shall provide public notice of each plan that will be voted on and provide at least 45 days for public comment on the proposed plan or plans. Each plan that will be voted on shall include such census data as is necessary to accurately describe the plan and verify the population of each district, and shall include the map and legal description required in part (9) of this section.

(c) A final decision of the commission to adopt a redistricting plan requires a majority vote of the commission, including at least two commissioners who affiliate with each major party, and at least two commissioners who do not affiliate with either major party. If no plan satisfies this requirement for a type of district, the commission shall use the following procedure to adopt a plan for that type of district:

(i) Each commissioner may submit one proposed plan for each type of district to the full commission for consideration.

(ii) Each commissioner shall rank the plans submitted according to preference. Each plan shall be assigned a point value inverse to its ranking among the number of choices, giving the lowest ranked plan one point and the highest ranked plan a point value equal to the number of plans submitted.

(iii) The commission shall adopt the plan receiving the highest total points, that is also ranked among the top half of plans by at least two commissioners not affiliated with the party of the commissioner submitting the plan, or in the case of a plan submitted by non-affiliated commissioners, is ranked among the top half of plans by at least two commissioners affiliated with a major party. If plans are tied for the highest point total, the secretary of state shall randomly select the final plan from those plans. If no plan meets the requirements of this subparagraph, the secretary of state shall randomly select the final plan from among all submitted plans pursuant to part (14)(c)(i).

(15) Within 30 days after adopting a plan, the commission shall publish the plan and the material reports, reference materials, and data used in drawing it, including any programming information used to produce and test the plan. The published materials shall be such that an independent person is able to replicate the conclusion without any modification of any of the published materials.

(16) For each adopted plan, the commission shall issue a report that explains the basis on which the commission made its decisions in achieving compliance with plan requirements and shall include the map and legal description required in part (9) of this section. A commissioner who votes against a redistricting plan may submit a dissenting report which shall be issued with the commission's report.

(17) An adopted redistricting plan shall become law 60 days after its publication. The secretary of state shall keep a public record of all proceedings of the commission and shall publish and distribute each plan and required documentation.

(18) The terms of the commissioners shall expire once the commission has completed its obligations for a census cycle but not before any judicial review of the redistricting plan is complete.

(19) The supreme court, in the exercise of original jurisdiction, shall direct the secretary of state or the commission to perform their respective duties, may review a challenge to any plan adopted by the commission, and shall remand a plan to the commission for further action if the plan fails to comply with the requirements of this constitution, the constitution of the United States or superseding federal law. In no event shall any body, except the independent citizens redistricting commission acting pursuant to this section, promulgate and adopt a redistricting plan or plans for this state.

(20) This section is self-executing. If a final court decision holds any part or parts of this section to be in conflict with the United States constitution or federal law, the section shall be implemented to the maximum extent that the United States constitution and federal law permit. Any provision held invalid is severable from the remaining portions of this section.

(21) Notwithstanding any other provision of law, no employer shall discharge, threaten to discharge, intimidate, coerce, or retaliate against any employee because of the employee's membership on the commission or attendance or scheduled attendance at any meeting of the commission.

(22) Notwithstanding any other provision of this constitution, or any prior judicial decision, as of the effective date of the constitutional amendment adding this provision, which amends article IV, sections 1 through 6, article V, sections 1, 2 and 4, and article VI, sections 1 and 4, including this provision, for purposes of interpreting this constitutional amendment the people declare that the powers granted to the commission are legislative functions not subject to the control or approval of the legislature, and are exclusively reserved to the commission. The commission, and all of its responsibilities, operations, functions, contractors, consultants and employees are not subject to change, transfer, reorganization, or reassignment, and shall not be altered or abrogated in any manner whatsoever, by the legislature. No other body shall be established by law to perform functions that are the same or similar to those granted to the commission in this section.

History: Const. 1963, Art. IV, §6, Eff. Jan. 1, 1964;—Am. Init., approved Nov. 6, 2018, Eff. Dec. 22, 2018.
Transfer of powers: See §16.132.

Legislators; qualifications, removal from district.

Sec. 7. Each senator and representative must be a citizen of the United States, at least 21 years of age, and an elector of the district he represents. The removal of his domicile from the district shall be deemed a vacation of the office. No person who has been convicted of subversion or who has within the preceding 20 years been convicted of a felony involving a breach of public trust shall be eligible for either house of the legislature.

History: Const. 1963, Art. IV, §7, Eff. Jan. 1, 1964.
Former constitution: See Const. 1908, Art. V, §5.

Ineligibility of government officers and employees.

Sec. 8. No person holding any office, employment or position under the United States or this state or a political subdivision thereof, except notaries public and members of the armed forces reserve, may be a member of either house of the legislature.

History: Const. 1963, Art. IV, §8, Eff. Jan. 1, 1964.
Former constitution: See Const. 1908, Art. V, §6.

Civil appointments, ineligibility of legislators.

Sec. 9. No person elected to the legislature shall receive any civil appointment within this state from the governor, except notaries public, from the legislature, or from any other state authority, during the term for which he is elected.

History: Const. 1963, Art. IV, §9, Eff. Jan. 1, 1964.
Former constitution: See Const. 1908, Art. V, §7.

Legislators and state officers, government contracts, conflict of interest.

Sec. 10. No member of the legislature nor any state officer shall be interested directly or indirectly in any contract with the state or any political subdivision thereof which shall cause a substantial conflict of interest. The legislature shall further implement this provision by appropriate legislation.

History: Const. 1963, Art. IV, §10, Eff. Jan. 1, 1964.
Former constitution: See Const. 1908, Art. V, §§7, 25.

Legislators privileged from civil arrest and civil process; limitation; questioning for speech in either house prohibited.

Sec. 11. Except as provided by law, senators and representatives shall be privileged from civil arrest and civil process during sessions of the legislature and for five days next before the commencement and after the termination thereof. They shall not be questioned in any other place for any speech in either house.

History: Const. 1963, Art. IV, §11, Eff. Jan. 1, 1964;—Am. S.J.R. A, approved Nov. 2, 1982, Eff. Dec. 18, 1982.
Former constitution: See Const. 1908, Art. V, §8.

State officers compensation commission.

Sec. 12. The state officers compensation commission is created which subject to this section shall determine the salaries and expense allowances of the members of the legislature, the governor, the lieutenant governor, the attorney general, the secretary of state, and the justices of the supreme court.

The commission shall consist of 7 members appointed by the governor whose qualifications may be determined by law. Subject to the legislature's ability to amend the commission's determinations as provided in this section, the commission shall determine the salaries and expense allowances of the members of the legislature, the governor, the lieutenant governor, the attorney general, the secretary of state, and the justices of the supreme court which determinations shall be the salaries and expense allowances only if the legislature by concurrent resolution adopted by a majority of the members elected to and serving in each house of the legislature approve them. The senate and house of representatives shall alternate on which house of the legislature shall originate the concurrent resolution, with the senate originating the first concurrent resolution.

The concurrent resolution may amend the salary and expense determinations of the state officers compensation commission to reduce the salary and expense determinations by the same proportion for members of the legislature, the governor, the lieutenant governor, the attorney general, the secretary of state, and the justices of the supreme court. The legislature shall not amend the salary and expense determinations to reduce them to below the salary and expense level that members of the legislature, the governor, the lieutenant governor, the attorney general, the secretary of state, and the justices of the supreme court receive on the date the salary and expense determinations are made. If the salary and expense determinations are approved or amended as provided in this section, the salary and expense determinations shall become effective for the legislative session immediately following the next general election. The commission shall meet each 2 years for no more than 15 session days. The legislature shall implement this section by law.

History: Const. 1963, Art. IV, §12, Eff. Jan. 1, 1964;—Am. H.J.R. AAA, approved Aug. 6, 1968, Eff. Sept. 21, 1968;—Am. H.J.R. E, approved Aug. 6, 2002, Eff. Sept. 21, 2002.

Legislature; time of convening, sine die adjournment, measures carried over.

Sec. 13. The legislature shall meet at the seat of government on the second Wednesday in January of each year at twelve o'clock noon. Each regular session shall adjourn without day, on a day determined by concurrent resolution, at twelve o'clock noon. Any business, bill or joint resolution pending at the final adjournment of a regular session held in an odd numbered year shall carry over with the same status to the next regular session.

History: Const. 1963, Art. IV, §13, Eff. Jan. 1, 1964.
Former constitution: See Const. 1908, Art. V, §13.

Quorum; powers of less than quorum.

Sec. 14. A majority of the members elected to and serving in each house shall constitute a quorum to do business. A smaller number in each house may adjourn from day to day, and may compel the attendance of absent members in the manner and with penalties as each house may prescribe.

History: Const. 1963, Art. IV, §14, Eff. Jan. 1, 1964.
Former constitution: See Const. 1908, Art. V, §14.

Legislative council.

Sec. 15. There shall be a bi-partisan legislative council consisting of legislators appointed in the manner prescribed by law. The legislature shall appropriate funds for the council's operations and provide for its staff which shall maintain bill drafting, research and other services for the members of the legislature. The council shall periodically examine and recommend to the legislature revision of the various laws of the state.

History: Const. 1963, Art. IV, §15, Eff. Jan. 1, 1964.

Legislature; officers, rules of procedure, expulsion of members.

Sec. 16. Each house, except as otherwise provided in this constitution, shall choose its own officers and determine the rules of its proceedings, but shall not adopt any rule that will prevent a majority of the members elected thereto and serving therein from discharging a committee from the further consideration of any measure. Each house shall be the sole judge of the qualifications, elections and returns of its members, and may, with the concurrence of two-thirds of all the members elected thereto and serving therein, expel a member. The reasons for such expulsion shall be entered in the journal, with the votes and names of the members voting upon the question. No member shall be expelled a second time for the same cause.

History: Const. 1963, Art. IV, §16, Eff. Jan. 1, 1964.
Former constitution: See Const. 1908, Art. V, §15.

Committees; record of votes, public inspection, notice of hearings.

Sec. 17. Each house of the legislature may establish the committees necessary for the efficient conduct of its business and the legislature may create joint committees. On all actions on bills and resolutions in each committee, names and votes of members shall be recorded. Such vote shall be available for public inspection. Notice of all committee hearings and a clear statement of all subjects to be considered at each hearing shall be published in the journal in advance of the hearing.

History: Const. 1963, Art. IV, §17, Eff. Jan. 1, 1964.

Journal of proceedings; record of votes, dissents.

Sec. 18. Each house shall keep a journal of its proceedings, and publish the same unless the public security otherwise requires. The record of the vote and name of the members of either house voting on any question shall be entered in the journal at the request of one-fifth of the members present. Any member of either house may dissent from and protest against any act, proceeding or resolution which he deems injurious to any person or the public, and have the reason for his dissent entered in the journal.

History: Const. 1963, Art. IV, §18, Eff. Jan. 1, 1964.
Former constitution: See Const. 1908, Art. V, §16.

Record of votes on elections and advice and consent.

Sec. 19. All elections in either house or in joint convention and all votes on appointments submitted to the senate for advice and consent shall be published by vote and name in the journal.

History: Const. 1963, Art. IV, §19, Eff. Jan. 1, 1964.
Former constitution: See Const. 1908, Art. V, §17.

Open meetings.

Sec. 20. The doors of each house shall be open unless the public security otherwise requires.

History: Const. 1963, Art. IV, §20, Eff. Jan. 1, 1964.
Former constitution: See Const. 1908, Art. V, §18.

Adjournments, limitations.

Sec. 21. Neither house shall, without the consent of the other, adjourn for more than two intervening calendar days, nor to any place other than where the legislature may then be in session.

History: Const. 1963, Art. IV, §21, Eff. Jan. 1, 1964.
Former constitution: See Const. 1908, Art. V, §18.

Bills.

Sec. 22. All legislation shall be by bill and may originate in either house.

History: Const. 1963, Art. IV, §22, Eff. Jan. 1, 1964.
Former constitution: See Const. 1908, Art. V, §19.

Style of laws.

Sec. 23. The style of the laws shall be: The People of the State of Michigan enact.

History: Const. 1963, Art. IV, §23, Eff. Jan. 1, 1964.
Former constitution: See Const. 1908, Art. V, §20.

Laws; object, title, amendments changing purpose.

Sec. 24. No law shall embrace more than one object, which shall be expressed in its title. No bill shall be altered or amended on its passage through either house so as to change its original purpose as determined by its total content and not alone by its title.

History: Const. 1963, Art. IV, §24, Eff. Jan. 1, 1964.
Former constitution: See Const. 1908, Art. V, §§21, 22.

Revision and amendment of laws; title references, publication of entire sections.

Sec. 25. No law shall be revised, altered or amended by reference to its title only. The section or sections of the act altered or amended shall be re-enacted and published at length.

History: Const. 1963, Art. IV, §25, Eff. Jan. 1, 1964.
Former constitution: See Const. 1908, Art. V, §21.

Bills; printing, possession, reading, vote on passage.

Sec. 26. No bill shall be passed or become a law at any regular session of the legislature until it has been printed or reproduced and in the possession of each house for at least five days. Every bill shall be read three times in each house before the final passage thereof. No bill shall become a law without the concurrence of a majority of the members elected to and serving in each house. On the final passage of bills, the votes and names of the members voting thereon shall be entered in the journal.

History: Const. 1963, Art. IV, §26, Eff. Jan. 1, 1964.
Compiler's note: In Advisory Opinion on Constitutionality of 1978 PA 426, 403 Mich. 631, 272 N.W.2d 495 (1978), the Michigan supreme court held that the lieutenant governor may cast a tie-breaking vote during the final consideration of a bill when the senate is equally divided, and 1978 PA 426 was constitutionally enacted.
Former constitution: See Const. 1908, Art. V, §§22, 23.

Laws, effective date.

Sec. 27. No act shall take effect until the expiration of 90 days from the end of the session at which it was passed, but the legislature may give immediate effect to acts by a two-thirds vote of the members elected to and serving in each house.

History: Const. 1963, Art. IV, §27, Eff. Jan. 1, 1964.
Constitutionality: A law proposed by initiative petition which is enacted by the Legislature without change or amendment within forty days of its reception takes effect ninety days after the end of the session in which it was enacted unless two-thirds of the members of each house of the Legislature vote to give it immediate effect. Frey v. Department of Management and Budget, 429 Mich. 315, 414 N.W.2d 873 (1987).
Former constitution: See Const. 1908, Art. V, §21.

Bills, subjects at special session.

Sec. 28. When the legislature is convened on extraordinary occasions in special session no bill shall be passed on any subjects other than those expressly stated in the governor's proclamation or submitted by special message.

History: Const. 1963, Art. IV, §28, Eff. Jan. 1, 1964.
Former constitution: See Const. 1908, Art. V, §22.

Local or special acts.

Sec. 29. The legislature shall pass no local or special act in any case where a general act can be made applicable, and whether a general act can be made applicable shall be a judicial question. No local or special act shall take effect until approved by two-thirds of the members elected to and serving in each house and by a majority of the electors voting thereon in the district affected. Any act repealing local or special acts shall require only a majority of the members elected to and serving in each house and shall not require submission to the electors of such district.

History: Const. 1963, Art. IV, §29, Eff. Jan. 1, 1964.
Former constitution: See Const. 1908, Art. V, §30.

Appropriations; local or private purposes.

Sec. 30. The assent of two-thirds of the members elected to and serving in each house of the legislature shall be required for the appropriation of public money or property for local or private purposes.

History: Const. 1963, Art. IV, §30, Eff. Jan. 1, 1964.
Former constitution: See Const. 1908, Art. V, §24.

General appropriation bills; priority, statement of estimated revenue.

Sec. 31. The general appropriation bills for the succeeding fiscal period covering items set forth in the budget shall be passed or rejected in either house of the legislature before that house passes any appropriation bill for items not in the budget except bills supplementing appropriations for the current fiscal year's operation. Any bill requiring an appropriation to carry out its purpose shall be considered an appropriation bill. One of the general appropriation bills as passed by the legislature shall contain an itemized statement of estimated revenue by major source in each operating fund for the ensuing fiscal period, the total of which shall not be less than the total of all appropriations made from each fund in the general appropriation bills as passed.

History: Const. 1963, Art. IV, §31, Eff. Jan. 1, 1964.

Laws imposing taxes.

Sec. 32. Every law which imposes, continues or revives a tax shall distinctly state the tax.

History: Const. 1963, Art. IV, §32, Eff. Jan. 1, 1964.
Former constitution: See Const. 1908, Art. X, §6.

Bills passed; approval by governor or veto, reconsideration by legislature.

Sec. 33. Every bill passed by the legislature shall be presented to the governor before it becomes law, and the governor shall have 14 days measured in hours and minutes from the time of presentation in which to consider it. If he approves, he shall within that time sign and file it with the secretary of state and it shall become law. If he does not approve, and the legislature has within that time finally adjourned the session at which the bill was passed, it shall not become law. If he disapproves, and the legislature continues the session at which the bill was passed, he shall return it within such 14-day period with his objections, to the house in which it originated. That house shall enter such objections in full in its journal and reconsider the bill. If two-thirds of the members elected to and serving in that house pass the bill notwithstanding the objections of the governor, it shall be sent with the objections to the other house for reconsideration. The bill shall become law if passed by two-thirds of the members elected to and serving in that house. The vote of each house shall be entered in the journal with the votes and names of the members voting thereon. If any bill is not returned by the governor within such 14-day period, the legislature continuing in session, it shall become law as if he had signed it.

History: Const. 1963, Art. IV, §33, Eff. Jan. 1, 1964.
Former constitution: See Const. 1908, Art. V, §36.

Bills, referendum.

Sec. 34. Any bill passed by the legislature and approved by the governor, except a bill appropriating money, may provide that it will not become law unless approved by a majority of the electors voting thereon.

History: Const. 1963, Art. IV, §34, Eff. Jan. 1, 1964.
Former constitution: See Const. 1908, Art. V, §38.

Publication and distribution of laws and judicial decisions.

Sec. 35. All laws enacted at any session of the legislature shall be published in book form within 60 days after final adjournment of the session, and shall be distributed in the manner provided by law. The prompt publication of judicial decisions shall be provided by law. All laws and judicial decisions shall be free for publication by any person.

History: Const. 1963, Art. IV, §35, Eff. Jan. 1, 1964.
Former constitution: See Const. 1908, Art. V, §39.

General revision of laws; compilation of laws.

Sec. 36. No general revision of the laws shall be made. The legislature may provide for a compilation of the laws in force, arranged without alteration, under appropriate heads and titles.

History: Const. 1963, Art. IV, §36, Eff. Jan. 1, 1964.
Former constitution: See Const. 1908, Art. V, §40.

Administrative rules, suspension by legislative committee.

Sec. 37. The legislature may by concurrent resolution empower a joint committee of the legislature, acting between sessions, to suspend any rule or regulation promulgated by an administrative agency subsequent to the adjournment of the last preceding regular legislative session. Such suspension shall continue no longer than the end of the next regular legislative session.

History: Const. 1963, Art. IV, §37, Eff. Jan. 1, 1964.

Vacancies in office.

Sec. 38. The legislature may provide by law the cases in which any office shall be vacant and the manner of filling vacancies where no provision is made in this constitution.

History: Const. 1963, Art. IV, §38, Eff. Jan. 1, 1964.
Former constitution: See Const. 1908, Art. XVI, §5.

Continuity of government in emergencies.

Sec. 39. In order to insure continuity of state and local governmental operations in periods of emergency only, resulting from disasters occurring in this state caused by enemy attack on the United States, the legislature may provide by law for prompt and temporary succession to the powers and duties of public offices, of whatever nature and whether filled by election or appointment, the incumbents of which may become unavailable for carrying on the powers and duties of such offices; and enact other laws necessary and proper for insuring the continuity of governmental operations. Notwithstanding the power conferred by this section, elections shall always be called as soon as possible to fill any vacancies in elective offices temporarily occupied by operation of any legislation enacted pursuant to the provisions of this section.

History: Const. 1963, Art. IV, §39, Eff. Jan. 1, 1964.
Former constitution: See Const. 1908, Art. XVI, §5.

Alcoholic beverages; age requirement; liquor control commission; excise tax; local option.

Sec. 40. A person shall not sell or give any alcoholic beverage to any person who has not reached the age of 21 years. A person who has not reached the age of 21 years shall not possess any alcoholic beverage for the purpose of personal consumption. An alcoholic beverage is any beverage containing one-half of one percent or more alcohol by volume.

Except as prohibited by this section, (t)he legislature may by law establish a liquor control commission which, subject to statutory limitations, shall exercise complete control of the alcoholic beverage traffic within this state, including the retail sales thereof. The legislature may provide for an excise tax on such sales. Neither the legislature nor the commission may authorize the manufacture or sale of alcoholic beverages in any county in which a majority of the electors voting thereon shall prohibit the same.

History: Const. 1963, Art. IV, §40, Eff. Jan. 1, 1964;—Am. Init., approved Nov. 7, 1978, Eff. Dec. 23, 1978.
Former constitution: See Const. 1908, Art. XVI, §11.

Lotteries.

Sec. 41. The legislature may authorize lotteries and permit the sale of lottery tickets in the manner provided by law. No law enacted after January 1, 2004, that authorizes any form of gambling shall be effective, nor after January 1, 2004, shall any new state lottery games utilizing table games or player operated mechanical or electronic devices be established, without the approval of a majority of electors voting in a statewide general election and a majority of electors voting in the township or city where gambling will take place. This section shall not apply to gambling in up to three casinos in the City of Detroit or to Indian tribal gaming.

History: Const. 1963, Art. IV, §41, Eff. Jan. 1, 1964;—Am. H.J.R. V, approved May 16, 1972, Eff. July 1, 1972;—Am. Init., approved Nov. 2, 2004, Eff. Dec. 18, 2004.
Former constitution: See Const. 1908, Art. V, §33.

Ports and port districts; incorporation, internal.

Sec. 42. The legislature may provide for the incorporation of ports and port districts, and confer power and authority upon them to engage in work of internal improvements in connection therewith.

History: Const. 1963, Art. IV, §42, Eff. Jan. 1, 1964.
Former constitution: See Const. 1908, Art. VIII, §30.

Bank and trust company laws.

Sec. 43. No general law providing for the incorporation of trust companies or corporations for banking purposes, or regulating the business thereof, shall be enacted, amended or repealed except by a vote of two-thirds of the members elected to and serving in each house.

History: Const. 1963, Art. IV, §43, Eff. Jan. 1, 1964.
Former constitution: See Const. 1908, Art. XII, §9.

Trial by jury in civil cases.

Sec. 44. The legislature may authorize a trial by a jury of less than 12 jurors in civil cases.

History: Const. 1963, Art. IV, §44, Eff. Jan. 1, 1964.
Former constitution: See Const. 1908, Art. V, §27.

Indeterminate sentences.

Sec. 45. The legislature may provide for indeterminate sentences as punishment for crime and for the detention and release of persons imprisoned or detained under such sentences.

History: Const. 1963, Art. IV, §45, Eff. Jan. 1, 1964.
Former constitution: See Const. 1908, Art. V, §28.

Death penalty.

Sec. 46. No law shall be enacted providing for the penalty of death.

History: Const. 1963, Art. IV, §46, Eff. Jan. 1, 1964.

Chaplains in state institutions.

Sec. 47. The legislature may authorize the employment of chaplains in state institutions of detention or confinement.

History: Const. 1963, Art. IV, §47, Eff. Jan. 1, 1964.
Former constitution: See Const. 1908, Art. V, §26.

Disputes concerning public employees.

Sec. 48. The legislature may enact laws providing for the resolution of disputes concerning public employees, except those in the state classified civil service.

History: Const. 1963, Art. IV, §48, Eff. Jan. 1, 1964.
Former constitution: See Const. 1908, Art. XVI, §7.

Hours and conditions of employment.

Sec. 49. The legislature may enact laws relative to the hours and conditions of employment.

History: Const. 1963, Art. IV, §49, Eff. Jan. 1, 1964.
Former constitution: See Const. 1908, Art. V, §29.

Atomic and new forms of energy.

Sec. 50. The legislature may provide safety measures and regulate the use of atomic energy and forms of energy developed in the future, having in view the general welfare of the people of this state.

History: Const. 1963, Art. IV, §50, Eff. Jan. 1, 1964.

Public health and general welfare.

Sec. 51. The public health and general welfare of the people of the state are hereby declared to be matters of primary public concern. The legislature shall pass suitable laws for the protection and promotion of the public health.

History: Const. 1963, Art. IV, §51, Eff. Jan. 1, 1964.

Natural resources; conservation, pollution, impairment, destruction.

Sec. 52. The conservation and development of the natural resources of the state are hereby declared to be of paramount public concern in the interest of the health, safety and general welfare of the people. The legislature shall provide for the protection of the air, water and other natural resources of the state from pollution, impairment and destruction.

History: Const. 1963, Art. IV, §52, Eff. Jan. 1, 1964.

Auditor general; appointment, qualifications, term, removal, post audits.

Sec. 53. The legislature by a majority vote of the members elected to and serving in each house, shall appoint an auditor general, who shall be a certified public accountant licensed to practice in this state, to serve for a term of eight years. He shall be ineligible for appointment or election to any other public office in this state from which compensation is derived while serving as auditor general and for two years following the termination of his service. He may be removed for cause at any time by a two-thirds vote of the members elected to and serving in each house. The auditor general shall conduct post audits of financial transactions and accounts of the state and of all branches, departments, offices, boards, commissions, agencies, authorities and institutions of the state established by this constitution or by law, and performance post audits thereof.

Independent investigations; reports.

The auditor general upon direction by the legislature may employ independent accounting firms or legal counsel and may make investigations pertinent to the conduct of audits. He shall report annually to the legislature and to the governor and at such other times as he deems necessary or as required by the legislature. He shall be assigned no duties other than those specified in this section.

Governing boards of institutions of higher education.

Nothing in this section shall be construed in any way to infringe the responsibility and constitutional authority of the governing boards of the institutions of higher education to be solely responsible for the control and direction of all expenditures from the institutions' funds.

Staff members, civil service.

The auditor general, his deputy and one other member of his staff shall be exempt from classified civil service. All other members of his staff shall have classified civil service status.

History: Const. 1963, Art. IV, §53, Eff. Jan. 1, 1964.

Limitations on terms of office of state legislators.

Sec. 54. No person shall be elected to the office of state representative more than three times. No person shall be elected to the office of state senate more than two times. Any person appointed or elected to fill a vacancy in the house of representatives or the state senate for a period greater than one half of a term of such office, shall be considered to have been elected to serve one time in that office for purposes of this section. This limitation on the number of times a person shall be elected to office shall apply to terms of office beginning on or after January 1, 1993.

This section shall be self-executing. Legislation may be enacted to facilitate operation of this section, but no law shall limit or restrict the application of this section. If any part of this section is held to be invalid or unconstitutional, the remaining parts of this section shall not be affected but will remain in full force and effect.

History: Add. Init. approved Nov. 3, 1992, Eff. Dec. 19, 1992.

ARTICLE V
EXECUTIVE BRANCH

Executive power.

Sec. 1. Except to the extent limited or abrogated by article V, section 2, or article IV, section 6, the executive power is vested in the governor.

History: Const. 1963, Art. V, §1, Eff. Jan. 1, 1964;—Am. Init., approved Nov. 6, 2018, Eff. Dec. 22, 2018.
Former constitution: See Const. 1908, Art. VI, §2.

Principal departments.

Sec. 2. All executive and administrative offices, agencies and instrumentalities of the executive branch of state government and their respective functions, powers and duties, except for the office of governor and lieutenant governor and the governing bodies of institutions of higher education provided for in this constitution, shall be allocated by law among and within not more than 20 principal departments. They shall be grouped as far as practicable according to major purposes.

Organization of executive branch; assignment of functions; submission to legislature.

Subsequent to the initial allocation, the governor may make changes in the organization of the executive branch or in the assignment of functions among its units which he considers necessary for efficient administration. Where these changes require the force of law, they shall be set forth in executive orders and submitted to the legislature. Thereafter the legislature shall have 60 calendar days of a regular session, or a full regular session if of shorter duration, to disapprove each executive order. Unless disapproved in both houses by a resolution concurred in by a majority of the members elected to and serving in each house, each order shall become effective at a date thereafter to be designated by the governor.

Exemption for independent citizens redistricting commission for state legislative and congressional districts.

Notwithstanding any other provision of this constitution or any prior judicial decision, as of the effective date of the constitutional amendment adding this provision, which amends article IV, sections 1 through 6, article V, sections 1, 2 and 4, and article VI, sections 1 and 4, including this provision, for purposes of interpreting this constitutional amendment the people declare that the powers granted to independent citizens redistricting commission for state and congressional districts (hereinafter, "commission") are legislative functions not subject to the control or approval of the governor, and are exclusively reserved to the commission. The commission, and all of its responsibilities, operations, functions, contractors, consultants and employees are not subject to change, transfer, reorganization, or reassignment, and shall not be altered or abrogated in any manner whatsoever, by the governor. No other body shall be established by law to perform functions that are the same or similar to those granted to the commission in article IV, section 6.

History: Const. 1963, Art. V, §2, Eff. Jan. 1, 1964;—Am. Init., approved Nov. 6, 2018, Eff. Dec. 22, 2018.

Single heads of departments; appointment, term.

Sec. 3. The head of each principal department shall be a single executive unless otherwise provided in this constitution or by law. The single executives heading principal departments shall include a secretary of state, a state treasurer and an attorney general. When a single executive is the head of a principal department, unless elected or appointed as otherwise provided in this constitution, he shall be appointed by the governor by and with the advice and consent of the senate and he shall serve at the pleasure of the governor.

Boards heading departments; appointment, term, removal.

When a board or commission is at the head of a principal department, unless elected or appointed as otherwise provided in this constitution, the members thereof shall be appointed by the governor by and with the advice and consent of the senate. The term of office and procedure for removal of such members shall be as prescribed in this constitution or by law.

Boards and commissions, maximum term.

Terms of office of any board or commission created or enlarged after the effective date of this constitution shall not exceed four years except as otherwise authorized in this constitution. The terms of office of existing boards and commissions which are longer than four years shall not be further extended except as provided in this constitution.

History: Const. 1963, Art. V, §3, Eff. Jan. 1, 1964.

Commissions or agencies for less than 2 years.

Sec. 4. Except to the extent limited or abrogated by article V, section 2 or article IV, section 6, temporary commissions or agencies for special purposes with a life of no more than two years may be established by law and need not be allocated within a principal department.

History: Const. 1963, Art. V, §4, Eff. Jan. 1, 1964;—Am. Init., approved Nov. 6, 2018, Eff. Dec. 22, 2018.

Examining or licensing board members, qualifications.

Sec. 5. A majority of the members of an appointed examining or licensing board of a profession shall be members of that profession.

History: Const. 1963, Art. V, §5, Eff. Jan. 1, 1964.

Advice and consent to appointments.

Sec. 6. Appointment by and with the advice and consent of the senate when used in this constitution or laws in effect or hereafter enacted means appointment subject to disapproval by a majority vote of the members elected to and serving in the senate if such action is taken within 60 session days after the date of such appointment. Any appointment not disapproved within such period shall stand confirmed.

History: Const. 1963, Art. V, §6, Eff. Jan. 1, 1964.

Vacancies in office; filling, senatorial disapproval of appointees.

Sec. 7. Vacancies in any office, appointment to which requires advice and consent of the senate, shall be filled by the governor by and with the advice and consent of the senate. A person whose appointment has been disapproved by the senate shall not be eligible for an interim appointment to the same office.

History: Const. 1963, Art. V, §7, Eff. Jan. 1, 1964.
Former constitution: See Const. 1908, Art. VI, §10.

Principal departments, supervision of governor; information from state officers.

Sec. 8. Each principal department shall be under the supervision of the governor unless otherwise provided by this constitution. The governor shall take care that the laws be faithfully executed. He shall transact all necessary business with the officers of government and may require information in writing from all executive and administrative state officers, elective and appointive, upon any subject relating to the duties of their respective offices.

Court enforcement of constitutional or legislative mandate.

The governor may initiate court proceedings in the name of the state to enforce compliance with any constitutional or legislative mandate, or to restrain violations of any constitutional or legislative power, duty or right by any officer, department or agency of the state or any of its political subdivisions. This authority shall not be construed to authorize court proceedings against the legislature.

History: Const. 1963, Art. V, §8, Eff. Jan. 1, 1964.
Former constitution: See Const. 1908, Art. VI, §3.

Principal departments, location.

Sec. 9. Single executives heading principal departments and the chief executive officers of principal departments headed by boards or commissions shall keep their offices at the seat of government except as otherwise provided by law, superintend them in person and perform duties prescribed by law.

History: Const. 1963, Art. V, §9, Eff. Jan. 1, 1964.
Former constitution: See Const. 1908, Art. VI, §1.

Removal or suspension of officers; grounds, report.

Sec. 10. The governor shall have power and it shall be his duty to inquire into the condition and administration of any public office and the acts of any public officer, elective or appointive. He may remove or suspend from office for gross neglect of duty or for corrupt conduct in office, or for any other misfeasance or malfeasance therein, any elective or appointive state officer, except legislative or judicial, and shall report the reasons for such removal or suspension to the legislature.

History: Const. 1963, Art. V, §10, Eff. Jan. 1, 1964.
Former constitution: See Const. 1908, Art. IX, §7.

Provisional appointments to fill vacancies due to suspension.

Sec. 11. The governor may make a provisional appointment to fill a vacancy occasioned by the suspension of an appointed or elected officer, other than a legislative or judicial officer, until he is reinstated or until the vacancy is filled in the manner prescribed by law or this constitution.

History: Const. 1963, Art. V, §11, Eff. Jan. 1, 1964.
Former constitution: See Const. 1908, Art. IX, §5.

Military powers.

Sec. 12. The governor shall be commander-in-chief of the armed forces and may call them out to execute the laws, suppress insurrection and repel invasion.

History: Const. 1963, Art. V, §12, Eff. Jan. 1, 1964.
Former constitution: See Const. 1908, Art. VI, §4.

Elections to fill vacancies in legislature.

Sec. 13. The governor shall issue writs of election to fill vacancies in the senate or house of representatives. Any such election shall be held in a manner prescribed by law.

History: Const. 1963, Art. V, §13, Eff. Jan. 1, 1964.
Former constitution: See Const. 1908, Art. VI, §6.

Reprieves, commutations and pardons.

Sec. 14. The governor shall have power to grant reprieves, commutations and pardons after convictions for all offenses, except cases of impeachment, upon such conditions and limitations as he may direct, subject to procedures and regulations prescribed by law. He shall inform the legislature annually of each reprieve, commutation and pardon granted, stating reasons therefor.

History: Const. 1963, Art. V, §14, Eff. Jan. 1, 1964.
Former constitution: See Const. 1908, Art. VI, §9.

Extra sessions of legislature.

Sec. 15. The governor may convene the legislature on extraordinary occasions.

History: Const. 1963, Art. V, §15, Eff. Jan. 1, 1964.
Former constitution: See Const. 1908, Art. VI, §7.

Legislature other than at seat of government.

Sec. 16. The governor may convene the legislature at some other place when the seat of government becomes dangerous from any cause.

History: Const. 1963, Art. V, §16, Eff. Jan. 1, 1964.
Former constitution: See Const. 1908, Art. VI, §8.

Messages and recommendations to legislature.

Sec. 17. The governor shall communicate by message to the legislature at the beginning of each session and may at other times present to the legislature information as to the affairs of the state and recommend measures he considers necessary or desirable.

History: Const. 1963, Art. V, §17, Eff. Jan. 1, 1964.
Former constitution: See Const. 1908, Art. VI, §5.

Budget; general and deficiency appropriation bills.

Sec. 18. The governor shall submit to the legislature at a time fixed by law, a budget for the ensuing fiscal period setting forth in detail, for all operating funds, the proposed expenditures and estimated revenue of the state. Proposed expenditures from any fund shall not exceed the estimated revenue thereof. On the same date, the governor shall submit to the legislature general appropriation bills to embody the proposed expenditures and any necessary bill or bills to provide new or additional revenues to meet proposed expenditures. The amount of any surplus created or deficit incurred in any fund during the last preceding fiscal period shall be entered as an item in the budget and in one of the appropriation bills. The governor may submit amendments to appropriation bills to be offered in either house during consideration of the bill by that house, and shall submit bills to meet deficiencies in current appropriations.

History: Const. 1963, Art. V, §18, Eff. Jan. 1, 1964.

Disapproval of items in appropriation bills.

Sec. 19. The governor may disapprove any distinct item or items appropriating moneys in any appropriation bill. The part or parts approved shall become law, and the item or items disapproved shall be void unless re-passed according to the method prescribed for the passage of other bills over the executive veto.

History: Const. 1963, Art. V, §19, Eff. Jan. 1, 1964.
Former constitution: See Const. 1908, Art. V, §37.

Reductions in expenditures.

Sec. 20. No appropriation shall be a mandate to spend. The governor, with the approval of the appropriating committees of the house and senate, shall reduce expenditures authorized by appropriations whenever it appears that actual revenues for a fiscal period will fall below the revenue estimates on which appropriations for that period were based. Reductions in expenditures shall be made in accordance with procedures prescribed by law. The governor may not reduce expenditures of the legislative and judicial branches or from funds constitutionally dedicated for specific purposes.

History: Const. 1963, Art. V, §20, Eff. Jan. 1, 1964.

State elective executive officers; term, election.

Sec. 21. The governor, lieutenant governor, secretary of state and attorney general shall be elected for four-year terms at the general election in each alternate even-numbered year.

Lieutenant governor, secretary of state and attorney general, nomination.

The lieutenant governor, secretary of state and attorney general shall be nominated by party conventions in a manner prescribed by law. In the general election one vote shall be cast jointly for the candidates for governor and lieutenant governor nominated by the same party.

Secretary of state and attorney general, vacancies in office.

Vacancies in the office of the secretary of state and attorney general shall be filled by appointment by the governor.

History: Const. 1963, Art. V, §21, Eff. Jan. 1, 1964.
Former constitution: See Const. 1908, Art. VI, §1.

Governor and lieutenant governor, qualifications.

Sec. 22. To be eligible for the office of governor or lieutenant governor a person must have attained the age of 30 years, and have been a registered elector in this state for four years next preceding his election.

History: Const. 1963, Art. V, §22, Eff. Jan. 1, 1964.
Former constitution: See Const. 1908, Art. VI, §13.

State elective executive officers, compensation.

Sec. 23. The governor, lieutenant governor, secretary of state and attorney general shall each receive the compensation provided by law in full payment for all services performed and expenses incurred during his term of office. Such compensation shall not be changed during the term of office except as otherwise provided in this constitution.

History: Const. 1963, Art. V, §23, Eff. Jan. 1, 1964.
Former constitution: See Const. 1908, Art. VI, §21.

Executive residence.

Sec. 24. An executive residence suitably furnished shall be provided at the seat of government for the use of the governor. He shall receive an allowance for its maintenance as provided by law.

History: Const. 1963, Art. V, §24, Eff. Jan. 1, 1964.

Lieutenant governor; president of senate, tie vote, duties.

Sec. 25. The lieutenant governor shall be president of the senate, but shall have no vote, unless they be equally divided. He may perform duties requested of him by the governor, but no power vested in the governor shall be delegated.

History: Const. 1963, Art. V, §25, Eff. Jan. 1, 1964.
Compiler's note: In Advisory Opinion on Constitutionality of 1978 PA 426, 403 Mich. 631, 272 N.W.2d 495 (1978), the Michigan supreme court held that the lieutenant governor may cast a tie-breaking vote during the final consideration of a bill when the senate is equally divided, and 1978 PA 426 was constitutionally enacted.
Former constitution: See Const. 1908, Art. VI, §19.

Succession to governorship.

Sec. 26. In case of the conviction of the governor on impeachment, his removal from office, his resignation or his death, the lieutenant governor, the elected secretary of state, the elected attorney general and such other persons designated by law shall in that order be governor for the remainder of the governor's term.

Death of governor-elect.

In case of the death of the governor-elect, the lieutenant governor-elect, the secretary of state-elect, the attorney general-elect and such other persons designated by law shall become governor in that order at the commencement of the governor-elect's term.

Duration of successor's term as governor.

If the governor or the person in line of succession to serve as governor is absent from the state, or suffering under an inability, the powers and duties of the office of the governor shall devolve in order of precedence until the absence or inability giving rise to the devolution of powers ceases.

Determination of inability.

The inability of the governor or person acting as governor shall be determined by a majority of the supreme court on joint request of the president pro tempore of the senate and the speaker of the house of representatives. Such determination shall be final and conclusive. The supreme court shall upon its own initiative determine if and when the inability ceases.

History: Const. 1963, Art. V, §26, Eff. Jan. 1, 1964.
Former constitution: See Const. 1908, Art. VI, §§16, 17.

Salary of successor.

Sec. 27. The legislature shall provide that the salary of any state officer while acting as governor shall be equal to that of the governor.

History: Const. 1963, Art. V, §27, Eff. Jan. 1, 1964.
Former constitution: See Const. 1908, Art. VI, §18.

State transportation commission; establishment; purpose; appointment, qualifications, and terms of members; director of state transportation department.

Sec. 28. There is hereby established a state transportation commission, which shall establish policy for the state transportation department transportation programs and facilities, and such other public works of the state, as provided by law.

The state transportation commission shall consist of six members, not more than three of whom shall be members of the same political party. They shall be appointed by the governor by and with the advice and consent of the senate for three-year terms, no three of which shall expire in the same year, as provided by law.

The director of the state transportation department shall be appointed as provided by law and shall be the principal executive officer of the state transportation department and shall be responsible for executing the policy of the state transportation commission.

History: Const. 1963, Art. V, §28, Eff. Jan. 1, 1964;—Am. H.J.R. F, approved Nov. 7, 1978, Eff. Dec. 23, 1978.

Civil rights commission; members, term, duties, appropriation.

Sec. 29. There is hereby established a civil rights commission which shall consist of eight persons, not more than four of whom shall be members of the same political party, who shall be appointed by the governor, by and with the advice and consent of the senate, for four-year terms not more than two of which shall expire in the same year. It shall be the duty of the commission in a manner which may be prescribed by law to investigate alleged discrimination against any person because of religion, race, color or national origin in the enjoyment of the civil rights guaranteed by law and by this constitution, and to secure the equal protection of such civil rights without such discrimination. The legislature shall provide an annual appropriation for the effective operation of the commission.

Rules and regulations; hearings, orders.

The commission shall have power, in accordance with the provisions of this constitution and of general laws governing administrative agencies, to promulgate rules and regulations for its own procedures, to hold hearings, administer oaths, through court authorization to require the attendance of witnesses and the submission of records, to take testimony, and to issue appropriate orders. The commission shall have other powers provided by law to carry out its purposes. Nothing contained in this section shall be construed to diminish the right of any party to direct and immediate legal or equitable remedies in the courts of this state.

Appeals.

Appeals from final orders of the commission, including cease and desist orders and refusals to issue complaints, shall be tried de novo before the circuit court having jurisdiction provided by law.

History: Const. 1963, Art. V, §29, Eff. Jan. 1, 1964.
Administrative rules: R 37.1 et seq. and R 37.101 of the Michigan Administrative Code.

Limitations on terms of executive officers.

Sec. 30. No person shall be elected more than two times to each office of the executive branch of government: governor, lieutenant governor, secretary of state or attorney general. Any person appointed or elected to fill a vacancy in the office of governor, lieutenant governor, secretary of state or attorney general for a period greater than one half of a term of such office, shall be considered to have been elected to serve one time in that office for purposes of this section. This limitation on the number of times a person shall be elected to office shall apply to terms of office beginning on or after January 1, 1993.

This section shall be self-executing. Legislation may be enacted to facilitate operation of this section, but no law shall limit or restrict the application of this section. If any part of this section is held to be invalid or unconstitutional, the remaining parts of this section shall not be affected but will remain in full force and effect.

History: Add. Init. approved Nov. 3, 1992, Eff. Dec. 19, 1992.

ARTICLE VI
JUDICIAL BRANCH

Judicial power in court of justice; divisions.

Sec. 1. Except to the extent limited or abrogated by article IV, section 6, or article V, section 2, the judicial power of the state is vested exclusively in one court of justice which shall be divided into one supreme court, one court of appeals, one trial court of general jurisdiction known as the circuit court, one probate court, and courts of limited jurisdiction that the legislature may establish by a two-thirds vote of the members elected to and serving in each house.

History: Const. 1963, Art. VI, §1, Eff. Jan. 1, 1964;—Am. Init., approved Nov. 6, 2018, Eff. Dec. 22, 2018.
Former constitution: See Const. 1908, Art. VII, §1.

Justices of the supreme court; number, term, nomination, election.

Sec. 2. The supreme court shall consist of seven justices elected at non-partisan elections as provided by law. The term of office shall be eight years and not more than two terms of office shall expire at the same time. Nominations for justices of the supreme court shall be in the manner prescribed by law. Any incumbent justice whose term is to expire may become a candidate for re-election by filing an affidavit of candidacy, in the form and manner prescribed by law, not less than 180 days prior to the expiration of his term.

History: Const. 1963, Art. VI, §2, Eff. Jan. 1, 1964.
Former constitution: See Const. 1908, Art. VII, §2.

Chief justice; court administrator; other assistants.

Sec. 3. One justice of the supreme court shall be selected by the court as its chief justice as provided by rules of the court. He shall perform duties required by the court. The supreme court shall appoint an administrator of the courts and other assistants of the supreme court as may be necessary to aid in the administration of the courts of this state. The administrator shall perform administrative duties assigned by the court.

History: Const. 1963, Art. VI, §3, Eff. Jan. 1, 1964.

General superintending control over courts; writs; appellate jurisdiction.

Sec. 4. Except to the extent limited or abrogated by article IV, section 6, or article V, section 2, the supreme court shall have general superintending control over all courts; power to issue, hear and determine prerogative and remedial writs; and appellate jurisdiction as provided by rules of the supreme court. The supreme court shall not have the power to remove a judge.

History: Const. 1963, Art. VI, §4, Eff. Jan. 1, 1964;—Am. Init., approved Nov. 6, 2018, Eff. Dec. 22, 2018.
Former constitution: See Const. 1908, Art. VII, §4.

Court rules; distinctions between law and equity; master in chancery.

Sec. 5. The supreme court shall by general rules establish, modify, amend and simplify the practice and procedure in all courts of this state. The distinctions between law and equity proceedings shall, as far as practicable, be abolished. The office of master in chancery is prohibited.

History: Const. 1963, Art. VI, §5, Eff. Jan. 1, 1964.
Constitutionality: The State of Michigan, through the combined actions of the Supreme Court, the Legislature, and the State Bar, may compulsorily exact dues, and require association of attorneys, to support only those duties and functions of the State Bar which serve a compelling state interest and which cannot be accomplished by means less intrusive upon the First Amendment rights of objecting attorneys. Falk v. State Bar, 418 Mich. 270, 342 N.W.2d 504 (1983).

The regulation of the practice of law, the maintenance of high standards in the legal profession, and the discharge of the profession's duty to protect and inform the public are purposes in which the State of Michigan has a compelling interest justifying unavoidable intrusions on the First Amendment rights of attorneys; on the other hand, political and legislative activities are impermissible intrusions, as are activities designed to further commercial and economic interests of the members of the bar. Falk v. State Bar, 418 Mich. 270, 342 N.W.2d 504 (1983).

Former constitution: See Const. 1908, Art. VII, §5.

Decisions and dissents; writing, contents.

Sec. 6. Decisions of the supreme court, including all decisions on prerogative writs, shall be in writing and shall contain a concise statement of the facts and reasons for each decision and reasons for each denial of leave to appeal. When a judge dissents in whole or in part he shall give in writing the reasons for his dissent.

History: Const. 1963, Art. VI, §6, Eff. Jan. 1, 1964.
Former constitution: See Const. 1908, Art. VII, §7.

Staff; budget; salaries of justices; fees.

Sec. 7. The supreme court may appoint, may remove, and shall have general supervision of its staff. It shall have control of the preparation of its budget recommendations and the expenditure of moneys appropriated for any purpose pertaining to the operation of the court or the performance of activities of its staff except that the salaries of the justices shall be established by law. All fees and perquisites collected by the court staff shall be turned over to the state treasury and credited to the general fund.

History: Const. 1963, Art. VI, §7, Eff. Jan. 1, 1964.
Former constitution: See Const. 1908, Art. VII, §6.

Court of appeals; election of judges, divisions.

Sec. 8. The court of appeals shall consist initially of nine judges who shall be nominated and elected at non-partisan elections from districts drawn on county lines and as nearly as possible of equal population, as provided by law. The supreme court may prescribe by rule that the court of appeals sit in divisions and for the terms of court and the times and places thereof. Each such division shall consist of not fewer than three judges. The number of judges comprising the court of appeals may be increased, and the districts from which they are elected may be changed by law.

History: Const. 1963, Art. VI, §8, Eff. Jan. 1, 1964.

Judges of court of appeals, terms.

Sec. 9. Judges of the court of appeals shall hold office for a term of six years and until their successors are elected and qualified. The terms of office for the judges in each district shall be arranged by law to provide that not all terms will expire at the same time.

History: Const. 1963, Art. VI, §9, Eff. Jan. 1, 1964.

Jurisdiction, practice and procedure of court of appeals.

Sec. 10. The jurisdiction of the court of appeals shall be provided by law and the practice and procedure therein shall be prescribed by rules of the supreme court.

History: Const. 1963, Art. VI, §10, Eff. Jan. 1, 1964.

Circuit courts; judicial circuits, sessions, number of judges.

Sec. 11. The state shall be divided into judicial circuits along county lines in each of which there shall be elected one or more circuit judges as provided by law. Sessions of the circuit court shall be held at least four times in each year in every county organized for judicial purposes. Each circuit judge shall hold court in the county or counties within the circuit in which he is elected, and in other circuits as may be provided by rules of the supreme court. The number of judges may be changed and circuits may be created, altered and discontinued by law and the number of judges shall be changed and circuits shall be created, altered and discontinued on recommendation of the supreme court to reflect changes in judicial activity. No change in the number of judges or alteration or discontinuance of a circuit shall have the effect of removing a judge from office during his term.

History: Const. 1963, Art. VI, §11, Eff. Jan. 1, 1964.
Former constitution: See Const. 1908, Art. VII, §8.

Circuit judges; nomination, election, term.

Sec. 12. Circuit judges shall be nominated and elected at non-partisan elections in the circuit in which they reside, and shall hold office for a term of six years and until their successors are elected and qualified. In circuits having more than one circuit judge their terms of office shall be arranged by law to provide that not all terms will expire at the same time.

History: Const. 1963, Art. VI, §12, Eff. Jan. 1, 1964.
Former constitution: See Const. 1908, Art. VII, §9.

Circuit courts; jurisdiction, writs, supervisory control over inferior courts.

Sec. 13. The circuit court shall have original jurisdiction in all matters not prohibited by law; appellate jurisdiction from all inferior courts and tribunals except as otherwise provided by law; power to issue, hear and determine prerogative and remedial writs; supervisory and general control over inferior courts and tribunals within their respective jurisdictions in accordance with rules of the supreme court; and jurisdiction of other cases and matters as provided by rules of the supreme court.

History: Const. 1963, Art. VI, §13, Eff. Jan. 1, 1964.
Former constitution: See Const. 1908, Art. VII, §10.

County clerks; duties, vacancies; prosecuting attorneys, vacancies.

Sec. 14. The clerk of each county organized for judicial purposes or other officer performing the duties of such office as provided in a county charter shall be clerk of the circuit court for such county. The judges of the circuit court may fill a vacancy in an elective office of county clerk or prosecuting attorney within their respective jurisdictions.

History: Const. 1963, Art. VI, §14, Eff. Jan. 1, 1964.
Former constitution: See Const. 1908, Art. VII, §11.

Probate courts; districts, jurisdiction.

Sec. 15. In each county organized for judicial purposes there shall be a probate court. The legislature may create or alter probate court districts of more than one county if approved in each affected county by a majority of the electors voting on the question. The legislature may provide for the combination of the office of probate judge with any judicial office of limited jurisdiction within a county with supplemental salary as provided by law. The jurisdiction, powers and duties of the probate court and of the judges thereof shall be provided by law. They shall have original jurisdiction in all cases of juvenile delinquents and dependents, except as otherwise provided by law.

History: Const. 1963, Art. VI, §15, Eff. Jan. 1, 1964.
Former constitution: See Const. 1908, Art. VII, §13.

Probate judges; nomination, election, terms.

Sec. 16. One or more judges of probate as provided by law shall be nominated and elected at non-partisan elections in the counties or the probate districts in which they reside and shall hold office for terms of six years and until their successors are elected and qualified. In counties or districts with more than one judge the terms of office shall be arranged by law to provide that not all terms will expire at the same time.

History: Const. 1963, Art. VI, §16, Eff. Jan. 1, 1964.
Former constitution: See Const. 1908, Art. VII, §14.

Judicial salaries and fees.

Sec. 17. No judge or justice of any court of this state shall be paid from the fees of his office nor shall the amount of his salary be measured by fees, other moneys received or the amount of judicial activity of his office.

History: Const. 1963, Art. VI, §17, Eff. Jan. 1, 1964.

Salaries; uniformity, changes during term.

Sec. 18. Salaries of justices of the supreme court, of the judges of the court of appeals, of the circuit judges within a circuit, and of the probate judges within a county or district, shall be uniform, and may be increased but shall not be decreased during a term of office except and only to the extent of a general salary reduction in all other branches of government.

Circuit judges, additional salary from county.

Each of the judges of the circuit court shall receive an annual salary as provided by law. In addition to the salary received from the state, each circuit judge may receive from any county in which he regularly holds court an additional salary as determined from time to time by the board of supervisors of the county. In any county where an additional salary is granted, it shall be paid at the same rate to all circuit judges regularly holding court therein.

History: Const. 1963, Art. VI, §18, Eff. Jan. 1, 1964.
Former constitution: See Const. 1908, Art. VII, §12; Art. XVI, §3.

Courts of record; seal, qualifications of judges.

Sec. 19. (1) The supreme court, the court of appeals, the circuit court, the probate court and other courts designated as such by the legislature shall be courts of record and each shall have a common seal. Justices and judges of courts of record must be persons who are licensed to practice law in this state.

(2) To be qualified to serve as a judge of a trial court, a judge of the court of appeals, or a justice of the supreme court, a person shall have been admitted to the practice of law for at least 5 years. This subsection shall not apply to any judge or justice appointed or elected to judicial office prior to the date on which this subsection becomes part of the constitution.

(3) No person shall be elected or appointed to a judicial office after reaching the age of 70 years.

History: Const. 1963, Art. VI, §19, Eff. Jan. 1, 1964;—Am. S.J.R. D, approved Nov. 5, 1996, Eff. Dec. 21, 1996.
Former constitution: See Const. 1908, Art. VII, §17.

Removal of domicile of judge.

Sec. 20. Whenever a justice or judge removes his domicile beyond the limits of the territory from which he was elected or appointed, he shall have vacated his office.

History: Const. 1963, Art. VI, §20, Eff. Jan. 1, 1964;—Am. H.J.R. F, approved Aug. 6, 1968, Eff. Sept. 21, 1968.
Former constitution: See Const. 1908, Art. VII, §19.

Ineligibility for other office.

Sec. 21. Any justice or judge of a court of record shall be ineligible to be nominated for or elected to an elective office other than a judicial office during the period of his service and for one year thereafter.

History: Const. 1963, Art. VI, §21, Eff. Jan. 1, 1964.
Former constitution: See Const. 1908, Art. VII, §9.

Incumbent judges, affidavit of candidacy.

Sec. 22. Any judge of the court of appeals, circuit court or probate court may become a candidate in the primary election for the office of which he is the incumbent by filing an affidavit of candidacy in the form and manner prescribed by law.

History: Const. 1963, Art. VI, §22, Eff. Jan. 1, 1964;—Am. H.J.R. F, approved Aug. 6, 1968, Eff. Sept. 21, 1968.

Judicial vacancies, filling; appointee, term; successor; new offices.

Sec. 23. A vacancy shall occur in the office of judge of any court of record or in the district court by death, removal, resignation or vacating of the office, and such vacancy shall be filled by appointment by the governor. The person appointed by the governor shall hold office until 12 noon of the first day of January next succeeding the first general election held after the vacancy occurs, at which election a successor shall be elected for the remainder of the unexpired term. Whenever a new office of judge in a court of record, or the district court, is created by law, it shall be filled by election as provided by law. The supreme court may authorize persons who have been elected and served as judges to perform judicial duties for limited periods or specific assignments.

History: Const. 1963, Art. VI, §23, Eff. Jan. 1, 1964;—Am. H.J.R. F, approved Aug. 6, 1968, Eff. Sept. 21, 1968.
Former constitution: See Const. 1908, Art. VII, §20.

Incumbent judges, ballot designation.

Sec. 24. There shall be printed upon the ballot under the name of each incumbent justice or judge who is a candidate for nomination or election to the same office the designation of that office.

History: Const. 1963, Art. VI, §24, Eff. Jan. 1, 1964;—Am. H.J.R. F, approved Aug. 6, 1968, Eff. Sept. 21, 1968.
Former constitution: See Const. 1908, Art. VII, §23.

Removal of judges from office.

Sec. 25. For reasonable cause, which is not sufficient ground for impeachment, the governor shall remove any judge on a concurrent resolution of two-thirds of the members elected to and serving in each house of the legislature. The cause for removal shall be stated at length in the resolution.

History: Const. 1963, Art. VI, §25, Eff. Jan. 1, 1964.
Former constitution: See Const. 1908, Art. IX, §6.

Circuit court commissioners and justices of the peace, abolition; courts of limited jurisdiction.

Sec. 26. The offices of circuit court commissioner and justice of the peace are abolished at the expiration of five years from the date this constitution becomes effective or may within this period be abolished by law. Their jurisdiction, compensation and powers within this period shall be as provided by law. Within this five-year period, the legislature shall establish a court or courts of limited jurisdiction with powers and jurisdiction defined by law. The location of such court or courts, and the qualifications, tenure, method of election and salary of the judges of such court or courts, and by what governmental units the judges shall be paid, shall be provided by law, subject to the limitations contained in this article.

Present statutory courts.

Statutory courts in existence at the time this constitution becomes effective shall retain their powers and jurisdiction, except as provided by law, until they are abolished by law.

History: Const. 1963, Art. VI, §26, Eff. Jan. 1, 1964.

Power of appointment to public office.

Sec. 27. The supreme court, the court of appeals, the circuit court, or any justices or judges thereof, shall not exercise any power of appointment to public office except as provided in this constitution.

History: Const. 1963, Art. VI, §27, Eff. Jan. 1, 1964.
Former constitution: See Const. 1908, Art. VII, §11.

Administrative action, review.

Sec. 28. All final decisions, findings, rulings and orders of any administrative officer or agency existing under the constitution or by law, which are judicial or quasi-judicial and affect private rights or licenses, shall be subject to direct review by the courts as provided by law. This review shall include, as a minimum, the determination whether such final decisions, findings, rulings and orders are authorized by law; and, in cases in which a hearing is required, whether the same are supported by competent, material and substantial evidence on the whole record. Findings of fact in workmen's compensation proceedings shall be conclusive in the absence of fraud unless otherwise provided by law.

Property tax valuation or allocation; review.

In the absence of fraud, error of law or the adoption of wrong principles, no appeal may be taken to any court from any final agency provided for the administration of property tax laws from any decision relating to valuation or allocation.

History: Const. 1963, Art. VI, §28, Eff. Jan. 1, 1964.

Conservators of the peace.

Sec. 29. Justices of the supreme court, judges of the court of appeals, circuit judges and other judges as provided by law shall be conservators of the peace within their respective jurisdictions.

History: Const. 1963, Art. VI, §29, Eff. Jan. 1, 1964.
Former constitution: See Const. 1908, Art. VII, §18.

Judicial tenure commission; selection; terms; duties; power of supreme court.

Sec. 30. (1) A judicial tenure commission is established consisting of nine persons selected for three-year terms as follows: Four members shall be judges elected by the judges of the courts in which they serve; one shall be a court of appeals judge, one a circuit judge, one a probate judge and one a judge of a court of limited jurisdiction. Three shall be members of the state bar who shall be elected by the members of the state bar of whom one shall be a judge and two shall not be judges. Two shall be appointed by the governor; the members appointed by the governor shall not be judges, retired judges or members of the state bar. Terms shall be staggered as provided by rule of the supreme court. Vacancies shall be filled by the appointing power.

(2) On recommendation of the judicial tenure commission, the supreme court may censure, suspend with or without salary, retire or remove a judge for conviction of a felony, physical or mental disability which prevents the performance of judicial duties, misconduct in office, persistent failure to perform his duties, habitual intemperance or conduct that is clearly prejudicial to the administration of justice. The supreme court shall make rules implementing this section and providing for confidentiality and privilege of proceedings.

History: Add. H.J.R. PP, approved Aug. 6, 1968, Eff. Sept. 21, 1968.

ARTICLE VII
LOCAL GOVERNMENT

Counties; corporate character, powers and immunities.

Sec. 1. Each organized county shall be a body corporate with powers and immunities provided by law.
History: Const. 1963, Art. VII, §1, Eff. Jan. 1, 1964.
Former constitution: See Const. 1908, Art. VIII, §1.

County charters.

Sec. 2. Any county may frame, adopt, amend or repeal a county charter in a manner and with powers and limitations to be provided by general law, which shall among other things provide for the election of a charter commission. The law may permit the organization of county government in form different from that set forth in this constitution and shall limit the rate of ad valorem property taxation for county purposes, and restrict the powers of charter counties to borrow money and contract debts. Each charter county is hereby granted power to levy other taxes for county purposes subject to limitations and prohibitions set forth in this constitution or law. Subject to law, a county charter may authorize the county through its regularly constituted authority to adopt resolutions and ordinances relating to its concerns.

Election of charter commissions.

The board of supervisors by a majority vote of its members may, and upon petition of five percent of the electors shall, place upon the ballot the question of electing a commission to frame a charter.

Approval of electors.

No county charter shall be adopted, amended or repealed until approved by a majority of electors voting on the question.
History: Const. 1963, Art. VII, §2, Eff. Jan. 1, 1964.

Reduction of size of county.

Sec. 3. No organized county shall be reduced by the organization of new counties to less than 16 townships as surveyed by the United States, unless approved in the manner prescribed by law by a majority of electors voting thereon in each county to be affected.
History: Const. 1963, Art. VII, §3, Eff. Jan. 1, 1964.
Former constitution: See Const. 1908, Art. VIII, §2.

County officers; terms, combination.

Sec. 4. There shall be elected for four-year terms in each organized county a sheriff, a county clerk, a county treasurer, a register of deeds and a prosecuting attorney, whose duties and powers shall be provided by law. The board of supervisors in any county may combine the offices of county clerk and register of deeds in one office or separate the same at pleasure.
History: Const. 1963, Art. VII, §4, Eff. Jan. 1, 1964.
Former constitution: See Const. 1908, Art. VIII, §3.

Offices at county seat.

Sec. 5. The sheriff, county clerk, county treasurer and register of deeds shall hold their principal offices at the county seat.
History: Const. 1963, Art. VII, §5, Eff. Jan. 1, 1964.
Former constitution: See Const. 1908, Art. VIII, §4.

Sheriffs; security, responsibility for acts, ineligibility for other office.

Sec. 6. The sheriff may be required by law to renew his security periodically and in default of giving such security, his office shall be vacant. The county shall never be responsible for his acts, except that the board of supervisors may protect him against claims by prisoners for unintentional injuries received while in his custody. He shall not hold any other office except in civil defense.

History: Const. 1963, Art. VII, §6, Eff. Jan. 1, 1964.
Former constitution: See Const. 1908, Art. VIII, §5.

Boards of supervisors; members.

Sec. 7. A board of supervisors shall be established in each organized county consisting of one member from each organized township and such representation from cities as provided by law.

History: Const. 1963, Art. VII, §7, Eff. Jan. 1, 1964.
Constitutionality: Section held invalid under federal constitution. Advisory Opinion re Constitutionality of P.A. 1966, No. 261, 380 Mich. 736, 158 N.W. 2d 497 (1968); In re Apportionment of Ontonagon County Board of Supervisors, 11 Mich. App. 348, 157 N.W. 2d 698 (1967).
Former constitution: See Const. 1908, Art. VIII, §7.

Legislative, administrative, and other powers and duties of boards.

Sec. 8. Boards of supervisors shall have legislative, administrative and such other powers and duties as provided by law.

History: Const. 1963, Art. VII, §8, Eff. Jan. 1, 1964.
Former constitution: See Const. 1908, Art. VIII, §8.

Compensation of county officers.

Sec. 9. Boards of supervisors shall have exclusive power to fix the compensation of county officers not otherwise provided by law.

History: Const. 1963, Art. VII, §9, Eff. Jan. 1, 1964.
Former constitution: See Const. 1908, Art. VIII, §9.

Removal of county seat.

Sec. 10. A county seat once established shall not be removed until the place to which it is proposed to be moved shall be designated by two-thirds of the members of the board of supervisors and a majority of the electors voting thereon shall have approved the proposed location in the manner prescribed by law.

History: Const. 1963, Art. VII, §10, Eff. Jan. 1, 1964.
Former constitution: See Const. 1908, Art. VIII, §13.

Indebtedness, limitation.

Sec. 11. No county shall incur any indebtedness which shall increase its total debt beyond 10 percent of its assessed valuation.

History: Const. 1963, Art. VII, §11, Eff. Jan. 1, 1964.
Former constitution: See Const. 1908, Art. VIII, §12.

Navigable streams, permission to bridge or dam.

Sec. 12. A navigable stream shall not be bridged or dammed without permission granted by the board of supervisors of the county as provided by law, which permission shall be subject to such reasonable compensation and other conditions as may seem best suited to safeguard the rights and interests of the county and political subdivisions therein.

History: Const. 1963, Art. VII, §12, Eff. Jan. 1, 1964.
Former constitution: See Const. 1908, Art. VIII, §14.

Consolidation of counties, approval by electors.

Sec. 13. Two or more contiguous counties may combine into a single county if approved in each affected county by a majority of the electors voting on the question.

History: Const. 1963, Art. VII, §13, Eff. Jan. 1, 1964.

Organization and consolidation of townships.

Sec. 14. The board of supervisors of each organized county may organize and consolidate townships under restrictions and limitations provided by law.

History: Const. 1963, Art. VII, §14, Eff. Jan. 1, 1964.
Former constitution: See Const. 1908, Art. VIII, §15.

County intervention in public utility service and rate proceedings.

Sec. 15. Any county, when authorized by its board of supervisors shall have the authority to enter or to intervene in any action or certificate proceeding involving the services, charges or rates of any privately owned public utility furnishing services or commodities to rate payers within the county.

History: Const. 1963, Art. VII, §15, Eff. Jan. 1, 1964.

Highways, bridges, culverts, airports; road tax limitation.

Sec. 16. The legislature may provide for the laying out, construction, improvement and maintenance of highways, bridges, culverts and airports by the state and by the counties and townships thereof; and may authorize counties to take charge and control of any highway within their limits for such purposes. The legislature may provide the powers and duties of counties in relation to highways, bridges, culverts and airports; may provide for county road commissioners to be appointed or elected, with powers and duties provided by law. The ad valorem property tax imposed for road purposes by any county shall not exceed in any year one-half of one percent of the assessed valuation for the preceding year.

History: Const. 1963, Art. VII, §16, Eff. Jan. 1, 1964.
Former constitution: See Const. 1908, Art. VIII, §26.

Townships; corporate character, powers and immunities.

Sec. 17. Each organized township shall be a body corporate with powers and immunities provided by law.

History: Const. 1963, Art. VII, §17, Eff. Jan. 1, 1964.
Former constitution: See Const. 1908, Art. VIII, §16.

Township officers; term, powers and duties.

Sec. 18. In each organized township there shall be elected for terms of not less than two nor more than four years as prescribed by law a supervisor, a clerk, a treasurer, and not to exceed four trustees, whose legislative and administrative powers and duties shall be provided by law.

History: Const. 1963, Art. VII, §18, Eff. Jan. 1, 1964.
Former constitution: See Const. 1908, Art. VIII, §18.

Township public utility franchises.

Sec. 19. No organized township shall grant any public utility franchise which is not subject to revocation at the will of the township, unless the proposition shall first have been approved by a majority of the electors of such township voting thereon at a regular or special election.

History: Const. 1963, Art. VII, §19, Eff. Jan. 1, 1964.
Former constitution: See Const. 1908, Art. VIII, §19.

Townships, dissolution; villages as cities.

Sec. 20. The legislature shall provide by law for the dissolution of township government whenever all the territory of an organized township is included within the boundaries of a village or villages notwithstanding that a village may include territory within another organized township and provide by law for the classification of such village or villages as cities.

History: Const. 1963, Art. VII, §20, Eff. Jan. 1, 1964.

Cities and villages; incorporation, taxes, indebtedness.

Sec. 21. The legislature shall provide by general laws for the incorporation of cities and villages. Such laws shall limit their rate of ad valorem property taxation for municipal purposes, and restrict the powers of cities and villages to borrow money and contract debts. Each city and village is granted power to levy other taxes for public purposes, subject to limitations and prohibitions provided by this constitution or by law.

History: Const. 1963, Art. VII, §21, Eff. Jan. 1, 1964.
Former constitution: See Const. 1908, Art. VIII, §20.

Charters, resolutions, ordinances; enumeration of powers.

Sec. 22. Under general laws the electors of each city and village shall have the power and authority to frame, adopt and amend its charter, and to amend an existing charter of the city or village heretofore granted or enacted by the legislature for the government of the city or village. Each such city and village shall have power to adopt resolutions and ordinances relating to its municipal concerns, property and government, subject to the constitution and law. No enumeration of powers granted to cities and villages in this constitution shall limit or restrict the general grant of authority conferred by this section.

History: Const. 1963, Art. VII, §22, Eff. Jan. 1, 1964.
Former constitution: See Const. 1908, Art. VIII, §21.

Parks, boulevards, cemeteries, hospitals.

Sec. 23. Any city or village may acquire, own, establish and maintain, within or without its corporate limits, parks, boulevards, cemeteries, hospitals and all works which involve the public health or safety.
History: Const. 1963, Art. VII, §23, Eff. Jan. 1, 1964.
Former constitution: See Const. 1908, Art. VIII, §22.

Public service facilities.

Sec. 24. Subject to this constitution, any city or village may acquire, own or operate, within or without its corporate limits, public service facilities for supplying water, light, heat, power, sewage disposal and transportation to the municipality and the inhabitants thereof.

Services outside corporate limits.

Any city or village may sell and deliver heat, power or light without its corporate limits in an amount not exceeding 25 percent of that furnished by it within the corporate limits, except as greater amounts may be permitted by law; may sell and deliver water and provide sewage disposal services outside of its corporate limits in such amount as may be determined by the legislative body of the city or village; and may operate transportation lines outside the municipality within such limits as may be prescribed by law.
History: Const. 1963, Art. VII, §24, Eff. Jan. 1, 1964.
Former constitution: See Const. 1908, Art. VIII, §23.

Public utilities; acquisition, franchises, sale.

Sec. 25. No city or village shall acquire any public utility furnishing light, heat or power, or grant any public utility franchise which is not subject to revocation at the will of the city or village, unless the proposition shall first have been approved by three-fifths of the electors voting thereon. No city or village may sell any public utility unless the proposition shall first have been approved by a majority of the electors voting thereon, or a greater number if the charter shall so provide.
History: Const. 1963, Art. VII, §25, Eff. Jan. 1, 1964.
Former constitution: See Const. 1908, Art. VIII, §25.

Cities and villages, loan of credit.

Sec. 26. Except as otherwise provided in this constitution, no city or village shall have the power to loan its credit for any private purpose or, except as provided by law, for any public purpose.
History: Const. 1963, Art. VII, §26, Eff. Jan. 1, 1964.

Metropolitan governments and authorities.

Sec. 27. Notwithstanding any other provision of this constitution the legislature may establish in metropolitan areas additional forms of government or authorities with powers, duties and jurisdictions as the legislature shall provide. Wherever possible, such additional forms of government or authorities shall be designed to perform multipurpose functions rather than a single function.
History: Const. 1963, Art. VII, §27, Eff. Jan. 1, 1964.
Former constitution: See Const. 1908, Art. VIII, §31.

Governmental functions and powers; joint administration, costs and credits, transfers.

Sec. 28. The legislature by general law shall authorize two or more counties, townships, cities, villages or districts, or any combination thereof among other things to: enter into contractual undertakings or agreements with one another or with the state or with any combination thereof for the joint administration of any of the functions or powers which each would have the power to perform separately; share the costs and responsibilities of functions and services with one another or with the state or with any combination thereof which each would have the power to perform separately; transfer functions or responsibilities to one another or any combination thereof upon the consent of each unit involved; cooperate with one another and with state government; lend their credit to one another or any combination thereof as provided by law in connection with any authorized publicly owned undertaking.

Officers, eligibility.

Any other provision of this constitution notwithstanding, an officer or employee of the state or any such unit of government or subdivision or agency thereof, except members of the legislature, may serve on or with any governmental body established for the purposes set forth in this section and shall not be required to relinquish his office or employment by reason of such service.
History: Const. 1963, Art. VII, §28, Eff. Jan. 1, 1964.

Highways, streets, alleys, public places; control, use by public utilities.

Sec. 29. No person, partnership, association or corporation, public or private, operating a public utility shall have the right to the use of the highways, streets, alleys or other public places of any county, township, city or village for wires, poles, pipes, tracks, conduits or other utility facilities, without the consent of the duly constituted authority of the county, township, city or village; or to transact local business therein without first obtaining a franchise from the township, city or village. Except as otherwise provided in this constitution the right of all counties, townships, cities and villages to the reasonable control of their highways, streets, alleys and public places is hereby reserved to such local units of government.

History: Const. 1963, Art. VII, §29, Eff. Jan. 1, 1964.
Former constitution: See Const. 1908, Art. VIII, §28.

Franchises and licenses, duration.

Sec. 30. No franchise or license shall be granted by any township, city or village for a period longer than 30 years.

History: Const. 1963, Art. VII, §30, Eff. Jan. 1, 1964.
Former constitution: See Const. 1908, Art. VIII, §29.

Vacation or alteration of roads, streets, alleys, public places.

Sec. 31. The legislature shall not vacate or alter any road, street, alley or public place under the jurisdiction of any county, township, city or village.

History: Const. 1963, Art. VII, §31, Eff. Jan. 1, 1964.
Former constitution: See Const. 1908, Art. VIII, §27.

Budgets, public hearing.

Sec. 32. Any county, township, city, village, authority or school district empowered by the legislature or by this constitution to prepare budgets of estimated expenditures and revenues shall adopt such budgets only after a public hearing in a manner prescribed by law.

History: Const. 1963, Art. VII, §32, Eff. Jan. 1, 1964.

Removal of elected officers.

Sec. 33. Any elected officer of a political subdivision may be removed from office in the manner and for the causes provided by law.

History: Const. 1963, Art. VII, §33, Eff. Jan. 1, 1964.
Former constitution: See Const. 1908, Art. IX, §8.

Construction of constitution and law concerning counties, townships, cities, villages.

Sec. 34. The provisions of this constitution and law concerning counties, townships, cities and villages shall be liberally construed in their favor. Powers granted to counties and townships by this constitution and by law shall include those fairly implied and not prohibited by this constitution.

History: Const. 1963, Art. VII, §34, Eff. Jan. 1, 1964.

ARTICLE VIII
EDUCATION

Encouragement of education.

Sec. 1. Religion, morality and knowledge being necessary to good government and the happiness of mankind, schools and the means of education shall forever be encouraged.

History: Const. 1963, Art. VIII, §1, Eff. Jan. 1, 1964.
Former constitution: See Const. 1908, Art. XI, §1.

Free public elementary and secondary schools; discrimination.

Sec. 2. The legislature shall maintain and support a system of free public elementary and secondary schools as defined by law. Every school district shall provide for the education of its pupils without discrimination as to religion, creed, race, color or national origin.

Nonpublic schools, prohibited aid.

No public monies or property shall be appropriated or paid or any public credit utilized, by the legislature or any other political subdivision or agency of the state directly or indirectly to aid or maintain any private, denominational or other nonpublic, pre-elementary, elementary, or secondary school. No payment, credit, tax benefit, exemption or deductions, tuition voucher, subsidy, grant or loan of public monies or property shall be provided, directly or indirectly, to support the attendance of any student or the employment of any person at any such nonpublic school or at any location or institution where instruction is offered in whole or in part to such nonpublic school students. The legislature may provide for the transportation of students to and from any school.

History: Const. 1963, Art. VIII, §2, Eff. Jan. 1, 1964;—Am. Init., approved Nov. 3, 1970, Eff. Dec. 19, 1970.

Constitutionality: That portion of second sentence of second paragraph of this section, prohibiting use of public money to support attendance of any student or employment of any person at any location or institution where instruction is offered in whole or in part to nonpublic students, was held unconstitutional, void, and unenforceable because it contravened free exercise of religion guaranteed by the United States Constitution and was violative of equal protection of laws provisions of United States Constitution. Traverse City School District v. Attorney General, 384 Mich. 390, 185 N.W. 2d 9 (1971).

Former constitution: See Const. 1908, Art. XI, §9.

State board of education; duties.

Sec. 3. Leadership and general supervision over all public education, including adult education and instructional programs in state institutions, except as to institutions of higher education granting baccalaureate degrees, is vested in a state board of education. It shall serve as the general planning and coordinating body for all public education, including higher education, and shall advise the legislature as to the financial requirements in connection therewith.

Superintendent of public instruction; appointment, powers, duties.

The state board of education shall appoint a superintendent of public instruction whose term of office shall be determined by the board. He shall be the chairman of the board without the right to vote, and shall be responsible for the execution of its policies. He shall be the principal executive officer of a state department of education which shall have powers and duties provided by law.

State board of education; members, nomination, election, term.

The state board of education shall consist of eight members who shall be nominated by party conventions and elected at large for terms of eight years as prescribed by law. The governor shall fill any vacancy by appointment for the unexpired term. The governor shall be ex-officio a member of the state board of education without the right to vote.

Boards of institutions of higher education, limitation.

The power of the boards of institutions of higher education provided in this constitution to supervise their respective institutions and control and direct the expenditure of the institutions' funds shall not be limited by this section.

History: Const. 1963, Art. VIII, §3, Eff. Jan. 1, 1964.
Former constitution: See Const. 1908, Art. XI, §§2, 6.

Higher education institutions; appropriations, accounting, public sessions of boards.

Sec. 4. The legislature shall appropriate moneys to maintain the University of Michigan, Michigan State University, Wayne State University, Eastern Michigan University, Michigan College of Science and Technology, Central Michigan University, Northern Michigan University, Western Michigan University, Ferris Institute, Grand Valley State College, by whatever names such institutions may hereafter be known, and other institutions of higher education established by law. The legislature shall be given an annual accounting of all income and expenditures by each of these educational institutions. Formal sessions of governing boards of such institutions shall be open to the public.

History: Const. 1963, Art. VIII, §4, Eff. Jan. 1, 1964.
Former constitution: See Const. 1908, Art. XI, §10.

University of Michigan, Michigan State University, Wayne State University; controlling boards.

Sec. 5. The regents of the University of Michigan and their successors in office shall constitute a body corporate known as the Regents of the University of Michigan; the trustees of Michigan State University and their successors in office shall constitute a body corporate known as the Board of Trustees of Michigan State University; the governors of Wayne State University and their successors in office shall constitute a body corporate known as the Board of Governors of Wayne State University. Each board shall have general supervision of its institution and the control and direction of all expenditures from the institution's funds. Each board shall, as often as necessary, elect a president of the institution under its supervision. He shall be the principal executive officer of the institution, be ex-officio a member of the board without the right to vote and preside at meetings of the board. The board of each institution shall consist of eight members who shall hold office for terms of eight years and who shall be elected as provided by law. The governor shall fill board vacancies by appointment. Each appointee shall hold office until a successor has been nominated and elected as provided by law.

History: Const. 1963, Art. VIII, §5, Eff. Jan. 1, 1964.
Former constitution: See Const. 1908, Art. XI, §§3, 4, 5, 7, 8, 16.

Other institutions of higher education, controlling boards.

Sec. 6. Other institutions of higher education established by law having authority to grant baccalaureate degrees shall each be governed by a board of control which shall be a body corporate. The board shall have general supervision of the institution and the control and direction of all expenditures from the institution's funds. It shall, as often as necessary, elect a president of the institution under its supervision. He shall be the principal executive officer of the institution and be ex-officio a member of the board without the right to vote. The board may elect one of its members or may designate the president, to preside at board meetings. Each board of control shall consist of eight members who shall hold office for terms of eight years, not more than two of which shall expire in the same year, and who shall be appointed by the governor by and with the advice and consent of the senate. Vacancies shall be filled in like manner.

History: Const. 1963, Art. VIII, §6, Eff. Jan. 1, 1964.

Community and junior colleges; state board, members, terms, vacancies.

Sec. 7. The legislature shall provide by law for the establishment and financial support of public community and junior colleges which shall be supervised and controlled by locally elected boards. The legislature shall provide by law for a state board for public community and junior colleges which shall advise the state board of education concerning general supervision and planning for such colleges and requests for annual appropriations for their support. The board shall consist of eight members who shall hold office for terms of eight years, not more than two of which shall expire in the same year, and who shall be appointed by the state board of education. Vacancies shall be filled in like manner. The superintendent of public instruction shall be ex-officio a member of this board without the right to vote.

History: Const. 1963, Art. VIII, §7, Eff. Jan. 1, 1964.

Services for disabled persons.

Sec. 8. Institutions, programs, and services for the care, treatment, education, or rehabilitation of those inhabitants who are physically, mentally, or otherwise seriously disabled shall always be fostered and supported.

History: Const. 1963, Art. VIII, §8, Eff. Jan. 1, 1964;—Am. S.J.R. I, approved Nov. 3, 1998, Eff. Dec. 19, 1998.
Former constitution: See Const. 1908, Art. XI, §15.

Public libraries, fines.

Sec. 9. The legislature shall provide by law for the establishment and support of public libraries which shall be available to all residents of the state under regulations adopted by the governing bodies thereof. All fines assessed and collected in the several counties, townships and cities for any breach of the penal laws shall be exclusively applied to the support of such public libraries, and county law libraries as provided by law.

History: Const. 1963, Art. VIII, §9, Eff. Jan. 1, 1964.
Former constitution: See Const. 1908, Art. XI, §14.

ARTICLE IX
FINANCE AND TAXATION

Taxes for state expenses.

Sec. 1. The legislature shall impose taxes sufficient with other resources to pay the expenses of state government.

History: Const. 1963, Art. IX, §1, Eff. Jan. 1, 1964.
Former constitution: See Const. 1908, Art. X, §2.

Power of taxation, relinquishment.

Sec. 2. The power of taxation shall never be surrendered, suspended or contracted away.

History: Const. 1963, Art. IX, §2, Eff. Jan. 1, 1964.
Former constitution: See Const. 1908, Art. X, §9.

Property taxation; uniformity; assessments; limitations; classes; approval of legislature.

Sec. 3. The legislature shall provide for the uniform general ad valorem taxation of real and tangible personal property not exempt by law except for taxes levied for school operating purposes. The legislature shall provide for the determination of true cash value of such property; the proportion of true cash value at which such property shall be uniformly assessed, which shall not, after January 1, 1966, exceed 50 percent; and for a system of equalization of assessments. For taxes levied in 1995 and each year thereafter, the legislature shall provide that the taxable value of each parcel of property adjusted for additions and losses, shall not increase each year by more than the increase in the immediately preceding year in the general price level, as defined in section 33 of this article, or 5 percent, whichever is less until ownership of the parcel of property is transferred. When ownership of the parcel of property is transferred as defined by law, the parcel shall be assessed at the applicable proportion of current true cash value. The legislature may provide for alternative means of taxation of designated real and tangible personal property in lieu of general ad valorem taxation. Every tax other than the general ad valorem property tax shall be uniform upon the class or classes on which it operates. A law that increases the statutory limits in effect as of February 1, 1994 on the maximum amount of ad valorem property taxes that may be levied for school district operating purposes requires the approval of 3/4 of the members elected to and serving in the Senate and in the House of Representatives.

History: Const. 1963, Art. IX, §3, Eff. Jan. 1, 1964;—Am. S.J.R. S, approved Mar. 15, 1994, Eff. Apr. 30, 1994.
Former constitution: See Const. 1908, Art. X, §§3, 4, 7, 8.

Exemption of religious or educational nonprofit organizations.

Sec. 4. Property owned and occupied by non-profit religious or educational organizations and used exclusively for religious or educational purposes, as defined by law, shall be exempt from real and personal property taxes.

History: Const. 1963, Art. IX, §4, Eff. Jan. 1, 1964.

Assessment of property of public service businesses.

Sec. 5. The legislature shall provide for the assessment by the state of the property of those public service businesses assessed by the state at the date this constitution becomes effective, and of other property as designated by the legislature, and for the imposition and collection of taxes thereon. Property assessed by the state shall be assessed at the same proportion of its true cash value as the legislature shall specify for property subject to general ad valorem taxation. The rate of taxation on such property shall be the average rate levied upon other commercial, industrial, and utility property in this state under the general ad valorem tax law, or, if the legislature provides, the rate of tax applicable to the property of each business enterprise assessed by the state shall be the average rate of ad valorem taxation levied upon other commercial, industrial, and utility property in all counties in which any of such property is situated.

History: Const. 1963, Art. IX, §5, Eff. Jan. 1, 1964;—Am. S.J.R. S, approved Mar. 15, 1994, Eff. Apr. 30, 1994.

Real and tangible personal property; limitation on general ad valorem taxes; adoption and alteration of separate tax limitations; exceptions to limitations; property tax on school district extending into 2 or more counties.

Section 6. Except as otherwise provided in this constitution, the total amount of general ad valorem taxes imposed upon real and tangible personal property for all purposes in any one year shall not exceed 15 mills on each dollar of the assessed valuation of property as finally equalized. Under procedures provided by law, which shall guarantee the right of initiative, separate tax limitations for any county and for the townships and for school districts therein, the aggregate of which shall not exceed 18 mills on each dollar of such valuation, may be adopted and thereafter altered by the vote of a majority of the qualified electors of such county voting thereon, in lieu of the limitation hereinbefore established. These limitations may be increased to an aggregate of not to exceed 50 mills on each dollar of valuation, for a period of not to exceed 20 years at any one time, if approved by a majority of the electors, qualified under Section 6 of Article II of this constitution, voting on the question.

The foregoing limitations shall not apply to taxes imposed for the payment of principal and interest on bonds approved by the electors or other evidences of indebtedness approved by the electors or for the payment of assessments or contract obligations in anticipation of which bonds are issued approved by the electors, which taxes may be imposed without limitation as to rate or amount; or, subject to the provisions of Section 25 through 34 of this article, to taxes imposed for any other purpose by any city, village, charter county, charter township, charter authority or other authority, the tax limitations of which are provided by charter or by general law.

In any school district which extends into two or more counties, property taxes at the highest rate available in the county which contains the greatest part of the area of the district may be imposed and collected for school purposes throughout the district.

History: Const. 1963, Art. IX, §6, Eff. Jan. 1, 1964;—Am. Init., approved Nov. 7, 1978, Eff. Dec. 23, 1978.
Former constitution: See Const. 1908, Art. X, §21.

Income tax.

Sec. 7. No income tax graduated as to rate or base shall be imposed by the state or any of its subdivisions.

History: Const. 1963, Art. IX, §7, Eff. Jan. 1, 1964.

Sales and use taxes.

Sec. 8. Except as provided in this section, the Legislature shall not impose a sales tax on retailers at a rate of more than 4% of their gross taxable sales of tangible personal property.

Beginning May 1, 1994, the sales tax shall be imposed on retailers at an additional rate of 2% of their gross taxable sales of tangible personal property not exempt by law and the use tax at an additional rate of 2%. The proceeds of the sales and use taxes imposed at the additional rate of 2% shall be deposited in the state school aid fund established in section 11 of this article. The allocation of sales tax revenue required or authorized by sections 9 and 10 of this article does not apply to the revenue from the sales tax imposed at the additional rate of 2%.

No sales tax or use tax shall be charged or collected from and after January 1, 1975 on the sale or use of prescription drugs for human use, or on the sale or use of food for human consumption except in the case of prepared food intended for immediate consumption as defined by law. This provision shall not apply to alcoholic beverages.

History: Const. 1963, Art. IX, §8, Eff. Jan. 1, 1964;—Am. Init., approved Nov. 5, 1974, Eff. Dec. 21, 1974;—Am. S.J.R. S, approved Mar. 15, 1994, Eff. Apr. 30, 1994.
Former constitution: See Const. 1908, Art. X, §23.

Use of specific taxes on fuels for transportation purposes; authorization of indebtedness and issuance of obligations.

Sec. 9. All specific taxes, except general sales and use taxes and regulatory fees, imposed directly or indirectly on fuels sold or used to propel motor vehicles upon highways and to propel aircraft and on registered motor vehicles and aircraft shall, after the payment of necessary collection expenses, be used exclusively for transportation purposes as set forth in this section.

Not less than 90 percent of the specific taxes, except general sales and use taxes and regulatory fees, imposed directly or indirectly on fuels sold or used to propel motor vehicles upon highways and on registered motor vehicles shall, after the payment of necessary collection expenses, be used exclusively for the transportation purposes of planning, administering, constructing, reconstructing, financing, and maintaining state, county, city, and village roads, streets, and bridges designed primarily for the use of motor vehicles using tires, and reasonable appurtenances to those state, county, city, and village roads, streets, and bridges.

The balance, if any, of the specific taxes, except general sales and use taxes and regulatory fees, imposed directly or indirectly on fuels sold or used to propel motor vehicles upon highways and on registered motor vehicles, after the payment of necessary collection expenses; 100 percent of the specific taxes, except general sales and use taxes and regulatory fees, imposed directly or indirectly on fuels sold or used to propel aircraft and on registered aircraft, after the payment of necessary collection expenses; and not more than 25 percent of the general sales taxes, imposed directly or indirectly on fuels sold to propel motor vehicles upon highways, on the sale of motor vehicles, and on the sale of the parts and accessories of motor vehicles, after the payment of necessary collection expenses; shall be used exclusively for the transportation purposes of comprehensive transportation purposes as defined by law.

The legislature may authorize the incurrence of indebtedness and the issuance of obligations pledging the taxes allocated or authorized to be allocated by this section, which obligations shall not be construed to be evidences of state indebtedness under this constitution.

History: Const. 1963, Art. IX, §9, Eff. Jan. 1, 1964;—Am. H.J.R. F, approved Nov. 7, 1978, Eff. Dec. 23, 1978.
Former constitution: See Const. 1908, Art. X, §22.

Sales tax; distribution to local governments.

Sec. 10. Fifteen percent of all taxes imposed on retailers on taxable sales at retail of tangible personal property at a rate of not more than 4% shall be used exclusively for assistance to townships, cities and villages, on a population basis as provided by law. In determining population the legislature may exclude any portion of the total number of persons who are wards, patients or convicts in any tax supported institution.

History: Const. 1963, Art. IX, §10, Eff. Jan. 1, 1964;—Am. S.J.R. S, approved Mar. 15, 1994, Eff. Apr. 30, 1994.
Former constitution: See Const. 1908, Art. X, §23.

State school aid fund; source; distribution; guarantee to local school district.

Sec. 11. There shall be established a state school aid fund which shall be used exclusively for aid to school districts, higher education, and school employees' retirement systems, as provided by law. Sixty percent of all taxes imposed at a rate of 4% on retailers on taxable sales at retail of tangible personal property, 100% of the proceeds of the sales and use taxes imposed at the additional rate of 2% provided for in section 8 of this article, and other tax revenues provided by law, shall be dedicated to this fund. Payments from this fund shall be made in full on a scheduled basis, as provided by law. Beginning in the 1995-96 state fiscal year and each state fiscal year after 1995-96, the state shall guarantee that the total state and local per pupil revenue for school operating purposes for each local school district shall not be less than the 1994-95 total state and local per pupil revenue for school operating purposes for that local school district, as adjusted for consolidations, annexations, or other boundary changes. However, this guarantee does not apply in a year in which the local school district levies a millage rate for school district operating purposes less than it levied in 1994.

History: Const. 1963, Art. IX, §11, Eff. Jan. 1, 1964—Am. S.J.R. S, approved Mar. 15, 1994, Eff. Apr. 30, 1994.

Evidence of state indebtedness.

Sec. 12. No evidence of state indebtedness shall be issued except for debts authorized pursuant to this constitution.

History: Const. 1963, Art. IX, §12, Eff. Jan. 1, 1964.
Former constitution: See Const. 1908, Art. X, §11.

Public bodies, borrowing power.

Sec. 13. Public bodies corporate shall have power to borrow money and to issue their securities evidencing debt, subject to this constitution and law.

History: Const. 1963, Art. IX, §13, Eff. Jan. 1, 1964.

State borrowing; short term.

Sec. 14. To meet obligations incurred pursuant to appropriations for any fiscal year, the legislature may by law authorize the state to issue its full faith and credit notes in which case it shall pledge undedicated revenues to be received within the same fiscal year for the repayment thereof. Such indebtedness in any fiscal year shall not exceed 15 percent of undedicated revenues received by the state during the preceding fiscal year and such debts shall be repaid at the time the revenues so pledged are received, but not later than the end of the same fiscal year.

History: Const. 1963, Art. IX, §14, Eff. Jan. 1, 1964.

Long term borrowing by state.

Sec. 15. The state may borrow money for specific purposes in amounts as may be provided by acts of the legislature adopted by a vote of two-thirds of the members elected to and serving in each house, and approved by a majority of the electors voting thereon at any general election. The question submitted to the electors shall state the amount to be borrowed, the specific purpose to which the funds shall be devoted, and the method of repayment.

History: Const. 1963, Art. IX, §15, Eff. Jan. 1, 1964.

State loans to school districts.

Sec. 16. The state, in addition to any other borrowing power, may borrow from time to time such amounts as shall be required, pledge its faith and credit and issue its notes or bonds therefor, for the purpose of making loans to school districts as provided in this section.

Amount of loans.

If the minimum amount which would otherwise be necessary for a school district to levy in any year to pay principal and interest on its qualified bonds, including any necessary allowances for estimated tax delinquencies, exceeds 13 mills on each dollar of its assessed valuation as finally equalized, or such lower millage as the legislature may prescribe, then the school district may elect to borrow all or any part of the excess from the state. In that event the state shall lend the excess amount to the school district for the payment of principal and interest. If for any reason any school district will be or is unable to pay the principal and interest on its qualified bonds when due, then the school district shall borrow and the state shall lend to it an amount sufficient to enable the school district to make the payment.

Qualified bonds.

The term "qualified bonds" means general obligation bonds of school districts issued for capital expenditures, including refunding bonds, issued prior to May 4, 1955, or issued thereafter and qualified as provided by law pursuant to Section 27 or Section 28 of Article X of the Constitution of 1908 or pursuant to this section.

Repayment of loans, tax levy by school district.

After a school district has received loans from the state, each year thereafter it shall levy for debt service, exclusive of levies for nonqualified bonds, not less than 13 mills or such lower millage as the legislature may prescribe, until the amount loaned has been repaid, and any tax collections therefrom in any year over and above the minimum requirements for principal and interest on qualified bonds shall be used toward the repayment of state loans. In any year when such levy would produce an amount in excess of the requirements and the amount due to the state, the levy may be reduced by the amount of the excess.

Bonds, state loans, repayment.

Subject to the foregoing provisions, the legislature shall have the power to prescribe and to limit the procedure, terms and conditions for the qualification of bonds, for obtaining and making state loans, and for the repayment of loans.

Power to tax unlimited.

The power to tax for the payment of principal and interest on bonds hereafter issued which are the general obligations of any school district, including refunding bonds, and for repayment of any state loans made to school districts, shall be without limitation as to rate or amount.

Rights and obligations to remain unimpaired.

All rights acquired under Sections 27 and 28 of Article X of the Constitution of 1908, by holders of bonds heretofore issued, and all obligations assumed by the state or any school district under these sections, shall remain unimpaired.

History: Const. 1963, Art. IX, §16, Eff. Jan. 1, 1964.
Former constitution: See Const. 1908, Art. X, §§27, 28.

Payments from state treasury.

Sec. 17. No money shall be paid out of the state treasury except in pursuance of appropriations made by law.

History: Const. 1963, Art. IX, §17, Eff. Jan. 1, 1964.
Former constitution: See Const. 1908, Art. X, §16.

State credit.

Sec. 18. The credit of the state shall not be granted to, nor in aid of any person, association or corporation, public or private, except as authorized in this constitution.

Investment of public funds.

This section shall not be construed to prohibit the investment of public funds until needed for current requirements or the investment of funds accumulated to provide retirement or pension benefits for public officials and employees, as provided by law.

History: Const. 1963, Art. IX, §18, Eff. Jan. 1, 1964.
Former constitution: See Const. 1908, Art. X, §12.

Subscription to or interest in stock by state prohibited; exceptions.

Sec. 19. The state shall not subscribe to, nor be interested in the stock of any company, association or corporation, except as follows:

(a) Funds accumulated to provide retirement or pension benefits for public officials and employees may be invested as provided by law.

(b) Endowment funds created for charitable or educational purposes may be invested as provided by law governing the investment of funds held in trust by trustees.

(c) Funds held as permanent funds or endowment funds other than those described in subdivision (b) may be invested as provided by law.

Except as otherwise provided in this section, other state funds or money may be invested in accounts of a bank, savings and loan association, or credit union organized under the laws of this state or federal law, as provided by law.

History: Const. 1963, Art. IX, §19, Eff. Jan. 1, 1964;—Am. H.J.R. GG, approved Nov. 7, 1978, Eff. Dec. 23, 1978;—Am. S.J.R. T, approved Aug. 6, 2002, Eff. Sept. 21, 2002.
Former constitution: See Const. 1908, Art. X, §13.

Deposit of state money in certain financial institutions; requirements.

Sec. 20. No state money shall be deposited in banks, savings and loan associations, or credit unions, other than those organized under the law of this state or federal law. No state money shall be deposited in any bank, savings and loan association, or credit union, in excess of 50 percent of the net worth of the bank, savings and loan association, or credit union. Any bank, savings and loan association, or credit union, receiving deposits of state money shall show the amount of state money so deposited as a separate item in all published statements.

History: Const. 1963, Art. IX, §20, Eff. Jan. 1, 1964;—Am. H.J.R. GG, approved Nov. 7, 1978, Eff. Dec. 23, 1978.
Former constitution: See Const. 1908, Art. X, §15.

Accounting for public moneys.

Sec. 21. The legislature shall provide by law for the annual accounting for all public moneys, state and local, and may provide by law for interim accounting.

Accounting and auditing for local governments.

The legislature shall provide by law for the maintenance of uniform accounting systems by units of local government and the auditing of county accounts by competent state authority and other units of government as provided by law.

History: Const. 1963, Art. IX, §21, Eff. Jan. 1, 1964.
Former constitution: See Const. 1908, Art. X, §18.

Examination and adjustment of claims against state.

Sec. 22. Procedures for the examination and adjustment of claims against the state shall be prescribed by law.

History: Const. 1963, Art. IX, §22, Eff. Jan. 1, 1964.
Former constitution: See Const. 1908, Art. VI, §20.

Financial records; statement of revenues and expenditures.

Sec. 23. All financial records, accountings, audit reports and other reports of public moneys shall be public records and open to inspection. A statement of all revenues and expenditures of public moneys shall be published and distributed annually, as provided by law.

History: Const. 1963, Art. IX, §23, Eff. Jan. 1, 1964.
Former constitution: See Const. 1908, Art. X, §17.

Public pension plans and retirement systems, obligation.

Sec. 24. The accrued financial benefits of each pension plan and retirement system of the state and its political subdivisions shall be a contractual obligation thereof which shall not be diminished or impaired thereby.

Financial benefits, annual funding.

Financial benefits arising on account of service rendered in each fiscal year shall be funded during that year and such funding shall not be used for financing unfunded accrued liabilities.

History: Const. 1963, Art. IX, §24, Eff. Jan. 1, 1964.

Voter approval of increased local taxes; prohibitions; emergency conditions; repayment of bonded indebtedness guaranteed; implementation of section.

Sec. 25. Property taxes and other local taxes and state taxation and spending may not be increased above the limitations specified herein without direct voter approval. The state is prohibited from requiring any new or expanded activities by local governments without full state financing, from reducing the proportion of state spending in the form of aid to local governments, or from shifting the tax burden to local government. A provision for emergency conditions is established and the repayment of voter approved bonded indebtedness is guaranteed. Implementation of this section is specified in Sections 26 through 34, inclusive, of this Article.

History: Add. Init., approved Nov. 7, 1978, Eff. Dec. 23, 1978.

Limitation on taxes; revenue limit; refunding or transferring excess revenues; exceptions to revenue limitation; adjustment of state revenue and spending limits.

Sec. 26. There is hereby established a limit on the total amount of taxes which may be imposed by the legislature in any fiscal year on the taxpayers of this state. This limit shall not be changed without approval of the majority of the qualified electors voting thereon, as provided for in Article 12 of the Constitution. Effective with fiscal year 1979-1980, and for each fiscal year thereafter, the legislature shall not impose taxes of any kind which, together with all other revenues of the state, federal aid excluded, exceed the revenue limit established in this section. The revenue limit shall be equal to the product of the ratio of Total State Revenues in fiscal year 1978-79 divided by the Personal Income of Michigan in calendar year 1977 multiplied by the Personal Income of Michigan in either the prior calendar year or the average of Personal Income of Michigan in the previous three calendar years, whichever is greater.

For any fiscal year in the event that Total State Revenues exceed the revenue limit established in this section by 1% or more, the excess revenues shall be refunded pro rata based on the liability reported on the Michigan income tax and single business tax (or its successor tax or taxes) annual returns filed following the close of such fiscal year. If the excess is less than 1%, this excess may be transferred to the State Budget Stabilization Fund.

The revenue limitation established in this section shall not apply to taxes imposed for the payment of principal and interest on bonds, approved by the voters and authorized under Section 15 of this Article, and loans to school districts authorized under Section 16 of this Article.

If responsibility for funding a program or programs is transferred from one level of government to another, as a consequence of constitutional amendment, the state revenue and spending limits may be adjusted to accommodate such change, provided that the total revenue authorized for collection by both state and local governments does not exceed that amount which would have been authorized without such change.

History: Add. Init., approved Nov. 7, 1978, Eff. Dec. 23, 1978.

Exceeding revenue limit; conditions.

Sec. 27. The revenue limit of Section 26 of this Article may be exceeded only if all of the following conditions are met: (1) The governor requests the legislature to declare an emergency; (2) the request is specific as to the nature of the emergency, the dollar amount of the emergency, and the method by which the emergency will be funded; and (3) the legislature thereafter declares an emergency in accordance with the specific of the governor's request by a two-thirds vote of the members elected to and serving in each house. The emergency must be declared in accordance with this section prior to incurring any of the expenses which constitute the emergency request. The revenue limit may be exceeded only during the fiscal year for which the emergency is declared. In no event shall any part of the amount representing a refund under Section 26 of this Article be the subject of an emergency request.

History: Add. Init., approved Nov. 7, 1978, Eff. Dec. 23, 1978.

Limitation on expenses of state government.

Sec. 28. No expenses of state government shall be incurred in any fiscal year which exceed the sum of the revenue limit established in Sections 26 and 27 of this Article plus federal aid and any surplus from a previous fiscal year.

History: Add. Init., approved Nov. 7, 1978, Eff. Dec. 23, 1978.

State financing of activities or services required of local government by state law.

Sec. 29. The state is hereby prohibited from reducing the state financed proportion of the necessary costs of any existing activity or service required of units of Local Government by state law. A new activity or service or an increase in the level of any activity or service beyond that required by existing law shall not be required by the legislature or any state agency of units of Local Government, unless a state appropriation is made and disbursed to pay the unit of Local Government for any necessary increased costs. The provision of this section shall not apply to costs incurred pursuant to Article VI, Section 18.

History: Add. Init., approved Nov. 7, 1978, Eff. Dec. 23, 1978.

Reduction of state spending paid to units of local government.

Sec. 30. The proportion of total state spending paid to all units of Local Government, taken as a group, shall not be reduced below that proportion in effect in fiscal year 1978-79.

History: Add. Init., approved Nov. 7, 1978, Eff. Dec. 23, 1978.

Levying tax or increasing rate of existing tax; maximum tax rate on new base; increase in assessed valuation of property; exceptions to limitations.

Sec. 31. Units of Local Government are hereby prohibited from levying any tax not authorized by law or charter when this section is ratified or from increasing the rate of an existing tax above that rate authorized by law or charter when this section is ratified, without the approval of a majority of the qualified electors of that unit of Local Government voting thereon. If the definition of the base of an existing tax is broadened, the maximum authorized rate of taxation on the new base in each unit of Local Government shall be reduced to yield the same estimated gross revenue as on the prior base. If the assessed valuation of property as finally equalized, excluding the value of new construction and improvements, increases by a larger percentage than the increase in the General Price Level from the previous year, the maximum authorized rate applied thereto in each unit of Local Government shall be reduced to yield the same gross revenue from existing property, adjusted for changes in the General Price Level, as could have been collected at the existing authorized rate on the prior assessed value.

The limitations of this section shall not apply to taxes imposed for the payment of principal and interest on bonds or other evidence of indebtedness or for the payment of assessments on contract obligations in anticipation of which bonds are issued which were authorized prior to the effective date of this amendment.

History: Add. Init., approved Nov. 7, 1978, Eff. Dec. 23, 1978.

Suit to enforce sections 25 to 31.

Sec. 32. Any taxpayer of the state shall have standing to bring suit in the Michigan State Court of Appeals to enforce the provisions of Sections 25 through 31, inclusive, of this Article and, if the suit is sustained, shall receive from the applicable unit of government his costs incurred in maintaining such suit.

History: Add. Init., approved Nov. 7, 1978, Eff. Dec. 23, 1978.

Definitions applicable to sections 25 to 32.

Sec. 33. Definitions. The definitions of this section shall apply to Section 25 through 32 of Article IX, inclusive.

"Total State Revenues" includes all general and special revenues, excluding federal aid, as defined in the budget message of the governor for fiscal year 1978-1979. Total State Revenues shall exclude the amount of any credits based on actual tax liabilities or the imputed tax components of rental payments, but shall include the amount of any credits not related to actual tax liabilities. "Personal Income of Michigan" is the total income received by persons in Michigan from all sources, as defined and officially reported by the United States Department of Commerce or its successor agency. "Local Government" means any political subdivision of the state, including, but not restricted to, school districts, cities, villages, townships, charter townships, counties, charter counties, authorities created by the state, and authorities created by other units of local government. "General Price Level" means the Consumer Price Index for the United States as defined and officially reported by the United States Department of Labor or its successor agency.

History: Add. Init., approved Nov. 7, 1978, Eff. Dec. 23, 1978.

Implementation of sections 25 to 33.

Sec. 34. The Legislature shall implement the provisions of Sections 25 through 33, inclusive, of this Article.

History: Add. Init., approved Nov. 7, 1978, Eff. Dec. 23, 1978.

Michigan natural resources trust fund.

Sec. 35. There is hereby established the Michigan natural resources trust fund. The trust fund shall consist of all bonuses, rentals, delayed rentals, and royalties collected or reserved by the state under provisions of leases for the extraction of nonrenewable resources from state owned lands, except such revenues accruing under leases of state owned lands acquired with money from state or federal game and fish protection funds or revenues accruing from lands purchased with such revenues. The trust fund may receive appropriations, money, or other things of value. The assets of the trust fund shall be invested as provided by law.

Until the trust fund reaches an accumulated principal of $500,000,000.00, $10,000,000.00 of the revenues from bonuses, rentals, delayed rentals, and royalties described in this section otherwise dedicated to the trust fund that are received by the state each state fiscal year shall be deposited into the Michigan state parks endowment fund. However, until the trust fund reaches an accumulated principal of $500,000,000.00, in any state fiscal year, not more than 50 percent of the total revenues from bonuses, rentals, delayed rentals, and royalties described in this section otherwise dedicated to the trust fund that are received by the state each state fiscal year shall be deposited into the Michigan state parks endowment fund.

The amount accumulated in the trust fund in any state fiscal year shall not exceed $500,000,000.00, exclusive of interest and earnings and amounts authorized for expenditure pursuant to this section. When the accumulated principal of the trust fund reaches $500,000,000.00, all revenue from bonuses, rentals, delayed rentals, and royalties described in this section that would be received by the trust fund but for this limitation shall be deposited into the Michigan state parks endowment fund until the Michigan state parks endowment fund reaches an accumulated principal of $800,000,000.00. When the Michigan state parks endowment fund reaches an accumulated principal of $800,000,000.00, all revenues from bonuses, rentals, delayed rentals, and royalties described in this section shall be distributed as provided by law.

The interest and earnings of the trust fund shall be expended for the acquisition of land or rights in land for recreational uses or protection of the land because of its environmental importance or its scenic beauty, for the development of public recreation facilities, and for the administration of the trust fund, which may include payments in lieu of taxes on state owned land purchased through the trust fund. The trust fund may provide grants to units of local government or public authorities which shall be used for the purposes of this section. The legislature shall provide that a portion of the cost of a project funded by such grants be provided by the local unit of government or public authority.

Until the trust fund reaches an accumulated principal of $500,000,000.00, the legislature may provide, in addition to the expenditure of interest and earnings authorized by this section, that a portion, not to exceed 33-1/3 percent, of the revenues from bonuses, rentals, delayed rentals, and royalties described in this section received by the trust fund during each state fiscal year may be expended during subsequent state fiscal years for the purposes of this section.

Not less than 25 percent of the total amounts made available for expenditure from the trust fund from any state fiscal year shall be expended for acquisition of land and rights in land and not more than 25 percent of the total amounts made available for expenditure from the trust fund from any state fiscal year shall be expended for development of public recreation facilities.

The legislature shall provide by law for the establishment of a trust fund board within the department of natural resources. The trust fund board shall recommend the projects to be funded. The board shall submit its recommendations to the governor who shall submit the board's recommendations to the legislature in an appropriations bill.

The legislature shall provide by law for the implementation of this section.

History: Add. H.J.R. M, approved Nov. 6, 1984, Eff. Dec. 22, 1984;—Am. S.J.R. E, approved Nov. 8, 1994, Eff. Dec. 24, 1994;—Am. S.J.R. T, approved Aug. 6, 2002, Eff. Sept. 21, 2002.

Michigan state parks endowment fund.

Sec. 35a. There is hereby established the Michigan state parks endowment fund. The endowment fund shall consist of revenues as provided in section 35 of this article, and as provided by law. The endowment fund may also receive private contributions of money or other things of value. All money in the Genevieve Gillette state parks endowment fund shall be transferred to the endowment fund. The assets of the endowment fund shall be invested as provided by law.

The accumulated principal of the endowment fund shall not exceed $800,000,000.00, which amount shall be annually adjusted pursuant to the rate of inflation beginning when the endowment fund reaches $800,000,000.00. This annually adjusted figure is the accumulated principal limit of the endowment fund.

Money available for expenditure from the endowment fund as provided in this section shall be expended for operations, maintenance, and capital improvements at Michigan state parks and for the acquisition of land or rights in land for Michigan state parks.

Money in the endowment fund shall be expended as follows:

(1) Until the endowment fund reaches an accumulated principal of $800,000,000.00, each state fiscal year the legislature may appropriate not more than 50 percent of the money received under section 35 of this article plus interest and earnings and any private contributions or other revenue to the endowment fund.

(2) Once the accumulated principal in the endowment fund reaches $800,000,000.00, only the interest and earnings of the endowment fund in excess of the amount necessary to maintain the endowment fund's accumulated principal limit may be made available for expenditure.

Unexpended appropriations of the endowment fund from any state fiscal year as authorized by this section may be carried forward or may be appropriated as determined by the legislature for purposes of this section.

The legislature shall provide by law for implementation of this section.

History: Add. S.J.R. E, approved Nov. 8, 1994, Eff. Dec. 24, 1994;—Am. S.J.R. T, approved Aug. 6, 2002, Eff. Sept. 21, 2002.

Compiler's note: This section was originally added to the Constitution by S.J.R. E as section 36, effective Dec. 24, 1994, but was compiled as §36[1] to distinguish it from another section 36 added to Article 9, effective April 30, 1994, which pertained to a tax on tobacco products. When this section (§36[1]) was amended by S.J.R. T, effective September 21, 2002, it was renumbered as section 35a.

Tax on tobacco products; dedication of proceeds.

Sec. 36. Six percent of the proceeds of the tax on tobacco products shall be dedicated to improving the quality of health care of the residents of this state.

History: Add. S.J.R. S, approved Mar. 15, 1994, Eff. Apr. 30, 1994.

Michigan veterans' trust fund.

Sec. 37. The Michigan veterans' trust fund is established within the department of treasury. All money in the fund established by 1946 (1st Ex Sess) PA 9 shall be transferred to the Michigan veterans' trust fund. The trust fund may additionally receive appropriations, money, or other things of value. The state treasurer shall direct investment of the fund as provided by law, and credit interest and earnings of the fund to the fund. Except for the state treasurer's actions authorized under this section, an expenditure or transfer of a trust fund asset, interest, or earnings may be made only upon the authorization of a majority of the members of the Michigan veterans' trust fund board of trustees.

History: Add. H.J.R. H, approved Nov. 5, 1996, Eff. Dec. 21, 1996;—Am. S.J.R. T, approved Aug. 6, 2002, Eff. Sept. 21, 2002.

Michigan veterans' trust fund board of trustees; establishment.

Sec. 38. The Michigan veterans' trust fund board of trustees is established and consists of veterans honorably discharged from the armed services and appointed by the governor as prescribed by law.

History: Add. H.J.R. H, approved Nov. 5, 1996, Eff. Dec. 21, 1996.

Michigan veterans' trust fund board of trustees; administration of trust fund.

Sec. 39. The Michigan veterans' trust fund board of trustees shall administer the Michigan veterans' trust fund. The board of trustees shall not authorize the expenditure or transfer of a trust fund asset, interest, or earnings unless the board of trustees determines in its discretion and by a majority vote that the expenditure or transfer is for the benefit of veterans or their spouses or dependents.

History: Add. H.J.R. H, approved Nov. 5, 1996, Eff. Dec. 21, 1996.

Michigan conservation and recreation legacy fund.

Sec. 40. The Michigan conservation and recreation legacy fund is established. The state treasurer shall direct the investment of the legacy fund. The state treasurer shall establish within the legacy fund restricted accounts as authorized by this section and may establish additional subaccounts as authorized by law. The state treasurer may receive gifts, grants, bequests, or assets from any source for deposit into a particular account or subaccount. The assets of the legacy fund shall be invested as provided by law. Interest and earnings accruing from each account or subaccount shall be credited to that account or subaccount.

The forest recreation account is established as an account within the legacy fund. The forest recreation account shall consist of revenue derived from concessions, leases, contracts, and fees from recreational activities on state forestlands and other revenues as authorized by law. Money in the forest recreation account shall be expended only for the following:

(a) The development, improvement, operation, promotion, and maintenance of forest recreation activities.

(b) Grants to state colleges and universities to implement programs funded by the forest recreation account.

(c) The administration of the forest recreation account.

The game and fish protection account is established as an account within the legacy fund. The game and fish protection account shall consist of revenue derived from hunting and fishing licenses, passbooks, permits, fees, concessions, leases, contracts, and activities; damages paid for the illegal taking of game and fish; revenue derived from fees, licenses, and permits related to game, game areas, and game fish; and other revenues as authorized by law. Money in the game and fish protection account shall be expended only for the following:

(a) The development, improvement, operation, promotion, and maintenance of wildlife and fisheries programs and facilities.

(b) The acquisition of land and rights in land that support wildlife and fisheries programs.

(c) Research to support wildlife and fisheries programs.

(d) The enforcement and administration of the wildlife and fisheries laws of the state, including the necessary equipment and apparatus incident to the operation and enforcement of wildlife and fisheries laws.

(e) The protection, propagation, distribution, and control of wildlife and fish.

(f) Grants to state colleges and universities to implement programs funded by the game and fish protection account.

(g) The administration of the game and fish protection account, which may include payments in lieu of taxes on state owned land that has been or will be purchased through the game and fish protection fund or account.

The off-road vehicle account is established as an account within the legacy fund. The off-road vehicle account shall consist of revenue derived from fees imposed upon the use or registration of off-road vehicles and other revenues as authorized by law. Money in the off-road vehicle account shall be expended only for the following:

(a) Signage for and the improvement, maintenance, and construction of off-road vehicle trails, routes, or areas.

(b) The administration and enforcement of state regulations related to off-road vehicles.

(c) The leasing of land for use by off-road vehicles.

(d) The acquisition of easements, permits, or other agreements for the use of land for off-road vehicle trails, routes, or areas.

(e) The restoration of any of the natural resources of the state on public land that are damaged due to off-road vehicle use.

(f) Safety education programs related to the operation of off-road vehicles.

(g) Other uses as provided by law as long as the uses are consistent with the development, improvement, operation, promotion, and maintenance of the state's off-road vehicle programs.

(h) Grants to state colleges and universities to implement programs funded by the off-road vehicle account.

(i) The administration of the off-road vehicle account.

The recreation improvement account is established as an account within the legacy fund. The recreation improvement account shall consist of all tax revenue derived from the sale of two percent of the gasoline sold in this state for consumption in internal combustion engines and other revenues as authorized by law. Money in the recreation improvement account shall be distributed as follows:

(a) Eighty percent of the money shall be annually transferred to the waterways account to be used for the purposes of that account.

(b) Fourteen percent of the money shall be annually transferred to the snowmobile account to be used for the purposes of that account.

(c) The remainder of the money that is not transferred under this section shall be used, upon appropriation, for recreation projects, including grants to state colleges and universities to implement recreation projects, and for the administration of the recreation improvement account. Of the amount that is credited to recreational projects in a fiscal year, not less than twenty-five percent of any funds designated for projects intended for off-road vehicles shall be expended on projects to repair damages as a result of pollution, impairment, or destruction of air, water, or other natural resources, or the public trust, in air, water, or other natural resources, as a result of the use of off-road vehicles.

The snowmobile account is established as an account within the legacy fund. The snowmobile account shall consist of revenue derived from fees imposed for the registration or use of snowmobiles; revenue derived from the use of snowmobile trails; transfers from the recreation improvement account; and other revenues as authorized by law. Money in the snowmobile account shall be expended only for the following:

(a) Planning, construction, maintenance, and acquisition of trails and areas for the use of snowmobiles.

(b) Providing access to trails and areas for the use of snowmobiles.

(c) Providing basic snowmobile facilities.

(d) The administration and enforcement of state regulations related to snowmobiles.

(e) Safety education programs related to the operation of snowmobiles.

(f) Other uses as provided by law as long as the uses are consistent with the development, improvement, operation, promotion, and maintenance of the state's snowmobile programs.

(g) Grants to state colleges and universities to implement programs funded by the snowmobile account.

(h) The administration of the snowmobile account, which may include payments in lieu of taxes on state owned land that has been or will be purchased through the recreational snowmobile trail improvement fund or snowmobile account.

The state park improvement account is established as an account within the legacy fund. The state park improvement account shall consist of revenue derived from concessions, leases, contracts, fees, and permits for activities in state parks and recreation areas; damages paid to the state for illegal activities in state parks and recreation areas; and other revenues as authorized by law. Money in the state park improvement account shall be expended only for the following:

(a) The development, improvement, operation, promotion, and maintenance of state parks and recreation areas.

(b) Grants to state colleges and universities to implement programs funded by the state park improvement account.

(c) The administration of the state park improvement account.

The waterways account is established as an account within the legacy fund. The waterways account shall consist of revenue derived from watercraft registration fees assessed on the ownership or operation of watercraft in the state; revenue derived from fees charged for the moorage of watercraft at state-operated mooring facilities; revenue derived from fees charged for the use of state-operated public access sites; transfers from the recreation improvement account; all tax revenue derived from the sale of diesel fuel in this state that is used to generate power for the operation or propulsion of vessels on the waterways of the state; and other revenues as authorized by law. Money in the waterways account shall be expended only for the following:

(a) The construction, operation, and maintenance of recreational boating facilities that provide public access to waterways or moorage of watercraft.

(b) The acquisition of property for the purpose of paragraph (a).

(c) Grants to local units of government and state colleges and universities for the provision of public access or moorage of watercraft and law enforcement or boating education to recreational watercraft operators.

(d) The acquisition and development of harbors and public access sites.

(e) The enforcement of laws related to the operation of watercraft and education related to the operation of watercraft. Not less than forty-nine percent of revenues from watercraft registration fees received by the waterways account shall be used for the purposes of this subdivision.

(f) The administration of programs funded by the waterways account.

(g) Other uses as provided by law as long as the uses are consistent with the development, improvement, operation, promotion, and maintenance of the state's waterways programs.

(h) The administration of the waterways account, which may include payments in lieu of taxes on state owned land that has been or will be purchased through the Michigan state waterways fund or waterways account.

The legislature shall provide by law for the implementation of this section.

History: Add. H.J.R. Z, approved Nov. 7, 2006, Eff. Dec. 23, 2006.

Michigan game and fish protection trust fund.

Sec. 41. The Michigan game and fish protection trust fund is established. The Michigan game and fish protection trust fund shall consist of revenue derived from bonuses, rentals, delayed rentals, royalties, and other revenues collected or reserved by the state under leases or direct sale contracts accruing from state owned lands acquired with money from state or federal game and fish protection funds or revenues accruing from lands purchased with such revenues. The Michigan game and fish protection trust fund may also receive gifts, grants, bequests, or assets from any source and may receive other revenues as authorized by law.

The assets of the Michigan game and fish protection trust fund shall be invested as provided by law. The interest and earnings from these investments shall be credited to the Michigan game and fish protection trust fund.

The accumulated interest and earnings of the Michigan game and fish protection trust fund and not more than $6,000,000.00 of the principal of the Michigan game and fish protection trust fund may be expended in any year for the purposes of the game and fish protection account of the Michigan conservation and recreation legacy fund established in section 40.

The legislature shall provide by law for the implementation of this section.

History: Add. H.J.R. Z, approved Nov. 7, 2006, Eff. Dec. 23, 2006.

Michigan nongame fish and wildlife trust fund.

Sec. 42. The Michigan nongame fish and wildlife trust fund is established. The Michigan nongame fish and wildlife trust fund shall consist of revenue designated by a member of the public for the benefit of nongame fish and wildlife.

The Michigan nongame fish and wildlife trust fund may also receive gifts, grants, bequests, or assets from any source and may receive other revenues as authorized by law.

The assets of the Michigan nongame fish and wildlife trust fund shall be invested as provided by law. The interest and earnings from these investments shall be credited to the Michigan nongame fish and wildlife trust fund.

The Michigan nongame fish and wildlife trust fund shall maintain a principal balance of not less than $6,000,000.00.

The interest and earnings of the Michigan nongame fish and wildlife trust fund and other revenues not retained on a permanent basis shall be expended only for the following:

(a) The management of nongame fish and wildlife species consistent with a long-range plan for the management of Michigan's nongame fish and wildlife resources.

(b) Grants to state colleges and universities to implement programs funded by the Michigan nongame fish and wildlife trust fund.

(c) The administration of the Michigan nongame fish and wildlife trust fund.

History: Add. H.J.R. Z, approved Nov. 7, 2006, Eff. Dec. 23, 2006.

ARTICLE X
PROPERTY

Disabilities of coverture abolished; separate property of wife; dower.

Sec. 1. The disabilities of coverture as to property are abolished. The real and personal estate of every woman acquired before marriage and all real and personal property to which she may afterwards become entitled shall be and remain the estate and property of such woman, and shall not be liable for the debts, obligations or engagements of her husband, and may be dealt with and disposed of by her as if she were unmarried. Dower may be relinquished or conveyed as provided by law.

History: Const. 1963, Art. X, §1, Eff. Jan. 1, 1964.
Former constitution: See Const. 1908, Art. XVI, §8.

Eminent domain; compensation.

Sec. 2. Private property shall not be taken for public use without just compensation therefore being first made or secured in a manner prescribed by law. If private property consisting of an individual's principal residence is taken for public use, the amount of compensation made and determined for that taking shall be not less than 125% of that property's fair market value, in addition to any other reimbursement allowed by law. Compensation shall be determined in proceedings in a court of record.

"Public use" does not include the taking of private property for transfer to a private entity for the purpose of economic development or enhancement of tax revenues. Private property otherwise may be taken for reasons of public use as that term is understood on the effective date of the amendment to this constitution that added this paragraph.

In a condemnation action, the burden of proof is on the condemning authority to demonstrate, by the preponderance of the evidence, that the taking of a private property is for a public use, unless the condemnation action involves a taking for the eradication of blight, in which case the burden of proof is on the condemning authority to demonstrate, by clear and convincing evidence, that the taking of that property is for a public use.

Any existing right, grant, or benefit afforded to property owners as of November 1, 2005, whether provided by this section, by statute, or otherwise, shall be preserved and shall not be abrogated or impaired by the constitutional amendment that added this paragraph.

History: Const. 1963, Art. X, § 2, Eff. Jan. 1, 1964;—Am. S.J.R. E, approved Nov. 7, 2006, Eff. Dec. 23, 2006.
Former constitution: See Const. 1908, Art. XIII, §§ 1-5.

Homestead and personalty, exemption from process.

Sec. 3. A homestead in the amount of not less than $3,500 and personal property of every resident of this state in the amount of not less than $750, as defined by law, shall be exempt from forced sale on execution or other process of any court. Such exemptions shall not extend to any lien thereon excluded from exemption by law.

History: Const. 1963, Art. X, §3, Eff. Jan. 1, 1964.
Former constitution: See Const. 1908, Art. XIV, §§1-4.

Escheats.

Sec. 4. Procedures relating to escheats and to the custody and disposition of escheated property shall be prescribed by law.

History: Const. 1963, Art. X, §4, Eff. Jan. 1, 1964.
Former constitution: See Const. 1908, Art. VI, §20.

State lands.

Sec. 5. The legislature shall have general supervisory jurisdiction over all state owned lands useful for forest preserves, game areas and recreational purposes; shall require annual reports as to such lands from all departments having supervision or control thereof; and shall by general law provide for the sale, lease or other disposition of such lands.

State land reserve.

The legislature by an act adopted by two-thirds of the members elected to and serving in each house may designate any part of such lands as a state land reserve. No lands in the state land reserve may be removed from the reserve, sold, leased or otherwise disposed of except by an act of the legislature.

History: Const. 1963, Art. X, §5, Eff. Jan. 1, 1964.

Resident aliens, property rights.

Sec. 6. Aliens who are residents of this state shall enjoy the same rights and privileges in property as citizens of this state.

History: Const. 1963, Art. X, §6, Eff. Jan. 1, 1964.
Former constitution: See Const. 1908, Art. XVI, §9.

ARTICLE XI
PUBLIC OFFICERS AND EMPLOYMENT

Oath of public officers.

Sec. 1. All officers, legislative, executive and judicial, before entering upon the duties of their respective offices, shall take and subscribe the following oath or affirmation: I do solemnly swear (or affirm) that I will support the Constitution of the United States and the constitution of this state, and that I will faithfully discharge the duties of the office of .... according to the best of my ability. No other oath, affirmation, or any religious test shall be required as a qualification for any office or public trust.

History: Const. 1963, Art. XI, §1, Eff. Jan. 1, 1964.
Former constitution: See Const. 1908, Art. XVI, §2.

Terms of office of state and county officers.

Sec. 2. The terms of office of elective state officers, members of the legislature and justices and judges of courts of record shall begin at twelve o'clock noon on the first day of January next succeeding their election, except as otherwise provided in this constitution. The terms of office of county officers shall begin on the first day of January next succeeding their election, except as otherwise provided by law.

History: Const. 1963, Art. XI, §2, Eff. Jan. 1, 1964.
Former constitution: See Const. 1908, Art. XVI, §1.

Extra compensation.

Sec. 3. Neither the legislature nor any political subdivision of this state shall grant or authorize extra compensation to any public officer, agent or contractor after the service has been rendered or the contract entered into.

History: Const. 1963, Art. XI, §3, Eff. Jan. 1, 1964.
Former constitution: See Const. 1908, Art. XVI, §3.

Custodian of public moneys; eligibility to office, accounting.

Sec. 4. No person having custody or control of public moneys shall be a member of the legislature, or be eligible to any office of trust or profit under this state, until he shall have made an accounting, as provided by law, of all sums for which he may be liable.

History: Const. 1963, Art. XI, §4, Eff. Jan. 1, 1964.
Former constitution: See Const. 1908, Art. X, §19.

Classified state civil service; scope; exempted positions; appointment and terms of members of state civil service commission; state personnel director; duties of commission; collective bargaining for state police troopers and sergeants; appointments, promotions, demotions, or removals; increases or reductions in compensation; creating or abolishing positions; recommending compensation for unclassified service; appropriation; reports of expenditures; annual audit; payment for personal services; violation; injunctive or mandamus proceedings.

Sec. 5. The classified state civil service shall consist of all positions in the state service except those filled by popular election, heads of principal departments, members of boards and commissions, the principal executive officer of boards and commissions heading principal departments, employees of courts of record, employees of the legislature, employees of the state institutions of higher education, all persons in the armed forces of the state, eight exempt positions in the office of the governor, and within each principal department, when requested by the department head, two other exempt positions, one of which shall be policy-making. The civil service commission may exempt three additional positions of a policy-making nature within each principal department.

The civil service commission shall be non-salaried and shall consist of four persons, not more than two of whom shall be members of the same political party, appointed by the governor for terms of eight years, no two of which shall expire in the same year.

The administration of the commission's powers shall be vested in a state personnel director who shall be a member of the classified service and who shall be responsible to and selected by the commission after open competitive examination.

The commission shall classify all positions in the classified service according to their respective duties and responsibilities, fix rates of compensation for all classes of positions, approve or disapprove disbursements for all personal services, determine by competitive examination and performance exclusively on the basis of merit, efficiency and fitness the qualifications of all candidates for positions in the classified service, make rules and regulations covering all personnel transactions, and regulate all conditions of employment in the classified service.

State Police Troopers and Sergeants shall, through their elected representative designated by 50% of such troopers and sergeants, have the right to bargain collectively with their employer concerning conditions of their employment, compensation, hours, working conditions, retirement, pensions, and other aspects of employment except promotions which will be determined by competitive examination and performance on the basis of merit, efficiency and fitness; and they shall have the right 30 days after commencement of such bargaining to submit any unresolved disputes to binding arbitration for the resolution thereof the same as now provided by law for Public Police and Fire Departments.

No person shall be appointed to or promoted in the classified service who has not been certified by the commission as qualified for such appointment or promotion. No appointments, promotions, demotions or removals in the classified service shall be made for religious, racial or partisan considerations.

Increases in rates of compensation authorized by the commission may be effective only at the start of a fiscal year and shall require prior notice to the governor, who shall transmit such increases to the legislature as part of his budget. The legislature may, by a majority vote of the members elected to and serving in each house, waive the notice and permit increases in rates of compensation to be effective at a time other than the start of a fiscal year. Within 60 calendar days following such transmission, the legislature may, by a two-thirds vote of the members elected to and serving in each house, reject or reduce increases in rates of compensation authorized by the commission. Any reduction ordered by the legislature shall apply uniformly to all classes of employees affected by the increases and shall not adjust pay differentials already established by the civil service commission. The legislature may not reduce rates of compensation below those in effect at the time of the transmission of increases authorized by the commission.

The appointing authorities may create or abolish positions for reasons of administrative efficiency without the approval of the commission. Positions shall not be created nor abolished except for reasons of administrative efficiency. Any employee considering himself aggrieved by the abolition or creation of a position shall have a right of appeal to the commission through established grievance procedures.

The civil service commission shall recommend to the governor and to the legislature rates of compensation for all appointed positions within the executive department not a part of the classified service.

To enable the commission to exercise its powers, the legislature shall appropriate to the commission for the ensuing fiscal year a sum not less than one percent of the aggregate payroll of the classified service for the preceding fiscal year, as certified by the commission. Within six months after the conclusion of each fiscal year the commission shall return to the state treasury all moneys unexpended for that fiscal year.

The commission shall furnish reports of expenditures, at least annually, to the governor and the legislature and shall be subject to annual audit as provided by law.

No payment for personal services shall be made or authorized until the provisions of this constitution pertaining to civil service have been complied with in every particular. Violation of any of the provisions hereof may be restrained or observance compelled by injunctive or mandamus proceedings brought by any citizen of the state.

History: Const. 1963, Art. XI, §5, Eff. Jan. 1, 1964;—Am. Init., approved Nov. 7, 1978, Eff. Dec. 23, 1978.
Former constitution: See Const. 1908, Art. VI, §22.

Merit systems for local governments.

Sec. 6. By ordinance or resolution of its governing body which shall not take effect until approved by a majority of the electors voting thereon, unless otherwise provided by charter, each county, township, city, village, school district and other governmental unit or authority may establish, modify or discontinue a merit system for its employees other than teachers under contract or tenure. The state civil service commission may on request furnish technical services to any such unit on a reimbursable basis.

History: Const. 1963, Art. XI, §6, Eff. Jan. 1, 1964.

Impeachment of civil officers.

Sec. 7. The house of representatives shall have the sole power of impeaching civil officers for corrupt conduct in office or for crimes or misdemeanors, but a majority of the members elected thereto and serving therein shall be necessary to direct an impeachment.

Prosecution by 3 members of house of representatives.

When an impeachment is directed, the house of representatives shall elect three of its members to prosecute the impeachment.

Trial by senate; oath, presiding officer.

Every impeachment shall be tried by the senate immediately after the final adjournment of the legislature. The senators shall take an oath or affirmation truly and impartially to try and determine the impeachment according to the evidence. When the governor or lieutenant governor is tried, the chief justice of the supreme court shall preside.

Conviction; vote, penalty.

No person shall be convicted without the concurrence of two-thirds of the senators elected and serving. Judgment in case of conviction shall not extend further than removal from office, but the person convicted shall be liable to punishment according to law.

Judicial officers, functions after impeachment.

No judicial officer shall exercise any of the functions of his office after an impeachment is directed until he is acquitted.

History: Const. 1963, Art. XI, §7, Eff. Jan. 1, 1964.
Former constitution: See Const. 1908, Art. IX, §§1-4.

Convictions for certain felonies; eligibility for elective office or certain positions of public employment.

Sec. 8. A person is ineligible for election or appointment to any state or local elective office of this state and ineligible to hold a position in public employment in this state that is policy-making or that has discretionary authority over public assets if, within the immediately preceding 20 years, the person was convicted of a felony involving dishonesty, deceit, fraud, or a breach of the public trust and the conviction was related to the person's official capacity while the person was holding any elective office or position of employment in local, state, or federal government. This requirement is in addition to any other qualification required under this constitution or by law.

The legislature shall prescribe by law for the implementation of this section.

History: Add. S.J.R. V, approved Nov. 2, 2010, Eff. Dec. 18, 2010.

ARTICLE XII
AMENDMENT AND REVISION

Amendment by legislative proposal and vote of electors.

Sec. 1. Amendments to this constitution may be proposed in the senate or house of representatives. Proposed amendments agreed to by two-thirds of the members elected to and serving in each house on a vote with the names and vote of those voting entered in the respective journals shall be submitted, not less than 60 days thereafter, to the electors at the next general election or special election as the legislature shall direct. If a majority of electors voting on a proposed amendment approve the same, it shall become part of the constitution and shall abrogate or amend existing provisions of the constitution at the end of 45 days after the date of the election at which it was approved.

History: Const. 1963, Art. XII, §1, Eff. Jan. 1, 1964.
Former constitution: See Const. 1908, Art. XVII, §1.

Amendment by petition and vote of electors.

Sec. 2. Amendments may be proposed to this constitution by petition of the registered electors of this state. Every petition shall include the full text of the proposed amendment, and be signed by registered electors of the state equal in number to at least 10 percent of the total vote cast for all candidates for governor at the last preceding general election at which a governor was elected. Such petitions shall be filed with the person authorized by law to receive the same at least 120 days before the election at which the proposed amendment is to be voted upon. Any such petition shall be in the form, and shall be signed and circulated in such manner, as prescribed by law. The person authorized by law to receive such petition shall upon its receipt determine, as provided by law, the validity and sufficiency of the signatures on the petition, and make an official announcement thereof at least 60 days prior to the election at which the proposed amendment is to be voted upon.

Submission of proposal; publication.

Any amendment proposed by such petition shall be submitted, not less than 120 days after it was filed, to the electors at the next general election. Such proposed amendment, existing provisions of the constitution which would be altered or abrogated thereby, and the question as it shall appear on the ballot shall be published in full as provided by law. Copies of such publication shall be posted in each polling place and furnished to news media as provided by law.

Ballot, statement of purpose.

The ballot to be used in such election shall contain a statement of the purpose of the proposed amendment, expressed in not more than 100 words, exclusive of caption. Such statement of purpose and caption shall be prepared by the person authorized by law, and shall consist of a true and impartial statement of the purpose of the amendment in such language as shall create no prejudice for or against the proposed amendment.

Approval of proposal, effective date; conflicting amendments.

If the proposed amendment is approved by a majority of the electors voting on the question, it shall become part of the constitution, and shall abrogate or amend existing provisions of the constitution at the end of 45 days after the date of the election at which it was approved. If two or more amendments approved by the electors at the same election conflict, that amendment receiving the highest affirmative vote shall prevail.

History: Const. 1963, Art. XII, §2, Eff. Jan. 1, 1964.
Former constitution: See Const. 1908, Art. XVII, §§2, 3.

General revision of constitution; submission of question, convention delegates and meeting.

Sec. 3. At the general election to be held in the year 1978, and in each 16th year thereafter and at such times as may be provided by law, the question of a general revision of the constitution shall be submitted to the electors of the state. If a majority of the electors voting on the question decide in favor of a convention for such purpose, at an election to be held not later than six months after the proposal was certified as approved, the electors of each representative district as then organized shall elect one delegate and the electors of each senatorial district as then organized shall elect one delegate at a partisan election. The delegates so elected shall convene at the seat of government on the first Tuesday in October next succeeding such election or at an earlier date if provided by law.

Convention officers, rules, membership, personnel, publications.

The convention shall choose its own officers, determine the rules of its proceedings and judge the qualifications, elections and returns of its members. To fill a vacancy in the office of any delegate, the governor shall appoint a qualified resident of the same district who shall be a member of the same party as the delegate vacating the office. The convention shall have power to appoint such officers, employees and assistants as it deems necessary and to fix their compensation; to provide for the printing and distribution of its documents, journals and proceedings; to explain and disseminate information about the proposed constitution and to complete the business of the convention in an orderly manner. Each delegate shall receive for his services compensation provided by law.

Submission of proposed constitution or amendment.

No proposed constitution or amendment adopted by such convention shall be submitted to the electors for approval as hereinafter provided unless by the assent of a majority of all the delegates elected to and serving in the convention, with the names and vote of those voting entered in the journal. Any proposed constitution or amendments adopted by such convention shall be submitted to the qualified electors in the manner and at the time provided by such convention not less than 90 days after final adjournment of the convention. Upon the approval of such constitution or amendments by a majority of the qualified electors voting thereon the constitution or amendments shall take effect as provided by the convention.

History: Const. 1963, Art. XII, §3, Eff. Jan. 1, 1964.
Former constitution: See Const. 1908, Art. XVII, §4.

Severability.

Sec. 4. If any section, subsection or part of Article 2, Section 10, Article 4, Section 54 or Article 5, Section 30 is for any reason held to be invalid or unconstitutional, the remaining sections, subsections or parts of those sections shall not be affected but will remain in full force and effect.

History: Add. Init., approved Nov. 3, 1992, Eff. Dec. 19, 1992.

SCHEDULE AND TEMPORARY PROVISIONS

To insure the orderly transition from the constitution of 1908 to this constitution the following schedule and temporary provisions are set forth to be effective for such period as are thereby required.

Recommendations by attorney general for changes in laws.

Sec. 1. The attorney general shall recommend to the legislature as soon as practicable such changes as may be necessary to adapt existing laws to this constitution.

History: Const. 1963, Schedule, §1, Eff. Jan. 1, 1964.
Former constitution: See Const. 1908, Schedule, §8.

Existing public and private rights, continuance.

Sec. 2. All writs, actions, suits, proceedings, civil or criminal liabilities, prosecutions, judgments, sentences, orders, decrees, appeals, causes of action, contracts, claims, demands, titles and rights existing on the effective date of this constitution shall continue unaffected except as modified in accordance with the provisions of this constitution.

History: Const. 1963, Schedule, §2, Eff. Jan. 1, 1964.
Former constitution: See Const. 1908, Schedule, §2.

Officers, continuance in office.

Sec. 3. Except as otherwise provided in this constitution, all officers filling any office by election or appointment shall continue to exercise their powers and duties until their offices shall have been abolished or their successors selected and qualified in accordance with this constitution or the laws enacted pursuant thereto.

Terms of office.

No provision of this constitution, or of law or of executive order authorized by this constitution shall shorten the term of any person elected to state office at a statewide election on or prior to the date on which this constitution is submitted to a vote. In the event the duties of any such officers shall not have been abolished or incorporated into one or more of the principal departments at the expiration of his term, such officer shall continue to serve until his duties are so incorporated or abolished.

History: Const. 1963, Schedule, §3, Eff. Jan. 1, 1964.
Former constitution: See Const. 1908, Schedule, §5.

Officers elected in spring of 1963, term.

Sec. 4. All officers elected at the same election that this constitution is submitted to the people for adoption shall take office and complete the term to which they were elected under the 1908 constitution and existing laws and continue to serve until their successors are elected and qualified pursuant to this constitution or law.

History: Const. 1963, Schedule, §4, Eff. Jan. 1, 1964.
Former constitution: See Const. 1908, Schedule, §6.

State elective executive officers and senators, 2 and 4 year terms.

Sec. 5. Notwithstanding any other provision in this constitution, the governor, the lieutenant governor, the secretary of state, the attorney general and state senators shall be elected at the general election in 1964 to serve for two-year terms beginning on the first day of January next succeeding their election. The first election of such officers for four-year terms under this constitution shall be held at the general election in 1966.

History: Const. 1963, Schedule, §5, Eff. Jan. 1, 1964.

Supreme court, reduction to 7 justices.

Sec. 6. Notwithstanding the provisions of this constitution that the supreme court shall consist of seven justices it shall consist of eight justices until the time that a vacancy occurs as a result of death, retirement or resignation of a justice. The first such vacancy shall not be filled.

History: Const. 1963, Schedule, §6, Eff. Jan. 1, 1964.

Judges of probate, eligibility for re-election.

Sec. 7. Any judge of probate serving on the effective date of this constitution may serve the remainder of the term and be eligible to succeed himself for election regardless of other provisions in this constitution requiring him to be licensed to practice law in this state.

History: Const. 1963, Schedule, §7, Eff. Jan. 1, 1964.

Judicial officers, staggered terms.

Sec. 8. The provisions of Article VI providing that terms of judicial offices shall not all expire at the same time, shall be implemented by law providing that at the next election for such offices judges shall be elected for terms of varying length, none of which shall be shorter than the regular term provided for the office.

History: Const. 1963, Schedule, §8, Eff. Jan. 1, 1964.

State board of education; first election, terms.

Sec. 9. The members of the state board of education provided for in Section 3 of Article VIII of this constitution shall first be elected at the first general election after the effective date of this constitution for the following terms: two shall be elected for two years, two for four years, two for six years, and two for eight years as prescribed by law.

Abolition of existing state board of education.

The state board of education provided for in the constitution of 1908 is abolished at twelve o'clock noon January 1 of the year following the first general election under this constitution and the terms of members thereof shall then expire.

History: Const. 1963, Schedule, §9, Eff. Jan. 1, 1964.

Boards controlling higher education institutions and state board of public community and junior colleges, terms.

Sec. 10. The provisions of this constitution providing for members of boards of control of institutions of higher education and the state board of public community and junior colleges shall be implemented by law. The law may provide that the term of each member in office on the date of the vote on this constitution may be extended, and may further provide that the initial terms of office of members may be less than eight years.

History: Const. 1963, Schedule, §10, Eff. Jan. 1, 1964.

Michigan State University trustees and Wayne State University governors, terms.

Sec. 11. The provisions of this constitution increasing the number of members of the Board of Trustees of Michigan State University and the Board of Governors of Wayne State University to eight, and of their term of office to eight years, shall be implemented by law. The law may provide that the term of each member in office on the date of the vote on this constitution may be extended one year, and may further provide that the initial terms of office of the additional members may be less than eight years.

History: Const. 1963, Schedule, §11, Eff. Jan. 1, 1964.

Initial allocation of departments by law or executive order.

Sec. 12. The initial allocation of departments by law pursuant to Section 2 of Article V of this constitution, shall be completed within two years after the effective date of this constitution. If such allocation shall not have been completed within such period, the governor, within one year thereafter, by executive order, shall make the initial allocation.

History: Const. 1963, Schedule, §12, Eff. Jan. 1, 1964.

State contracts, continuance.

Sec. 13. Contractual obligations of the state incurred pursuant to the constitution of 1908 shall continue to be obligations of the state.

Korean service bonus bonds, appropriation.

For the retirement of notes and bonds issued under Section 26 of Article X of the 1908 constitution, there is hereby appropriated from the general fund each year during their life a sum equal to the amount of principal and interest payments due and payable in each year.

History: Const. 1963, Schedule, §13, Eff. Jan. 1, 1964.

Mackinac Bridge Authority; refunding of bonds, transfer of functions to highway department.

Sec. 14. The legislature by a vote of two-thirds of the members elected to and serving in each house may provide that the state may borrow money and may pledge its full faith and credit for refunding any bonds issued by the Mackinac Bridge Authority and at the time of refunding the Mackinac Bridge Authority shall be abolished and the operation of the bridge shall be assumed by the state highway department. The legislature may implement this section by law.

History: Const. 1963, Schedule, §14, Eff. Jan. 1, 1964.

Submission of constitution; time, notice.

Sec. 15. This constitution shall be submitted to the people for their adoption or rejection at the general election to be held on the first Monday in April, 1963. It shall be the duty of the secretary of state forthwith to give notice of such submission to all other officers required to give or publish any notice in regard to a general election. He shall give notice that this constitution will be duly submitted to the electors at such election. The notice shall be given in the manner required for the election of governor.

History: Const. 1963, Schedule, §15, Eff. Jan. 1, 1964.
Former constitution: See Const. 1908, Schedule, §10.

Voters, ballots, effective date.

Sec. 16. Every registered elector may vote on the adoption of the constitution. The board of election commissioners in each county shall cause to be printed on a ballot separate from the ballot containing the names of the nominees for office, the words: Shall the revised constitution be adopted? ( ) Yes. ( ) No. All votes cast at the election shall be taken, counted, canvassed and returned as provided by law for the election of state officers. If the revised constitution so submitted receives more votes in its favor than were cast against it, it shall be the supreme law of the state on and after the first day of January of the year following its adoption.

History: Const. 1963, Schedule, §16, Eff. Jan. 1, 1964.
Former constitution: See Const. 1908, Schedule, §11.

SS { Adopted by the Constitutional Convention of nineteen hundred sixty-one at Constitution Hall in Lansing on the first day of August, nineteen hundred sixty-two.

Stephen S. Nisbet, President
Fred I. Chase, Secretary

The vote on the Constitution of 1963, as certified by the Board of State Canvassers on June 20, 1963, was 810,860 to 803,436 in favor of adoption.

PROPOSED AMENDMENTS TO THE CONSTITUTION OF 1963 — SUMMARY OF ADOPTION OR REJECTION

Subject of Amendment	Article	Section	Method of Proposal*	Year of Election	Action	Vote	
						For	Against
Lower minimum voting age from 21 to 18 years	2	1	Senate Joint Resolution "A" of 1966	Nov. 1966	Rejected	703,076	1,267,872
Establish judicial tenure commission	6	30	House Joint Resolution "PP" of 1968	Aug. 1968	Approved	553,182	228,738
Require legislature to create state officers compensation commission	4	12	House Joint Resolution "AAA" of 1968	Aug. 1968	Approved	417,393	346,839
Define manner of filling judicial vacancies	6	20,22, 23,24	House Joint Resolution "F" of 1968	Aug. 1968	Approved	494,512	266,561
Permit election of members of legislature to another state office during their term of office	4	9	Senate Joint Resolution "Q" of 1968	Nov. 1968	Rejected	778,388	1,783,186
Permit state to impose a graduated income tax	9	7	Senate Joint Resolution "G" of 1967	Nov. 1968	Rejected	614,826	2,025,052
Prohibit public aid to nonpublic schools and students	8	2	Initiatory Petition of 1970	Nov. 1970	Approved	1,416,838	1,078,740
Lower minimum voting age from 21 to 18 years	2	1	House Joint Resolution "A" of 1970	Nov. 1970	Rejected	924,981	1,446,884
Allow legislature to authorize lotteries and the sale of lottery tickets	4	41	House Joint Resolution "V" of 1972	May 1972	Approved	1,352,768	506,778
Permit members of legislature to resign and accept another office to which they have been elected or appointed	4	9	Senate Joint Resolution "DD" of 1972	May 1972	Rejected	866,593	915,312
Allow trial by jury of less than 12 jurors in all prosecutions for misdemeanors punishable by imprisonment for not less than 1 year	1	20	House Joint Resolution "M" of 1972	Aug. 1972	Approved	696,570	357,186
Limit property tax for school, county, and township purposes and require legislature to establish a state tax program for support of schools	9	6	Initiatory Petition	Nov. 1972	Rejected	1,324,702	1,815,126
Permit state to impose graduated income tax and allow legislature to authorize political subdivisions to levy graduated income tax	9	7	Initiatory Petition	Nov. 1972	Rejected	959,286	2,102,744

* See Const. 1963, art. XII, §§ 1 and 2.

PROPOSED AMENDMENTS TO THE CONSTITUTION OF 1963 — SUMMARY OF ADOPTION OR REJECTION (*Cont.*)

Subject of Amendment	Article	Section	Method of Proposal	Year of Election	Action	Vote For	Vote Against
Limit use of motor fuel tax fund	9	9	Senate Joint Resolution "LL" of 1972	Nov. 1974	Rejected	1,091,938	1,146,109
Eliminate sales tax and use tax on food and prescription drugs	9	8	Initiatory Petition of 1974	Nov. 1974	Approved	1,337,609	1,071,253
Lower minimum age of eligibility for office of state representative or state senator from 21 to 18 years . . .	4	7	House Joint Resolution "B" of 1976	Nov. 1976	Rejected	698,993	2,580,945
Limit taxation imposed by legislature to 8.3% of state personal income	9	25,26,27, 28,29,30, 31	Initiatory Petition	Nov. 1976	Rejected	1,407,438	1,866,620
Permit state to impose a graduated income tax	9	7	Initiatory Petition	Nov. 1976	Rejected	897,780	2,332,513
Call for constitutional convention			Required by Const. 1963, art. 12, § 3 . . .	Nov. 1978	Rejected	640,286	2,112,549
Authorize deposit of state funds in savings and loan associations and credit unions, as well as banks . . .	9	19,20	House Joint Resolution "GG" of 1978	Nov. 1978	Approved	1,819,847	933,101
Prohibit alcoholic beverages from being sold to, or possessed by, a person under the age of 21	4	40	Initiatory Petition of 1978	Nov. 1978	Approved	1,609,589	1,208,497
Establish limits on taxes imposed by legislature and units of local government (Headlee Amendment)	9	6, 25,26,27, 28,29,30, 31,32,33, 34	Initiatory Petition	Nov. 1978	Approved	1,450,150	1,313,984
Grant Michigan state troopers and sergeants right to collective bargaining and binding arbitration	11	5	Initiatory Petition	Nov. 1978	Approved	1,535,023	1,203,930
Prohibit use of property taxes for school operating expenses and establish a voucher system for financing education of students at public and nonpublic schools	9 8	6 2	Initiatory Petition	Nov. 1978	Rejected	718,440	2,075,583
Reduce property tax assessments to establish a maximum of 5.6% on the rate of the state income tax; prohibit legislature from requiring new or expanded local programs without state funding; and allow school income tax with voter approval (Tisch Amendment I)	9	3; 3(a),7(a), 7(b),25(a), 25(b),26	Initiatory Petition	Nov. 1978	Rejected	1,032,343	1,737,133

Subject of Amendment	Article	Section	Method of Proposal	Year of Election	Action	Vote For	Vote Against
Allow courts to deny bail under certain circumstances involving violent crimes; provide for commencement of trial within 90 days	1	15	House Joint Resolution "Q" of 1978	Nov. 1978	Approved	2,307,038	458,357
Allocate at least 90% of gas tax revenues for general road purposes and the remainder for other transportation purposes; and replace state highway commission with transportation commission	5 9	28 9	House Joint Resolution "F" of 1978	Nov. 1978	Approved	1,478,316	1,233,196
Require legislature to create a railroad redevelopment authority to make loans to railroads with trackage in Michigan and to authorize authority to issue general obligation bonds in amount not to exceed 175 million dollars	4	54	House Joint Resolution "OO" of 1978	Nov. 1978	Rejected	1,257,606	1,415,441
Make local school boards responsible for school personnel and programs, reduce local property tax maximums for operational purposes, provide additional property tax relief for senior retirees, and require the state to raise revenues necessary for equal per pupil funding of public schools	8 9	2 6,31, 6a,26a	Initiatory Petition	Nov. 1980	Rejected	746,027	2,769,497
Lower minimum legal age for possession or consumption of alcoholic beverages from 21 to 19 years	4	40	House Joint Resolution "S" of 1980	Nov. 1980	Rejected	1,403,935	2,250,873
Provide property tax relief; reimburse local and state governments with additional sales tax; require net state lottery revenues be deposited in school aid fund; and mandate creation of state "rainy day" fund	4 9	41,54 2,3,8,30, 31	Senate Joint Resolution "X" of 1980	Nov. 1980	Rejected	894,441	2,583,253
Decrease property taxes and prohibit new types of homestead taxes; require 60% voter approval to raise state taxes or fees; require partial state reimbursement to local units for lost income; limit legislature's ability to change tax exemptions or credits or change per pupil formula (Tisch Amendment II)	9	1,2,3,31, 2a,3a,3b, 3c,3d,3e, 3f,33a, 33b	Initiatory Petition	Nov. 1980	Rejected	1,622,301	2,051,008

PROPOSED AMENDMENTS TO THE CONSTITUTION OF 1963 — SUMMARY OF ADOPTION OR REJECTION (*Cont.*)

Subject of Amendment	Article	Section	Method of Proposal	Year of Election	Action	Vote	
						For	Against
Allow the legislature to pass laws relating to members' immunity from civil arrest and process during legislative sessions.	4	11	Senate Joint Resolution "L" of 1980	Nov. 1980	Rejected	1,287,172	2,134,546
Restrict authority of lieutenant governor and establish a procedure to fill a vacancy in the office of the lieutenant governor.	4 5	9 25,26	Senate Joint Resolution "K" of 1980	Nov. 1980	Rejected	1,410,912	1,927,001
Reduce property taxes and city income taxes; limit growth of property tax revenues; return additional sales tax to local governments and schools; and require net lottery revenues be deposited in school aid fund.	4 9	41 3,8,30,31	House Joint Resolution "G" of 1981	May 1981	Rejected	560,924	1,451,305
Allow the legislature to pass laws to reform members' immunity from civil arrest and process during legislative sessions.	4	11	Senate Joint Resolution "A" of 1981	Nov. 1982	Approved	1,804,728	1,029,743
Create a Michigan department of state police; provide for its personnel; prescribe its duties; and require minimum staffing.	5	2,30	Initiatory Petition	Nov. 1982	Rejected	720,915	2,111,802
Provide for an elected public service commission.	5	30	Initiatory Petition	Nov. 1982	Rejected	1,026,160	1,771,098
Allow legislature to approve or disapprove administrative rules proposed by state agencies.	4	37	House Joint Resolution "P" of 1984	Nov. 1984	Rejected	1,280,948	1,827,677
Establish a natural resources trust fund and a board to administer it; to provide revenues for the fund from natural resources leases and existing funds; specify and limit expenditures therefrom.	9	35	House Joint Resolution "M" of 1984	Nov. 1984	Approved	2,066,554	1,120,794
Amend constitution relating to taxes, other revenues and voter or legislative approval for same.	9	1,2	Initiatory Petition	Nov. 1984	Rejected	1,376,141	2,035,867
Allow establishment of the library of Michigan within the legislative branch.	4	54	House Joint Resolution "V" of 1986	Nov. 1986	Rejected	908,627	936,643
Allow for approval or rejection of administrative rules by the legislature.	4	37	House Joint Resolution "W" of 1986	Nov. 1986	Rejected	648,116	1,136,721
Expand authority of state officers compensation commission to determine compensation of attorney general and secretary of state.	4	12	House Joint Resolution "U" of 1986	Nov. 1986	Rejected	905,767	910,297

PROPOSED AMENDMENTS TO THE CONSTITUTION OF 1963 — SUMMARY OF ADOPTION OR REJECTION (*Cont.*)

Subject of Amendment	Article	Section	Method of Proposal	Year of Election	Action	Vote For	Against
Provide for rights of crime victims	1	24	House Joint Resolution "P" of 1988	Nov. 1988	Approved	2,662,796	650,515
Increase the sales/use tax from 4¢ to 4½¢ and dedicate funds for local schools	4 9	41 8,10,11	House Joint Resolution "I" of 1989	Nov. 1989	Rejected	514,407	1,341,292
Increase the sales/use tax from 4¢ to 6¢, reduce school property taxes, set permanent school operating millages not subject to voter renewal, and dedicate funds for local schools	4 9	41 3,5,6,8, 10,11,14	House Joint Resolution "I" of 1989	Nov. 1989	Rejected	436,958	1,392,053
Limit annual increases in homestead property tax assessments and provide separate tax limitations for different property classifications	9	3,31	House Joint Resolution "H" of 1991	Nov. 1992	Rejected	1,433,354	2,384,777
Restrict/limit the number of times a person can be elected to congressional, state executive and state legislative offices	2 4 5 12	10 54 30 4	Initiatory Petition	Nov. 1992	Approved	2,295,904	1,613,404
Exempt property from a portion of school operating property taxes and limit annual increases in all property tax assessments	9	3	Initiatory Petition	Nov. 1992	Rejected	1,552,119	2,276,360
Limit property tax assessments and increase sales tax	4 9	41 3,6,8, 10,11	House Joint Resolution "G" of 1993	June 1993	Rejected	1,008,425	1,164,468
Increase sales and use tax rates from 4% to 6%; limit annual increases in property tax assessments, exempt school operating millages from uniform taxation requirement, and require 3/4 vote of legislature to exceed statutorily established school operating millage rates	9	3,5,8, 11,36	Senate Joint Resolution "S" of 1993	March 1994	Approved	1,684,541	750,952
Call for constitutional convention			Required by Const. 1963, art. 12, sec. 3.	Nov. 1994	Rejected	777,779	2,008,070
Limit criminal appeals	1	20	Senate Joint Resolution "D" of 1994	Nov. 1994	Approved	2,118,734	761,784
Establish a Michigan state parks endowment fund, increase maximum allowable funds in Michigan natural resources trust fund, and eliminate diversion of dedicated revenue from Michigan natural resources trust fund	9	35,36	Senate Joint Resolution "E" of 1994	Nov. 1994	Approved	2,007,097	806,888

PROPOSED AMENDMENTS TO THE CONSTITUTION OF 1963 — SUMMARY OF ADOPTION OR REJECTION (Cont.)

Subject of Amendment	Article	Section	Method of Proposal	Year of Election	Action	Vote For	Vote Against
Establish qualifications for judicial offices.	6	19	Senate Joint Resolution "D" of 1995	Nov. 1996	Approved	2,806,833	629,402
Establish the current Michigan Veterans' Trust Fund in the state constitution and require that expenditures from the fund be made solely for purposes authorized by the trust fund's board of trustees.	9	37,38,39	House Joint Resolution "H" of 1995	Nov. 1996	Approved	2,447,905	849,525
Change the word "handicapped" to "disabled" in the state constitution	8	8	Senate Joint Resolution "I" of 1998	Nov. 1998	Approved	1,708,873	1,181,138
Permit the state to indirectly support nonpublic school students	8	2,10	Initiatory Petition	Nov. 2000	Rejected	1,235,533	2,767,320
Require a 2/3 legislative vote to enact laws affecting local governments	4	55	Initiatory Petition	Nov. 2000	Rejected	1,242,516	2,548,995
Amend the provision of the state constitution governing the operation of the state officers compensation commission (SOCC)	4	12	House Joint Resolution "E" of 2001	Aug. 2002	Approved	1,057,503	404,682
Allow certain permanent and endowment funds to be invested as provided by law and increase allowed spending for state parks, local parks and outdoor recreation	9	19,35,35a, 36(1).37	Senate Joint Resolution "T" of 2002	Aug. 2002	Approved	925,475	565,971
Grant state classified employees the constitutional right to collective bargaining with binding arbitration	11	5	Initiatory Petition	Nov. 2002	Rejected	1,336,249	1,591,756
Reallocate the tobacco settlement revenue received by the state from cigarette manufacturers	9	36	Initiatory Petition	Nov. 2002	Rejected	1,018,644	2,011,105
Require voter approval for any new gambling authorization, with exceptions	4	41	Initiatory Petition	Nov. 2004	Approved	2,689,448	1,926,721
Provide that marriage may only be the union of a man and woman	1	25	Initiatory Petition	Nov. 2004	Approved	2,698,077	1,904,319
Require that conservation/recreation funds be used only for intended purposes	9	40,41,42	House Joint Resolution "Z" of 2004	Nov. 2006	Approved	2,915,106	680,859
Ban affirmative action programs for public employment, education, and contracting	1	26	Initiatory Petition	Nov. 2006	Approved	2,141,010	1,555,691
Restrict use of eminent domain	10	2	Senate Joint Resolution "E" of 2005	Nov. 2006	Approved	2,914,214	724,573
Permit stem cell research under certain conditions	1	27	Initiatory Petition	Nov. 2008	Approved	2,521,026	2,271,083

Subject of Amendment	Article	Section	Method of Proposal	Year of Election	Action	Vote For	Vote Against
Call for constitutional convention			Required by Const. 1963, art. 12, sec. 3.	Nov. 2010	Rejected	983,019	1,960,573
Ban felons from public office/positions	11	8	Senate Joint Resolution "V" of 2010	Nov. 2010	Approved	2,270,657	760,586
Grant public and private employees the constitutional right to organize and bargain collectively through labor unions	1 11	28 5	Initiatory Petition	Nov. 2012	Rejected	1,949,513	2,626,731
Require electric utilities to provide at least 25% of their annual retail sales of electricity from renewable energy sources by 2025	4	55	Initiatory Petition	Nov. 2012	Rejected	1,721,279	2,842,000
Establish the Michigan Quality Home Care Council and provide collective bargaining for in-home care workers	5 11	31 5	Initiatory Petition	Nov. 2012	Rejected	1,985,595	2,550,420
Require a 2/3 majority of each house of the legislature or statewide election to impose new state taxes	9	26a	Initiatory Petition	Nov. 2012	Rejected	1,410,944	3,105,649
Require the approval of voters in a statewide election and in affected municipalities for the state to build an international bridge or tunnel	3	6a	Initiatory Petition	Nov. 2012	Rejected	1,853,127	2,699,558
Increase the sales/use tax from 6% to 7%. Replace and supplement reduced revenue to the school aid fund and local units of government caused by the elimination of the sales/use tax on gasoline and diesel fuel for vehicles operating on public roads. Give effect to laws that provide additional money for roads and other transportation purposes by increasing the gas tax and vehicle registration fees.	9	8,10,11	House Joint Resolution "UU" of 2014	May 2015	Rejected	349,862	1,406,019
Establish a commission of citizens with exclusive authority to adopt district boundaries for the Michigan Senate, Michigan House of Representatives and U.S. Congress, every 10 years	4 5 6	1,2,3,4 5,6 1,2,4 1,4	Initiatory Petition	Nov. 2018	Approved	2,522,355	1,593,556
Authorize automatic and Election Day voter registration, no-reason absentee voting, and straight ticket voting; and add current legal requirements for military and overseas voting and postelection audits to the Michigan Constitution.	2	4	Initiatory Petition	Nov. 2018	Approved	2,777,998	1,373,636

CONSTITUTION
OF THE
UNITED STATES

CONSTITUTION OF
THE UNITED STATES OF AMERICA

PREAMBLE

WE THE PEOPLE of the United States, in Order to form a more perfect Union, establish Justice, insure domestic Tranquility, provide for the common defence, promote the general Welfare, and secure the Blessings of Liberty to ourselves and our posterity, do ordain and establish this Constitution for the United States of America.

ARTICLE I.

Grant of legislative power.

Section 1. All legislative Powers herein granted shall be vested in a Congress of the United States, which shall consist of a Senate and House of Representatives.

House of representatives; qualifications of electors.

Section 2. The House of Representatives shall be composed of Members chosen every second Year by the People of the several States, and the Electors in each State shall have the Qualifications requisite for Electors of the most numerous Branch of the State Legislature.

Qualifications of representative.

No person shall be a Representative who shall not have attained to the Age of twenty five Years, and been seven Years a Citizen of the United States, and who shall not, when elected, be an Inhabitant of that State in which he shall be chosen.

Apportionment of representatives and direct taxes; census; first apportionment.

[1] Representatives and direct Taxes shall be apportioned among the several States which may be included within this Union, according to their respective Numbers, which shall be determined by adding to the whole Number of free Persons, including those bound to Service for a Term of Years, and excluding Indians not taxed, three fifths of all other Persons. The actual Enumeration shall be made within three Years after the first Meeting of the Congress of the United States, and within every subsequent Term of ten Years, in such Manner as they shall by Law direct. The Number of Representatives shall not exceed one for every thirty Thousand, but each State shall have at Least one Representative; and until such enumeration shall be made, the State of New Hampshire shall be entitled to chuse three, Massachusetts eight, Rhode-Island and Providence Plantations one, Connecticut five, New-York six, New Jersey four, Pennsylvania eight, Delaware one, Maryland six, Virginia ten, North Carolina five, South Carolina five, and Georgia three.

Vacancies.

When vacancies happen in the Representation from any State, the Executive Authority thereof shall issue Writs of Election to fill such Vacancies.

Officers of the House; impeachments.

The House of Representatives shall chuse their Speaker and other Officers; and shall have the sole Power of Impeachment.

Senate.

[2] Section 3. The Senate of the United States shall be composed of two Senators from each State, chosen by the Legislature thereof, for six Years; and each Senator shall have one Vote.

Classification of members; vacancies.

Immediately after they shall be assembled in Consequence of the first Election, they shall be divided as equally as may be into three Classes. The Seats of the Senators of the first Class shall be vacated at the Expiration of the second Year, of the second Class at the Expiration of the fourth Year, and of the third Class at the Expiration of the sixth Year, so that one third may be chosen every second Year; and if Vacancies happen by Resignation, or otherwise, during the Recess of the Legislature of any State, the Executive thereof may make temporary Appointments until the next Meeting of the Legislature, which shall then fill such Vacancies.

Qualifications of members.

No Person shall be a Senator who shall not have attained to the Age of thirty Years, and been nine Years a Citizen of the United States, and who shall not, when elected, be an Inhabitant of that State for which he shall be chosen.

Vice president to be president of the senate.

The Vice President of the United States shall be President of the Senate, but shall have no Vote, unless they be equally divided.

Other officers of the senate.

The Senate shall chuse their other Officers, and also a President pro tempore, in the Absence of the Vice President, or when he shall exercise the Office of President of the United States.

Trial of impeachments.

The Senate shall have the sole Power to try all Impeachments. When sitting for that Purpose, they shall be on Oath or Affirmation. When the President of the United States is tried, the Chief Justice shall preside: And no Person shall be convicted without the Concurrence of two thirds of the Members present.

Judgment in impeachment.

Judgment in Cases of Impeachment shall not extend further than to removal from Office, and disqualification to hold and enjoy any Office of honor, Trust or Profit under the United States: but the Party convicted shall nevertheless be liable and subject to Indictment, Trial, Judgment and Punishment, according to Law.

Election of members of congress.

[3] Section 4. The Times, Places and Manner of holding Elections for Senators and Representatives, shall be prescribed in each State by the Legislature thereof; but the Congress may at any time by Law make or alter such Regulations, except as to the Places of chusing Senators.

Meetings of congress.

The Congress shall assemble at least once in every Year, and such Meeting shall be on the first Monday in December, unless they shall by Law appoint a different Day.

Powers of each house; quorum.

Section 5. Each House shall be the Judge of the Elections, Returns and Qualifications of its own Members, and a Majority of each shall constitute a Quorum to do Business; but a smaller Number may adjourn from day to day, and may be authorized to compel the Attendance of absent Members, in such Manner, and under such Penalties as each House may provide.

Rules of proceedings; expulsion of members.

Each House may determine the Rules of its Proceedings, punish its Members for disorderly Behaviour, and, with the Concurrence of two thirds, expel a Member.

Journal.

Each House shall keep a Journal of its Proceedings, and from time to time publish the same, excepting such Parts as may in their Judgment require Secrecy; and the Yeas and Nays of the Members of either House on any question shall, at the Desire of one fifth of those present, be entered on the Journal.

Adjournment.

Neither House, during the Session of Congress, shall, without the Consent of the other, adjourn for more than three days, nor to any other Place than that in which the two Houses shall be sitting.

Compensation and privileges of members.

Section 6. The Senators and Representatives shall receive a Compensation for their Services, to be ascertained by Law, and paid out of the Treasury of the United States. They shall in all Cases, except Treason, Felony and Breach of the Peace, be privileged from Arrest during their Attendance at the Session of their respective Houses, and in going to and returning from the same; and for any Speech or Debate in either House, they shall not be questioned in any other Place.

Disabilities of members.

No Senator or Representative shall, during the Time for which he was elected, be appointed to any civil Office under the Authority of the United States, which shall have been created, or the Emoluments whereof shall have been encreased during such time; and no Person holding any Office under the United States, shall be a Member of either House during his Continuance in Office.

Revenue bills.

Section 7. All Bills for raising Revenue shall originate in the House of Representatives; but the Senate may propose or concur with Amendments as on other Bills.

Passage and approval of bills; return with objections; reconsideration; pocket veto.

Every Bill which shall have passed the House of Representatives and the Senate, shall, before it become a Law, be presented to the President of the United States; if he approves he shall sign it, but if not he shall return it, with his Objections to that House in which it shall have originated, who shall enter the Objections at large on their Journal, and proceed to reconsider it. If after such Reconsideration two thirds of that House shall agree to pass the Bill, it shall be sent, together with the Objections, to the other House, by which it shall likewise be reconsidered, and if approved by two thirds of that House, it shall become a Law. But in all such Cases the Votes of both Houses shall be determined by Yeas and Nays, and the Names of the Persons voting for and against the Bill shall be entered on the Journal of each House respectively. If any Bill shall not be returned by the President within ten Days (Sundays excepted) after it shall have been presented to him, the Same shall be a Law, in like Manner as if he had signed it, unless the Congress by their Adjournment prevent its Return, in which Case it shall not be a Law.

Concurrent action to be presented for approval.

Every Order, Resolution, or Vote to which the Concurrence of the Senate and House of Representatives may be necessary (except on a question of Adjournment) shall be presented to the President of the United States; and before the Same shall take Effect, shall be approved by him, or, being disapproved by him, shall be repassed by two thirds of the Senate and House of Representatives, according to the Rules and Limitations prescribed in the Case of a Bill.

Power of congress as to taxation, uniformity.

Section 8. The Congress shall have Power To lay and collect Taxes, Duties, Imposts and Excises, to pay the Debts and provide for the common Defence and general Welfare of the United States; but all Duties, Imposts and Excises shall be uniform throughout the United States;

Loans.

To borrow Money on the credit of the United States;

Commerce.

To regulate Commerce with foreign Nations, and among the several States, and with the Indian Tribes;

Naturalization; bankruptcies.

To establish a uniform Rule of Naturalization, and uniform Laws on the subject of Bankruptcies throughout the United States;

Money; weights; measures.

To coin Money, regulate the Value thereof, and of foreign Coin, and fix the Standard of Weights and Measures;

Counterfeiting.

To provide for the Punishment of counterfeiting the Securities and current Coin of the United States;

Postoffices.

To establish Post Offices and post Roads;

Patents; copyrights.

To promote the Progress of Science and useful Arts, by securing for limited Times to Authors and Inventors the exclusive Right to their respective Writings and Discoveries;

Inferior courts.

To constitute Tribunals inferior to the supreme Court;

Piracies; felonies.

To define and punish Piracies and Felonies committed on the high Seas, and Offences against the Law of Nations;

War.

To declare War, grant Letters of Marque and Reprisal, and make Rules concerning Captures on Land and Water;

Army; appropriations.

To raise and support Armies, but no Appropriation of Money to that Use shall be for a longer Term than two Years;

Navy.

To provide and maintain a Navy;

Military affairs.

To make Rules for the Government and Regulation of the land and naval Forces;

Militia.

To provide for calling forth the Militia to execute the Laws of the Union, suppress Insurrections and repel Invasions;

Organization, arming and discipline of militia.

To provide for organizing, arming, and disciplining, the Militia, and for governing such Part of them as may be employed in the Service of the United States, reserving to the States respectively, the Appointment of the Officers, and the Authority of training the Militia according to the discipline prescribed by Congress;

Exclusive legislation over seat of government, other places.

To exercise exclusive Legislation in all Cases whatsoever, over such District (not exceeding ten Miles square) as may, by Cession of particular States, and the Acceptance of Congress, become the Seat of the Government of the United States, and to exercise like Authority over all Places purchased by the Consent of the Legislature of the State in which the Same shall be, for the Erection of Forts, Magazines, Arsenals, dock-Yards, and other needful Buildings; — And

Execution of powers granted.

To make all Laws which shall be necessary and proper for carrying into Execution the foregoing Powers, and all other Powers vested by this Constitution in the Government of the United States, or in any Department or Officer thereof.

Limitations of the powers of congress; importation of certain persons.

Section 9. The Migration or Importation of such Persons as any of the States now existing shall think proper to admit, shall not be prohibited by the Congress prior to the Year one thousand eight hundred and eight, but a Tax or duty may be imposed on such Importation, not exceeding ten dollars for each Person.

Same; habeas corpus.

The Privilege of the Writ of Habeas Corpus shall not be suspended, unless when in Cases of Rebellion or Invasion the public Safety may require it.

Same; bill of attainder; ex post facto.

No Bill of Attainder or ex post facto Law shall be passed.

Same; direct tax.

No Capitation, or other direct, Tax shall be laid, unless in Proportion to the Census or Enumeration herein before directed to be taken.[4]

Same; exportations from states.

No Tax or Duty shall be laid on Articles exported from any State.

Same; preference in interstate commerce.

No Preference shall be given by any Regulation of Commerce or Revenue to the Ports of one State over those of another: nor shall Vessels bound to, or from, one State, be obliged to enter, clear, or pay Duties in another.

Same; expenditures from treasury.

No Money shall be drawn from the Treasury, but in Consequence of Appropriations made by Law; and a regular Statement and Account of the Receipts and Expenditures of all public Money shall be published from time to time.

Same; titles of nobility; gifts from foreign states.

No Title of Nobility shall be granted by the United States: And no Person holding any Office of Profit or Trust under them, shall, without the Consent of the Congress, accept of any present, Emolument, Office, or Title, of any kind whatever, from any King, Prince, or foreign State.

Limitations of powers of individual states; prohibited powers.

Section 10. No State shall enter into any Treaty, Alliance, or Confederation; grant Letters of Marque and Reprisal; coin Money; emit Bills of Credit; make any Thing but gold and silver Coin a Tender in Payment of Debts; pass any Bill of Attainder, ex post facto Law, or Law impairing the Obligation of Contracts, or grant any Title of Nobility.

Same; concurrent powers; duties.

No State shall, without the Consent of the Congress, lay any Imposts or Duties on Imports or Exports, except what may be absolutely necessary for executing its inspection Laws: and the net Produce of all Duties and Imposts, laid by any State on Imports or Exports, shall be for the Use of the Treasury of the United States; and all such Laws shall be subject to the Revision and Controul of the Congress.

Same; other concurrent powers.

No State shall, without the Consent of Congress, lay any Duty of Tonnage, keep Troops, or Ships of War in time of Peace, enter into any Agreement or Compact with another State, or with a foreign Power, or engage in War, unless actually invaded, or in such imminent Danger as will not admit of delay.

ARTICLE II.

Executive power; term of president.

Section 1. The executive Power shall be vested in a President of the United States of America. He shall hold his Office during the Term of four Years, and, together with the Vice President, chosen for the same Term, be elected as follows

Electors; manner of choice, persons disqualified.

Each State shall appoint, in such Manner as the Legislature thereof may direct, a Number of Electors, equal to the whole Number of Senators and Representatives to which the State may be entitled in the Congress: but no Senator or Representative, or Person holding an Office of Trust or Profit under the United States, shall be appointed an Elector.

Same; meeting and proceedings.

[5] The Electors shall meet in their respective States, and vote by Ballot for two Persons, of whom one at least shall not be an Inhabitant of the same State with themselves. And they shall make a List of all the Persons voted for, and of the Number of Votes for each; which List they shall sign and certify, and transmit sealed to the Seat of the Government of the United States, directed to the President of the Senate. The President of the Senate shall, in the Presence of the Senate and House of Representatives, open all the Certificates, and the Votes shall then be counted. The Person having the greatest Number of Votes shall be the President, if such Number be a Majority of the whole Number of Electors appointed; and if there be more than one who have such Majority, and have an equal Number of Votes, then the House of Representatives shall immediately chuse by Ballot one of them for President; and if no Person have a Majority, then from the five highest on the List the said House shall in like Manner chuse the President. But in chusing the President, the Votes shall be taken by States, the Representation from each State having one Vote; A quorum for this Purpose shall consist of a Member or Members from two thirds of the States, and a Majority of all the States shall be necessary to a Choice. In every Case, after the Choice of the President, the Person having the greatest Number of Votes of the Electors shall be the Vice President. But if there should remain two or more who have equal Votes, the Senate shall chuse from them by Ballot the Vice President.

Same; time of choice.

The Congress may determine the Time of chusing the Electors, and the Day on which they shall give their Votes; which Day shall be the same throughout the United States.

Qualifications of president.

No Person except a natural born Citizen, or a Citizen of the United States, at the time of the Adoption of this Constitution, shall be eligible to the Office of President; neither shall any Person be eligible to that Office who shall not have attained to the Age of thirty five Years, and been fourteen Years a Resident within the United States.

Devolution of powers upon vice president.

In Case of the Removal of the President from Office, or of his Death, Resignation, or Inability to discharge the Powers and Duties of the said Office, the same shall devolve on the Vice President, and the Congress may by Law provide for the Case of Removal, Death, Resignation or Inability, both of the President and Vice President, declaring what Officer shall then act as President, and such Officer shall act accordingly, until the Disability be removed, or a President shall be elected.

Compensation of president.

The President shall, at stated Times, receive for his Services, a Compensation, which shall neither be increased nor diminished during the Period for which he shall have been elected, and he shall not receive within that Period any other Emolument from the United States, or any of them.

Oath of office.

Before he enter on the Execution of his Office, he shall take the following Oath or Affirmation: —
"I do solemnly swear (or affirm) that I will faithfully execute the Office of President of the United States, and will to the best of my Ability, preserve, protect and defend the Constitution of the United States."

Powers of president.

Section 2. The President shall be Commander in Chief of the Army and Navy of the United States, and of the Militia of the several States, when called into the actual Service of the United States; he may require the Opinion, in writing, of the principal Officer in each of the executive Departments, upon any Subject relating to the Duties of their respective Offices, and he shall have Power to grant Reprieves and Pardons for Offences against the United States, except in Cases of Impeachment.

Treaties and appointments.

He shall have Power, by and with the Advice and Consent of the Senate, to make Treaties, provided two thirds of the Senators present concur; and he shall nominate, and by and with the Advice and Consent of the Senate, shall appoint Ambassadors, other public Ministers and Consuls, Judges of the supreme Court, and all other Officers of the United States, whose Appointments are not herein otherwise provided for, and which shall be established by Law: but the Congress may by Law vest the Appointment of such inferior Officers, as they think proper, in the President alone, in the Courts of Law, or in the Heads of Departments.

Filling vacancies.

The President shall have Power to fill up all Vacancies that may happen during the Recess of the Senate, by granting Commissions which shall expire at the End of their next Session.

Messages to congress; extra sessions; ambassadors; laws; execution; commissioning officers.

Section 3. He shall from time to time give to the Congress Information of the State of the Union, and recommend to their Consideration such Measures as he shall judge necessary and expedient; he may, on extraordinary Occasions, convene both Houses, or either of them, and in Case of Disagreement between them, with Respect to the Time of Adjournment, he may adjourn them to such Time as he shall think proper; he shall receive Ambassadors and other public Ministers; he shall take Care that the Laws be faithfully executed, and shall Commission all the Officers of the United States.

Officers liable to impeachment.

Section 4. The President, Vice President and all civil Officers of the United States, shall be removed from Office on Impeachment for, and Conviction of, Treason, Bribery, or other high Crimes and Misdemeanors.

ARTICLE III.

Judicial power; judges, term, compensation.

Section 1. The judicial Power of the United States, shall be vested in one supreme Court, and in such inferior Courts as the Congress may from time to time ordain and establish. The Judges, both of the supreme and inferior Courts, shall hold their Offices during good Behaviour, and shall, at stated Times, receive for their Services, a Compensation, which shall not be diminished during their Continuance in Office.

Extent of judicial power.

[6] Section 2. The judicial Power shall extend to all Cases, in Law and Equity, arising under this Constitution, the Laws of the United States, and Treaties made, or which shall be made, under their Authority; — to all Cases affecting Ambassadors, other public Ministers and Consuls; — to all Cases of admiralty and maritime Jurisdiction; — to Controversies to which the United States shall be a Party; — to Controversies between two or more States; — between a State and Citizens of another State; — between Citizens of different States, between Citizens of the same State claiming Lands under Grants of different States, and between a State, or the Citizens thereof, and foreign States, Citizens or Subjects.

Original and appellate jurisdiction of supreme court.

In all Cases affecting Ambassadors, other public Ministers and Consuls, and those in which a State shall be Party, the supreme Court shall have original Jurisdiction. In all the other Cases before mentioned, the supreme Court shall have appellate Jurisdiction, both as to Law and Fact, with such Exceptions, and under such Regulations as the Congress shall make.

Jury trials for crimes.

The Trial of all Crimes, except in Cases of Impeachment, shall be by Jury; and such Trial shall be held in the State where the said Crimes shall have been committed; but when not committed within any State, the Trial shall be at such Place or Places as the Congress may by Law have directed.

Treason; defined; trial.

Section 3. Treason against the United States, shall consist only in levying War against them, or in adhering to their Enemies, giving them Aid and Comfort. No Person shall be convicted of Treason unless on the Testimony of two Witnesses to the same overt Act, or on Confession in open Court.

Same; punishment.

The Congress shall have Power to declare the Punishment of Treason, but no Attainder of Treason shall work Corruption of Blood, or Forfeiture except during the Life of the Person attainted.

ARTICLE IV.

Full faith and credit of public acts, records, etc., of each state; proof; effect.

Section 1. Full Faith and Credit shall be given in each State to the public Acts, Records, and judicial Proceedings of every other State. And the Congress may by general Laws prescribe the Manner in which such Acts, Records and Proceedings shall be proved, and the Effect thereof.

Citizenship; privileges and immunities.

Section 2. The Citizens of each State shall be entitled to all Privileges and Immunities of Citizens in the several States.

Extradition; fugitives from justice.

A Person charged in any State with Treason, Felony, or other Crime, who shall flee from Justice, and be found in another State, shall, on Demand of the executive Authority of the State from which he fled, be delivered up, to be removed to the State having Jurisdiction of the Crime.

Same; fugitive slaves.

No Person held to Service or Labour in one State, under the Laws thereof, escaping into another, shall, in Consequence of any Law or Regulation therein, be discharged from such Service or Labour, but shall be delivered up on Claim of the Party to whom such Service or Labour may be due.[7]

Admission of new states.

Section 3. New States may be admitted by the Congress into this Union; but no new State shall be formed or erected within the Jurisdiction of any other State; nor any State be formed by the Junction of two or more States, or Parts of States, without the Consent of the Legislatures of the States concerned as well as of the Congress.

Power of congress over federal territory and property.

The Congress shall have Power to dispose of and make all needful Rules and Regulations respecting the Territory or other Property belonging to the United States; and nothing in this Constitution shall be so construed as to Prejudice any Claims of the United States, or of any particular State.

Republican form of government guaranteed; protection from invasion and domestic violence.

Section 4. The United States shall guarantee to every State in this Union a Republican Form of Government, and shall protect each of them against Invasion; and on Application of the Legislature, or of the Executive (when the Legislature cannot be convened) against domestic Violence.

ARTICLE V.

Amendment of the constitution, procedure.

The Congress, whenever two thirds of both Houses shall deem it necessary, shall propose Amendments to this Constitution, or on the Application of the Legislatures of two thirds of the several States, shall call a Convention for proposing Amendments, which, in either Case, shall be valid to all Intents and Purposes, as Part of this Constitution, when ratified by the Legislatures of three fourths of the several States, or by Conventions in three fourths thereof, as the one or the other Mode of Ratification may be proposed by the Congress; Provided that no Amendment which may be made prior to the Year One thousand eight hundred and eight shall in any Manner affect the first and fourth Clauses in the Ninth Section of the first Article; and that no State, without its Consent, shall be deprived of its equal Suffrage in the Senate.

ARTICLE VI.

Public debt.

All Debts contracted and Engagements entered into, before the Adoption of this Constitution, shall be as valid against the United States under this Constitution, as under the Confederation.

Constitution, supreme law of land.

This Constitution, and the laws of the United States which shall be made in Pursuance thereof; and all Treaties made, or which shall be made, under the Authority of the United States, shall be the supreme Law of the Land; and the Judges in every State shall be found thereby, any Thing in the Constitution or Laws of any State to the Contrary notwithstanding.

Oath of office; religious test prohibited.

The Senators and Representatives before mentioned, and the Members of the several State Legislatures, and all executive and judicial Officers, both of the United States and of the several States, shall be bound by Oath or Affirmation, to support this Constitution; but no religious Test shall ever be required as a Qualification to any Office or public Trust under the United States.

ARTICLE VII.

Ratification of Constitution.

The Ratification of the Conventions of nine States, shall be sufficient for the Establishment of this Constitution between the States so ratifying the Same.

DONE in Convention by the Unanimous Consent of the States present the Seventeenth Day of September in the Year of our Lord one thousand seven hundred and Eighty seven and of the Independence of the United States of America the Twelfth. IN WITNESS whereof we have hereunto subscribed our Names.

G°. WASHINGTON - Presd't
and deputy from Virginia
Attest William Jackson *Secretary*

NEW HAMPSHIRE
JOHN LANGDON
NICHOLAS GILMAN

MASSACHUSETTS
NATHANIEL GORHAM
RUFUS KING

CONNECTICUT
WM. SAML. JOHNSON
ROGER SHERMAN

NEW YORK
ALEXANDER HAMILTON

NEW JERSEY
WIL. LIVINGSTON
DAVID BREARLEY
WM. PATERSON
JONA. DAYTON

VIRGINIA
JOHN BLAIR —
JAMES MADISON JR.

NORTH CAROLINA
WM. BLOUNT
RICHD. DOBBS SPAIGHT
HU. WILLIAMSON

PENNSYLVANIA
B. FRANKLIN
THOMAS MIFFLIN
ROBT. MORRIS
GEO. CLYMER
THOS. FITZSIMONS
JARED INGERSOLL
JAMES WILSON
GOUV. MORRIS

DELAWARE
GEO. READ
GUNNING BEDFORD jun
JOHN DICKINSON
RICHARD BASSETT
JACO. BROOM

MARYLAND
JAMES MCHENRY
DAN OF ST. THOS. JENIFER
DANL. CARROLL

SOUTH CAROLINA
J. RUTLEDGE
CHARLES COTESWORTH PINCKNEY
CHARLES PINCKNEY
PIERCE BUTLER

GEORGIA
WILLIAM FEW
ABR. BALDWIN

AMENDMENTS
TO THE CONSTITUTION

ARTICLES IN ADDITION TO, AND AMENDMENT OF THE CONSTITUTION OF THE UNITED STATES OF AMERICA, PROPOSED BY CONGRESS, AND RATIFIED BY THE LEGISLATURES OF THE SEVERAL STATES, PURSUANT TO THE FIFTH ARTICLE OF THE ORIGINAL CONSTITUTION.

ARTICLE I.[8]

Religious freedom; freedom of speech and press; right to peaceably assemble and petition.

Congress shall make no law respecting an establishment of religion, or prohibiting the free exercise thereof; or abridging the freedom of speech, or of the press; or the right of the people peaceably to assemble, and to petition the Government for a redress of grievances.

ARTICLE II.

Right to bear arms.

A well regulated militia, being necessary to the security of a free State, the right of the people to keep and bear arms, shall not be infringed.

ARTICLE III.

Quartering soldiers.

No Soldier shall, in time of peace be quartered in any house, without the consent of the owner, nor in time of war, but in a manner to be prescribed by law.

ARTICLE IV.

Unreasonable searches and seizures; search warrants.

The right of the people to be secure in their persons, houses, papers, and effects, against unreasonable searches and seizures, shall not be violated, and no warrants shall issue, but upon probable cause, supported by oath or affirmation, and particularly describing the place to be searched, and the persons or things to be seized.

ARTICLE V.

Rights of persons charged with crimes; guaranty of life, liberty and property.

No person shall be held to answer for a capital, or otherwise infamous crime, unless on a presentment or indictment of a Grand Jury, except in cases arising in the land or naval forces, or in the militia, when in actual service in time of war or public danger; nor shall any person be subject for the same offence to be twice put in jeopardy of life or limb; nor shall be compelled in any criminal case to be a witness against himself, nor be deprived of life, liberty, or property, without due process of law; nor shall private property be taken for public use, without just compensation.

ARTICLE VI.

Trials of criminal cases; rights of accused.

In all criminal prosecutions, the accused shall enjoy the right to a speedy and public trial, by an impartial jury of the State and district wherein the crime shall have been committed, which district shall have been previously ascertained by law, and to be informed of the nature and cause of the accusation; to be confronted with the witnesses against him; to have compulsory process for obtaining witnesses in his favor, and to have the assistance of counsel for his defence.

ARTICLE VII.

Trial by jury in civil cases.

In Suits at common law, where the value in controversy shall exceed twenty dollars, the right of trial by jury shall be preserved, and no fact tried by a jury, shall be otherwise reexamined in any Court of the United States, than according to the rules of the common law.

ARTICLE VIII.

Excessive bail, fines and punishments.

Excessive bail shall not be required, nor excessive fines imposed, nor cruel and unusual punishments inflicted.

ARTICLE IX.

Rights of people.

The enumeration in the Constitution, of certain rights, shall not be construed to deny or disparage others retained by the people.

ARTICLE X.

Powers reserved to the states, people.

The powers not delegated to the United States by the Constitution, nor prohibited by it to the States, are reserved to the States respectively, or to the people.

ARTICLE XI.

Limitation of judicial powers.

The Judicial power of the United States shall not be construed to extend to any suit in law or equity, commenced or prosecuted against one of the United States by Citizens of another State, or by Citizens or Subjects of any Foreign State.

The eleventh amendment to the Constitution of the United States was proposed to the legislatures of the several States by the Third Congress, on the 4th of March 1794; and was declared in a message from the President to Congress, dated the 8th of January, 1798, to have been ratified by the legislatures of three-fourths of the States.

ARTICLE XII.[9]

Manner of electing president and vice president; qualifications of vice president.

The Electors shall meet in their respective states, and vote by ballot for President and Vice-President, one of whom, at least, shall not be an inhabitant of the same state with themselves; they shall name in their ballots the person voted for as President, and in distinct ballots the persons voted for as Vice-President, and they shall make distinct lists of all persons voted for as President, and of all persons voted for a Vice-President, and of the number of votes for each, which lists they shall sign and certify, and transmit sealed to the seat of the government of the United States, directed to the President of the Senate; — The President of the Senate shall, in the presence of the Senate and House of Representatives, open all the certificates and the votes shall then be counted; — The person having the greatest number of votes for President, shall be the President, if such number be a majority of the whole number of Electors appointed; and if no person have such majority, then from the persons having the highest numbers not exceeding three on the list of those voted for as President, the House of Representatives shall choose immediately, by ballot, the President. But in choosing the President, the votes shall be taken by states, the representation from each state having one vote; a quorum for this purpose shall consist of a member or members from two-thirds of the states, and a majority of all the states shall be necessary to a choice. And if the House of Representatives shall not choose a President whenever the right of choice shall devolve upon them, before the fourth day of March next following, then the Vice-President shall act as President, as in the case of the death or other constitutional disability of the President. — The person having the greatest number of votes as Vice-President, shall be the Vice-President, if such number be a majority of the whole number of Electors appointed, and if no person have a majority, then from the two highest numbers on the list, the Senate shall choose the Vice-President; a quorum for the purpose shall consist of two-thirds of the whole number of Senators, and a majority of the whole number shall be necessary to a choice. But no person constitutionally ineligible to the office of President shall be eligible to that of Vice-President of the United States.

The twelfth amendment to the Constitution of the United States was proposed to the legislatures of the several States by the Eighth Congress, on the 9th of December, 1803, in lieu of the original third paragraph of the first section of the second article; and was declared in a proclamation of the Secretary of State, dated the 25th of September, 1804, to have been ratified by the legislatures of three-fourths of the States.

ARTICLE XIII.

Prohibition of slavery.

Section 1. Neither slavery nor involuntary servitude, except as a punishment for crime whereof the party shall have been duly convicted, shall exist within the United States, or any place subject to their jurisdiction.

Power of congress.

Section 2. Congress shall have power to enforce this article by appropriate legislation.

The thirteenth amendment to the Constitution of the United States was proposed to the legislatures of the several States by the Thirty-eighth Congress, on the 31st day of January, 1865, and was declared, in a proclamation of the Secretary of State, dated the 18th of December, 1865, to have been ratified by the legislatures of twenty-seven of the thirty-six States, viz: Illinois, Rhode Island, Michigan, Maryland, New York, West Virginia, Maine, Kansas, Massachusetts, Pennsylvania, Virginia, Ohio, Missouri, Nevada, Indiana, Louisiana, Minnesota, Wisconsin, Vermont, Tennessee, Arkansas, Connecticut, New Hampshire, South Carolina, Alabama, North Carolina, and Georgia.

ARTICLE XIV.

Citizenship; security of persons and property, due process and equal protection clauses.

Section 1. All persons born or naturalized in the United States, and subject to the jurisdiction thereof, are citizens of the United States and of the State wherein they reside. No State shall make or enforce any law which shall abridge the privileges or immunities of citizens of the United States; nor shall any State deprive any person of life, liberty, or property, without due process of law; nor deny to any person within its jurisdiction the equal protection of the laws.

Apportionment of representatives.

Section 2. Representatives shall be apportioned among the several States according to their respective numbers, counting the whole number of persons in each State, excluding Indians not taxed. But when the right to vote at any election for the choice of electors for President and Vice President of the United States, Representatives in Congress, the Executive and Judicial officers of a State, or the members of the Legislature thereof, is denied to any of the male inhabitants of such State, being twenty-one years of age, and citizens of the United States, or in any way abridged, except for participation in rebellion, or other crime, the basis of representation therein shall be reduced in the proportion which the number of such male citizens shall bear to the whole number of male citizens twenty-one years of age in such State.

Disability to hold office, removal.

Section 3. No person shall be a Senator or Representative in Congress, or elector of President and Vice President, or hold any office, civil or military, under the United States, or under any State, who, having previously taken an oath, as a member of Congress, or as an officer of the United States, or as a member of any State legislature, or as an executive or judicial officer of any State, to support the Constitution of the United States, shall have engaged in insurrection or rebellion against the same, or given aid or comfort to the enemies thereof. But Congress may by a vote of two-thirds of each House, remove such disability.

Validity of public debt; void obligations.

Section 4. The validity of the public debt of the United States, authorized by law, including debts incurred for payment of pensions and bounties for services in suppressing insurrection or rebellion, shall not be questioned. But neither the United States nor any State shall assume or pay any debt or obligation incurred in aid of insurrection or rebellion against the United States, or any claim for the loss or emancipation of any slave; but all such debts, obligations and claims shall be held illegal and void.

Power of congress.

Section 5. The Congress shall have power to enforce, by appropriate legislation, the provisions of this article.

The fourteenth amendment to the Constitution of the United States was proposed to the legislatures of the several States by the Thirty-ninth Congress, on the 13th of June, 1866. On the 21st of July, 1868, Congress adopted and transmitted to the Department of State a concurrent resolution, declaring that "the legislatures of the States of Connecticut, Tennessee, New Jersey, Oregon, Vermont, New York, Ohio, Illinois, West Virginia, Kansas, Maine, Nevada, Missouri, Indiana, Minnesota, New Hampshire, Massachusetts, Nebraska, Iowa, Arkansas, Florida, North Carolina, Alabama, South Carolina, and Louisiana, being three-fourths and more of the several States of the Union, have ratified the fourteenth article of amendment to the Constitution of the United States, duly proposed by two-thirds of each House of the Thirty-ninth Congress: Therefore, *Resolved,* That said fourteenth article is hereby declared to be a part of the Constitution of the United States, and it shall be duly promulgated as such by the Secretary of State." The Secretary of State accordingly issued a proclamation, dated the 28th of July, 1868, declaring that the proposed fourteenth amendment had been ratified, in the manner hereafter mentioned, by the legislatures of thirty of the thirty-six States, viz; Connecticut, June 25, 1866; New Hampshire, July 6, 1866; Tennessee, July 19, 1866; New Jersey, September 11, 1866 (and the legislature of the same State passed a resolution in April 1868, to withdraw its consent to it;) Oregon, September 19, 1866; Vermont, October 30, 1866; Georgia rejected it November 13, 1866, and ratified it July 21, 1868; North Carolina rejected it December 4, 1866, and ratified it July 4, 1868; South Carolina rejected it December 20, 1866, and ratified it July 9, 1868; New York ratified it January 10, 1867; Ohio ratified it January 4, 1867 (and the legislature of the same State passed a resolution in January 1868, to withdraw its consent to it;) Illinois ratified it January 15, 1867; West Virginia, January 16, 1867; Kansas, January 11, 1867; Maine, January 19, 1867; Nevada, January 22, 1867; Missouri, January 25, 1867; Indiana, January 23, 1867; Minnesota, January 16, 1867; Rhode Island, February 7, 1867; Wisconsin, February 17, 1867; Pennsylvania, February 12, 1867; Michigan, January 16, 1867; Massachusetts, March 20, 1867; Nebraska, June 15, 1867; Iowa, March 16, 1868; Arkansas, April 6, 1868; Florida, June 9, 1868; Louisiana, July 9, 1868; and Alabama, July 13, 1868. Georgia again ratified the amendment February 2, 1870. Texas rejected it November 1, 1866, and ratified it February 18, 1870. Virginia rejected it January 9, 1867, and ratified it October 8, 1869. The amendment was rejected by Kentucky January 10, 1867; by Delaware February 8, 1867, but subsequently ratified February 12, 1901; by Maryland March 23, 1867, but subsequently ratified April 4, 1959.

California ratified this amendment May 6, 1959.

ARTICLE XV.

Right of citizens to vote; race; color.

Section 1. The right of citizens of the United States to vote shall not be denied or abridged by the United States or by any State on account of race, color, or previous condition of servitude.

Power of congress.

Section 2. The Congress shall have power to enforce this article by appropriate legislation.

The fifteenth amendment to the Constitution of the United States was proposed to the legislatures of the several States by the Fortieth Congress, on the 26th of February, 1869, and was declared, in a proclamation of the Secretary of State, dated March 30, 1870, to have been ratified by the legislatures of twenty-nine of the thirty-seven States. The dates of these ratifications (arranged in the order of their reception at the Department of State) were: from North Carolina, March 5, 1869; West Virginia, March 3, 1869; Massachusetts, March 12, 1869; Wisconsin, March 9, 1869; Maine, March 11, 1869; Louisiana, March 5, 1869; Michigan, March 8, 1869; South Carolina, March 15, 1869; Pennsylvania, March 25, 1869; Arkansas, March 15, 1869; Connecticut, May 19, 1869; Florida, June 14, 1869; Illinois, March 5, 1869; Indiana, May 14, 1869; New York, March 17-April 14, 1869 (and the legislature of the same State passed a resolution January 5, 1870, to withdraw its consent to it, which action it rescinded on March 30, 1970); New Hampshire, July 1, 1869; Nevada, March 1, 1869; Vermont, October 20, 1869; Virginia, October 8, 1869; Missouri, January 7, 1870; Mississippi, January 17, 1870; Ohio, January 27, 1870; Iowa, February 3, 1870; Kansas, January 19, 1870; Minnesota, January 13, 1870; Rhode Island, January 18, 1870; Nebraska, February 17, 1870; Texas, February 18, 1870. The State of Georgia also ratified the amendment February 2, 1870.

The amendment was subsequently ratified by Texas, February 18, 1870; New Jersey, February 15, 1871; Delaware, February 12, 1901; California, April 3, 1962; Oregon, February 24, 1969.

ARTICLE XVI.

Income tax.

The Congress shall have power to lay and collect taxes on incomes, from whatever source derived, without apportionment among the several States, and without regard to any census or enumeration.

The sixteenth amendment to the Constitution of the United States was proposed to the legislatures of the several States by the Sixty-first Congress on the 12th of July, 1909, and was declared, in a proclamation of the Secretary of State, dated the 25th of February, 1913, to have been ratified by the Legislatures of the States of Alabama, Kentucky, South Carolina, Illinois, Mississippi, Oklahoma, Maryland, Georgia, Texas, Ohio, Idaho, Oregon, Washington, California, Montana, Indiana, Nevada, North Carolina, Nebraska, Kansas, Colorado, North Dakota, Michigan, Iowa, Missouri, Maine, Tennessee, Arkansas, Wisconsin, New York, South Dakota, Arizona, Minnesota, Louisiana, Delaware, and Wyoming; in all, thirty-six.

ARTICLE XVII.

United States senate; membership, election, term, vote.

The Senate of the United States shall be composed of two Senators from each State, elected by the people thereof, for six years; and each Senator shall have one vote. The electors in each State shall have the qualifications requisite for electors of the most numerous branch of the State legislatures.

Same; filling of vacancies.

When vacancies happen in the representation of any State in the Senate, the executive authority of such State shall issue writs of election to fill such vacancies: *Provided,* That the legislature of any State may empower the executive thereof to make temporary appointments until the people fill the vacancies by election as the legislature may direct.

Application of amendment.

This amendment shall not be so construed as to affect the election or term of any Senator chosen before it becomes valid as part of the Constitution.

The seventeenth amendment to the Constitution of the United States was proposed to the legislatures of the several States by the Sixty-second Congress on the 13th of May, 1912, and was declared, in a proclamation of the Secretary of State, dated the 31st of May, 1913, to have been ratified by the legislatures of the States of Massachusetts, Arizona, Minnesota, New York, Kansas, Oregon, North Carolina, California, Michigan, Idaho, West Virginia, Nebraska, Iowa, Montana, Texas, Washington, Wyoming, Colorado, Illinois, North Dakota, Nevada, Vermont, Maine, New Hampshire, Oklahoma, Ohio, South Dakota, Indiana, Missouri, New Mexico, New Jersey, Tennessee, Arkansas, Connecticut, Pennsylvania, and Wisconsin.

ARTICLE XVIII.[10]

Section 1. After one year from the ratification of this article the manufacture, sale, or transportation of intoxicating liquors within, the importation thereof into, or the exportation thereof from the United States and all territory subject to the jurisdiction thereof for beverage purposes is hereby prohibited.

Sec. 2. The Congress and the several States shall have concurrent power to enforce this article by appropriate legislation.

Sec. 3. This article shall be inoperative unless it shall have been ratified as an amendment to the Constitution by the legislatures of the several States, as provided in the Constitution, within seven years from the date of the submission hereof to the States by the Congress.

The eighteenth amendment to the Constitution of the United States was proposed to the legislatures of the several States by the Sixty-fifth Congress, on the 18th of December, 1917, and was declared, in a proclamation of the Secretary of State, dated the 29th of January, 1919, to have been ratified by the Legislatures of the States of Alabama, Arizona, California, Colorado, Delaware, Florida, Georgia, Idaho, Illinois, Indiana, Kansas, Kentucky, Louisiana, Maine, Maryland, Massachusetts, Michigan, Minnesota, Mississippi, Montana, Nebraska, New Hampshire, North Carolina, North Dakota, Ohio, Oklahoma, Oregon, South Dakota, South Carolina, Texas, Utah, Virginia, Washington, West Virginia, Wisconsin, and Wyoming.

ARTICLE XIX.

Right to vote; sex; enforcement.

The right of citizens of the United States to vote shall not be denied or abridged by the United States or by any State on account of sex.

Congress shall have power to enforce this article by appropriate legislation.

The nineteenth amendment to the Constitution of the United States was proposed to the legislatures of the several States by the Sixty-sixth Congress, on the 4th of May, 1919, and was declared, in a proclamation of the Secretary of State, dated the 26th of August, 1920, to have been ratified by the Legislatures of the States of Arizona, Arkansas, California, Colorado, Idaho, Illinois, Indiana, Iowa, Kansas, Kentucky, Maine, Massachusetts, Michigan, Minnesota, Missouri, Montana, Nebraska, Nevada, New Hampshire, New Jersey, New Mexico, North Dakota, New York, Ohio, Oklahoma, Oregon, Pennsylvania, Rhode Island, South Dakota, Tennessee, Texas, Utah, Washington, West Virginia, Wisconsin and Wyoming.

This amendment was ratified by Virginia, February 21, 1952 (after having rejected it on February 12, 1920); Florida, May 13, 1969; Georgia, February 20, 1970 (after having rejected it on July 25, 1919); Louisiana, June 11, 1970 (after having rejected it on July 1, 1920).

ARTICLE XX.

Terms of office, commencement.

Section 1. The terms of the President and Vice President shall end at noon on the 20th day of January, and the terms of Senators and Representatives at noon on the 3rd day of January, of the years in which such terms would have ended if this article had not been ratified; and the terms of their successors shall then begin.

Congress, time of assembly.

Sec. 2. The Congress shall assemble at least once in every year, and such meeting shall begin at noon on the 3rd day of January, unless they shall by law appoint a different day.

President elect, death, etc., order of succession.

Sec. 3. If, at the time fixed for the beginning of the term of the President, the President elect shall have died, the Vice President elect shall become President. If a President shall not have been chosen before the time fixed for the beginning of his term, or if the President elect shall have failed to qualify, then the Vice President elect shall act as President until a President shall have qualified; and the Congress may by law provide for the case wherein neither a President elect nor a Vice President elect shall have qualified, declaring who shall then act as President, or the manner in which one who is to act shall be selected, and such person shall act accordingly until a President or Vice President shall have qualified.

Same; congressional act.

Sec. 4. The Congress may by law provide for the case of the death of any of the persons from whom the House of Representatives may choose a President whenever the right of choice shall have devolved upon them, and for the case of the death of any of the persons from whom the Senate may choose a Vice President whenever the right of choice shall have devolved upon them.

Sec. 5. Sections 1 and 2 shall take effect on the 15th day of October following the ratification of this article.

Sec. 6. This article shall be inoperative unless it shall have been ratified as an amendment to the Constitution by the legislatures of three-fourths of the several States within seven years from the date of its submission.

The twentieth amendment to the Constitution was proposed to the legislatures of the several states by the Seventy-Second Congress, on the 2nd day of March, 1932, and was declared, in a proclamation by the Secretary of State, dated on the 6th day of February, 1933, to have been ratified by the legislatures of the states of Alabama, Arizona, Arkansas, California, Delaware, Georgia, Idaho, Illinois, Indiana, Kansas, Kentucky, Louisiana, Maine, Michigan, Minnesota, Mississippi, Missouri, Montana, Nebraska, New Jersey, New York, North Carolina, North Dakota, Ohio, Oklahoma, Pennsylvania, Rhode Island, South Carolina, South Dakota, Texas, Utah, Virginia, Washington, West Virginia, and Wyoming — said states constituting three-fourths of the whole number of states in the United States, and certified as valid to all intents and purposes as a part of the Constitution of the United States.

The amendment was subsequently ratified by Massachusetts, Wisconsin, Colorado, Nevada, Connecticut, New Hampshire, Vermont, Maryland, and Florida.

ARTICLE XXI.

Repeal of 18th amendment.

Section 1. The eighteenth article of amendment to the Constitution of the United States is hereby repealed.

Transportation or importation of intoxicating liquors.

Sec. 2. The transportation or importation into any State, Territory, or possession of the United States for delivery or use therein of intoxicating liquors, in violation of the laws thereof, is hereby prohibited.

Sec. 3. This article shall be inoperative unless it shall have been ratified as an amendment to the Constitution by conventions in the several States, as provided in the Constitution, within seven years from the date of the submission hereof to the States by the Congress.

The twenty-first amendment to the Constitution was proposed to the several states by the Seventy-Second Congress, on the 20th day of February, 1933, and was declared, in a proclamation by the Secretary of State, dated on the 5th day of December, 1933, to have been ratified by conventions in the States of Arizona, Alabama, Arkansas, California, Colorado, Connecticut, Delaware, Florida, Idaho, Illinois, Indiana, Iowa, Kentucky, Maryland, Massachusetts, Michigan, Minnesota, Missouri, Nevada, New Hampshire, New Jersey, New Mexico, New York, Ohio, Oregon, Pennsylvania, Rhode Island, Tennessee, Texas, Utah, Vermont, Virginia, Washington, West Virginia, Wisconsin and Wyoming — said states constituting three-fourths of the whole number of states in the United States, and certified as valid to all intents and purposes as a part of the Constitution of the United States.

The amendment was subsequently ratified by Maine and Montana.

ARTICLE XXII.

Limitation of presidential terms.

Section 1. No person shall be elected to the office of the President more than twice, and no person who has held the office of President, or acted as President, for more than two years of a term to which some other person was elected President shall be elected to the office of the President more than once. But this Article shall not apply to any person holding the office of President when this Article was proposed by the Congress, and shall not prevent any person who may be holding the office of President, or acting as President, during the term within which this Article becomes operative from holding the office of President or acting as President during the remainder of such term.

Sec. 2. This article shall be inoperative unless it shall have been ratified as an amendment to the Constitution by the legislatures of three-fourths of the several States within seven years from the date of its submission to the States by the Congress.

PROPOSAL AND RATIFICATION

This amendment was proposed to the legislatures of the several States by the Eightieth Congress on Mar. 21, 1947 by House Joint Res. No. 27, and was declared by the Administrator of General Services, on Mar. 3, 1951, to have been ratified by the following State legislatures: Arkansas, California, Colorado, Connecticut, Delaware, Georgia, Idaho, Illinois, Indiana, Iowa, Kansas, Louisiana, Maine, Michigan, Mississippi, Missouri, Montana, Nebraska, Nevada, New Hampshire, New Jersey, New Mexico, New York, North Carolina, North Dakota, Ohio, Oregon, Pennsylvania, South Dakota, Tennessee, Texas, Utah, Vermont, Virginia, Wisconsin, and Wyoming.

The amendment was subsequently ratified by North Carolina, South Carolina, Maryland, Florida, and Alabama.

CERTIFICATION OF VALIDITY

Publication of the certifying statement of the Administrator of General Services that the Amendment had become valid was made on Mar. 1, 1951, F.R. Doc. 51-2940, 16 F.R. 2019.

ARTICLE XXIII.

Presidential electors for District of Columbia.

Section 1. The District constituting the seat of Government of the United States shall appoint in such manner as the Congress may direct:

A number of electors as President and Vice President equal to the whole number of Senators and Representatives in Congress to which the District would be entitled if it were a State, but in no event more than the least populous State; they shall be in addition to those appointed by the States, but they shall be considered, for the purposes of the election of President and Vice President, to be electors appointed by a State; and they shall meet in the District and perform such duties as provided by the twelfth article of amendment.

Power of Congress.

Section 2. The Congress shall have power to enforce this article by appropriate legislation.

PROPOSAL AND RATIFICATION

This amendment was proposed by the Eighty-sixth Congress on June 17, 1960 and was declared by the Administrator of General Services on Apr. 3, 1961, to have been ratified.

The amendment was ratified by the following States: Hawaii, June 23, 1960; Massachusetts, Aug. 22, 1960; New Jersey, Dec. 19, 1960; New York, Jan. 17, 1961; California, Jan. 19, 1961; Oregon, Jan. 27, 1961; Maryland, Jan. 30, 1961; Idaho, Jan. 31, 1961; Maine, Jan. 31, 1961; Minnesota, Jan. 31, 1961; New Mexico, Feb. 1, 1961; Nevada, Feb. 2, 1961; Montana, Feb. 6, 1961; South Dakota, Feb. 6, 1961; Colorado, Feb. 8, 1961; Washington, Feb. 9, 1961; West Virginia, Feb. 9, 1961; Alaska, Feb. 10, 1961; Wyoming, Feb. 13, 1961; Utah, Feb. 20, 1961; Delaware, Feb. 20, 1961; Utah, Feb. 23, 1961; Wisconsin, Feb. 21, 1961; Pennsylvania, Feb. 28, 1961; Indiana, Mar. 3, 1961; North Dakota, Mar. 3, 1961; Tennessee, Mar. 6, 1961; Michigan, Mar. 8, 1961; Connecticut, Mar. 9, 1961; Arizona, Mar. 10, 1961; Illinois, Mar. 14, 1961; Nebraska, Mar. 15, 1961; Vermont, Mar. 15, 1961; Iowa, Mar. 16, 1961; Missouri, Mar. 20, 1961; Oklahoma, Mar. 21, 1961; Rhode Island, Mar. 22, 1961; Kansas, Mar. 29, 1961; Ohio, Mar. 29, 1961, and New Hampshire, Mar. 30, 1961.

CERTIFICATION OF VALIDITY

Publication of the certifying statement of the Administrator of General Services that the Amendment had become valid was made on Apr. 3, 1961, F.R. Doc. 61-3017, 26 F.R. 2808.

ARTICLE XXIV.

Right to vote in federal election not to be denied because of failure to pay poll or other tax.

Section 1. The right of citizens of the United States to vote in any primary or other election for President or Vice President, for electors for President or Vice President, or for Senator or Representative in Congress, shall not be denied or abridged by the United States or any State by reason of failure to pay any poll tax or other tax.

Power of Congress.

Section 2. The Congress shall have power to enforce this article by appropriate legislation.

PROPOSAL AND RATIFICATION

This amendment was proposed by the Eighty-seventh Congress by Senate Joint Resolution No. 29, which was approved by the Senate on Mar. 27, 1962, and by the House of Representatives on Aug. 27, 1962. It was declared by the Administrator of General Services on Feb. 4, 1964, to have been ratified.

This amendment was ratified by the following States: Illinois, Nov. 14, 1962; New Jersey, Dec. 3, 1962; Oregon, Jan. 25, 1963; Montana, Jan. 28, 1963; West Virginia, Feb. 1, 1963; New York, Feb. 4, 1963; Maryland, Feb. 6, 1963; California, Feb. 7, 1963; Alaska, Feb. 11, 1963; Rhode Island, Feb. 14, 1963; Indiana, Feb. 19, 1963; Utah, Feb. 20, 1963; Michigan, Feb. 20, 1963; Colorado, Feb. 21,

1963; Ohio, Feb. 27, 1963; Minnesota, Feb. 27, 1963; New Mexico, Mar. 5, 1963, Hawaii, Mar. 6, 1963; North Dakota, Mar. 7, 1963; Idaho, Mar. 8, 1963; Washington, Mar. 14, 1963; Vermont, Mar. 15, 1963; Nevada, Mar. 19, 1963; Connecticut, Mar. 20, 1963; Tennessee, Mar. 21, 1963; Pennsylvania, Mar. 25, 1963; Wisconsin, Mar. 26, 1963; Kansas, Mar. 28, 1963; Massachusetts, Mar. 28, 1963; Nebraska, Apr. 4, 1963; Florida, Apr. 18, 1963; Iowa, Apr. 24, 1963; Delaware, May 1, 1963; Missouri, May 13, 1963; New Hampshire, June 12, 1963; Kentucky, June 27, 1963; Maine, Jan. 16, 1964; South Dakota, Jan. 23, 1964.

ARTICLE XXV.

Succession to Presidency.

Section 1. In case of the removal of the President from office or of his death or resignation, the Vice President shall become President.

Succession to Vice Presidency.

Sec. 2. Whenever there is a vacancy in the office of the Vice President, the President shall nominate a Vice President who shall take office upon confirmation by a majority vote of both Houses of Congress.

Disability of President; declaration of President.

Sec. 3. Whenever the President transmits to the President pro tempore of the Senate and the Speaker of the House of Representatives his written declaration that he is unable to discharge the powers and duties of his office, and until he transmits to them a written declaration to the contrary, such powers and duties shall be discharged by the Vice President as Acting President.

Disability of President; declaration by Vice President and officers of executive departments; removal of disability.

Sec. 4. Whenever the Vice President and a majority of either the principal officers of the executive departments or of such other body as Congress may by law provide, transmit to the President pro tempore of the Senate and the Speaker of the House of Representatives their written declaration that the President is unable to discharge the powers and duties of his office, the Vice President shall immediately assume the powers and duties of the office as Acting President.

Thereafter, when the President transmits to the President pro tempore of the Senate and the Speaker of the House of Representatives his written declaration that no inability exists, he shall resume the powers and duties of his office unless the Vice President and a majority of either the principal officers of the executive department or of such other body as Congress may by law provide, transmit within four days to the President pro tempore of the Senate and the Speaker of the House of Representatives their written declaration that the President is unable to discharge the powers and duties of his office. Thereupon Congress shall decide the issue, assembling within forty-eight hours for that purpose if not in session. If the Congress, within twenty-one days after receipt of the latter written declaration, or, if Congress is not in session, within twenty-one days after Congress is required to assemble, determines by two-thirds vote of both Houses that the President is unable to discharge the powers and duties of his office, the Vice President shall continue to discharge the same as Acting President; otherwise, the President shall resume the powers and duties of his office.

ARTICLE XXVI.

Right to vote; citizens eighteen years of age or older.

Section 1. The right of citizens of the United States, who are eighteen years of age or older, to vote shall not be denied or abridged by the United States or by any State on account of age.

Power of Congress.

Sec. 2. The Congress shall have power to enforce this article by appropriate legislation.

PROPOSAL AND RATIFICATION

This amendment was proposed by the Ninety-second Congress by Senate Joint Resolution No. 7, which was approved by the Senate on Mar. 10, 1971, and by the House of Representatives on Mar. 23, 1971. It was declared by the Administrator of General Services on July 5, 1971, to have been ratified.

This amendment was ratified by the following States: Connecticut, March 23, 1971; Delaware, March 23, 1971; Minnesota, March 23, 1971; Tennessee, March 23, 1971; Washington, March 23, 1971; Hawaii, March 24, 1971; Massachusetts, March 24, 1971; Montana, March 29, 1971; Arkansas, March 30, 1971; Idaho, March 30, 1971; Iowa, March 30, 1971; Nebraska, April 2, 1971; New Jersey, April 3, 1971; Kansas, April 7, 1971; Michigan, April 7, 1971; Alaska, April 8, 1971; Maryland, April 8, 1971; Indiana, April 8, 1971; Maine, April 9, 1971; Vermont, April 16, 1971; Louisiana, April 17, 1971; California, April 19, 1971; Colorado, April 27, 1971; Pennsylvania, April 27, 1971; Texas, April 27, 1971; South Carolina, April 28, 1971; West Virginia, April 28, 1971; New Hampshire, May 13, 1971; Arizona, May 14, 1971; Rhode Island, May 27, 1971; New York, June 2, 1971; Oregon, June 4, 1971; Missouri, June 14, 1971; Wisconsin, June 22, 1971; Illinois, June 29, 1971; Alabama, June 30, 1971; Ohio, June 30, 1971; North Carolina, July 1, 1971; Oklahoma, July 1, 1971.

Ratification was completed on July 1, 1971.

The amendment was subsequently ratified by Virginia, July 8, 1971; Wyoming, July 8, 1971; Georgia, October 4, 1971.

CERTIFICATION OF VALIDITY

Publication of the certifying statement of the Administrator of General Services that the Amendment had become valid was made on July 7, 1971, F.R. Doc. 71-9691, 36 F.R. 12725.

ARTICLE XXVII.

Senators and Representatives; compensation.

No law, varying the compensation for the services of the Senators and Representatives, shall take effect, until an election of Representatives shall have intervened.

Compiler's note: Congress submitted the text of the Twenty-Seventh Amendment to the States as part of the proposed Bill of Rights on September 25, 1789. The Amendment was not ratified together with the first ten Amendments, which became effective on December 15, 1791. The Twenty-Seventh Amendment to the Constitution of the United States of America was ratified on May 7, 1992, by the vote of Michigan.

---

[1] This clause has been affected by the 14th and 16th amendments.

[2] This section has been affected by the 17th amendment.

[3] This section has been affected by the 20th amendment.

[4] This clause has been affected by the 16th amendment.

[5] This clause has been affected by the 12th amendment.

[6] This section has been affected by the 11th amendment.

[7] This clause has been affected by the 13th amendment.

[8] The first ten amendments to the Constitution of the United States were proposed to the legislatures of the several States by the First Congress, on the 25th of September, 1789. They were ratified by the following States, and the notifications of ratification by the governors thereof were successively communicated by the President to Congress: New Jersey, November 20, 1789; Maryland, December 19, 1789; North Carolina, December 22, 1789; South Carolina, January 19, 1790; New Hampshire, January 25, 1790; Delaware, January 28, 1790; Pennsylvania, March 10, 1790; New York, March 27, 1790; Rhode Island, June 7, 1790; Vermont, November 3, 1791, and Virginia, December 15, 1791. The legislatures of Connecticut, Georgia and Massachusetts ratified them on April 19, 1939, March 18, 1939 and March 2, 1939, respectively.

[9] This amendment has been affected by the 20th amendment.

[10] Repealed. See Article XXI.

Chapter III

THE LEGISLATIVE BRANCH

2019–2020

PROFILE OF THE MICHIGAN LEGISLATURE

The legislative power of the state of Michigan is vested in a **bicameral** (two chamber) body comprised of a senate and a house of representatives. The **senate** consists of 38 members who are elected by the qualified electors of districts that have an average of 260,095 residents each (under a redistricting plan enacted in 2011). Senators are elected at the same time as the governor and serve four-year terms concurrent with the governor's term of office. The **house of representatives** consists of 110 members who are elected by the qualified electors of districts that have an average of 89,851 residents each (under a redistricting plan enacted in 2011). Representatives are elected in even-numbered years to two-year terms. Legislative districts are drawn on the basis of population figures obtained through the federal decennial census. Terms for senators and representatives begin on January 1, following the November general election. Effective with terms of office beginning on or after January 1, 1993, state legislators (as well as the governor, lieutenant governor, secretary of state, and attorney general) are subject to **term limitations**. State senators may not be elected more than two times and state representatives may not be elected more than three times. (Partial terms that are less than half of a full term are not counted as one of these terms.)

The state legislature **enacts the laws of Michigan**; levies taxes and appropriates funds from money collected for the support of public institutions and the administration of the affairs of state government; proposes amendments to the state constitution, which must be approved by a majority vote of the electors; and considers legislation proposed by initiatory petitions. The legislature also provides **oversight of the executive branch** of government through the administrative rules and audit processes, committees, and the budget process; advises and consents, through the senate, on gubernatorial appointments; and considers proposed amendments to the Constitution of the United States. The majority of the legislature's work, however, entails lawmaking. Through a process defined by the state constitution, statute, and legislative rules, the legislature considers thousands of bills (proposed laws) during each two-year session.

Senate Chamber

House Chamber

THE MICHIGAN LEGISLATURE

MEMBERS OF THE LEGISLATURE

Qualifications

In order to qualify as a member of the Michigan Legislature, a person:

- Must be a citizen of the United States, at least 21 years of age, and an elector of the district he or she represents.

- Must not have been convicted of subversion or, within the past 20 years, have been convicted of a felony involving a breach of the public trust.

- Must not hold any office, employment, or position under the United States, the state of Michigan, or any political subdivisions thereof. A person may, however, be a notary public or a member of the armed forces reserve. This constitutional provision allows people holding offices or positions to run for the legislature, but since dual office holding is prohibited, a legislator-elect must resign the prior office or employment as a condition of taking a seat in the legislature.

- Must have had an accounting, in the manner prescribed by law, of all sums for which the person may be liable if the person has custody or control of public money.

Members-elect, before entering upon the duties of office, are required to take and subscribe to the oath of office set forth in the Constitution of 1963, article XI, section 1.

Restrictions of Office

Once elected to the legislature, a member is not eligible to receive any appointment, except as a notary public, within this state from the governor, the legislature, or from any other state authority during the term for which the member was elected. In addition, an amendment to the state constitution adopted by the voters limits state representatives to three terms (six years) in the House of Representatives and state senators (for terms starting January 1, 1995, and after) to two terms (eight years) in the Michigan Senate.

A member of the legislature cannot have an interest, either directly or indirectly, in any contract with the state of Michigan or any political subdivision which would cause a substantial conflict of interest. This constitutional provision was implemented by Public Act 318 of 1968.

The senate and house rules also contain provisions related to legislative conduct and ethics.

Under the Constitution of 1963, each house of the legislature is the sole judge of the qualifications, elections, and returns of its members.

Each chamber also has authority to expel a member with the concurrence of two-thirds of its members. The reasons for an expulsion must be entered in the journal along with the votes and names of the members voting on the expulsion. The constitution prohibits a member from being expelled a second time for the same reason.

Legislative Privileges

Senators and representatives are privileged from civil arrest and civil process during sessions of the legislature and for five days before the commencement and after the termination of session. A constitutional amendment approved at the November 1982 general election authorized the legislature to pass laws to reform this exemption. Subsequently, statutes were enacted that prohibit legislators from being made party to civil actions or to contested cases under the Administrative Procedures Act of 1969 for actions pursuant to duties as a legislator. Certain legislative records are exempted from subpoena. In certain administrative proceedings and civil actions, exceptions were made to service of process requirements and provision was made for continuances to a nonsession day. Members cannot be questioned in any other place for any speech made in either house. Legislators are not immune from arrest on criminal charges.

The Constitution of 1963 also affords legislators the privilege of dissenting from, and protesting against, any act, proceeding, or resolution which the members deem injurious to any person or the public and to have the reason for the dissent entered into the journal.

Vacancies in Office

Under the Michigan Constitution, the Governor is responsible for determining whether a special election will be held to fill a vacancy in a legislative office or if the vacancy will be filled at the next general election. The election procedures for filling the vacancy are prescribed by law (Constitution of 1963, art. V, sec. 13).

Legislator Compensation

Legislators' salaries and expense allowances are determined by the State Officers Compensation Commission, which was established in the Constitution of 1963. The commission meets every two years. The commission's determinations shall be the salaries and expense allowances only if the legislature, by concurrent resolution adopted by a majority of the members elected to and serving in each house of the legislature, approves them. The concurrent resolution may amend the determinations to reduce them by the same proportion for members of the legislature, the governor, the lieutenant governor, the attorney general, the secretary of state, and the justices of the supreme court. However, the legislature may not reduce the determinations to below the levels members receive on the date the determinations are made. If the salary and expense determinations are approved or amended, they become effective for the legislative session immediately following the next general election.

The annual salary remains unchanged for legislators for 2019-2020 at $71,685, with an expense allowance of $10,800. Current supplemental salaries are also unchanged as follows: speaker of the house, $24,300; senate majority leader, $23,400; house and senate minority leaders, $19,800; house and senate majority floor leaders, $10,800; house and senate minority floor leaders, $9,000; house and senate appropriations committee chairs, $6,300; and house speaker pro tempore and senate president pro tempore, $4,962 (these figures for salaries, expenses, and supplemental salaries represent a 10 percent reduction from the 2009-2010 Legislature). In addition, each legislator may claim reimbursement for certain travel undertaken in the conduct of official legislative business.

LEGISLATIVE OFFICERS, RULES, AND PROCEDURES

Except as provided in the state constitution, each house of the state legislature chooses its own officers and determines the rules of its proceedings.

Officers of the Senate

By virtue of office, the lieutenant governor, who is not an elected member of the senate, is the president (presiding officer) of the senate. In addition to calling each senate session to order and instructing the secretary of the senate to call the roll and announce the attendance, the lieutenant governor has general control over order and decorum within the senate chamber. The lieutenant governor may vote only when senators are equally divided.

Prior to the commencement of the first session of a quadrennium (four-year term), the senate and each party caucus elect other officers. The senate elects a president pro tempore, assistant president pro tempore, and associate president pro tempore. One of these officers presides in the absence of the lieutenant governor.

In an organizational caucus, each party elects a leader, floor leader, whip, assistant leader, caucus chair, assistant floor leader, assistant whip, and assistant caucus chair.

The senate majority leader appoints all committees and has supervisory control over the administration and office budget of the senate, refers bills to committees, and develops and disseminates guidelines on a variety of senate operations.

The majority floor leader is responsible for scheduling and managing the day-to-day business of the senate. During session, the majority floor leader keeps members informed on the order of business and the progress of measures that may be considered for a final vote.

The principal duty of the whips is to ensure that the members of their respective caucuses will be present to vote on a given bill. The caucus officers conduct and preside over caucus meetings and are influential in caucus decisions.

As the senate parliamentarian, the secretary of the senate advises the senate on questions relating to parliamentary law and procedure. The secretary, who is not a member of the senate, is elected by the members of the senate. Among the duties assigned to this officer are keeping a journal of the daily proceedings, providing for the printing of bills, assigning bill numbers, and maintaining an official record of all bills received by the senate. The secretary of the senate also exercises supervisory control over the senate chamber, committee rooms, pages, and the senate's computer system.

Officers of the House

The presiding officer of the Michigan House of Representatives is the speaker, who is elected at the beginning of the biennium (two-year term) by the members of the house and serves as the caucus leader of the majority party. As the presiding officer, the speaker calls the house to order, maintains decorum, decides on questions of order, recognizes who shall speak, and settles points of order that arise during session. The speaker also appoints all committees and most employees of the house, refers bills to appropriate committees, and controls the order in which bills are considered. As an elected member of the house, the speaker is entitled to vote on all questions.

The speaker pro tempore and associate speaker pro tempore are elected by the majority party caucus. One of these officers presides if the speaker is absent or chooses to participate in floor debate. While presiding, they can generally exercise the same powers as the speaker (i.e., recognize speakers, settle points of order, etc.).

The floor leaders and their assistants are the primary strategists for their respective caucuses. During session the floor leader keeps the session agenda moving with regular statements regarding the daily calendar.

As in the senate, the various caucus officers are responsible for conducting party caucus meetings that are often held to develop strategy on a specific measure or package of bills. In turn, the whips serve their respective caucuses by making certain that members are present for key votes.

The clerk of the house is not a member of the house of representatives, but is elected by the members to serve as the manager of the "housekeeping" details. The clerk calls the roll, announces a quorum, keeps the journal, numbers and distributes the bills, and serves as the chief parliamentary officer of the house.

Standing Rules

The senate adopts its standing rules every four years, and the house of representatives adopts its rules every two years.

In the senate, amending or repealing a rule is proposed by resolution which is referred to a standing committee for review. The amendment or repeal of a rule requires an affirmative vote of a majority of those elected and serving. A rule may be suspended by a majority of the members elected and serving.

House rules may be altered by a majority vote of the members elected and serving, but any proposed changes must be made in writing and in the possession of the house five days prior to its consideration. A rule may be suspended by a vote of three-fifths of the representatives present. Suspension of the rules on matters related to the order of business, schedule of legislative sessions, and adjournment may be by majority vote of the members elected and serving.

Parliamentary Procedure

In the Senate, the Senate Rules identify the sources of legal authority. This includes the Michigan Constitution, fundamental legal principles, statutory rules, Senate rules and adopted parliamentary authority. The Senate uses as its parliamentary authority *Mason's Manual of Legislative Procedure*. Senators' inquiries as to parliamentary procedure during session are directed to the presiding officer. It should also be noted that, by senate rule, the secretary of the senate or a member of the staff of the secretary of the senate serves as the senate parliamentarian to advise the senate on questions relating to parliamentary law and procedure.

In the house, in cases not provided for by the state constitution, the Standing Rules of the House of Representatives, or by the Joint Rules of the Senate and House of Representatives, the authority is *Mason's Manual of Legislative Procedure*. In the house, members' inquiries are directed to the presiding officer.

LEGISLATIVE SESSIONS

Biennial Sessions

Meetings of the Michigan Legislature are on a two-year basis. Any business or legislation pending at the final adjournment of a regular session held in an odd-numbered year carries over with the same status until the next regular session. However, under the Joint Rules of the Senate and House of Representatives, either house is prohibited from reconsidering in a subsequent year the vote by which any business, bill, or joint resolution was defeated or vetoed during the previous year.

Regular Sessions

In accordance with the state constitution, the Michigan Legislature is required to meet at the seat of government (Lansing) on the second Wednesday in January of each year at 12:00 noon.

The daily sessions of the legislature are normally held, unless either house designates a different hour for convening, on Tuesday, Wednesday, and Thursday at 10:00 a.m. in the senate; Tuesday and Wednesday at 1:30 p.m. and Thursday at 12:00 noon in the house.

Quorums

A majority of the members elected to and serving in each house constitutes a quorum to conduct business. In the senate, 20 members constitute a quorum, while in the house, 56 members may conduct business. If a legislative seat has been vacated for any reason, and is not filled, it is not counted in computing a quorum.

Calls of the House or Senate

In either house, if a quorum is not present, the members present may adjourn from day-to-day and may compel the attendance of absent members in the manner and with penalties as each house prescribes. For example, a call of the senate may be ordered by a majority of Senators voting and at least 1/5 of members elected and serving. To order a call in the house of representatives, at least 15 members must vote in favor of the motion. Once a call is ordered, the doors of the house or senate are closed and the members are prohibited from leaving the floor of the chambers without permission of the body. The sergeant-at-arms or other authorized person may be dispatched after absentees.

Recesses and Adjournments

Neither house can adjourn, without the consent of the other, for more than two intervening calendar days, nor adjourn to any place other than where the legislature may then be in session.

Regular sessions are adjourned sine die (without day) at twelve o'clock noon on a day determined by concurrent resolution. Usually, the sine die or final adjournment occurs during the last week of the year.

Special Sessions

The governor is authorized by the state constitution to convene the legislature on extraordinary occasions. The governor may also convene the legislature at some other place if it becomes dangerous to meet at the seat of government. During a special session, the legislature cannot pass bills on any subject other than those expressly stated in the governor's proclamation or those submitted by special message.

Under the joint rules, if either or both houses have adjourned for more than two days until a specific date, a committee composed of the senate majority leader and the speaker may, by unanimous vote, convene either or both houses at any time in case of emergency.

Open Meetings

Under the state constitution, the doors of each house must be kept open unless the public security requires otherwise. The sessions of the legislature must also be held in compliance with the provisions of the Michigan Open Meetings Act (Public Act 267 of 1976). Exceptions to this law applicable to the legislature include the following:

- The right to address or speak at a meeting of the legislature or either house may be limited to prescribed times at hearings and committee meetings only.

- Partisan caucuses of members of the legislature may be held in closed session.
- The 18-hour public notice for rescheduled meetings does not apply to conference committees. These committees are required to give a six-hour notice. A second conference committee has to give only a one-hour notice. The conference committee meeting notice must include written notice to each committee member and the majority and minority leaders of each house of the time and place of the meeting.

HOW A BILL BECOMES A LAW

Introduction of Bills

Bills may be introduced in either house of the legislature. Senate bills are filed with the secretary of the senate and house bills with the clerk of the house. Upon introduction, bills are assigned a number. At the beginning of each biennial session, house bills are numbered consecutively starting with House Bill No. 4001 and senate bills are numbered starting with Senate Bill No. 1. In both houses, joint resolutions are assigned a letter designation.

Title Reading

Under the state constitution, every bill must be read three times before it may be passed. The courts have held, however, that this requirement can be satisfied by reading the bill's title. Upon introduction, the bill's title is read a first and a second time in the senate and is read once in the house. The bill is then ordered to be printed.

Referral to Committee

Upon introduction, a bill is referred to a standing committee in the senate by the majority leader. In the house of representatives the speaker of the house refers bills to the standing committee. All bills involving an appropriation must be referred either directly to the appropriations committee or to an appropriate standing committee and then to the appropriations committee.

Committee Review

Committee members consider a bill by discussing and debating the bill. The committee may also hold public hearings on the bill.

Committee Action

A standing committee may act on a bill in various ways. The committee may:
- Report the bill with favorable recommendation.
- Report the bill with amendments with favorable recommendation.
- Report the bill with the recommendation that a substitute be adopted.
- Report the bill without recommendation.
- Report the bill with amendments but without recommendation.
- Report the bill with the recommendation that the bill be referred to another committee.
- Take no action on a bill.
- Vote to not report a bill out of committee.

Reported with recommendation. If a bill is reported from committee favorably with or without amendment or in the form of a substitute bill, the committee report is printed in the journal, with a list of how committee members voted on reporting the bill. On being reported favorably from committee, the bill and recommended committee amendments (if any) are placed on the order of "General Orders" in the Senate. In the House, the bill and amendments (if any) are referred to the order of "Second Reading."

Reported without recommendation. The bill, upon being reported from committee, is tabled (temporarily removed from consideration) on the floor. A majority vote of the members present and voting in the chamber where the bill is tabled is required to remove the bill from the table before it may be given further consideration.

Failing to report a bill. In both chambers, a majority vote of the members serving on a committee is necessary to report a bill. If a committee fails to report a bill, a motion to discharge the committee from consideration of the bill may be offered in the chamber having possession of the bill. If this motion is approved by a vote of a majority of the members elected and serving, the bill is then placed in position on the calendar for floor action. In the House, at least a one-day prior notice of the motion to discharge must be given to the Clerk of the House.

Committee Reports

If a bill is reported from committee favorably with or without amendment or in the form of a substitute bill, the committee report is printed in the journal under the order of business entitled "Reports of Standing Committees" in the house. On being reported favorably from committee, the bill and recommended committee amendments, if any, are placed on the order of "General Orders" in the senate. In the house, the bill and amendments are referred to the order of "Second Reading."

General Orders or Second Reading

For the purpose of considering the standing committee recommendations on a bill, the senate resolves itself into the committee of the whole and the house assumes the order of Second Reading. Amendments to the bill may be offered by any member when the bill is being considered at this stage of the legislative process. In the senate, a simple majority of members present and voting may recommend adoption of amendments to the bill and recommend a bill be advanced to Third Reading. In the house, amendments may be adopted by a majority serving, and a majority voting may advance the bill to Third Reading. In the house, a bill may be placed on Third Reading for a specified date.

Third Reading

While there are provisions in the Standing Rules of the House of Representatives and the Senate Rules for reading bills unless exception is made, in practice, bills are not read in full in either chamber. In both chambers, amendments must be approved by a majority vote of the members serving and the previous question may be moved and debate cut off by a vote of a majority of the members present and voting. At the conclusion of Third Reading, the bill is either passed or defeated by a roll call vote of the majority of the members elected and serving (pursuant to the state constitution, approval of certain measures requires a "supermajority" of a two-thirds or three-fourths vote) or one of the following four options is exercised to delay final action on the bill: (a) the bill is returned to committee for further consideration; (b) consideration of the bill is postponed indefinitely; (c) consideration is postponed until a certain date; or (d) the bill is tabled.

Following either passage or defeat of a bill, a legislator may move for reconsideration of the vote by which the bill was passed or defeated. (A motion to reconsider can be made for any question.) In the senate, the motion for reconsideration must be made within the following two session days; in the house, the motion must be made within the next succeeding session day.

Five-Day Rule

No bill can become law at any regular session of the legislature until it has been printed and reproduced and in the possession of each house for at least five days (Constitution of 1963, art. IV, sec. 26).

Immediate Effect

No act shall take effect until the expiration of 90 days from the end of the session at which the measure was enacted. The legislature may give immediate effect to an act by a two-thirds vote of the members elected and serving in each house (Constitution of 1963, art. IV, sec. 27).

Enactment by the Legislature

If a bill passes, it is sent to the other house of the legislature where the bill follows the procedure outlined above, resulting in defeat or passage.

If a bill is passed by both houses in identical form, the bill is ordered enrolled by the house in which the bill originated. Following enrollment and printing, the bill is sent to the governor.

If a bill is passed in a different form by the second house, the bill must be returned to the house of origin and one of the following occurs:

- If the amendment(s) or substitute bill of the second house is accepted in the house of origin, the bill is enrolled, printed, and sent to the governor. It should also be noted that either house may amend an amendment made by the other to a bill or joint resolution. At any time while in possession of the bill, either house may recede from its position in whole or in part and the bill may be returned to the other house for this purpose. If this further action is agreed to by both houses, the bill is ordered enrolled.

- If the amendment(s) or substitute proposal of the second house is rejected in the house of origin, the bill is then either:
  - Sent to a conference committee (a committee composed of three legislators from the senate and three legislators from the house) which attempts to reconcile differences between the two versions of the bill. The conference committee can consider only issues in the bill upon which there is disagreement between the two houses. However, when the agreement arrived at by the conferees is such that it affects other parts of the bill, such as in an appropriations measure, the conferees may recommend further amendments to conform with the agreement. The conferees may also recommend corrections to any errors in the bill. The conference committee may reach a compromise approved by at least a majority of the conferees from each house and submit a report to the house of origin. If adopted, the report and bill are transmitted to the second house. If the conference committee report is approved in the second house, the bill is then enrolled, printed, and sent to the governor. A conference report may not be amended by either house. If the conference committee is not able to agree, or if the report is rejected by either house, a second conference committee is appointed. When a second conference has met and the two houses are still unable to agree, no further conference is in order; or
  - Amended by the house of origin and sent back to the second house for further consideration.

Approval by Governor

Upon receipt of an enrolled bill, the governor has 14 days to consider the bill. The governor may:

- Sign the bill, which then either becomes law at the expiration of 90 days after the legislature adjourns sine die or on a date beyond the ninetieth day specified in the bill. If the bill has been given immediate effect by a two-thirds vote of the members elected to, and serving in, each house, the bill will become law after the governor signs the bill and files it with the secretary of state or on a day specified in the bill.
- Veto the bill and return it to the house of origin with a message stating the governor's objections.
- Choose not to sign or veto the bill. If the bill is neither signed nor vetoed and the legislature is in session or in recess, the bill becomes law 14 days after having reached the governor's desk. If the legislature should adjourn sine die before the end of the 14 days, the unsigned bill does not become law. If the legislature has adjourned before the bill reaches the governor, he or she has 14 days to consider the bill. If the governor fails to approve the bill, it does not become law.

Legislative Veto Response

If the governor vetoes a bill while the legislature is in session or recess, one of the following actions may occur:

- The legislature may override the veto by a two-thirds vote of the members elected to and serving in each house. The bill then becomes law.
- The bill may not receive the necessary two-thirds vote and thus the attempt to override the veto will fail.
- The bill may be tabled.
- The bill may be re-referred to a committee.
- Consideration of the veto override may be postponed indefinitely or to a definite time.

THE COMMITTEE SYSTEM

The committee system has evolved in response to the great number and diversity of issues that must be considered by the Michigan Legislature. Without being divided into committees, it would be difficult for either the senate or the house to effectively or efficiently evaluate the thousands of proposals that are introduced each biennial session. The committee system distributes the workload; in many instances, the critical decisions regarding legislation are made in a committee or in a subcommittee.

Legal Authority for Legislative Committees

The Constitution of Michigan of 1963 is the ultimate authority by which the legislature creates and acts through committees. Constitution of 1963, art. IV, sec. 17, provides that "Each house of the legislature may establish the committees necessary for the conduct of its business . . ." including joint committees. The constitution makes certain stipulations governing committees, including the right of the members of a house to discharge a committee from further consideration of a bill (art. IV, sec. 16) and the maintaining of votes and actions taken and the notification of meetings (art. IV, sec. 17).

The constitution also provides specifically for the Legislative Council, a bipartisan joint committee charged with providing various services supporting the operations of the legislature (art. IV, sec. 15).

Many functions of committees are provided for by statute, including provisions relating to expenses, the administering of oaths to witnesses, subpoena power, contempt, the inspection of state agency records, and other matters.

The rules of each house create the standing committees and govern most of the activities of committees. The procedures followed by the respective houses in considering bills and exercising oversight of the executive branch departments are, for the most part, set forth in these rules. The number of members on each committee, the names of the committees, the responsibilities of committee members and chairs, staffing and expenses, procedures, reports, and parliamentary practices are contained in the rules.

Standing Committees

Standing committees are the principal bodies that scrutinize, debate, and modify legislation. Standing committees are created by the rules of each chamber. For 2019, there are 19 standing committees in the senate and 21 standing committees in the house. House and senate rules specify the number of legislators that serve on each committee. Committee assignments are made by the majority leader in the senate and by the speaker of the house, unless otherwise directed. In the senate, appointments to committees are subject to approval by the senate. The senate rules provide that appointments of minority party members must be made from a list submitted by the minority leader and must consider the preferences, seniority, and experience of the members. If the majority leader rejects names on the list and their corresponding committee assignments, the minority leader submits replacement nominations. In both houses, the first member named to the committee is the chairperson and the second named is the vice chairperson. By tradition, the first named member of the minority party is the minority vice chairperson.

Legislation is referred to the standing committees by the Senate Majority Leader or the Speaker of the House. With a few exceptions, the rules of the Senate and House generally do not describe the jurisdictions of the individual standing committees, but the assignment of bills traditionally follows topical lines. All Senate bills involving an appropriation must be referred either directly to the Appropriations Committee or to an appropriate standing committee and then to the Appropriations Committee. Additionally, the House Rules require that most committees refer legislation to a second committee before it can be reported to the House floor. Bills containing appropriations must be referred to the Appropriations Committee, bills creating or revising a criminal offense must be referred to the Judiciary Committee, and all other bills must be referred to the Ways and Means Committee. Those three committees, the Government Operations Committee, and any select committees may refer bills directly to the floor.

While the primary function of the standing committees is to consider legislation, there are a few specific exceptions. For example, the appropriations committees in the House and Senate have the added responsibility under the state constitution of approving or disapproving gubernatorial executive orders that propose reductions of expenditures authorized by appropriation. The Senate Advice and Consent Committee is the committee to which nominations to office submitted by the governor requiring advice and consent are referred. All other executive business in the Senate is referred to the Government Operations Committee. This committee also responds to questions relating to the interpretation and enforcement of Senate Rules concerning legislative conduct and ethics. Reports issued by the Auditor General are referred to the oversight committees in both the House and Senate.

Standing committees are empowered to review legislation, hear testimony, and may, by resolution, be authorized to administer oaths, subpoena witnesses, and examine the books and records of any persons, partnerships, or corporations involved in a matter properly before any committee. The legislature may punish witnesses who neglect or refuse to obey committee subpoenas, or who refuse to be sworn or testify, or who fail, upon demand, to produce necessary materials relative to an investigation. The legislature may also punish witnesses or attorneys who are guilty of contempt while in attendance at any hearing before any committee.

Committees operate under the applicable committee rules of their respective houses and the state constitution, which requires committees to keep an action journal recording the date and time of each meeting, the members present and absent, and all action on legislation with the names and votes of the members.

Standing committees generally have a regular schedule indicating the day and time the committees will meet each week. In the house, the schedule is adopted by the committee at the beginning of each term and is printed in the journal. Notices of committee meetings in the senate are printed in the journal, on the calendar, and are posted in various capitol complex locations. Verbal notice of the meeting is also given during session by the chairperson of the committee. If the legislature is in recess, the meeting notice must be filed at least 10 days prior to the meeting. A standing committee in either house may also hold public hearings on bills referred to that committee. Notice of the hearing, its subject, time and place is also printed in the journal, on the calendar, and is posted. Committees cannot meet during session unless authorized by the entire body.

Special Committees

Special committees, sometimes called ad hoc or select committees, are established by legislative resolution or by leadership and may consist of members of one or both houses. The number of members who serve on these committees varies according to the provisions of the resolution creating the committee. Special committees are generally appointed to serve for a specified period of time. For the most part, the purpose of a special committee is to study and investigate topics of special interest, such as fire safety needs, oil and gas extraction on public lands, and health care costs.

Joint Committees

In addition to the special committees which may consist of members from both houses, there are two permanent joint committees created by state statute:

Legislative Council — a constitutionally created committee responsible for maintaining bill drafting, research, and other services for members of the legislature.

Joint Committee on Administrative Rules — a statutorily created bipartisan legislative committee, comprised of five house and five senate members, which is responsible for the legislative oversight of administrative rules proposed by state agencies. Legislative Council staff provide needed services to the committee.

Other Committees

Certain committees are created by the legislature for parliamentary purposes. These committees include the committee of the whole, which includes all of the members of a house sitting as a committee. The committee of the whole is established on General Orders in the senate and on the order of Second Reading in the house to consider the recommendations made by a standing committee. The committee of the whole may also adopt amendments to the bill. This parliamentary device generally offers greater informality and freedom of discussion and action than is possible at other stages of the legislative process. Another type of committee that plays an integral part in the legislative process is the conference committee. Conference committees consist of members from each house and are assigned the responsibility of resolving differences between versions of the same bill passed by both houses.

THE ONE HUNDREDTH LEGISLATURE

SENATE, 2019-2020

LEADERS

MIKE SHIRKEY, *Majority Leader*
WAYNE SCHMIDT, *Assistant Majority Leader*
PETER MACGREGOR, *Majority Floor Leader*
DAN LAUWERS, *Assistant Majority Floor Leader*
JIM ANANICH, *Minority Leader*
STEPHANIE CHANG, *Minority Floor Leader*

OFFICERS

GARLIN GILCHRIST II, *President*
ARIC NESBITT, *President Pro Tempore*
LANA THEIS, *Assistant President Pro Tempore*
MARSHALL BULLOCK II, *Associate President Pro Tempore*
MARGARET E. O'BRIEN, *Secretary of the Senate*
ADAM W. REAMES, *Assistant Secretary of the Senate*

District	Name, Party	Post Office	Occupation
1	Stephanie Chang, D	Detroit	Community organizer
2	Adam Hollier, D	Detroit	U.S. Army/public policy
3	Sylvia Santana, D	Detroit	Finance
4	Marshall Bullock II, D	Detroit	Local government
5	Betty Jean Alexander, D	Detroit	Local government
6	Erika Geiss, D	Taylor	Small business owner/writer/educator
7	Dayna Polehanki, D	Livonia	Teacher
8	Pete Lucido, R	Shelby Twp.	Attorney/insurance agent/realtor
9	Paul J. Wojno, D	Warren	Local government/Legislative staff
10	Michael MacDonald, R	Macomb Twp.	Health care/finance
11	Jeremy Moss, D	Southfield	Local government
12	Rosemary Bayer, D	Beverly Hills	Small business owner/computer engineer
13	Mallory McMorrow, D	Royal Oak	Product design/advertising
14	Ruth Johnson, R	Groveland Twp.	Secretary of State/local government/ small business owner
15	Jim Runestad, R	White Lake	Insurance/local government
16	Mike Shirkey, R	Liberty Twp.	Engineer/small business owner
17	Dale W. Zorn, R	Ida	Small business owner/local government
18	Jeff Irwin, D	Ann Arbor	Local government
19	John Bizon, R	Battle Creek	Physician/U.S. Air Force
20	Sean McCann, D	Kalamazoo	Local government/community development
21	Kim LaSata, R	Bainbridge Twp.	Teacher
22	Lana Theis, R	Brighton	Local government
23	Curtis Hertel Jr., D	East Lansing	Local government
24	Tom Barrett, R	Charlotte	U.S. Army/Department of Treasury
25	Dan Lauwers, R	Brockway	Agricultural business owner
26	Aric Nesbitt, R	Lawton	Congressional staff
27	Jim Ananich, D	Flint	Teacher/education coordinator
28	Peter MacGregor, R	Cannon Twp.	Business owner/local government
29	Winnie Brinks, D	Grand Rapids	Non-profit workforce development
30	Roger Victory, R	Georgetown Twp.	Agricultural business owner
31	Kevin Daley, R	Lum	Dairy farmer/local government
32	Ken Horn, R	Frankenmuth	Small business owner/local government
33	Rick Outman, R	Six Lakes	U.S. Army/National Guard/small business owner
34	Jon Bumstead, R	Newaygo	Small business owner
35	Curtis S. VanderWall, R	Ludington	Small business owner/local government
36	Jim Stamas, R	Midland	Small Business owner
37	Wayne Schmidt, R	Traverse City	Business/local government
38	Ed McBroom, R	Waucedah Twp.	Dairy farmer

MICHIGAN SENATE DISTRICTS — 2010 CENSUS

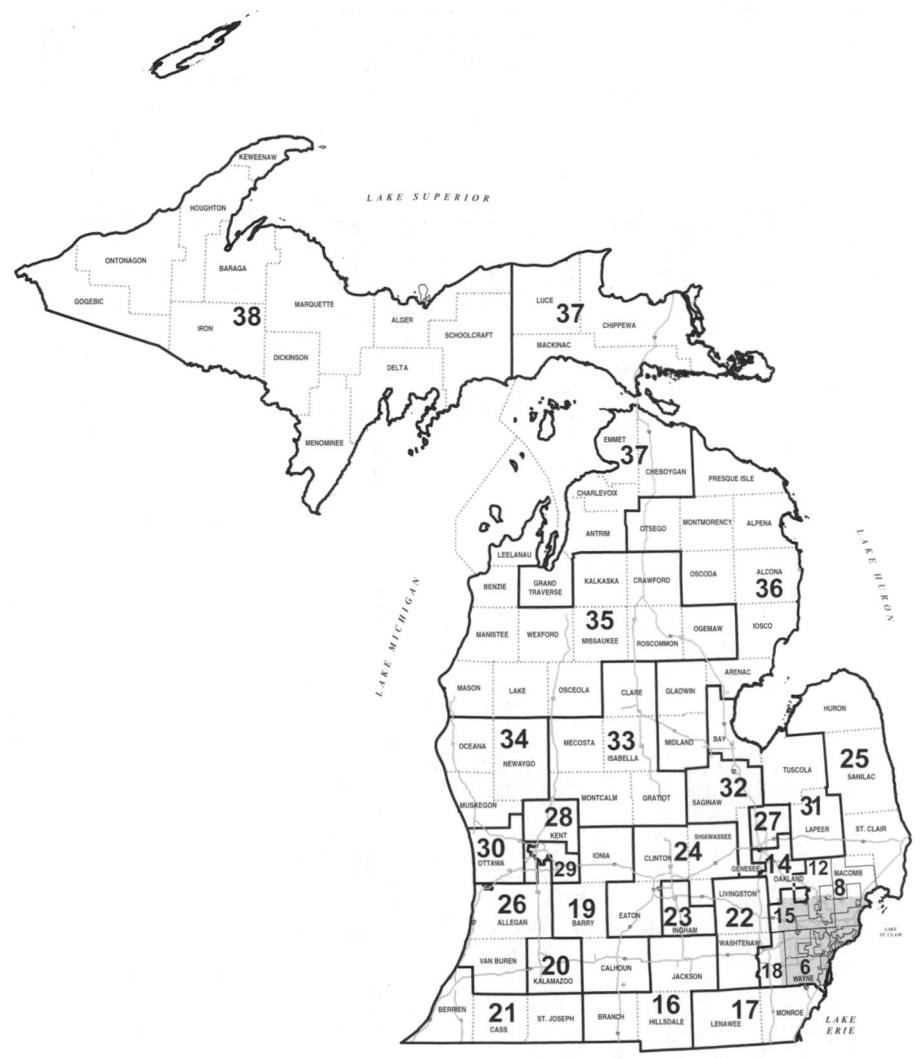

MICHIGAN SENATE DISTRICTS — 2010 CENSUS
METROPOLITAN DETROIT AREA — Wayne/Oakland/Macomb Counties

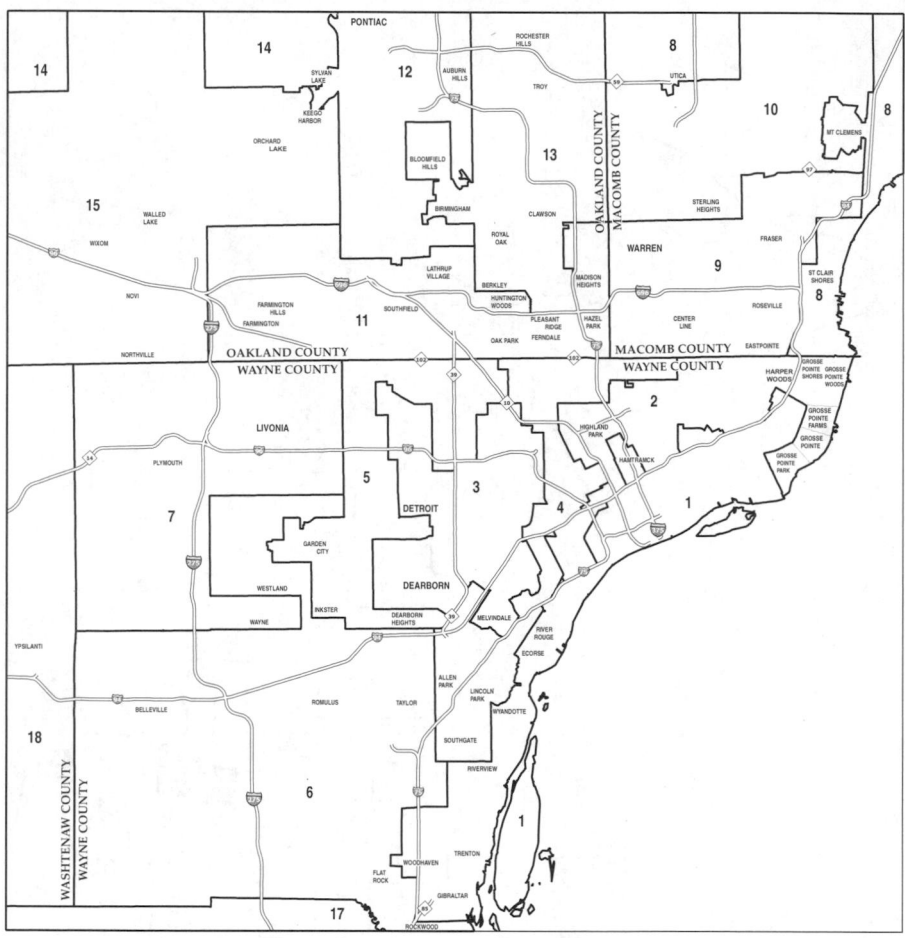

SENATE DISTRICT POPULATIONS

District	2010 Population
1	254,865
2	254,991
3	255,006
4	255,037
5	260,337
6	267,741
7	272,600
8	270,685
9	271,123
10	271,486
11	272,444
12	255,623
13	272,733
14	248,755
15	258,160
16	252,184
17	251,920
18	272,716
19	259,224
20	250,331
21	270,401
22	253,042
23	265,110
24	269,574
25	266,956
26	261,519
27	252,657
28	257,945
29	270,824
30	263,801
31	251,819
32	267,949
33	249,853
34	247,218
35	252,697
36	247,592
37	251,625
38	255,097

SENATE
STANDING COMMITTEES

ADVICE AND CONSENT:
Senators Lucido (C), LaSata (VC), Nesbitt, McBroom, Hertel (Min. VC).

AGRICULTURE:
Senators Daley (C), Victory (VC), Lauwers, Ananich (Min. VC), Polehanki.

APPROPRIATIONS:
Senators Stamas (C), Bumstead (VC), Barrett, Bizon, LaSata, MacDonald, MacGregor, Nesbitt, Outman, Runestad, Schmidt, Victory, Hertel (Min. VC), Bayer, Hollier, Irwin, McCann, Santana.

ECONOMIC AND SMALL BUSINESS DEVELOPMENT:
Senators Horn (C), VanderWall (VC), MacGregor, Theis, Lauwers, Schmidt, McMorrow (Min. VC), Geiss, Moss.

EDUCATION AND CAREER READINESS:
Senators Theis (C), Horn (VC), Bumstead, Runestad, Daley, Polehanki (Min. VC), Geiss.

ELECTIONS:
Senators Johnson (C), McBroom (VC), Lucido, VanderWall, Wojno (Min. VC).

ENERGY AND TECHNOLOGY:
Senators Lauwers (C), Horn (VC), LaSata, Nesbitt, Barrett, Bumstead, Outman, McCann (Min. VC), Brinks, McMorrow.

ENVIRONMENTAL QUALITY:
Senators Outman (C), Daley (VC), Johnson, VanderWall, McBroom, Bayer (Min. VC), Brinks.

FAMILIES, SENIORS, AND VETERANS:
Senators Bizon (C), Barrett (VC), Runestad, Johnson, Zorn, Bullock II (Min. VC), Alexander.

FINANCE:
Senators Runestad (C), Nesbitt (VC), Daley, Bumstead, VanderWall, Chang (Min. VC), Alexander.

GOVERNMENT OPERATIONS:
Senators Shirkey (C), Lauwers (VC), Nesbitt, Ananich (Min. VC), Chang.

HEALTH POLICY AND HUMAN SERVICES:
Senators VanderWall (C), Bizon (VC), Johnson, LaSata, MacDonald, Theis, Brinks (Min. VC), Hertel, Santana, Wojno.

INSURANCE AND BANKING:
Senators Theis (C), Lauwers (VC), LaSata, Nesbitt, Daley, Barrett, Horn, Geiss (Min. VC), Bullock II, McMorrow.

JUDICIARY AND PUBLIC SAFETY:
Senators Lucido (C), VanderWall (VC), Barrett, Johnson, Runestad, Chang (Min. VC), Irwin.

LOCAL GOVERNMENT:
Senators Zorn (C), Johnson (VC), Daley, Alexander (Min. VC), Moss.

NATURAL RESOURCES:
Senators McBroom (C), Bumstead (VC), Outman, Schmidt, McCann (Min. VC).

OVERSIGHT:
Senators McBroom (C), Lucido (VC), Theis, MacDonald, Irwin (Min. VC).

REGULATORY REFORM:
Senators Nesbitt (C), Theis (VC), Johnson, Lauwers, VanderWall, Zorn, Moss (Min. VC), Polehanki, Wojno.

TRANSPORTATION AND INFRASTRUCTURE:
Senators Barrett (C), LaSata (VC), McBroom, Victory, Outman, Lauwers, Geiss (Min. VC), Bullock II, Hollier.

SENATE APPROPRIATIONS SUBCOMMITTEES

AGRICULTURE AND RURAL DEVELOPMENT:
Senators Victory (C), Daley (VC), McCann.

CAPITAL OUTLAY:
Senators Horn (C), Outman (VC), Zorn, Runestad, Bizon, Schmidt, Santana (Min. VC), Hertel, McCann.

COMMUNITY HEALTH/HUMAN SERVICES:
Senators MacGregor (C), Bizon (VC), Schmidt, LaSata, MacDonald, Barrett, Hertel (Min. VC), Irwin, Santana.

GENERAL GOVERNMENT:
Senators Stamas (C), Victory (VC), Bumstead, Irwin.

JUSTICE AND PUBLIC SAFETY:
Senators Barrett (C), Runestad (VC), Hollier.

K-12 AND MICHIGAN DEPARTMENT OF EDUCATION:
Senators Schmidt (C), Outman (VC), Bumstead, Daley, Bayer (Min. VC).

LICENSING AND REGULATORY AFFAIRS (LARA)/DEPARTMENT OF INSURANCE AND FINANCIAL SERVICES (DIFS):
Senators Nesbitt (C), MacDonald (VC), Santana.

NATURAL RESOURCES AND ENVIRONMENTAL QUALITY:
Senators Bumstead (C), Outman (VC), Victory, McCann (Min. VC), Bayer.

TALENT AND ECONOMIC DEVELOPMENT/MEDC:
Senators Horn (C), Schmidt (VC), Hollier.

TRANSPORTATION:
Senators Schmidt (C), Victory (VC), MacGregor, MacDonald, Zorn, Hollier (Min. VC), Bayer.

UNIVERSITIES AND COMMUNITY COLLEGES:
Senators LaSata (C), Horn (VC), Bizon, MacDonald, Zorn, Irwin (Min. VC), Hertel.

JOINT STATUTORY STANDING COMMITTEES

(Senate members only listed)

JOINT COMMITTEE ON ADMINISTRATIVE RULES:
Senators Lucido (C), McBroom (VC), Theis, Hollier (Min. VC), Irwin.

LEGISLATIVE COUNCIL:
Senators Shirkey (C), Stamas, Schmidt, Horn, Ananich, Chang.
Alternates: Senators Bizon, MacDonald, Moss.

MICHIGAN SENATE
BIOGRAPHICAL SKETCHES OF MEMBERS

THE ONE HUNDREDTH LEGISLATURE
2019-2020

State Senator
BETTY JEAN ALEXANDER
D–5th Senate District

Office: Room 4300, Binsfeld Office Bldg., P.O. Box 30036, Lansing, MI 48909, (517) 373-0994

Committees: Families, Seniors, and Veterans; Finance; Local Government (Minority Vice Chair)

Biography: Democrat, of Detroit; two children; attended Albuquerque Technical Vocational Institute and Rio Grande High School; former clerical specialist, Wayne County Clerk's Office, former administrative assistant with two foster care agencies: Starr Commonwealth and Holy Cross Children's Services; enjoys bowling and traveling; member, the American Federation of State, County, and Municipal Employees (AFSCME), local Detroit-PTA, the Sportsman Caucus, Progressive Women's Caucus, Labor Caucus, the Detroit Caucus, and Michigan Legislative Black Caucus; elected to the State Senate, 2018.

State Senator
JIM ANANICH
D–27th Senate District

Office: Room S-105, Capitol Bldg., P.O. Box 30036, Lansing, MI 48909, (517) 373-0142, Toll-Free: (855) 347-8027, Fax: (517) 373-3938, E-Mail: senjananich@senate.michigan.gov

Committees: Agriculture (Minority Vice Chair); Government Operations (Minority Vice Chair)

Biography: Democrat, of Flint; born September 20, 1975, in Flint; spouse, Andrea; son, Jacob; bachelor's degree in political economics and secondary education certificate in social studies, Michigan State University; master's degree in public administration, University of Michigan-Flint; former teacher, Carmen-Ainsworth Schools and Flint Community Schools; education coordinator for Priority Children, helping Flint-area youth secure jobs and internships; four years, Flint City Council, one year as president; member, Legislative Council and Senate Fiscal Agency Governing Board; elected to the House of Representatives, 2010, 2012; elected to the State Senate in a special election, May 2013, reelected in 2014 and 2018, Senate Minority Leader, 2015 to present.

State Senator
TOM BARRETT
R–24th Senate District

Office: Room 3200, Binsfeld Office Bldg., P.O. Box 30036, Lansing, MI 48909, (517) 373-3447

Committees: Appropriations (Subcommittees: Community Health/Human Services; Justice and Public Safety (Chair)); Energy and Technology; Families, Seniors, and Veterans (Vice Chair); Insurance and Banking; Judiciary and Public Safety; Transportation and Infrastructure (Chair)

Biography: Republican, of Charlotte; born April 30, 1981, in Southfield; spouse, Ashley; children, Patrick, Eleanora, and Gwendolyn; attends St. Mary's Catholic Church; bachelor's degree in political science, Western Michigan University; U.S. Army, 18 years; aviator, Michigan Army National Guard assigned to Grand Ledge; analyst, Michigan Department of Treasury; member, Veterans of Foreign Wars, and American Legion; elected to the House of Representatives, 2014 and 2016, elected to the State Senate, 2018.

State Senator
ROSEMARY BAYER
D–12th Senate District

Office: Room 3600, Binsfeld Office Bldg., P.O. Box 30036, Lansing, MI 48909, (517) 373-2417

Committees: Appropriations (Subcommittees: K-12 and Michigan Department of Education (Minority Vice Chair); Natural Resources and Environmental Quality; Transportation); Environmental Quality (Minority Vice Chair)

Biography: Democrat, of Beverly Hills; born January 2, 1959, in Royal Oak; spouse, John Lisiecki; child, Erin Mack; bachelor's degree, Computer Science with math and chemistry minors, Central Michigan University; masters of business administration, Lawrence Technological University; co-founder and co-owner, ardentCause L3C; co-founder, Michigan Council of Women in Technology; longtime computer software engineer and inventor of software products; engineering and business management, Sun Microsystems for 15 years; Oakland County Girl Scout Leader for 10 years; board member at Oakland County Girl Scout Council, The SheHive, NEW Solutions for Nonprofits; former board member, the Birmingham Area Cable Board; elected to the State Senate, 2018.

State Senator
JOHN BIZON, M.D.
R–19th Senate District

Office: Room 3400, Binsfeld Office Bldg., P.O. Box 30036, Lansing, MI 48909, (517) 373-2426

Committees: Appropriations (Subcommittees: Capital Outlay; Community Health/Human Services (Vice Chair); Universities and Community Colleges); Families, Seniors, and Veterans (Chair); Health Policy and Human Services (Vice Chair)

Biography: Republican, of Battle Creek; born September 1, 1951, in Detroit; spouse, Debbie; four children; member, St. Joseph Catholic Church; bachelor's degree, Michigan State University, Doctor of Medicine, Wayne State University; lieutenant colonel, United States Air Force, 11 years; ear, nose, and throat specialist; former member, State Board of Audiology; clinical assistant professor of surgery, Western Michigan University School of Medicine; member, Calhoun County Medical Society, Michigan State Medical Society, Calhoun Farm Bureau, and Chamber of Commerce; alternate member, Legislative Council; elected to the House of Representatives, 2014 and 2016, elected to the State Senate, 2018.

State Senator
WINNIE BRINKS
D–29th Senate District

Office: Room 6500, Binsfeld Office Bldg., P.O. Box 30036, Lansing, MI 48909, (517) 373-1801

Committees: Energy and Technology; Environmental Quality; Health Policy and Human Services (Minority Vice Chair)

Biography: Democrat, of Grand Rapids; born February 17, 1968 in Mount Vernon, Washington; married to Steve, three children, Olivia, Annalise, and Emma; parents, Raymond and Alice (Wind) DeVries, immigrants from the province of Friesland, Netherlands; bachelor's degree in Spanish, Calvin College; executive director, One Way House Inc.; educator in Grand Rapids Christian Schools and Godfrey-Lee public schools; caseworker at The Source; chair, East Grand Rapids Parent-Teacher Association's Legislative Committee; member, Christian Reformed Church; elected to the House of Representatives, 2012, 2014, and 2016; policy chair, Democratic Caucus, 2015 to 2018; elected to the State Senate, 2018; Senate Democratic Whip, 2019.

State Senator
MARSHALL BULLOCK II
D–4th Senate District

Office: Room 3500, Binsfeld Office Bldg., P.O. Box 30036, Lansing, MI 48909, (517) 373-7918

Committees: Families, Seniors, and Veterans (Minority Vice Chair); Insurance and Banking; Transportation and Infrastructure

Biography: Democrat, of Detroit; born July 4, 1967 in Detroit; spouse, Angela; children, Maya, and twins Marshall III and Layla: Christian; bachelor's degree in human services, University of Phoenix; 30 years of public health and service experience in juvenile justice, foster care, health department, and the City of Detroit; five years as the district manager, Department of Neighborhoods, City of Detroit and community and legislative affairs manager for the Mayor's office (2014 to 2018); frequently engages in mentorship and community service through various volunteer organizations including Omega Academy; elected to the State Senate, 2018, Associate President Pro Tempore.

State Senator
JON BUMSTEAD
R–34th Senate District

Office: Room 4600, Binsfeld Office Bldg., P.O. Box 30036, Lansing, MI 48909, (517) 373-1635

Committees: Appropriations (Vice Chair) (Subcommittees: General Government; K-12 and Michigan Department of Education; Natural Resources and Environmental Quality (Chair)); Education and Career Readiness; Energy and Technology; Finance; Natural Resources (Vice Chair)

Biography: Republican, of Newaygo; born July 30, 1957, in Fremont; children, Belinda, Ray, and Jona, four grandchildren; Newaygo United Methodist Church; graduate, Newaygo High School; 30 years as owner-operator of his own home-building/remodeling business, Bumstead Construction; charter member, Newaygo Jaycees; member, Chamber of Commerce, Michigan Home Builders Association, Newaygo County Building Review Board, NRA, Right to Life, Michigan United Conservation Corps, and Michigan Sheriffs' Association; past president, Safari Club International; member, Brooks Township Planning Commission; elected to the House of Representatives, 2010, 2012, and 2014, elected to the State Senate, 2018.

State Senator
STEPHANIE CHANG
D–1st Senate District

Office: Room S-9, Capitol Bldg., P.O. Box 30036, Lansing, MI 48909, (517) 373-7346

Committees: Finance (Minority Vice Chair); Government Operations; Judiciary and Public Safety (Minority Vice Chair)

Biography: Democrat, of Detroit; born October 24, 1983, in Detroit; spouse, Sean Gray; two young daughters; bachelor's degree in Psychology (2005), minor in Asian/Pacific Islander American Studies, Master of Public Policy and Master of Social Work (2014), University of Michigan; Unitarian Universalist; community engagement coordinator, James and Grace Boggs School; alumni engagement and evaluation coordinator, Center for Progressive Leadership in Michigan; deputy director, Campaign for Justice; organizer for Michigan United/One United Michigan; co-founder and past president of APIAVote-Michigan; former assistant to Grace Lee Boggs; mentor, Detroit Asian Youth Project; advisory board, New American Leaders Project; Legislator of the Year, Michigan Association of School Social Workers (2015); Health Care Hero Award, MichUHCAN (2016); Champion Award, Michigan Coalition for Immigrant and Refugee Rights (2016); Legislator of the Year, Michigan League of Conservation Voters (2017); Friend of Nursing Award, Michigan Nurses Association (2017); Constituent Services Chair, House Democratic Caucus; chair, Progressive Women's Caucus; co-founder, Asian Pacific American Legislative Caucus; elected to the House of Representatives, 2014 and 2016; elected to the State Senate, 2018, Democratic Floor Leader, 2019; member, Legislative Council.

State Senator
KEVIN DALEY
R–31st Senate District

Office: Room 5200, Binsfeld Office Bldg., P.O. Box 30036, Lansing, MI 48909, (517) 373-1777

Committees: Agriculture (Chair); Education and Career Readiness; Environmental Quality (Vice Chair); Finance; Insurance and Banking; Local Government; Appropriations Subcommittees: Agriculture and Rural Development (Vice Chair), K-12 and Michigan Department of Education

Biography: Republican, of Lum; wife, Debbie (nee Spurleon); children, Michael, Elizabeth, Thomas (deceased 2011); parents, J. Clifford and Marian; member, Immaculate Conception Catholic Church and Knights of Columbus; owner-operator of family farm; former chair, Lapeer County E.M.S. Board of Directors; former president, Michigan Milk Producers Association Tri-County Local; 41-year member, Farm Bureau; member, Lapeer County Agriculture Preservation Board; 4-H Dairy supervisor; Arcadia Township supervisor, treasurer, trustee, and planning commissioner; elected to the House of Representatives, 2008, 2010 and 2012, elected to the State Senate, 2018.

State Senator
ERIKA GEISS
D–6th Senate District

Office: Room 5500, Binsfeld Office Bldg., P.O. Box 30036, Lansing, MI 48909, (517) 373-7800

Committees: Economic and Small Business Development; Education and Career Readiness; Insurance and Banking (Minority Vice Chair); Transportation and Infrastructure (Minority Vice Chair)

Biography: Democrat, of Taylor, City of Birth; spouse, Doug Geiss; two children; second-generation American with family from Panama and the Caribbean; bachelor's degree Developmental Psychology, Brandeis University, 1993; master's degree in Art and Architectural History, Tufts University, 1998; formerly employed at the Museum of Fine Arts – Boston, Isabella Stewart Gardner Museum, Rose Art Museum At Brandeis University as Director of Education, and the Charles H. Wright Museum of African American History; published author and editor; founded and operates small editing and publishing service; author; adjunct professor/instructor, University of New Hampshire-Durham and Wayne County Community College District; elected to the House of Representatives, 2014 and 2016; elected to the State Senate, 2018.

State Senator
CURTIS HERTEL JR.
D–23rd Senate District

Office: Room 7600, Binsfeld Office Bldg., P.O. Box 30036, Lansing, MI 48909, (517) 373-1734, E-Mail: senchertel@senate.michigan.gov

Committees: Advice and Consent (Minority Vice Chair); Appropriations (Minority Vice Chair) (Subcommittees: Capital Outlay; Community Health/Human Services (Minority Vice Chair); Universities and Community Colleges); Health Policy and Human Services

Biography: Democrat, of East Lansing; born January 9, 1978 in Detroit; son of Curtis Hertel; parishioner, St. Thomas Church; spouse, Elizabeth; children, CJ, Nathan, Hailey, and Jack; bachelor's degree in social relations, James Madison College at Michigan State University; staff, Michigan House Democratic Caucus, 2001 to 2003; policy analyst, Department of Community Health, 2004 to 2005; legislative liaison, Department of Community Health, 2005 to 2008; elected to Ingham County Board of Commissioners, 2001 to 2008; elected to Ingham County Register of Deeds, 2008 to 2014; elected to the State Senate, 2014 and 2018.

State Senator
ADAM HOLLIER
D–2nd Senate District

Office: Room 3300, Binsfeld Office Bldg., P.O. Box 30036, Lansing, MI 48909, (517) 373-7748

Committees: Appropriations (Subcommittees: Justice and Public Safety; Talent and Economic Development/MEDC; Transportation (Minority Vice Chair)); Transportation and Infrastructure

Biography: Democrat, of Detroit; born September 26, 1985, in Detroit; spouse, Krystle; daughter, Lillian; Catholic; member of Muscogee Creek nation; bachelor's degree in industrial and labor relations, Cornell University and master's degree in urban planning, University of Michigan; 1st Lieutenant, 412th Civil Affairs BN, Public Works Officer United States Army Reserves, former director of government and community relations at the Michigan Fitness Foundation, former vice president of Hantz Woodlands; City of Detroit legislative liaison for Mayor Dave Bing, chief of staff for Senator Bert Johnson and district director, Senator Buzz Thomas; volunteer coordinator, East Biloxi Relief and Recovery Center in Biloxi, Mississippi after Hurricane Katrina; former member, Ann Arbor Public School Board; elected to the Senate in a special election held November 2018 to fill the remaining six weeks of the legislative session; elected to a full term in the State Senate, November 2018; Minority Vice Chair, Joint Committee on Administrative Rules.

State Senator
KEN HORN
R–32nd Senate District

Office: Room 7100, Binsfeld Office Bldg., P.O. Box 30036, Lansing, MI 48909, (517) 373-1760, Toll-Free: (855) 347-8032, E-Mail: senkhorn@senate.michigan.gov

Committees: Economic and Small Business Development (Chair); Education and Career Readiness (Vice Chair); Energy and Technology (Vice Chair); Insurance and Banking; Appropriations Subcommittees: Capital Outlay (Chair), Talent and Economic Development/MEDC (Chair), Universities and Community Colleges (Vice Chair)

Biography: Republican, of Frankenmuth; born July 10, 1959, in Detroit; spouse, Veronica; two children, Kevin (Ruth) and Andrea (Anton), grandchildren, Liam and our angel Zellie, who is terribly missed; bachelor's degree in criminal justice from Concordia University; completed Michigan State University Political Leadership Program; small business owner, nearly 15 years, Horn's Restaurant in Frankenmuth; substitute teacher; vice president for donor services at Saginaw Community Foundation; appointed by Governor John Engler to Michigan Travel Commission; served on White House Conference on Tourism; Habitat for Humanity, Saginaw Field and Stream, Frankenmuth Conservation Club; Saginaw County commissioner, 16 years; 2020 chair, Council of State Governments Midwestern Legislative Conference; member, Legislative Council; elected to the House of Representatives, 2006, 2008, and 2010; elected to the State Senate, 2014 and 2018.

State Senator
JEFF IRWIN
D–18th Senate District

Office: Room 5300, Binsfeld Office Bldg., P.O. Box 30036, Lansing, MI 48909, (517) 373-2406

Committees: Appropriations (Subcommittees: Community Health/Human Services; General Government; Universities and Community Colleges (Minority Vice Chair)); Judiciary and Public Safety; Oversight

Biography: Democrat, of Ann Arbor; born June 19, 1977, in Petoskey; spouse, Kathryn; daughter, Sylvia, son, Mackinac; bachelor's degree, University of Michigan; staff, League of Conservation Voters Education Fund; executive director, Michigan League of Conservation Voters; staff, State Senator Alma Wheeler Smith; Washtenaw County Commissioner, 1999 to 2010, chair, 2007 to 2008; elected to the House of Representatives, 2010, 2012, 2014, elected to the State Senate, 2018; member, Joint Committee on Administrative Rules.

State Senator
RUTH JOHNSON
R–14th Senate District

Office: Room 7300, Binsfeld Office Bldg., P.O. Box 30036, Lansing, MI 48909, (517) 373-1636

Committees: Elections (Chair); Local Government (Vice Chair); Environmental Quality; Families, Seniors, and Veterans; Health Policy and Human Services; Judiciary and Public Safety; Regulatory Reform

Biography: Republican, of Groveland Township; born January 8, 1955; daughter, Emily; associate's degree, Oakland Community College; bachelor's degree, Oakland University; master's degree, Wayne State University; former small business owner; served ten years as an Oakland County commissioner, six years as vice chair; eight years as Michigan Secretary of State; elected to the House of Representatives, 1998, reelected 2000 and 2002; elected to the State Senate, 2018.

State Senator
Kim LASATA
R–21st Senate District

Office: Room S-310, Capitol Bldg., P.O. Box 30036, Lansing, MI 48909, (517) 373-6960

Committees: Advice and Consent (Vice Chair); Appropriations (Subcommittees: Community Health/ Human Services; Universities and Community Colleges (Chair)); Energy and Technology; Health Policy and Human Services; Insurance and Banking; Transportation and Infrastructure (Vice Chair)

Biography: Republican, of Bainbridge Township; born April 20, in St. Joseph; Roman Catholic; spouse, Charles; children, Sarah, Anna, Chas, Claire; bachelor's degree in education, graduated *cum laude* and master's degree in literacy studies, Western Michigan University, graduated *summa cum laude*; fifth grade teacher, Lake Michigan Catholic Elementary School; Republican precinct delegate, Berrien County; secretary, Berrien County Republican Women's Club; past president, Berrien County Guardianship Services, Inc., Capstone Center, and Women's Service League; past vice chair, Child and Family Services, Inc.; elected to the House of Representatives, 2016, elected to the State Senate, 2018.

State Senator
DAN LAUWERS
R–25th Senate District

Office: Room S-2, Capitol Bldg., P.O. Box 30036, Lansing, MI 48909, (517) 373-7708

Committees: Agriculture; Economic and Small Business Development; Energy and Technology (Chair); Government Operations (Vice Chair); Insurance and Banking (Vice Chair); Regulatory Reform; Transportation and Infrastructure

Biography: Republican, of Brockway; born January 15, 1963 in Almont; married to Kellie; children, Jonathan, Lauren Mary, and Nicholas; Catholic; bachelor's degree, agricultural economics, Michigan State University; Michigan State University Extension Agent, former legislative assistant to U.S. Representative Bill Schuette; legislative representative for the National Milk Producers Federation; program director, W.K. Kellogg Foundation; owner and general manager, Eastern Michigan Grain; precinct delegate, Brockway Township, St. Clair County; member, Knights of Columbus, Yale/Brockway recreation council, and Soil Conservation Board; usher, Yale Sacred Heart Church; member, House Fiscal Agency Governing Committee; elected to the House of Representatives, 2012, 2014, and 2016, Majority Floor Leader, 2016 to 2018; elected to the State Senate, 2018.

State Senator
PETE LUCIDO
R–8th Senate District

Office: Room 3100, Binsfeld Office Bldg., P.O. Box 30036, Lansing, MI 48909, (517) 373-7670

Committees: Advice and Consent (Chair); Elections; Judiciary and Public Safety (Chair); Oversight (Vice Chair)

Biography: Republican, of Shelby Township; born July 31, 1960, in Detroit; Catholic; spouse, AnnMarie; children, Briana, Nina, and Peter III; associate's degree, Macomb Community College; bachelor's degree in public administration and business, Central Michigan University; master's degree in business administration; juris doctor, Detroit College of Law (now known as Michigan State University College of Law); practicing attorney, over 30 years; founder, president and counsel, Lucido & Manzella, P.C.; licensed insurance agent and realtor, over 40 years; security register representative; founder and publisher emeritus, *Macomb Now Magazine*; chairman, Macomb Foundation; Macomb Hall of Fame Inductee; member, Macomb County Chamber of Commerce, Greater Romeo-Washington Chamber of Commerce, Italian American Chamber of Commerce, Macomb County Republican Party, and Republican Committee of Northern Macomb County, Italian American Cultural Center, Kiwanis Club of Shelby Golden K, Michigan Farm Bureau, Knights of Columbus, Italian American Bar Association, Michigan Bar Association, American Bar Association, Federal Bar Association, and Patriot Life Member National Rifle Association; member and former board member, Ambassador Club of Henry Ford Macomb Hospitals; former member board of trustees, De La Salle Collegiate; founding member of De La Salle Pilot Bar Association; Oakland University Foundation member and former board member; member, Michigan Law Revision Commission, 2014 to 2018; member, Attorney General's Elder Abuse Taskforce, Criminal Justice Policy Commission, Michigan Commission on Uniform State Laws, National Uniform Law Commission, and Macomb County Prosecutor's Protecting Animal Welfare Taskforce; elected to the House of Representatives, 2014 and 2016; elected to the State Senate, 2018; chair, Joint Committee on Administrative Rules.

State Senator
MIKE MacDONALD
R–10th Senate District

Office: Room 4200, Binsfeld Office Bldg., P.O. Box 30036, Lansing, MI 48909, (517) 373-7315

Committees: Appropriations (Subcommittees: Community Health/Human Services; Licensing and Regulatory Affairs (LARA)/Department of Insurance and Financial Services (DIFS) (Vice Chair); Transportation; Universities and Community Colleges); Health Policy and Human Services; Oversight

Biography: Republican, of Macomb Township; born March 11, 1980, in Mount Clemens; Christian; spouse, Lauraanne; bachelor's degree in exercise science, Western Michigan University (2000 to 2004); master's degree in business administration, Oakland University (2005 to 2008); doctorate in health administration, University of Phoenix (2009 to 2015); vice president, Michigan Air Force Association (2018); financial representative, Northwestern Mutual (2015 to 2018); personal trainer, Detroit Metropolitan YMCA (2008 to 2014); exercise physiologist, Henry Ford Health System (2004 to 2007); computer technician, Computer Dimensions (1998 to 2000); active with Clinton Township Kiwanis Club, Sterling Heights Chamber of Commerce, The Selfridge Base Council; program founder, Doctoral Alumni Ambassador and Doctoral Mentor; elected to the State Senate, 2018.

State Senator
PETER MacGREGOR
R–28th Senate District

Office: Room S-132, Capitol Bldg., Lansing, MI 48909, (517) 373-0797,
E-Mail: senpmacgregor@senate.michigan.gov

Committees: Appropriations (Subcommittees: Community Health/Human Services (Chair); Transportation); Economic and Small Business Development

Biography: Republican, of Cannon Township; born February 24, 1966, in Detroit; spouse, Christine; three sons; attends Blythefield Hills Baptist Church, Rockford; graduate, Michigan State University School of Business; former small-business owner; avid sportsman; former president and member, Rockford Lions Club; founder and co-director, Volley for Mitchell Charity raising funds for Duchenne Muscular Dystrophy research; former Cannon Township supervisor, trustee, planning commissioner; member, Senate Fiscal Agency Governing Board; elected to the House of Representatives, 2010 and 2012; elected to the State Senate, 2014 and 2018, Majority Floor Leader, 2019.

State Senator
ED McBROOM
R–38th Senate District

Office: Room 7200, Binsfeld Office Bldg., P.O. Box 30036, Lansing, MI 48909, (517) 373-7840

Committees: Advice and Consent; Elections (Vice Chair); Environmental Quality; Natural Resources (Chair); Oversight (Chair); Transportation and Infrastructure

Biography: Republican, of Waucedah Township; born May 30, 1981, in Waucedah Township; wife, Sarah; children, Helen, Eddie, Esther, Kenny Jack and Edith; First Baptist Church of Norway; Norway High School, 1999; Northern Michigan University, 2005; bachelor's degrees in music education, instrumental/piano specialization and secondary education social studies, history minor; dairy farmer; member, Iron-Range Farm Bureau; served on State Policy Development and State Young Farmer committees; member, Upper Peninsula State Fair Authority; chair, Livestock Advisory Committee and milkhouse superintendent; director and horn player, Norway City Band; Waucedah Township Zoning Board of Appeals, 2010; elected to the House of Representatives 2010, 2012, and 2014; Assistant Whip, 2011 to 2012; elected to the State Senate 2018; Caucus Dean, Vice Chair, Joint Committee on Administrative Rules.

State Senator
SEAN McCANN
D–20th Senate District

Office: Room 6600, Binsfeld Office Bldg., P.O. Box 30036, Lansing, MI 48909, (517) 373-5100

Committees: Appropriations (Subcommittees: Agriculture and Rural Development; Capital Outlay; Natural Resources and Environmental Quality (Minority Vice Chair)); Energy and Technology (Minority Vice Chair); Natural Resources (Minority Vice Chair)

Biography: Democrat, of Kalamazoo; born September 21, 1971, in Detroit; wife, Priscilla Lambert; son, Alexander and daughter, Lauren; bachelor's degree in political science, Western Michigan University in 1993; executive director, Vine Neighborhood Association, 1995 to 2002; director of financial development, Greater Kalamazoo Area American Red Cross, 2002 to 2009; Kalamazoo City Commission, 1999 to 2009; member, Kalamazoo Irish-American Club, and Kalamazoo NAACP; former executive director, Kalamazoo Friends of Recreation; Michigan Association of State and Federal Program Specialists Legislative Award, 2013; ISAAC, Elected Ally of the Year 2012; Michigan Citizens Action Public Service Award, 2010; Michigan Political Leadership Program, 1999; Leadership Michigan, 1998; Leadership Kalamazoo, 1996 to 1997; elected to the House of Representatives, 2010 and 2012; elected to the State Senate, 2018.

State Senator
MALLORY McMORROW
D–13th Senate District

Office: Room 6200, Binsfeld Office Bldg., P.O. Box 30036, Lansing, MI 48909, (517) 373-2523, E-Mail: senmmcmorrow@senate.michigan.gov

Committees: Economic and Small Business Development (Minority Vice Chair); Energy and Technology; Insurance and Banking

Biography: Democrat, of Royal Oak; born August 23, 1986, in New Jersey; spouse, Ray Wert; bachelor's degree in industrial design, University of Notre Dame, 2004 to 2008; previously held roles as designer and creative director at Mattel, Gawker Media, Mazda; writer covering automotive industry for *Road & Track*, *Jalopnik*, and *Jezebel*; founder/owner of Ginger Haus consultancy providing branding, creative strategy for local businesses, and automotive trend analysis and forecasting; member, Freelancer's Union, Freelancer's Guild of Detroit; vice chair, Automotive Caucus; member, Progressive Women's Caucus; elected to the State Senate, 2018; youngest woman elected to the Michigan Senate.

State Senator
JEREMY MOSS
D–11th Senate District

Office: Room 6400, Binsfeld Office Bldg., P.O. Box 30036, Lansing, MI 48909, (517) 373-7888

Committees: Economic and Small Business Development; Local Government; Regulatory Reform (Minority Vice Chair)

Biography: Democrat, of Southfield; born June 23, 1986, in Detroit; Judaism; bachelor's degrees in journalism and political science, Michigan State University; legislative aide, Representative Paul Condino, two years; district director, Representative Rudy Hobbs, two years; freelance graphic designer, 2012 to present; board trustee, congregation Beth Ahm; member, Greater Southfield/Farmington NAACP, Martin Luther King Task Force, and Magnolia Homeowners Association; past president, Phi Sigma Pi National Honors Fraternity, MSU Chapter; former committeeman, Michigan Democratic Party State Central; former board officer, Oakland County Democratic Party; Oakland County Democratic Party Young Democrat of the Year, 2011; Michigan Political Leadership Program, class of 2013; member, Southfield City Council, 2011 to 2014; elected to the House of Representatives, 2014 and 2016; House Democratic Whip, 2017 to 2018; elected to the State Senate, 2018, Assistant Democratic Leader, 2019.

State Senator
ARIC NESBITT
R–26th Senate District

Office: Room 6100, Binsfeld Office Bldg., P.O. Box 30036, Lansing, MI 48909, (517) 373-0793

Committees: Advice and Consent; Appropriations (Subcommittees: Licensing and Regulatory Affairs (LARA)/Department of Insurance and Financial Services (DIFS) (Chair)); Energy and Technology; Finance (Vice Chair); Government Operations; Insurance and Banking; Regulatory Reform (Chair)

Biography: Republican, of Lawton; born January 25, 1980, in Kalamazoo; grew up on a family farm south of Lawton in Porter Township; spouse, Trisha; daughter, Catherine Barbara; attended Kalamazoo Valley Community College, bachelor's degree in economics, Hillsdale College, master's degree in international business, Norwegian School of Economics; page in the U.S. House of Representatives; staff member, Representative and Senator Tom George; legislative director, Michigan Congressman Tim Walberg; lead Republican staff person, bipartisan Congressional Natural Gas Caucus and Congressional Steel Caucus; commissioner, Michigan Lottery 2017 to 2018; life member, National Rifle Association; member, Van Buren County Farm Bureau, Michigan Right to Life, Michigan Steelhead and Salmon Fishermen's Association - South Haven Chapter, Paw Paw and South Haven Chambers of Commerce, and Van Buren County Republican Party; Hillsdale College Alumnus of the Year for being a conservative reformer, 2017; chair, House Republican Campaign Committee, 2014 to 2016; executive committee, Republican Legislative Campaign Committee; state committee member, Michigan Republican Party, 2017 to 2018; elected to the House of Representatives, 2010, 2012, and 2014; Republican Floor Leader, 2015 to 2016; elected to the State Senate, 2018, President Pro Tempore, 2019.

State Senator
RICK OUTMAN
R–33rd Senate District

Office: Room 4400, Binsfeld Office Bldg., P.O. Box 30036, Lansing, MI 48909, (517) 373-3760

Committees: Appropriations (Subcommittees: Capital Outlay (Vice Chair); K-12 and Michigan Department of Education (Vice Chair); Natural Resources and Environmental Quality (Vice Chair)); Energy and Technology; Environmental Quality (Chair); Natural Resources; Transportation and Infrastructure

Biography: Republican, of Six Lakes; born December 15, 1963, in Lakeview; spouse, Kris; three children, two grandchildren; member, Mt. Pleasant Community Church; bachelor of science, with major in biology and secondary education concentration, Grand Valley State University; U.S. Army combat veteran, Beirut, Lebanon; member, 1073rd National Guard unit in Greenville; owner/operator, Outman Excavating; substitute teacher; member, National Rifle Association, Right to Life of Michigan, Six Lakes Chamber of Commerce, Montcalm County Farm Bureau, Hough-Pontius #3701 VFW post in Lakeview; former board member, Montcalm County Soil and Conservation District; member, Austin Hunting Club in Atlanta, Michigan; elected to the House of Representatives, 2010, 2012, 2014, elected to the State Senate, 2018.

State Senator
DAYNA POLEHANKI
D–7th Senate District

Office: Room 5400, Binsfeld Office Bldg., P.O. Box 30036, Lansing, MI 48909, (517) 373-7350

Committees: Agriculture; Education and Career Readiness (Minority Vice Chair); Regulatory Reform

Biography: Democrat, of Livonia; born December 3, 1969, in Flint; spouse, Joseph Walkup; bachelor's degree, Central Michigan University; Michigan Professional Educator Certification/English Major, Alma College; master's degree in teaching, Marygrove College; K-12 Michigan School Administrator Certification, Michigan Association of Secondary School Principals; manager of Features Casting, Paramount Pictures, 1995 to 1998; teacher, New Haven Community Schools, 2002 to 2018; owner, Detroit Casting Company, 2009 to present; member, Livonia Chapter of American Association of University Women, and Casting Society of America; elected to the State Senate, 2018.

State Senator
JIM RUNESTAD
R–15th Senate District

Office: Room 7500, Binsfeld Office Bldg., P.O. Box 30036, Lansing, MI 48909, (517) 373-1758

Committees: Appropriations (Subcommittees: Capitol Outlay; Justice and Public Safety (Vice Chair)); Education and Career Readiness; Families, Seniors, and Veterans; Finance (Chair); Judiciary and Public Safety

Biography: Republican, of White Lake; born March 1, 1959, in Flint; spouse, Kathy; children, Joel, Justin, Lena, Lee, and Kayla; Christian; bachelor's degree in education, Central Michigan University; owner, Runestad Financial Associates since 2004; foster parent; member Highland-White Lake Business Association, Oakland County Business Round Table, Huron Valley Chamber of Commerce, North Oakland Board of Realtors, Citizen's Advisory Committee for the Friend of the Court, Michigan Association of Counties Judicial Committee, and Family Rights Coalition of Michigan; involved with the Farm Bureau in southeastern Michigan, Meals on Wheels, and the Lions Club; past president, North Oakland Republican Club; former chair, Waterford Republican Caucus, seven years; editor and publisher, *The Michigan Conservative Banner*, two years; Oakland County commissioner, 6 years; elected to the House of Representatives, 2014 and 2016; elected to the State Senate, 2018; Assistant Caucus Chair, 2019.

State Senator
SYLVIA SANTANA
D–3rd Senate District

Office: Room 5600, Binsfeld Office Bldg., P.O. Box 30036, Lansing, MI 48909, (517) 373-0990

Committees: Appropriations (Subcommittees: Capitol Outlay (Minority Vice Chair); Community Health/Human Services; Licensing and Regulatory Affairs (LARA)/Department of Insurance and Financial Services (DIFS)); Health Policy and Human Services

Biography: Democrat, of Detroit; born November 23, 1979, in Cincinnati, Ohio; husband, Harvey Santana; three children; Christian; bachelor's degree, Eastern Michigan University; employed 15 years in the financial sector; fellow, Michigan Political Leadership Program, 2015, and Center for Progressive Leadership, 2012; OFA volunteer, 2012; Warrendale Community Organization, 2007 to 2016; Neighborhood Partners Organization, 2012 to 2015; Cody Rouge Community Action Alliance, 2010 to present; elected to the House of Representatives, 2016; elected to the State Senate, 2018.

State Senator
WAYNE SCHMIDT
R–37th Senate District

Office: Room S-8, Capitol Bldg., Lansing, MI 48909, (517) 373-2413,
E-Mail: senwschmidt@senate.michigan.gov

Committees: Appropriations (Subcommittees: Capital Outlay; Community Health/Human Services; K-12 and Michigan Department of Education (Chair); Talent and Economic Development/MEDC; Transportation (Chair)); Economic and Small Business Development; Natural Resources

Biography: Republican, of Traverse City; born October 6, 1966, in Cleveland, Ohio, and life-long resident of Traverse City; spouse, Kathleen; children, Danny and Ryan; majored in economics and public policy, University of Chicago; graduate of Michigan State University Political Leadership Program; general manager, Captain's Quarters, men's clothing business in Traverse City; member, Grand Traverse County Economic Development Corporation and Brownfield Redevelopment Authority, Traverse City Area Chamber of Commerce Government Affairs Committee, Bay Area Transit Authority, Michigan Association of Counties Human Services Committee (chair), Grand Traverse County Land Use and Transportation Study Group - Grand Vision, Grand Traverse County Republican Party (vice chair and membership chair), Big Brothers/Big Sisters of Northwest Michigan, National Cherry Festival, Trout Unlimited, Economic Club of Traverse City, Kiwanis Noon Club, Boardman Neighborhood Association, Great Lakes Community Mental Health Authority (vice chair); chair, Traverse City Zoning Board of Appeals, Downtown Traverse City Association; elected five times to Grand Traverse County Board of Commissioners; member, Legislative Council; elected to the House of Representatives, 2008, 2010, and 2012; elected to the State Senate, 2014 and 2018, Assistant Majority Leader, 2019.

State Senator
MIKE SHIRKEY
R–16th Senate District

Office: Room S-106, Capitol Bldg., P.O. Box 30036, Lansing, MI 48909, (517) 373-5932

Committee: Government Operations (Chair)

Biography: Republican, from Liberty Township; born December 5, 1954, in Jackson; wife, Sue; three children David (Kelly), Marilyn (Kent), and Daniel (Mary); grandchildren, Andrew, Karter, Micah, Alyssia, Tyler, Benjamin, Gracelyn, Hazel, Nora, Ruby, Colin, and Ella; Jackson Free Methodist Church; bachelor's degree, General Motors Institute; master's degree, University of Wisconsin, Madison; 13 years, General Motors, various engineering and management positions; owner and cofounder, Orbitform, engineering and manufacturing company specializing in forming, fastening, and riveting applications; member, Columbia Central School Board; board chair, 14 years Allegiance Health System; avid outdoor enthusiast; enjoys woodworking and furniture building; elected to the House of Representatives, 2010 and 2012; elected to the State Senate, 2014 and 2018, Majority Leader, 2019; chair and alternate chair, Legislative Council.

State Senator
JIM STAMAS
R–36th Senate District

Office: Room S-324, Capitol Bldg., Lansing, MI 48909, (517) 373-7946,
Toll-Free: (855) 347-8036, E-Mail: senjstamas@senate.michigan.gov,
Website: senatorjimstamas.com

Committees: Appropriations (Chair), (Subcommittee: General Government (Chair))

Biography: Republican, of Midland; born February 17, 1967, in Midland; spouse, Marsha; two children; bachelor's degree, Northwood University; served in Michigan National Guard and United States Army; former realtor; former case project manager, Case Systems; owner, Pizza Sam's, long-time family business; former member, Midland Downtown Development Authority, and Midland Downtown Business Association; former member, Midland County Planning Commission; two terms on Midland County Board of Commissioners; Midland Township trustee, 1997 to 2004; elected to the House of Representatives, 2008, 2010, and 2012; Majority Floor Leader, 2011 to 2014; elected to the State Senate, 2014 and 2018.

State Senator
LANA THEIS
R–22nd Senate District

Office: Room 7400, Binsfeld Office Bldg., P.O. Box 30036, Lansing, MI 48909, (517) 373-2420

Committees: Economic and Small Business Development; Education and Career Readiness (Chair); Health Policy and Human Services; Insurance and Banking (Chair); Oversight; Regulatory Reform (Vice Chair)

Biography: Republican, of Brighton; born June 23, 1965, in Sturgis; spouse, Samuel; children, Jacob and Gabrielle; Christian; bachelor's degree in biology, minor in chemistry, California State University-Fullerton; co-owner, Cornerstone Associates; member and former chair, Brighton Area Fire Authority Board and Livingston County Treasurer's Association; member and former chair, Livingston County Republican Party; president, CARE for Brighton referendum; president, Michigan Association for Prosperity 2/3 ballot initiative; treasurer, Brighton Township, 2008 to 2014; elected to the House of Representatives, 2014 and 2016, elected to the State Senate, 2018, Assistant President Pro Tempore, 2019; member, Joint Committee on Administrative Rules.

State Senator
Curtis S. VanderWall
R–35th Senate District

Office: Room 4500, Binsfeld Office Bldg., P.O. Box 30036, Lansing, MI 48909, (517) 373-1725

Committees: Economic and Small Business Development (Vice Chair); Elections; Environmental Quality; Finance; Health Policy and Human Services (Chair); Judiciary and Public Safety (Vice Chair); Regulatory Reform

Biography: Republican, of Ludington; born November 3, 1961, in Grand Rapids; Christian, active member of Mason County Reform Church; spouse, Diane; children, Nick (Holly), Alyssa, and Hunter; granddaughter Kelsey; attended Grand Rapids Community College; employed 20 years in the grocery business, Eberhard Foods and Prevo's Family Market as store director/supervisor; owner, Turf Care Mole Man, 15 years; Mason County Commission, past chair; hunter safety and snowmobile safety instructor; volunteer, United Way; chair, Suds on the Shore; chair, Women's Jericho House; member, Right to Life, National Rifle Association, Michigan Snowmobile Association, Whitetails Unlimited; elected to the House of Representatives, 2016, elected to the State Senate, 2018.

State Senator
ROGER VICTORY
R–30th Senate District

Office: Room 4100, Binsfeld Office Bldg., P.O. Box 30036, Lansing, MI 48909, (517) 373-6920

Committees: Agriculture (Vice Chair); Appropriations (Subcommittees: Agriculture and Rural Development (Chair); General Government (Vice Chair); Natural Resources and Environmental Quality; Transportation (Vice Chair)); Transportation and Infrastructure

Biography: Republican, resident of Georgetown Township; bachelor's degree, business management, Davenport University; owner and chief operator, Victory Farms and Victory Sales LLC; former president, Ottawa County Farm Bureau; board member, Ottawa County Careerline Technical Center, Michigan Vegetable Council, former elder and deacon, current member, First Hudsonville Christian Reformed Church; elected to the House of Representatives, 2012, 2014, and 2016, elected to the State Senate, 2018.

State Senator
PAUL J. WOJNO
D–9th Senate District

Office: Room 6300, Binsfeld Office Bldg., P.O. Box 30036, Lansing, MI 48909, (517) 373-8360

Committees: Elections (Minority Vice Chair); Health Policy and Human Services; Regulatory Reform

Biography: Democrat, of Warren; born March 30, 1956, in Detroit; ethnicity, Polish, Irish, Welsh, Scottish, Baltic and Balkan States; Roman Catholic; spouse Lisa Wojno; three children, Kennedy, Bradley, and Audrey; graduated Center Line High School; attended Macomb Community College, University of Michigan, and Wayne State University; B.A. 1979; executive administrator and assistant personnel director, City of Warren; clerk, City of Warren 2008 to 2018; selected as one of five top municipal clerks in the state of Michigan in 2012 by the Michigan Municipal Clerks Association; member, Michigan Democratic Party, Great Lakes-St. Lawrence Legislative Caucus, Fraternal Order of Police, Knights of Columbus, Center Line Grant Foundation Committee, American Cancer Society, and American Polish Cultural Center; member, St. Anne Parish; Democrat of the Year, 1998; Legislator of the Year, Michigan Library Association, 2019; member, Auto, Criminal Justice, Labor, Sportsman's, Fire, National Labor of State Agencies, and Aerospace and Defense caucuses; elected to the House of Representatives 1996, 1998, and 2000; appointed House Majority and Minority Whip; elected to the Michigan Senate, 2018.

State Senator
DALE W. ZORN
R–17th Senate District

Office: Room 5100, Binsfeld Office Bldg., Lansing, MI 48909, (517) 373-3543,
Toll-free: (855) 347-8017, Fax: (517) 373-0927, E-Mail: sendzorn@senate.michigan.gov

Committees: Families, Seniors, and Veterans; Local Government (Chair); Regulatory Reform; Appropriations Subcommittees: Capital Outlay, Transportation, Universities and Community Colleges

Biography: Republican, of Ida; born December 31, 1953; spouse, Cindy, four children, 11 grandchildren; member, Ida United Methodist Church; co-owner, automotive business, Zorn's Service, Inc.; member, Ida Civic Club, Monroe County Vietnam Veterans Chapter 142, Monroe County Chamber of Commerce, National Rifle Association, Roselawn Memorial Park Board of Directors, Fraternal Order of Police Lodge 113, executive director, Christmas in Ida Festival and Parade of Lights; Raisinville Township, constable, four years, trustee, six years; Monroe County commissioner, 20 years, including four as chair; elected to the House of Representatives, 2010 and 2012; elected to the State Senate, 2014 and 2018.

HOUSE OF REPRESENTATIVES, 2019-2020

OFFICERS AND LEADERS

LEE CHATFIELD, *Speaker*
JASON WENTWORTH, *Speaker Pro Tempore*
PAMELA HORNBERGER AND JIM LILLY, *Associate Speakers Pro Tempore*
CHRISTINE GREIG, *Minority Leader*
TRISTON COLE, *Majority Floor Leader*
YOUSEF RABHI, *Minority Floor Leader*
GARY L. RANDALL, *Clerk*
RICHARD J. BROWN, *Assistant Clerk*

District	Name, Party	Post Office	Occupation
1	Tenisha Yancey, D	Detroit	Assistant prosecuting attorney/local government
2	Joseph Tate, D	Detroit	Professional football player/U.S. Marine Corps/economic development
3	Wendell Byrd, D	Detroit	Accountant/auditor
4	Isaac Robinson, D	Detroit	Attorney/organizer/Legislative staff
5	Cynthia A. Johnson, D	Detroit	Corrections/parole/probation officer
6	Tyrone Carter, D	Detroit	Law enforcement
7	LaTanya Garrett, D	Detroit	First responder/small business owner
8	Sherry Gay-Dagnogo, D	Detroit	Teacher
9	Karen Whitsett, D	Detroit	Community organizer
10	Leslie Love, D	Detroit	Professor
11	Jewell Jones, D	Inkster	Local government
12	Alex Garza, D	Taylor	Local government/Legislative staff
13	Frank Liberati, D	Allen Park	Small business owner
14	Cara Clemente, D	Lincoln Park	Teacher
15	Abdullah Hammoud, D	Dearborn	Health care consultant
16	Kevin Coleman, D	Westland	Local government
17	Joseph N. Bellino, R	Monroe	Small business owner
18	Kevin Hertel, D	St. Clair Shores	Analyst/consultant BCBS
19	Laurie Pohutsky, D	Livonia	Scientist
20	Matt Koleszar, D	Plymouth	Teacher/coach
21	Kristy Pagan, D	Canton	Congressional staff/small business owner
22	John Chirkun, D	Roseville	Law enforcement/local government
23	Darrin Camilleri, D	Brownstown	Teacher
24	Steve Marino, R	Harrison Twp.	Local government/small business owner
25	Nate Shannon, D	Sterling Heights	Teacher/local government
26	Jim Ellison, D	Royal Oak	Local government
27	Robert Wittenberg, D	Oak Park	Insurance agent
28	Lori Stone, D	Warren	Teacher
29	Brenda Carter, D	Pontiac	Community activist
30	Diana Farrington, R	Utica	Mortgage auditor/photographer
31	Bill Sowerby, D	Clinton Twp.	Local government
32	Pamela Hornberger, R	Chesterfield	Teacher
33	Jeff Yaroch, R	Richmond	Firefighter/paramedic/attorney
34	Sheldon Neeley, D	Flint	Broadcast engineer/local government
35	Kyra Harris Bolden, D	Southfield	Attorney
36	Douglas Wozniak, R	Shelby Twp.	Attorney/small business owner
37	Christine Greig, D	Farmington Hills	Consultant/business owner
38	Kathy Crawford, R	Novi	Local government/small business owner
39	Ryan Berman, R	Commerce Twp.	Attorney/Law enforcement
40	Mari Manoogian, D	Birmingham	International relations
41	Padma Kuppa, D	Troy	Engineer
42	Ann Bollin, R	Brighton Twp.	Local government
43	Andrea K. Schroeder, R	Independence Twp.	Teacher/consultant/local government
44	Matt Maddock, R	Milford	Small business owner
45	Michael Webber, R	Rochester Hills	Insurance agent/Legislative staff
46	John Reilly, R	Oakland Twp.	Small business owner
47	Henry Vaupel, R	Fowlerville	Veterinarian
48	Sheryl Y. Kennedy, D	Davison	School administrator
49	John Cherry, D	Flint	DNR staff/small business owner
50	Tim Sneller, D	Burton	Legislative staff
51	Mike Mueller, R	Linden	Law enforcement
52	Donna Lasinski, D	Scio Twp.	Small business owner

District	Name, Party	Post Office	Occupation
53	Yousef Rabhi, D.	Ann Arbor	Local government
54	Ronnie D. Peterson, D	Ypsilanti	Local government
55	Rebekah Warren, D	Ann Arbor	Legislative staff/public policy
56	Jason Sheppard, R	Temperance	Business owner/commercial real estate agent
57	Bronna Kahle, R.	Adrian	Small business owner
58	Eric Leutheuser, R	Hillsdale	Car dealership owner
59	Aaron Miller, R.	Sturgis	Teacher/coach
60	Jon Hoadley, D	Kalamazoo	Consultant/public policy
61	Brandt Iden, R.	Portage	Real estate/local government
62	Jim Haadsma, D.	Battle Creek	Attorney/local government
63	Matt Hall, R	Emmet Twp.	Attorney
64	Julie Alexander, R	Hanover	Teacher/dairy farmer/local government
65	Sarah Lightner, R	Springport	Paralegal/farmer/local government
66	Beth Griffin, R.	Mattawan	Teacher
67	Kara Hope, D	Holt	Attorney/local government
68	Sarah Anthony, D.	Lansing	Legislative staff/local government/ public policy
69	Julie Brixie, D	Okemos	Scientist/local government
70	James Lower, R	Greenville	Legislative staff/consultant
71	Angela Witwer, D.	Delta Twp.	Health care/public policy
72	Steve Johnson, R	Wayland	U.S. Air Force
73	Lynn Afendoulis, R.	Grand Rapids Twp.	Business
74	Mark E. Huizenga, R	Walker.	Consultant/health care management
75	David LaGrand, D	Grand Rapids.	Small business owner/attorney/local government
76	Rachel Hood, D.	Grand Rapids.	Health care/advocacy
77	Tommy Brann, R	Wyoming.	Small business owner
78	Brad Paquette, R	Niles	Teacher
79	Pauline Wendzel, R	Watervliet	Business/local government
80	Mary Whiteford, R	Plainwell	Nurse/financial planning
81	Gary Eisen, R.	St. Clair Twp.	Small business owner
82	Gary Howell, R	North Branch.	Farmer/attorney/local government
83	Shane Hernandez, R.	Port Huron	Architect
84	Phil Green, R.	Millington	Pastor
85	Ben Frederick, R	Owosso.	Legislative staff/local government
86	Thomas A. Albert, R.	Lowell	U.S. Marine Corps/state retirement system
87	Julie Calley, R	Portland	Real estate management/local government
88	Luke Meerman, R.	Coopersville	Small business owner/farmer/local government
89	Jim Lilly, R.	Park Twp.	Banking and finance
90	Bradley Slagh, R.	Zeeland.	Banking and finance/local government
91	Greg VanWoerkom, R.	Norton Shores	Congressional staff
92	Terry J. Sabo, D	Muskegon	Firefighter/local government/U.S. Air Force
93	Graham Filler, R.	DeWitt	Attorney/Assistant Attorney General
94	Rodney Wakeman, R	Saginaw Twp.	Funeral home owner
95	Vanessa Guerra, D	Saginaw	Attorney
96	Brian K. Elder, D	Bay City	Attorney/local government
97	Jason Wentworth, R	Clare	Law enforcement/U.S. Army
98	Annette Glenn, R	Midland.	Legislative staff/public policy
99	Roger Hauck, R	Mt. Pleasant.	Small business owner/local government
100	Scott VanSingel, R	Grant	Finance and accounting
101	Jack O'Malley, R.	Lake Ann.	Broadcaster
102	Michele Hoitenga, R.	Manton	Local government/small business owner
103	Daire Rendon, R	Lake City.	Small business owner
104	Larry Inman, R.	Williamsburg	Banking/local government
105	Triston Cole, R.	Mancelona.	Agriculture/small business owner
106	Sue Allor, R	Wolverine	Nurse/small business owner/local government
107	Lee Chatfield, R	Levering	Teacher/athletic director
108	Beau LaFave, R	Iron Mountain	Legislator
109	Sara Cambensy, D	Marquette	Education/local government
110	Greg Markkanen, R	Hancock	Teacher/U.S. Army/National Guard/ local government

MICHIGAN HOUSE DISTRICTS — 2010 CENSUS

MICHIGAN HOUSE DISTRICTS — 2010 CENSUS
METROPOLITAN DETROIT AREA — Wayne/Oakland/Macomb Counties

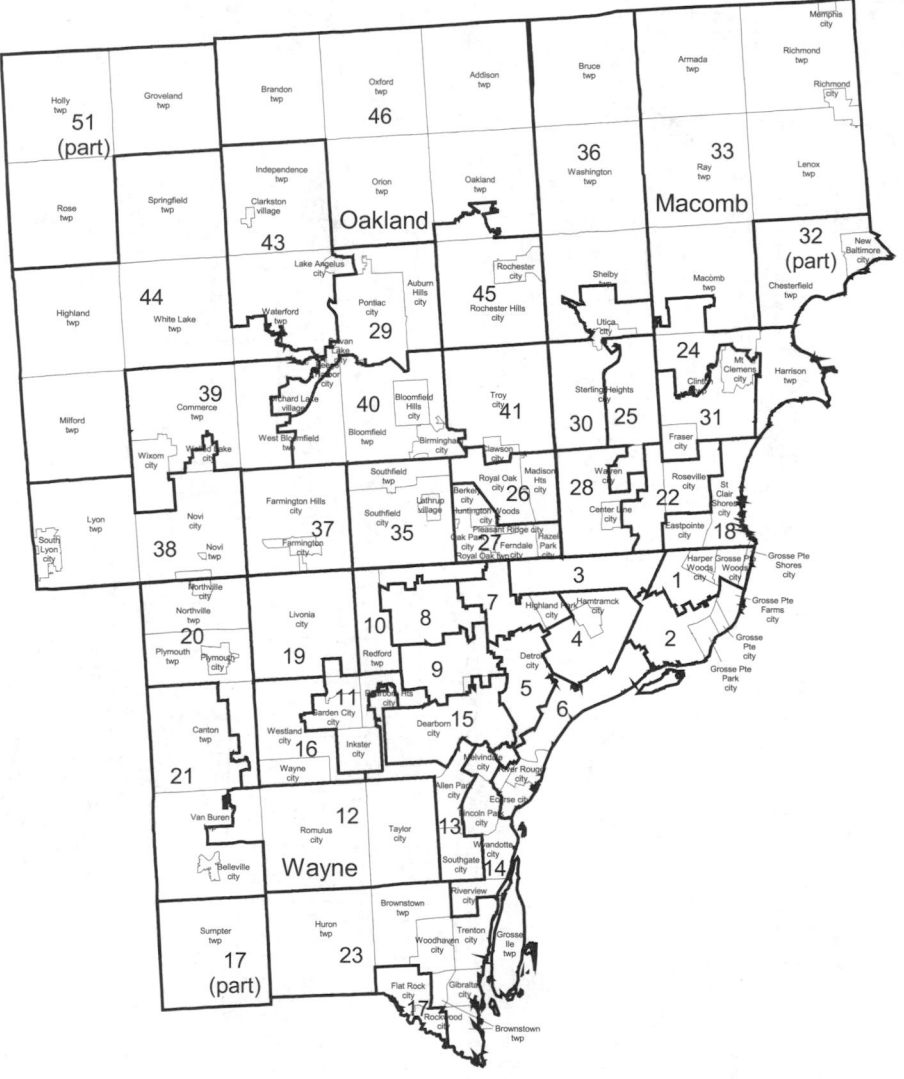

MICHIGAN HOUSE DISTRICTS — 2010 CENSUS
SELECTED COUNTIES

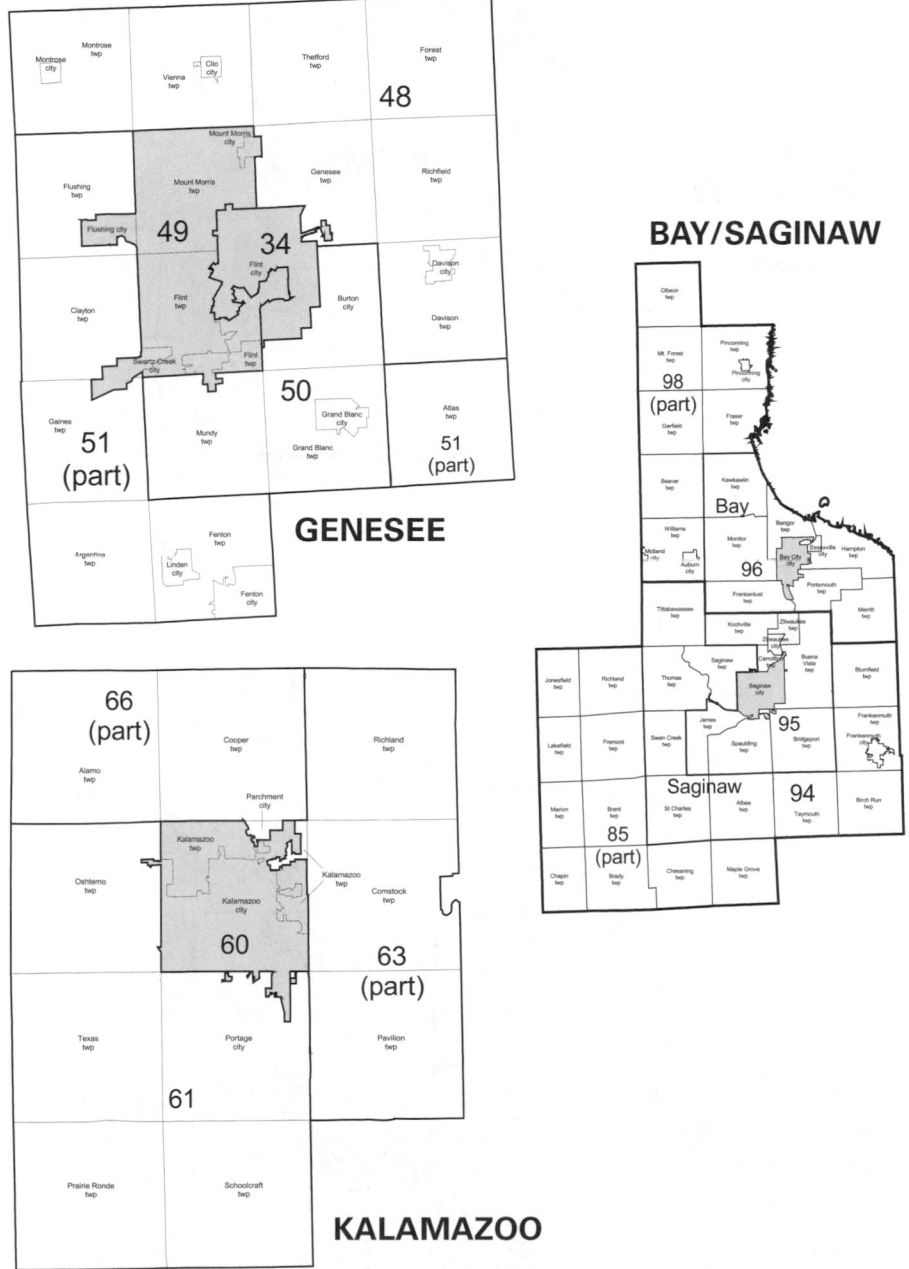

BAY/SAGINAW

GENESEE

KALAMAZOO

MICHIGAN HOUSE DISTRICTS — 2010 CENSUS
SELECTED COUNTIES

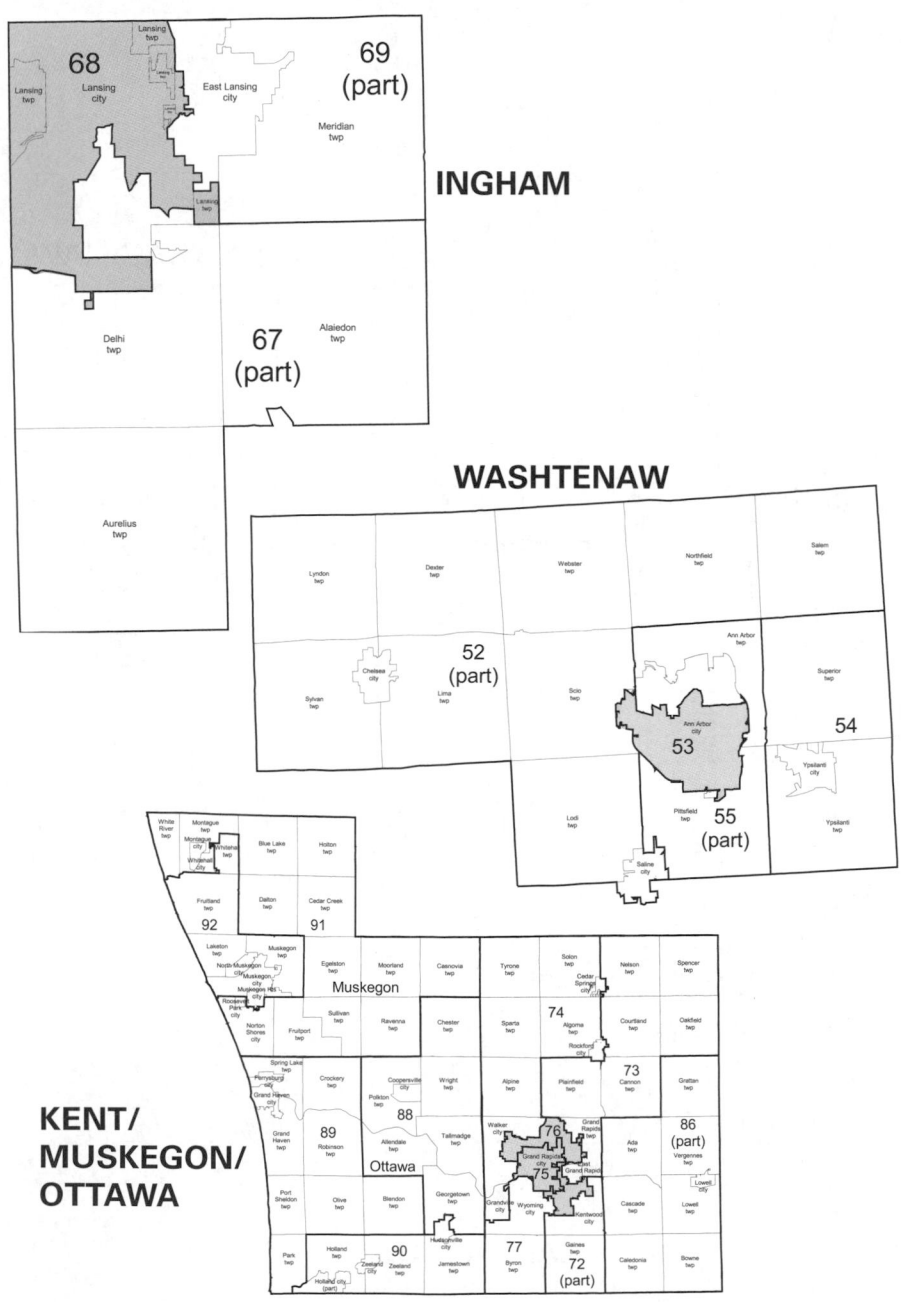

HOUSE DISTRICT POPULATIONS

District	2010 Population	District	2010 Population
1	87,768	56	86,534
2	87,186	57	94,159
3	87,906	58	91,936
4	88,168	59	93,735
5	87,306	60	94,090
6	89,423	61	91,735
7	88,564	62	92,488
8	87,850	63	92,487
9	89,598	64	86,288
10	87,869	65	93,807
11	92,260	66	91,935
12	92,972	67	93,456
13	91,612	68	94,139
14	87,299	69	93,300
15	89,952	70	87,024
16	91,519	71	93,645
17	88,203	72	93,393
18	92,236	73	93,757
19	92,330	74	91,218
20	92,769	75	93,805
21	92,256	76	94,318
22	86,238	77	92,437
23	93,261	78	90,881
24	86,068	79	85,785
25	85,781	80	91,868
26	86,930	81	85,568
27	91,794	82	88,319
28	86,089	83	88,442
29	87,812	84	88,847
30	87,305	85	93,124
31	88,987	86	92,271
32	87,609	87	94,041
33	86,511	88	87,130
34	86,516	89	85,375
35	90,361	90	91,296
36	86,298	91	86,460
37	90,112	92	85,728
38	91,466	93	94,176
39	92,083	94	89,912
40	91,523	95	87,781
41	92,805	96	86,595
42	91,923	97	85,628
43	93,724	98	85,899
44	92,733	99	89,217
45	88,602	100	86,569
46	89,329	101	92,671
47	89,044	102	85,950
48	90,592	103	92,224
49	86,567	104	86,986
50	90,865	105	92,098
51	94,338	106	94,220
52	86,541	107	94,062
53	85,745	108	87,266
54	85,855	109	87,465
55	86,650	110	86,997

HOUSE OF REPRESENTATIVES
STANDING COMMITTEES

AGRICULTURE:
Reps. Alexander (C), Meerman (VC), LaFave, Eisen, Mueller, Wendzel, Elder (Min. VC), Coleman, Garza, C. Johnson, Witwer.

APPROPRIATIONS:
Reps. Hernandez (C), Miller (VC), Sheppard, Albert, Allor, Brann, VanSingel, Whiteford, Yaroch, Bollin, Glenn, Green, Huizenga, Lightner, Maddock, Slagh, VanWoerkom, Hoadley (Min. VC), Love, Pagan, Hammoud, Peterson, Sabo, Anthony, Brixie, Cherry, Hood, Kennedy, Tate.

COMMERCE AND TOURISM:
Reps. Marino (C), Wendzel (VC), Reilly, Meerman, Schroeder, Wakeman, Cambensy (Min. VC), Camilleri, Hope, Manoogian, Robinson.

COMMUNICATIONS AND TECHNOLOGY:
Reps. Hoitenga (C), S. Johnson (VC), Wozniak, Coleman (Min. VC), Chirkun.

EDUCATION:
Reps. Hornberger (C), Paquette (VC), Crawford, Vaupel, Reilly, Hall, Markkanen, O'Malley, Wakeman, Camilleri (Min. VC), Sowerby, B. Carter, T. Carter, Koleszar, Stone.

ELECTIONS AND ETHICS:
Reps. Calley (C), Sheppard (VC), Hornberger, Marino, Paquette, Guerra (Min. VC), Hope.

ENERGY:
Reps. Bellino (C), Wendzel (VC), Alexander, Frederick, Lower, Filler, Markkanen, Mueller, O'Malley, Schroeder, Lasinski (Min. VC), Sneller, T. Carter, Haadsma, Kuppa, Manoogian, Shannon.

FAMILIES, CHILDREN, AND SENIORS:
Reps. Crawford (C), Rendon (VC), Hoitenga, Meerman, Wozniak, Garrett (Min. VC), Liberati, B. Carter, C. Johnson.

FINANCIAL SERVICES:
Reps. Farrington (C), Schroeder (VC), Sheppard, Bellino, Berman, Wakeman, Gay-Dagnogo (Min. VC), Wittenberg, Clemente, Stone, Whitsett.

GOVERNMENT OPERATIONS:
Reps. Sheppard (C), Cole (VC), Lilly, Greig (Min. VC), Rabhi.

HEALTH POLICY:
Reps. Vaupel (C), Frederick (VC), Alexander, Calley, Hornberger, Lower, Whiteford, Afendoulis, Filler, Mueller, Wozniak, Liberati (Min. VC), Garrett, Clemente, Ellison, Koleszar, Pohutsky, Stone, Witwer.

INSURANCE:
Reps. Rendon (C), Markkanen (VC), Webber, Vaupel, Bellino, Frederick, Hoitenga, LaFave, Berman, Paquette, Wittenberg (Min. VC), Gay-Dagnogo, Lasinski, Sneller, Bolden, B. Carter, Coleman.

JUDICIARY:
Reps. Filler (C), LaFave (VC), Farrington, Howell, S. Johnson, Rendon, Berman, Wozniak, LaGrand (Min VC), Guerra, Elder, Yancey, Bolden.

LOCAL GOVERNMENT AND MUNICIPAL FINANCE:
Reps. Lower (C), Marino (VC), Crawford, Calley, Howell, Eisen, Meerman, Paquette, Ellison (Min. VC), Sowerby, Garza, Hope, Kuppa.

MILITARY, VETERANS AND HOMELAND SECURITY:
Reps. LaFave (C), Mueller (VC), Marino, Afendoulis, Markkanen, Jones (Min. VC), Chirkun, T. Carter, Manoogian.

NATURAL RESOURCES AND OUTDOOR RECREATION:
Reps. Howell (C), Wakeman (VC), Calley, Reilly, Rendon, Eisen, Sowerby (Min. VC), Cambensy, Pohutsky.

OVERSIGHT:

Reps. Hall (C), Reilly (VC), Webber, S. Johnson, LaFave, Schroeder, C. Johnson (Min. VC), Camilleri, LaGrand.

REGULATORY REFORM:

Reps. Webber (C), Berman (VC), Crawford, Farrington, Frederick, Hoitenga, Filler, Hall, Wendzel, Chirkun (Min. VC), Liberati, Cambensy, Jones, Garza, Robinson.

TAX POLICY:

Reps. Afendoulis (C), Lower (VC), Vaupel, Webber, Farrington, S. Johnson, Hall, O'Malley, Schroeder, Yancey (Min. VC), Wittenberg, Ellison, Lasinski, Robinson, Whitsett.

TRANSPORTATION:

Reps. O'Malley (C), Eisen (VC), Cole, Sheppard, Alexander, Bellino, Howell, Afendoulis, Sneller (Min. VC), Clemente, Yancey, Haadsma, Shannon.

WAYS AND MEANS:

Reps. Iden (C), Lilly (VC), Leutheuser, Griffin, Hauck, Kahle, Wentworth, Warren (Min. VC), Byrd, Neeley, Hertel.

APPROPRIATIONS SUBCOMMITTEES

AGRICULTURE AND RURAL DEVELOPMENT:
Reps. VanWoerkom (C), Bollin (VC), Albert, Green, Kennedy (Min. VC), Sabo, Brixie.

CORRECTIONS:
Reps. Albert (C), Slagh (VC), VanSingel, Lightner, Maddock, Pagan (Min. VC), Sabo, Anthony, Kennedy.

GENERAL GOVERNMENT:
Reps. Huizenga (C), Lightner (VC), Allor, Brann, Bollin, VanWoerkom, Sabo (Min. VC), Hoadley, Tate.

HEALTH AND HUMAN SERVICES:
Reps. Whiteford (C), Green (VC), Allor, Yaroch, Bollin, Glenn, Huizenga, VanWoerkom, Hammoud (Min. VC), Hoadley, Love, Brixie, Cherry.

HIGHER EDUCATION AND COMMUNITY COLLEGES:
Reps. VanSingel (C), Bollin (VC), Green, Huizenga, Slagh, Anthony (Min. VC), Hoadley.

JOINT CAPITAL OUTLAY:
Reps. Slagh (C), Hernandez (VC), Sheppard, Maddock, Whiteford, Bollin, Love (Min. VC), Cherry, Hood.

JUDICIARY:
Reps. Brann (C), Lightner (VC), Yaroch, Maddock, Brixie (Min. VC), Pagan, Hammoud.

LICENSING AND REGULATORY AFFAIRS AND INSURANCE AND FINANCIAL SERVICES:
Reps. Yaroch (C), Glenn (VC), VanSingel, Lightner, Peterson (Min. VC), Hammoud, Anthony.

MILITARY AND VETERANS AFFAIRS AND STATE POLICE:
Reps. Miller (C), VanWoerkom (VC), Albert, Brann, Tate (Min. VC), Peterson, Hood.

NATURAL RESOURCES AND ENVIRONMENTAL QUALITY:
Reps. Allor (C), Glenn (VC), VanSingel, Green, Slagh, Cherry (Min. VC), Hood.

SCHOOL AID AND DEPARTMENT OF EDUCATION:
Reps. Miller (C), Hornberger (VC), Albert, Allor, Huizenga, Glenn, Green, Pagan (Min. VC), Hood, Kennedy, Tate.

TRANSPORTATION:
Reps. Maddock (C), Yaroch (VC), Miller, Brann, Bollin, Peterson (Min. VC), Love.

JOINT STATUTORY STANDING COMMITTEES

(House members only listed)

JOINT COMMITTEE ON ADMINISTRATIVE RULES:
Reps. Maddock (C), Wozniak, S. Johnson, Bolden (Min. VC), Garrett.

LEGISLATIVE COUNCIL:
Reps. Chatfield (Alt. C), Hernandez, Lilly, Wentworth, Clemente (Min. VC), Rabhi.
Alternates: Reps. Cole, Whiteford, Garrett.

MICHIGAN HOUSE OF REPRESENTATIVES
BIOGRAPHICAL SKETCHES OF MEMBERS

THE ONE HUNDREDTH LEGISLATURE
2019-2020

State Representative
LYNN AFENDOULIS
R–73rd Representative District

Office: Room N-1092, Cora B. Anderson House Office Bldg., P.O. Box 30014, Lansing, MI 48909, (517) 373-0218, Toll-Free: (855) 347-8073, E-Mail: lynnafendoulis@house.mi.gov

Committees: Health Policy; Military, Veterans and Homeland Security; Tax Policy (Chair); Transportation

Biography: Republican, of Grand Rapids Township; born November 3, 1958 in Grand Rapids; Greek Orthodox; children, Katharine, and Evan; bachelor's degree from Michigan State University, attended Miami University, Oxford, Ohio; employed more than 37 years in journalism and communications; employed at Universal Forest Products, 25 years, 15 years as director of corporate communications and community relations; board member, Economic Club of Grand Rapids; past board member of the Grand Rapids Area Chamber of Commerce; chair, Grand Rapids Student Advancement Foundation; member, Grand Rapids Youth Commonwealth, Opera Grand Rapids, Circle Theatre and the parish council, Holy Trinity Greek Orthodox Church; former commissioner, Michigan Transportation Commission, 2013 to 2018; elected to the House of Representatives, 2018; member, Select Committee on Reducing Car Insurance Rates, 2019.

State Representative
THOMAS A. ALBERT
R–86th Representative District

Office: Room N-1190, Cora B. Anderson House Office Bldg., P.O. Box 30014, Lansing, MI 48909, (517) 373-0846, Toll-Free: (844) 925-2378, E-Mail: thomasalbert@house.mi.gov

Committees: Appropriations (Subcommittees: Agriculture and Rural Development; Corrections (Chair); Military and Veterans Affairs and State Police; School Aid and Department of Education)

Biography: Republican, of Lowell; born April 12, 1985 in Grand Rapids; Catholic; spouse, Erica; three children; bachelor's degree in political science and history, University of Michigan; master of business administration in finance, Michigan State University; United States Marine Corps, 2007 to 2010 and United States Marine Corps Reserve, 2011 to 2013; employed by the State of Michigan, Bureau of Investments, 2013 to 2016; elected to the House of Representatives, 2016 and 2018.

State Representative
JULIE ALEXANDER
R–64th Representative District

Office: Room N-998, Cora B. Anderson House Office Bldg., P.O. Box 30014, Lansing, MI 48909, (517) 373-1795, E-Mail: juliealexander@house.mi.gov

Committees: Agriculture (Chair); Energy; Health Policy; Transportation

Biography: Republican, of Hanover; born November 23, 1962 in Saginaw; Lutheran; spouse, Jeff; children, Andrew, Adam, Anna, and Jared; bachelor's degree, Western Michigan University; graduate studies, Michigan State University; teacher, Hanover Horton Schools, East Jackson Community Schools, Jackson Public Schools, and Grass Lake Schools, 1984 to 2011; Jackson County Commissioner, 2011 to 2016; current or former member: Jackson County Republicans Party Executive Board, Republican Women's Federation of Michigan, American 1 Credit Union Board of Directors, Jackson County Parks, Cradle to Career (C2C), SCMWorks!, Land Bank Authority, Region 2 Planning Commission, Board of Public Works, and Hanover Horton Hometown Celebration, Marine Corps League; elected to the House of Representatives, 2016 and 2018.

State Representative
SUE ALLOR
R–106th Representative District

Office: Room S-1485, Cora B. Anderson House Office Bldg., P.O. Box 30014, Lansing, MI 48909, (517) 373-0833, E-Mail: sueallor@house.mi.gov

Committees: Appropriations (Subcommittees: General Government; Health and Human Services; Natural Resources and Environmental Quality (Chair); School Aid and Department of Education)

Biography: Republican, of Wolverine; born December 31, 1954 in Detroit; Lutheran; spouse, Patrick; three children and four grandchildren; bachelor of science in nursing, University of Detroit-Mercy; master of business administration degree, Lawrence Technological University; formerly employed in hospital settings, medical/surgical, cardiac step-down units, and maternity/nursery; strategic consultant advising in operations and finances for several businesses; board of commissioners, Cheboygan County, 2010 to 2016; board of review, Wilmot Township, 2006 to 2010; several positions with Cheboygan County Republican Party including executive committee, secretary, treasurer, and events committee chair; delegate, Republican Party state conventions; member, Indian River and Petoskey chambers of commerce; elected to the House of Representatives, 2016 and 2018.

State Representative
SARAH ANTHONY
D–68th Representative District

Office: Room S-1087, Cora B. Anderson House Office Bldg., P.O. Box 30014, Lansing, MI 48909, (517) 373-0826, Fax: (517) 373-5698, E-Mail: sarahanthony@house.mi.gov

Committees: Appropriations (Subcommittees: Corrections; Higher Education and Community Colleges (Minority Vice Chair); Licensing and Regulatory Affairs and Insurance and Financial Services)

Biography: Democrat, of Lansing; born December 2, 1983 in Lansing; Christian; bachelor's degree in political science, Central Michigan University; master's degree in public administration, Western Michigan University; New Leadership Academy Fellowship, University of Michigan; legislative aide, former Representative Joan Bauer; deputy director, Michigan College Access Network; member of Alpha Kappa Alpha Sorority, Inc. and National Association for the Advancement of Colored People; past member, Capital Area Michigan Works! Administrative Board, Capital Area United Way Community Investment Committee, Greater Lansing Food Bank Board; Lansing Economic Area Partnership Board; Michigan League of Conservation Voters; commissioner, Ingham County Board, 2013 to 2018; elected to the House of Representatives in a special election held November 2018 to fill the remaining six weeks of legislative session; elected to a full term in the House of Representatives, November 2018; Democratic Caucus chair.

State Representative
JOSEPH N. BELLINO
R–17th Representative District

Office: Room N-696, Cora B. Anderson House Office Bldg., P.O. Box 30014, Lansing, MI 48909, (517) 373-1530, Toll-Free: (855) 417-2355, E-Mail: josephbellino@house.mi.gov

Committees: Energy (Chair); Financial Services; Insurance; Transportation

Biography: Republican, of Monroe; born June 10, 1958 in Monroe; spouse, Margaret; children, Mary Bezeau, Annie Sullivan, and Meg Bellino; Catholic; associate's of science degree, Monroe County Community College; employed at Bellino's Quality Beverage, Society of St. Vincent de Paul, Joe Lake Tire and Auto; owner, Broadway Market, 1998 to present, Monroe County Community College Board of Trustees, 16 years (two as chair); member, Knights of Columbus, Exchange Club, and St. Mary Church choir; elected to the House of Representatives, 2016 and 2018.

State Representative
RYAN BERMAN
R–39th Representative District

Office: Room S-888, Cora B. Anderson House Office Bldg., P.O. Box 30014, Lansing, MI 48909, (517) 373-1799, Fax: (517) 373-8361, E-Mail: ryanberman@house.mi.gov

Committees: Financial Services, Insurance, Judiciary, Regulatory Reform (Vice Chair)

Biography: Republican, of Commerce Township; born October 2, 1980 in Detroit; Jewish; spouse, Stacie; children, Sloane and Morgan; bachelor's degree, psychology from Michigan State University, juris doctor from Wayne State University Law School, reserve police academy graduate, Oakland Police Academy; attorney and counselor at law, Berman Law; reserve police officer, Sylvan Lake Police Department; special prosecutor, Palm Beach County State Attorney's Office; special deputy, Oakland County Sheriff's Office; outreach chair, 11th Congressional District Republican Committee; president and vice president, homeowners association, member, board of trustees for the Crohn's and Colitis Foundation Michigan Chapter, young leadership, Friends of the Israeli Defense Forces, member, Oakland County Sportsman's Club; elected to the House of Representatives, 2018.

State Representative
KYRA HARRIS BOLDEN
D–35th Representative District

Office: Room N-799, Cora B. Anderson House Office Bldg., P.O. Box 30014, Lansing, MI 48909, (517) 373-1788, Toll-Free: (877) DIST-035, E-Mail: kyrabolden@house.mi.gov

Committees: Insurance; Judiciary

Biography: Democrat, of Southfield; born July 31, 1988; Christian; spouse, Dr. Gregory Bolden II; bachelor's degree in psychology, Grand Valley State University and juris doctor, University of Detroit-Mercy School of Law; appointed defense attorney with the 46th District Court, staff attorney with the Wayne County 3rd Circuit Court; civil litigation attorney, Lewis and Munday; commissioner, Southfield Total Living Commission; member, Alpha Kappa Alpha Sorority, Inc.; National Congress of Black Women, Oakland County Chapter, State Bar of Michigan, Wolverine Bar, Straker Bar, and the Women Lawyers Association of Michigan, Oakland County; elected to the House of Representatives, 2018, Minority Vice Chair, Joint Committee on Administrative Rules; member, Select Committee on Reducing Car Insurance Rates.

State Representative
ANN BOLLIN
R–42nd Representative District

Office: Room N-891, Cora B. Anderson House Office Bldg., P.O. Box 30014, Lansing, MI 48909, (517) 373-1784, Toll-Free: (800) 295-0066, E-Mail: annbollin@house.mi.gov

Committees: Appropriations (Subcommittees: Agriculture and Rural Development (Vice Chair); General Government; Health and Human Services; Higher Education and Community Colleges (Vice Chair); Joint Capital Outlay; Transportation

Biography: Republican, Brighton Township; born August 1960 in Detroit; Catholic; spouse, Tim; three sons, Derrick, Kyle, and Bryan; attended Central Michigan University; Harvard University, John F. Kennedy School of Government, Taubman Fellow, Senior Executives in State and Local Government Program; fellow, Michigan Political Leadership Program; clerk, Charter Township of Brighton, 2003 to 2018; marketing manager/coordinator, ALNM/The Keith Companies, 1994 to 2002; executive director, Western Townships Utilities Authority, 1989 to 1990; executive director, Conference of Western Wayne, 1983 to 1988; member Greater Brighton Area Chamber of Commerce board of directors; Michigan Townships Association, board of directors; Michigan Association of Municipal Clerks, Legislative Committee and Council of Election Officials, voting alternate; Holy Spirit Catholic Church, Parish Council; Livingston County Community Alliance; elected to the House of Representatives, 2018.

State Representative
TOMMY BRANN
R–77th Representative District

Office: Room N-1096, Cora B. Anderson House Office Bldg., P.O. Box 30014, Lansing, MI 48909, (517) 373-2277, Toll-Free: (855) 866-4077, E-Mail: tommybrann@house.mi.gov

Committees: Appropriations (Subcommittees: General Government; Judiciary (Chair); Military and Veterans Affairs and State Police; Transportation)

Biography: Republican, of Wyoming; born December 23, 1951 in Grand Rapids; Catholic; spouse, Sue; high school graduate; restaurant owner for over 45 years; member, Mero Health Foundation Board; past chairperson and board member, Wyoming Kentwood Chamber of Commerce; member, Grand Rapids Chamber of Commerce tax committee; past chairman, Grand Rapids Community College culinary advisory committee; past board member, Michigan Restaurant Association; past advisory chairperson, Godwin Heights High School; former president, Division Avenue Business Association; former president, Wyoming Economic Development Corporation; past mentor, Wyoming-Gateway Project Innovator; author, *Mind Your Own Business: Lessons from a Hardworking Restaurateur* and the children's book *Taking Care of Business*; elected to the House of Representatives, 2016 and 2018.

State Representative
JULIE BRIXIE
D–69th Representative District

Office: Room S-1088, Cora B. Anderson House Office Bldg., P.O. Box 30014, Lansing, MI 48909, (517) 373-1786, Fax: (517) 373-5717, E-Mail: juliebrixie@house.mi.gov

Committees: Appropriations (Subcommittees: Agriculture and Rural Development; Health and Human Services; Judiciary (Minority Vice Chair))

Biography: Democrat, of Meridian Township; born May 7, 1966 in Chicago, Illinois; Catholic; spouse, Randy Schaetzl; children, Madeline, Annika, and Heidi Schaetzl; bachelor's degree in physical geography, University of Illinois; master's degree in crop and soil sciences with a specialization in environmental toxicology, Michigan State University; employed as an environmental chemist with Fishbeck, Thompson, Carr, and Huber, 1991 to 1994 and as an environmental consultant with Michigan Biotechnology Institute, 1994 to 1996; member, Chippewa Parent Group for Okemos Public Schools, Michigan Recycling Coalition; board member, Meridian Township Zoning Board of Appeals, 1998, Capital Area Transportation Authority, 2013 to 2016, Meridian Township Land Preservation Board, 2012 to 2018; commissioner, Meridian Township Planning Commission, 1999; trustee, Meridian Township, 2000 to 2008; treasurer, Meridian Township, 2008 to 2018, Meridian Township Economic Development Corporation, 2008 to 2018; vice president, Okemos Public Schools Parent Council, 2007 to 2008; former president, Haslett-Okemos Rotary Club; co-founder and chair, Capital Area Treasurers Association, 2008 to 2018; elected to the House of Representatives, 2018.

State Representative
WENDELL BYRD
D–3rd Representative District

Office: Room S-587, Cora B. Anderson House Office Bldg., P.O. Box 30014, Lansing, MI 48909, (517) 373-0144, Toll-Free: (855) 564-4673, Fax: (517) 373-8929, E-Mail: wendellbyrd@house.mi.gov

Committee: Ways and Means

Biography: Democrat, of Detroit; born July 12, 1945; son, Phillip; graduated from Detroit College of Business; tax accountant auditor, state of Michigan; deputy comptroller, city of Ecorse; tax accounting business owner; elected to the House of Representatives, 2014, 2016, and 2018.

State Representative
JULIE CALLEY
R–87th Representative District

Office: Room N-1191, Cora B. Anderson House Office Bldg., P.O. Box 30014, Lansing, MI 48909, (517) 373-0842, E-Mail: juliecalley@house.mi.gov

Committees: Elections and Ethics (Chair); Health Policy; Local Government and Municipal Finance; Natural Resources and Outdoor Recreation

Biography: Republican, of Portland; born August 19, 1975 in Grand Rapids; Christian; spouse, Brian; children, Collin, Reagan and Karagan; bachelor of business administration, Northwood University; Ionia County commissioner, 2009 to 2016, three years as chair; employed in property management, Eyde Company, 1998 to 2008; Michigan Republican State Committee, two terms; executive committee member, Ionia County Republican Party; member, Republican Women's Federation of Michigan; precinct delegate; chair, Michigan Community Service Commission; vice chair, The Right Door; vice chair, ACSET Governing Board; member, Ionia County Board of Public Works; member, Ionia County Tax Allocation Board; active member, South Church, Lansing; elected to the House of Representatives, 2016 and 2018.

State Representative
SARA CAMBENSY
D–109th Representative District

Office: Room S-1488, Cora B. Anderson House Office Bldg., P.O. Box 30014, Lansing, MI 48909, (517) 373-0498

Committees: Commerce and Tourism (Minority Vice Chair); Natural Resources and Outdoor Recreation; Regulatory Reform

Biography: Democrat, of Marquette; bachelor's degree in education and a master's degree in public administration, Northern Michigan University; currently working on a Ph.D. in environmental and energy policy; director, adult education, Marquette Public Schools; Marquette city commissioner, 2012 to 2017; elected to the House of Representatives in a special election, November 7, 2017, reelected in 2018.

State Representative
DARRIN CAMILLERI
D–23rd Representative District

Office: Room S-787, Cora B. Anderson House Office Bldg., P.O. Box 30014, Lansing, MI 48909, (517) 373-0855, E-Mail: darrincamilleri@house.mi.gov

Committees: Commerce and Tourism; Education (Minority Vice Chair); Oversight

Biography: Democrat, of Brownstown; born January 28, 1992 in Dearborn; Catholic; bachelor of arts degree in political science, Kalamazoo College; Spanish immersion, Universidad San Francisco de Quito; co-chair, Michigan Latino Legislative Caucus; formerly employed by Brownstown Township as recreation commissioner; Social Studies teacher, team leader, and Freshman advisor, Consortium College Prep High School, 2014 to 2016; past state president, Michigan Federation of College Democrats; advisor, YMCA Michigan Youth in Government; intern, former U.S. Representative John D. Dingell; elected to the House of Representatives, 2016 and 2018; Democratic Whip.

State Representative
BRENDA CARTER
D–29th Representative District

Office: Room N-793, Cora B. Anderson House Office Bldg., P.O. Box 30014, Lansing, MI 48909, (517) 373-0475, Toll-Free: (855) 473-4635, Fax: (517) 373-5061, E-Mail: brendacarter@house.mi.gov

Committees: Education; Families, Children, and Seniors; Insurance

Biography: Democrat, of Pontiac; born September 10, 1954 in Detroit; spouse, Randy; six children; bachelor's degree in business administration from Spring Arbor University, master's degree in public administration, Oakland University; employed with General Motors; president, Pontiac Public Schools Board of Education; president, Michigan Association of School Boards; member, Benevolent Protective Order of Elks; elected to the House of Representatives, 2018.

State Representative
TYRONE CARTER
D–6th Representative District

Office: Room S-685, Cora B. Anderson House Office Bldg., P.O. Box 30014, Lansing, MI 48909, (517) 373-0823, Toll-Free: (844) 672-4264, E-Mail: tyronecarter@house.mi.gov

Committees: Education; Energy; Military, Veterans and Homeland Security

Biography: Democrat, of Detroit; born May 24, 1962 in River Rouge; Protestant; spouse, Lisa; children, Tyrone II (deceased) and Tyler; associate's degree from Henry Ford College and a bachelor's degree from Central Michigan University; employed with the Wayne County Sheriff's Office, 1984 to 2008, Wayne County Community College District, 2009 to 2010, Detroit Public Schools, 2011 to 2012, and Wayne State University Center for Urban Studies, 2015 to 2018; president, Original United Citizens of Southwest Detroit; board member, Adult Well Being Services; member, Downriver Delta; small business owner; elected to the House of Representatives, 2018.

State Representative
LEE CHATFIELD
R–107th Representative District

Office: Room 162, Capitol Bldg., P.O. Box 30014, Lansing, MI 48909, (517) 373-2629, Toll-Free: (855) 737-4107, E-Mail: leechatfield@house.mi.gov

Biography: Republican, of Levering; spouse, Stephanie; five children; bachelor's degree in history education, Northland International University; master's degree in public policy, Liberty University; high school teacher, coach, and athletic director, Northern Michigan Christian Academy in Burt Lake; member, Right to Life of Michigan, National Rifle Association, Michigan Coalition for Responsible Gun Owners, and Michigan Farm Bureau; vice chair, House Fiscal Agency Board of Governors; elected to the House of Representatives, 2014, 2016, and 2018; Speaker Pro Tempore, 2017 to 2018; Speaker of the House 2019; chair and alternate chair, Legislative Council.

State Representative
JOHN CHERRY
D–49th Representative District

Office: Room N-898, Cora B. Anderson House Office Bldg., P.O. Box 30014, Lansing, MI 48909, (517) 373-7515, Fax: (517) 373-5817, E-Mail: johncherry@house.mi.gov

Committees: Appropriations (Subcommittees: Health and Human Services; Joint Capital Outlay; Natural Resources and Environmental Quality (Minority Vice Chair))

Biography: Democrat, of Flint; born May 30, 1985 in Clio; Episcopalian; spouse, Teresa; child, Diana; bachelor's degree in environmental studies, University of Michigan, master's degree in public policy, Ford School, University of Michigan; performance management coordinator, 2012 to 2018, grants management, 2011 to 2012, and Office of Science and Policy, 2010 to 2011 in the Michigan Department of Natural Resources; owner, Flint Coffee Company; vice chair, Flint Charter Commission; member, College Cultural Neighborhood Association, past secretary, Flint Master Plan Advisory Committee; elected to the House of Representatives, 2018.

State Representative
JOHN CHIRKUN
D–22nd Representative District

Office: Room S-786, Cora B. Anderson House Office Bldg., P.O. Box 30014, Lansing, MI 48909, (517) 373-0854, Toll-Free: (844) 992-4475, E-Mail: johnchirkun@house.mi.gov

Committees: Communications and Technology; Military, Veterans and Homeland Security; Regulatory Reform (Minority Vice Chair)

Biography: Democrat, of Roseville; born September 11, 1952 in Detroit; spouse, Sharon; children, Jon and Denise; foster children, River and Cody; two grandchildren; Methodist; attended Macomb Community College and Highland Park Community College; graduate, State Police Instructor's School and Wayne County Police Academy; served in the United States Air Force, 1971 to 1977; Wayne County Sheriff's Department, 29 years; executive sergeant and commanding officer, Sheriff's Internet Crimes Unit and Special Operations Division; member, Roseville Optimist Club, Roseville Goodfellows, Friends of the Roseville Public Library, Roseville Historical and Genealogical Society, and Nautical Mile Handicapped Fishing Derby; member, Wayne County Police Lieutenants and Sergeants Association, Richmond Sportsmen's Club; former chair, Southeast Macomb Sanitary District and South Macomb Disposal Authority; member, Roseville City Council, 1995 to 2009; mayor, city of Roseville, 2009 to 2014; elected to the House of Representatives, 2014, 2016, and 2018.

State Representative
CARA CLEMENTE
D–14th Representative District

Office: Room N-693, Cora B. Anderson House Office Bldg., P.O. Box 30014, Lansing, MI 48909, (517) 373-0140, E-Mail: caraclemente@house.mi.gov

Committees: Financial Services; Health Policy; Transportation

Biography: Democrat, of Lincoln Park; born October 2, 1966; spouse, Paul; children, Joseph, Nathan and Emma; Roman Catholic; member, St. Frances Cabrini Parish, parish/school volunteer; bachelor's degree in elementary education, Master of Arts degree with an emphasis on reading, Eastern Michigan University; teacher, academic development coordinator, manager, Clemente's Restaurant Bar and Bowling; elected to the House of Representatives, 2016 and 2018; member, Legislative Council.

State Representative
TRISTON COLE
R–105th Representative District

Office: Room 153, Capitol Bldg., P.O. Box 30014, Lansing, MI 48909, (517) 373-0829, Toll-Free: (855) 347-8105, E-Mail: tristoncole@house.mi.gov

Committees: Government Operations (Vice Chair); Transportation

Biography: Republican, of Mancelona; born January 4, 1976 in Michigan; spouse, Stacy; children, Etta, Adalynne, and Ruby; attended Northwestern Michigan College and Ferris State University; small-business farm owner providing produce for local markets; semi-truck driver; 15 years experience in hunting and guiding industry; former chair, Antrim County Republican Party; past president, Antrim County Farm Bureau; member, East Port Baptist Church; House Fiscal Agency Board of Governors, 2019 to present; elected to the House of Representatives, 2014, 2016, and 2018. Majority Floor Leader 2019.

State Representative
KEVIN COLEMAN
D–16th Representative District

Office: Room N-695, Cora B. Anderson House Office Bldg., P.O. Box 30014, Lansing, MI 48909, (517) 373-2576, Fax: (517) 373-5962, E-Mail: kevincoleman@house.mi.gov

Committees: Agriculture; Communications and Technology (Minority Vice Chair); Insurance

Biography: Democrat, of Westland; born June 30, 1983 in Redford; Catholic; bachelor's degree, Western Michigan University; previously employed as a music instructor; member Westland City Council 2014 to 2017; member Westland Festival Committee and Westland Veterans Association; elected to the House of Representatives, 2018.

State Representative
KATHY CRAWFORD
R–38th Representative District

Office: Room S-887, Cora B. Anderson House Office Bldg., P.O. Box 30014, Lansing, MI 48909, (517) 373-0827, E-Mail: kathycrawford@house.mi.gov

Committees: Education; Families, Children, and Seniors (Chair); Local Government and Municipal Finance; Regulatory Reform

Biography: Republican, of Novi; born March 15, 1942 in Northville; spouse Hugh; children, Doug, Amy, and Kelly; four grandchildren; Protestant; senior citizen director, City of Novi, 27 years; small business owner; author; member, Novi Oaks American Business Women, Optimist International, Pavilion Shores Conservancy, and Michigan State Fair Steering Committee; chair, Novi Historical Commission; chair, West Oakland Republican Club, Oakland County Republican Executive Committee; member, Novi City Council, 2007 to 2010; commissioner, Oakland County, 2011 to 2014; elected to the House of Representatives, 2014, 2016, and 2018.

State Representative
GARY EISEN
R–81st Representative District

Office: Room S-1185, Cora B. Anderson House Office Bldg., P.O. Box 30014, Lansing, MI 48909, (517) 373-1790, Toll-Free: (855) REP-8181, Fax: (517) 373-9983, E-Mail: GaryEisen@house.mi.gov

Committees: Agriculture; Local Government and Local Municipal Finance; Natural Resources and Outdoor Recreation; Transportation (Vice Chair)

Biography: Republican, of St. Clair Township; born February 1, 1955 in City of St. Clair; spouse, Annie; children, Zachary and Bethany; attended Winona Technical College; owner, Eisen Inc., a welding and fabricating business; owner, Michigan Personal Protection Training; holds a 7th Dan Black Belt in martial arts, teaches martial arts; competitive shooter; national sport chair, AAU Target Shooting; St. Peter's Church, four years on church council; elected to the House of Representatives, 2018.

State Representative
BRIAN K. ELDER
D–96th Representative District

Office: Room S-1285, Cora B. Anderson House Office Bldg., P.O. Box 30014, Lansing, MI 48909, (517) 373-0158, Toll-Free: (866) 737-0096, E-Mail: brianelder@house.mi.gov

Committees: Agriculture (Minority Vice Chair); Judiciary

Biography: Democrat, of Bay City; born January 2, 1973 in Flint; Catholic; spouse, Susan; children, Brian, Daniel and Johanna; bachelor of arts degree in history, Wayne State University; juris doctorate, UCLA School of Law; owner, Brian K. Elder, PLC, 2006 to present, private practice attorney since 1998; Bay County Board of Commissioners, 2003 to 2010; Bay County Democratic Party, 17 years; member, Ancient Order of Hibernians, Knights of Columbus, and All Saints Catholic Parish; board of directors, Salvation Army; chair and cofounder of the Michigan Legislative Labor Caucus; elected to the House of Representatives, 2016 and 2018; member, Michigan Law Revision Commission.

State Representative
JIM ELLISON
D–26th Representative District

Office: Room N-790, Cora B. Anderson House Office Bldg., P.O. Box 30014, Lansing, MI 48909, (517) 373-3818, Toll-Free: (866) 585-2471, E-Mail: jimellison@house.mi.gov

Committees: Health Policy; Local Government and Municipal Finance (Minority Vice Chair); Tax Policy

Biography: Democrat, of Royal Oak; born January 7, 1952 in Royal Oak; spouse, Jodie; children, Emilie, Brian, Bradley, Sarah, Jonathan, Jacob, Madeline, and Isaac; 13 grandchildren; construction cost estimator, Ronnisch Construction Group and Barton Malow Company; business development, Royal Oak Storage; commissioner, City of Royal Oak, 1991 to 1995; mayor, City of Royal Oak, 2003 to 2016; member, Royal Oak Planning Commission, 2000 to 2016; chairman, Royal Oak Planning Commission, 2002 to 2003; chairman, Woodward Dream Cruise Liaison; president, Royal Oak Housing Commission; member, Greater Royal Oak Democratic Club, Oakland County Democratic Party, and Michigan Democratic Party; past president, Stagecrafters Community Theatre; past vice president, Royal Oak Longfellow School PTA; elected to the House of Representatives, 2016 and 2018.

State Representative
DIANA FARRINGTON
R–30th Representative District

Office: Room N-794, Cora B. Anderson House Office Bldg., P.O. Box 30014, Lansing, MI 48909, (517) 373-7768, E-Mail: dianafarrington@house.mi.gov

Committees: Financial Services (Chair); Judiciary; Regulatory Reform; Tax Policy

Biography: Republican, of Utica; born March 9, 1965 in Flint; member, Trinity Lutheran Church; spouse, Jeff; two sons; attended Macomb Community College and Oakland University; small business owner; mortgage quality control specialist; volunteer for church, school activities, and community groups; elected to the House of Representatives, 2016 and 2018.

State Representative
GRAHAM FILLER
R–93rd Representative District

Office: Room N-1197, Cora B. Anderson House Office Bldg., P.O. Box 30014, Lansing, MI 48909, (517) 373-1778, E-Mail: grahamfiller@house.mi.gov

Committees: Energy; Health Policy; Judiciary (Chair); Regulatory Reform

Biography: Republican, of DeWitt; born August 13, 1983 in Ovid; Protestant; spouse, Alicia; child, Claire; bachelor's degree in law, politics, history, Miami University, Ohio; juris doctor, Detroit Mercy Law School; Michigan Assistant Attorney General, 2011 to 2018; member, Farm Bureau, NRA, Right to Life of Clinton County, Northpointe Community Church; active with the Kiwanis, SafeCenter organization, and Big Brothers Big Sisters; elected to the House of Representatives, 2018.

State Representative
BEN FREDERICK
R–85th Representative District

Office: Room S-1189, Cora B. Anderson House Office Bldg., P.O. Box 30014, Lansing, MI 48909, (517) 373-0841, E-Mail: benfrederick@house.mi.gov

Committees: Energy; Health Policy (Vice Chair); Insurance; Regulatory Reform

Biography: Republican, of Owosso; born July 8, 1982 in Owosso; Presbyterian; spouse, Lydia; children, Devlin and Katie; bachelors in interdisciplinary studies, Liberty University; legislative staff for various Michigan legislators, 2002 to 2016; Owosso City council member, 2007 to 2016, mayor for seven years; managed several state-level election campaigns; member, Shiawassee Farm Bureau and Shiawassee and Saginaw Right to Life; Champion for Life, Shiawassee Pregnancy Center; member and 2012 Citizen of the Year, Shiawassee Regional Chamber of Commerce; life member, NRA; Shiawassee Conservation Association, Welcome Home Veterans, Inc., MCRGO, Friends of the Shiawassee River; member, Select Committee on Reducing Car Insurance Rates; elected to the House of Representatives, 2016 and 2018.

State Representative
LaTANYA GARRETT
D–7th Representative District

Office: Room S-686, Cora B. Anderson House Office Bldg., P.O. Box 30014, Lansing, MI 48909, (517) 373-2276, Toll-Free: (855) 647-3707, E-Mail: latanyagarrett@house.mi.gov

Committees: Families, Children, and Seniors (Minority Vice Chair); Health Policy

Biography: Democrat, of Detroit; born February 20, 1975; married, three children; graduate of Life Support Training Institute and Wayne County Community College; bachelor's degree from Davenport University; licensed first responder, community activist, and small business owner; elected to the House of Representatives, 2014, 2016, and 2018. Serves on the Legislative Council and Joint Committee on Administrative Rules.

State Representative
ALEX GARZA
D–12th Representative District

Office: Room N-691, Cora B. Anderson House Office Bldg., P.O. Box 30014, Lansing, MI 48909, (517) 373-0852, Toll-Free: (888) 737-4347, E-Mail: alexgarza@house.mi.gov

Committees: Agriculture; Local Government and Local Municipal Finance; Regulatory Reform

Biography: Democrat, of Taylor; born February 13, 1994 in Detroit; Catholic; associates degree from Baker College and bachelor's degree in political science from University of Michigan; legislative aide, Detroit City Council; field organizer, Organizing for America; director of constituent relations, Representative Stephanie Chang; elected to the Taylor City Council in 2013, president, Taylor City Council 2017 to 2018; member Taylor Rotary Club and Taylor Goodfellows; elected to the House of Representatives, 2018.

State Representative
SHERRY GAY-DAGNOGO
D–8th Representative District

Office: Room S-687, Cora B. Anderson House Office Bldg., P.O. Box 30014, Lansing, MI 48909, (517) 373-3815, Toll-Free: (888) 347-8008, E-Mail: sherrygay-dagnogo@house.mi.gov, Website: gay-dagnogo.housedems.com

Committees: Financial Services (Minority Vice Chair); Insurance

Biography: Democrat, of Detroit; born January 30, 1967 in Detroit; child, Jordan; Pentecostal; bachelor's and master's degrees in education, Wayne State University; education consultant; Detroit city council aide; former director of educational performance for United Way; member, Detroit public schools Board of Education; community organizer and public education advocate; education chair, National Congress of Black Women, Greater Detroit Chapter; vice president, North Rosedale Park Civic Association; steering committee member, Coalition of Labor Union Women; member, Fannie Lou Hamer; member, NAACP; elected to the House of Representatives, 2014, 2016, and 2018.

State Representative
ANNETTE GLENN
R–98th Representative District

Office: Room S-1287, Cora B. Anderson House Office Bldg., P.O. Box 30014, Lansing, MI 48909, (517) 373-1791, E-Mail: annetteglenn@house.mi.gov

Committees: Appropriations (Subcommittees: Health and Human Services; Licensing and Regulatory Affairs and Insurance and Financial Services (Vice Chair); Natural Resources and Environmental Quality (Vice Chair); School Aid and Department of Education)

Biography: Republican, of Midland; born November 19, 1963 in Boise, Idaho; Christian; spouse, Gary; five children and six grandchildren; bachelor's degree in public administration from Boise State University; former state high school champion in mile relay; former state Senate intern; state chair and national vice chair of College Republicans; former Congressional staff in the U.S. House of Representatives; former manager of Congressional, state Supreme Court, Lt. Governor, and multiple state House and Senate campaigns, regional coordinator for U.S. Senate campaign, and staff of Senator Bob Dole's 1988 presidential campaign; board member, Marketing Research Foundation; commercial real estate developer; former volunteer with Boy Scouts of America as den leader, cub master, committee member, and merit badge counselor; former treasurer, Midland Fleet Feet track team, Midland Flames basketball team, and Kairos Debate Club; member of Auburn Lions Club, associate member of Midland Blue Star Mothers, member of American Legion Auxiliary, Midland and Bay City post, and member of Midland, Pinconning-Linwood, and Sanford chambers of commerce; elected to the House of Representatives, 2018.

State Representative
PHIL GREEN
R–84th Representative District

Office: Room S-1188, Cora B. Anderson House Office Bldg., P.O. Box 30014, Lansing, MI 48909, (517) 373-0476, Toll-Free: (888) 254-5284, E-Mail: repphilgreen@house.mi.gov

Committees: Appropriations (Subcommittees: Agriculture and Rural Development; Health and Human Services (Vice Chair); Higher Education and Community Colleges; Natural Resources and Environmental Quality; School Aid and Department of Education)

Biography: Republican, of Millington; born June 11, 1977 in Flint; Baptist; spouse, Marun; children, Anthony, Tyler, and Laci K; bachelor's degree in Bible with a concentration in youth ministries and emphasis in sacred music from Pensacola Christian College; master's degree in Biblical Exposition from Pensacola Theological Seminary; doctorate work at Northland International University, Dunbar, Wisconsin in Sacred Ministry and Pensacola Graduate School in Education, Strategic Leadership; employed as assistant pastor/school administrator, Juniata Baptist Church and Christian School, Vassar, 2012 to 2018; senior pastor, First Baptist Church of Pavilion, New York, 2003 to 2012; coach, Pavilion Central School District, New York, 2004 to 2012; youth pastor, Wyldewood Baptist Church Wisconsin, 1999 to 2003; director, Upward Basketball league, K4-6th grade; coach, Upward Basketball; former board member, Tonawanda Valley Federal Credit Union, New York; chaplain, Genesee County Sheriff's Office and 2011 National Sheriff's Association Chaplin of the Year; former coach and official, AYSO; elected to the House of Representatives, 2018.

State Representative
CHRISTINE GREIG
D–37th Representative District

Office: Room 167, Capitol Bldg., P.O. Box 30014, Lansing, MI 48909, (517) 373-1793, Toll-Free: (888) 642-4037, E-Mail: christinegreig@house.mi.gov

Committee: Government Operations (Minority Vice Chair)

Biography: Democrat, of Farmington Hills; born January 11, 1963 in Plymouth, Indiana; spouse, Robert; children, Alexander, Andrew, and William; Roman Catholic; Bachelor's degree in American studies and computer applications, University of Notre Dame; formerly employed, Andersen Consulting, Chicago, Kmart Corporation, Troy, and Fulcrum Computer Services, Inc., Farmington Hills; member, St. Gerald Church, Detroit Duchess Club, USTA, Farmington/Farmington Hills Education Foundation, National Board of Advisors for Let America Vote, American Association of University Women, and League of Women Voters; member, Pentathlon Institute Board Member, Farmington/Farmington Hills Democratic Club, Oakland County Democratic Party, and Michigan Democratic Party; member, House Fiscal Agency Board of Governors; elected to the House of Representatives, 2014, 2016, and 2018; House Democratic Floor Leader, 2016 to 2017; House Democratic Leader, 2019.

State Representative
BETH GRIFFIN
R–66th Representative District

Office: Room S-1085, Cora B. Anderson House Office Bldg., P.O. Box 30014, Lansing, MI 48909, (517) 373-0839, Toll-Free: (800) 577-6212, E-Mail: bethgriffin@house.mi.gov

Committee: Ways and Means

Biography: Republican, of Mattawan; born June 14, 1967; spouse, Greg; two children; Christian; bachelor's degree in psychology, Indiana-Purdue at Fort Wayne University; master's degree in education and English, Old Dominion University; Michigan Excellence in Public Service series, certificate, 2013; teacher, special education and English, Parchment Middle School, 1999 to 2005; guest teacher, Mattawan Consolidated Schools, 2010 to 2015; Van Buren County Commissioner, 2012 to 2016; chair, Area Agency on Aging, Region IV, 2013 to 2016; board member, Southwest Michigan Planning Commission and Kalamazoo Area Transportation Study MPO, 2013 to 2016; Van Buren County drug treatment and mental health specialty courts, 2014 to 2016; precinct delegate, member, and executive committee member, Van Buren County Republican Party; member, Van Buren County Right to Life, Van Buren County Farm Bureau, Van Buren County Conservation Club, Paw Paw and South Haven Chambers of Commerce, Mattawan Lions Club; religious education teacher, St. John Bosco church; Wings of God; chair, Mattawan Area Food Pantry, 2010 to present; elected to the House of Representatives, 2016 and 2018.

State Representative
VANESSA GUERRA
D–95th Representative District

Office: Room N-1199, Cora B. Anderson House Office Bldg., P.O. Box 30014, Lansing, MI 48909, (517) 373-0152, Toll-Free: (855) 347-8095, E-Mail: vanessaguerra@house.mi.gov

Committees: Elections and Ethics (Minority Vice Chair); Judiciary

Biography: Democrat, of Saginaw; born September 14, 1989 in Saginaw; Catholic; bachelor's degrees in political science and Latino studies, University of Michigan; juris doctorate, University of Detroit Mercy School of Law; academic advisor, Delta Community College; member, Saginaw Chapter of the American GI Forum; member, Saginaw County Democratic Party; elected to the Bridgeport Charter Township Board, 2012; elected to the House of Representatives, 2014, 2016, and 2018.

State Representative
JIM HAADSMA
D–62nd Representative District

Office: Room N-996, Cora B. Anderson House Office Bldg., P.O. Box 30014, Lansing, MI 48909, (517) 373-0555, E-Mail: jimhaadsma@house.mi.gov

Committees: Energy; Transportation and Infrastructure

Biography: Democrat, of Battle Creek; born January 27, 1958 in Grand Rapids; Methodist; children, Tess, Stewart, Jon, and Jerry; bachelor's degree, Michigan State University; attended University of Denver; juris doctorate, Wayne State University Law School; legal aid of Western Michigan, 1984 to 1987; McCroskey Law PLC, 1987 to 2018; member, Calhoun County Board of Commissioners, four terms, 2009 to 2016; board member Kiwanis Club of Battle Creek, Art Center of Battle Creek, Haven of Rest Ministries, Urban League of Battle Creek, and Salvation Army; member, Calhoun County Bar Association, Battle Creek NAACP Legal Redress Chair; elected to the House of Representatives, 2018.

State Representative
MATT HALL
R–63rd Representative District

Office: Room N-997, Cora B. Anderson House Office Bldg., P.O. Box 30014, Lansing, MI 48909, (517) 373-1787, E-Mail: matthall@house.mi.gov, Website: www.repmatthall.com

Committees: Education; Oversight (Chair); Regulatory Reform; Tax Policy

Biography: Republican, of Emmett Township; born July 25, 1983; Christian; *cum laude*, bachelor's degree in business management and public administration, Western Michigan University; *magna cum laude*, juris doctor in Advanced Constitutional Advocacy, Western Michigan University Cooley Law School; member, Uniform Law Commission; business development representative, L-3 Combat Propulsion Systems, 2007 to 2011; West Michigan liaison, Michigan Attorney General's Office, 2011 to 2015; constitutional law attorney, 2018; elected to the House of Representatives, 2018.

State Representative
ABDULLAH HAMMOUD
D–15th Representative District

Office: Room N-694, Cora B. Anderson House Office Bldg., P.O. Box 30014, Lansing, MI 48909, (517) 373-0847, Toll-Free: (855) 775-1515, E-Mail: abdullahhammoud@house.mi.gov

Committees: Appropriations (Subcommittees: Health and Human Services (Minority Vice Chair); Judiciary; Licensing and Regulatory Affairs and Insurance and Financial Services)

Biography: Democrat, of Dearborn; born March 19, 1990 in Dearborn; Muslim; bachelor of science, University of Michigan, Dearborn; master of public health, University of Michigan, Ann Arbor; master of business administration, University of Michigan, Ross School of Business; lead analyst with Blue Care Network of Michigan, 2011 to 2012; health care consultant with the Center for Healthcare Research and Transformation, 2012 to 2014; senior strategic intelligence consultant with Health Alliance Plan/Henry Ford Health System, 2014 to 2016; member of the bylaws committee; chair, Arab American Democratic Caucus; member, Arab American Political Action Committee; elected to the House of Representatives, 2016 and 2018; Assistant Caucus Whip and Deputy Policy Chair 2017 to 2018; Policy and Messaging Chair 2019.

State Representative
ROGER HAUCK
R–99th Representative District

Office: Room S-1288, Cora B. Anderson House Office Bldg., P.O. Box 30014, Lansing, MI 48909, (517) 373-1789, E-Mail: rogerhauck@house.mi.gov

Committee: Ways and Means

Biography: Republican, of Mt. Pleasant; born October 8, 1961 in Beal City; Catholic; spouse, Raschelle; children, Matthew and Stacey; attended Central Michigan University; employed by Delfield for 24 years; owner, Quality Housing; trustee, Union Township, 2013 to 2016; assisted with campaigning for various individuals running for statewide office; member, Sacred Heart Catholic church; elected to the House of Representatives, 2016 and 2018.

State Representative
SHANE HERNANDEZ
R–83rd Representative District

Office: Room 351 Capitol Bldg., P.O. Box 30014, Lansing, MI 48909, (517) 373-0835, Fax: (517) 373-9876, E-Mail: shanehernandez@house.mi.gov

Committees: Appropriations (Chair), Joint Capital Outlay

Biography: Republican, of Port Huron; born August 23, 1982 in Port Huron; Christian; spouse, Renee; children, Kelsey and Kara; bachelor of science degree in architecture and masters of architecture with distinction, Lawrence Technological University; architectural designer, 2005 to 2013 and vice president of design since 2013 with SyDesign Architects; chair, St. Clair County Republican Party, 2013 to 2014; member, executive committee of 10th Congressional District Republican Party, 2013 to 2016; member, Michigan Republican Party State Committee, 2013 to 2016; treasurer, Blue Water District United Methodist Men; vice chair, Port Huron Housing Commission, 2014 to 2017; member; House Fiscal Agency Board of Governors Chair, 2019; member, Legislative Council; elected to the House of Representatives, 2016 and 2018.

State Representative
KEVIN HERTEL
D–18th Representative District

Office: Room N-697, Cora B. Anderson House Office Bldg., P.O. Box 30014, Lansing, MI 48909, (517) 373-1180, E-Mail: kevinhertel@house.mi.gov

Committee: Ways and Means

Biography: Democrat, of St. Clair Shores; born in 1985; spouse, Ann; Michigan State University; legislative analyst for Blue Cross Blue Shield of Michigan, 2004 to 2011; special assistant in the office of the president, Blue Cross Blue Shield of Michigan, 2011 to 2016; member, St. Clair Shores Waterfront Environmental Committee, St. Clair Shores Democratic Club; executive board member, 9th Congressional District Democratic Party; board of directors, Macomb County Care House; volunteer, Macomb County Special Olympics; elected to the House of Representatives, 2016 and 2018.

State Representative
JON HOADLEY
D–60th Representative District

Office: Room N-994, Cora B. Anderson House Office Bldg., P.O. Box 30014, Lansing, MI 48909, (517) 373-1785, Toll-Free: (888) 833-6636, E-Mail: jonhoadley@house.mi.gov

Committees: Appropriations (Minority Vice Chair) (Subcommittees: General Government; Health and Human Services; Higher Education and Community Colleges)

Biography: Democrat, of Kalamazoo; born August 14, 1983 in Vermillion, South Dakota; partner, Kris; bachelor's degree from James Madison College in social relations and bachelor's degree from the College of Arts and Letters in women's studies from Michigan State University; former executive director, National Stonewall Democrats; named 2015 Young Democrat of the Year; 2015 Friend of Nursing, 2015-2016 Legislative Session Conservation Champion from the Michigan League of Conservation Voters, 2016 ISAAC Public Ally of the Year, 2019 Jean Chabut Health Policy Champion, House Fiscal Agency Board of Governors, Minority Vice Chair, 2019; elected to the House of Representatives, 2014, 2016, and 2018.

State Representative
MICHELE HOITENGA
R–102nd Representative District

Office: Room S-1386, Cora B. Anderson House Office Bldg., P.O. Box 30014, Lansing, MI 48909, (517) 373-1747, E-Mail: michelehoitenga@house.mi.gov

Committees: Communications and Technology (Chair); Families, Children and Seniors; Insurance; Regulatory Reform

Biography: Republican, of Manton; born July 25, 1969 in Cadillac; Christian, spouse, Phil; children, Gregory and Tyler; degree in human service from Baker College; owner, oil and gas consulting business; mayor, city of Manton, 2013 to 2016, commissioner, Wexford County Planning Board; vice chair, Wexford County Republican Party; former treasurer and president, Manton Chamber of Commerce; elected to the House of Representatives, 2016 and 2018.

State Representative
RACHEL HOOD
D–76th Representative District

Office: Room N-1095, Cora B. Anderson House Office Bldg., P.O. Box 30014, Lansing, MI 48909, (517) 373-0822, Toll-Free: (855) 747-4946, Fax: (517) 373-5276, E-Mail: RachelHood@house.mi.gov

Committees: Appropriations (Subcommittees: Joint Capital Outlay, Military and Veterans Affairs and State Police; Natural Resources and Environmental Quality; School Aid and Department of Education)

Biography: Democrat, of Grand Rapids; born October 12, 1976 in Livonia; Presbyterian; spouse, David Petroelje; children, Evelyn and Ineke; bachelor's degree in social relations from James Madison College, Michigan State University; formerly employed by Dig Deep, a consulting firm; former executive director, West Michigan Environmental Action Council; former community relations manager, Metro Health Hospital; elected to the House of Representatives, 2018.

State Representative
KARA HOPE
D–67th Representative District

Office: Room S-1086, Cora B. Anderson House Office Bldg., P.O. Box 30014, Lansing, MI 48909, (517) 373-0587, Fax: (517) 373-9430, E-Mail: karahope@house.mi.gov

Committees: Commerce and Tourism; Elections and Ethics; Local Government and Municipal Finance

Biography: Democrat, of Holt; born Kara Margaret Henigan, April 9, 1974 in Ypsilanti; spouse Evan Hope; bachelor's degree Michigan State University, Phi Beta Kappa graduate, juris doctor Western Michigan University Cooley Law School; employed with the Ionia Sentinel-Standard, 1998 to 2000, Michigan Court of Appeals Prehearing Division, 2003 to 2005, defense litigation firm, 2005 to 2006, Cooley Law School, 2006 to 2012, solo law practice, 2015 to 2018; commissioner, Ingham County Board of Commissioners, 2012 to 2018; founding president and board member, Holt Community Arts Council; past board member, Mid-Michigan Environmental Action Council; executive board member, Capital Area College Access Network, 2013 to present; volunteer Holt Education Foundation, Sam Corey Senior Center Club, Elder Law of Michigan; elected to the House of Representatives, 2018.

State Representative
PAMELA HORNBERGER
R–32nd Representative District

Office: Room N-796, Cora B. Anderson House Office Bldg., P.O. Box 30014, Lansing, MI 48909, (517) 373-8931, E-Mail: pamelahornberger@house.mi.gov

Committees: Appropriations Subcommittee School Aid and Department of Education (Vice Chair); Education (Chair); Elections and Ethics; Health Policy

Biography: Republican, of Chesterfield Township; born May 17, 1968 in Mt. Clemens; Catholic; one daughter; bachelor's degree, Michigan State University; teacher certification, Wayne State University; master's of education, leadership, Saginaw Valley State University; employed, East China Public Schools, 1994 to 2016; Metrics Unlimited, Inc.; trustee, L'Anse Creuse Public Schools Board of Education, 2010 to 2016; elected to the House of Representatives, 2016 and 2018.

State Representative
GARY HOWELL
R–82nd Representative District

Office: Room S-1186, Cora B. Anderson House Office Bldg., P.O. Box 30014, Lansing, MI 48909, (517) 373-1800

Committees: Judiciary; Local Government and Municipal Finance; Natural Resources and Outdoor Recreation (Chair); Transportation

Biography: Republican, of North Branch; born October 27, 1947 in Swartz Creek; spouse, Cheryl; three children and four grandchildren; United Methodist; U.S. Army veteran (overseas duty in Korea); BA in economics and government, Michigan State University; J.D., University of Michigan Law School; retired township and village attorney; lifelong farmer, owner of Howell Farms Ltd.; member, Farm Bureau for 40 years; active supporter, 4-H and FFA; chairman, Lapeer County Road Commission, 2013 to 2016; past president, Lapeer County Intermediate Board of Education, 1998 to 2016, North Branch School Board, 1995 to 2000, and Lapeer County Bar Association, 1993 to 1994; chair, Republican State Policy Committee, 2015 to present; charter member, Lapeer County Economic Club; member, Lapeer County Historical Society, Lapeer and Imlay City Chambers of Commerce; life member, Lapeer American Legion Post 16 and Veterans of Foreign Wars Post 4139; elected to the House of Representatives in a special election in March 2016; reelected in November 2016 and 2018.

State Representative
MARK E. HUIZENGA
R–74th Representative District

Office: Room N-1093, Cora B. Anderson House Office Bldg., P.O. Box 30014, Lansing, MI 48909, (517) 373-8900, Fax: (517) 373-8697, E-Mail: markhuizenga@house.mi.gov

Committees: Appropriations (Subcommittees: General Government (Chair); Health and Human Services; Higher Education and Community Colleges; School Aid and Department of Education)

Biography: Republican, of Walker; born July 21, 1967 in Grand Rapids; Christian Reformed; spouse, Kristine; children, Elaina, Olivia, and Blake; bachelor's degree, business administration from Calvin College and master's degree, management from Aquinas College; board certified Medical Practice Executive, American College of Medical Practice Executives; Mark Huizenga Systems Consulting, LLC, 1997 to present; managing partner and founder, Key Green Solutions, LLC; director of Pediatrics Practices, Spectrum Health, Helen DeVos Children's Hospital, 2000 to 2002; director of reimbursement, ProCare Systems Inc., 2002 to 2003; risk group coordinator, Spectrum Health Care Management Group, 1998 to 2000; practice manager, Associates Family Medicine PC, 1993 to 1998; systems consultant, Schellenberg and Evers PC, 1992 to 1993; accounting systems manager, Van's Delivery Service, Inc., 1990 to 1993; commissioner, Walker City, 2011 to 2013, and mayor, Walker City, 2013 to 2018; elected to the House of Representatives, 2018.

State Representative
BRANDT IDEN
R–61st Representative District

Office: Room 372, Capitol Bldg., P.O. Box 30014, Lansing, MI 48909, (517) 373-1774, E-Mail: brandtiden@house.mi.gov

Committee: Ways and Means (Chair)

Biography: Republican, of Portage; born July 5, 1983 in Battle Creek; Catholic; bachelor's degrees in political science and economics, Kalamazoo College; president, Identity Management and Consulting Inc.; partner, Baron Builders Inc.; past board member, Discover Kalamazoo and Big Brothers Big Sisters; board member, Junior Achievement of Southwest Michigan; chairman emeritus, Kalamazoo Regional Chamber PAC; elected to Kalamazoo County Commission, two terms, 2010 to 2014; elected to the House of Representatives, 2014, 2016, and 2018.

State Representative
LARRY INMAN
R–104th Representative District

Office: Room S-1388 Cora B. Anderson House Office Bldg., P.O. Box 30014, Lansing, MI 48909, (517) 373-1766, Toll-Free: (800) 737-1046, E-Mail: larryinman@house.mi.gov

Biography: Republican, of Williamsburg; born April 10, 1954; member, Christ the King Church; associate's degree, Northwestern Michigan College; bachelor's degree, Northern Michigan University; retired vice president, Huntington National Bank, Traverse City; served on the Northwest Regional Airport Commission of Cherry Capital Airport, seven years, board chairman in 2008 and 2011; member, State of Michigan Community Corrections Board, ten years, board chairman from 1999 to 2014; member, Northwest Michigan Council of Governments Board of Directors, 16 years, board chairman from 2003 to 2014; Northern Michigan University Board of Trustees, six years; Michigan Association of Counties Board of Directors, six years, president, 2002 to 2003; National Association of Counties Finance and Intergovernmental Affairs Board, nine years, chair, five years; elected to the Grand Traverse County Board of Commissioners 1992 to 2014; elected to the House of Representatives, 2014, 2016, and 2018.

State Representative
CYNTHIA A. JOHNSON
D–5th Representative District

Office: Room S-589, Cora B. Anderson House Office Bldg., P.O. Box 30014, Lansing, MI 48909, (517) 373-0844, Toll-Free: (877) 877-9007, E-Mail: cynthiaajohnson@house.mi.gov

Committees: Agriculture; Families, Children and Seniors; Oversight (Minority Vice Chair)

Biography: Democrat, of Detroit; born August 19, 1958 in Detroit; lifelong Detroiter; mother of three children, Wallace, Tyhecia, and Henry Hoskins; bachelor's degree in business management, Walsh College, 1992; associates degree in general studies, Wayne County Community College; host of Stand Up Now with Cynthia A. Johnson, 2013 to present; corrections officer and probation and parole agent with the Michigan Department of Corrections, 1999 to 2012; elected to the House of Representatives, 2018.

State Representative
STEVE JOHNSON
R–72nd Representative District

Office: Room N-1091, Cora B. Anderson House Office Bldg., P.O. Box 30014, Lansing, MI 48909, (517) 373-0840, Toll-Free: (888) 347-8072, E-Mail: stevenjohnson@house.mi.gov

Committees: Communications and Technology (Vice Chair); Judiciary; Oversight; Tax Policy

Biography: Republican, of Wayland; born December 2, 1990 in Grand Rapids; Christian; associates degree, electronic systems technology, Community College of the Air Force; currently pursuing a M.A. in Public Policy, Liberty University; U.S. Air Force, nuclear missile maintenance, four years; deacon, Wayland Christian Reformed Church; Joint Committee on Administrative Rules; elected to the House of Representatives, 2016 and 2018.

State Representative
JEWELL JONES
D–11th Representative District

Office: Room N-690, Cora B. Anderson House Office Bldg., P.O. Box 30014, Lansing, MI 48909, (517) 373-0849, E-Mail: jewelljones@house.mi.gov

Committees: Military, Veterans and Homeland Security (Minority Vice Chair); Regulatory Reform

Biography: Democrat, of Inkster; born April 11, 1995 in Wayne; Spiritual Israelite; currently attending the University of Michigan, Dearborn; member of the 210th Military Police Battalion, Michigan Army National Guard; member, Inkster City Council, 2015 to 2016; Senior Deacon at the Spiritual Israel Church and Its Army; strategic consultant at the Coup Group; owner, HOLLA LLC; member, Inkster Task Force, Inkster Youth Coalition, Inkster Chamber of Commerce, Army Reserve Officers' Training Corps, the University of Michigan, Dearborn Black Student Union, and the Student Veteran Association; co-founder of DuBois Club; Executive Board member of UMD's National Society of Leadership and Success; elected to the House of Representatives, 2016 and 2018.

State Representative
BRONNA KAHLE
R–57th Representative District

Office: Room N-991, Cora B. Anderson House Office Bldg., P.O. Box 30014, Lansing, MI 48909, (517) 373-1706, E-Mail: bronnakahle@house.mi.gov

Committee: Ways and Means

Biography: Republican, of Adrian; born June 23, 1968 in Washington, D.C.; Christian, member Grace Point Church; spouse, Patrick; children, Benjamin (Savanna) and Rebekah; bachelor of science in business administration, Salisbury State University, Maryland; masters of business administration, Baker College; sales consultant, Pitney Bowes; sales manager, WOLC Radio; owner and operator of Partners at Home Senior Care; director, Adrian Senior Center; member, Habitat for Humanity Neighborhood Rehabilitation Initiative, Associated Charities of Lenawee, Lenawee Walk to End Alzheimer's; board member and vice chair, Adrian Symphony Orchestra; member, Adrian Area Chamber of Commerce and Zonta of Lenawee; elected to the House of Representatives, 2016 and 2018.

State Representative
SHERYL Y. KENNEDY
D–48th Representative District

Office: Room N-897, Cora B. Anderson House Office Bldg., P.O. Box 30014, Lansing, MI 48909, (517) 373-7557, Toll-Free: (888) 347-8048, Fax: (517) 373-5953, E-Mail: sherylkennedy@house.mi.gov

Committees: Appropriations (Subcommittees: Agriculture and Rural Development (Minority Vice Chair); Corrections; School Aid and Department of Education)

Biography: Democrat, of Davison; born August 6, 1966 in Flint; Episcopalian; spouse, Michael; children, David, Joe, and Karissa; attended Seattle Pacific University, bachelor's degree, Marygrove College, master's degree and Ph.D., Oakland University; K-12 music teacher, Armada Area Schools, 1988; secondary choral music, Davison Community Schools, 2001; assistant principal, Birmingham Public Schools, 2010; principal, Walled Lake Consolidated Schools, 2012 to 2018; lecturer, University of Michigan, Flint, 2010 to present; member, Foundation for Excellence, Walled Lake; member, St. Paul's Episcopal Church, Flint; elected to the House of Representatives, 2018.

State Representative
MATT KOLESZAR
D–20th Representative District

Office: Room N-699, Cora B. Anderson House Office Bldg., P.O. Box 30014, Lansing, MI 48909, (517) 373-3816, E-Mail: mattkoleszar@house.mi.gov

Committees: Education; Health Policy

Biography: Democrat, of Plymouth; born September 21, 1981 in Royal Oak; spouse, Kimberly; bachelor's degree in secondary education from Saginaw Valley State University and a master's degree in English studies for teachers from Eastern Michigan University; teacher with Airport Community Schools, 2006 to 2018; elected to the House of Representatives, 2018.

State Representative
PADMA KUPPA
D–41st Representative District

Office: Room N-890, Cora B. Anderson House Office Bldg., P.O. Box 30014, Lansing, MI 48909, (517) 373-1783, Toll-Free: (877) 248-0001, E-Mail: padmakuppa@house.mi.gov, Website: kuppa.housedems.com

Committees: Energy; Local Government and Municipal Finance

Biography: Democrat, of Troy; born August 10, 1965 in Bhilai, India; spouse, Sudhakar Tadepalli; daughter Shreekari and son Shreyas; Hindu; bachelor's degree in mechanical engineering, National Institute of Technology, Warangal, 1988; formerly employed, Faculty Student Association, SUNY Stony Brook; Carlson Marketing, Troy; Group-41 Online Marketing, Troy; Fiat Chrysler Automotive, Auburn Hills, TEK Systems/Ally Financial, Troy; member, Bharatiya Temple of Metropolitan Detroit; member, India Caucus/MIADC, Troy Democratic Club; Michigan Roundtable for Diversity and Inclusion, board member; Troy Historic Society, board president; co-founder and secretary, Troy-area Interfaith Group, 2005 to 2010; Women's Interfaith Solutions for Dialogue and Outreach in Metro Detroit, board and advisory board member, 2008 to 2017; MI-India Hall of Fame Inductee 2015; co-chair APA Caucus; MLBC Historian; Assistant Democratic Whip; planning commissioner, City of Troy, 2015 to 2018; zoning board of appeals, City of Troy, 2016 to 2017; Progressive Women's Caucus Equal Pay Taskforce, cochair; Bowhay Institute for Legislative Leadership Development fellow, 2019; elected to the House of Representatives, 2018.

State Representative
BEAU LaFAVE
R–108th Representative District

Office: Room S-1487, Cora B. Anderson House Office Bldg., P.O. Box 30014, Lansing, MI 48909, (517) 373-0156, E-Mail: beaulafave@house.mi.gov

Committees: Agriculture; Insurance; Judiciary (Vice Chair); Military, Veterans and Homeland Security (Chair); Oversight

Biography: Republican, of Iron Mountain; born June 27, 1992 in Iron Mountain; Catholic, bachelor's degree international relations/political economy, James Madison College, Michigan State University; one year, Wayne State Law School; formerly employed by Lakeside Builders; precinct delegate, Breitung Township, 2012 to present; intern, Michigan Republican Party and Dickinson County GOP; former voting member, Dickinson Area Community Foundation; former alter server, Immaculate Conception Parish; member, Select Committee on Reducing Car Insurance Rates; elected to the House of Representatives, 2016 and 2018.

State Representative
DAVID LaGRAND
D–75th Representative District

Office: Room N-1094, Cora B. Anderson House Office Bldg., P.O. Box 30014, Lansing, MI 48909, (517) 373-2668, Toll-Free: (888) 750-3326, E-Mail: davidlagrand@house.mi.gov

Committees: Judiciary (Minority Vice Chair); Oversight

Biography: Democrat, of Grand Rapids; spouse Melissa, four children; Eastern Avenue Christian Reform church; bachelor's degree in history, Calvin College; attended University of Michigan; law degree, University of Chicago; small business owner, construction, coffee shop and bakery, law firm, farm, distillery; worked as a lawyer at Warner, Norcross and Judd; Kent County assistant prosecutor; Grand Rapids City Commission, Grand Rapids Board of Education; elected to the House of Representatives in a special election March 2016, reelected November 2016 and 2018.

State Representative
DONNA LASINSKI
D–52nd Representative District

Office: Room S-986, Cora B. Anderson House Office Bldg., P.O. Box 30014, Lansing, MI 48909, (517) 373-0828, Toll-Free: (855) 627-5052, E-Mail: donnalasinski@house.mi.gov

Committees: Energy (Minority Vice Chair); Insurance; Tax Policy

Biography: Democrat, of Scio Township; born November 3, 1968 in Detroit; spouse, Mike; children, Alec, Nate, and Jack; bachelor's degree in business administration, University of Michigan, master of business administration, Northwestern University; professional management consultant, owner of ThinkStretch, serving schools in 38 states with a summer learning program; Treasurer, Ann Arbor public schools board of trustees; Friends of Education, Washtenaw County; Granholm Appointee, Early Learning Advisory Council, Great Start Collaborative; Michigan Political Leadership Program, 2011; Select Committee on Reducing Car Insurance Rates, Minority Vice Chair, 2019; elected to the House of Representatives, 2016 and 2018.

State Representative
ERIC LEUTHEUSER
R–58th Representative District

Office: Room N-992, Cora B. Anderson House Office Bldg., P.O. Box 30014, Lansing, MI 48909, (517) 373-1794, Toll-Free: (866) 362-8812, E-Mail: ericleutheuser@house.mi.gov

Committee: Ways and Means

Biography: Republican, of Hillsdale; born October 8, 1959 in Hillsdale; spouse, Laura; children, Anna, Clara, and Grace; multiple grandchildren; member, St. Anthony Catholic Church; bachelor's degree in political economy, Hillsdale College; former president, Leutheuser Buick GMC; member of Hillsdale County Rotary Club, member of Hillsdale County Right to Life; previously served on board of Hillsdale County Community Foundation and Hillsdale Economic Development Commission; elected to the House of Representatives, 2014, 2016, and 2018.

State Representative
FRANK LIBERATI
D–13th Representative District

Office: Room S-692, Cora B. Anderson House Office Bldg., P.O. Box 30014, Lansing, MI 48909, (517) 373-0845, Toll-Free: (866) 737-1313, E-Mail: frankliberati@house.mi.gov

Committees: Families, Children, and Seniors; Health Policy (Minority Vice Chair); Regulatory Reform

Biography: Democrat, of Allen Park; born February 7, 1964; spouse, Nina; children, Nick, Angelo, and Antonio; member, St. Frances Cabrini Parish; bachelor's degree, Michigan State University; president, Allen Park school board, 2004 to 2012, president, Allen Park School Board, 2006 to 2012; owner of Liberati's Italian Deli and Bakery; board of directors, Fragile X Association of Michigan; elected to the House of Representatives, 2014, 2016, and 2018.

State Representative
SARAH LIGHTNER
R–65th Representative District

Office: Room N-999, Cora B. Anderson House Office Bldg., P.O. Box 30014, Lansing, MI 48909, (517) 373-1775, E-Mail: sarahlightner@house.mi.gov

Committees: Appropriations (Subcommittees: Corrections; General Government (Vice Chair); Judiciary (Vice Chair); Licensing and Regulatory Affairs and Insurance and Financial Services)

Biography: Republican, of Springport; born April 15, 1982 in Lansing; Christian; spouse David; children, Eli and Gavin; paralegal program, Lansing Community College; criminal defense paralegal, Wm. Burt Burleson, PLLC, 2004 to 2015; commissioner, Jackson County, three terms; member, Springport FFA Alumni and Boosters, Jackson County Fair Board, and Farm Bureau Young Farmer; elected to the House of Representatives, 2018.

State Representative
JIM LILLY
R–89th Representative District

Office: Room 374 Capitol Bldg., P.O. Box 30014, Lansing, MI 48909, (517) 373-0838, E-Mail: jimlilly@house.mi.gov

Committees: Government Operations; Ways and Means (Vice Chair)

Biography: Republican, of Park Township; born September 30, 1981 in Ypsilanti; Christian; spouse, Sarah; bachelor's degree in economics, John Carroll University; currently attending Grand Valley State University, master's of business administration; commercial banker, Macatawa Bank and Bank of Holland; involved with Greater Ottawa County United Way, Community Foundation of the Holland Zeeland Area, West Coast Chamber of Commerce, and Holland Young Professionals; former board member of the Lakeshore 504 Certified Development Corporation, the Holland Professional Club, and the Holland Area Arts Council; member, Legislative Council; elected to the House of Representatives, 2016 and 2018.

State Representative
LESLIE LOVE
D–10th Representative District

Office: Room S-689, Cora B. Anderson House Office Bldg., P.O. Box 30014, Lansing, MI 48909, (517) 373-0857, Toll-Free: (855) 568-3010, E-Mail: leslielove@house.mi.gov

Committees: Appropriations (Subcommittees: Health and Human Services; Transportation; Joint Capitol Outlay (Minority Vice Chair)

Biography: Democrat, of Detroit; born July 8 in Detroit; United Church of Christ; bachelor's degree, Siena Heights University; master's degrees in human resources management and fine arts, Marygrove College and Wayne State University; theater operations director and adjunct professor, Marygrove College; adjunct professor, Wayne County Community College District; co-chair. Michigan Legislative Sportsmen's Caucus; member, Progressive Women's Caucus; executive vice chair, Michigan Legislative Black Caucus; member, Detroit Caucus, Greater Wayne County Caucus, Michigan Labor Caucus, Great Lakes – St. Lawrence Legislative Caucus, Michigan Democratic Party State Central Alternate, Detroit Wayne Port Authority Committee, and 14th Congressional District Party Organization; National Conference of State Legislatures Labor and Economic Development Committee; elected to the House of Representatives, 2014, 2016, and 2018.

State Representative
JAMES LOWER
R–70th Representative District

Office: Room S-1089, Cora B. Anderson House Office Bldg., P.O. Box 30014, Lansing, MI 48909, (517) 373-0834, Toll-Free: (866) 347-8070, E-Mail: jameslower@house.mi.gov

Committees: Energy; Health Policy; Local Government and Municipal Finance (Chair); Tax Policy (Vice Chair)

Biography: Republican, of Greenville; born April 10, 1989 in Grand Rapids; Catholic, parishioner, Nativity of the Lord Parish; spouse, Kristen; bachelor's of arts in economics, Michigan State University; master's degree in business administration, Grand Valley State University; director of operations, Mitchell Research and Communications; village manager, village of Edmore; vice chair, Ionia County Board of Commissioners; legislative director, Senator Judy Emmons; legislative staff, Michigan House of Representatives; Montcalm County Republican Party; campaign manager, senate page, and house intern; executive committee member, Montcalm Economic Alliance; lifetime member, NRA; member, Michigan Capitol Committee; elected to the House of Representatives, 2016 and 2018.

State Representative
MATT MADDOCK
R–44th Representative District

Office: Room N-893, Cora B. Anderson House Office Bldg., P.O. Box 30014, Lansing, MI 48909, (517) 373-2616

Committees: Appropriations (Subcommittees: Corrections; Joint Capital Outlay; Judiciary; Transportation (Chair))

Biography: Republican, of Milford; born December 10, 1965; Christian; spouse, Meshawn; children, Gunther, Winsome, and Parker; attended Oakland Community College; private investigator, bail bondsman, small business owner, 28 years; founder, the Michigan Conservative Coalition; member, Milford Men's club and Cornerstone Highland Church; chair, Joint Committee on Administrative Rules; elected to the House of Representatives, 2018.

State Representative
MARI MANOOGIAN
D–40th Representative District

Office: Room S-889, Cora B. Anderson House Office Bldg., P.O. Box 30014, Lansing, MI 48909, (517) 373-8670, Toll-Free: (855) 373-8670, Fax: (517) 373-5868, E-Mail: marimanoogian@house.mi.gov, Website: manoogian.housedems.com

Committees: Commerce and Tourism; Energy; Military, Veterans and Homeland Security

Biography: Democrat, of Birmingham, born September 3, 1992 in Birmingham; Armenian Apostolic Orthodox; bachelor's degree, international affairs and security policy, master's degree global communication and public diplomacy, The George Washington University; attended Michigan State University; intern, U.S. Representative John Dingell and U.S. Mission to the United Nations; office coordinator and digital engagement manager, U.S. Department of State; former director of operations, Washington Area Model UN Conference; former delegate, Stanford U.S.-Russia Forum; member, Oakland Democratic Party, ACLU, Sierra Club, Moms Demand Action; elected to the House of Representatives, 2018.

State Representative
STEVE MARINO
R–24th Representative District

Office: Room S-788, Cora B. Anderson House Office Bldg., P.O. Box 30014, Lansing, MI 48909, (517) 373-0113, E-Mail: stevemarino@house.mi.gov

Committees: Commerce and Tourism (Chair); Elections and Ethics; Local Government and Municipal Finance (Vice Chair); Military, Veterans and Homeland Security

Biography: Republican, of Harrison Township; born March 24, 1989 in Detroit; Catholic; bachelor of arts degrees in economics, public policy and public administration, and political theory and constitutional democracy, Michigan State University; president, Campaign Finance Strategies; government relations coordinator, Delta Dental of Michigan, Ohio, and Indiana; Macomb County Board of Commissioners, 2014 to 2016; Harrison Township Zoning Board of Appeals; co-chair, Operation Rx, Legislative Steering Committee; and member, Public Policy Committee; Macomb County Chamber of Commerce; board of directors, L'Anse Creuse Foundation; co-chair, L'Anse Creuse Community Action Coalition; elected to the House of Representatives, 2016 and 2018.

State Representative
GREG MARKKANEN
R–110th Representative District

Office: Room S-1489, Cora B. Anderson House Office Bldg., P.O. Box 30014, Lansing, MI 48909, (517) 373-0850, Toll-Free: (888) 663-4031, Fax: (517) 373-9303, E-Mail: gregmarkkanen@house.mi.gov

Committees: Education; Energy; Insurance (Vice Chair); Military, Veterans and Homeland Security

Biography: Republican, of Hancock; born March 7, 1958 in Cloquet, Minnesota; Lutheran; spouse, Jane; children, Kalle, and Maija; bachelor's degrees in biology and social sciences from Michigan Technological University, bachelor's degrees in history and political science from Northern Michigan University; has taught special education and social studies; social science and biology instructor, Gogebic Community College; served as a Teacher-Ranger-Teacher with Keweenaw National Historical Park working directly with its Youth Conservation Corps; United States Army, 82nd Airborne Division, 452nd Combat Support Hospital and Michigan Army National Guard's 107th Engineer Battalion (combined 26 years); member, Hancock City Council, 2015 to 2016; member, Gloria Dei Lutheran Church; served with the Copper County AmeriCorps Program; coach, Copper Country History SmackDown; elected to the House of Representatives, 2018.

State Representative
LUKE MEERMAN
R–88th Representative District

Office: Room N-1192, Cora B. Anderson House Office Bldg., P.O. Box 30014, Lansing, MI 48909, (517) 373-1830, Toll-Free: (888) MICH-088, Fax: (517) 373-0292, E-Mail: lukemeerman@house.mi.gov

Committees: Agriculture (Vice Chair); Commerce and Tourism; Families, Children and Seniors, Local Government and Municipal Finance

Biography: Republican, of Coopersville; born March 8, 1975 in Coopersville; Baptist; spouse, Victoria; children, Julie, Esther, Anthony, Samantha, and Kennett, Michigan State University Great Lakes Leadership Academy, 2011 to 2012; dairy farmer; owner, A&L Machinery and Repair; member, executive committee, Ottawa County Republican Party, 2013 to 2018; member, board of directors, Healthy Water Rural Pride, 2012 to present; member, Ottawa County Republican Party executive board of directors, 2012 to present; former trustee, Polkton Township, 2012 to 2018; member, Ottawa County Farmland Preservation board, 2011 to present; member, Critter Barn Zeeland Board, 2009 to present; member, Ottawa County Farm Bureau, 2007 to present; member, Ottawa County Farmland Preservation, 2001 to present; former co-chair, Committee on Communication, Ottawa County Farm Bureau; member, American Cheese Society; member, Michigan Farm Bureau; former chair, Outreach Committee, Ottawa County Republican Party; vice president, Ottawa County Farm Bureau board of directors, 2007 to 2013; co-chair, Breakfast on the Farm, 2011; elected to the House of Representatives, 2018.

State Representative
AARON MILLER
R–59th Representative District

Office: Room N-993, Cora B. Anderson House Office Bldg., P.O. Box 30014, Lansing, MI 48909, (517) 373-0832, Toll-Free: (877) 262-5959, E-Mail: aaronmiller@house.mi.gov

Committees: Appropriations (Vice Chair) (Subcommittees: School Aid and Department of Education (Chair); Transportation)

Biography: Republican, of Sturgis; born June 14, 1987 in Sturgis; spouse, Alexandria; daughters, Jael, Leah, and Anna; attends Grace Christian Fellowship; bachelor's degrees in political science, social studies and mathematics secondary education, Western Michigan University; master's degree in school administration, Bethel College, Indiana; mathematics teacher, Northridge High School, Middlebury, Indiana; former tennis, track, and cross country coach; elected to the House of Representatives, 2014, 2016, and 2018.

State Representative
MIKE MUELLER
R–51st Representative District

Office: Room S-985, Cora B. Anderson House Office Bldg., P.O. Box 30014, Lansing, MI 48909, (517) 373-1780, Toll-Free: (866) 989-5151, Fax: (517) 373-5810, E-Mail: mikemueller@house.mi.gov

Committees: Agriculture; Energy; Health Policy; Military, Veterans and Homeland Security (Vice Chair)

Biography: Republican, of Linden; born September 30, 1974 in Linden; Christian; Spouse, Angela Acox Mueller; four children, Olivia, Owen, Cole, and Ryan; Bachelor of Science in Criminology from Eastern Michigan University; U.S. Navy veteran, 1993 to 1997; employed as a Sheriff Deputy with Livingston and Washtenaw counties, 2000 to 2018; fruit grower, Mueller's Orchard and Cider Mill; elected to the House of Representatives, 2018.

State Representative
SHELDON NEELEY
D–34th Representative District

Office: Room N-798, Cora B. Anderson House Office Bldg., P.O. Box 30014, Lansing, MI 48909, (517) 373-8808, E-Mail: sheldonneeley@house.mi.gov

Committee: Ways and Means

Biography: Democrat, of Flint; born September 20, 1968; Baptist; bachelor of arts, Saginaw Valley State University; associates degree, Delta College; retired broadcast engineer, WJRT-TV12; member, Flint Civil Service Commission, four years; member, Flint City Council, three terms; elected to the House of Representatives, 2014, 2016, and 2018.

State Representative
JACK O'MALLEY
R–101st Representative District

Office: Room S-1385, Cora B. Anderson House Office Bldg., P.O. Box 30014, Lansing, MI 48909, (517) 373-0825, Toll Free: (855) 347-8101

Committees: Education; Energy; Tax Policy; Transportation (Chair)

Biography: Republican, of Lake Ann; born September 9, 1959 in Detroit; Christian; spouse, Robin; children, Beth, Grace, and Zane; attended Henry Ford Community College and Wayne State University; graduated from Specs Howard School of Media Arts; has worked in radio since 1980; member, community corrections board; charter member, Silent Observer Board; chair of local July 4th celebration committee; coach, high school softball; volunteer, Hospice of Michigan and Child and Family Services of Northwest Michigan; Chaplin, the Sons of the American Legion Squadron Post 531, Copemish; elected to the House of Representatives, 2018.

State Representative
KRISTY PAGAN
D–21st Representative District

Office: Room S-785, Cora B. Anderson House Office Bldg., P.O. Box 30014, Lansing, MI 48909, (517) 373-2575, E-Mail: kristypagan@house.mi.gov

Committees: Appropriations (Subcommittees: Corrections (Minority Vice Chair); Judiciary; School Aid and Department of Education (Minority Vice Chair)

Biography: Democrat, of Canton; born September 5, 1982 in Belleville; bachelor's degrees in health education and women's studies, Western Michigan University; master's degree in political management, The George Washington University; associate director of development, Wayne State University Law School; owner, KP Consulting, LLC, in Canton; legislative aide for U.S. Senator Debbie Stabenow; board of directors, Canton Community Foundation; Advisory Council of Youth Leadership Canton; advisor, Lead Like a Girl, Canton; volunteer, STEM program Canton High School; chair, Women's Information Network; elected to the House of Representatives, 2014, 2016, and 2018; chair, Michigan Legislative Progressive Women's Caucus.

State Representative
BRAD PAQUETTE
R–78th Representative District

Office: Room N-1097, Cora B. Anderson House Office Bldg., P.O. Box 30014, Lansing, MI 48909, (517) 373-1796, Toll-Free: (888) 373-0078, Fax: (517) 373-5918, E-Mail: bradpaquette@house.mi.gov

Committees: Education (Vice Chair); Elections and Ethics; Insurance; Local Government and Municipal Finance

Biography: Republican, of Niles; born May 24, 1987 in Marquette; Christian; bachelor's degree, political science/prelaw, Northern Michigan University; master's degree, art of teaching from Andrews University; civics and Spanish teacher, Niles New Tech at Niles Community Schools for six years; planning commission, City of Niles; elected to the House of Representatives, 2018.

State Representative
RONNIE D. PETERSON
D–54th Representative District

Office: Room S-988, Cora B. Anderson House Office Bldg., P.O. Box 30014, Lansing, MI 48909, (517) 373-1771, Toll-Free: (855) 347-8054, E-Mail: ronniepeterson@house.mi.gov

Committees: Appropriations (Subcommittees: Licensing and Regulatory Affairs and Insurance and Financial Services (Minority Vice Chair); Military and Veterans Affairs and State Police; Transportation (Minority Vice Chair))

Biography: Democrat, of Ypsilanti; born July 7, 1952 in Ypsilanti; bachelor's degree in Community Development/Public Administration from Central Michigan University; Washtenaw County Commissioner, 2001 to 2016; former member, Ypsilanti City Council; former President of the Ypsilanti Breakfast Optimist Club; former Vice President and Treasurer of the Ypsilanti Area Jaycees; board member, Washtenaw County United Way; advisory council member, Foster Grandparents Program; policy council member, Washtenaw County Head Start; member, The Corner Health Center, Full Circle Community Center, and Washtenaw County Council for Children; elected to the House of Representatives, 2016 and 2018.

State Representative
LAURIE POHUTSKY
D–19th Representative District

Office: Room N-698, Cora B. Anderson House Office Bldg., P.O. Box 30014, Lansing, MI 48909, (517) 373-3920, E-Mail: lauriepohutsky@house.mi.gov

Committees: Health Policy; Natural Resources and Outdoor Recreation

Biography: Democrat, of Livonia; born April 28, 1988 in Detroit; bachelor's degree in microbiology, Michigan State University; employed in food safety, health care and drug testing commercial and clinical laboratories; member, Livonia Democratic Club, Indivisible Michigan, and Indivisible District 11; volunteer, Angela Hospice; elected to the House of Representatives, 2018.

State Representative
YOUSEF RABHI
D–53rd Representative District

Office: Room 141, Capitol Bldg., P.O. Box 30014, Lansing, MI 48909, (517) 373-2577, E-Mail: yousefrabhi@house.mi.gov, Website: rabhi.housedems.com

Committee: Government Operations

Biography: Democrat, of Ann Arbor; born June 9, 1988 in Ypsilanti; bachelors of science in environmental science, University of Michigan, 2010; outreach assistant, city of Ann Arbor Natural Area Preservation, 2012 to 2014; volunteer coordinator, University of Michigan Matthaei Botanical Gardens and Nichols Arboretum, 2014 to 2016; Washtenaw County Commissioner, working session chair, 2011 to 2012, chairman of the board, 2013 to 2014; and vice chairman of the board, 2015 to 2016; Washtenaw County Agricultural Lands Preservation Advisory Committee, six years; Washtenaw County Brownfield Redevelopment Authority, six years; Southeast Michigan Council of Governments, six years; Washtenaw Area Transportation Study Committee, six years; Washtenaw County Board of Public Works, five years; Washtenaw County Food Policy Council, four years; Washtenaw County Statutory Drainage Board, four years; chairman, Washtenaw Urban County, four years; member, House Fiscal Agency Board of Governors, 2019; and Legislative Council; elected to the House of Representatives, 2016 and 2018. Elected House Democratic Floor Leader, 2018.

State Representative
JOHN REILLY
R–46th Representative District

Office: Room N-895, Cora B. Anderson House Office Bldg., P.O. Box 30014, Lansing, MI 48909, (517) 373-1798, E-Mail: johnreilly@house.mi.gov

Committees: Commerce and Tourism; Education; Natural Resources and Outdoor Recreation; Oversight (Vice Chair)

Biography: Republican, of Oakland Township; born January 31, 1958 in Detroit; Roman Catholic; spouse, Karen, four adult children, two grandchildren; associates degree, automotive technology engineering, Oakland Community College; business owner, Log Cabin Handyman, 12 years; former automotive engineer, 20 years; precinct delegate, member, Oakland County Republican Party; elected to the House of Representatives, 2016 and 2018.

State Representative
DAIRE RENDON
R–103rd Representative District

Office: Room S-1387, Cora B. Anderson House Office Bldg., P.O. Box 30014, Lansing, MI 48909, (517) 373-3817, E-Mail: dairerendon@house.mi.gov

Committees: Families, Children and Seniors (Vice Chair); Insurance (Chair); Judiciary; Natural Resources and Outdoor Recreation

Biography: Republican, of Lake City; born May 26, 1952 in Camp LeJeune, North Carolina; Catholic; spouse, Bruce; two daughters, three grandchildren; attended Grand Rapids Community College, Northwestern Michigan College, and Mid-Michigan Community College; formerly employed by the Social Security Administration and the Cadillac Credit Bureau; owner, Check Alert Systems, 1988 to 2012; owner, Dragon Payment Systems, Inc. since 2001; former chair, Missaukee County Republican Party and current precinct delegate, Lake Township; Vice Chair, Select Committee on Reducing Car Insurance Rates, 2019; elected to the House of Representatives, 2016 and 2018.

State Representative
ISAAC ROBINSON
D–4th Representative District

Office: Room S-588, Cora B. Anderson House Office Bldg., P.O. Box 30014, Lansing, MI 48909, (517) 373-1008, Toll-Free: (855) 654-0404, Fax: (517) 373-5995

Committees: Commerce and Tourism; Regulatory Reform; Tax Policy

Biography: Democrat, of Detroit; born August 21, 1975 in Eloise; Catholic; attended University of Michigan-Dearborn and University of Michigan-Ann Arbor; graduate Northwestern Law, attorney at law; advisory board chair, American Human Rights Council; member, Phi Beta Sigma Fraternity, Inc.; volunteer, ARC Detroit; former political director, Michigan Teamsters Union; lifetime member Detroit branch NAACP, elected to the House of Representatives, 2018.

State Representative
TERRY J. SABO
D–92nd Representative District

Office: Room N-1196, Cora B. Anderson House Office Bldg., P.O. Box 30014, Lansing, MI 48909, (517) 373-2646, Toll-Free: (877) 411-3684, E-Mail: terrysabo@house.mi.gov

Committees: Appropriations (Subcommittees: Agriculture and Rural Development; Corrections; General Government (Minority Vice Chair));

Biography: Democrat, of Muskegon; born November 8, 1966 in Ravenna; spouse, Denise; children, Ryan, Bianca, Aubree, and Garret; seven grandchildren; United States Air Force, security policeman; fire fighter and police officer, City of Muskegon Heights, 25 years; employed part-time, City of North Muskegon Police Department and the Muskegon County Sheriff's Department; four years, Muskegon County Commissioner, chair, 2015 to 2016; Muskegon County Road Commissioner; member, Veterans of Foreign Wars Auxiliary Post 8846, American Legion Post 9, Muskegon Northside Lions Club, and Muskegon Heights Optimist Club; served on WWII Legends Flight committee in 2014; member, Select Committee on Reducing Car Insurance Rates, 2019; elected to the House of Representatives, 2016 and 2018.

State Representative
ANDREA K. SCHROEDER
R–43rd Representative District

Office: Room N-892, Cora B. Anderson House Office Bldg., P.O. Box 30014, Lansing, MI 48909, (517) 373-0615, Toll-Free: (888) 737-4043, E-Mail: andreaschroeder@house.mi.gov

Committees: Commerce and Tourism; Energy; Financial Services (Vice Chair); Oversight; Tax Policy

Biography: Republican, of Independence Township; born June 2, 1964 in Detroit; Catholic; spouse, Mark; children, Maggie, Luke, and Grace; bachelor's degree in education, Miami University, 1982 to 1986; master's degree coursework in education, Wheelock College; Michigan Political Leadership Program, Michigan State University, 2006; kindergarten teacher, 1987 to 1990; global director of strategic alliances, Oakwood Worldwide, 1991 to 2001; vice president of business development, Knowledge Management Group, 2002 to 2003; director of investor relations, Blackford Capital, 2013 to 2014; partner, Strategic Five Business Solutions, 2003 to 2018; trustee, Independence Township, 2012 to 2018; vice chair, ACE Academy SDA, charter school, Highland Park; president, Clarkston Area Optimists; former president, Clarkston District PTA Council; Distinguished Service Award, Clarkston Community Schools; former legislative liaison, Michigan PTA; pre-K and kindergarten teacher, Christ the Redeemer Catholic Church, 2002 to present; elected to the House of Representatives, 2018.

State Representative
NATE SHANNON
D–25th Representative District

Office: Room S-789, Cora B. Anderson House Office Bldg., P.O. Box 30014, Lansing, MI 48909, (517) 373-2275, Fax: (517) 373-5910, E-Mail: nateshannon@house.mi.gov

Committees: Energy; Transportation

Biography: Democrat, of Sterling Heights; born December 10, 1974 in Pocahontas, Iowa; Lutheran; spouse, Lori; children, Madilyn, Brodie, and Elisabeth; bachelor's degree in political science from Oakland University; master's degree in teaching from Wayne State University; teacher, L'Anse Creuse Public Schools, 2010 to 2018; elected to the House of Representatives, 2018.

State Representative
JASON SHEPPARD
R–56th Representative District

Office: Room H-375 Capitol Bldg., P.O. Box 30014, Lansing, MI 48909, (517) 373-2617, E-Mail: jasonsheppard@house.mi.gov

Committees: Appropriations (Subcommittee: Joint Capital Outlay); Elections and Ethics (Vice Chair); Financial Services; Government Operations (Chair); Transportation

Biography: Republican, of Temperance; born August 25, 1978 in Toledo, Ohio; spouse Melissa; member, Wyldewood Baptist Church; attended Michigan State University and University of Toledo; owner, Husky Snow Removal; commercial real estate agent, Signature Associates, 2009 to present; Monroe County Commissioner, 2011 to 2014; member, Bedford Business Association, Exchange Club, Monroe County Chamber of Commerce, and Hungarian American Fellowship; member, Monroe County Republican Party; elected to Monroe County Commission, two terms; elected to the House of Representatives, 2014, 2016, and 2018.

State Representative
BRADLEY SLAGH
R–90th Representative District

Office: Room N-1194, Cora B. Anderson House Office Bldg., P.O. Box 30014, Lansing, MI 48909, (517) 373-0830, E-Mail: bradleyslagh@house.mi.gov

Committees: Appropriations (Subcommittees: Corrections (Vice Chair); Higher Education and Community Colleges; Joint Capital Outlay (Chair); Natural Resources and Environmental Quality

Biography: Republican, of Zeeland; born February 21, 1957 in Kalamazoo; Protestant; spouse, Carol; children, Rachel, Katie, and Phillip; bachelor's degree in business administration from Hope College; secondary education teaching credential, Davenport College; employed with Twin Falls Reformed Church, Idaho, 1982 to 1984; First Michigan Bank Corporation, 1984 to 1997; Byron Center Bank, 1997 to 2003; supervisor, Zeeland Township, 2001 to 2007; treasurer, Ottawa County, 2007 to 2018; member, First Reformed Church and Zeeland Chamber of Commerce; elected to the House of Representatives, 2018.

State Representative
TIM SNELLER
D–50th Representative District

Office: Room N-899, Cora B. Anderson House Office Bldg., P.O. Box 30014, Lansing, MI 48909, (517) 373-3906, Toll-Free: (844) 763-5537, E-Mail: timsneller@house.mi.gov

Committees: Energy; Insurance; Transportation (Minority Vice Chair)

Biography: Democrat, of Burton; born June 20, 1956 in Flint; Baptist; bachelor's degree in political science and secondary teaching certificate in social studies and English, University of Michigan-Flint; formerly employed at Flint Truck and Bus Assembly, served as alternate committeeman, UAW Local 598; substitute/teacher, Burton-Bentley schools, 2003 to 2005; legislative assistant to several Michigan legislators over a period of 30 years; member, Michigan Democratic Party and Genesee County Democratic Party; elected to the House of Representatives, 2016 and 2018.

State Representative
BILL SOWERBY
D–31st Representative District

Office: Room N-795, Cora B. Anderson House Office Bldg., P.O. Box 30014, Lansing, MI 48909, (517) 373-0159, Toll-Free: (877) 347-8031, E-Mail: billsowerby@house.mi.gov

Committees: Education; Local Government and Municipal Finance; Natural Resources and Outdoor Recreation (Minority Vice Chair)

Biography: Democrat, of Clinton Township; born September 16, 1956 in St. Clair Shores; Christian; spouse, Martha Higgins; son Brad and daughter-in-law Briana; bachelor's degree double major in psychology and sociology, Wayne State University, 1978; automotive sales representative, 17 years; treasurer, Charter Township of Clinton, 1996 to 2016; Macomb County Commissioner, 1989 to 1996; member, Michigan Democratic Party and Macomb County Democratic Party; organizer, Macomb County Charter County Executive petition drive; past officer, Michigan Townships Association Macomb Chapter; member, Mount Clemens Optimist Club; past chairperson, Clinton Township Community Blood Drive; senior member, Clinton Valley Kiwanis Club; past board member, Grosse Pointes Clinton Refuse Disposal Authority and SMART; elected to the House of Representatives, 2016 and 2018.

State Representative
LORI STONE
D–28th Representative District

Office: Room N-792, Cora B. Anderson House Office Bldg., P.O. Box 30014, Lansing, MI 48909, (517) 373-1772, Toll-Free: (888) 347-8028, E-Mail: loristone@house.mi.gov

Committees: Education; Financial Services; Health Policy

Biography: Democrat, of Warren; born January 3, 1980; bachelor's degree in political theory and constitutional democracy, James Madison College, Michigan State University, bachelor's degree, elementary education and master's degree in science education, Michigan State University; elementary school teacher, Fitzgerald Public Schools, 2003 to 2018; member, Michigan Education Association, Fitzgerald Education Association, American Cancer Society Relay for Life of Warren, Warren Civic Theatre; elected to the House of Representatives, 2018.

State Representative
JOSEPH TATE
D–2nd Representative District

Office: Room S-586, Cora B. Anderson House Office Bldg., P.O. Box 30014, Lansing, MI 48909, (517) 373-1776

Committees: Appropriations (Subcommittees: General Government; Military and Veterans Affairs and State Police (Minority Vice Chair); School Aid and Department of Education)

Biography: Democrat, of Detroit; born December 13, 1980 in Grosse Pointe; Christian; bachelor's degree, public policy and master's degree, kinesiology from Michigan State University; master's degree, environmental policy and planning and MBA from the University of Michigan; program manager, Detroit Economic Growth Corporation; infantry officer in the United States Marine Corps; professional athlete, National Football League; member, Creekside Community Development Corporation, Grosse Pointe Democratic Club, Southeast Waterfront Neighborhood Association, NFL Players Association, Sierra Club; elected to the House of Representatives, 2018.

State Representative
SCOTT VanSINGEL
R–100th Representative District

Office: Room S-1289, Cora B. Anderson House Office Bldg., P.O. Box 30014, Lansing, MI 48909, (517) 373-7317, E-Mail: scottvansingel@house.mi.gov

Committees: Appropriations (Subcommittees: Corrections; Higher Education and Community Colleges (Chair); Licensing and Regulatory Affairs and Insurance and Financial Services; Natural Resources and Environmental Quality)

Biography: Republican, of Grant; born October 5, 1979 in Grand Rapids; Christian; child, Sophia; bachelor's degree in business administration, finance, and accounting, Central Michigan University; master's degree in business administration, Cornerstone University; auditor, Pricewaterhouse Coopers, 2004 to 2006; financial analyst, Dematic Corporation, 2006 to 2016; served as treasurer for an election campaign and the Newaygo County Republican Party; treasurer, National Wild Turkey Federation, former treasurer, Grant Gobblers Chapter; deacon, Grant Reformed Church; volunteer, Fremont Community Foundation Scholarship committee; elected to the House of Representatives, 2016 and 2018.

State Representative
GREG VanWOERKOM
R–91st Representative District

Office: Room N-1195, Cora B. Anderson House Office Bldg., P.O. Box 30014, Lansing, MI 48909, (517) 373-3436, Toll-Free: (877) 633-0331, Fax: (517) 373-9698, E-Mail: gregvanwoerkom@house.mi.gov

Committees: Appropriations (Subcommittees: Agriculture and Rural Development (Chair); General Government; Health and Human Services; Military and Veterans Affairs and State Police (Vice Chair))

Biography: Republican, of Norton Shores; born July 24, 1980; Christian Reformed Church; spouse, Wendy; children, Noah, Rowan, and Ewan; bachelor's degree political science and public administration, Calvin College and master's degree, The George Washington University; director of public policy for U.S. Representative Pete Hoekstra, district director for U.S. Representative Bill Huizenga; president, Western Michigan Christian High and Middle School Board; member, United Way of the Lakeshore and Muskegon Rotary Club; elected to the House of Representatives, 2018.

State Representative
HENRY VAUPEL
R–47th Representative District

Office: Room N-896, Cora B. Anderson House Office Bldg., P.O. Box 30014, Lansing, MI 48909, (517) 373-8835, Toll-Free: (866) 828-4863, E-Mail: hankvaupel@house.mi.gov

Committees: Education; Health Policy (Chair); Insurance; Tax Policy

Biography: Republican, of Fowlerville; born December 11, 1943 in Detroit; spouse, Cathy; children, Matthew and Zachary; three grandchildren; Lutheran; bachelor's degree and doctorate of Veterinary Medicine, Michigan State University; U.S. Army Veterinary Corps, 1968 to 1971; owner, Kern Road Veterinary Clinic, 1972 to 2001; member, St. John's Lutheran Church, Michigan Veterinary Medical Association, Fowlerville Community Fire Authority Board, Fowlerville DDA, Howell Chamber of Commerce, Hartland Chamber of Commerce, and Fowlerville Rotary; elected to Fowlerville Community School Board; trustee and supervisor, Handy Township; elected to the House of Representatives, 2014, 2016, and 2018.

State Representative
RODNEY WAKEMAN
R–94th Representative District

Office: Room N-1198, Cora B. Anderson House Office Bldg., P.O. Box 30014, Lansing, MI 48909, (517) 373-0837, Fax: (517) 373-3589, E-Mail: rodneywakeman@house.mi.gov

Committees: Commerce and Tourism; Education; Financial Services; Natural Resources and Outdoor Recreation (Vice Chair)

Biography: Republican, of Saginaw Township; born October 18, 1966 in Saginaw; Protestant; spouse, Johanna; child, Kayla; associate degree, arts, Delta College, University Center; Certificate of Mortuary Science, Eugene Applebaum College of Pharmacy and Health Sciences, Wayne State University; owner, Wakeman Funeral Home, Inc.; member of Holy Cross Lutheran Church, Saginaw; president, Valley Lutheran High School Foundation; member, Wayne State University School of Mortuary Science Advisory Committee; past president of the Saginaw Lions Club; Michigan Funeral Directors Association, former chairman of the Michigan Board of Examiners in Mortuary Science; former member, Lutheran Education Advancement Plan (LEAP) implementation team of the Great Lakes Bay Region; former chairman of the Valley Lutheran High School Alumni Association Scholarship Committee; elected to the House of Representatives, 2018.

State Representative
REBEKAH WARREN
D–55th Representative District

Office: Room S-989, Cora B. Anderson House Office Bldg., P.O. Box 30014, Lansing, MI 48909, (517) 373-1792, Toll-Free: (855) 936-5355, Fax: (517) 373-7757, E-Mail: rebekahwarren@house.mi.gov

Committee: Ways and Means (Minority Vice Chair)

Biography: Democrat, of Ann Arbor; born November 25, 1971 in Owosso; graduated from University of Michigan with a Bachelor of Arts in Political Science; graduate studies in child and family ecology at Michigan State University and business administration at Harvard University; former legislative assistant to State Representative Mary Schroer and State Representative Hubert Price for six years; previously executive director of MARAL Pro-Choice Michigan; recipient, 2010 Legislative Conservationist of the Year from the Michigan United Conservation Clubs (MUCC), 2010 Susan B. Anthony Award from the Wayne County Chapter of the National Organization for Women (NOW), 2011 Elected Official of the Year Award from the Michigan Recreation and Parks Association, 2011 Partners in Conservation Award from Trout Unlimited, 2011 Public Official of the Year Award from Habitat for Humanity of Michigan, 2012 Health Policy Champion Award from the Michigan Department of Community Health, 2012 Legislator of the Year Award from Police Officers Association of Michigan (POAM), 2014 Michigan Legislator of the Year Award from Michigan Association of Social Workers, 2014 Legislator of the Year Award from Michigan Council for Maternal and Child Health, 2014 Legislator of the Year Award from Michigan Association of Health Plans, 2016 Woman of Excellence Award from National Foundation for Women Legislators, 2018 honoree of the Michigan Music Therapy Association, 2018 Michigan Nonprofit Champion award from the Michigan Nonprofit Association and Council of Michigan Foundations, 2018 Champion of Justice Award from the Michigan Domestic and Sexual Violence Prevention and Treatment Board; 2019 MICHauto Legislator of the year; former member, Responsible Retirement Reform for Local Government Task Force, Commission on Human Trafficking, Mental Health and Wellness Commission, Healthcare Cost and Quality Advisory Committee; member, Michigan Council on Future Mobility and Great Lakes Commission; founding co-chair of Cancer Caucus and Legislative Biotechnology Caucus; member, Progressive Women's Caucus, Asian Pacific American Caucus, Labor Caucus, Auto Caucus, Gun Violence Prevention Caucus; legislative co-chair of Let's End Campus Sexual Assault summit; former state director for WiLL/WAND; state lead for National Conference of Environmental Legislators; state director, Women in Government; member, National Conference of State Legislatures, Council of State Governments Midwestern Legislative Conference (MLC) and MLC Agriculture and Natural Resources Committee and Health & Human Services Committee; elected to the House of Representatives, 2006, 2008, and 2018; elected to the State Senate, 2010 and 2014.

State Representative
MICHAEL WEBBER
R–45th Representative District

Office: Room N-894, Cora B. Anderson House Office Bldg., P.O. Box 30014, Lansing, MI 48909, (517) 373-1773, E-Mail: michaelwebber@house.mi.gov

Committees: Insurance; Oversight; Regulatory Reform (Chair); Tax policy

Biography: Republican, of Rochester Hills; born March 7, 1978 in Santa Monica, California; spouse, Julia; son, James; Catholic; bachelor's degree in international relations, Michigan State University; legislative aide, 2001 to 2010; licensed insurance agent, 2010 to present; member, Rochester Area Jaycees and Rochester Regional Chamber of Commerce; member, Oakland County Republican Party Executive Committee; elected to Rochester Hills City Council, 2007 and 2011; elected to the House of Representatives, 2014, 2016, and 2018.

State Representative
PAULINE WENDZEL
R–79th Representative District

Office: Room N-1098, Cora B. Anderson House Office Bldg., P.O. Box 30014, Lansing, MI 48909, (517) 373-1403, E-Mail: paulinewendzel@house.mi.gov

Committees: Agriculture; Commerce and Tourism (Vice Chair); Energy (Vice Chair); Regulatory Reform

Biography: Republican, of Watervliet; born December 18, 1989 in St. Joseph; Christian; bachelor's degree in anthropology from Michigan State University, minor in food industry management; programs director, North Berrien Historical Museum, product development manager, Coloma Frozen Foods; assistant deputy clerk, Bainbridge Township; active in 4-H Berrien County Youth Fair and JDRF Coastline Children's Film Festival; elected to the House of Representatives, 2018.

State Representative
JASON WENTWORTH
R–97th Representative District

Office: Room 251, Capitol Bldg., P.O. Box 30014, Lansing, MI 48909, (517) 373-8962,
E-Mail: jasonwentworth@house.mi.gov

Committee: Ways and Means

Biography: Republican, of Clare; born September 23, 1982 in Clare; Non-denominational Christian; spouse, Heather; children, Kiley, Makayla, and Alexa; attended Central Michigan University; Master of Science Administration, Leadership, St. Petersburg College; United States Army, military police officer, 2001 to 2006; formerly employed in law enforcement; formerly managed the Michigan Veteran Resource Service Center and was the regional coordinator for the Michigan Veterans Affairs Agency in the east central region of Michigan; Chair, Select Committee on Reducing Car Insurance Rates, 2019; member, Legislative Council; elected to the House of Representatives, 2016 and 2018.

State Representative
MARY WHITEFORD
R–80th Representative District

Office: Room N-1099, Cora B. Anderson House Office Bldg., P.O. Box 30014, Lansing, MI 48909, (517) 373-0836, Toll-Free: (855) 737-0080, E-Mail: marywhiteford@house.mi.gov

Committees: Appropriations (Subcommittees: Health and Human Services (Chair), Joint Capital Outlay); Health Policy

Biography: Republican, of Casco Township; spouse, Kevin; three adult children; Bachelor of Science in Nursing, Northern Illinois University; worked in pediatric neurosurgery and pediatric emergency units; owner, financial planning firm; member, Michigan Human Trafficking Task Force, 2013 to 2014; elected to the House of Representatives in a special election March 2016, reelected in November 2016 and 2018.

State Representative
KAREN WHITSETT
D–9th Representative District

Office: Room S-688, Cora B. Anderson House Office Bldg., P.O. Box 30014, Lansing, MI 48909, (517) 373-6990, E-Mail: karenwhitsett@house.mi.gov

Committees: Financial Services; Tax policy

Biography: Democrat, of Detroit, born November 8, 1967 in Detroit; Christian; husband Jason and son Chris; graduate, Cody High School; block club organizer; member, Select Committee on Reducing Car Insurance Rates; elected to the House of Representatives, 2018.

State Representative
ROBERT WITTENBERG
D–27th Representative District

Office: Room N-791, Cora B. Anderson House Office Bldg., P.O. Box 30014, Lansing, MI 48909, (517) 373-0478, Toll-Free: (855) REP-WITT, E-Mail: robertwittenberg@house.mi.gov

Committees: Financial Services; Insurance (Minority Vice Chair); Tax Policy

Biography: Democrat, of Huntington Woods; born January 20, 1981 in Detroit; Judaism; bachelor's degree in business management, Indiana University; licensed agent, life and health insurance for 14 years; member, Oak Park-Huntington Woods Democratic Club, Berkley Democratic Club, Southeast Oakland Democratic Club, and Ferndale Area Democratic Club; treasurer, Tri-Community Coalition of Berkley, Huntington Woods, and Oak Park; member, American Civil Liberties Union of Michigan, Sierra Club, American State Legislators for Gun Violence Prevention, National Caucus of Environmental Legislators, and National Association of Jewish Legislators; founder and chair, Michigan Gun Violence Prevention Caucus; elected to the House of Representatives, 2014, 2016, and 2018.

State Representative
ANGELA WITWER
D–71st Representative District

Office: Room N-1090, Cora B. Anderson House Office Bldg., P.O. Box 30014, Lansing, MI 48909, (517) 373-0853, Toll-Free: (855) 328-6671, E-Mail: angelawitwer@house.mi.gov

Committees: Agriculture; Health Policy

Biography: Democrat, of Delta Township; born July 25, 1962 in Traverse City; Catholic; spouse, Bruce; children, J.R. (Lindsey) Artibee and Danielle (David) Lenz; four granddaughters, Alivia, Lily, Charlotte, and Rosalyn; bachelor's degree from Northwood University; employed Sparrow Health System, 22 years and Edge Partnerships, 11 years; member, Waverly Community Schools Board of Education, 2012 to December 2018; active with the McLaren Greater Lansing Foundation Board, Volunteers of America Hungry No More, Wharton Center Advisory Committee, Food Bank Council of Michigan, Capital Area Humane Society, Children's Trust Fund, Cristo Rey Community Center, Lansing Regional Chamber of Commerce Economic Club, and Michigan Society for Health Care Planning and Marketing; elected to the House of Representatives, 2018.

State Representative
DOUGLAS WOZNIAK
R–36th Representative District

Office: Room S-885, Cora B. Anderson House Office Bldg., P.O. Box 30014, Lansing, MI 48909, (517) 373-0843, Toll-Free: (888) 642-4737, E-Mail: douglaswozniak@house.mi.gov

Committees: Communications and Technology; Families, Children and Seniors; Health Policy; Judiciary

Biography: Republican, of Shelby Township; born January 17, 1947 in Hamtramck; Catholic; spouse, Pamela; child, Lauren DeRosa (Wozniak); degree in mathematics, University of Michigan and law degree, Michigan State University, College of Law; founder and owner, Law Offices of Douglas C. Wozniak, PLC, Wozniak Law Office, and Wozniak Realty Associates; trustee, Shelby Township, 2008 to 2018; former member, downtown development authority, planning commission, construction board of appeals, Macomb board of canvassers; member, Daybreakers Kiwanis, Shelby Optimists, St. Kieran's Knights of Columbus, Shelby Lions; elected to the House of Representatives, 2018; Vice Chair, Joint Committee on Administrative Rules.

State Representative
TENISHA YANCEY
D–1st Representative District

Office: Room S-585, Cora B. Anderson House Office Bldg., P.O. Box 30014, Lansing, MI 48909, (517) 373-0154

Committees: Judiciary; Tax Policy (Minority Vice Chair); Transportation

Biography: Democrat, of Harper Woods; one son; bachelor's degree, Eastern Michigan University; law degree, University of Detroit Mercy School of Law; project manager, Wayne County Land Bank, government relations executive and community outreach program coordinator, Wayne County executive's office; assistant prosecuting attorney, Wayne County prosecutor's office; Harper Woods board of education; attends Olive Tree Ministries in Detroit; elected to the House of Representatives in a special election, November 7, 2017, reelected in 2018.

State Representative
JEFF YAROCH
R–33rd Representative District

Office: Room N-797, Cora B. Anderson House Office Bldg., P.O. Box 30014, Lansing, MI 48909, (517) 373-0820, Toll-Free: (800) 209-3330, E-Mail: jeffyaroch@house.mi.gov

Committees: Appropriations (Subcommittees: Health and Human Services; Judiciary; Licensing and Regulatory Affairs and Insurance and Financial Services (Chair); Transportation (Vice Chair))

Biography: Republican, of Richmond; born October 18, 1970 in Mt. Clemens; spouse, Sara; daughters, Reagan and Madison; associate's degree, fire science, Macomb Community College; bachelor's degree, human resources management, Baker College; law degree, Western Michigan University Cooley Law School; former firefighter, attaining rank of Batallion Chief; paramedic; attorney; Eagle Scout; member, Lions Club; member, Richmond City Council, 1999 to 2016; elected to the House of Representatives, 2016 and 2018.

LEGISLATIVE AND CONGRESSIONAL REPRESENTATION BY COUNTY, 2019-2020

County	Representative in Congress	District	State Senator	District	State Representative	District
Alcona	Jack Bergman, R	1	Jim Stamas, R	36	Sue Allor, R	106
Alger	Jack Bergman, R	1	Ed McBroom, R	38	Sara Cambensy, D	109
Allegan	Bill Huizenga, R Fred S. Upton, R	2 6	Aric Nesbitt, R	26	Steve Johnson, R Mary Whiteford, R	72 80
Alpena	Jack Bergman, R	1	Jim Stamas, R	36	Sue Allor, R	106
Antrim	Jack Bergman, R	1	Wayne Schmidt, R	37	Triston Cole, R	105
Arenac	Daniel T. Kildee, D	5	Jim Stamas, R	36	Jason Wentworth, R	97
Baraga	Jack Bergman, R	1	Ed McBroom, R	38	Greg Markkanen, R	110
Barry	Justin Amash, I	3	John Bizon, R	19	Julie Calley, R	87
Bay	Daniel T. Kildee, D	5	Kevin Daley, R	31	Brian K. Elder, D Annette Glenn, R	96 98
Benzie	Jack Bergman, R	1	Curtis S. VanderWall, R	35	Jack O'Malley, R	101
Berrien	Fred S. Upton, R	6	Kim LaSata, R	21	Brad Paquette, R Pauline Wendzel, R	78 79
Branch	Tim Walberg, R	7	Mike Shirkey, R	16	Eric Leutheuser, R	58
Calhoun	Justin Amash, I	3	John Bizon, R	19	Jim Haadsma, D Matt Hall, R	62 63
Cass	Fred S. Upton, R	6	Kim LaSata, R	21	Aaron Miller, R Brad Paquette, R	59 78
Charlevoix	Jack Bergman, R	1	Wayne Schmidt, R	37	Triston Cole, R	105
Cheboygan	Jack Bergman, R	1	Wayne Schmidt, R	37	Sue Allor, R Lee Chatfield, R	106 107
Chippewa	Jack Bergman, R	1	Wayne Schmidt, R	37	Lee Chatfield, R	107
Clare	John Moolenaar, R	4	Rick Outman, R	33	Jason Wentworth, R	97
Clinton	John Moolenaar, R	4	Tom Barrett, R	24	Graham Filler, R	93
Crawford	Jack Bergman, R	1	Curtis S. VanderWall, R	35	Daire Rendon, R	103

County	Representative in Congress	District	State Senator	District	State Representative	District
Delta	Jack Bergman, R	1	Ed McBroom, R	38	Beau LaFave, R	108
Dickinson	Jack Bergman, R	1	Ed McBroom, R	38	Beau LaFave, R	108
Eaton	Tim Walberg, R	7	Tom Barrett, R	24	Sarah Lightner, R	65
					Angela Witwer, D	71
Emmet	Jack Bergman, R	1	Wayne Schmidt, R	37	Lee Chatfield, R	107
Genesee	Daniel T. Kildee, D	5	Ruth Johnson, R	14	Sheldon Neeley, D	34
			Jim Ananich, D	27	Sheryl Y. Kennedy, D	48
			Ken Horn, R	32	John Cherry, D	49
					Tim Sneller, D	50
					Mike Mueller, R	51
Gladwin	John Moolenaar, R	4	Jim Stamas, R	36	Jason Wentworth, R	97
Gogebic	Jack Bergman, R	1	Ed McBroom, R	38	Greg Markkanen, R	110
Grand Traverse	Jack Bergman, R	1	Wayne Schmidt, R	37	Larry Inman, R	104
Gratiot	John Moolenaar, R	4	Rick Outman, R	33	James Lower, R	70
					Graham Filler, R	93
Hillsdale	Tim Walberg, R	7	Mike Shirkey, R	16	Eric Leutheuser, R	58
Houghton	Jack Bergman, R	1	Ed McBroom, R	38	Greg Markkanen, R	110
Huron	Paul Mitchell, R	10	Dan Lauwers, R	25	Phil Green, R	84
Ingham	Elissa Slotkin, D	8	Tom Barrett, R	24	Kara Hope, D	67
			Curtis Hertel, Jr., D	23	Sarah Anthony, D	68
					Julie Brixie, D	69
Ionia	Justin Amash, I	3	John Bizon, R	19	Thomas A. Albert, R	86
					Julie Calley, R	87
Iosco	Daniel T. Kildee, D	5	Jim Stamas, R	36	Sue Allor, R	106
Iron	Jack Bergman, R	1	Ed McBroom, R	38	Greg Markkanen, R	110
Isabella	John Moolenaar, R	4	Rick Outman, R	33	Roger Hauck, R	99
Jackson	Tim Walberg, R	7	Mike Shirkey, R	16	Julie Alexander, R	64
					Sarah Lightner, R	65

LEGISLATIVE AND CONGRESSIONAL REPRESENTATION BY COUNTY, 2019-2020 (Cont.)

County	Representative in Congress	District	State Senator	District	State Representative	District
Kalamazoo	Fred S. Upton, R.	6	Sean McCann, D	20	Jon Hoadley, D.	60
					Brandt Iden, R.	61
					Matt Hall, R.	63
					Beth Griffin, R.	66
Kalkaska	Jack Bergman, R.	1	Curtis S. VanderWall, R.	35	Daire Rendon, R.	103
Kent	Bill Huizenga, R.	2	Aric Nesbitt, R.	26	Steve Johnson, R.	72
	Justin Amash, I.	3	Peter MacGregor, R.	28	Lynn Afendoulis, R.	73
			Winnie Brinks, D.	29	Mark E. Huizenga, R.	74
					David LaGrand, D.	75
					Rachel Hood, D.	76
					Tommy Brann, R.	77
					Thomas A. Albert, R.	86
Keweenaw	Jack Bergman, R.	1	Ed McBroom, R.	38	Greg Markkanen, R.	110
Lake	Bill Huizenga, R.	2	Curtis S. VanderWall, R.	35	Scott VanSingel, R.	100
Lapeer	Paul Mitchell, R.	10	Kevin Daley, R.	31	Gary Howell, R.	82
Leelanau	Jack Bergman, R.	1	Curtis S. VanderWall, R.	35	Jack O'Malley, R.	101
Lenawee	Tim Walberg, R.	7	Dale W. Zorn, R.	17	Bronna Kahle, R.	57
					Sarah Lightner, R.	65
Livingston	Elissa Slotkin, D	8	Lana Theis, R.	22	Ann Bollin, R.	42
					Henry Vaupel, R.	47
Luce	Jack Bergman, R.	1	Wayne Schmidt, R.	37	Sara Cambensy, D.	109
Mackinac	Jack Bergman, R.	1	Wayne Schmidt, R.	37	Lee Chatfield, R.	107
Macomb	Andy Levin, D	9	Pete Lucido, R.	8	Kevin Hertel, D	18
	Paul Mitchell, R	10	Paul Wojno, D.	9	John Chirkun, D.	22
			Mike MacDonald, R.	10	Steve Marino, R	24
			Dan Lauwers, R.	25	Nate Shannon, D	25
					Lori Stone, D	28
					Diana Farrington, R.	30
					Bill Sowerby, D	31
					Pamela Hornberger, R.	32
					Jeff Yaroch, R.	33
					Douglas Wozniak, R.	36

Chapter III – THE LEGISLATIVE BRANCH •

County	Representative in Congress	District	State Senator	District	State Representative	District
Manistee	Jack Bergman, R	1	Curtis S. VanderWall, R	35	Jack O'Malley, R	101
Marquette	Jack Bergman, R	1	Ed McBroom, R	38	Sara Cambensy, D	109
					Greg Markkanen, R	110
Mason	Jack Bergman, R	1	Curtis S. VanderWall, R	35	Jack O'Malley, R	101
	Bill Huizenga, R	2				
Mecosta	John Moolenaar, R	4	Rick Outman, R	33	Michele Hoitenga, R	102
Menominee	Jack Bergman, R	1	Ed McBroom, R	38	Beau LaFave, R	108
Midland	John Moolenaar, R	4	Jim Stamas, R	36	Annette Glenn, R	98
					Roger Hauck, R	99
Missaukee	John Moolenaar, R	4	Curtis S. VanderWall, R	35	Daire Rendon, R	103
Monroe	Tim Walberg, R	7	Dale W. Zorn, R	17	Joseph N. Bellino, R	17
					Jason Sheppard, R	56
Montcalm	Justin Amash, I	3	Rick Outman, R	33	James Lower, R	70
	John Moolenaar, R	4				
Montmorency	Jack Bergman, R	1	Jim Stamas, R	36	Triston Cole, R	105
Muskegon	Bill Huizenga, R	2	Jon Bumstead, R	34	Greg VanWoerkom, R	91
					Terry J. Sabo, D	92
Newaygo	Bill Huizenga, R	2	Jon Bumstead, R	34	Scott VanSingel, R	100
Oakland	Elissa Slotkin, D	8	Jeremy Moss, D	11	Jim Ellison, D	26
	Andy Levin, D	9	Rosemary Bayer, D	12	Robert Wittenberg, D	27
	Haley Stevens, D	11	Mallory McMorrow, D	13	Brenda Carter, D	29
	Brenda L. Lawrence, D	14	Ruth Johnson, R	14	Kyra Harris Bolden, D	35
			Jim Runestad, R	15	Christine Greig, D	37
					Kathy Crawford, R	38
					Ryan Berman, R	39
					Mari Manoogian, D	40
					Padma Kuppa, D	41
					Andrea K. Schroeder, R	43
					Matt Maddock, R	44
					Michael Webber, R	45
					John Reilly, R	46
					Mike Mueller, R	51
Oceana	Bill Huizenga, R	2	Jon Bumstead, R	34	Scott VanSingel, R	100

LEGISLATIVE AND CONGRESSIONAL REPRESENTATION BY COUNTY, 2019-2020 (Cont.)

County	Representative in Congress	District	State Senator	District	State Representative	District
Ogemaw	John Moolenaar, R	4	Curtis S. VanderWall, R	35	Daire Rendon, R	103
Ontonagon	Jack Bergman, R	1	Ed McBroom, R	38	Greg Markkanen, R	110
Osceola	John Moolenaar, R	4	Curtis S. VanderWall, R	35	Jason Wentworth, R Michele Hoitenga, R	97 102
Oscoda	Jack Bergman, R	1	Jim Stamas, R	36	Triston Cole, R	105
Otsego	Jack Bergman, R	1	Jim Stamas, R	36	Triston Cole, R	105
Ottawa	Bill Huizenga, R	2	Roger Victory, R	30	Luke Meerman, R Jim Lilly, R Bradley Slagh, R	88 89 90
Presque Isle	Jack Bergman, R	1	Jim Stamas, R	36	Sue Allor, R	106
Roscommon	John Moolenaar, R	4	Curtis S. VanderWall, R	35	Daire Rendon, R	103
Saginaw	John Moolenaar, R Daniel T. Kildee, D	4 5	Ken Horn, R	32	Ben Frederick, R Rodney Wakeman, R Vanessa Guerra, D	85 94 95
St. Clair	Paul Mitchell, R	10	Dan Lauwers, R	25	Pamela Hornberger, R Gary Eisen, R Shane Hernandez, R	32 81 83
St. Joseph	Fred S. Upton, R	6	Kim LaSata, R	21	Aaron Miller, R	59
Sanilac	Paul Mitchell, R	10	Dan Lauwers, R	25	Shane Hernandez, R	83
Schoolcraft	Jack Bergman, R	1	Ed McBroom, R	38	Sara Cambensy, D	109
Shiawassee	John Moolenaar, R	4	Tom Barrett, R	24	Ben Frederick, R	85
Tuscola	Daniel T. Kildee, D Paul Mitchell, R	5 10	Kevin Daley, R	31	Phil Green, R	84
Van Buren	Fred S. Upton, R	6	Aric Nesbitt, R	26	Beth Griffin, R	66
Washtenaw	Tim Walberg, R Debbie Dingell, D	7 12	Jeff Irwin, D Lana Theis, R	18 22	Donna Lasinski, D Yousef Rabhi, D Ronnie D. Peterson, D Rebekah Warren, D	52 53 54 55

LEGISLATIVE AND CONGRESSIONAL REPRESENTATION BY COUNTY, 2019-2020 *(Cont.)*

County	Representative in Congress	District	State Senator	District	State Representative	District
Wayne	Haley Stevens, D	11	Stephanie Chang, D	1	Tenisha Yancey, D	1
	Debbie Dingell, D	12	Adam Hollier, D	2	Joseph Tate, D	2
	Rashida Tlaib, D	13	Sylvia Santana, D	3	Wendell Byrd, D	3
	Brenda L. Lawrence, D	14	Marshall Bullock II, D	4	Isaac Robinson, D	4
			Betty Jean Alexander, D	5	Cynthia Johnson, D	5
			Erika Geiss, D	6	Tyrone Carter, D	6
			Dayna Polehanki, D	7	LaTanya Garrett, D	7
					Sherry Gay-Dagnogo, D	8
					Karen Whitsett, D	9
					Leslie Love, D	10
					Jewell Jones, D	11
					Alex Garza, D	12
					Frank Liberati, D	13
					Cara Clemente, D	14
					Abdullah Hammoud, D	15
					Kevin Coleman, D	16
					Joseph N. Bellino, R	17
					Laurie Pohutsky, D	19
					Matt Koleszar, D	20
					Kristy Pagan, D	21
					Darrin Camilleri, D	23
Wexford	John Moolenaar, R	4	Curtis S. VanderWall, R	35	Michele Hoitenga, R	102

LEGISLATIVE BRANCH AGENCIES

In addition to the legislators who are elected to serve in the House of Representatives and the Senate, the legislative branch also contains permanent offices, agencies, commissions, and committees designed to enable Michigan's Legislature to carry out its functions and duties. These entities support the Legislature by providing procedural assistance, fiscal analysis, security, building maintenance, bill drafting, research, oversight and auditing of government agencies, and investigation and study of important policy issues.

MARGARET E. O'BRIEN
Secretary of the Senate

ADAM W. REAMES
Assistant Secretary of the Senate

Secretary of the Senate

Margaret E. O'Brien, Secretary of the Senate
Adam W. Reames, Assistant Secretary of the Senate

The Secretary of the Senate is elected by the Senators as a statutory officer at the beginning of each 4-year Senate term. As the parliamentarian and record keeper of the Senate, the Secretary fulfills many constitutional requirements of the Senate. These duties are assigned in statute, Joint rules and Senate rules and include the "care and preservation" of bills and Senate records; recording and validating official Senate actions; enrolling of bills; preparing the journal of each day's proceedings; disseminating of bills, resolutions and amendments to Senators; noticing of committee meetings; maintaining and recording of committee actions; and presenting bills to the Governor.

The Secretary's most visible role is the work on the podium during session — announcing the proceedings, reading in communications and bills, recording votes, and presiding in the absence of designated presiding officers. The Secretary's office is also responsible for management of session staff, committee clerks, Senate Media Services and special projects. Additionally, the Secretary serves on the Michigan State Capitol Commission which governs the Michigan State Capitol Historic Site, maintains and restores the State Capitol Building, and maintains and improves the grounds of the site. The Secretary of the Senate's office is located in Room S-5, State Capitol, Lansing, MI 48933. Phone: (517) 373-2400.

―――◈―◈―◈―――

Senate Fiscal Agency

Christopher Harkins, Director

The Senate Fiscal Agency is a nonpartisan legislative agency that was formed by state statute to provide assistance through research and analysis to the Michigan Senate. The staff provides technical, analytical, and preparatory support for all appropriations and retirement bills. The agency also prepares an objective written analysis of all bills and administrative rules under consideration by the Senate.

Fiscal analysts of the Senate Fiscal Agency review and evaluate state programs, proposed policies, proposed rules, budgetary requests, and the fiscal impact of all bills before the Senate. The fiscal analysts serve as the primary staff to the Senate Appropriations Committee and the subcommittees of the Senate Appropriations Committee. The agency also provides economic and revenue analysis and forecasting, analyzes the impact of federal budget decisions on the state, tracks state and national economic conditions, and monitors the state's compliance with constitutional and statutory fiscal requirements. The agency's economic and revenue forecasts are used as the official Senate forecasts at the Consensus Revenue Estimating Conference

Legislative analysts of the Senate Fiscal Agency are responsible for providing objective bill analysis for all bills considered by Senate standing committees, other than the Senate Appropriations Committee. Legislative analysts prepare summaries of bills in committee, and bills reported from committee, to provide a straightforward explanation of the changes a bill would make to present law. Once a bill is reported from committee, the analyst also may prepare a detailed analysis describing the reason for the bill's introduction, the changes the bill would make in present law, background information, supporting and opposing arguments, and fiscal implications. Analyses are updated as bills are amended throughout the legislative process.

The Senate Fiscal Agency is located in the Victor Center, 8th Floor, 201 N. Washington Square, Lansing, MI 48933. Phone: (517) 373-2768. Reports and publications of the Senate Fiscal Agency can be found on the agency's website at www.senate.michigan.gov/sfa.

SENATE FISCAL AGENCY BOARD OF GOVERNORS

Senators Shirkey (C), Stamas, Bumstead, Ananich, Hertel Jr.

GARY L. RANDALL
Clerk

RICHARD J. BROWN
Assistant Clerk

Clerk of the House of Representatives

Gary L. Randall, Clerk
Richard J. Brown, Assistant Clerk

The Office of the Clerk of the House of Representatives is the parliamentary office for this chamber of the Michigan legislature.

The Clerk of the House oversees a wide range of operations in the House of Representatives. These responsibilities include direct supervision of the preparation of various legislative documents, including the House journal and the daily calendar, which specifies the order of pending business; the printing and reproduction of bills, acts, or other documents; and the responsibility for the care and preservation of each bill introduced in the House or received from the Senate.

The Clerk of the House, whose duties are stipulated in statute, House Rules, and Joint Rules, and at the direction of the membership, is elected by the members of the House of Representatives. The clerk has an active parliamentary role during legislative sessions. The clerk calls the roll, announces the proceedings of the House, records votes, and serves as parliamentarian and presides in the absence of a designated presiding officer. Assisting the clerk at the podium during session are the assistant clerk and the clerks responsible for bill amendments, bills and resolutions, and the journal.

The Clerk of the House is also the administrator of the House Sergeant-at-Arms police agency and is a statutory member of the Michigan State Capitol Commission. The clerk's offices are located in the State Capitol. Phone: (517) 373-0135.

House Fiscal Agency

Mary Ann Cleary, Director

The House Fiscal Agency is a nonpartisan agency within the Michigan House of Representatives. Agency personnel provide confidential, nonpartisan assistance to the House Appropriations Committee and all other members of the House on legislative fiscal matters. The agency also provides objective, nonpartisan explanations of bills before House standing committees and bills being considered by the full House.

Fiscal Analysts assist legislators with developing the state budget; review and prepare budget and supplemental appropriations bills and certain transfer requests; provide fiscal impact statements on proposed legislation; monitor, research, and analyze fiscal issues; and prepare reports and documents to assist legislative deliberations. *Economists* analyze legislation related to tax and lottery issues, monitor state revenue, track state and national economic conditions, and prepare reports on revenue and other economic issues. *Legislative Analysts* prepare nonpartisan summaries and analyses of bills. Summaries, completed prior to committee deliberations, describe how a bill would change current law, including any fiscal impact. Analyses are prepared for bills reported from committee and typically include, in addition to the information included in a summary, a description of the problem being addressed, arguments for and against the bill, and positions of interested parties. The Agency *Director*, by statute, is one of three state officials charged with forecasting state revenues at Consensus Revenue Estimating Conferences.

Reports and publications prepared by the House Fiscal Agency are available on the agency's website at www.house.mi.gov/hfa; bill summaries and analyses are available on the Michigan Legislative Information System website at www.legislature.mi.gov. The House Fiscal Agency is located on the 4th floor of the North Tower of the Anderson House Office Building, 124 N. Capitol Avenue, Lansing, MI 48933. Phone: (517) 373-8080. Fax: (517) 373-5874.

HOUSE FISCAL AGENCY GOVERNING COMMITTEE

Reps. Hernandez (C), Chatfield (VC), Cole, Hoadley (Min. VC), Greig, Rabhi.

MICHAEL FERLAND
Chief Sergeant-at-Arms
Senate

DAVID D. DICKSON JR.
Chief Sergeant-at-Arms
House

Senate/House Sergeants-at-Arms

Michael Ferland, Chief Sergeant-at-Arms, Senate
David D. Dickson Jr., Chief Sergeant-at-Arms, House of Representatives

The **Senate Sergeant-at-Arms** is the chief security officer of the Senate. Under the direction of the Senate Majority Leader, the Director of the Senate Business Office supervises and directs the Senate Police Department, the work of the Sergeant-at-Arms, and Assistant Sergeants-at-Arms.

The Sergeant-at-Arms attends the Senate during its sessions and maintains order under the direction of the presiding officer. The Sergeant-at-Arms executes the commands of the presiding officer and of the Senate and all processes issued by their authority.

The Sergeant-at-Arms has general charge of, and maintains order in, the gallery, chamber, and committee rooms of the Senate. The Sergeant-at-Arms ensures that all staff and visitors are seated. The Sergeants carry out police responsibilities to provide for the safety and security for all members of the Senate, Senate staff, and visitors to the Senate areas of the Capitol, the Senate Office Building, and areas the Senate occupies in the Boji Tower.

The **House Sergeant-at-Arms** is the chief security officer of the House of Representatives. Under the direction of the Speaker's Office, the Clerk of the House supervises and directs the work of the Sergeant-at-Arms, Assistant Sergeant-at-Arms, and session interns. The Sergeant-at-Arms Office is a police agency, designated to serve and protect citizens, staff members, and state representatives. The Sergeant-at-Arms executes the commands of the presiding officer of the House and has general charge of, and maintains order in, the gallery, chamber, and committee rooms of the House of Representatives during session. The Sergeant-at-Arms has arrest powers and authority to serve subpoenas and warrants issued by the House, any duly authorized officer, or Committee and ensures that all visitors comply with all rules and regulations while visiting the Capitol Building or other state legislative facilities.

DOUG A. RINGLER
Auditor General

Office of the Auditor General

Doug A. Ringler, Auditor General

The independent audit function in Michigan is vested in the legislative branch of government, and the Auditor General is appointed to serve an 8-year term by a majority vote of members of the House and Senate.

The Auditor General is the principal executive responsible for the **Office of the Auditor General** policies and practices, day-to-day audit operations, and liaison with the legislature. The Office of the Auditor General conducts post-financial and performance audits of state government operations. These include financial audits of the State of Michigan Comprehensive Annual Financial Report, federal funds subject to the Federal Single Audit Act of 1984, and individual departments and agencies. Additionally, the office conducts performance audits of state programs and operations, using risk-based selection criteria, and in response to legislative requests. All audit reports are public documents.

Doug A. Ringler was appointed Auditor General by the Michigan Legislature effective June 9, 2014. Mr. Ringler has held a variety of positions within State government for the past 30 years, most recently as the Director of Internal Audit within the executive branch. Mr. Ringler is a member of the American Institute of Certified Public Accountants and the Institute of Internal Auditors. He is a past recipient of the "Internal Auditor of the Year" Award, presented by the Institute's Lansing Chapter.

Mr. Ringler graduated from Ferris State University and is a native of Reed City.

Michigan State Capitol Commission

The Michigan State Capitol Commission is created by the *Michigan State Capitol Historic Site Act* (PA 240 of 2013) to manage the Michigan State Capitol Historic Site, maintain and restore the State Capitol Building, and maintain and improve the grounds of the site. The commission consists of the Secretary of the Senate; the Clerk of the House of Representatives; two individuals jointly appointed by the Secretary of the Senate and the Clerk of the House; and two individuals appointed by the Governor.

GARY L. RANDALL (Chair)
JOHN TRUSCOTT (Vice-Chair)
JOAN BAUER
KERRY CHARTKOFF
WILLIAM C. KANDLER
MARGARET E. O'BRIEN

Michigan Capitol Building
P.O. Box 30014
Lansing, MI 48909-7514
CapitolFacilities@legislature.mi.gov

⋙◆⋘

Michigan Legislative Retirement Board

The Michigan Legislative Retirement System was created by Public Act 261 of 1957 for the maintenance, and administration of a legislative members' and presiding officers' retirement system within the legislature. The system's health plan provides its members with health, dental, vision and hearing insurance coverage.

MICHIGAN LEGISLATIVE RETIREMENT SYSTEM
BOARD OF TRUSTEES

THE HONORABLE R. ROBERT GEAKE
Retiree Member (Chair)

THE HONORABLE J. MICHAEL BUSCH
Retiree Member

THE HONORABLE DEBORAH L. CHERRY
Retiree Member

THE HONORABLE JOHN D. CHERRY JR.
Retiree Member

THE HONORABLE PHILIP E. HOFFMAN
Retiree Member

THE HONORABLE JOSEPH PALAMARA
Retiree Member

THE HONORABLE GARY L. RANDALL
Retiree Member

THE HONORABLE MARK SCHAUER
Retiree Member

THE HONORABLE JOHN J. H. SCHWARZ
Defined Contribution Plan Member

THE HONORABLE ALMA WHEELER SMITH
Retiree Member (Vice-Chair)

⋙◆⋘

The Legislative Council

The **Legislative Council** is a bipartisan committee of the House and Senate, consisting of 12 regular and six alternate members, established pursuant to the Constitution of 1963, art. IV, sec. 15. The primary responsibility of the council is to maintain bill drafting, research, and other services for legislators. The council appoints the Legislative Council Administrator, who is the chief executive officer of all Legislative Council agencies. The council may create subcommittees that include members of the legislature who are not council members.

MICHIGAN LEGISLATIVE COUNCIL

SENATOR MIKE SHIRKEY, Chair in 2019, Alternate Chair in 2020
SPEAKER LEE CHATFIELD, Alternate Chair in 2019, Chair in 2020
SENATOR JIM ANANICH
SENATOR STEPHANIE CHANG
SENATOR KEN HORN
SENATOR WAYNE SCHMIDT
SENATOR JIM STAMAS
REPRESENTATIVE CARA CLEMENTE
REPRESENTATIVE SHANE HERNANDEZ
REPRESENTATIVE JIM LILLY
REPRESENTATIVE YOUSEF RABHI
REPRESENTATIVE JASON WENTWORTH

Alternate Members

SENATOR JOHN BIZON, M.D.
SENATOR MIKE MACDONALD
SENATOR JEREMY MOSS
REPRESENTATIVE TRISTON COLE
REPRESENTATIVE LATANYA GARRETT
REPRESENTATIVE MARY WHITEFORD

Legislative Council Administrator

JENNIFER DETTLOFF

JENNIFER DETTLOFF
Legislative Council Administrator

Legislative Council Administrator

Jennifer Dettloff

The **Legislative Council Administrator** position was created by Public Act 189 of 1995. The Council Administrator is responsible for supervisory oversight for all Legislative Council agencies:

- The Legislative Service Bureau
- The Legislative Corrections Ombudsman
- The Michigan Veterans' Facility Ombudsman
- The Michigan Law Revision Commission
- The Michigan Commission on Uniform State Laws
- The Joint Committee on Administrative Rules
- The State Drug Treatment Advisory Committee
- The Criminal Justice Policy Commission

The Legislative Council Administrator has the following duties and responsibilities:

- To provide personnel policy oversight and development for all Legislative Council agencies
- To develop, prepare, and present Legislative Council agency budgets
- To review quarterly financial statements of Legislative Council agencies and monitor budgetary compliance
- To act as secretary to the council
- To perform other duties and responsibilities as determined and assigned by the Legislative Council.

In addition, the Council Administrator is a member of the Law Revision Commission and the Michigan Commission on Uniform State Laws.

More specific duties of the Administrator are set forth in the rules established by the Legislative Council.

The Office of the Legislative Council Administrator is located in the Boji Tower, 124 W. Allegan, Lansing, MI 48909. Phone: (517) 373-0212.

⟩⟩◆⟨⟨

Jennifer Dettloff was appointed Legislative Council Administrator on November 9th, 2016. Prior to being appointed to the Legislative Council, Ms. Dettloff served as Legal Counsel for two Senate Majority Leaders. She had previously served for legislators in both the House and Senate in numerous capacities.

Ms. Dettloff is a member of the State Bar of Michigan. She holds a B.A. from James Madison College at Michigan State University in Social Relations and a J.D. from Thomas M. Cooley Law School.

Ms. Dettloff and her husband Robert Snyder live in Williamston with their triplets, Madeline, Jack, and William.

⟩⟩◆⟨⟨

Legislative Council Agencies

Legislative Service Bureau

The Legislative Service Bureau is a nonpartisan agency providing all members of the Michigan Legislature with a variety of services on a confidential basis. With oversight by the legislative council administrator and pursuant to policies adopted by the Legislative Council, the Bureau provides legal counsel on bill drafting and other legislative drafting matters, research services, printing services, and telecommunications operations for all legislators and legislative staff. The Legislative Service Bureau's main operations are located in the Boji Tower, 124 W. Allegan, Lansing, MI 48909. Phone: (517) 373-0170. Jennifer Dettloff, Legislative Council Administrator.

Legislative Corrections Ombudsman

Public Act 46 of 1975, being sec. 4.351 to 4.364 of the Michigan Compiled Laws, provides for the creation of a corrections ombudsman within the structure of the legislative branch. The ombudsman, who is appointed by the Legislative Council on recommendation of the council administrator, is authorized to investigate complaints of administrative actions by the Department of Corrections which are alleged to be contrary to law, contrary to departmental policy, unaccompanied by an adequate statement of reason, or based on irrelevant, immaterial, or erroneous grounds. The Office of the Legislative Corrections Ombudsman is located in the Boji Tower, 124 W. Allegan, Lansing, MI 48909. Phone: (517) 373-8573. E-mail: ombudsman@legislature.mi.gov. Keith Barber, Legislative Corrections Ombudsman.

Joint Committee on Administrative Rules (Staff)

The Joint Committee on Administrative Rules is a statutorily created bipartisan legislative committee, comprised of five House and five Senate members, and is responsible for the legislative oversight of administrative rules proposed by state agencies. The staff assigned to assist the committee is responsible for processing rules transmitted to the committee by state agencies, scheduling committee hearings at the direction of the committee chair, providing members with the background and legal analysis of the rules, and reviewing proposed legislation to determine whether rulemaking authority is, or should be, necessary to carry out the legislative intent of proposed legislation. The staff falls under the Legislative Council for supervisory and budgetary functions and is located in the Boji Tower, 124 W. Allegan, Lansing, MI 48909. Phone: (517) 373-6476. Jennifer Dettloff, Legislative Council Administrator.

Veterans' Facility Ombudsman

The Veterans' Facility Ombudsman was established within the Legislative Council by Public Act 198 of 2016 to investigate concerns regarding the Michigan veterans' facilities. The Veterans' Facility Ombudsman investigates alleged violations of state law or issues concerning an administrative act, medical treatment of a facility resident, or a condition existing at a facility that poses a significant health or safety issue for which there is no effective administrative remedy or is alleged to be contrary to law or policy. The Office of the Veterans' Facility Ombudsman is located in the Boji Tower, 124 W. Allegan, Lansing, MI 48909. Phone: (517) 373-1347. E-mail: MVFO@legislature.mi.gov. Kellie Cody, Veterans Facility Ombudsman.

Michigan Commission on Uniform State Laws

Two legislative members appointed by the Senate Majority Leader, two legislative members appointed by the Speaker of the House, the director of the Legislative Service Bureau or the director's designee, and three non-legislative members appointed by the Legislative Council serve as Michigan's delegation to the National Conference of Commissioners on Uniform State Laws pursuant to Public Act 268 of 1986.

Michigan's delegation meets and confers with commissioners from other states to bring about uniformity of state law in instances where wide variations in state law could tend to complicate the resolution of interstate problems. In addition to "uniform acts" such as the Uniform Commercial Code, which every state is urged to adopt, the National Conference of Commissioners on Uniform State Laws also drafts "model acts" to guide legislatures dealing with issues that need not be treated uniformly by all states. Some models, such as the Model State Administrative Procedures Act, have been adopted for use by most states. The commission's address is 124 W. Allegan, Lansing, MI 48909-7536. Phone: (517) 373-0212. Jennifer Dettloff, Legislative Liaison.

MICHIGAN COMMISSION ON UNIFORM STATE LAWS

Appointed by Legislative Council
THOMAS J. BUITEWEG (Chair)
KIERAN MARION
JAMES P. SPICA

Appointed by Senate Majority Leader
SENATOR PETE LUCIDO
SENATOR JEFF IRWIN

Appointed by Speaker of the House
REPRESENTATIVE MATT HALL
REPRESENTATIVE TENISHA YANCEY

Designated Under Public Act 268 of 1986
JENNIFER DETTLOFF, Legislative Council Administrator

Michigan Law Revision Commission

Legislation enacted in 1965 establishing the Legislative Council, Public Act 412 of 1965 (since superseded by Public Act 268 of 1986), also authorized the creation of a law revision commission to "examine the common law and statutes of the state and current judicial decisions for the purpose of discovering defects and anachronisms in the law and recommending needed reforms." The commission makes an annual report to the Legislative Council. The Office of the Legislative Council Administrator organizes and coordinates commission activities and provides staff assistance when needed. Jane Wilensky, Executive Secretary. Phone: (517) 373-0212. Legislative contact: Jennifer Dettloff.

MICHIGAN LAW REVISION COMMISSION

Appointed by Legislative Council
RICHARD D. MCLELLAN (Chair)
ANTHONY DEREZINSKI (Vice Chair)
GEORGE WARD
BRIAN A. LAVICTOIRE

Appointed by Senate Majority Leader
SENATOR PETE LUCIDO
SENATOR STEPHANIE CHANG

Appointed by Speaker of the House
REPRESENTATIVE RYAN BERMAN
REPRESENTATIVE BRIAN K. ELDER

ex officio
JENNIFER DETTLOFF, Legislative Council Administrator

State Drug Treatment Court Advisory Committee

Public Act 224 of 2004 provided for the creation of the State Drug Treatment Court Advisory Committee in the Legislative Council and went into effect on January 1, 2005. Comprised of 18 members, with the State Court Administrator (or his/her designee) being one member, and the Speaker of the House and Senate Majority Leader jointly appointing the other 17 members, the advisory committee monitors the effectiveness of drug treatment courts and veterans treatment courts and the availability of funding for those courts.

The State Drug Treatment Court Advisory Committee is statutorily required to meet at least quarterly and presents recommendations regarding proposed statutory changes for drug treatment courts to the Legislature and the Supreme Court in the form of an annual report. The Office of the Legislative Council Administrator organizes and coordinates committee activities and provides staff assistance when needed.

STATE DRUG TREATMENT COURT ADVISORY COMMITTEE

Appointed by Senate Majority Leader and Speaker of the House

THE HONORABLE AMY RONAYNE KRAUSE (Chair)
THE HONORABLE RAYMOND P. VOET (Vice Chair)
THE HONORABLE LOUISE ALDERSON
HEIDI CANNON
THE HONORABLE SUSAN L. DOBRICH
ANDREW KONWIAK
THE HONORABLE MARK W. LATCHANA
DOUGLAS R. LLOYD
SHERIFF MICHAEL MAIN
CHRISTINA NICHOLAS
THE HONORABLE JULIA B. OWDZIEJ
MARK RISK
THE HONORABLE GENO SALOMONE
STACY SALON
GARY P. SECOR
ALMA VALENZUELA

Designated Under Public Act 224 of 2004

ANDREW SMITH

Criminal Justice Policy Commission

Public Act 465 of 2014 provided for the creation of the Criminal Justice Policy Commission within the Legislative Council. This 17-member commission is to review and analyze information regarding state and local sentencing and proposed release policies and practices. The Commission is to develop modifications to the sentencing guidelines for recommendation to the legislature. The Office of the Legislative Council Administrator coordinates commission activities and provides staff assistance when needed. The Commission's statute was repealed by Public Act 576 of 2018 effective September 30, 2019.

AMANDA BURGESS-PROCTOR (Chair)
LINUS BANGHART-LINN
RONALD BRETZ
HONORABLE CHUCK GOEDERT
D.J. HILSON
KYLE D. KAMINSKI
SHERYL KUBIAK
REPRESENTATIVE BEAU LAFAVE
SHERIFF MICHELLE LAJOYE-YOUNG
BARBARA LEVINE
SENATOR PETE LUCIDO
KENNETH B. MITCHELL
REPRESENTATIVE ISAAC ROBINSON
SENATOR SYLVIA SANTANA
JENNIFER STRANGE
THE HONORABLE PAUL E. STUTESMAN
ANDREW G. VERHEEK

Michigan Consumers Council

Public Act 277 of 1966, being sec. 445.821 to 445.829 of the Michigan Compiled Laws, provides for the Michigan Consumers Council to "formulate and direct a program for the protection of individual consumers from harmful products and merchandise, false advertising, and deceptive sales practices."

The council is composed of three nonlegislators appointed by the Legislative Council, three members appointed by the governor, as well as the secretary of state, the attorney general, and the head of the Department of Commerce. The agency has not received funding since 1991 and is currently unstaffed for budgetary reasons.

FORMER LEGISLATURES AND LEGISLATIVE OFFICERS
TERRITORIAL LEGISLATURES
1824-1835
FIRST LEGISLATIVE COUNCIL — FIRST AND SECOND SESSIONS[1]

1st Session
June 7, 1824 - August 5, 1824

2nd Session
January 17, 1825 - April 21, 1825

OFFICERS
Abraham Edwards, *President*
John P. Sheldon, George A. O'Keefe, Edmund A. Brush, *Clerks*
Morris Jackson, *Sergeant-at-Arms*

County	Member	County	Member
Brown	Robert Irwin, Jr.	Oakland	{ Stephen Mack
Macomb	{ John Stockton		{ Roger Sprague
	{ Joseph Miller	St. Clair	Zephaniah W. Bunce
Michilimackinac	William H. Puthuff	Wayne	Abraham Edwards
Monroe	{ Hubert Lacroix		
	{ Wolcott Lawrence		

[1] See An Ordinance for the government of the Territory of the United States, northwest of the river Ohio (1787), amended by An Act to provide for the Government of the Territory Northwest of the river Ohio, 1 Stat. 50 (1789) and An Act respecting the government of the territories of the United States northwest and south of the river Ohio, 1 Stat. 285 (1792); An Act to divide the Indiana Territory into two separate governments, 2 Stat. 309 (1805); An Act to amend the ordinance and acts of Congress for the government of the territory of Michigan, and for other purposes, 3 Stat. 769 (1823).

SECOND LEGISLATIVE COUNCIL — FIRST AND SECOND SESSIONS[1]

1st Session
November 2, 1826 - December 30, 1826

2nd Session
January 1, 1827 - April 13, 1827

OFFICERS
Abraham Edwards, *President*
John P. Sheldon, Edmund A. Brush, Randall S. Rice, *Clerks*
William Meldrum, *Sergeant-at-Arms*

District	County	Member	District	County	Member
1	Wayne	{ Abraham Edwards	4	Macomb	{ John Stockton
		{ Henry Connor			{ William A. Burt
		{ Robert A. Forsyth	5	St. Clair	Zephaniah W. Bunce[4]
		{ John McDonell[2]	6	Brown	
2	Monroe	{ Hubert Lacroix		Crawford	} Robert Irwin, Jr.[5]
		{ Wolcott Lawrence		Michilimackinac	
		{ Laurent Durocher			
3	Oakland	{ Sidney Dole			
		{ William F. Mosely[3]			

[1] First council whose membership elected by district. See An Act in addition to an act, entitled "An act to amend the ordinance and acts of Congress for the government of the territory of Michigan," and for other purposes, 4 Stat. 80 (1825); An Act to provide for the election of members of the Legislative Council, approved April 13, 1825, Laws of the Territory of Michigan.

[2] Presented credentials and took seat November 16, 1826.

[3] Presented credentials and took seat November 6, 1826.

[4] Presented credentials and took seat November 21, 1826.

[5] Presented credentials and took seat November 10, 1826.

THIRD LEGISLATIVE COUNCIL — FIRST AND SECOND SESSIONS[1]

1st Session
May 5, 1828 - July 3, 1828

2nd Session
September 7, 1829 - November 5, 1829

OFFICERS

Abraham Edwards, *President*
John P. Sheldon, Samuel Satterlee, Seneca Allen, *Clerks*
William Meldrum, *Sergeant-at-Arms*

County	Member	County	Member
Brown Chippewa Crawford Michilimackinac	Henry R. Schoolcraft[2] Robert Irwin, Jr.[2]	Oakland	Thomas J. Drake Stephen V. R. Trowbridge
Macomb St. Clair	John Stockton	Washtenaw	Henry Rumsey
Monroe	Laurent Durocher Wolcott Lawrence Charles Noble	Wayne	William Brown Henry Connor Abraham Edwards John McDonell

[1] First council directly elected by the eligible voters of that period. See An Act to allow the citizens of the territory of Michigan to elect members of their legislative council, and for other purposes, 4 Stat. 200 (1827); An Act to apportion the membership of the Legislative Council among the several districts of the Territory, approved April 13, 1827, Laws of the Territory of Michigan.
[2] Presented credentials and took seat May 16, 1828.

FOURTH LEGISLATIVE COUNCIL — FIRST AND SECOND SESSIONS[1]

1st Session
May 11, 1830 - July 31, 1830

2nd Session
January 4, 1831 - March 4, 1831

OFFICERS

Abraham Edwards, *President*
Edmund A. Brush, *Secretary*
William Meldrum, *Sergeant-at-Arms*

District	County	Member	District	County	Member
1	Wayne	William Brown William Bartow John McDonell William A. Fletcher	4	Oakland	Daniel LeRoy Thomas J. Drake
2	Monroe Lenawee	Wolcott Lawrence Abraham Edwards Laurent Durocher	5	Washtenaw	James Kingsley
3	Macomb St. Clair	John Stockton	6	Brown Chippewa Crawford Michilimackinac	Robert Irwin, Jr.[2] Henry R. Schoolcraft

[1] See An Act to district the Territory of Michigan, and to provide for the Election of members of the Legislative Council, approved July 3, 1828, Laws of the Territory of Michigan.
[2] Did not attend second session.

FIFTH LEGISLATIVE COUNCIL — FIRST AND SECOND SESSIONS[1]

1st Session
May 1, 1832 - June 29, 1832

2nd Session
January 1, 1833 - April 23, 1833[2]

OFFICERS

John McDonell, *President*
Edmund A. Brush, *Secretary*
James T. Allen, *Sergeant-at-Arms*

District	County	Member	District	County	Member
1	Wayne	John McDonell Joseph W. Torrey Charles Moran	5	Monroe Lenawee	Daniel Bacon Laurent Durocher
2	Macomb St. Clair	Alfred Ashley	6	Cass St. Joseph Kalamazoo	Calvin Britain
3	Oakland	Charles C. Hascall Roger Sprague	7	Chippewa Brown	Henry Dodge[3] Morgan L. Martin
4	Washtenaw	James Kingsley George Renwick		Crawford Iowa Michilimackinac	

[1] See An Act to amend the act entitled "An act to district the Territory of Michigan, and to provide for the election of the members of the Legislative Council," approved July three, one thousand eight hundred and twenty-eight, and for other purposes, approved March 4, 1831, Laws of the Territory of Michigan.
[2] See An Act prolonging the second session of the fifth legislative council of the territory of Michigan, 4 Stat. 650 (1833).
[3] Did not attend either session.

SIXTH LEGISLATIVE COUNCIL — FIRST AND SECOND SESSIONS

1st Session
January 7, 1834 - March 7, 1834

Extra Session
September 1, 1834 - September 8, 1834[1]

Adjourned Session
November 11, 1834 - December 31, 1834

2nd Session
January 12, 1835 - March 28, 1835

Special Session
August 17, 1835 - August 25, 1835

OFFICERS

John McDonell, *President*
John Norvell, *Secretary*[2]
Elisha L. Atkins, *Sergeant-at-Arms*

District	County	Member	District	County	Member
1	Wayne	John McDonell Charles Moran Elon Farnsworth	5	Monroe Lenawee	Daniel Bacon Laurent Durocher
2	Macomb St. Clair	John Stockton	6	Cass St. Joseph Kalamazoo	Calvin Britain
3	Oakland	Charles C. Hascall Samuel Satterlee	7	Brown Chippewa	James D. Doty Morgan L. Martin[3]
4	Washtenaw	George Renwick Abel Millington		Crawford Iowa Michilimackinac	

[1] See An Act to authorize an extra session of the legislative council of the territory of Michigan, 4 Stat. 724 (1834).
[2] Resigned; succeeded by Charles W. Whipple at second session.
[3] Elected president at the second annual session.

FORMER STATE LEGISLATURES, 1835-2018

No.[1]	Session Year	Meeting/Adjournment Dates[2]	Session Days[3]	Public Acts	Local Acts	Resolutions Adopted[5]	Senators	Representatives
				Laws Enacted[4]			Membership[6]	
1	1835	Nov. 2/Nov. 14	13	7		2	16[7]	50[7]
	1836	Feb. 1/Mar. 28	57	83		7	16	50
		July 11/July 26	16	30		3		
2	1837	Jan. 2/Mar. 22	80	111		16	16	50
		June 12/June 22	11	19		3		
		Nov. 9/Dec. 30	52	14		5		
3	1838	Jan. 1/Apr. 6	96	126		23	16	50
4	1839	Jan. 7/Apr. 20	104	117		35	17[8]	52[8]
5	1840	Jan. 6/Apr. 1	87	127		27	17	52
6	1841	Jan. 4/Apr. 13	100	90		30	17	52
7	1842	Jan. 3/Feb. 17	46	89		42	18[9]	53[9]
8	1843	Jan. 2/Mar. 9	67	98		25	18	53
9	1844	Jan. 1/Mar. 12	72	96		34	18	53
10	1845	Jan. 6/Mar. 24	78	115		30	18	53
11	1846	Jan. 5/May 18	134	160		30	18	53
12	1847	Jan. 4/Mar. 17	73	110		38	22[10]	66[10]
13	1848	Jan. 3/Apr. 3	92	295		52	22	66
14	1849	Jan. 1/Apr. 2	92	267		41	22	66
15	1850	Jan. 7/Apr. 2	86	346		33	22	63
16	1851	Feb. 5/Apr. 5	60	157		18	22	63[11]
		June 9/June 28	20	38		1		
17	1853	Jan. 5/Feb. 14	41	97		25	32[12]	71[12]

No.[1]	Session Year	Meeting/Adjournment Dates[2]	Session Days[3]	Public Acts	Local Acts	Resolutions Adopted[5]	Sen. Dem.	Sen. Rep.	Rep. Dem.	Rep. Rep.
18	1855	Jan. 3/Feb. 13	42	174		32	7	25	24	48
19	1857	Jan. 7/Feb. 17	42	195		31	3	29	17[13]	63[13]
	1858	Jan. 20/Feb. 4	16	32		10				
20	1859	Jan. 5/Feb. 16	43	263		29	8	24	25[14]	56[14]
21	1861	Jan. 2/Mar. 16	74	265		19	2	30	11[15]	72[15]
		May 7/May 11	4	10		2				
	1862	Jan. 2/Jan. 20	19	26		16				
22	1863	Jan. 7/Mar. 23	76	243		26	14 (D&U)[16]	18	39[17]	60[17]
	1864	Jan. 19/Feb. 6	19	71		9	14	18	39	
23	1865	Jan. 4/Mar. 23	79	365		58	11 (D&U)	21	27	73
24	1867	Jan. 2/Mar. 28	86	520		47	1	30	21	79
25	1869	Jan. 6/Apr. 5	90	486		56	5	27	25	75
	1870	July 27/Aug. 10	15	8		4				
26	1871	Jan. 4/Apr. 18	105	197[18]	297[18]	52	5	27	29	71
	1872	Mar. 13/Apr. 11	30[19]	64	0	14				
		Apr. 11/May 24[20]	44							
27	1873	Jan. 1/May 1	121	199[18]	197[18]	43	1	31	5	95
	1874	Mar. 3/Mar. 26	24	7	15	11				
28	1875	Jan. 6/May 4	119	234	166	48	15	17	46	54
29	1877	Jan. 3/May 22	140	207[21]	157[21]	49	9	23	25	75
30	1879	Jan. 1/May 31	151	268	140	53	9 (D&N)[22]	23	35	65
31	1881	Jan. 5/June 11	158	290	142	43	2 (D&N)	30	14[23]	86
	1882	Feb. 23/Mar. 14	20	27	21	5				
32	1883	Jan. 3/June 9	158	197	144	28	13 (D&N)[24]	19	38	62
33	1885	Jan. 7/June 20	165	234	165	42	14 (D&N)[25]	18	48	52
34	1887	Jan. 5/June 29	176	317	248	36	10 (D&N)	22	37[26]	63
35	1889	Jan. 2/July 3	183	277	207	42	8 (D&N)	24	30	70
36	1891	Jan. 7/July 3	178	200	198	22	17 (D&N)	15[27]	66[28]	34
	1892	Aug. 5/Aug. 8	4	2	0	2				
37	1893	Jan. 4/May 29	146	213	209	34	10 (D&N)[29]	22	31[30]	69
38	1895	Jan. 2/May 31	150	271	198	33	0	32	1	99

FORMER STATE LEGISLATURES, 1835-2018 *(Cont.)*

No.[1]	Session Year	Meeting/ Adjournment Dates[2]	Session Days[3]	Laws Enacted[4] Public Acts	Laws Enacted[4] Local Acts	Resolutions Adopted[5]	Membership[6] Senators Dem.	Senators Rep.	Representatives Dem.	Representatives Rep.
39	1897	Jan. 6/May 31	146	289	190	37	6 (D&N)[31]	26	19[31]	81
	1898	Mar. 22/Apr. 13	23	8	0	3				
40	1899	Jan. 4/June 24	172	273	190	37	5	27	8	92
		Dec. 18/Jan. 6	19	3	4	2				
	1900	Oct. 10/Oct. 15	6	6	0	2				
		Dec. 12/Dec. 22	11	0	0	0				
41	1901	Jan. 2/June 6	156	242	244	31	1	31	10	90
42	1903	Jan. 7/June 18	107	257	293	27	1	31	10	90
43	1905	Jan. 4/June 17	97	332	339	21	0	32	0	100
44	1907	Jan. 2/June 29	106	340	414	36	0	32	5	95
		Oct. 7/Oct. 26	10	7	2	2				
45	1909	Jan. 6/June 2	87	322	5	4	0	32	2	98
46	1911	Jan. 4/May 2	73	299	12	1	4	28	12	88
	1912	Feb. 26/Mar. 20	15	12	0	0	4	28	12	88
		Mar. 20/Apr. 10	12	9	0	2				
47	1913	Jan. 1/May 15	86	407	10	9	5	27[32]	35	65[33]
48	1915	Jan. 6/May 25	82	314	11	2	3	29	5	95
49	1917	Jan. 3/May 11	75	387	4	8	5	27	12	88
50	1919	Jan. 1/May 15	82	421	11	5	0	32	2	98
		June 3/June 26	12	26	0	1				
51	1921	Jan. 5/May 19	77	404	6	3	0	32	0	100
		May 24/June 20	13	31	0	2				
		June 30/July 26	5	5	0	0				
	1922	Oct. 10/Oct. 20	5	1	0	0	0	32	0	100
52	1923	Jan. 3/May 31	81	323	0	1	0	32	5	95
		Dec. 4/Dec. 19	13	0	5	0				
53	1925	Jan. 7/May 28	79	393	3	5	0	32	0	100
	1926	Feb. 16/Mar. 15	13	21	0	0	0	32	0	100
54	1927	Jan. 5/June 6	82	408	9	4	0	32	2	98
55	1929	Jan. 2/May 29	85	326	8	3	0	32	2	98
56	1931	Jan. 7/June 19	93	336	11	5	1	31	2	98
	1932	Mar. 29/May 21	29	42	0	0	1	31	2	98
		Dec. 27/Dec. 31	4	1	0	0				
57	1933	Jan. 4/July 18	118	270	6	1	17	15	55	45
		Nov. 22/Jan. 4	21	19	0	0				
	1934	Feb. 19/Apr. 4	22	40	0	0	17	15	55	45
		Dec. 10/Dec. 31	8	0	0	0				
58	1935	Jan. 2/June 22	97	258	6	3	11	21	49	51
	1936	Dec. 21/Dec. 29	3	1	0	0	11	21	49	51
59	1937	Jan. 6/July 30	110	350	8	1	17	15	60	40
		July 30/Aug. 1	12	4	0	0				
	1938	Aug. 29/Sept. 16	5	9	0	0	17	15	60	40
60	1939	Jan. 4/June 30	100	346	4	2	9	23	27	73
61	1941	Jan. 1/Oct. 11	100	384	6	2	10	22	32	68
	1942	Jan. 19/Jan. 27	6	16	0	0	10	22	32	68
		Feb. 9/Feb. 27	12	22	0	0				
62	1943	Jan. 6/Apr. 30	58	250	6	5	7	25	26	74
		Apr. 30/May 20[34]	5							
	1944	Jan. 31/Mar. 14	17	59	0	0	7	25	26	74
		June 19/June 20	2	1	0	0				
		Nov. 3/Nov. 4	2	3	0	0				
63	1945	Jan. 3/June 7	79	345	32	2	8	24	34	66
	1946	Feb. 4/Mar. 8	16	29	0	1	8	24	34	66
		July 9/July 26	5	4	0	1				
64	1947	Jan. 1/July 12	97	360	11	4	4	28	5	95
		Sept. 29/Sept. 30	2	1	0	0				
		Nov. 5/Nov. 12	4	4	0	0				
	1948	Mar. 16/May 21	27	51	0	2	4	28	5	95
		Dec. 6/Dec. 15	3	11	0	0				
65	1949	Jan. 5/June 24	91	317	5	1	9	23	39	61
	1950	Mar. 15/Dec. 30	102	43	0	2	9	23	39	61
66	1951	Jan. 3/June 29	95	279	6	3	7	25	34	66
		Aug. 20/Aug. 22	3	5	0	0				
		Oct. 23/Oct. 24	2	2	0	0				
	1952	Jan. 9/June 19	76	280	5	1	7	25	34	66
		Dec. 18/Dec. 23	2	4	0	0				

No.[1]	Session Year	Meeting/ Adjournment Dates[2]	Session Days[3]	Laws Enacted[4] Public Acts	Local Acts	Resolutions Adopted[5]	Membership[6] Senators Dem.	Rep.	Representatives Dem.	Rep.
67	1953	Jan. 14/July 3	87	234	5	1	8	24	34	66
	1954	Jan. 13/May 14	65	217	5	2	8	24	34	66
		Aug. 18/Aug. 19	2	3	0	0				
68	1955	Jan. 12/July 15	97	283	6	4	11[35]	23[35]	51[35]	59[35]
		Nov. 1/Nov. 4	4	11	0	0				
		Nov. 7/Dec. 14	18	1	0	0				
	1956	Jan. 11/May 12	64	230	1	1	11	23	51	59
		June 13/Nov. 8	10	14	6	0				
69	1957	Jan. 9/June 28	92	315	10	0	11	23	49	61
	1958	Jan. 8/June 14	74	230	1	0	11	23	49	61
		June 19/June 19	1	1	0	0				
70	1959	Jan. 14/Dec. 19	175	277	1	3	12	22	55	55
	1960	Jan. 13/May 18	63	163	1	2	12	22	55	55
		Sept. 22/Sept. 23	2	2	0	0				
		Dec. 7/Dec. 22	2	2	0	0				
71	1961	Jan. 11/June 9	78	239	2	3	12	22	54	56
		June 15/June 15	1	0	0	0				
	1962	Jan. 10/Dec. 27	104	242	1	0	12	22	54	56
72	1963	Jan. 9/June 7	74	249	2	1	11	23	52	58
		Sept. 11/Nov. 14	24	2	0	0				
		Dec. 3/Dec. 24	14	68	1	0				
	1964	Jan. 8/May 29	88	290	3	0	11	23	52	58

No.[1]	Session Year	Meeting/ Adjournment Dates[2]	Sen.	Hse.	Public Acts	Local Acts	Resolutions Adopted[5]	Senators Dem.	Rep.	Representatives Dem.	Rep.
73	1965	Jan. 13/Dec. 30	126	126	413	3	1	23[36]	15[36]	73	37
	1966	Jan. 12/Dec. 9	118	120	351	1	1	23	15	73	37
74	1967	Jan. 11/Aug. 3	112	118	306	1	1	18	20	54	56
		Oct. 10/Dec. 22	29	33	12	0	0				
	1968	Jan. 10/Aug. 16	101	104	358	2	4	18	20	54	56
75	1969	Jan. 8/Dec. 19	146	142	346	0	0	18	20	57	53
	1970	Jan. 14/Dec. 31	120	128	252	1	1	18	20	57	53
76	1971	Jan. 13/Dec. 30	144	155	233	0	1	19	19	58	52
	1972	Jan. 12/Dec. 29	119	120	382	1	5	19	19	58	52
77	1973	Jan. 10/Dec. 28	127	126	208	2	0	19	19	60	50
	1974	Jan. 9/Dec. 31	116	121	387	1	0	19	19	60	50
78	1975	Jan. 8/Dec. 31	141	142	336	0	0	24	14	66	44
	1976	Jan. 14/Dec. 30	122	128	454	0	1	24	14	66	44
79	1977	Jan. 12/Dec. 29	134	133	319	1	0	24	14	68	42
	1978	Jan. 11/Dec. 29	125	127	642	0	5	24	14	70	40
80	1979	Jan. 10/Dec. 27	128	136	220	0	0	24	14	70	40
	1980	Jan. 9/Dec. 30	133	134	524	0	4	24	14	70	40
81	1981	Jan. 14/Dec. 30	123	129	232	0	2	24	14	64	46
	1982	Jan. 13/Dec. 29	110	116	541	0	0	24	14	64	46
82	1983	Jan. 12/Dec. 29	123	120	259	0	0	20	18	63	47
	1984	Jan. 11/Dec. 28	90	102	432	0	2	18[37]	20[37]	63	47
83	1985	Jan. 9/Dec. 30	107	126	227	0	0	18	20	57	53
	1986	Jan. 8/Dec. 30	81	94	322	0	3	18	20	57	53
84	1987	Jan. 14/Dec. 30	99	110	286	0	0	18	20	64	46
	1988	Jan. 13/Dec. 29	87	97	521	0	1	18	20	64	46
85	1989	Jan. 11/Dec. 28	81	119	306	1	1	18	20	61	49
	1990	Jan. 10/Dec. 27	75	97	360	0	0	18	20	61	49
86	1991	Jan. 9/Dec. 30	100	121	201	0	1	18	20	61	49
	1992	Jan. 8/Dec. 30	78	92	309	0	1	18	20	61	49
87	1993	Jan. 13/Dec. 31	112	117	362	0	2	16	22	55	55
	1994	Jan. 12/Dec. 29	67	74	451	0	2	16	22	55	55
88	1995	Jan. 11/Dec. 28	92	94	291	0	2	16	22	54	56
	1996	Jan. 10/Dec. 30	80	84	594	0	0	16	22	54	56
89	1997	Jan. 8/Dec. 30	93	97	202	0	0	16	22	58	52
	1998	Jan. 14/Dec. 22	77	85	553	0	1	16	22	58	52
90	1999	Jan. 13/Dec. 10	87	87	276	0	0	15	23	52	58
	2000	Jan. 12/Dec. 29	80	74	506	0	0	15	23	52	58
91	2001	Jan. 10/Dec. 21	91	89	280	0	1	15	23	52	58
	2002	Jan. 9/Dec. 30	76	77	747	0	1	15	23	52	58
92	2003	Jan. 8/Dec. 30	107	97	322	0	0	16	22	48	62
	2004	Jan. 14/Dec. 29	109	93	596	0	1	16	22	48	62

No.[1]	Session Year	Meeting/ Adjournment Dates[2]	Session Days[3]	Laws Enacted[4]		Resolutions Adopted[5]	Membership[6]			
				Public Acts	Local Acts		Senators		Representatives	
							Dem.	Rep.	Dem.	Rep.
93	2005	Jan. 12/Dec. 29	113	110	340	0	1	16	22	52	58
	2006	Jan. 11/Dec. 29	98	97	682	0	0	16	22	52	58
94	2007	Jan. 10/Dec. 27	132	134	221	0	0	17	21	58	52
	2008	Jan. 9/Dec. 30	95	96	586	0	0	17	21	58	52
95	2009	Jan. 14/Dec. 30	107	113	242	0	0	16	22	67	43
	2010	Jan. 13/Dec. 29	99	99	383	0	1	16	22	66	44[38]
96	2011	Jan. 12/Dec. 28	101	103	323	0	0	12	26	47	63
	2012	Jan. 11/Dec. 27	82	84	625	0	0	12	26	47	63
97	2013	Jan. 9/Dec. 13	103	107	277	0	0	12	26	51[39]	59
	2014	Jan. 8/Dec. 30	86	88	572	0	2	12	26	51[39]	59
98	2015	Jan. 14/Dec. 18	104	112	269	0	0	11	27	48	62
	2016	Jan. 13/Dec. 28	80	81	563	0	0	11	27	48	62
99	2017	Jan. 11/Dec. 28	103	98	267	0	0	11	27	47	63
	2018	Jan. 10/Dec. 28	84	85	690	0	1	11	27	47	63

[1] The provisions of the Constitution of 1835 governed the 1st through the 15th legislatures, while the Constitution of 1850 regulated the actions of the 16th through the 44th legislatures. The 45th through the 3rd session of the 72nd legislature acted under the terms of the Constitution of 1908. The 1964 session of the 72nd legislature and all subsequent sessions have been governed by the provisions of the Constitution of 1963.

The 1st through the 12th legislatures also met in Detroit, then the capital of the state. Beginning with the 13th legislature, all subsequent sessions have convened in Lansing, designated Michigan's capital by Public Act 60 of 1847, Laws of Michigan.

[2] The date listed is that of the last adjourning house, if applicable.

[3] The length of the sessions of the 1st through the 41st legislatures is calculated in calendar days from the opening to the adjournment of each session. Beginning with the 42nd and ending with the 72nd legislature, the number listed is the actual number of session days of the last adjourning house.

[4] The 1st through the 25th legislatures made no distinction between a public act or a local act; all were published as "acts of the legislature" in a single volume. Public Act 97 of 1871, Laws of Michigan, first required the publication of public acts and local acts as separate volumes.

[5] For the 1st through the 44th legislatures, the number of resolutions listed may include joint, concurrent, or regular resolutions, as the legislature did not distinguish among the types of resolutions in the same manner as the legislature has done since the adoption of the 1908 constitution. Beginning in 1909, the list includes resolutions used to propose amendments to the state constitution, ratify amendments to the U.S. constitution, and to carry out other similar business. For the 45th through the 47th legislatures, the legislature referred to these resolutions as concurrent resolutions. Beginning with the 48th legislature, the legislature referred to these resolutions as joint resolutions, with one exception in 1925.

[6] Political data has been included in the table since 1885. The political make-up of the earlier legislatures was ascertained as nearly as possible by researching newspapers of the period, of which 1850 was the earliest obtainable.

[7] As Allegan County was organized by an act of the territorial council after adoption of the proposed constitution for submission to a vote and before actual adoption by the voters, the county was entitled to one representative in the house upon the effective date of the constitution. Therefore, the house of representatives admitted the Allegan County delegate, increasing its membership to 50. See Const. 1835, art. IV, §4, and Sched. §12.

[8] Under the terms of the Constitution of 1835, art. IV, §3, the legislature enacted Public Act 82 of 1838, Laws of Michigan, apportioning house of representatives members and arranging senate districts.

[9] See Public Act 61 of 1841, Laws of Michigan, reapportioning house of representatives membership and senate districts.

[10] See Public Act 25 of 1846, Laws of Michigan, reapportioning house of representatives membership and senate districts.

[11] Organized as counties in March 1850, prior to the adoption of the Constitution of 1850, both Tuscola and Montcalm Counties were entitled to one representative each under the provisions of the Constitution of 1835, art. IV, §4. The house of representatives admitted both delegates to increase its membership to 68.

[12] The Constitution of 1850, art. IV, §2, increased the number of senators to 32. Art. IV, §3, established a range in the number of representatives. Public Act 167 of the Extra Session of 1851, Laws of Michigan, reapportioned house membership within that range.

[13] See Public Act 104 of 1855, Laws of Michigan, reapportioning house of representatives membership. Saginaw County was inadvertently omitted from the reapportionment act, but was entitled to one seat in the house.

[14] Bay County was organized in 1857. Having met the requirements for representation of the Constitution of 1850, art. IV, §3, the house of representatives admitted its delegate, increasing membership to 81.

[15] Alpena County, organized in 1857 and originally a part of another district, met the population requirements of the Constitution of 1850, art. IV, §3, thereby entitling it to one representative. Muskegon County was organized in 1859 under the terms of the Constitution of 1850. Therefore, the house of representatives admitted both delegates to increase its membership to 83.

[16] Democratic and Union.

[17] See Public Act 116 of 1861, Laws of Michigan, reapportioning house of representatives membership and increasing it to the constitutional limit.

[18] Public Act 97 of 1871 and Public Act 157 of 1873, Laws of Michigan, authorized the publication of acts enacted by the legislature into three volumes: acts of a general nature; charters from cities, villages and other municipal bodies, and all acts of a local or personal nature. The charters of cities, villages and municipal bodies are included in the local act total.

[19] Both the house and senate voted to extend the extra session beyond its 20-day constitutional limit to allow members of the senate to return home before organizing as a court of impeachment.

[20] Session of the senate sitting as a court of impeachment for the trial of Charles A. Edmonds, commissioner of the state land office.

[21] Public Act 170 of 1877 repealed the 1871 and 1873 acts on publication of laws enacted and authorized the publication of acts enacted into two volumes: acts of a general nature and all acts of a local nature.

[22] Democratic and National.

FORMER STATE LEGISLATURES, 1835-2018 *(Cont.)*

[23] One Independent.

[24] Democratic, Fusionist and Greenback.

[25] Greenback and Republican, one; Labor and Fusionist, one; Labor and Republican, one.

[26] Labor Republican, four; Labor and Fusionist, three; Greenback and Labor, one; Labor, Greenback and Republican, one; Patrons of Industry, three.

[27] Three Patrons of Industry.

[28] Four Patrons of Industry and three Industrial.

[29] One Democratic and Populist.

[30] Three Populists.

[31] Democratic, Populist and Silverite.

[32] Six National Progressives.

[33] Eleven National Progressives.

[34] Session of the senate sitting as a court of impeachment for the trial of Michael E. Nolan, judge of probate for the County of Gogebic.

[35] An amendment to sections 2, 3, and 4 of article 5 of the Constitution of 1908, proposed by initiative petition and approved November 1952, increased the number of senators to 34 and the number of representatives to 110.

[36] The Constitution of 1963, art. 4, §2, increased the number of senators to 38.

[37] Voters recalled Democratic senators representing the 8th and 9th senate districts in November 1983. Republican candidates won both seats.

[38] The 65th house district, previously held by a Democrat, was vacant from the commencement of the 2010 Regular Session until a special election on November 7, 2010, when the seat was won by a Republican.

[39] One Independent Urban Democracy Caucus member.

| Name[2] | Post Office[3] | Session Years[4] | |
		House	Senate
Abbott, Adrian O.	Hudson, Lenawee	1887-1890	
Abbott, Isaac C.	Pine Creek, Calhoun	1863-1864	
Abbott, Joshua K.	Grand Blanc, Genesee	1850	
Abbott, William L.	Goodland, Lapeer	1877-1880	
Abed, Theresa	Grand Ledge, Eaton	2013-2014	
Abel, Sylvester	Ann Arbor, Washtenaw		1857-1858
Abell, Oliver C.	Wayne, Wayne		1867-1868
Abrams, Edward T.	Dollar Bay, Houghton	1907-1908	
Accavitti, Frank, Jr.	Eastpointe, Macomb	2003-2008	
Acciavatti, Daniel Joseph	Chesterfield, Macomb	2003-2008	
	New Baltimore, Macomb		
Achard, Anton Emil	Clare, Clare		1929-1930
Acker, Henry	Jackson, Jackson	1839-1840	
Acker, Ural Stebbins	Kalamazoo, Kalamazoo	1939-1950	
Ackley, Francis	St. Charles, Saginaw	1873-1874	
Adair, William	Detroit, Wayne		1861-1866; 1869-1870; 1875-1878
Adam, John Johnstone	Clinton, Lenawee	1839;1847;1871-1872	1840-1841
Adamini, Stephen F.	Marquette, Marquette	2001-2006	
Adams, Calvin Spencer	Lawton, Van Buren	1901-1904	
Adams, Charles Parmenio	Howell, Livingston	1935-1944	
Adams, Clark J.	Pontiac, Oakland	1937-1944	
Adams, Edgar J.	Grand Rapids, Kent	1897-1900	
Adams, Ezra Chadwick	Alamo, Kalamazoo	1861-1862; 1885-1886	
Adams, Isaac	Troy, Oakland	1838	
Adams, John Quincy	Negaunee, Marquette	1883	
Adams, Oliver	Utica, Macomb	1853-1854	
Adams, Oliver Holt	Mount Pleasant, Isabella	1905-1908	
Adams, Oscar	Flint, Genesee	1871-1872	
Adams, Robert Newton	Sault Saint Marie, Chippewa	1903-1906	
Adams, Wales	Prairie River, Branch	1844-1845	
Adsit, Allen Clark	Spring Lake, Ottawa	1871-1872	
Afendoulis, Chris	Grand Rapids, Kent	2015-2018	
Afendoulis, Lynn	Grand Rapids Township, Kent	2019-	
Agee, James G.	Muskegon, Muskegon	1993-1998	
Agema, David	Grandville, Kent	2007-2012	
Agens, M. Livy	Ludington, Mason	1905-1910	
Aitkin, Robert P.	Flint, Genesee	1865-1866	
Aitkin, William H.	Croswell, Sanilac		1909-1910
Albert, Thomas	Grattan Township, Kent	2017-	
Albosta, Donald Joseph	St. Charles, Saginaw	1975-1976	
Alden, Hiram	Coldwater, Branch	1835-1837	
Aldrich, Ezra F.	Hiawatha, Alger	1935-1938	
Aldrich, Frank	Detroit, Wayne	1899-1900	
Aldrich, Frank B.	Longpoint, Cheboygan	1919-1922	
Aldrich, Levi	Edwardsburg, Cass	1863-1864	1865-1866
Aleshire, Oscar Emmet	Buchanan, Berrien	1889-1890	
Alexander, Betty Jean	Detroit, Wayne		2019-
Alexander, Julie	Hanover, Jackson	2017-	
Alexander, Lorenzo P.	Buchanan, Berrien	1861-1862	1871-1872
Alexander, Sydney U.	DeWitt, Clinton	1867-1868	
Alexander, Sylvanus	Wexford, Wexford	1889-1892	
Allard, Homer Layton	Sturgis, St. Joseph	1919-1922; 1935-1944	
Allbritten, Drew William	Grand Rapids, Kent	1979-1980	
Allen, Abram	Commerce, Oakland	1865-1866	
Allen, Artemas	Medina, Lenawee	1839	
Allen, Dick	Fairgrove, Tuscola	1983-1994	
Allen, Edward Payson	Ypsilanti, Washtenaw	1877-1880	
Allen, George Washington	Grand Rapids, Kent	1859-1860; 1865-1866	
Allen, Giles Bertram	Charlotte, Eaton	1895-1896	
Allen, Harmon	Milan, Monroe	1857-1858	
Allen, Hiram Murray	Bellevue, Eaton	1887-1888	
Allen, Jason	Traverse City, Grand Traverse	1999-2002	2003-2010
Allen, John	Ann Arbor, Washtenaw		1845-1848

Name[2]	Post Office[3]	House	Senate
			Session Years[4]
Allen, Lester J.	Ithaca, Gratiot	1957-1968	
Allen, Lewis	Manchester, Washtenaw	1839	
Allen, Lovatus C.	York, Washtenaw	1863-1864	
Allen, Morris S.	DeWitt, Clinton	1849	
Allen, Richard John	Ithaca, Gratiot	1969-1972	1975-1982
	Alma, Gratiot		
Allen, Thomas J.	Flint, Genesee		1907-1908
Alley, Tom	West Branch, Ogemaw	1979-1998	
Allison, Freeman W.	Pinckney, Livingston	1897-1898	
Allman, William	Sturgis, St. Joseph	1857-1858; 1877-1878	
Allor, Sue	Wolverine, Cheboygan	2017-	
Allswede, William H.	Sanford, Midland		1913-1914
Almy, John	Grand Rapids, Kent	1837	
Alvord, Charles H.	Camden, Hillsdale	1907-1908	
Alvord, Henry Jones	Lapeer, Lapeer		1855-1856
Alvord, Nathan A.	Camden, Hillsdale	1881-1884	
Alward, Robert	Hudsonville, Ottawa	1897-1902	
Amash, Justin	Cascade, Kent	2009-2010	
Amberson, Verne Clarence	Blissfield, Lenawee		1913-1914
Ambler, William E.	Pentwater, Oceana		1879-1882
Amerson, Harvey S.	Elk Rapids, Antrim	1911-1912	
Ames, James W.	Detroit, Wayne	1901-1902	
Ames, Joseph G.	Bertrand, Berrien	1844	
Ames, Michael E.	Plymouth, Wayne	1846	
Amidon, Edmund Sumner	Sturgis, St. Joseph	1895-1896	
Amon, Aaron	Remus, Mecosta	1915-1918	1919-1922
Amos, Fran	Waterford, Oakland	2003-2008	
Ananich, Jim	Flint, Genesee	2011-2013	2013-
Anderson, Andrew F.	Omena, Leelanau	1915-1918	
Anderson, Cora Reynolds	L'Anse, Baraga	1925-1926	
Anderson, David	Bear Lake Mills, Van Buren		1873-1874
Anderson, Glenn S.	Westland, Wayne	2001-2006	2007-2014
Anderson, Jeremiah H.	Grand Rapids, Kent	1893-1894; 1897-1900; 1903-1904; 1907-1908	
Anderson, Lloyd L.	Pontiac, Oakland	1957-1964	
Anderson, Loren D.	Pontiac, Oakland	1967-1974	
Anderson, Louis Edwin	Northport, Leelanau	1929-1932; 1941-1954	
Anderson, Samuel Finley	Cassopolis, Cass	1842-1843	
Anderson, Thomas Jefferson	Southgate, Wayne	1965-1980	
Anderson, William A.	Fremont, Newaygo	1887-1888	
Andrews, Charles	Armada, Macomb		1867-1870
Andrews, Frank	Hillman, Montmorency		1949-1960
Andrews, John	Lawrence, Van Buren	1843; 1845; 1849	
Andrews, John L.	Milford, Oakland	1871-1872	
Andrews, Josiah	Paw Paw, Van Buren	1846	
Andrews, Steve	Wolverine, Cheboygan	1979-1980	
Andrus, Wesley P.	Cedar Springs, Kent		1877-1878
Andrus, William W.	Utica, Macomb		1881-1882
Angel, Dan	Marshall, Calhoun	1973-1978	
Angerer, Charles	Scofield, Monroe	1889-1890	
Angerer, Kathy	Dundee, Monroe	2005-2010	
Anhut, John N.	Detroit, Wayne		1909-1910
Annable, Fernando C.	Paw Paw, Van Buren	1842	
Anthony, David	Escanaba, Delta	1991-1998	
Anthony, Sarah	Lansing, Ingham	2018-	
Apley, Raymond J., Jr.	Mount Clemens, Macomb	1959-1962	
Aplin, Henry Harrison	West Bay City, Bay	1895-1896	
Armbruster, Loren Simon	Kalamazoo, Kalamazoo	1973-1980	
	Caro, Tuscola		
Arms, Willard B.	White Lake, Oakland		1855-1858; 1867-1868
	Fenton, Genesee		
Armstrong, John H.	Hillsdale, Hillsdale	1870	
Armstrong, Joseph C.	Detroit, Wayne	1925-1932	
Armstrong, Sullivan	Ashland, Newaygo	1873-1876	

Name[2]	Post Office[3]	House	Session Years[4]
			Senate
Arnett, Homer	Kalamazoo, Kalamazoo	1957-1966	
Arnold, Joseph	Lakeville, Oakland	1842	
Arnold, Paul	Detroit, Wayne	1947-1948	
Arnold, Seymour	Lakeville, Oakland	1845	
Arnold, William P.	Quincy, Branch	1853-1854	
Arthurhultz, Phillip J.	Whitehall, Muskegon		1979-1994
Arzeno, Alexander M.	Newport, Monroe	1847	1863-1864
Ashley, James	Adamsville, Cass	1869-1870	
Ashley, Noble	Detroit, Wayne	1903-1904; 1911-1916	1905-1906
Ashman, Samuel	Sault Saint Marie, Chippewa	1840	
Ashmun, Henry C.	Midland City, Midland	1855-1858	
Ashton, Benjamin D.	Traverse City, Grand Traverse	1887-1888	
Asselin, Charles B.	Bay City, Bay		1933-1934
Atkinson, John	Detroit, Wayne	1897-1898	
Attridge, Robert	Brown City, Sanilac	1905-1908	
Atwood, Henry P.	Vassar, Tuscola	1855-1856	
Atwood, Marcus M.	Dansville, Ingham	1861-1862; 1871-1872	
Atwood, Orville E.	Newaygo, Newaygo	1919-1922	1923-1926; 1929-1930
Atwood, Theron W.	Caro, Tuscola		1899-1902
Atwood, William A.	Flint, Genesee		1887-1888
Austin, Andrew V.	Milford, Oakland	1903-1906	
Austin, Charles	Battle Creek, Calhoun	1881-1882	1883-1886
Austin, Charles W.	Detroit, Wayne	1909-1912	
Austin, Daniel	Ludington, Mason	1889-1890	
Austin, William A.	Muskegon, Muskegon	1953-1954	
Averill, Harrison H.	Coopersville, Ottawa	1919-1922	
Averill, Paul J.	Grand Rapids, Kent	1911-1912; 1915-1916	
Avery, John	Greenville, Montcalm	1869-1870	
Axford, Samuel	Oxford, Oakland	1839-1840; 1842-1843	1851-1852
	Shelby, Macomb		
Axford, William	Clarkston, Oakland	1850	
Baade, Paul T.	Roosevelt Park, Muskegon	1991-1998	
Babcock, Charles Volney	Southfield, Oakland		1863-1864; 1875-1876
Babcock, Christopher G.	East Gilead, Branch	1897-1900	
Babcock, Edwin Green	Coldwater, Branch	1933-1934	
Babcock, Henry S.	Southfield, Oakland	1842	
Babcock, Herbert	Woodbury, Eaton	1897-1898	
Babcock, Jonathan W.	Lexington, Sanilac		1887-1888
Babcock, W. Irving	Niles, Berrien		1887-1890
Backus, Henry Titus	Detroit, Wayne	1840	1861-1862
Backus, Ira C.	Jackson, Jackson		1859-1860
Backus, William	Greenville, Montcalm	1875-1876	
Bacon, Cyrus	Edwardsburg, Cass	1849	
Bacon, Daniel S.	Monroe, Monroe	1839	
Bacon, John	Eagle River, Keweenaw	1851-1852	
Bacon, Levi, Jr.	Pontiac, Oakland	1857-1858	
Baginski, Martin W.	Detroit, Wayne	1933-1936	
Bagley, Walter	Wilson, Menominee	1943-1944	
Bagot, Richard W.	Elk Rapids, Antrim	1893-1894	
Bahorski, Joseph	Detroit, Wayne		1923-1928
Bailey, Alvin W.	Hastings, Barry	1853-1854	
Bailey, Charles A.	Port Huron, St. Clair	1893-1894	
Bailey, Frederick G.	Vernon, Shiawassee	1873-1876	
Bailey, Isaac G.	Fort Pleasant, St. Joseph	1840	
Bailey, John W.	Grand Rapids, Kent	1929-1930	
Bailey, Norman	Hastings, Barry		1861-1862
Baillie, Thomas Gilbert	Saginaw, Saginaw	1905-1906	
Baird, John	Zilwaukee, Saginaw	1895-1896	1901-1906
Baird, Laura L.	Okemos, Ingham	1995-2002	
Baird, William Bayley	Detroit, Wayne	1955-1964	
Baker, Edward L.	Detroit, Wayne	1947-1948	
Baker, Francis	Groveland, Oakland	1848	
Baker, Fred A.	Detroit, Wayne	1877-1878	
Baker, Frederick Kessler	Menominee, Menominee		1899-1902

Name[2]	Post Office[3]	House	Session Years[4] Senate
Baker, Herbert F.	Weadock, Cheboygan	1907-1912	1919-1922
Baker, Lewis C.	Adrian, Lenawee	1891-1892	
Baker, Milo S.	Portland, Ionia	1861-1862	
Baker, Newton	St. Johns, Clinton	1877-1878	
Baker, Raymond L.	Berkley, Oakland	1961-1974	
	Farmington, Oakland		
Baker, Seward	Newport, Monroe	1885-1888	
Baker, William A.	Coloma, Berrien	1887-1890	
Baker, William, Jr.	Hudson, Lenawee		1861-1862
Balch, Nathaniel A.	Kalamazoo, Kalamazoo		1847-1848
Balcombe, John L.	Battle Creek, Calhoun	1851-1852	
Baldwin, Augustus Carpenter	Milford, Oakland	1844; 1846	
Baldwin, Charles	Rochester, Oakland	1846; 1879-1882	
	Pontiac, Oakland		
Baldwin, Elias Jones	Morenci, Lenawee	1851-1852	
Baldwin, Ezra P.	Birmingham, Oakland	1848	
Baldwin, Frank Augustus	Gaylord, Otsego	1887-1888	
Baldwin, Gaylord M.	Hopkins, Allegan	1889-1890	
Baldwin, Henry Porter	Detroit, Wayne		1861-1862
Baldwin, James M.	Hopkins, Allegan	1859-1860	
Baldwin, Joseph A.	Albion, Calhoun		1935-1936; 1939-1944
Baldwin, Levi W.	Fowler, Clinton	1891-1892	
Baldwin, Robert W.	Albion, Calhoun	1945-1948	
Baldwin, Simeon Lathrop	Grand Rapids, Kent	1877-1878	
Baldwin, William L.	Palmyra, Lenawee	1909-1912	
Ball, Byron D.	Grand Rapids, Kent		1871-1872
Ball, John	Grand Rapids, Kent	1838	
Ball, John C.	Tecumseh, Lenawee	1842	
Ball, Richard J.	Laingsburg, Shiawassee	2005-2010	
Ball, William	Hamburg, Livingston	1865-1868; 1881-1882	1889-1890
Ball, William Hazen	Coloma, Berrien	1909-1912	
Ballantine, Mary Keith	Jackson, Jackson	1979-1980	
Ballard, Jesse	Tecumseh, Lenawee	1837	
Ballenger, William S., III.	Lansing, Ingham	1969-1970	1971-1974
	Ovid, Clinton		
Ballentine, Silas L.	Port Huron, St. Clair	1901-1902	
Ballentine, William H.	Brockway, St. Clair	1881-1882	
Bancroft, Edward C.	Port Huron, St. Clair	1845	
Bancroft, William Lyman	Port Huron, St. Clair	1859-1860	1865-1866
Bandstra, Richard A.	Grand Rapids, Kent	1985-1994	
Bangham, Arthur D.	Homer, Calhoun		1901-1904
Bankes, Lyn R.	Livonia, Wayne	1985-1998	
Banks, Brian	Grosse Pointe Woods, Wayne	2013-2017	
Bannasch, John Walford	Jackson, Jackson	1943-1950	
Barbeau, Peter B.	Fort Brady, Chippewa	1845	
Barber, Daniel	Eaton, Eaton	1840	
Barber, Homer Griswold	Vermontville, Eaton		1871-1872
Barber, John	Adrian, Lenawee		1851-1852
Barber, Julius S.	Coldwater, Branch	1867-1868	
Barber, Leslie T.	Edmore, Montcalm	1933-1934	
Barbour, John	Battle Creek, Calhoun	1846	
Barcia, James A.	Bay City, Bay	1977-1980	1983-1993; 2003-2010
Barclay, Jonathan S.	Hampton, Saginaw	1855-1856	
Bardwell, Hiram H.	Mount Morris, Genesee	1885-1888	
Barker, Richard P.	Niles, Berrien	1847	
Barkworth, Thomas E.	Jackson, Jackson	1891-1894	
Barlow, Nathan	Yankee Springs, Barry	1841; 1848	
Barlow, Nathan, Jr.	Hastings, Barry	1850	
Barnaby, Horace T.	Pompeii, Gratiot	1869-1872	
Barnaby, Horace Thomas, Jr.	Grand Rapids, Kent	1901-1904	1909-1912
Barnard, Edmund M.	Grand Rapids, Kent	1891-1892	1893-1898
Barnard, Ely	Howell, Livingston	1843-1844	
Barnard, George S.	Benton Harbor, Berrien	1919-1924	1927-1930
Barnard, Harry E.	Jackson, Jackson	1929-1932	

Name[2]	Post Office[3]	Session Years[4]	
		House	Senate
Barnard, Newell Oliver	Saginaw, Saginaw	1883-1884	
Barnes, Eleazar	London, Monroe	1851-1852	
Barnes, George	Howell, Livingston		1903-1904
Barnes, George Albert	Flint, Genesee		1915-1916
Barnes, Henry	Detroit, Wayne		1859-1860
Barnes, Norman	LaSalle, Monroe	1850	
Barnes, Orlando Mack	Mason, Ingham	1863-1864	
Barnes, Orsamus S.	Roxand, Eaton	1879-1880	
Barnett, Vicki L.	Farmington Hills, Oakland	2009-2014	
Barns, Justine	Westland, Wayne	1983-1994	
Barnum, Ezra Castle	Petoskey, Emmet		1895-1898
Barr, Adrian C.	Shepherd, Isabella	1933-1934	
Barrett, Hiram	Walled Lake, Oakland	1846	
Barrett, Ray M.	Muskegon, Muskegon	1937-1940	
Barrett, Tom	Potterville, Eaton	2015-2018	2019-
Barringer, John E.	Armada, Macomb		1887-1890
Barry, John Allison	Harrietta, Wexford	1907-1908	
Barry, John Stewart	Constantine, St. Joseph		1835-1838; 1841
Barry, Thomas B.	East Saginaw, Saginaw	1885-1886	
Bartholomew, Ira H.	Lansing, Ingham	1873-1874	
Bartlett, Charles Edward	Detroit, Wayne	1923-1932	
Bartlett, Wallace R.	Watrousville, Tuscola	1857-1858	
Bartnik, Jerry Carl	Temperance, Monroe	1983-1992	
Barton, Walter W.	Leland, Leelanau	1881-1882	1887-1888
Bartow, John	Flint, Genesee		1838
Bartow, Moses	Westphalia, Clinton	1865; 1875-1876	
Basham, Raymond E.	Taylor, Wayne	1997-2002	2003-2010
Bassett, Wilfred G.	Jackson, Jackson	1951-1964	
Bastone, John	Caro, Tuscola		1891
Batchelder, John Lawrence	Detroit, Wayne	1903-1904	
Bates, Alfred G.	Monroe, Monroe	1853-1854	
Bates, Bion Lamott	Ovid, Clinton		1947-1950
Bates, Erastus Newton	Moline, Allegan	1885-1888	1907-1910
Bates, William R.	Au Gres, Bay	1871; 1897-1898	
	Flint, Genesee		
Bathey, Fred H.	Smiths Creek, St. Clair	1891-1894	
Bauer, Homer L.	Charlotte, Eaton	1943-1952	
Bauer, Joan	Lansing, Ingham	2007-2012	
Baum, William B.	Saginaw, Saginaw	1893-1894	
Baumann, Jacob	Detroit, Wayne	1901-1902	
Baumgaertner, Leonard	Saginaw, Saginaw	1899-1904	
Baumgardner, William G.	Filer City, Manistee	1887-1888	
Baxter, Benjamin L.	Tecumseh, Lenawee	1869-1870	
Baxter, Howard F.	Grand Rapids, Kent	1923-1924	1925-1928
Baxter, Levi	Jonesville, Hillsdale		1849-1850
Baxter, Rick	Hanover, Jackson	2005-2006	
Baxter, Witter J.	Jonesville, Hillsdale		1877-1878
Bayer, Rosemary	Beverly Hills, Oakland		2019-
Bayley, James	Big Beaver, Oakland	1865-1866	
Bayliss, Joseph Edward	Sault Saint Marie, Chippewa	1913-1914	
Beach, Joseph P.	Battle Creek, Calhoun	1865-1866	
Beach, Noah	Bridgeport, Saginaw	1843	1850-1852
Beadle, Frank D.	St. Clair, St. Clair		1951-1968
Beadle, Harvey J.	Detroit, Wayne	1959-1962	
Beakes, Hiram J.	Ann Arbor, Washtenaw	1863-1864	
Beal, Junius Emery	Ann Arbor, Washtenaw	1905-1906	
Beall, Isaac D.	Colon, St. Joseph	1867-1870	
Beam, Warren Barnhart	Mancelona, Antrim	1925-1926	
Beamer, George K.	Irving, Barry	1861-1862	
Beardsley, Fred G.	Oxford, Oakland	1949-1956	
Beattie, Adam	Ovid, Clinton		1873-1874
Beaufait, Louis	Detroit, Wayne	1838-1839	
Beck, John J.	Detroit, Wayne	1953-1954	
Becker, James	Detroit, Wayne	1945-1946	

| Name[2] | Post Office[3] | House | Session Years[4] |
			Senate
Beckwith, Jefferson H.	Lyons, Ionia		1855-1856
Bedtelyon, Jacob	Goodrich, Genesee	1879-1880	
Beebe, Joseph E.	Jackson, Jackson	1855-1856	1857-1858
Beebe, N. Lorraine	Dearborn, Wayne		1967-1970
Beebe, Uriah	Orion, Oakland	1859-1860	
Beecher, Charles N.	Genesee, Genesee	1851-1852; 1857-1858	
	Flint, Genesee		
Beecher, Norman A.	Flushing, Genesee	1885-1888	
Beecher, Robert R.	Adrian, Lenawee	1855-1856	
Beedon, Francis W.	Muskegon, Muskegon	1963-1968	
Beekman, Benjamin F.	Vermontville, Eaton	1885-1886	
Beeman, Alonzo P.	Jones, Cass	1907-1910	
Beers, John S.	Stevensville, Berrien		1891-1892
Beers, Philo	Courtland, Kent	1850; 1859-1860	
	Northport, Leelanau		
Beeson, Jesse G.	Dowagiac, Cass		1853-1854
Beeson, William B.	Niles, Berrien	1859-1860	
Begick, Adolph	Bay City, Bay	1943-1944	
Begick, Lester O.	Bay City, Bay	1961-1962	1963-1964
Begick, Paul	Bay City, Bay	1939-1941	
Begole, Josiah Williams	Flint, Genesee		1871-1872
Belden, Eugene H.	Horton, Jackson	1881-1882	
Belding, Friend	Birmingham, Oakland	1849	
Belen, Elizabeth Lehman	Lansing, Ingham	1937-1938	
Belknap, James William	Greenville, Montcalm		1883-1886
Belknap, Lyman E.	Mayville, Tuscola	1895-1898	
Bell, Alexander F.	Ionia, Ionia	1847	
Bell, Digby V.	Ada, Kent	1840	1842-1843
Bell, George William	Cheboygan, Cheboygan		1879-1880
Bellino, Joseph N.	Monroe, Monroe	2017-	
Bellows, Harold Cagwin	Bay City, Bay	1933-1936	
Bement, Rufus Budd	Dexter, Washtenaw	1838	
Bemis, Arthur L.	Carson City, Montcalm	1897-1898	
Bender, Robert G.	Middleville, Barry	1983-1994	
Benedict, Alexander H.	Fowlerville, Livingston	1867-1868	
Benedict, Jacob M.	Portland, Ionia	1875-1876	
Benedict, Peter H.	Lexington, Sanilac	1853-1854	
Benedict, Stanley Carleton	Port Huron, St. Clair	1941-1942	
Benjamin, Fay E.	Cedar Springs, Kent	1949	
Benjamin, William H. P.	Bridgeport, Saginaw	1875-1876	1879-1880
Bennane, Michael J.	Detroit, Wayne	1977-1996	
Bennett, Adam	New Haven, Macomb	1893-1895	
Bennett, Alonzo	Berrien, Berrien	1842	
Bennett, Charles H	Plymouth, Wayne	1870	
Bennett, Davis D.	Fairfield, Lenawee	1848	
Bennett, Doug	Muskegon, Muskegon	2005-2010	
Bennett, Frank Tripp	Jackson, Jackson	1907-1908	
Bennett, James T.	Sault Saint Marie, Chippewa	1907-1908	
Bennett, John	Redford Township, Wayne	1965-1992	
	Redford, Wayne		
Bennett, John H.	Coldwater, Branch	1881-1884	
Bennett, Loren N.	Canton, Wayne		1995-2002
Bennett, Stillman W.	Fairfield, Lenawee	1879-1880	
Bennett, Theodore G.	Jackson, Jackson		1871-1872
Benoit, Charles P.	Detroit, Wayne	1893-1896	
Benson, John R.	Mount Morris, Genesee		1891-1892
Benson, Victor	Iron River, Iron	1939	
Bentley, Elijah	Napoleon, Jackson	1863-1864	
Bentley, John Westcott	Mendon, St. Joseph	1883-1888	
Benton, Cassius R.	Northville, Wayne	1905-1908	
Benzie, D. Stephen	Norway, Dickinson		1939-1942
Berk, John	Belle River, St. Clair	1875	
Berka, Frank Joseph	Saginaw, Saginaw	1933-1938	
Berman, Maxine L.	Southfield, Oakland	1983-1996	

Name[2]	Post Office[3]	Session Years[4] House	Senate
Berman, Ryan	Commerce Township, Oakland	2019-	
Bernero, Virg	Lansing, Ingham	2001-2002	2003-2005
Berrick, Francis H.	Buchanan, Berrien		1875-1876
Berry, Enos G.	Quincy, Branch	1842	1848-1849
Berry, John G.	Berryville, Otsego		1889-1890
Berry, Jonathan	Adrian, Lenawee	1844	
Berry, Langford G.	Adrian, Lenawee	1857-1858	
Berryman, Jim	Adrian, Lenawee		1991-1998
Bettinger, Conrad	Detroit, Wayne	1883-1884; 1887-1888	
Betts, Charles	Burr Oak, St. Joseph	1863-1864	
Betz, Eugene C.	Monroe, Monroe	1945-1954	
Bialy, Mendel J.	Bay City, Bay		1895-1896
Biddle, John	Detroit, Wayne	1841	
Bidelman, Samuel J.	Hastings, Barry	1881-1882	
Bieda, Steven M.	Warren, Macomb	2003-2008	2011-2018
Bielawski, Albert M.	Hamtramck, Wayne Detroit, Wayne	1929-1930; 1935-1936	
Bierd, William J.	Auburn, Bay	1907-1914	1919-1920
Biggerstaff, John M.	Kalamazoo, Kalamazoo	1915-1916	
Bignall, Solomon L.	Fowlerville, Livingston	1889-1890	
Billings, Samuel Mead	Marquette, Marquette	1897-1898	
Billings, Simeon R.	Flint, Genesee	1875-1878	1879-1882
Bills, Perley	Tecumseh, Lenawee		1855-1856
Bingham, Henry H.	Grass Lake, Jackson	1848	
Bingham, Kinsley Scott	Green Oak, Livingston	1837-1839; 1841-1842	
Binning, Jay	Jackson, Jackson	1925-1926	1927-1932
Binsfeld, Connie Berube	Maple City, Leelanau	1975-1980	1983-1990
Bird, John M.	Unionville, Tuscola	1840	
Bird, William C.	Hesperia, Newaygo	1939-1946	
Birk, William C.	Baraga, Baraga	1927-1934	1941-1942
Birkholm, Clarence Dickinson	Eau Claire, Berrien	1925-1932	
Birkholz, Patricia L.	Saugatuck Township, Allegan	1997-2002	2003-2010
Birney, James	Bay City, Bay		1859-1860
Bisbee, Clark E.	Jackson, Jackson	1999-2004	
Bischoff, Carl W.	Detroit, Wayne	1933-1934	1939-1940
Bishop, Donald E.	Rochester, Oakland	1967-1970	1971-1982
Bishop, James C.	Burr Oak, St. Joseph	1881-1882	
Bishop, Michael D.	Rochester, Oakland	1999-2002	2003-2010
Bishop, Otto William	Alpena, Alpena		1935-1948
Bishop, Roswell Peter	Ludington, Mason	1883-1884; 1893-1894	
Bitely, Nathan H.	Lawton, Van Buren		1867-1870
Bixby, David A.	Adrian, Lenawee	1883-1884	
Bizon, John	Battle Creek, Calhoun	2015-2018	2019-
Black, Cyrenius Penny	Caro, Tuscola	1883-1886	
Black, Douglas	Twining, Arenac	1925-1928	
Blacker, Robert R.	Manistee, Manistee	1883-1886	
Blackman, Henry Elijah	Allegan, Allegan	1879-1880	
Blackman, Samuel H.	Paw Paw, Van Buren	1873-1874	1863-1864
Blackwell, Albert O.	Gladstone, Delta		1889-1890
Blades, William	Flint, Genesee	1848	
Blair, Austin	Jackson, Jackson	1846	1855-1856
Blair, Charles	Tipton, Lenawee	1842; 1845	
Blake, John E.	Lamont, Ottawa	1869-1870	
Blake, William A.	Galesburg, Kalamazoo	1891-1892	
Blakeslee, Edwin A.	Galien, Berrien		1897-1900
Blakeslee, George	Birmingham, Oakland	1861-1862	
Blakley, Abram Randolph	Alpena, Alpena	1893-1894	
Blanchard, Adolph	Bay City, Bay	1957-1960	
Bland, Joseph Edward	Detroit, Wayne	1901-1906	1907-1908
Bledsoe, Timothy	Grosse Pointe, Wayne	2009-2012	
Blindbury, John	Detroit, Wayne	1844	
Blinn, Charles Oscar	Caro, Tuscola	1917-1920	
Bliss, Aaron T.	Midland, Midland	1935-1936	
Bliss, Aaron Thomas	Saginaw, Saginaw		1883-1884

Name[2]	Post Office[3]	House	Senate
Bliss, Solomon B.	East Saginaw, Saginaw	1863-1864	
Block, Charles H.	Wyandotte, Wayne	1945-1948	
Blodgett, Amos Crippen	Ypsilanti, Washtenaw	1857-1858	
Blondy, Allen H.	Detroit, Wayne		1953-1954
Blondy, Charles S.	Detroit, Wayne		1941-1964
Blood, Calvin A.	Marine City, St. Clair	1881-1882	
Bloom, Adam E.	Detroit, Wayne	1881-1882	
Bobier, William	Hesperia, Oceana	1991-1998	
Bodem, Beverly A.	Alpena, Alpena	1991-1998	
Bogardus, Rose.	Davison, Genesee	1997-2002	
Bohn, Frank Probasco	Newberry, Luce		1923-1926
Boies, Henry M.	Hudson, Lenawee		1855-1858
Boies, John K.	Hudson, Lenawee	1865-1868	1869-1870; 1875-1876
Bolden, Kyra Harris	Southfield, Oakland	2019-	
Bolen, George Lewis	Battle Creek, Calhoun		1917-1918
Bolger, Jase.	Marshall, Calhoun	2009-2014	
Bolger, Robert E.	Detroit, Wayne	1881-1884	
Bollin, Ann.	Brighton, Livingston	2019-	
Bolt, Andrew.	Grand Rapids, Kent	1939-1964	
Bolt, Arthur J.	Muskegon, Muskegon		1921-1922
Bolt, Tom J. G.	Ravenna, Muskegon		1909-1910
Bolton, Abraham F.	Jackson, Jackson	1836	
Bolton, Earl B.	Gaylord, Otsego	1901-1904	
Bond, William S.	Detroit, Wayne	1865-1866	
Bonham, Asher	Centerville, St. Joseph	1850	
Bonine, Evan J.	Niles, Berrien	1853-1854; 1865-1868;	1869-1870
	Vandalia, Cass	1873	
Bonine, Gordon Elwood.	Vandalia, Cass		1943-1952
Bonine, James Gordon	Cassopolis, Cass		1931-1932
Bonior, David Edward	Mount Clemens, Macomb	1973-1974; 1976	
Bonnell, Benjamin C.	Pioneer, Missaukee	1883-1884	
Bonser, John Edward	Pinconning, Bay	1901-1902	
Booher, Darwin L.	Evart, Osceola	2005-2010	2011-2018
Boos, William A., Jr.	Saginaw, Saginaw	1961-1966	
Borgman, Edward A.	Grand Rapids, Kent	1949-1964	
Borgman, Martin V.	Detroit, Wayne	1881-1882	
Bosch, Albert H.	Jamestown, Ottawa	1915-1918	
Bosley, William Edwin	Marshall, Calhoun	1905-1906	
Boss, Alfred J.	Pontiac, Oakland		1855-1856
Bostwick, Edward E.	Union City, Branch		1897-1898
Bostwick, Ezra	Union City, Branch	1869-1870	
Botsford, Philip V. M.	Pittsburg, Shiawassee	1891-1892	
Bottomley, Thomas H.	Capac, St. Clair	1873-1874	
Bouchard, Michael J.	Birmingham, Oakland	1991	1991-1999
Boughner, Charles Bartolette	Pontiac, Oakland		1891-1892
Boussum, Charles O.	Colon, St. Joseph	1909-1910	
Bouwsma, Oscar E.	Muskegon, Muskegon	1961-1964	1967-1974
Bovin, Douglas R.	Gladstone, Delta	1999-2002	
Bowen, Casper L.	Nashville, Barry	1891-1892	
Bowen, Jesse.	Quincy, Branch	1863-1864	
Bowen, Ozro A.	Lansing, Ingham	1879-1880	
Bowerman, Willard I., Jr.	Lansing, Ingham	1953-1960	
Bowman, John H.	Three Rivers, St. Joseph	1838; 1845	
Bowman, John T.	Roseville, Macomb	1955-1962	1963-1977
Bowne, John	Hickory Corners, Barry	1849	1850-1852
	Fulton, Barry		
Boyd, James L.	Ecorse, Wayne	1957-1958	
Boyd, William	Albion, Calhoun	1901-1902	
Boyer, Charles A.	Manistee, Manistee.	1955-1962	
Boyle, Jesse George.	Buchanan, Berrien	1927-1932	
Boynton, Daniel	Leoni, Jackson	1885-1886	
Boynton, Nathan Smith.	Marine City, St. Clair	1869	
Brackenridge, Robert	St. Joseph, Berrien	1991-1998	
Bradbury, Samuel K.	Bay City, Bay	1895-1896	

Name[2]	Post Office[3]	House	Senate
			Session Years[4]
Bradfield, Thomas Deane	Copper Falls, Keweenaw	1875-1876; 1879-1880	
Bradford, Vincent L.	Niles, Berrien		1838-1839
Bradley, Edward	Marshall, Calhoun		1843
Bradley, Harmon	Battle Creek, Calhoun	1879-1880	
Bradley, James	Detroit, Wayne	1955-1974	
Bradley, Martin R.	Hermansville, Menominee	1923-1924; 1927-1934	
Bradley, Nathan Ball	Bay City, Bay		1867-1868
Bradley, William Herbert	Greenville, Montcalm		1909-1912
Bradley, William M.	Detroit, Wayne		1937-1940
Bradshaw, Elias	Van Buren, Wayne	1835-1836	
Bradstreet, Ken	Gaylord, Otsego	1999-2004	
Brady, Walter B.	Detroit, Wayne	1927-1932	
Brainerd, Erastus C.	Vassar, Tuscola	1925-1928	
Brake, D. Hale	Stanton, Montcalm		1935-1942
Brake, David H.	Fremont, Newaygo	1923-1928; 1931-1932	
Braman, Oscar W.	Grand Rapids, Kent	1919-1924	
Branch, Norris H.	Jackson, Jackson	1901-1902	
Brandenburg, Jack	Harrison Township, Macomb	2003-2008	2011-2018
Brandon, Calvin Knox	Detroit, Wayne	1885-1886	
Brann, Tommy	Wyoming, Kent	2017-	
Branson, Edward L.	Battle Creek, Calhoun		1929-1932
Brant, Lyman A.	Detroit, Wayne	1883-1886	
Brater, Elizabeth S.	Ann Arbor, Washtenaw	1995-2000	2003-2010
Braun, Gus A.	Elkton, Huron	1923-1930	
Braun, Virgil Otto	Owosso, Shiawassee	1939-1944	
Breen, Bartley	Menominee, Menominee	1887-1888	
Breitung, Edward	Negaunee, Marquette	1873	1877-1878
Brennan, Bert C.	Saginaw, Saginaw	1969-1974	
Brennan, Vincent Morrison	Detroit, Wayne		1919-1920
Brenner, Charles E.	Saginaw, Saginaw	1893-1894	
Bresnahan, John Thomas	River Rouge, Wayne	1945-1946	
Brewer, John	Ypsilanti, Washtenaw	1835-1836	
Brewer, Lingg	Holt, Ingham	1995-2000	
Brewer, Mark Spencer	Pontiac, Oakland		1873-1874
Brewster, William W.	Cass, Hillsdale	1859-1860	
Bricker, Willis Fillmore	Belding, Ionia	1897-1898; 1911-1914	
Bridge, Henry P.	Kent, Kent		1840-1841
Briggs, Charles	Calumet, Houghton	1879-1880	
Briggs, Edward L.	Grand Rapids, Kent	1873-1876	
Briggs, Franklin Markham	Plymouth, Wayne		1895-1896
Briggs, George G.	Grand Rapids, Kent	1869-1870	
Briggs, Henry C.	Allegan, Allegan		1861
Briggs, Robert V.	Wyandotte, Wayne	1869-1870	1871-1872
Brigham, Roy H.	Battle Creek, Calhoun	1949-1964	
Brinks, Winnie	Grand Rapids, Kent	2013-2018	2019-
Briske, John	Bay City, Bay	1889-1890	
Bristol, Eli H.	Commerce, Oakland	1853-1854	
Bristow, Fred W.	Highland Park, Wayne	1923-1926	
Britain, Calvin	St. Joseph, Berrien	1847; 1850-1852	1835-1837
Britton, Roswell	Grandville, Kent	1835-1836	
Brixie, Julie	Okemos, Ingham	2019-	
Brock, Martin W.	West Bay City, Bay	1887-1888	
Brockway, James E.	Bay City, Bay	1905-1906	
Brockway, William H.	Albion, Calhoun	1865-1866; 1871-1872	1855-1856
Brodhead, Thornton Fleming	Pontiac, Oakland; Trenton, Wayne		1850; 1859-1860
Brodhead, William M.	Detroit, Wayne	1971-1974	
Brooks, Earnest C.	Holland, Ottawa		1937-1938; 1941-1942
Brooks, John Adams	Newaygo, Newaygo	1857-1860	
Brooks, Nathaniel W.	Algonac, St. Clair	1847	
Broomfield, William S.	Royal Oak, Oakland	1949-1954	1955-1956
Brotherson, P. C. H.	Manchester, Washtenaw	1846	
Brotherton, Wilbur V.	Farmington, Oakland	1975-1988	
Brott, Charles A.	South Boardman, Missaukee	1907-1908	

Name[2]	Post Office[3]	House	Senate
			Session Years[4]
Brouwer, Edward	Holland, Ottawa	1933-1936	
Brower, Burney Eslie	Jackson, Jackson	1917-1920	1921-1926
Brown, Aaron B.	Sheridan, Montcalm		1891-1892
Brown, Addison Makepeace	Schoolcraft, Kalamazoo		1899-1900
Brown, Alvarado	Quincy, Branch	1847-1848	
Brown, Ammon	Nankin, Wayne	1835-1837	
Brown, Amos S.	Breedsville, Van Buren	1867-1868	
Brown, Asahel	Algansee, Branch		1857-1860
	Coldwater, Branch		
Brown, Basil W.	Detroit, Wayne		1957-1988
Brown, Benjamin	Walled Lake, Oakland	1859-1860	
Brown, Bob	Dearborn Heights, Wayne	1997-2002	
Brown, Cameron S.	Fawn River Township, St. Joseph	1999-2002	2003-2010
Brown, Charles	Medina, Lenawee	1875-1876	
Brown, Charles	Vicksburg, Kalamazoo	1883-1886	
Brown, Charles A.	Flint, Genesee	1921-1922	
Brown, Charles H.	Greenland, Ontonagon	1903-1904	
Brown, Charles R.	St. Joseph, Berrien	1867-1868	
Brown, Cora M.	Detroit, Wayne		1953-1956
Brown, David E.	Schoolcraft, Kalamazoo	1839-1840	
Brown, Donald A.	Royal Oak, Oakland	1957-1958	
Brown, Ebenezer Lakin	Schoolcraft, Kalamazoo	1841	1855-1856; 1879-1880
Brown, Ethan A.	Berrien Springs, Berrien	1874-1875	
Brown, Frank D.	Bellevue, Eaton	1931-1932	
Brown, Garry Eldridge	Schoolcraft, Kalamazoo		1963-1966
Brown, George	Fulton, Barry	1855-1856	
Brown, George	Detroit, Wayne	1919-1920; 1923-1924	
Brown, George I.	Battle Creek, Calhoun	1871-1872	
Brown, George W.	Jackson, Jackson	1859-1860	
Brown, Giles T.	Ithaca, Gratiot		1881-1882
Brown, Jim N.	Okemos, Ingham	1969-1972	
Brown, John S.	Hillsdale, Hillsdale	1843	
Brown, Joseph A.	Detroit, Wayne		1947-1948
Brown, Lisa	West Bloomfield, Oakland	2009-2012	
Brown, Mary Carney	Kalamazoo, Kalamazoo	1977-1994	
Brown, Norris J.	Stanton, Montcalm	1889-1890	
Brown, Rich	Bessemer, Gogebic	2001-2006	
Brown, Robert	Dushville, Isabella	1895-1896	
Brown, Robert Peter	Detroit, Wayne	1947-1948	
Brown, Samuel B.	Ransom, Hillsdale	1877-1880	
Brown, Stephen F.	Schoolcraft, Kalamazoo	1857-1860	1861-1862; 1865-1866; 1885-1886
Brown, Terry L.	Pigeon, Huron	2007-2010; 2013-2014	
Brown, Thomas H.	Highland Park, Wayne	1909-1912	
Brown, Thomas H.	Westland, Wayne	1971-1980	
Brown, Thomas J.	Houghton, Houghton		1867-1868
Brown, Thomas L.	Lansing, Ingham	1967-1970	
Brown, Vernon J.	Mason, Ingham	1929-1938	
Brown, William E.	Lapeer, Lapeer		1903-1906
Brown, William G.	Parma, Jackson	1867-1868	
Browne, Henry Wheelock	Hubbardston, Ionia	1889-1890	
Browne, William S.	Utica, Macomb	1987-1988	
Brownell, Edmund	Thomas, Lapeer	1898-1900	
Brownell, Ellery A.	Metamora, Lapeer	1867-1870	
Brownell, Franklin	Dowagiac, Cass	1855-1856	
Brownell, George	East Farmington, Oakland	1835-1836	
Brownell, Seymour	Utica, Macomb		1872
Brownell, William	Utica, Macomb	1857-1862	
Bruce, Helmer	Bark River, Delta	1931-1932	
Brundage, Charles LeRoy	Muskegon, Muskegon		1893-1896
Brunner, Charles M.	Bay City, Bay	2011-2016	
Brunson, John C.	Victor, Clinton	1873-1874	
Bryan, Edward C.	Wyandotte, Wayne	1897-1900	
Bryan, Simon D.	Charlotte, Eaton	1919-1924	

Name[2]	Post Office[3]	Session Years[4] House	Senate
Bryant, Bristoe	Detroit, Wayne		1951-1952
Bryant, Ernest J.	Sand Creek, Lenawee	1907-1910	1917-1922
Bryant, Milton Daniel	Traverse City, Grand Traverse	1925-1928	
Bryant, William R., Jr.	Grosse Pointe Farms, Wayne	1971-1996	
Brzostowski, Joseph Stanley	Detroit, Wayne	1933-1934	
Buck, Philip H.	Sturgis, St. Joseph	1849	
Buckbee, Walter A.	Ypsilanti, Washtenaw	1838	
Buckley, Chester	Battle Creek, Calhoun	1857-1864	
Buckley, William G.	Detroit, Wayne	1933-1934; 1937-1944	
Budge, Laurin J.	Beaverton, Gladwin	1927-1930	
Budlong, Philo H.	Marshall, Calhoun	1875-1876	
Buel, Alexander Woodruff	Detroit, Wayne	1838;1848; 1859-1860	
Buel, Henry S.	Franklin, Oakland	1859-1860	
Buell, Ahasuerus W.	Holly, Oakland	1863-1864	
Buell, Darius D.	Union City, Branch	1891-1894	
Buell, Emmons	Little Prairie Ronde, Cass		1863-1864
Buell, John L.	Menominee, Menominee	1873-1874	
Bullard, Bill, Jr.	Milford, Oakland	1983-1996	1996-2002
	Highland, Oakland		
Bullard, Perry	Ann Arbor, Washtenaw	1973-1992	
Bullock, Frederick G.	Lapeer, Lapeer	1891-1892	
Bullock, Marshall	Detroit, Wayne		2019-
Bumstead, Jon	Newaygo, Newaygo	2011-2016	2019-
Bunce, Horace E.	Port Huron, St. Clair	1861-1862	
Bunting, Archibald F.	Empire, Leelanau	1905-1908	
Burbank, William	Rochester, Oakland	1837	
Burch, John	Monroe, Monroe		1842-1843
Burch, Lou J.	Detroit, Wayne	1899-1900	
Burch, Marsden C.	Hersey, Osceola		1877-1878
Burdick, Cyren	Bronson, Kalamazoo	1835-1836	
Burdick, Noah Whittier	Mancelona, Antrim	1899-1900; 1907-1910	
Burfoot, Edmund	Grand Rapids, Kent	1899-1900	
Burhans, Earl L.	Paw Paw, Van Buren	1931-1934	1937-1942
Burk, Andrew L.	Berrien Springs, Berrien	1849	
Burke, Francis X.	River Rouge, Wayne	1913-1914	
Burke, Tom	Detroit, Wayne		1937-1938
Burke, William	Summerville, Cass	1837-1838	
Burkhalter, Larry E.	Lapeer, Lapeer	1977-1980	
Burleigh, John L.	Ann Arbor, Washtenaw		1877-1878
Burleson, Edward G.	Grand Rapids, Kent	1931-1934	
Burnett, William	Scio, Washtenaw	1848	
Burnham, Charles F.	Amadore, Sanilac	1921-1922	
Burnham, Fred J.	New Boston, Wayne	1909-1912	
Burns, David E.	Grand Rapids, Kent	1901-1902	1903-1904
Burns, James	Detroit, Wayne	1873-1874	
Burns, James A.	Detroit, Wayne	1923-1924	1937-1938; 1941-1942
Burns, Thomas M.	Saginaw, Saginaw	1953-1956	
Burns, William R.	Munising, Alger	1909-1910; 1915-1916	
Burr, Henry	Strickland, Isabella	1887-1888	
Burr, Redmond Morris	Ann Arbor, Washtenaw	1935-1936	
Burritt, Fred W.	Houghton, Houghton		1943-1948
Burroughs, Delebar	Fentonville, Oakland	1850	
Bursley, Gilbert Everette	Ann Arbor, Washtenaw	1961-1964	1975-1978
Burt, Edwin	Isabella City, Isabella	1863-1864	
Burt, Wellington R.	Saginaw, Saginaw		1893-1894
Burt, William Austin	Mount Vernon, Macomb	1853-1854	
Burton, Claude E.	Bellevue, Eaton	1965-1966	
Burton, Porter	Hastings, Barry	1879-1880	
Busch, J. Michael	Saginaw, Saginaw	1975-1996	
Bush, Charles P.	Genoa, Livingston	1840-1843	1846-1847; 1855-1856
	Lansing, Ingham		
Bush, David	Fowlerville, Livingston	1859-1860	
Bush, Eric Thomas	Battle Creek, Calhoun	1995-1996	
Bushnell, Ambrose G.	Bronson, Branch	1929-1932; 1935-1936	

Name[2]	Post Office[3]	Session Years[4]	
		House	Senate
Bushnell, Daniel P.	Detroit, Wayne	1859-1860	
Bushnell, William B.	Bronson, Branch	1901-1902	
Buskirk, Henry F.	Wayland, Allegan	1897-1900	
Buth, Martin D.	Comstock Park, Kent	1959-1980	
Buth, Richard D.	Belmont, Kent	1973-1974	
Butler, Abram G.	Bellevue, Eaton	1893-1894	
Butler, David H.	Fostoria, Tuscola	1921-1924	1925-1926
Butler, Orange	Adrian, Lenawee	1837	
Butler, Richard	Mount Clemens, Macomb	1838	
Buttars, Archibald	Charlevoix, Charlevoix		1881-1884
Butterfield, Ira H.	Utica, Macomb		1861-1862; 1873-1874
	Lapeer, Lapeer		
Butterfield, John W.	Niles, Berrien	1851-1852	
Button, John H.	Farmington, Oakland	1840	
Buys, Edward J.	Three Rivers, St. Joseph	1929-1932	
Buza, Frank P.	Rogers City, Presque Isle	1937-1938	
Buzzell, Fred C.	Romeo, Macomb	1893-1894	
Byker, Gary	Hudsonville, Ottawa		1968-1978
Bykowski, Clement	Detroit, Wayne	1982	
Byl, William R.	Grand Rapids, Kent	1995-2002	
Byrd, Wendell	Detroit, Wayne	2015-	
Byrnes, Pam	Chelsea, Washtenaw	2005-2010	
Byrns, Charles J.	Ishpeming, Marquette	1901-1908	
Byrum, Barb	Lansing, Ingham	2007-2012	
Byrum, Dianne	Onondaga, Ingham	1991-1994; 2003-2006	1995-2002
Byrum, Warren D.	Leslie, Ingham	1919-1924	
Cady, Burt Duward	Port Huron, St. Clair		1907-1908
Cady, Charles H.	Wayne, Wayne	1887-1888	
Cady, Charles T.	Dundee, Monroe	1855-1856	
Cady, Chauncey G.	Mount Clemens, Macomb	1849	
Cady, Horace H.	Mount Clemens, Macomb	1843; 1865-1866; 1873-1874	
Cahoon, David J.	Mount Pleasant, Isabella	1897-1898	
Caldwell, John	Manton, Wexford	1897-1900	
Calhoun, Norman	Clinton, Lenawee	1857-1858	
Calkin, Ephraim	Utica, Macomb	1837	
Calkins, Alanson	Worth, Tuscola	1851-1852	
Callaghan, Miles Morris	Reed City, Osceola	1929-1936; 1943-1944	1937-1940
Callahan, James N.	Mount Morris, Genesee	1967-1970	
Callahan, John H.	Detroit, Wayne	1929-1932	
Callahan, Matthew F.	Detroit, Wayne	1927-1928	1947-1948
Callahan, William J.	St. Clair Shores, Macomb	1997-2002	
Callender, Sherman D.	Detroit, Wayne	1925-1926	
Calley, Brian N.	Portland, Ionia	2007-2010	
Calley, Julie	Portland, Ionia	2017-	
Callton, Mike	Nashville, Barry	2011-2016	
Calvert, Frank J.	Highland Park, Wayne	1929-1947	
Cambensy, Sara	Marquette, Marquette	2017-	
Camburn, Levi	Stanton, Montcalm	1865-1868	
Camburn, Thomas M.	Tipton, Lenawee	1895-1898	
Cameron, Alexander	Kalamazoo, Kalamazoo	1869-1872	
Cameron, Burton Gordon	Charlotte, Eaton	1927-1928	
Cameron, Duncan Alex	Alpena, Alpena	1933-1934	
Camilleri, Darrin	Brownstown, Wayne	2017-	
Camp, David Lee	Midland, Midland	1989-1990	
Campau, Theodore J.	Detroit, Wayne	1859-1860	
Campbell, Abner E.	Battle Creek, Calhoun	1848	
Campbell, Allen	Groveland, Oakland	1875-1876	
Campbell, Andrew	Ypsilanti, Washtenaw		1897-1898
Campbell, Bradford	Brighton, Livingston	1849	
Campbell, Calvin Albert	Indian River, Cheboygan		1927-1934
Campbell, Colin Percy	Grand Rapids, Kent	1907-1910	
Campbell, Daniel	Bay City, Bay		1887-1888
Campbell, David L.	Clawson, Oakland	1977-1980	

Name[2]	Post Office[3]	Session Years[4] House	Senate
Campbell, H. Frank	Sherman, Wexford	1893-1896	
Campbell, James H.	Marshall, Calhoun	1879-1882	
Campbell, Job T.	Mason, Ingham	1893-1896	
Campbell, John K.	Ypsilanti, Washtenaw	1897-1898	
Campbell, Joseph L.	Hastings, Barry	1925-1928	
Campbell, Milo Dewitt	Quincy, Branch	1885-1886	
Campbell, Thomas G.	Gladwin, Gladwin	1901-1904	
Campbell, Walter Moore	Gladwin, Gladwin	1943-1944	
Campbell, William Bert	Detroit, Wayne	1925-1932	
Canby, Israel	Harbor Springs, Emmet	1883-1884	
Canfield, Edward J.	Sebewaing, Huron	2015-2018	
Canfield, Irvin S.	Alpena, Alpena	1905-1906	
Canfield, Lucius H.	New Haven, Macomb	1877-1892	
Canfield, Samuel P.	New Haven, Macomb	1853-1854	
Canfield, William	Mount Clemens, Macomb		1857-1860
Canniff, Stephen	Litchfield, Hillsdale	1867-1868	
Cannon, Ellery Channing	Evart, Osceola	1885-1888	1901-1904
Caplis, James	Detroit, Wayne	1873-1874	1881-1882
Carey, Edward	Detroit, Wayne	1945-1946; 1949-1957	
Carl, Douglas	Mount Clemens, Macomb	1985-1986	1987-1997
Carleton, Israel E.	Mears, Oceana	1865-1866	1867-1870
	Whitehall, Muskegon		
Carlton, Aubern D.	Dimondale, Eaton	1885-1886	
Carlton, Palmer S.	St. Clair, St. Clair	1879-1880	
Carmer, Sherlock Houston	Lansing, Ingham	1881-1882	
Carpenter, Ben	Harrison, Clare		1931-1936; 1941-1946
Carpenter, Charles K.	Orion, Oakland	1859-1860	
Carpenter, Guy	Blissfield, Lenawee	1843	
Carpenter, Henry D.	Detroit, Wayne	1850	
Carpenter, Joel	Blissfield, Lenawee		1859-1862
Carpenter, Manson	Woodbridge, Lenawee	1879-1882	1885-1886
Carpenter, William Elmore	Pontiac, Oakland	1883-1884; 1891-1892	
Carr, Nathan Tracy	Midland City, Midland	1859-1860	
Carr, William S.	Manchester, Washtenaw	1840	
Carroll, Howard Robert	Van Dyke, Macomb	1943-1944; 1947-1954	
	Mount Clemens, Macomb		
Carter, Brenda	Pontiac, Oakland	2019-	
Carter, Edward Ross	Gladstone, Delta	1923-1926	
Carter, John	Milford, Oakland	1873-1874	
Carter, Tyrone	Detroit, Wayne	2019-	
Cartier, Charles Ernest	Ludington, Mason		1911-1912
Carton, Augustus C.	East Tawas, Iosco		1907-1908
Carton, John Jay	Flint, Genesee	1899-1904	
Cartter, Harleigh	Utica, Macomb	1845; 1850	
Cartwright, Arthur	Detroit, Wayne	1963-1964	1967-1978
Cartwright, John F.	Davison, Genesee	1893-1894	
Caruss, Richard B.	St. Johns, Clinton	1881-1882	
Carver, Lyman	Saline, Washtenaw	1848	
Carveth, John	Middleville, Barry		1885-1886
Case, Arthur T.	Homestead, Leelanau	1885-1888	
Case, Barnabas	Manchester, Washtenaw		1851-1852
Case, Bernie L.	Ithaca, Gratiot		1923-1926
Case, Daniel L.	Portland, Ionia	1851-1852	
Case, Emanuel	Manchester, Washtenaw	1837	
Case, James A.	Alpena, Alpena	1885-1886	
Case, Leon D.	Watervliet, Berrien		1913-1914; 1933-1936
Case, Ovid Nathan	Detroit, Wayne	1883-1886	
Case, Spaulding M.	Brighton, Livingston	1851-1852	
Case, William L.	Benzonia, Benzie	1919-1922	1923-1926
Casperson, Tom	Escanaba, Delta	2003-2008	2011-2018
Cassis, Nancy C.	Novi, Oakland	1996-2002	2003-2010
Castle, Lemuel	Owosso, Shiawassee	1840-1841	
Caswell, Bruce E.	Hillsdale, Hillsdale	2003-2008	2011-2014
Cater, Eugene R.	Ludington, Mason	1965-1966	

Name[2]	Post Office[3]	House	Session Years[4]	
				Senate
Cathcart, John G.	Constantine, St. Joseph	1840		
Cathro, John J.	Alpena, Alpena	1895-1896		
Catlin, Ashmon H.	Webberville, Ingham	1911-1914		
Caukin, Volney Worden	White Swan, Kent	1857-1858		
Caul, Bill	Mount Pleasant, Isabella	2005-2010		
Caul, Sandy	Mount Pleasant, Isabella	1999-2004		
Cavanagh, Joseph A.	Midland, Midland	1949-1956		
Cavanagh, Philip M.	Redford Township, Wayne	2011-2014		
Cawley, James P.	Morenci, Lenawee			1871-1872
Cawthorne, Dennis O.	Manistee, Manistee	1967-1978		
Chafey, Merritt N.	Manistee, Manistee	1873		
Chamberlain, Eli B.	St. Ignace, Mackinac	1887-1888		
Chamberlain, Frank	Wayland, Allegan	1911-1914		
Chamberlain, Fremont C.	Bessemer, Gogebic	1893-1900		
Chamberlain, Harmon	St. Clair, St. Clair	1850		
Chamberlain, Henry	New Buffalo, Berrien	1849		
Chamberlain, William	Three Oaks, Berrien	1871-1874		1877-1880
Chamberlin, Samuel	Pontiac, Oakland	1855-1856		
Chambers, Clifton J.	Ithaca, Gratiot	1907-1912		
Chambers, Michael	St. Ignace, Mackinac	1889-1890		
Champion, Schuyler	Lansing, Ingham			1893-1894
Champlin, Elisha Powell	Jonesville, Hillsdale	1838; 1840		1841; 1842
Chandler, David Green	Traverse City, Grand Traverse	1909-1912		
Chandler, George	Romeo, Macomb	1851-1852		
Chandler, Joseph H.	Hancock, Houghton			1881-1882
Chandler, Paul M.	Livonia, Wayne	1963-1964		
Chandler, William	Sault Saint Marie, Chippewa	1899-1902		
Chang, Stephanie	Detroit, Wayne	2015-2018		2019-
Chapel, Caleb M.	Gidley's Station, Jackson	1853-1854		
Chapel, Charles W.	Sault Saint Marie, Chippewa	1855-1856		
Chapin, Samuel A.	White Pigeon, St. Joseph	1839		
Chapin, Theodore N.	Bellaire, Antrim	1915-1920		
Chapman, Adelbert R.	Reading, Hillsdale	1885-1888		1889-1890
Chapman, Delmont L., Jr.	Newport, Monroe	1957-1958		
Chapman, Ira Gardner	Utica, Macomb	1901-1904		
Chapman, Leander	Jackson, Jackson	1849		
Chapman, Warren	St. Joseph, Berrien			1865-1868
Chapoton, Alexander	Detroit, Wayne	1863-1864		
Chapoton, William	Detroit, Wayne	1861-1862		
Chappell, Worden R.	Corunna, Shiawassee	1887-1888		
Charron, Sanford E.	Pinconning, Bay	1965-1966		
Charter, Francis	LaSalle, Monroe	1835-1836; 1838		
Chartrand, Joseph Daniel	Muskegon, Muskegon	1945-1946		
Chase, Eugene V.	Elsie, Clinton	1877-1880		
Chase, Irvin	Evart, Osceola	1919-1922		
Chase, Jonathan	Royal Oak, Oakland	1839		
Chase, Marcus A.	Detroit, Wayne	1857-1858		
Chase, Robert J.	Flint, Genesee	1949-1950		
Chase, William	Kinderhook, Branch	1861-1862		
Chatfield, Chester C.	Eaton Rapids, Eaton	1855-1856		
Chatfield, Lee	Levering, Emmet	2015-		
Chauvin, Charles B.	Detroit, Wayne	1867-1868		
Cheeks, Marsha G.	Detroit, Wayne	2003-2008		
Cheeney, Charles W.	Chesaning, Saginaw	1929-1932		
Cheever, Henry Martyn	Detroit, Wayne	1899-1900		
Cheney, Amherst B.	Sparta, Kent	1877-1880		
Cherry, Deborah L.	Burton, Genesee	1995-2002		2003-2010
Cherry, Henry P.	Johnstown, Barry	1871-1872		
Cherry, John	Flint, Genesee	2019-		
Cherry, John D. Jr.	Clio, Genesee	1983-1986		1987-2002
Chester, Easton T.	Camden, Hillsdale	1844		
Chew, Jacob E.	East Jordan, Charlevoix	1917-1920		
Childs, Aaron	Ypsilanti, Washtenaw	1871-1872		
Childs, Augustus W.	Hudson, Lenawee	1851		

Name[2]	Post Office[3]	House	Senate
		Session Years[4]	
Childs, James Webster	Ypsilanti, Washtenaw	1859-1862	1865-1868; 1873-1874;
	Paint Creek, Washtenaw		1879-1880
Chilver, Arthur H.	Grand Rapids, Kent	1895-1896	
Chipman, John Logan	Detroit, Wayne	1865-1866	
Chipman, John Smith	Centerville, St. Joseph	1842	
Chipman, Joseph S.	Niles, Berrien		1845; 1846
Chirkun, John	Roseville, Macomb	2015-	
Chisholm, Hugh	Breckenridge, Gratiot	1891-1892	
Chittenden, Clyde C.	Cadillac, Wexford		1895-1896
Chittenden, William F.	Detroit, Wayne	1849; 1853-1854	
Choate, Emerson	Monroe, Monroe	1861-1862	
Christiancy, Isaac Peckman	Monroe, Monroe		1850-1852
Christman, Lewis G.	Ann Arbor, Washtenaw	1945-1954	1955-1960
Chubb, Harvey	Ann Arbor, Washtenaw	1846-1847	
Church, Lucius L.	Howard City, Montcalm	1891-1894	
Church, Thomas Brownell	Grand Rapids, Kent	1851-1852; 1855-1856	
Churchill, Worthy L.	Alpena, Alpena	1875-1876	
Ciaramitaro, Nick	Roseville, Macomb	1979-1998	
Cihak, Joseph Frank, Jr.	Muskegon, Muskegon	1943-1944; 1947-1948	
Cisky, Jon Ayres	Thomas Township, Saginaw		1991-1998
Clack, Brenda J.	Flint, Genesee	2003-2008	
Clack, Floyd E.	Flint, Genesee	1983-1996	
Clancy, Denis G.	Hillsdale, Hillsdale	1925-1928	
Clancy, Michael J.	Detroit, Wayne	1937-1940	
Clapp, Frank W.	Battle Creek, Calhoun	1891-1892	1893-1896
Clark, Albert K.	Saline, Washtenaw	1875-1876	
Clark, Benjamin	Albion, Calhoun	1869-1870	
Clark, Charles Wilbur	Dansville, Ingham	1915-1918	
Clark, Darius	Marshall, Calhoun	1851	
Clark, David	Eagle, Clinton	1851	
Clark, Edwin G.	Clarkston, Oakland	1877-1878	
Clark, Elihu L.	Adrian, Lenawee	1848	
Clark, Elijah B.	New Canandaigua, Oakland	1847	
Clark, Frederick Owen	Escanaba, Delta	1875-1876	
Clark, Harold B.	Warren, Macomb	1965-1972	
Clark, Jasper N.	Poulson, Mason	1895-1898	
Clark, Jeremiah	Clarkston, Oakland	1839; 1841	
Clark, John	China, St. Clair	1857-1858	1835-1838
Clark, John R.	Adrian, Lenawee	1859-1860	
Clark, Judson Beecher	St. Ignace, Mackinac	1905-1906	
Clark, Myron W.	Parma, Jackson		1893-1894
Clark, Newcomb	West Bay City, Bay	1883-1886	
Clark, Orman	Chelsea, Washtenaw	1869-1870	
Clark, Robert E.	Belleville, Wayne	1863-1864	
Clark, Roy	Eau Claire, Berrien		1919-1922
Clark, Walter H.	Grand Haven, Ottawa	1911-1914	
Clark, William A.	Howell, Livingston		1863-1864
Clark-Coleman, Irma	Detroit, Wayne	1999-2002	2003-2010
Clarke, Hansen	Detroit, Wayne	1991-1992; 1999-2002	2003-2010
Clarke, Hovey K.	Marshall, Calhoun	1850	
Clarke, Luther W.	Eagle River, Keweenaw		1853-1854
Clarken, John	Detroit, Wayne	1909-1910	
Clarkson, S. James	Southfield, Oakland	1959-1960	
Cleary, William J.	Benton Harbor, Berrien	1943-1950	
Clement, John R.	Albion, Calhoun	1925-1930	
Clement, Joshua	Leoni, Jackson	1871-1872	
Clemente, Cara	Lincoln Park, Wayne	2017-	
Clemente, Ed	Lincoln Park, Wayne	2005-2010	
Clemente, Paul D.	Lincoln Park, Wayne	2011-2016	
Clements, Herb	Deckerville, Sanilac	1951-1956	
Clements, James	Ann Arbor, Washtenaw	1865-1866	
Climie, Andrew	Leonidas, St. Joseph	1871-1874	
Cline, William M.	Port Huron, St. Clair		1885-1886
Clines, Hans Ole	Ludington, Mason	1933-1938	

Name[2]	Post Office[3]	House	Session Years[4]
			Senate
Clisbee, Charles W.	Cassopolis, Cass		1867-1868
Clodfelter, Mark	Flint, Genesee	1975-1980	
Cloon, Joseph P.	Wakefield, Gogebic		1943-1944; 1947-1948; 1951-1954
Clothier, Bruce F.	North Branch, Lapeer		1947-1950
Clubb, Henry S.	Grand Haven, Ottawa		1873-1874
Clute, Henry Alson	Marshall, Calhoun	1897-1898	
Clyburn, William L.	Summerville, Cass	1851-1852	
Coad, Mathias	Williamston, Ingham	1897-1898	
Coates, Claude W.	Munising, Alger	1929-1932	
Coates, Joseph	Pine Lake, Oakland	1841	
Coates, Lintsford B.	Otsego, Allegan	1847	
Cobb, Andrew Whitney	Elsie, Clinton	1950-1964	
Cobb, George Pomroy	Bay City, Bay	1881-1882	
Cobb, James B.	Kalamazoo, Kalamazoo	1863-1866	
Cobb, Thomas S.	Kalamazoo, Kalamazoo	1873-1874	1875-1876
Cochran, James B.	Detroit, Wayne	1947-1948	
Cochran, Tom	Mason, Ingham	2013-2018	
Cochrane, James Winslow	Midland, Midland		1879-1880
Cochrane, Lyman	Detroit, Wayne	1871-1872	
Coe, George Alonzo	Coldwater, Branch	1849	1846-1847
Cogshall, Bela	Holly, Oakland	1869-1870	
Cohen, Alex	Lansing, Ingham	1907	
Colbath, Lemuel	Erie, Monroe	1837	
Colbeck, Patrick	Canton, Wayne		2011-2018
Colby, Sheridan J.	Detroit, Wayne	1899-1904; 1907-1909	
Cole, Ezra	Three Rivers, St. Joseph	1846	
Cole, Miner T.	Palmyra, Lenawee	1887-1890	
Cole, Triston	Mancelona, Antrim	2015-	
Cole, William B.	Ludington, Mason	1875-1876	
Coleman, Creighton R.	Marshall, Calhoun		1949-1956
Coleman, George	Howell, Livingston	1883-1886	
Coleman, Hammond J.	Marshall, Calhoun	1919-1921	
Coleman, Henry	Kendall, Van Buren	1840	
Coleman, Kevin	Westland, Wayne	2019-	
Coleman, Sheldon	Lawton, Van Buren	1927-1930	
Colgrove, Philip T.	Hastings, Barry		1889-1890
Collier, Victory Phelps	Battle Creek, Calhoun		1865-1868
Collingwood, Charles Barnard	Lansing, Ingham		1899-1890
Collins, Barbara-Rose	Detroit, Wayne	1975-1980	
Collins, David	Croton, Newaygo	1889-1892	
Collins, Frederick W.	Middleville, Barry	1873-1874	
Collins, James J.	Flint, Genesee	1949-1950; 1953-1956	
Collins, John Price	Negaunee, Marquette	1933-1934	
Collins, Lucius Henry	Detroit, Wayne	1885-1886	
Collins, Samuel B.	Jackson, Jackson	1899-1900	
Collins, William A.	Bay City, Bay		1909-1912
Colman, Hutson Benedict	Kalamazoo, Kalamazoo		1897-1898
Colvin, Benjamin	St. Charles, Saginaw	1897-1900	
Colvin, Oliver D.	Kinderhook, Branch	1850	
Colwell, David G.	Fenton, Livingston	1865-1866	
Colwell, Henry J.	Marquette, Marquette	1874	
Colwell, William M.	Manistique, Schoolcraft	1883-1884	
Coman, Russell	Cass, Hillsdale	1849	
Combs, Henry P.	Rome, Lenawee	1857-1858; 1863-1864	
Combs, John H.	Adrian, Lenawee	1901-1904	
Compson, Evo Sanford	Remus, Mecosta	1935-1936	
Compton, Henry	Ypsilanti, Washtenaw	1845	1843-1844
Comstock, Horace H.	Comstock, Kalamazoo	1849	1835-1838
	Otsego, Allegan		
Comstock, Oliver Cromwell	Coldwater, Branch	1849	
Conant, Harry Armitage	Monroe, Monroe		1879-1880
Condino, Paul	Southfield, Oakland	2003-2008	
Condon, George M. Dallas	Detroit, Wayne		1917-1930

Name[2]	Post Office[3]	House	Senate
			Session Years[4]
Conely, Edwin F.	Detroit, Wayne	1877-1878	
Congdon, Elisha	Chelsea, Washtenaw	1863-1864	
Congdon, James M.	Chelsea, Washtenaw	1871-1872	
Conger, Omar Dwight	Port Huron, St. Clair		1855-1860
Conkling, Henry C.	Tecumseh, Lenawee		1869-1870
Conley, John	Lapeer, Lapeer		1911-1912
Conlin, Michael H.	Jackson, Jackson	1975-1978	
Conlin, Rollo G.	Tipton, Lenawee	1945-1966	
Conlon, Ernest Thomas	Grand Rapids, Kent		1929-1932
Connelly, William M.	Spring Lake, Ottawa		1919-1920; 1923-1924
Connor, Richard H.	Grosse Pointe, Wayne	1859-1860	
Connor, Rowland	East Saginaw, Saginaw	1889-1892	
Connors, James	St. Ignace, Mackinac	1897-1898	
Connors, Jim	Iron Mountain, Dickinson	1985-1988	
Connors, John Patrick	Detroit, Wayne	1933-1934	
Conrad, Charles O.	Jackson, Jackson	1965-1966	
Conrad, Luther Fitch	Wacousta, Clinton	1885-1886	
Conroy, Joe	Flint, Genesee	1977-1980	1983-1998
Constan, Bob	Dearborn Heights, Wayne	2007-2012	
Constantini, James K.	Iron Mountain, Dickinson	1961-1962; 1965-1966	
Convis, Ezra	Battle Creek, Calhoun	1835-1837	
Conyers, Ian	Detroit, Wayne		2016-2018
Cook, Albert Balwin	Owosso, Shiawassee		1903-1906
Cook, Asa Brigs	Marshall, Calhoun	1857-1858	
Cook, August Charles	Iron Mountain, Dickinson	1895-1896	
Cook, David R.	Hastings, Barry		1877-1878; 1881-1882
Cook, Elijah F.	Farmington, Oakland		1838-1839
Cook, Francis W.	Muskegon, Muskegon	1883-1884; 1891-1892	
Cook, Hervey	Homer, Calhoun	1840	
Cook, Jacob	Saline, Washtenaw	1841	
Cook, John P.	Hillsdale, Hillsdale	1846	1847-1848; 1874
Cook, Levi	Detroit, Wayne	1838	
Cook, Peter	Saline, Washtenaw	1873-1874	
Cook, Peter J.	Saugatuck, Allegan	1845	
Cook, Warren J.	Grand Rapids, Kent	1927-1928	
Cook, William	Homer, Calhoun	1861-1864	1875-1878
Cooley, Anthony	Kalamazoo, Kalamazoo	1838	
Cooley, Sloan	Oakwood, Oakland	1861-1862	
Coomer, George W.	Wyandotte, Wayne	1885-1886	
Coon, Myron	Greenfield, Wayne	1877-1878	
Cooper, Clyde Eugene	White Cloud, Newaygo	1947-1960	
Cooper, Daniel S.	Oak Park, Oakland	1965-1970	1971-1978
Cooper, George Byran	Jacksonopolis, Jackson / Jackson, Jackson	1842	1837-1838
Cooper, George H.	Vernon, Shiawassee	1881-1882	
Coots, Walter Henry	Detroit, Wayne	1883-1884	
Copeland, Benjamin	Brooklyn, Jackson	1839; 1841	
Copeland, Joseph T.	St. Clair, St. Clair		1850-1851
Copeland, William R.	Wyandotte, Wayne	1953-1974	
Copley, Alexander B.	Decatur, Van Buren	1865-1866; 1871-1872; 1875-1876; 1881-1882	
Copley, Almon Ward	Detroit, Wayne	1909-1914; 1917-1922	
Corbin, Gary George	Clio, Genesee		1975-1986
Corbin, Sanford H.	Armada, Macomb	1851-1852	
Corbin, William	Petersburg, Monroe / Adrian, Lenawee	1881-1882	1863-1864
Corey, Jeremiah D.	Manchester, Washtenaw	1867-1868	1875-1876
Corliss, John Blaisdell, Jr.	Detroit, Wayne	1923-1924	
Corliss, Terry T.	Mayville, Tuscola		1913-1916
Cornell, Jerry G.	Spring Arbor, Jackson	1837	
Cornell, Thurber	Howell, Livingston	1945-1948	
Corrigan, Patrick	East Exeter, Monroe	1851-1852	
Corriveau, Marc R.	Northville, Wayne	2007-2010	
Corwin, Alvah H.	Marion, Osceola	1901-1902	

Name[2]	Post Office[3]	House	Session Years[4] Senate
Cossitt, Charles H.	Owosso, Shiawassee	1885-1886	
Cotter, Gerald J.	Mount Pleasant, Isabella		1935-1936
Cotter, Kevin	Mount Pleasant, Isabella	2011-2016	
Cottrell, Eber Ward	Detroit, Wayne	1879-1882	
Coulouris, Andy	Saginaw, Saginaw	2007-2010	
Coulter, John F.	Niles, Berrien	1871-1872	
Coulter, Joseph	Ontonagon, Ontonagon		1861
Coumans, Joseph Vincent	Bay City, Bay	1933-1936	1937-1938
Courser, Todd	Silverwood, Lapeer	2015	
Courter, Byron W.	Imlay City, Lapeer	1935-1948	
Cousins, James	Pittsford, Hillsdale	1895-1898	
Covell, George Gary	Traverse City, Grand Traverse	1893-1896	1897
Covert, Frank L.	Pontiac, Oakland		1915-1918
Covert, Lewis M.	Waterford Center, Oakland	1851-1852	
Cowan, Alex	North Street, St. Clair Port Huron, St. Clair	1915-1918; 1925-1928	1929-1932
Cowan, George Y.	Eaton Rapids, Eaton	1863-1864	
Cowdin, George D.	Oxford, Oakland	1907-1908	
Cox, Laura	Livonia, Wayne	2015-2018	
Cox, Robert	Hudson, Lenawee	1861-1862	
Craig, James	Detroit, Wayne	1875-1876	
Craig, Roger E.	Dearborn, Wayne		1965-1970
Cramton, Louis Convers	Lapeer, Lapeer	1909-1910; 1949-1960	
Cramton, Louis K.	Midland, Midland	1971-1980	
Crandall, Nancy	Muskegon, Muskegon	1989-1990	
Crandall, Tracy F.	Howell, Livingston	1931-1932	
Crandell, George W.	Dearborn, Wayne	1877-1878	
Crane, Archer H.	Blissfield, Lenawee	1869-1872	
Crane, Flavius J. B.	Howell, Livingston	1838	
Crane, George	Adrian, Lenawee	1851-1852	
Crane, George L.	Adrian, Lenawee	1863-1864	
Crane, Jesse D.	Fenton, Genesee		1893-1894
Crapo, Henry Howland	Flint, Genesee		1863-1864
Crapser, Bert F.	Swartz Creek, Genesee	1913-1914	
Crary, Isaac Edwin	Marshall, Calhoun	1842; 1846	
Cravath, Isaac M.	Lansing, Ingham		1871-1872
Craven, Robert E.	Duplain, Clinton	1853-1854	
Crawford, Hugh D.	Novi, Oakland	2009-2014	
Crawford, John G.	Holly, Oakland		1865-1866
Crawford, Kathy	Novi, Oakland	2015-	
Crawford, Mark L.	Coldwater, Branch		1937-1938
Crawford, Samuel E.	Ypsilanti, Washtenaw	1917-1920	
Creen, George J.	Saginaw, Saginaw	1933-1934	
Crego, Richard J.	Brooklyn, Jackson South Jackson, Jackson	1861-1864	1865-1866
Cressy, Alonzo	Hillsdale, Hillsdale Clinton, Lenawee	1837	1855-1856
Crim, Bobby D.	Davison, Genesee	1965-1966; 1973-1982	
Crippen, George D.	Stambaugh, Iron	1897-1898	
Crippen, William W.	Milford, Oakland	1893-1894	
Crissman, Penny M.	Rochester, Oakland	1993-1998	
Crocker, Martin	Mount Clemens, Macomb	1887-1888	1891-1892
Crofoot, George W.	Pinckney, Livingston	1871-1872	
Croll, Henry, Jr.	Beaverton, Gladwin	1913-1920	
Cropsey, Alan Lee	DeWitt, Clinton	1979-1982; 1993-1998	1983-1986; 2003-2010
Cropsey, Harmon George	Decatur, Van Buren	1981-1982	1983-1990
Cropsey, Jesse R.	Vicksburg, Kalamazoo		1905-1908
Crosby, Calvin B.	Plymouth, Wayne		1887-1888
Crosby, Daniel W.	Elbridge, Oceana	1889-1890	
Crosby, Hale E.	New Buffalo, Berrien	1857-1858	
Crosby, Moreau S.	Grand Rapids, Kent		1873-1874
Crosby, Will Antony	Battle Creek, Calhoun	1899-1900	
Cross, John S.	Bangor, Van Buren	1885-1888	
Crossman, Alanson	Dexter, Washtenaw	1835-1836	

Name[2]	Post Office[3]	Session Years[4]	
		House	Senate
Crossman, Daniel L.	Dansville, Ingham	1867-1870	
Crossman, John S.	Ingham Center, Ingham	1851-1852	
Croswell, Charles M.	Adrian, Lenawee	1873-1874	1863-1868
Crouse, Robert	Hartland, Livingston	1848	1859-1860
Crowley, Francis A.	Clarkston, Oakland	1965-1966	
Crozer, James A.	Menominee, Menominee	1885-1886	
Cruce, Doug	Troy, Oakland	1981-1982	1983-1991
Crutchfield, John B.	Saginaw, Saginaw	1925-1926	
Culver, Charles Herbert	Detroit, Wayne	1915-1918; 1921-1932	
Culver, Jonathan H.	Colon, St. Joseph	1847	
Cumings, Charles Begole	Flint, Genesee	1939-1940	
Cummings, Frank S.	Centreville, St. Joseph		1925-1928
Cummins, George Johnson	Harrison, Clare	1909-1912	
Currie, Edgar C.	Detroit, Wayne	1949-1962	
Currie, Gilbert Archibald	Midland, Midland	1909-1914	
Curry, James L.	Clio, Genesee	1869-1870	1873-1874
Curry, Solomon S.	Ishpeming, Marquette	1875-1876	
Curtenius, Frederick W.	Kalamazoo, Kalamazoo		1853-1854; 1867-1868
Curtis, Candace A.	Swartz Creek, Genesee	1993-1998	
Curtis, George Mason	Flint, Genesee	1893-1896	
Curtis, Israel	Erin Corners, Macomb	1849	
Curtis, James B. F.	New Lothrop, Shiawassee	1889-1890	
Curtis, John L.	Grand Rapids, Kent		1885-1886
Curtis, Miles S.	Battle Creek, Calhoun	1895-1896; 1917-1926	
Curtis, Norman D.	Monroe, Monroe		1838-1839
Curtis, Thomas	Kensington, Oakland	1841	
Curtis, William H.	Hanley, Ottawa	1873-1874; 1878-1880	
Curtis, William L.	Petoskey, Emmet	1901-1902	1903-1906
Curtiss, Darwin Z.	Detroit, Wayne	1909-1910	
Curtiss, John W.	Dushville, Isabella	1891-1894	
Curtiss, Lester	Ishpeming, Marquette	1877-1878	
Curts, Edwin J.	Flint, Genesee		1913-1914
Cushingberry, George, Jr.	Detroit, Wayne	1975-1980; 2005-2010	
Cust, Edwin M.	Hamburg, Livingston		1842-1845
Cutcheon, Otis E. M.	Oscoda, Iosco	1879-1882	
Cutcheon, Sullivan M.	Ypsilanti, Washtenaw	1861-1864	
Cuthbertson, Alexander D.	Flint, Genesee	1929-1932	
Cuthbertson, Willis Earle	Flint, Genesee	1933-1936	
Cutler, George	Luther, Lake		1933-1934
Dacey, Clarence Joseph	Detroit, Wayne	1929-1930	1931-1932
Dacey, Vincent Paul	Detroit, Wayne	1921-1924; 1929-1932	
Dafoe, Lemuel Grant	Alpena, Alpena	1891-1892; 1919-1922	
Daigneau, Samuel E.	Benton Harbor, Berrien	1915-1918	
Dakin, Milo H.	Saginaw, Saginaw	1885-1887	
Daley, Kevin	Attica, Lapeer Lum, Lapeer	2009-2014	2019-
Dalman, Jessie F.	Holland, Ottawa	1991-1998	
Dalton, James I., Jr.	Dalton's Mills, Ottawa	1859-1860	
Dalton, John W.	Adrian, Lenawee	1889-1890	
Dalton, Lawrence	Dalton's Corner, Wayne	1871-1872	
Daly, James	Detroit, Wayne	1875-1876	
Damman, James J.	Troy, Oakland	1971-1974	
Damon, John Adams	Mount Pleasant, Isabella	1887-1890	1915-1918
Damrow, Kurt	Port Austin, Huron	2011-2012	
Danforth, Ephraim B.	Mason, Ingham		1847-1848
Danforth, George	Ann Arbor, Washtenaw		1851-1852
Daniels, David I.	Wacousta, Clinton	1859-1860	
Daniels, Ebenezer	Medina, Lenawee	1841	
Daniels, Kenneth R.	Detroit, Wayne	1999-2004	
Danz, George	Monroe, Monroe	1921-1922	
Daprato, John	Iron Mountain, Dickinson	1913-1920; 1931-1934	
Darany, George T.	Dearborn, Wayne	2011-2016	
Darin, Frank P.	River Rouge, Wayne	1925-1932	
Darling, Henry	Tecumseh, Lenawee	1851-1852	

Name[2]	Post Office[3]	House	Session Years[4] Senate
Darragh, Archibald Bard	St. Louis, Gratiot	1883-1884	
Darrah, Lewis	La Salle, Monroe	1847	
Daugherty, Samuel J.	Caro, Tuscola	1907-1908	
Davenport, George	Hadley, Lapeer	1881-1884	
Davenport, George	Saginaw, Saginaw		1885-1886
David, James I.	Ecorse, Wayne	1859-1860	1875-1876
David, Orin	Trenton, Wayne	1849	
Davidson, John B.	Eaton Rapids, Eaton	1929-1930	1931-1932
Davidson, Robert D.	Hersey, Osceola	1949-1950	
Davis, Alexander P.	Flint, Genesee		1859-1860; 1865-1866
Davis, Alexander W.	Grand Blanc, Genesee	1861-1862	
Davis, Alonzo C.	Minong, Isle Royale	1877-1878; 1885-1886	
	L'Anse, Baraga		
Davis, Ammos	Southfield, Oakland	1839-1840	
Davis, Bayard G.	Lawton, Van Buren		1919-1922
Davis, Calvin	Macomb, Macomb	1845	
Davis, Charles J.	Onondaga, Ingham	1962-1968	
Davis, Chauncey	Muskegon, Muskegon	1861-1863	
Davis, Clarke Edwin	Vermontville, Eaton	1953-1954	
Davis, George Burlingham	Utica, Macomb	1895-1898	1899-1900
Davis, Henry	Pennsylvania, Branch	1853-1854	
Davis, Ira	Trenton, Kalamazoo	1861-1862	
Davis, James M.	Kalamazoo, Kalamazoo	1899-1900	
Davis, John	Birmingham, Oakland	1844; 1846	
Davis, John M.	Detroit, Wayne	1857-1858	
Davis, Jonathan D.	Plymouth, Wayne		1835-1837
Davis, Lewis C.	Vassar, Tuscola		1885-1886
Davis, Robert W.	Oxford, Oakland	1849	
Davis, Robert William	Gaylord, Otsego	1967-1970	1971-1978
	St. Ignace, Mackinac		
Davis, Stanley J.	Grand Rapids, Kent	1965-1972	
Davis, Willard	Vermontville, Eaton	1857-1858	
Davis, William	Fremont, Newaygo	1907-1910	
Davis, William R.	Oakfield, Kent	1869-1870	
Davison, Oliver Perry	Highland, Oakland	1847	
Davock, Harlow Palmer	Detroit, Wayne	1893-1894	
Dawe, Denias	Monroe, Monroe	1923-1924	1935-1936
Dayton, Daniel	Davisonville, Genesee	1849	
De Young, Cornelius	Crystal, Montcalm	1909-1910	
Deadman, Richard Hector	Alpena, Alpena	1939-1950	
Dean, John G.	Bay City, Bay	1919-1922; 1943-1944	
Dean, Robert	Grand Rapids, Kent	2007-2010	
Deane, Charles Werden	Pentwater, Oceana	1867-1868	
Deare, Henry W.	Detroit, Wayne	1863-1864	
DeBeaussaert, Kenneth Joseph	Washington, Macomb	1979-1984; 1987-1992	1995-2002
	New Baltimore, Macomb		
DeBoer, William	Grand Rapids, Kent	1915-1916; 1925-1928	
deBoom, Adrian	Owosso, Shiawassee	1949-1958	
Decker, Alpheus P.	Deckerville, Sanilac	1935-1950	1951-1954
Decker, Freeman L.	Lake City, Missaukee	1905-1906; 1909-1912	
Decker, Jesse	Orion, Oakland	1838-1839	
DeClaire, Benjamin Harrison	St. Clair Shores, Macomb	1929-1930	
Dee, Patrick	Detroit, Wayne	1889-1890	
Defebaugh, James E.	Birmingham, Oakland	1971-1980	
Defer, George	Detroit, Wayne		1927
DeFoe, Murl Holcomb	Charlotte, Eaton		1919-1920; 1943-1946
DeGrow, Alvin J.	Pigeon, Huron		1968-1984
DeGrow, Dan L.	Port Huron, St. Clair	1981-1982	1985-2002
DeHart, Eileen	Westland, Wayne	1995-2002	
Dehmel, Arthur A.	Unionville, Tuscola		1955-1964
Del Rio, James	Detroit, Wayne	1965-1972	
Delamatter, Anson H.	Columbia, Jackson	1844	
DeLand, Charles Johnson	Jackson, Jackson	1929-1930	1915-1920
	Detroit, Wayne		

Name[2]	Post Office[3]	House	Senate
DeLand, Charles V.	Jackson, Jackson		1861-1862; 1873-1874
	East Saginaw, Saginaw		
DeLange, Walter J.	Kentwood, Kent	1983-1996	
DeLano, Carl F.	Kalamazoo, Kalamazoo	1931-1938	1939-1945
DeLisle, Peter Bienvenu	Delray, Wayne	1903-1904	
DeMars, Robert A.	Lincoln Park, Wayne	1983-1996	
DeMaso, Harry A.	Battle Creek, Calhoun	1957-1966	1967-1986
Deming, Daniel H.	Dover , Lenawee	1847; 1849	
Deming, David Ebenezer	Kalamazoo, Kalamazoo		1841-1842
Deming, Theodore E.	Wayne, Wayne	1889-1890	
Dempsey, James Ward	Manistee, Manistee	1893-1894	
Den Herder, Jacob	Zeeland, Ottawa		1889-1890
Denby, Cindy	Handy Township, Livingston	2009-2014	
Denby, Edwin	Detroit, Wayne	1903-1904	
Denman, Henry B.	Dowagiac, Cass	1863-1864	
Denning, Moses R.	Manistee, Manistee	1891	
Dennis, David B.	Adrian, Lenawee	1848; 1850	
Dennis, Julie	Muskegon, Muskegon	1999-2004	
Dennis, Orville	Lake City, Missaukee	1901-1904	
Denton, Samuel	Ann Arbor, Washtenaw		1845-1848
Denton, Solomon W.	Pontiac, Oakland	1848	
Derezinski, Anthony A.	Muskegon, Muskegon		1975-1978
Derham, Ray	Iron Mountain, Dickinson		1933-1934
DeRoche, Craig M.	Novi, Oakland	2003-2008	
DeRossett, Gene	Manchester, Washtenaw	1999-2004	
DeSana, James R.	Wyandotte, Wayne		1976-1984
Deshano, William J.	Auburn, Bay	1923-1930	
DeShazor, Larry	Portage, Kalamazoo	2009-2010	
DeStigter, Melvin John	Hudsonville, Ottawa	1965-1978	
Deuel, Andrew L.	Harbor Springs, Emmet	1917-1920	
Devlin, John	Detroit, Wayne	1883-1884	
DeVuyst, Larry L.	Alma, Gratiot	1997-2002	
DeWeese, Paul N.	Williamston, Ingham	1999-2002	
Dewey, George Ensign	Shelby, Oceana	1905-1908	
Dewey, George M.	Hastings, Barry		1873-1874
Dewey, Hezekiah Ranney	Grand Blanc, Genesee	1889-1890	
Dewey, John W.	Owosso, Shiawassee	1881-1882	
Dewitt, Francis Byron	Standish, Arenac	1921-1922	
Dexter, Ernest Ransom	Mount Pleasant, Isabella	1923-1928	
Dexter, George W.	Ionia, Ionia	1842	
Dexter, John C.	Ionia, Ionia		1871-1872
Deyo, Charles I.	Oxford, Oakland		1887-1888
Dianda, Scott	Calumet, Houghton	2013-2018	
Dickerman, Albert	Hillsdale, Hillsdale		1881-1882
Dickerson, Bert Andrew	Constantine, St. Joseph	1949-1951	
Dickey, Charles	Marshall, Calhoun	1859-1860	1850-1854
Dickinson, Joseph H.	Detroit, Wayne	1897-1900	
Dickinson, Luren D.	Charlotte, Eaton	1897-1898; 1905-1908	1909-1910
Dickinson, William Edmund	Clifton, Keweenaw		1859-1860
Dickson, Robinson J.	Dowagiac, Cass	1883-1888	
Diehl, Barney	Mount Clemens, Macomb	1917-1918	
Diehl, Harry Leo	Monroe, Monroe	1935-1938	
Diekema, Gerrit John	Holland, Ottawa	1885-1892	
Diggs, Charles Coles, Jr.	Detroit, Wayne		1951-1954
Diggs, Charles Coles, Sr.	Detroit, Wayne		1937-1944
Diggs, Charles M.	Detroit, Wayne	1955-1958	
Diggs, O. Roosevelt	Detroit, Wayne	1959-1962	
Dignan, Herman Henry	Owosso, Shiawassee	1935-1938	1939-1942
Diller, Henry B.	Mount Morris, Genesee	1881-1884	
Dillingham, Frederick P.	Fowlerville, Livingston	1979-1986	1987-1994
Dillmann, Louis	Detroit, Wayne	1877-1878	
Dillon, Andy	Redford Township, Wayne	2004-2010	
Dillon, Brandon	Grand Rapids, Kent	2011-2015	
Dillon, Joseph	Grand Rapids, Kent	1887-1888	

Name[2]	Post Office[3]	House	Session Years[4] Senate
Dimmers Jr., Albert Worthington	Hillsdale, Hillsdale	1945-1948	
Dimond, Reuben B.	Lexington, Sanilac	1848	
DiNello, Gilbert J.	East Detroit, Macomb	1973-1978	1979-1994
Dingell, Christopher Dennis	Trenton, Wayne		1987-2002
Dingley, Edward Nelson	Kalamazoo, Kalamazoo	1899-1902	
Dingman, Fred R.	Detroit, Wayne	1941-1944; 1949-1959	
Dingwell, Robert E.	Lansing, Ingham	1965-1966	
Dinturff, Daniel W.	Fowlerville, Livingston	1873-1874	
Dively, Michael A.	Traverse City, Grand Traverse	1969-1974	
Divine, John	Lexington, Sanilac	1855-1856	
Divine, Joseph	Cambria, Hillsdale	1885-1886	
Divine, Rosekrans K.	Eureka, Montcalm	1855-1856	
Divine, Westbrook	Greenville, Montcalm		1863-1866
Dixon, John Sargent	Charlevoix, Charlevoix	1863-1864	
Dobb, Barbara Jeane	Union Lake, Oakland	1991-1998	
Dobronski, Agnes M.	Dearborn, Wayne	1987-1988; 1991-1998	
Docherty, James A.	Port Huron, St. Clair	1983-1984; 1987-1988	
Dockeray, James	Laphamville, Kent	1863-1864	
Dodak, Lewis N.	Birch Run, Saginaw Montrose, Genesee	1977-1992	
Dodge, Charles D.	London, Monroe	1891-1894	
Dodge, Frank Luke	Lansing, Ingham	1883-1886	
Dodge, Hiram	Clinton, Lenawee	1835-1836	
Dohany, John Seymour	Greenfield, Wayne	1903-1904	
Doherty, Alfred James	Clare, Clare		1901-1906
Dolan, Jan Clark	Farmington Hills, Oakland	1989-1996	
Doll, Tracy M.	Detroit, Wayne	1945-1946; 1949-1950	
Dolsen, Levi E.	Detroit, Wayne	1841	
Dombrowski, Stanley J.	Detroit, Wayne	1935-1944	
Dongvillo, Jeff	Scottville, Mason	1979-1980	
Donigan, Marie	Royal Oak, Oakland	2005-2010	
Donnelly, John C.	Detroit, Wayne	1879-1880	
Donnelly, William Minton	Detroit, Wayne	1933-1934; 1945-1946	
Donovan, John	Bay City, Bay	1895-1898	
Doorn, William	Grand Rapids, Kent	1961-1964	
Doran, Peter	Grand Rapids, Kent		1891-1894
Doremus, Frank Ellsworth	Portland, Ionia	1891-1892	
Dorsey, Andrew	Homer, Calhoun	1838	
Dort, Titus	Dearborn, Wayne	1839; 1842; 1865-1866	1849-1852
Dotsch, James D.	Garden, Delta		1937-1940
Doty, Philo	Eagle, Clinton	1869-1872	
Doty, Samuel	Ann Arbor, Washtenaw	1838	
Double, Thomas E.	Vienna, Monroe	1905-1908	
Dougherty, Archibald K.	Elk Rapids, Antrim	1887-1888	
Douglas, Columbus C.	Houghton, Houghton	1861-1862	
Douglass, Frank A.	Houghton, Houghton	1887-1888	
Douma, Robert	Whitehall, Muskegon	1941-1942	
Douville, Henry	Alpena, Alpena	1931-1932; 1935-1938	
Dovel, Andrew J.	Manistee, Manistee	1874	
Dow, John	Sunfield, Eaton	1863-1864	
Dow, Peter	Pontiac, Oakland	1875-1876	1863-1864; 1879-1882
Dowling, Michael Angelo	Wenona, Bay	1877-1878	
Dowling, Thomas J.	Detroit, Wayne	1947-1948	
Down, Edgar Fielding	Pleasant Ridge, Oakland		1947-1948
Downing, Alonzo	Downington, Sanilac	1891-1892	
Downing, Charles E.	Romulus, Wayne	1913-1914	
Dox, Peter	Birmingham, Oakland	1850	
Doyle, Dale D.	Saginaw, Saginaw		1935-1936
Doyle, Leo J.	Flint, Genesee	1949-1952	
Doyle, Michael J.	Sault Saint Marie, Chippewa	1891	
Doyle, Michael S.	Elsie, Clinton	1899-1902	
Doyle, Patrick J.	Dearborn, Wayne	1945-1954	1955-1962
Doyle, W. F.	Menominee, Menominee		1933-1934
Drake, Thomas J.	Flint, Genesee		1839-1841

Name[2]	Post Office[3]	House	Senate
		Session Years[4]	
Drake, William P.	Amboy, Hillsdale	1873-1874	
Draper, Charles.	Pontiac, Oakland		1867-1868
Draper, William P.	Lapeer, Lapeer	1838	
Dresch, Stephen Paul	Hancock, Houghton	1991-1992	
Dressel, James K.	Holland, Ottawa	1979-1980	
Drew, John A.	Mackinac, Mackinac	1841	
Drew, John F.	Jackson, Jackson	1873-1874	
Driggs, Alfred L.	Constantine, St. Joseph	1847	
Driggs, John Fletcher	East Saginaw, Saginaw	1859-1860	
Driskell, Gretchen	Saline, Washtenaw	2013-2016	
Drolet, Leon C.	Clinton Township, Macomb	2001-2006	
Drummond, Hugh.	Flint, Genesee	1919-1920	
Dudgeon, Anthony	Detroit, Wayne		1859-1860
Dudley, Harlan J.	Fremont, Newaygo	1897-1900	
Duff, William James	Port Huron, St. Clair	1899-1900	
Duffield, William Ward	Inkster, Wayne		1879-1880
Dunakin, Daniel	Homer, Calhoun	1855-1856	
Dunaskiss, Mat J.	Lake Orion, Oakland	1981-1990	1991-2002
Dunbar, Addison Edwin	Monroe, Monroe	1885-1858	
Dunbar, William	Monroe, Monroe	1857-1860	
Duncan, Delamore	Schoolcraft, Kalamazoo	1850	
Duncan, George W.	Detroit, Wayne	1903-1908	
Duncan, Lawson A.	Niles, Berrien		1883-1884
Duncan, Robert W.	Grand Haven, Ottawa	1855-1856	
Duncan, William Chamberlain	Detroit, Wayne		1863-1864
Dunckel, Miller	Three Rivers, St. Joseph		1935-1938
Dundass, Robert F.	Ludington, Mason	1881-1882	
Dunham, Nelson	Dundee, Monroe	1840; 1844; 1846	1848-1849
Dunlap, Abijah Barnum	Traverse City, Grand Traverse	1865-1868	
Dunlop, John W.	Clare, Clare	1941-1942	
Dunn, Fred E.	Croswell, Sanilac	1911-1914; 1919-1922	
	Highland Park, Wayne		
Dunn, George	Pigeon, Huron	1953-1960	
Dunn, Gerald Raymond	Flushing, Genesee		1965-1966
Dunn, James	Emmett, St. Clair	1901-1904	
Dunning, William M.	Blaine, St. Clair	1907-1910	
Dunstan, James C.	Dollar Bay, Houghton	1903-1906	
Dunstan, Thomas B.	Hancock, Houghton		
	Central Mine, Keweenaw	1883-1884	1889-1890
Dupont, Charles	Detroit, Wayne	1901-1902	
DuPuy, James	Spring Arbor, Jackson	1855-1856	
Durhal, Fred, III	Detroit, Wayne	2015-2018	
Durhal, Fred, Jr.	Detroit, Wayne	2002; 2009-2014	
Durham, Millard	Coopersville, Ottawa	1903-1906	
Durkee, Lewis	Nashville, Barry		1881
Durocher, Laurent H.	Monroe, Monroe	1839	1835-1836
	Brest, Monroe		
Dusenbury, Frank H.	Mount Pleasant, Isabella	1909-1912	
Dusseau, Joel J.	Loranger, Monroe	1867-1868	
Dusseau, Victor A.	Erie, Monroe	1865-1866; 1869-1870	
Dust, William T.	Detroit, Wayne	1907-1908	
Dutko, Dennis Marcie	Warren, Macomb	1975-1989	
Dyckman, Evert B.	Schoolcraft, Kalamazoo	1847	
Dyer, Walter Richardson	Standish, Arenac	1889-1890	
Dykstra, Ate	Grand Rapids, Kent	1923-1934; 1939-1942;	
		1945-1946	
Dykstra, John	Muskegon, Muskegon	1927-1934	
Dzendzel, Raymond D.	Detroit, Wayne	1955-1958	1959-1970
Dziengielewski, J. A.	Hamtramck, Wayne	1927	
Eakins, James	Port Crescent, Huron	1881-1882	
Earl, Barney	Cooper, Kalamazoo	1849; 1851-1852	
Earle, Horatio Sawyer	Detroit, Wayne		1901-1902
Earle, J. Milton	Belding, Ionia		1893-1896
Earle, Nathaniel A.	Grand Rapids, Kent	1881-1882	

Name[2]	Post Office[3]	House	Senate
		Session Years[4]	
Eastman, Ahira G.	Adrian, Lenawee	1845	
Easton, David J.	Union City, Branch	1881-1882	
Eaton, Charles L.	Paw Paw, Van Buren	1889-1892	
Eaton, Crosby.	South Haven, Van Buren	1877-1882	
Eaton, Ebenezer C.	Rawsonville, Wayne	1839; 1847	
Eaton, Edwin.	Hudson, Lenawee		1895-1896
Eaton, Elton R.	Plymouth, Wayne	1937-1940; 1945-1948	
Eaton, Fred Lloyd	Saginaw, Saginaw	1917-1918	
Eaton, Jerome B.	Jackson, Jackson	1851-1852; 1869-1870	
Eaton, Levi	Romulus, Wayne	1851-1852	
Eaton, Royal C.	Bravo, Allegan	1891-1894	
Eaton, Sterling	Plymouth, Wayne	1957-1958	
Ebli, Kate M.	Monroe, Monroe	2006-2010	
Eck, William R.	Colon, St. Joseph	1867-1870	
Ecklee, George.	Rollin, Lenawee	1845	
Eddy, Hiram S.	Fairfield, Lenawee	1855-1856	
Edgar, William R.	Blissfield, Lenawee	1895-1898	
Edinborough, Frank Lewis	Bay City, Bay		1907-1908
Edmunds, James M.	Ypsilanti, Washtenaw	1846-1847	1840-1841
Edsell, Wilson C.	Otsego, Allegan		1865-1866; 1877-1878; 1881-1882
Edwards, Adelbert D.	Atlantic Mine, Houghton	1907-1918	
Edwards, Arthur.	Trenton, Wayne	1855-1856	
Edwards, Edward E.	Fremont, Newaygo	1881-1882	1885-1888
Edwards, F. Robert.	Flint, Genesee	1971-1976	
Edwards, George F.	Niles, Berrien	1877-1878	
Edwards, George H.	Detroit, Wayne	1955-1978	
Edwards, Henry D.	Detroit, Wayne	1873-1874	
Edwards, Norma Dee	Detroit, Wayne	1949-1950	
Edwards, William J.	Niles, Berrien	1871-1872	
Egan, Francis B.	Detroit, Wayne	1885-1886	
Eggleston, Ebenezer S.	Grand Rapids, Kent	1873-1874	
Eggleston, James.	Monterey, Allegan	1875-1876	
Ehardt, Stephen R.	Lexington, Sanilac	1999-2004	
Ehlers, Vernon James	Grand Rapids, Kent	1983-1985	1985-1994
Eichhorn, Philip.	Port Huron, St. Clair	1903-1906	
Eikhoff, Henry J.	Detroit, Wayne	1897-1900	
Eisen, Gary.	St. Clair Township, St. Clair	2019-	
Eisenmann, George J.	Temperance, Monroe	1913-1914	
Eisenmann, John C.	Erie, Monroe	1881-1882	
Elder, Brian K.	Bay City, Bay	2017-	
Elder, Stanley.	Marquette, Marquette	1943-1944	
Eldred, Alvah D.	Tekonsha, Calhoun	1885-1888	
Eldred, Caleb	Climax Prairie, Kalamazoo	1837	
Eldred, Foss Oscar	Ionia, Ionia		1921-1924
Eldredge, James B.	Mount Clemens, Macomb	1863-1864	
Eldredge, Nathaniel Buel.	Dryden, Lapeer	1848	
Eldredge, Robert P.	Mount Clemens, Macomb		1847-1848
Elkins, Jennifer J.	Lake, Clare	2003-2004	
Ellenwood, John	Pine Lake, Oakland	1835-1836	
Elliott, Adam	Hickory Corners, Barry	1869-1870	
Elliott, Daisy.	Detroit, Wayne	1963-1978; 1981-1982	
Elliott, Marcus D.	Holly, Oakland	1877-1878	
Ellis, Edward D.	Monroe, Monroe		1835-1837
Ellis, George Edwin	Grand Rapids, Kent	1905-1906	
Ellis, Myron H.	New Boston, Wayne	1883-1884	
Ellison, Jim.	Royal Oak, Oakland	2017-	
Ellstein, Jack.	Detroit, Wayne	1945-1946	
Ellsworth, Charles Clinton	Greenville, Montcalm	1853-1854	
Ellsworth, William A.	St. Ignace, Mackinac		1949-1954
Elsenheimer, Kevin A.	Bellaire, Antrim	2005-2010	
Ely, Elisha	Allegan, Allegan	1835-1837	
Ely, Heman B.	Carp River, Marquette	1853-1854	
Ely, Ralph.	Alma, Gratiot		1873-1874

Name[2]	Post Office[3]	House	Senate
		Session Years[4]	
Ely, Townsend A.	Alma, Gratiot		1905-1908
Emerson, Luther G.	Rockland, Ontonagon	1867-1868	
Emerson, Philip H.	Battle Creek, Calhoun		1871-1874
Emerson, Richard	Clare, Clare	1921-1924; 1927-1928	
Emerson, Robert L.	Flint, Genesee	1980-1998	1999-2006
Emery, Jared H.	Burnside, Lapeer	1867-1868	
Emmons, Harry T.	Byron Center, Kent	1951-1960	
Emmons, Jedidiah Philo Clark	Detroit, Wayne	1848	
Emmons, Joanne G.	Big Rapids, Mecosta	1987-1990	1991-2002
Emmons, Judy K.	Sheridan, Montcalm	2003-2008	2011-2018
Empson, George Raymond	Gladstone, Delta	1915-1916	
Emunson, Chester Philip	Manistee, Manistee	1933-1936	
Engel, Albert Joseph	Lake City, Missaukee		1921-1922; 1927-1932
Engel, Charles	Minden City, Sanilac	1909-1910	
Engle, Ernest C.	Centerville, St. Joseph	1933-1934	
Englemann, Hieronymus	Center Line, Macomb	1885-1888	
Engler, Colleen House	Mount Pleasant, Isabella	1974-1986	
Engler, John M.	Mount Pleasant, Isabella	1971-1978	1979-1990
Engstrom, Arnell	Traverse City, Grand Traverse	1941-1968	
Enos, Jehiel	St. Joseph, Berrien	1848; 1857-1858	
	Benton, Berrien		
Enos, Morgan	Pipestone, Berrien	1859-1860	
Enos, Uriel	Edwardsburgh, Cass	1855-1856	
Ensign, W. Scott	Battle Creek, Calhoun	1965-1966	
Erickson, Ole	Escanaba, Delta	1905-1908	
Erlandsen, Einar E.	Escanaba, Delta	1949-1966	
Erskine, James	Port Sanilac, Sanilac	1857-1858; 1863-1864	
Esch, Marvin Lionel	Ann Arbor, Washtenaw	1965-1966	
Espie, John Paxton	Eagle, Clinton	1923-1932; 1935-1949	
Espinoza, John	Croswell, Sanilac	2005-2010	
Estabrook, John S.	East Saginaw, Saginaw	1879-1882	
Estee, Free	Mount Pleasant, Isabella	1885-1886	
Estes, Howard Robert	Birmingham, Oakland	1945-1953	
Etheridge, Samuel	Coldwater, Branch		1839-1840
Evans, Charles	Tipton, Lenawee	1917-1926	
Evans, Charles A.	Saginaw, Saginaw	1913-1914	
Evans, David H.	Mount Clemens, Macomb	1977-1984	
Evens, M. L.	Coldwater, Branch	1915-1916	
Ewell, Philander	Utica, Macomb	1855-1856	
Ewers, Charles	Detroit, Wayne	1881-1882	
Ewing, Alexander Dexter	Dexter, Washtenaw	1853-1854	
Ewing, Alvin Enoch	White, Hillsdale	1893-1894	
Ewing, William Shaw	Marquette, Marquette	1911-1922	
Fairbank, Merton W.	Mount Morris, Genesee	1905-1908	
Fairbanks, Earl S.	Luther, Lake	1903-1906	1907-1910
Faircloth, Ernest Edward	Onaway, Presque Isle	1933-1938	
Fairfield, Ebenezer W.	Adrian, Lenawee	1844	
Fairfield, Edmund Burke	Hillsdale, Hillsdale		1857-1858
Fallass, Silas S.	Fallassburg, Kent	1859-1862	
Fancher, Isaac Alger	Mount Pleasant, Isabella	1873-1874	1875-1876
Fargo, John D.	Granville, Montcalm	1857-1858	
Farhat, David	Muskegon, Muskegon	2003-2006	
Farhat, Debbie	Muskegon, Muskegon	1987-1988	
Faris, Pam	Clio, Genesee	2013-2018	
Farmer, Edwin	Stockbridge, Ingham	1907-1914	
Farmer, John Webster	Stockbridge, Ingham	1883-1884	
Farnsworth, James S.	Allegan, Allegan	1963-1974	
	Plainwell, Allegan		
Farr, Augustine W.	Onekama, Manistee	1877-1878	1901-1906
Farr, George A.	Grand Haven, Ottawa		1879-1882
Farrah, Barbara A.	Southgate, Wayne	2003-2008	
Farrand, William R.	Detroit, Wayne	1925-1930	
Farrell, Charles H.	Kalamazoo, Kalamazoo	1907-1908	
Farrier, Nelson G.	Hillman, Montmorency	1917-1928	

Name[2]	Post Office[3]	Session Years[4] House	Senate
Farrington, Diana	Utica, Macomb	2017-	
Farrington, Jeff	Utica, Macomb	2011-2016	
Farrington, Thomas	London, Monroe	1837	
Fast, Orlando J.	Mendon, St. Joseph		1883-1884
Faulkner, Ellis E.	Delton, Barry	1935-1944	
Faulkner, Robert E.	Coloma, Berrien	1951-1952	1953-1958
Faunce, Jennifer	Warren, Macomb	1999-2002	
Faust, William Paul	Westland, Wayne		1967-1994
Faxon, Jack	Detroit, Wayne	1965-1970	1971-1994
Faxon, Thomas J.	Tecumseh, Lenawee	1847	
Fay, Jonathan P.	Detroit, Wayne	1835-1836	
Feenstra, Charles R.	Grand Rapids, Kent	1935-1948	1951-1962
Fehling, Edward William	St. Johns, Clinton		1935-1938
Feighner, Len W.	Nashville, Barry	1929-1932	
Felch, Alpheus	Monroe, Monroe	1835-1837	
Fellows, Orville H.	Schoolcraft, Kalamazoo	1863-1868	
Felt, Dorman	Felts, Ingham	1859-1860	
Fenlon, Edward H.	St. Ignace, Mackinac	1933-1938	
Fenner, Clyde V.	Highland Park, Wayne		1939-1940
Fenner, George H.	Marlette, Sanilac	1869-1870	
Fenton, Charles B.	Mackinac, Mackinac	1867-1868; 1871-1872	
Fenton, Joseph S.	Fenton, Genesee	1851-1852	
Fenton, William M.	Fentonville, Genesee		1846-1847
	Flint, Genesee		
Ferguson, Augustus F.	Okemos, Ingham	1889-1892	
Ferguson, Daniel, Jr.	DeWitt, Clinton	1844	
Ferguson, Fenner	Albion, Calhoun	1849	
Ferguson, James E.	Bangor, Van Buren	1877-1880	
Ferguson, Marvin	Marshall, Calhoun	1891-1894	
Ferguson, Rosetta A.	Detroit, Wayne	1965-1978	
Ferguson, Thomas A.	Sherman, Wexford	1873-1876	
Ferguson, William Webb	Detroit, Wayne	1893-1896	
Ferrington, George W.	Redford, Wayne	1835-1837; 1847	
Ferris, Benjamin F.	Sherwood, Branch	1848	
Ferris, Chester A.	Detroit, Wayne	1923-1924; 1947-1948	
Ferris, Jacob	Greenville, Montcalm	1859-1860	
Ferris, Richard	Bear Lake Mills, Van Buren	1871-1872	
Ferry, Asa P.	Rockford, Kent	1871-1872	
Ferry, Dexter Mason, Jr.	Detroit, Wayne	1901-1904	
Ferry, Thomas White	Grand Haven, Ottawa	1851-1852	1857-1858
Fessenden, C. B. H.	Utica, Macomb	1842	
Fessler, Richard D.	Union Lake, Oakland	1975-1980	1983-1990
Fey, Conrad	East Saginaw, Saginaw	1873-1874	
Field, James	,	1837	
Field, Nathaniel L.	Rudyard, Chippewa	1909-1912	
Fifield, Francis W.	Pontiac, Oakland	1863-1864	
Fildew, Francis	Detroit, Wayne	1891-1892	
Filler, Graham	DeWitt, Clinton	2019-	
Finch, Asahel, Jr.	Adrian, Lenawee	1837	
Finch, Silas	Saline, Washtenaw		1835-1836
Finley, William	Ann Arbor, Washtenaw		1849-1850
Finney, Noble H.	Grand Rapids, Kent	1839	
Fish, George W.	Flint, Genesee		1875-1876
Fisher, Alonzo W.	Fennville, Allegan	1903-1906	
Fisher, Delos	Jackson, Jackson	1865-1866	
Fisher, Edward F.	Dearborn, Wayne	1929-1936; 1941-1944	
Fisk, Charles H.	Detroit, Wayne	1895-1896	
Fisk, J. Russell	Rives Junction, Jackson	1903-1906; 1911-1912	
Fitch, Charles C.	Mason, Ingham	1889-1892	
Fitch, Ferris S.	Bunker Hill, Ingham	1853-1856	
Fitch, Lyman A.	Mattawan, Van Buren		1855-1856
Fitch, Morgan L.	Paw Paw, Van Buren	1851-1852	
Fitch, Nathan	Niles, Berrien	1863-1864	
Fitch, Norton	Sparta, Kent	1891-1894	

Name[2]	Post Office[3]	House	Session Years[4]	
				Senate
Fitch, Virgil A.	Ludington, Mason	1919-1920; 1925-1928		
Fitzgerald, Chester B.	Detroit, Wayne	1933-1940		
Fitzgerald, Frank M.	Grand Ledge, Eaton	1987-1998		
Fitzgerald, George S.	Grosse Pointe Park, Wayne			1965-1974
Fitzgerald, Jerome B.	St. Joseph, Berrien			1847-1848
FitzGerald, John Chaplain	Marshall, Calhoun			1869-1870
Fitzgerald, John P.	Detroit, Wayne	1919-1920; 1947-1948		
Fitzgerald, John Warner	Grand Ledge, Eaton			1959-1964
Fitzgerald, John Wesley	Grand Ledge, Eaton	1895-1896		
Fitzgerald, Lee Gerald	Flint, Genesee	1961-1964		
Fitzgerald, Thomas	Niles, Berrien	1839		
Fitzgerald, William B.	Detroit, Wayne	1965-1970		
Fitzgerald, William B., Jr.	Detroit, Wayne	1971-1974		1975-1978
Fitzgerald, William L.	Kalamazoo, Kalamazoo	1913-1914		
Fitzgibbon, David Augustus	Port Huron, St. Clair	1911-1912		1913-1916
FitzPatrick, Edwin A.	Detroit, Wayne	1955-1964		
Fitzpatrick, John J.	Detroit, Wayne	1949-1966		
Fitzpatrick, Richard G.	Battle Creek, Calhoun	1979-1986		
Fitzsimmons, George	Reading, Hillsdale	1853-1854		
Flanigan, Joseph T.	Centreville, St. Joseph	1951-1952		
Flavin, Ray M.	Swartz Creek, Genesee	1965-1966		
Fleischhauer, Alfred M.	Reed City, Osceola	1897-1900		
Fleming, James G.	Jackson, Jackson			1967-1974
Flesheim, Joseph	Menominee, Menominee			1891-1894
Fletcher, John W.	Marshall, Calhoun	1877-1878		
Fletcher, John W.	Centreville, St. Joseph	1952-1958		1945-1948
Fletcher, Niram A.	Grand Rapids, Kent	1883-1884		
Flood, James K.	Hart, Oceana	1895-1896		1897-1900
Flower, James	Armada, Macomb	1849		
Flowers, Charles	Detroit, Wayne	1909-1918		
Flynn, Felix H. H.	Cadillac, Wexford			1933-1940; 1951-1953
Folks, Charles	Pulaski, Jackson	1907-1910		
Folks, James N.	Horton, Jackson	1955-1972		
Follett, Elwin B.	Hale, Iosco	1913-1916		
Follett, Martin P.	Fair Plain, Montcalm	1861-1862		
Foote, Charles E.	Kalamazoo, Kalamazoo	1895-1898		
Foote, Charles R.	Walled Lake, Oakland	1837; 1840; 1861-1862		
	Milford, Oakland			
Foote, Dan P.	Saginaw City, Saginaw			1877-1878
Foote, Henry K.	Walled Lake, Oakland	1837; 1840; 1861-1862		
	Milford, Oakland			
Forbes, John	Brownstown, Wayne	1840		
Forbes, Joseph	Detroit, Wayne	1971-1984		
Forbes, Joshua	Saline, Washtenaw	1865-1866		
Ford, Henry	Lawton, Van Buren			1881-1882
Ford, Melbourne Haddock	Grand Rapids, Kent	1885-1886		
Ford, Ransom L.	Montrose, Genesee	1915-1918		
Ford, Sheridan D.	Detroit, Wayne	1915-1918		
Ford, Thomas G.	Grand Rapids, Kent	1965-1972		
Ford, William David	Taylor, Wayne			1963-1964
Forlini, Anthony	Harrison Township, Macomb	2011-2016		
Forrester, George B.	Deckerville, Sanilac			1917-1922
Forster, John H.	Houghton, Houghton			1865-1866
Forsyth, Alexander	Standish, Arenac			1897-1898
Foster, Charles Woodworth	Lansing, Ingham			1915-1918
Foster, Eugene	Gladwin, Gladwin			1909-1912
Foster, Frank D.	Pellston, Emmet	2011-2014		
Foster, Joe C.	East Lansing, Ingham			1931-1934
Foster, Seymour	Lansing, Ingham	1895-1896		
Foster, Wilder De Ayr	Grand Rapids, Kent			1855-1856
Foster, William Henry	Traverse City, Grand Traverse	1897-1900		
Foster, William J.	Battle Creek, Calhoun	1901-1904		
Fouch, Perle L.	Allegan, Allegan	1907-1910		
Fowle, James	Camden, Hillsdale	1850; 1861-1864		

Name[2]	Post Office[3]	Session Years[4]	
		House	Senate
Fowle, Otto	Sault Saint Marie, Chippewa		1909-1912
Fowler, Frederick	Reading, Hillsdale	1859-1860	1865-1866
Fowler, Ralph	Cedar, Livingston	1845; 1851-1852	
Fowler, Smith W.	Charlotte, Eaton		1863-1864
Fox, Aaron O.	Batavia, Branch	1917-1918	
Fox, Benjamin F.	Waterloo, Jackson	1849	
Fox, Edwin G.	Mayville, Tuscola		1887-1890; 1893-1894; 1909-1910
Fralick, Henry	Plymouth, Wayne	1847	1853-1854
Fralick, Thomas Tracy	Copemish, Manistee	1911-1914	
Francis, James	Alpena, Alpena	1903-1904	
Francis, Lynn O.	Midland, Midland		1955-1962
Francis, Thomas F.	Ishpeming, Marquette	1915-1918; 1921-1922	
Francis, William H.	Frankfort, Benzie	1879-1880	1885-1886
Frank, A. T.	Saginaw, Saginaw	1997-2002	
Franz, Ray A.	Onekama, Manistee	2011-2016	
Fraser, Charles L.	Petoskey, Emmet	1881-1882	
Frazer, Murdoch	Saginaw, Saginaw	1848	
Frederick, Ben	Owosso, Shiawassee	2017-	
Fredricks, Ed	Holland, Ottawa	1975-1978	1985-1990
Freeman, Chandler	Maple Rapids, Clinton	1863-1864	
Freeman, Charles Huse	Highland Park, Wayne	1913-1914	
Freeman, Franklin S.	Ionia, Ionia		1877-1878
Freeman, John F.	Madison Heights, Oakland	1993-1998	
Freeman, Leonard	Fenton, Genesee		1911-1912
Frees, Retire Whittimore	Sand Creek, Lenawee	1923-1924	
French, Alfred	Bronson, Branch		1850-1851
French, Charles B.	Petersburg, Monroe	1901-1902	
French, George H.	Homer, Calhoun		1861-1864
French, John M.	Eaton Rapids, Eaton	1842	
French, Robert Edmund	Fort Gratiot, St. Clair		1893-1896
French, William A.	Dundee, Monroe	1883-1884	
Frey, Edward W.	Detroit, Wayne	1947-1948	
Frey, James G.	Battle Creek, Calhoun	1929-1936	
Frey, John W.	Three Rivers, St. Joseph	1853-1854	
Freye, Louis Herbert	Muskegon, Muskegon	1943-1948; 1951-1952	
Frick, G. Oliver	Detroit, Wayne	1921-1922	
Fridlender, Charles A.	Oscoda, Iosco		1891-1892
Frisbee, Alonzo Thompson	Oak Grove, Livingston		1883-1884
Frisbee, Philip S.	Davisburg, Oakland	1859-1860	
Friske, Richard	Charlevoix, Charlevoix	1971-1972	
Frost, Almon B.	Oakland, Oakland	1871-1872	
Frost, Joseph James	Grand Rapids, Kent	1917-1918	
Fuller, Ceylon Canfield	Big Rapids, Mecosta	1869-1870	
Fuller, Clarence J.	Fowlerville, Livingston	1921-1924	
Fuller, Edward L.	Ann Arbor, Washtenaw	1840	1841-1842
Fuller, Jack	Detroit, Wayne	1945-1946; 1949-1950	
Fuller, Jesse E.	Alma, Gratiot	1925-1932	
Fuller, Oramel Baum	Ford River, Delta	1893-1898	1901-1904; 1907-1908
Fuller, Philo C.	Adrian, Lenawee	1841	
Funston, George A.	Capac, St. Clair	1867-1868	
Furton, George C.	Mount Clemens, Macomb	1985-1986	
Fyfe, Andrew	Grand Rapids, Kent		1905-1908
Fyfe, Lawrence C.	St. Joseph, Berrien	1881-1884	
Gaffney, Edward J.	Grosse Pointe Farms, Wayne	2003-2008	
Gage, Henry Thurston	Grosse Pointe, Wayne	1947-1948	
Gage, John L.	Flint, Genesee	1843	
Gage, Seneca H.	Bellevue, Eaton	1859-1860	
Gage, William	Holly, Oakland	1843	
Gagliardi, Pat	Drummond Island, Chippewa	1983-1998	
Gahagan, George M.	Hudson, Lenawee	1913-1914	
Gaige, Joseph Moss	Croswell, Sanilac		1895-1896
Galbraith, Franklin B.	Pontiac, Oakland		1889-1890
Galbraith, William J.	Calumet, Houghton	1903-1908	

Name[2]	Post Office[3]	Session Years[4] House	Senate
Gale, Elbridge E.	Goodrich, Genesee	1853-1854	1861-1862
	Davisonville, Genesee		
Gale, Martin P.	Big Rapids, Mecosta	1881-1882	
Gallagher, Earl C.	Detroit, Wayne	1937-1944	
Galloway, David N.	White Lake, Oakland	1993-1998	
Galloway, Edward R.	Reading, Hillsdale	1917-1920	
Galloway, John	Waterford Center, Oakland	1845	
Galloway, John H.	Howell, Livingston		1861-1862
Gallup, Caleb H.	Port Austin, Huron	1867-1868	
Gallup, George	Excanaba, Delta	1903-1904	
Gamrat, Cindy	Plainwell, Allegan	2015	
Gansser, Augustus Herbert	Bay City, Bay	1911-1912	1915-1918; 1923-1932
Gantt, Samuel N.	Pontiac, Oakland	1838	
Garcia, Daniela	Holland, Ottawa	2015-2018	
Garcia, Valde	Howell, Livingston	1999-2001	2001-2010
	St. Johns, Clinton		
Gard, George W.	Cassopolis, Cass	1911-1912	
Gardner, Amos	Matteson, Branch	1885-1886	
Gardner, James H.	Flint, Genesee	1947-1948	
Gardner, Lynn Cleveland	Stockbridge, Ingham	1925-1930	
Gardner, Ransom	Jonesville, Hillsdale		1853-1854
Garfield, Charles William	Grand Rapids, Kent	1881-1882	
Garfield, John P.	Rochester Hills, Oakland	2003-2008	
Garfield, Samuel M.	Grand Rapids, Kent	1871-1876	
Gargett, James	Alma, Gratiot	1863-1864	
Garrett, LaTanya	Detroit, Wayne	2015-	
Garrison, William D.	Vernon, Shiawassee	1871-1872	
Gartner, Frederick J.	Wyandotte, Wayne	1935-1944	
Garvelink, Jan Willem	Graafschap, Allegan	1873-1874; 1883-1884	1891-1894
Garvey, Matthew T.	Cassopolis, Cass		1875-1876
Garvey, Raymond Earl	Ironwood, Gogebic	1939-1940	
Garwood, Alonzo	Cassopolis, Cass		1857-1858
Gary, Clifford D.	Detroit, Wayne	1982	
Garza, Alex	Taylor, Wayne	2019-	
Garza, Belda	Detroit, Wayne	1999-2002	
Gast, Harry	St. Joseph, Berrien	1971-1978	1979-2002
Gay, Mylo L.	Howell, Livingston	1869-1870	1871-1872
Gay-Dagnogo, Sherry	Detroit, Wayne	2015-	
Gayde, Edward	Plymouth, Wayne	1915-1918	
Gaylord, Augustine Smith	Saginaw City, Saginaw	1863-1864	
Geake, R. Robert	Northville, Wayne	1973-1977	1977-1998
Gedda, Michael A.	Bessemer, Gogebic	1935-1936	
Geddes, John	Ann Arbor, Washtenaw	1841	
Gee, James J.	Whitehall, Muskegon	1901-1902	
Geerlings, Clyde H.	Holland, Ottawa		1951-1964
Geerlings, Edgar A.	Muskegon, Muskegon	1967-1986	
Geerlings, Henry	Holland, Ottawa	1945-1950	
Geiger, Terry	Lake Odessa, Ionia	1995-2002	
Geiss, Douglas A.	Taylor, Wayne	2009-2014	
Geiss, Erika	Taylor, Wayne	2015-2018	2019-
Gelinas, Ludger A.	Saginaw, Saginaw	1909-1910	
Genetski, Bob	Saugatuck, Allegan	2009-2014	
George, Tom M.	Kalamazoo, Kalamazoo	2001-2002	2003-2010
Geralds, Monte R.	Madison Heights, Oakland	1975-1978	
Germain, George W.	North Plains, Ionia	1857-1858	
Gernaat, John	McBain, Antrim	1991-1998	
Gerrish, Nathaniel L.	Hersey, Osceola	1875-1876	
Gettel, Godfried	Sebewaing, Huron	1915-1918; 1921-1922	1923-1926
Giachino, Joseph J.	Iron Mountain, Dickinson	1959-1960	
Gibbons, Joseph	Blaine, St. Clair	1889-1892	
Gibbs, Adoniram J.	Portland, Ionia	1881-1882	
Gibbs, Edward H.	Perkins, Delta		1955-1956
Gibbs, George C.	Marshall, Calhoun	1839	
Gibbs, James L.	Mayfield, Grand Traverse	1877-1878; 1885-1886	

Name[2]	Post Office[3]	Session Years[4] House	Senate
Gibbs, Lloyd W.	Portland, Ionia	1951-1964	
Gibson, Charles F.	Bay City, Bay		1881-1882; 1893-1894
	Detroit, Wayne		
Gibson, John	Detroit, Wayne	1871-1872	
Gibson, Samuel	Constantine, St. Joseph	1897-1898	
Giddings, Charles W.	St. Louis, Gratiot		1899-1900
Giddings, Jabez Wight	Cadillac, Wexford		1887-1890
Giddings, Marsh	Galesburg, Kalamazoo	1849	
Giddings, Orrin N.	Charleston, Kalamazoo	1846	
Gidley, Townsend E.	Barry, Jackson	1835-1836; 1838; 1850	1839-1842; 1863-1864
	Parma, Jackson		
Gieleghem, Paul	Clinton Township, Macomb	1999-2004	
Gies, Paul	Detroit, Wayne	1859-1860; 1865-1866; 1877-1878	1867-1868
Giese, Edgar W.	Manistee, Manistee	1981-1990	
Gifford, Milo E.	Plainwell, Allegan	1869-1870	
Gilbert, Donald W.	Saginaw, Saginaw		1951-1954
Gilbert, Jud	Algonac, St. Clair	1999-2002; 2011-2012	2003-2010
Gilbert, Linus S.	Romeo, Macomb	1837	
Gilbert, Peter	Sterling, Arenac		1891-1894
Gilbert, Robert S.	Saginaw, Saginaw	1957-1960	
Gilbert, Roy T.	Algonac, St. Clair	1939-1944	
Gilbert, Thomas D.	Grand Rapids, Kent	1861-1862	
Gilday, John F.	Yargerville, Monroe	1893-1894	
Giles, Charles I.	Muskegon, Muskegon	1909-1912	
Gill, Frank H.	Grand Rapids, Kent	1889-1890	
Gillam, George Edwin	Harrisville, Alcona	1897-1900	
Gillam, George F.	Bronson, Branch	1871-1872	
Gillard, Matthew O.	Alpena, Alpena	2003-2008	
Gillespie, George A.	Gaines, Genesee	1939-1940; 1943-1948; 1951-1960	
Gillett, Amasa	Manchester, Washtenaw	1849	
Gillett, John E.	Rapid City, Kalkaska	1923-1930	
Gillett, Martin S.	Port Huron, St. Clair	1849	
Gillett, Shadrach	Detroit, Wayne	1841	
Gillette, Joel H.	Niles, Berrien	1899-1902	
Gillis, Joseph A.	Detroit, Wayne	1959-1964	
Gilluly, John	Brighton, Livingston	1859-1860	
Gilman, Joseph	Paw Paw, Van Buren	1855-1856	
Gilmer, Donald H.	Augusta, Kalamazoo	1977-1998	
Gilmore, Arthur D.	Blissfield, Lenawee	1873-1874	1889-1890
Gingrass, Jack L.	Iron Mountain, Dickinson	1967-1968; 1973-1984	
Girardin, Joseph E.	Detroit, Wayne	1879-1880	
Gire, Sharon L.	Mount Clemens, Macomb	1987-1998	
Girrbach, George	Sault Saint Marie, Chippewa		1945-1948
Gittins, Clarence E.	Highland Park, Wayne		1913-1914
Glardon, Ben	Owosso, Shiawassee	2011-2016	
Glasgow, Cassius L.	Nashville, Barry		1903-1906
Glasner, Henry C.	Nashville, Barry	1911-1914	1933-1934
	Charlotte, Eaton		
Glaspie, Andrew Bird	Oxford, Oakland	1917-1922	1923-1924
Glass, Harry, Jr.	Grand Rapids, Kent	1935-1938	
Glavin, John Maurice	New Buffalo, Berrien	1867-1868	
Glazier, Frank Porter	Chelsea, Washtenaw		1903-1904
Gleason, Daniel G.	Richmond, Macomb	1883-1886	
Gleason, James	Hartland, Livingston	1853-1854	
Gleason, John J.	Flushing, Genesee	2003-2006	2007-2013
Gleason, John P.	Memphis, St. Clair	1853-1854	
Glenn, Annette	Larkin Township, Midland	2019-	
Glenn, Gary	Midland, Midland	2015-2018	
Glenn, James L.	Edwardsburgh, Cass	1846-1847	
Glessner, Augustus S.	Coldwater, Branch	1859-1860	
Gluecklich, Anthony	Detroit, Wayne	1893-1894	
Gnodtke, Carl F.	Sawyer, Berrien	1979-1996	

Name[2]	Post Office[3]	Session Years[4]	
		House	Senate
Godchaux, Pan	Birmingham, Oakland	1997-2002	
Godfrey, Joseph	Detroit, Wayne		1865-1866
Godfroy, James J.	Monroe, Monroe	1835-1836	
Godfroy, Peter	Springwells, Wayne	1843-1844	
Goebel, August	Detroit, Wayne	1879-1880	
Goemaere, Warren N.	Roseville, Macomb	1965-1978	
Goff, Sewell S.	Blissfield, Lenawee	1853-1854	
Goike, Ken	Ray Township, Macomb	2011-2016	
Golden, Charles J.	Monroe, Monroe	1955-1956	
Gonzales, Lee	Flushing, Genesee	2005-2010	
	Flint, Genesee		
Good, Chester A.	Highland Park, Wayne	1927-1928	
Good, Edmund	Gagetown, Huron	1961-1964	
Goodell, Alfred	Armada, Macomb	1847	
Goodell, Daniel	Detroit, Wayne	1843	
Goodell, James M.	Corunna, Shiawassee		1873-1874
Goodell, Solon	Denton, Wayne	1897-1900	1901-1904
Goodman, Alonzo A.	Mount Clemens, Macomb	1857-1858	
Goodman, Francis	Burnips Corners, Allegan	1881-1884	
Goodman, Lowell	Detroit, Wayne	1838	
Goodrich, Chauncey	Lansing, Ingham	1861-1862	
Goodrich, Chauncey B.	Ganges, Allegan	1857-1858	
Goodrich, Enos	Goodrich, Genesee	1847	1853-1854
	Atlas, Genesee		
Goodrich, John V. B.	Coopersville, Ottawa	1887-1890	
Goodrich, Lester Adoran	Hillsdale, Hillsdale	1899-1902	
Goodrich, Levi N.	Concord, Jackson	1869-1870; 1873-1874	
Goodrich, Reuben	Goodrich, Genesee	1857-1858	1855-1856
Goodwin, Justus	Burlington, Calhoun	1839; 1842-1843; 1847	
	Union City, Branch		
Goodwin, William F.	Concord, Jackson	1857-1860	1881-1882
Goodwine, John W.	Marlette, Sanilac	1927-1934	
Goodyear, Henry A.	Hastings, Barry	1847; 1875-1876	1885-1886
Goodyear, Samuel C.	Swartz Creek, Genesee	1897-1900	
Gordon, Don	Leland, Leelanau	1963-1964	
Gordon, Henry	Flat Rock, Wayne	1873-1874	
Gordon, James Wright	Marshall, Calhoun		1839
Gordon, John R.	Marquette, Marquette	1899-1902; 1905-1908	
Gordon, William D.	Midland, Midland	1893-1898	
Gorham, Charles T.	Marshall, Calhoun		1859-1860
Gorman, James Sedgwick	Chelsea, Washtenaw	1881-1882	1887-1890
	Dexter, Washtenaw		
Gorman, Lee A.	Detroit, Wayne		1933-1936
Gorman, Patrick	Grafton, Monroe	1871-1872	
Goschka, Michael John	Brant, Saginaw	1993-1998	1999-2006
Goss, Georgina F.	Northville, Wayne	1991-1992	
Gosselin, Robert M.	Troy, Oakland	1999-2002; 2005-2006	
Gougeon, Joel	Bay City, Bay		1993-2002
Gould, Amos	Owosso, Shiawassee		1853-1854
Gould, James	Jackson, Jackson	1879-1880	
Gould, James J.	Kalamo, Eaton	1877-1878	
Goulette, James	Iron Mountain, Dickinson	1939-1948; 1951-1958	
Gowdy, Herbert W.	Union Pier, Berrien	1919-1922	
Grace, Benjamin	Fenton, Genesee	1859-1860	
Grace, William Charles	Kalamazoo, Kalamazoo		1913-1914
Graebner, Clarence F.	Saginaw, Saginaw	1947-1954	1955-1958
Graebner, Henry J.P.	Saginaw, Saginaw	1939-1946	
Graham, James	Berrien Springs, Berrien	1865-1866	
Graham, James Franklin	Freeland, Saginaw	1939-1942	
Graham, James W.	St. Charles, Saginaw	1891-1892	
Graham, Jonathan B.	Jonesville, Hillsdale	1846	
Graham, Robert Darwin	Grand Rapids, Kent	1895-1898	1899-1900
Grajewski, Michael J., Jr.	Hamtramck, Wayne	1933-1934	
Granger, Elihu	Berlin, St. Clair	1848	

Name[2]	Post Office[3]	House	Senate
		Session Years[4]	
Granger, George H.	Unionville, Tuscola	1879-1882	
Granger, Lyman	Columbus, St. Clair		1842-1843
Grant, Alexander	Utica, Macomb	1881-1884	
Grant, Claudius Buchanan	Ann Arbor, Washtenaw	1871-1874	
Grant, Robert J.	Hastings, Barry	1869-1872	
Graveraet, Robert J.	Marquette, Marquette		1857-1858
Graves, Benjamin F.	Adrian, Lenawee	1911-1912	
Graves, Carl Raymond	Hazel Park, Oakland	1945-1948	
Graves, Gerald William	Alpena, Alpena	1951-1954	
Graves, Joseph	Argentine Township, Genesee	2012-2018	
Gray, Charles F.	Ypsilanti, Washtenaw	1965-1966	
Gray, Edgar L.	Newaygo, Newaygo	1871-1872	1873-1876
Gray, Humphrey Snell	Ludington, Mason	1899-1900	
Gray, James D.	Warren, Macomb		1967-1974
Gray, James S.	Troy, Oakland	1883-1884	
Gray, Myles F.	Lansing, Ingham	1909-1910	
Gray, Neil, Jr.	Ray, Macomb		1843-1844
Gray, Sidney C.	Detroit, Wayne		1935-1936
Gray, Thomas	Ridgeway, Lenawee	1851-1852	
Gray, Thomas	Rosebush, Isabella	1913-1914	
Green, Albertus L.	Olivet, Eaton	1861-1862; 1865-1866; 1870	1867-1868
Green, Allison	Kingston, Tuscola	1951-1964	
Green, Alonzo B.	Hillman, Montmorency	1915-1918; 1923-1930	
Green, Charles M.	Port Huron, St. Clair	1897-1898	
Green, Cogswell K.	Niles, Berrien	1835-1836	
Green, David A.	Pontiac, Oakland	1909-1912; 1921-1922	
Green, Edbert B.	Alma, Gratiot		1889-1890
Green, Edward Heistand	Charlevoix, Charlevoix	1873-1876	
Green, George C.	Detroit, Wayne	1893-1894	
Green, Isaac	Forestville, Sanilac	1875-1876	
Green, James A.	Bay City, Bay	1887-1888	
Green, Joseph	Crystal Falls, Iron	1929-1936	
Green, Kevin	Wyoming, Kent	2005-2010	
Green, Mike	Mayville, Tuscola	1995-2002	2011-2018
Green, Nelson	White River, Muskegon	1853-1854	1861-1864
Green, Noah K.	Clay Bank, Oceana Addison, Lenawee Medina, Lenawee Morenci, Lenawee	1850; 1861-1864	
Green, Orson	Geneva, Lenawee	1859-1860; 1871-1872	
Green, Patrick	Warren, Macomb	2016-2018	
Green, Phil	Millington, Tuscola	2019-	
Green, Sanford Moon	Owosso, Shiawassee Pontiac, Oakland		1843-1844; 1846-1847
Green, William	Hillman, Montmorency	1929-1936; 1939-1944	
Greene, Charles E.	Richmond, Macomb		1925-1928
Greene, Daniel Carroll	Romeo, Macomb	1879-1880	
Greene, Perry William	Grand Rapids, Kent		1945-1962
Greenfield, Alson	Vassar, Tuscola	1867-1868	
Greenfield, John	Ontonagon, Ontonagon	1859-1860	
Greenly, William L.	Adrian, Lenawee		1839-1840; 1842-1843
Gregory, Charles	Jonesville, Hillsdale	1851-1852	
Gregory, Charles Seymour	Dexter, Washtenaw	1861-1862; 1883-1884	
Gregory, John Van Nest	Dexter, Washtenaw	1889-1892	
Gregory, Vincent	Southfield, Oakland	2009-2010	2011-2018
Gregory, William H.	Plymouth, Wayne	1853-1858	
Gregory, William S.	Plymouth, Wayne	1840	
Greig, Christine	Farmington Hills, Oakland	2015-	
Greimel, Tim	Auburn Hills, Oakland	2012-2018	
Greiner, Michael	Connor's Creek, Wayne	1875-1876	1885-1886
Grenell, Judson	Detroit, Wayne	1887-1888	
Greusel, John	Detroit, Wayne	1871-1874	1875-1876; 1881-1884
Greusel, Joseph	Detroit, Wayne	1903-1908; 1913-1914	

Name[2]	Post Office[3]	House	Session Years[4] Senate
Grier, Theophilus C.	Bay City, Bay	1867-1868	
Griffey, Clinton G.	Negaunee, Marquette	1879-1880	1889-1890
Griffin, Beth	Mattawan, Van Buren	2017-	
Griffin, James W.	Adamsville, Cass	1844	
Griffin, Martin J.	Jackson, Jackson	2007-2010	
Griffin, Michael J.	Jackson, Jackson	1973-1998	
Griffin, Thomas Michael	Flint, Genesee	1945-1946	
Griffiths, Martha Wright	Detroit, Wayne	1949-1952	
Griggs, Albert G.	Pontiac, Oakland	1913-1920	
Grimes, Thompson	Pinckney, Livingston	1879-1880	
Grinnell, John	Brockway, St. Clair	1863-1864	
Griswold, Augustus D.	Grand Rapids, Kent	1863-1866	
Griswold, George R.	Detroit, Wayne		1848-1849; 1853-1854
Griswold, Harrison W.	Niles, Berrien	1853-1854	
Groat, Gustave J.	Battle Creek, Calhoun	1967-1972	
Groesbeck, Charles C.	Warren, Macomb	1863-1864	
Groger, Frank Alphonso	Brooklyn, Jackson		1915-1916
Grosfield, Anthony	Detroit, Wayne		1889-1890
Grosvenor, Ebenezer Oliver	Jonesville, Hillsdale		1859-1860; 1863-1864
Grosvenor, Ira Rufus	Monroe, Monroe	1871-1872	
Groves, John	Niles, Berrien	1845-1846	
Grovier, Isaac J.	Mount Clemens, Macomb	1839	
Gruse, Gregory G.	Madison Heights, Oakland	1985-1986	
Guastello, Thomas	Utica, Macomb	1969-1974	1975-1982
	Sterling Heights, Macomb		
Gubow, David M.	Huntington Woods, Oakland	1985-1998	
Guerra, Vanessa	Saginaw, Saginaw	2015-	
Guggisberg, John Christian	Gaylord, Otsego	1939-1944	
Gulick, Nicholas	Byron, Shiawassee	1853-1854	
Gulley, Alfred	Dearbornville, Wayne	1857-1858	
Gulley, Alfred B.	Dearbornville, Wayne	1851-1852	
Gullifer, Freeman O.	Au Sable, Iosco		1883-1884
Gunning, James	Livonia, Wayne	1842	
Gurney, Theron S.	Hart, Oceana		1889-1890
Gustafson, Dan	Haslett, Ingham	1993-1998	
Gustin, Henry K.	Alpena, Alpena	1897-1900	
Guzowski, Richard A. H. J.	Detroit, Wayne	1963-1964	
Haack, Bernard	Blumfield, Saginaw	1871-1872	
Haadsma, Jim	Battle Creek, Calhoun	2019-	
Haan, William A.	Grand Rapids, Kent	1919-1922	
Haase, Jennifer	Richmond, Macomb	2009-2010	
Hackett, Walter	Monroe, Monroe	1881-1882	
Hackett, William B.	Saginaw, Saginaw	1933-1934	
Hadden, James E.	Adrian, Lenawee	1979-1980	
Hadden, Joseph B.	Holland, Ottawa		1913-1914
Hadley, John, Jr.	Holly, Oakland	1861-1862	
Hadsall, Henry S.	Owosso, Shiawassee		1897-1898
Hagaman, Francis H.	Medina, Lenawee	1843	
Hager, Lauren M.	Port Huron, St. Clair	1999-2004	
Hager, Marie L.	Lansing, Ingham	1961-1964	
Haggerty, Robert A.	Detroit, Wayne		1949-1954
Haight, Charles F.	Lansing, Ingham	1923-1932; 1935-1936	
Haight, Salmon L.	Saline, Washtenaw	1849; 1853-1854	
Hailwood, James W.	Grand Rapids, Kent	1937-1938	
Haines, Gail	Waterford, Oakland	2009-2014	
Haire, Elias	Manchester, Washtenaw	1865-1866	
Haire, John	Grandville, Kent	1861-1862	
Haire, Robert A.	Spring Lake, Ottawa	1873-1874	
Halbert, Horace	Fowlerville, Livingston		1879-1880
Hale, David B.	Eaton Rapids, Eaton	1875-1876	
Hale, Derrick F.	Detroit, Wayne	1997-2002	
Hale, Will Erwin	Eaton Rapids, Eaton	1909-1912	
Hale, William	Detroit, Wayne		1845-1846
Haley, G. Kirk	Bad Axe, Huron	1947-1950	

Name[2]	Post Office[3]	House	Session Years[4] Senate
Hall, Adney Adelbert	Stockbridge, Ingham	1899-1900	
Hall, Alfred D.	Tecumseh, Lenawee	1877-1880	
Hall, DeVere	West Branch, Ogemaw	1891	
Hall, Ezra S.	Lake City, Missaukee	1917-1922	
Hall, Frederick	Ionia, Ionia	1850	
Hall, Henry	Dexter, Washtenaw	1844	1853-1854
Hall, Henry C.	Battle Creek, Calhoun	1889-1890	
Hall, Horatio	Bellevue, Eaton	1851-1852	
Hall, Luther E.	Ionia, Ionia	1927-1930	
Hall, Matt	Emmet Township, Calhoun	2019-	
Hall, Moses	Battle Creek, Calhoun	1844	
Hall, Salmon C.	Richland, Kalamazoo	1851-1852	
Hall, Talman W.	Battle Creek, Calhoun	1855-1856	
Halladay, Frayer	Ashton, Osceola	1903-1904	
Hallenbeck, Cornelius A.	Vermontville, Eaton	1901-1904	
Hallett, William B.	Kalamazoo, Kalamazoo	1917-1918	
Hamilton, Eva McCall	Grand Rapids, Kent		1921-1922
Hamilton, John	Constantine, St. Joseph	1879-1880	
Hamilton, John F.	Detroit, Wayne	1937-1940	
Hamilton, Nathaniel A.	St. Joseph, Berrien	1877-1878	
Hamilton, Robert J.	Battle Creek, Calhoun		1945-1948
Hammel, Richard E.	Flushing, Genesee	2007-2012	
Hammerstrom, Beverly Swoish	Temperance, Monroe	1993-1998	1999-2006
Hammon, Ted	Burton, Genesee	2007-2008	
Hammond, Andrew G.	Kalamazoo, Kalamazoo	1839	
Hammond, Charles F.	Lansing, Ingham	1893-1894	
Hammond, Charles G.	Union City, Branch	1840-1841	
Hammond, D. Judson	Pontiac, Oakland	1897-1900	
Hammond, Horace Nelson	St. Clair, St. Clair	1885-1886	
Hammond, John Tedford	Benton Harbor, Berrien		1939-1942
Hammond, William	Charlotte, Eaton	1849	
Hammoud, Abdullah	Dearborn, Wayne	2017-	
Hampton, Alvin C.	Negaunee, Marquette		1945-1946
Hampton, Bernie Franklin	Harrison, Clare	1937-1940	
Hampton, Charles S.	Harbor Springs, Emmet	1885-1886	
Hampton, William P.	Birmingham, Oakland	1965-1970	
Hance, John W.	Mount Pleasant, Isabella		1883-1884
Hand, George E.	Detroit, Wayne	1846	
Hand, Michael	Berrien Springs, Berrien	1853-1854	
Handy, Gail R.	Eau Claire, Berrien	1939-1942; 1959-1964	
Handy, Sherman T.	Crystal Falls, Iron	1899-1902	
Hankerd, Patrick	Henrietta, Jackson	1877-1878; 1883-1886	
Hanley, James W.	Detroit, Wayne		1913-1918
Hanley, Michael Joseph	Saginaw, Saginaw	1995-2002	
Hanlon, Martin	Williamston, Ingham	1905-1908	
Hanna, D. Knox	Caro, Tuscola	1933-1934	
Hannah, Perry	Traverse City, Grand Traverse	1857-1858	
Hannahs, George	South Haven, Van Buren		1871-1872
Hannan, James P.	Detroit, Wayne		1949-1950
Hanscom, Alfred H.	Pontiac, Oakland	1842; 1845	
Hanscom, Charles A.	Ironwood, Gogebic	1889-1890	
Hansen, Goeff	Hart, Oceana	2005-2010	2011-2018
Hansen, John P.	Dexter, Washtenaw	1999-2002	
Harbaugh, David E.	Detroit, Wayne	1840	
Harden, William F.	Martin, Allegan	1874-1876	
Harder, Clark A.	Owosso, Shiawassee	1991-1998	
Hardiman, Bill	Kentwood, Kent		2003-2010
Harding, Fisher A.	Detroit, Wayne	1841	
Harding, Fred W.	Grosse Pointe, Wayne		1929-1932
Hardman, Artina Tinsley	Detroit, Wayne	1999-2004	
Hardy, Anson R.	Lansing, Ingham	1901-1902	
Harford, William M.	Muskegon, Muskegon	1881-1882	
Harger, Seeley	West Bloomfield, Oakland	1849	
Harkness, John Underwood	Rollin, Lenawee	1883-1884	

Name[2]	Post Office[3]	House	Session Years[4] Senate
Harley, Charles I.	Riverton, Mason	1901-1904	
Harley, William	Scottville, Mason	1891-1892	
Harma, George Oscar	Atlantic Mine, Houghton	1935-1944	
Harmon, Henry H.	Howell, Livingston	1863-1864	
Harnly, Andrew H.	Saginaw, Saginaw	1927-1932	
Harper, Egbert P.	Saline, Washtenaw	1885-1888	
Harper, William	Madison, Livingston	1891-1892	
Harrelson, Leaun	Pontiac, Oakland	1949-1954	
Harrington, Anson R.	Comstock Park, Kent		1917-1918
Harrington, Charles F.	Port Huron, St. Clair	1877-1878	
Harrington, Daniel B.	Port Huron, St. Clair	1847	1853-1854
Harrington, Ebenezer B.	Port Huron, St. Clair		1839
Harrington, Patrick L.	Monroe, Monroe	1981-1982	
Harris, Israel V.	Tallmadge, Ottawa		1853-1854
Harris, James A.	Saginaw, Saginaw	1919-1922	
Harris, John M.	Boyne City, Charlevoix	1925-1928	
Harris, Michael	Harris, Menominee	1905-1910; 1917-1918	
Harris, Myron	Tallmadge, Ottawa	1875-1876	
Harris, Silas G.	Tallmadge, Ottawa	1847-1848; 1850	
Harris, Thomas W.	Detroit, Wayne	1869-1870	
Harris, Wilbur J.	Bay City, Bay	1939-1940	
Harris, William	Norwood, Antrim	1889-1890; 1895-1898	
Harris, William	Rockland, Ontonagon	1871-1874	
Harrison, Charlie James, Jr.	Pontiac, Oakland	1973-1993	
Harry, William	Hancock, Houghton	1891-1892	
Harshaw, Andrew	Alpena, Alpena		1887-1890
Hart, Alvin N.	Lapeer, Lapeer Whiteville, Lapeer Lansing, Ingham	1835-1836; 1871-1872	1844-1845; 1848-1850
Hart, Burton Lloyd	Morenci, Lenawee	1899-1900	
Hart, Doug	Rockford, Kent	1999-2004	
Hart, George Zaven	Dearborn, Wayne		1979-1982; 1987-2002
Hart, Henry	Midland City, Midland	1875-1876	
Hart, Jerome Thomas	Saginaw, Saginaw		1965-1990
Hart, Jonathan	Battle Creek, Calhoun	1840	
Hart, Kay M.	Swartz Creek, Genesee	1987-1990	
Hart, Noah H.	Lapeer, Lapeer	1851-1852	
Hart, Patrick	Battle Creek, Calhoun	1893-1894	
Hart, Russell A.	Detroit, Wayne	1921-1922	
Hart, William	Detroit, Wayne	1927-1928	
Hartman, Gus Theodore	Houghton, Houghton	1925-1934	
Hartson, William W.	Wales Center, St. Clair Port Huron, St. Clair	1869-1870; 1893-1894	
Hartsuff, Joseph L.	Unadilla, Livingston	1849	
Hartway, Will C.	Mount Clemens, Macomb	1919-1922	
Hartzog, William B.	Mason, Ingham	1925-1928	
Harvey, Barzilla J.	Adrian, Lenawee	1857-1858	
Harvey, James Mark	Constantine, St. Joseph		1919-1920
Harvie, Andrew	Detroit, Wayne	1845	1850-1852
Harwood, Willard	Imlay City, Lapeer	1891-1894	
Hascall, Charles C.	Flint, Genesee		1835-1836
Haskin, Nelson	Imlay City, Lapeer	1887-1888	
Haskins, Haran	Pine Lake, Oakland	1837	
Hasper, Gerrit C.	Muskegon, Muskegon	1969-1980	
Hassenger, Franklin A.	Constantine, St. Joseph	1917-1918	
Hastings, Ernest W.	Traverse City, Grand Traverse	1901-1902	
Hatch, Barnabas C.	Bennett's Corners, Jackson	1849	
Hatch, Hazen Jesse	Marshall, Calhoun	1931-1932	
Hatch, Jesse Monroe	Marshall, Calhoun	1909-1910	
Hatch, Laverne	Horton, Jackson	1933-1934; 1937-1938	
Hathaway, Hiram	Ray, Macomb Armada, Macomb	1842; 1855-1856	
Hathaway, Manning	Detroit, Wayne	1955-1956	
Hatheway, Gilbert	New Baltimore, Macomb		1871

Name[2]	Post Office[3]	House	Session Years[4] Senate
Hatzenbuhler, Otto	Detroit, Wayne	1899-1900	
Hauck, Roger	Union Township, Isabella	2017-	
Hauffe, Arthur Carl	Saginaw, Saginaw	1947-1952	
Haugh, Harold L.	Roseville, Macomb	2009-2014	
Haveman, Joseph H.	Holland, Ottawa	2009-2014	
Haven, Martin	Albion, Calhoun	1867-1868	
Haviland, James Matthew	Richmond, St. Clair	1909-1912; 1915-1916	
Hawkins, Duane	Vermontville, Eaton	1881-1882	
Hawkins, Lucius D.	Parma, Jackson		1875-1876
Hawkins, Olney	Ann Arbor, Washtenaw		1839-1840
Hawley, Augustus D.	Jackson, Jackson	1841	
Hawley, Chauncey	Napoleon, Jackson	1842	
Hawley, Elijah, Jr.	South Nankin, Wayne	1844; 1846; 1849	
Hawley, Richard	Detroit, Wayne	1865-1866; 1877-1878	
Hawley, Thomas DeRiemer	Detroit, Wayne	1867-1868	1885-1886
Hawley, Willard	Saranac, Ionia	1889-1892	
Hayden, Henry	Portsmouth, Bay	1863-1864	
Hayden, Henry A.	Jackson, Jackson	1863-1864	
Hayden, James G.	Cassopolis, Cass		1905-1906
Haydon, Philotus	Hamilton, Allegan	1844; 1847; 1850	1851-1852; 1859-1860
	Decatur, Van Buren		
	Keelersville, Van Buren		
Hayes, Eleazar B.	Watrousville, Tuscola	1883-1886	
Hayes, Michael D.	Midland, Midland	1981-1988	
Hayes, Nathan Bradley	Muir, Ionia	1877-1878	
Hayes, Walter John	Grosse Pointe, Wayne		1919-1924
	Detroit, Wayne		
Haynes, Harvey	Coldwater, Branch	1865-1866; 1871-1872	
Haynes, John	Midland City, Midland	1871-1872	
Hays, Andrew L.	Marshall, Calhoun	1845	
Hayward, John W.	Grand Rapids, Kent	1891-1892	
Hayward, William	Royal Oak, Oakland	1959-1976	
Haywood, James E.	Port Hope, Huron	1871-1874	
Hazard, Chester	Howell, Livingston	1848	
Haze, Charles W.	Pinckney, Livingston	1853	
Haze, William H.	Farmington, Oakland	1857-1858; 1863-1864	
Hazelton, George H.	Flint, Genesee	1845-1846	
Hazen, Ezra	Memphis, St. Clair	1865-1866; 1871-1872	1861-1862
Hazen, Luke	Sylvanus, Hillsdale	1848	
Heald, Henry T.	Grand Rapids, Kent	1905-1906	
Heald, Perley C.	Midland, Midland		1899-1900
Healey, William P.	Negaunee, Marquette	1867-1868	
Heath, Frank	Bay City, Bay		1945-1954
Heath, John S.	Desmond, St. Clair	1835-1837	
Hebard, Charles A.	Lapeer, Lapeer	1844; 1847	
Hebert, Earl	Ecorse, Wayne	1949-1954	
Heck, George Rowland	Lansing, Ingham	1899-1900	
Heckert, Benjamin Franklin	Paw Paw, Van Buren	1909-1911	
Heidkamp, Adolph Francis	Lake Linden, Houghton		1929-1936
Heine, Albert Oscar	Bay City, Bay		1905-1906
Heineman, David Emil	Detroit, Wayne	1899-1900	
Heinemann, August	Port Hope, Huron	1889-1890	
Heinze, James H.	Battle Creek, Calhoun	1967-1972	
Heise, Kurt	Plymouth, Wayne	2011-2016	
Heisterman, Carl	Bad Axe, Huron		1885-1886
Hellman, Russell	Dollar Bay, Houghton	1961-1980	
Helme, James W., Jr.	Adrian, Lenawee	1931-1938	1899-1902
Hemans, Lawton Thomas	Mason, Ingham	1901-1904	
Hemingway, George F.	Midland City, Midland	1861-1862	
Hemingway, William	Lapeer, Lapeer	1863-1864	
Henderson, Donald E.	Saginaw, Saginaw	1895-1896	
Henderson, Eden Foster	Battle Creek, Calhoun	1861-1862	
Henderson, Henry P.	Mason, Ingham	1879-1880	
Henderson, Robert J.	Detroit, Wayne	1947-1948	

Name[2]	Post Office[3]	House	Session Years[4] Senate
Henry, Charles R.	Au Sable, Iosco		1885-1886
Henry, James	Battle Creek, Calhoun	1907-1916	1919-1925
Henry, John	Saginaw, Saginaw	1901-1902	
Henry, John F.	Saugatuck, Allegan	1893-1896	
Henry, Paul Brentwood	Grand Rapids, Kent	1979-1980	1983-1984
Henze, Walter A.	Iron Mountain, Dickinson	1921-1924	
Henze, William E.	Detroit, Wayne	1891-1892	
Herald, Roy	Highland Park, Wayne		1925-1926
Herkimer, Henry H.	Maybee, Monroe	1903-1906	
Hermann, Harry	Laurium, Houghton	1939-1944; 1947-1954	
Hernandez, Shane	Port Huron, St. Clair	2017-	
Herrick, Charles R.	Fenwick, Montcalm		1925-1928
Herrick, Walter Grant	Hubbardston, Ionia Carson City, Montcalm	1935-1949	
Herrig, Peter	Saginaw, Saginaw	1895-1900	
Herrington, Caleb	Northville, Wayne	1837	
Herrington, Cass E.	Pontiac, Oakland	1887-1888	
Hertel, Curtis	Detroit, Wayne	1981-1998	
Hertel, Curtis, Jr.	East Lansing, Ingham		2015-
Hertel, Dennis Mark	Detroit, Wayne	1975-1980	
Hertel, John Charles	Harper Woods, Wayne		1974-1982
Hertel, Kevin	St. Clair Shores, Macomb	2017-	
Hertzler, Christian	Erie, Monroe	1873-1876	1885-1886
Herz, John M.	Detroit, Wayne	1891-1892	
Hewitt, Alexander	Hillsdale, Hillsdale	1873-1876	1879-1880
Hewitt, Henry	Marshall, Calhoun		1842
Hewitt, Lauren K.	Lansing, Ingham		1863-1864
Hewitt, Walter B.	Ypsilanti, Washtenaw	1842	
Hewitt, William F.	Marshall, Calhoun		1874
Hewlett, Ray L.	Jackson, Jackson	1923-1924	
Hickner, Thomas L.	Bay City, Bay	1978-1992	
Hickock, James W.	Walton, Grand Traverse		1853-1854
Hicks, Byron P.	Durand, Shiawassee Owosso, Shiawassee		1919-1922
Hicks, Eugene	Brighton, Livingston	1893-1896	
Hicks, John Fullerton	Menominee, Menominee	1893-1894	
Hicks, Melancton W.	Southfield, Oakland	1851-1852	
Hicks, Orren V.	Edwardsburg, Cass	1913-1914	
Higgins, George Neil	Ferndale, Oakland	1939-1944	1945-1946; 1949-1954
Higgins, Thomas T.	Cassopolis, Cass	1903-1906	
High, Hiram M.	Ovid, Clinton		1901-1902
High, Oliver	Manchester, Washtenaw	1857-1858	
Higley, Hiram	Rochester, Oakland	1835-1836	
Hilbert, Frederic	Wayland, Allegan		1961-1964
Hildenbrand, Dave	Lowell, Kent	2005-2010	2011-2018
Hill, Benjamin L.	St. Charles, Saginaw	1861-1862	
Hill, E. Parker	Decatur, Van Buren	1877-1880	
Hill, Fitch	Ann Arbor, Washtenaw	1845	
Hill, Frederick H.	Attica, Lapeer	1882	
Hill, James W.	Columbia Lake, Washtenaw	1835-1836	
Hill, Loyal W.	Eagle, Clinton	1887-1888	
Hill, Nicholas R.	Cedar Springs, Kent	1871-1872	
Hill, Samuel Worth	Eagle River, Keweenaw	1867-1868; 1871-1872	
Hill, Sandra J.	Montrose, Genesee	1993-1996	
Hillegonds, Paul	Holland, Ottawa	1979-1996	
Hilsendegen, Louis N.	Grosse Pointe, Wayne		1915-1916
Hilton, George E.	Fremont, Newaygo	1893-1896	
Himebaugh, Emanuel	Burr Oak, St. Joseph	1883-1884	
Hinchman, Theodore H.	Detroit, Wayne		1877-1878
Hinds, Henry Harrison	Stanton, Montcalm		1873-1874
Hine, James W.	Lowell, Kent		1883-1884
Hine, Milton B.	Austerlitz, Kent		1879-1880
Hinkley, Dana Harrison	Petoskey, Emmet	1911-1916; 1931-1933	
Hinkley, Warren J.	Flushing, Genesee		1925-1926

Name[2]	Post Office[3]	House	Session Years[4] Senate
Hinkson, George	Amadore, Sanilac	1889-1890	
Hitchcock, John C.	Hazel Park, Oakland	1959-1962	
Hitchcox, James H.	Union, Cass	1881-1882	
Hitchings, John P.	Concord, Jackson	1851-1852	
Hittle, Harry Faron	East Lansing, Ingham		1935-1957
	Lansing, Ingham		
Hixson, Daniel	Clinton, Lenawee	1843;1855-1856	1853-1854
	Bridgewater, Washtenaw		
Hoadley, Jon	Kalamazoo, Kalamazoo	2015-	
Hoaglin, Frederick F.	Albion, Calhoun	1887-1890	
Hoar, Richard M.	Houghton, Houghton	1873-1874	
Hobart, David	Holly, Oakland	1889-1890	
Hobart, Norton P.	Athens, Calhoun	1849	
Hobbs, Rudy	Lathrup Village, Oakland	2011-2014	
Hodge, Hiram C.	Concord, Jackson	1872	1879-1880
Hodges, Israel S.	Ogden, Lenawee	1861-1862	
Hodgkinson, Bradshaw	Wayne, Wayne	1863-1864	
Hoeft, John	Rogers, Presque Isle	1909-1910	
Hoekman, Alvin J.	Holland, Ottawa	1985-1992	
Hoffman, Clarence E.	Detroit, Wayne	1947-1948	
Hoffman, Herbert H.	Sandusky, Sanilac	1915-1916	
Hoffman, Philip E.	Horton, Jackson	1983-1993	1993-2002
Hoffman, Quincy P.	Applegate, Sanilac	1965-1980	
Hofma, Edward	Grand Haven, Ottawa		1915-1916
Hofmeister, Charles A.	Unionville, Tuscola	1897-1900	
Hogan, Henry M.	Birmingham, Oakland	1961-1964	
Hoitenga, Michele	Manton, Wexford	2017-	
Holbeck, Frederick Charles	East Tawas, Iosco	1929-1936	
Holbrook, Donald E.	Clare, Clare	1965-1972	
Holbrook, John	Lansing, Ingham		1887-1890
Holcomb, James E.	Wolverine, Cheboygan		1891-1892
Holcomb, Martin H.	Pierson, Montcalm	1911-1914	
Holcomb, Thomas M.	Lansing, Ingham	1975-1978	
Holden, Charles Wayne	Grand Rapids, Kent	1895-1896	
Holden, Dennison F.	Oviatt, Leelanau	1891-1892	
Holdridge, Horace	Tecumseh, Lenawee	1893-1894	
Holland, Charles E.	Hancock, Houghton	1871-1872	
Holland, John	Bessemer, Gogebic	1911-1914; 1919-1930	
Hollier, Adam	Detroit, Wayne		2018-
Hollister, David C.	Lansing, Ingham	1975-1993	
Hollister, Fred W.	Saginaw, Saginaw	1889-1890	
Hollister, Hannibal	Port Huron, St. Clair	1846	
Hollister, Henry S.	Gidley's Station, Jackson	1847	
Hollister, Isaac T.	Victor, Clinton		1857-1858
Hollon, Joseph A.	East Saginaw, Saginaw	1875-1876	
Hollway, George R.	Grand Rapids, Kent	1913-1914	
Holman, Joseph H.	Rochester, Oakland	1885-1886	
Holmes, Alfred	Worth, Tuscola	1849	
Holmes, Arthur L.	Detroit, Wayne	1895-1896	1897-1898; 1901-1902
Holmes, David S., Jr.	Detroit, Wayne	1959-1974	1974-1994
Holmes, John H.	Bay City, Bay	1893-1894	
Holmes, John W.	Alma, Gratiot	1901-1906	
Holmes, Kirby	Utica, Macomb	1973-1978	1984-1986
Holmes, Lyman A.	Romeo, Macomb		1917-1920
Holmes, Patricia	Detroit, Wayne		1994
Holt, Henry H.	Muskegon, Muskegon	1867-1872; 1879-1880; 1887-1888	
Holton, William Marcy	Dearborn, Wayne	1891-1892	
Honigman, David M.	West Bloomfield, Oakland	1985-1990	1991-1996
Hoobler, Samuel R.	Worth, Tuscola	1887-1888	
Hood, John G.	Grafton, Monroe	1861-1864	
Hood, Morris W., III	Detroit, Wayne	2003-2008	2011-2018
Hood, Morris, Jr.	Detroit, Wayne	1971-1998	
Hood, Rachel	Grand Rapids, Kent	2019-	

		Session Years⁴	
Name²	Post Office³	House	Senate
Hood, Raymond W.	Detroit, Wayne	1965-1980	
Hoogendyk, Jacob W., Jr.	Portage, Kalamazoo	2003-2008	
	Kalamazoo, Kalamazoo		
Hooker, Azel	Summerfield, Monroe	1839	
Hooker, Cortez P.	Ashley, Macomb	1850	1855-1856
	Romeo, Macomb		
Hooker, Thomas B	Byron Center, Kent	2011-2016	
Hooper, Warren Green	Albion, Calhoun	1939-1944	1945
Hope, Kara	Holt, Ingham	2019-	
Hopgood, Hoon-Yung	Taylor, Wayne	2003-2008	2011-2018
Hopkins, Arlie L.	Bear Lake, Manistee	1915-1922	
Hopkins, George H.	Detroit, Wayne	1879-1884	
Hopkins, Harvey J.	Chesaning, Saginaw	1881-1882	
Hopkins, Mordecai L.	Millpoint, Ottawa		1855-1856
Hopkins, Moses B.	Grand Haven, Ottawa	1867-1868	
Hopkins, R. Henry	Augusta, Kalamazoo	1913-1914	
Hopkins, Samuel Whaley	Mount Pleasant, Isabella	1877-1880	1893-1894
Horn, Kenneth B.	Frankenmuth, Saginaw	2007-2012	2015-
Horn, Vernald E.	Royal Oak, Oakland	1955-1956	
Hornberger, Pamela	Chesterfield, Macomb	2017-	
Horrigan, Albert Raymond	Flint, Genesee	1953-1970	
Horton, Benjamin S.	Bell River, St. Clair	1865-1866	
Horton, Dexter	Fenton, Genesee	1869-1870	
Horton, Jack	Alpine Township, Kent	1991-1992; 1995-1998	
Horton, Norman B.	Fruit Ridge, Lenawee		1923-1932
Hosford, Franklin H.	Detroit, Wayne	1887-1888	
Hosking, John	Ishpeming, Marquette	1923-1926	
Hosner, Orcott V.	Frankfort, Benzie	1873-1874	
Hotchkiss, Lauren	Medina, Lenawee	1838	
Hough, Lewis Cass	Plymouth, Wayne		1893-1894
Hough, Olmstead	Tecumseh, Lenawee		1835-1837
Houghton, Charles A.	Bay City, Bay	1917-1918	
Houghton, George E.	Swartz Creek, Genesee	1891-1892	
Houk, Theodore Graves	Elbridge, Oceana	1885-1888	
House, Elisha J.	Paw Paw, Van Buren	1857-1858	
Houseman, Fred J.	Albion, Calhoun	1935-1936	
Houseman, Julius	Grand Rapids, Kent	1871-1872	
Houston, John	Dearborn, Wayne	1875-1876	
Hovey-Wright, Marcia	Muskegon, Muskegon	2011-2016	
Howard, Cyrus	Dearborn, Wayne	1848	
Howard, Harvey Hinkley	Bloomingdale, Van Buren	1881-1884	
Howard, Henry	Port Huron, St. Clair	1873-1876	
Howard, Jacob Merritt	Detroit, Wayne	1838	
Howard, Joshua	Dearborn, Wayne	1838; 1840	
Howard, Manly D.	Holland, Ottawa	1863-1866	
Howard, Orrin F.	Three Rivers, St. Joseph	1865-1868	
Howard, Sumner	Flint, Genesee	1883-1884	
Howarth, Elijah B., Jr.	Royal Oak, Oakland	1923-1924	1925-1926
Howarth, Spencer C.	Lake Orion, Oakland	1945-1948	
Howe, Abel N.	Horton, Jackson	1883-1884	
Howe, George	Clinton, Lenawee	1835-1836	
Howe, John	Deer Creek, Livingston	1857-1858	
Howe, M. J.	Azalia, Monroe	1919-1920	
Howe, Orrin	Lodi, Washtenaw	1835-1837; 1843	
Howell, Andrew	Adrian, Lenawee		1865-1868
Howell, Chester Milton	Saginaw, Saginaw	1923-1926	1927-1932; 1939-1945
Howell, Gary K.	Lapeer, Lapeer	2016-	
	Silverwood, Lapeer		
Howell, George	Tecumseh, Lenawee	1883-1886; 1899-1900	1887-1888
Howell, Jim	St. Charles, Saginaw	1999-2004	
Howell, William T.	Hillsdale, Hillsdale	1842; 1861-1864	1843-1846
	Jonesville, Hillsdale		
	Newaygo, Newaygo		
Howland, Nathaniel	Bristol, Lapeer	1839	

Name[2]	Post Office[3]	House	Session Years[4] Senate
Howland, Simpson	Galesburg, Kalamazoo	1875-1878	
Howlett, T. Henry	Gregory, Livingston	1933-1934	
Howrylak, Martin	Troy, Oakland	2013-2018	
Howze, Lisa	Detroit, Wayne	2011-2012	
Hoxie, T. Jefferson	St. Louis, Gratiot	1943-1956	
Hoyt, Charles Keeler	Hudsonville, Ottawa	1893-1896	
Hoyt, Herbert H.	East Saginaw, Saginaw	1877-1878	
Hoyt, James M.	Walled Lake, Oakland		1859-1860
Hoyt, John P.	Vassar, Tuscola	1873-1876	
Hoyt, Marcus	Suttons Bay, Leelanau	1923-1926	
Hoyt, William C.	Detroit, Wayne	1871-1872	
Hubbard, A. B.	Clarkston, Oakland	1923-1924	
Hubbard, Collins B.	Detroit, Wayne	1881-1882	
Hubbard, Edward R.	Stephenson, Menominee	1921-1922	
Hubbard, Giles	Mount Clemens, Macomb		1865-1866
Hubbard, John H.	Waterloo, Jackson	1869-1870	
Hubbard, Leonidas	South Wright, Hillsdale	1875-1876	
Hubbell, Holly Eugene	Saginaw, Saginaw	1951-1960	
Hubbell, Jay Abel	Houghton, Houghton		1885-1888
Hubbell, Sardis F.	Milford, Oakland	1851-1852	
Huber, Robert James	Birmingham, Oakland		1965-1970
Huckins, Israel	Lexington, Sanilac	1867-1868	
Huckleberry, Mike	Greenville, Montcalm	2009-2010	
Hudson, Bradley P.	Marshall, Calhoun	1853-1854	
Hudson, Grant Martin	Schoolcraft, Kalamazoo	1905-1908	
Hudson, Jonathan	Brownstown, Wayne	1850	
Hudson, Leslie H.	Pontiac, Oakland	1955-1958	
Huebner, George C.	Detroit, Wayne	1889-1890	
Hueston, James M.	Northville, Wayne		1883-1886
Huff, Henry	Jonesville, Hillsdale	1871-1872	
Huff, Otis	Marcellus, Cass	1927-1932	
Huffman, Bill S.	Madison Heights, Oakland	1963-1974	1975-1982
Huggett, David	Bellevue, Eaton	1893-1896	
Huggett, George	Bellevue, Eaton	1875-1876	
Hughes, Arthur D.	Irving, Barry		1897-1898
Hughes, Harold B.	Clare, Clare		1961-1964
Hughes, Holly	Montague, Muskegon	2011-2012; 2015-2018	
Hughes, Rossel B.	Bellevue, Eaton	1871-1872	
Hughes, Theodore F.	Berkley, Oakland	1955-1958	
Huizenga, Bill	Zeeland, Ottawa	2003-2008	
Huizenga, Mark	Walker, Kent	2019-	
Hulbert, Edwin J.	Houghton, Houghton	1875-1876	
Hulett, Orvy	Armada, Macomb	1923-1928	
Hull, Oscar C.	Detroit, Wayne	1929-1932	
Hull, Tyler B.	Dimondale, Eaton	1883-1884	
Hull, William	Centerville, St. Joseph	1875-1876	
Hulse, Charles A.	St. Johns, Clinton	1913-1918	
Hummel, Scott	DeWitt, Clinton	2001-2006	
Humphrey, Elijah O.	Kalamazoo, Kalamazoo		1863-1864
Humphrey, James W.	Wayland, Allegan		1899-1902
Humphrey, John	Wheatland, Hillsdale	1845	
Humphrey, Levi S.	Monroe, Monroe	1841-1842	
Hune, Joe R.	Fowlerville, Livingston Hamburg, Livingston	2003-2008	2011-2018
Hungerford, Harold W.	Lansing, Ingham	1947-1964	1967-1970
Hunsberger, Glenn	Grand Rapids, Kent	1955-1959	
Hunsinger, Josephine Drivinsky	Detroit, Wayne	1955-1976	
Hunt, Cleveland	Detroit, Wayne	1875-1876	
Hunt, Edmund W.	Windsor, Eaton	1869-1870	
Hunt, Fred A.	Detroit, Wayne	1901-1906	
Hunt, Leonard H.	Lowell, Kent	1887-1888	
Hunter, George G.	Ovid, Clinton St. Johns, Clinton	1919-1922	1923-1926
Hunter, Teola Pearl	Detroit, Wayne	1981-1992	

Name[2]	Post Office[3]	House	Senate
Hunter, Tupac A.	Detroit, Wayne	2003-2006	2007-2014
Huntington, George M.	Mason, Ingham		1875-1876
Huntley, Victor F.	Manton, Wexford	1909-1910	
Hupert, Paul Alfred	Mount Clemens, Macomb	1933-1934	
Hurd, Homer C.	Union City, Branch	1855-1856; 1861-1862	
Hurd, John S.	Jackson, Jackson	1857-1858	
Hurlbut, William H.	South Haven, Van Buren	1869-1872	
Hurst, William A.	Detroit, Wayne	1901-1902	
Hussey, Erastus	Battle Creek, Calhoun	1850	1855-1856
Huston, Benjamin W., Jr.	Vassar, Tuscola	1869-1872	1879-1880
Hutchins, Allen	Adrian, Lenawee	1835-1836	
Hutchins, J. Weston	Hanover, Jackson		1913-1914
Hutchinson, Edward	Fennville, Allegan	1947-1950	1951-1960
Hutchinson, Loomis	Ceresco, Calhoun	1869-1870	
Huuki, Matt	Atlantic Mine, Houghton	2011-2012	
Hyde, Benjamin F.	Detroit, Wayne	1851-1852	
Hyso, Walter J.	Hamtramck, Wayne	1963-1964	
Iden, Brandt	Kalamazoo, Kalamazoo	2015-	
Ingalls, Charles W.	Portland, Ionia	1853-1854	
Ingalls, Daniel F.	Oxford, Oakland	1840	
Ingersoll, John N.	Owosso, Shiawassee	1849; 1869-1870	1861-1862
	Sault Saint Marie, Chippewa		
	Corunna, Shiawassee		
Inman, Larry	Williamsburg, Grand Traverse	2015-	
Ireland, Silas	Summerville, Cass	1877-1878	
Irvine, John D.	Mackinac, Mackinac	1850-1852	
Irwin, Jeff	Ann Arbor, Washtenaw	2011-2016	2019-
Irwin, Mitch	Sault Saint Marie, Chippewa		1979-1990
Irwin, William W.	Detroit, Wayne	1853-1854	
Isbell, Nelson Gordon	Howell, Livingston		1848-1852
Isbister, Gilbert H.	Port Huron, St. Clair		1939-1942
Isham, Edwin B.	Negaunee, Marquette		1873-1874
Ives, Friend	Plainwell, Allegan	1850	
Ives, Samuel G.	Unadilla, Livingston	1855-1858	
Ivory, William E.	Elba, Lapeer	1905-1908; 1917-1920	
Jackson, Andrew	Sault Saint Marie, Chippewa	1879-1880	
Jackson, Chester E.	Ovid, Clinton	1897-1898	
Jackson, John W.	Chesaning, Saginaw	1917-1920	
Jackson, Joseph	Perry's Grove, Monroe	1835-1836	
Jackson, Joseph Ingram	Highland Park, Wayne	1955-1962	
Jackson, Samuel P.	Monroe, Monroe	1889-1892	
Jackson, Shanelle	Detroit, Wayne	2007-2012	
Jackson, Walter F.	Big Rapids, Mecosta	1929-1932	
Jackson, William B.	Detroit, Wayne	1891-1892	
Jacobetti, Dominic J.	Negaunee, Marquette	1955-1994	
Jacobs, Gilda Z.	Huntington Woods, Oakland	1999-2002	2003-2010
Jacobsen, Bradford C.	Oxford, Oakland	2011-2016	
Jahnke, William Frederick	Saginaw, Saginaw	1927-1932	
Jakway, James J.	Benton Harbor, Berrien	1913-1914	
James, Delbert C.	Detroit, Wayne	1919-1920	
James, Walter J.	Flint, Genesee	1939-1940	
James, William Francis	Hancock, Houghton		1911-1914
Jamian, John E.	Bloomfield Hills, Oakland	1991-1996	
Jamison, James K.	Ontonagon, Ontonagon	1935-1936	
Jamison, Julius MacLain	Grand Rapids, Kent		1895-1896
Jamnick, Ruth Ann	Ypsilanti, Washtenaw	1999-2004	
Janes, Oscar Albartus	Hillsdale, Hillsdale		1895-1896
Jankowski, Cass J.	Detroit, Wayne		1927-1930
Jansen, Mark C.	Grand Rapids, Kent	1997-2002	2007-2014
January, William Louis	Detroit, Wayne	1897-1898	
Jarvis, Harvey Hope	Benton Harbor, Berrien	1933-1936	
Jarvis, W. J. Bryan	Benton Harbor, Berrien	1937-1938	
Jasnowski, Adolph	Detroit, Wayne	1889-1890	
Jay, William	Whitmore Lake, Washtenaw		1863-1866

Name[2]	Post Office[3]	House	Session Years[4] Senate
Jaye, David	Utica, Macomb	1989-1997	1998-2001
Jeffries, Edward H.	Detroit, Wayne	1941-1944; 1951-1962	
Jeffries, J. R.	Detroit, Wayne	1931-1932	
Jelinek, Ron	Three Oaks, Berrien	1997-2002	2003-2010
Jellema, Jon	Grand Haven, Ottawa	1995-2000	
Jenema, Mark	Falmouth, Missaukee	1939-1948	
Jenison, Henry Hamilton	Eagle, Clinton		1883-1884
Jenison, William F.	Eagle, Clinton	1863-1864	
Jenkins, Nancy E.	Clayton, Lenawee	2011-2016	
Jenks, Bela W.	Harbor Beach, Huron		1905-1908
Jenks, Bela W.	St. Clair, St. Clair		1869-1872
Jenks, Cassius M.	Jackson, Jackson	1903-1904	
Jenks, Jeremiah	Rock Falls, Huron		1875-1876
Jenness, John S.	Ypsilanti, Washtenaw	1867-1868	
Jenness, John Smith	Almont, Lapeer	1865-1866	1867-1868
Jenney, William, Jr.	Mount Clemens, Macomb		1877-1878
Jennings, Ira M.	Brighton, Livingston	1839; 1847	
Jennison, Hiram	Granville, Ottawa	1853-1854	
Jensen, Peter	Escanaba, Delta	1909-1914; 1919-1922	
Jensen, Roy Albert	Escanaba, Delta	1947-1948	
Jerome, David Howell	Saginaw, Saginaw		1863-1868
Jerome, George	Detroit, Wayne		1855-1858
Jerome, James D.	Detroit, Wayne	1905-1908; 1911-1922	
Jerome, Timothy	Saginaw City, Saginaw	1857-1858	
Jerome, William F.	Hillsdale, Hillsdale	1915-1916	
Jersevic, Roland J.	Saginaw Township, Saginaw	1993-1996	
Jesperson, Yorgen	Petoskey, Emmet	1939-1944	
Jewell, Augustus	Dowagiac, Cass		1893-1896
Jewell, Charles A.	Medina, Lenawee	1869-1870	
Jewell, Edward	Cedar Springs, Kent	1865-1868	
Jewell, James Franklin	Hubbell, Houghton	1921-1926; 1931-1934	
Jewell, Joseph B.	Fremont, Newaygo	1877-1878	
Jibb, William	Maybee, Monroe		1897-1898
Johnson, Andrew	Beulah, Wexford	1943-1944	
Johnson, Augustus S.	Springfield, Oakland	1845	
Johnson, Bert	Highland Park, Wayne	2007-2010	2011-2018
Johnson, Charles C.	Barryton, Mecosta	1909-1910	
Johnson, Cynthia	Detroit, Wayne	2019-	
Johnson, Daniel F.	Groveland, Oakland	1840	
Johnson, Daniel S.	Zilwaukee, Saginaw		1853-1854
Johnson, David	Jackson, Jackson	1845; 1847	
Johnson, Hiram	Lennon, Shiawassee	1891-1892	
Johnson, James	Sturgis, St. Joseph	1883-1886	
Johnson, James Lawrence	Plymouth, Wayne	1925-1928	
Johnson, Joel	Clare, Clare	2011-2016	
Johnson, Luke S.	Caseville, Huron	1891-1892	
Johnson, Milo Amble	Greenville, Montcalm	1929-1932	1951-1954
Johnson, Milo N.	Northville, Wayne	1919-1924	
Johnson, Oren G.	Fostoria, Tuscola		1921-1924
Johnson, Ransom C.	Flint, Genesee		1895-1896
Johnson, Rick	LeRoy, Osceola	1999-2004	
Johnson, Roger	Marshall, Calhoun		1965-1966
Johnson, Ruth A.	Holly, Oakland	1999-2004	2019-
	Groveland Township, Oakland		
Johnson, Samuel	Dowagiac, Cass	1877-1880	
Johnson, Shirley	Royal Oak, Oakland	1981-1998	1999-2006
Johnson, Simeon M.	Grand Rapids, Kent	1843	
Johnson, Steve	Wayland, Allegan	2017-	
Johnson, Welcome W.	Grand Rapids, Kent	1877-1878	
Johnston, Hugh H.	Rosebush, Isabella	1949-1956	
Johnston, Ivan A.	Mount Clemens, Macomb		1943-1946
Jolly, Carlos J.	South Range, Houghton	1923-1924	
Jondahl, H. Lynn	East Lansing, Ingham	1973-1994	
	Okemos, Ingham		
Jones, Carroll Brewster	Marcellus, Cass		1937-1938

Name[2]	Post Office[3]	Session Years[4]	
		House	Senate
Jones, Coulter W.	Midland, Midland	1923-1924	
Jones, DeGarmo	Detroit, Wayne		1840-1841
Jones, Edward H.	Constantine, St. Joseph	1861-1862	
Jones, Edward L.	Jackson, Jackson	1850	
Jones, George	Grand Ledge, Eaton	1853-1854	
Jones, George C.	Ontonagon, Ontonagon	1865-1866	
Jones, George N.	Marine City, St. Clair		1903-1906
Jones, Gilman C.	Dowagiac, Cass		1861-1862
Jones, Hayes	Pontiac, Oakland	2006	
Jones, Jewell	Inkster, Wayne	2017-	
Jones, John	Ishpeming, Marquette	1893-1896	
Jones, John D.	Brockway Center, St. Clair	1877-1878	
Jones, John H.	Quincy, Branch	1865-1868	1869-1870; 1875-1876
Jones, Loss E.	Brooklyn, Jackson	1847	
Jones, Richard	Assyria, Barry	1867-1868	
Jones, Rick	Grand Ledge, Eaton	2005-2010	2011-2018
Jones, Robert B.	Kalamazoo, Kalamazoo	2007-2010	
Jones, Whitney	Lansing, Ingham	1845-1846	1859-1860
	Delta, Eaton		
Jones, William H.	Detroit, Wayne	1915-1918	
Jones, William T.	Morley, Mecosta	1885-1888	
Jonker, Nate	Clio, Genesee	1987-1992	
Joslin, Chauncey	Ypsilanti, Washtenaw	1844	
Jowett, William L.	Port Huron, St. Clair	1967-1980	
Joy, James Frederic	Detroit, Wayne	1861-1862	
Judd, Ethel	North Adams, Hillsdale	1855-1858	
Judd, George E.	McCords, Kent	1889-1890	
Judson, Ephraim	Durand, Shiawassee	1933-1934	
Julian, Larry	Lennon, Shiawassee	1999-2004	
Jurkiewicz, Leonard A.	Detroit, Wayne	1933-1936	
Kahle, Bronna	Adrian, Lenawee	2017-	
Kahn, Roger N.	Saginaw, Saginaw	2005-2006	2007-2014
Kallander, Martin	Bessemer, Gogebic	1887-1888	
Kalmbach, John	Chelsea, Washtenaw	1911-1912	
Kaminski, Joseph Lawrence	Detroit, Wayne	1935-1940	
Kammer, Kerry Kenneth	Pontiac, Oakland		1975-1982
Kanar, Walter	Hamtramck, Wayne	1931-1932	
Kandrevas, Andrew J.	Southgate, Wayne	2009-2014	
Kane, Harry J.	Mount Pleasant, Isabella		1905-1908
Kanouse, Jacob	Byron, Shiawassee	1861-1862	
Kanouse, Luther C.	Byron, Shiawassee	1901-1902	
Kanter, Edward	Detroit, Wayne	1857-1858	
Kappler, Frederick	Lake Linden, Houghton	1909-1914; 1919-1920; 1935-1938; 1945-1946	
Karcher, Horatio S.	Rose City, Ogemaw		1923-1928
Karel, John D.	Grand Rapids, Kent	1945-1950	
Karoub, James H.	Highland Park, Wayne	1963-1968	
Karwick, Leo G.	Hamtramck, Wayne		1933-1934
Kaza, Greg	Rochester Hills, Oakland	1993-1998	
Kedzie, Robert C.	Lansing, Ingham	1867-1868	
Keeler, Lucius	Union, Cass	1865-1866	
Keeler, Miner S.	Middleville, Barry		1895-1896
Keeler, Richard	Battle Creek, Calhoun	1877-1878	
Keen, Walter A.	Mount Pleasant, Isabella	1915-1916	
Keeney, Andrew J.	Erie, Monroe	1863-1864	
Keep, Edward P.	Tekonsha, Calhoun	1899-1900	
Kehres, Raymond C.	Monroe, Monroe	1965-1980	
Kehrl, Herb	Monroe, Monroe	2005	
Keith, William A.	Sawyer, Berrien	1883-1884	
Keith, William R.	Garden City, Wayne	1973-1994	
Kelley, Harrison	Sturgis, St. Joseph	1859-1860	
Kelley, Louis L.	Farwell, Clare	1905-1908	1913-1916
Kelley, Mark N.	Metamora, Lapeer	1885-1888	
Kelley, Robert J.	Alpena, Alpena	1877-1878	

Name[2]	Post Office[3]	Session Years[4]	
		House	Senate
Kelley, Samuel Harlan	Benton Harbor, Berrien	1905-1908	
Kellogg, Charles Burnell	Constantine, St. Joseph	1893-1894	
Kellogg, Edwin	White Pigeon, St. Joseph	1850	
Kellogg, Francis William	Kelloggsville, Kent	1857-1858	
Kellogg, John R.	Allegan, Allegan	1838	
Kellogg, Keith	Ithaca, Gratiot	1933-1934	
Kellogg, Oliver	Sharon, Washtenaw	1837	
Kellogg, Shiverick	Ionia, Ionia	1871-1874	
Kelly, John Francis	Detroit, Wayne		1979-1994
Kelly, Peter J.	Detroit, Wayne	1945-1946; 1949-1958	
Kelly, Thomas H.	Wayne, Wayne	1995-2000	
Kelly, Tim	Saginaw Township, Saginaw	2013-2018	
Kelly, William D.	Muskegon, Muskegon	1895-1900	1901-1904
Kelly, William J.	La Salle, Monroe	1895-1896	
Kelsey, John T.	Warren, Macomb	1965-1982	
Kelsey, Newell James	West Le Roy, Calhoun	1883-1884	
Kelsey, Sullivan R.	Byron, Shiawassee	1847; 1859-1862	
Kemmerling, Charles Wesley	Monroe, Monroe	1909-1912; 1915-1916	
Kempf, Reuben	Ann Arbor, Washtenaw	1895-1896	1885-1886
Kendrick, Frank	Dryden, Lapeer	1881	
Kendrick, Frederick Guntherodt	Roseville, Macomb	1869-1870	
Kendrick, Lucius	Dryden, Lapeer	1869-1870	
Kennedy, Bela E.	Bangor, Van Buren	1971-1980	
Kennedy, Bert S.	Detroit, Wayne	1933-1934	
Kennedy, Deb	Brownstown Township, Wayne	2009-2010	
Kennedy, Frederick A., Jr.	Hanover, Jackson	1846	
Kennedy, Frederick A., Sr.	Ridgeway, Lenawee	1850	
Kennedy, Sheryl	Davison, Genesee	2019-	
Kenny, Casper Patrick	Flint, Genesee	1945-1946	
Kenny, Munnis	Webster, Washtenaw	1840	
Kenny, Myron C.	Lapeer, Lapeer	1865-1866	
Kent, Henry	Greenville, Montcalm	1895-1896	
Kent, Richard	Adrian, Lenawee		1853-1854
Kent, William A.	Prairie River, Branch	1838	
Kenyon, John, Jr.	Tyrone, Livingston	1850	1855-1856
	Hartland, Livingston		
Kercheval, Benjamin B.	Detroit, Wayne		1838-1839
Kerns, Joseph W.	Saginaw, Saginaw	1911-1912	
Kerr, Angus W.	Calumet, Houghton	1899-1902	
Kerr, James	Taymouth, Saginaw	1897-1898	
Kessel, John Francis	Saginaw, Saginaw	1937-1938	
Kesto, Klint	Commerce Township, Oakland	2013-2018	
Keyes, Danforth	Clinton, Lenawee	1875-1876	
Keyes, Karl D.	Olivet, Eaton		1907-1908
Kibbee, Henry C.	Mount Clemens, Macomb		1851-1852
Kibbee, Rufus	Medina, Lenawee		1846-1847
Kidder, Charles B.	Almont, Lapeer	1901-1904	
Kilborn, John	Petoskey, Emmet	1955-1962	
Kilborn, Joseph H.	Okemos, Ingham	1847-1850	
Kilbourne, Samuel L.	Lansing, Ingham	1875-1876	
Kildee, Dale Edward	Flint, Genesee	1965-1974	1975-1977
Killean, John	Grand Rapids, Kent	1887-1890	
Kilpatrick, Carolyn Cheeks	Detroit, Wayne	1979-1996	
Kilpatrick, Kwame M.	Detroit, Wayne	1997-2001	
Kilpatrick, William Marvin	Owosso, Shiawassee		1881-1882; 1895-1896
Kilstrom, Oscar Edward	Grand Rapids, Kent	1939-1943	
Kimball, Charles T.	Jonesville, Hillsdale	1931-1934	
Kimberly, Ebenezer C.	Corunna, Shiawassee	1851-1852	
Kimmis, Austin Noble, Jr.	Wixom, Oakland	1895-1898	
King, Edward	Ypsilanti, Washtenaw	1881-1884	
King, Francis	Alma, Gratiot		1913-1914
King, Gideon G.	Bird, Hillsdale	1855-1856	
King, John	Whitmore Lake, Washtenaw	1843	
King, John B.	East Raisinville, Monroe	1850	

Name[2]	Post Office[3]	House	Senate
			Session Years[4]
King, Jonathan P.	Mackinac, Mackinac	1837-1839; 1842; 1848	1849-1850
King, Nathan G.	Brooklyn, Jackson		1873-1874
Kingman, Albert Charles	Battle Creek, Calhoun		1909-1912
Kingott, John	Capac, St. Clair	1899-1900	
Kingsbury, Solomon O.	Grand Rapids, Kent	1867-1868	
Kingsland, Edward Leonard	Benton Harbor, Berrien	1893-1896	
Kingsley, James	Ann Arbor, Washtenaw	1837; 1848; 1869-1870	1838-1839; 1842
Kingsley, Samuel R., Jr.	Romulus, Wayne	1893-1896	
Kinnane, James H.	Dowagiac, Cass		1907-1908
Kinne, Daniel	Reading, Hillsdale	1847	
Kinne, Edward Dewitt	Ann Arbor, Washtenaw	1881-1882	
Kipp, George	Goodrich, Genesee	1873-1874	
Kipp, James	DuPlain, Clinton	1857-1858	
Kirby, Eugene J.	Covert, Van Buren	1921-1926	
Kirby, John W.	Galesburg, Kalamazoo	1889-1890	
Kirby, William J.	Pavilion, Kalamazoo	1887-1888	
Kircher, Fred L.	Lansing, Ingham	1939-1946	
Kircher, Samuel W.	Kawkawlin, Bay	1937	
Kirk, James	Fair Grove, Tuscola	1891	
Kirk, James	Vassar, Tuscola	1943-1950	
Kirk, John Patrick	Ypsilanti, Washtenaw	1903-1904	
Kirk, William	Caro, Tuscola	1901-1904	
Kirkland, George	Erie, Monroe	1855-1856	
Kirkpatrick, William M.	Palmer, Marquette	1885-1886	
Kirksey, Jack E.	Livonia, Wayne	1977-1984	
Kirkwood, Edward B.	Grand Rapids, Kent	1931-1934	
Kirkwood, John	Dowagiac, Cass	1893-1894	
Kistler, Clarence E.	Ludington, Mason	1917-1918; 1929-1932	
Kivela, John	Marquette, Marquette	2013-2017	
Klei, Henry	Detroit, Wayne	1881-1882	
Klein, Peter	Detroit, Wayne	1869-1870; 1875-1876	
Klein, Vincent	Detroit, Wayne	1945-1946	
Kline, Charles H.	Ann Arbor, Washtenaw	1893-1894	
Kline, Fred B.	Addison, Lenawee		1907-1912
Klump, Edwin William	Harbor Beach, Huron		1947-1950
Knabusch, Milton J. H.	Monroe, Monroe	1963-1964	
Knaggs, Daniel A.	Monroe, Monroe	1943-1944	
Knapp, Alonzo S.	South Lyon, Oakland	1873-1874	
Knapp, Cornelius	Rome Center, Lenawee	1871-1872	
Knapp, Jacob	Saginaw, Saginaw	1881-1882	
Kneeland, George W.	Howell, Livingston	1850	
Knezek, David	Dearborn Heights, Wayne	2013-2014	2015-2018
Knight, Benjamin	Eaton Rapids, Eaton	1844; 1847	
Knight, Birdsey	Bay City, Bay	1891-1894	
Knight, Godfrey E.	Schoolcraft, Kalamazoo	1875-1876	
Knight, James Brooks	Norway, Dickinson	1903-1908; 1911-1912	
Knight, Marvin L. Mickey	Muskegon, Muskegon	1981-1992	
Knight, Nathan	Bay City, Bay	1877-1880	
Knight, Richard	Atwood, Antrim	1883-1884	
Knight, Willard A.	Battle Creek, Calhoun	1905-1906	
Knollenberg, Marty	Troy, Oakland	2007-2012	2015-2018
Knowlton, Elbridge G.	Groveland, Oakland	1844	
Knox, Victor Alfred	Sault Saint Marie, Chippewa	1937-1952	
Koehler, Herman L.	Detroit, Wayne	1913-1916	1917-1918
Koetje, James L.	Walker, Kent	1999-2004	
	Grandville, Kent		
Kohn, George A.	Fenwick, Montcalm	1950-1954	
Koivisto, Donald W.	Mass City, Ontonagon	1981-1986	1990-2002
	Ironwood, Gogebic		
Kok, Peter	Grand Rapids, Kent	1965-1978	
Kolb, Chris	Ann Arbor, Washtenaw	2001-2006	
Kolderman, Johannes C., Jr.	Wyoming, Kent	1967-1968	
Koleszar, Matt	Plymouth, Wayne	2019-	
Kolowich, George J.	Hamtramck, Wayne		1929-1930

| Name[2] | Post Office[3] | Session Years[4] | |
		House	Senate
Kolvoord, John........................	Hamilton, Allegan...............................	1891-1892	
Kooiman, Jerry O.	Grand Rapids, Kent	2001-2006	
Koon, Ezra L.	Hillsdale, Hillsdale..		1869-1870; 1883-1884
Kooyers, Gerrit W.	Holland, Ottawa	1915-1926	
Kore, Jacob C.	Hadley, Lapeer	1859-1860	
Kosowski, Robert L.	Westland, Wayne	2013-2018	
Kosteva, James A.	Canton, Wayne	1985-1992	
Kowall, Eileen	White Lake, Oakland	2009-2014	
Kowall, Mike...........................	White Lake, Oakland	1999-2002	2011-2018
Kowalski, Joseph J.	Detroit, Wayne	1939-1944	
Kowalski, Joseph J.	Detroit, Wayne	1949-1967	
Kozak, Henry Raymond..................	Hamtramck, Wayne		1945-1950
Kramer, Albert A.	Oak Park, Oakland.............................	1965-1970	
Kramer, Herman	Detroit, Wayne	1933-1934	
Kratz, Jerry.............................	Grass Lake, Jackson	2003	
Krause, Victor C.	Rockford, Kent	1983-1990	
Kronk, Martin Anthony..................	Detroit, Wayne	1937-1944	
Krueger, Gustav A.	Detroit, Wayne		1909-1910
Kruse, John D.	Manistee, Manistee..............................	1943-1954	
Kuhn, George W.	Birmingham, Oakland...........................		1967-1970
Kuhn, Joseph Herman	Detroit, Wayne	1879-1880	
Kuipers, Wayne D.	Holland, Ottawa	1999-2002	2003-2010
Kukuk, Alvin H.	Macomb Township, Macomb	1993-1998	
Kukuk, Janet L.	Macomb Township, Macomb	1999-2000	
Kulchitsky, D. Roman	Warren, Macomb	1990	
Kulp, Francis A.	Battle Creek, Calhoun...............................		1933-1934
Kuppa, Padma..........................	Troy, Oakland....................................	2019-	
Kurth, Frederick William August	Springwells, Wayne	1879-1880	
Kurtz, Arthur...........................	Detroit, Wayne	1947-1948	
Kurtz, Kenneth	Coldwater, Branch	2009-2014	
Lacey, Elijah............................	Niles, Berrien.....................1838..............................		1840-1841; 1861-1862
Lacey, Obed P.	Niles, Berrien....................................	1843	
Ladd, Emmor Otis......................	Old Mission, Grand Traverse	1919-1924	
Ladd, Nathaniel	Dearborn, Wayne		1855-1856
Ladner, Frank	Ada, Kent	1903-1906	
LaDu, Stallham Williams	Coral, Montcalm	1881-1884	
LaFave, Beau	Iron Mountain, Dickinson......................	2017-	
Laflamboy, Charles H., NW	McBridges, Montcalm	1899-1902	1903-1904
Lafler, Warren Brainerd	Dundee, Monroe	1901-1902	
LaFontaine, Andrea......................	Richmond, Macomb...........................	2011-2016	
LaForge, Edward........................	Kalamazoo, Kalamazoo.........................	1995-2000	
LaFramboise, Joseph A.	Gladstone, Delta		1941-1944
LaGrand, David	Grand Rapids, Kent	2016-	
Lahti, Michael..........................	Hancock, Houghton	2007-2010	
LaHuis, Albert	Zeeland, Ottawa	1887-1888	
Laing, William Paisley	Perry, Shiawassee...............................	1865-1866	
Laing, William S.	Iron Mountain, Dickinson...........................		1887-1888
LaJoy, Philip J.	Canton, Wayne	2003-2008	
Lakey, Albert L.	Kalamazoo, Kalamazoo.........................	1887-1888	
Lalonde, Leo R.	East Detroit, Macomb...........................	1979-1980	
Lamb, Jacob C.	Dryden, Lapeer	1871-1874	
Lamb, John Merritt	Dryden, Lapeer ....1841-483..................		1857-1858; 1863-1864
	Look's Corners, Lapeer		
Lambert, George A.	Niles, Berrien....................................	1891-1892	
Lamond, Robert D.	Flint, Genesee....................................	1844	
Lamonte, Collene	Montague, Muskegon...........................	2013-2014	
Lamoreaux, James Neal..................	Comstock Park, Kent...............................		1933-1934; 1937-1938
Lamphere, Allan L.	Redford, Wayne.................................	1915-1918	
Lancaster, Columbia.....................	Centerville, St. Joseph...........................	1838	
Landon, John	Parma, Jackson..............1865-1866; 1871		
Landon, Palmer	Mount Pleasant, Isabella	1939-1948	
Landon, Reynolds	Elk Rapids, Antrim	1891-1892	
Landon, Rufus Wharton	Niles, Berrien...		1863-1864
Lane, Garland Bearl	Flint, Genesee..		1949-1974

Name[2]	Post Office[3]	House	Session Years[4] Senate
Lane, John	St. Joseph, Berrien	1901-1904	
Lane, Marilyn	Fraser, Macomb	2011-2016	
Lane, Minot Thayer	Romeo, Macomb	1838; 1848	
Lane, Orville B.	Pittsford, Hillsdale	1903-1906	
Lane, Peter	Saginaw, Saginaw	1869-1870	
Lane, Robert H.	Bay City, Bay	1931-1932	
Lane, Thomas D.	South Lyon, Oakland	1859-1860	1861-1862
Lane, Thomas Michael	Detroit, Wayne	1947-1948	
Langdon, Nathaniel	Ida, Monroe		1865-1866
Langsford, Fred	Iron Mountain, Dickinson	1925-1928	
Lapham, Leander	Maple Grove, Barry	1865-1866	
Lapham, Smith	Laphamville, Kent	1855-1856	1857-1858
Larsen, Melvin L.	Oxford, Oakland	1973-1978	
Larue, James B.	St. Joseph, Berrien	1840-1841	
LaSata, Charles T.	St. Joseph, Berrien	1999-2004	
LaSata, Kim	Benton Harbor, Berrien Bainbridge Township, Berrien	2017-2018	2019-
Lasinski, Donna	Scio Township, Washtenaw	2017-	
Lathrop, Henry B.	Jackson, Jackson	1840	1847
Lathrop, Horace Newton	Lapeer, Lapeer	1853-1854	
Latimer, William Irving	Big Rapids, Mecosta	1895-1896	1897-1900
Latourette, David Lewis	Fenton, Genesee		1867-1868
Laubach, Benjamin	Berlin, Ottawa	1877-1880	
Lauwers, Dan	Brockway Township, St. Clair	2013-2018	2019-
LaVoy, Bill	Monroe, Monroe	2013-2016	
Law, Arthur James	Pontiac, Oakland	1959-1972	
Law, David	West Bloomfield, Oakland Commerce Township, Oakland	2005-2008	
Law, Gerald H.	Plymouth, Wayne	1983-1991	
Law, Kathleen	Gibralter, Wayne	2003-2008	
Law, Robert C.	Livonia, Wayne	1977-1980	
Lawrence, Edwin	Ann Arbor, Washtenaw	1848	
Lawrence, Peter E.	Leoni, Jackson	1843	
Lawrence, Samuel J.	Wyandotte, Wayne		1897-1898
Lawrence, Solomon L.	Girard, Branch	1851-1852	
Lawson, James Earl	Royal Oak, Oakland	1925-1930	1931-1932
Lay, Ezra Dennison	Ypsilanti, Washtenaw	1875-1876	
Le Baron, Sirrell C.	Tecumseh, Lenawee	1840	
Leach, DeWitt Clinton	Mundy, Genesee	1850	
Leach, Travis Francis	Ellington, Tuscola	1891-1892	
Leavitt, Charles Wirt	Stetson, Oceana	1893-1894	
Leavitt, Roswell	Bellaire, Antrim		1889-1890
LeBlanc, Richard	Westland, Wayne	2007-2012	
Ledyard, Henry	Detroit, Wayne		1857-1858
Lee, Benn Hubbard	Grand Rapids, Kent	1913-1914	
Lee, Daniel S.	Novi, Oakland	1843	
Lee, Henry	Lapeer, Lapeer	1895-1898	
Lee, James	Sutton's Bay, Leelanau	1875-1878	
Lee, James Barker	Brighton, Livingston	1869-1870	
Lee, James Henderson	Detroit, Wayne		1911-1912
Lee, Josiah	Ray, Macomb	1841	
Lee, Melvin H.	Royal Oak, Oakland	1931-1938	
Lee, Thomas	Dexter, Washtenaw	1837	
Lee, William O.	Port Huron, St. Clair	1921-1924	
Lee, William Wells	Saginaw, Saginaw		1945-1946
Leech, Gurdon C.	Utica, Macomb	1841	
Leech, Payne Kenyon, Jr.	Utica, Macomb	1846	
Leedy, David Warner	Scottville, Mason	1921-1924	
Leetch, Andrew J.	Ypsilanti, Washtenaw	1861-1862	
Legel, Jack	Detroit, Wayne	1975-1980	
Legg, Peter Rugby	Escanaba, Delta	1933-1946	
Leidlein, John	Saginaw, Saginaw		1899-1900; 1911-1912; 1933-1934
Leighton, William	Grand Marais, Schoolcraft	1917-1919	

Name[2]	Post Office[3]	House	Session Years[4] Senate
Leitch, John	Deckerville, Sanilac	1883-1884	
Leland, Burton	Detroit, Wayne	1981-1998	1999-2006
Leland, Elijah	Quincy, Branch	1857-1858	
Leland, Gabe Daniel	Detroit, Wayne	2005-2010	
Leland, George	Fennville, Allegan	1915-1920	1923-1934
Leland, Joshua G.	Lucerne, Washtenaw	1844; 1846	
Lemire, William A.	Escanaba, Delta	1917-1918	1919-1922
Lemmons, LaMar, III	Detroit, Wayne	1999-2002; 2005-2006	
Lemmons, LaMar, Jr.	Detroit, Wayne	2005-2010	
Lennon, Peter B.	Lennon, Shiawassee	1919-1924	1927-1932
Leonard, Joseph C.	Union City, Branch		1853-1854
Leonard, Orvice R.	Detroit, Wayne	1911-1914	
Leonard, Tom	DeWitt Township, Clinton	2013-2018	
Lepczyk, Joseph A.	Bay City, Bay	1937-1938	
Leppien, William J.	Saginaw, Saginaw		1963-1964
LeRoy, John P.	Pontiac, Oakland		1840-1841; 1851-1852
Lesinski, Edmond	Detroit, Wayne	1963-1964	
Lesinski, T. John	Detroit, Wayne	1951-1960	
L'Esperance, David Andre, Jr.	Detroit, Wayne	1907-1908	
Lester, George H.	Crystal, Montcalm	1891-1892	
Lester, George S.	Lexington, Sanilac	1850	
Leszynski, Joseph J.	Detroit, Wayne	1943-1946	
LeTarte, Clyde	Horton, Jackson	1993-1998	
Leutheuser, Eric	Hillsdale, Hillsdale	2015-	
Levake, Henry A.	Sault Saint Marie, Chippewa	1836-1839	
Leveque, David J.	Lake Linden, Houghton	1917-1918	
Levin, Sander Martin	Berkley, Oakland		1965-1970
Lewandowski, Chester	Detroit, Wayne	1949-1954	
Lewis, Amos	Shelby, Oceana	1879-1880	
Lewis, Charles F.	Pentwater, Oceana	1923-1926; 1929-1930	
Lewis, George	Bay City, Bay	1873-1874	
Lewis, John Denison	Bay City, Bay Vassar, Tuscola	1865-1866	1874
Lewis, Lynn J.	Bangor, Van Buren	1915-1920	
Lewis, Nathaniel W.	Ganges, Allegan		1879-1880
Lewis, Rollie L.	Charlevoix, Charlevoix	1921-1924	
Lewis, Thomas	Monguagon, Wayne	1842; 1846	
Lewis, William	Yankee Springs, Barry	1846	
Lewis, William F.	Shelby, Oceana	1891-1892	
Liberati, Frank	Allen Park, Wayne	2015-	
Licata, Anthony C.	Detroit, Wayne	1967-1968	
Liddy, Ralph William	Detroit, Wayne	1919-1922	
Lightner, Sarah	Springport, Jackson	2019-	
Lilly, Jim	Park Township, Ottawa	2017-	
Lincoln, Everitt F.	Albion, Calhoun	1978-1980	
Lincoln, Lansing Edgar	Sand Beach, Huron	1885-1888	
Lindberg, Steven W.	Marquette, Marquette	2007-2012	
Lindemer, Lawrence B.	Stockbridge, Ingham	1951-1952	
Linderman, Albert T.	Whitehall, Muskegon	1893-1896	
Linderman, Peter	Mason, Ingham	1857-1858	
Lindow, Frederick	Marine City, St. Clair	1889	
Lindquist, Carl Gottfred	Iron River, Iron	1941-1954	
Lindsay, David L.	Detroit, Wayne	1949-1960	
Lingeman, Caspar J.	Grosse Pointe, Wayne	1935-1936	
Lingemann, Adrian A.	St. Clair Shores, Macomb	1931-1932	
Linsley, Edward Baldwin	Three Rivers, St. Joseph		1905-1908
Linton, William Seelye	East Saginaw, Saginaw	1887-1888	
Lipsey, Alexander C.	Kalamazoo, Kalamazoo	2001-2006	
Lipton, Ellen Cogen	Huntington Woods, Oakland	2009-2014	
Liss, Lesia	Warren, Macomb	2009-2012	
Litowich, Harry	Benton Harbor, Berrien	1953-1958	1959-1964
Littell, William E.	Orion, Oakland	1879-1882	
Little, Carl O.	Saginaw, Saginaw	1961-1968	
Little, Charles D.	Saginaw City, Saginaw	1871-1872; 1875-1878	

Name[2]	Post Office[3]	Session Years[4] House	Senate
Little, Lloyd S.	Tawas City, Iosco	1923-1924	
Little, Norman	Saginaw City, Saginaw	1839; 1842	
Littlefield, Sherman	Detroit, Wayne	1947-1948	
Littlejohn, David	Bridgman, Berrien	1917-1918	
Littlejohn, Flavius J.	Allegan, Allegan	1842-1843; 1848; 1855-1856	1845-1846
Littlejohn, Philetus Orville	Allegan, Allegan	1863-1864	
Littlewood, William P.	Wayndotte, Wayne	1951-1952	
Livermore, Fidus	Jackson, Jackson	1843-1844	
Livermore, John S.	Rochester, Oakland	1839; 1842	
Livingston, William, Jr.	Detroit, Wayne	1875-1876	
Llewellyn, John T.	Fremont, Newaygo	1993-1998	
Locher, Joseph A.	Saranac, Ionia	1899-1900	
Locke, Charles	Perry, Shiawassee	1867-1868	
Locke, David Guy	Carson City, Montcalm	1921-1922	
Lockerby, William H.	Quincy, Branch		1901-1904
Lockwood, Emil	St. Louis, Gratiot		1963-1970
Lockwood, James Kent	Alpena, Alpena	1867-1868; 1873-1874	
Lockwood, Major Ferris	Milford, Oakland	1849	
Lockwood, Patricia A.	Fenton, Genesee	1999-2002	
Lockwood, Thomas W.	Detroit, Wayne	1861-1864	
Lodge, John Christian	Detroit, Wayne	1909-1910	
Lodge, L. Harvey	Pontiac, Oakland; Drayton Plains, Oakland	1947-1948	1957-1960; 1967-1974
Loeser, Hugo Charles	Jackson, Jackson		1901-1902
Logie, Jerry Thompson	Bay City, Bay		1939-1944
Lohman, Ben E.	Allegan, Allegan; Hamilton, Allegan	1951-1962	
Lomison, John	Parkville, St. Joseph	1855-1856	
London, Terry	Marysville, St. Clair	1985-1986; 1989-1998	
Long, George Marsh	Pompeii, Gratiot	1923-1924	
Long, Jeremiah D.	Detroit, Wayne	1885-1886	
Long, Joseph A.	Milford, Oakland	1935-1936	
Lonsbury, Philo Miner	Reed City, Osceola	1895-1896	
Look, Dexter G.	Lowell, Kent	1923-1934	
Look, Henry M.	Pontiac, Oakland	1865-1866	
Loomis, Charles A.	St. Clair, St. Clair		1848-1849
Loomis, Dewey William	Wellston, Manistee	1939-1942	
Loomis, Peter Burr	Jackson, Jackson	1859-1860	
Loomis, Robert B.	Grand Rapids, Kent		1897-1902
Loomis, Thomas N.	Oxford, Oakland	1847	
Lord, George	Detroit, Wayne	1905-1908; 1911-1912; 1921-1922	
Lori, Matt	Constantine, St. Joseph	2009-2014	
Lothrop, Edwin H.	Schoolcraft, Kalamazoo	1835-1837; 1842-1844; 1848	
Loupee, Sherman L.	Dowagiac, Cass	1939-1948	
Love, Leslie	Detroit, Wayne	2015-	
Lovell, Cyrus	Ionia, Ionia	1849; 1855-1856	
Lovell, Enos T.	Climax, Kalamazoo	1867-1870	1881-1882
Lovell, George W.	Climax, Kalamazoo	1853-1856	
Lovell, Lafayette Washington	Climax, Kalamazoo		1857-1858
Lovell, Nathan V.	Eau Claire, Berrien	1903-1906	
Lowden, James L.	Ypsilanti, Washtenaw	1889-1892	
Lowe, Allen L.	Grayling, Crawford	1993-1998	
Lower, James	Cedar Lake, Montcalm	2017-	
Lowrey, Berry John	Howard City, Montcalm	1901-1902	
Lowry, John Peter	Lodi, Washtenaw	1889-1890	
Lucas, Anthony Joseph	Calumet, Houghton	1911-1912	
Luce, Charles D.	Osseo, Hillsdale	1873-1874	
Luce, Cyrus Gray	Gilead, Branch	1855-1856	1865-1868
Lucido, Peter	Shelby Township, Macomb	2015-2018	2019-
Ludington, Allen G.	Detroit, Wayne		1939-1940
Ludington, Jeremiah, Jr.	Verona Mills, Huron	1875-1876; 1879-1880	

Name[2]	Post Office[3]	House	Session Years[4] Senate
Ludlow, Luther H.	Parma, Jackson	1877-1878	
Ludlow, Samuel	Springwells, Wayne	1857-1858	
Luecke, John Frederick	Escanaba, Delta		1935-1936
Lugers, Luke	Holland, Ottawa	1899-1902	1907-1908
Lund, Peter J.	Shelby Township, Macomb	2009-2014	
Lundgren, Kent T.	Menominee, Menominee		1962-1964
Lusk, George Lathrop	West Bay City, Bay	1897-1900	
Lusk, John J.	Kalamazoo, Kalamazoo	1889-1892	
Luther, George	Lamont, Ottawa	1863-1865	
Lyon, Frank A.	Hillsdale, Hillsdale		1899-1900
Lyon, Frank B.	Calumet, Houghton	1893-1894	
Lyon, Truman H.	Grand Rapids, Kent		1853-1854
Lyons, Lisa Posthumus	Alto, Kent	2011-2016	
Maas, Joseph P.	Detroit, Wayne	1913-1914	
MacDonald, Allan A.	Lansing, Ingham	1933-1934	
MacDonald, Michael	Macomb Township, Macomb		2019-
MacDonald, Robert Bruce	Laurium, Houghton	1919-1930	
MacDonald, Robert J.	Flint, Genesee	1941-1944	1945-1946
MacGregor, Peter	Rockford, Kent	2011-2014	2015-
Mack, Almon	Rochester, Oakland	1848	
Mack, Andrew	Detroit, Wayne	1839	
Mack, Joseph Samuel	Ironwood, Gogebic	1961-1964	1965-1990
MacKay, Alexander M.	West Branch, Ogemaw	1937-1952	
MacKay, John Donald M.	Detroit, Wayne		1905-1910
MacKinnon, Arthur Custer	Bay City, Bay	1923-1932; 1941-1948; 1951-1952	
MacMaster, Greg	Kewadin, Antrim	2011-2014	
MacNaughton, Thomas Henry	Ada, Kent	1909-1912	1913-1914; 1919-1924
MacRae, Richard Andrew	Detroit, Wayne	1929-1932	
Maddock, Matt	Milford, Oakland	2019-	
Madill, Joshua Benjamin	Ubly, Huron	1895-1898	
Madill, Leslie D.	Midland, Midland	1925-1926	
Magnotta, Alfonso A.	Albion, Calhoun	1937-1938	
Magoon, Isaac	Silver Lake, Washtenaw	1842; 1845	
Mahalak, Edward E.	Romulus, Wayne	1965-1984	
Mahoney, Frank A.	Detroit, Wayne	1949-1964	
Mahoney, Robert Daniel	Detroit, Wayne	1955-1972	
Main, Verner Wright	Battle Creek, Calhoun	1927-1928	
Maitland, Alexander	Negaunee, Marquette		1897-1900
Makelin, John	Valley Center, Sanilac	1885-1888	
Makley, Peter D.	Oxford, Oakland	1847	
Malcolm, Robert W.	Commerce, Oakland	1885-1886	
Mallary, Charles F.	Romeo, Macomb	1863-1866	
Mallett, Charles G.	Lambertville, Monroe	1867-1868	
Mandigo, James W.	White Pigeon, St. Joseph	1869-1879	
Mankowski, John	Hamtramck, Wayne		1935-1936
Manly, Charles H.	Ann Arbor, Washtenaw	1887-1888	
Mann, Emanuel	Ann Arbor, Washtenaw		1871-1872
Manning, Randolph	Pontiac, Oakland		1837
Manoogian, Mari	Birmingham, Oakland	2019-	
Mans, George W.	Trenton, Wayne	1997-2002	
Mansour, Theodore P.	Flint, Genesee	1971-1972	
Manwaring, Edward B.	Ann Arbor, Washtenaw	1921-1924	
Manwaring, Joseph	Dryden, Lapeer	1885-1886	
Manwaring, Joshua	Lapeer, Lapeer		1883-1886
Manzelmann, Charles	Detroit, Wayne	1905-1906	
Mapes, Carl Edgar	Grand Rapids, Kent	1905-1906	1909-1912
Marantette, Patrick	Nottawa, St. Joseph	1847	
Marino, Steve	Harrison Township, Macomb	2017-	
Marion, Adolph N.	Detroit, Wayne	1891-1892	
Markes, John F.	Westland, Wayne	1973-1976	
Markey, Daniel P.	West Branch, Ogemaw	1885-1888	
Markey, Matthew	Wayne, Wayne; Springwells, Wayne	1873-1874	1877-1878

Name[2]	Post Office[3]	House	Session Years[4] Senate
Markham, Giles B.	White Pigeon, St. Joseph	1877-1878; 1881-1882	
Markkanen, Gregory	Hancock, Houghton	2019-	
Marks, Herman	Detroit, Wayne	1901-1902	
Marleau, Jim	Lake Orion, Oakland	2005-2010	2011-2018
Mars, Thomas	Berrien Center, Berrien		1881-1882
Marsh, Lester M.	Gilead, Branch	1895-1896	
Marsh, William D.	Midland, Midland	1891-1892	
Marsh, William R.	White Lake, Oakland	1853-1854	
Marshall, Frederic J.	Allen, Hillsdale	1951-1968	
Marsilje, Isaac	Holland, Ottawa	1895-1898	
Marston, Isaac	Bay City, Bay	1872	
Martin, Bill	Battle Creek, Calhoun	1987-1994	
Martin, Chester William	Ithaca, Gratiot		1895-1896
Martin, David Mackenzie	Flint, Genesee	1937-1938	1939-1940
Martin, E. Broox	Reed City, Osceola	1881-1884	
Martin, George	Detroit, Wayne	1851-1852	
Martin, Jacob	Monroe, Monroe	1927-1928	
Martin, John	Detroit, Wayne	1837	
Martin, John B., Jr.	Grand Rapids, Kent		1949-1950
Martin, John Y.	Corunna, Shiawassee	1915-1920	
Martin, Joseph F., Jr.	Detroit, Wayne	1935-1938	
Martin, Mortimer B.	Fremont, Shiawassee	1848; 1850	
Martin, Stephen	Detroit, Wayne	1877-1878	
Martin, Vincent A.	Fruitport, Muskegon		1917-1918; 1925-1928
Martin, Wells R.	Vermontville, Eaton	1848	
Martindale, Frederick C.	Greenfield, Wayne Detroit, Wayne	1901-1902	1905-1908
Martinez, Lynne	Lansing, Ingham	1994-2000	
Martz, William H.	Detroit, Wayne	1911-1918	
Marvin, Dighton R.	Hersey, Osceola	1905-1906	
Marvin, Jarvis E.	Ypsilanti, Washtenaw	1851-1852	
Mason, Anthony L.	Galesburg, Kalamazoo	1867-1868	
Mason, Edward M.	Flint, Genesee	1869-1870	
Mason, George T.	Owosso, Shiawassee	1899-1902	
Mason, Henry	Lambertville, Monroe	1845	
Mason, Henry M.	St. Ignace, Mackinac	1885-1886	
Mason, Lorenzo M.	Port Huron, St. Clair Detroit, Wayne	1863-1864	1844-1845; 1869-1872
Mason, Richard	Gladstone, Delta		1895-1898
Massoglia, D. J.	Laurium, Houghton	1955-1958	
Master, Sheridan F.	Kalamazoo, Kalamazoo	1903-1906	
Mastin, Philip O., Jr.	Hazel Park, Oakland Dearborn, Wayne	1971-1976	1983
Mather, Alonzo T.	Dearbornville, Wayne	1841	
Mathews, George	Mason, Ingham	1848	
Mathews, Levi C.	Colon, St. Joseph	1849	
Mathews, Rufus	Dixborough, Washtenaw	1835-1836	
Mathews, Thomas P.	Redford, Wayne	1853-1854	
Mathieson, George	Royal Oak, Oakland	1945-1948	
Mathieu, Thomas C.	Grand Rapids, Kent	1975-1998	
Mattheeussen, Floyd J.	Benton Harbor, Berrien	1965-1966	
Matthews, Charles W.	Buchanan, Berrien	1915-1916	
Matthews, Christian F.	Mount Clemens, Macomb		1935-1938
Matthews, John A.	Detroit, Wayne	1895-1896	
Matthews, Maurice Reid	Fenton, Genesee	1935-1936	
Maturen, David	Vicksburg, Kalamazoo	2015-2018	
Maurer, John	Detroit, Wayne	1947-1948	
Maxey, John O.	L'Anse, Baraga	1909-1910	
Maxwell, Andrew C.	Bay City, Bay	1865-1866	
May, Benjamin	Detroit, Wayne	1865-1866	
May, Henry Frank	Cadillac, Wexford	1879-1880	
Mayer, Samuel W.	Holt, Ingham	1897-1898	
Mayes, Jeff	Bay City, Bay	2005-2010	
Maynard, John M.	St. Clair Shores, Macomb	1975-1990	

Name[2]	Post Office[3]	Session Years[4] House	Senate
Maynard, Loren	Marengo, Calhoun		1846-1847
Mayo, Perry	Battle Creek, Calhoun		1887-1888
McAllister, George C.	Gull Lake, Barry	1879-1880	
McArthur, George Elmer	Eaton Rapids, Eaton	1917-1918	1921-1922
McArthur, William	Cheboygan, Cheboygan	1877-1878	
McAuley, James H.	Detroit, Wayne	1905-1906	
McBride, Charles Hamilton	Holland, Ottawa	1911-1914	
McBride, James N.	Burton, Shiawassee	1913-1914; 1929-1932	
McBroom, Ed	Vulcan, Dickinson	2011-2016	2019-
McBryde, Jim	Mount Pleasant, Isabella	1991-1998	
McCabe, Charles R.	Marquette, Marquette	1909-1910	
McCabe, James	Pontiac, Oakland		1848-1849
McCain, Arthur	Jackson, Jackson	1905-1906	
McCall, Lyman Hakes	Charlotte, Eaton	1899-1902	
McCall, Thomas W.	Memphis, St. Clair	1905-1908	
McCallum, George P.	Ann Arbor, Washtenaw	1899-1902	1937-1944
	Thompson, Schoolcraft		
McCallum, John H.	Manistique, Schoolcraft	1907-1908	
McCamly, Sands	Battle Creek, Calhoun	1837; 1843	1839-1840
McCann, Sean	Kalamazoo, Kalamazoo	2011-2014	2019-
McCarthy, John J.	Standish, Arenac	1903-1908	
McCarty, Thomas	Saginaw City, Saginaw	1850	
McCauley, John E.	Wyandotte, Wayne		1965-1975
McCauley, William	Brighton, Livingston		1853-1854
McCleland, Hugh	Detroit, Wayne	1885-1886	
McClelland, Robert	Monroe, Monroe	1838; 1840; 1843	
McCloy, James	Wyandotte, Wayne	1891-1892	
McColl, Duncan John, Jr.	Port Huron, St. Clair	1929-1935	
McCollough, Lucille H.	Dearborn, Wayne	1955-1980	
McCollough, Patrick H.	Dearborn, Wayne		1971-1978; 1983-1986
McConico, Bill	Detroit, Wayne	2001-2006	
McCormick, Augustin C.	Grafton, Monroe		1891-1892
McCormick, Henry F.	Grand Rapids, Kent	1879-1880	
McCormick, James W.	Fennville, Allegan	1885-1888	1889-1890
McCotter, Thaddeus G.	Livonia, Wayne		1999-2002
McCowen, Henry	Moscow, Hillsdale	1869-1870	
McCracken, Harry N.	Farmington, Oakland	1905-1908	
McCready, Mike	Bloomfield Hills, Oakland	2013-2018	
McCune, John J.	East Lansing, Ingham	1953-1956	
McCurdy, Hugh	Corunna, Shiawassee		1865-1866
McCutcheon, Warren	Ransom, Hillsdale	1867-1868	
McDermid, John	Cambria Mills, Hillsdale		1861-1862
McDermott, John	Detroit, Wayne	1859-1860	
McDonald, Elmer B.	Port Hope, Huron	1931-1934	
McDonald, Harry A., Jr.	Detroit, Wayne	1947-1948	
McDonald, James	Clinton, Lenawee	1840; 1846	
McDonell, John	Detroit, Wayne		1835-1838
McDougall, Malcomb	Clinton, Lenawee	1853-1854	
McDowell, Gary	Rudyard, Chippewa	2005-2010	
McEachern, Archibald	Gould City, Mackinac	1903-1904; 1911-1912	
McEachron, Fred F.	Hudsonville, Ottawa	1923-1932	
McElroy, Crockett	St. Clair, St. Clair		1877-1880
McElroy, Frank	Marine City, St. Clair	1889-1890	
McEwen, Earl W., Sr.	Flint, Genesee	1941-1942	
McFadzen, William H.	Oak Hill, Manistee	1909-1910	
McFarlan, James	Detroit, Wayne	1847	
McFarlane, Duncan	Detroit, Wayne	1901-1902	
McGaffey, Neal	White Pigeon, St. Joseph	1837	
McGee, Edward L.	Ecorse, Wayne	1955-1956	
McGee, Robert D.	Union Lake, Oakland	1983-1984	
McGill, Charles William	Grand Rapids, Kent	1897-1898	
McGillivray, Will	Oscoda, Iosco	1917-1920	
McGinley, Charles H.	Minden City, Sanilac		1893-1894
McGinnis, Patrick	Detroit, Wayne	1877-1878	

Name[2]	Post Office[3]	House	Session Years[4] Senate
McGonegal, James	Detroit, Wayne	1871-1872	
McGovern, Daniel	Tustin, Osceola	1891-1892	
McGowan, Jonas Hartzell	Coldwater, Branch		1873-1874
McGraw, Homer	Detroit, Wayne	1915-1916	
McGraw, Thomas	Pontiac, Oakland	1847	
McGraw, William T.	Detroit, Wayne		1899-1900
McGregor, James E.	Ypsilanti, Washtenaw		1913-1914
McGregor, John A.	Freeland, Saginaw	1885-1890	
McGurk, James R.	Capac, St. Clair	1879-1880	1881-1882
McInerney, John R.	Wyandotte, Wayne	1933-1934	
McIntosh, William J.	Port Huron, St. Clair	1939-1940	
McIntyre, Donald	Ann Arbor, Washtenaw	1855-1856	
McIntyre, Dugald	Cumber, Sanilac	1881-1882	
McKay, George R.	Marshall, Calhoun	1865-1866	
McKay, John	Romeo, Macomb	1909-1912	
McKay, William	Caro, Tuscola	1889-1890; 1899-1902;	1907-1908
	East Dayton, Tuscola	1905-1906	
McKee, Frank Eugene	Muskegon, Muskegon		1943-1944; 1951
McKee, Robert G.	DeWitt, Clinton	1839	
McKeen, Silas D.	Lapeer, Lapeer	1837	
McKenna, Edward B.	Detroit, Wayne		1933-1934
McKenzie, Frank W.	Concord, Jackson	1925-1926	
McKeon, James E.	Pinconning, Bay	1919-1922	
McKernan, John Q.	Houghton, Houghton	1863-1870	
McKey, Anthony	Deerfield, Lenawee		1837-1838
McKibbin, Roy B.	Beaverton, Gladwin	1925-1926	
McKie, James L.	Three Oaks, Berrien	1885-1888	
McKinlay, John F.	Detroit, Wayne	1893-1894	
McKinley, Peter	St. James, Manitou	1857-1860	
McKinney, John	Paw Paw, Van Buren	1848	1849-1850
McKinstry, William H.	Muskegon, Muskegon	1889-1890; 1893-1894	
McKnight, Sheldon	Detroit, Wayne	1857-1858	
McLachlan, Donald P.	Milan, Washtenaw	1913-1914	
McLachlin, Dyckes	Petersburgh, Monroe	1875-1876	
McLain, Richard Waln	Quincy, Branch	1925-1928	
McLaughlin, Joseph Rogers	Detroit, Wayne		1893-1896
McLaughlin, Robert B.	Flint, Genesee		1941-1944
McLean, Joseph	Bay City, Bay	1899-1900	
McLeod, Malcolm J.	Detroit, Wayne	1899-1900	
McLeod, William Norman	Mackinac, Mackinac	1843-1845	
McMahon, James	Ann Arbor, Washtenaw	1857-1860	
McMahon, Joel W.	Marlette, Sanilac		1883-1884
McMahon, Walter T.	Hazel Park, Oakland	1949-1958	
McManiman, Charles O'Brien	Houghton, Houghton		1959-1964
McMann, Clifford	Grand Rapids, Kent	1935-1936	
McManus, George A,, Jr.	Traverse City, Grand Traverse		1991-2002
McManus, Michelle Ann	Traverse City, Grand Traverse	1993-1998	2003-2010
	Lake Leelanau, Leelanau		
McMartin, Daniel D.	Martin, Allegan	1863-1864	
McMillan, Herman I.	East Jordan, Charlevoix	1913-1916	
McMillan, Neal	Rockford, Kent	1887-1890	
McMillin, Tom E.	Rochester Hills, Oakland	2009-2014	
McMorrow, Mallory	Royal Oak, Oakland		2019-
McMullen, Daniel P.	Cheboygan, Cheboygan		1899-1902
McNabb, John W.	Fremont, Newaygo	1879-1880; 1885-1886	
McNair, William	Tecumseh, Lenawee	1849	
McNall, B. Frank	LaFayette, Gratiot	1895-1896	
McNamee, Ruth B.	Birmingham, Oakland	1975-1984	
McNaughton, Moses Archibald	Jackson, Jackson		1853-1854
McNeeley, Hiram	Inkster, Wayne	1955-1964	
McNeely, Matthew	Detroit, Wayne	1965-1986	
McNeil, John L.	Atlas, Genesee	1849	
McNitt, H. Clay	Cadillac, Wexford	1911-1914	
McNitt, H. Earl	Cadillac, Wexford	1925-1936	

Name[2]	Post Office[3]	House	Session Years[4] Senate
McNutt, James	Midland, Midland	1991-1998	
McPeek, Jacob L.	Grand Ledge, Eaton		1879-1880
McPhillips, Frank H.	Saginaw, Saginaw	1913-1914	1915-1916
McRae, Duncan	Greenbush, Alcona		1917-1922
	Harrisville, Alcona		
McReynolds, Andrew T.	Detroit, Wayne	1840	1847
McWhorter, David	Grass Lake, Jackson	1853-1854	
Meacham, George	Union, Cass	1839	1859-1860
Mead, Darius	Blissfield, Lenawee	1835-1836	
Mead, David C.	Frankfort, Benzie	1999-2002	
Mead, Elisha F.	Romeo, Macomb	1867-1870	
Mead, Henry S.	Hillsdale, Hillsdale	1850	1851-1852
Mead, Stephen	Paint Creek, Washtenaw	1839	
Meadows, Mark	East Lansing, Ingham	2006-2012	
Mears, Charles	Lincoln, Mason		1863-1864
Mears, William J.	Boyne Falls, Charlevoix		1893-1894
Meekhof, Arlan B.	West Olive, Ottawa	2007-2010	2011-2018
Meerman, Luke	Coopersville, Ottawa	2019-	
Meggison, Clarence Buell	Charlevoix, Charlevoix	1955-1962	
Meggison, Thomas D.	Central Lake, Antrim	1921-1924	
Meisner, Andrew E.	Ferndale, Oakland	2003-2008	
Mellen, Harvey	Romeo, Macomb	1889-1892	1893-1894
Mellen, John N.	Romeo, Macomb		1873-1876
Melton, Tim W.	Auburn Hills, Oakland	2007-2011	
Meltzer, Kim	Clinton Township, Macomb	2007-2010	
Menerey, Martin	Mount Pleasant, Isabella	1921-1922	
Menzie, David	Concord, Jackson	1845	
Mercer, James	Ontonagon, Ontonagon	1881-1882	1883-1884
Mercer, William	Saranac, Ionia	1875-1876	
Merrill, Elias W.	Muskegon, Muskegon	1857-1858	1865-1866
Merriman, George W.	Hartford, Van Buren		1895-1898
Merriman, Joel C.	Deckerville, Sanilac	1917-1920	
Merritt, Adolphus	Detroit, Wayne	1905-1906	
Merritt, Nelson B.	Midland, Midland	1947-1948	
Metcalf, Abraham T.	Kalamazoo, Kalamazoo	1875-1876	
Metcalf, Alfred R.	Constantine, St. Joseph	1841	
Metcalfe, E. W.	Detroit, Wayne	1947-1948	
Meyer, Henry	Fair Haven, St. Clair	1883-1884	
Meyer, Louis	Brighton, Livingston	1875-1876	
Meyer, Tom	Bad Axe, Huron	2001-2006	
Mezzano, Louis A.	Wakefield, Gogebic	1945-1960	
Michalski, Edward K.	Detroit, Wayne	1961-1966	
Mick, John	Clarksville, Ionia	1901-1902	
Mickle, John	Reading, Hillsdale	1842	
Mickley, Charles E.	Adrian, Lenawee	1865-1868	1873-1874
Middaugh, James Mick	Paw Paw, Van Buren	1975-1998	
Middaugh, Mary Ann	Paw Paw, Van Buren	1999-2004	
Middlesworth, Abraham	Argentine, Genesee	1855-1856	
Middleton, Emery T.	Flint, Genesee	1913-1914	
Middleton, Thomas F.	Ortonville, Oakland	1991-1998	
Mielock, James P.	Whittemore, Iosco	1955-1964	
Miles, Aaron W.	Big Rapids, Mecosta	1919-1924	
Miles, Cyrus	Port Huron, St. Clair	1865-1866; 1869-1870	
Miles, Fabius	Lawrence, Van Buren	1859-1860	
Miles, Frederick T.	Saugatuck, Allegan	1943-1946	
Miles, Marcus H.	St. Clair, St. Clair	1867-1868	
Miles, Nelson A.	Holland, Ottawa	1937-1944	
Millard, Winfield S.	Niles, Berrien	1881-1882	
Millen, George W.	Ann Arbor, Washtenaw		1919-1920
Miller, Aaron	Sturgis, St. Joseph	2015-	
Miller, Albert	Saginaw, Saginaw	1847	
Miller, Arthur J., Jr.	Warren, Macomb		1977-2002
Miller, Charles L.	Colon, St. Joseph	1853-1856	
Miller, Chester A.	Greenville, Montcalm	1897-1900	

Name[2]	Post Office[3]	House	Senate
		Session Years[4]	
Miller, Derek E.	Warren, Macomb	2015-2016	
Miller, Eli R.	Richland, Kalamazoo	1871-1874	
Miller, Frank C.	Ionia, Ionia	1909-1910	
Miller, Fred	Mount Clemens, Macomb	2005-2010	
Miller, George H.	East Grand Rapids, Kent	1919-1922	
Miller, George W.	Greenville, Montcalm	1915-1916	1917-1920
Miller, Gilbert E.	Detroit, Wayne	1927-1928	
Miller, Guy Alonzo	Detroit, Wayne	1907-1910	1911-1912
Miller, Henry	Rochester, Oakland	1853-1854; 1863-1864	
Miller, Hiram L.	Saginaw City, Saginaw	1841; 1844	
Miller, Jesse	Norwalk, Manistee	1937-1938	
Miller, John	Port Huron, St. Clair	1857-1858; 1863-1864	
Miller, John C.	New Buffalo, Berrien	1863-1864	
Miller, Joseph	Richland, Kalamazoo	1840-1841	
Miller, Judith	Birmingham, Oakland	1985-1990	
Miller, Leo	Jackson, Jackson	1950-1955	
Miller, Leonard	Jonesville, Hillsdale	1861-1862	
Miller, Lewis T.	Moscow, Hillsdale	1835-1836	
Miller, Lucien B.	La Salle, Monroe	1877-1880	
Miller, Norton L.	Mount Clemens, Macomb	1869-1872	
Miller, Ole Herman	Manistee, Manistee	1923-1924	
Miller, Oliver	Ridgeway, Lenawee	1844	
Miller, Philemon J.	Walled Lake, Oakland	1925-1932	
Miller, Philip Derr	Schoolcraft, Kalamazoo	1893-1896	
Miller, Richard C.	Greenville, Montcalm	1871-1874	
Miller, Samuel	Eaton Rapids, Eaton	1891-1892	
Miller, William	Eaton Rapids, Eaton		1891-1892
Miller, William F.	Houghton, Houghton	1921-1922	
Milliken, James T.	Traverse City, Grand Traverse		1941-1950
Milliken, James W.	Traverse City, Grand Traverse		1898-1900
Milliken, William G.	Traverse City, Grand Traverse		1961-1964
Millikin, James H.	Caro, Tuscola	1909-1912	
Milliman, Claude Henry	Iron Mountain, Dickinson	1929-1930	
Millington, Charles R.	Constantine, St. Joseph	1869-1872	
Mills, Charles Blunt	Mayville, Tuscola	1877-1878	1869-1870
Mills, Frank E.	Ann Arbor, Washtenaw	1893-1894	
Mills, John W.	Leoni, Jackson	1855-1856	
Mills, William S.	Lexington, Sanilac		1859-1860
Mills, Willis N.	Menominee, Menominee		1905-1906
Millspaugh, Hiram	Belleville, Wayne	1850	
Milnes, Alfred	Coldwater, Branch		1889-1892
Milosch, Matt	Lambertville, Monroe	2003-2004	
Miner, John	Detroit, Wayne	1891-1892	
Miner, Leon F.	Owosso, Shiawassee		1929-1930
Ming, Fred R.	Cheboygan, Cheboygan	1905-1906; 1923-1932	1907-1910
Minne, Joseph P.	Port Huron, St. Clair	1851-1852	
Minne, Joseph Theodore Standard	St. Clair, St. Clair	1871-1872	
Minnema, John	Traverse City, Grand Traverse		1954-1960
Minnis, Adam	Wayne, Wayne		1865-1866
Minore, Jack D.	Flint, Genesee	1999-2004	
Miron, William E.	Escanaba, Delta		1957-1962
Mitchell, Preston	Marshall, Calhoun	1871-1874	
Mitchell, Thomas	Constantine, St. Joseph	1859-1860	
Mitchell, William H. C.	East Traverse Bay, Grand Traverse	1869-1872	1873-1876
Mitchell, William T.	Port Huron, St. Clair	1853-1854	
Mittan, Ray C.	Benton Harbor, Berrien	1969-1978	
Moe, Otho	Sturgis, St. Joseph	1879-1880	
Moffatt, Orlando	Battle Creek, Calhoun	1849	
Moffatt, Orlando C.	Traverse City, Grand Traverse		1903-1906
Moffatt, Seth Crittenden	Northport, Leelanau Traverse City, Grand Traverse	1881-1882	1871-1872
Mohr, Christopher	West Bay City, Bay	1893-1894	
Mol, James	Grand Rapids, Kent	1919-1920	

Name[2]	Post Office[3]	House	Session Years[4] Senate
Moll, John A.	Forestville, Sanilac	1893-1894	
Molster, Walter E.	Detroit, Wayne	1897-1898	
Monaghan, George Francis	Detroit, Wayne		1899-1900
Monfore, Isaac	Ray, Macomb	1835-1837	
Monks, Bruce L.	Mount Clemens, Macomb	1965-1966	
Monroe, Charles Jay	South Haven, Van Buren		1883-1888
Monroe, Darius	Bronson's Prairie, Branch	1865-1866	1861-1864
Monroe, James	Albion, Calhoun	1857-1860	
Monroe, James H.	Traverse City, Grand Traverse	1903-1908	
Monroe, James Smith	Ironwood, Gogebic	1901-1910	
Monsma, Stephen V.	Grand Rapids, Kent	1975-1978	1979-1982
Montague, Daniel N.	Thetford, Genesee	1855-1856	
Montague, Henry	Kalamazoo, Kalamazoo	1855-1856	
Monteith, David T.	Port Huron, St. Clair	1913-1914	
Montgomery, George	Detroit, Wayne	1945-1946; 1959-1980	
Montgomery, George F.	Detroit, Wayne	1965-1970	
Montgomery, John	Eaton Rapids, Eaton	1850	
Montgomery, Martin V.	Eaton Rapids, Eaton	1871-1872	
Montgomery, Robert M.	Lansing, Ingham	1945-1952	
Montgomery, Stanley D.	Lansing, Ingham	1907	
Montgomery, William H.	Ida, Monroe; Monroe, Monroe	1838	1855-1856
Montgomery, William R.	Hillsdale, Hillsdale	1851-1852	
Moody, Silas	Forest Hill, Gratiot	1893-1894	
Moody, William J.	Jackson, Jackson		1835-1836; 1843-1844
Moolenaar, John	Midland, Midland	2003-2008	2011-2014
Moon, John W.	Muskegon, Muskegon		1885-1888
Moore, Alexander H.	Mottville, St. Joseph	1851-1852	
Moore, Andrew L.	Pontiac, Oakland		1933-1936
Moore, Charles Freeman	St. Clair, St. Clair	1877-1878	
Moore, Charles W.	Detroit, Wayne	1893-1894	1897-1898
Moore, Edward S.	Three Rivers, St. Joseph		1853-1854
Moore, Ephraim W.	Battle Creek, Calhoun	1897-1898	
Moore, Franklin	St. Clair, St. Clair	1899-1902	
Moore, Franklin	St. Clair, St. Clair	1917-1922	
Moore, George W.	Brownstown, Wayne	1847	
Moore, George W.	Detroit, Wayne	1879-1880	
Moore, George W.	Port Huron, St. Clair		1899-1902
Moore, Henry M.	Greenville, Montcalm	1851-1852	
Moore, Hiram	Climax, Kalamazoo	1850	
Moore, John W.	Houghton, Houghton	1919-1920	
Moore, Joseph B.	Lapeer, Lapeer		1879-1880
Moore, Miller G.	Detroit, Wayne	1895-1898	
Moore, Thomas F.	Adrian, Lenawee	1861-1862	1863-1864
Moore, Tim	Farwell, Clare	2005-2010	
Moore, William	York, Washtenaw	1843	1837-1838
Moore, William H.	Palmyra, Lenawee	1913-1916	
Moorman, Asa P.	Detroit, Wayne	1855-1856	
Moran, Charles	Detroit, Wayne	1836; 1838; 1840	
Moran, George	Hamtramck, Wayne	1846; 1849	
Morcom, Elisha	Quinnesec, Menominee	1883-1884	
Morford, J. Lee	Gaylord, Otsego	1911-1914	1915-1918
Morgan, David T.	Ishpeming, Marquette	1909-1914	
Morgan, Franklin E.	Coldwater, Branch		1877-1878
Morgan, Thomas C.	Battle Creek, Calhoun	1943-1950	
Moriarty, Michael H.	Crystal Falls, Iron		1903-1912
Morley, F. Dean	New Troy, Berrien	1933-1938	
Morrice, James L.	Harbor Springs, Emmet	1903-1910	
Morris, Carlton H.	Kalamazoo, Kalamazoo		1949-1962
Morris, John C.	Midland, Midland	1957-1960	
Morris, William	Sturgis, St. Joseph	1848	
Morrison, Alexander Hamilton	St. Joseph, Berrien	1861-1862	1857-1858
Morrison, Clayton T.	Pickford, Chippewa	1953-1966	
Morrison, David F.	Germfask, Schoolcraft	1921-1928; 1943-1950	

Name[2]	Post Office[3]	House	Senate
		Session Years[4]	
Morrison, Dwight S.	St. Johns, Clinton	1909-1912	
Morrison, Edward C.	Columbiaville, Lapeer	1925-1934	
Morrison, Thomas	Wayne, Wayne	1877-1878	1881-1882
Morrow, James H.	Adrian, Lenawee		1891-1894
Morse, Allen Benton	Ionia, Ionia		1875-1876
Morse, Charles H.	New Haven Center, Gratiot	1873-1876	1877-1878
Morse, John L.	Otisco, Ionia	1846	
Morse, Joseph D.	Otisco, Ionia	1893-1896	
Morse, Richard E.	Ypsilanti, Washtenaw	1835-1836	
Mortimer, Leslie	Jackson, Jackson	2005-2006	
Mortimer, Mickey	Horton, Jackson	1999-2004	
Morton, Edward G.	Monroe, Monroe	1849-1850; 1853-1854; 1863-1866	1869-1872
Morton, Eurotas	Rawsonville, Wayne	1841	
Morton, Frank	Lakeview, Mecosta	1889-1890	
Morton, Henry C.	St. Joseph, Berrien	1863-1864	
Mosely, William F.	Saginaw, Saginaw	1837	
Mosher, Charles	Hillsdale, Hillsdale	1863-1864; 1877-1880	
Mosher, Jabez S.	Jackson Mills, Lenawee	1849	
Mosher, Thomas H.	Springville, Lenawee	1844	
Moshier, James B.	Linden, Genesee	1871-1872; 1875-1876	
Mosier, Frank R.	Bravo, Allegan Fennville, Allegan	1919-1922	1935-1936
Moss, Chuck	Birmingham, Oakland	2007-2012	
Moss, Jeremy	Southfield, Oakland	2015-2018	2019-
Most, Clark F.	Alanson, Emmet	1963-1964	
Mottram, William	Nottawa, St. Joseph	1843	
Moulton, Luther V.	Grand Rapids, Kent	1879-1880	
Movius, Julius	Ypsilanti, Washtenaw	1850	
Mowat, John S., Jr.	Adrian, Lenawee	1971-1978	1979-1982
Mower, Horace	Kalamazoo, Kalamazoo	1847	
Mowry, Zebina M.	Milford, Oakland	1848	
Moyers, Gilbert	Allegan, Allegan		1857-1858
Mrozowski, Ted	Hamtramck, Wayne	1969-1972	
Mudge, Elisha	Maple Rapids, Clinton		1897-1898
Mudge, Julian Scott	Grand Ledge, Eaton	1893-1894	
Mueller, Charles L.	Linden, Genesee	1977-1986	
Mueller, Mike	Linden, Genesee	2019-	
Mugford, Enoch T.	Hart, Oceana		1891-1894
Mulholland, James	Erie, Monroe	1840; 1848	
Mulholland, Samuel	Vienna, Monroe Erie, Monroe	1849	1861-1862
Mullen, Joseph G.	Wallace, Menominee	1935-1938	
Mulvey, John	Negaunee, Marquette	1881-1882; 1887-1888; 1895-1896	
Munger, Orrin W.	St. Johns, Clinton	1865-1866	
Munger, William	Flat Rock, Wayne	1837; 1845; 1857-1858	
Munsell, Silas H.	Fowlerville, Livingston	1903-1904	
Munsell, Susan Grimes	Howell, Livingston	1987-1996	
Munshaw, Earl Wright	Grand Rapids, Kent		1933-1944
Munthe, Louis W.	Ironwood, Gogebic	1891-1892	
Murdoch, John J.	Caseville, Huron	1899-1902	
Murfin, James O.	Detroit, Wayne		1901-1902
Murphy, Christopher	Sanilac Centre, Sanilac	1899-1902	
Murphy, Ernest	Detroit, Wayne	1957-1964	
Murphy, Frank	Detroit, Wayne	1937-1940	
Murphy, Frank E.	Detroit, Wayne	1925-1926	
Murphy, Gerald L.	Detroit, Wayne	1941-1946; 1951-1954	
Murphy, Harry L.	St. Joseph, Berrien	1911-1914	
Murphy, James A.	Detroit, Wayne		1933-1939
Murphy, James J.	Detroit, Wayne	1941-1945	
Murphy, John	Gun Plain, Allegan	1883-1884	
Murphy, John B.	Detroit, Wayne	1933-1944	
Murphy, Joseph C.	Grosse Pointe Park, Wayne	1933-1940	

Name[2]	Post Office[3]	House	Session Years[4] Senate
Murphy, Michael C.	Lansing, Ingham	2001-2006	
Murphy, Nicholas	Mount Morris, Genesee	1937-1938	
Murphy, Raymond M.	Detroit, Wayne	1983-1998	1998-2002
Murphy, Seba	Monroe, Monroe		1840-1841
Murphy, William F.	Detroit, Wayne	1927-1928; 1931-1932	
Murphy, William W.	Jonesville, Hillsdale	1844	
Murray, Andrew	St. Joseph, Berrien	1848	
Murray, Archibald Y.	Borodino, Wayne	1843; 1845	
Murray, Dennis	Grand Rapids, Kent	1907-1908	
Murray, Lyman	Grand Rapids, Kent	1867-1870	1875-1876
	Lisbon, Kent		
Murtagh, James P.	Detroit, Wayne	1889-1890	
Murtha, James Alfred	Detroit, Wayne		1911-1918
Muscott, Newton N.	Williamston, Ingham	1857-1858	
Mussey, Dexter	Romeo, Macomb	1855-1862	
Musson, Thomas William	Edmore, Montcalm	1925-1928	
Muxlow, Keith David	Brown City, Sanilac	1981-1992	
Muxlow, Paul	Brown City, Sanilac	2011-2016	
Muzzy, Franklin	Niles, Berrien		1859-1860
Myers, Charles M.	Dowagiac, Cass	1933-1938	
Myers, George C.	Flint, Genesee	1911-1912	
Nagel, Ernest George	Detroit, Wayne	1933-1940	1941-1942
Nagel, Joseph F.	Detroit, Wayne	1935-1946	
Nagel, Joseph Franz Aloysius	Detroit, Wayne		1889-1890
Nagel, Nathan	Detroit, Wayne	1919-1920	
Nakkula, Walter G.	Gladwin, Gladwin	1953-1964	
Nank, William F.	Mount Clemens, Macomb	1905-1907; 1913-1916	
Nash, Edward P.	Grattan, Kent	1899-1902	
Nash, Ernest W.	Dimondale, Eaton	1975-1986	
Nash, Willard J.	St. Charles, Saginaw	1913-1914	
Nathan, David	Detroit, Wayne	2009-2014	
Neal, Frank S.	Northville, Wayne	1901-1904	
Near, John L.	Brownstown, Wayne	1839	1857-1862
	Detroit, Wayne		
Neasmith, James M.	Schoolcraft, Kalamazoo		1871-1874
Neeley, Sheldon	Flint, Genesee	2015-	
Neff, Cady	Trenton, Wayne	1875-1876	
Neller, F. Jack	Battle Creek, Calhoun	1939-1942	
Neller, Louis	Lansing, Ingham	1913-1914	
Nelson, Charles D.	Muskegon, Muskegon		1875-1878
Nelson, Earl E.	Lansing, Ingham	1971-1974	1975-1978
Nelson, Edward D.	Ishpeming, Marquette	1881-1882	
Nelson, Hugo A.	Indian River, Cheboygan	1945-1954	
Nelson, Sigurd G.	Ironwood, Gogebic	1915-1918	
Nelson, Wilbur	Ithaca, Gratiot	1881-1882	
Nerat, Judy	Wallace, Menominee	2009-2010	
Nesbitt, Aric	Lawton, Van Buren	2011-2016	2019-
Netting, Conrad John	Detroit, Wayne	1925-1932	
Neumann, Andy	Alpena, Alpena	1999-2002; 2009-2010	
Nevins, Alfred M.	Doster, Barry	1921-1924	
Nevins, Bartlett A.	Otsego, Allegan	1899-1902	
Nevins, John M.	Hastings, Barry	1857-1858	1865-1866
Newberry, Frank D.	Coldwater, Branch	1903-1904	
Newberry, Seneca	Rochester, Oakland		1853-1854
Newcomb, Roland B. C.	Blissfield, Lenawee	1865-1866	1877-1878
Newcombe, George K.	East Saginaw, Saginaw	1867-1868	
Newell, Gary A.	Saranac, Ionia	2001-2006	
Newell, John L.	Port Huron, St. Clair	1867-1868	
Newkirk, Henry Wirt	Luther, Lake	1893-1894; 1907-1910;	
	Ann Arbor, Washtenaw	1917-1918	
Newman, Almeron	Portland, Ionia	1859-1860	
Newman, Orlando	East Tawas, Iosco	1869-1870	
Newton, Carroll Cecil	Delton, Barry	1955-1964	
Newton, Frank T.	Ypsilanti, Washtenaw		1909-1912

Name[2]	Post Office[3]	Session Years[4]	
		House	Senate
Newton, George	Pickett's Corners, Cass	1859-1860	
Newton, James	La Grange, Cass	1839-1840	
Nichczynski, John F.	Detroit, Wayne		1933-1934
Nichols, Edward T.	Detroit, Wayne	1929-1932	
Nichols, George Ellsworth	Ionia, Ionia		1901-1902
Nichols, Haskell Linton	Jackson, Jackson	1933-1936; 1939-1942	1943-1966
Nichols, Lewis A.	Orangeville Mills, Barry	1881-1882	
Nichols, Rudy J.	Waterford, Oakland	1983	1984-1990
Nicholson, Fred	Warren, Macomb		1955-1956
Niedermeier, August	South Rockwood, Monroe	1897-1900	
Niederstadt, Roland G.	Saginaw, Saginaw	1987-1992	
Niles, Johnson	Troy, Oakland	1835-1836	1844-1845
Nill, Walter H.	Muskegon, Muskegon	1949-1962	
Nims, Jerome W.	Romeo, Macomb		1901-1902
Nims, William R.	Lexington, Sanilac		1865-1866
Nitz, Neal	Baroda, Berrien	2003-2008	
Nixon, Charles H.	Cadillac, Wexford	1937-1942	
Nixon, Robert	Oneida, Eaton	1865-1866	
Nixon, Samuel	Grand Ledge, Eaton	1877-1878	
Noah, Frank A.	Detroit, Wayne	1879-1880	
Noble, Charles	Nankin, Wayne	1855-1856	
Noble, David Addison	Monroe, Monroe	1846-1847	
Noble, Herman C.	Byron, Shiawassee	1849	
Noble, Jeff	Plymouth, Wayne	2017-2018	
Noeker, Frank	Westphalia, Clinton	1879-1880; 1883-1884	
Nofs, Mike	Battle Creek, Calhoun	2003-2008	2009-2018
Nolan, Lawrence	Detroit, Wayne	1891-1892	
Noll, John	Cheboygan, Cheboygan	1913-1914	
Norman, John Wells	Lexington, Sanilac	1893-1896	
Norrington, John W.	West Olive, Ottawa	1893-1894	
Norris, Ezra B.	Manchester, Washtenaw	1877-1878	
Norris, Jason B.	Cambria Mills, Hillsdale	1871-1872	
Norris, Lyman D.	Ypsilanti, Washtenaw		1869-1870
North, Seth D.	Hancock, Houghton	1877-1878; 1881-1886	1879-1880
North, Townsend	Vassar, Tuscola		1875-1876
North, Walter H.	St. Ignace, Mackinac		1995-2002
Northrop, Darwin B.	Northville, Wayne	1875-1876	
Northrop, Elijah S.	Hancock, Houghton		1863-1864
Northup, Alonzo R.	Escanaba, Delta	1889-1892	
Northwood, John	New Lothrop, Shiawassee	1885-1886	
Norton, Henry A.	Berlin, Ottawa	1869-1870	
Norton, John D	Pontiac, Oakland	1875-1878	
Norton, John Martin	Rochester, Oakland		1883-1884
Norton, Pleasant	Cassopolis, Cass	1850; 1853-1854	
Norton, William A.	St. Johns, Clinton	1907-1908	
Norvell, John	Detroit, Wayne	1842	
Nottingham, David M.	Lansing, Ingham	1903-1906	
Novak, Michael	Detroit, Wayne	1943-1946; 1949-1964; 1967-1976	
Novak, Stanley	Detroit, Wayne	1949-1954	
Novak, Stanley J.	Detroit, Wayne		1955-1974
Nowak, Evelyn M.	Detroit, Wayne	1945-1946	
Nowak, Francis J.	Detroit, Wayne	1939-1944	
Nowak, Stanley	Detroit, Wayne		1939-1948
Nowland, Moses R.	Catville, Wayne	1865-1866	
Noyes, Bethuel	Plymouth, Wayne	1848; 1850	
Noyes, Horace A.	Plymouth, Wayne	1835-1836	
Noyes, Michael J.	Chelsea, Washtenaw	1873-1874	
Nugent, Howard	Bad Axe, Huron	1935-1946; 1951-1952	
Nunneley, James S.	Mount Clemens, Macomb	1967	
Nye, Michael Earl	Litchfield, Hillsdale	1983-1998	
Oakes, Stacy Erwin	Saginaw, Saginaw	2010-2014	
Oakley, Marshall A.	Bay City, Bay	1913-1916	
Oates, William Richard	Laurium, Houghton	1909-1910	

| Name[2] | Post Office[3] | Session Years[4] | |
		House	Senate
O'Beirne, Nelson M.	Clarksville, Ionia	1923-1926	
Oberdorffer, William J.	Stephenson, Menominee	1897-1900; 1925-1926	
O'Brien, Bernard Francis, Jr.	Detroit, Wayne		1965-1966
O'Brien, Bernard Francis, Sr.	Detroit, Wayne	1945-1946	
O'Brien, Carl W.	Pontiac, Oakland		1965-1966
O'Brien, E. D.	Detroit, Wayne	1957-1972	
O'Brien, Frank J.	Detroit, Wayne	1955-1964	
O'Brien, Margaret E.	Portage, Kalamazoo	2011-2014	2015-2018
O'Brien, Michael J.	Detroit, Wayne		1974-1998
O'Brien, Michael J.	Detroit, Wayne	1941-1946; 1949-1964	1965-1974
O'Brien, Patrick	Iron River, Iron	1915-1924	
O'Brien, Thomas Cornelius	Detroit, Wayne	1945-1946; 1949-1951	
O'Brien, Warren	Warren, Macomb	1973-1974	
O'Callaghan, Jeremiah	Detroit, Wayne	1853-1854	
Ocobock, Horace N.	Wyandotte, Wayne	1875-1876	
O'Connell, Philip	McGregor, Sanilac	1923-1926	1927-1930
O'Connor, Joseph Garrett	Detroit, Wayne	1949-1962	
O'Connor, Margaret	Ann Arbor, Washtenaw	1983-1992	
Odell, Arthur U.	Allegan, Allegan	1911-1914; 1923-1928; 1933-1942	
O'Dell, James	Cassopolis, Cass	1835-1836; 1838	
Odell, Samuel	Shelby, Oceana	1909-1912	1913-1914
O'Dell, Thomas	Shelby, Oceana	1873-1874	
O'Dett, Lewis	Avoca, St. Clair	1897-1898	
O'Flynn, Cornelius	Detroit, Wayne	1857-1858	
Ogg, Robert Y.	Detroit, Wayne	1887-1888; 1909-1912	1913-1916
Ogonowski, Casmer P.	Detroit, Wayne	1969-1980	
O'Grady, James	Marquette, Marquette	1865-1866	
O'Keefe, George A.	Detroit, Wayne	1843	
O'Keefe, Richard D.	Carsonville, Sanilac	1885-1890	
Olds, Martin	Branch, Branch	1843	
Olin, Charles	Marshall, Calhoun	1841	
Oliver, John Freeman	Kalamazoo, Kalamazoo	1879-1882	
Olmsted, Clifford George	Midland, Midland	1915-1922	
Olsen, Fred O.	Sheridan, Montcalm	1955-1964	
Olshove, Dennis G.	Warren, Macomb	1991-1998	2003-2010
Olson, Rick	Saline, Washtenaw	2011-2012	
Olumba, John	Detroit, Wayne	2011-2014	
O'Malley, Charles M.	Mackinac, Mackinac	1846-1847; 1849	
O'Malley, Jack	Lake Ann, Benzie	2019-	
O'Malley, Patrick James	Detroit, Wayne	1949-1950	
O'Neil, William J.	Allen Park, Wayne	1999-2004	
O'Neill, James E., Jr.	Saginaw, Saginaw	1967-1994	
O'Neill, Lawrence	Paris, Mecosta	1933-1934	
Oppenborn, Christian Augustus	Alpena, Alpena	1911-1912	
Opsommer, Paul E.	DeWitt, Clinton	2007-2012	
Ord, Placidus	Sault Saint Marie, Chippewa	1846	
O'Reilly, Bernard	Detroit, Wayne		1887-1888
Ormsbee, Ira G.	Flint, Genesee	1909-1910	
Ormsbee, William B.	Flint, Genesee	1915-1918; 1923-1926	
Ormsby, Caleb N.	Ann Arbor, Washtenaw	1839	
Orr, Herbert Pritcgard	Caro, Tuscola		1931-1934
Orr, W. Reed	Battle Creek, Calhoun	1951-1954	
Orth, George	Au Sable, Iosco	1891-1892	
Osborn, Donald C.	Kalamazoo, Kalamazoo		1921-1924
Osborn, Frank A.	Kalamazoo, Kalamazoo	1901-1904	
Osborn, George W.	Parkville, St. Joseph	1891-1892	
Osborn, Henry Alfred	Sault Saint Marie, Chippewa	1921-1936	
Osborn, John M	Hudson, Lenawee	1869-1872	1875-1876
Osborn, William H.	Tecumseh, Lenawee	1865-1868	
Osburn, Charles Y.	Owosso, Shiawassee	1871-1872	
Osburn, Leander D.	Vandalia, Cass	1867-1868	
Osburn, Reuben Howard	Calumet, Houghton		1877-1878
Ostling, Ralph A.	Roscommon, Roscommon	1973-1992	

Name[2]	Post Office[3]	House	Senate
			Session Years[4]
Otis, Asa H.	Detroit, Wayne	1850	
Otis, Lauren Ford	Kibbie, Allegan	1895-1898	
Otterbacher, John R.	Grand Rapids, Kent	1973-1974	1975-1978
Ouimet, Mark	Ann Arbor, Washtenaw	2011-2012	
Outman, Rick	Six Lakes, Montcalm	2011-2016	2019-
Ouwinga, Sidney	Marion, Osceola	1983-1991	
Oviatt, Daniel Barber	Alden, Antrim	1903-1906	
Oviatt, George W. B.	Chase, Lake	1885-1888	
Owen, Gary Mack	Ypsilanti, Washtenaw	1973-1988	
Owen, John E.	Detroit, Wayne	1929	
Owen, John G.	Clarkston, Oakland		1861-1862
Owen, Lynn F.	Maybee, Monroe	1985-1998	
Owen, Tubal C.	Marine City, St. Clair	1870	
Oxender, Glenn S.	Sturgis, St. Joseph	1983-1998	
Pack, Albert	Lexington, Sanilac	1865-1866	
Pack, Philip Clarkson	Ann Arbor, Washtenaw	1931-1934	
Pack, William F.	Centerville, St. Joseph	1899-1900	
Packard, Franklin S.	Sturgis, St. Joseph	1875-1876	
Packard, William	New Casco, Allegan	1865-1868	
Packard, William Oscar	Covert, Van Buren		1877-1878
Packer, Henry	Litchfield, Hillsdale	1845	
Padden, Jeffrey D.	Wyandotte, Wayne	1975-1984	
Paddock, Alfred	Concord, Jackson		1853-1854
Paddock, Robert W.	Charlevoix, Charlevoix	1903-1904	
Pagan, Kristy	Canton, Wayne	2015-	
Pagel, Dave	Berrien Springs, Berrien	2013-2018	
Pailthorp, Charles J.	Petoskey, Emmet	1879-1880	
Paine, Rodney C.	Niles, Berrien		1855-1856
Palamara, Joseph	Wyandotte, Wayne	1985-1998	
Paletko, Daniel S.	Dearborn Heights, Wayne	2003-2004	
Palmer, Ambrose E.	Kalkaska, Kalkaska		1901-1902
Palmer, Brian P.	Romeo, Macomb	2002-2008	
Palmer, Charles S.	Saginaw, Saginaw	1846	
Palmer, George Perry	Detroit, Wayne	1913-1916	
Palmer, John R.	Albion, Calhoun	1853-1854	
Palmer, Lewis G.	Big Rapids, Mecosta		1887-1890
Palmer, Milton R.	Detroit, Wayne	1921-1932	
Palmer, Oscar	Grayling, Crawford	1883-1884	
Palmer, Samuel H.	Jackson, Jackson	1848	
Palmer, Thomas Witherell	Detroit, Wayne		1879-1880
Palmer, Walter H.	Reed City, Osceola	1877-1880	
Palmer, William	Flint, Genesee		1933-1938
Palmerlee, Heman	Grand Rapids, Kent	1881-1882	
Palsrok, David W.	Manistee, Manistee	2003-2008	
Pangborn, Samuel H.	Bad Axe, Huron		1935-1938
Pappageorge, John	Troy, Oakland	1999-2004	2007-2014
Paquette, Brad	Niles, Berrien	2019-	
Pardee, Amaziah B.	Saranac, Ionia	1887-1888	
Park, Peter E.	Detroit, Wayne		1891-1892
Parker, Burton	Monroe, Monroe	1883-1884	
Parker, Charles D.	Otisville, Genesee	1933-1934	
Parker, Charles Frederick	Middleville, Barry	1933-1934	
Parker, James H.	Rome Center, Lenawee	1855-1856	
Parker, John	Portage, Kalamazoo		1859-1860
Parker, Leonard B.	Newport, Monroe		1863-1864
Parker, Leroy	Flint, Genesee	1874-1876	
Parker, Paul John	Flint, Genesee	1957-1960	
Parker, Sampson	Dexter, Washtenaw	1867-1868	
Parker, Warren	Milton, Macomb	1879-1882	
Parker, Warren J.	Cement City, Lenawee	1905-1908	
Parkhurst, Jonathan G.	Decatur, Van Buren	1885-1886	
Parkhurst, Nathan C.	Pontiac, Oakland	1849; 1853-1854	
Parkill, Charles P.	Hartwellville, Shiawassee	1857-1858	
Parkinson, Thomas Hamilton	Yale, St. Clair	1895-1896	

Name[2]	Post Office[3]	Session Years[4]	
		House	Senate
Parks, Byron F.	Wales, St. Clair	1883-1884	
Parks, John Hunter	Crystal Falls, Iron	1911-1912	
Parks, Mary Lou	Detroit, Wayne	1993-1998	
Parmalee, Linus S.	Reading, Hillsdale	1867-1868	
Parmelee, Abner C.	Hastings, Barry	1844	
Parrott, Mary Ellen	Utica, Macomb	1983-1984	
Parsons, Andrew	Corunna, Shiawassee	1855-1856	1847-1848
Parsons, Fayette	Burr Oak, St. Joseph	1873-1874	
Parsons, Jonathan	Kalamazoo, Kalamazoo	1877-1882	
Parsons, Orrin	Saline, Washtenaw	1846	
Parsons, S. Titus	Corunna, Shiawassee	1863-1864; 1867-1868	
Partlow, Levi P.	Grand Ledge, Eaton	1903-1906	
Partridge, Azariah S.	Flushing, Genesee	1881-1882	
Partridge, Benjamin F.	Bay City, Bay	1881-1882	
Partridge, George W.	Detroit, Wayne	1895-1896	
Pascoe, John J.	Ishpeming, Marquette	1919-1920	
Pascoe, Peter	Republic, Marquette		1893-1896
Pastor, John R.	Livonia, Wayne	2003-2008	
Patchen, Levi	Centerville, St. Joseph	1848	
Paterson, Leonard J.	Sandusky, Sanilac		1939-1942
Pattengill, Orlando R.	Plymouth, Wayne	1871-1872	
Patterson, Bruce	Canton, Wayne	1999-2002	2003-2010
Patterson, James	Fenton, Oakland	1851-1852	
Patterson, John C.	Marshall, Calhoun		1879-1882
Patterson, Joseph H.	Adrian, Lenawee	1839; 1843; 1848	
Patterson, Michael A.	Tecumseh, Lenawee	1846	1844-1845
Patterson, Neil A.	Detroit, Wayne	1947-1948	
Pattison, William H.	Saline, Washtenaw		1855-1858
Paul, John	East Grand Rapids, Kent		1915-1916
Pavlov, Phillip	St. Clair Township, St. Clair	2005-2010	2011-2018
Payant, John D.	Kinsford, Dickinson	1969-1972	
Payne, Jira	Clinton, Lenawee	1838	
Peabody, James H.	Birmingham, Oakland	1889-1890	
Pealer, Russel R.	Three Rivers, St. Joseph	1889-1890	
Pearce, Tom	Rockford, Kent	2005-2010	
Pearl, Perry Diamond	Belleville, Wayne	1871-1872	
Pearl, Stephen	DuPlain, Clinton	1867-1868	1869-1870
Pears, Don R.	Buchanan, Berrien	1951-1962; 1965-1970	
Pearson, Richard	Urban, Sanilac	1895-1900	
Pearson, William J.	Boyne Falls, Charlevoix	1909-1912	1923-1926
Pease, William H.	Grass Lake, Jackson	1845	
Peck, George Washington	Brighton, Livingston	1846-1847	
Peckham, William	Albion, Calhoun	1913-1914	
Peek, Archibald J.	Jackson, Jackson	1897-1898	1905-1908
Peer, George W.	Rankin, Genesee	1895-1896	
Peltz, Emil Albert	Rogers City, Presque Isle	1945-1960	
Penczak, John Joseph	Detroit, Wayne	1949-1964	
Pendill, James P.	Marquette, Marquette	1863-1864	
Pendleton, Edward W.	Sturgis, St. Joseph		1879-1880
Pengra, Olin	Sebewaing, Huron	1883-1884	
Pennell, Orrin G.	DeWitt, Clinton		1885-1886
Penney, Harvey A.	Saginaw, Saginaw	1915-1916	1917-1926
Pennington, Henry F.	Charlotte, Eaton		1883-1884
Pennington, Irving	Sparta, Kent	1950-1954	
Pennoyer, Henry	Grand Haven, Ottawa	1849	1859-1860
Perakis, Robert A.	Mount Clemens, Macomb	1985-1986	
Perham, John B.	Spring Lake, Ottawa	1881-1884	
Perkins, Edwin Zina	Cheboygan, Cheboygan	1887-1888	
Perkins, Jabez	Springville, Lenawee	1859-1860	
Perkins, John	Norway, Menominee	1891-1892	
Perkins, John J.	Prairieville, Barry	1901-1904	
Perkins, Sanford S.	Saginaw, Saginaw	1893-1894	
Perras, Clifford E.	Nadeau, Menominee	1963-1964	
Perren, John J.	Detroit, Wayne		1899-1900

Name[2]	Post Office[3]	House	Senate
			Session Years[4]
Perricone, Charles R.	Kalamazoo, Kalamazoo	1995-2000	
Perrin, Henry M.	St. Johns, Clinton		1865-1866
Perrin, Porter K.	St. Johns, Clinton		1877-1878
Perrizo, Paul	Daggett, Menominee	1913-1914	
Perry, Aaron	Oakland, Oakland	1873-1874	
Perry, Charles W.	Pierport, Manistee	1895-1898	
Perry, Edwin	Union City, Branch	1857-1860	
Perry, Gideon Durfee	Tecumseh, Lenawee	1857-1858	1859-1860
Perry, Henry E.	Newberry, Luce	1933-1934	
Perry, John M.	Tustin, Osceola	1907-1912	
Person, Seymour Howe	Lansing, Ingham	1915-1920	1927-1930
Persons, Alonzo E.	Alpena, Alpena	1861-1862	
Pestka, Steve	Grand Rapids, Kent	1999-2002	
Petermann, Albert Edward	Calumet, Houghton	1913-1918	
Peters, Gary C.	Bloomfield Township, Oakland, Pontiac, Oakland		1995-2002
Peters, George	Petersburgh, Monroe	1861-1862	1867-1868
Peters, Walter Clarence	Monroe, Monroe	1925-1926; 1929-1930	
Peters, William	Ishpeming, Marquette	1897-1898	
Peterson, Frank W.	Rockford, Kent	1917-1918	
Peterson, Jens G.	Detroit, Wayne	1861-1862	
Peterson, Ronnie	Ypsilanti, Washtenaw	2017-	
Petit, Timothy H.	Essex, Clinton	1855-1856	
Petitpren, Vincent J.	Wayne, Wayne	1965-1970	
Petri, Alexander	Ecorse, Wayne	1959-1964	
Petrowsky, Charles Henry	Detroit, Wayne	1897-1898	
Pettalia, Peter	Presque Isle, Presque Isle	2011-2016	
Pettit, Alvin D.	Hancock, Houghton	1903-1906	
Pettit, William H. H.	Ransom, Hillsdale	1887-1888	
Phelps, Fitch	Big Rapids, Mecosta	1877-1880	1883-1886
Phelps, John W.	Mason, Ingham	1859-1860	
Phelps, Phil K.	Flushing, Genesee	2013-2018	
Phelps, William	Detroit, Wayne	1861-1862	
Philbrick, Nathan S.	Farmington, Oakland	1841	
Phillips, Charles Curtiss	Bangor, Van Buren	1897-1900	
Phillips, Clarence E.	Pontiac, Oakland	2001-2006	
Phillips, Delos	Kalamazoo, Kalamazoo		1869-1870
Phillips, Frank E.	Mount Pleasant, Isabella	1929-1932	
Phillips, Harry J.	Port Huron, St. Clair	1943-1962	
Phillips, John I.	Pine Run, Genesee	1871	
Phillips, Millard F.	Dowagiac, Cass	1897-1898	
Phillips, Nathaniel G.	North Newburgh, Shiawassee	1865-1866	
Phillips, Pitts	Southfield, Oakland	1837	
Phillips, Ralph William	Bay City, Bay		1921-1922
Phinney, Edwin R.	East Saginaw, Saginaw	1883-1884	
Pierce, Ansel B.	Belle Branch, Wayne	1887-1888	
Pierce, Charles Sumner	Oscoda, Iosco		1893-1894
Pierce, Darius	Lima, Washtenaw	1846-1847	
Pierce, Edgar	Big Rapids, Mecosta	1883-1884	
Pierce, Edward Charles	Ann Arbor, Washtenaw		1979-1982
Pierce, John Davis	Marshall, Calhoun	1847-1848	
Pierce, Joseph B.	Jackson, Jackson	1850	
Pierce, Nathan	Marengo, Calhoun, Pierceville, Washtenaw	1839-1841; 1850-1851	1853-1854; 1857-1858
Pierce, Onesimus O.	Redford, Wayne	1873-1874	
Pierce, Peter R. L.	Grand Rapids, Kent		1869-1870
Pierson, Benjamin	Farmington, Oakland	1871-1872	
Pierson, William S.	Flint, Genesee		1901-1902
Pilch, Alex	Dearborn, Wayne	1967-1972	
Piper, Daniel D.	Clinton, Lenawee	1861-1864	
Pitcher, Washington	Constantine, St. Joseph	1845	
Pitkin, Clarence G.	Whitehall, Muskegon	1921-1924	
Pitoniak, Gregory E.	Taylor, Wayne	1989-1997	
Pitt, Frederick	Ionia, Ionia	1883-1884	

Name[2]	Post Office[3]	Session Years[4] House	Senate
Pittenger, Philip O.	Lansing, Ingham	1967-1970	1971-1974
Pitts, Charles M.	Monroe, Monroe	1865-1866	
Place, Lester B.	Three Rivers, St. Joseph	1915-1916	
Place, William Dallas	Ionia, Ionia	1893-1896	
Plakas, Jim A.	Garden City, Wayne	2001-2006	
Planck, Edgar Allan	Union, Cass		1915-1918
Plawecki, David A.	Dearborn Heights, Wayne		1971-1982
Plawecki, Julie	Dearborn Heights, Wayne	2015-2016	
Plawecki, Lauren	Dearborn Heights, Wayne	2016	
Plimpton, Emory M.	Buchanan, Berrien	1869-1870	
Plumley, Benjamin Franklin	Harbor Beach, Huron	1913-1914	
Pohutsky, Laurie	Livonia, Wayne	2019-	
Points, David S.	Highland Park, Wayne	1993-1994	
Polehanki, Dayna	Livonia, Wayne		2019-
Poleski, Earl	Jackson, Jackson	2011-2016	
Poleski, John J.	Detroit, Wayne	1941-1942	
Polidori, Gino H.	Dearborn, Wayne	2005-2010	
Polk, Alex J.	Detroit, Wayne	1947-1948	
Pollack, Lana	Ann Arbor, Washtenaw		1983-1994
Pomroy, Enos A.	Litchfield, Hillsdale	1881-1882	
Pond, Alfred	Flushing, Genesee	1847	
Pond, Elihu B.	Ann Arbor, Washtenaw		1859-1860
Pond, Jared	Branch, Branch	1839	
Poppleton, Orrin	Birmingham, Oakland	1853-1854	
Poppleton, William	Birmingham, Oakland	1843	
Porreca, Vincent "Joe"	Trenton, Wayne	1983-1996	
Porter, Elmer R.	Blissfield, Lenawee		1937-1964
Porter, George Ford	Gooding, Ottawa		1891-1892
Porter, Ira	Port Huron, St. Clair	1841	
Porter, John	Grand Rapids, Kent	1863-1864	
Porter, Lewis	Grand Rapids, Kent	1857-1858	1859-1860
Porter, Micah	Sharon, Washtenaw	1844	
Porter, Paul	Quincy, Branch	1975-1978	
Post, Floyd Lewelleyn	Coleman, Midland	1885-1886	1887-1888
Post, James I.	Hillsdale, Hillsdale	1935-1944; 1949-1950	
Post, Maurice E.	Rockford, Kent	1933-1948	
Post, Samuel	Ypsilanti, Washtenaw	1871-1872	
Posthumus, Dick	Lowell, Kent Alto, Kent		1983-1998
Potter, Allen	Kalamazoo, Kalamazoo	1857-1858	
Potter, Calvin B.	St. Joseph, Berrien	1875-1876	
Potter, Edward K.	Alpena, Alpena	1889-1890	
Potter, Fordyce H.	Bancroft, Shiawassee	1883-1886	
Potter, George N.	Potterville, Eaton		1887-1888
Potter, S. Don	Lansing, Ingham		1965-1966
Potter, William W.	Hastings, Barry		1899-1900
Potvin, Phil	Cadillac, Wexford	2011-2016	
Poucher, Anthony	Columbia Lake, Washtenaw	1838	
Powell, Gardner	Constantine, St. Joseph	1903-1904	
Powell, Herbert Ernest	Ionia, Ionia	1901-1904	1913-1916
Powell, Milo	Constantine, St. Joseph	1848	
Powell, Stanley M.	Ionia, Ionia	1931-1932; 1965-1978	
Power, Nathan	Farmington, Oakland	1855-1856	
Power, Pliny	Oxford, Oakland Detroit, Wayne	1844; 1855-1856	
Power, Robert D.	Brighton, Livingston	1844-1845	
Power, Thomas G.	Traverse City, Grand Traverse	1983-1992	
Powers, James	Scotts, Kalamazoo	1897-1898	
Powers, Randall D.	Bronson, Branch	1905-1908	
Powers, William	Emmett, St. Clair	1885-1888	
Powers, William H.	Grand Rapids, Kent	1879-1880	
Pratt, Abner	Marshall, Calhoun	1863-1864	1844-1845
Pratt, Foster	Kalamazoo, Kalamazoo	1859-1860	
Pratt, Gilbert E.	Ithaca, Gratiot	1861-1862	

Name[2]	Post Office[3]	House	Senate
			Session Years[4]
Pratt, William A.	Franklin, Oakland	1843-1845	
Pray, Ernest George	Dimondale, Eaton	1913-1916	
Pray, Esek	Dixborough, Washtenaw	1838	
Pray, George	Wood's Corners, Ionia	1879-1880	
Prescott, Charles Test	Prescott, Ogemaw		1947-1961
Prescott, George A.	Tawas City, Iosco	1967-1978	
Prescott, George Allen	Tawas City, Iosco		1895-1898
Preston, Almon E.	Battle Creek, Calhoun	1875-1876	
Preston, John L.	Columbiaville, Lapeer	1889-1890	1895-1898
Preston, Loomis King	St. Joseph, Berrien	1923-1926; 1939-1950	
Preston, Otis	White Pigeon, St. Joseph	1842	
Preston, S. Horace	Lansing, Ingham	1887-1888	
Preston, Wallace W.	Mount Pleasant, Isabella	1889-1890	
Price, Amanda	Park Township, Ottawa	2011-2016	
Price, Hubert, Jr.	Pontiac, Oakland	1994-2000	
Price, Jacob	Brandon, Oakland	1850	
Price, Layman B.	Lakeville, Oakland	1847	1871-1872
	Utica, Macomb		
Pridnia, John D.	Harrisville, Alcona	1983-1990	1991-1994
	Hubbard Lake, Alcona		
Priehs, Louis	Mount Clemens, Macomb	1937-1938; 1941-1942	
Priest, Deliverance S.	Romeo, Macomb	1871-1874	
Priest, Franklin Charles	Mancelona, Antrim	1933-1938	
Prindle, Clarence W.	Grand Rapids, Kent	1877-1878; 1881-1882	
Prindle, Frank L.	Gladwin, Gladwin		1891-1892
Pringle, Eugene A.	Jackson, Jackson	1861-1862	1867-1868
Probert, William	Bear Lake, Manistee	1879-1880; 1889-1890	
Profit, Kirk A.	Ypsilanti, Washtenaw	1989-1998	
Proos, John	St. Joseph, Berrien	2005-2010	2011-2018
Prosser, Halley H.	Flushing, Genesee	1905-1908	
Provost, Francis J.	Byron, Shiawassee	1843	
Prusi, Michael	Ishpeming, Marquette	1995-2000	2003-2010
	National Mine, Marquette		
Prutzman, Abraham Clifford	Three Rivers, St. Joseph		1869-1874
Pscholka, Al	Stevensville, Berrien	2011-2016	
Ptaszkiewicz, John Stanley	Detroit, Wayne	1947-1950	
Pullen, Charles Dwight	Mount Pleasant, Isabella	1935-1936	
Pullen, Nicholas W.	Romulus, Wayne	1845	
Pulver, Henry H.	Laingsburg, Shiawassee		1885-1886
Pulver, Seth Q.	Owosso, Shiawassee		1927-1928
Pumford, Mike	Newaygo, Newaygo	1999-2004	
Purcell, William	Detroit, Wayne	1869	
Purdy, Robert	Summit, Washtenaw	1837; 1843	
Pursell, Carl Duane	Plymouth, Wayne		1971-1976
Putnam, Uzziel, Jr.	Pokagon, Cass	1869-1870	1871-1872
Putney, Charles G.	Sandusky, Sanilac		1911-1912
Putney, Elmore	Speaker, Sanilac	1897-1898	
Quackenboss, Daniel G.	Tecumseh, Lenawee	1848; 1850; 1853-1854	
Quarles, Nancy L.	Southfield, Oakland	1997-2002	
Quinlan, James C.	Grand Rapids, Kent		1925-1928; 1947-1948
Quinn, Cornelius Patrick	Detroit, Wayne	1945-1946	
Quintel, August	Bay City, Bay	1915-1918	
Raap, F. Charles	Twin Lake, Muskegon	1955-1960; 1965-1966	
	Muskegon, Muskegon		
Rabhi, Yousef	Ann Arbor, Washtenaw	2017-	
Raczkowski, Andrew	Farmington Hills, Oakland	1997-2002	
Rahoi, Philip Joseph	Iron Mountain, Dickinson	1935-1938	1955-1964
Rairden, John	Detroit, Wayne		1887-1888
Ralph, Stillman	Scipio, Hillsdale	1837; 1855-1856	
	Jonesville, Hillsdale		
Ramsdell, Norton R.	Ann Arbor, Washtenaw	1844	
Ramsdell, Thomas Jefferson	Manistee, Manistee	1861-1862	
Ramsey, Edwin Boyd	Lansing, Ingham	1921-1922	
Randall, Caleb Dwinell	Coldwater, Branch		1871-1872

Name[2]	Post Office[3]	House	Session Years[4] Senate
Randall, Edmond S.	New Era, Oceana	1899-1904	
Randall, Gary Lee	Elwell, Gratiot	1979-1996	
Randall, Harvey	Tekonsha, Calhoun	1867-1868	
Randall, James Andrus	Detroit, Wayne	1889-1890	
Rankin, Daniel D.	Shelby, Oceana	1921	
Rankin, Francis Hamilton	Flint, Genesee	1861-1864	1877-1878
Rankin, Henry C.	Ypsilanti, Washtenaw	1911-1912	
Ranney, Lemuel S.	Hillsdale, Hillsdale	1875-1876	
Ranney, Peyton	Kalamazoo, Kalamazoo	1883-1884	1889-1890
Ransom, Epaphroditus	Kalamazoo, Kalamazoo	1853-1854	
Ransom, Fletcher	Alamo, Kalamazoo	1845-1846	
Ransom, James Walter	Grand Rapids, Kent	1875-1876	
Rasmussen, Hans Christian	Ludington, Mason	1957-1964	
Rasmussen, William Erastus	Stanton, Montcalm	1921-1924	
Rathke, Erwin	Bay City, Bay	1949-1950	
Rauchholz, John C.	Hemlock, Saginaw	1921-1928	
Raudabaugh, Richard	Lansing, Ingham	1911-1912	
Rawson, Audley	Cass City, Tuscola	1935-1942	1943-1946
Rayburn, Robert H.	Alpena, Alpena	1913-1914	
Raymond, Henry	Bay City, Bay	1859-1860	
Raymond, Hiram	Tecumseh, Lenawee	1863-1864	
Raymond, Mahlon H.	Grass Lake, Jackson	1879-1880	
Raymond, Samuel William	Adrian, Lenawee		1933-1934
Raymond, Selah H.	Manitou Beach, Lenawee	1891-1894	
	Town House, Lenawee		
Raynale, Ebenezer	Franklin, Oakland		1835-1837
Read, Edward G.	Richland, Kalamazoo	1919-1924	
Read, Gilbert E.	Richland, Kalamazoo	1861-1866	1877-1878
Read, J. Herbert	Copemish, Manistee	1899-1906; 1925-1930	
Read, Thomas	Shelby, Oceana	1915-1920	1927-1928
Reader, George H.	Scottville, Mason	1887-1888	
Redfern, Francis William	Maple Rapids, Clinton	1893-1896	
Redfield, Alexander Hamilton	Cassopolis, Cass		1848-1849; 1857
	Detroit, Wayne		
Redfield, George A.	Adamsville, Cass	1841	1842-1844
Redfield, Heman J.	Monroe, Monroe		1875-1878
Reed, Charles H.	Clio, Genesee	1925-1932	
Reed, Charles P.	Ravenna, Muskegon	1883-1884	
Reed, Clarence J.	Spring Arbor, Jackson	1915-1918	
Reed, George W.	Stanwood, Mecosta	1897-1900	
Reed, Lucien	Mason, Ingham	1865-1866	
Reed, Marshall	Springville, Lenawee	1875-1876	
Reed, Rasselas	Vernon, Shiawassee	1877-1880	
Reed, William A.	Horton, Jackson	1899-1902	
Reeves, Henry L.	Roseville, Macomb	1859-1860	
Reeves, Triette E. Lipsey	Detroit, Wayne	1992; 1999-2004	
Reid, Archie Miller	Detroit, Wayne	1925-1928	
Reid, Clarence A.	Detroit, Wayne		1941-1948; 1951-1952
Reid, D. Neil	Detroit, Wayne	1947-1948	
Reid, John Wheeler	Highland Park, Wayne		1933-1936
Reilly, John	Oakland, Oakland	2017-	
Remer, Lawrence T.	East China, St. Clair	1873-1876	
Remer, Walter F.	Saginaw, Saginaw	1935-1936; 1939-1942	
Remick, George Bradford	Detroit, Wayne	1881-1882	
Rendon, Bruce R.	Lake City, Missaukee	2011-2016	
Rendon, Daire	Lake City, Missaukee	2017-	
Reno, John	Detroit, Wayne	1853-1854	
Rentz, Theodore	Detroit, Wayne	1887-1888	1889-1890
Renwick, George	Rider, Washtenaw	1839-1841; 1847-1848	
	Salem, Washtenaw		
Renwick, John	Lucerne, Washtenaw	1850; 1853-1854	
Reutter, Albert H.	Detroit, Wayne	1919-1922	
Rexford, Roswell B.	Napoleon, Jackson		1855-1856
Reynolds, Asa	Rose, Oakland	1855-1856	

Name[2]	Post Office[3]	House	Session Years[4] Senate
Reynolds, Edwin W.	Adamsville, Cass	1859-1860	
Reynolds, Richard B.	Inland, Leelanau	1903-1904	
Reynolds, Rush W.	Waldron, Hillsdale	1909-1912	
Rhead, Kim A.	Sandusky, Sanilac	1993-1998	
Rice, John A.	Adrian, Lenawee	1846	
Rice, Justin	Port Huron, St. Clair		1840-1841
Rice, Nelson C.	St. Joseph, Berrien	1907-1910	
Rice, Thomas J.	Scio, Washtenaw	1842-1843	
Rice, Wayne Remington	White Cloud, Newaygo	1913-1918	
Rice, William Elmer	Rogers City, Presque Isle	1895-1896	
Rich, Arthur Lawrence	Ashland, Newaygo	1901-1902	
Rich, Hampton	Ionia, Ionia		1867-1870
Rich, Irving B.	Jackson, Jackson	1895-1896	
Rich, John Tyler	Elba, Lapeer	1873-1876; 1877-1880	1881
Richards, Alvin E.	Marquette, Marquette	1947-1954	
Richards, George D.	Wolverine, Cheboygan	1903-1904	
Richards, James A.	Albion, Calhoun	1923-1924	
Richards, William P.	Somerset, Hillsdale	1859-1860	
Richardson, Charles W.	Marquette, Marquette	1913-1914; 1923-1928	1929-1932
Richardson, David M.	Detroit, Wayne		1873-1874
Richardson, George Frederick	Hudsonville, Ottawa	1885-1886; 1891-1892	
Richardson, George W.	Dundee, Monroe	1895-1896	
Richardson, John H.	Tuscola, Tuscola		1883-1884
Richardson, Origen D.	Pontiac, Oakland	1835-1836; 1841	
Richardson, Paschal D.	Worth, Tuscola	1853-1854; 1859-1860	
Richardson, Robert	Saginaw, Saginaw		1965-1974
Richardville, Randy	Monroe, Monroe	1999-2004	2007-2014
Richmond, Charles H.	Ann Arbor, Washtenaw		1883-1884
Richmond, Charles Lott	Saginaw, Saginaw	1845	
Richmond, William Almy	Grand Rapids, Kent		1844-1845
Richner, Andrew C.	Grosse Pointe Park, Wayne	1997-2002	
Rider, Ira	Plymouth, Wayne	1853-1854	
Riegel, John Michael	West Bay City, Bay	1901-1902	
Riford, Almond B.	Benton Harbor, Berrien	1869-1872	
Riley, Henry H.	Constantine, St. Joseph		1850-1852; 1862
Riopelle, Claude N.	Detroit, Wayne	1869-1870	
Riopelle, Hyacinthe F.	Ecorse, Wayne	1883-1884	
Riopelle, Oscar A.	Detroit, Wayne		1921-1924
Ripley, Montague W.	Montague, Muskegon	1931-1932	
Ripley, Thomas C.	Saginaw, Saginaw	1873-1874	
Risdon, Orange	Saline, Washtenaw	1838	
Rison, Vera B.	Flint, Genesee	1997-2002	
Rivers, Lynn Nancy	Ann Arbor, Washtenaw	1993-1994	
Rivet, Joseph L.	Bay City, Bay	1999-2004	
Rix, Oel	Richmond, St. Clair	1843-1844	1846-1847
Robbins, Richard B.	Adrian, Lenawee	1875-1878	1879-1878
Roberts, Alton T.	Marquette, Marquette		1915-1918
Roberts, Brett	Charlotte, Eaton	2015-2018	
Roberts, Christopher T.	Crystal Falls, Iron	1893-1894	
Roberts, Elijah J.	Eagle River, Houghton	1850	1851
Roberts, Farrell E.	Hancock, Houghton	1957-1960	1961-1966
	Pontiac, Oakland		
Roberts, John	Hastings, Barry		1857-1858
Roberts, Sarah B.	St. Clair Shores, Macomb	2009-2010; 2013-2016	
Robertson, Alexander	Pokagon, Cass	1873-1874	
Robertson, Andrew S.	Mount Clemens, Macomb		1863-1864
Robertson, Archibald	Saginaw, Saginaw	1915-1916; 1923-1924	
Robertson, David B.	Grand Blanc, Genesee	1991-1992; 2003-2008	2011-2018
Robertson, Ernest C.	Fostoria, Tuscola	1929-1932	
Robertson, George	Albion, Calhoun	1879-1882	
Robertson, John M.	Algonac, St. Clair	1895-1896	
Robinson, Alfred T.	Saginaw, Saginaw	1919-1922	
Robinson, Carl A.	Marshall, Calhoun	1917-1918	
Robinson, Edward J.	Dearborn, Wayne		1965-1966

Name[2]	Post Office[3]	House	Session Years[4]	Senate
Robinson, George J.	Alpena, Alpena	1883-1884		
Robinson, George P.	Noble Center, Branch	1875-1876		
Robinson, Glenn B.	South Haven, Van Buren	1947-1952		
Robinson, Hiram White	Bridgeport, Saginaw	1889-1891		
Robinson, Isaac	Detroit, Wayne	2019-		
Robinson, James L.	Vandalia, Cass	1899-1902		
Robinson, James Willin	Vestaburgh, Montcalm	1887-1888		
Robinson, Lote C.	Eckford, Calhoun	1903-1904		
Robinson, Orrin Williams	Chassell, Houghton	1895-1896		1897-1898
Robinson, Rix	Ada, Kent			1846-1849
Robinson, Robert	Trent, Muskegon	1887-1890		
Robinson, Rose Mary	Detroit, Wayne	2013-2018		
Robinson, Solon E.	Marshall, Calhoun	1873-1874		
Robinson, Walter	Adrian, Lenawee	1867-1868		
Robinson, Walter Clarence	Detroit, Wayne	1903-1906		
Robison, Andrew	Machester, Washtenaw	1859-1860		
Robison, John J.	Manchester, Washtenaw	1879-1880		1863-1864
Robson, John	Lansing, Ingham			1901-1902
Rocca, Sal	Sterling Heights, Macomb	1975-1994; 2001-2004		
Rocca, Sue	Sterling Heights, Macomb	1995-2000		
Rocca, Tory	Sterling Heights, Macomb	2005-2010		2011-2018
Rockwell, Gordon	Mount Morris, Genesee	1960-1964		1967-1974
Rockwell, Hewlett C.	Benton Harbor, Berrien	1891-1892		
Rockwood, Chandler H.	Flint, Genesee	1867-1868		
Rodesiler, Fred	Riga, Lenawee	1939-1944		
Rodgers, Lincoln	Muskegon, Muskegon	1901-1904		
Rogers, Bill	Brighton, Livingston	2009-2014		
Rogers, Jeremiah M.	Hastings, Barry	1887-1890		
Rogers, Levi	Fredonia, Washtenaw	1841		
Rogers, Mike J.	Howell, Livingston			1995-2000
Rogers, Tom F.	Ravenna, Muskegon	1915-1916		
Rogner, John Jacob	Richville, Tuscola	1893-1896		
Rohlfs, Harry Edward	Akron, Tuscola	1965-1970		
Romano, William	Van Dyke, Macomb	1945-1964		1965-1966
	Warren, Macomb			
Romanski, Stanley J.	Detroit, Wayne	1935-1936		
Romeyn, James Woodruff	Detroit, Wayne	1869-1870		1871-1872; 1883-1884
Rood, Horace D.	Lapeer, Lapeer	1871-1872		
Roof, Adam L.	Lyons, Ionia	1845		1849-1850
Roof, Albert K.	Lyons, Ionia	1871-1872		1887-1888
Roosevelt, Joseph C.	Detroit, Wayne	1933-1936		1937-1938
Roost, John	Holland, Ottawa	1871-1872		1883-1884
Root, Amos	Jackson, Jackson	1853-1854		
Root, Claude Boone	Greenville, Montcalm			1933-1934
Root, Cyril H.	Kalamazoo, Kalamazoo	1950-1968		
Root, Edson V., Jr.	Bangor, Van Buren	1953-1971		
Root, Edson V., Sr.	Paw Paw, Van Buren	1935-1947		
Root, Lyman C.	Allegan, Allegan	1915-1918		
Root, Roland	Coldwater, Branch	1850-1852		
Root, Roswell	Plymouth, Wayne	1841		
Root, William W.	Mason, Ingham	1881-1882		
Rorick, John Porter	Adrian, Lenawee	1925-1930		
Rork, Asa D.	Hastings, Barry	1877-1878		
Rose, Allen S.	Rose City, Ogemaw	1893-1896		
Rose, David G.	Manchester, Washtenaw			1881-1882
Rose, Elias O.	Big Rapids, Mecosta	1873-1874		
Rose, Harry C.	Ashley, Gratiot	1917-1920		
Rose, Henry L.	Excanaba, Delta	1927-1930		
Rose, William H.	Bath, Clinton	1881-1884		
Rose, William O.	Roseville, Macomb	1845		
Rosenbaum, Paul A.	Battle Creek, Calhoun	1973-1978		
Rosenkrans, William A.	Corunna, Shiawassee			1911-1914
Ross, Doug	Oak Park, Oakland			1979-1982
Ross, Giles	Highland, Oakland	1871-1872; 1877		

Name[2]	Post Office[3]	House	Session Years[4] Senate
Ross, Henry T.	Milford, Oakland	1915-1920	1921-1924
Ross, John D.	Buchanan, Berrien	1855-1856	
Ross, John D.	Ford River, Delta	1879-1880	
Rounsville, Frank G.	Fowlerville, Livingston	1887-1888	
Routhier, Henry	Ishpeming, Marquette	1889-1890	
Rowden, John C.	Auburn, Bay	1891-1892	
Rowe, Floyd W.	Camden, Hillsdale	1921-1924	
Rowe, Frederick C.	Detroit, Wayne		1919-1920
Rowe, Squire W.	Highland, Oakland	1865-1866	
Rowell, Ralph Clarence	Ironwood, Gogebic	1937-1938	
Rowland, David H.	Northville, Wayne	1843-1844	
Rowley, William A.	Mount Clemens, Macomb	1895-1898	
Rowlson, Harvey B.	Hillsdale, Hillsdale	1869-1870	
Roxborough, Charles A.	Detroit, Wayne		1931-1932
Roxburgh, George F.	Reed City, Osceola	1923-1926	
Roy, Leo H.	Hancock, Houghton		1949-1958
Royce, Arthur	Mecosta, Mecosta	1937-1940	
Rozycki, Stanley F.	Detroit, Wayne		1955-1974
Ruehle, John V., Jr.	Detroit, Wayne	1844	
Ruff, Theodore Christian	St. Clair, St. Clair	1913-1914	1933-1934
Rulison, George W.	Hancock, Houghton	1897-1902	
Rulison, John G.	Lansing, Ingham	1933	
Rumer, James Fulton	Davison, Genesee		1905-1906
Rummel, Alvin L.	Ironwood, Gogebic	1931-1934	
Rummel, John G.	Frankenmuth, Saginaw	1883-1884	
Rumsey, Henry	Ann Arbor, Washtenaw		1835-1837
Rumsey, Marshall E.	Leslie, Ingham	1885-1888	
Runco, William J.	Dearborn, Wayne	1983-1986; 1989-1990	
Runestad, Jim	White Lake, Oakland	2015-2018	2019-
Runyan, Hiram D.	Disco, Macomb	1871-1872	
Runyan, John G.	Carlton Center, Barry	1865-1866	
Runyan, Philip E.	White Pigeon, St. Joseph	1844	
Rush, Allen F.	Lake Orion, Oakland	1967-1968	
Rushton, Herbert J.	Escanaba, Delta		1927-1932
Russ, Lucius E.	North Adams, Hillsdale	1889-1890	
Russell, Henry C.	Cedar Springs, Kent		1881-1882
Russell, Huntley	Soldiers' Home, Kent		1905-1908
Russell, James I.	Summerfield, Monroe	1841; 1848	
Russell, Josiah	Greenville, Montcalm		1853-1854
Russell, Orlando D.	Sturgis, St. Joseph	1911-1912	
Rutledge, David	Ypsilanti, Washtenaw	2011-2016	
Ryan, Daniel J.	Detroit, Wayne		1945-1946
Ryan, Harold Martin	Detroit, Wayne		1949-1962
Ryan, James Rogers	Redford, Wayne	1995-1996	
Ryan, William A.	Detroit, Wayne	1958-1980	
Ryland, Frank J.	Peck, Sanilac	1891-1892	
Sabin, Marden	Centerville, St. Joseph		1891-1894
Sabo, Terry	Muskegon, Muskegon	2017-	
Sabol, John	Ironwood, Gogebic	1941-1944	
Sackett, David	Redford, Wayne	1850	
Sackett, Wayne B.	Portage, Kalamazoo	1969-1976	
Sackrider, George W.	Oakley, Saginaw	1877-1878	
Sadowski, George G.	Detroit, Wayne		1931-1932
Sak, Michael G.	Grand Rapids, Kent	2003-2008	
Salisbury, Abiram D.	Midland, Midland	1889-1890	
Sallade, George Wahr	Ann Arbor, Washtenaw	1955-1960	
Salyer, Nathan	Lucerne, Washtenaw	1849	
Sanborn, Alan Bruce	Richmond, Macomb	1998-2001	2001-2010
Sanborn, Cummings	Port Huron, St. Clair	1842	
Sanborn, James L.	Ossineke, Alpena	1907-1910	
Sanborn, James W.	Demingsburg, Lapeer	1840; 1846; 1855-1856	
	Port Huron, St. Clair		
	Metamora, Lapeer		
Sanborn, Kenneth N.	Mount Clemens, Macomb	1957-1958	
Sanborn, William	Port Huron, St. Clair		1867-1868

Name[2]	Post Office[3]	Session Years[4]	
		House	Senate
Sanders, Garry E.	Mason, Ingham	1909-1910	
Sanderson, Asa T.	St. Charles, Saginaw	1901-1904	
Sanderson, Rodolphus	Battle Creek, Calhoun	1865-1866; 1873-1874	
Sanford, George P.	Lansing, Ingham	1869-1870	
Sanson, William C.	Caro, Tuscola	1921-1924	
Santana, Harvey	Detroit, Wayne	2011-2016	
Santana, Sylvia	Detroit, Wayne	2017-2018	2019-
Santo, John Randle	Traverse City, Grand Traverse	1913-1914	
Sargent, Edward L.	Levering, Emmet	1921-1924; 1927-1930	
Saul, John	Munising, Alger	1939-1942	
Saunders, Harry	Monguagon, Wayne	1839; 1844	
Saunders, Nelis J.	Detroit, Wayne	1969-1972	
Saunders, Nelson W.	Detroit, Wayne	1983-1996	
Saur, M. Harold	Kent City, Kent		1935-1936; 1939-1946
Savage, Hiram A.	Saginaw, Saginaw	1897-1898	
Savidge, William	Spring Lake, Ottawa		1897-1898
Sawyer, Andrew J.	Ann Arbor, Washtenaw	1877-1880; 1897-1898	
Sawyer, Jacob C.	Hudson, Lenawee	1877-1878	
Sawyer, Meredith P.	Menominee, Menominee	1919-1920	
Sawyer, Robert Nute	Monroe, Monroe	1939-1942	
Sawyer, Willis F.	Ontonagon, Ontonagon		1893-1894
Saxton, Arthur Wilmot	Henrietta, Jackson	1895-1896	
Sayre, Ira Terry	Flushing, Genesee		1899-1900
Schaeffer, George W.	Sturgis, St. Joseph	1913-1914	
Schantz, William H.	Hastings, Barry	1905-1910	
Schars, Peter	New Baltimore, Macomb	1865-1868	
Schattler, Casper F.	Roseville, Macomb	1875-1876	
Schauer, Mark H.	Battle Creek, Calhoun	1997-2002	2003-2009
Schellberg, Bernhard F.	Detroit, Wayne	1893-1894	
Schepers, Jacob	East Lansing, Ingham	1947-1950	
Scherer, Milton E.	Muskegon, Muskegon	1941-1942	
Schermerhorn, Barth W.	Dowagiac, Cass	1857-1858	
Schermesser, Gloria	Lincoln Park, Wayne	1996-2002	
Schmidt, Henry L.	Grand Rapids, Kent	1917-1918	
Schmidt, Henry M.	Saginaw, Saginaw	1899-1900	
Schmidt, John	Reed City, Osceola	1913-1918	
Schmidt, Louis E.	Livonia, Wayne	1967-1968	
Schmidt, Roy	Grand Rapids, Kent	2009-2012	
Schmidt, Wayne A.	Traverse City, Grand Traverse	2009-2014	2015-
Schneider, Albert W.	Detroit, Wayne	1937-1938	
Schneider, Louis James	Detroit, Wayne	1933-1936	
Schoenhals, George H.	St. Johns, Clinton	1933-1934	
Schoolcraft, James L.	Fort Brady, Chippewa	1843-1844	
Schooley, Louis G.	Grandville, Kent	1949-1950	
Schor, Andy	Lansing, Ingham	2013-2017	
Schriber, Frederick R.	Grand Rapids, Kent	1935-1938	
Schroeder, Andrea	Independence Township, Oakland	2019-	
Schroeder, George A.	Detroit, Wayne	1933-1938	
Schroer, Mary B.	Ann Arbor, Washtenaw	1993-1998	
Schuch, John Philip	Saginaw, Saginaw	1943-1946	1947-1950
Schuette, Bill	Midland, Midland		1995-2002
Schuitmaker, Tonya	Lawton, Van Buren	2005-2010	2011-2018
Schumaker, Anthony B.	Grand Ledge, Eaton		1901-1902
Schwartz, John E.	Detroit, Wayne	1845	1847-1848
Schwarz, John	Battle Creek, Calhoun		1987-2002
Schweigert, Thomas F.	Petoskey, Emmet		1961-1970
Schwinger, Louis C.	Saginaw, Saginaw	1937-1938	
Scidmore, Arthur W.	Three Rivers, St. Joseph	1905-1908	
Scott, Andrew J.	Saginaw, Saginaw	1901-1904	
Scott, Bettie Cook	Detroit, Wayne	2007-2010; 2017-2018	
Scott, Frank Douglas	Alpena, Alpena		1911-1914
Scott, George G.	Detroit, Wayne; Delray, Wayne	1905-1908	1909-1918

Name[2]	Post Office[3]	House	Senate
			Session Years[4]
Scott, Harold Joseph	Flint, Genesee	1973-1977	1977-1982
Scott, John	Detroit, Wayne	1842	
Scott, John Sr.	Iron River, Iron	1937-1938	
Scott, Martha G.	Highland Park, Wayne	1995-2000	2001-2010
Scott, Orville W.	McBain, Antrim	1931-1932	
Scott, Paul	Grand Blanc, Genesee	2009-2011	
Scott, Samuel M.	DeWitt, Clinton	1846; 1848; 1850	
	Essex, Clinton		
Scott, Thomas E.	Flint, Genesee	1977-1994	
	Burton, Genesee		
Scott, Winfield	Northville, Wayne	1873-1874	
Scranton, Judith L.	Brighton, Livingston	1997-2002	
Scripps, Dan	Leland, Leelanau	2009-2010	
Scripps, James Edmund	Detroit, Wayne		1903-1904
Scullen, William P.	Detroit, Wayne		1903-1904
Scully, Charles B.	Almont, Lapeer		1917-1920
Scully, James	Ionia, Ionia	1897-1900	
Sederburg, William Albert	East Lansing, Ingham		1979-1990
Sedgwick, George	Ann Arbor, Washtenaw	1850	
Seeley, Elijah B.	Lanesville, Hillsdale	1839	
Seeley, Harvey	Pontiac, Oakland	1843	
Seeley, Jesse	White Lake, Oakland	1847	
Seeley, Marvin L.	Mount Morris, Genesee	1891-1892	
Seeley, Thaddeus D.	Pontiac, Oakland	1901-1904	1905-1908
Segal, Kate	Battle Creek, Calhoun	2009-2014	
Sellers, Leonard McKnight	Cedar Springs, Kent	1883-1886	
Serotkin, David M.	Mount Clemens, Macomb	1967-1972	1983
Sessions, Alonzo	Ionia, Ionia	1857-1862	
Sessions, William	Ionia, Ionia	1873-1874	
Seward, Julian M.	Niles, Berrien	1869-1870	
Sexton, Jared	Dearbornville, Wayne	1851-1852	
Sexton, Jared A.	Taylor, Wayne	1867-1868	
Seymour, Elisha G.	Sault Saint Marie, Chippewa	1847	
Seymour, Henry	Grand Rapids, Kent	1865-1866	1867-1868
Seymour, Henry William	Sault Saint Marie, Chippewa	1881-1882	1883-1884; 1887-1888
Seymour, James	Flushing, Genesee	1853-1854	1857
Shackleton, Scott A.	Sault Saint Marie, Chippewa	1999-2004	
Shaffer, Rick S.	Three Rivers, St. Joseph	2003-2008	
Shanahan, Edward	Edwardsburgh, Cass	1861-1862	
Shank, Hulbert B.	Lansing, Ingham	1861-1862	
Shannon, Nate	Sterling Heights, Macomb	2019-	
Sharp, George W.	Newberry, Luce		1891-1892
Sharp, James Everette	Grant, Newaygo	1911-1912	
Sharp, John C.	Jackson, Jackson		1887-1888
Sharpe, Albert E.	East Tawas, Iosco	1901-1902	
Sharpe, Peter	Ridgeway, Lenawee	1859-1860	
Sharpe, Thomas George	Howell, Livingston	1963-1978	
Sharts, Derwin W.	Owosso, Shiawassee	1877-1880	
Shattuck, Gilbert	Ypsilanti, Washtenaw	1837	
Shattuck, Willard	Saginaw, Saginaw	1879-1880	
Shaughnessy, Deb	Charlotte, Eaton	2011-2012	
Shaw, Brackley	Clayton, Lenawee	1869-1870	1881-1884
Shaw, Edwin O.	Newaygo, Newaygo		1895-1896
Shaw, Henry A.	Eaton Rapids, Eaton	1857-1860; 1873-1874	
Shaw, James	Niles, Berrien	1845; 1847	
Shea, Henry F.	Laurium, Houghton		1937-1940
Shea, John	Detroit, Wayne	1903-1904	
Shearer, Jonathan	Plymouth, Wayne	1851-1852	1842-1844
Sheen, Fulton J.	Plainwell, Allegan	2003-2008	
Shelden, Carlos Douglas	Houghton, Houghton	1893-1894	1895-1896
Sheldon, Charles P.	Lawrence, Van Buren	1853-1854	
Sheldon, Clarence Leander	Bay, Bay	1903-1904	
Sheldon, James	Albion, Calhoun	1844	
Sheldon, Newton	Union District, Washtenaw	1842; 1869-1870	

Name[2]	Post Office[3]	Session Years[4] House	Senate
	Saline, Washtenaw		
Sheldon, Orson	Utica, Macomb	1838	
Sheldon, Suel Andrews	Berlin, Ottawa		1899-1900; 1905-1906
Sheldon, Timothy F.	South Plymouth, Wayne	1839	
Sheley, Alanson	Detroit, Wayne		1867-1868; 1871-1872
Shellhouse, Martin G.	Colon, St. Joseph	1837	
Sheltrown, Dale E.	West Branch, Ogemaw	1999-2004	
Sheltrown, Joel A.	West Branch, Ogemaw	2005-2010	
Shepard, Francis Marion	Owosso, Shiawassee	1897-1898	
Shepard, James M.	Cassopolis, Cass		1879-1880
Shepard, Luman	Olivet, Eaton	1883-1884	
Shepherd, Frank	Cheboygan, Cheboygan	1897-1900	
Shepherd, Thomas	Martin, Allegan	1867-1868	
Shepich, Stephen V.	Iron River, Iron	1993-1994	
Sheppard, Jason	Temperance, Monroe	2015-	
Sherbeck, Otto	Mount Clemens, Macomb	1945-1946	
Sheridan, Alfred A.	Taylor, Wayne	1965-1982	
Sherman, Abner	Ontonagon, Ontonagon	1853-1858; 1863-1864	
Sherman, Albert Alonzo	Coldwater, Branch	1913-1914	
Sherman, Alonzo J.	Fostoria, Tuscola	1913-1916	
Sherman, Benjamin	Centerville, St. Joseph	1835-1836	
Sherman, Cyrus	Ovid, Clinton	1889-1890	
Sherman, Roger	Bancroft, Shiawassee	1893-1894	
Sherwood, Alonzo	New Troy, Berrien	1879-1880	
Sherwood, Eleazer	St. Ignace, Mackinac	1895-1896	
Sherwood, George	Cassopolis, Cass	1851-1852	
Sherwood, Harvey Campbell	Watervliet, Berrien		1885-1886
Shetterly, Seth K.	Utica, Macomb	1869-1870; 1877-1878	
Shields, Francis J.	Howell, Livingston		1909-1910
Shields, Joseph A.	Lake Linden, Houghton	1915-1916	
Shier, Charles	Ypsilanti, Washtenaw	1855-1856; 1865-1866; 1869-1870	
Shinkle, Norman Douglas	Lambertville, Monroe		1983-1990
Shirkey, Mike	Clarklake, Jackson	2010-2014	2015-
Shisler, John W.	Caledonia, Kent	1897-1900	
Shoemaker, DeWitt	Grand Rapids, Kent	1853-1854	
Shoemaker, Joseph P.	Amsden, Montcalm		1879-1880
Shoemaker, Michael	Michigan Center, Jackson Jackson, Jackson		1848-1852; 1877-1878; 1883-1886
Shook, Abram N.	Coral, Montcalm	1903-1908	
Shook, David	Mount Clemens, Macomb	1851-1852	
Shook, Jacob	Mount Clemens, Macomb	1847	
Shorts, Philip P.	Ludington, Mason	1885-1886	
Shugars, Dale L.	Portage, Kalamazoo	1991-1994	1995-2002
Shull, John D.	Tecumseh, Lenawee	1891-1892	
Shulman, Marc	West Bloomfield, Oakland	1999-2004	
Shurtz, Frederick	White Pigeon, St. Joseph Three Rivers, St. Joseph	1839; 1844	1857-1858
Sias, Donald E.	Midland, Midland	1931-1934	
Sibley, Harry	Muskegon, Muskegon	1949-1950	
Sickles, Aaron	Elsie, Clinton	1869-1870	
Sienkiewicz, Paul N.	Detroit, Wayne	1945-1946	
Sietsema, George	Wyoming, Kent	1965-1966	
Sietsema, Jelt	Grand Rapids, Kent Wyoming, Kent	1969-1986	
Siggins, William N.	Detroit, Wayne	1903-1904	
Sikkema, Ken	Grandville, Kent Wyoming, Kent	1987-1996	1999-2006
Siljander, Mark Deli	Three Rivers, St. Joseph	1977-1981	
Simons, Charles C.	Detroit, Wayne		1903-1904
Simonson, James Bradford	Springfield, Oakland	1857-1858	
Simpson, Emery H.	Hartford, Van Buren	1873-1874; 1887-1888	
Simpson, John	Jackson, Jackson	1927-1928	
Simpson, Mike	Jackson, Jackson	2007-2009	

Name[2]	Post Office[3]	House	Senate
			Session Years[4]
Simpson, Nathan F.	Hartford, Van Buren	1905-1908	
Sinclair, Daniel D.	Adrian, Lenawee		1848
Singh, Samir	East Lansing, Ingham	2013-2018	
Sink, Charles Albert	Ann Arbor, Washtenaw	1919-1920; 1925-1926	1921-1922; 1927-1930
Sitz, Rick C.	Taylor, Wayne	1982-1988	
Skeels, Edward D.	Whitehall, Muskegon	1925-1931	
Skeels, Rufus F.	Hart, Oceana	1913-1914	
Skinner, James Abner	Cedar Springs, Kent		1929-1932
Skrel, Sylvia	Livonia, Wayne	1980	
Slafter, David G.	Worth, Tuscola	1863-1864	
Slagh, Bradley	Zeeland, Ottawa	2019-	
Slavens, Dian	Canton Township, Wayne	2009-2014	
Slayton, Thomas J.	Lowell, Kent	1867-1870	
Sleeper, Albert Edson	Lexington, Sanilac		1901-1904
Slezak, Jim	Davison, Genesee	2009-2010	
Sligh, Charles Robert	Grand Rapids, Kent		1923-1924
Slingerlend, Robert James	Lake Orion, Oakland	1965-1966	
Sloan, Daniel D.	Base Lake, Washtenaw	1850	
Slocum, Albert B.	Hudson, Lenawee	1865-1866	
Slocum, Elliott T.	Trenton, Wayne		1869-1870
Slosson, Willis M.	Reed City, Osceola	1889-1890	
Sly, Alexander	Gould City, Mackinac	1915-1916	
Smale, Hugh	Detroit, Wayne	1959-1962	
Smalley, Herbert	Detroit, Wayne	1893-1894	1895-1896
Smart, Clifford H.	Walled Lake, Oakland	1965-1974	
Smedley, Harold Hinsdill	Grand Rapids, Kent	1925-1926	
Smeekens, John P.	Coldwater, Branch	1969-1974	1957-1964
	Sherwood, Branch		
Smiley, Charles	Burton, Genesee	2011-2016	
Smiley, James Francis	Marshall, Calhoun	1895-1896	
Smit, Raymond J.	Ann Arbor, Washtenaw	1967-1974	
Smith, Abner C.	Mount Clemens, Macomb		1845-1846
Smith, Abram	Algonac, St. Clair	1863-1864	
Smith, Alma Wheeler	South Lyon, Oakland	2005-2010	1995-2002
	Ypsilanti, Washtenaw		
Smith, Alvah G.	Lake City, Missaukee		1899-1900
Smith, Amos	Vandalia, Cass		1869-1870
Smith, Aura	Girard, Branch	1863-1864	
Smith, Avery Almon	Hillsdale, Hillsdale	1889-1892	
Smith, C. Clifford	Redford, Wayne	1867-1868	
Smith, Carmie R.	Niles, Berrien	1898	
Smith, Charles	Hubbell, Houghton	1895-1898	1899-1910
	South Lake Linden, Houghton		
Smith, Charles H.	Jackson, Jackson		1895-1896
Smith, Charles Wallace	Lapeer, Lapeer	1911-1916	
Smith, Colin L.	Big Rapids, Mecosta	1941-1944	1945-1950
Smith, Davis	Tecumseh, Lenawee	1839	
Smith, Donald E.	Owosso, Shiawassee		1955-1958
Smith, Edward L.	Grand Rapids, Kent	1929-1930	
Smith, Elbert V.	Nashville, Barry		1915-1918
Smith, Ezekiel C.	Niles, Berrien	1850	
Smith, F. Hart	Somerset, Hillsdale	1891-1892	
Smith, Frank	Detroit, Wayne		1891-1892
Smith, Frank A.	Luther, Lake	1915-1924	1931-1932
	Cadillac, Wexford		
Smith, Frank L.	Jackson, Jackson	1871-1872	
Smith, Gad	Marquette, Marquette		1901-1902
Smith, George A.	Somerset, Hillsdale	1863-1864	1867-1868; 1885-1886
Smith, George Mortimer	Whitehall, Muskegon	1877-1878	
Smith, Henry	Monroe, Monroe	1838; 1841	
Smith, Henry C.	Austerlitz, Kent	1849; 1853-1854	
Smith, Hiram	Homer, Calhoun	1848	
Smith, Hiram Horton	Mason, Ingham	1843	
Smith, James F.	Davison, Genesee	1967-1976	

Name[2]	Post Office[3]	House	Session Years[4] Senate
Smith, James L.	Lexington, Sanilac	1851-1852	
Smith, Jeremiah R.	Grand Blanc, Genesee	1838; 1842	
Smith, Job	Van Buren, Wayne	1837	
Smith, John B.	Alma, Gratiot	1935-1942	1943-1944
Smith, John S.	Armada, Macomb		1853-1854
Smith, John W.	Port Huron, St. Clair	1919-1920	1921-1924
Smith, John William	Detroit, Wayne		1921-1922
Smith, Joseph	Edwardsburgh, Cass	1835-1837	
Smith, LeGrand J.	Addison, Lenawee	1873-1874	
Smith, Luther	St. Louis, Gratiot	1865-1868	
Smith, Milton H.	Ida, Monroe	1917-1918	
Smith, Morgan L.	Milford, Oakland	1855-1856	
Smith, Nathan D.	Algonac, St. Clair	1861-1862	
Smith, Newel	St. Louis, Gratiot	1913-1916	
Smith, Newman	Detroit, Wayne	1919-1920	
Smith, Nick H.	Addison, Lenawee	1979-1980	1983-1992
Smith, Oliver S.	Owosso, Shiawassee	1889-1890	
Smith, Oliver Saxton	Detroit, Wayne	1945-1946	
Smith, Richard G.	Bay City, Bay	1953-1956	
Smith, Robert Bruce	Portland, Ionia	1867-1870	
Smith, Roy	Ypsilanti, Washtenaw	1967-1972; 1975-1980	
Smith, Samuel J.	Mackinaw, Cheboygan	1915-1918	
Smith, Samuel L.	Algonac, St. Clair	1859-1860	
Smith, Samuel William	Pontiac, Oakland		1885-1886
Smith, Sheldon Ogden	Detroit, Wayne	1905-1906	
Smith, Sidney T.	Grass Lake, Jackson	1857-1858	
Smith, Thaddeus G.	Fentonville, Genesee	1863-1864	1869-1870
	Fenton, Genesee		
Smith, Thomas L.	Battle Creek, Calhoun	1937-1938	
Smith, Virgil Clark	Detroit, Wayne	2003-2008	2011-2016
Smith, Virgil Clark	Detroit, Wayne	1977-1988	1988-2000
Smith, Walker O.	Crapo, Mecosta	1891-1894	
Smith, William H.	Grass Lake, Jackson	1875-1876	
Smith, William M.	St. Johns , Clinton		1913-1914
Smith, William T.	White Pigeon, St. Joseph	1865-1866	
Smith, William Wallace	Traverse City, Grand Traverse		1917-1920
Snell, Joseph W.	Ora Labor, Huron	1869-1870	
Snell, Lawrence W.	Highland Park, Wayne	1905-1908	1909-1912
Snell, William	Rochester, Oakland	1843-1844	
Sneller, Tim	Burton, Genesee	2017-	
Snow, Byron A.	Chesaning, Saginaw	1887-1888	
Snow, Charles Warren Jr.	Jackson, Jackson	1937-1938	
Snow, Fielder S.	Clinton, Lenawee	1843	1849-1850; 1853-1854
Snow, Milo A.	Richland, Kalamazoo	1915-1916	
Snow, Raymond J.	Flint, Genesee	1941-1946	
Snow, Wilber B.	Comstock, Kalamazoo	1925-1930	
Snow, William T.	Lakeville, Oakland	1850	
Snyder, Joseph M.	St. Clair Shores, Macomb	1963-1974	1975-1978
Snyder, Stephen F.	Marshall, Calhoun	1883-1886	
Sobieski, John M.	Detroit, Wayne	1955-1964	
Sofio, Richard A.	Bessemer, Gogebic	1987-1990	
Somerville, Pat	New Boston, Wayne	2011-2016	
Soper, Julius Mason	Delta, Eaton	1899-1900	
Sorenson, Cleveland	Manistee, Manistee	1931-1932	
Sours, Lowell	Elk Rapids, Antrim	1915-1918	
Southworth, Harry C.	Hancock, Houghton	1889-1890	
Southworth, Tracy Waters	Monroe, Monroe	1931-1934	
Sovereign, Frederick F.	Three Oaks, Berrien		1901-1904
Sowerby, William	Clinton Township, Macomb	2017-	
Spade, Doug	Adrian, Lenawee	1999-2004	
Spade, Dudley	Tipton, Lenawee	2005-2010	
Spafford, Charles	Tecumseh, Lenawee	1838	
Spalding, Erastus	Pontiac, Oakland	1867-1868	
Spaniola, Francis Richard	Corunna, Shiawassee	1975-1990	

Name[2]	Post Office[3]	Session Years[4] House	Senate
Sparks, Gordon R.	Troy, Oakland	1983-1992	
Sparks, Levi	Buchanan, Berrien		1873-1874
Sparling, John	Ubly, Huron	1893-1894	
Spaulding, Phineas S.	Elmira, Eaton	1867-1868	
Speed, John J.	Detroit, Wayne	1873-1874	
Speer, Cameron C.	New Lothrop, Shiawassee	1905-1910	
Spence, Thomas R.	Detroit, Wayne	1867-1868	
Spencer, Asa	Smyrna, Ionia	1863-1864	
Spencer, Edward R.	Dowagiac, Cass	1889-1892	
Spencer, Grove	Ypsilanti, Washtenaw	1840-1841; 1848; 1850	
Spencer, Horace C.	Flint, Genesee		1885-1886
Spencer, James W.	Caro, Tuscola	1887-1888	
Spencer, Michael	Andover, Calhoun	1841	
Spencer, Newton C.	Stephenson, Menominee	1901-1902	
Spencer, Roy L.	Attica, Lapeer	1961-1976	
Spies, James A.	Menominee, Menominee	1941-1942	
Sprague, Paul S.	Nebraska, Shiawassee	1863-1864	
Sprague, Rollin	Rochester, Oakland	1840	
Sprague, William	Clinton, Lenawee	1841	
Sprague, William B.	Coldwater, Branch	1846	
Sproat, Will J.	Grand Rapids, Kent	1913-1914	
St. Aubin, Francis C.	Detroit, Wayne	1855-1856	
St. Clair, Eugene G.	Ishpeming, Marquette	1891-1892	
St. Clair, William M.	Algonac, St. Clair	1849	
St. John, John B.	Plumb Brook, Macomb	1848	
Stabenow, Debbie Ann	Lansing, Ingham	1979-1990	1991-1994
Stacey, Lad S.	Berrien Springs, Berrien	1979-1990	
Stacey, Lionel J.	Benton Harbor, Berrien	1967-1968	
Stackable, Frederick L.	Lansing, Ingham	1971-1974	
Stafford, Henry H.	Marquette, Marquette	1877-1878	
Stahl, John E.	North Branch, Lapeer	2003-2008	
Stahlin, John H.	Belding, Ionia		1959-1962
Stakoe, John P.	Highland, Oakland	2003-2008	
Stallings, Henry Edward, II	Detroit, Wayne		1995-1998
Stallworth, Alma Grace	Detroit, Wayne	1971-1974; 1982-1996; 2003-2004	
Stallworth, Keith B.	Detroit, Wayne	1997-2002	
Stallworth, Thomas F., III	Detroit, Wayne	2011-2014	
Stamas, Jim	Midland, Midland	2009-2014	2015-
Stamas, Tony	Midland, Midland	1999-2002	2003-2010
Stamm, Anthony	Kalamazoo, Kalamazoo		1967-1974
Stanchfield, Oliver O.	Ludington, Mason	1877-1880	
Standart, Joseph Gardner	Detroit, Wayne	1907-1908	
Standish, John H.	Newaygo, Newaygo		1867-1870
Stanislaw, Coleman A.	Dearborn, Wayne	1955-1958	
Stanley, James Benjamin	Kalamazoo, Kalamazoo	1937-1946	
Stanley, Woodrow	Flint, Genesee	2009-2014	
Stannard, Abiel S.	South Boston, Ionia	1867-1870	
Stannard, William Linus	Greenland, Ontonagon	1905-1906	
Stanton, Erastus H.	Ionia, Ionia		1881-1882
Staples, Hiram Edward	Whitehall, Muskegon	1885-1886	
Stapleton, Maureen L.	Detroit, Wayne	2011-2012	
Stark, George P.	Cascade, Kent	1885-1886	1887-1888
Starkey, Lewis F.	Kalamazoo, Kalamazoo		1843-1844
Starkweather, George A.	Plymouth, Wayne	1859-1860	
Starr, H. James	Lansing, Ingham	1965-1966	
Stearns, Benton R.	Galien, Berrien	1879-1880	
Stearns, Wesley J.	Stanton, Montcalm	1917-1920	
Steeh, George C.	Mount Clemens, Macomb	1955-1956	1957-1962
Steeh, Victor R.	Mount Clemens, Macomb	1965-1966	
Steel, George A.	St. Johns, Clinton		1893-1894
Steele, Amos E.	Onondaga, Ingham	1840	
Steele, Frank Nelson	Muskegon, Muskegon	1935-1938	
Steele, George E.	Elk Rapids, Antrim	1877-1878	

Name[2]	Post Office[3]	Session Years[4]	
		House	Senate
Steil, Glenn D.	Grand Rapids, Kent		1994-2002
Steil, Glenn D., Jr.	Grand Rapids, Kent	2003-2008	
Stempien, Marvin R.	Livonia, Wayne	1965-1966; 1969-1972	
Stenson, William C.	Greenland, Ontonagon	1941-1944	
Stephens, Charles E.	Detroit, Wayne	1947-1948	
Stephens, Lloyd A.	Scottville, Mason		1957-1964
Stephens, Rupert, Sr.	Scottville, Mason	1939-1948	
Stephens, William M.	Stockbridge, Ingham	1875-1876	
Stephenson, Robert	Menominee, Menominee	1881-1882	
Stephenson, Samuel Merritt	Menominee, Menominee	1877-1878	1879-1880; 1885-1886
Sterling, Lewis Thomas	Iron Mountain, Dickinson	1909-1910	
Sterling, William C.	Monroe, Monroe	1959-1962	
Stetson, Ezra	Galesburg, Kalamazoo	1851-1852	
Stevens, Amos	South Plymouth, Wayne	1849	
Stevens, Appleton	Portsmouth, Bay	1861-1862	
Stevens, Claude H.	Highland Park, Wayne		1929-1932
Stevens, E. Dan	Atlanta, Montmorency	1975-1978	
Stevens, Fitz H.	Paw Paw, Van Buren		1853-1854
Stevens, Horace	Waterford, Oakland	1845	
Stevens, J. Frank	Star City, Missaukee	1913-1916	
Stevens, J. Harold	Detroit, Wayne	1965-1968	
Stevens, John H. D.	Iron Wood, Gogebic		1891-1892
Stevens, John J.	Monroe, Monroe	1867-1868	
Stevens, Ross O.	Atlanta, Montmorency	1960-1964	
Stevens, Stephen R.	Greenville, Montcalm	1877-1880	
Stevens, William N.	Whitmore Lake, Washtenaw	1861-1862	
Stevenson, John	Detroit, Wayne	1909-1912; 1915-1918; 1921-1924	
Stewart, Albert E.	Detroit, Wayne	1897-1900	
Stewart, Earl Ruthven	Grand Rapids, Kent	1909-1912	
Stewart, Edwin	Mendon, St. Joseph	1861-1866	
Stewart, Hugh A.	Flint, Genesee		1917-1918
Stewart, James	Belleville, Wayne	1869-1870	
Stewart, John C.	Plymouth, Wayne	2001-2006	
Stille, Leon E.	Spring Lake, Ottawa Ferrysburg, Ottawa	1993-1994	1995-2002
Stillson, Eli L.	Battle Creek, Calhoun	1845	
Stinchcomb, Joseph W.	Woodland, Barry	1877-1878	
Stites, Robert C.	Manitou Beach, Lenawee	1967-1970	
Stockbridge, Francis Brown	Saugatuck, Allegan	1869-1870	1871-1872
Stockdale, David	Wayland, Allegan	1905-1908	
Stockfish, Walter N.	Hamtramck, Wayne	1935-1944	
Stockman, Dora H.	East Lansing, Ingham	1939-1946	
Stockton, John	Mount Clemens, Macomb	1840; 1841; 1850	1835-1836
Stoddard, Cameron C.	Fair Grove, Tuscola	1861-1862	
Stoddard, Claude Manuel	Davison, Genesee		1919-1920
Stoddard, Jesse	Cass, Hillsdale	1849	
Stoddard, William R.	Litchfield, Hillsdale	1857-1858	1871-1873
Stoflet, Henry L.	Flat Rock, Wayne	1889-1890	
Stoll, Albert	Detroit, Wayne		1899-1900
Stoll, Harold E.	Detroit, Wayne		1927-1928
Stoll, Otto	Detroit, Wayne	1895-1896	
Stone, Alvah Gardner	Medina, Lenawee	1901-1906	
Stone, Charles W.	Newaygo, Newaygo	1883-1884	
Stone, Clement W.	Houghton Lake, Roscommon	1877-1878	
Stone, Edward L.	Saginaw, Saginaw	1891	
Stone, Hiram	Monroe, Monroe	1844; 1845; 1848	
Stone, Hiram H.	Dearbornville, Wayne	1848	
Stone, Lori	Warren, Macomb	2019-	
Stoneman, Lewis A.	Detroit, Wayne	1897-1898	
Stopczynski, Stanley	Detroit, Wayne	1979-1990	
Stopczynski, Stephen	Detroit, Wayne	1965-1978	
Stopczynski, Thaddeus Casimir	Detroit, Wayne	1973-1980	
Storey, Bert J.	Belding, Ionia	1939-1950	1955-1958

Name[2]	Post Office[3]	Session Years[4] House	Senate
Storrs, Wales Fisher	Coopersville, Ottawa	1867-1868	1871-1872
Stout, Byron Gray	Pontiac, Oakland	1855-1858	1861-1862
	Troy, Oakland		
Stout, David B.	Allegan, Allegan	1839	
Stout, M. Clyde	Ionia, Ionia	1933-1938	
Stout, Stephen S.	Cheshire, Allegan	1889-1890	
Stow, Isaac	Iosco, Livingston	1875	
Stowell, Alexander H.	Detroit, Wayne		1853-1854
Straight, Henry E.	Coldwater, Branch	1909-1912	1913-1916
Strand, John Gregory	Lapeer, Lapeer	1981-1992	
Strang, DeForrest	Sturgis, St. Joseph	1967-1976	
Strang, James J.	St. James, Manitou	1853-1856	
Strange, John B.	Grand Ledge, Eaton	1933-1934	
Strange, Russell H.	Clare, Clare	1957-1970	
	Mount Pleasant, Isabella		
Strauch, William P.	Durand, Shiawassee	1921-1928	
	Vernon, Shiawassee		
Street, Samuel	Niles, Berrien	1850	
Strickland, Randolph	DeWitt, Clinton		1861-1862
Striker, Gilbert	Hastings, Barry	1873-1874	
Strom, Edward B.	Grand Rapids, Kent	1921-1922	
Strong, John	Detroit, Wayne	1835; 1836	
Strong, John, Jr.	South Rockwood, Monroe	1861-1862; 1879	1881-1884
	Greenfield, Wayne		
Strong, Myron	Edwardsburgh, Cass	1841	
Strong, Simeon G.	Gidley's Station, Jackson	1848	
Strong, Sylvester A.	Horton, Jackson	1879-1880; 1893-1894	
Stroud, Alonzo J.	Horton Bay, Charlevoix	1905-1908	
Strowbridge, Oliver P.	Almont, Lapeer	1850	
Struble, John	Volinia, Cass	1875-1876	
Stuart, Charles Edward	Kalamazoo, Kalamazoo	1842	
Stuart, Patrick	Detroit, Wayne	1887-1888	
Stumpenhusen, Henry	Rawsonville, Washtenaw	1899-1902	
Stupak, Bart T.	Menominee, Menominee	1989-1990	
Sturgis, David	DeWitt, Clinton		1851-1852
Sullivan, Frank P.	Sault Saint Marie, Chippewa	1893-1894	
Sullivan, James	Dowagiac, Cass		1855-1856
Sullivan, Richard F.	New Boston, Wayne	1983-1984	
Sumeracki, Adam William	Detroit, Wayne	1939-1944; 1955-1964	
Summers, Jacob	Utica, Macomb	1835-1836	1837-1840; 1849-1850
Sumner, John Dunklee	Kalamazoo, Kalamazoo	1893-1894	
Sumner, John J.	Lambertville, Monroe	1871-1872	1873-1874
Sundstrom, Charles F.	Michigamme, Marquette	1935-1942; 1945-1946	
Suski, Edward	Flint, Genesee	1965-1972	
Sutherland, Jabez Gridley	Saginaw, Saginaw	1853-1854	
Sutherland, James B.	St. Joseph, Berrien	1855-1856	
Sutherland, William	Kawkawlin, Bay	1899-1900	
Sutton, Daniel B.	Ann Arbor, Washtenaw	1913-1916	
Sutton, Edwin	Adamsville, Cass	1857-1858	
Sutton, George	Ann Arbor, Washtenaw	1875-1876	
Sutton, Nathan Esek	Ann Arbor, Washtenaw	1885-1886	
Sutton, William C.	Dearborn, Wayne		1873-1874
Swain, James	Coldwater, Branch	1937-1940	
Swainson, John Burley	Detroit, Wayne		1955-1958
Swallow, Joseph Patrick	Alpena, Alpena	1965-1972	
Sweeney, James H.	Morenci, Lenawee	1846	
Sweetland, John B.	Edwardsburgh, Cass	1875-1876	
Sweezey, James Albert	Hastings, Barry	1863-1864; 1867-1868	
Swift, Alden B.	Kalamo, Eaton	1889-1892	
Swift, George W.	Perrinsville, Wayne	1867-1869	
Swift, John M.	Northville, Wayne	1865	
Swift, Orson	Maple Grove, Barry	1885-1886	
Swift, William F.	Ishpeming, Marquette		1881-1882
Swineford, Alfred P.	Marquette, Marquette	1871-1872	

Name[2]	Post Office[3]	House	Session Years[4]	
			House	Senate
Switalski, Jon M.	Warren, Macomb	2009-2014		
Switalski, Michael N.	Roseville, Macomb	1999-2002		2003-2010
Symonds, Charles D.	Powers, Menominee	1911-1912; 1915-1916		
Symons, Joyce	Allen Park, Wayne	1965-1980		
Tabor, Susan L.	Delta Township, Eaton	1999-2004		
Tacels, Alexander	Romeo, Macomb	1835-1836; 1839		
Tate, Joseph	Detroit, Wayne	2019-		
Tateum, William Aldrich	Grand Rapids, Kent	1893-1894		
Taub, Shelley Goodman	Bloomfield Hills, Oakland	2003-2006		
	Bloomfield Township, Oakland			
Taube, Leo	Detroit, Wayne	1917-1918		
Taylor, Charles H.	Grand Rapids, Kent	1847-1848		
Taylor, Daniel W.	Look's Corners, Lapeer	1845		
Taylor, Edward Bancroft	Port Huron, St. Clair	1895-1896		
Taylor, George E.	Flint, Genesee			1883-1884
Taylor, Henry Wyllys	Marshall, Calhoun	1847		
Taylor, Lorison J.	Laingsburg, Shiawassee	1874-1876		1877-1878
Taylor, Robert L.	Lapeer, Lapeer			1889-1892
Taylor, Thaddeus Blake	Cedar Springs, Kent	1911-1914		
Taylor, Thomas Chalmers	Almont, Lapeer	1889-1890		
Taylor, Walter Ross	Kalamazoo, Kalamazoo			1909-1916
Taylor, William H	Saginaw, Saginaw	1865-1868		
Taylor, William H.	Sparta, Kent	1861-1862		
Taziman, James B.	Howell, Livingston	1899-1900		
Teachout, George Leo	Flint, Genesee	1933-1938		
Teagan, Robert J.	Detroit, Wayne	1927-1932		
Teahen, James M., Jr.	Owosso, Shiawassee			1951-1954
Tedder, Jim	Clarkston, Oakland	2015-2018		
Teeple, George W.	Pinckney, Livingston			1897-1898
Tefft, Henry M.	Spring Arbor, Jackson	1897-1898		
Ten Eyck, Conrad	Dearborn, Wayne	1846		1835-1837
Terbush, Jay Murray, Jr.	Owosso, Shiawassee	1959-1962		
Ternes, Peter	Yew, Wayne	1869-1870		
Terrell, Ethel	Highland Park, Wayne	1979-1990		
Terry, Henry D.	Mount Clemens, Macomb	1848		
Tesanovich, Paul	L'Anse, Baraga	1994-2000		
Thatcher, Frank E.	Ravenna, Muskegon	1891-1892		
Thatcher, T. Thomas	Ravenna, Muskegon	1933-1936		
Thayer, George W.	Flint, Genesee	1863-1866		
Thayer, Nahum P.	Detroit, Wayne	1837		
Thayer, Simeon M.	Minden, Sanilac	1871-1872		
Thayer, Stanley G.	Ann Arbor, Washtenaw			1961-1964
Theis, Lana	Brighton, Livingston	2015-2018		2019-
Thomas, George	Yorkville, Kalamazoo	1859-1860; 1863-1864		1851-1852; 1869-1870
	Gull Lake, Barry			
	Richland, Kalamazoo			
Thomas, Henry Franklin	Allegan, Allegan	1873-1874		1875-1876
Thomas, John	Farmington, Oakland	1846		
Thomas, Leonard R.	Bad Axe, Huron	1903-1908		
Thomas, Samuel Buzz, III	Detroit, Wayne	1997-2002		2003-2010
Thomas, Walter Joseph	Constantine, St. Joseph	1923-1928		
Thomas, William	Hartford, Van Buren	1875-1876		
Thomas, William J.	Cannonsburg, Kent	1925-1932		
Thomas, Zimri D.	Hillsdale, Hillsdale	1865-1866		
Thompson, Albert	South Haven, Van Buren			1875-1876
Thompson, Almon A.	Vermontville, Eaton	1869		
Thompson, Charles C.	Whitehall, Muskegon	1873-1874		
Thompson, George Washington	Grand Rapids, Kent	1883-1884		
Thompson, Henry Wallbridge	Escanaba, Delta	1887-1888		
Thompson, James B.	Niles, Berrien	1893-1894		
Thompson, Jeremiah Deuell	Adrian, Lenawee	1838; 1853-1854		
Thompson, Mark L.	Rogers City, Presque Isle	1973-1974		
Thompson, Robert	New Baltimore, Macomb	1859-1860		
Thompson, Robert R.	Corunna, Shiawassee	1845		

Name[2]	Post Office[3]	House	Session Years[4]
			House	Senate

Name[2]	Post Office[3]	House	Senate
Thompson, Ruth	Muskegon, Muskegon	1939-1940	
Thompson, Stacy C.	Manistee, Manistee	1907-1908	
Thompson, William G.	Detroit, Wayne		1895-1898
Thomson, Edward H.	Flint, Genesee	1859-1860	1848-1849
Thomson, James F.	Parma, Jackson	1929-1930	
Thomson, John S.	Port Sanilac, Sanilac	1877-1880	
Thomson, John W.	Midland, Midland	1935-1936; 1939-1942; 1945-1946	
Thomson, Richard L.	Highland Park, Wayne	1947-1954	
Thorington, Justus	Midland, Midland	1903-1904	
Thorne, William H.	Dearborn, Wayne	1959-1966	
Thorpe, Calvin J.	Sherwood, Branch	1879-1880	
Throop, George B.	Detroit, Wayne	1847	
Thurber, Jefferson G.	Monroe, Monroe	1851-1852	1844-1847
Tibbits, Douglas Deforest	Boyne City, Charlevoix	1933-1940	
Tibbits, John S.	Nankin, Wayne	1861-1862	
Tierney, James T.	Garden City, Wayne	1965-1972	
Tiffany, Alexander R.	Palmyra, Lenawee	1855-1856	
Tiffany, Harlow A.	Chippewa Lake, Mecosta	1905-1908	
Tilden, Junius	Dundee, Monroe	1849	
Tillson, Philo	Mount Clemens, Macomb	1844	
Tindall, Jefferson K.	Davisburg, Oakland	1887-1888	
Tinham, Alexander	Livonia, Wayne	1863-1864; 1883-1884	
Tinklepaugh, Jacob N.	Kalkaska, Kalkaska	1889-1892	
Tinney, Rufus	Highland, Oakland	1841	
Tinsley-Talabi, Alberta	Detroit, Wayne	2011-2016	
Tisdale, Nelson G.	Midland, Midland	1960-1970	
Titus, Albion B.	Kalamazoo, Kalamazoo	1921-1924	
Tlaib, Rashida	Detroit, Wayne	2009-2014	
Toan, William	Portland, Ionia		1899-1902
Tobey, Bracey	Sturgis, St. Joseph	1871-1872	
Tobocman, Steve H.	Detroit, Wayne	2003-2008	
Toepel, Andrew F.	Detroit, Wayne	1917-1920	
Toepp, John F.	Cadillac, Wexford	1963-1964	1967-1978
Toll, Alexander	Mackinac, Mackinac	1853-1854; 1861-1864	
Toll, Isaac DeGraaf	Fawn River, St. Joseph	1846	1847
Tomboulian, Alice W.	Rochester, Oakland	1979-1980	
Tomlin, Mervin Wilford	Port Huron, St. Clair	1935-1938	
Tompkins, James B.	Girard, Branch	1855-1856	
Tompkins, William M.	Eaton Rapids, Eaton	1867-1868	
Tooker, John S.	Lansing, Ingham		1879-1882
Totten, William D.	Kalkaska, Kalkaska	1901-1902	
Tower, Osmond	Ionia, Ionia		1859-1862
Town, Calvin Jay	Parma, Jackson North Adams, Hillsdale Springport, Jackson	1919-1924; 1927-1928	1933-1942
Town, Floyd E.	Jackson, Jackson	1931-1932; 1935-1936; 1939-1949	
Town, Oka	Otsego, Allegan	1851-1852	
Town, William B.	Geneva, Lenawee	1885-1886	
Towne, Amos C.	Gull Lake, Barry	1875-1876	
Towner, Cassius B.	Byron Center, Kent	1905-1908	
Towner, Charles R.	Mount Clemens, Macomb	1963-1964	
Townsend, Emory	Saginaw, Saginaw		1895-1896
Townsend, George H.	Jackson, Jackson	1921-1922	
Townsend, Jim	Royal Oak, Oakland	2011-2016	
Townsend, Roger B.	Flint, Genesee	1953-1964	
Townsend, Uriel	Almont, Lapeer	1875-1876	
Toy, Laura M.	Livonia, Wayne	1999-2002	2003-2006
Trabbic, Flagget H.	Erie, Monroe	1907-1908	
Train, Jarvis Clement	Lowell, Kent	1883-1884	
Traver, Seneca Chamberlain	River Rouge, Wayne		1905-1908
Traver, William R.	Litchfield, Hillsdale	1853-1854	
Traxler, Jerome Rober	Bay City, Bay	1963-1974	

| Name[2] | Post Office[3] | House | Session Years[4] |
			Senate
Treat, Loren L.	Oxford, Oakland		1865-1866
Trembley, M. Bushnell	Flint, Genesee	1947-1948	
Trestrail, Albert H.	Caspian, Iron	1927-1928	
Trezise, R. Douglas	Owosso, Shiawassee	1971-1974	
Trim, Claude A.	Davisburg, Oakland	1975-1980; 1985-1992	
	Waterford, Oakland		
Tripp, Arthur Rollin	Pontiac, Oakland	1891-1894	
Tripp, Burrell	Allegan, Allegan		1915-1918
Tripp, Charles	Ann Arbor, Washtenaw		1855-1856
Tripp, Harold D.	Allegan, Allegan		1943-1950
Trombley, David J.	Detroit, Wayne	1949-1952	
Troutt, Terry L.	Romulus, Wayne		1965-1966
Trowbridge, Rowland Ebenezer	Birmingham, Oakland		1857-1860
Trowbridge, Stephen Van Rensselaer	Birmingham, Oakland		1839-1842
Trucks, Kenneth O.	Baldwin, Lake	1951-1956	
Truesdell, Aaron D.	Bridgewater, Washtenaw	1847; 1851-1852	
Truettner, Walter F.	Bessemer, Gogebic		1923-1928
Tubbs, Charles Walter	Ann Arbor, Washtenaw	1909-1910	
Tucker, True Paoli	St. Clair, St. Clair	1839-1840	
Tufts, Charles A.	Ludington, Mason	1911-1916	1917-1922
Tupper, Myron	South Cass, Ionia	1865-1866	
Turck, William S.	Ithaca, Gratiot	1877-1880	
Turnbull, James D.	Alpena, Alpena	1879-1882	1893-1894
Turner, George B.	Cassopolis, Cass	1848-1849	
Turner, James	Lansing, Ingham		1867-1868
Turner, James Munroe	Lansing, Ingham	1877-1878	
Turner, Jerome E.	Muskegon, Muskegon	1905-1908	
Turner, Jerome W.	Corunna, Shiawassee		1869-1870
Turner, Jesse F.	DeWitt, Clinton		1844-1845
Turner, John W.	Hudson, Lenawee	1847; 1849; 1851-1852	
	Northampton, Saginaw		
Turner, Milo H.	DeWitt, Clinton	1842	
Turner, Reuben D.	Mackinac, Mackinac	1840	
Turner, Stanley W.	Mason, Ingham	1877-1878; 1889-1890	
	Roscommon, Roscommon		
Turner, William F.	Morley, Mecosta	1927-1928	1929-1932
Turrill, James	Lapeer, Lapeer	1849	
Tuttle, Arthur J.	Leslie, Ingham		1907-1910
Tuttle, Warren	Nankin, Wayne	1849	
Twadell, Rodney K.	Quincy, Branch	1877-1880	
Twombly, Royal T.	Niles, Berrien		1853-1854
Tyler, Columbus V.	Bay City, Bay		1877-1880; 1889-1890
Tyler, Comfort	Oporto, St. Joseph	1841	1859-1860
Tyler, Sharon	Niles, Berrien	2009-2012	
Tyrrell, John Edward	Jackson, Jackson	1889-1890	
Ullman, Isaac J.	Constantine, St. Joseph	1835-1836	
Ulrich, Madison J.	Grand Rapids, Kent	1885-1886	
Underwood, Daniel K.	Adrian, Lenawee	1840	
Unsoeld, G. Joseph	Detroit, Wayne	1909-1914	
Upham, Edward W.	Williams, Kalamazoo	1917-1918	
Upjohn, James T.	Kalamazoo, Kalamazoo	1925-1928	1929-1934
Upson, A. I.	Eagle Harbor, Keweenaw		1855-1856
Upson, Charles	Centerville, St. Joseph		1855-1856; 1881-1882
	Coldwater, Branch		
Upton, Daniel	Jackson, Jackson	1867-1868	
Upton, David Frederick	St. Joseph, Berrien	1963-1964	
Upton, William W.	DeWitt, Clinton	1847	
Utley, William Sidney	Big Prairie, Newaygo	1865-1866	
Vagnozzi, Aldo	Farmington Hills, Oakland	2003-2008	
Valade, Joseph L.	Newport, Monroe	1877-1878	
Valenti, Guido D.	Iron Mountain, Dickinson	1949-1950	
Valentine, Mary	Muskegon, Muskegon	2007-2010	
Van Aken, George W.	Coldwater, Branch	1873-1876	
Van Akin, Simeon	Ida, Monroe		1903-1906

Name[2]	Post Office[3]	Session Years[4] House	Senate
Van Antwerp, Herbert Adelbert	Rockford, Kent.....................................	1915-1916	
Van Brocklin, John Franklin	Marquette, Marquette.........................	1929-1932	
Van Camp, Saunders Leroy.................	Benton Harbor, Berrien	1897-1900	
Van Dusen, Lawrence........................	Owosso, Shiawassee...........................	1883-1884	
Van Duser, Zachariah........................	Adams, Hillsdale 1847		
Van Eenenaam, Gordon F.	Muskegon, Muskegon		1929-1936
Van Every, Peter	Hamtramck, Wayne............................	1835-1836	
Van Husen, Caleb	Saline, Washtenaw...............................1844		
Van Keuren, Charles..........................	Howell, Livingston..............................	1905-1906	
Van Kleeck, James............................	Midland City, Midland	1883-1884	
Van Loo, Cornelius	Zeeland, Ottawa	1881-1884	
Van Orthwick, Aaron A.	Quincy, Branch	1887-1890	
Van Peursem, George M.	Zeeland, Ottawa	1951-1959	
Van Raalte, Dirk B. K.	Holland, Ottawa 1875-1878; 1909-1910		
Van Regenmorter, William.................	Jenison, Ottawa 1983-1990; 2003-2006		1991-2002
	Georgetown Township, Ottawa		
Van Scoy, Rowland S.	Maple Rapids, Clinton	1871-1874	
Van Singel, Donald............................	Grant, Newaygo	1973-1992	
Van Valkenburg, Wade	Kalamazoo, Kalamazoo......................	1947-1956	
Van Vleet, James	Gaines Station, Genesee......................	1865-1868	
Van Woerkom, Gerald........................	Muskegon, Muskegon	1999-2002	2003-2010
Van Zoeren, Jacob J.	Grand Rapids, Kent	1901-1904	
Vance, Henry	Saginaw, Saginaw	1905-1906	
Vandenberg, William C.	Holland, Ottawa		1945-1950
Vandenboom, Frank H.	Marquette, Marquette.........................		1919-1922
Vander Jagt, Guy	Cadillac, Wexford..............................		1965-1966
Vander Roest, Jerry............................	Charleston Township, Kalamazoo	1999-2002	
Vander Veen, Barb	Allendale, Ottawa	2001-2006	
Vander Veen, Harry...........................	Grand Rapids, Kent	1907-1910	
Vander Werp, Don	Fremont, Newaygo................... 1933-1934;1961-1964		1935-1956
Vandercook, Henry B.	Grand Rapids, Kent	1901-1904	
VanderLaan, Robert	Grand Rapids, Kent		1963-1982
Vanderploeg, Jan B.	North Muskegon, Muskegon		1965-1966
VanderWall, Curt..............................	Ludington, Mason ....2017-2018..........................		2019-
Vanderwerp, John	Muskegon, Muskegon		1911-1912; 1939-1940
VanDusen, Richard C.	Birmingham, Oakland.........................	1954-1956	
Vanek, Gary M.	Royal Oak, Oakland	1978-1980	
VanEvery, Albert E............................	Petoskey, Emmet	1925-1926	
VanSingel, Scott	Grant, Newaygo	2017-	
VanTil, Riemer	Holland, Ottawa	1959-1964	
VanWoerkom, Greg...........................	Norton Shores, Muskegon....................	2019-	
Varga, Ilona	Detroit, Wayne	1987-1998	
Varnum, Charles H.	Manistique, Schoolcraft......................	1967-1980	
Vaughan, Coleman C.	St. Johns, Clinton		1903-1904; 1911-1912
Vaughn, Edward................................	Detroit, Wayne 1979-1980; 1995-2000		
Vaughn, Jackie, III	Detroit, Wayne .... 1967-1978..........................		1978-2002
Vaughn, James C.	Rawsonville, Wayne............................1843		
Vaupel, Henry	Fowlerville, Livingston.......................	2015-	
Vear, Steve.......................................	Hillsdale, Hillsdale	1999-2002	
Veenfleet, George F.	Frostville, Saginaw.............................	1879-1880	
Verdier, Leonard D.	Grand Rapids, Kent	1909-1912	1913-1916
VerHeulen, Rob	Walker, Kent....................................	2013-2018	
Vickary, Walter................................	Ishpeming, Marquette.........................	1887-1888	
Vickery, Stephen	Schoolcraft, Kalamazoo.............. 1838; 1843-1845; 1848		
Victory, Roger	Hudsonville, Ottawa ....2013-2018..........................		2019-
Videto, James	Spring Arbor, Jackson	1842-1844	1845-1846
Vincent, Edward................................	Port Huron, St. Clair..........................	1883-1884	
Vine, John R.	Weston, Lenawee................................	1915-1922	
Vinton, David, Jr.	Williamsburg, Grand Traverse	1883-1884	
Volkema, Harold J.	Holland, Ottawa		1965-1967
Voorhees, Emory B.	Ovid, Clinton	1885-1886	
Voorhees, Harold J.	Wyoming, Kent	1993-1998	
Voorhees, Joanne..............................	Wyoming, Kent	1999-2004	
Voorhees, Vern	Albion, Calhoun	1933-1934	

Name[2]	Post Office[3]	House	Session Years[4] Senate
Voorheis, Hiram	New Canandaigua, Oakland	1851-1852	
Voorheis, Isaac I.	Pontiac, Oakland	1835-1836; 1848	
Voorheis, Peter	Pontiac, Oakland	1895-1896	
Voorheis, Sebring	White Lake, Oakland	1863-1864	
Vorva, Jerry	Plymouth, Wayne	1993-1994	
Vought, Dewitt	Alma, Gratiot	1897-1898	
Vowles, George	New Hudson, Oakland	1869-1870	
Vroman, John J.	Belden, Wayne	1887-1888	
Wachtel, Philip B.	Petoskey, Emmet	1893-1894	
Wade, Cerrel Blakely	Brooklyn, Jackson	1861-1862	
Wade, Frank B.	Flint, Genesee	1927-1932	
Wade, Fred	Saugatuck, Allegan	1921-1926; 1929-1932	
Wade, Silas A.	Florida, Hillsdale	1857-1858	
Wade, Theodosius	Fennville, Allegan	1901-1904	
Wadhams, Ralph	Port Huron, St. Clair	1838	
Wagar, Edgar Shaw	Edmore, Montcalm	1893-1896	1897-1900
Wagner, Albert A.	Mount Clemens, Macomb	1935-1936	
Wagner, Floyd E.	Cassopolis, Cass	1959-1966	
Wagner, George	Marquette, Marquette	1889-1894	
Wagner, John	East Le Roy, Calhoun	1869-1870	
Wagner, Leo Pierre	Saginaw, Saginaw	1917-1918	
Wagner, Matthew D.	Sand Beach, Huron		1897-1900
Wait, Jonathan G.	Sturgis, St. Joseph	1851-1852	1863-1868
Waite, Benjamin W.	Scio, Washtenaw	1849	
Waite, Byron S.	Menominee, Menominee	1889-1890; 1895-1896	
Wakefield, Daniel B.	Grand Blanc, Genesee Springfield, Oakland	1838	1842-1843
Wakeman, Marcus	Jackson, Jackson	1846	
Wakeman, Rodney	Saginaw Township, Saginaw	2019-	
Walberg, Tim	Tipton, Lenawee	1983-1998	
Walbridge, David Safford	Kalamazoo, Kalamazoo		1849-1850
Waldo, Campbell	Albion, Calhoun		1848-1849
Waldo, George H.	Detroit, Wayne	1895-1896	
Waldron, Henry	Hillsdale, Hillsdale	1843	
Waldron, Robert Edwin	Grosse Pointe, Wayne	1955-1970	
Wales, Gilbert L.	Stambaugh, Iron	1955-1964	
Walker, Adam W.	West Bay City, Bay Bay City, Bay	1905-1908	
Walker, Arnold	Leslie, Ingham	1873-1874	
Walker, Benjamin	Perry, Shiawassee	1873	
Walker, Charles Irish	Grand Rapids, Kent	1841	
Walker, Cyrus A.	Kalamazoo, Kalamazoo	1909-1912	
Walker, Dewitt C.	Romeo, Macomb	1840; 1844; 1846	1841-1842
Walker, Edward A.	Montrose, Genesee	1901-1904	
Walker, Edward C.	Detroit, Wayne	1867-1868	
Walker, Frederick	Mount Morris, Genesee	1872-1874	
Walker, Henry N.	Detroit, Wayne	1844	
Walker, Henry T.	Summit, Washtenaw	1842; 1845	
Walker, Howard C.	Traverse City, Grand Traverse	2003-2008	2011-2014
Walker, James B.	Benzonia, Benzie		1865-1866
Walker, John	Cooper, Kalamazoo	1869-1874	
Walker, Levi	Flint, Genesee	1873	
Walker, Samuel S.	St. Johns, Clinton	1875-1876	
Walker, Sylvester	Cambridge, Lenawee	1847	
Walkinshaw, James	Marshall, Calhoun	1877-1878	
Wallace, John B.	Dearbornville, Wayne	1859-1860	
Wallace, Robert C.	Grant, Newaygo	1903-1906	
Wallace, Robert N.	Bay Port, Huron	1919-1920	
Wallace, Ted	Detroit, Wayne	1988-1998	
Wallin, Franklin B.	Saugatuck, Allegan	1861-1862	
Walsh, Edward John	Detroit, Wayne	1933-1944	
Walsh, John J.	Livonia, Wayne	2009-2014	
Walsh, Patrick	Detroit, Wayne		1949-1954
Walter, Robert E.	Traverse City, Grand Traverse		1911-1916

Name[2]	Post Office[3]	House	Senate
			Session Years[4]
Walters, William G.	Detroit, Wayne	1925-1928	
Walthew, George W.	Detroit, Wayne	1885-1886	
Walton, Andrew	Bay City, Bay	1875-1876; 1879-1880	
Walton, Jacob	Adrian, Lenawee	1869-1874	
Walton, Leonard S.	Detroit, Wayne	1963-1972	
Waltz, Joseph	Waltz, Wayne	1879-1880; 1885-1886	
Ward, Arthur N.	Mount Pleasant, Isabella	1917-1920	
Ward, Charles A.	Ann Arbor, Washtenaw		1899-1900
Ward, Charles E.	Bancroft, Shiawassee	1903-1908	
Ward, Chris	Brighton, Livingston	2003-2008	
Ward, Edgar B.	Laingsburg, Shiawassee	1869-1870	
Ward, George A.	Brant, Saginaw	1911-1912; 1915-1916	
Ward, Lyman M.	Benton Harbor, Berrien	1879-1882	
Ward, Newton O.	Stanwood, Mecosta	1901-1904	1909-1912
Ward, Robert E.	Berrien, Berrien	1837	
Ward, William A.	Nessen City, Grand Traverse	1929-1937	
	Thompsonville, Grand Traverse		
Ward, Zael	Belle River, St. Clair	1855-1856	
Wardell, Robert D.	Detroit, Wayne	1923-1924; 1927-1932	
Ware, Joseph Bruff	Grand Rapids, Kent	1895-1896	
Waring, Guernsey P.	Ridgeway, Lenawee	1881-1882	
Warner, Dale	Eaton Rapids, Eaton	1967-1974	
Warner, Dwight G. F.	Frankfort, Benzie	1909-1914	
Warner, Ebenezer A.	Sault Saint Marie, Chippewa	1859-1862	
Warner, Edward A.	Coldwater, Branch		1842-1843
Warner, Fred Lee	Belding, Ionia	1915-1922	
Warner, Fred Maltby	Farmington, Oakland		1895-1898
Warner, James F.	Ypsilanti, Washtenaw	1957-1964	
Warner, Joseph Edwin	Ypsilanti, Washtenaw	1921-1930; 1937-1956	
Warner, P. Dean	Farmington, Oakland	1851-1852; 1865-1868	1869-1870
Warner, William	Dexter, Washtenaw	1851-1852	
Warner, William	Detroit, Wayne	1863-1864; 1867-1868	
Warner, William E.	Rawsonville, Wayne	1853-1854	1859-1860; 1863-1864
Warren, Asa K.	Olivet, Eaton	1873-1874	1875-1876
Warren, Rebekah	Ann Arbor, Washtenaw	2007-2010; 2019-	2011-2018
Warren, Robert L.	Decatur, Van Buren	1883-1884	
Warren, Samuel N.	Fenton, Genesee	1848	
Warren, Stephen H.	Eureka, Montcalm		1857-1858
Wartner, Paul	Portage, Kalamazoo	1983-1990	1991-1994
Washburn, Norman B.	Adrian, Lenawee	1887-1888	
Washer, John	West Bay City, Bay	1897-1898; 1903-1904	
Waterbury, I. Roy	Highland Station, Oakland	1899-1902	1903-1904
Waterbury, John C.	Lexington, Sanilac	1861-1862	1871-1872; 1877-1878
Waters, Arthur J.	Manchester, Washtenaw	1905-1908	
Waters, Charles H.	Saginaw, Saginaw	1907-1912	
Waters, Mary D.	Detroit, Wayne	2001-2006	
Watkins, Charles W.	Wayland, Allegan	1871-1873	
Watkins, Erwin C.	Rockford, Kent	1873-1876	
Watkins, Frank B.	Hopkins, Allegan	1909-1910	
Watkins, Fred E.	Pontiac, Oakland	1933-1934	
Watkins, Freeman C.	Brooklyn, Jackson	1851-1852	
Watkins, Juanita	Detroit, Wayne	1979-1990	
Watkins, Lucius Whitney	Manchester, Washtenaw		1909-1912
Watkins, Milton C.	Ashley, Kent	1859-1860	1863-1866
	Grattan, Kent		
Watkins, Roy Milton	Grand Rapids, Kent	1915-1916	1919-1920
Watson, Bernice M.	Flint, Genesee	1947-1948	
Watson, Frank H.	Owosso, Shiawassee	1887-1888	
Watson, George C.	Capac, St. Clair	1923-1938	
Watson, George Crittenden	Caro, Tuscola	1893-1894	
Watson, Henry	Greenville, Montcalm	1885-1890	
Watson, Joseph E.	Bronson, Branch	1919-1924	1925-1928
Watt, J. Clyde	Saranac, Ionia	1905-1908	
Watters, Mathew H.	Ishpeming, Marquette	1899-1900	

Name[2]	Post Office[3]	House	Session Years[4] Senate
Watts, John W.	Jackson, Jackson	1887-1892	1895
Wayne, Duncan Anderson	Bradford, Midland	1905-1908	
	Gordonville, Midland		
Weadock, George Leo	Saginaw, Saginaw		1913-1914
Weadock, George W., II	Saginaw, Saginaw		1937-1938
Weatherby, Charles W.	Gilead, Branch	1861-1864	
	Bronson, Branch		
Webb, Dwight	Ann Arbor, Washtenaw		1849-1850
Webb, Nathan	Ypsilanti, Washtenaw		1861-1862
Webb, Wilfred D.	Hazel Park, Oakland	1982-1984; 1987-1992	
Webber, Andrew J.	Ionia, Ionia	1885-1888	
Webber, Michael	Rochester Hills, Oakland	2015-	
Webber, William L.	East Saginaw, Saginaw		1875-1876
Weber, William V.	Kalamazoo, Kalamazoo	1967-1972	
Webster, Alanson J.	Pontiac, Oakland	1871-1872	
Webster, James	Groveland, Oakland	1846	
Wedge, Stanley E.	Coldwater, Branch	1941-1944	
Weeks, Augustus W.	Lowell, Kent	1893-1896	1901-1904
Weeks, Lloyd "Pete" F.	Warren, Macomb	1983-1994	
Weideman, Arnold Joseph	Mount Pleasant, Isabella	1937-1938	
Weidenfeller, Charles A.	Bloomingdale, Van Buren	1913-1914; 1919-1920	
	Kalamazoo, Kalamazoo		
Weier, August John	Monroe, Monroe	1897-1900	
Weier, Joseph	Monroe, Monroe	1869-1870	
Weir, James Douglas	Detroit, Wayne		1879-1880
Weiss, Henry A.	Elm Hall, Gratiot	1885-1886	
Weiss, Joseph M.	Detroit, Wayne	1907-1908	1891-1894
Weissert, Charles A.	Hastings, Barry	1915-1918	
Welborn, Jack	Kalamazoo, Kalamazoo	1973-1974	1974-1982; 1985-1994
Welborn, Robert A.	Kalamazoo, Kalamazoo	1974-1982	1983-1985
Welch, Henry B.	Monroe, Monroe	1873-1874	
Welch, John	East Saginaw, Saginaw		1881-1882
Welch, John B.	Ionia, Ionia	1863-1866	
Welch, Lewis	Exeter, Monroe		1857-1860
Weld, Washington	Centerville, St. Joseph	1843	
Welker, Erastus J.	Kinderhook, Branch	1873-1874; 1877-1878	
Welles, Marshall M.	Kensington, Oakland	1850	
Wellman, Charles	Port Huron, St. Clair	1885-1888	
Wellman, Homer E.	Mancelona, Antrim	1913-1914	
Wells, Frank C.	Warren, Macomb	1899-1900	
Wells, Fred B.	Cassopolis, Cass	1915-1926	
	Dowagiac, Cass		
Wells, Frederick L.	Port Huron, St. Clair	1871-1872	1873-1876
Wells, Hayes E.	Charlotte, Eaton	1925-1926	
Wells, Henry B.	Dowagiac, Cass	1867-1868	
Wells, Henry H.	Detroit, Wayne	1855	
Wells, John Tyler	Detroit, Wayne	1889-1890	
Wells, Thomas M.	Negaunee, Marquette	1903-1904	
Wells, William P.	Detroit, Wayne	1865-1866	
Welsh, George Wilson	Grand Rapids, Kent	1917-1924	
Welsh, Stanton	St. Clair Shores, Macomb	1939-1940	
Wendell, George T.	Mackinac, Mackinac	1857-1860	
Wendell, Jacob A. T.	Mackinac, Mackinac	1855-1856; 1865-1866; 1869-1870	
Wendell, John A.	Rose, Oakland	1842	
Wendell, W. Worth	Northville, Wayne	1891-1892	
Wendzel, Pauline	Watervliet, Berrien	2019-	
Wenke, Lorence R.	Richland, Kalamazoo	2003-2008	
Wenting, Peter	Muskegon, Muskegon	1913-1914	
Wentworth, Jason	Clare, Clare	2017-	
Werline, Gideon T.	Nadeau, Menominee	1903-1904	
Werner, Harry B.	LeRoy, Osceola	1949-1954	
Wesselius, Sybrant	Grand Rapids, Kent		1889-1890
Wesson, William Bingham	Detroit, Wayne		1873-1874

Name[2]	Post Office[3]	House	Session Years[4] Senate
West, Daniel W.	Detroit, Wayne	1963-1964	
West, Thomas J.	Coloma, Berrien	1873-1876	
Westcott, Charles Henry	St. Clair, St. Clair		1897-1898
Westcott, Frank	Vernon, Shiawassee	1895-1896	
Westgate, Ansel W.	Cheboygan, Cheboygan		1887-1888
Westover, Frank L.	Bay City, Bay		1901-1904
Westover, Luther	Bay City, Bay	1869-1870	
Weter, James E.	Richmond, Macomb	1899-1902	1909-1912
Wetherbee, Hezekiah	Three Rivers, St. Joseph	1857-1858	
Wetherbee, William H.	Detroit, Wayne	1897-1898	
Wetmore, Fred C.	Cadillac, Wexford		1907-1910
Wetters, Howard	Kawkawlin, Bay	1993-1998	
Wettlaufer, August F.	Detroit, Wayne	1889-1890	
Weza, Isadore A.	Ontonagon, Ontonagon	1937-1940	
Wheaton, William Wallace	Detroit, Wayne	1889-1890	
Wheeler, A. Oren	Manistee, Manistee		1891-1892; 1895-1896
Wheeler, Amos R.	Benona, Oceana	1873-1876	
Wheeler, Calvin	Summit, Washtenaw	1851-1852	
Wheeler, Charles P.	Three Rivers, St. Joseph	1901-1902	
Wheeler, Elmer G.	Davison, Genesee	1909-1912	
Wheeler, George S.	Salem, Washtenaw	1899-1900	
Wheeler, Harrison H.	Wenona, Bay		1871-1874
Wheeler, Isaac P.	Pulaski, Jackson	1875-1876	
Wheeler, James	Tecumseh, Lenawee	1835-1836	
Wheeler, Lycurgus J.	Nashville, Barry	1883-1884	
Wheeler, Neil	Shelby, Oceana	1935-1938	
Wheeler, William	Flowerfield, St. Joseph	1861-1864	
Whelan, Bion	Hillsdale, Hillsdale	1913-1914	
Whelan, John Jeffers	Vernon, Shiawassee	1909-1912	
Whelan, Nicholas J.	Holland, Ottawa	1903-1908	
Whinery, Thomas J.	Grand Rapids, Kent	1943-1944; 1947-1948; 1951-1964	
Whipple, Charles W.	Detroit, Wayne	1835-1837	
Whitaker, Byron C.	Dexter, Washtenaw	1901-1904	
White, Arthur Scott	Grand Rapids, Kent	1891-1894	
White, Charles E.	Niles, Berrien		1909-1912
White, Charline	Detroit, Wayne	1951-1959	
White, Darwin O.	Southfield, Oakland	1869-1872	
White, Frank G.	Calumet, Houghton		1871-1872
White, Fred J.	Detroit, Wayne	1919-1920	
White, George H.	Grand Rapids, Kent	1863-1864	
White, Harry Clark	Grand Rapids, Kent		1917-1918
White, Horace Alton	Detroit, Wayne	1941-1942	
White, Jacob W.	Clio, Genesee	1889-1890	
White, James Ezra	Pentwater, Oceana	1881-1884	
White, James H.	Port Huron, St. Clair	1879-1882	
White, Jonathan R.	Lapeer, Lapeer	1855-1856	
White, Oliver K.	New Era, Oceana	1877-1878	
White, Orrin	Ann Arbor, Washtenaw	1842	
White, Peter	Marquette, Marquette	1857-1858	1875-1876
White, Shubael F.	Ludington, Mason		1883-1884
White, Thomas	Ann Arbor, Washtenaw	1867-1868	
White, Thomas W.	Detroit, Wayne	1965-1968	
White, Thomas W.	Grand Haven, Ottawa	1844	
White, William E.	Wayland, Allegan	1865-1866	
Whiteford, Mary	Caso Township, Allegan Plainwell, Allegan	2016-	
Whiteley, Harry H.	Millersburg, Presque Isle Dowagiac, Cass	1915-1916	1923-1926
Whiting, Justin Rice	St. Clair, St. Clair		1883-1884
Whitmer, Gretchen	East Lansing, Ingham	2001-2006	2006-2014
Whitmore, Ezra W.	Ann Arbor, Washtenaw	1855-1856	
Whitney, Charles E.	Muskegon Heights, Muskegon	1897-1900	
Whitney, Joseph Herbert	Merrill, Saginaw	1895-1896	1907-1910

Name[2]	Post Office[3]	Session Years[4] House	Senate
Whitney, Luther D.	Hadley, Lapeer	1857-1858	
Whitney, Nathan	Trent, Muskegon	1875-1876	
Whitney, Thomas	East Saginaw, Saginaw		1857-1858
Whitsett, Karen	Detroit, Wayne	2019-	
Whyman, Deborah	Canton Township, Wayne	1993-1998	
Wickman, Arthur H.	Carney, Menominee	1939-1940	
Wickstrom, John C.	Norway, Dickinson		1935-1938
Widoe, John F.	Hart, Oceana	1897-1898	
Wieland, Frederick	Orion, Oakland	1913-1916	
Wierzbicki, Frank V.	Detroit, Wayne	1967-1980	
Wiggins, Milan D.	Bloomingdale, Van Buren	1889-1892	1911-1914
Wiggins, William H.	Adrian, Lenawee	1885-1886	
Wight, Buckminster	Detroit, Wayne		1855-1856
Wight, Stanley G.	Detroit, Wayne	1863-1864	
Wilber, Mark D.	Allegan, Allegan		1873-1874
Wilbur, Charles A.	Howell, Livingston	1855-1856	
Wilcox, Albert	Cambridge, Lenawee	1841	
Wilcox, Elliot R.	Pontiac, Oakland Rochester, Oakland	1869-1870	1877-1878
Wilcox, James M.	Calumet, Houghton Ontonagon, Ontonagon	1913-1914	1917-1928
Wilcox, Marcus	Corunna, Shiawassee		1891-1892
Wilcox, Marcus B.	Pinckney, Livingston		1857-1858
Wilcox, William S.	Adrian, Lenawee	1865-1868	1871-1872
Wilder, Daniel G.	Watrousville, Tuscola		1861-1862
Wildey, Edwin A.	Paw Paw, Van Buren	1893-1896	
Wiley, David W.	Douglas, Allegan	1875-1876	
Wiley, Jefferson	Detroit, Wayne	1867-1868	
Wiley, Merlin	Sault Saint Marie, Chippewa	1915-1920	
Wilk, Theodore J.	Detroit, Wayne	1949-1954	
Wilke, Albert J.	Iron Mountain, Dickinson		1949-1950
Wilkerson, Alfred	Dundee, Monroe	1859-1860	
Wilkins, Samuel M.	Eaton Rapids, Eaton	1879-1882	1893-1894
Wilkinson, Daniel S.	Adrian, Lenawee	1849	
Wilkinson, Robert R.	Eastport, Antrim		1891-1892
Wilkowski, Anthony J.	Detroit, Wayne		1933-1938; 1945-1946; 1949-1950
Wilkowski, Leo Joseph	Detroit, Wayne		1939-1944
Willard, George	Battle Creek, Calhoun	1867-1868	
Willard, Karen S.	Clay Township, St. Clair	1993-1998	
Willard, William, Jr.	Ontonagon, Ontonagon		1869-1870
Willett, A. Milan	Muir, Ionia	1881-1884	
Willett, John	Flint, Genesee	1877-1880	
Williams, Anthony	Attica, Lapeer	1883-1884	
Williams, Asa	Lima, Washtenaw	1845	
Williams, Buel M.	Lawrence, Van Buren	1863-1866	
Williams, Cleveland Dodge	Charlotte, Eaton	1935-1942	
Williams, Carl M.	Saginaw, Saginaw	2001-2006	
Williams, Charles W.	Kassan, Leelanau	1889-1890	
Williams, Edwin R.	Ionia, Ionia	1885-1886	
Williams, Edwin S.	Niles, Berrien	1895-1898	
Williams, Fitch R.	Elk Rapids, Antrim		1877-1878
Williams, Frank Donald	Detroit, Wayne	1953-1960	
Williams, Gardner D.	Saginaw, Saginaw	1835-1836; 1840	1845-1846
Williams, George	Calumet, Houghton		1915-1916
Williams, Harvey	Charlotte, Eaton		1859-1860
Williams, Hubert G.	Marquette, Marquette	1869	
Williams, James A.	Quincy, Branch	1869-1872	
Williams, Jeremiah D.	Dexter, Washtenaw	1855-1856	
Williams, John M.	North Adams, Hillsdale	1929-1930	
Williams, Joseph R.	Constantine, St. Joseph		1861
Williams, Philip John	Detroit, Wayne	1947-1948	
Williams, Theodore	Detroit, Wayne	1838	
Williams, Thomas H.	Jackson, Jackson	1887-1888	

Name[2]	Post Office[3]	House	Session Years[4] Senate
Williams, Walter W.	Eaton Rapids, Eaton	1887-1890	
Williams, William Brewster	Allegan, Allegan		1867-1870
Williams, William D.	Ontonagon, Ontonagon	1869-1870	
Williams, Zebulon	Rolland, Hillsdale	1848	
Willis, George W.	Bay City, Bay	1901-1902	
Willis, Mark	Applegate, Sanilac	1901-1904	
Willison, Frank Leslie	Climax, Kalamazoo		1917-1918
Willits, Baron B.	Jonesville, Hillsdale	1841; 1865-1866	
	Hillsdale, Hillsdale		
Willits, Warren J.	Three Rivers, St. Joseph		1887-1888
Willitts, George E.	Marshall, Calhoun	1907-1908	
Willoughby, George	Clyde , Oakland	1909-1912	
Willoughby, L. Jean	Bloomfield Hills, Oakland	1981-1982	
Wilson, Dana F.	Hazel Park, Oakland	1977-1982	1982
Wilson, Farwell A.	Harrison, Clare	1887-1888	
Wilson, James M.	Kalamazoo, Kalamazoo	1929-1936	
Wilson, Jeremiah C.	Rochester, Oakland	1867-1868	
Wilson, John B.	Lapeer, Lapeer	1861-1864	
Wilson, Louis T. N.	Coldwater, Branch		1855-1856
Wilson, Philo	Medina, Lenawee	1842; 1850	
Wilson, Robert S.	Ann Arbor, Washtenaw		1843-1844
Wilson, Thomas M.	New Baltimore, Macomb	1861-1862; 1875-1876	
Wilson, William B.	Muskegon, Muskegon	1885-1886	
Wiltse, Jacob M.	Frost, Saginaw	1883-1884	
Winans, Edwin Baruch	Hamburg, Livingston	1861-1864	
Winchell, Amaziah	Ingham, Ingham	1850	
Winchell, Jerome	Plainwell, Allegan	1877-1878	
Winegar, Charles T.	Iron Mountain, Dickinson		1913-1914
Wing, Austin E.	Monroe, Monroe	1842	
Wing, Giles M.	Manistee, Manistee	1881-1882	
Wing, Myron	Hickory Corners, Barry	1897-1900	
Wing, Warner	Monroe, Monroe	1837	1838-1839
Wing, Washington	Howell, Livingston	1846	
Winsor, Richard	Port Austin, Huron	1863-1866	1869-1870; 1881-1882
	Huron City, Huron		
Winters, James	Pine Creek, Calhoun	1853-1854	
Wismer, Donald M., Jr.	Port Huron, St. Clair	1963-1964	
Wisner, Chauncey W.	Saginaw, Saginaw	1893-1894	1887-1891
Wisner, George W.	Pontiac, Oakland	1837	
Wisti, Andrew H.	Chassell, Houghton	1959-1960	
Witherbee, Elijah B.	Flint, Genesee		1847
Witherell, Benjamin Franklin Hawkins	Detroit, Wayne		1840-1841
Withey, Solomon L.	Grand Rapids, Kent		1861-1862
Withington, William Herbert	Jackson, Jackson	1873-1874	1891-1892
Wittenberg, Robert	Oak Park, Oakland	2015-	
Witwer, Angela	Delta Township, Eaton	2019-	
Wixom, Isaac	Farmington, Oakland	1838; 1839	1842-1843
Wixson, Daniel	Lexington, Sanilac	1859-1860; 1873-1874	
Wixson, Joshua	Lexington, Sanilac	1883-1884	
Wojcik, Louis F.	Detroit, Wayne	1927-1928	
Wojno, Lisa	Warren, Macomb	2003-2008	
Wojno, Paul J.	Warren, Macomb	1997-2002	2019-
Wolcott, Grove Henry	Jackson, Jackson	1881-1882	
Wolcott, L. J.	Albion, Calhoun	1911-1916	
Wolpe, Howard Eliot	Kalamazoo, Kalamazoo	1973-1976	
Wolter, Theodore Mathew	Detroit, Wayne	1895-1896	
Womack, Jimmy	Detroit, Wayne	2009-2012	
Wood, Alfred B.	East Saginaw, Saginaw		1869-1872
Wood, Arthur E.	Detroit, Wayne	1923-1924	
Wood, Arthur E.	Detroit, Wayne	1917-1918	1919-1932; 1935-1936; 1943-1944; 1947-1948
Wood, Charles M.	Pinckney, Livingston		1875-1876
Wood, Edwin Kleber	Stanton, Montcalm	1885-1886	
Wood, Emory J.	Jackson, Jackson	1909-1916	

Name[2]	Post Office[3]	Session Years[4] House	Senate
Wood, Henry L.	St. Louis, Gratiot	1887-1890; 1899-1900	
Wood, James C.	Jackson, Jackson	1875-1878	
Wood, James C.	Manistique, Schoolcraft		1913-1918
Wood, John F.	Manistique, Schoolcraft	1951-1954	
Wood, Leonard E.	Detroit, Wayne	1953-1956	
Wood, Lucian Eby	Pokagon, Cass	1895-1896	
Wood, Stephen R.	Sault Saint Marie, Chippewa	1841	
Wood, Thomas	Saline, Washtenaw	1845	
Woodard, David A.	Milan, Monroe	1869-1870	
Woodbridge, William	Detroit, Wayne		1838-1839
Woodbury, James H.	Adrian, Lenawee	1842	
Woodman, Blair G.	Owosso, Shiawassee	1965-1968	
Woodman, Jason	Paw Paw, Van Buren		1903-1906
Woodman, Jonathan J.	Paw Paw, Van Buren	1861-1872	
Woodruff, Albert N.	Watervliet, Berrien	1885-1886	
Woodruff, Ari E.	Wyandotte, Wayne	1893-1896; 1907-1912	
Woodruff, Ari Harrison	Wyandotte, Wayne Ford, Wayne	1915-1924	1925-1932
Woodruff, Edwin W.	Winn, Isabella	1899-1900	
Woodruff, Henry	Farwell, Clare	1881-1884	1885-1886
Woodruff, Newton R.	Watervliet, Berrien	1865-1866	
Woodward, David T.	Madison Heights, Oakland	1999-2004	
Woodward, Hiel	Brooklyn, Jackson	1865-1868	1869-1870
Woodward, Lysander	Rochester, Oakland	1861-1862	
Woodworth, Fred Langdon	Caseville, Huron	1909-1912	1913-1916
Woodworth, John D.	Leslie, Ingham	1863-1866	
Woodworth, Thomas B.	Caseville, Huron	1877-1878	
Woolley, Delbert Ernest	Flint, Genesee	1927-1928	
Woolnough, Walter Waters	Battle Creek, Calhoun	1859-1860	
Worden, Ananias	Montcalm, Ionia	1848	
Worden, Robert	Hudson, Lenawee	1853-1854	
Woronchak, Gary	Dearborn, Wayne	1999-2004	
Wortley, Jabez B.	Ypsilanti, Washtenaw	1895-1896	
Wozniak, Chester	Hamtramck, Wayne	1953-1962, 1991-1992	
Wozniak, Douglas	Shelby Township, Macomb	2019-	
Wreford, William Baxter	Detroit, Wayne	1931-1932	
Wright, Charles R.	St. James, Manitou	1861-1862	
Wright, David A.	Taylorville, Oakland Austin, Oakland	1849	1853-1854
Wright, George S.	Milan, Washtenaw	1915-1916	
Wright, Hamilton Mercer	Bay City, Bay	1883-1886	
Wright, Henry D.	Broomfield, Isabella	1901-1904	
Wright, Horatio	Austin, Oakland	1867-1868	
Wright, John A.	Flint, Genesee		1947-1948
Wurzel, Raymond C.	North Street, St. Clair	1957-1966	
Wyckoff, Herman A.	White Lake, Oakland	1881-1882	
Wyllis, George C.	Moscow, Hillsdale	1883-1884	
Wyman, Henry	Blissfield, Lenawee	1845	
Yaeger, Charles Edmund	Pontiac, Oakland	1945-1946	
Yancey, Tenisha	Detroit, Wayne	2017-	
Yanez, Henry	Sterling Heights, Macomb	2013-2018	
Yaple, Edward Lewis	Kalamazoo, Kalamazoo	1909-1912	
Yaroch, Jeffrey	Richmond, Macomb	2017-	
Yarrington, Charles Theodore Halsey	Norvell, Jackson	1881-1882	
Yates, Frederick	Detroit, Wayne	1955-1962	
Yawkey, Samuel W.	Saginaw, Saginaw	1865-1866; 1869	
Yeager, Weldon Osborne	Detroit, Wayne	1969-1970	
Yeckley, George G. B.	Decatur, Van Buren	1875	
Yeo, William T.	West Branch, Ogemaw	1909-1912	
Yeomans, Sanford A.	Ionia, Ionia	1877-1880	
Yeomans, Walter	Ionia, Ionia		1905-1908
Yerkes, George	Novi, Oakland	1879-1880	
Yerkes, William	West Farmington, Oakland Northville, Wayne	1837; 1857-1858	

Name[2]	Post Office[3]	Session Years[4] House	Senate
Yocum, John K.	Waterloo, Jackson	1851-1852	
Yokich, Tracey A.	St. Clair Shores, Macomb	1991-1996	
Yonker, Ken	Caledonia, Kent	2011-2016	
Yost, Chester L.	Ypsilanti, Washtenaw		1859-1860
Youmans, Henry Melville	Bridgeport, Saginaw		1897-1898
Young, Alexander Vincent	Big Rapids, Mecosta	1911-1914	
Young, Ambrose P.	Romulus, Wayne	1848; 1881-1882	
Young, Carl	Muskegon, Muskegon	1917-1920	
Young, Coleman A., II	Detroit, Wayne	2007-2010	2011-2018
Young, Coleman Alexander	Detroit, Wayne		1965-1974
Young, David E.	Saginaw, Saginaw	1943-1950	
Young, Frank Landon	Lansing, Ingham		1923-1926
Young, Fred W.	Bay City, Bay	1909-1910	
Young, H. Olin	Ishpeming, Marquette	1879-1880	
Young, John F.	Flint, Genesee	1949-1952	
Young, Joseph F., Jr.	Detroit, Wayne	1979-1994	1995-2002
Young, Joseph F., Sr.	Detroit, Wayne	1974-1993	
Young, Maxcine	Detroit, Wayne	1960-1966	
Young, Ralph H.	East Lansing, Ingham	1957-1962	
Young, Richard Arthur	Dearborn Heights, Wayne	1965-1994	
Young, Robert D.	Saginaw, Saginaw	1971-1974	1975-1982
Youngblood, Charles N., Jr.	Detroit, Wayne		1963-1974
Youngblood, Charles Nicholas	Detroit, Wayne		1943-1946
Younger, Paul C.	Lansing, Ingham		1957-1962
Younglove, George	North Raisinville, Monroe	1843	
Youngs, S. Perry	Stanton, Montcalm	1883-1884	
Zaagman, Milton	Grand Rapids, Kent		1963-1974
Zacharias, Henry Joseph	Saginaw, Saginaw	1907-1908	
Zagelmeyer, Alexander	West Bay City, Bay	1889-1890	
Zak, Albert J.	Hamtramck, Wayne	1945-1946; 1951-1952	
Zanglin, Joseph Richard	Wyandotte, Wayne	1949-1950	
Zelenko, Paula	Burton, Genesee	2001-2006	
Zemke, Adam	Ann Arbor, Washtenaw	2013-2018	
Ziegler, Hal Walter	Jackson, Jackson	1967-1974	1975-1978
Zimmerman, Elisha	Pontiac, Oakland	1873-1874	
Zimmerman, Henry Martin	Marine City, St. Clair	1897-1989	
Zimmerman, John	Detroit, Wayne	1893-1894	
Zimmerman, Lewis William	Traverse City, Grand Traverse	1939-1940	
Zinn, Frederick W.	Battle Creek, Calhoun	1955-1956	
Zollar, Charles O.	Benton Harbor, Berrien		1965-1978
Zorn, Dale W.	Ida, Monroe	2011-2014	2015-

[1] This table was compiled using previous editions of the Michigan Manual, the Library of Michigan's legislator database, and other primary sources. In some cases, inaccuracies and conflicting information were identified in the original sources about particular legislators. While attempts were made to resolve inaccuracies and conflicts found in other sources, errors may still exist in this table.

[2] This table includes the most complete version of a legislator's name possible but uses shortened versions of first and middle names in some cases. Different historical records may use different versions of individual legislators' names (e.g. nicknames, initials).

[3] The post offices listed in this table represent the municipality listed in the Michigan Manual as the legislator's post office address during their time in the Legislature and the county in which that post office was in at that time. The post office addresses listed in this table may not reflect the municipality in which a legislator actually lived and the closest post office to a legislator's home may have been outside of the district they served. The post office addresses listed in this table also may not conform to present day locations. Over the course of the state's history, post office locations have changed; municipalities and counties have changed names; and municipalities and counties have been established, changed, or eliminated.

[4] The years listed in this table are intended to reflect the years in which a legislator was an elected member of the House of Representatives or Senate. As a result, years are included as part of a legislator's service in which the Legislature did not convene (e.g., 1940) because they were an elected member of the Legislature during that time and would have served if the Legislature had met. The table intends to reflect partial terms due to death, resignation, and other causes, but the historical records used to compile this table may have been incomplete.

SENATE MAJORITY LEADERS, 1959-2019[1]

Senator	Hometown	District	Session Years
Frank D. Beadle	St. Clair	34	1959-1962
Stanley G. Thayer	Ann Arbor	33	1963-1964
Raymond D. Dzendzel	Detroit	7	1965-1966
Emil Lockwood	St. Louis	30	1967-1970
Robert VanderLaan	Kentwood	31	1971-1974
Milton Zaagman	Grand Rapids	32	1974
William B. Fitzgerald	Detroit	1	1975-1976
William Faust	Westland	13	1976-1984
John M. Engler	Mt. Pleasant	35	1984-1990
Richard Posthumus	Alto	31	1991-1998
Dan L. DeGrow	Port Huron	27	1999-2002
Ken Sikkema	Grandville	28	2003-2006
Michael D. Bishop	Rochester	12	2007-2010
Randy Richardville	Monroe	17	2011-2014
Arlan B. Meekhof	West Olive	30	2015-2018
Mike Shirkey	Liberty Township	16	2019-

[1] The Standing Rules of the Senate adopted in January 1959 were the first rules to provide for the election of a Majority Leader by the majority caucus. The rules adopted in 1961 and 1963 changed the position's name to Majority Caucus Chairman, but subsequent rules once again referred to Majority Leader. Not until 1979, with a revision of the Senate Rules, did the Senate Majority Leader gain the authority to name the members to committees.

PRESIDENTS PRO TEMPORE
OF THE STATE SENATE, 1835-2019[1]

Senator	County of Residence	District	Session Years
John S. Barry	St. Joseph	3	1835-1836
Jonathan D. Davis	Wayne	1	1837
John S. Barry	St. Joseph	3	1838
Benjamin B. Kercheval[2]	Wayne	1	1839
Thomas J. Drake[3]	Genesee	3	1840-1841
James Kingsley	Washtenaw	2	1842
William L. Greenly	Lenawee	3	1842-1843
Edwin M. Cust	Livingston	2	1844
William T. Howell	Hillsdale	3	1845
Flavius J. Littlejohn	Allegan	5	1846
Charles P. Bush[4]	Livingston	2	1847
Samuel Denton	Washtenaw	2	1848
Alvin N. Hart	Lapeer	6	1849
Jonathan P. King	Mackinac	6	1850
Michael Shoemaker	Jackson	2	1851
George R. Griswold[5]	Wayne	1	1853
Alonzo Cressy	Hillsdale	15	1855
Perley Bills	Lenawee	11	1857-1858
Omar D. Conger	St. Clair	26	1859
Joseph R. Williams[6]	St. Joseph	16	1861
Henry T. Backus	Wayne	3	1861
Byron G. Stout	Oakland	5	1862
Charles M. Croswell	Lenawee	10, 8[7]	1863-1867
William B. Williams	Allegan	17	1869-1870
Alfred B. Wood[8]	Saginaw	26	1871
Philip H. Emerson	Calhoun	11	1872
J. Webster Childs	Washtenaw	4	1873-1874
John K. Boies	Lenawee	6	1875
Charles D. Nelson	Muskegon	26	1877
William Chamberlain	Berrien	13	1879
William E. Ambler	Oceana	27	1881-1882
Archibald Buttars	Charlevoix	28	1883
James W. Belknap	Montcalm	21	1885
Charles J. Monroe	Montcalm	10	1887
William Ball[9]	Livingston	13	1889
Chauncey W. Wisner[10]	Saginaw	18	1891
Aaron B. Brown	Montcalm	23	1892
Samuel W. Hopkins	Isabella	25	1893
Joseph R. McLaughlin[11]	Wayne	3	1895
John L. Preston	Lapeer	21	1897-1898

PRESIDENTS PRO TEMPORE
OF THE STATE SENATE, 1835-2019 *(Cont.)*

Senator	County of Residence	District	Session Years
Robert B. Loomis	Kent	16	1899-1901
Oramel B. Fuller	Delta	30	1903
Cassius L. Glasgow	Barry	15	1905
Michael H. Moriarty	Iron	31	1907
Fred R. Ming	Cheboygan	29	1909
Fred B. Kline	Lenawee	19	1911-1912
Frank D. Scott	Alpena	29	1913
Walter Ross Taylor	Kalamazoo	6	1915
J. Lee Morford	Otsego	29	1917
Charles B. Scully	Lapeer	21	1919
Walter J. Hayes	Wayne	1	1921-1923
George M. Condon	Wayne	4	1925-1926
Augustus H. Gansser	Bay	24	1927-1929
Norman B. Horton	Lenawee	19	1931-1932
Leon D. Case	Berrien	7	1933-1934
Adolph F. Heidkamp	Houghton	32	1935-1936
William Palmer	Genesee	13	1937-1938
Felix H. H. Flynn	Wexford	27	1939
D. Hale Brake	Montcalm	25	1941-1942
George P. McCallum	Washtenaw	12	1943-1944
Harry F. Hittle	Ingham	14	1945-1948, 1953-1956
Harold D. Tripp	Allegan	8	1949-1950
Don Vander Werp	Newaygo	26	1951-1952
Frank Andrews	Montmorency	29	1957-1958
Charles T. Prescott	Ogemaw	28	1959-1960
Perry W. Greene	Kent	16	1961-1962
John P. Smeekens	Branch	9	1963-1964
John T. Bowman	Macomb	26	1965-1966
Thomas F. Schweigert[12]	Emmet	37	1967-1970
Milton Zaagman[13]	Kent	32	1971-1974
L. Harvey Lodge	Oakland	17	1974
John T. Bowman[14]	Macomb	27	1975-1977
Jack Faxon	Wayne	7	1977-1982
Jackie Vaughn III	Wayne	3	1983
Harry A. DeMaso	Calhoun	20	1984-1986
Nick H. Smith	Hillsdale	19	1987-1990
Vernon J. Ehlers[15]	Kent	32	1991-1994
John J. H. Schwarz, M.D.[16]	Calhoun	24	1994-2002
Patricia L. Birkholz	Allegan	24	2003-2006
Randy Richardville	Monroe	17	2007-2010
Tonya L. Schuitmaker	Van Buren	20	2011-2018
Aric Nesbitt	Lawton	26	2019-

[1] The president pro tem acts as the presiding officer of the state senate in the absence of the president of the senate, the lieutenant governor. Chosen by senate peers, the president pro tem is currently elected at the first session of the quadrennium. When acting as the presiding officer, the powers and duties of the post are defined by the adopted rules of the senate.

[2] Elected April 20, 1839, last day of the session year.

[3] Elected April 1, 1840, last day of session year; assumed duties of president of senate when Lieutenant Governor James Wright Gordon became acting governor February 24, 1841.

[4] Assumed duties of president of senate when Lieutenant Governor William L. Greenly became acting governor March 4, 1847.

[5] Assumed duties of president of senate when Lieutenant Governor Andrew Parsons became acting governor March 7, 1853.

[6] Assumed duties of president of senate upon resignation of James Birney as lieutenant governor April 3, 1861; died 1861, and succeeded by Henry T. Backus May 8, 1861.

[7] Act 162 of 1861, Laws of Michigan, apportioned a section of Lenawee County into District 10; that same portion of Lenawee County was apportioned as District 8 by Act 220 of 1865, Laws of Michigan.

[8] Resigned March 29, 1872; succeeded by Philip H. Emerson.

[9] Assumed duties of president of senate upon death of Lieutenant Governor James H. MacDonald.

[10] Resigned July 3, 1891; succeeded by Aaron B. Brown August 6, 1892.

[11] Assumed duties of president of senate upon resignation of Lieutenant Governor Alfred Milnes May 31, 1895.

[12] See Opinion of the Attorney General, No. 4625, April 22, 1968, and Act 8 of 1969. Assumed title of president of senate and acting lieutenant governor March 20, 1970.

[13] Resigned January 22, 1974, and succeeded by L. Harvey Lodge.

[14] Resigned from senate February 1, 1977; succeeded by Jack Faxon.

[15] Resigned from senate effective January 13, 1994.

[16] Elected president pro tempore of the senate February 3, 1994.

SECRETARIES OF THE STATE SENATE, 1835-2019[1]

Session Years	Name and Address	Session Years	Name and Address
1835-1838	John J. Adam, Clinton	1885-1889	Lewis M. Miller, Muskegon
1839	Samuel Yorke At Lee, Kalamazoo	1891-1892	Alfred J. Murphy, Detroit
1840-1841	Dan W. Kellogg, Ann Arbor	1893-1895	Dennis E. Alward, Clare
1842	Samuel Yorke At Lee, Detroit	1897-1900	Charles S. Pierce, Oscoda
1843-1844	James E. Platt, Ann Arbor	1901-1912	Elbert V. Chilson, Lansing
1845	Thornton F. Brodhead, Pontiac	1913-1929	Dennis E. Alward, Clare
1846-1847	James E. Platt, Ann Arbor	1931-1932	Fred I. Chase, Lansing
1848	John N. Ingersoll,[2] Sault Ste. Marie	1933-1934	Don W. Canfield, Detroit
	Charles Smith, Adrian	1935-1961	Fred I. Chase,[3] Lansing
1849	William L. Bancroft, Port Huron	1962-1965	Beryl I. Kenyon,[4] Lansing
1850-1853	Oliver W. Moore, Ann Arbor	1966	Eugene B. Farnum, Lansing
1855-1858	Isaac W. Wilder, Ann Arbor	1967-1975	Beryl I. Kenyon, Lansing
1859-1862	Aaron B. Turner, Grand Rapids	1975-1979	Billie S. Farnum,[5] Lansing
1863-1864	William A. Bryce, Bay City	1979-1986	William C. Kandler, Lansing
1865-1867	Thomas H. Glenn, Niles	1987-1994	Willis H. Snow, Lansing
1869-1872	Henry S. Sleeper, Galesburg	1995-2014	Carol Morey Viventi, Okemos
1873-1877	James H. Stone, Kalamazoo	2015-2018	Jeffrey Fetzer Cobb, Lansing
1879-1883	Edwin S. Hoskins, Bellevue	2019-	Margaret E. O'Brien, Portage

[1] The position of secretary of the senate is an elective one, by members of the senate, currently at the commencement of each quadrennium of the legislature. The powers and duties of the post are defined by the adopted rules of the senate, which govern the day-to-day operations of that house.

[2] Resigned January 5, 1848; succeeded by Charles Smith January 21, 1848.

[3] Resigned December 31, 1961; succeeded by Beryl I. Kenyon January 11, 1962.

[4] Resigned December 31, 1965; succeeded by Eugene B. Farnum.

[5] Elected pursuant to Senate Resolution No. 190, June 30, 1975; died November 18, 1979; succeeded by William C. Kandler December 6, 1979.

SPEAKERS OF THE HOUSE OF REPRESENTATIVES, 1835-2019[1]

Representative	County of Residence	District	Session Years
Ezra Convis	Calhoun	Calhoun	1835-1836
Charles W. Whipple	Wayne	Wayne	1837
Kinsley S. Bingham	Livingston	Livingston	1838-1839
Henry Acker	Jackson	Jackson	1840
Philo C. Fuller[2]	Lenawee	Lenawee	1841
John Biddle	Wayne	Wayne	1841
Kinsley S. Bingham	Livingston	Livingston	1842
Robert McClelland	Monroe	Monroe	1843
Edwin H. Lothrop	Kalamazoo	Kalamazoo	1844
Alfred H. Hanscom	Oakland	Oakland	1845
Isaac E. Crary	Calhoun	Calhoun	1846
George W. Peck	Livingston	Livingston	1847
Alexander W. Buel	Wayne	Wayne	1848
Leander Chapman	Jackson	Jackson	1849
Silas G. Harris	Ottawa	Ottawa/Kent	1850
Jefferson G. Thurber	Monroe	Monroe	1851
Daniel G. Quackenboss	Lenawee	1st Lenawee	1853
Cyrus Lovell	Ionia	Ionia	1855
Byron G. Stout	Oakland	1st Oakland	1857-1858
Henry A. Shaw	Eaton	1st Eaton	1859
Dexter Mussey	Macomb	3rd Macomb	1861-1862
Sullivan M. Cutcheon	Washtenaw	1st Washtenaw	1863-1864
Gilbert E. Read	Kalamazoo	1st Kalamazoo	1865
P. Dean Warner	Oakland	3rd Oakland	1867
Jonathan J. Woodman	Van Buren	1st Van Buren	1869-1872
Charles M. Croswell	Lenawee	4th Lenawee	1873-1874
John P. Hoyt	Tuscola	Tuscola	1875
John T. Rich	Lapeer	1st Lapeer	1877-1879
Seth C. Moffatt	Gd. Traverse	Gd. Traverse/Wexford	1881-1882
Sumner Howard	Genesee	1st Genesee	1883
Newcomb Clark	Bay	2nd Bay	1885
Daniel P. Markey	Ogemaw	Ogemaw	1887
Gerrit J. Diekema	Ottawa	1st Ottawa	1889
Philip B. Wachtel	Cheboygan	Cheboygan	1891-1892
William A. Tateum	Kent	1st Kent	1893
William D. Gordon	Midland	Midland	1895-1898
Edgar J. Adams	Kent	1st Kent	1899-1900
John J. Carton	Genesee	2nd Genesee	1901-1903
Sheridan F. Master	Kalamazoo	1st Kalamazoo	1905
Nicholas J. Whelan	Ottawa	1st Ottawa	1907
Colin P. Campbell	Kent	3rd Kent	1909
Herbert F. Baker	Cheboygan	Cheboygan	1911-1912
Gilbert Archibald Currie	Midland	Midland	1913
Charles Wallace Smith	Lapeer	Lapeer	1915
Wayne R. Rice	Newaygo	Newaygo	1917
Thomas Read	Oceana	Oceana	1919
Fred L. Warner	Ionia	Ionia	1921-1922
George W. Welsh	Kent	1st Kent	1923
Fred B. Wells	Cass	Cass	1925-1926
Lynn C. Gardner	Livingston	Livingston	1927
Fred R. Ming	Cheboygan	Cheboygan	1929-1932
Martin R. Bradley	Menominee	Menominee	1933-1934
George A. Schroeder	Wayne	1st Wayne	1935-1938
Howard Nugent	Huron	Huron	1939-1946
Victor A. Knox	Chippewa	Chippewa	1947-1952
Wade Van Valkenburg	Kalamazoo	1st Kalamazoo	1953-1956
George M. Van Peursem	Ottawa	Ottawa	1957-1958
Don R. Pears	Berrien	1st Berrien	1959-1962
Allison Green	Tuscola	Tuscola	1963-1964
Joseph J. Kowalski	Wayne	19[3]	1965-1966
Robert E. Waldron	Wayne	1	1967-1968
William A. Ryan	Wayne	3	1969-1974
Bobby D. Crim	Genesee	82	1975-1982
Gary Owen	Washtenaw	22	1983-1988
Lewis N. Dodak	Saginaw	86	1989-1992

SPEAKERS OF THE HOUSE OF REPRESENTATIVES,
1835-2019 *(Cont.)*

Representative	County of Residence	District	Session Years
Curtis Hertel[4]	Wayne	2	1993-1994
Paul Hillegonds[4,5]	Allegan	88	1993-1996
Curtis Hertel	Wayne	2	1997-1998
Charles R. Perricone	Kalamazoo	61	1999-2000
Rick Johnson	Osceola	102	2001-2004
Craig M. DeRoche	Oakland	38	2005-2006
Andy Dillon	Wayne	17	2007-2010
Jase Bolger	Calhoun	63	2011-2014
Kevin Cotter	Isabella	99	2015-2016
Tom Leonard	DeWitt	93	2017-2018
Lee Chatfield	Levering	107	2019-

[1] Elected by house peers, the speaker of the house of representatives is the presiding officer of that body. In addition to duties as chair, the adopted rules of the house of representatives specify other powers and duties of the post. The speaker is currently elected for a two-year term in the odd-numbered years in which the legislature convenes.

[2] Resigned April 3, 1841; succeeded by John Biddle.

[3] The Apportionment and Districting Plan of 1964 changed the method of naming legislative districts by counties to a numbering system. Under the previous system, the county was the basis for the district name, and each county, if qualified, had numbered districts within its borders. See Constitution of 1835, art. IV, secs. 3, 4; Constitution of 1850, art. IV, secs. 3, 4; Constitution of 1963, art. IV, sec. 3.

[4] Elected co-speaker of the house January 13, 1993. Pursuant to the Standing Rules of the House of Representatives and the *Democratic/Republican Leadership Agreement re Organization of the Michigan House of Representatives,* both ratified by resolutions adopted January 13, 1993, Democratic and Republican co-speakers were elected by the Michigan House of Representatives and authorized to act as presiding officer of the house during alternating months until the election of a speaker by at least 56 votes or the conclusion of the 87th Legislature on December 31, 1994. See 1993 Journal of the House (No. 1, January 13, 1993).

[5] Elected speaker of the house January 11, 1995.

SPEAKERS PRO TEMPORE OF
THE HOUSE OF REPRESENTATIVES, 1835-2019[1]

Representative	County of Residence	District	Session Years
Orrin Howe	Washtenaw	Washtenaw	1835
Hiram Alden	Branch	Branch	1837
Alexander W. Buel	Wayne	Wayne	1838
Isaac Wixom	Oakland	Oakland	1839
Henry Acker[2]	Jackson	Jackson	1840
Philo C. Fuller[3]	Lenawee	Lenawee	1841
James B. Larue[4]	Berrien	Berrien	1841
Edwin H. Lothrop	Kalamazoo	Kalamazoo	1842-1843
Dewitt C. Walker	Macomb	Macomb	1844
William A. Pratt	Oakland	Oakland	1845
Augustus C. Baldwin	Oakland	Oakland	1846
James L. Glenn	Cass	Cass	1847
Hiram Stone	Monroe	Monroe	1848
Charles M. O'Malley	Mackinac	Mackinac	1849
Oliver C. Comstock[5]	Branch	Branch	1849
John Stockton	Macomb	Macomb	1850
Calvin Britain	Berrien	Berrien	1851
Edward G. Morton	Monroe	2nd Monroe	1853
Robert R. Beecher	Lenawee	3rd Lenawee	1855
William H. Gregory	Wayne	4th Wayne	1857
Charles Dickey	Calhoun	2nd Calhoun	1859
William T. Howell	Newaygo	Newaygo	1861-1863
Augustus D. Griswold	Kent	3rd Kent	1865
Jonathan J. Woodman	Van Buren	1st Van Buren	1867
Benjamin W. Huston, Jr.	Tuscola	Tuscola	1869-1872
Claudius B. Grant	Washtenaw	1st Washtenaw	1873-1874
Erwin C. Watkins	Kent	4th Kent	1875
Nathaniel A. Hamilton	Berrien	2nd Berrien	1877
Edward P. Allen	Washtenaw	1st Washtenaw	1879
William Ball	Livingston	Livingston	1881-1882
George H. Hopkins	Wayne	1st Wayne	1883
Leonard M. Sellers	Kent	3rd Kent	1885
Erastus N. Bates	Allegan	2nd Allegan	1887
Walter W. Williams	Eaton	1st Eaton	1889
George F. Richardson	Ottawa	2nd Ottawa	1891
Charles W. Moore	Wayne	1st Wayne	1893
George W. Partridge	Wayne	1st Wayne	1895
Oramel B. Fuller	Delta	Delta	1897-1898
George E. Gillam	Alcona	Iosco	1899-1900
Sherman T. Handy	Iron	Dickinson	1901
Sheridan J. Colby	Wayne	1st Wayne	1903
Nicholas J. Whelan	Ottawa	1st Ottawa	1905
Charles E. Ward	Shiawassee	Shiawassee	1907
James M. Monroe	Gogebic	Gogebic	1909
John M. Perry	Osceola	Osceola	1911-1912
Charles H. McBride	Ottawa	1st Ottawa	1913
Wayne R. Rice	Newaygo	Newaygo	1915
Lynn J. Lewis	Van Buren	Van Buren	1917
Franklin Moore	St. Clair	2nd St. Clair	1919
Fred E. Dunn	Wayne	2nd Wayne	1921-1922
Thomas D. Meggison	Antrim	Antrim	1923
Robert Bruce MacDonald	Houghton	1st Houghton	1925-1926
Milton R. Palmer	Wayne	1st Wayne	1927
William J. Thomas	Kent	3rd Kent	1929
Vincent P. Dacey	Wayne	1st Wayne	1931-1932
Tracy W. Southworth	Monroe	Monroe	1933-1934
Carl DeLano	Kalamazoo	2nd Kalamazoo	1935-1936
Frank Berka	Saginaw	1st Saginaw	1937-1938
Maurice E. Post	Kent	3rd Kent	1939-1942
Victor A. Knox	Chippewa	Chippewa	1943-1946
Bert J. Storey	Ionia	Ionia	1947-1948
Robert M. Montgomery	Ingham	1st Ingham	1949-1952
William S. Broomfield	Oakland	4th Oakland	1953-1954
Andrew Bolt	Kent	1st Kent	1955-1956
Don R. Pears	Berrien	1st Berrien	1957-1958
Charles A. Boyer	Manistee	Wexford	1959-1960
Wilfred G. Bassett	Jackson	1st Jackson	1961-1964

SPEAKERS PRO TEMPORE OF
THE HOUSE OF REPRESENTATIVES, 1835-2019 *(Cont.)*

Representative	County of Residence	District	Session Years
Albert R. Horrigan	Genesee	19[6]	1965-1966
Martin D. Buth	Kent	90	1967-1968
Stanley J. Davis	Kent	92	1969-1972
Matthew McNeely	Wayne	16	1973-1986
Teola P. Hunter[7]	Wayne	5	1987-1992
Raymond M. Murphy	Wayne	7	1992-1994
Frank M. Fitzgerald[8,9]	Eaton	71	1993-1996
Raymond M. Murphy	Wayne	7	1997-1998
Patricia L. Birkholz	Allegan	88	1999-2002
Larry Julian	Shiawassee	85	2003-2004
Jerry O. Kooiman	Kent	75	2005-2006
Michael G. Sak	Kent	76	2007-2008
Pam Byrnes	Washtenaw	52	2009-2010
John Walsh	Wayne	19	2011-2014
Tom Leonard	Clinton	93	2015-2016
Lee Chatfield	Levering	107	2017-2018
Jason Wentworth	Clare	97	2019-

[1] The speaker pro tem of the house of representatives acts as the presiding officer of that body in the absence of the speaker.

[2] Elected speaker of the house of representatives January 8, 1840.

[3] Elected speaker of the house of representatives January 6, 1841.

[4] Elected speaker pro tem April 3, 1841.

[5] Elected February 12, 1849, to preside in speaker's three-day absence.

[6] The Apportionment and Districting Plan of 1964 changed the method of naming legislative districts by counties to a numbering system. Under the previous system, the county was the basis for the district name, and each county, if qualified, had numbered districts within its borders. See Constitution of 1835, art. IV, secs. 3, 4; Constitution of 1850, art. IV, secs. 3, 4; Constitution of 1963, art. IV, sec. 3.

[7] Resigned from the house of representatives January 17, 1992.

[8] Elected co-speaker pro tem January 13, 1993. Pursuant to the Standing Rules of the House of Representatives and the *Democratic/Republican Leadership Agreement re Organization of the Michigan House of Representatives*, both ratified by resolutions adopted January 13, 1993, Democratic and Republican co-speakers pro tem were elected by the house of representatives and authorized to preside during alternating months. See 1993 Journal of the House (No. 1, January 13, 1993).

[9] Elected speaker pro tempore January 11, 1995.

CLERKS OF THE HOUSE OF REPRESENTATIVES, 1835-2019[1]

Session Years	Name and Address	Session Years	Name and Address
1835-1836	George R. Griswold, Detroit	1903-1907	Charles S. Pierce,[2] Oscoda
1837	Anthony Ten Eyck, Detroit	1907-1912	Paul H. King,[3] Lansing
1838	Jed P. C. Emmons, Detroit	1912-1927	Charles S. Pierce, Lansing
1839	Elijah J. Roberts, Detroit	1929-1936	Myles F. Gray, Lansing
1840-1841	Mark Howard, Ann Arbor	1937-1938	T. Thomas Thatcher, Ravenna
1841-1843	Elijah J. Roberts, Detroit	1939-1944	Myles F. Gray, Lansing
1844	Augustine W. Hovey, Pontiac	1945-1965	Norman E. Philleo,[4] Lansing
1845	Ezra Williams	1966-1980	T. Thomas Thatcher, Lansing
1846-1849	Augustine W. Hovey, Pontiac	1981-1983	Thomas S. Husband,[5] East Lansing
1850-1853	Daniel P. Bushnell, Detroit	1983-1984	William A. Ryan, Detroit
1855	Henry Barns, Detroit	1985-1994	David H. Evans,[6] Haslett
1857-1859	Charles V. DeLand, Jackson	1993-1996	Melvin DeStigter,[6,7] Hudsonville
1861-1863	Edward W. Barber, Charlotte	1997-1998	Mary Kay Scullion, Lansing
1864-1872	Nelson B. Jones, Lansing	1999-2006	Gary L. Randall, Elwell
1873-1889	Daniel L. Crossman, Williamston	2007-2010	Richard J. Brown, Bessemer
1891-1892	Lyman A. Brant, Detroit	2011-	Gary L. Randall, Elwell
1893-1901	Lewis M. Miller, Lansing		

[1] The office of clerk of the house of representatives is an elective position, by members of the house, in each odd-numbered year in which the legislature meets. The powers and duties of the post are established by the adopted rules of the house of representatives, which govern the day-to-day operations of that body.

[2] Resigned October 7, 1907; succeeded by Paul H. King.

[3] Resigned February 26, 1912; succeeded by Charles S. Pierce.

[4] Resigned January 1, 1966; succeeded by T. Thomas Thatcher.

[5] Resigned May 2, 1983; succeeded by William A. Ryan.

[6] Elected co-clerk of the house January 13, 1993. Pursuant to the Standing Rules of the House of Representatives and the *Democratic/Republican Leadership Agreement re Organization of the Michigan House of Representatives*, both ratified by resolutions adopted January 13, 1993, Democratic and Republican co-clerks of the house were elected by the house of representatives and authorized to act during the periods prescribed in the agreement and the rules. See 1993 Journal of the House (No. 1, January 13, 1993).

[7] Elected clerk of the house January 11, 1995.

AUDITORS GENERAL, 1836-2019[1]

Robert Abbott[2]	1836-1839	Perry F. Powers	1901-1904
Henry Howard[3]	1839-1840	James B. Bradley	1905-1908
Eurotas P. Hastings	1840-1842	Oramel B. Fuller	1909-1932
Alpheus Felch[4]	1842	John K. Stack, Jr.[10]	1933-1935
Henry L. Whipple[5]	1842	John J. O'Hara[11]	1935-1936
Charles G. Hammond[6]	1842-1845	George T. Gundry	1937-1938
John J. Adam[7]	1845-1846	Vernon J. Brown	1939-1944
Digby V. Bell[8]	1846-1848	John D. Morrison	1945-1946
John J. Adam[9]	1848-1851	Murl K. Aten	1947-1950
John Swegles, Jr.	1851-1854	John B. Martin, Jr.	1951-1954
Whitney Jones	1855-1858	Victor Targonski[12]	1955-1956
Daniel L. Case	1859-1860	Frank S. Szymanski[13]	1956-1959
Langford G. Berry	1861-1862	William R. Hart (acting)[14]	1959
Emil Anneke	1863-1866	Otis M. Smith[15]	1959-1961
William Humphrey	1867-1874	William A. Burgett (acting)[16]	1961
Ralph Ely	1875-1878	Billie S. Farnum[17]	1961-1964
W. Irving Latimer	1879-1882	Allison Green (acting)[18]	1965
William C. Stevens	1883-1886	Albert Lee[19]	1965-1982
Henry H. Aplin	1887-1890	Franklin C. Pinkelman[20]	1982-1989
George W. Stone	1891-1892	Charles S. Jones (acting)[21]	1989
Stanley W. Turner	1893-1896	Thomas H. McTavish[22]	1989-2014
Roscoe D. Dix	1897-1900	Doug A. Ringler[23]	2014-

[1] Auditors general were appointed by the governor for two-year terms prior to the adoption of the Constitution of 1850 which established the position as a statewide elected office. The Constitution of 1963 granted appointment authority to the legislature by concurrent resolution and extended the term to eight years.

[2] Resigned May 1, 1839.

[3] Appointed by the governor following the resignation of Robert Abbot.

[4] Resigned April 1, 1842 following appointment to the Michigan Supreme Court.

[5] Appointed by the governor April 4, 1842 to serve in a temporary capacity following the resignation of Alpheus Felch.

[6] Appointed by the governor April 13, 1842 following the resignation of Alpheus Felch; Resigned May 31, 1845.

[7] Appointed by the governor following the resignation of Charles G. Hammond.

[8] Resigned March 20, 1848.

[9] Appointed by the governor following the resignation of Digby V. Bell.

[10] Died January 18, 1935.

[11] Appointed by the governor January 22, 1935 following the death of John K. Stack.

[12] Resigned May 17, 1956.

[13] Appointed by the governor June 7, 1956 following the resignation of Victor Targonski; Resigned October 11, 1959.

[14] Appointed acting auditor general by the governor October 12, 1959.

[15] Appointed by the governor October 21, 1959; Resigned October 9, 1961.

[16] Appointed acting auditor general by the governor October 10, 1961.

[17] Appointed by the governor October 23, 1961.

[18] Appointed acting auditor general by the governor to assume responsibilities that had previously belonged to the elected auditor general but had not been transferred to the legislatively-appointed auditor general created by the Constitution of 1963. Served until the adoption of the Executive Reorganization Act of 1965 which transferred those duties to the Department of Treasury.

[19] Appointed by the legislature February 4, 1965. See House Concurrent Resolution No. 24.

[20] Appointed acting auditor general by the legislature September 17, 1982; Appointed auditor general by the legislature December 8, 1982. See Senate Concurrent Resolution No. 825 and House Concurrent Resolution No. 940.

[21] Appointed acting auditor general by the legislature February 6, 1989; Appointment extended through November 1, 1989. See Senate Concurrent Resolution No. 20 and Senate Concurrent Resolution No. 275.

[22] Appointed by the legislature November 2, 1989. See House Concurrent Resolution No. 416.

[23] Appointed by the legislature June 9, 2014. See House Concurrent Resolution No. 28.

SOURCES OF MICHIGAN LEGISLATIVE INFORMATION

Introduction

Many sources are available for people wishing to follow or research the legislative process. Materials are available in paper form as well as online. More recent editions of the key components of the legislative process — the journals of the house and senate, the bills considered, and bills enacted into public acts — are available online. Some of these documents are eventually provided in traditional book form, while older materials are maintained in their hard copy originals.

A review of the many sources available can provide a person with useful background information on a law in Michigan. Analyses of proposed and adopted amendments, arguments for and against, and individual viewpoints on legislation may lend some insight into the reasons behind the passage of a bill.

www.legislature.mi.gov

This website is maintained by the Michigan Legislative Council, the Michigan House of Representatives, and the Michigan Senate and administered by the Legislative Internet Technology Team. The home page has fields to search for current session bills and to search the Michigan Compiled Laws (MCL), the state's body of permanent laws. The site allows a researcher to examine currently pending legislation and what was considered in prior legislatures (back to 1995) and to examine the state's compiled laws and its constitution.

Additional materials can be found on this site, including the house rules, senate rules, and joint rules; several informational booklets; nine complete volumes of the *Michigan Manual*; and yearly volumes of the Public Acts and Journals.

The legislature's website also has links to the home pages of the house and senate, which open a wealth of information pertinent to the current session, including individual legislator websites.

House and Senate Journals

In Michigan, the house and senate journals are the first sources of background material that should be examined by persons seeking information on the history of legislation. The journals are the official record of action taken on legislation by the house and senate, but are not a verbatim record of the proceedings. They contain essential research information such as citations, sponsors' names, the committees that considered the bill, dates when action was taken, and roll call votes. In addition, the journals contain floor amendments that were offered but defeated, "no vote" explanations by members, and titles of reports filed by committees. The house and senate journals are available online back to 1997. Although no longer printed, older bound copies of the journals can be found at the Library of Michigan (517/373-1300), law libraries across Michigan, numerous local libraries (especially Michigan documents depository libraries), and county libraries throughout the state.

To locate and trace a bill through the various steps of the legislative process, a researcher can use the indices of the house and senate journals for the year a law was enacted. It may also be necessary to check either the preceding or subsequent year's journals, since a bill can take up to two years to progress through each legislature. Using the bill and joint resolution index and/or the general index for each house's journals, one can find the bill number. The final journals for each year also contain a table of acts and corresponding bill numbers. With the bill number, one can use the bill histories to track the actions taken during the enactment process. This bill history section of the index will reference the house or senate journal for the day on which the action took place and the page number of the journal where the action is recorded.

Bills

Online versions of many of these documents are available from the Michigan Legislature's home page, from 1995 to the present, in either PDF or text format. Bills, substitute bills, and public acts from prior sessions may be obtained in hard copy from a law library, including the Library of Michigan's law library.

Text of Laws

The first avenue followed by most researchers examining the permanent body of state law, the Michigan Compiled Laws (MCLs), is the MCL database found at the legislature's website. With few exceptions (such as may occur at the end of session, when the number of bills signed into law may cause a delay) the Michigan Compiled Laws are updated within days or even hours of any amendatory act or new statute added to the state's laws. The website offers both a basic search capability and advanced search tools. Searches can be conducted in a number of different ways, including statute citation, popular name, chapter number, or by words or phrases.

It is helpful for a person to understand that a bill enacted into law, which becomes a public act of that specific year, is either a new act or an act to amend an existing act. Most enacted bills amend already existing law.

The Public Act Tables for 1998 and subsequent years are available online on the Michigan Legislature's website. These tables provide not only public act numbers for each year, but the corresponding bill numbers, effective dates, and general description.

Several private entities provide information on the state's laws. These include **Michigan Legislative Service**, a compilation published by the West Group and issued periodically during the legislative year and containing most of the same information found in the *Public and Local Acts of the Legislature of the State of Michigan*. Since 2000, West Group has also published **Michigan Session Laws** on an annual basis. The **Advance Legislative Service** for **Michigan Compiled Laws Service** is published by LexisNexis. These sets are indexed and contain tables that indicate the public acts of that year that amend any section of the **Michigan Compiled Laws**. A major advantage of the commercial publications is that changes in the text of a law made by an amendatory act are indicated by the insertion of an underline under the new language, and deletions of existing law are noted by the insertion of deletion marks to indicate deleted language.

Two other versions of the state's statutes, **Michigan Compiled Laws Annotated (MCLA)**, prepared by the West Group, and **Michigan Compiled Laws Service (MCLS)**, prepared by LexisNexis, contain a number of additional editorial features which can be of particular value to a researcher. Both are kept current through the preceding calendar year by the use of annual pocket parts and pamphlet supplements which reflect any changes in the text of the law made during the years succeeding the printing of each volume of these sets. Catchlines (which are not part of the law) at the beginning of each statute help identify the subject of a section. History notes follow each section, indicating the origination of each statute and a list of subsequent amendatory acts.

Committee Records

Legislative committee records may provide another source of background material. For the house, some materials for certain committees are available for the period 1965 to 1998 in the state archives (517/373-1408). At the beginning of each odd-numbered year, the previous biennial session's house committee records are boxed and handed over to the office of clerk of the house, which sends them to the state archives after being microfilmed by the state records center. These microfilmed records are available to the public immediately after the microfilming process is completed. Current house committee records are available by calling the house committee rooms (517/373-0135).

The Senate maintains past and present committee records on its website starting with the 2009-2010 term. Each January of an odd-numbered year, the Senate sends committee records for the previous term to the state record retention center. After four years, the documents are transferred to the State Archives. Contact the secretary of the senate's office to access available paper records at (517/373-2400).

These committee records may include minutes (date, time, place of meeting, decisions made, and roll call votes), bill analyses, and letters and written position statements that may have been submitted to the committee by interested parties. Tape recordings of meetings and public hearings conducted by committees may also be available. Video recordings of certain senate committee meetings may be available for a nominal fee from the secretary of the senate.

A variety of current committee record information is available through the "committee bill records" link at **www.legislature.mi.gov**.

Recordings of Session

For the period 1968 to 1998, audio tape recordings of most house sessions are available at the state archives. Additionally, audio recordings of senate sessions are available for the current session, through the office of the secretary of the senate. Video recordings of recent house and senate sessions are also available on the house and senate websites. It should be noted, however, that the journals of the senate and the house of representatives are the only official record of each session.

Appropriations Acts

Because they are not part of the permanent body of state law (because they pertain to a given fiscal year), appropriations acts are not included in the Michigan Compiled Laws. They can be found online or in print as public acts.

Legislative Studies and Reports

Legislative studies or reports are another source of information. Depending upon the subject, a researcher may want to contact special or interim committees, caucus and standing committee staffs, individual legislators, the house and senate fiscal agencies, the Auditor General, the Law Revision Commission, the Michigan Commission on Uniform State Laws, as well as other legislative agencies for specific documents. The Library of Michigan maintains *Michigan Documents*, an index for legislative documents which may identify useful materials. The Library of Michigan may also know of executive agency reports such as those prepared by a governor's task force or commission. One note of caution: generally, legislative reports or studies examine a particular issue rather than a specific bill and thus are indexed by subject rather than by bill or act number. The Library of Michigan's online catalog can be a useful source for background material and reports.

Both the House Fiscal Agency and the Senate Fiscal Agency have prepared various reports and publications over the years providing background information on appropriations bills and topics of legislative interest. They can also be accessed through the legislature's website, under the links for the house and the senate (under "Related Sites").

Bill Analyses

Bill analyses, which typically include a description of the problem being addressed, arguments for and against, and other background information on legislation, can be informative. The explanations presented often clarify complex legalities that may be difficult to understand from the bill itself. Both the house and the senate have legislative analysis units that prepare these documents.

The Library of Michigan (517/373-1300) and its law library (517/373-0630) maintain an analysis collection dating from 1969, with some analyses available for 1968. These include some analyses prepared by various state departments and agencies as well as by the analysis units of the house (1973 to present) and the senate (1980 to present). House and senate summaries and analyses for bills of the current and previous legislatures back to 1997 can be found online at the legislature's website through the bill search section.

Other Sources of Information

Nongovernmental information may be valuable to a research effort. Newspaper accounts, Gongwer News Service's *Michigan Report*, Michigan Information & Research Service's *Capitol Capsule*, the *Michigan Bar Journal*, and law journal articles are examples of such materials. Some of these are also available through online subscription. Libraries maintaining *Michigan Report* may also have a paper index covering articles from 1993 to present. If an issue has been in the news recently, this may quickly provide background or explanatory material. Newspapers can also be useful in providing coverage of the lawmaking process on specific issues. A researcher may also find it useful to contact lobbying groups that may have been involved in the passage of legislation, as these groups may have compiled and retained information on a particular issue or bill.

Another source of information may be found in **Attorney General opinions**. Cumulative indices are available at various libraries throughout the state. Attorney General opinions from 1963 to the present are available at the Attorney General's webpage. The state archives maintains a file containing the donated records of various state officials.

Chapter IV

THE EXECUTIVE BRANCH

2019–2020

PROFILE OF THE EXECUTIVE BRANCH

The executive power is vested in the governor, who is responsible for the faithful execution of the laws of the state. Elected by the people to a 4-year term, the **governor**:

- Supervises the principal departments of the executive branch and appoints members to state boards and commissions;

- May direct an investigation of any department of state government and may require written information from executive and administrative state officers on any subject relating to the performance of their duties;

- May remove elective and appointive officers of the executive branch for cause, as well as elective county, city, township, and village officers;

- Submits messages to the legislature and recommends measures considered necessary or desirable;

- Submits an annual state budget to the legislature, recommending sufficient revenues to meet proposed expenditures;

- May convene the legislature in extraordinary session;

- May call a special election to fill a vacancy in the legislature or the U.S. House of Representatives, and may fill a vacancy in the U.S. Senate by appointment;

- May grant reprieves, commutations of sentences, and pardons;

- May seek extradition of fugitives from justice who have left the state and may issue warrants at the request of other governors for fugitives who may be found within this state;

- Signs all commissions, patents for state lands, and appoints notaries public and commissioners in other states to take acknowledgements of deeds for this state;

- Serves as chairperson of the State Administrative Board, which supervises and approves certain state expenditures, and has veto power over its actions; and

- Serves as commander-in-chief of the state's armed forces.

The **lieutenant governor** is nominated at the party convention and elected with the governor. The term of office, beginning in 1966, changed from two years to four years. The lieutenant governor serves as President of the Michigan Senate, but may vote only in the case of a tie. The lieutenant governor may perform duties requested by the governor, but no power vested in the governor by the Constitution of 1963 may be delegated to the lieutenant governor. The lieutenant governor is a member of the State Administrative Board and would succeed the governor in case of death, impeachment, removal from office, or resignation.

ORGANIZATION OF THE EXECUTIVE BRANCH

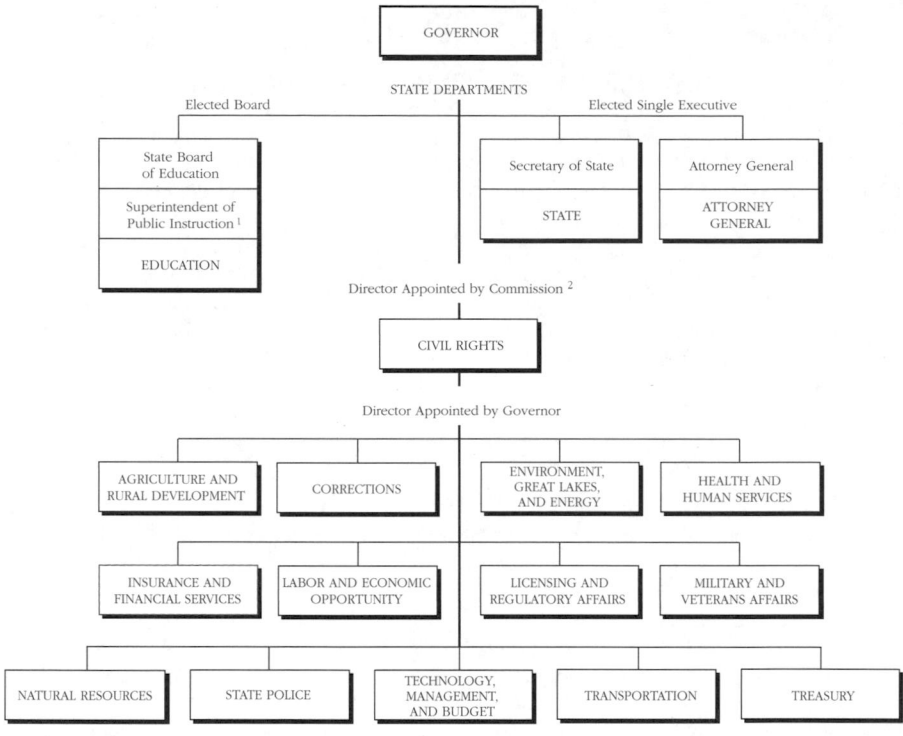

NOTE: Section 2 of Article V of the Constitution of the State of Michigan of 1963 provides that all executive offices, agencies and instrumentalities of the executive branch of state government and their respective functions, powers, and duties, except for the office of governor and lieutenant governor and the governing bodies of institutions of higher education, shall be "allocated by law among and within not more than 20 principal departments." The initial allocation of departments "by law" was completed with the enactment of the Executive Organization Act of 1965, Act 380 of 1965, being 16.101 to 16.113 of the Michigan Compiled Laws.

[1] The Superintendent of Public Instruction is appointed by the State Board of Education pursuant to Const. 1963, art. VIII, sec. 3.

[2] The members of the Civil Rights Commission are appointed by the governor, by and with the advice and consent of the Senate.

EXECUTIVE BRANCH REORGANIZATION

Early Efforts

One of Michigan's earliest attempts at reorganizing and integrating the growing number of state agencies, boards, and commissions was initiated by Governor Alexander J. Groesbeck in 1920. At his urging, the legislature enacted a statute creating the State Administrative Board to set administrative policy for more than 100 independent departments, bureaus, commissions, and agencies. The board, which consisted of the governor, secretary of state, state treasurer, auditor general, attorney general, highway commissioner, and superintendent of public instruction, merged 33 boards and agencies into five new departments — Agriculture, Conservation, Labor, Public Safety, and Welfare. Other efforts at administrative consolidation were initiated by Governor Frank Murphy in 1936, under the Commission on Reform and Modernization of Government. And in 1949, the Joint Legislative Committee on Reorganization of State Government, sometimes referred to as the "little Hoover commission," was created to study the issue of executive branch reorganization. One of the committee's recommendations — allowing the governor to propose a reorganization subject to legislative disapproval — was later embodied in Public Act 125 of 1958, which established a method by which the governor could submit plans for the reorganization of executive agencies to the legislature, subject to disapproval by either house:

> Sec. 1. Within the first 30 days of any regular legislative session, the governor may submit to both houses of the legislature at the same time, 1 or more formal and specific plans for the reorganization of executive agencies of state government.
> Sec. 2. A reorganization plan so submitted shall become effective by executive order not sooner than 90 days after the final adjournment of the session of the legislature to which it is submitted, unless it is disapproved within 60 legislative days of its submission by a senate or house resolution adopted by a majority vote of the respective members-elect thereof.
> Sec. 3. The presiding officer of the house in which a resolution disapproving a reorganization plan has been introduced, unless the resolution has been previously accepted or rejected by that house, shall submit it to a vote of the membership not later than 60 legislative days after the submission by the governor to that house of the reorganization plan to which the resolution pertains.

A reorganization plan not disapproved by one or the other house of the legislature in the manner set forth in the act was to be considered for all purposes as the equivalent in force, effect, and intent of a public act of the state upon its taking effect by executive order. In addition, a reorganization plan not disapproved by one or the other house of the legislature was to be subject to the provisions of the state constitution respecting the exercise of the referendum power reserved to the people in the same manner as prescribed for the approval or rejection of any legislative enactment subject to the referendum power.

Both Governor G. Mennen Williams and Governor John B. Swainson submitted reorganization plans to the legislature under authority of Public Act 125 of 1958, but, with one exception, all were rejected by the legislature.

The Constitution of 1963

Concerns over what many considered an unwieldy structure of state government under the Constitution of 1908 were cited by advocates of a new constitution. The question of what authority should be granted the governor to reorganize state government was debated again at the Constitutional Convention of 1961. After debate in which some delegates were concerned about how to balance the "tremendous political power" that could result from reorganization authority, the constitution was adopted with a process that gave responsibility to both the executive and the legislative branches.

The legislature was given the authority to undertake the initial reorganization. If the legislature failed to complete the reassignments in two years, the governor was authorized to make the initial reorganization within one year thereafter. The mandatory reorganization of executive offices and agencies into no more than 20 principal departments was to follow these provisions:

> All executive and administrative offices, agencies and instrumentalities of the executive branch of state government and their respective functions, powers and duties, except for the office of governor and lieutenant governor and the governing bodies of institutions of higher education provided for in this constitution, shall be allocated

by law among and within not more than 20 principal departments. They shall be grouped as far as practicable according to major purposes (Constitution of 1963, Schedule and Temporary Provisions, sec. 12).

After that "initial allocation" of agencies by law, the governor

. . . may make changes in the organization of the executive branch or in the assignment of functions among its units which he considers necessary for efficient administration. Where these changes require the force of law, they shall be set forth in executive orders and submitted to the legislature. Thereafter the legislature shall have 60 calendar days of a regular session, or a full regular session if of shorter duration, to disapprove each executive order. Unless disapproved in both houses by a resolution concurred in by a majority of the members elected to and serving in each house, each order shall become effective at a date thereafter to be designated by the governor. (Constitution of 1963, art. V, sec. 2).

Executive Organization Act of 1965

In fact, the initial allocation of executive branch offices, agencies, and instrumentalities among 19 principal departments was effected by the legislature through the enactment of the Executive Organization Act of 1965, MCL 16.101 to 16.113. Consequently, the governor was never required to undertake the allocation of agencies, although on several occasions, our governors have used this reorganization power to make changes in the organization of the executive branch.

The act provides a general mechanism for placing existing agencies into the framework of the 19 principal departments. Three types of transfers could be effectuated. Under a Type I transfer, an agency is merely identified as being within a particular department; the agency continues to perform its functions as prescribed by statute. Under a Type II transfer, the agency loses autonomous control of its functions — "all its statutory authority, powers, duties and functions, records, personnel, property, unexpended balances of appropriations, allocations or other funds, including the functions of budgeting and procurement [are] transferred to that principal department." Under a Type III transfer, the agency is abolished, (MCL 16.103).

Notable Reorganization Efforts

Although previous governors made use of the executive reorganization power, none used it more frequently or as extensively as Governor John Engler to reshape the executive branch of state government. During his tenure as governor, 1991 to 2002, he issued more than 100 executive reorganization orders considered necessary for efficient administration. These included orders to revamp the state's job-creating agencies and orders to create entirely new departments, including the Department of Information Technology and the Department of History, Arts and Libraries in 2001.

In 1991, Governor Engler issued Executive Order No. 1991-31 essentially abolishing the existing Department of Natural Resources and creating a "new" Department of Natural Resources, with the head of the new department continuing to be the Commission of Natural Resources, but the governor having authority to appoint the chair of the commission; abolishing several legislatively-established boards and commissions and transferring their authority over natural resources and environmental protection to the director of the "new" Department of Natural Resources. The executive order was challenged by the Speaker of the House and two not-for-profit corporate plaintiffs on the grounds that the order exceeded the governor's limited legislative authority under the Constitution of 1963, art. V, sec. 2. The case ultimately required the Michigan Supreme Court to determine the scope of authority granted to the governor to effect subsequent changes in the structure of the executive branch; specifically, whether the governor, through an executive order not disapproved by the legislature, could constitutionally transfer the authority, powers, and duties of the legislatively created Department of Natural Resources to a new, gubernatorially created Department of Natural Resources. The court found that the Constitution of 1963, art. V, sec. 2, authorized the governor to make such broad changes in the organization of the executive branch and that neither the separation of powers doctrine nor the Executive Organization Act of 1965 could be interpreted to prevent the governor from exercising his constitutionally mandated powers (See *House Speaker* v *Governor*, 443 Mich 560 (1993)).

Governor Jennifer Granholm utilized the reorganization authority to reshape the executive branch to reflect changed conditions in the state. Executive Order No. 2003-18, creation of the Department of Labor and Economic Growth, which was renamed the Department of Energy, Labor and Economic Growth by Executive Order 2008-20, brought about major changes among the agencies faced with responsibilities involving the work place, regulatory matters, and the state's economic development and work force training efforts. Executive Order No. 2007-30 consolidated human resources services, abolished the Department of Civil Service, and transferred the functions of the Civil Service Commission and the State Personnel Director to the Department of Management and Budget.

In 2009, Executive Order 2009-36, amended by Executive Order 2009-43, abolished the Department of History, Arts and Libraries and transferred its responsibilities and agencies to various departments. Executive Order 2009-45 combined the Department of Natural Resources and the Department of Environmental Quality to create the new Department of Natural Resources and Environment. Executive Order 2009-55 combined the Department of Management and Budget and the Department of Information Technology to create the new Department of Technology, Management, and Budget.

Governor Rick Snyder continued the tradition of aligning the executive departments to suit his strategy and style of management. Shortly after taking office, Executive Order 2011-1 split the Department of Natural Resources and the Department of Environmental Quality into two units. They had been combined into a single department by Executive Orders in 2009. He also established the Department of Licensing and Regulatory Affairs (Executive Order 2011-4) and the Department of Insurance and Financial Services (Executive Order 2013-1) and abolished the Department of Energy, Labor and Economic Growth. After being reelected in 2014, the Governor made additional changes by combining the Departments of Community Health and Human Services into one department renamed Health and Human Services (Executive Order 2015-5). This new department is the state's largest with more than 14,000 employees. The Governor also created the Department of Talent and Economic Development by Executive Order 2014-12.

GUBERNATORIAL APPOINTMENT PROCESS

The selection of qualified individuals to serve in state governmental positions excepted or exempted from state civil service is a responsibility shared by the executive and the legislative branches of government. This joint participation in the appointment process is mandated by the Constitution of the State of Michigan of 1963, which accords the governor certain powers to appoint officials subject to the advice and consent of the Michigan Senate.

Historical Developments

To gain a broader perspective of the governor's appointment powers and the use of advice and consent, it is useful to trace the historical development of the executive/legislative relationship regarding appointments. Due to the deep-seated distrust of, and contempt for, British-imposed colonial governors, many early state constitutions greatly limited the power of the office of the governor. Michigan's first constitution (1835), however, did not follow that pattern — it gave the governor substantial power. The governor had the power to appoint the secretary of state, judges of the supreme court, the auditor general, the attorney general, and prosecuting attorneys for each county. These appointments were subject to Senate confirmation. The only state officers popularly elected were the governor, lieutenant governor, and state legislators.

In contrast, the 1850 constitution reflected the influence of "Jacksonian democracy," ultimately producing the so-called "long ballot." Among the principles of Jacksonian democracy was the belief that public officials should be chosen by election rather than by appointment. The 1850 constitution provided for the election of all principal state officials, including the secretary of state, state treasurer, attorney general, auditor general, superintendent of public instruction, regents of the University of Michigan, state board of education, and supreme court justices. Accordingly, the governor's appointment power was reduced to filling vacancies.

While the adoption of a new constitution in 1908 did little to either erode or enhance the governor's appointment power, other developments led to a substantial increase in the number of state officials appointed by the governor. Ironically, it was the legislature that played the most significant role in expanding the gubernatorial appointment power. Of the more than 2,000 appointments for which the governor is responsible today, most are to the more than 200 boards, commissions, and other advisory bodies, which, in most cases, have been established by statutes enacted by the legislature. Some are created on an ad hoc basis, but many are permanent. As rapidly changing social and economic conditions brought about the emergence of new and more complex problems, state government began to expand. Prior to the adoption of the 1963 constitution, there were no limitations on the number of state agencies that could be established and no restrictions on the power of the legislature to assign administrative duties to newly created agencies or positions independent of gubernatorial supervision. Even the 1963 constitution does not preclude the creation of new agencies. However, article V, section 2 of that document does limit the number of principal departments to ". . . not more than 20 . . . ." Moreover, all executive offices, excluding the offices of governor and lieutenant governor and the university governing boards, are to be allocated within those principal departments.

Many newly created agencies were responsible to boards or commissions comprised of individuals appointed by the governor. Boards and commissions are common to the administrative structure of many businesses as well as to all levels of government. Proponents of the system argue that by creating a degree of independence, a board or commission can be insulated from political manipulation. The use of staggered or overlapping terms for the members of a board encourages continuity of policy while making it difficult for an executive to appoint a majority of board members during any one term. In addition, the application of bipartisan representation on these bodies ensures some degree of minority representation and input.

Critics of the board or commission role in government object to the lack of accountability of appointees and the possibility of stalemates in the decision-making process. Moreover, perhaps due to the fact that boards and commissions in Michigan state government have evolved gradually over the years, there appears to be little consistency in the internal structure of these bodies, the method used to appoint members, or their functions.

Types of Appointments

In addition to appointing a personal executive staff, the governor currently appoints most executive department heads with the advice and consent of the Senate. Two department heads, the secretary of state and attorney general, are popularly elected. The remaining department directors are appointed by the respective board or commission that heads the department.

The governor is also authorized to appoint a limited number of other positions, particularly of a policymaking nature, within most of the principal departments. Those positions, along with the positions within the Office of the Governor, are exempted from civil service. Certain regulatory officials, such as the racing commissioner, are also appointed by the governor with Senate confirmation. The members of the boards or commissions that head departments are appointed by the governor with Senate confirmation, but the terms for these officials overlap so that a majority of the members cannot be appointed in any one year.

In some cases the governor serves as an ex officio member of a board or commission. For example, the governor serves as an ex officio member of the State Board of Education. On a number of boards, the heads of executive departments serve as ex officio members.

The governor also appoints the heads of other autonomous agencies such as the lottery commissioner. Most of these appointments require Senate confirmation.

Pursuant to Sec. 1104 of the Revised Judicature Act (MCL 600.1104), stenographers for each circuit court of the state ". . . shall be appointed by the governor after having first been recommended by the judge or judges of the court to which he is appointed . . . ." Senate confirmation is not required.

Limitations on Gubernatorial Appointment Power

The common requirement that gubernatorial appointments be confirmed by the Senate is the most significant limitation imposed on the appointment power. In addition, in some cases the legislature has brought both the speaker of the House and the Senate majority leader into the appointment process.

There are a number of other ways in which a governor is limited in appointing individuals to boards and commissions. Many limitations relate to statutory conditions regarding those eligible for appointment. For instance, pursuant to art. V, sec. 5, of the state constitution, ". . . A majority of the members of an appointed examining or licensing board of a profession shall be members of that profession." Furthermore, during the mid-1970s, the legislature amended various laws establishing licensing boards to assure each board had at least one member representing the interests of the general public.

Some of the statutes creating boards and commissions are very specific in dictating the membership qualifications and experiences required. Some sections of law require the governor to appoint members from a list of nominees submitted by nongovernmental groups. Also, certain territorial divisions of the state must be represented on certain boards and commissions.

Advice and Consent

A primary concern of the framers of the U.S. Constitution was preventing a concentration of power in any one branch of government. Accordingly, a system of checks and balances was incorporated into the federal constitution. A key component of this is legislative review of appointments through the mechanism of advice and consent. In Michigan, this is provided for in the state constitution. Art. V, sec. 6, states:

> Appointment by and with the advice and consent of the senate when used in this constitution or laws in effect or hereafter enacted means appointment subject to disapproval by a majority vote of the members elected to and serving in the senate if such action is taken within 60 session days after the date of such appointment. Any appointment not disapproved within such period shall stand confirmed.

The incorporation of this provision in the 1963 constitution effectively reversed the advice and consent process practiced under previous constitutions, none of which provided a definition of advice and consent. Rather than the Senate approving an appointment by positive action, this provision requires the Senate to disapprove an appointment within 60 session days after submission for consideration. In other words, no action by the Senate constitutes a confirmation of an appointment after 60 session days. The count of 60 session days commences when the secretary of the Senate receives written notification of an appointment from the governor's office.

The advice and consent provision incorporated into the 1963 constitution was designed to provide the Senate with reasonable time to reject an appointee while at the same time making confirmation definite should the Senate choose not to act on an appointment.

Michigan's advice and consent process contrasts with the concept as practiced by the U.S. Senate. Individuals named to federal positions cannot assume the office until they are confirmed. On the federal level, the President nominates, and the U.S. Senate appoints. In Michigan, the governor appoints, and the Senate confirms or rejects the appointment.

CONSTITUTIONAL EXECUTIVE OFFICERS

ELECTED OFFICERS
(Terms Expire January 1, 2023)

Governor
GRETCHEN WHITMER, East Lansing

Lieutenant Governor
GARLIN GILCHRIST II, Detroit

Secretary of State
JOCELYN BENSON, Detroit

Attorney General
DANA NESSEL, Plymouth Township

APPOINTED OFFICERS

State Treasurer
RACHAEL EUBANKS, East Lansing

Superintendent of Public Instruction
MICHAEL F. RICE, Kalamazoo

GOVERNOR
GRETCHEN WHITMER

Gretchen Whitmer was sworn in as the 49th governor of Michigan on January 1, 2019.

A lifelong Michigander, Governor Whitmer grew up in Grand Rapids and East Lansing. Her parents instilled in her and her siblings a strong work ethic and the deep belief that everyone is important. She started her first job at age 15 at Burlingame Lumber, and later worked the line at the Royal Fork Buffet and stocked shelves at Target.

Governor Whitmer is a proud product of Michigan's public school system and a graduate of Michigan State University and the Michigan State University College of Law, where she graduated *Magna Cum Laude*.

Governor Whitmer served in the Michigan Legislature, elected to the House of Representatives in 2000, 2002, and 2004, and to the State Senate in a special election in March of 2006. She was reelected in November 2006 and 2010, and served as the Senate Democratic Leader in the State Senate.

During her time in the Michigan Legislature, Governor Whitmer negotiated an increase in the minimum wage with a cost-of-living adjustment, and because of that bipartisan work, the minimum wage went up for the fourth time in 2018. As Senate Democratic Leader, she brought workers, labor unions, and businesses together to fight anti-worker legislation.

In addition to her service to the state, Governor Whitmer taught at the University of Michigan and Michigan State University, and in 2016 she stepped up to serve as Ingham County Prosecutor, restoring faith in the office after it had been hit by scandal. In that role, she established a new Domestic Violence and Sexual Assault Unit to go after abusers, sped up the rehabilitation of non-violent first-time offenders, and asked the Michigan State Police to investigate the integrity of the county's evidence room.

Governor Whitmer is committed to expanding access to affordable healthcare, improving education and skills training, respecting working families, cleaning up Michigan's drinking water, and of course, fixing the roads.

Governor Whitmer has two daughters, Sherry and Sydney, and her husband Marc Mallory has three sons, Alex, Mason and Winston.

LIEUTENANT GOVERNOR
GARLIN GILCHRIST II

Lt. Governor Garlin Gilchrist has dedicated his career to fixing problems for hardworking families. From spearheading campaigns for equality and justice to harnessing technology to solve everyday problems for Detroiters, his focus has consistently remained on serving the public by getting things done.

Bringing Michigan's state government fully into the 21st century is a top priority for Lt. Governor Gilchrist. He studied computer engineering and computer science at the University of Michigan, graduating with honors, and later had a successful career as a software engineer at Microsoft, helping to build SharePoint into the fastest growing product in the company's history.

Lt. Governor Gilchrist served as Social Media Manager for the 2008 Obama campaign in Washington, where he helped launch a national text message program to recruit volunteers. He later served as the first Director of New Media at the Center for Community Change in Washington, D.C., and spent three years as National Campaign Director at MoveOn.org, where he spearheaded equity and justice campaigns.

This eventually led to his serving as the first ever Director of Innovation & Emerging Technology for the city of Detroit, where he used public data and technology to address every day concerns the community was facing – including an app to report issues such as broken fire hydrants, potholes and broken street lights. This mindset of harnessing technology to solve problems will play a critical role in finding solutions to improve the lives of people across the state.

Lt. Governor Gilchrist and his wife Ellen are the proud parents of twins, Garlin III and Emily Grace.

SECRETARY OF STATE
JOCELYN BENSON

Jocelyn Benson was sworn in as Michigan's 43rd secretary of state January 1, 2019, after being elected November 6, 2018, to a 4-year term.

A national leader in election law, Ms. Benson is the author of *State Secretaries of State: Guardians of the Democratic Process.* It is the first major book on the role of the secretary of state in enforcing election and campaign finance laws.

An expert on civil rights law, education law and election law, Ms. Benson served as dean of Wayne State University Law School in Detroit. When she was appointed dean at age 36, she became the youngest woman in U.S. history to lead a top-100, accredited law school. She continues to serve as vice chair of the advisory board for the Levin Center at Wayne Law, which she founded with former U.S. Senator Carl Levin. She served as director of the center from fall 2016 until August 2017. Previously, Ms. Benson was an associate professor and associate director of the Damon J. Keith Center for Civil Rights at Wayne State University Law School.

Prior to her election, she served as CEO of the Ross Initiative in Sports for Equality (RISE), a national nonprofit organization using the unifying power of sports to improve race relations. She continues to serve on the RISE Board of Directors and as cochair of the RISE to Vote initiative, a nonpartisan effort to register professional and college athletes to vote and encourage them to lead their fans in becoming informed and engaged citizens.

Ms. Benson is the founder of the nonpartisan Michigan Center for Election Law, which hosts projects that support transparency and integrity in elections, and cofounder and former president of Military Spouses of Michigan, a network dedicated to providing support and services to military spouses and their children.

In 2015, Ms. Benson became one of the youngest women in history to be inducted into the Michigan Women's Hall of Fame.

She earned a bachelor of arts from Wellesley College, master of philosophy from Oxford University and a law degree from Harvard Law School. Ms. Benson and her husband Ryan reside in Detroit.

ATTORNEY GENERAL
DANA NESSEL

Dana Nessel, Michigan's 54th Attorney General, began her legal career as an Assistant Prosecutor in the Wayne County Prosecutor's Office. For more than a decade, she was assigned to a number of elite units within the office and handled some of Wayne County's most difficult cases in the Child and Family Abuse Bureau, Police Conduct Review Team, and Auto Theft Unit. Nessel was specially assigned to try homicide, arson, criminal sexual conduct and gang-related conspiracy cases, among many others.

In 2005, Nessel left the Prosecutor's Office to open her own legal firm. In her criminal practice, she vigorously defended the rights of indigent defendants on hundreds of criminal cases, from petty theft to first degree murder. She also handled civil rights actions for plaintiffs against police departments and government agencies that have committed transgressions against community residents. Nessel has petitioned courts across Michigan on behalf of dozens of victims of domestic violence who sought Personal Protection Orders against their abusers. She has also handled a myriad of other disciplines, ranging from family law, probate matters, and driver license restoration cases.

Dana Nessel is also recognized as a premier litigator of LGBTQ issues in Michigan. In 2010, she brought the matter of *Harmon* v. *Davis*, in which a Michigan court, for the first time, held that a non-biological parent in a same-sex couple could establish custodial rights to the couple's children. Nessel also successfully petitioned for the first second-parent adoptions for same-sex couples in Oakland and Wayne Counties. She has defended and acquired exonerations for scores of defendants wrongly targeted for prosecution based on sexual orientation and gender identity and have represented various clients terminated from employment based upon those classifications.

In 2012, Nessel spearheaded the precedent-setting case, *DeBoer* v. *Snyder*, which challenged the bans on adoption and marriage for same-sex couples in Michigan. DeBoer was later consolidated with its affiliated U.S. Sixth Circuit cases into *Obergefell* v. *Hodges* in the United States Supreme Court. This landmark case legalized same-sex marriage nationwide.

Nessel is the founder and first president of the Fair Michigan Foundation. In 2016, she and Wayne County Prosecutor Kym L. Worthy created the Fair Michigan Justice Project, a first of its kind task force which investigates and prosecutes hate crimes committed against the LGBTQ community. In the first few years of existence, the Justice Project had charged more than 20 capital offenses including homicides, sexual assaults, armed robberies, child abuse, attempted murder, and car-jackings. The Fair Michigan Justice Project has a 100 percent conviction rate.

Nessel has received numerous awards for her civil rights initiatives, including the "Champion of Justice" award from the Michigan State Bar Association, "Woman of the Year" from *Michigan Lawyers Weekly* and the "Treasure of Detroit" award from Wayne State University Law school. Nessel lives in southeast Michigan with her wife, Alanna Maguire, and her twin sons, Alex and Zach, along with various cats.

STATE TREASURER
RACHAEL EUBANKS

Rachael Eubanks was appointed as Michigan's 47th State Treasurer by Governor Gretchen Whitmer in January of 2019.

In 2016, she was appointed by Governor Rick Snyder, and reappointed in 2017 to serve on the Michigan Public Service Commission as a utility regulatory commissioner. In that capacity she reviewed and voted on hundreds of orders that helped shape Michigan's energy future. In particular, the Commission had regulatory oversight over the implementation of two comprehensive energy law changes during her tenure. She served on several national organizations, including as Vice President to the Organization of PJM States, Inc., and was on the Board of Directors of the National Association of Regulatory Utility Commissioners, where she was chair of the Supplier and Workforce Development Subcommittee.

Prior to that role, Ms. Eubanks structured more than $25 billion in bond financings for public entities — primarily the state of Michigan, State Building Authority, Michigan Finance Authority and the Michigan Strategic Fund. Treasurer Eubanks also served as point of contact for credit rating agencies on state credit matters for ten years.

Ms. Eubanks serves on the National Association of State Treasurers' State Debt Management Network and Legislative Committees. She was on the Board of Michigan Women in Finance from 2008 to 2013 and was elected treasurer and president.

She obtained her bachelor's in economics from the University of Michigan.

Ms. Eubanks is a resident of East Lansing.

SUPERINTENDENT OF PUBLIC INSTRUCTION
DR. MICHAEL F. RICE

Dr. Michael F. Rice was appointed Superintendent of Public Instruction in May 2019 by Michigan's State Board of Education.

He served as the superintendent of the Kalamazoo Public Schools from 2007 to 2019, where he supported full-day pre-kindergarten; improved student achievement in reading, writing, and math; and encouraged student participation in Advanced Placement courses.

Prior to serving as Kalamazoo's superintendent, Dr. Rice served five years as superintendent of the Clifton Public Schools in Clifton, New Jersey.

Dr. Rice began his career in the Washington, D.C. Public Schools, where he taught high school French, and founded and coached an award-winning speech and debate program. He earned a bachelor's degree in psychology with honors from Yale University and a master's degree and doctorate in public administration with honors from New York University.

He was president of the Middle Cities Education Association, 2013 to 2014 and received the Michigan Superintendent of the Year Award from the Michigan Association of Superintendents and Administrators in 2016.

His most personally rewarding work is his steady mentoring and teaching of, and informal discussions with, school children — which he continues to do as Michigan's State Superintendent.

STATE BOARD OF EDUCATION

CASANDRA E. ULBRICH

PAMELA PUGH

MICHELLE FECTEAU

TOM McMILLIN

JUDITH PRITCHETT

LUPE RAMOS-MONTIGNY

NIKKI SNYDER

TIFFANY TILLEY

Members	*Term expires*
CASANDRA E. ULBRICH, *President*, Rochester Hills	Jan. 1, 2023
PAMELA PUGH, *Vice President*, Saginaw	Jan. 1, 2023
MICHELLE FECTEAU, *Secretary*, Detroit	Jan. 1, 2021
TOM McMILLIN, *Treasurer*, Oakland Township	Jan. 1, 2025
JUDITH PRITCHETT, Washington Township	Jan. 1, 2027
LUPE RAMOS-MONTIGNY, Grand Rapids	Jan. 1, 2021
NIKKI SNYDER, Dexter	Jan. 1, 2025
TIFFANY TILLEY, *NASBE Delegate*, Southfield	Jan. 1, 2027

ex officio
GRETCHEN WHITMER, Governor
MICHAEL F. RICE, Superintendent of Public Instruction

STATE BOARD OF EDUCATION

Members

The eight voting members of the **Michigan State Board of Education** are elected at-large on the partisan statewide ballot for 8-year terms. Two are elected every two years in the general election. In addition, there are two nonvoting, ex officio members — the governor and the state superintendent of public instruction, who is the chair of the board. Any vacancies on the board which occur between elections are filled through appointment by the governor for the remainder of the term.

The state board elects its own officers for 2-year terms. It also selects and appoints the state superintendent of public instruction, who administers the Michigan Department of Education.

The state board of education is at the core of an unusual state education system which seeks to carry out Michigan's long tradition of local control balanced against the overall needs of the people statewide.

Historical Background

The Northwest Ordinance in 1787 encouraged schools and the means of education.

In 1809, nearly three decades before statehood, Michigan territorial law directed each judicial district to start schools and collect a tax for them. The **territorial council** made it mandatory in 1829 to divide the townships into school districts and gave the state the right to inspect and supervise schools and to set the length of time each would be open.

Michigan's first constitution, in 1835, created the office of superintendent of public instruction. **John D. Pierce**, a New England clergyman who had come to Michigan as a frontier missionary, was named the first superintendent, becoming the first independent administrator of education under a state constitution in the United States.

Michigan became a state in 1837 and adopted a new constitution in 1850 which formalized the state board of education as a constitutional body. The state board of education was created by the Michigan Legislature in 1849 to administer what is now Eastern Michigan University. Many duties were extended to the board over the years, but the current responsibilities were established in the 1963 state constitution.

Constitutional Powers

The state board of education exercises its constitutional **duties** of leadership and general supervision over all public education, including adult education and instructional programs in state institutions, except for institutions of higher education granting baccalaureate degrees. It serves as the general planning and coordinating body for all public education and advises the legislature as to the financial requirements for public education.

Among their several duties, the state board of education and Department of Education distribute state funds to local school districts; reimburse schools for certain programs such as school lunches, bus transportation, and remedial and special education; administer federal aid programs; and provide student financial aid. In addition, the state board appoints advisory councils and committees from the education community and general public to investigate, review, or make recommendations.

DEPARTMENT OF
AGRICULTURE AND RURAL DEVELOPMENT

GARY MCDOWELL, DIRECTOR
Constitution Hall
P.O. Box 30017, Lansing, MI 48909
www.michigan.gov/mdard

The Department of Agriculture was established under Public Act 13 of 1921 and was reorganized under Public Act 380 of 1965. In January 2011, "rural development" was added to the department's name. A 5-member Commission of Agriculture and Rural Development, appointed by the Governor, with the advice and consent of the Senate, provides policy development for the department. Commission members are appointed for terms of four years.

COMMISSION OF AGRICULTURE AND RURAL DEVELOPMENT

Term expires

PATRICIA BERGDAHL, Skandia	Dec. 31, 2022
TREVER MEACHUM, Hartford	Dec. 31, 2019
CHARLIE MEINTZ, Stephenson	Dec. 31, 2022
DRU MONTRI, Bath	Dec. 31, 2021
BRIAN PRIDGEON, Montgomery	Dec. 31, 2020

The Department of Agriculture and Rural Development (MDARD) promotes agricultural interests of the state and develops safeguards to protect the public from disease and unsanitary conditions in connection with food production and food handling, product labeling, dairy products, animals, and plants. The department also protects consumers by enforcing laws relating to food safety, standard weights and measures, farm produce storage, and dairy products; inspection and enforcement of animal health; control of plant pests and diseases; and perishable fruits and vegetables.

The department is composed of the Executive Office and six divisions: Agriculture Development, Animal Industry, Environmental Stewardship, Food and Dairy, Laboratory, and Pesticide and Plant Pest Management.

The **Executive Office** houses the Office of the Director, who is responsible for policy development, department strategic planning, daily operations, and more. The following department functions also fall under the Executive Office: budget, emergency management, communications, legislative liaison, and support for the Michigan Commission of Agriculture and Rural Development.

The **Agriculture Development Division** delivers expertise and leadership to support economic prosperity in Michigan's food and agriculture sector through industry-focused economic development, export assistance, and grant management. The division also administers the Grain Dealers Act and the Farm Produce Insurance Act.

The **Animal Industry Division** is responsible for programs to control and eradicate reportable contagious, infectious, and communicable diseases of livestock, poultry, and equine and companion animals; controlling contamination from toxic substances; enforcing the humane treatment of animals; and promoting Michigan animal industries.

The **Environmental Stewardship Division** provides assistance and support to soil conservation districts, drainage boards, and land users, enabling them to carry out programs maintaining Michigan's food and fiber productivity and environmental sustainability, control erosion, protect water quality, and protect groundwater.

The **Food and Dairy Division** administers programs that enforce laws and regulations governing the safety and wholesomeness of food and food products; regulates the commercial handling of farm produce; administers food sanitation programs; and assures a safe, high-quality supply of dairy products.

The **Laboratory Division** provides analytical, diagnostic, and technical support to the regulatory divisions of the department and to other state and federal agencies. The division also prevents economic fraud and deception in the area of weights and measures, labeling, and advertising. It also regulates the sale and quality of motor fuel.

The **Pesticide and Plant Pest Management Division** administers programs to enforce laws and regulations to prevent the introduction and dissemination of serious plant and bee pests; to prevent the adulteration of animal food, unsanitary grain storage facilities, and misuse of pesticides; and to provide assurance that animal feeds and remedies, fertilizers, seeds, and pesticides are accurately labeled. It also provides for grading, inspection, and certification of fruits and vegetables.

DEPARTMENT OF
ATTORNEY GENERAL

DANA NESSEL, ATTORNEY GENERAL
G. Mennen Williams Building
P.O. Box 30212, Lansing, MI 48909
www.michigan.gov/ag

The Attorney General is a constitutional officer, the chief law enforcement officer of the state and the head of the state's executive branch Department of Attorney General. The duties of the Attorney General are prescribed by constitution, statute, court decisions, and tradition. The department predates statehood, having been established by an 1807 territorial act and it has been preserved in every constitution of this state since then.

The Attorney General is the lawyer for the state of Michigan. When public legal matters arise, she renders opinions on matters of law and provides legal counsel for the Legislature and for each officer, department, board and commission of state government. She provides legal representation in court actions and assists in the conduct of official hearings held by state agencies.

The Attorney General's Office is also the People's Law Firm and may intervene in any lawsuit, criminal or civil, when the interest of the people of the state of Michigan require. She advises and supervises prosecuting attorneys throughout Michigan and possesses certain investigative powers, including the power to investigate allegations of election fraud and complaints for the removal of public officials. She also may request grand jury investigations of crime in Michigan.

By virtue of the office, the Attorney General is a member of various state boards and commissions, including, but not limited to, the State Administrative Board, State Employees' Retirement Board, Judges' Retirement Board and the Michigan Commission on Law Enforcement Standards.

While the Attorney General is responsible for representing various state agencies and officials, there is no law that authorizes her to provide legal services to private individuals or appear in court on their behalf.

To assist in the myriad functions of the department, the Attorney General employs a staff of more than 250 assistant attorneys general, who must be members of the State Bar of Michigan and appointed under Michigan Civil Service rules. In addition, the Attorney General has a staff of more than 125 investigators and support staff to assist in carrying out the mandate of the office. All legal work is performed by the assistant attorneys general, including drafting of opinions and legal documents and representation of client agencies, is done in the name of the Attorney General and with her approval or the approval of her designee.

The department is organized into five bureaus: Criminal Justice, Consumer Protection, Civil Rights and Civil Litigation, Environmental and Real Property, and State Government. It also has four newly established units, including the Hate Crimes Unit, Payroll Fraud Unit, Auto-Insurance Fraud Unit, and Conviction Integrity Unit. Additionally, the department includes the Prosecuting Attorneys Coordinating Council, an autonomous entity.

The Attorney General maintains offices in Lansing and Detroit.

DEPARTMENT OF
CIVIL RIGHTS

MARY ENGELMAN, INTERIM DIRECTOR
Executive Office, Capitol Tower Building
110 W. Michigan Avenue, Suite 800
Lansing, MI 48933
www.michigan.gov/mdcr

The Michigan Civil Rights Commission was created by the Michigan Constitution of 1963 to carry out the guarantees against discrimination articulated in Article I, Section 2. As further stated in Art. V, Sec. 29, the state constitution directs the commission to investigate alleged discrimination against any person because of religion, race, color, or national origin and to "secure the equal protection of such civil rights without such discrimination." Public Acts 453 and 220 of 1976 and subsequent amendments have added sex, age, marital status, height, weight, arrest record, genetic disposition, and physical and mental disabilities to the original four protected categories.

The Michigan Department of Civil Rights (MDCR) was established in 1965 to provide a staff complement to the policy-making responsibilities of the commission. In 1991, the department was expanded when the Michigan Women's Commission was transferred from the Department of Management and Budget to this agency by executive order. In April 2011, the Asian Pacific American Affairs Commission, the Hispanic/Latino Commission and the Division on Deaf, Deafblind, and Hard of Hearing were moved to MDCR, also through executive order. In 2014, the State Americans with Disabilities Act Compliance Director and staff were transferred to MDCR from the Department of Technology, Management and Budget.

The Department of Civil Rights enforces the state's protections against illegal discrimination primarily by investigating discrimination complaints. The department works to prevent discrimination through programs that promote voluntary compliance with civil rights laws and provides information and services to businesses on diversity initiatives, procurement opportunities and equal employment law. Staff and allies also work to prevent discrimination through statewide educational initiatives on bullying awareness, eradicating hate crimes, building community response to bias-related incidents, improving living and working conditions for migrant and seasonal farmworkers, and through the Advocates and Leaders for Police and Community Trust groups across Michigan.

The department has offices in Detroit, Flint, Grand Rapids, Lansing and Marquette. A complaint may be filed at any of the department's offices, if the alleged discrimination has occurred within the past 180 days; complaints may also be filed online.

DEPARTMENT OF
CORRECTIONS

HEIDI E. WASHINGTON, DIRECTOR

Grandview Plaza
P.O. Box 30003, Lansing, MI 48909
www.michigan.gov/corrections

The Department of Corrections is one of the principal state departments. Final responsibility for operation of the department rests with the governor, who appoints the director, with the advice and consent of the Michigan Senate. The director serves at the pleasure of the governor and is the department's chief administrative officer. The director has full power and authority in the supervision and control of the department's affairs. The office of the director includes:

The **Legislative Affairs Section** coordinates legislative activities. The legislative liaison acts as liaison to the legislature on matters of department policy and procedure and other areas of concern to the department.

The **Office of Public Information and Communications** coordinates contacts with the news media and provides employees and the general public information regarding department activities.

The **Office of Executive Affairs** oversees the Discipline Section which is responsible for all employee discipline; the Internal Affairs Section which is responsible for investigating allegations of staff misconduct and the Effective Process Improvement and Communication Section which is responsible for evaluating and monitoring process improvement, communication, score-card activities, strategic planning, and serving as liaison with the Office of Good Government.

The **Offender Success Administration** is responsible for prisoner and community-based reentry programs and services and includes the Office of Community Corrections, which is responsible for implementation of the Community Corrections Act, and the Education Section which provides programming in the areas of adult basic education, general education development, and special education, in addition to offering a variety of vocational programs.

The **Correctional Facilities Administration** is responsible for the oversight of all prisons operated by the department, including the reception and classification process, the treatment and transfer of prisoners, and the special alternative incarceration facilities. The prisons are supervised by two assistant deputy directors.

The **Operations Division** is responsible for providing programming support to the prisons and consists of the Records Administration, the Classification and Placement Section, the Emergency Management Section, the Transportation Section, and the Special Activities Coordinator.

The **Bureau of Health Care Services** is responsible for the coordination and monitoring of health care services for prisoners, including the treatment of seriously mentally ill prisoners. The chief medical officer is responsible for oversight and direction regarding the medical and clinical practice of prisoner health care. Substance Abuse Services is responsible for the overall planning, monitoring and evaluation of prisoner substance abuse programming and testing.

The **Field Operations Administration** (FOA) is responsible for providing investigative support, information and sentencing recommendations to the courts in criminal cases, as well as supervising probationers and parolees following their release from prison. The FOA is divided into regions — the metropolitan territory and the outstate territory. Each territory is headed by an assistant deputy director responsible for oversight of the field operations within each geographic region.

The **Office of Parole and Probation Services** is headed by an assistant deputy director who is responsible for oversight of the Parole Services Section, which provides investigative support and information to the parole board in the parole revocation, supervision, and discharge processes; the Program Services Section, which is responsible for oversight of the intensive detention reentry program, sex offender management, and the Interstate Compact Unit, which implements the interstate compact for parolees and probationers; and the Electronic Monitoring Center, which monitors parolees and probationers on tether and discharged sex offenders for whom electronic monitoring is required.

The **Parole Board** is composed of ten members appointed by the director, one of whom is designated as the chairperson. The board is responsible for parole decisions, including establishing the terms and conditions of parole and the processing of cases for reprieve, commutation and pardon. The Office of the Parole Board provides administrative and support services to the board, including in the parole and lifer consideration process. The office is also responsible for operation of the crime victim notification process.

The **Absconder Recovery Unit** is responsible for locating and arresting escapees, parole violators, and probationers.

The **Budget and Operations Administration** (BOA) provides oversight of central office staff support functions and provides internal organizational support to the department's operational unit. The BOA is comprised of the following areas:

The **Budget and Projections Division** coordinates the budget development process and financial management for the department.

The **Physical Plant Division** is responsible for new construction, remodeling and major maintenance programs, fire safety standards, and environmental affairs. This division also provides a mechanism for auditing county jails.

The **Procurement, Monitoring, and Compliance Division** is responsible for procurement functions and contract management and also includes the Prison Rape Elimination Act unit which is responsible for ensuring the department's compliance with the *Prohibited Sexual Conduct Involving Prisoners* policy directive. The unit reports data to the United States Department of Justice in regard to prisoner-on-prisoner sexual violence, staff sexual misconduct, and staff sexual harassment.

The **Office of Legal Affairs** coordinates communication with the Department of Attorney General regarding legal issues and litigation activities. The FOIA Section coordinates compliance with the Freedom of Information Act; the Policy and Rules Development Section handles policy and administrative rules development; and the Grievance Section coordinates prisoner property reimbursement with the State Administrative Board, coordinating investigations and decisions of third-step prisoner grievances. The Litigation Section is responsible for coordinating litigation against the department or its employees and oversees department compliance with court orders. The Rehearings Section is responsible for the major misconduct and formal hearing process within the department and reviews requests for rehearing from all formal administrative hearings.

Personnel Services provides oversight of all human resource services and equal employment opportunity services provided to department staff by the Civil Service Commission. The Labor Relations Section is responsible for responding to staff grievances and unfair labor practice charges and representation at related conferences, hearings, arbitration, and contract disputes.

The **Office of Research and Planning** provides corrections research, statistical analyses, legislative impact studies, and prisoner population projections in support of strategic and operational planning, and also manages the enterprise-wide automated data systems oversight, development, maintenance, and security. In addition, the office responds to emergency and ad hoc requests from throughout state and federal government, other agencies and organizations, the media, and the public for data, analysis, information, and statistical reporting.

Michigan State Industries is responsible for the overall control, management, and supervision of prison industry programs.

The **Training Division** is responsible for new employee, in-service, and leadership training for staff, the recruitment of new employees, and the Ordnance Unit.

DEPARTMENT OF CORRECTIONS
STATE INSTITUTIONAL FACILITIES

	FISCAL YEAR 2018	FISCAL YEAR 2019

ALGER CORRECTIONAL FACILITY

Acting Warden Scott Sprader
Population: 874

Appropriations	$30,945,800	$31,189,400
Expenditures		
State employee wages and benefits	$28,000,100	$28,601,700
Materials, equipment, facilities	$2,670,200	$2,331,700
Other[1]	$275,500	$256,000
Total	$30,945,800	$31,189,400

BARAGA CORRECTIONAL FACILITY

Warden Daniel Lesatz
Population: 828

Appropriations	$35,688,200	$36,021,600
Expenditures		
State employee wages and benefits	$32,572,000	$33,020,000
Materials, equipment, facilities	$2,448,800	$2,622,500
Other	$667,400	$379,100
Total	$35,688,200	$36,021,600

BELLAMY CREEK CORRECTIONAL FACILITY

Acting Warden Matt Macauley
Population: 1,786

Appropriations	$44,219,200	$45,003,600
Expenditures		
State employee wages and benefits	$39,775,500	$40,825,800
Materials, equipment, facilities	$2,618,000	$1,850,300
Other	$1,825,700	$2,327,500
Total	$44,219,200	$45,003,600

CARSON CITY CORRECTIONAL FACILITY

Warden Randee Rewerts
Population: 2,380

Appropriations	$47,451,300	$49,613,500
Expenditures		
State employee wages and benefits	$43,454,300	$44,833,200
Materials, equipment, facilities	$2,476,500	$3,397,500
Other	$1,520,500	$1,382,800
Total	$47,451,300	$49,613,500

CENTRAL MICHIGAN CORRECTIONAL FACILITY

Warden John Christiansen
Population: 2,542

Appropriations	$46,460,300	$47,009,300
Expenditures		
State employee wages and benefits	$41,915,000	$42,834,700
Materials, equipment, facilities	$3,991,800	$3,538,600
Other	$553,500	$636,000
Total	$46,460,300	$47,009,300

CHARLES E. EGELER RECEPTION AND GUIDANCE CENTER

Warden Jeremy Bush
Population: 1,171

Appropriations	$45,255,200	$46,366,300
Expenditures		
State employee wages and benefits	$42,011,500	$43,658,900
Materials, equipment, facilities	$2,853,700	$2,354,800
Other	$390,000	$352,600
Total	$45,255,200	$46,366,300

CHIPPEWA CORRECTIONAL FACILITY

Warden Connie Horton
Population: 2,327

Appropriations	$51,628,100	$52,230,000
Expenditures		
State employee wages and benefits	$46,856,200	$47,876,400
Materials, equipment, facilities	$3,983,900	$3,586,500
Other	$788,000	$767,100
Total	$51,628,100	$52,230,000

COOPER STREET CORRECTIONAL FACILITY

Acting Warden Michelle Floyd
Population: 1,718

Appropriations	$29,999,800	$30,325,000
Expenditures		
State employee wages and benefits	$27,954,200	$27,670,100
Materials, equipment, facilities	$1,725,800	$1,990,700
Other	$319,800	$664,200
Total	$29,999,800	$30,325,000

EARNEST C. BROOKS CORRECTIONAL FACILITY

Warden Shane Jackson
Population: 1,212

Appropriations	$51,192,500	$30,604,700
Expenditures		
State employee wages and benefits	$46,571,500	$27,997,900
Materials, equipment, facilities	$3,674,000	$2,263,800
Other	$947,000	$343,000
Total	$51,192,500	$30,604,700

G. ROBERT COTTON CORRECTIONAL FACILITY

Warden Kevin Lindsey
Population: 1,769

Appropriations	$44,304,100	$45,634,700
Expenditures		
State employee wages and benefits	$41,013,500	$42,743,900
Materials, equipment, facilities	$2,770,800	$2,478,000
Other	$519,800	$412,800
Total	$44,304,100	$45,634,700

GUS HARRISON CORRECTIONAL FACILITY

Warden Sherman Campbell
Population: 2,025

Appropriations	$48,770,900	$50,857,600
Expenditures		
State employee wages and benefits	$44,646,800	$46,098,400
Materials, equipment, facilities	$3,691,400	$4,242,100
Other	$432,700	$517,100
Total	$48,770,900	$50,857,600

IONIA CORRECTIONAL FACILITY

Warden John Davids
Population: 598

Appropriations	$34,259,900	$34,886,000
Expenditures		
State employee wages and benefits	$31,464,900	$32,133,600
Materials, equipment, facilities	$2,090,900	$2,157,100
Other	$704,100	$595,300
Total	$34,259,900	$34,886,000

KINROSS CORRECTIONAL FACILITY

Warden Jack Kowalski
Population: 1,562

Appropriations	$32,747,300	$33,008,100
Expenditures		
State employee wages and benefits	$29,750,900	$29,930,600
Materials, equipment, facilities	$2,492,800	$2,401,800
Other	$503,600	$675,700
Total	$32,747,300	$33,008,100

LAKELAND CORRECTIONAL FACILITY

Warden Noah Nagy
Population: 1,452

Appropriations	$33,505,000	$33,619,700
Expenditures		
State employee wages and benefits	$29,404,500	$29,586,000
Materials, equipment, facilities	$3,508,900	$3,129,200
Other	$591,600	$904,500
Total	$33,505,000	$33,619,700

MACOMB CORRECTIONAL FACILITY

Warden Pat Warren
Population: 1,383

Appropriations	$35,016,900	$35,285,600
Expenditures		
State employee wages and benefits	$31,917,900	$32,570,400
Materials, equipment, facilities	$2,575,100	$2,191,300
Other	$523,900	$523,900
Total	$35,016,900	$35,285,600

MARQUETTE BRANCH PRISON

Warden Erica Huss
Population: 1,021

Appropriations	$37,588,100	$38,697,200
Expenditures		
State employee wages and benefits	$33,807,800	$34,803,900
Materials, equipment, facilities	$3,503,800	$3,500,700
Other	$276,500	$392,600
Total	$37,588,100	$38,697,200

MICHIGAN REFORMATORY

Warden Gregory Skipper
Population: 1,209

Appropriations	$34,519,200	$36,034,000
Expenditures		
State employee wages and benefits	$31,948,500	$33,212,300
Materials, equipment, facilities	$1,908,900	$2,100,200
Other	$661,800	$721,500
Total	$34,519,200	$36,034,000

MUSKEGON CORRECTIONAL FACILITY

Warden Sherry Burt
Population: 1,297

Appropriations	$25,637,900	$26,109,600
Expenditures		
State employee wages and benefits	$23,073,100	$23,594,000
Materials, equipment, facilities	$2,005,600	$1,986,300
Other	$559,200	$529,300
Total	$25,637,900	$26,109,600

NEWBERRY CORRECTIONAL FACILITY

Warden Catherine Bauman
Population: 1,089

Appropriations	$24,618,700	$24,673,000
Expenditures		
State employee wages and benefits	$22,310,900	$22,045,700
Materials, equipment, facilities	$2,032,900	$2,288,600
Other	$274,900	$338,700
Total	$24,618,700	$24,673,000

OAKS CORRECTIONAL FACILITY

Warden Les Parish
Population: 1,066

Appropriations	$34,425,900	$34,862,600
Expenditures		
State employee wages and benefits	$31,483,700	$32,110,000
Materials, equipment, facilities	$2,759,500	$2,428,700
Other	$182,700	$323,900
Total	$34,425,900	$34,862,600

PARNALL CORRECTIONAL FACILITY

Warden Melinda Braman
Population: 1,659

Appropriations	$28,947,300	$29,475,600
Expenditures		
State employee wages and benefits	$26,925,300	$27,340,200
Materials, equipment, facilities	$1,614,800	$1,542,700
Other	$407,200	$592,700
Total	$28,947,300	$29,475,600

RICHARD A. HANDLON CORRECTIONAL FACILITY

Warden Dewayne Burton
Population: 1,253

Appropriations	$30,442,600	$30,762,400
Expenditures		
State employee wages and benefits	$27,558,400	$27,821,100
Materials, equipment, facilities	$1,774,000	$1,744,000
Other	$1,110,200	$1,197,300
Total	$30,442,600	$30,762,400

SAGINAW CORRECTIONAL FACILITY

Warden Tom Winn
Population: 1,454

Appropriations	$33,291,500	$33,835,800
Expenditures		
State employee wages and benefits	$30,489,700	$31,258,800
Materials, equipment, facilities	$2,527,800	$2,246,500
Other	$274,000	$330,500
Total	$33,291,500	$33,835,800

SPECIAL ALTERNATIVE INCARCERATION PROGRAM

Acting Warden Michelle Floyd
Population: 147

Appropriations	$13,842,300	$14,179,300
Expenditures		
State employee wages and benefits	$12,820,000	$12,797,200
Materials, equipment, facilities	$929,300	$1,034,500
Other	$93,000	$347,600
Total	$13,842,300	$14,179,300

ST. LOUIS CORRECTIONAL FACILITY

Acting Warden Bob Vashaw
Population: 1,122

Appropriations	$37,497,500	$37,907,700
Expenditures		
State employee wages and benefits	$34,294,900	$34,505,600
Materials, equipment, facilities	$2,980,000	$3,090,100
Other	$222,600	$312,000
Total	$37,497,500	$37,907,700

THUMB CORRECTIONAL FACILITY

Warden Willis Chapman
Population: 1,039

Appropriations	$33,353,100	$33,809,700
Expenditures		
State employee wages and benefits	$30,408,800	$30,981,600
Materials, equipment, facilities	$2,317,800	$2,191,500
Other	$626,500	$636,600
Total	$33,353,100	$33,809,700

WOMEN'S HURON VALLEY CORRECTIONAL FACILITY

Warden Shawn Brewer
Population: 2,048

Appropriations	$60,163,400	$60,568,400
Expenditures		
State employee wages and benefits	$53,229,300	$54,011,000
Materials, equipment, facilities	$5,760,800	$5,407,700
Other	$1,173,300	$1,149,700
Total	$60,163,400	$60,568,400

WOODLAND CORRECTIONAL FACILITY

Warden Jodi DeAngelo
Population: 345

Appropriations	$32,824,200	$33,169,100
Expenditures		
State employee wages and benefits	$29,842,200	$30,142,600
Materials, equipment, facilities	$2,621,500	$2,519,500
Other	$360,500	$507,000
Total	$32,824,200	$33,169,100

DETROIT DETENTION CENTER

Acting Warden Lee McRoberts
Population: N/A

Appropriations	$8,567,400	$8,685,100
Expenditures		
State employee wages and benefits	$7,649,900	$7,816,800
Materials, equipment, facilities	$841,600	$842,500
Other	$75,900	$25,800
Total	$8,567,400	$8,685,100

DETROIT REENTRY CENTER

Acting Warden Lee McRoberts
Population: 622

	FISCAL YEAR 2018	FISCAL YEAR 2019
Appropriations	$28,129,400	$29,989,600
Expenditures		
State employee wages and benefits	$25,575,100	$26,651,500
Materials, equipment, facilities	$2,340,800	$3,017,000
Other	$213,500	$321,100
Total	$28,129,400	$29,989,600

Source: Michigan Department of Corrections, Director's Office, June 2019.

---

[1] Other includes direct payments to clients, medical payments on behalf of clients, educational expenses on behalf of clients or students, other contracts, and all other costs.

DEPARTMENT OF
EDUCATION

MICHAEL F. RICE,
SUPERINTENDENT OF PUBLIC INSTRUCTION
John A. Hannah Building
P.O. Box 30008, Lansing, MI 48909
www.michigan.gov/mde

The State Board of Education was first provided for in the Constitution of 1850 and currently exists through the provisions of Article VIII, Section 3, of the Constitution of 1963. The state board is composed of eight members nominated by party conventions and elected at-large for terms of eight years, with two members being elected at each biennial state general election. The governor is authorized to fill vacancies on the state board and also serves as an ex officio member of the state board, without the right to vote. The Superintendent of Public Instruction is appointed by the board for a term to be determined by the board, to serve as its chair, without the right to vote.

STATE BOARD OF EDUCATION
www.michigan.gov/sbe

	Term expires
CASANDRA E. ULBRICH, *President*, Rochester Hills	Jan. 1, 2023
PAMELA PUGH, *Vice President*, Saginaw	Jan. 1, 2023
MICHELLE FECTEAU, *Secretary*, Detroit	Jan. 1, 2021
TOM MCMILLIN, *Treasurer*, Oakland Township	Jan. 1, 2025
JUDITH PRITCHETT, Washington Township	Jan. 1, 2027
LUPE RAMOS-MONTIGNY, Grand Rapids	Jan. 1, 2021
NIKKI SNYDER, Dexter	Jan. 1, 2025
TIFFANY TILLEY, *NASBE Delegate*, Southfield	Jan. 1, 2027

ex officio
GRETCHEN WHITMER, Governor
MICHAEL F. RICE, Superintendent of Public Instruction

The State Board of Education exercises its constitutional duties of leadership and general supervision over all public education, including adult education and instructional programs in state institutions, except for institutions of higher education granting baccalaureate degrees. It serves as the general planning and coordinating body for all public education, including higher education, and advises the legislature as to the financial requirements for public education.

The **Office of the State Board of Education** is responsible for supervising, managing, and coordinating all activities of the State Board of Education, including policy development, operations, and communications.

The **State Board Executive** is responsible as the legal repository of all State Board of Education activities and records. The State Board Executive prepares all State Board of Education correspondence, expenses, budget, and scheduling; and prepares all State Board of Education meeting agendas, minutes, and follow-up materials.

The State Board of Education and Michigan Department of Education's Mission is: "Supporting Learning and Learners."

The **Superintendent of Public Instruction** is appointed by and responsible to the State Board of Education. The superintendent is the principal executive officer of the Department of Education and is a member of the State Administrative Board. The superintendent is the chair and a nonvoting member of the State Board of Education. The superintendent also serves on the Public School Employees' Retirement Board, the Library of Michigan Board, and the Michigan State Safety Commission. The superintendent is an ex officio member of the State Tenure Commission.

As the principal executive officer of the Department of Education, the superintendent of public instruction is responsible for assisting the State Board of Education in advising the legislature. The superintendent is responsible for the day-to-day management, supervision, and leadership of the department.

Major departmental responsibilities include: educator preparation and certification; providing technical assistance to schools in the areas of education improvement and innovation, special education, grants, transportation, health, and food programs; statewide student assessment; school accountability; career and technical education; early childhood learning; distribution of state school aid; and overseeing the distribution and use of federal education program funding. The department also operates the Library of Michigan and the Michigan School for the Deaf in Flint.

The **Office of the Superintendent of Public Instruction** includes a chief deputy superintendent; a deputy superintendent for finance and operations; a deputy superintendent for P-20 system and student transitions; a deputy superintendent for educator, student, and school supports; the State Board Office; and the director of the Office of Public and Governmental Affairs.

The Department of Education also includes the Michigan Interagency Coordinating Council, the Michigan Special Education Advisory Committee, State Tenure Commission, and the Library of Michigan Board.

MICHIGAN SCHOOL FOR THE DEAF

The Michigan School for the Deaf (MSD) is a state-run agency for deaf and hard of hearing students. The MSD has both an academic and residential component. Students are placed at the school through the individualized educational program team process in their resident districts.

The MSD is a bilingual program that provides instruction in American Sign Language and English. A general education curriculum is provided, based on Michigan Merit Curriculum requirements.

The school was founded in 1848 and opened its doors to the first pupil in 1854.

	FISCAL YEAR 2017	FISCAL YEAR 2018
Average Number of Students	165	156
Legislative Appropriation[1]	$11,395,800	$12,351,600
Expenditures		
Salary of Principal	$97,837	$99,304
Salaries, wages, fringe benefits	5,281,529	5,114,763
Contractual services, supplies, materials	4,597,302	4,379,501
Travel	22,918	10,008
Total	$9,999,587	$9,603,577

[1] Michigan School for the Deaf (MSD) shares its operations appropriation with the Low Incidence Outreach Program (former Michigan School for the Blind). Amounts shown are for MSD use only.

DEPARTMENT OF
ENVIRONMENT, GREAT LAKES, AND ENERGY

LIESL EICHLER CLARK, DIRECTOR

Constitution Hall, 6th Floor South
P.O. Box 30473
Lansing, MI 48909-7973
www.Michigan.gov/EGLE

The Department of Environment, Great Lakes, and Energy (EGLE) protects Michigan's environment and public health by managing air, water, land, and energy resources.

Governor Gretchen Whitmer created EGLE in February 2019 by signing Executive Order No. 2019-6. In addition to renaming the former Department of Environmental Quality as EGLE, the order established the Office of Clean Water Public Advocate, the Office of Environmental Justice Public Advocate, and the Office of Climate and Energy within the new department. It also reestablished the Office of the Great Lakes in EGLE.

Consistent with Article V, Section 3, of the Michigan Constitution of 1963, the director of EGLE is appointed by and serves at the pleasure of the governor, subject to the advice and consent process. Executive Order No. 2019-6 establishes the director as the governor's chief advisor on policies and programs relating to energy, freshwater, and the Great Lakes. It also vests the director with a full complement of chief executive authorities, including allocating and reallocating duties, delegating powers to deputies, and setting the department's internal organization to promote "economic and efficient administration and operation."

Through its transition to EGLE, the department has retained its previous programmatic divisions focused on air quality, materials management, water resources, remediation and redevelopment, drinking water and environmental health, and oil, gas, and minerals. Much of EGLE's statutory authority is provided by the Natural Resources and Environmental Protection Act, 1994 PA 451, as amended. EGLE has also created three new divisions to assist with meeting the department's mission, optimizing performance, and supporting staff.

The **Air Quality Division** (AQD) supports efforts to maintain clean air and minimize adverse impacts on human health and the environment. AQD staff work to reduce existing outdoor air pollution and prevent deterioration of air quality through air emission control programs, air monitoring, control strategy planning, permit issuance, and inspection of air emission sources.

The **Drinking Water and Environmental Health Division** (DWEHD) oversees Michigan's public water supplies to ensure safe drinking water. The DWEHD is involved in source water protection, operator certification and training, water well construction, registration of water well drilling contractors, assisting local health departments in conducting drinking water quality investigations, approving and licensing the handling of domestic septage, and oversight of the on-site wastewater program. The DWEHD is also responsible for the approval and licensing of campgrounds and public swimming pools.

The **Environmental Support Division** (ESD) is responsible for EGLE's proactive outreach efforts and support functions necessary to maintain an effective organization. The ESD prepares professional materials to support EGLE's communication strategy. The ESD also hosts live events, coordinates webinars, produces videos, and develops publications. Working with program staff, the ESD assures public meetings and public hearings are professionally conducted. In addition, the ESD operates the call center, coordinates emergency response efforts, oversees EGLE's facilities, and provides training opportunities to staff.

The **Finance Division** (FD) is responsible for all financial aspects of EGLE from budget development to year-end closing. The FD Director serves as EGLE's Chief Financial Officer. The FD oversees the Michigan Underground Storage Tank Authority and the Water Infrastructure Financing Section. The Michigan Underground Storage Tank Authority assures underground storage tank owners and operators can meet federal financial requirements necessary to operate in Michigan and provides a funding mechanism to address environmental issues. The Water Infrastructure Financing Section is responsible for providing funding mechanisms to assist communities with meeting water infrastructure needs.

The **Information Management Division** (IMD) is responsible for establishing and implementing coordinated EGLE data management standards and processes for information tracking to support transparency and effective internal processes. The goal of the IMD is to implement processes that allow program staff more time to address program issues and less time on non-programmatic functions. The IMD is responsible for assessing information technology tools and strategies to meet the ever-changing business needs of EGLE. In addition, the IMD is responsible for coordinating EGLE's geographic infomation system initiatives, maintaining EGLE's website, and overseeing Freedom of Information Act responses. The IMD contains a Performance Optimization Section responsible for evaluating EGLE processes, updating department procedures, tracking audits, assuring corrective action plans are implemented, and coordinating appointments and other tasks for EGLE's various commissions.

The **Materials Management Division** (MMD) oversees the solid and hazardous waste programs, radioactive materials activities, radon awareness program, and energy program. The MMD oversees waste disposal, transportation, and storage, as well as implementing strategies to support pollution prevention and beneficial uses of waste materials. Activities in the radiological area include coordinating with nuclear power plants, local emergency responders, and the federal government to ensure that Michigan has sufficient resources in the event of a radioactive material release.

The **Oil, Gas, and Minerals Division** (OGMD) oversees the development of fossil fuels and minerals while ensuring the protection of natural resources, the environment, property, and public health and safety. The OGMD regulates the locating, drilling, operating, and plugging of wells used for exploration and production of oil, gas, brine, and minerals, as well as for underground storage and waste disposal. It also regulates mines for metallic minerals and industrial sand. Additionally, the OGMD maintains a variety of maps and data on Michigan geology, fossil fuels, and minerals for industry and public use.

The **Remediation and Redevelopment Division** (RRD) oversees the remediation and redevelopment of contaminated properties in Michigan. The RRD administers two environmental cleanup programs: the Environmental Remediation Program and the Leaking Underground Storage Tank Program. In addition, the RRD coordinates the implementation of brownfield redevelopment financing for environmental response activities. The RRD also manages portions of the federal Superfund Program and oversees EGLE's laboratory responsible for drinking water and environmental testing.

The **Water Resources Division** (WRD) protects and monitors Michigan's waters by establishing water quality standards, assessing the health of aquatic communities, issuing permits to regulate wastewater dischargers, and overseeing aquatic invasive species concerns and water withdrawals. The WRD processes permit applications and provides technical assistance to local soil erosion and sedimentation control programs, as well as activities like dredging or filling; constructing or dismantling dams; constructing marinas, seawalls, or docks; building in a designated critical sand dune, wetland, or floodplain; and protecting underwater shipwreck resources. The WRD oversees and issues construction permits for all public wastewater infrastructure, requires asset management in National Pollutant Discharge Elimination System permits to ensure proper maintenance, and oversees critical large-scale infrastructure improvements in the area of combined sewer overflow and sanitary sewer overflow control vital to the health of Michigan's waterways.

DEPARTMENT OF
HEALTH AND
HUMAN SERVICES

ROBERT GORDON, DIRECTOR
South Grand Building
333 S. Grand Avenue Lansing, MI 48933
www.michigan.gov/mdhhs

The Michigan Department of Health and Human Services (MDHHS) is the largest of the executive branch departments. The department provides opportunities, services, and programs that promote a healthy, safe and stable environment for residents to be self-sufficient.

MDHHS is responsible for health policy; management of the state's health, mental health, and substance abuse care systems; the Medicaid program; the child welfare system; and assisting children, families, and vulnerable adults to be safe, stable, and self-supporting through the distribution of public assistance and service programs in every county statewide.

Services provided by the department include:

The **Population Health Administration** protects and improves the health of Michigan individuals, families, communities, and populations. The Population Health Administration is responsible for many public health programs, including communicable disease surveillance and outbreak investigation; control and prevention of chronic diseases such as cancer, cardiovascular disease, diabetes, and injuries; health statistics compilation and dissemination; HIV and sexually transmitted disease prevention and care; immunizations; lead abatement; newborn screenings; and vital records collection and maintenance. The administration coordinates this work through contracts with local public health departments that serve all the jurisdictions in Michigan, as well as community-based and private health care organizations that support population health initiatives. The administration also serves Michigan residents through the Women, Infants, and Children program and is responsible for ensuring capacity and quality improvement among Michigan's local health departments, health care agencies, and community-based organizations.

The **Bureau of Emergency Medical Services, Trauma, and Preparedness** serves to better protect the health and well-being of Michigan residents through the administration and continuous improvement of emergency medical services, trauma system, and all-hazards preparedness planning and response.

The **Bureau of Epidemiology and Population Health** ensures the health and well-being of Michigan residents through education, technology, and the epidemiological process. It helps detect and prevent communicable diseases; tracks infectious diseases; addresses environmental dangers such as lead; and responds to outbreaks and prepares for public health emergencies. The bureau also maintains records for births, deaths, and marriages that occurred in Michigan and manages several disease registries.

The **Bureau of Health and Wellness** serves Michigan residents through a range of programs focused on disease prevention; chronic disease management; and the prevention, care, and treatment of HIV and sexually transmitted diseases.

The **Bureau of Family Health Services** promotes and improves the health and well-being of women, children, and families in Michigan by providing leadership in accessing services and supporting health equity. It serves Michigan residents through the Immunization Program, Maternal and Infant Health Program, and Child and Adolescent Health Program.

The **Bureau of Laboratories** manages one of the nation's leading public health laboratories. It serves Michigan residents by providing the following: essential public health laboratory testing services; support for public health programs at the state, local, and federal levels; laboratory results needed by health care providers, public health partners, epidemiologists, and researchers to advance public health services in their communities; and testing of all newborns for rare congenital disorders to prevent and treat serious health problems.

The **Office of Local Health Services** supports Michigan's 45 local health departments through funding and technical assistance. It also provides systematic review and assessment of jurisdictional capacity to meet program standards through the state accreditation process.

The **Medical Services Administration** (MSA) provides oversight of Michigan's Medicaid program. Medicaid provides medical assistance for low-income residents who meet certain eligibility criteria. The program pays for a broad range of services, such as inpatient and outpatient hospital care, physician visits, drugs, long-term care, durable medical equipment, and behavioral health services. MSA also administers the MIChild program — a comprehensive benefits package for the children of Michigan's eligible working families. The current Medicaid caseload is more than 2.4 million people. Approximately 43 percent of the Medicaid beneficiaries receiving services are children. The administration also operates the Healthy Michigan Plan, providing health care coverage at a low cost to approximately 680,000 eligible adults. Approximately 80 percent of Michigan's Medicaid population is enrolled or is required to enroll in a managed care organization.

The public **Behavioral Health and Developmental Disabilities Administration** (BHDDA) operates under the authority of the Michigan Mental Health Code. As such, the code charges MDHHS to provide and administer services and support to children and youth with serious emotional disturbance, adults with serious mental illness, and persons with intellectual/developmental disability, and/or substance use disorders. BHDDA is comprised of the following organizational units: Bureau of Community Based Services, Bureau of State Hospitals, Children and Adults with Autism Spectrum Disorder Section, and the Michigan Developmental Disabilities Council.

The **Bureau of Community-Based Services**, under contracts with BHDDA, delivers publicly funded mental health services through a system of 46 county-based Community Mental Health Services Programs (CMHSPs). These CMHSPs provide a comprehensive set of prevention, treatment, and support services to Michigan's 83 counties. For Medicaid beneficiaries, specialty behavioral health and intellectual/developmental disability services are funded and delivered through specialty behavioral health managed care plans called Prepaid Inpatient Health Plans (PIHPs). PIHPs receive capitated funding from MDHHS to administer Medicaid specialty services to Medicaid beneficiaries through the CMHSP system and other contracted providers. In addition, PIHPs assume the role of department-designated "Community Mental Health Entities" and are charged with the provision of services to individuals with substance use disorders.

Through the **Bureau of State Hospitals**, BHDDA directly operates five state psychiatric inpatient facilities to supplement the primary inpatient hospital programs that are part of the local PIHP/CMHSP service network. These facilities serve the most severely mentally ill children and adults, including those with criminal justice and forensic involvement.

The **Children and Adults with Autism Spectrum Disorder Section** coordinates autism spectrum disorder efforts between state agencies and administers the MDHHS Autism Council, MDHHS autism contracts granted to universities, and behavior analysis services for those with autism spectrum disorder.

The **Michigan Developmental Disabilities Council**, authorized under Executive Order 2006-12 and the Developmental Disabilities Assistance and Bill of Rights Act of 2000, is a gubernatorial-appointed body that advocates for those with developmental disabilities in the state.

The **Aging and Adult Services Agency** promotes and enhances the dignity and independence of older and vulnerable adults in Michigan. It allocates and monitors state and federal funds to Michigan's area agencies on aging for all Older Americans Act services, including nutrition, community services, caregiver support, legal services, elder abuse prevention, and care management. It also handles adult services policy and long-term care policy at the state level, and oversees the Michigan Long-Term Care Ombudsman program.

The **Children's Services Agency** investigates complaints of child abuse and neglect, intervenes to ensure child safety and provides a continuum of statewide services to strengthen families so they can remain together safely. Through its local offices and private child placing agencies, the Children's

Services Agency supervises about 13,500 children placed in foster care and refers children and their families to services to meet their unique needs — including medical and mental health needs — and helps them overcome trauma, build resilience, and be safely reunified. When children cannot be safely reunified with their parents, the agency works to develop permanent relationships through adoption and guardianship. The Children's Services Agency administers grants and contracts for community-based prevention, homeless youth and runaway programs, recruitment of foster and adoptive homes, and independent living programs. The agency regulates all licensed child placing agencies that provide foster care and residential services and oversees the operation of state juvenile justice programs and facilities.

MDHHS staff and contractors deliver a wide range of services for families and children of Michigan. They include protective and preventive services for children who are neglected, abused, or exploited. The agency provides a range of institutional and noninstitutional social services for the care, training, and treatment of neglected and delinquent children committed to the department as state wards and temporary court wards. Such services include casework and counseling, adoption, foster care, and the operation of centers for institutional residential care and group homes. In addition, the Children's Services Agency offers consultation on general child welfare issues to private and public agencies throughout the state and offers services through an interstate compact.

Field Operations provides safety-net services and temporary public assistance to families and individuals statewide, as there are offices for all 83 counties. Field Operations also handles applications for public assistance, including financial assistance through the Family Independence Program; State Disability Assistance, Food Assistance Program; state emergency relief; child development and care; refugee assistance services; migrant services; disability determination service; and the Office of Child Support. Caseworkers are assigned to more than 200 schools so that they are more accessible to children and families in need and are better positioned to help customers remove barriers to success.

The **Financial Operations Administration** is responsible for the overall financial and central operations administration for the department, which includes the Bureau of Finance and Accounting, the Bureau of Budget, the Bureau of Grants and Purchasing, the Bureau of Internal Audit, the Bureau of IT Support Services, and the Bureau of Organizational Services, providing statewide operational and building oversight for all local department offices.

The **Office of Recipient Rights.** The Office of Recipient Rights provides rights protection services to individuals admitted to state psychiatric hospitals and centers. It also has a mandate to assess and monitor the quality and effectiveness of the rights protection systems in the community mental health service programs and to provide education and training to both the community mental health service programs and licensed private psychiatric hospitals.

The **Office of Inspector General** (OIG) is an independent and autonomous criminal justice agency within the Department. The OIG is committed to the mission of detecting, investigating, and preventing fraud and abuse and promoting efficiency and effectiveness of MDHHS programs and operations. The office makes referrals for prosecution and disposition of appropriate cases as determined by the inspector general; reviews administrative policies, practices, and procedures; and makes recommendations to improve program integrity and accountability. Areas of oversight include but are not limited to: Health Services Programs (Medicaid, Mental Health, MIChild, the Healthy Michigan Plan, Children's Special Healthcare Services), the Food Assistance Program, the Family Independence Program (cash assistance), Children's Services, Aging and Adult Services, and other program areas as deemed necessary.

The **Strategic Integration Administration** (SIA) supports MDHHS's business needs by ensuring initiatives align with the strategic priorities and direction of the department; providing structure and governance to keep projects on schedule while mitigating issues and risks; and identifying ways to achieve efficiencies by reusing technology and data readily available to us and avoiding duplication. In addition, SIA is the designated authority for the development, education, and enforcement of policies, standards, and procedures to ensure the protection, governance, and sharing of data and information, as well as, promoting the rights of individuals, families, and children who access our services and programs.

The **Legal Affairs Administration** office for MDHHS assists the department's staff in carrying out responsibilities in accordance with applicable laws, provides legal research and input, and ensures compliance with the Freedom of Information Act. The office also oversees and coordinates rulemaking under the Administrative Procedures Act; administrates the department's Institutional Review Board; represents the department in administrative hearings involving assistance programs; and responds to subpoenas. Working closely with the Department of Attorney General, the legal office coordinates the department's administrative hearings, litigation, and requests for legal advice.

The **Office of External Relations and Communications** is responsible for the internal and external engagement and communication with department stakeholders.

The **Michigan Community Services Commission** promotes service as a strategy to address the state's most pressing issues and empowers volunteers to strengthen communities through programs such as Michigan's AmeriCorps, Mentor Michigan, Volunteer Michigan, and the Governor's Service Awards.

The **Office of Faith and Community Engagement** promotes collaboration between state departments and faith- and community-based agencies to improve the quality of life for Michigan residents.

The **Workforce Engagement and Transformation** works within MDHHS to inform, engage, and empower department employees and improve program efficiency and operations.

The **Office of Communication** is responsible for all MDHHS internal and external communications, including responding to news media requests, communicating with the department's 14,000 employees, and keeping stakeholders informed.

Policy and Planning Services administration includes Michigan Rehabilitation Services, the Bureau of Community Services, the Office of Planning, and the Policy and Innovation Division.

The **Policy and Innovation Division** provides policy analysis, strategic alignment, and program management support for crosscutting departmental priorities, and leads efforts around health disparities reduction and data-sharing.

The **Office of Planning** plans for and manages the state's medical facilities and equipment needs through the Certificate of Need program and supports the healthcare workforce through programs like loan forgiveness for medical professionals working in underserved areas. It also manages Pathways to Potential, which places caseworkers in schools to remove barriers to success for children and families.

The **Bureau of Community Services** oversees the department's housing and homelessness funding and programs and the Division of Victim Services. It also manages the Division of Community Action and Economic Opportunity, which supports weatherization programs, distributes grants, and works with local Community Action Agencies to reduce poverty and empower low-income people.

The **Michigan Rehabilitation Services** provides specialized employment and education-related services and training to assist teens and adults with disabilities in becoming employed or retaining employment and also works with employers to support them in attracting, retaining and supporting workers with disabilities.

The **Legislative, Appropriations and Constituent Services** works with constituents and members of the Michigan Legislature and their offices and focuses on appropriations and policy.

STATISITICAL DATA FOR THE FIVE STATE-RUN PSYCHIATRIC HOSPITALS FOR ADULTS AND CHILDREN WHO HAVE A MENTAL ILLNESS

	FISCAL YEAR 2017	FISCAL YEAR 2018
CARO CENTER		
Director - Rose Laskowski		
Salary	$133,427	$136,096
Residents	146	147
Appropriations	$57,270,900	$59,211,600
Expenditures		
Salaries and wages	$42,062,348	$40,321,552
Other operating costs	$6,030,868	$9,270,949
Total	$48,093,216	$49,592,501
CENTER FOR FORENSIC PSYCHIATRY		
Director - Estelle Horne (acting)[1]		
Salary	$239,269	$244,054
Residents	248	259
Appropriations	$81,702,000	$82,823,400
Expenditures		
Salaries and wages	$71,162,642	$73,674,562
Other operating costs	$12,114,719	$11,056,326
Total	$83,277,361	$84,730,888
HAWTHORN CENTER		
Director - Andrea VanDenBergh (acting)[1]		
Salary	$239,269	$283,523
Residents	47	53
Appropriations	$29,142,500	$31,793,100
Expenditures		
Salaries and wages	$26,247,274	$27,433,909
Other operating costs	$2,826,640	$5,488,880
Total	$29,073,914	$32,922,789
KALAMAZOO PSYCHIATRIC HOSPITAL		
Director - Jill Krause		
Salary	$133,427	$136,096
Residents	141	139
Appropriations	$65,674,600	$68,057,700
Expenditures		
Salaries and wages	$54,497,402	$53,479,060
Other operating costs	$6,495,090	$9,460,151
Total	$60,992,492	$62,939,211
WALTER REUTHER PSYCHIATRIC HOSPITAL		
Director - Mary Clare Solky		
Salary	$239,269	$244,054
Residents	170	166
Appropriations	$56,872,000	$59,603,400
Expenditures		
Salaries and wages	$43,705,880	$42,316,659
Other operating costs	$9,574,307	$13,349,489
Total	$53,280,187	$55,666,148

[1] Salary may not reflect actual data for an acting director.

Source: Michigan Department of Health and Human Services, September 30, 2019.

DEPARTMENT OF
INSURANCE AND FINANCIAL SERVICES

ANITA G. FOX, DIRECTOR
530 W. Allegan Street
P.O. Box 30220, Lansing, MI 48909
www.michigan.gov/difs

Consisting of approximately 345 professionals, the Department of Insurance and Financial Services (DIFS) administers 40 public acts and regulates a variety of individual licensees and entities, including: HMOs, domestic and foreign insurance companies, banks, credit unions, insurance agents, agencies, adjusters, solicitors and counselors, mortgage licensees and registrants, deferred presentment companies, and other consumer finance-related entities.

The department is composed of nine program and regulatory offices: Banking; Consumer Finance; Consumer Services; Credit Unions; Fraud Investigation; General Counsel; Insurance Evaluation; Insurance Rates and Forms; Insurance Licensing and Market Conduct; and Policy, Research, and Communications.

The **Office of Banking** is responsible for all aspects of the supervision, regulation, and examination of state-chartered banks, savings banks, trust-only banks, and trust departments, including processing related corporate applications and requests. The office is also responsible for examining business and industrial development companies.

The **Office of Consumer Finance** is responsible for the licensing, regulation, and examination of entities and individuals doing business under various Michigan consumer finance statutes, including mortgage brokers, lenders, and servicers, mortgage loan originators, money transmitters, deferred presentment providers, direct loan companies, motor vehicle installment sellers and sales finance companies, and other consumer finance providers.

The **Office of Consumer Services** is responsible for managing consumer information, inquiries, and complaints. This office is also responsible for overseeing the communication center, which serves as the initial point of contact for all incoming calls and visitors.

The **Office of Credit Unions** is dedicated to maintaining the public confidence in Michigan state-chartered credit unions, and to ensuring Michigan state-chartered credit unions provide safe, sound, and reliable financial services to their members.

The **Office of General Counsel** is responsible for providing legal advice and representation to the Director and DIFS staff with respect to: enforcement actions, formal administrative hearings, receivership proceedings, orders, rules, statutes, regulations, bulletins, declaratory rulings, health benefit claims, special projects, legislative research and analysis, and processing Patient's Right to Independent Review Act appeals. The general counsel serves as FOIA coordinator and acts as liaison with the Attorney General and other state/federal agencies. The Fraud Investigation Unit is also housed within the Office of General Counsel and is responsible for performing the collection, analysis and investigations of complaints alleging fraudulent activities in Michigan's insurance and financial services markets and coordinating DIFS' investigative efforts with the Attorney General's Office and law enforcement.

The **Office of Insurance Evaluation** is responsible for all aspects of monitoring and regulating the financial condition of risk bearing insurance entities including: the processing of applications for licensure filed by insurance companies, on-site financial examinations of domestic insurance companies, ongoing financial monitoring of licensed insurance companies, and working with insurance companies reporting negative trends to take appropriate corrective measures. The office is also responsible for the licensing, monitoring, and examination of captive insurers.

The **Office of Insurance Rates and Forms** is responsible for enforcing Michigan insurance statutes and regulations pertaining to rates and forms submitted by insurance companies and other licensed entities. The office is also responsible for reviewing all filings relative to the Patient Protection and Affordable Care Act.

The **Office of Insurance Licensing and Market Conduct** is responsible for licensing individual and agency insurance producers (agents), solicitors, counselors, adjusters, foreign risk retention groups, premium finance companies, purchasing groups, reinsurance intermediaries, and third-party administrators. The office is also responsible for market conduct examinations of insurers, investigations and audits of insurance agents/entities, and monitoring of all surplus lines tax filings and payments.

The **Office of Policy, Research, and Communications** is responsible for creating, researching, and advancing the legislative agenda and communications efforts on behalf of the Department. The office oversees contact with legislators, committee activity, legislative tracking, research, and analyses. The office also oversees contact with the media, external communications including social and digital media, publication management, and education and outreach along with management of internal office communication. Additionally, it houses the Insurance Innovation Hotline.

DEPARTMENT OF
LABOR AND ECONOMIC OPPORTUNITY

JEFFREY M. DONOFRIO, DIRECTOR
105 W. Allegan St.
Lansing, MI 48933
www.michigan.gov/leo

The Department of Labor and Economic Opportunity (LEO) was created under Executive Order 2019-13 by Governor Gretchen Whitmer to streamline and better coordinate efforts within state government to meet the state's business and labor needs by consolidating workforce and economic development functions in one department. LEO includes the Michigan State Housing Development Authority, the Michigan Strategic Fund, and the Michigan Office for Global Michigan (formerly known as the Office for New Americans). LEO also houses two new commissions: the Workers' Disability Compensation Appeals Commission and the Unemployment Insurance Appeals Commission.

The **Michigan State Housing Development Authority** provides financial and technical assistance through public and private partnerships to create and preserve safe and decent affordable housing.

The **Michigan Strategic Fund** (MSF) was created by Public Act 270 of 1984 and has broad authority to promote economic development and create jobs. The MSF board has the following responsibilities:

- Approve grants and loans under the Michigan Business Development Program.
- Approve grants and loans under the Michigan Community Revitalization Program.
- Approve the use of Private Activity Revenue Bonds.
- Authorize the submittal by local units of government of Community Development Block Grant applications.
- Recommend to the State Administrative Board Agricultural Processing, Renewable Energy, and Forest Products Processing Renaissance Zone designations.
- Approve Tool and Die Renaissance Recovery Zones.
- Act as the fiduciary agent with respect to the 21st Century Jobs Fund investments.
- Pursuant to statute, the Chief Compliance Officer provides advice and guidance in regard to the 21st Century Jobs Fund.

The **Michigan Occupational Safety and Health Administration** protects Michigan workers by promoting workplace safety and health through outreach training services, fair enforcement, and cooperative agreements.

The **Unemployment Insurance Agency** provides temporary income to jobless workers while they are seeking employment.

The **Michigan Office of Global Michigan** helps grow Michigan's economy by attracting global talent to our state and promoting the skills, energy, and entrepreneurial spirit of our immigrant communities.

The **Workforce Development Agency's** vision is to promote a flexible, innovative, and effective workforce system within the State of Michigan.

The **Michigan Land Bank Authority** promotes economic growth in this state through the acquisition, assembly and disposal of public property, including tax reverted property, in a coordinated manner to foster the development of that property, and to promote and support land bank operations at the county and local levels.

The **Bureau of Services for Blind Persons** (BSBP) assists more than 4,500 blind and visually impaired individuals annually to achieve employment and independence, and helps employers find and retain qualified workers. BSBP serves people of all ages.

The **Workers' Compensation Agency** administers the Workers' Disability Compensation Act, which provides wage replacement, medical, and vocational rehabilitation benefits to men and women who suffer work-related injuries and disabilities. The agency also ensures compliance with the mandatory insurance provisions of the act to protect injured workers and to protect Michigan employers from unfair competition by those who are not in compliance.

Other bureaus and agencies located within LEO include the Bureau of Employment Relations, MiSTEM Network, Michigan Economic Development Corporation, Michigan Economic Development Corporation, Michigan Occupational Safety and Health Administration, Michigan Rehabilitation Services, Nonincorporated Private Educational Institutions, the State Historic Preservation Office, Wage and Hour Division of Employment Relations, and Workforce Development.

DEPARTMENT OF
LICENSING AND REGULATORY AFFAIRS

ORLENE HAWKS, DIRECTOR
611 W. Ottawa, 4th Floor
P.O. Box 30004, Lansing, MI 48909
www.michigan.gov/lara

The Department of Licensing and Regulatory Affairs (LARA) is composed of the following agencies, bureaus, and commissions that promote business growth and job creation through streamlined, simple, fair, and efficient regulation, and at the same time protect the health and safety of Michigan's citizens.

Agencies, Bureaus, and Commissions

The **Corporations, Securities and Commercial Licensing Bureau** (CSCL) supports business growth and job creation while protecting the health, safety, and welfare of Michigan's citizens through a simple, fair, efficient, and transparent regulatory structure. CSCL protects consumers through the licensing and regulation of certain professions, occupations, businesses, and services. While the bureau does not have the authority to enforce the ethical standards of a profession, or to handle fee disputes, it does have the authority to investigate and to pursue disciplinary action against a license, registration, or permit issued by the bureau.

CSCL performs the public facing duties of helping to grow business activity in Michigan through the Corporations division, and by protecting the health, welfare, and safety of Michigan citizens through regulatory and licensing functions of the Securities and Audit, Licensing, and Regulatory Compliance divisions. In addition to the divisions listed below, the bureau also includes the IT and Web Development Section.

The **Corporations Division** promotes economic development and growth by facilitating the formation and development of business entities in the state. The division enables domestic and foreign corporations, limited partnerships, and limited liability companies to transact business in the state.

The **Securities and Audit Division** administers the Michigan Uniform Securities Act and the Living Care Disclosure Act, regulating securities offerings, broker-dealers, securities agents, investment advisers, investment adviser representatives, and living care facilities. The division is committed to educating and protecting Michigan investors and consumers while fostering efficient capital formation in Michigan. The Audit Section conducts audits of the financial records of licensees who maintain trust or escrow accounts on behalf of the public in professions under our jurisdiction. These professions include real estate brokers, prepaid funeral contractors, collection agencies, and privately-owned cemeteries. The audits are conducted on a complaint, routine, or random basis.

The **Licensing Division** protects the health, safety, and welfare of the public by ensuring that applicants, licensees, and registrants meet reasonable and appropriate legal requirements for the practice of 17 professions, while providing businesses the opportunity to flourish without having to navigate a web of complex and confusing regulations. Professions/occupations that are handled by the Schools and Licensing Section include: Cemetery, Cemetery Renewals, Commission Support, Midwestern State Authorization Reciprocity Agreement, Mortuary Science,

Polygraph, Prepaid Funerals, Private Colleges & Universities, Professional Employer Organizations, Professional Investigators, Proprietary Schools, Security Alarms, Security Alarm Systems, Security Guards, Student Transcripts, Transportation Network Companies, and Vehicle Protection Warrantors.

The **Regulatory Compliance Division** provides fair and uniform access to the bureau's public records, and fair and equal due process to licensees and registrants accused of violating the statutes and rules administered by CSCL, by conducting compliance conferences and coordinating or undertaking legal representation of the bureau at contested case proceedings. The division also timely, accurately, and effectively drafts and serves CSCL's administrative complaints, subpoenas, and other legal pleadings or orders. It assists the bureau director in tracking and analyzing proposed legislation, responding to legislative inquiries, and promulgating administrative rules. Finally, the division provides prompt, thorough, and polite customer service with an emphasis on respect for others, uniformity, inclusiveness, honesty, and integrity.

The **Office of Communications** responds to inquiries from the news media, issues news releases about important developments in programs and services, and provides public information and news of internal departmental events and policies. The office ensures that key information is communicated to both the internal and external customers of LARA.

The **Bureau of Community and Health Systems** (BCHS) is responsible for state licensing and regulation of facilities, agencies, and programs under the Michigan Public Health Code, Mental Health Code, Adult Foster Care Facility Licensing Act, and the Child Care Organizations Act. BCHS is also the State Survey Agency (SA) for the federal Centers for Medicare and Medicaid Services (CMS) under the Social Security Act §1864 agreement with the U.S. Secretary of Health and Human Services. As the SA, BCHS monitors and determines regulatory compliance of CMS-certified facilities/agencies under federal law and regulations. The mission of BCHS is to protect the health, safety, and welfare of individuals receiving services from state licensed and federally certified providers. A major part of regulatory and licensing activities is performed by field staff statewide, who conduct routine inspections and complaint investigations, and educate providers and the public. The bureau's divisions are: Federal Survey and Certification, Child Care Licensing, Adult Foster Care Facility Licensing and Children's Camps Division, Health Facility State Licensing, Permits, and Support Division.

The **Bureau of Construction Codes** (BCC) is responsible for the construction code enforcement and licensing of those individuals working in boiler, building, code inspection, electrical, elevator, mechanical, plumbing, and ski/amusement trades as well as overseeing the manufactured housing program. BCC also ensures an orderly and consistent review of subdivision plats and administers the statewide program of monumenting and remonumenting the original U.S. government public land survey property. The State Boundary Commission within the bureau is responsible for adjudicating many types of municipal boundary adjustments.

The **Bureau of Employment Relations** (BER) The Michigan Employment Relations Commission (MERC) housed within the BER resolves labor disputes involving public and private sector employees by appointing mediators, arbitrators and fact finders, conducting union representation elections, determining appropriate bargaining units, and adjudicating unfair labor practice cases.

Wage & Hour administers the laws that protect the wages and fringe benefits of Michigan's workers and ensures compliance with the requirement that certain entities post notices related to human trafficking. The division investigates complaints alleging non-payment of wages and fringe benefits, state minimum wage, overtime, equal pay, prevailing wage disputes, and not displaying human trafficking notifications. The Wage and Hour Division also educates employers and employees in the areas covered by these labor standards.

Ethnic Commissions The Michigan Asian Pacific American Affairs Commission, the Commission on Middle Eastern American Affairs, and the Hispanic/Latino Commission are housed in LARA.

The **Bureau of Fire Services** (BFS) serves the training needs of Michigan firefighters; reviews, plans, and inspects state-regulated facilities for fire and life safety.

The **Aboveground and Underground Storage Tank Program** protects the public health, environment, and natural resources of Michigan from environmental contamination and fire safety hazards associated with storage tanks.

627 Tank Truck Program Rule 627 Tank Truck Test Program (Part 55 of the Natural Resources and Protection Act; 1994 PA 451), requires that all delivery vessels perform a pressure/vacuum test annually as performed by LARA.

The **Office of Human Resources** provides a full range of human resources services for all LARA employees, and follows the guiding principles of collaboration, inclusion, integrity, and measurable outcomes to guide LARA in its mission.

The **Marijuana Regulatory Agency** (MRA) oversees the licensing of adult-use marijuana and medical marijuana in Michigan. MRA regulates the state's marijuana facilities and licensees, and tracks marijuana product from seed to sale. The bureau also oversees the state's patient registry program and administers the Michigan Medical Marihuana Act.

The **Michigan Administrative Hearing System** centralizes state government functions related to conducting administrative hearings and includes the Michigan Compensation Appellate Commission, the Michigan Tax Tribunal, Workers' Compensation Board of Magistrates, and the Qualifications Advisory Committee.

The **Michigan Indigent Defense Commission** develops and oversees the implementation, enforcement, and modification of minimum standards, rules, and procedures to ensure that indigent criminal defense services providing effective assistance of counsel are delivered to all indigent adults in this state consistent with the safeguards of the United States Constitution, the Constitution of Michigan of 1963, and with the Michigan Indigent Defense Commission Act.

The **Michigan Liquor Control Commission** regulates availability of alcoholic beverages for consumption while protecting consumers and the general public through regulation of the related industries.

The **Michigan Office of Administrative Hearings and Rules** (MOAHR) is a Type I Agency, created by EO 2019-06. MOAHR includes a Central Panel Administrative Hearing System housed in offices across the state, as well as the agency that oversees administrative rulemaking for the state departments. Administrative hearings handled by MOAHR include benefits issues, regulatory issues, and licensing issues. The state agencies that refer matters for hearing include the bureaus of Community and Health Systems, Marijuana Regulatory Agency, and Professional Licensing; the Department of Health and Human Services; the Public Service Commission; the Unemployment Insurance Agency; and the Workers' Compensation Agency. In addition to several divisions of administrative law judges, the Michigan Compensation Appellate Commission, the Michigan Tax Tribunal, and the Workers' Compensation Board of Magistrates are also part of MOAHR. The organizational mission is to provide all parties in need of administrative hearings and rules with a timely, professional, sound, and respectful process.

The **Michigan Public Service Commission** regulates electric and natural gas utilities, as well as many telecommunications services, to ensure safe, reliable, and accessible energy and telecommunication services at reasonable rates for Michigan's residents.

The **Office of Policy and Legislative Affairs** coordinates legislative activity for the department including monitoring legislation and reviewing and advising on legislative proposals as well as serving as a liaison to the Office of Regulatory Reinvention.

The **Bureau of Professional Licensing** (BPL) is responsible for licensing and regulating more than 700,000 individuals who are regulated by either the Michigan Occupational Code or the Public Health Code. BPL is also responsible for maintaining the Health Professional Recovery Program the Michigan Automated Prescription System and overseeing the certification and regulation of qualified sign language interpreters. The mission of BPL is to protect, preserve and improve the health, safety and welfare of Michigan's citizens through the licensing and regulation of occupational and health professionals. BPL is designed to make the regulatory system simple, fair and efficient. BPL divisions and sections are: Enforcement, Licensing, Investigations and Inspections, Drug Monitoring, Boards and Committees, Michigan Professional Licensing User System and Information Technology.

DEPARTMENT OF
MILITARY AND VETERANS AFFAIRS

MAJOR GENERAL PAUL D. ROGERS, DIRECTOR/ ADJUTANT GENERAL OF MICHIGAN

Headquarters Building
3411 N. Martin Luther King Jr. Boulevard, Lansing, MI 48906
www.michigan.gov/dmva

The Department of Military and Veterans Affairs, also known as the state military establishment, has three primary missions: to execute the duties required by various statutes and the Governor, to administer state-supported veterans programming, and to assist both state and federal authorities with military preparedness. The Michigan Army and Air National Guard constitute the armed forces of the state and serve under the orders of the Governor as commander-in-chief. The Governor appoints an adjutant general to serve as commanding general of the Michigan National Guard and as director of the Department of Military and Veterans Affairs.

The primary military mission of the department is to recruit, train, and maintain the Michigan Army and Air National Guard as reserve components of the United States Army and Air Force for federal mobilization.

The state military mission of the department is to train and maintain National Guard forces for the protection of life and property of Michigan citizens in natural disasters and the preservation of peace, order, and public safety.

The Department of Military and Veterans Affairs provides support services for the approximately 11,000 military personnel constituting the Michigan National Guard. Approximately 3,000 full-time employees (state and federal) are assigned to various divisions, sections, and units located across the state, including 41 armories, two air bases (Selfridge Air National Guard Base and Battle Creek Air National Guard Base), and two army training Centers (Camp Grayling which has 146,000 acres and Fort Custer Training Center in Augusta which has 7,500 acres).

The department, through the **Michigan Veterans Affairs Agency**, provides executive oversight and coordination for state veterans programming. Operations encompass the Service Administration with oversight of the Grand Rapids and D.J. Jacobetti (Marquette) Veterans Homes, the Michigan Veterans Trust Fund, and the Michigan Veterans Homeowners Assistance Program. The Targeted Initiatives Administration is responsible for the agency's strategy development, internal and external communications, the Veterans Resource Service Center — a 24/7 resource for Michigan's veterans, family members and service providers, and the administration of annual grants to veterans service organizations who assist veterans in processing claims with the federal government.

D.J. JACOBETTI VETERANS HOME

425 Fisher Street
Marquette, MI 49855

Established in 1981, the DJ. Jacobetti Veterans Home provides dignified service and quality care in a homelike environment full of activity. Located in Marquette near the shores of Lake Superior, the Jacobetti Home provides skilled nursing care, a memory care unit and domiciliary care services. The Home offers physician coverage as well as the following services: pharmacy, respiratory therapy, physical therapy, in-patient rehabilitation, mental health, social work, routine dental examination, speech therapy, occupational therapy, laboratory services, recreation therapy, EKG, and specialty clinics.

	FISCAL YEAR 2016-2017	FISCAL YEAR 2017-2018
Salary Administrator	$114,561	$119,716
Population[1]	181	175
Revenues[2]	$23,329,034	$24,411,272
Expenditures	$22,147,203	$23,984,251

GRAND RAPIDS VETERANS HOME

3000 Monroe Ave NE
Grand Rapids MI 49505

The Grand Rapids Home for Veterans is a long-term care state veterans home located on 90 beautifully wooded and landscaped acres near the Grand River. The campus first opened in 1885 and has received many upgrades and new facilities over the years, including the current construction of a new 128-bed facility (opening 2021). The Grand Rapids Veterans Home provides skilled nursing care, specialized units for memory care and individuals with dual diagnoses and domiciliary care services. Health care services are extensive including a psychiatric program, pharmacy, rehabilitation therapy, and specialty clinics.

	FISCAL YEAR 2016-2017	FISCAL YEAR 2017-2018
Salary Chief Operating Officer	$120,000	$122,000
Population[1]	357	271
Revenues[2]	$43,450,614	$41,890,151
Expenditures	$44,557,159	$42,517,868

---

[1] End of Fiscal Year population includes skilled nursing and domiciliary.
[2] Posted revenue plus general funds spent.

Source: Michigan Department of Military and Veterans Affairs, September, 2019.

DEPARTMENT OF
NATURAL RESOURCES

DAN EICHINGER, DIRECTOR

Constitution Hall
525 West Allegan Street
P.O. Box 30028, Lansing, MI 48909-7528
www.michigan.gov/dnr

The Department of Natural Resources (DNR) is committed to the conservation, protection, management, use, and enjoyment of the state's natural and cultural resources for current and future generations — a role it has embraced since the creation of Michigan's original Conservation Department in 1921.

The director serves as the department's chief executive officer, monitors program activities to ensure efficiency and effectiveness of department operations, and ensures that the department's mission, policies, and statutory mandates are met. The director's primary authority flows from the Natural Resources and Environmental Protection Act (Public Act 451 of 1994, as amended) and is authorized by Executive Order 1991-31 to delegate decision-making authorities to appropriate levels within the department. DNR divisions, programs, and offices are housed within two main bureaus, Resource and Administration, while some other positions report directly to the department director.

Resource Bureau

The Resource Bureau includes the Fisheries Division, the Forest Resources Division, the Law Enforcement Division, the Parks and Recreation Division, the Wildlife Division and the Office of Minerals Management.

The **Fisheries Division** is mandated to protect and manage the state's aquatic resources, including fish populations, other aquatic life, and habitats that are held in trust for all Michigan citizens. The division promotes the wise use of these resources for the benefit of current and future generations. Online at: www.michigan.gov/fishing.

Michigan offers a wealth of fishing opportunities with its two peninsulas that touch four of the five Great Lakes. The state has more than 11,000 inland lakes and tens of thousands of miles of rivers and streams. Michigan has 3,000 miles of freshwater shoreline — more than any other state.

Fish populations and other forms of aquatic life are monitored and studied by biologists to ensure these resources' long-term protection. Up to 12 fish species are hatched and reared at six state hatcheries, which have state-of-the-art facilities to produce fish of very high quality. These fish are stocked annually into designated public waters throughout the state to maintain or improve fish populations. Michigan ranks fifth in the nation in fishing participation, with 1.1 million licensed anglers who annually contribute $2.3 billion to the state economy.

The **Forest Resources Division** manages, protects, and provides for the sustainable use of Michigan's forest resources. Michigan has one of the largest dedicated state forest systems in the nation, spanning four million acres. This division sustainably manages those acres to provide critical habitat for wildlife, valuable resources for a thriving timber products industry, and outdoor spaces for recreation. Michigan's forests and other land-based industries play a crucial role in supporting regional and rural economies. Online at: www.michigan.gov/forestry.

Forest health program staff and DNR partners work to ensure forest vitality by detecting, monitoring, and managing forest health issues. Private landowners, cities, and rural communities benefit from programs that leverage federal dollars to help create sustainable landscapes across the state. The Forests Resources Division also houses the Resource Assessment Section, which uses state-of-the-art mapping techniques to aid in managing various resources.

The division is also charged with protecting state forest resources and private land across the state through its nationally recognized wildfire suppression program.

The **Law Enforcement Division** is home to Michigan's conservation officers. It is Michigan's oldest statewide law enforcement agency, created in 1887. Conservation officers use law enforcement and education to protect Michigan's natural resources and environment for the health, safety, and enjoyment of the public. They are state-licensed law enforcement officers with authority to enforce all criminal and civil laws in Michigan. While primarily enforcing regulations for outdoor recreation activities such as off-road vehicle use, snowmobiling, boating, hunting, and fishing, they also provide traditional law enforcement assistance, when needed, to communities across the state and often serve as first responders. The Law Enforcement Division handles many other responsibilities, including education, recreational safety, and public outreach. The division provides investigative and enforcement services and coordinates emergency management and homeland security responsibilities for the department. Online at: www.michigan.gov/conservationofficers.

The division continually evolves to meet new challenges and deliver more effective service. Additional staffing, harnessing technology, and training in the latest investigative techniques are key drivers of its success. New officers have been hired each year since Fiscal Year 2014 thanks to funding investments by the state. Now, more than 240 sworn officers fill its ranks. To stay on the cutting edge of technology, the division enhanced its Report All Poaching system in 2017 to accept text messages, including photographs.

The **Parks and Recreation Division** protects, preserves, acquires, and manages Michigan's state parks, cultural, and historic resources within state parks, trails, state forests, and more than 1,300 boat launches. The division also operates 19 state harbors and partners with 63 locally-operated public harbors that make up the Harbors of Refuge system along the Great Lakes. Michigan's 103 state parks annually host more than 28 million visitors and are a major attraction for Michigan's tourism industry, contributing $650 million to the state's economy in day-use visits and camping alone. Online at: www.michigan.gov/stateparks.

The **Recreation Passport** grants Michigan residents vehicle access to Michigan state parks, recreation areas, state trailhead parking, and fee-based boat launches, while also helping to sustain the natural, historic, and cultural places of Michigan. The Recreation Passport is purchased when residents renew a Michigan license plate through the Secretary of State. The current fee is $11 for vehicles and $6 for motorcycles. In addition to supporting statewide recreation, the Recreation Passport also provides communities with recreation development grants for projects that provide health benefits, enhance property values, drive local economies, and improve quality of life. Online at: www.michigan.gov/recreationpassport.

Michigan's more than 12,500 miles of state-designated trails connect hikers, bicyclists, equestrians, off-road vehicle users, kayakers, and snowmobilers to Michigan's great outdoors. In addition, Michigan is home to the Iron Belle Trail — the longest state-designated trail in the nation — encompassing more than 2,000 miles with a route for hiking and a route for biking. It extends from Belle Isle in Detroit to Ironwood in the western Upper Peninsula. The trail is more than 70 percent complete and funding is still being secured to complete the trail.

The **Wildlife Division's** mission is "to enhance, restore, and conserve the state's wildlife resources, natural communities, and ecosystems for the benefit of Michigan's citizens, visitors, and future generations." The conservation of more than 400 species of animals — the birds and mammals that sustain our state's hunting heritage, as well as nongame wildlife, including threatened and endangered plant and animal species — is part of that mission. Michigan is among the top states in the nation in almost every hunting category, with more than 700,000 licensed hunters contributing $8.9 billion annually to the state economy. Online at: www.michigan.gov/wildlife.

The Wildlife Division continues to be a national leader in wildlife disease management. Monitoring the health of Michigan's wildlife is a critical component of the division's mission. With the finding of chronic wasting disease in a free-ranging deer herd in May 2015, the division has spent enormous time and resources understanding the extent of this fatal disease while working to slow its spread. In addition, bovine tuberculosis continues to be a disease that affects the state's free-ranging deer and livestock industry.

The Michigan DNR's Wildlife Division comanages the state forests with the DNR Forest Resources Division and directly administers approximately 400,000 acres of state game and wildlife management areas. In addition to this, an extensive network of partnerships and grant opportunities significantly expands the division's conservation reach and impact throughout the State of Michigan.

The **Office of Minerals Management** manages 6.4 million acres of Michigan's mineral estate, which includes leasing the rights to explore and pursue development of state-owned metallic, nonmetallic, and oil and gas minerals, as well as underground natural gas storage areas. Royalty revenue from these leases typically contributes between $30 million and $60 million annually to the Michigan State Parks Endowment Fund for parks improvement and to the Game and Fish Protection Trust Fund for game and fish management. Online at: www.michigan.gov/minerals.

This office also provides geological and mineral resource evaluation services for department land transactions and works closely with other state agencies, industry and environmental groups and the public on matters related to these vital natural resources-based economies.

Administration Bureau

The Administration Bureau includes the Finance and Operations Division, the Marketing and Outreach Division and the Michigan History Center.

The **Finance and Operations Division** provides budget and financial services, facilities and infrastructure management, construction of shooting ranges, real estate, grants management, purchasing, field operations support, and business operations.

The **Marketing and Outreach Division** works to find creative, new ways to get more residents and visitors outside, taking advantage of a variety of recreation opportunities in Michigan. The division provides expertise and services including website administration, visual and written communications, customer systems, marketing, technology, license sales, recreational skills, and educational programs for all ages and experience levels. Its staff works to help people understand natural and cultural resources management and why it matters.

The **Michigan History Center** fosters curiosity, enjoyment, and inspiration rooted in Michigan's stories. Community engagement includes outreach, education, special programs, marketing and visitor services. The Archives of Michigan makes more than 150 million records available to the public for research. The Michigan History Museum in Lansing (MHM), ten regional historic sites and museums, and the Thunder Bay National Marine Sanctuary and Underwater Preserve interpret Michigan's stories. The center's programs and sites annually welcome more than 380,000 visitors, including more than 65,000 school children who explore the MHM. The center also manages the Michigan Historical Marker program and a heritage trails program. It works with the Michigan Historical Commission, Michigan Freedom Trail Commission, Iron Industry Museum Advisory Board, State Historic Records Advisory Board, and Underwater Salvage and Preserve Committee. Online at: www.michigan.gov/mhc.

The DNR also encompasses several entities, offices, committees, and commissions that provide essential support and guidance to the above-referenced programs and help preserve, promote, and interpret Michigan's natural, historic and cultural resources. They include:

The **Upper Peninsula Regional Office** serves to represent the department and director in the Upper Peninsula by working closely with stakeholders, media outlets, community organizations, local units of government, elected officials, and the public to build awareness and understanding of department policies and programs, natural resource-related issues, and outdoor recreation opportunities.

The **Public Information Office** works closely with the Executive Office and department divisions to coordinate the communication of core DNR messages to a variety of statewide audiences, serves as primary contact for media representatives, and partners in the marketing of department initiatives, programs, and services — all in an effort to strengthen the public's connection to Michigan's natural and cultural resources.

The **Legislative and Legal Affairs Office** works with the Office of Attorney General on litigation involving state properties, employees, and natural resource-related issues. Staff also focus its efforts on administrative rules and regulations and emerging natural and cultural resources issues, strengthening the department's relationship with the Legislature, helping to evaluate and set department policy, and assisting the director and management team with strategic planning, implementation of department priorities, and special assignments. The office provides guidance in response to Freedom of Information Act requests and assists in drafting and updating department policies and procedures, administrative rules, and DNR director's orders for land use, fisheries, and wildlife conservation.

The office maintains original, signed memoranda of understanding and other interagency agreements and makes recommendations on contract and grant agreement language.

This office also manages tribal coordination efforts and works to develop and sustain positive and mutually beneficial, cooperative relationships with Michigan's tribal governments, with emphasis on the natural resource provisions related to the 1836 Treaty and its associated Great Lakes and Inland Consent Decrees and the 1842 Treaty's natural resource components.

The **Michigan Natural Resources Commission** is a 7-member public body whose members are appointed by the governor and subject to the advice and consent of the Senate. The commission has the exclusive authority to regulate the taking of game and sportfish and is authorized to designate game species and the establishment of the first open season for animals. Residents are encouraged to attend and become actively involved in the commission's regularly scheduled public meetings. Online at: www.michigan.gov/nrc.

The **Michigan Natural Resources Trust Fund** (MNRTF) was established under the Kammer Recreational Land Trust Fund Act of 1976 to provide a permanent funding source for the public acquisition of land for resource protection and public outdoor recreation. Funding was provided by revenue derived from royalties on the sale and lease of state-owned oil, gas and mineral rights. In 1984, the MNRTF was expanded to allow funding of development of public land. Per the state constitution, the maximum amount of the accumulation of nonrenewable mineral royalties in the MNRTF is $500 million. This level was reached in 2011 and represents the permanent investment corpus. Today, the MNRTF functions as a permanent endowment and funds grants, administration and payments in lieu of taxes (PILT). Online at: www.michigan.gov/mnrtf.

To date, the MNRTF has awarded over $1.1 billion in grants to local units of government and state agencies for projects throughout all 83 Michigan counties. Of this total, $245 million has been invested in trails. In excess of 1,000 public parks have been acquired and/or developed. Other projects funded include ball fields, boat launches, trailheads, restrooms and other amenities, for a total of 2,497 MNRTF-assisted projects since 1976.

The **Mackinac Island State Park Commission** is an autonomous entity with authority to acquire, construct, maintain, and improve property related to the historic Straits of Mackinac. The commission was formed in 1895 and is responsible for all aspects of managing Mackinac State Historic Parks. It meets approximately five times a year and is made up of seven members appointed by the governor and confirmed by the Senate. Commissioners serve 6-year terms. Online at: www.mackinacparks.com.

Additionally, there are other committees and councils that advise the department. These include, but are not limited to:

- Michigan Trails Advisory Council
- Forest Management Advisory Committee
- Belle Isle Park Advisory Committee
- Michigan State Waterways Commission
- Timber Advisory Council
- Upper Peninsula Citizens' Advisory Councils

DEPARTMENT OF
STATE

JOCELYN BENSON, SECRETARY OF STATE
Richard H. Austin Building
P.O. Box 30045, Lansing, MI 48918-9900
www.michigan.gov/sos

The Department of State is the oldest department within Michigan state government and is administered by the secretary of state. Elected to a 4-year term with a maximum of two terms, the secretary of state is a member of the executive branch and has constitutional as well as statutory duties.

In the event of concurrent vacancies in the office of governor and lieutenant governor, including absence from the state, the secretary of state serves as governor. The secretary of state is the chief motor vehicle administrator and chief election officer for the state's ten million residents and is a voting member of several state boards and commissions, including the State Administrative Board, Governor's Traffic Safety Advisory Commission, and Michigan Truck Safety Commission.

Michigan is one of two states where the secretary of state has authority over election processes as well as vehicle registrations and the licensing of drivers. Other duties include administration of driver education and traffic safety programs; document certification as Keeper of the Great Seal, which provides the highest level of document certification in the state; and management of the notary public program. The department also maintains the state's official repository of records, including state and local government records, state statutes and commercial financing statements. Additionally, the department administers the state's organ donor registry.

The Department of State's organizational structure includes the Bureau of Elections, Customer Services Administration, Legal Services Administration, and several offices administered by the department's chief of staff.

The **Bureau of Elections** is responsible for overseeing elections in Michigan and relevant programs, including campaign-finance and lobbyist disclosure. The bureau oversees the coordination of 83 county clerks, county canvassing boards, election commissions, and 1,500 city and township clerks. The elections director serves as secretary to the Board of State Canvassers, a constitutional body responsible for canvassing petitions to place statewide ballot questions before voters and for canvassing nominating petitions and election results for all statewide offices, certain congressional and legislative offices, and all judicial offices.

The **Customer Services Administration** (CSA) includes the Office of Continuous Improvement and Transformation, Bureau of Traffic Safety, Office of Customer Service, Branch Office Support Services, Office of Customer Records, and Office of Occupancy Services. CSA operates a network of 131 branch offices providing driver's licensing, vehicle titling and registration and voter registration. The Office of Continuous Improvement and Transformation focuses on improving the customer experience and the employee experience through insights and data-driven decisions. The Bureau of Traffic Safety manages and oversees driver and vehicle records; traffic safety initiatives; and driver licensing, assessment and education. The Office of Customer Service oversees uniform commercial code services and serves international registration plan vehicle owners. Branch Office Support Services provides assistance to secretary of state offices across the state in serving customers. The Office of Occupancy Services oversees the department's facilities located in every county of the state.

The **Legal Services Administration** (LSA) provides legal support to the secretary of state, and includes the Office of Legal Policy, Office of Hearings and Administrative Oversight, and Office of Investigative Services. The LSA also supports the Independent Citizens Redistricting Commission. The Office of Legal Policy oversees implementation of Proposal 18-3 and other policy initiatives and provides legal support. The Office of Hearings and Administrative Oversight employs hearing officers who hold hearings on driver's license appeals as well as administrative hearings for business licenses and certifications. It also administers the Breath Alcohol Ignition Interlock Device Program. The Office of Investigative Services is made up of the Business Compliance and Regulation Division which covers automotive business licensing and compliance; the Regulatory Monitoring Division, which investigates licensed and registered automotive-related businesses and other vehicle-related regulatory issues; and the Enforcement Division, which contains the Fraud Investigation Section, Investigative Analytics Section and Branch Review, and Special Programs Section. The Department of State is responsible for implementing the application process for the new Independent Citizens Re-districting Commission that now exists in the state constitution to oversee the redrawing of congressional and state legislative districts after every decennial census. The Secretary of State serves as the secretary of the Commission.

Chief of Staff-administered offices include the Bureau of Programs, Integration and Delivery; Office of Human Resources; Office of Communications; the Legislative Liaison; and Office of Public Engagement. The Bureau of Programs, Integration and Delivery includes the Office of Program Support, Information Security and Control Division, Technology and Project Services Division, and Financial Services Division.

DEPARTMENT OF
STATE POLICE

COL. JOSEPH M. GASPER, DIRECTOR
7150 Harris Dr.
Dimondale, MI 48821
www.michigan.gov/msp

The Michigan Department of State Police began as a temporary, wartime emergency force for the purpose of domestic security during World War I. On April 19, 1917, Governor Albert Sleeper created the Michigan State Troops, also known as the Michigan State Constabulary. This new force consisted of five troops of mounted, dismounted, and motorized units, totaling 300 men. Public Act 26 of 1919 and Public Act 59 of 1935 reorganized the Michigan State Constabulary as the permanent, peace-time Michigan State Police (MSP). When Michigan citizens adopted a new constitution authorizing up to 20 state departments, Public Act 380 of 1965 established the MSP as one of the departments. Today, the MSP consists of approximately 3,000 enlisted and civilian employees.

The director of the MSP holds the rank of colonel and is appointed by the governor. The director serves as State Director of Emergency Management and as Michigan's Homeland Security Director. In addition, either the director or his designee is a member of the Michigan Homeland Protection Board, Michigan Public Safety Interoperability Board, Michigan Intelligence Operations Center Advisory Board, State 9-1-1 Committee, Governor's Traffic Safety Advisory Commission, Michigan Truck Safety Commission, School Safety Commission, Auto Theft Prevention Authority, and Michigan Commission on Law Enforcement Standards.

According to MCL 28.6, enlisted members of the MSP "...may serve and execute all criminal and civil process, when directed to do so by the Governor or the Attorney General, in actions and matters in which the state is a party." In addition to the department's responsibility for directly providing general police services statewide, the MSP is statutorily mandated to provide traffic patrol on freeways and state trunk lines. The MSP also has hundreds of other significant statutory responsibilities in areas such as crime reporting, traffic safety, and forensic science.

The MSP is a full-service law enforcement agency providing over 60 different services either directly to citizens or in support of other law enforcement agencies. The MSP personnel most visible to the public are the uniform troopers whose primary responsibilities include investigating crimes, deterring criminal activity, apprehending criminals and fugitives, conducting traffic enforcement to increase traffic safety, and participating in community outreach and prevention services activities. The MSP also has a cadre of highly trained detectives who conduct investigations in specialized fields such as homicides, fraud, felonious assault, computer crimes, fire investigation, and criminal sexual conduct.

The MSP has a variety of specialized teams that each receive advanced training and equipment and are available to provide direct service or to assist other law enforcement agencies. These teams include the Bomb Squad, Canine Unit, Marine Services Team, Aviation Unit, Emergency Support Team, Motor Unit, and Tactical Bike Team. The MSP also provides leadership for over 20 multijurisdictional teams in areas including narcotics, auto theft, computer crimes, and cold cases. In addition, MSP motor carrier officers perform commercial motor vehicle enforcement and truck safety initiatives statewide.

The MSP provides 24-hour, forensic science services from eight regional laboratories to all police agencies in the state. Each laboratory meets the Federal Bureau of Investigation's Quality Assurance Standards and is accredited by the American National Standards Institute-American Society of Quality National Accreditation Board.

The MSP is the repository for criminal justice records including criminal history records, traffic crash records, firearms records, concealed pistol registrations, sex offender registry, missing persons, stolen property, mug shots, and fingerprints. The department also administers the Law Enforcement Information Network (LEIN) to provide criminal justice agencies access to this information. In addition, the MSP uses Michigan Incident Crime Reporting to prepare the annual Uniform Crime Report that provides both a local-level and statewide description of crime in Michigan.

The **State Emergency Operations Center** (SEOC) is managed and maintained by the MSP Emergency Management and Homeland Security Division. The SEOC is responsible for facilitating the coordination of all state agency activities and resources during an emergency or disaster ensuring an effective and efficient state response. In addition to helping local governments plan and prepare for both man-made and natural disasters, the MSP coordinates state and federal resources to assist local jurisdictions with response and relief activities in the event of an emergency or disaster. The MSP coordinates all state-level homeland security initiatives and serves as the State Administrative Agency for federal homeland security grants. Michigan's Homeland Security Advisor is the MSP Director.

The **MSP Training Academy** located in Dimondale provides learning opportunities and training programs for both MSP employees and the broader criminal justice community in areas such as leadership development, narcotics investigation, pursuit driving, first aid, marksmanship, and Michigan law. The MSP's Precision Driving Unit is internationally recognized for its annual Police Vehicle Evaluation program.

Agencies housed within the MSP include the Auto Theft Prevention Authority, Michigan Commission on Law Enforcement Standards, and Michigan Office of Highway Safety Planning.

DEPARTMENT OF
TECHNOLOGY, MANAGEMENT AND BUDGET

TRICIA FOSTER, CPM, ACoM, DIRECTOR

Lewis Cass Building
320 S. Walnut St.
Lansing, MI 48909
www.michigan.gov/dtmb

The Michigan Department of Technology, Management and Budget (DTMB) provides financial, administrative, and technology services and information to Michigan's state agencies, citizens, businesses, local governments, and universities. With nearly 2,800 employees, DTMB is responsible for 41 DTMB-managed facilities that total 9.8 million square feet and more than 480 leased locations that total more than 5 million square feet of space, almost 55,000 desktop, laptop, and tablet computers as well as five retirement systems that serve one in nine Michigan households. DTMB is also responsible for state government's procurement portfolio of about 800 contracts worth billions of dollars.

DTMB's fully unified services structure, advanced IT infrastructure, and long-standing relationships across government boundaries place Michigan in a unique position to serve its residents. A commitment of more than $40 million in ongoing base funding is helping modernize state legacy systems and increase online and self-service resources for Michigan residents. This strong foundation supports DTMB's commitment to Michiganders and ensures customers can find the resources they need, quickly and easily.

The department derives its legal authority from the Management and Budget Act, Public Act 431 of 1984, as amended, and several executive orders. It is the summation of the former Department of Administration, which was created by Public Act 51 of 1948, as well as functions that had been under the office of the governor, such as budgeting, that were transferred by Executive Order No. 1973-7. Executive Order 2009-55, issued December 30, 2009, and effective March 21, 2010, combined the former Departments of Management and Budget and Information Technology into the Department of Technology, Management and Budget.

The DTMB **Director's Office** provides direct management and oversight for strategic planning, public information, enterprise security, and enterprise development. The critical functional areas within the department include:

The **State Budget Office** coordinates all executive budget activities, including development of the executive budget recommendation, presentation of the budget to the Legislature and implementation of the budget after enactment. The state budget director is appointed by the governor and is a member of the governor's cabinet. The state budget director serves as the governor's adviser on fiscal matters and oversees the state's accounting and payroll functions, its financial management system, internal audit services, and the collection and reporting of data about the performance of Michigan's public schools and students.

The state's **chief information officer** (CIO) is responsible for the information technology services for state government. Areas and services overseen by the CIO include the following:

Cybersecurity and Infrastructure Protection is under the direction of Michigan's chief security officer and is organized into two divisions: Michigan Cyber Security (MCS) and the Office of Infrastructure Protection (OIP). MCS provides cybersecurity services and protections for state of Michigan executive branch agencies. OIP provides physical security measures and emergency management for DTMB-managed buildings. This includes access control and security services to DTMB offices and state facilities, employee ID and access card services, 24/7 systems monitoring and camera program, and emergency response coordination and management.

The **Agency Services Division** serves as the liaison between the department and individual executive branch agencies. This team maintains the technology and business relationships between DTMB and its agency partners. The services include managing agency information technology plans and ensuring the timely delivery of agreed-upon IT services. The staff members work across all agencies to identify common technology needs.

DTMB's **Office of the Chief Technology Officer** provides enterprise network, telecommunications, data center services, enterprise architecture, office automation, and technical services. With almost 55,000 laptops, desktops, and tablets in operation, DTMB works to provide a single end-user technology environment that supports the business needs of the different state agencies and departments. The office is responsible for the acquisition of hardware and software and provision of operational and technical support for a mainframe computer, more than 3,700 servers, data storage, and monitoring systems for the state's data centers. The office is also responsible for managing the network connectivity, Wi-Fi, telephones, email, and back-office services for all executive branch agencies and departments.

The DTMB is the responsible agent of the **Office of Michigan's Public Safety Communications System** (MPSCS) within the Center for Shared Solutions. The MPSCS provides statewide public safety communications resources for more than 1,825 state, local, federal, tribal, and private public safety agencies. The system spans 59,415 square miles and includes 259 tower sites and more than 81 state and local public safety dispatch centers with 415 dispatch consoles and 59 computer-aided dispatch consoles. The MPSCS Network Communication Center handles 11.5 million push-to-talk transmissions per month for more than 99,145 radios and 4,568 fire pagers.

The DTMB **chief deputy director** oversees the department areas that provide management and administrative services. These offices and their functions include:

The **Office of Retirement Services** (ORS) is responsible for the 18th largest public pension system in the United States and the 47th largest pension system in the world. The office administers retirement programs for Michigan's state employees, public school employees, judges, state police and National Guard members. ORS serves 570,000 active and retired customers representing approximately one out of every nine Michigan households. Within these systems, ORS administers defined benefit, defined contribution, deferred compensation, hybrid, and retiree healthcare plans. ORS has combined net assets of $80.8 billion. The State Employees' Retirement System is administered under the provision of Public Act 240 of 1943. The Michigan Public School Employee's Retirement System is administered under the provisions of Public Act 300 of 1980. The Michigan State Police Retirement System is administered under Public Act 182 of 1986. The Judges Retirement System is administered under Public Act 234 of 1992. Finally, the Military Retirement Provisions are administered under Public Act 150 of 1967.

Central Procurement Services is responsible for purchasing goods, services, and information technology resources on behalf of all state agencies and sets procurement policies and procedures for most state departments. Its mission is to provide state agencies with the mechanism to purchase the products and services required to serve the citizens of the state of Michigan on time, of good quality, and at a reasonable price. Central Procurement Services manages a portfolio of about 800 contracts worth billions of dollars and an extended purchasing program, MiDeal, which allows more than 1,100 local units of government to purchase goods and services using these competitively bid contracts.

The **State Facilities Administration** (SFA) manages and maintains 41 state-owned facilities that total 9.8 million square feet on 906 acres. It is responsible for all day-to-day operations that include building maintenance, infrastructure, energy management, HVAC, and landscaping services. The SFA also provides design and construction management services for all state agencies as well as universities and colleges that are implementing infrastructure improvement or new construction projects. The SFA provides and is responsible for more than 480 leases totaling more than 5 million square feet of space, allowing agencies to meet changing space requirements and locations. State Facilities Administration also manages all land acquisitions and surplus property dispositions, including working with the Michigan Land Bank as determined. The SFA provides Health and Safety Program management and consultation services, which includes training to ensure that work places are free of hazards, accidents, and injuries.

Financial Services (FS) provides a broad range of services, including accounting services, departmental procurement and accounts payable processing, financial analysis, business planning, management-level reporting, automated billings, data collection and interfaces, as well as financial system security access. FS provides accounting services to all organizations within DTMB, including the Offices of the State Employer, State Budget, and Children's Ombudsman, the Civil Service Commission, Department of Civil Rights, Department of Military and Veterans Affairs, Grand Rapids Home for Veterans, Michigan State Police, and the Executive Office. FS also is responsible for service rate development and financial analysis and serves as audit liaison with the Office of the Auditor General and the Office of Internal Audit Services in the State Budget Office. In addition, DTMB's information security officer position is organizationally located within Financial Services.

The **Bureau of Labor Market Information and Strategic Initiatives** (LMISI) is a one-stop shop for information and analysis on Michigan's population, labor market, and more. Its Federal-State Programs Division runs the state's cooperative agreements with the U.S. Department of Labor, Bureau of Labor Statistics, and the U.S. Census Bureau, making LMISI the official sources for this information. The Research and Evaluation Division conducts workforce research and program evaluation.

The **Office of Performance Management** works to continually enhance department performance through a variety of services, including process improvement, IT governance, metrics consulting, employee engagement, customer satisfaction, administration of policies and forms, and other strategic initiatives.

The **Office of Support Services** provides customers with a wide range of business services, allowing state agencies, colleges, universities, and local units of government to focus on their primary missions. Its Mailing Services Division offers a full range of automated and manual mail handling. Printing Services offers design, digital printing, and high-volume mainframe and variable data printing. Delivery Services operates statewide, providing delivery and freight services and transportation of U.S. and interdepartmental mail. The State Surplus Program manages disposal of all state surplus personal property through reutilization, donation, remarketing, and recycling. The Federal Surplus Property Program facilitates reutilization of federal surplus property to eligible recipients. Warehouse Services offers comprehensive inventory and warehouse storage services, including management of IT hardware. Records Management Services stores and manages official state records and provides electronic document management and imaging services. It also establishes retention and disposal schedules for all public records. Vehicle and Travel Services manages a centralized fleet and is responsible for travel policy and travel reimbursement rates.

Under Article XI, Section 5, of the Michigan Constitution, the **Civil Service Commission** operates as an autonomous entity. Its administrative powers are vested in the state personnel director, who is the commission's principal executive officer. The Civil Service Commission, through the state personnel director and staff, has overall responsibility to regulate conditions of employment for classified civil servants in all departments of the executive branch of state government and for staff of the Auditor General. Under Executive Order 2007-30, the commission also provides human resources services to most executive branch departments.

Under Executive Order 1979-5, the **Office of the State Employer** operates as a Type I autonomous entity within DTMB. The office director is appointed by the governor and is a member of the governor's cabinet. The Office of the State Employer is the governor's designated representative in recognized employee organization negotiations and developing and implementing employment relations policy for the executive branch. The office is also responsible for administering the state of Michigan's Workers' Compensation Program, the state of Michigan's Drug and Alcohol testing program, transitional employment and statewide safety and health systems, covering active state employees of the executive branch.

The **Office of Children's Ombudsman** (OCO), established in 1994 by PA 204, is an autonomous entity housed within DTMB. The children's ombudsman is appointed by the governor with the advice and consent of the Michigan Senate. The office independently investigates complaints about children involved with protective services, foster care, adoption services, and juvenile justice. OCO makes recommendations to the governor, Legislature and the director of the Department of Health and Human Services to improve the child welfare system.

The multidisciplinary team of professionals determines if an action or decision was made according to the laws, rules, and policies governing the Department of Health and Human Services and private child-placing agencies. The office takes necessary action, including legal action, to protect the rights and welfare of a child. That action also includes investigation of cases involving children who have died as a result of child abuse or neglect when there has been previous agency involvement. The office also works to educate the public about child welfare laws and policies.

DEPARTMENT OF
TRANSPORTATION

PAUL C. AJEGBA, DIRECTOR

Transportation Building
P.O. Box 30050, Lansing, MI 48909
www.michigan.gov/mdot

On Dec. 22, 1978, the Department of State Highways and Transportation became the Michigan Department of Transportation (MDOT). Also in 1978, the State Transportation Commission was created through a constitutional amendment to direct policy for the department.

MDOT's primary functions are constructing, improving, and maintaining the 9,664 miles of interstate, M-numbered and U.S. routes; developing and implementing comprehensive transportation plans for the entire state, including all modes of public transit, providing professional and technical assistance; and administering state and federal funds allocated for these programs. The governor appoints the department director with the advice and consent of the Senate.

The **State Transportation Commission** (STC) establishes policy for MDOT, its programs and facilities, and other such public works of the state, as provided by law. The governor appoints the six commission members, with the advice and consent of the Senate, for 3-year terms. No more than three members may be from the same political party. Upon expiration of a term, a member may continue to serve until a successor is appointed.

The **Aeronautics Commission** provides policy direction on state aviation regulations and funding of airport development programs relevant to the location, design, building, equipping, and operation of all airports and other aeronautical facilities. The commission also provides guidance for the registration of aircraft and licensing of airports, flight schools, airport managers, and aircraft dealers meeting the requirements of the Aeronautics Code and federal regulations and standards.

MDOT works closely with the Aeronautics Commission and the STC, along with the Mackinac Bridge Authority in St. Ignace and the Sault Ste. Marie Bridge Authority in Sault Ste. Marie.

Organizationally, MDOT comprises four bureaus and nine offices. The four bureaus are Finance and Administration, Development, Field Services, and Transportation Planning. MDOT's nine offices are Aeronautics, Business Development, Communications, Economic Development, Governmental Affairs, Human Resources, Operations Administrative Services, Passenger Transportation, and Rail.

The **Bureau of Finance and Administration** provides internal support for departmental operations. It is responsible for accounting services, fiscal reporting, fiscal planning, budgeting, cash management, contracting, bond financing, property leasing, purchasing, stores control, office space management, and all related financial functions.

The **Bureau of Development** and the **Bureau of Field Services** are responsible for designing, constructing, operating, and maintaining a statewide system of trunkline highways, welcome centers, roadside parks, and rest areas. They also provide administrative and technical assistance in designing, constructing, and maintaining city and village streets and county roads.

The **Bureau of Development** comprises the Design and Development Services divisions, as well as the Environmental Services Section and Performance Excellence.

The **Design Division** prepares construction plans and engineering data for state highways, bridges, and related structures. It ensures compliance with Federal Highway

Administration, American Association of State Highway and Transportation Officials and MDOT design procedures, principal standards, and specifications. The division also houses the Traffic and Safety Section, which oversees the sign, pavement marking, and safety programs.

The **Development Services Division** oversees the following for the state trunkline system: real property appraisal, acquisition, condemnation, clearance, relocation, management and disposal of excess property, and related appurtenances. The division also coordinates utility, highway advertisement, non-MDOT construction and utility installation permitting, and oversize/overweight commercial vehicle transport permitting. Additionally, the division administers the federal and state aid programs for local agencies.

The **Environmental Services Section** provides support and expertise on environmental issues in all aspects of state highway planning, design, construction, and operation.

The **Bureau of Field Services** includes the Construction Field Services Division, the Transportation Systems Management Division, the Research Administration, and the Safety and Security Administration.

The **Construction Field Services Division** provides statewide support for engineering guidance and technical expertise for pavements, bridges, materials, specifications, geotechnical design, traffic control, environmental mitigation, and system preservation. The division also provides engineering, materials control, and testing oversight for the concrete and bituminous paving and bridge fabrication programs.

The **Transportation Systems Management Division** provides statewide support for winter operations, roadway surface, and roadside facilities. It also provides bridge repair crews and oversees the statewide bridge inspection program. Other responsibilities include traffic incident management, congestion and mobility, work zone management, traffic signal operations, and the statewide traffic operations center. Intelligent Transportation Systems (ITS) focuses on coordinating the ITS program, MDOT's autonomous vehicle activities, and MDOT's connected vehicle strategies.

The **Research Administration** manages MDOT research, which includes research funded with federal and state funds. Projects focus on MDOT's research needs and are typically contracted to universities or consultants with MDOT managing each project.

The **Safety and Security Administration** is responsible for emergency management, homeland security, occupational safety and health, and environmental audits and hazardous materials.

The **Bureau of Transportation Planning** is primarily responsible for maintaining MDOT's federal aid eligibility by developing and implementing a comprehensive transportation planning process. This results in transportation investments that are consistent with the STC's financial, social, economic, and environmental policies. Other major responsibilities include strategic planning and policy development, multi-modal planning, program management, security and mobility planning, economic development, strategic information technology/tools, asset management, and operations-oriented process support.

MDOT field operations are conducted from seven regional offices and 22 transportation service centers. The regional offices are located in Escanaba, Gaylord, Grand Rapids, Jackson, Kalamazoo, Saginaw, and Southfield, the latter serving metro Detroit. The department operates 77 freeway rest areas and 82 roadside parks across Michigan on interstate and M-numbered and U.S. routes. In Addition, MDOT operates 14 welcome centers across the state, which promote Michigan's myriad tourism destinations and travel-related businesses.

DEPARTMENT OF
TREASURY

RACHAEL EUBANKS, STATE TREASURER
Richard H. Austin Building
P.O. Box 30716, Lansing, MI 48909
www.michigan.gov/treasury

The Office of State Treasurer is provided for by Article V, Section 3, of the Michigan Constitution of 1963. The state treasurer is appointed by the governor, with the advice and consent of the senate, and serves at the pleasure of the governor.

The department was established by the Executive Organization Act of 1965, as a result of merging the operations of six agencies: State Treasurer, Department of Revenue, Municipal Finance Commission, Board of Tax Appeals, State Tax Commission, and Auditor General (except the state audit function). In addition, the Board of Equalization and Board of Escheats were abolished and their functions were absorbed by the new department.

Effective July 1, 1984, the Municipal Finance Commission was abolished, which transferred all powers and duties to the state treasurer. Effective August 1991, the Michigan Tax Tribunal was transferred to the Department of Commerce (now Licensing and Regulatory Affairs) pursuant to Executive Order No. 1991-18. Effective May 1992, the Michigan Higher Education Facilities Commission and Michigan Higher Education Facilities Authority were transferred from the Department of Education to the Department of Treasury pursuant to Executive Order No. 1992-2. Effective April 8, 1995, the Michigan Higher Education Assistance Authority and Michigan Higher Education Student Loan Authority were transferred from the Department of Education to the Department of Treasury pursuant to Executive Order No. 1995-3. Effective January 1, 2000, all administrative responsibilities related to statewide educational assessments were transferred from the Department of Education to the Department of Treasury pursuant to Executive Order No. 1999-12. Effective December 21, 2003, the administration of the Michigan Educational Assessment Program tests was transferred to the superintendent of public instruction. Effective March 4, 2010, ten public finance authorities were consolidated into the Michigan Finance Authority, an autonomous entity within Treasury, pursuant to Executive Order 2010-2.

The **state treasurer** acts as principal advisor to the governor on tax and fiscal policy issues. The state treasurer is the chairperson of the Michigan Education Trust and the Michigan Finance Authority. The state treasurer serves as chair of the State of Michigan Investment Board which serves as custodian of the judges, public school employees, state employees, and state police retirement funds. The state treasurer also serves as treasurer of the retirement systems, the Legislative Retirement System, and the Mackinac Bridge Authority. The state treasurer is also a member of the following boards and commissions: Michigan Education Trust, Michigan State Finance Authority, Michigan State Housing Development Authority, Local Emergency Financial Assistance Loan Board, Michigan Early Stage Venture Investment Corporation Board, Michigan Economic Development Corporation Corporate Board, Michigan Strategic Fund, State of Michigan Retirement Board, Michigan State Police Retirement Board, State Administrative Board, Michigan Legislative Retirement System, Detroit Financial Review Commission, and Michigan Land Bank.

Executive Office
Operational responsibilities of the department are handled by the **Executive Office**, which consists of the state treasurer; the chief deputy treasurer; chief investment officer; deputy treasurers for Tax

Administration, Tax Policy, Financial and Administrative Services, State/Local Finance, and Executive Operations. Executive Operations includes Budget, Information Technology, Communications, and Continuous Improvement and Engagement.

Investments

Pursuant to state law, the 5-person **State of Michigan Investment Board** is the investment fiduciary for the state's defined benefit pension plans, the State of Michigan Retirement System (SMRS), and the State of Michigan 401(k) and 457 defined contribution plans (DC Plans). The state treasurer is appointed as the permanent chairperson of the Board. Additionally, state law grants the state treasurer with specific fiduciary and/or investment authority over other various state trust and agency funds.

Total defined benefit pension assets managed as of December 31, 2018, were $69.5 billion, making the SMRS the 18th largest defined benefit, public pension fund in the United States. The SMRS includes the Michigan Public School Employees' Retirement System, State Employees' Retirement System, Michigan State Police Retirement System, and Michigan Judges Retirement System. The SMRS services a total of more than 530,000 members, which includes vested working employees and retired members.

The Board's investment oversight responsibilities for the DC Plans are accomplished in consultation with the Department of Technology, Management, and Budget (DTMB), with total assets amounting to $7.8 billion within the 401(k) and 457 plans. The state treasurer is also responsible for investing state operating and other state trust and agency funds, with total assets of these funds in excess of $8.5 billion.

The **Bureau of Investments** (BOI) performs all investment functions, and associated accounting and compliance functions, on behalf of the board and state treasurer. The SMRS investment portfolio is diversified and includes domestic and international stock exposure, corporate and government bonds, real estate, and alternative investments. The bureau is organized by major investment disciplines as follows: Private Equity Division; Venture Capital Division, Real, Opportunistic and Absolute Return Division; Fixed Income Division; Real Estate and Infrastructure Division; International Equity Division; Defined Contribution, Trust, and Agencies Division; and Domestic Equity Division. The Trust Accounting Division works directly with each investment division to account for and settle investment transactions on a daily basis. The Compliance and Corporate Governance Division is responsible for overseeing: (i) the timely filing of all proof of claim forms for securities litigation; (ii) timely voting of proxies; (iii) compliance with divestment mandates; and (iv) disclosure events of external managers.

The BOI's primary goal is to invest each fund prudently and in accordance with state law, taking into account the purpose of a particular fund and applicable authorizing statutes. Therefore, asset allocations differ between funds depending upon the type of liability structure or purpose for a particular fund.

Tax Policy

Tax Policy includes the Office of Legislative Affairs, Office of Legal Affairs, Bureau of Tax Policy, Office of Taxpayer Advocate, and Office of Revenue and Tax Analysis.

Legislative Affairs works with the state legislature and with internal Treasury stakeholders to ensure that legislative initiatives are administrable and fit with the governor's policy objectives. It works with legislators to clarify and solve problems and provides information to policymakers to aid in decision making.

The **Bureau of Tax Policy** consists of the Tax Policy Division and the Hearings Division. The **Tax Policy Division** helps ensure the consistent application of tax laws and existing departmental policies, as well as identifying and developing new policies. Policies are usually of a tax technical nature and relate to other revenue bureaus in the areas of tax compliance, customer contact, and return processing. The Tax Policy Division provides guidance pertaining to tax statutes through the drafting of revenue administrative bulletins, internal policy directives, and technical advice letters. The division also provides support to the Office of Legislative Affairs by providing bill language and bill analyses, when needed. It also provides support to the Attorney General's staff in substantive tax litigation as it relates to their understanding and presentation of tax laws and departmental tax policies.

The **Hearings Division** provides informal conferences mandated by the Revenue Act on disputed tax matters, including assessments, credit audits, and refund denials. Informal conferences are also provided for principal residence exemption denials.

Decisions are signed on behalf of the state treasurer by the division administrator or the bureau director. Decisions and orders issued by the division are subject to further appeal to the Michigan Tax Tribunal or Court of Claims as provided by statute.

The **Office of the Taxpayer Advocate** serves as an ombudsman within the Department of Treasury to ensure taxpayer's rights are protected and Treasury's processes are fairly administered. As the resource of last resort, the advocate office assists individual and business taxpayers by clarifying and resolving account specific issues that have not been resolved through Treasury's normal channels. The advocate has the ability to review and grant requests for penalty waivers within guidelines established by Treasury. The advocate office is the referral point for taxpayer issues that come from the governor's office, the legislature, congressional delegation, and tax practitioners. Using information gathered in the resolution of customer inquiries, the advocate office provides feedback to other areas of Treasury in order to improve and increase customer service.

The **Office of Revenue and Tax Analysis** (ORTA) is the forecasting, revenue analysis, and local government revenue sharing section of the Michigan Department of Treasury. ORTA advises the governor, lieutenant governor, treasurer, and state budget director on issues dealing with the economy, revenues, and the state's tax structure, and is responsible for preparing the official economic forecast and revenue estimates for the administration. ORTA also represents the administration at the consensus revenue estimating conferences. In addition to estimating revenues generated by state taxes, fees, and other sources, ORTA is also responsible for estimating and analyzing the cost of existing tax exclusions, deductions, exemptions, and credits, and the potential fiscal implications of legislatively proposed tax law changes. ORTA also administers and distributes more than $1 billion annually to local governments through the constitutional revenue sharing program; City, Village and Township Revenue Sharing Program; county revenue sharing programs; Financially Distressed City, Village and Township Grant Program; Convention Facility Development Fund; airport parking tax; Health and Safety Fund; and the Emergency 9-1-1 Fund.

Tax Administration

Tax Administration includes the Tax Compliance Bureau, Tax Administrative Services Bureau, Quality Assurance, and Tax Technical and Outreach Section.

The purpose of the **Tax Compliance Bureau** (TCB) is to increase compliance with state of Michigan tax statutes while concurrently providing improved taxpayer service by effectively managing the Taxpayer Bill of Rights. The TCB combines an audit function with discovery and tax enforcement functions and is comprised of four divisions, including Field Audit 1 (instate), Field Audit 2 (IP and outstate), Discovery and Tax Enforcement, and Operations. The Michigan Department of Treasury administers tax programs in a manner that recognizes that most taxes are reported and paid through a voluntary compliance system, with no direct enforcement and minimal interaction between Treasury and taxpayers. Compliant taxpayers effectively make up for the shortfall caused by noncompliant taxpayers that do not pay or under report tax.

The **Tax Administrative Services Bureau** is responsible for reviewing and processing all major Michigan tax returns and related forms. Annually, more than 8 million individual and business tax returns are processed by the bureau. All tax returns are reviewed for accuracy. The review may result in the issuance of refunds, requests for additional information, adjustments, or assessments as appropriate. The bureau also administers certain licensing functions, registers taxpayers, engages in quality assurance controls, and responds to millions of taxpayer inquiries received through correspondence, phone calls, and web-based contacts. The Tax Administrative Services Bureau includes three divisions: Business Taxes, Individual Income Taxes, and Special Taxes.

Financial and Administrative Services

The **Financial and Administrative Services** mission is to provide centralized financial and administrative services to the Michigan Department of Treasury, other state departments, and external stakeholders through Accounting Services, Collection Services Bureau, Departmental Services, Financial Services, and Privacy and Security.

The **Office of Accounting Services** (OAS) is responsible for overall monitoring and control of the department's accounting system. This includes coordination and oversight of the year-end closing, accrual processes, account balances, and acting as the department liaison with the Office of Financial Management for the Comprehensive Annual Financial Report. The office is responsible for issuing payments in lieu of taxes for certain eligible senior citizen facilities and Department of Natural Resources' managed state land. Staff oversees the processes related to Treasury's central control agency function.

The **Collection Services Bureau** is responsible for the centralized collection of all overdue assessed taxes administered by Treasury and delinquent, nontax debts owed to state agencies, including oversight of private collection agency contracts. The bureau also administers the service of garnishments and legal offset orders served on the state treasurer.

The **Office of Departmental Services** (ODS) oversees facility, mail, and data operations functions; unclaimed property; purchasing; and forms, documentation, and e-file services. This office is also responsible for management of the department's relationship with the Office of Internal Audit Services and the Office of the Auditor General and facilitates completion of the bi-annual internal control evaluation process. ODS manages Treasury's real estate leases and maintains building occupancy agreements.

The **Office of Financial Services** serves as the central service agency to all state agencies for the administration of all statewide banking activity, related banking contracts, cash receipting, and disbursements. The office administers the receipting of a majority of state and federal funds. The office also manages the disbursement of state funds including wire transfers, warrants, electronic funds transfers, payment adjustments (e.g., cancels, undeliverables, reversals, stop payments), and forgery claims.

The **Office of Privacy and Security** (OPS) establishes policies and enforces practices to ensure the privacy, confidentiality, integrity, and availability of information collected, used, and retained by the department through prevention, detection, and enforcement practices in compliance with applicable laws, regulations, standards, and industry best practices. The OPS administers the disclosure provisions of the Revenue Act, Internal Revenue Code 6103, and other applicable laws for securing and protecting confidential information of the department.

State/Local Finance

State/Local Finance consists of the Bureau of State and Authority Finance, Bureau of Local Government and School Services, Student Financial Services Bureau, and Michigan Infrastructure Council.

The **Bureau of State and Authority Finance** coordinates the issuance of state and authority bonds and notes, including state general obligation issues and assists the state treasurer in managing the state's common cash and cash flow activity, compliance with federal tax laws, and federal disclosure requirements. The bureau performs fiscal agent and trust services for various bond issues and public finance programs, carries out oversight of compliance with the Federal Cash Management Improvement Act requirements for drawing federal funds, and administers the state's School Bond Qualification and Loan Program.

The **Michigan Finance Authority** (MFA) was established by Executive Order 2010-2 to further improve efficiency in state government by consolidating ten public finance authorities into one. The MFA offers effective, low cost financing to public and private entities that provide essential services to the citizens of Michigan. These include municipalities; healthcare providers; public, private, and charter schools; and higher education loans to college students.

The **State Building Authority** (SBA) provides capital financing to acquire, construct, furnish, equip, and/or renovate buildings for the use of the state, including public universities and community colleges pursuant to Public Act 183 of 1964. Since its creation, the SBA has financed approximately 300 projects, approaching $5.1 billion in construction costs. SBA bond issues permit the construction of needed capital outlay projects, which otherwise might be delayed or canceled due to state fiscal constraints, by spreading costs over a portion of the project's useful life. In addition to outlay financing, the SBA houses nonemployee risk management functions for the state. It provides state agencies with commercial property, general liability, aviation, and builder's risk insurance, as well as other needed insurance coverage. The SBA also administers the state's Vehicle Self Insurance Fund, which covers liabilities arising from accidents involving the state vehicle fleet, which numbers in excess of 10,000 vehicles.

The **Student Financial Services Bureau** is comprised of three divisions: Student Scholarships and Grants, 529 College Savings Plans, and the Student Loan Repayment Division.

The **529 College Savings Plans Division** includes the Michigan Education Trust (MET) which provides a method for families to prepay a student's future Michigan college tuition costs. The trust offers contracts to purchasers, collects and invests the funds, and pays out tuition to colleges and universities when enrollees attend college. The Michigan Education Savings Program (MESP) was created to provide families with a flexible way to save for future education expenses through a choice of investment options and is also administered by the state treasurer. The Michigan 529 Advisor Plan provides families with a flexible way to save for future education expenses through an advisor-sold program.

The **Student Scholarships and Grants Division** administers ten state and federal aid programs that assist students with tuition and fee expenses at Michigan colleges and universities. The division also provides multiple outreach and support services to students, families, and high school counselors. Programs administered include: Children of Veterans Tuition Grant, Dual Enrollment for Private Colleges, Fostering Futures Scholarships, Michigan Competitive Scholarship (MCS), Michigan Nursing Scholarship, Merit Award, Michigan Tuition Grant, Police Officers and Fire Fighters Survivors Tuition Grant, Talent for Tomorrow Scholarship (TTS), and the Tuition Incentive Program. The MI GEAR UP scholarship is a federally funded program administered at the state level.

The bureau's **Student Loan Repayment Division** no longer issues student loans. The Federal Family Education Loan Program (FFELP) discontinued new loans in 2010. The state's alternative loan program, MI-LOAN, ceased making new loans in 2008. The division is responsible for monitoring its contracted servicer for compliance with federal laws, rules, and regulations governing loans made under FFELP. It is also responsible for required federal reporting and budgeting. The Michigan Guaranty Agency (MGA) is the state designated guarantor for Michigan. The MGA administers guarantees of loans made by various financial lending institutions and administers its outstanding federal loan portfolio in compliance with federal laws, rules, and regulations. MGA continues to provide default prevention assistance and other types of assistance to students with various issues related to the repayment of their outstanding loans.

In addition, the bureau is responsible for the administration of the Michigan Achieving a Better Life Experience (MiABLE) program. MiABLE is a savings and investment program for individuals who were diagnosed with a disability prior to the age of 26. MiABLE allows individuals to save up to $15,000 annually for future qualified disability expenses without jeopardizing state and federal means-tested benefits.

The **Bureau of Local Government Services** is responsible for the administration and enforcement of state laws that implement provisions of the Michigan Constitution requiring taxation of real and tangible personal property, a uniform system of accounting and auditing for units of local government, and the preservation of the credit of the state. The bureau is responsible for the administration of Public Act 436 of 2012, the Local Financial Stability and Choice Act; Public Act 2 of 1968, the Uniform Budgeting and Accounting Act; Public Act 34 of 2001, the revived Municipal Finance Act; Public Act 202 of 2017, the Protecting Local Government Retirement and Benefits Act; Public Acts 92 and 93 of 2014, the State Essential Services Assessment Act and the Alternative State Essential Services Act; and Public Acts 109 to 113 of 2015, the Revised School Code and the State School Aid Act, which provide early warning and technical assistance to Michigan school districts.

The **Property Services Division's** main function is to provide staff services for the State Tax Commission and assistance to local assessing officers. The State Tax Commission, which was created by Public Act 360 of 1927, is charged with providing general supervision of the administration of property tax laws of the State of Michigan and to render assistance to assessing officers of the state to ensure proper administration of the laws governing assessments and the levying of taxes in this state. The Commission establishes the state equalized value for each class of property for each county total; prepares assessment rolls for state assessed public utilities; approves applications for exemptions for air and water pollution control facilities and neighborhood enterprise zones and industrial property abatements; adds omitted property to local assessment rolls and corrects erroneous personal property statements under MCL 211.154; arbitrates petitions for change of classification; certifies valuation and assessment of lands purchased by the DNR; assumes superintending control over uncertified local assessment rolls; and provides general supervision of all assessing officers. The Commission also provides education, training, examinations, and certification of assessing officers and receives and acts upon disciplinary complaints filed against assessing officers. Staff provides support for all duties that were transferred to the Commission by the 2009 executive reorganization order that abolished the former State Assessors Board.

The Property Services Division staff also receives, reviews, and prepares recommendations for approval of applications for various tax exemption programs, such as the Industrial Facilities Tax, Air, and Water Pollution Control; Charitable Nonprofit Housing; Neighborhood Enterprise Zone; Obsolete Property Rehabilitation; Commercial Redevelopment Act; and New Personal Property. Of significance, the division conducts audits of claims for the principal residence exemption and reviews appeals of principal residence exemption denials.

The **Essential Services Assessment Section** (ESA) is housed within the Property Services Division and is responsible for the administration of the State Essential Services Assessment Act and the Alternative State Essential Services Assessment Act, which is the specific tax authorized under these acts for eligible manufacturing personal property that is exempt from taxation under the General Property Tax Act. In addition to the collection of the ESA tax, the division provides policy guidance for taxpayers and practitioners. The ESA Division is responsible for auditing claims and submissions, as well as defending related actions required in the administration of the acts.

The **Community Engagement and Finance Division** provides regulatory support services for local units of governments. The state of Michigan has passed several laws that are intended to protect the fiscal health of our communities. This division sets standards, checks for compliance, and provides approvals to local units to ensure they are in accordance with these regulatory requirements. Staff performs both contracted audit services as well as delinquent audits, approves or denies the issuance of debt, and supports the Municipal Stability Board. As part of this regulatory role, the division collects data that is used to analyze and monitor the overall financial position of units of local government. Local units with potential for fiscal distress are identified and staff provides direct and indirect community assistance. Additionally, the division works to raise the fiscal fluency of local unit elected and appointed officials through conferences and education programs.

The **Office of School Review and Fiscal Accountability** is responsible for improving the financial health of Michigan school districts, intermediate school districts, and public school academies as authorized by Public Acts 109 to 114 of 2015, Public Act 436 of 2012, and Public Act 181 of 2014. This includes promoting resources and best practices, providing early warning oversight, assisting the enhanced deficit elimination plans of districts with rapidly deteriorating financial conditions or deficits exceeding five years, and working with the Emergency Financial Assistance Loan Board and Detroit Financial Review Commission to resolve financial emergencies.

Support provided by the Office of School Review and Fiscal Accountability includes hosting conferences for financial best practices, identifying potential fiscal stress using financial projection models and budget reviews, developing peer-to-peer comparisons and financial summaries, evaluating budgetary assumptions, visiting districts to develop financial strategies, and guiding districts toward helpful resources.

Bureau of State Lottery

The **Bureau of State Lottery** is an autonomous entity within the Department of Treasury created by Public Act 239 of 1972. State law requires that all net proceeds from lottery games go to the state School Aid Fund.

The **Michigan Lottery** provided more than $941.3 million to the School Aid Fund in Fiscal Year 2018 and $924.1 million in Fiscal Year 2017. Contributions for the last four years exceed $3.5 billion, about 16 percent of the $22.4 billion that the Lottery has provided for Michigan schools in its 46-year history.

The **Bureau of State Lottery's Charitable Gaming Division** is responsible for the licensing and regulation of non-profit organizations operating bingo games, raffles, and selling charity game tickets. In fiscal year 2018, non-profits licensed by the Charitable Gaming Division raised $60.8 million to support a variety of activities and services in their communities.

Michigan Gaming Control Board

In November 1996, Michigan voters approved Proposal E, effectively authorizing three licensed casinos to be built in the city of Detroit. Proposal E was adopted into law as the Michigan Gaming Control and Revenue Act (Initiated Law 1 of 1996). Created by Public Act 69 of 1997, the **Michigan Gaming Control Board** (MGCB) is responsible for implementing, administering, and enforcing the provisions of the initiated law related to licensing, regulating, and collecting taxes and fees from the three authorized Detroit casinos. In calendar year 2018, the combined state wagering taxes paid by the three Detroit casinos and deposited into the School Aid Fund totaled $116.9 million. The three casinos also paid $182.9 million in wagering tax and development agreement payments to the city of Detroit. MGCB's executive director also is responsible for the licensing and regulation of Michigan horse racing and charitable gaming millionaire party events and suppliers along with providing oversight of the 12 tribal-state compacts for the 24 tribal casinos throughout Michigan.

BOARDS AND COMMISSIONS IN THE STATE OF MICHIGAN

Board or Commission	Description	Authority for Creation
Accountancy, State Board of	This board is responsible for the certification, licensure, and regulation of certified public accountants and public accounting firms. **Members:** Jennifer Kluge, Grosse Pointe Shores Dr. Ola M. Smith, Kalamazoo Barbra Homier, Ada James Bayson, Kewadin Paul Balas, Troy Shelly Gower, Farmington Hills David Barrons, Rockford Matthew Roling, Detroit Teressa Keena, Ada	Act 299 of 1980
Acupuncture, Board of	The board ascertains minimal entry level competency of acupuncturists and takes disciplinary action against registrants who have adversely affected the public's health, safety, and welfare. **Members:** Beth Converse, West Bloomfield Renee Hubbs, Lansing Jonell Underwood, Dansville Julie Silver, Royal Oak Jonathan Zaidan, Bloomfield Hills Xiaohong Tan, East Lansing David Krofcheck, Richland Sheryl Blanchard, Okemos Anne Biris, Ann Arbor John Sealey, Orchard Lake Zhiling Trowbridge, Grand Rapids Liz Lukasik, East Lansing Jeffrey Rogers, Royal Oak	Act 30 of 2006
Aeronautics Commission	Responsible for the general supervision of all aeronautics within the state. **Members:** Russell A. Kavalhuna, Dearborn Roger Salo, Plymouth Rick Fiddler, Ada F/Lt. Brian Bahlau, Lansing Major General Len Isabelle, Lansing Kevin Jacobs, Roscommon Laura Mester, Lansing Michael Trout, Clarklake Kelly Burris, Pleasant Ridge Brian Smith, Grand Ledge	Act 327 of 1945
Agricultural Preservation Fund Board	The board is charged with managing the distribution of grants to preserve farmland and help conserve Michigan's agricultural heritage. **Members:** Gordon Wenk, Williamston Scott Goeman, Lansing Margaret Kohring, Sawyer Carl Bednarski, Pigeon Brian Bourdages, Traverse City Jonathan Jarosz, Bay City Kenneth DeCock, Armada Township	Executive Order 2009-54

BOARDS AND COMMISSIONS IN THE STATE OF MICHIGAN *(Cont.)*

Board or Commission	Description	Authority for Creation
Agriculture and Rural Development Commission	Provides oversight and executive direction for the programs of the Department of Agriculture and Rural Development and approves rules and regulations that the department promulgates. **Members:** Dru Montri, Bath Charlie Meintz, Stephenson Trever Meachum, Hartford Patricia Bergdahl, Skandia Brian Pridgeon, Montgomery	Act 380 of 1965
Appellate Defender Commission	Responsible for the development of a system of indigent appellate defense services. **Members:** William Caprathe, Bay City Judith Gracey, West Bloomfield Douglas Messing, Wixom Douglas Mains, Lansing Thomas W. Cranmer, Bloomfield Hills Thomas Adams, Detroit Thomas G. McNeill, Grosse Pointe	Act 620 of 1978
Apple Committee	An organization dedicated to improving the profitability of Michigan's fresh and processed apple industries. **Members:** Robert Gregory, Leland Michael Dietrich, Conklin Mark Youngquist, Kent City Kimberly Kropf, Lowell Jeremy Shank, Dowagiac Caleb Coulter, New Era Damon Glei, Hillsdale	Act 232 of 1965
Architects, Board of	Regulates the practice of architecture. **Members:** Joseph Welmers, Brighton Scott Gustafson, Ypsilanti Dan Lamble, Troy Matthew Slagle, Grand Rapids Patrick Barry, New Hudson Deveron Sanders, Flint Gilbert Barish, DeWitt Jennifer Myers, Troy Jay Larson, Marshall	Act 299 of 1980

BOARDS AND COMMISSIONS IN THE STATE OF MICHIGAN *(Cont.)*

Board or Commission	Description	Authority for Creation
Arts and Cultural Affairs, Michigan Council for	Serves to encourage, develop and facilitate an enriched environment of creative and cultural activity in Michigan. **Members:** W. Omari Rush, Chair, Ann Arbor Anne Belanger, Rogers City Darryl Brown, St. Ignace Cezanne Charles, Ann Arbor Gretchen Gonzales Davidson, Birmingham Joshua Davis, Lake Leelanau Lilian Demas, Bruce Township Sigal Hemy, Pleasant Ridge Nheena Ittner, Marquette Joori Jung, Detroit Deborah Mikula, Howell Tyler Rossmaessler, Fenton Eric David Treur, Grand Rapids Ara Topouzian, Farmington Hills Xavier Verna, Bear Lake	Act 48 of 1966
Asian Pacific American Affairs Commission	Adds value to the State of Michigan and the Asian Pacific American community by fully engaging Asian Pacific Americans across the state. **Members:** Ryan Rosario, Rochester Hills Grace Lee, Bloomfield Hills Joe Tasma, Livonia Lisa Gray, Northville Toshiki Masaki, Canton Kaushik Nag, Grand Rapids Jamie Hsu, Troy Jianli Wang, Superior Township Anthony Chang, Grand Rapids Wei-Chein Dow, Rochester Hills Asim Alavi, Ann Arbor Mi Kyung Dong, Northville Kavy Lenon, West Olive Adi Sathi, Novi Chandragupta Acharya, Canton Angela Wang, Fenton David Han, Plymouth Leena Mangrulkar, Ann Arbor Reginald Pacis, Ferndale Hoa Dinh, Shelby Township Suchiraphon McKeithen-Polish, Sterling Heights	Executive Order 2009-21
Asparagus Advisory Board	This board seeks to promote the production and consumption of asparagus grown in Michigan and to assist in the research and development of asparagus farming. **Members:** Victor Lee Shank, Dowagiac Tracey Butler, Shelby Nick Oomen, Hart Thomas John Oomen, Hart Dwight Fuehring, Mears Kyle Weber, Watervliet Sarah Greiner, Hart Eric Herrygers, Hart John Williams, Hart	Act 232 of 1965

BOARDS AND COMMISSIONS IN THE STATE OF MICHIGAN *(Cont.)*

Board or Commission	Description	Authority for Creation
Athletic Trainers, Board of	The board ascertains minimal entry level competency of health practitioners and verifies continuing education during licensure. The board also takes disciplinary action against licensees who have adversely affected the public's health, safety, and welfare. **Members:** Daniel Tinkey, St. Joseph James Winkler Jr., Allendale Jeremy Marra, Saline Christina Marie Eyers, Holt Michael Kolinski, Kalamazoo Thye Fischman, Jackson Felix Valbuena Jr., Bloomfield Hills Lisa Kravitz, Farmington Hills Morgan McCaul, Lake Odessa Michael Braid, Twin Lake Megan Snow, Jenison	Act 54 of 2006
Audiology, Board of	The board ascertains minimal entry level competency of health practitioners and verifies continuing education during licensure. The board also takes disciplinary action against licensees who have adversely affected the public's health, safety, and welfare. **Members:** Nicole Ferguson, Mount Pleasant Teresa Zwolan, Ann Arbor Melissa Somers, Petoskey Sharon Blackburn, Cadillac Lisa Brennan, Grand Rapids Richard Baldwin, Haslett Robert Borenitsch, Saginaw Teresa Zwolan, Ann Arbor Stylianos Dokianakis, Saugatuck	Act 97 of 2004
Autism Council	The Autism Council is charged with overseeing Michigan's Autism Spectrum Disorders State Plan. **Members:** George Mellos, Farmington Hills Mary Chaliman, Holt Joanne Winkelman, Bloomfield Anthony Ianni, East Lansing Christopher Pinter, Kawkawlin Amy Matthews, Grand Haven Stacie Rulison, St. Johns Krista Clancy, Commerce Township Colleen Allen, Detroit Rhonda Fossitt Stefani Hines, Farmington Krista Boe, Traverse City Kent Rehmann, Lansing Jenny Piatt, Chelsea Brian DeBano, Laingsburg Amy Miilu, Portland Lauren Ringle, Petoskey	Executive Order 2012-11

BOARDS AND COMMISSIONS IN THE STATE OF MICHIGAN *(Cont.)*

Board or Commission	Description	Authority for Creation
Automobile Theft Prevention Authority Board	Awards grants to law enforcement agencies, prosecutors' offices, and nonprofit community organizations to be used for auto theft prevention. **Members:** Michael Thompson, Mason William Patterson, Marshall Lori Davis, Wixom Gene Adamczyck, Saugatuck Daniel Pfannes, Canton Curtis Caid, Brighton Col. Joseph M. Gasper, Lansing	Act 218 of 1956
Barber Examiners, Board of	Regulates the services of barbers, barber students, barber colleges, barber instructors, student instructors, and barbershops in Michigan. **Members:** Phillip Smith III, Brooklyn Micaela Reardon, Grosse Pointe Woods Kelly Mitchell, Grand Rapids Eric Dimoff, Williamston Perry Vitto, Canton Michel Bigelow, Brooklyn Jeffrey Jenson, Traverse City Peter Dellisse, Menominee	Act 299 of 1980
Barrier Free Design Board	The board has the responsibility to receive, review, and process requests for exceptions to the barrier free design specifications; require appropriate equivalent alternatives when exceptions are granted; receive, process, and make recommendations for barrier free design rules. **Members:** Ronald Campbell, Flint Jason Turkish, Southfield Aaron Besmer, Caledonia Chris MacKay, Petoskey Jamie Spore, Ludington David Mollitor, DeWitt Eric Thomas, Flint Jeffrey Eischen, Clarkston	Act 1 of 1966
Bean Commission	The primary objectives of the commission are research and promotion. **Members:** Clinton Stoutenburg, Sandusky Greg Ackerman, Vassar Neil French, Reese Kevin Noffsiner, Pinconning Brian Stratton, Edmore Mark Reif, Saginaw Stephen Ewald, Unionville Allen Bischer, Minden City Ross Voelker, Pigeon	Act 114 of 1965
Beef Industry Commission	The purpose of the commission is to promote the sale of beef and beef products. **Members:** Bret Schapman, Almont Garry Lee Wiley, Gladwin Leonard Brown, Sandusky Dale Oeschger, Bay Port Jon Haindl, Cooks Jill Sears, Horton Travis Schunk, Clare Dave Clark, Clifford David Neitzel, Kentwood	Act 291 of 1972

Board or Commission	Description	Authority for Creation
Blind Persons, Commission for	Advises the department director and governor on the coordination and administration of programs and policies concerning the state's blind community. **Members:** John Charles Scott, Detroit Larry Posont, Dearborn Heights Lydia Schuck, Mason	Executive Order 2012-10
Blue Cross Blue Shield Board of Directors	Governing board of Blue Cross Blue Shield. **Members:** James Agee Melvin Larsen Peter Ajluni, D.O. Daniel Loepp Reneé Axt Christopher Maksym, Pharm.D. Ronald Bieber Gary McInerney William Black Anne Mervenne Darrell Burks William Meyers Terry Burns R. Daniel Musser III Robert Casalou Phillip Pierce Patrick J. Devlin Brian Peters Sarah Doyle Jean Rose Linda Forte James Settles Jr. Joseph Garcia F. Remington Sprague, M.D. Yousif Ghafari Gregory Sudderth Diane Goddeeris, R.N., B.S.N. Laura Swartzmiller James Grant, M.D. Brad Thompson Paula Herbart Gary Torgow Gary Jones Renee Turner-Bailey Kerry Kaysserian	Act 350 of 1980
Boiler Rules, Board of	The responsibilities of the board are to prescribe uniform rules for boilers; provide for the licensing of boiler inspectors, installers, and repairers; set fees for licenses, permits, inspections, and certificates; and to provide penalties for violation of the act. **Members:** Ryan Randazzo, Brownstown James Lewis, Jackson David Robin, Howell Robert David Hutsell, Dearborn Dale Palmer, Byron Center Jim Arini, St. Clair Shores Lawrence Black, Pinckney Garret Jackson, Zeeland Chris Lanzon, Harrison Township Michael Horton, Swartz Creek Lucas Liedel, Howell Brian Zyler, Greenville	Act 290 of 1965

BOARDS AND COMMISSIONS IN THE STATE OF MICHIGAN *(Cont.)*

Board or Commission	Description		Authority for Creation
Building Authority Board of Trustees, State	The purpose of the authority is to acquire, construct, furnish, equip, and renovate buildings and equipment for the use of the state, including public universities and community colleges.		Act 183 of 1964
	Members:		
	Dale Zahn, Holland	Ehrlich Crain, Detroit	
	Peter F. Schwartz	Patrick J. Devlin, Livonia	
	Jimmy Greene, Saginaw		
Capitol Commission, Michigan State	Manages the Michigan State Capitol Historic Site, maintains and restores the Capitol Building, and maintains and improves the grounds.		Act 240 of 2013
	Members:		
	Gary Randall, Elwell	Kerry Charkoff, East Lansing	
	John Truscott, Lansing	Margaret E. O'Brien, Portage	
	William C. Kandler, Lansing	Joan Bauer, Lansing	
Carrot Commission, Michigan	Seeks to promote the production and consumption of carrots grown in Michigan.		Act 232 of 1965
	Members:		
	Ralph Oomen, Hart	Jared Oomen, Hart	
	Glenn Vogel, Fremont	Ryan Malburg, Hart	
	Nathan Schwass, Scottville		
Central Michigan University Board of Trustees	The board governs the business and affairs of the university.		Act 48 of 1963
	Members:		
	Edward J. Plawecki Jr., Plymouth	Robert F. Wardrop II, Grand Rapids	
	Todd J. Anson, Charlevoix	Richard K. Studley, Grand Ledge	
	Tricia A. Keith, Royal Oak	Joseph A. Anderson Jr., Bloomfield Hills	
	William H. Weideman, Midland	Michael A. Sandler, West Bloomfield	
Certificate of Need Commission	Certificate of Need is a state regulatory program intended to balance the cost, quality, and access of Michigan's health care system.		Act 368 of 1978
	Members:		
	Tom Mittelbrun, Lake Orion	Tressa Gardner, Waterford	
	Debra Guido-Allen, Sterling Heights	Steward Wang, Ann Arbor	
	James B. Falahee Jr., Kalamazoo	Amy McKenzie, Washington Township	
	Denise Brooks-Williams, Detroit	John Lindsey Dood, Interlochen	
	Robert L. Hughes, Grand Rapids	Melisa Oca, Ann Arbor	
	Melanie Lalonde, Grosse Pointe Park		

BOARDS AND COMMISSIONS IN THE STATE OF MICHIGAN *(Cont.)*

Board or Commission	Description		Authority for Creation
Cherry Committee	Charged with development of a marketing program and developing methods for collecting and auditing assessments.		Act 232 of 1965
	Members:		
	Mark Schilling, Benton Harbor	Daryl Peterson, Ludington	
	Greg Shooks, Central Lake	David Smeltzer, Bear Lake	
	Benjamin LaCross, Lake Leelenau	Isaiah Wunsch, Traverse City	
	Michael DeRuitter, Hart	Andrew Riley, Mears	
	Joseph Muvrin, Paw Paw		
Child Abuse and Neglect Prevention Board	Serves as a voice for Michigan's children and families and promotes their health, safety, and welfare.		Act 50 of 1982
	Members:		
	Lauren Rakolta, Birmingham	Roxanna Duntley-Matos, Kalamazoo	
	Stanley Hannah, Novi	Michael Talbot, Plymouth	
	Willie Dubas, Howell	Reginald Bluestein, East Pointe	
	Krista Beach, Byron Center	Kathleen Trott, Birmingham	
	Sean Bertolino, Williamston	David Zyble, DeWitt	
	Randy Richardville, Monroe		
Child Abuse and Neglect, Governor's Task Force	A multidisciplinary task force to serve the purposes of the federal Child Abuse Prevention and Treatment Act.		Executive Order 2013-4
	Members:		
	Lisa Niergarth, Cedar	Tana Bridge, Canton	
	Danita Echols, Ann Arbor	Lori Budnik, Rogers City	
	Jennifer Pintar, Tawas City	Veda D. Thompkins, Detroit	
	Shannon Lowder, Jackson	Daniel Babin, Grandville	
	Julie Nakfoor Pratt, Hastings	Bethany Mohr, Ann Arbor	
	Kelly Ann Ramsey, Livonia	Racheal Rancilio, Fennville	
	Frederick Gruber, Riverview	Cynthia Smith, Williamsburg	
	Colin Parks, DeWitt	Christopher Wirth, Hudsonville	
	Cheryl Lohmeyer, Monroe		

BOARDS AND COMMISSIONS IN THE STATE OF MICHIGAN *(Cont.)*

Board or Commission	Description	Authority for Creation
Chiropractic, Board of	The board ascertains minimal entry level competency of health practitioners and verifying continuing education during licensure. The board also has the obligation to take disciplinary action against licensees who have adversely affected the public's health, safety, and welfare. **Members:** Robert Maciolek, Macomb Robyn Wilson Peake, Paw Paw Beau Taylor, Sterling Heights Leigh Elceser, Clarkston Robert Huta, Gaylord Donald Reno, Harrison Township Ronald Wilcox, Wyoming Lewis Squires, Scottville Ryan Thornton, Byron Center	Act 368 of 1978
Citizen - Community Emergency Response Coordinating Council, Michigan	Assists in developing, maintaining, and implementing this plan and in supporting and promoting emergency response principles, strategies and practices within governmental agencies and private sector organizations in Michigan. **Members:** Kerry Minshall, Mason Michael Bradley, Dowagiac Steven Frisbie, Battle Creek Brad Smith, Carleton Marc Breckenridge, Ypsilanti Michael Yankowski, DeWitt Phillip Schertzing, Lansing S. Tutt Gorman, Portland Kerry Minshall, Mason Bradley Deacon, Department of Agriculture Kevin Sehlmeyer, State Fire Marshal Krystal A. Fields, Detroit Hasson Hammoud, Detroit Jay Eickholt, Department of Environment, Great Lakes, and Energy Virginia Holmes, Michigan Community Service Commission Eileen Phifer, Michigan Department of Transportation Capt. Emmitt McGowan, Lansing, Department of the State Police Linda Scott, Department of Health and Human Services Col. Sean Southworth, Department of Military and Veterans Affairs Sara Stoddard, Pontiac Michael Yankowski, Lansing	Executive Order 2007-18
Civil Rights Commission	Carries out the guarantees against discrimination articulated in the state constitution and investigates alleged discrimination against any person because of religion, race, color or national origin. Subsequent amendments have added sex, age, marital status, height, weight, arrest record and physical and mental disabilities as protected categories. **Members:** Alma Wheeler Smith, South Lyon Rasha Demashkieh, Fort Gratiot Laura Reyes-Kopack, Livonia Jeffrey Sakwa, Birmingham Stacie Clayton, Detroit Ira Combs, Jackson Regina Gasco-Bentley, Petoskey Denise Grim, Novi	Article 5, Section 29, 1963 Constitution

BOARDS AND COMMISSIONS IN THE STATE OF MICHIGAN *(Cont.)*

Board or Commission	Description		Authority for Creation
Civil Service Commission	Charged with classifying all positions in the classified service according to their respective duties and responsibilities; fixing rates of compensation for all classes of positions; regulating all conditions of employment in the classified service; and other duties.		Act 30 of 1965
	Members:		
	Jeff Steffel, Springport	Janet McClelland, Lansing	
	James Barrett, Perry	Jase Bolger, Grand Rapids	
Collection Practices Board	This board was created to license and regulate collection agencies operating in Michigan.		Act 299 of 1980
	Members:		
	Thomas Oldani, Ann Arbor	Nicholas Dondzila, Kentwood	
	Thomas Matonican, Midland	Kirstin Demaio, Whitehall	
	Terry Lutz, Pigeon	Michael Hiller, Brighton	
	John Garret Angelo, Bloomfield Hills	Lorray Brown, Ypsilanti	
	Rebecca Roberts, Jackson		
Community Action and Economic Opportunity Commission	In part, this commission is charged with reducing the causes, conditions, and effects of poverty and promoting social and economic opportunities that foster self-sufficiency for low-income people.		Act 230 of 1981; Executive Order 2014-9
	Members:		
	Fran Amos, Waterford	Matthew Purcell, Burton	
	James T. Borchard, Frankenmuth	Bob Scolnik, Norton Shores	
	Jill Edwards-Sutton, Mt. Pleasant	Joelle-Jude Fontaine, Troy	
	LaTarro Traylor, Grand Rapids	Miguel Limon Rodriguez Jr., Jackson	
	Luke Shaefer, Ann Arbor	Mykale Garrett, Lathrup Village	
	Jessica Taylor, Detroit	Theresa May Thompson, Dafter	
Community Corrections Board	This board is charged with approving many components of community corrections programs including: goals, eligibility criteria, program guidelines, program standards and policies, the application process, procedures for funding, and criteria for evaluation.		Act 511 of 1988
	Members:		
	The Honorable Martha Anderson, Troy	Keith Turpel, Kalamazoo	
	Bobby J. Hopewell, Kalamazoo	Todd Woodcox, Macomb	
	Deborah Smith-Olson, Baldwin	The Honorable Bradley S. Knoll, Holland	
	L. Paul Bailey, Berrien Center	Jennifer C. Janetsky, Flushing	
	Heidi E. Washington, Lansing	Anna R. Kohn, Detroit	
	William DeBoer, Byron Center	Jake W. Smith, Battle Creek	
	Cory Chavis, Canton		

BOARDS AND COMMISSIONS IN THE STATE OF MICHIGAN *(Cont.)*

Board or Commission	Description	Authority for Creation
Community Service Commission	This commission strives to build a culture of service by providing vision and resources to strengthen communities through volunteerism. **Members:** Sheila A. Alles, Northville Maria Holmes, Belleville Judith Watson-Olson, Gwinn Beverly Grant, Grand Rapids Anne Mervenne, Royal Oak Aubrey Moon, Macomb Township Angela Ayers, Bloomfield Hills Corey Utley, Okemos Michelle Rabideau, Grand Rapids Heidi Magyar, Laingsburg Katharine Janes, Mt. Pleasant Kathy Wilbur, Okemos David Parent, Ann Arbor Diana Veronica Rodriguez-Algra, Lansing Peter Lemmer, East Lansing Lorna Utley, Grosse Pointe Woods Kelsey Snyder, Ann Arbor Jessica Ives, Grass Lake Scott Hiipakka, Milford Dan Olsen, Charlotte Kathleen Cain-Babbitt, Kalamazoo John Graham, New Boston Peter Spadafore, Lansing Douglas Ferrick, Northville Township Cathy Sharp	Act 219 of 1994
Compensation Appellate Commission	Judiciously serves Michigan's employees, employers and insurers by expeditiously addressing and impartially resolving appeals of decisions and orders involving the award of workers' compensation and unemployment insurance benefits. **Members:** Phil Hendges, Lansing Jack Wheatley, Royal Oak George Wyatt III, East Lansing Kevin Weise, Mason William J. Runco, Dearborn Lester Owczarski, West Bloomfield Garry Goolsby, Lansing David DeGraw, Grand Rapids Duncan McMillan, East Grand Rapids	Executive Order 2011-6
Construction Code Commission, State	Improves the quality of housing for Michigan residents while assisting the housing industry. **Members:** William E. Duffield, West Bloomfield Joseph Sucher, Grosse Pointe Woods Matt Zurbrick, Ortonville Michael Boss, Kalkaska Daryl Gallant, Brighton Adam Krouse, Lansing Thomas Erdman, Vassar Greg Pollock, Midland Kenneth Misiewicz, Lake Odessa Anthony D'Ascenzo, Northville Jeffrey Spencer, Davisburg Frank Bayer, Clinton Township Brad Bartholomew, Kalamazoo Mark Lee, Kalamazoo David Thomlinson, Metamora Glenn Davis, Bloomfield Hills Jonathon Jackson, Carleton	Act 230 of 1972

BOARDS AND COMMISSIONS IN THE STATE OF MICHIGAN (*Cont.*)

Board or Commission	Description		Authority for Creation
Corn Marketing Program Committee	Enhances the economic position of Michigan corn growers by providing for the growth and expansion of the corn industry in Michigan. **Members:**		Act 232 of 1965
	John Burk, Bay City Blaine Baker, Clayton Paul Wagner, Grawn Steve Lonier, Lansing Matthew Holyz, Vicksburg	Ned-Wyse, Camden Tom Durand, Croswell Brett Brink, Hamilton Scott Miller, Elsie Kory Brodbeck, Woodland	
Correctional Officers' Training Council	Develops, approves, and updates vocational certificate program; minimum requirements for recruitment and selection; and standards for certification of state corrections officers. **Members:**		Act 415 of 1982
	Matthew Fedorchuk, Okemos Francine Marie Wresinski, Holt Reverend Robert Davis, Saginaw Sherman Campbell, Jackson	William Henderson, Freeland Christopher Mills, Grand Rapids Tamara McDiarmid, Ionia Juliette Roddy, Berkley	
Cosmetology, Board of	Licenses and regulates the practice of cosmetology in Michigan. **Members:**		Act 299 of 1980
	Linda Ward, Big Rapids Scott Weaver, Okemos Gabriella Abel, Okemos Cindy Straley, Alpena Kelly Coffee-Tavi, East Lansing	Kathleen Skipper-Stong, Ida Sally Pittsenbarger, Ferndale Kathryn Wilkinson, Howell Danielle Kruithoff, Holland	
Counseling, Board of	The board ascertains minimal entry level competency of health practitioners and verifying continuing education during licensure. The board also has the obligation to take disciplinary action against licensees who have adversely affected the public's health, safety, and welfare. **Members:**		Act 368 of 1978
	Jana Simmons, Ferndale Katie Bozek, Grand Rapids Mary Billman, Kentwood Walter Harper, Rose City Robyn Emde, St. Joseph Gerald Papazian, Lake Ann	Harold Love, Clarkston Stephen Craig, Grand Rapids Harold Koviak, Cheboygan Charles Hughes, Gaylord Janet Glaes, Vicksburg	

BOARDS AND COMMISSIONS IN THE STATE OF MICHIGAN (*Cont.*)

Board or Commission	Description	Authority for Creation
Craft Beverage Council, Michigan	The Michigan Craft Beverage Council replaced the Grape and Wine Industry Council created by Executive Reorganization Order No. 2014-2. The Council will award grants for research into winemaking, hops, barley, beer and spirits; conduct market surveys and analysis; and offer other programs that encourage the agricultural elements related to Michigan's craft beverage industries. The council's activities are funded exclusively by non-retail, non-wholesale liquor license fees.	Executive Order 2014-6
	The Council is comprised of nine members appointed by the Governor. Members serve 3-year terms.	
	Members:	
	Dustin Stabile, Boyne Falls Rosalind Mayberry, Grand Haven Zachary Owen, Temperance Jim Holton, Mount Pleasant Scott Graham, Lansing	Bradley Stevenson, Grand Rapids Brian Lesperance, Fennville Michael Beck, St. Johns Richard Anderson, Thompsonville
Crime Victim Services Commission	Provides reimbursement expenses to innocent crime victims who suffer a physical injury.	Act 223 of 1976; Executive Order 1997-10
	Members:	
	William Fales, Kalamazoo Victor Fitz, Cassopolis Karen Gray Sheffield, Detroit	Brian Mackie, Ann Arbor Annie Harrison, Lansing
Criminal Justice Policy Commission	Established to collect, prepare, analyze, and disseminate information regarding state and local sentencing and proposed release policies for felonies and the use of prisons and jails and conduct ongoing research on several corrections issues.	Act 465 of 2014; Repealed by Act 576 of 2018, effective September 30, 2019
	Members:	
	Amanda Burgess-Proctor, Chair Linus Banghart-Linn Ronald Bretz Honorable Chuck Goedert D.J. Hilson Kyle D. Kaminski Sheryl Kubiak Representative Beau LaFave Sheriff Michelle LaJoye-Young	Barbara Levine Senator Pete Lucido Kenneth B. Mitchell Representative Isaac Robinson Senator Sylvia Santana Jennifer Strange The Honorable Paul E. Stutesman Andrew G. Verheek

BOARDS AND COMMISSIONS IN THE STATE OF MICHIGAN (*Cont.*)

Board or Commission	Description		Authority for Creation
Dairy Market Program Committee	Promote milk and milk products produced within the State of Michigan.		Act 232 of 1965
	Members:		
	Brian Preston, Quincy	Jeffrey Horning, Manchester	
	Rodney Daniels, Whitemore	Corby Werth, Alpena	
	Bryan Hull, Fenwick	Carol Marz-Evans, Litchfield	
	Dwight Nash, Elsie	Daniel Van Dyke, Marne	
	Timothy Charles Hood, Paw Paw	Renee McCauley, Lowell	
	Kenneth Paul Nobis, St. Johns	Amy Martin, Leroy	
	Eric J. Frahm, Frankenmuth		
Data Collection Agency Governing Board	This board is responsible for the determination of workers' compensation data requirements for establishing workers' disability compensation insurance rates.		Act 281 of 1956
	Member:		
	Emily McDonough, Williamston		
Deaf, Deafblind, and Hard of Hearing Advisory Council	Advises the department on matters pertaining to hearing impaired persons.		Act 72 of 1937
	Members:		
	KT Maviglia, Dundee	Michael McKee, Dexter	
	Jill Gaus, Jackson	Cynthia Caldwell, Springport	
	Elizabeth Bystrycki, Otsego	Thomas Shields, DeWitt	
	Todd Morrison, Fowlerville	Matthew Stephens, Taylor	
	Christopher Hunter, Holt	Debbi Mitre-Smith, Novi	
	Ann Liming, Lansing	Joanne Forbes, Royal Oak	
	Elizabeth Kobylak, Troy		
Dentistry, Board of	The board works with the department to oversee the practice of dentists, dental specialists, hygienists, and dental assistants.		Act 122 of 1919
	Members:		
	Mark Johnston, Lansing	Peter Chiaravalli, DeWitt	
	Patricia Roels, Caledonia	Rita Hale, Munising	
	Kathleen Inman, Croswell	Paula Weidig, Fort Gratiot	
	Sandra Franklin, St. Clair Shores	Timothy Schmakel, Bloomfield Hills	
	William Perrone, East Lansing	Vaijanthi Oza. West Bloomfield	
	Joshua Goodrich, Constantine	Cheryl Bentley, Grand Rapids	
	Lori Barnhart, Lennon	Martha Morgan, Royal Oak	
	Irene Tseng, Livonia	Hassan Yehia, Dearborn	
	Grace Curcuru, New Baltimore	Deborah Brown, Grand Rapids	
	Kathleen Weber, Ann Arbor	Kristi Thomas, Lathrup Village	

BOARDS AND COMMISSIONS IN THE STATE OF MICHIGAN *(Cont.)*

Board or Commission	Description	Authority for Creation
Detroit Financial Review Commission	The Financial Review Commission is responsible for oversight of the City of Detroit and the Detroit Public Schools Community District. It ensures both are meeting statutory requirements, reviews and approves their budgets, and establishes programs and requirements for prudent fiscal management, among other roles and responsibilities. **Members:** Stacy Fox, Detroit David A. Nicholson, Grosse Pointe Isaiah McKinnon, Detroit Ronald Rose, Birmingham John Walsh, Livonia	Act 181 of 2014
Detroit/Wayne County Port Authority	Mission is to plan, develop, and promote Detroit as a freight transportation and distribution hub for U.S. Midwest and Southwestern Ontario businesses and their customers and vendors, for the purpose of fostering economic growth in the City of Detroit, Wayne County, and the State of Michigan. **Members:** Andy Doctoroff, Huntington Woods Tom Orzechowski Jr. Jonathan C. Kinloch The Honorable Alisha Bell Lorron James	Act 639 of 1978
Developmental Disabilities Council	This council acts as an advocate for people with developmental disabilities, as a strong voice working on behalf of those citizens. **Members:** Mark McWilliams, Lansing Sharon Milberger, Farmington Hills Deborah Rock, Pewamo Steve Johnson, West Olive Richard Kline, Grand Rapids Colleen Allen, Southfield Jamie Junior, Detroit Bonnie Gonzalez, Muskegon Price Pullins, Kalamazoo Janet Timbs, Mount Morris David Taylor, Ferndale Matt Bolger, Lansing Denise Simmons, Oak Park Tammy Yeomans, Grand Rapids Kelly Rockwell, West Bloomfield Brad Rivard, Rockford Todd Koopmans, Fremont Karsten Bekemeir, East Lansing	Executive Order 2006-12
Domestic and Sexual Violence Prevention and Treatment Board	This board coordinates and monitors programs and services for the prevention of domestic and sexual violence and the treatment of victims of domestic and sexual violence. **Members:** Sue Snyder, Ann Arbor Yvonne Brantley, Bay City Elizabeth Pollard Hines, Ann Arbor Thomas C. Cameron, Northville Township Jeffrie Cape, West Bloomfield James Fink, Ypsilanti Cris Mary Sullivan, Potterville	Executive Order 2012-17

BOARDS AND COMMISSIONS IN THE STATE OF MICHIGAN *(Cont.)*

Board or Commission	Description	Authority for Creation
Early Childhood Investment Corporation	Created to be the state's focal point for information and investment in early childhood in Michigan. **Members:** Kristen McDonald, Bay City Hiram Fitzgerald, DeWitt Sharyl Smith, Farmington Hills Jason Gold, Belleville Beverly Burns, Grosse Pointe Judith O'Neill, Grosse Pointe Farms Leslie Murphy, Ann Arbor Shauna Barbeau, Midland Judy Freeman, East Grand Rapids Carol Paine-McGovern, Grand Rapids Luanne Ewald, Royal Oak Laurie Linscott, East Lansing Scott Menzel, Whitmore Lake Jennifer Archey, Rochester Hills	Interlocal Agreement between the State of Michigan and Intermediate School Districts
Early Stage Venture Investment Corporation Board of Directors	Promotes a healthy economic climate by fostering job creation, retention, and expansion through the promotion of investment in venture capital businesses specializing in early stage and seed investments. **Members:** Peter Cracchiolo, Grosse Pointe Shores Scott Idle, East Lansing Robert Manilla, Clarkston Jeb Burns, Okemos Thomas Clifford Kinnear, Ann Arbor Rachael Eubanks, East Lansing	Act 296 of 2003
Eastern Michigan University Board of Regents	The governing body of Eastern Michigan University. **Members:** Michael Hawks, East Lansing Richard L. Baird, Bath Mary Treder Lang, Grosse Pointe Farms James Webb, Farmington Dennis Beagen, Northville Michelle Crumm, Ann Arbor Eunice Jeffries, Farmington Hills Alexander Simpson, Southfield	Act 48 of 1963
Economic Development Corporation Executive Committee	Provides policy direction and guidance to the Michigan Economic Development Corporation regarding economic development programs and initiatives. **Members:** David Meador, Troy Scott Newman-Bale, Traverse City Jeff Noel, Benton Harbor Lizabeth Ardisana, Orchard Lake Christina MacInnes, Beulah Fritz J. Erickson, Marquette Karen Weaver, Flint Mike McLauchlan, Detroit Dr. Robert K. McMahan Jr., Flint Fay Beydoun, Dearborn Kyle D. Caldwell, Rockford Awenate Cobbina, Detroit April Clobes, Bath Jeffrey M. Donofrio, Lansing Krista Flynn, Ada Bobby J. Hopewell, Kalamazoo Thomas Lutz, Garden City	Interlocal Agreement between Michigan Strategic Fund and various public agencies

BOARDS AND COMMISSIONS IN THE STATE OF MICHIGAN *(Cont.)*

Board or Commission	Description	Authority for Creation
Education Council	Considers any matters relating to recommendations of the Education Commission of the States and the activities of the members in representing Michigan. **Members:** Eileen L. Weiser, Ann Arbor Kellie Dean, Okemos Sheila A. Alles, Lansing Tyler Sawher Gretchen Whitmer, Lansing	Act 359 of 1972
Education Trust Board of Directors, Michigan	Is responsible for policy development, investment initiatives, program development and implementation. **Members:** Robert A. Bowman Virinder Moudgil, Rochester Hills Cheryl Bartholic, East Lansing Dr. Glenn D. Mroz, Houghton Robert Ferrentino, Greenville Ronald Wiser, South Haven Michael Flynn, Shelby Township Rachael Eubanks, East Lansing Kristin Beltzer, Haslett	Act 316 of 1986
Electrical Administrative Board	This board makes recommendations for electrical code rules; grants annual licenses and certificates to qualified applicants; and makes all orders, rules, and regulations necessary for the enforcement and carrying out of the provisions of the act. **Members:** Joseph Gillespie, Newaygo Alan Kuipers, Portage Scott Weaver, Sunfield David Iverson, Mason Marshell Carissimi, St. Clair Shores Aaron Cooper, Middleville Robert Werbrouck, Wyoming Matthew Wolterstorff, Ada Brian Williams Keith Lambert, Lansing	Act 217 of 1956
Electronic Recording Commission	Keeps the standards and practices and technology of county registers of deeds in this state in harmony with the standards and practices of offices of county registers of deeds in other jurisdictions. **Members:** Donna Krall, Royal Oak Christian Meyer, Grand Rapids Thomas Richardson, Ann Arbor Teresa Walker, Atlanta Patricia Niepoth, Central Lake Justin Roebuck, Zeeland Brandon Denby, Howell	Act 123 of 2010

BOARDS AND COMMISSIONS IN THE STATE OF MICHIGAN (Cont.)

Board or Commission	Description	Authority for Creation
Elevator Safety Board	Promulgates rules, prepares exams, and issues elevator contractor licenses. **Members:** Douglas Datema, Grand Rapids Mike Nelson, Springport Michael Vandervennet, Dearborn Heights Domenic Policicchio III, Novi Terri Flint, Fenton Mark Smith, Muskegon John Vitale, Grosse Pointe Woods Michael Janca, Roscommon Orlene Hawks, Lansing Richard Knott, Grosse Pointe Woods	Act 227 of 1967
Employment Relations Commission	This commission resolves labor disputes involving public and private sector employees. **Members:** Edward D. Callaghan, Royal Oak Bob LaBrant, Perry Natalie Yaw, Detroit	Act 176 of 1939
Ethics, State Board of	It is this board's jurisdiction to determine the ethical conduct of classified or unclassified state employees, and public officers of the executive branch of Michigan state government who are appointed by the Governor or another executive department official. **Members:** The Honorable Lawrence M. Glazer, Okemos Patrick Barrett, Birmingham Albert Taylor Nelson Jr., Troy The Honorable Richard A. Bandstra, Grand Rapids Thomas C. Phillips, Okemos Leslee Fritz, Albion Catherine McClure, Chelsea	Act 196 of 1973
Examiners in Mortuary Science, State Board of	The board works with the department to oversee the practice of mortuary science licensees, residential trainees, and funeral homes. **Members:** Mark Canale, Marquette Thomas Chrzanowski, Taylor Kathleen Barone, Coldwater Mary Ochalek, Milan Ronald Karelse, Belmont Stephen Linder, Okemos Patrick Miller, Troy Mark Ransford, Caro Harold Rediske II, Brownstown	Act 299 of 1980
Farm Produce Insurance Authority	Has the responsibility of establishing, administering and promoting the Farm Produce Insurance Fund. **Members:** William Willson, Perry Mark Metz, Ida Steven Kluemper, Williamston James Howe, Frankenmuth Mark Kies, Allen Theodore Crowley, Ravenna Stephen Ewald, Unionville Jason Haag, Unionville Rita Herford, Pigeon	Act 198 of 2003

BOARDS AND COMMISSIONS IN THE STATE OF MICHIGAN *(Cont.)*

Board or Commission	Description	Authority for Creation
Ferris State University Board of Control	The board shall have general control, supervision, and management of the University and control and direction of all expenditures from the funds of the University. **Members:** Kari Sederburg, East Lansing Kurt A. Hofman, Grand Rapids Robert J. Hegbloom, Clarkston Lori A. Gwizdala, Bay City Ana L. Ramirez-Saenz, Rockford Rupesh K. Srivastava, Franklin Village Amna P. Seibold, East Grand Rapids LaShanda R. Thomas, Grosse Pointe	Act 114 of 1949
Film Office Advisory Council	Advises the office, the fund, the governor, and the legislature on how to promote and market this state's locations, crews, facilities, and technical production facilities and other services used by film, television, digital media, and related industries. **Members:** Terry Terry, East Lansing Brian Winn, Okemos Niki Adams, Mason Bill Ludwig, Birmingham Timothy Pietryga, Grand Rapids Michael Mittelstaedt, Traverse City Richard Hert, Ada Dan Lemieux, Plymouth Andriy B. Pereklita, Ann Arbor Joe Voss, Kalamazoo Skot Welch, Kentwood Dori DePree, Saugatuck Eric Kuiper, Grand Rapids Larry Fouts, Flint	Act 380 of 1965
Finance Authority Board of Directors	Improves efficiency in state government by consolidating ten public finance authorities. **Members:** Travis Jones, Owosso William Beekman, East Lansing Timothy Hoffman, DeWitt Murray David Wikol, Bloomfield Hills Luke Forest, Ann Arbor Anna E. Heaton, Lansing	Executive Order 2010-2
Fire Fighters Training Council	Serves the training and certification needs of the state's fire departments and fire fighters and officers. **Members:** Aileen Pettinger, Saginaw Terrence Blackmer, Mayville Brian Blomstrom, Sheridan Chad Tackett, Otsego Lynnae White, Allegan Jacob Steichen, Ann Arbor Alan Styles, Twin Lake Gregory Janik, Saugatuck	Act 291 of 1966

BOARDS AND COMMISSIONS IN THE STATE OF MICHIGAN (*Cont.*)

Board or Commission	Description	Authority for Creation
Fire Safety Board, State	Mission of protecting life and property from fire, smoke, hazardous materials and fire-related panic in specific types of public facilities in cooperation with the Bureau of Fire Services and other fire organizations within the state. **Members:** Paul Korte, Southfield Michael W. Powers, Rockford Andrew Lenaghan, Dearborn Jullie Bulson, Grand Rapids Lynn Artman, Chassell Kevin Sehlmeyer, Lansing John Enkemann, Northville Jeramie Morris, Saginaw Kassandra Renneberg, Riverdale Lindsey Haley, Ada David Piche, White Lake Tina Kerr, Eaton Rapids Ron Sabin, Byron Center Robert Williams III, Dexter Mark Jensen, Millington Kenneth Letts, Marshall Jeffery Green, Marquette	Act 207 of 1941
Flint Water Interagency Coordinating Committee	This committee brings together a wide range of experts to work on long-term solutions to the Flint water situation and ongoing public health concerns affecting residents. **Members:** Karen Weaver, Flint Mona Hanna-Attisha, West Bloomfield Laura Sullivan, Flint Lawrence Reynolds, Flint Gen. Michael McDaniel, East Lansing Santino Guerra, Flint Jim Koski, Saginaw Pamela Pugh, Saginaw Bryant Nolden, Flint Mark Young, Grand Blanc Marc Edwards, Blacksburg, VA	Executive Order 2016-1
Freedom Trail Commission	Directed to preserve, protect and promote the legacy of the Freedom Trail in Michigan. **Members:** Juanita Moore, Detroit Amanda Campbell, Oscoda Ronald Brown, Ypsilanti Michael Nassaney, Kalamazoo C. David Teeter, Detroit Kevin Turman, Detroit Roy Eugene Finkenbine, Livonia Kerry Baldwin, Grand Rapids	Act 409 of 1998

BOARDS AND COMMISSIONS IN THE STATE OF MICHIGAN (*Cont.*)

Board or Commission	Description		Authority for Creation
Future Talent Council, Michigan	Focuses on job creation and building a strong workforce in Michigan.		Executive Order 2011-13
	Members:		
	Marcus James, Jackson	Tony Day, Athens	
	Helen Dietrich, Conklin	Stephanie Beckhorn, Okemos	
	Douglas Parkes, Manistee	Kenyatta Brame, Grand Rapids	
	Brad Rusthoven, DeWitt	Mark Alyea, Jackson	
	Al Haidous, Wayne	John Moll, North Branch	
	Marilyn Moran, Onaway	Paul Arsenault, Ishpeming	
	Darcy Kerr, Sunfield	Joseph Billig, Mason	
	Dennis Argyle, Freeland	Representative Brandt Iden	
	Tony Retaskie, Marquette	Senator Ken Horn	
	Bill Peterson, Harrison Township	William Robinson, Lansing	
	Gregory Winter, Alpena	Steven Claywell, Battle Creek	
	Sharon Miller, Sylvan Lake	Lee Graham, Fenton	
	Conan Smith, Ann Arbor	Kristin Beltzer, Haslett	
	Doug Chaffin, Monroe	Marisue Moreau, Onaway	
Gaming Control Board	This board licenses and regulates the Detroit commercial casinos and their suppliers.		Initiated Law 1 of 1996
	Members:		
	Robert Anthony IV, Northville	Carla Walker-Miller, Detroit	
	Andrew Palms, Chelsea	Barbara Smith, Bloomfield Hills	
	Patrick McQueen, Bloomfield Hills		
Grand Rapids - Kent County Convention/ Arena Authority	The authority administers Van Andel Arena, DeVos Place and DeVos Performance Hall.		Act 203 of 1999
	Members:		
	Steven R. Heacock, Grand Rapids	Charles Secchia	
	Birgit M. Klohs, Grand Rapids	The Honorable Rosalynn Bliss,	
	Richard Winn, Grand Rapids	Grand Rapids	
	Floyd Wilson Jr.	Lew Chamberlin	
Grand Valley State University Board of Trustees	Governs the business and affairs of the university.		Act 120 of 1960
	Members:		
	Mary L. Kramer, Detroit	Randall S. Damstra, Ada	
	John G. Russell, East Lansing	Kate Pew Wolters, Grand Rapids	
	Victor M. Cardenas, Novi	Susan M. Jandernoa, West Olive	
	Megan S. Sall, Grand Rapids	Elizabeth C. Emmitt, Byron Center	

BOARDS AND COMMISSIONS IN THE STATE OF MICHIGAN *(Cont.)*

Board or Commission	Description	Authority for Creation
Great Lakes Water Authority	An agreement between the City of Detroit, the counties of Macomb, Oakland, and Wayne, and the State of Michigan to create a regional authority designed to leverage the assets of the Detroit-owned water and sewerage system. **Members:** Craig Hupy, Ypsilanti Gary Brown, Detroit Robert Daddow, Oakland County Freman Hendrix, Detroit Brian Baker, Macomb County Abe Munfakh, P.E., Wayne County	Memorandum of Understanding
Health and Safety Compliance and Appeals, Board of	Reviews all contested Michigan Occupational Safety and Health Administration (MIOSHA) cases involving safety and health citations, orders, and appeals. **Members:** Kim Dennison, Laingsburg Craig Chunchick, Shelby Township George Van Coppenolle, Adrian Daniel Kozakiewicz, Midland Kevin Lepak, West Bloomfield John Rupp, West Bloomfield D. Lynn Coleman, Ashley	Act 154 of 1974
Health Endowment Fund Board	Administers the fund to benefit health and wellness of minor children and seniors through the state with a significant focus on infant mortality, wellness and fitness programs, access to healthy food, technology enhancements, health-related transportation needs and foodborne illness prevention. **Members:** Tim Damschroder, Ann Arbor Michael Williams, Westland Keith A. Pretty, Midland Lynn Alexander, Bloomfield Hills Rob Fowler, Haslett Henry Veenstra, Zeeland Susan M. Jandernoa, West Olive Tina Reynolds, East Lansing Alexis Wiley, Detroit	Act 4 of 2013
Health Information Technology (HIT) Commission	The commission's mission is to facilitate and promote the design, implementation, operation, and maintenance of an interoperable health care information infrastructure in Michigan. **Members:** Patricia Rinvelt, Ann Arbor Jack Harris, Lansing Karen Parker, Webberville Thomas Simmer, Ann Arbor Rozelle Hegeman-Dingle, Rochester Hills Jim VanderMey, Byron Center Jonathan Kufahl, Jackson Michael Zaroukian, Okemos Norman J. Beauchamp, Grand Rapids Renee Smiddy, Howell Heather Somand, Ann Arbor Paul LaCasse, West Bloomfield Nicholas D'Isa, Haslett	Act 137 of 2006

BOARDS AND COMMISSIONS IN THE STATE OF MICHIGAN (*Cont.*)

Board or Commission	Description		Authority for Creation
Hispanic/Latino Commission of Michigan	Develops a unified policy and plan of action to serve the needs of Michigan's Hispanic and Latino people.		Act 164 of 1975
	Members:		
	Juan Marinez, Okemos	Jose Lopez, Detroit	
	Jesse Venegas, Royal Oak	Carlos Pava, Grand Rapids	
	Ivonne Soler, Livonia	Juanita Bocanegra, Holland	
	Sonya Hernandez, Muskegon	Angela Baldwin, Farmington Hills	
	Anthony Garcia-Rubio, Cadillac	Jessica Cruz, Marquette	
	Jeremiah Hernandez, DeWitt	Keysha Camps, Franklin	
	Esperanza Cantu, Berkley	Jesse Bernal, Grand Rapids	
	Monica Reyes, Saginaw		
Historic Preservation Review Board, State	Reviews and approves each national register nomination prior to submission to the Keeper of the National Register.		Executive Order 2007-53
	Members:		
	Misty Jackson, Leslie	Krystal Ryzewski, Ypsilanti	
	Dale Gyure, Farmington Hills	Janet Kreger, Ann Arbor	
	Rhonda Baker, Caledonia	Lane Demas, Mount Pleasant	
	Brian Rebain, Detroit	Kemba Braynon, Ypsilanti	
	Grace A.M. Smith, Rockford		
Historical Commission, Michigan	Advises the director of the Michigan Department of Natural Resources on the museum, archival and other programs of the Michigan Historical Center.		Act 271 of 1913
	Members:		
	Thomas Truscott, Lansing	Timothy Chester, Grand Rapids	
	Joseph Calvaruso, Galesburg	Eric Hemenway, Harbor Springs	
	Brian Egen, Monroe	Laura Ashlee, Okemos	
	Susan Safford, Mackinaw City	Delia Fernandez, Lansing	
	Larry Wagenaar, Ada		
Historical Records Advisory Board	The board acts as a coordinating body to facilitate cooperation and communication among historical records repositories and information agencies within the state.		Executive Order 2007-54
	Members:		
	Cynthia Ghering, East Lansing	Marian Matyn, Clare	
	James Cameron, Saline	Lindsay Hiltunen, Hancock	
	Katheryn Kelly, Saginaw		

Board or Commission	Description		Authority for Creation
Horse Racing Advisory Commission	Created to establish procedure governing the operation and promotion of horse racing in this state. **Members:** Thomas Barrett, Novi Mike Carlo, Northville George Kutlenios, Holly Frank Nickels, Haslett	Don Ryker, Ortonville Ladd Biro, Warren James Kober, West Olive	Public Act 271 of 2016
Housing Development Authority, Michigan State	Provides financial and technical assistance through public and private partnerships to create and preserve safe and decent affordable housing. **Members:** Tyrone Hamilton, Belleville Carl English, Bingham Farms Deborah Muchmore, Laingsburg	Luke Terry, Haslett Jennifer Grau, Lansing	Act 346 of 1966
Human Trafficking Commission	Identifies sources for grants that will assist in examining and countering human trafficking, funds research programs, provides information and training to appropriate personnel, and establishes a program for victims of human trafficking. **Members:** Hassan Beydoun, Novi David Leyton, Flint Deborah Monroe, Madison Heights Kelly Carter, Lansing Cheryl Pezon, Michigan Center D/Sgt. Tracey Walton, Lansing Matt Lori, Constantine	Liz Lukasik, East Lansing Judith K. Emmons, Sheridan Shari Montgomery, Eaton Rapids Elizabeth Moon Carter, Ferndale Fadowa Harrel, Farmington Hills Chad Baugh, Canton	Act 325 of 2014
Human Trafficking Health Advisory Board	Established in the Department of Health and Human Services to collect and analyze information concerning medical and mental health services available to survivors of human trafficking, identify state, federal and local agencies that are involved with issues relating to human trafficking, and coordinate the dissemination of information concerning medical and mental health services available to survivors of human trafficking in this state. **Members:** Subburaman Sivakumar, Northville Township Jayashree Kommareddi, Grand Blanc Sheila Meshinski, Macomb	Brigette Robarge, Belleville Ruth Rondon, Wyoming James Blessman, Detroit Stacy Doctoroff, Huntington Woods	Act 461 of 2014

BOARDS AND COMMISSIONS IN THE STATE OF MICHIGAN *(Cont.)*

Board or Commission	Description		Authority for Creation
Humanities Council, Michigan	Connects people and communities by fostering and supporting quality cultural programs.		Federal/State Partnership
	Members:		
	Margaret Stephanak, Portage	April Clobes, Bath	
	Jade Sims, Okemos	James Napolitano, Dryden	
	Glenn Stevens, Beverly Hills	Jenell Leonard, DeWitt	
Indiana-Michigan Boundary Line Commission	Established to administer a survey and remonumentation of the Indiana-Michigan border.		Act 259 of 2010
	Members:		
	John Kamer, Eau Claire	David Mostrom, St. Joseph County	
	Michael Lodzinski, Cement City	Ed Reed, Quincy	
	Chris Marbach, Edwardsburg		
Indigent Defense Commission, Michigan	Collects and compiles data necessary for the review of indigent defense services, creates standards to ensure constitutional obligations are met, and implements plans to meet standards.		Act 93 of 2013
	Members:		
	Michael Puerner, Ada	Frank Eaman, Huntington Woods	
	Thomas McMillin, Rochester Hills	Brandy Robinson, Detroit	
	Thomas P. Boyd, Mason	William Swor, Grosse Pointe Woods	
	Nancy J. Diehl, Detroit	John Shea, Chelsea	
	James Fisher, Grand Rapids	Joseph Haveman, Holland	
	Gary Walker, Marquette	Kristina Robinson, Detroit	
	Derek King, Ceresco	Jeffrey Collins, Detroit	
	David Schuringa, Grandville		
Intelligence Operations Center for Homeland Security Advisory Board	Collects, evaluates, collates, and analyzes information and intelligence and disseminates this information so that any threat of terrorism or criminal activity will be successfully identified and addressed.		Executive Order 2012-5
	Members:		
	Tom Reich, Eaton Rapids	Kimberly Buddin, Novi	
	Richard A. Fenton, Ann Arbor	Chief William T. Riley, Inkster	
	Daniel Levy, Lansing	Col. Joseph M. Gasper, Lansing	
	Edward Mize, Lansing	Brian Slocum, Novi	
	Mark Reene, Vassar	Major General Paul D. Rogers, Lansing	

BOARDS AND COMMISSIONS IN THE STATE OF MICHIGAN (*Cont.*)

Board or Commission	Description		Authority for Creation
Interagency Coordinating Council for Infants and Toddlers with Developmental Disabilities	Strengthens and supports Michigan families of children ages birth to five with special needs.		Executive Order 2007-43
	Members:		
	Kristina Donaldson, Caledonia	Tiffany Kostelec, Lansing	
	Nolana Bandy, Detroit	Rachel Harmon, Lansing	
	Laura McKechnie, Sault Ste. Marie	Deb Canja, Lansing	
	Judy Goth-Owens, East Lansing	M. Jennifer Forsthoff, Fenton	
	Barbara Anne Corbin, Jenison	Anne Blankenhorn, Haslett	
	Prachi Shah, Ann Arbor	Karin Nanos, Huntington Woods	
	Deana Strudwick, White Pigeon	Victoria Martinez, Dearborn Heights	
	Stephanie Peters, Eaton Rapids	Paula Johnson, Lansing	
	Cheryl Granzo, Belding	Melissa Epstein, Ann Arbor	
	Fred Williams, Lansing	Andrea Caron, Negaunee	
	Renee DeMars-Johnson, Lansing		
Interagency Council on Homelessness	Charged with developing, adopting, and updating a 10-year plan to end homelessness.		Executive Order 2015-2
	Members:		
	Patrick Patterson, DeWitt	Dennis Sturtevant, West Olive	
	Kristin Brady, Traverse City	Rachel Poole, Sunfield	
	Mark Hoffman, Mason	Kelly Rose, DeWitt	
	Philip M. Cavanagh, Redford	Kristina Leonardi, Davison	
	Tom Combs, Highland	Pam Kies-Lowe, Lansing	
	Janet Kaley, East Lansing	Cylenthia LaToye Miller, Detroit	
	Paul Kaiser VanDam, East Lansing		
Interstate Adult Offender Supervision, State Council	Guides the transfer of offenders in a manner that promotes effective supervision strategies consistent with public safety, offender accountability, and victim's rights.		Act 40 of 2002
	Members:		
	Matt Lori, Constantine	Russ Marlan, DeWitt	
	The Honorable Joseph F. Burke, Ann Arbor	Amna Osman, Grand Blanc	
	Cheri Arwood, St. Johns		
Interstate Juvenile Supervision, Michigan State Council	A formal agreement between member states with the goal of preserving child welfare and promoting public safety interests of citizens, including victims of juvenile offenders.		Executive Order 2013-5
	Members:		
	John Tomlinson, Fort Gratiot	Johanna Marie Delp, Grosse Pointe Park	
	Cheri Arwood, St. Johns	Roy Yaple, Brighton	

BOARDS AND COMMISSIONS IN THE STATE OF MICHIGAN *(Cont.)*

Board or Commission	Description	Authority for Creation
Investment Board, State of Michigan	Reviews investments, goals, and objectives of each of the retirement funds and may submit recommendations. **Members:** Reginald Sanders, Portage James B. Nicholson, Detroit Dina Richard, Northville Rachael Eubanks, East Lansing Chris Kolb, Lansing	Act 380 of 1965
Iron Industry Museum Advisory Board	Advises the Michigan Department of Natural Resources on policies, plans and programs concerning the Michigan Iron Industry Museum. **Members:** Victoria Leonhardt, Marquette Susan Hornbogen Justin Carlson, Negaunee James Paquette, Negaunee Gregory Montgomery, Negaunee Joseph Derocha, Marquette Allen Koski, Negaunee Michael Gregory, Ishpeming	Act 152 of 1984
Judicial Tenure Commission	Serves to promote the integrity of the judicial process and preserve public confidence in the courts. **Members:** The Honorable Pablo Cortes Thomas J. Ryan, Esq. The Honorable Monte Burmeister Nancy J. Diehl, Esq. The Honorable Nanci J. Grant The Honorable Lawrence S. Talon Missy Spickler, Bloomfield Hills The Honorable Karen Fort Hood Ari Adler, Okemos	Michigan State Constitution of 1963, Article 6, Section 30
Juvenile Justice Committee	The committee advises on juvenile justice issues and guides effective implementation of juvenile justice policies and programs. **Members:** MaryAnn Sarosi, Ann Arbor Terri Gilbert, Ann Arbor Larry Emig, Reed City Mary Beth Kelly, Grosse Ile Nancy Becker Bennett, Okemos Sandra Metcalf, Grand Haven Joseph Ryan, Ann Arbor Bob Higgins, Portage Thomas Jay Weichel, Spruce Jessica Black, Mount Pleasant Cory Haines, Madison Heights Marquaun Kane, Ann Arbor Antonio Leija, Greenville Sara McCauley, Traverse City Kathleen Bailey, Plainwell Shenette Coleman, Redford Township Sandra Lindsey, Lathrup Village Cameron Clark, Beulah Kenyatta Stephens, Farmington Hills	Executive Order 2012-1

BOARDS AND COMMISSIONS IN THE STATE OF MICHIGAN (*Cont.*)

Board or Commission	Description	Authority for Creation
Lake Superior State University Board of Trustees	The board is granted the power of control and direction of all expenditures from the university's funds. **Members:** Ann Parker, East Lansing Rodney Nelson, St. Ignace Dr. Mark W. Mercer, Harbor Springs Sandi Frost Steensma, Grand Rapids Thomas Bailey, Petoskey Randy Pingatore, Sault Ste. Marie Timothy Lukenda, Brimley Richard Barch, Ann Arbor	Act 26 of 1969
Law Enforcement Officers Memorial Monument Fund Commission	Established to oversee the financing, design and construction of Michigan's Law Enforcement Officers Memorial. **Members:** Diane Philpot, Detroit Mary Johnson, Okemos Ken Rochell, Ann Arbor Linda Emmert, Omena Katy Sherwood, Farwell John Szczubelek, Lansing	Act 177 of 2004
Law Enforcement Standards, Michigan Commission	Sets standards for selection, employment, licensing, license revocation, and funding in law enforcement and criminal justice, in both the public and private sectors. **Members:** Richard Heins, Sterling Heights Donald Mawer, Frankenmuth Arthur Weiss, Farmington Hills Thomas Adams, Detroit Michael Wendling, Goodells Mark Diaz, Holly Timothy Donnellon, Emmett Kenneth Grabowski, Livonia Nathan Johnson, Vermontville David Molloy, Novi Matthew Saxton, Battle Creek Duane Smith, Saline Karianne Thomas, Scotts Matthew Hartig, Marshall Michael Sauger, Sterling Heights Gregory Zyburt, Marquette	Executive Order 2001-5; Executive Order 2008-19
Law Examiners Board	The board is in charge of the investigation and examination of all persons who initially apply for admission to the bar of this state. **Members:** Eric Pelton The Honorable Brian R. Sullivan Jeffery Stuckey The Honorable Christopher M. Murray Candice Moore	Act 236 of 1961
Library of Michigan Board of Trustees	The board shall make recommendations to the department concerning library services. **Members:** Stacy Nowicki, Kalamazoo Elaine Didier, Plymouth Jennifer Crowley, Grand Rapids Pamela Christensen, Marquette Randy Riley, Lansing Barbara Bonge, Lansing Trisha Deming-Burns, Linwood Beata Kica, Lansing Kyle Guerrant, Lansing Nancy Hmayed, Dearborn	Act 540 of 1982

BOARDS AND COMMISSIONS IN THE STATE OF MICHIGAN *(Cont.)*

Board or Commission	Description	Authority for Creation
Liquor Control Commission	Responsible for being the sole wholesaler for all spirit products in the state and for the enforcement of the state's liquor laws. **Members:** Dennis Olshove Andy Deloney Teri Quimby	Ed Clemente Bradford Jacobsen	Act 58 of 1998
Local Community Stabilization Authority Council	Coordinates access to public rights-of-way and the payment of maintenance fees by telecommunications providers to municipalities and is responsible for distributing personal property tax replacement revenue to municipalities throughout the state according to specific statutory formulas. **Members:** Donald Rogers, Coldwater Mary Anne Jones, Rockford Scott Erbisch, Marquette	Devid Keenan, Auburn Steven Ezikian, Howell	Acts 86 and 88 of 2014
Logistics and Supply Chain Collaboration, Commission for	This commission is charged with advising appropriate state agencies on methods, proposals, programs, and initiatives involving freight transportation and supply chain management in this state that may stimulate state economies and provide additional employment opportunities for Michigan. **Members:** Leslie Brand, Holland Roger Huff, Farmington Hills Robert Boehm, Grand Ledge Dr. David Closs, Williamston	Dr. Pasi Lautula, Hancock Frederick Schlemmer, Novi Janice Walsh, Livonia	Act 76 of 2013
Mackinac Bridge Authority	Preserve and maintain the Mackinac Bridge. **Members:** Matthew McLogan, Grand Rapids Barbara J. Brown, St. Ignace Patrick F. Gleason, Davison Kirk T. Steudle, South Lyon	Brad Canale, Marquette Tricia Kinley, Lansing Paul C. Ajeba, Ann Arbor	Act 21 of 1950
Mackinac Island State Park Commission	The commission is responsible for all aspects of managing Mackinac State Historic Parks. **Members:** William Marvin, Mackinaw City Dan Loepp, Birmingham Richard A. Manoogian, Grosse Pointe Park	Richard Posthumus, Alto Marlee Brown, Mackinac Island Rachel Bendit, Ann Arbor	Act 451 of 1994

BOARDS AND COMMISSIONS IN THE STATE OF MICHIGAN *(Cont.)*

Board or Commission	Description	Authority for Creation
Manufactured Housing Commission	Responsible for establishing uniform policy relating to all phases of manufactured housing, business, manufactured housing parks, and seasonal manufactured housing parks. **Members:** Phil Copeland, Holly William Lettinga, Byron Center Steve Karbal, Bloomfield Hills Bryan Davis, Redford Margaret R. Mularoni-Burns, Detroit Patti Jo Schafer, Eagle Kevin Baker, Belmont Alicia Dashevskiy, East Lansing	Act 96 of 1987
Marriage and Family Therapy, Board of	The board licenses and regulates the practice of marriage and family therapy in Michigan and takes disciplinary action against licensees who have adversely affected the public's health, safety, and welfare. **Members:** Laura Mammen, Grand Rapids Sara Dupuis, East Lansing Samantha West, Lansing Amy Campbell, Lansing Madeline Timmer, Portland Andrea Wittenborn, Okemos Silvia Leija, Troy Emily Short, Burton Karol Ross, West Bloomfield	Act 368 of 1978
Massage Therapy Board	Provides for licensing of massage therapists. **Members:** Beth Miazga, Fenton Charlie Franklin, Southfield Katie Kiter, Lansing Lynn Wolf, Petoskey Tiffany Gennety, Roseville JT Stout, Lansing Teri Hunter, Grosse Ile Tina Latham-Enix, St. Joseph Carolyn Harden, Haslett Stacey Murray, Williamston Jodi Wiley, Lansing	Act 368 of 1978
Mechanical Rules, Board of	This board makes recommendations for mechanical code rules, issues mechanical contractor's licenses to qualified applicants, and makes all orders, rules, and regulations necessary for enforcement of the provisions of the act. **Members:** Christopher Freeman, South Lyon Catherine Gay, Troy Robert Fosburg, Caledonia Robert Logan, Battle Creek Kenneth Misiewicz, Lake Odessa Daniel Grafmiller, Fenton Mark Riley, Berkley Matt Marsiglio, St. Clair Shores Bruce Seiler, Roseville Craig Howson, Midland Terry Gilligan, Livonia David Galbreath, Lowell Gerald Philo, Northville Timothy Sweeney, Belmont	Act 192 of 1984

BOARDS AND COMMISSIONS IN THE STATE OF MICHIGAN *(Cont.)*

Board or Commission	Description		Authority for Creation
Medicine, Board of	Oversees the practice of medical doctors in the state.		Act 368 of 1978
	Members:		
	Renee Johnston, Saginaw	James Rogers, Williamsburg	
	Terri Tahnoose, West Bloomfield	Louis Prues, Grosse Pointe Park	
	Richard Bates, Ossineke	Rosalie Tocco-Bradley, Ann Arbor	
	James Sondheimer, West Bloomfield	Eric Stocker, Marysville	
	Michael Chafry, Kalamazoo	Venkat Rao, Grand Blanc	
	Paul E. Sophiea, Dearborn	Cara Poland, Alto	
	Stacey Frankovich, Clawson	Shereen Tabrizi, Okemos	
	Dennis Szymanski, Benton Harbor	Traci Ruiz, Bath	
	Mohammed Arsiwala, Novi	John McGinnity, Attica	
	Michael Chrissos, Ann Arbor		
Mental Health Diversion Council	This council advises and assists in the implantation of the Diversion Action Plan and provides recommendations for statutory, contractual or procedural changes to improve diversion.		Executive Order 2013-7
	Members:		
	Michele Bell, Midland	Ross Buitendorp, Grand Rapids	
	Soleil Campbell, Okemos	Curtis J. Bell, Kalamazoo	
	Ronald Derrer, Grand Rapids	Christopher Becker, Ada	
	John Searles, Wheeler	George Strander, Albion	
	Brian N. Calley, Portland	Larry Cameron, Southfield	
	Lia Gulick, Wheeler	Jon Gale, Twin Lake	
	Steve Kempker, Zeeland	Christopher Cooke, Traverse City	
	Betsy Hardwick, Horton	Debra Pinals, Ann Arbor	
	Milton L. Mack, Wayne	Willie Brooks, Rochester Hills	
Michigan Humanities Council	Connects people and communities by fostering and supporting quality cultural programs.		Federal/State Partnership
	Members:		
	Jade Sims, Okemos	April Clobes, Bath	
	Glenn Stevens, Beverly Hills	James Napolitano, Dryden	
	Margaret Stephanak, Portage	Jenell Leonard, DeWitt	

BOARDS AND COMMISSIONS IN THE STATE OF MICHIGAN *(Cont.)*

Board or Commission	Description		Authority for Creation
Michigan Municipal Services Authority	Encourages best practices, teamwork and inter-local cooperation between municipalities and school districts.		Interlocal Agreement
	Members:		
	Donald Snider, Franklin	James Cambridge, Livonia	
	Doug Smith, Bloomfield Hills	Dominic Pallone, DeWitt	
	Peggy Jury, Davison	Phil Bertolini, Clarkston	
	Scott Buhrer, Grand Rapids	Kelli Scott, Battle Creek	
	Eric DeLong, Grand Rapids	Jessica Moy, Okemos	
	Brian Meakin, Livonia		
Michigan Pre-K-12 Literacy Commission	Advises and assists in matters relating to the assessment, professional development, education programming, socioeconomic challenges, best practices, collaboration, parental engagement, and teaching of literacy.		Executive Order 2016-18
	Members:		
	Susan Medendorp, Lansing	Jeremy Reuter, Haslett	
	Denise Smith, Detroit	Lois Bader, East Lansing	
	John C. Kennedy, Kentwood	Steve Goodman, Grand Haven	
	Naomi Norman, Ann Arbor	Nadra Shami, Dearborn	
	Ja'Nel Jamerson, Flint	Cynthia Pape, Saginaw	
	Amanda Price, Holland	Punita Dani Thurman, Novi	
	Kyle Mayer, Grand Haven		
Michigan Technological University Board of Control	The board governs the business and affairs of the university.		Act 70 of 1885
	Members:		
	Robert Jacquart, Ironwood	Derhun Sanders, Redford Township	
	Linda Kennedy, Troy	Steven M. Tomaszewski, Howell	
	Brenda Ryan, Commerce Township	Jeffrey C. Littmann, Grosse Pointe Park	
	William Johnson, Newaygo	John Bacon, Ann Arbor	
Middle Eastern American Affairs, Commission on	Advises the Governor and the Director of the Department of Civil Rights on the state's policies concerning the Middle-Eastern American Community and on the full range of issues facing the community, and promotes public awareness of Middle-Eastern American culture.		Executive Order 2015-6
	Members:		
	Michael Romaya, West Bloomfield	Susan Dabaja, Dearborn	
	Manal Saab, Fenton	Ronald Haddad, Dearborn	
	Suzanne Sukkar, Ypsilanti	Sharif Hussein, Grand Ledge	
	Fay Beydoun, Dearborn	Adel Mozip, Dearborn	
	Haifa Fakhouri, Troy	Nabeel R. Obeid, Ann Arbor	
	Lina Haraji, Dearborn	Fadwa Hammoud, Dearborn	
	Abe Munfakh, Plymouth	Martin Manna, Bloomfield Hills	
	Dave Abdallah, Dearborn Heights		

BOARDS AND COMMISSIONS IN THE STATE OF MICHIGAN *(Cont.)*

Board or Commission	Description		Authority for Creation
Midwifery, Board of Licensed	Establishes and implements the licensing program for the practice of midwifery in Michigan. **Members:** Deborah Fisch, Ann Arbor Amanda Howell, Clinton Tami Michele, Fremont Geradine Simkins, Maple City Nichole White, Detroit Stacia Proefrock, Ann Arbor	Heather Robinson, Detroit Connie Perkins, Mason Katheryn Mazzara, Howell Patrice Bobier, Hesperia Donald Greydanus, Portage Claretta Duckett-Freeman, Lansing	Act 417 of 2016
Military Appeals Tribunal	Has appellate jurisdiction, upon petition of an accused, to hear and review the record in all decisions of a court-martial after the review provided in the Michigan code of military justice. **Members:** Robert C. Gardella, Brighton Bradley L. Smith, Addison Kyle R. Dufrane, Macomb	Thomas Bourque, Ann Arbor Gaetan Gerville-Reache, Ada	Act 523 of 1980
MiSTEM Advisory Council	Advises the Governor, Legislature, and the Departments of Talent and Economic Development and Education with recommendations designed to improve and promote innovation and collaboration in STEM education and prepare students for careers in science, technology, engineering, and mathematics. **Members:** Gail S. Alpert, West Bloomfield Mary K. Bacon, Paris Lee Graham, Holly Jacqueline Huntoon, Ph.D., Houghton Tonya M. Matthes, Ph.D., Detroit	Christian A. Velasquez, Midland Daniel Williams, Ph.D., Grand Rapids Wendy A. Winston, Grand Rapids Adam F. Zemke, Ypsilanti	Act 94 of 1979
Natural Resources Commission	Has exclusive authority to regulate the taking of game and fish has been vested with the NRC. **Members:** Vicki Pontz, Portland Rex Schlaybaugh Jr., Birmingham Christopher Tracy, Richland Louise Klarr, Bloomfield	Keith Creagh, Williamston Dave Nyberg, Skandia John Walters, Vanderbilt	Act 380 of 1965; Ballot proposal G in 1996; Act 21 of 2013
Natural Resources Trust Fund Board, Michigan	Oversees the Michigan Natural Resource Trust Fund. **Members:** Erin McDonough, Williamston Samuel Cummings, Grand Rapids Steve Hamp, Ann Arbor	William R. Rustem, Mason Keith Creagh, Williamston	Act 451 of 1994

BOARDS AND COMMISSIONS IN THE STATE OF MICHIGAN *(Cont.)*

Board or Commission	Description		Authority for Creation
Northern Michigan University Board of Trustees	Governing authority of the university.		Act 48 of 1963, 2nd extra session
	Members:		
	Steven Mitchell, West Bloomfield	Lisa Fittante, Kingsfrod	
	James K. Haveman, Grand Haven	Alexis Hart, Royal Oak	
	Robert E. Mahaney, Marquette	Travis Weber, Detroit	
	Tami M. Seavoy, Marquette	Stephen E. Young, Lansing	
Nursing, Board of	Acts upon all matters except those that relate to standards for the education and training of RNs. Decisions on such matters are concurred in solely by a majority of the RN and public board members.		Act 368 of 1978
	Members:		
	Glenn O'Connor, Grosse Pointe Woods	Joshua Meringa, RN, Grandville	
	Tiffany McDonald, Flint	Jackeline Iseler, Grand Rapids	
	Tori Sachs, Okemos	Cerise Tounsel, West Bloomfield	
	Cynthia Fenske, Ann Arbor	Scott Richardson, East Grand Rapids	
	Elizabeth Horton, Fenton	Maureen Saxton, DeWitt	
	Kathy Bouchard-Wyant, RN, East Lansing	Kristin Ahrens, Wixom	
	Deborah Vendittelli, Novi	Tatyana Chatman, Hudsonville	
	Patricia Harney, Grand Haven	Lori Glenn, White Lake	
	Ron Basso, Iron River	Sarah Coker, Clare	
	Paula Hopper, Concord	Jason Puscas, Detroit	
	Jill DeVries, LPN, Zeeland	Alana Thomas, Lansing	
	Mary Vander Kolk, RN, Traverse City		
Nursing Home Administrators, Board of	Licenses nursing home administrators in Michigan.		Act 368 of 1978
	Members:		
	Ricky Ackerman, Ada	Pegi Chatti, East Lansing	
	Paul Barber, Freeport	Kristine Dozeman, Grand Rapids	
	Ian Koffler, Grand Rapids	Cheryl Bray, Norway	
	Jana Broughton, Grand Rapids	Helen Hartwell, Lansing	
	Kimberly Kimbrough-Wozniak, Muskegon		
Oakland University Board of Control	Governing authority of the university.		Act 35 of 1970
	Members:		
	Marianne Fey, Birmingham	Tonya Allen, Troy	
	Richard L. DeVore, Bloomfield Hills	Robert I. Schostak, Bloomfield Hills	
	Melissa Stolicker, Haslett	Dennis Muchmore	
	David W. Tull, Birmingham	Brian N. Calley, Portland	

BOARDS AND COMMISSIONS IN THE STATE OF MICHIGAN *(Cont.)*

Board or Commission	Description	Authority for Creation
Occupational Therapists, Board of	The board ascertains minimal entry level competency of health practitioners and verifies continuing education during licensure. The board also takes disciplinary action against licensees who have adversely affected the public's health, safety, and welfare. **Members:** Lynn Kaiser, Flat Rock Gregory Zimmerman, Big Rapids Janet Santos, Saline Richard Bryce, Royal Oak Valerie Palmer, Kalamazoo Matthew Swan, Eaton Rapids Kelly King, OTR, Wyoming David Oh, West Bloomfield Mary Jo Vaughn, Wetmore	Act 473 of 1988 amended the Public Health Code, Public Act 368 of 1978
Onion Committee	This commission seeks to promote the production and consumption of onions and to assist in the agricultural research and development of onion farming. **Members:** Michael Bosch, Hamilton Kristin Oomen, Scottville Bruce J. Klamer, Byron Center Eric Schreur, Hudsonville Dan Steenwyk, Dorr	Act 232 of 1965
Optometry Board	Allows optometrists to be certified to administer topical ocular diagnostic pharmaceutical agents to the anterior segment of the human eye. **Members:** Sandra Doud, Brighton Teresa Seim, Lawton John Kaminski, Midland Thomas Terres, Bath Nancy Peterson-Klein, Mecosta Virginia Manolakoudis, Lansing Carl Powers, Petoskey Lisa Webb, Okemos Hrisais Skorna, Lansing	Act 368 of 1978
Organized Retail Crime Advisory Board	Develops a database of organized retail crimes, compiles annual statistics on organized retail crime acts, and recommends actions to be taken by the department and law enforcement to further combat organized retail crime. **Members:** William Hallan, Okemos Joshua Meier, Canton Douglas R. Lloyd, Lansing Shannon Simon, Byron Center	Act 455 of 2012

BOARDS AND COMMISSIONS IN THE STATE OF MICHIGAN *(Cont.)*

Board or Commission	Description		Authority for Creation
Osteopathic Medicine and Surgery, Board of	Regulates the practice of osteopathic medicine and surgery in the state of Michigan; provides for the examination, licensing and registration of osteopathic physicians and surgeons; and provides for the discipline of offenders against the act.		Act 368 of 1978
	Members:		
	Diane Parrett, Norton Shores	Molly McLogan, Grand Rapids	
	Craig Glines, Riverview	Jesse Guasco, East Lansing	
	Kathleen Kudray, Flint	Matthew Hauser, Redford	
	James Kilmark, Belleville	Walker Foland, Grand Blanc	
	Sheryl Thompson, Reed City	Stephen Bell, Carleton	
	Stacey Beltz, Troy		
Pharmacy and Therapeutics Committee	Advises the department on issues affecting prescription drug coverage for its various health care programs.		Act 368 of 1978 and Executive Order 2001-8
	Members:		
	Margo Farber, Grosse Pointe Park	Brian Peltz, Dearborn Heights	
	Anthony Ognjan, Shelby	Jayne Courts, Caledonia	
	Bradley Uren, Pinckney	Rony Fournia, Commerce Township	
	Victoria Tutag Lehr, Birmingham	Andrew Adair, Ferndale	
	Debera H. Eggleston, Ada	Melanie Manary, Petoskey	
	Andrew Mac, Plymouth		
Pharmacy, Board of	The board regulates, controls, and inspects the character and standards of pharmacy practice and of drugs manufactured, distributed, prescribed, dispensed, and administered or issued in this state. The board also has the obligation to discipline licensees who have adversely affected the public's health, safety, and welfare.		Act 368 of 1978
	Members:		
	Kathleen Burgess, Grosse Pointe Farms	Charles Mollien, Wyoming	
	Cynthia Boston, Utica	Kelli Oldham, East Lansing	
	David Hills, St. Joseph	Grace Sesi	
	James Stevenson, RPh, Northville	Sandra Taylor	
	Kathleen Pawlicki, Novi	Maria Young	
	Mary Ann Victor, Shelby Township		

Board or Commission	Description	Authority for Creation
Physical Fitness, Health and Sports, Governor's Council on	The council is charged with improving the health of, and increasing physical activity among, Michigan residents. **Members:** Scott Przystas, Grand Haven Edwin Kornoelje, Grand Rapids Justin Zatkoff, West Bloomfield Wayman Britt, Grand Rapids Andy Younger, Fenton Rick Ferkel, Mount Pleasant Nolan Moody, Ann Arbor Cameron Gordon, West Bloomfield Florine Mark, Farmington Hills Andre Hutson, East Lansing Warde Manuel Brigitte LaPointe, Marquette Laurie Rospond, DeWitt Dexter Mason, Detroit Nick Payne, Lansing Mary Patay, Mackinac Island	Executive Order 1992-5
Physical Therapy, Board of	The board ascertains minimal entry level competency of health practitioners. The board also has the obligation to take disciplinary action against licensees who have adversely affected the public's health, safety, and welfare. **Members:** Sarah McAllister, Saline Morgan Kennedy, Ann Arbor Adam Swain, Plainwell Whitney Shaffer, Lansing Ajay Middha, Midland Syed Rob, Hamtramck Brian Gilbert, Grand Rapids Michael Winkler, Hamilton Matthew McFadden, East Lansing Craig Miller, Macomb Allison Ives, Marcellus	Act 368 of 1978
Physician's Assistants Task Force	Develops and approves the qualifications of physician's assistants, develops guidelines on the appropriate delegation of functions, and directs the department to issue licenses to applicants who meet the requirements. **Members:** Susan Laham, Grand Rapids Lara Davis, Fenton CaShanda Range, Belleville Maryam Komejan, Holland William Palazzolo, Dexter Heather Kloop, Grand Ledge James Rogers, MD, Williamsburg Ali Safiedine, Southfield Sara Basso, JD, Iron River Adam Carlson, Muskegon Megan Dietrich, Royal Oak Christina Hopps, Rockford	Act 386 of 1978

BOARDS AND COMMISSIONS IN THE STATE OF MICHIGAN *(Cont.)*

Board or Commission	Description	Authority for Creation
Pipeline Safety Advisory Board	The board will ensure safety, upkeep, and transparency of issues related to the state's network of pipelines. **Members:** C. Heidi Grether, Lansing Matthew Schneider, Lansing Keith Creagh, Williamston Capt. Chris Kelenske, Lansing Sally Talberg, Williamston Jerome Popiel, Avon Lake, OH Jennifer McKay, Petoskey Michael Shriberg, Ann Arbor Brad Shamala, Eden Prairie, MN Shawn Lyon, Findley, OH Christopher Shepler, Harbor Springs Jeffrey Pillon, East Lansing Craig Hupp, Grosse Pointe Homer Mandoka, Bronson Anne Armstrong Cusack Anthony England, Ypsilanti	Executive Order 2015-12
Plumbing Board	Makes recommendations for plumbing code rules; licensing plumbers; and making all orders, rules, and regulations necessary for the enforcement of the provisions of the act. **Members:** Scott Kalchik, Northville Paul Lemley, Ada Mark Wiseley, Whitmore Lake Timothy Danielak, Beaverton Paul Kurtzhals, Wolverine Lake	Act 733 of 2002
Podiatric Medicine and Surgery, Board of	The board ascertains minimal entry level competency of health practitioners and verifying continuing education during licensure. The board also has the obligation to take disciplinary action against licensees who have adversely affected the public's health, safety, and welfare. **Members:** Vicki Anton-Athens, Grosse Ile Jay Meyer, Okemos Cyrus Farrehi, Grand Blanc Ali Safiedine, Southfield Deborah Maciolek, Macomb Joseph Martin, Holt Brandon Weber, Kerley Harvey Lefkowitz Erik Kissel, Bloomfield Township	Act 368 of 1978
Port Authority Advisory Committee	Recommends projects to the Michigan Strategic Fund Board of Directors related to port facilities. **Members:** Kyle Burleson, Grosse Pointe Woods Erin Kuhn, Norton Shores Paul LaMarre, Newport Gabe Schneider, Traverse City Charles Squires, Sebewaing Rodney Stokes, Holt Paul Sirpko, Big Rapids Robert Innis, Canton Mark Pontti, Iron Mountain	Act 90 of 2014

BOARDS AND COMMISSIONS IN THE STATE OF MICHIGAN *(Cont.)*

Board or Commission	Description	Authority for Creation
Potato Industry Commission	The commission provides leadership in disseminating information to foster the growth and well-being of the potato industry. **Members:** Guthry Laurie, Caro Jonathan Yoder, Sturgis Rebecca Johnson, Grand Rapids Benjamin Sklarczyk, Johannesburg Travis Horkey, Dundee Mathew Skogman, Foster City Philip Gusmano, Grosse Pointe Farms Donald Kitchen, Elmira Matt Wilkes, Rockford	Act 29 of 1970
Professional Engineers, State Board of	Licenses and regulates the practice of professional engineering in Michigan. **Members:** Charles Hookham, Ann Arbor James Stevens, Farmington Hills Michael Drewyor, Houghton Daniel J. Acciavatti, Chesterfield Lori Fobes, Jackson Kelly Fedele, Southgate Patrick Barry, New Hudson Brett Karl, White Lake Deveron Sanders, Flint	Act 299 of 1980
Professional Surveyors, State Board of	Licenses and regulates the practice of land surveying in Michigan. **Members:** Michael Drewyor, Houghton Ginger Michalski-Wallace, Whitmore Lake Jeffrey D. Bartlett, Standish Gilbert Barish, DeWitt Nick Darin, Allen Park Timothy Platz, Sand Lake Andrew Kurncz, St. Johns James Hollandsworth Jennifer Myers, Troy	Act 299 of 1980
Psychology, Board of	The board ascertains minimal entry level competency of health practitioners. The board also has the obligation to take disciplinary action against licensees who have adversely affected the public's health, safety, and welfare. **Members:** Mindy Fernandes, Walled Lake Valencia Agnew, Grand Rapids Eric Ozkan, PhD, Midland Valerie Shebroe, Haslett Lt. Col. Michael Connelly, East Lansing Sara Van Wormer, LLP, Ferndale Gail Majcher, Northville Sarah Eckenwiler, Fowlerville Mindy Brandish-Orta, Leslie	Act 368 of 1978

BOARDS AND COMMISSIONS IN THE STATE OF MICHIGAN *(Cont.)*

Board or Commission	Description	Authority for Creation
Public Safety Communications Interoperability Board	The board may establish advisory workgroups or task forces composed of persons representing law enforcement or other governmental or tribal public safety agencies or organizations that operate or utilize public safety communications systems in this state. **Members:** Bryce Tracy, St. Ignace Kenneth Morris, Lowell Troy A. Stern, Tecumseh Bradley Kersten, Emmet Lawrence Schloegl, Laingsburg John Unruh, Brighton Matthew Sahr Edwin Miller, Sterling Heights John Allen, Allen Park	Executive Order 2009-55
Public School Employees Retirement System Board	Provides oversight of the Michigan Public School Employees Retirement System. **Members:** Dan Christner, Brighton Timothy Raymer, Grand Rapids Steven Epstein, West Bloomfield Ann Gabrielle Kroneman, Okemos Kevin Phillips, East Grand Rapids Mike Engle, Hastings Liz Eastway, Cadillac Laura Colligan, Holt Jeffrey Mills, Allegan Alan Sonnanstine, Canton	Act 300 of 1980
Public Service Commission	The commission seeks to grow Michigan's economy and enhance the quality of life of its communities by assuring safe and reliable energy, telecommunications, and transportation services at reasonable rates. **Members:** Sally Talberg, Williamston Tremaine Phillips, Kentucky Dana Scripps, Northport	Act 3 of 1939
Real Estate Appraisers, Board of	The board works with the department to oversee the practice of limited real estate appraisers, state licensed appraisers, certified general appraisers and certified residential appraisers. **Members:** David Worthams, Kalamazoo Ronald Wheeler, DeWitt James Hartman, East Lansing Delbert Denkins, Niles Martin Wagar, Kalamazoo Mark Jenkins, Rockford Christine Rodriguez, East Lansing Thomas Watson, Midland Phyllis Howard, Muskegon	Act 299 of 1980

BOARDS AND COMMISSIONS IN THE STATE OF MICHIGAN *(Cont.)*

Board or Commission	Description		Authority for Creation
Real Estate Brokers and Salespersons, Board of	The board works with the department to oversee the practice of real estate salespersons, associate real estate brokers, real estate brokers, and branch offices.		Act 299 of 1980
	Members:		
	Ronald Zupko, Brighton	Natalie Rowe, Portage	
	Patrick Dean, East Lansing	Hassan Ahmad, Dearborn Heights	
	Karen Greenwood, Troy	Benjamin Smith, Farmington Hills	
	Robert Craig, St. Johns	Chase Cantrell, Detroit	
	Sara Storch-Lipnitz, Birmingham		
Regional Transit Authority Board of Directors	Plans for and coordinates public transportation in the Wayne, Oakland, Macomb, and Washtenaw Counties region, including the City of Detroit, and to deliver rapid transit system.		Act 387 of 2012
	Members:		
	Paul Hillegonds, Lansing	Sonya Mays, Wayne County	
	Alma Wheeler Smith, Washtenaw County	Roy Rose, Macomb County	
	Liz Gerber, Washtenaw County	Donald Morandini, Macomb County	
	Freman Hendrix, Detroit	Chuck Moss, Oakland County	
	Mark Gaffney, Wayne County	Timothy Soave, Oakland County	
Rehabilitation Services Council	Reviews, analyzes, and advises Michigan's rehabilitation programs and services, and advises the department director and governor.		Executive Order 2012-10
	Members:		
	Carol Bergquist, Escanaba	Jennipher Wiebold, Kalamazoo	
	Ed Benning, Clio	Sheryl Diamond, Lansing	
	Elaine Wood, Traverse City	Carrie Dudek, Davison	
	Michael Poyma, Williamston	Jacqueline Tahtinen, Pike	
	Anne Riddering, Novi	Michael Miller, Homer	
	Brian Sabourin, Midland	David Szydlowski, Alpena	
	Steve Perdue, Traverse City	Brenda Henige, East Lansing	
	Robin L. Bennett, Canton	Tiffany Guthrie, Alma	
	Trina Edmonson, Wyoming		

BOARDS AND COMMISSIONS IN THE STATE OF MICHIGAN *(Cont.)*

Board or Commission	Description	Authority for Creation
Residential Builders' and Maintenance and Alteration Contractors' Board	The board licenses and regulates persons engaged in the construction of a residential structure or combination residential and commercial structure, or persons who undertake the repair, alteration, addition, subtraction or improvement of a residential structure or combination residential and commercial structure. **Members:** William Adcock, Lansing Matthew Zalewski, Dearborn John Kelly, Bloomfield Hills Jeffrey Donius, Shelby Township Sidney Browne Jr., Marine City William Goble, Belleville Mark Wahl, Linwood Herman Harris, Ann Arbor Kenneth Calverley, Goodrich	Act 299 of 1980
Respiratory Care, Board of	Oversees the licensure requirements and standards for respiratory therapists. **Members:** Jonathan Vono, Shelby Township John Byrd, Marshall Veena Erinjeri, Flint Michael Dunn, Troy Shari Heydenburg, Jackson Laurie Niemer, Harrison Township Andrew Weirauch, Plymouth Elizabeth Weir, Lansing Elizabeth Glasser, Gaylord Helen Wiltse, Clinton Township Jeremy Bainbridge, Grand Rapids	Act 368 of 1978
Rural Development Fund Board	Oversees the Rural Development Fund within the Department of Agriculture and Rural Development. **Members:** Fred Taccolini, Marquette Laura Braun, Ovid Margaret Minerick, Sagola Justin Horvath, Owosso	Act 411 of 2012
Saginaw Valley State University Board of Control	Granted the power of control and direction of all expenditures from the university's funds. **Members:** Dennis Durco, Pinckney Raj Kumari Wiener, Williamston John Kunitzer, Saginaw John D. Cherry Jr., Clio Vicki L. Rupp, Saginaw Lindsey Eggers, Linwood JoAnn T. Crary, Frankenmuth	Act 278 of 1965
Sault Ste. Marie Bridge Authority	Committed to the safe and efficient movement of people and goods across the International Bridge between Sault Ste. Marie, Ontario and Sault Ste. Marie, Michigan. **Members:** Thomas Buckingham, Newberry Scott Shackleton, Sault Ste. Marie Linda Hoath, Sault Ste. Marie Nick White, Petoskey	Act 99 of 1954

BOARDS AND COMMISSIONS IN THE STATE OF MICHIGAN *(Cont.)*

Board or Commission	Description	Authority for Creation
Self-Insurers' Security, Second Injury Fund, Silicosis, Dust Disease, and Logging Industry Compensation Fund Board of Trustees	Oversees the Funds Administration, which is funded by insurers who write workers' compensation policies in the state of Michigan and employers who self-insure their workers' compensation liability. **Members:** Lee Anne Fontaine, Kalamazoo Jerome Harper, Roseville	Act 317 of 1969
Services to the Aging Commission	Advises the Governor and Legislature on coordination and administration of state programs, changes in federal and state programs, and the nature and magnitude of aging priorities. **Members:** Matthew Adeyanju, Big Rapids Kristie Zamora, Flint Dona Wishart, Gaylord Peter Lichtenberg, Farmington Linda Strohl, Sawyer Nancy Duncan, Lansing Mark Bomberg, Gladstone Renee Cortright, Troy Laura Kathleen LaTosch, Ferndale Jean Hall, East Lansing William Bupp, DeWitt Georgia Crawford-Cambell, Detroit Guillermo Lopez, Lansing Stephen Franko, Vassar Marshall Greenhut, North Muskegon	Act 180 of 1981
Ski Area Safety Board	The board works with the department to oversee the operation of ski areas, surface and chair lifts, and rope tows. **Members:** Timothy Meyer, Cadillac Jim Bartlett, Harbor Springs Nick Sirdenis, Houghton Charles Gano, Petoskey Jeff Cranson, Grand Rapids Matthew Torreano, Marquette Thomas Wheat, Kalamazoo	Act 199 of 1962
Social Work, Board of	The board ascertains minimal entry level competency of health practitioners. The board also has the obligation to take disciplinary action against licensees who have adversely affected the public's health, safety, and welfare. **Members:** Michael Fiorillo, Royal Oak Constance Squires, Rockford Shelley Ovink, Ishpeming Brittany Risk, Plymouth Brian Philson, Horton Marc J. Milburn, Houghton Lake Christine Nelson, Charlotte Larry Herren, Farmington Julian Diaz, Birmingham	Act 368 of 1978

Board or Commission	Description		Authority for Creation
Soybean Promotion Committee	Manages resources to increase return on investment for Michigan soybean farmers while enhancing sustainable soybean production.		Act 232 of 1965
	Members:		
	Laurie Isley, Palmyra	Dennis Gardner, Croswell	
	Sarah Peterson, Niles	Steven Koeman, Hamilton	
	Peter Crawford, Dansville	Robert Moore, Bannister	
	Michael Sahr, Saginaw		
Speech Language Pathology, Board of	The board ascertains minimal entry level competency of health practitioners. The board also has the obligation to take disciplinary action against licensees who have adversely affected the public's health, safety, and welfare.		Act 368 of 1978
	Members:		
	Jeffrey Weingarten, MD, Grosse Pointe Woods	Katie Wright, Battle Creek	
		Ryan Burklow, Livonia	
	Bradford Swartz, Mount Pleasant	Lawrence Prokop, Mason	
	Patricia Mervenne, Bloomfield Hills	Nick Carlson, Spring Lake	
	Jodi Waldman, Okemos	Denise Ludwig, Grand Rapids	
	Lorri Rishar Jandron, Lansing	Erika Shuptar, East Lansing	
State 9-1-1 Committee	The committee promotes the successful development, implementation, and operation of 9-1-1 systems across the state of Michigan.		Act 79 of 1999
	Members:		
	John Bawol, Saint Helen	Steven Berenbaum, Birmingham	
State Boundary Commission	Adjudicates many types of municipal boundary adjustments and recommends the approval or denial of petitions for incorporations of new Home Rule Cities, new Home Rule Villages, and municipal consolidations.		Act 191 of 1968
	Members:		
	Michael Rice, Williamston	Richard Datema, Petoskey	
	Robin Beltramini, Troy		
State Canvassers, Board of	Responsible for canvassing and certifying statewide elections, elections for legislative districts that cross county lines and all judicial offices except Judge of the Probate Court, conducting recounts for state-level offices, canvassing nominating petitions, canvassing state-level ballot proposal petitions, assigning ballot designations and adopting ballot language for statewide ballot proposals, and approving electronic voting systems for use in the state.		State of Michigan Constitution of 1963 (Article 2, Sec. 7)
	Members:		
	Norman Shinkle, Williamston	Jeannette Bradshaw, Ortonville	
	Julie Matuzak, Mount Clemens	Aaron Van Langevelde, Charlotte	

BOARDS AND COMMISSIONS IN THE STATE OF MICHIGAN *(Cont.)*

Board or Commission	Description	Authority for Creation
State Officers Compensation Commission	Determines the salaries and expense allowances of the members of the Legislature, the Governor, the Lieutenant Governor, the Attorney General, the Secretary of State, and the Justices of the Supreme Court. **Members:** James Hallan, East Lansing Nancy E. Jenkins, Manitou Beach Joseph Smalley, East Lansing Gerald Hildenbrand, Plainwell Dan L. DeGrow, Burtchville Phyllis Browne, DeWitt Osama Siblani, West Bloomfield	State of Michigan Constitution of 1963 (Article 4, Sec. 12)
State Police Retirement Board	Provides oversight of the Michigan State Police Retirement System. **Members:** Mitchell Stevens, Gaylord Steve O'Neill, Owosso Julie Darden Diane DeWitt, Howell	Act 182 of 1986
State Survey and Remonumentation Commission	Creates and distributes a model county plan that may be adopted by a county with any changes appropriate for that county. **Members:** Marvin Myers, Roscommon John Quine, Elsie Andrew Hartwick, Shelbyville William Karr, Pickford Karen Hahn, Big Rapids Jack Owens, Roscommon Roland Self, Saranac	Act 345 of 1990
Statewide Independent Living Council	Works cooperatively with several state departments to develop and submit the State Plan for Independent Living. **Members:** Gabriella Burman, Huntington Woods Kelsey Kleimola, Ypsilanti Mairead C. Warner, Melvin Alexander Darr, Brighton Aaron M. Andres, Marquette Theresa Metzmaker, Lansing Yvonne Fleener, Grand Ledge Patricia Sterling, Sault Ste. Marie Charles Williams Harrison Jr., Redford Mark Pierce, Holt Glen Ashlock, Brooklyn	Executive Order 2007-49, Executive Order 2012-15
Strategic Fund Board of Directors, Michigan	Authority to promote economic development and create jobs. **Members:** Jeff Mason, Lansing Paul C. Ajegba, Lansing Jeffrey M. Donofrio, Lansing Rachael Eubanks, East Lansing Paul V. Gentilozzi, Lansing Charles P. Rothstein, Farmington Hills Britany L. Affolter-Caine, Ypsilanti Ronald W. Beebe, Midland September Hargrove, Detroit Susan Tellier, Caledonia Cindy L. Warner, Traverse City	Act 270 of 1984

BOARDS AND COMMISSIONS IN THE STATE OF MICHIGAN (*Cont.*)

Board or Commission	Description		Authority for Creation
Tax Commission, State	Has general supervision of the administration of the Property Tax Laws in Michigan and shall render such assistance and give such advice to assessors, as they deem necessary. **Members:** William Howard Morris, Detroit Leonard Kutschman, Oakland	Nick Khouri, Plymouth	Executive Order 2009-51
Tax Tribunal, Michigan	An administrative court that hears tax appeals for all Michigan taxes. **Members:** Marcus Abood, Lansing Preeti Gadola, East Lansing Michelle Lange, East Lansing	Victoria Enyart, Jackson Steven Bieda, Warren Christine Schauer, Kalamazoo	Act 186 of 1973
Teacher Tenure Commission, State	Acts as a board of review for all cases appealed from the decision of a controlling board. **Members:** David Campbell, Kalamazoo Stephen Olsen, Chelsea William Wooster, Milford	Michael Richard, DeWitt Jeffrey Sewick, East Lansing	Act 4 of 1937
Traffic Safety Advisory Commission, Governor's	This commission shall identify traffic safety challenges, and develop, promote and implement strategies to address those challenges. **Members:** Linda Scarpetta, Lansing Kenneth Micklash, Lansing Carol Reagan, Lansing Michael L. Prince, Lansing F/Lt. Jim Flegel, Lansing Kim Avery, Lansing	Steven Kiefer, Northville Sheriff Michael Poulin, North Muskegon Ronald Wiles Jr., Grand Blanc Rachel Telder Hank Kelly, Grand Rapids	Executive Order 2002-6
Trails Advisory Council	Advises on the creation, development, operation, and maintenance of motorized and non-motorized trails in the state, including, but not limited to, snowmobile, biking, equestrian, hiking, off-road vehicle, and skiing trails. **Members:** Thomas M. Dunn, Lansing Jason Rolling, Negaunee William D. Manson Jr., Rockford Jenny Cook, Kalamazoo Bob Wilson, Lansing John Matonich, Marenisco	Steven Davis, Marquette Joe Kuchnicki, Alanson Patty Janes, Spring Lake Jessi Adler, Okemos Peggy McCaughn, White Pine	Act 451 of 1994

BOARDS AND COMMISSIONS IN THE STATE OF MICHIGAN *(Cont.)*

Board or Commission	Description	Authority for Creation
Transportation Asset Management Council	Collects physical inventory and information on the condition of all roads and bridges in Michigan. **Members:** Joanna I. Johnson, Kalamazoo County Bob Slattery, Burton Derek Bradshaw, Genesee County William McEntee, Lansing Jennifer Tubbs, Watertown Township Bradley Wieferich, Lansing Rob Surber, Lansing Jonathan Start, Kalamazoo County Roger Belknap, Lansing Gary Mekjian, Farmington Hills Christopher Bolt, Jackson Todd White, Lansing	Act 51 of 1951
Transportation Commission	Establishes policy for the Department of Transportation in relation to transportation programs and facilities and other such works as related to transportation development, as provided by law. **Members:** Michael D. Hayes, Midland George Heartwell, Newago Todd Wyett, Charlevoix Chuck Moser, Drummond Island Chris Yatooma, Bloomfield Hills Helen Zeerip, Allegan	Act 286 of 1964
Travel Commission	Promotes, maintains and develops the orderly growth of the Michigan travel product. **Members:** Stephen Kircher, Walloon Lake Camille Jourden-Mark, Muskegon William Parlberg, Frankenmuth Sally Laukitis, Holland John Madigan, Munising Charles Burns, Novi Jon Nunn, Grand Rapids Mike Busley, Traverse City Jerome Toney, Howell Julie Sprenger, Laurium Richard Owens, Lewiston Jennifer Zieger, Wyandotte Marsha Quebbeman, East Lansing	Act 106 of 1945
Tree Fruit Commission, Michigan	Charged with improving the economic position and competitiveness of the Michigan tree fruit industry. **Members:** James Nugent, Suttons Bay Christopher Kropf, Lowell Michael VanAgtmael, Hart Jim Engelsma, Walker Rick Sayler, Williamsburg Steve Thome, Comstock Park Fred Koenigshof, Coloma William Teichman, Eau Claire Travis Bratschi, Williamsburg	Act 232 of 1965

BOARDS AND COMMISSIONS IN THE STATE OF MICHIGAN *(Cont.)*

Board or Commission	Description	Authority for Creation
Truck Safety Commission, Michigan	Improves truck safety by providing Michigan's trucking industry and the citizens of Michigan with effective educational programs, and by addressing significant truck safety issues. **Members:** Kim Kelly, Dimondale Gregory Casuley, Saginaw Jeremy Worm, Ahmeek Jeffrey Lee, Canton Carol Heinowski, Grand Ledge James Shea, Waterford Michelle Taylor, Muskegon Capt. Harold Love, Lansing Fred Bueter, Lansing Chuck Moser, Drummond Island Michael L. Prince, Lansing	Act 51 of 1951
Unarmed Combat Commission	Responsible for the regulation of professional boxing and mixed martial arts under PA 403 of 2004, as amended. The commission is the successor to the Michigan Boxing Commission. **Members:** Bronco McKart, Monroe Bruce Hundley, Howell Teresa Graham, Owosso Chris DeRose, Ann Arbor Josh Bocks, New Hudson Ed Pigeon, Hopkins Vincent Philip Viviano, Shelby Township Jason Hanselman, DeWitt Jeff Styers, Northville Donald Weatherspoon, Haslett	Act 546 of 2012
Underground Storage Tank Authority Board	Manages the Underground Storage Tank Cleanup Fund. **Members:** Bill Saad, Grosse Ile Juman Doleh-Alomary, Detroit Greg Gould, Livonia Brian Eggers, Linwood Grenetta Thomassey, Petoskey Richard Bratschi, Williamston	Act 416 of 2014
Underwater Salvage and Preserve Committee	Provides technical and other advice with respect to maintaining Michigan's 13 underwater preserves. **Members:** James Nowka, Brutus Brian Abbott, Haslett Rob Campau, East Lansing Laurence Monshor, Gaylord Hannah MacDonald, Alpena	Act 451 of 1994

BOARDS AND COMMISSIONS IN THE STATE OF MICHIGAN (*Cont.*)

Board or Commission	Description	Authority for Creation
Unmanned Aircraft Systems Task Force	Created to develop statewide policy recommendations on the operation, use, and regulation of unmanned aircraft systems in Michigan. **Members:** Scott Baldwin, Fort Gratiot Township Jon Cool, Grand Rapids Katie Jones, Northville Michael Olson, Battle Creek Daniel Coffey, New Buffalo Charles Drayton, St. Paul, MN Eric Ebenstein, Annandale, VA John Flanagan, Midland John Hill, Traverse City Christopher Johnson, Northville Craig Amey, Shelby Township Richard Kathrens, St. Johns Kevin Klein, Traverse City Greg MacMaster, Kewadin Thomas Scott, Okemos Michael Trout, Clarklake Corbett Adkins, McBain Andrew Bordine, Jackson Bradley Chambers, Mackinac Island Julia Dale, Lansing Thomas Harrell, Gladstone Kevin Jacobs, Roscommon Kevin Lindsey, Jackson Matthew Rogers, Rockford Robert Sweeney, St. Ignace Brian Matchett, Traverse City Melinda Marion, Plymouth	Act 436 of 2016
Utility Consumer Participation Board	Provides grants to qualified applicants that represent the interests of Michigan's residential energy (gas, electric, and other fuel) utility customers at residential energy proceedings before the Michigan Public Service Commission. **Members:** James MacInnes, Beulah Paul Isely, Grand Rapids Samuel Passmore, Ann Arbor Brian Vilmont, Grand Rapids Elise Matz, Marquette	Act 3 of 1939
Veterans Facilities Board of Managers	Exercises certain regulatory and governance authority regarding admission and member affairs at Michigan's two veterans' homes. **Members:** James Ausdemore, Pinckney Ronald Schrieber, Roscommon Robert Johnson, Kingsley Adam Weiner, Rochester Harold Mast, Kentwood Shane Preston, Howell Deborah Chambers, Grand Rapids	Act 152 of 1985
Veterans Facility Authority Board of Directors	Governs the Michigan Veterans' Facility Authority. **Members:** David Rutledge, Ypsilanti Mary Kummer Naber, Grosse Pointe Park MaryAnne Shannon, Sault Ste. Marie David Henry, Fruitport Spencer Hoover, Grosse Pointe Park Larry Yachcik, Chelsea Henry Boutros, Ann Arbor Bradford Slagle, Marquette	Act 560 of 2016

BOARDS AND COMMISSIONS IN THE STATE OF MICHIGAN *(Cont.)*

Board or Commission	Description	Authority for Creation
Veterans' Memorial Park Commission	The commission provides advice on the development, management and maintenance of the Michigan Veterans' Memorial Park. **Members:** Jeffrey Schuett, Royal Oak Jim Dunn, Petoskey Lynn O'Brien, Milford John Juarez, Lansing	Executive Order 2001-10
Veterans Trust Fund Board of Directors	Provides grants for the emergency needs of veterans. **Members:** James Tighe, Birmingham Edward Hirsch, Farmington Hills Barry Wood, Hastings James Dempsey, Dexter Robert Williams, Benton Harbor Rachel Genier, Battle Creek Charles Kosal, Oxford	Act 9 of 1946
Veterinary Medicine, Board of	The board works with the department to oversee veterinarians and veterinary technicians. **Members:** Peter Levine, Flint Tracy Nyberg, Skandia Dwight McNally, Saginaw Jordan Kennedy, Lansing Amy Hicswa, Middleville Nancy Frank, Haslett Renee Werth, Eaton Rapids Jean Hudson, Haslett Marianne Tear, Chesterfield	Act 368 of 1978
Waterways Commission, Michigan State	Responsible for the acquisition, construction, and maintenance of recreational harbors, channels, docking and launching facilities, and administration of commercial docks in the Straits of Mackinac. **Members:** Dennis Nickels, Grand Haven Mary Rising, Fenton Nicki Polan, White Lake Peter Beauregard, Grosse Pointe Shores James R. Hansen, Escanaba Barb Brooks, Boyne City Steve Arwood, St. Johns	Act 451 of 1994
Western Michigan University Board of Control	Power and authority for general supervision of the institution and the control and direction of all expenditures from the institution's funds. **Members:** Lynn L. Chen-Zhang, Portage Ronald R. Kitchens, Portage James B. Bolger, Whitehall Shani J. Penn, Farmington Hills William D. Johnston, Portage David Behen, Saline Jeffrey A. Rinvelt, Ann Arbor Shelly Edgerton, Plainwell	Act 48 of 1963 (2nd Ex. Sess.)

BOARDS AND COMMISSIONS IN THE STATE OF MICHIGAN *(Cont.)*

Board or Commission	Description	Authority for Creation
Wheat Promotion Committee	The committee oversees the wheat marketing program. **Members:** William Hunt, Davison Art Loeffler, Frankenmuth Gerald Heck, Monroe Brent Wagner, Grawn Frank Vyskocil, New Lothrop Sally McConnachie, Deckerville Marc Hasenick, Springport David Milligan, Cass City Jason Dunning, Fremont	Act 232 of 1965
Wildlife Council, Michigan	Charged with protecting the environment and natural resources of the state. **Members:** Matt Pedigo, Howell Henry Stancato, Detroit Jeffrey Poet, Clare Carol Rose, Hillman Edgar Roy, Traverse City Jim Hammill, Crystal Falls Beth Gruden, Perrinton Nick Buggia, Mayville	Act 246 of 2013
Women's Commission	Mission of improving the lives of Michigan women. **Members:** Margaret Derrer, Grand Rapids Christine Etienne, Petoskey Krista Licata Haroutunian, Detroit Deidre Lambert-Bounds, Southfield Renee Haley, Harrison Cathleen Knauf, St. Joseph Joanne Dawley, Northville Jan Peabody, Lapeer Kathleen Vogelsang, Ada Mary Templeton, Plymouth Nicole DeMarco, East Lansing Catherine Hendrian, Plymouth Barbara Land, Waterford Kelli Saunders, Byron Center Alisha Meneely, Byron Center	Act 1 of 1968
Worker's Compensation Board of Magistrates	Hears administrative claims for benefits and resolves disputes arising under the Workers' Disability Compensation Act. **Members:** Louis Ognisanti, Saginaw David Grunewald, Grosse Pointe Chris D. Slater, Grand Rapids Luke McMurray, Grand Blanc Keith Castora, Canton Robert Timmons, Grand Rapids John Housefield, Haslett Jane Colombo, Grosse Pointe David Williams, Grosse Pointe Woods Lisa Woons, Grand Rapids Michael Heck, Troy Philip D. Santina, Howell John Sims, Marshall David DeGraw, Grand Rapids	Act 317 of 1969; Executive Order 2003-18; Executive Order 2009-53; Executive Order 2011-4

Source: http://www.michigan.gov/whitmer/0,9309,7-387-90501_90626-346537--,00.html and executive department websites as of October 1, 2019.

FORMER OFFICIALS OF MICHIGAN

FRENCH-CANADIAN GOVERNORS, 1603-1760

No.	Name	Title	Year
1	Aymar de Chastes, Sieur de Monts.		1603-12
2	Samuel de Champlain with Prince de Conde as acting governor . .		1612-19
3	Henry, Duke of Montmorenci, acting governor		1619-29
4	Samuel de Champlain[1]	Lieut. Gen. and Viceroy. .	1633
			1635
5	Marc Antoine de Bras-de-Fer de Chateaufort	Lieut. Gen. and Viceroy. .	1636
6	Charles Hualt de Montmagny	Gov. and Lieut. Gen. . . .	1636-47
7	Louis d'Ailleboust, Sieur de Coulonges	Governor	1648-51
8	Jean de Lauson.	Governor.	1651-55
9	Charles de Lauson-Charny[2]	Governor	1656-57
10	Louis d'Ailleboust, Sieur de Coulonges[3].	Governor.	1657-58
11	Pierre de Voyer, Viscount d'Argenson	Governor.	1658-61
12	Baron Dubois d'Avaugour.	Governor.	1661-63
13	Augustin de Saffray-Mezy	Governor.	1663-65
14	Alexandre de Prouville, Marquis de Tracy	Viceroy	1663
15	Daniel Remy, Sieur de Courcelles	Gov. and Lieut. Gen. . . .	1665-72
16	Louis de Buade, Count de Frontenac.	Governor.	1672-82
17	Antoine Joseph Le Febvre de la Barre	Governor.	1682-85
18	Jacques Rene de Brisay, Marquis de Denonville.	Governor.	1685-89
19	Louis de Buade, Count de Frontenac[4]	Governor.	1689-98
20	Louis Hector de Callieres	Governor.	1698
			1702
21	Philippe de Rigaud, Marquis de Vaudreuil.	Governor.	1703
22	Charles LeMoyne, Baron de Longueuil	Governor.	1725
23	Charles de la Boische, Marquis de Beauharnois.	Governor.	1726-47
24	Rolland Michel Barrin, Marquis de la Galissonniere	Governor	1747-49
25	Jacques Pierre de Taffanel, Marquis de la Jonquiere.	Governor.	1749-52
26	Charles LeMoyne, Baron de Longueuil[5]	Governor.	1752
27	Michel Ange Duquesne, Marquis de Menneville.	Governor.	1752-55
28	Pierre Rigaud, Marquis de Vaudreuil Cavagnal.	Governor.	1755-60

[1] The English held possession of Canada from 1629 to 1632.
[2] Son of No. 8.
[3] Same as No. 7.
[4] Same as No. 16.
[5] Son of No. 22.

BRITISH-CANADIAN GOVERNORS, 1760-1792

No.	Name	Title	Year
1	Sir Jeffrey Amherst	Maj. Gen. and Commander-in-Chief	1760-63
2	Sir James Murray	Governor of Quebec	1763-66
3	Palinus Emelius Irving	President of Elective Council for 3 months . .	1766
4	Brigadier Guy Carleton.	Lieut. Gov. and Commander-in-Chief	1766-70
5	Hector Theophilus Cramahe	Acting Governor	1770-74
6	Major General Guy Carleton[1]	Governor General	1774-78
7	Sir Frederick Haldimand	Governor General	1778-84
8	Henry Hamilton[2]	Lieut. Governor.	1784
9	Colonel Henry Hope	President of Council.	1785
10	Guy Carleton (as Lord Dorchester)[3].	Governor General	1785
11	John Graves Simcoe	Lieut. Governor of U.P. Canada	1792

[1] Same as No. 4.
[2] Captured at Vincennes, Ind., Feb. 24, 1778, by General George Rogers Clark, U.S.A.
[3] Same as No. 4.

GOVERNORS OF THE NORTHWEST TERRITORY, 1787-1800[1]

No.	Name	Title	Year
1	General Arthur St. Clair..............	Governor.........................	1787 1800
2	Winthrop Sargent..................	Secretary and Acting Governor...........	1796

[1] Ordinance of 1787 made Michigan part of the Northwest Territory.

GOVERNOR OF THE INDIANA TERRITORY, 1800-1805

No.	Name	Title	Year
1	General William Henry Harrison........	Governor.........................	1800 1805

GOVERNORS OF THE MICHIGAN TERRITORY, 1805-1835

No.	Governor	Date of Appointment
1	General William Hull, Governor	Mar. 1, 1805
	Stanley Griswold, Secretary and Acting Governor...............	1806
2	General William Hull, Governor	Apr. 1, 1808
3	General William Hull, Governor[1,2]	Jan. 11, 1811
	Reuben Atwatter, Acting Governor........................	1811-1812
4	General Lewis Cass, Governor...........................	Oct. 29, 1813
5	General Lewis Cass, Governor...........................	Jan. 21, 1817
	William Woodbridge, Secretary and Acting Governor...........	Aug. 17, 1818
6	General Lewis Cass, Governor...........................	Jan. 24, 1820
	William Woodbridge, Secretary and Acting Governor...........	Aug. 8, 1820; Sept. 18, 1821
7	General Lewis Cass, Governor...........................	Dec. 20, 1822
	William Woodbridge, Secretary and Acting Governor...........	Sept. 29, 1823; May 28, 1825
8	General Lewis Cass, Governor...........................	Dec. 22, 1825
	William Woodbridge, Secretary and Acting Governor...........	Aug. 31, 1826; Oct. 23, 1826; July 25, 1827
9	General Lewis Cass, Governor...........................	Dec. 24, 1828
	James Witherell, Secretary and Acting Governor................	Jan. 1, 1830 to Apr. 2, 1830
	General John T. Mason, Secretary and Acting Governor	Sept. 24, 1830 to Oct. 4, 1830; Apr. 4 to May 27, 1831
	Stevens T. Mason, Secretary and Acting Governor[3]	Aug. 1, 1831 to Sept. 17, 1831
10	George B. Porter, Governor[4]	Aug. 6, 1831
	Stevens T. Mason, Secretary and Acting Governor	Oct. 30, 1831 to June 11, 1832; May 23 to July 14, 1833; Aug. 13 to Aug. 28, 1833; Sept. 5 to Dec. 14, 1833; Feb. 1 to Feb. 7, 1834
11	Stevens T. Mason, ex officio Governor as Secretary of Territory[5]	July 6, 1834
	Charles Shaler[6]	Aug. 29, 1835
	John S. Horner, Secretary and Acting Governor[7]................	Sept. 8, 1835

[1] Court martialed at Albany, Jan. 3, 1814, for his surrender of Detroit, Aug. 16, 1812 and sentenced to be shot. Sentence remitted.

[2] Hull's appointment would have expired in 1814. The territorial records were destroyed by the British at the capture of Detroit, so no official data on that point exists.

[3] On the resignation of General Cass, Aug. 1, 1831, who was appointed Secretary of War by President Jackson, July, 1831.

[4] Died July 6, 1834.

[5] Henry D. Gilpin was appointed Governor by President Jackson, Nov. 5, 1834, but the nomination was rejected. No other appointment was made for the office while Michigan was a territory.

[6] To supersede Mason as secretary, but the appointment was declined.

[7] Appointed secretary of Wisconsin Territory by President Jackson, May 6, 1836.

GOVERNORS OF THE STATE OF MICHIGAN, 1835-2019[1]

D — Stevens T. Mason 1835-1840	R — Fred M. Warner[9] 1905-1910
W — William Woodbridge[2] 1840-1841	R — Chase S. Osborn 1911-1912
W — James Wright Gordon[3] 1841-1842	D — Woodbridge N. Ferris 1913-1916
D — John S. Barry 1842-1846	R — Albert E. Sleeper 1917-1920
D — Alpheus Felch[4] 1846-1847	R — Alexander J. Groesbeck 1921-1926
D — William L. Greenly[5] 1847-1848	R — Fred W. Green 1927-1930
D — Epaphroditus Ransom 1848-1850	R — Wilber M. Brucker 1931-1932
D — John S. Barry 1850-1851	D — William A. Comstock 1933-1934
D — Robert McClelland[6] 1852-1853	R — Frank D. Fitzgerald 1935-1936
D — Andrew Parsons[7] 1853-1854	D — Frank Murphy 1937-1938
R — Kinsley S. Bingham 1855-1858	R — Frank D. Fitzgerald[10] 1939
R — Moses Wisner 1859-1860	R — Luren D. Dickinson[11] 1939-1940
R — Austin Blair 1861-1864	D — Murray D. Van Wagoner 1941-1942
R — Henry H. Crapo 1865-1868	R — Harry F. Kelly 1943-1946
R — Henry P. Baldwin 1869-1872	R — Kim Sigler 1947-1948
R — John J. Bagley 1873-1876	D — G. Mennen Williams 1949-1960
R — Charles M. Croswell 1877-1880	D — John B. Swainson 1961-1962
R — David H. Jerome 1881-1882	R — George Romney[12] 1963-1969
D — Josiah Williams Begole[8] 1883-1884	R — William G. Milliken[13] 1969-1982
R — Russell A. Alger 1885-1886	D — James J. Blanchard 1983-1990
R — Cyrus G. Luce 1887-1890	R — John M. Engler 1991-2002
D — Edwin B. Winans 1891-1892	D — Jennifer M. Granholm 2003-2010
R — John T. Rich 1893-1896	R — Rick Snyder 2011-2018
R — Hazen S. Pingree 1897-1900	D — Gretchen Whitmer 2019-
R — Aaron T. Bliss 1901-1904	

Political Party Designations
D — Democrat
R — Republican
W — Whig

---

[1] Prior to the Constitution of 1963, governors were elected to 2-year terms. Governors began serving 4-year terms starting with the election held in 1966.

[2] Resigned February 23, 1841, to become U.S. senator.

[3] Assumed office February 24, 1841 following the resignation of William Woodbridge.

[4] Resigned March 3, 1847, to become U.S. senator.

[5] Assumed office March 4, 1847 following the resignation of Alpheus Felch.

[6] Elected to one-year term in 1851 and reelected to full 2-year term in 1852, under the provisions of the Constitution of 1850, art. IV, sec. 34, and art. V, sec. 3, and Act 175 of the Extra Session of 1851, Laws of Michigan; Resigned March 7, 1853, to become U.S. secretary of interior.

[7] Assumed office March 8, 1853 following the resignation of Robert McClelland.

[8] Fusionist.

[9] First governor to be nominated under direct, primary election system.

[10] Died March 16, 1939.

[11] Assumed office March 16, 1939 following the death of Frank D. Fitzgerald.

[12] First governor to be elected with lieutenant governor as a single ticket; Resigned January 22, 1969, to become U.S. secretary of housing and urban development.

[13] Assumed office January 22, 1969 following the resignation of George Romney.

LIEUTENANT GOVERNORS, 1835-2019[1]

D — Edward Mundy	1835-1840	
W — James Wright Gordon[2]	1840-1841	
W — Thomas J. Drake[3]	1841	
D — Origen D. Richardson	1842-1846	
D — William L. Greenly[4]	1846-1847	
D — Charles P. Bush[5]	1847	
D — William M. Fenton	1848-1851	
D — Calvin Britain[6]	1852	
D — Andrew Parsons[7]	1853	
D — George R. Griswold[8]	1853-1854	
R — George Alonzo Coe	1855-1858	
R — Edmund B. Fairfield	1859-1860	
R — James Birney[9]	1861	
R — Joseph R. Williams[10]	1861	
R — Henry T. Backus[11]	1861-1862	
R — Charles S. May	1863-1864	
R — Ebenezer O. Grosvenor	1865-1866	
R — Dwight May	1867-1868	
R — Morgan Bates	1869-1872	
R — Henry H. Holt	1873-1876	
R — Alonzo Sessions	1877-1880	
R — Moreau S. Crosby	1881-1884	
R — Archibald Buttars	1885-1886	
R — James H. MacDonald[12]	1889	
R — William Ball[13]	1889-1890	
D — John Strong	1891-1892	
R — J. Wight Giddings	1893-1894	
R — Alfred Milnes[14]	1895	
R — Joseph R. McLaughlin[15]	1895-1896	
R — Thomas B. Dunstan	1897-1898	
R — Orrin W. Robinson	1899-1902	
R — Alexander Maitland	1903-1906	
R — Patrick H. Kelley	1907-1910	
R — John Q. Ross	1911-1914	
R — Luren D. Dickinson	1915-1920	
R — Thomas Read	1921-1924	
R — George W. Welsh	1925-1926	
R — Luren D. Dickinson	1927-1932	
D — Allen E. Stebbins	1933-1934	
R — Thomas Read	1935-1936	
D — Leo J. Nowicki	1937-1938	
R — Luren D. Dickinson[16]	1939	
R — Matilda R. Wilson[17]	1940	
D — Frank Murphy	1941-1942	
R — Eugene C. Keyes	1943-1944	
R — Vernon J. Brown	1945-1946	
R — Eugene C. Keyes	1947-1948	
D — John W. Connolly	1949-1950	
R — William C. Vandenberg	1951-1952	
R — Clarence A. Reid	1953-1954	
D — Philip A. Hart	1955-1958	
D — John B. Swainson	1959-1960	
D — T. John Lesinski	1961-1964	
R — William G. Milliken[18]	1965-1969	
R — Thomas F. Schweigert[19]	1970	
R — James H. Brickley	1971-1974	
R — James J. Damman	1975-1978	
R — James H. Brickley	1979-1982	
D — Martha Wright Griffiths	1983-1990	
R — Connie B. Binsfeld	1991-1998	
R — Richard Posthumus	1999-2002	
D — John D. Cherry Jr.	2003-2010	
R — Brian N. Calley	2011-2018	
D — Garlin Gilchrist II	2019-	

Political Party Designations
D — Democrat
R — Republican
W — Whig

[1] Prior to the Constitution of 1963, lieutenant governors were elected to 2-year terms. Lieutenant governors began serving 4-year terms starting with the election held in 1966.

[2] Assumed office of governor February 24, 1841 following the resignation of William Woodbridge.

[3] Elected president pro tem of the senate to perform lieutenant governor's duties as president of the senate following vacancy created in the office of when James Wright Gordon became governor.

[4] Assumed office of governor March 4, 1847 following resignation of Alpheus Felch.

[5] Elected president pro tem of the senate to perform lieutenant governor's duties as president of the senate following vacancy created in the office of when William L. Greenly became governor.

[6] Elected to a one-year term only in 1851 under the provisions of the Constitution of 1850, art. IV, sec. 34, and art. V, sec. 3, and Act 175 of the Extra Session of 1851, Laws of Michigan.

[7] Assumed office of governor March 8, 1853 following the resignation of Robert McClelland.

[8] Elected president pro tem of the senate to perform lieutenant governor's duties as president of the senate following vacancy created in the office of when Andrew Parsons became governor.

[9] Resigned April 3, 1861.

[10] Elected president pro tem of the senate to perform lieutenant governor's duties as president of the senate following vacancy created in the office of when James Birney resigned; Died June 15, 1861.

[11] Elected president pro tem of the senate to perform lieutenant governor's duties as president of the senate following vacancy created in the office of when Joseph R. Williams died.

[12] Died January 19, 1889.

[13] Elected president pro tem of the senate to perform lieutenant governor's duties as president of the senate following vacancy created in the office of when James H. MacDonald died.

[14] Resigned May 31, 1895, to become U.S. representative to Congress.

[15] Elected president pro tem of the senate to perform lieutenant governor's duties as president of the senate following vacancy created in the office of when Alfred Milnes resigned.

[16] Assumed office of governor March 16, 1939 following the death of Frank D. Fitzgerald.

[17] Appointed November 14, 1940, by Governor Luren D. Dickinson. The Constitution of 1908 provided no specific guidance on whether a vacancy in the office of lieutenant governor could be filled by appointment, and after Luren D. Dickerson became governor and vacated the office of lieutenant governor, the attorney general issued an opinion stating that the governor did not have the power to appoint a lieutenant governor. Governor Dickerson disagreed with the attorney general and sought to test the opinion by appointing Matilda R. Wilson. The appointment was not challenged in court during the six weeks between her appointment and the end of the term. See Opinion of the Attorney General,1939-1940, p. 69.

[18] First lieutenant governor to be elected as part of a single party ticket; Assumed office of governor January 22, 1969 following the resignation of George Romney.

[19] Became "president of the senate and acting lieutenant governor" March 20, 1970 under Act 8 of 1969 after William G. Milliken became governor. See Opinion of the Attorney General, No. 4625, April 22, 1968.

SECRETARIES OF STATE, 1835-2019[1]

Kintzing Pritchette	1835-1838	Justus S. Stearns	1899-1900
Randolph Manning	1838-1840	Fred M. Warner	1901-1904
Thomas Rowland	1840-1842	George A. Prescott	1905-1908
Robert P. Eldredge	1842-1846	Frederick C. Martindale	1909-1914
Gideon O. Whittemore	1846-1848	Coleman C. Vaughan	1915-1920
George W. Peck	1848-1850	Charles J. DeLand	1921-1926
George R. Redfield[2]	1850	John S. Haggerty	1927-1930
Charles H. Taylor[3]	1850-1852	Frank D. Fitzgerald[8]	1931-1934
William Graves	1853-1854	Clarke W. Brown[9]	1934
John McKinney	1855-1858	Orville E. Atwood	1935-1936
Nelson G. Isbell	1859-1860	Leon D. Case	1937-1938
James B. Porter	1861-1866	Harry F. Kelly	1939-1942
Oliver L. Spaulding	1867-1870	Herman Henry Dignan	1943-1946
Daniel Striker	1871-1874	Fred M. Alger Jr.	1947-1952
Ebenezer G. D. Holden	1875-1878	Owen J. Cleary	1953-1954
William Jenney	1879-1882	James M. Hare	1955-1970
Harry A. Conant	1883-1886	Richard H. Austin	1971-1994
Gilbert R. Osmun	1887-1890	Candice S. Miller	1995-2002
Daniel E. Soper[4]	1891	Terri Lynn Land	2003-2010
Robert R. Blacker[5]	1891-1892	Ruth Johnson	2011-2018
John W. Jochim[6]	1893-1894	Jocelyn Benson	2019-
Washington Gardner[7]	1894-1898		

[1] Secretaries of state were appointed by the governor for 2-year terms prior to the adoption of the Constitution of 1850 which established the position as a statewide elected office. Secretaries of state began serving 4-year terms starting with the election held in 1966.
[2] Resigned April 11, 1850.
[3] Appointed by the governor following the resignation of George R. Redfield.
[4] Resigned December 19, 1891.
[5] Appointed by the governor December 24, 1891 following the resignation of Daniel E. Soper.
[6] Removed by governor March 20, 1894.
[7] Appointed by the governor March 20, 1894 following the removal of John W. Jochim.
[8] Resigned November 15, 1934.
[9] Appointed by the governor November 15, 1934 following the resignation of Frank D. Fitzgerald.

ATTORNEYS GENERAL, 1836-2019[1]

Daniel LeRoy	1836-1837	Roger I. Wykes[10]	1912
Peter Morey	1837-1841	Grant Fellows	1913-1916
Zephaniah Platt	1841-1843	Alexander J. Groesbeck	1917-1920
Elon Farnsworth	1843-1845	Merlin Wiley[11]	1921-1923
Henry N. Walker	1845-1847	Andrew B. Dougherty[12]	1923-1926
Edward Mundy[2]	1847-1848	Clare Retan[13]	1926
George V. N. Lothrop[3]	1848-1851	William W. Potter[14]	1927-1928
William Hale	1851-1854	Wilber M. Brucker[15]	1928-1930
Jacob M. Howard	1855-1860	Paul W. Voorhies	1931-1932
Charles Upson	1861-1862	Patrick H. O'Brien	1933-1934
Albert Williams	1863-1866	Harry S. Toy[16]	1935
William L. Stoughton	1867-1868	David H. Crowley[17]	1935-1936
Dwight May	1869-1872	Raymond W. Starr	1937-1938
Byron D. Ball[4]	1873-1874	Thomas Read	1939-1940
Isaac Marston[5]	1874	Herbert J. Rushton	1941-1944
Andrew J. Smith	1875-1876	John R. Dethmers[18]	1945-1946
Otto Kirchner	1877-1880	Foss O. Eldred[19]	1946
Jacob J. Van Riper	1881-1884	Eugene F. Black	1947-1948
Moses Taggart	1885-1888	Stephen J. Roth	1949-1950
Stephen V. R. Trowbridge[6]	1889-1890	Frank G. Millard	1951-1954
Benjamin W. Huston Jr.[7]	1890	Thomas M. Kavanagh[20]	1955-1957
Adolphus A. Ellis	1891-1894	Paul L. Adams[21]	1958-1961
Fred A. Maynard	1895-1898	Frank J. Kelley[22]	1961-1998
Horace M. Oren	1899-1902	Jennifer M. Granholm	1999-2002
Charles A. Blair	1903-1904	Mike Cox	2003-2010
John E. Bird[8]	1905-1910	Bill Schuette	2011-2018
Franz C. Kuhn[9]	1910-1912	Dana Nessel	2019-

---

[1] Attorneys general were appointed by the governor for 2-year terms prior to the adoption of the Constitution of 1850 which established the position as a statewide elected office. Attorneys general began serving 4-year terms starting with the election held in 1966.
[2] Resigned April 3, 1848 following appointment to the Michigan Supreme Court.
[3] Appointed by the governor following the resignation of Edward Mundy.
[4] Resigned April 1, 1874.
[5] Appointed by the governor following the resignation of Byron D. Ball.
[6] Resigned March 25, 1890.
[7] Appointed by the governor following the resignation of Stephen V. R. Trowbridge.
[8] Resigned June 6, 1910.
[9] Appointed by the governor following the resignation of John E. Bird; Resigned September 9, 1912.
[10] Appointed by the governor following the resignation of Franz C. Kuhn.
[11] Resigned January 4, 1923.
[12] Appointed by the governor January 9, 1923 following the resignation of Merlin Wiley; Resigned October 27, 1926.
[13] Appointed by the governor following the resignation of Andrew B. Dougherty.
[14] Resigned February 16, 1928.
[15] Appointed by the governor February 18, 1928 following the resignation of William W. Potter.
[16] Resigned October 24, 1935.
[17] Appointed by the governor following the resignation of Harry S. Toy.
[18] Resigned August 15, 1946.
[19] Appointed by the governor September 9, 1946 following the resignation of John R. Dethmers.
[20] Resigned December 4, 1957.
[21] Appointed by the governor January 1, 1958 following the resignation of Thomas M. Kavanagh; Resigned December 27, 1961 following appointment to the Michigan Supreme Court.
[22] Appointed by the governor December 28, 1961 following the resignation of Paul L. Adams.

STATE TREASURERS, 1836-2019[1]

Henry Howard[2]	1836-1839	Albert E. Sleeper	1909-1912
Peter Desnoyer[3]	1839-1840	John W. Haarer	1913-1916
Robert Stuart[4]	1840-1841	Samuel Odell[13]	1917-1919
George W. Jermain[5]	1841-1842	Frank E. Gorman[14]	1919-1924
John J. Adam[6]	1842-1845	Frank D. McKay	1925-1930
George R. Redfield[7]	1845-1846	Howard C. Lawrence	1931-1932
George B. Cooper[8]	1846-1850	Theodore I. Fry	1933-1938
Bernard C. Whittemore	1850-1854	Miller Dunckel	1939-1940
Silas M. Holmes	1855-1858	Theodore I. Fry	1941-1942
John McKinney	1859-1860	D. Hale Brake	1943-1954
John G. Owen	1861-1866	Sanford A. Brown	1955-1965
Ebenezer O. Grosvenor	1867-1870	Allison Green[15]	1965-1978
Victory P. Collier	1871-1874	Loren E. Monroe[16]	1978-1982
William B. McCreery	1875-1878	Robert A. Bowman[17]	1983-1991
Benjamin D. Pritchard	1879-1882	Douglas B. Roberts[18]	1991-1998
Edward H. Butler	1883-1886	Mark A. Murray[19]	1999-2001
George L. Maltz	1887-1890	Douglas B. Roberts[20]	2001-2002
Frederick Braastad	1891-1892	Jay B. Rising[21]	2003-2006
Joseph F. Hambitzer[9]	1893-1894	Robert J. Kleine[22]	2006-2010
James M. Wilkinson[10]	1894-1896	Andy Dillon[23]	2011-2013
George A. Steel	1897-1900	Kevin Clinton[24]	2013-2015
Daniel McCoy	1901-1904	Nick Khouri[25]	2015-2018
Frank P. Glazier[11]	1905-1908	Rachael Eubanks[26]	2019-
John T. Rich[12]	1908		

[1] Prior to 1850, the state treasurer was appointed by a joint vote of the House of Representatives and Senate for 2-year terms, however the governor was empowered to make interim appointments. Under the Constitution of 1850, the position of state treasurer became a statewide elected office. The Constitution of 1963 did not include the position as an elected office, giving the governor the authority to appoint the state treasurer as the head of the Department of Treasury.

[2] Resigned May 1, 1839.

[3] Appointed by the governor following the resignation of Henry Howard.

[4] Appointed by the legislature January 23, 1840; Resigned July 8, 1841.

[5] Appointed by the governor following the resignation of Robert Stuart.

[6] Appointed by the legislature January 13, 1842; Resigned May 31, 1845.

[7] Appointed by the governor following the resignation of John J. Adam.

[8] Appointed by the legislature March 12, 1846.

[9] Removed by the governor March 20, 1894.

[10] Appointed by the governor following the removal of Joseph F. Hambitzer.

[11] Resigned January 22, 1908.

[12] Appointed by the governor January 23, 1908 following the resignation of Frank P. Glazier.

[13] Resigned May 21, 1919.

[14] Appointed by the governor following the resignation of Samuel Odell.

[15] Appointed by the governor effective September 14, 1965.

[16] Appointed by the governor effective September 5, 1978.

[17] Appointed by the governor effective January 4, 1983.

[18] Appointed by the governor effective January 1, 1991.

[19] Appointed by the governor effective January 10, 1999.

[20] Appointed by the governor effective May 1, 2001.

[21] Appointed by the governor effective January 6, 2003.

[22] Appointed by the governor effective April 6, 2006.

[23] Appointed by the governor effective January 1, 2011.

[24] Appointed by the governor effective November 1, 2013.

[25] Appointed by the governor effective April 19, 2015.

[26] Appointed by the governor effective January 1, 2019.

SUPERINTENDENTS OF PUBLIC INSTRUCTION, 1836-2019[1]

John D. Pierce	1836-1841	Webster H. Pearce	1927-1933
Franklin Sawyer Jr.	1841-1843	Paul F. Voelker	1933-1935
Oliver C. Comstock	1843-1845	Maurice R. Keyworth[11]	
Ira Mayhew	1845-1849	Eugene B. Elliott[12]	1935-1948
Francis W. Shearman	1849-1854	Lee M. Thurston[13]	1948-1953
Ira Mayhew	1855-1858	Clair L. Taylor[14]	1953-1957
John M. Gregory	1859-1864	Lynn M. Bartlett	1957-1965
Oramel Hosford	1865-1872	Alexander J. Kloster (acting)[15]	1965-1966
Daniel B. Briggs	1873-1876	Ira Polley[16]	1966-1969
Horace S. Tarbell[2]	1877-1878	John W. Porter[17]	1969-1979
Cornelius A. Gower[3]	1878-1881	Eugene T. Paslov (interim)[18]	1979-1980
Varnum B. Cochran[4]	1881-1883	Phillip E. Runkel[19]	1980-1987
Herschel R. Gass[5]	1883-1885	Gary D. Hawks (interim)[20]	1987-1988
Theodore Nelson[6]	1885-1886	Donald L. Bemis[21]	1988-1991
Joseph Estabrook	1887-1890	Gary D. Hawks (interim)[22]	1991
Ferris S. Fitch	1891-1892	Robert E. Schiller[23]	1991-1995
Henry R. Pattengill	1893-1896	Arthur E. Ellis[24]	1995-2001
Jason E. Hammond	1897-1900	Thomas D. Watkins Jr.[25]	2001-2005
Delos Fall	1901-1904	Jeremy Hughes[26]	2005
Patrick H. Kelley	1905-1906	Michael P. Flanagan[27]	2005-2015
Luther L. Wright[7]	1907-1913	Brian J. Whiston[28]	2015-2018
Fred L. Keeler[8]	1913-1919	Sheila A. Alles (interim)[29]	2018-2019
Thomas E. Johnson[9]	1919-1926	Michael F. Rice[30]	2019-
Wilford L. Coffey[10]	1926-1927		

[1] Superintendents of public instruction were appointed by the governor for 2-year terms prior to the adoption of the Constitution of 1850 which established the position as a statewide elected office. The Constitution of 1963 granted appointment authority to the state board of education for a term subject to the board's discretion.

[2] Resigned August 31, 1878.

[3] Appointed by the governor September 3, 1878 following the resignation of Horace S. Tarbell; Resigned May 10, 1881.

[4] Appointed by the governor following the resignation of Cornelius A. Gower; Resigned February 21, 1883.

[5] Appointed by the governor following the resignation of Varnum B. Cochran; Resigned April 2, 1885.

[6] Appointed by the governor April 15, 1885 following the resignation of Herschel R. Gass.

[7] Resigned November 15, 1913.

[8] Appointed by the governor following the resignation of Luther L. Wright; Died April 4, 1919.

[9] Appointed by the governor April 9, 1919 following the death of Fred L. Keeler; Removed by governor November 6, 1926.

[10] Appointed by the governor November 16, 1926 following the removal of Thomas E. Johnson.

[11] Died June 22, 1935 prior to taking office.

[12] Appointed by the governor July 1, 1935 following the death of Maurice R. Keyworth; Resigned July 1, 1948.

[13] Appointed by the governor August 16, 1948 following the resignation of Eugene B. Elliot; Resigned June 30, 1953.

[14] Appointed by the governor following the resignation of Lee M. Thurston.

[15] Appointed by the state board of education effective July 1, 1965.

[16] Appointed by the state board of education effective April 29, 1966.

[17] Appointed acting superintendent of public instruction by the state board of education October 14, 1969; Appointed by the state board of education October 14, 1970; Resigned June 30, 1979.

[18] Appointed by the state board of education effective July 1, 1979.

[19] Appointed by the state board of education effective January 29, 1980.

[20] Appointed by the state board of education effective May 2, 1987.

[21] Appointed by the state board of education effective April 7, 1988; Granted leave of absence January 8, 1991; Resigned effective June 27, 1991.

[22] Appointed temporary acting superintendent of public instruction by the state board of education January 8, 1991; Appointed acting superintendent of public instruction by the state board of education March 5, 1991; Appointed interim superintendent of public instruction by the state board of education effective June 27, 1991.

[23] Appointed by the state board of education effective December 18, 1991.

[24] Appointed interim superintendent of public instruction by the state board of education effective August 7, 1995; Appointed superintendent of public instruction by the state board of education effective January 1, 1996.

[25] Appointed by the state board of education effective April 30, 2001.

[26] Appointed interim superintendent of public instruction by the state board of education effective March 10, 2005.

[27] Appointed by the state board of education effective July 12, 2005.

[28] Appointed by the state board of education effective July 1, 2015; Died May 2018.

[29] Appointed interim superintendent of public instruction by the state board of education effective May 2018.

[30] Appointed by the state board of education effective August 1, 2019.

STATE BOARD OF EDUCATION, 1849-2019[1]

Samuel Newberry	1849-1850
Samuel Barstow	1849-1851
Randolph Manning	1849-1850
Isaac E. Crary	1850-1854
George N. Skinner	1850-1851
Elias M. Skinner	1850-1851
Consider A. Stacy	1851-1852
Chauncey Joslin	1851-1854
Gideon O. Whittemore	1853-1856
Hiram L. Miller	1854-1857
John R. Kellogg	1855-1860
D. Bethune Duffield	1856
Witter J. Baxter	1857-1881
George Willard	1857-1862
Edwin Willits	1861-1872
Daniel E. Brown	1863-1874
Edward Dorsch	1873-1878
David P. Mayhew	1874
Edgar Rexford	1875-1886
George F. Edwards	1879-1884
Bela W. Jenks	1881-1888
James M. Ballou	1885-1890
Samuel S. Babcock	1887-1892
Perry F. Powers	1889-1900
David A. Hammond	1891-1896
Eugene A. Wilson	1893-1898
James W. Simmons	1896-1898
Elias F. Johnson	1898-1901
Frederick A. Platt	1899-1901
Lincoln Avery	1901
Luther L. Wright	1901-1907
James H. Thompson	1901-1905
Patrick H. Kelley	1901-1905
Edward C. Hinman	1905-1906
William J. McKone	1905-1915
Dexter Mason Ferry Jr.	1906-1912
William A. Cotton	1907-1911
Thomas W. Nadal	1911-1917
Frank Cody	1913-1943
Frederick A. Jeffers	1915-1933
Thomas E. Johnson	1917-1919
Allen M. Freeland	1919-1935
Edna C. Wilson	1933-1939
Wynard Wichers	1935-1945
Mary F. Farnsworth	1939-1945
Stephen S. Nisbet	1943-1961
Louisa I. Durham	1945-1953
Charles G. Burns	1945-1957
Walter F. Greis	1953-1959
Chris H. Magnusson	1957-1963
Cornelia A. Robinson	1959-1964
Frank Hartman	1961-1964
James F. O'Neil	1963-1964
	1967-1974
Leon Fill[2]	1965-1966
Donald M. D. Thurber[2]	1965-1966
Carmen L. DelliQuadri[2]	1965-1968
Peter Oppewall[2]	1965-1970
Charles E. Morton[2]	1965-1972
Edwin L. Novak[2]	1965-1972
Marilyn Jean Kelly[2]	1965-1976
Thomas J. Brennan[2]	1965-1972
Leroy G. Augenstein	1967-1969
Gorton Riethmiller[3]	1969-1976
Michael J. Deeb	1969-1974
Annetta Miller	1971-1994
Barbara A. Dumouchelle[4]	1973-1986
	1989-1992
William A. Sederburg	1973-1975
Edmund F. Vandette	1973-1988
Norman O. Stockmeyer Sr.[5]	1975-1988
Barbara Roberts Mason	1975-1998
Roger B. Tilles	1975
Paul B. Henry[6]	1975-1978
Gumecindo Salas	1977-1984
	1987-1994
John Watanen	1977-1984
Silverenia Q. Kanoyton[7]	1978-1981
David Laro[8]	1981-1982
Carroll M. Hutton	1983-1988
Dorothy Beardmore	1985-2000
Cherry Jacobus	1985-1992
Rollie Hopgood[9]	1988-1990
Marilyn Lundy	1989-1996
Richard DeVos	1991-1993
Katherine J. DeGrow[10]	1992-1995
Kathleen N. Straus	1993-2016
Gary Wolfram[11]	1993-1998
Clark Durant	1995-1999
Sharon Wise	1995-2002
Ruth A. Braun[12]	1995-1996
Louis Legg III[13]	1996
Herbert S. Moyer	1997-2004
Marianne Yared McGuire	1997-2012
Sharon L. Gire	1999-2003
Eileen L. Weiser	1999-2006
	2011-2018
Michael D. Warren Jr.[14]	1999-2002
John C. Austin	2001-2016
Elizabeth W. Bauer	2003-2010
Carolyn L. Curtin	2003-2010
Reginald M. Turner[15]	2003-2010
Nancy Danhof	2005-2012
Casandra E. Ulbrich	2007-
Daniel Varner	2010-2014
Richard Zeile	2011-2018
Michelle Fecteau	2013-
Lupe Ramos-Montigny	2013-
Pamela Pugh	2015-
Tom McMillin	2017-
Nikki Snyder	2017-
Judith Pritchett	2019-
Tiffany Tilley	2019-

---

[1] The Constitution of 1850 established the state board of education as a statewide elected office with three members serving six-year terms. The Constitution of 1908 expanded the board to four members. The Constitution of 1963 expanded the board to eight members serving eight-year terms. For information about exact dates of resignations and appointments for members elected prior to the adoption of the Constitution of 1963, see *2015-2016 Manual*.

[2] Under the provisions of the Constitution of 1963, Leon Fill and Donald M. D. Thurber were elected to 2-year terms, Carmen L. DelliQuadri and Marilyn Jean Kelly to 4-year terms, Peter Oppewall and Thomas J. Brennan to 6-year terms, and Charles E. Morton and Edwin L. Novak to 8-year terms, each beginning at noon on January 1, 1965.

[3] Appointed to fill vacancy December 2, 1969 following the death of Leroy G. Augenstein; Appointed to fill vacancy November 12, 1974 following the resignation of Michael J. Deeb.

[4] Appointed to fill vacancy January 1, 1973 following the resignation of Thomas J. Brennan.

[5] Appointed to fill vacancy January 13, 1975 following the resignation of William A. Sederburg.

[6] Appointed to fill vacancy August 26, 1975 following the resignation of Roger B. Tilles.

[7] Appointed to fill vacancy December 29, 1978 following the resignation of Paul B. Henry.

STATE BOARD OF EDUCATION, 1849-2019 *(Cont.)*

[8] Appointed to fill vacancy August 1, 1981 following the resignation of Silverenia Q. Kanoyton.

[9] Appointed to fill vacancy September 16, 1988 following the resignation of Carroll M. Hutton.

[10] Appointed to fill vacancy July 13, 1992 following the resignation of Barbara A. Dumouchelle.

[11] Appointed to fill vacancy January 22, 1993 following the resignation of Richard DeVos.

[12] Appointed to fill vacancy February 24, 1995 following the resignation of Katherine J. DeGrow.

[13] Appointed to fill vacancy August 21, 1996 following the resignation of Ruth A. Braun.

[14] Appointed to fill vacancy September 21, 1999 following the resignation of Clark Durant.

[15] Appointed to fill vacancy September 25, 2003 following the resignation of Sharon L. Gire.

STATE HIGHWAY COMMISSIONERS, 1903-1965[1]

Horatio S. Earle	1903-1909	G. Donald Kennedy[5]	1940-1942
Townsend A. Ely	1909-1913	Lloyd B. Reid[6]	1942-1943
Frank F. Rogers[2]	1913-1929	Charles M. Ziegler[7]	1943-1957
Grover C. Dillman[3]	1929-1933	John C. Mackie	1957-1965
Murray D. Van Wagoner[4]	1933-1940		

[1] The state highway department was originally established by Act 203 of 1903 with a commissioner of highways as the chief officer of the department. The commissioner was originally appointed by the governor for a 4-year term. Act 146 of 1905 changed the name of the office to state highway commissioner. The position became a statewide elective office following the enactment of Act 283 of 1909. The Constitution of 1963 established a state transportation commission and provided for the appointment of a director of the state transportation department. Act 286 of 1964 transferred the powers and duties of the state highway department to the state transportation commission and abolished the office of state highway commissioner effective July 1, 1965.

[2] Resigned December 21, 1928.

[3] Appointed by the governor January 17, 1929 following the resignation of Frank F. Rogers.

[4] Resigned.

[5] Appointed by the governor November 12, 1940 following the resignation of Murray D. Van Wagoner; Elected April 7, 1941 to unexpired term and full term; Resigned December 30, 1942.

[6] Appointed by the governor December 30, 1942 following the resignation of G. Donald Kennedy.

[7] Elected to unexpired term April 5, 1943.

Chapter V

THE JUDICIAL BRANCH

The Judicial Branch information is provided by the Michigan Supreme Court and Court Administrative Office, updated April 2019.

2019–2020

ORGANIZATION OF THE JUDICIAL BRANCH

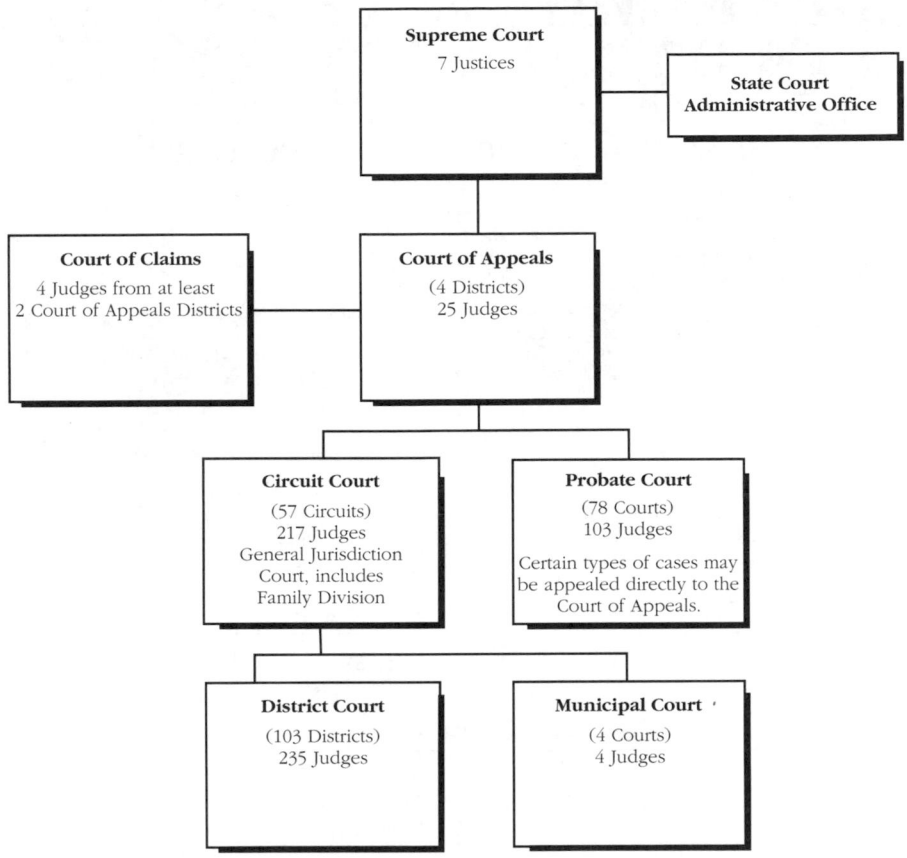

Supreme Court
7 Justices

State Court Administrative Office

Court of Claims
4 Judges from at least 2 Court of Appeals Districts

Court of Appeals
(4 Districts)
25 Judges

Circuit Court
(57 Circuits)
217 Judges
General Jurisdiction Court, includes Family Division

Probate Court
(78 Courts)
103 Judges

Certain types of cases may be appealed directly to the Court of Appeals.

District Court
(103 Districts)
235 Judges

Municipal Court
(4 Courts)
4 Judges

The *Constitution of the State of Michigan of 1963* provides that "The judicial power of the state is vested exclusively in one court of justice which shall be divided into one supreme court, one court of appeals, one trial court of general jurisdiction known as the circuit court, one probate court, and courts of limited jurisdiction that the legislature may establish by a two-thirds vote of the members elected to and serving in each house."

THE
SUPREME
COURT

JUSTICES OF THE MICHIGAN SUPREME COURT

Term expires

BRIDGET MARY McCORMACK, Chief Justice	Jan. 1, 2021
DAVID F. VIVIANO, Chief Justice Pro Tem	Jan. 1, 2025
RICHARD H. BERNSTEIN	Jan. 1, 2023
MEGAN KATHLEEN CAVANAGH	Jan. 1, 2027
ELIZABETH T. CLEMENT	Jan. 1, 2027
STEPHEN J. MARKMAN	Jan. 1, 2021
BRIAN K. ZAHRA	Jan. 1, 2023

www.courts.mi.gov/supremecourt

History

Under the **territorial government** of Michigan established in 1805, the supreme court consisted of a chief judge and two associate judges appointed by the President of the United States. Under the "second" grade of territorial government established in 1824, the term of office was limited to four years.

First Grade

Augustus B. Woodward	1805-1824	James Witherell	1805-1824
Frederick Bates	1805-1808	John Griffin	1806-1824

Second Grade

James Witherell	1824-1828	William Woodbridge	1828-1832
John Hunt	1824-1827	George Morrell	1832-1837
Solomon Sibley	1824-1837	Ross Wilkins	1832-1837
Henry Chipman	1827-1832		

The **Constitution of 1835** provided for a supreme court, the judges of which were appointed by the governor, by and with the advice and consent of the senate, for 7-year terms. In 1836 the legislature provided for a chief justice and two associate justices. The state was then divided into three circuits and the supreme court was required to hold an annual term in each circuit. The Revised Statutes of 1838 provided for a chief justice and three associate justices.

The **Constitution of 1850** provided for a term of six years and that the judges of the five circuit courts be judges of the supreme court. In 1857, the legislature reorganized the supreme court to consist of a chief justice and three associate justices to be elected for 8-year terms. The number of justices was increased to five by the legislature in 1887. Public Act 250 of 1903 increased the number of justices to eight.

The **Constitution of 1908** provided for the nomination of the justices at partisan conventions and election at nonpartisan elections.

The **Constitution of 1963** provides that "the judicial power of the state is vested exclusively in one court of justice which shall be divided into one supreme court, one court of appeals, one trial court of general jurisdiction known as the circuit court, one probate court, and the courts of limited jurisdiction that the legislature may establish by a two-thirds vote of the members elected to and serving in each house." Constitution of 1963, article VI, section 1.

"The supreme court shall consist of seven justices elected at nonpartisan elections as provided by law. The term of office shall be eight years and not more than two terms of office shall expire at the same time." Constitution of 1963, art. VI, sec. 2.

"One justice of the supreme court shall be selected by the court as its chief justice as provided by rules of the court. He shall perform duties required by the court. The supreme court shall appoint an administrator of the courts and other assistants of the supreme court as may be necessary to aid in the administration of the courts of this state. The administrator shall perform administrative duties assigned by the court." Constitution of 1963, art. VI, sec. 1.

The Michigan Supreme Court is the highest court in the state, hearing cases appealed to it from other state courts. Applications for "leave to appeal" are filed with the supreme court and the court decides whether to grant them. If an application is granted, the supreme court will hear the case; if denied, the decision of the lower court stands.

In addition to its judicial duties, the supreme court is charged with general administrative supervision of all courts in the state. This is referred to in the state constitution as "general superintending control." The supreme court is responsible for establishing rules for practice and procedure in all courts.

The supreme court consists of seven justices. One justice is selected every two years by the court as chief justice. Two justices are elected every two years (one in the eighth year) in the November election. Although nominated by political parties, the justices are elected on a nonpartisan ballot, separate from the ballot for other elective offices. Candidates for the supreme court must be qualified electors, licensed to practice law in Michigan, and, at the time of election, must be under 70 years of age. The salary of the justices is fixed by the State Officers Compensation Commission and paid by the state.

Administrative Functions

In addition to serving as the state's highest court, the Michigan Supreme Court administers the state court system. The State Court Administrative Office is the court's administrative agency and oversees Michigan's trial courts under the Supreme Court's direction.

The administrative activities include:

- drafting and promulgating state court rules, rules of evidence, and administrative orders;
- providing continuing education for state judges and court staff;
- overseeing courts' management of their caseloads, including tracking how long courts take to dispose of cases;
- informing the public about the justice system and the judiciary through the Court's Annual Report, the Michigan Supreme Court Learning Center, press releases, and educational events;
- monitoring courts' handling of child welfare cases, including addressing barriers to permanent placements for children;
- overseeing Michigan's friend of the court offices, that enforce court orders regarding child support, parenting time, and child custody;
- providing technological assistance to trial courts that request it;
- developing statewide court networks and databases for tracking case information;
- overseeing drug treatment courts throughout the state;
- improving collections of court-imposed fines, costs, and fees;
- maintaining the "One Court of Justice" website, which contains sites for the Supreme Court, Court of Appeals, State Court Administrative Office, Michigan trial courts, Michigan court rules, and other areas of interest;
- supporting community centers that provide mediation services and other alternatives to litigation; and
- proposing legislation to improve the administration of justice.

BIOGRAPHICAL SKETCHES OF JUSTICES

CHIEF JUSTICE
BRIDGET MARY McCORMACK

Term expires January 1, 2021

Chief Justice Bridget Mary McCormack joined the Michigan Supreme Court in January 2013, and became Chief Justice in January 2019.

Before her election to the Court in November 2012, she was a law professor and dean at the University of Michigan Law School. Since joining the Court, Chief Justice McCormack continues to teach at the Law School.

Chief Justice McCormack is a graduate of the New York University Law School, where she was a Root-Tilden scholar and won the Anne Petluck Poses Prize in Clinical Advocacy. She spent the first five years of her legal career in New York, first with the Legal Aid Society and then at the Office of the Appellate Defender. In 1996, she became a faculty fellow at the Yale Law School.

In 1998, she joined the University of Michigan Law School faculty. At Michigan Law, she taught criminal law, legal ethics, and various clinical courses. Her scholarship focused on the professional benefits of clinical legal education. She also created new clinics at the law school, including a Domestic Violence Clinic and a Pediatric Health Advocacy Clinic.

In 2002, she was named Associate Dean for Clinical Affairs. Responsible for the continuing development of the law school's practical education, she continued to expand the clinical offerings at Michigan Law School, launching a Mediation Clinic, a Low Income Taxpayer Clinic, an International Transactions Clinic, a Human Trafficking Clinic, a Juvenile Justice Clinic, and an Entrepreneurship Clinic. In her capacity as professor and associate dean, she conducted and supervised many types of civil and criminal litigation at all levels of the state and federal courts. The University of Michigan Law School's clinical programs are now recognized nationally as one of the best places to be trained as a lawyer.

In 2008, then-Associate Dean McCormack cofounded the Michigan Innocence Clinic, in which students represent wrongfully convicted Michiganders. The clinic has exonerated over 15 people so far, and has shined a light on the important justice issues underlying wrongful conviction. In 2010, McCormack won the "Justice for All" Award for the Clinic's work, and in 2011 the Washtenaw County Bar Association gave her the "Patriot Award." In 2012, she won the Cooley Law School's "Distinguished Brief Award" for the best brief filed in the Michigan Supreme Court during the term. Also in 2012, the Justice Caucus presented her with the Millie Jeffrey Award and the Washtenaw County Women Lawyers recognized her with the Mary Foster Award. In 2013, Chief Justice McCormack was honored with the Honorable Kaye Tertzag Purple Sport Coat Award. The American-Arab Anti-Discrimination Committee recognized her with its Guardian of Justice Award in 2014. She accepted the Impact Award from the Washtenaw County Dispute Resolution Center in 2017. In 2018, the Michigan Association for Justice honored Chief Justice McCormack with its Judicial Excellence Award.

Chief Justice McCormack previously chaired the Supreme Court's Limited English Proficiency Implementation Advisory Committee, and participates with a number of professional organizations including the American Bar Association Access to Justice committee, the American Bar Association Litigation Journal's Board of Editors (serving as an Associate Editor for *Litigation Magazine*), the American Bar Association Working Group on Pro Bono and Public Service, the National Conference of Bar Examiners Torts Drafting Committee, the advisory board of the Michigan Civil Rights Academy, the Board of the Washtenaw County Chapter of Families Against Narcotics, and serves as a board member of the National Board of Legal Specialty Certification. In 2013, Chief Justice McCormack was elected to The American Law Institute. In 2014, Chief Justice McCormack was appointed by the U.S. Department of Justice and the U.S. Department of Commerce's National Institute of Standards and Technology to a newly-created National Commission on Forensic Science. Chief Justice McCormack publishes on a broad range of topics in professional journals.

Chief Justice McCormack is married to Steven Croley, currently a partner at Latham and Watkins, and continues to teach at the University of Michigan Law School. They have four children attending college and enjoy frequent family trips to west Michigan.

JUSTICE
RICHARD H. BERNSTEIN

Term expires January 1, 2023

Justice Richard Bernstein became the first blind justice, elected by voters statewide, to the Michigan Supreme Court in November 2014. With a commitment to justice and fairness, Bernstein began his 8-year term in January 2015.

Prior to being elected to Michigan's highest court, Justice Bernstein was known as a tireless advocate for disabled rights as an attorney heading the public service division for The Sam Bernstein Law Firm in Farmington Hills, Michigan. Blind since birth, Justice Bernstein is a Phi Beta Kappa graduate of the University of Michigan and earned his juris doctorate from Northwestern University School of Law.

Committed to taking action to help clients who needed him, Justice Bernstein's cases often set national standards protecting the rights and safety of people with and without disabilities.

Among his cases in private practice, he represented the Paralyzed Veterans of America in partnership with the United States Department of Justice in an action against the University of Michigan to allow for safe access for disabled individuals when the university's alterations to the stadium failed to accommodate and represent disabled visitors. The case helped establish guidelines that are used by all commercial facilities across the country.

He also successfully partnered with the United States Department of Justice to force the City of Detroit to fix broken wheelchair lifts on its buses, establishing a precedent for accessibility in public transportation. Further, Bernstein represented disabled residents against the Oakland County Road Commission after "roundabout" traffic circles were built without disabled access, impacting future ADA compliance for road construction throughout the United States.

In a landmark settlement against Delta Airlines and Detroit Metro Airport, Bernstein gained accessibility for disabled fliers, helping set the standard for which airlines and airports are to be covered under the Americans with Disabilities Act of 1990. A proponent of education, he argued for, and won, preservation of special education funding throughout the state and filed a federal suit against the American Bar Association to put an end to its discriminatory practices toward blind students via requirement of the Law School Admissions Test. He also challenged the City of New York to make Central Park and all parks safer for visitors and accessible for disabled and visually impaired individuals.

Bernstein previously served an 8-year term on the Wayne State University Board of Governors, elected by voters statewide, serving as its Chair from 2009-2010. He also served as an adjunct professor in the political science department at the University of Michigan.

Honors Justice Bernstein has received include: "Michiganian of the Year" by the *Detroit News*, one of Crain's Detroit Business' "40 Under 40" and recognition on worldwide television by CNN as a leader in keeping government honest. He was selected by The Young Lawyers Section of the State Bar of Michigan as the 2003-2004 Regeana Myrick Outstanding Young Lawyer Award recipient for outstanding commitment to public service and is the recipient of the 2008 John W. Cummiskey Pro Bono Award from the State Bar of Michigan in recognition of his leadership as an advocate and activist.

Michigan Lawyers Weekly named Justice Bernstein a 2009 Leader in the Law, and the University of Michigan presented him with the James T. Neubacher Award in 2011 for his unwavering commitment to equal rights and opportunities for people with disabilities. Also in 2011, L. Brooks Patterson, Michigan's Oakland County Executive, selected Justice Bernstein as one of the region's Elite 40 Under 40. In 2013, Justice Bernstein was inducted into the National Jewish Sports Hall of Fame.

In his spare time, Justice Bernstein is an avid runner, completing 22 marathons – including 13 New York City marathons – the full Ironman triathlon in Coeur d'Alene, Idaho in 2008 and the Israman triathlon's half Ironman in Eilat, Israel in 2011. He also previously cohosted a 1-hour legal radio show called "Fighting for Justice" on WCHB-AM (1200) in Metro Detroit.

JUSTICE
MEGAN KATHLEEN CAVANAGH

Term expires January 1, 2027

Justice Megan Kathleen Cavanagh is a life-long Michigander who grew up in East Lansing and lives in metro Detroit. She is a graduate of the University of Michigan College of Engineering and Wayne State University Law School. Before joining the Michigan Supreme Court in January of 2019, she had over 15 years of experience as one of Michigan's top appellate attorneys and was a shareholder at Garan Lucow Miller P.C. in Detroit.

Justice Cavanagh is the Supreme Court Liaison to Tribal Courts, Child Welfare Services, the Attorney Grievance Commission and the Judicial Tenure Commission. She also serves on the Attorney General's Elder Abuse Task Force.

Justice Cavanagh has served as Chair of the Appellate Practice Section of the State Bar of Michigan, an organization focused on maintaining excellence and improving appellate jurisprudence and practice in Michigan. She served as a council person for the Negligence Section of the State Bar of Michigan, a diverse group of plaintiff and defense attorneys dedicated to finding consensus on important issues affecting citizens' fair and equal access to the courts. She has served many years as cochair of the Michigan Bench Bar Appellate Conference Foundation, organizing and participating in a truly unique educational opportunity for both judges and lawyers to constantly improve our state legal system. And she was a member of the Michigan Attorney Grievance Commission, charged with the responsibility of ensuring that attorneys maintain the highest standards of representation for their clients, other litigants, and the legal system.

Prior to her election to the Court, Justice Cavanagh was rated as one of Michigan's Super Lawyers. She was honored by *Michigan Lawyer's Weekly* as Lawyer of the Year in 2006 and a Woman in the Law in 2017.

Justice Cavanagh is the mother of two daughters, Georgia and Eloise.

JUSTICE
ELIZABETH T. CLEMENT

Term expires January 1, 2027

Justice Elizabeth T. Clement joined the Michigan Supreme Court on November 17, 2017, becoming the 113th Justice and the 11th woman to serve on the bench. Before her appointment by Governor Rick Snyder, she served as chief legal counsel for the Governor, advising him on a wide variety of legal, legislative, and policy matters.

Her duties as chief legal counsel also included working with the Attorney General's Office on litigation affecting the State of Michigan, negotiating tribal compacts and settlement agreements, and interviewing and recommending appointees to Court of Appeals and Supreme Court judicial vacancies.

She previously held the positions of cabinet secretary and deputy chief of staff, as well as deputy legal counsel in the Governor's Office.

Clement served as legal counsel for Senate Majority Leader Michael Bishop in 2010 where she provided legal research, analysis, and advice on legislation and management of the office. In addition, she was responsible for the State Senate advice and consent process including providing reports and recommendations on appointees.

As a policy advisor in the Senate Majority Policy Office from 2006 to 2010, Clement provided analysis and research to the Senate Judiciary Committee, Senate Health Policy Committee, and the Senate Local and State Affairs Committee.

Clement owned and operated Clement Law, PLLC, from 2002 to 2006, where she represented individuals and businesses primarily in the areas of family law, adoption, probate, estate planning, and criminal law.

Prior to working in private practice, Justice Clement worked as a legislative aide to State Senate Majority Floor Leader Mike Rogers.

Clement was licensed to the State Bar of Michigan in 2002. She graduated from the Michigan State University College of Law that same year, where she served as an executive member of the Moot Court Board. She attended Michigan State University on an academic scholarship and graduated in 1999 with a B.A. in political science.

Justice Clement lives with her husband and their four children in East Lansing.

JUSTICE
STEPHEN J. MARKMAN

Term expires January 1, 2021

Stephen Markman was appointed Justice of the Michigan Supreme Court on October 1, 1999. Before his appointment, he served as Judge on the Michigan Court of Appeals from 1995 to 1999. Prior to this, he practiced law with the firm of Miller, Canfield, Paddock & Stone in Detroit.

From 1989 to 1993, Justice Markman served as United States Attorney, or federal prosecutor, in Michigan, after having been nominated by President George H. W. Bush and confirmed by the United States Senate. From 1985 to 1989, he served as Assistant Attorney General of the United States, after having been nominated by President Ronald Reagan and confirmed by the United States Senate. In that position, he headed the Department of Justice's Office of Legal Policy, which served as the principal policy development office within the Department, and which coordinated the federal judicial selection process. Prior to this, he served for seven years as Chief Counsel of the United States Senate Subcommittee on the Constitution and as Deputy Chief Counsel of the United States Senate Judiciary Committee.

Justice Markman has authored articles for such publications as the *University of Michigan Journal of Law Reform*, the *Detroit College of Law Review*, the *Stanford Law Review*, the *University of Chicago Law Review*, the *American Criminal Justice Law Review*, the *Barrister's Law Journal*, the *Harvard Journal of Law & Public Policy*, and the *American University Law Review*. He has also served as a contributing editor of *National Review* magazine, and has authored chapters in such books as "In the Name of Justice: The Aims of the Criminal Law," "Still the Law of the Land," and "Originalism: A Quarter Century of Debate."

Justice Markman has taught constitutional law at Hillsdale College since 1993. He has traveled to Ukraine on two occasions on behalf of the State Department, to provide assistance in the development of that nation's post-Soviet constitution. He is a Fellow of the Michigan Bar Foundation, a Master of the Bench of the Inns of Court, and a member of the One Hundred Club. He has spoken before hundreds of youth, civic, charitable, and legal groups throughout Michigan and nationally, and has coached Little League baseball and basketball. He lives with his wife Mary Kathleen in Mason, and has two sons, James and Charles.

Justice Markman was reelected to the Supreme Court in 2000, 2004, and 2012. His present term expires January 1, 2021.

**JUSTICE
DAVID F. VIVIANO**

Term expires January 1, 2025

David F. Viviano joined the Michigan Supreme Court in 2013 and currently serves as the Court's Chief Justice Pro Tem.

Justice Viviano previously served as chief judge of the Macomb County Circuit and Probate Courts. As chief judge, he was responsible for the administration of one of the largest trial courts in Michigan.

Justice Viviano has participated in a number of initiatives to improve the administration of justice. In 2008, he worked with a small group of judges to test reforms to Michigan's jury system, many of which were adopted and are being used throughout Michigan. For their efforts, Justice Viviano and his colleagues received a national award for jury innovation. Justice Viviano also enjoys teaching Jury Management at the Michigan Judicial Institute's New Judges' School.

Justice Viviano is a strong advocate for technological innovation in the court system. He has long been a proponent of a statewide e-filing system and has worked to improve how our local courts manage electronic data and share it with the public and other units of government.

Before becoming a judge, Justice Viviano worked at two nationally-recognized law firms and then founded his own law firm in Mt. Clemens. Justice Viviano also served as City Attorney for the City of Center Line.

Justice Viviano received his bachelor of arts degree from Hillsdale College and his juris doctor from the University of Michigan Law School.

Justice Viviano and his wife, Neran, live in Sterling Heights with their four children.

JUSTICE
BRIAN K. ZAHRA

Term expires January 1, 2023

Justice Brian K. Zahra was appointed by Governor Rick Snyder to the Michigan Supreme Court on January 14, 2011. The people of Michigan subsequently elected him in November 2012 to a partial term and then reelected him in November 2014 to a full term.

Justice Zahra received his undergraduate degree in 1984 from Wayne State University. To finance his education, he opened and operated a small health and personal care retail store in downtown Detroit. Justice Zahra later opened a grocery outlet, also in Detroit, with two partners. In 1987, he graduated with honors from the University Of Detroit School Of Law, where he served as a member of the Law Review and as Articles Editor of the State Bar of Michigan's *Corporation and Finance Business Law Journal*. Upon graduation, he served as law clerk to Judge Lawrence P. Zatkoff of the U.S. District Court for the Eastern District of Michigan, before joining and eventually becoming a partner in the law firm of Dickinson, Wright, Moon, Van Dusen & Freeman. In 1994, Governor John M. Engler appointed him to the Wayne County Circuit Court where in 1996 he was elected to a 6-year term. In December of 1998, he was appointed to the Michigan Court of Appeals by Governor John M. Engler. He was elected to 6-year terms in 2000 and 2006. From December 2005 to January 2007, he served as the Court of Appeals' Chief Judge Pro Tem.

Justice Zahra has served on many professional and legislative committees, including the Michigan Civil Jury Instructions Committee, the Circuit Court Appellate Rules Committee, the Domestic Violence Legislation Implementation Task Force, and the advisory committee for the Michigan Judicial Institute Domestic Violence Benchbook. Justice Zahra also served on the Michigan Board of Law Examiners, which drafts and grades the examination that law school graduates must pass in order to become licensed attorneys. He is currently a Senior Fellow of Law and Public Policy at the University of Michigan-Dearborn campus, as well as a Distinguished Fellow at Hillsdale College, Hillsdale, Michigan. He previously served on the adjunct faculty at the University of Detroit-Mercy Law School.

Justice Zahra has been active in many civic and charitable organizations, including Boys and Girls Clubs of Southeastern Michigan, Kiwanis Club International, Leadership Detroit, the Knights of Columbus, the Maltese American Community Club, and the Maltese American Benevolent Society, of which he is a past officer. He is a former board member and officer of the Catholic Lawyers Society, and past officer of the Federalist Society, where he currently serves as a member of the advisory board to the Michigan chapter.

Justice Zahra resides in Northville Township with his wife, Suzanne, and their two children.

JUSTICES OF THE MICHIGAN SUPREME COURT, 1836-2019

Name	Residence	Term Years
William A. Fletcher	Ann Arbor	1836-1842
George Morrell	Detroit	1836-1843
Epaphroditus Ransom	Kalamazoo	1836-1848
Charles W. Whipple	Detroit	1839-1855
Daniel Goodwin	Detroit	1843-1850
Alpheus Felch	Monroe	1845-1852
Warner Wing	Monroe	1845-1856
George Miles	Ann Arbor	1846-1850
Sanford M. Green	Pontiac	1848-1857
Edward Mundy	Ann Arbor	1848-1851
Abner Pratt	Marshall	1850-1857
George Martin	Grand Rapids	1851-1867
Joseph T. Copeland	Port Huron	1852-1857
Samuel T. Douglass	Detroit	1852-1857
David Johnson	Jackson	1852-1857
Nathaniel Bacon	Niles	1855-1857
Edward H. C. Wilson	Hillsdale	1856-1857
Benjamin F. H. Witherell	Detroit	1857
Benjamin F. Graves	Battle Creek	1857, 1868-1881
Josiah Turner	Howell	1857
Edwin Lawrence	Ann Arbor	1857
Randolph Manning	Pontiac	1858-1869
James V. Campbell	Detroit	1858-1890
Thomas M. Cooley	Adrian-Ann Arbor	1863-1885
Isaac P. Christiancy	Monroe	1874-1881
Isaac Marston	Bay City-Detroit	1875-1889
Thomas R. Sherwood	Kalamazoo	1882-1889
John W. Champlin	Grand Rapids	1884-1891
Allen B. Morse	Ionia	1885-1893
Charles D. Long	Flint	1888-1907
Edward Cahill	Lansing	1890
Claudius B. Grant	Marquette	1890-1909
John W. McGrath	Detroit	1891-1895
Robert M. Montgomery	Grand Rapids	1892-1911
George H. Durand	Flint	1892
Frank A. Hooker	Charlotte	1894-1913
Joseph B. Moore[1]	Lapeer	1896-1926
William L. Carpenter	Detroit	1902-1908
Charles A. Blair[2]	Jackson	1905-1912
Russell C. Ostrander[3]	Lansing	1905-1919
Aaron V. McAlvay[4]	Manistee	1905-1915
Flavius L. Brooke[5]	Detroit	1908-1921
John W. Stone[6]	Marquette	1910-1922
John E. Bird[7]	Adrian	1910-1928
Joseph H. Steere[8]	Sault Ste. Marie	1911-1927
Franz C. Kuhn[9]	Mt. Clemens	1912-1919
Rollin H. Person	Lansing	1915-1916
Grant Fellows	Hudson	1916-1929
George M. Clark[10]	Bad Axe	1919-1933
Nelson Sharpe[11]	West Branch	1919-1935
Howard Wiest[12]	Lansing	1921-1945
John S. McDonald	Grand Rapids	1922-1933
Ernest A. Snow[13]	Saginaw	1926-1927
Richard H. Flannigan[14]	Norway	1927-1928
Louis H. Fead	Newberry	1928-1937
William W. Potter[15]	Hastings	1928-1940
Walter H. North[16]	Battle Creek	1928-1952
Henry M. Butzel	Detroit	1929-1955
Thomas A. E. Weadock	Detroit	1933
George E. Bushnell[17]	Detroit	1934-1957
Edward M. Sharpe	Bay City	1934-1957
Harry S. Toy	Detroit	1935-1936
Bert D. Chandler	Hudson	1936-1943
Thomas F. McAllister[18]	Grand Rapids	1938-1941
Emerson R. Boyles[19]	Charlotte	1940-1956
Raymond W. Starr[20]	Grand Rapids	1941-1946
Neil E. Reid[21]	Mt. Clemens	1944-1956
Leland W. Carr	Lansing	1945-1963
John R. Dethmers	Holland	1946-1971

Name	Residence	Years
Clark J. Adams	Pontiac	1952-1953
Harry F. Kelly	Detroit	1954-1971
Talbot Smith[22]	Ann Arbor	1955-1961
Eugene F. Black	Port Huron	1956-1973
John D. Voelker[23]	Ishpeming	1957-1959
George C. Edwards[24]	Detroit	1957-1961
Thomas M. Kavanagh[25]	Carson City	1958-1975
Theodore Souris	Grosse Pointe Farms	1960-1968
Otis M. Smith	Flint	1961-1967
Paul L. Adams	Sault Ste. Marie	1962, 1964-1973
Michael D. O'Hara	Menominee	1963-1969
Thomas E. Brennan[26]	Detroit	1967-1973
Thomas Giles Kavanagh	Birmingham	1969-1985
John B. Swainson[27]	Manchester	1971-1975
G. Mennen Williams	Grosse Pointe Farms	1971-1987
Mary Stallings Coleman[28]	Battle Creek	1973-1982
Charles L. Levin	Detroit	1973-1997
John W. Fitzgerald	Grand Ledge	1974-1983
Lawrence B. Lindemer	Stockbridge	1975-1977
James L. Ryan[29]	Detroit	1975-1986
Blair Moody Jr.[30]	Grosse Pointe Shores	1977-1982
Dorothy Comstock Riley[31, 34]	Grosse Pointe Farms	1982-1983, 1985-1997
James H. Brickley[32]	Traverse City	1982-1999
Michael F. Cavanagh	East Lansing	1983-2014
Patricia J. Boyle	Detroit	1983-1998
Dennis W. Archer[33]	Detroit	1986-1990
Robert P. Griffin	Traverse City	1987-1995
Conrad L. Mallett Jr.[35]	Detroit	1990-1999
Elizabeth A. Weaver	Glen Arbor	1995-2010
Marilyn Jean Kelly	Bloomfield Hills	1997-2012
Clifford W. Taylor	Laingsburg	1997-2009
Maura D. Corrigan	Grosse Pointe Park	1998-2011
Robert P. Young Jr.[36]	Grosse Pointe Park	1998-2017
Stephen J. Markman	Mason	1999-
Diane M. Hathaway[37]	Grosse Pointe Park	2009-2013
Mary Beth Kelly[38]	Grosse Ile	2011-2015
Brian K. Zahra	Northville	2011-
Bridget Mary McCormack	Ann Arbor	2013-
David F. Viviano	Sterling Heights	2013-
Richard H. Bernstein	Detroit	2015-
Joan L. Larsen[39]	Scio Township	2015-2017
Kurtis T. Wilder	Canton	2017-2018
Elizabeth T. Clement	East Lansing	2017-
Megan Kathleen Cavanagh	Birmingham	2019-

[1] Resigned; Ernest A. Snow appointed Jan. 1, 1926.
[2] Deceased; Franz C. Kuhn appointed Sept. 6, 1912.
[3] Deceased; Nelson Sharpe appointed Sept. 25, 1919.
[4] Died before taking office; Rollin H. Person appointed July 16, 1915.
[5] Deceased; Howard Wiest appointed Jan. 25, 1921.
[6] Deceased; John S. McDonald appointed Mar. 29, 1922.
[7] Deceased; William W. Potter appointed Feb. 14, 1928.
[8] Resigned; Richard H. Flannigan appointed Sept. 29, 1927.
[9] Resigned; George M. Clark appointed Dec. 30, 1919.
[10] Resigned; Thomas A. E. Weadock appointed Aug. 10, 1933 to Dec. 31, 1933.
[11] Deceased; Harry S. Toy appointed Oct. 24, 1935.
[12] Deceased; Leland W. Carr appointed Sept. 24, 1945.
[13] Deceased; Walter H. North appointed Oct. 24, 1927.
[14] Deceased; Louis H. Fead appointed Feb. 21, 1928.
[15] Deceased; Emerson R. Boyles appointed Aug. 8, 1940.
[16] Deceased; Clark J. Adams appointed Aug. 14, 1952 to Aug. 31, 1953.
[17] Resigned; Talbot Smith appointed Jan. 6, 1955.
[18] Resigned; Raymond W. Starr appointed June 2, 1941.
[19] Resigned; John D. Voelker appointed Dec. 31, 1956.
[20] Resigned; John R. Dethmers appointed Aug. 15, 1946.
[21] Deceased; George C. Edwards appointed May 15, 1956.
[22] Resigned; Otis M. Smith appointed Oct. 10, 1961.
[23] Resigned; Theodore Souris appointed Dec. 31, 1959.
[24] Resigned; Paul L. Adams appointed Dec. 27, 1961.

JUSTICES OF THE MICHIGAN SUPREME COURT,
1836-2019 *(Cont.)*

[25] Deceased; Lawrence B. Lindemer appointed May 5, 1975.
[26] Resigned; John W. Fitzgerald appointed Jan. 1, 1974.
[27] Resigned; James L. Ryan appointed Dec. 2, 1975.
[28] Resigned; James H. Brickley appointed Dec. 27, 1982.
[29] Resigned; Dennis W. Archer appointed Jan. 1, 1986.
[30] Deceased; Dorothy Comstock Riley appointed Dec. 9, 1982.
[31] Withdrawn; Patricia J. Boyle appointed April 20, 1983.
[32] Resigned; Stephen J. Markman appointed Oct. 1, 1999.
[33] Resigned; Conrad L. Mallett Jr. appointed Dec. 27, 1990.
[34] Resigned; Clifford W. Taylor appointed Aug. 21, 1997.
[35] Resigned; Robert P. Young Jr. appointed Dec. 30, 1998.
[36] Resigned; Kurtis T. Wilder appointed May 9, 2017.
[37] Resigned; David F. Viviano appointed Feb. 27, 2013.
[38] Resigned; Joan L. Larsen appointed Sept. 30, 2015.
[39] Resigned; Elizabeth T. Clement appointed Nov. 17, 2017.

MICHIGAN
COURT
OF APPEALS

JANE M. BECKERING, CHIEF JUDGE PRO TEM
CHRISTOPHER M. MURRAY, CHIEF JUDGE PRO TEM

925 W. Ottawa
P.O. Box 30022, Lansing, MI 48909
Phone: (517) 373-0786
courts.mi.gov/courts/coa

The court of appeals was created by the Constitution of 1963, art. VI, sec. 1, and began operation in 1965 with a bench of nine judges. The legislature increased the size of the bench to 12 judges in 1969, to 18 judges in 1974, to 24 judges in 1986, and to 28 judges in 1993. In 2012, legislation was enacted that will eventually reduce the court's size to 24 judges through attrition.

A candidate for the court of appeals must be a lawyer, under 70 years of age, a qualified elector, and a resident of the district in which he or she is running. Judges are elected in nonpartisan elections for 6-year terms. Their salaries are set by the legislature. The court is divided into four geographic districts for election purposes and has offices located in each district: Detroit (District I), Troy (District II), Grand Rapids (District III), and Lansing (District IV). Although elected by district, the judges sit statewide in panels of three, rotating with two different judges every month. The rotation of judges on panels encourages statewide uniformity in rulings by eliminating the likelihood of conflicting legal philosophies developing in specific geographical areas.

The court of appeals hears both civil and criminal cases. Cases may be initiated as discretionary appeals, appeals by right, or original actions (in limited case types as provided by the legislature). Published opinions of the court are controlling across all four districts, and decisions of the court are final unless and until reversed or overruled by a special conflict panel of the court or by the Supreme Court. The court sits year-round in Detroit, Lansing and Grand Rapids, or in another location as designated by the chief judge. At present, arguments are scheduled once a year in Marquette or the northern Lower Peninsula, usually Petoskey or Traverse City.

Every two years a chief judge is selected by the Supreme Court. In addition to hearing cases, the chief judge or his/her designee performs administrative duties and other assignments required by the Supreme Court.

THE COURT OF APPEALS — JUDICIAL DISTRICTS

(Pursuant to Public Act 40 of 2012)

County	Population in 2010	County	Population in 2010
1st District		**4th District**	
Branch	45,248	Alcona	10,942
Hillsdale	46,688	Alger	9,601
Kalamazoo	250,331	Alpena	29,598
Lenawee	99,892	Antrim	23,580
Monroe	152,021	Arenac	15,899
St. Joseph	61,295	Baraga	8,860
Wayne	1,820,584	Bay	107,771
		Benzie	17,525
Total	2,476,059	Charlevoix	25,949
		Cheboygan	26,152
		Chippewa	38,520
		Clare	30,926
		Clinton	75,382
		Crawford	14,074
2nd District		Delta	37,069
Genesee	425,790	Dickinson	26,168
Macomb	840,978	Emmet	32,694
Oakland	1,202,362	Gladwin	25,692
		Gogebic	16,427
Total	2,469,130	Grand Traverse	86,986
		Gratiot	42,476
		Houghton	36,628
		Huron	33,118
		Ingham	280,895
3rd District		Iosco	25,887
Allegan	111,408	Iron	11,817
Barry	59,173	Isabella	70,311
Berrien	156,813	Kalkaska	17,153
Calhoun	136,146	Keweenaw	2,156
Cass	52,293	Lake	11,539
Eaton	107,759	Lapeer	88,319
Ionia	63,905	Leelanau	21,708
Jackson	160,248	Livingston	180,967
Kent	602,622	Luce	6,631
Mason	28,705	Mackinac	11,113
Montcalm	63,342	Manistee	24,733
Muskegon	172,188	Marquette	67,077
Newaygo	48,460	Mecosta	42,798
Oceana	26,570	Menominee	24,029
Ottawa	263,801	Midland	83,629
Van Buren	76,258	Missaukee	14,849
Washtenaw	344,791	Montmorency	9,765
		Ogemaw	21,699
Total	2,474,482	Ontonagon	6,780
		Osceola	23,528
		Oscoda	8,640
		Otsego	24,164
		Presque Isle	13,376
		Roscommon	24,449
		Saginaw	200,169
		St. Clair	163,040
		Sanilac	43,114
		Schoolcraft	8,485
		Shiawassee	70,648
		Tuscola	55,729
		Wexford	32,735
		Total	2,463,969

NOTE: The state is divided into 4 judicial districts for the election of judges of the court of appeals. The districts are constituted and numbered in accordance with this table. See 2012 PA 40.

THE COURT OF APPEALS — JUDICIAL DISTRICTS

Constitution of Michigan of 1963, Article VI, Sec. 8

"The court of appeals shall consist initially of nine judges who shall be nominated and elected at non-partisan elections from districts drawn on county lines and as nearly as possible of equal population, as provided by law. The supreme court may prescribe by rule that the court of appeals sit in divisions and for the terms of court and the times and places thereof. Each such division shall consist of not fewer than three judges. The number of judges comprising the court of appeals may be increased, and the districts from which they are elected may be changed by law."

District **I**: Branch, Hillsdale, Kalamazoo, Lenawee, Monroe, St. Joseph, Wayne

District **II**: Genesee, Macomb, Oakland

District **III**: Allegan, Barry, Berrien, Calhoun, Cass, Eaton, Ionia, Jackson, Kent, Mason, Montcalm, Muskegon, Newaygo, Oceana, Ottawa, Van Buren, Washtenaw

District **IV**: Balance of counties for State of Michigan

JUDGES OF THE COURT OF APPEALS

1st District

Term expires

THOMAS C. CAMERON, Northville Township . . . . Jan. 1, 2023
KAREN FORT HOOD, Detroit . . . . Jan. 1, 2021
KIRSTEN FRANK KELLY, Grosse Pointe Park . . . . Jan. 1, 2025
ANICA LETICA, Canton . . . . Jan. 1, 2021
CHRISTOPHER M. MURRAY, Grosse Pointe Farms, Chief Judge . . Jan. 1, 2021
MICHAEL J. RIORDAN, Plymouth . . . . Jan. 1, 2025
CYNTHIA DIANE STEPHENS, Detroit . . . . Jan. 1, 2023

2nd District

MARK J. CAVANAGH, Royal Oak . . . . Jan. 1, 2021
ELIZABETH L. GLEICHER, Pleasant Ridge . . . . Jan. 1, 2025
KATHLEEN JANSEN, St. Clair Shores . . . . Jan. 1, 2025
COLLEEN A. O'BRIEN, Clarkston . . . . Jan. 1, 2023
DEBORAH A. SERVITTO, Royal Oak . . . . Jan. 1, 2025
JONATHAN TUKEL, Orchard Lake . . . . Jan. 1, 2021

3rd District

JANE M. BECKERING, Grand Rapids . . . . Jan. 1, 2025
MARK T. BOONSTRA, Holland . . . . Jan. 1, 2021
JANE E. MARKEY, Grand Rapids . . . . Jan. 1, 2021
JAMES ROBERT REDFORD, East Grand Rapids . . . . Jan. 1, 2021
DAVID H. SAWYER, East Grand Rapids . . . . Jan. 1, 2023
DOUGLAS B. SHAPIRO, Ann Arbor . . . . Jan. 1, 2025

4th District

STEPHEN L. BORRELLO, Saginaw . . . . Jan. 1, 2025
MICHAEL F. GADOLA, Haslett . . . . Jan. 1, 2023
MICHAEL J. KELLY, Maple City . . . . Jan. 1, 2021
AMY RONAYNE KRAUSE, Lansing . . . . Jan. 1, 2021
PATRICK M. METER, Saginaw . . . . Jan. 1, 2021
BROCK A. SWARTZLE, Okemos . . . . Jan. 1, 2023

BIOGRAPHICAL SKETCHES OF COURT OF APPEALS JUDGES

First District Judges

JUDGE
THOMAS C. CAMERON

Term expires January 1, 2023

Judge Thomas C. Cameron was appointed to the Michigan Court of Appeals in 2017, and previously served as a judge on the Wayne County Circuit Court bench from 2014 until his appointment to the Court of Appeals.

Previously, Judge Cameron worked for the Michigan Department of Attorney General where he supervised several large civil and criminal divisions for the Attorney General, including the Civil Rights Division, Corrections Division, Criminal Division, and Alcohol and Gambling Division. Prior to him serving as a senior manager, he served as an assistant Attorney General, where he litigated high-profile public corruption and cold-case homicides. He is the former chairman of the Michigan Commission on Law Enforcement Standards.

Judge Cameron currently serves on the Michigan Domestic Violence and Sexual Assault Treatment Board and also as co-chair of the Criminal Justice Committee for the Michigan Judges Association. He is a member of the Michigan Chapter of the Federalist Society, Detroit Metropolitan Bar Association, Catholic Lawyer's Society, the Incorporated Society of Irish-American Lawyers and a member of the University of Detroit Mercy Inns of Court. He serves as an adjunct professor for the University of Toledo School of Law.

Judge Cameron is a graduate of Western Michigan University and Wayne State University School of Law.

JUDGE
KAREN FORT HOOD

Term expires January 1, 2021

In November 2002, Judge Karen Fort Hood made history when she became the first black woman to be elected to the Michigan Court of Appeals. She was born in Detroit, Michigan, received her undergraduate degree in 1980 from the Regents College of the University of the State of New York at Albany, and her law degree in 1989 from the Detroit College of Law. Early in her career, Judge Hood worked as a teacher for the Detroit Public Schools, a probation officer, and served as a special assistant prosecutor and assistant prosecuting attorney for the Juvenile and Appellate divisions of the Wayne County Prosecutor's office. Judge Hood was elected to the Recorder's Court bench in 1992. In 1997, she was elected to the Wayne County Circuit Court, where she was appointed presiding judge over the Criminal Division in 1999. Judge Hood's professional affiliations include the Association of Black Judges of Michigan, the Wolverine Bar Association, and the National Bar Association.

JUDGE
KIRSTEN FRANK KELLY

Term expires January 1, 2025

Judge Kelly was elected to the Court in 2000 and reelected in 2006 and 2012. She graduated from Michigan State University and from the University of Detroit School of Law. After law school, Judge Kelly joined the Detroit law firm of Durant and Durant, where she practiced civil litigation, and became a partner in the firm.

In 1987, she was elected a municipal judge, and she was twice reelected to that position. She was appointed to the Wayne Circuit Court by Governor John M. Engler in 1994. In 1997, she was appointed presiding judge of the Family Division of the Wayne Circuit Court by the Supreme Court. In 1999, she was also appointed the presiding judge of Family Division - Juvenile Division.

Judge Kelly served two terms as president of the Michigan Association of Municipal Judges and served on the board of directors of the Michigan District Judges Association. She also serves on the Rules and Family Law committees of the Michigan Judges Association.

Judge Kelly's civic activities include being a member of Leadership Detroit XVII, National Kidney Foundation of Michigan, Detroit Executive Leadership Committee, KIDS-Talk Advisory Committee and DMBA Inns of Court. Judge Kelly and her husband, William B. Kelly, have three children.

JUDGE
ANICA LETICA

Term expires January 1, 2021

Judge Anica Letica was appointed to the Michigan Court of Appeals in 2018.

She first joined the Court of Appeals as a prehearing attorney in 1985. Thereafter, she clerked for the Honorable John H. Gillis.

Judge Letica then worked in the Appellate Division of the Oakland County Prosecutor's Office, handling hundreds of appeals and supporting legislation benefitting crime victims, law enforcement, and the public.

In 2009, the Michigan Attorney General appointed Judge Letica to serve as an Assistant Attorney General in the Department's Criminal Appellate Division. There, she supervised criminal appeals for 56 county prosecutors along with in-state prisoner litigation. Judge Letica also coordinated the Department's Sexual Assault Kit Initiative projects to investigate and prosecute cases arising from the testing of previously untested sexual assault kits. In addition, Judge Letica assisted the Human Trafficking Commission and represented the Attorney General on the Michigan Commission on Law Enforcement Standards.

Judge Letica is a member of the State Bar's Criminal Law and Appellate Practice Sections, previously serving on the latter's Council. For a number of years, she also served on the Standard Criminal Jury Instruction Committee and was a member of the workgroup responsible for proposing revisions to the court rules governing circuit-court appellate practice.

Judge Letica has lectured for the Michigan Judicial Institute and the Prosecuting Attorneys Association of Michigan. She contributed to the post-conviction and appellate chapters in *Michigan Criminal Procedure for the Institute of Continuing Legal Education* and served on the editorial advisory committee for the Michigan Judicial Institute's *Criminal Proceedings Benchbook, Volume 3*.

Judge Letica graduated from the University of Michigan with high distinction, receiving her bachelor of arts degree. She then graduated from the Wayne State University Law School, where she was elected to the Order of the Coif.

CHIEF JUDGE
CHRISTOPHER M. MURRAY

Term expires January 1, 2021

Judge Murray was appointed to the Court in 2002 to fill a term ending that year. He was then elected in 2002, and reelected in 2008 and 2014. Previously, he served as a judge on the Wayne Circuit Court in the Family Division, as Deputy Legal Counsel to Governor John M. Engler, and as an attorney in private practice. Judge Murray currently serves on the Board of Law Examiners and is the chair of the Board of Advisors for the Michigan Lawyers Division of the Federalist Society. Judge Murray was formerly the chair of the State Board of Ethics, previously served as a member of the Local Government Claims Review Board, the Committee on Model Civil Jury Instructions, and was on the board of directors for the Detroit Metropolitan Bar Association and the Catholic Lawyers Society.

JUDGE
MICHAEL J. RIORDAN

Term expires January 1, 2025

Michael J. Riordan was appointed to the Michigan Court of Appeals on March 16, 2012. In November 2012, Judge Riordan was elected to a full 6-year term. Previously, the Judge served as an Assistant United States Attorney for the Eastern District of Michigan, as assistant general counsel for the Northwestern Mutual Financial Network, and as senior attorney in the Enforcement Division of the United States Securities and Exchange Commission. Upon graduation from law school, Judge Riordan was a Federal Judicial Law Clerk for the Honorable Robert E. DeMascio, of the United States District Court for the Eastern District of Michigan. Judge Riordan is an adjunct professor of securities regulation and business organizations at the University of Detroit Mercy School of Law. He has been a member of the State Bar of Michigan's Board of Commissioners since 2006. He is a past-president of the Federal Bar Association of the Eastern District of Michigan and of the Incorporated Society of Irish American Lawyers. He is vice-president of the University of Detroit Mercy School of Law Alumni Association and is on the Board of Directors of the Catholic Lawyers' Society. Judge Riordan received his B.A. from Michigan State University and his J.D., *cum laude*, from the University of Detroit School of Law.

JUDGE
CYNTHIA DIANE STEPHENS

Term expires January 1, 2023

Judge Stephens was appointed to the Court of Appeals in 2008. Prior to that appointment, she served as a general jurisdiction trial judge for 23 years. She was appointed to the Wayne County Circuit Court in 1985, after serving as a judge of the 36th District Court. Judge Stephens was the Chief Judge Pro Tempore, Mediation Tribunal Chair and presiding civil division judge of Wayne County Circuit Court for eight years.

An Emory Law School graduate, Judge Stephens has been admitted to practice in Georgia, Texas, and Michigan. Prior to her election to the bench in 1981, she served as vice-chair of the Wayne County Charter Commission, Associate General Counsel to the Michigan Senate, Regional Director for the National Conference of Black Lawyers Atlanta office, and consultant to the National League of Cities Veterans Discharge Upgrade Project.

She has been active in bar work, including 16 years as a Commissioner of the State Bar of Michigan, chairing its Justice Initiatives Committee, Communications Committee, and Children's Task Force. Judge Stephens is a former chair of the Association of Black Judges of Michigan, a former member of the executive board of the National Bar Association and its Judicial Council and a member of the American Bar Association. She was awarded the State Bar of Michigan's highest honor, the Roberts P. Hudson Award, in 2005.

Judge Stephens has served as adjunct faculty at Wayne State University Law School, the Detroit College of Law, and the University of Detroit Mercy Law School. She has also served as a faculty member for the National Judicial College and the Michigan Judicial Institute. She was a contributing author to the *Lawyers Cooperative's Michigan Nonstandard Jury Instructions*, as well as numerous articles on subjects ranging from jury selection to ethics.

Judge Stephens has served on numerous civic boards and commissions, including New Detroit, the Inner City Business Improvement Forum, the Detroit Metropolitan Association Board of Trustees for the United Church of Christ, the Greater Detroit Area Health Care Council, and the Girl Scouts. She is a resident of Detroit.

Second District Judges

JUDGE
MARK J. CAVANAGH

Term expires January 1, 2021

Judge Cavanagh was elected to the Court in 1988. Previously, he worked as a special assistant attorney general, as an assistant Wayne County prosecutor, and as an attorney in private practice. Judge Cavanagh received his bachelor's degree from the University of Michigan and his law degree from the Detroit College of Law. Judge Cavanagh has two children.

JUDGE
ELIZABETH L. GLEICHER

Term expires January 1, 2025

Judge Gleicher was appointed to the Court in 2007. Previously, she was an attorney in private practice for 27 years. She began her career at Goodman, Eden, Millender & Bedrosian in Detroit and opened her own litigation practice in 1994. She is an elected Fellow of the International Society of Barristers, 2004 and the American College of Trial Lawyers, 2005. She received the Respected Advocate Award from the Michigan Defense Trial Counsel in 2005 and the State Bar of Michigan Champion of Justice Award in 2001. Judge Gleicher has served on the faculty of the Institute for Continuing Legal Education and as an adjunct professor at Wayne State University Law School. She received her bachelor's degree from Carleton College in Northfield, Minnesota, and her law degree from Wayne State University Law School.

JUDGE
KATHLEEN JANSEN

Term expires January 1, 2025

Judge Jansen was appointed to the Court of Appeals in 1989. In November 1982, she was the first woman ever to be elected to the Macomb County Probate Court. In November 1984, she was the first woman elected to the Macomb County Circuit Court. Prior to her elections, she worked as an attorney in private practice. Judge Jansen received her bachelor's degree from Michigan State University and attended Western Washington State University for graduate studies. She obtained her law degree from the University of Detroit Law School in 1982.

JUDGE
COLLEEN A. O'BRIEN

Term expires January 1, 2023

Judge Colleen O'Brien was appointed to the Court of Appeals October 2015, and was elected to a 6-year term in 2016. She graduated from the University of Michigan in 1978 with a bachelor's degree and from the Detroit College of Law with a juris doctor degree in 1981. Judge O'Brien practiced law for 17 years prior to being elected to the Oakland County Circuit Court in 1998. As a Circuit Judge, she served as the Presiding Judge of the Female Adult Treatment Court for 12 years and as the Presiding Judge of the Civil/Criminal Division for several years. Judge O'Brien is a long time member of the Michigan Judges Association and served as President in 2015. She has also served as President of the Oakland County Women's Bar Association and served on the Board of Directors of the Women Lawyers Association of Michigan. An active member of the Oakland County Bar Association, Judge O'Brien received the Distinguished Public Servant Award in 2011. Judge O'Brien's civic activities include serving on the Advisory Board to Crossroads for Youth, serving as a member of the Indigent Defense Advisory Commission, and serving as a member of the Interagency Council on Homelessness.

JUDGE
DEBORAH A. SERVITTO

Term expires January 1, 2025

Judge Deborah A. Servitto was born in Sewickley, Pennsylvania. She graduated from Oakland University in 1978 with a bachelor's degree in Political Science and from the Detroit College of Law with a juris doctor degree in 1982.

She served from 1982 to 1986 as the first female assistant city attorney for the city of Warren. In 1986, Judge Servitto was elected to the 37th District Court. Governor James J. Blanchard appointed Judge Servitto to the Macomb Circuit Court in 1990, and she subsequently was elected three times to that court. Governor Jennifer M. Granholm appointed Judge Servitto to the Court of Appeals effective March 23, 2006, to replace Judge Hilda R. Gage.

During her tenure as a circuit judge, Judge Servitto was instrumental in implementing innovative programs, such as a seminar for divorcing parents aimed at helping their children cope with divorce and a drug court program that provides treatment and intensive supervision to nonviolent, drug-addicted felons. She was also one of the founding directors of Care House, a child-friendly haven for young victims of sexual and physical abuse.

In November 2006, Judge Servitto was elected to a full 6-year term to the Court of Appeals, District 2, which includes the counties of Macomb, Oakland, and Genesee. She was reelected in 2012.

JUDGE
JONATHAN TUKEL

Term expires January 1, 2021

Jonathan Tukel was appointed to the Court of Appeals in December 2017. Prior to his appointment he worked for the United States Department of Justice in Detroit as an Assistant U.S. Attorney, where he handled a wide variety of cases, including public corruption, narcotics and fraud. For the ten years prior to his appointment to the bench, he supervised the National Security Unit, handling cases involving international and domestic terrorism and terrorist financing.

Since 2009, Judge Tukel has taught a seminar in Federal Criminal Prosecution and Defense at the University of Michigan Law School. He was voted a "Leader in the Law" for 2012 by the state-wide publication *Michigan Lawyers Weekly* and that same year was a recipient of the Attorney General

Award, the Department of Justice's highest, given in recognition of his "Excellence in Furthering the Interest in U.S. National Security." During his career at the Department of Justice he lectured at the National Counter Terrorism Center, the FBI Academy, the Department of Justice's National Security Conference, and at the Public Prosecution Service of Canada. He also has served as the chairman of a Michigan Attorney Discipline Board Hearing Panel.

Judge Tukel graduated from the University of Michigan in 1982, receiving a bachelor's degree with Honors in Philosophy. In 1988 he graduated from the University of Michigan Law School, *magna cum laude*, and was elected to the Order of the Coif. Judge Tukel and his wife live with their three children in Oakland County.

Third District Judges

JUDGE
JANE M. BECKERING

Term expires January 1, 2025

Judge Beckering was appointed to the Court of Appeals in 2007, and elected in 2008, with reelection in 2012. Before taking the bench, Judge Beckering was an attorney in private practice for 17 years. She began her career at McDermott, Will & Emery, P.C. in Chicago, Illinois, before she returned to her hometown of Grand Rapids, Michigan, and later founded the law firm of Buchanan & Beckering, P.L.C. She received her undergraduate degree, with distinction from the University of Michigan and her law degree, *cum laude* from the University of Wisconsin. Judge Beckering is a member of the Michigan Supreme Court Committee on Model Civil Jury Instructions and the Steering Committee for the Hillman Trial Advocacy Program. She is also co-editor of *Michigan Civil Procedure*, published by the Institute of Continuing Legal Education.

JUDGE
MARK T. BOONSTRA

Term expires January 1, 2021

Judge Boonstra was appointed to the Michigan Court of Appeals in March 2012, and subsequently was elected in 2012 and 2014. In addition to his appellate duties, Judge Boonstra began serving a 2-year term on the Michigan Court of Claims, by appointment of the Michigan Supreme Court, effective May 1, 2015. Before joining the Court of Appeals, Judge Boonstra was a senior principal in the law firm of Miller, Canfield, Paddock and Stone, P.L.C., where he practiced law for 27 years, including serving as a deputy chair of the firm's Litigation Practice Group and as co-chair of its Appellate Practice Section. At the time of his appointment, Judge Boonstra was recognized in *Best Lawyers in America* in the areas of Antitrust Law, Appellate Practice, Bet-the-Company Litigation, Commercial Litigation, Litigation — Antitrust, Litigation — First Amendment, and Litigation — Securities. He also served as a law clerk to the Honorable Ralph B. Guy Jr., of the United States District Court for the Eastern District of Michigan.

Judge Boonstra holds degrees from both Michigan State University, where he graduated Phi Beta Kappa with a bachelor's degree in Political Science, and the University of Michigan, where he graduated with both a juris doctor degree and a master of applied economics degree.

In addition to serving many community and civic organizations, Judge Boonstra has been active in the State Bar of Michigan — including serving in the Representative Assembly, 2005 to 2011 and as chair of the Antitrust, Franchising, and Trade Regulation Section, 2000 to 2001 — as well as the Federal Bar Association and various local bar associations, including as a founding member of the Washtenaw American Inn of Court, 2011. He currently serves as chair of the State of Michigan Supreme Court Committee on the Model Civil Jury Instructions and as vice chair of the State of Michigan Retirement Board. He has been an author of, or contributor to, a number of legal publications and presentations.

JUDGE
JANE E. MARKEY

Term expires January 1, 2021

Judge Markey was elected to the Court in 1994 and reelected in 2002, 2008 and 2014. Judge Markey received her B.A., with high honors in Spanish/Secondary Education, from Michigan

State University and her law degree, *cum laude*, from Thomas M. Cooley Law School. She served as the first Editor-in-Chief of Thomas M. Cooley Law School.

Judge Markey began her legal career as a prehearing attorney/law clerk for the Michigan Court of Appeals. She then entered private practice with the law firms of Baxter & Hammond and then Dykema Gossett, specializing in civil litigation.

She was elected to the 61st District Court serving the City of Grand Rapids in 1990 and reelected in 1992. Judge Markey is a member of the State Bar of Michigan and the Western Michigan University/TMC Board of Directors and Executive Committee, 1995 to present. She has previously served on the State Bar Grievance Committee, 1990 to 1992 and as a hearing panelist for the State of Michigan Attorney Discipline Board, 1989 to 1995, the Academic Advisory Committee for District Court, 1993 to 1995 and currently is assigned to the Quality Review, Personnel, and ACE Award Committees for the Court of Appeals.

Judge Markey is also a long-time member of the board of directors for Alternative Directions and has served as a speaker/faculty member for numerous entities, including the National Institute of Trial Advocacy, the Hillman Advocacy Program U.S. District Court, Western District, Michigan Judicial Institute, Institute of Continuing Legal Education, the Lawyers' Show, National Conference of Law Review Boards, Appellate Bench Bar Conferences and graduation commencement speaker for WMU/TMC. In 2012, Judge Markey was selected One of West Michigan's 50 Most Influential Women.

JUDGE
JAMES ROBERT REDFORD

Term expires January 1, 2021

Judge Redford was appointed to the Court of Appeals in 2018. Prior to his appointment, he was the Director of the Michigan Veterans Affairs Agency and previously served as Governor Rick Snyder's Chief Legal Counsel from January 2015 until February 2016.

Judge Redford was a Kent County Circuit Judge from 2003 until 2015. Prior to his election to the trial bench, he was in private practice with Plunkett Cooney and served as an Assistant United States Attorney in the U.S. Attorney's Office for the Western District of Michigan and on active duty in the United States Navy Judge Advocate General's Corps for five years. In addition to his active duty military service, he served in the Navy Reserves for 23 years in a variety of assignments including commanding officer of the Navy Reserve Trial Judiciary and five years as a trial judge in the Navy-Marine Corps Trial Judiciary. Judge Redford transferred to the retired – reserve list in August 2012 at the rank of Captain.

Judge Redford has been active in many Bar and community organizations. He has served on and been chair of the Michigan Supreme Court Model Civil Jury Instructions Committee. He is a lifelong member of the Boy Scouts of America. He has also served on several non-profit boards including the Boy Scouts of America, Gerald R. Ford Council and the West Michigan Shores Council of the Girl Scouts of America.

Judge Redford received his Bachelor of Science in Business Administration from John Carroll University in Cleveland, Ohio in 1982 and his juris doctor from the University of Detroit School of Law in 1985.

JUDGE
DAVID H. SAWYER

Term expires January 1, 2023

The Honorable David H. Sawyer was elected to the Court of Appeals in 1986. He was elected to the Judicial Tenure Commission by his fellow Court of Appeals judges for a term that began January 1, 2010. He has served as the commission's chairperson, vice-chairperson, and secretary. Judge Sawyer currently serves on the State of Michigan Retirement Board. He served as Chief Judge Pro Tem of the Michigan Court of Appeals from November 2009 through December 2014. Before being elected to the bench, he was the Kent County Prosecuting Attorney from 1977 to 1987. Judge Sawyer is a past president of the Michigan Prosecuting Attorneys Association. He received his bachelor of science degree from the University of Arizona in 1970 and received his law degree from Valparaiso University School of Law in 1973.

JUDGE
DOUGLAS B. SHAPIRO

Term expires January 1, 2025

Judge Shapiro was appointed to the Court in 2009. Before taking the bench, Judge Shapiro was a partner in the law firm of Muth and Shapiro, P.C., where he practiced civil litigation in both trial and appellate courts for 17 years. Earlier in his career he served as an assistant defender with the state Appellate Defender Office, focusing on criminal appeals. He began his career as a law clerk to state Supreme Court Justice James H. Brickley. Judge Shapiro received his undergraduate degree in history from the University of Michigan in 1983 and his law degree from the University of Michigan Law School in 1986.

Fourth District Judges

JUDGE
STEPHEN L. BORRELLO

Term expires January 1, 2025

Judge Borrello was appointed to the Court of Appeals in 2003, elected in 2004, and reelected in 2006 and 2012. He served as an attorney and partner with the law firm Gilbert, Smith & Borrello, P.C., in Saginaw, Michigan. Judge Borrello also served as an assistant prosecuting attorney from 1988 to 1990 in Saginaw County. He earned his B.A. from Albion College and his J.D. from the Detroit College of Law. He is currently an adjunct professor in the Department of Criminal Justice at Saginaw Valley State University where he teaches Criminal Procedure and Evidence.

JUDGE
MICHAEL F. GADOLA

Term expires January 1, 2023

Judge Gadola received a bachelor's degree from Michigan State University's James Madison College in 1985 and a juris doctor degree with honors from the Wayne State University Law School in 1990. He worked as deputy legal counsel and then as director of the Office of Regulatory Reform for Governor John M. Engler. He then worked at the Dickinson Wright law firm in Lansing, having previously worked for the firm in its Detroit office. He returned to work for Governor Engler as deputy legal counsel and counsel for the executive organization. He went on to serve as house majority counsel in the Michigan Legislature and as Michigan Supreme Court Counsel. He then served as legal counsel to Governor Rick Snyder. In December 2014, Governor Rick Snyder appointed him to fill a vacancy on the Michigan Court of Appeals in the fourth district, effective January 5, 2015.

JUDGE
MICHAEL J. KELLY

Term expires January 1, 2021

Judge Kelly was elected to the Court of Appeals in 2008. After serving as a judicial advisory assistant to a circuit court judge, he worked as a trial lawyer in private practice for 20 years. He attended Michigan State University and earned his B.A. from the University of Michigan – Flint in 1984. Following his enrollment at the Detroit College of Law, he was accepted as a participant in the London Law Program at Regents College in London, England in 1987 and received his juris doctor from the Detroit College of Law in 1988.

JUDGE
AMY RONAYNE KRAUSE

Term expires January 1, 2021

Judge Amy Ronayne Krause was appointed to the Court of Appeals in November of 2010. Previously, she served as a judge on the 54-A District Court in Lansing for nearly eight years. Judge Ronayne Krause received her bachelor of arts from the University of Michigan and her juris doctor from the University of Notre Dame.

Judge Ronayne Krause began her legal career as a litigation attorney for a private law firm and then served eight years as an assistant prosecuting attorney. In 1997, she was appointed an assistant attorney general by then Attorney General Frank J. Kelley and was the first recipient of the Frank J. Kelley Award for Excellence in Trial Advocacy. Judge Ronayne Krause worked for the attorney general's office for six years. Prior to taking the bench, Judge Ronayne Krause was elected to serve on the Ingham County Board of Commissioners, during which time she chaired the Law and Courts committee. She is an adjunct professor for the Thomas M. Cooley Law School and has lectured for the Prosecuting Attorney Association of Michigan. She has also taught for the Michigan Judicial Institute, including teaching other district judges at the New Judges Seminar in 2007 and 2009. Judge Ronayne Krause has also served as faculty for the National Council of Juvenile and Family Court Judges, training other judges on a national level.

In September 2007, Judge Ronayne Krause was recognized statewide for her outstanding work with the State Bar of Michigan's Champion of Justice Award. She has previously served her community as a board member with the Lansing Educational Advancement Foundation and the Uplift Our Youth Foundation. Currently, she serves on the American Red Cross board of directors for the Great Lakes Region. Judge Ronayne Krause was appointed in 2011 by the Speaker of the House and the Senate Majority Leader to the State Drug Treatment Court Advisory Committee and in 2013 became chair of the committee.

Judge Ronayne Krause and her husband, Kurt E. Krause, live in the mid-Michigan area.

JUDGE
PATRICK M. METER

Term expires January 1, 2021

Judge Meter was appointed to the Court of Appeals in 1999. Previously, he served as a judge of the Saginaw Circuit Court, and he worked as a prosecuting attorney for Saginaw County and as an attorney in private practice. Judge Meter received his bachelor's and law degrees from the University of Notre Dame. He serves as a lecturer at Notre Dame Law School's Advanced Trial Advocacy Program.

JUDGE
BROCK A. SWARTZLE

Term expires January 1, 2023

Judge Brock A. Swartzle was appointed to the court in 2017. Prior to joining the bench, Judge Swartzle was chief of staff for the Speaker of the Michigan House of Representatives, as well as general counsel for the House. Judge Swartzle was previously a litigation partner with Honigman Miller Schwartz and Cohn LLP, and he also clerked for three years in the Eastern District of Michigan and the Western District of Michigan, as well as four years with the Honorable David W. McKeague on the U.S. Court of Appeals for the Sixth Circuit.

Judge Swartzle has authored numerous legal articles as well as co-authored a chapter in the Practitioner Treatise, *Business and Commercial Litigation in Federal Courts.* Judge Swartzle received his B.S. with distinction from the University of Michigan and his J.D. with honors from George Mason University School of Law, where he served on the George Mason Law Review Board of Editors.

MICHIGAN TRIAL COURTS

www.courts.mi.gov/courts/trialcourts/pages/default.aspx

Circuit Court

The history of the circuit court dates back to 1824 when three judges of the Supreme Court held annual terms in the counties of Wayne, Monroe, Oakland, Macomb, and St. Clair and were authorized to hold special sessions in Crawford, Brown, and Michilimackinac counties. In 1835, circuit courts were established by name, but were presided over by the judges of the Supreme Court.

The county courts in all of the counties of the territory east of Lake Michigan, except Wayne, were abolished in 1833 and replaced by "The circuit court of the territory of Michigan." The state was divided into three circuits in 1836 and the judges of the supreme court performed the duties of circuit judges. The Revised Statutes of 1846 abolished the court of chancery, and the chancery powers were conferred upon the several circuit courts. The Constitution of 1850 made the office of circuit judge elective and the term of office six years.

The Constitution of 1908 provided for judicial circuits. At present, the state is divided into 57 judicial circuits along county lines. The number of judges within a circuit is established by the Legislature to accommodate required judicial activity. In multicounty circuits, judges travel from one county to another to hold court sessions. Circuit judges are elected for terms of six years in nonpartisan elections. A candidate must be a qualified elector, a resident of the judicial circuit, a lawyer, and under 70 years of age. The Legislature sets salaries for circuit judges, which may be supplemented by counties.

The circuit court is referred to as the trial court of general jurisdiction in Michigan because of its very broad powers. Circuit court has jurisdiction over all actions except those given by state law to another court. Generally speaking, circuit court has original jurisdiction in all civil cases involving more than $25,000; in all criminal cases where the offense involves a felony or certain serious misdemeanors; and in all family cases and domestic relations cases such as divorce, paternity actions, juvenile proceedings, and adoptions.

The **Family Division** is a division of circuit court. The Family Division has exclusive jurisdiction over all family matters such as divorce, custody, parenting time, support, paternity, adoptions, name changes, juvenile proceedings, emancipation of minors, parental consent, and personal protection proceedings. The Family Division also has ancillary jurisdiction over cases involving guardianships and conservatorships and proceedings involving the mentally ill or developmentally disabled.

The **Court of Claims** is a court of statewide, limited jurisdiction established to hear and determine all civil actions filed against the State of Michigan and its agencies. The Court of Claims is located in the Michigan Court of Appeals. Four Court of Appeals judges, including a chief judge, are assigned to the Court of Claims by the Michigan Supreme Court. Each Court of Claims case is heard by a single judge. The Court of Claims operates much like any other Michigan circuit court. In the Court of Claims, however, there is no right to a jury trial.

Probate Court

In 1818, the court of probate was established in each county, the members of which were appointed by the Governor, and from which appeals might be taken to the supreme court. These courts continued in operation until Michigan became a state. The Revised Statutes of 1838 made the office of Judge of Probate elective and the term of office four years. The Constitution of 1850 provided for a probate court in each county, and the Constitution of 1963 expanded the term of office to six years.

The probate court has jurisdiction over cases that involve the admission of wills, administration of estates and trusts, guardianships, conservatorships, and the treatment of mentally ill and developmentally disabled persons.

Each county has its own probate court, with the exception of ten northern counties that have consolidated to form five probate court districts. Each of those probate court districts has one judge. Other probate courts have one or more judges. Probate judges are elected to 6-year terms on a nonpartisan ballot, subject to the same requirements as other judges. The Legislature sets probate judges' salaries.

District Court

District courts were created by Public Act 154 of 1968, to commence functioning January 1, 1969. These courts replaced justice of the peace courts and circuit court commissioners, as mandated by the

Constitution of 1963. The act also abolished municipal and police courts, but contained provisions allowing certain municipalities to retain their municipal courts. Four municipal courts still exist.

The district court is often referred to as "The People's Court," because the public has more contact with the district court than with any other court in the state and because many people go to district court without an attorney.

The district court has exclusive jurisdiction over most traffic violations, civil cases where the amount in controversy does not exceed $25,000, landlord-tenant and land contract matters, and civil infractions. The court may also conduct marriages in a civil ceremony.

The district court's small claims division handles cases in which the amount in controversy is $3,000 or less. Small claims litigants represent themselves; they waive their right to be represented by an attorney, as well as the right to a jury trial. They also waive evidence rules and any right to appeal the district judge's decision. If either party objects, the case is heard in the court's general civil division, where the parties retain these rights. If a district court attorney magistrate enters the judgment, the decision may be appealed to the district judge.

District courts handle a wide range of criminal proceedings, including misdemeanors, offenses for which the maximum possible penalty does not exceed one year in jail. In misdemeanor cases, the district court judge arraigns the defendant, sets and accepts bail, presides at the trial, and sentences the defendant. Typical district court misdemeanor offenses include driving under the influence of intoxicants, driving on a suspended license, assault, shoplifting, and possession of marijuana. The district courts also conduct preliminary examinations in felony cases, after which, if the prosecutor provides sufficient proofs, the felony case is transferred to the circuit court for arraignment and trial. The district courts also handle extraditions to another state for a pending criminal charge, coroner inquests, and issuance of search warrants. The court may appoint an attorney for persons who cannot afford a lawyer and may go to jail if convicted.

District judges are elected to 6-year terms on a nonpartisan ballot, subject to the same requirements as other judges. The Legislature sets district judges' salaries.

Municipal Courts

Municipal courts were organized subject to Public Act 5 of 1956, although most were established under either Public Act 279 of 1909 or Public Act 269 of 1933. The District Court Act of 1968 abolished most of the municipal courts, but permitted some municipalities to retain their courts. Four municipal courts remain: Grosse Pointe, Grosse Pointe Farms, Grosse Pointe Park, and Grosse Pointe Woods, all in Wayne County.

The municipal courts have jurisdiction over most traffic violations, civil cases where the amount in controversy does not exceed $3,000, landlord-tenant matters, and civil infractions. Municipal courts' jurisdiction in criminal proceedings includes handling misdemeanors and conducting preliminary examinations in felony cases.

Municipal judges are elected to 4-year terms and are paid by the municipalities. Candidates must be lawyers, qualified electors, and residents of their municipalities.

CIRCUIT COURT — JUDICIAL CIRCUITS

(Pursuant to Public Act 236 of 1961, Chapter 5)

County	Population in 2010	County	Population in 2010
1st Circuit		**17th Circuit**	
Hillsdale	46,688	Kent	602,622
2nd Circuit		**18th Circuit**	
Berrien	156,813	Bay	107,771
3rd Circuit		**19th Circuit**	
Wayne	1,820,584	Benzie	17,525
		Manistee	24,733
4th Circuit		Total	42,258
Jackson	160,248		
		20th Circuit	
5th Circuit		Ottawa	263,801
Barry	59,173		
		21st Circuit	
6th Circuit		Isabella	70,311
Oakland	1,202,362		
		22nd Circuit	
7th Circuit		Washtenaw	344,791
Genesee	425,790		
		23rd Circuit	
8th Circuit		Alcona	10,942
Ionia	63,905	Arenac	15,899
Montcalm	63,342	Iosco	25,887
Total	127,427	Oscoda	8,640
		Total	61,368
9th Circuit			
Kalamazoo	250,331	**24th Circuit**	
		Sanilac	43,114
10th Circuit			
Saginaw	200,169	**25th Circuit**	
		Marquette	67,077
11th Circuit			
Alger	9,601	**26th Circuit**	
Luce	6,631	Alpena	29,598
Mackinac	11,113	Montmorency	9,765
Schoolcraft	8,485	Total	39,363
Total	35,830		
		27th Circuit	
12th Circuit		Newaygo	48,460
Baraga	8,860	Oceana	26,570
Houghton	36,628	Total	75,030
Keweenaw	2,156		
Total	47,644	**28th Circuit**	
		Missaukee	14,849
13th Circuit		Wexford	32,735
Antrim	23,580	Total	47,584
Grand Traverse	86,986		
Leelanau	21,708	**29th Circuit**	
Total	132,274	Clinton	75,382
		Gratiot	42,476
14th Circuit		Total	117,858
Muskegon	172,188		
		30th Circuit	
15th Circuit		Ingham	280,895
Branch	45,248		
		31st Circuit	
16th Circuit		St. Clair	163,040
Macomb	840,978		

County	Population in 2010	County	Population in 2010
32nd Circuit		**46th Circuit**	
Gogebic	16,427	Crawford	14,074
Ontonagon	6,780	Kalkaska	17,153
Total	23,207	Otsego	24,164
		Total	55,391
33rd Circuit			
Charlevoix	25,949	**47th Circuit**	
		Delta	37,069
34th Circuit			
Ogemaw	21,699	**48th Circuit**	
Roscommon	24,449	Allegan	111,408
Total	46,148		
		49th Circuit	
35th Circuit		Mecosta	42,798
Shiawassee	70,648	Osceola	23,528
		Total	66,326
36th Circuit			
Van Buren	76,258	**50th Circuit**	
		Chippewa	38,520
37th Circuit			
Calhoun	136,146	**51st Circuit**	
		Lake	11,539
38th Circuit		Mason	28,705
Monroe	152,021	Total	40,244
39th Circuit		**52nd Circuit**	
Lenawee	99,892	Huron	33,118
40th Circuit		**53rd Circuit**	
Lapeer	88,319	Cheboygan	26,152
		Presque Isle	13,376
41st Circuit		Total	39,528
Dickinson	26,168		
Iron	11,817	**54th Circuit**	
Menominee	24,029	Tuscola	55,729
Total	62,014		
		55th Circuit	
42nd Circuit		Clare	30,926
Midland	83,629	Gladwin	25,692
		Total	56,618
43rd Circuit			
Cass	52,293	**56th Circuit**	
		Eaton	107,759
44th Circuit			
Livingston	180,967	**57th Circuit**	
		Emmet	32,694
45th Circuit			
St. Joseph	61,295		

CIRCUIT COURT — JUDICIAL CIRCUITS

Constitution of Michigan of 1963, Article VI, Sec. 11

"The state shall be divided into judicial circuits along county lines in each of which there shall be elected one or more circuit judges as provided by law. Sessions of the circuit court shall be held at least four times in each year in every county organized for judicial purposes. Each circuit judge shall hold court in the county or counties within the circuit in which he is elected, and in other circuits as may be provided by rules of the supreme court. The number of judges may be changed and circuits may be created, altered and discontinued by law and the number of judges shall be changed and circuits shall be created, altered and discontinued on recommendation of the supreme court to reflect changes in judicial activity. No change in the number of judges or alteration or discontinuance of a circuit shall have the effect of removing a judge from office during his term."

2019 Courts and Judgeships

LEGEND	TOTALS
# - Circuit Court	217 - Judgeships
(#) - Number of Circuit Court Judgeships	57 - Number of Judicial Circuits

JUDGES OF THE CIRCUIT COURT

Circuit	County	Judge	Circuit	County	Judge
1	Hillsdale	Michael R. Smith	6	Oakland	James M. Alexander
					Martha Anderson
2	Berrien	Donna B. Howard			Leo Bowman
		Charles T. LaSata			Mary Ellen Brennan
		Angela M. Pasula			Rae Lee Chabot
		Jennifer L. Smith			Jacob James Cunningham
					Lisa Ortlieb Gorcyca
3	Wayne	David J. Allen			Nanci J. Grant
		Mariam Bazzi			Hala Y. Jarbou
		Annette J. Berry			Shalina D. Kumar
		Gregory D. Bill			Denise Langford-Morris
		Ulysses W. Boykin			Lisa Langton
		Karen Y. Braxton			Jeffery S. Matis
		Jerome C. Cavanagh			Cheryl A. Matthews
		Eric William Cholack			Julie A. McDonald
		James R. Chylinski			Karen D. McDonald
		Kevin J. Cox			Phyllis C. McMillen
		Melissa Anne Cox			Daniel Patrick O'Brien
		Paul John Cusick			Victoria Ann Valentine
		Christopher D. Dingell			Michael D. Warren Jr.
		Prentis Edwards Jr.	7	Genesee	Duncan M. Beagle
		Charlene M. Elder			Celeste D. Bell
		Vonda R. Evans			Joseph J. Farah
		Wanda A. Evans			John A. Gadola
		Edward Ewell Jr.			Elizabeth Anne Kelly
		Patricia Susan Fresard			David J. Newblatt
		Sheila Ann Gibson			Michael J. Theile
		John H. Gillis Jr.			Richard B. Yuille
		Alexis A. Glendening	8	Montcalm	Suzanne Kreeger
		Tracy E. Green		Ionia	Ronald J. Schafer
		David Alan Groner	9	Kalamazoo	Paul J. Bridenstine
		Adel A. Harb			Gary C. Giguere Jr.
		Bridget Mary Hathaway			Stephen D. Gorsalitz
		Cynthia Gray Hathaway			Pamela L. Lightvoet
		Dana Margaret Hathaway			Alexander C. Lipsey
		Daniel Arthur Hathaway	10	Saginaw	Janet M. Boes
		Thomas M.J. Hathaway			James T. Borchard
		Charles S. Hegarty			André R. Borrello
		Catherine L. Heise			Darnell Jackson
		Susan L. Hubbard			Manvel Trice III
		Muriel Diane Hughes	11	Alger	William W. Carmody
		Edward Joseph		Luce	
		Timothy Michael Kenny		Mackinac	
		Donald Knapp		Schoolcraft	
		Qiana Denise Lillard	12	Baraga	Charles R. Goodman
		Kathleen M. McCarthy		Houghton	
		Cylenthia LaToye Miller		Keweenaw	
		Bruce Underwood Morrow	13	Gd. Traverse	Kevin A. Elsenheimer
		John A. Murphy		Antrim	Thomas G. Power
		Lynne A. Pierce		Leelanau	
		Lita Masini Popke	14	Muskegon	Timothy G. Hicks
		Kelly Anne Ramsey			Kathy L. Hoogstra
		Mark T. Slavens			William C. Marietti
		Leslie Kim Smith			Annette Rose Smedley
		Martha M. Snow	15	Branch	Patrick W. O'Grady
		Craig S. Strong	16	Macomb	James M. Biernat Jr.
		Brian R. Sullivan			Richard L. Caretti
		Lawrence S. Talon			Diane M. Druzinski
		Carla Testani			Jennifer Faunce
		Deborah A. Thomas			Julie Lynn Gatti
		Regina Daniels Thomas			James M. Maceroni
		Margaret M. VanHouten			Carl J. Marlinga
		Shannon N. Walker			Racheal Rancilio
4	Jackson	Susan Esther Beebe Jordan			Edward A. Servitto Jr.
		Richard N. LaFlamme			Michael E. Servitto
		John G. McBain Jr.			Mark S. Switalski
		Thomas D. Wilson			Matthew S. Switalski
					Joseph Toia
5	Barry	Amy McDowell			Kathryn A. Viviano
					Tracey A. Yokich

Circuit	County	Judge
17	Kent	Curt A. Benson Paul J. Denenfeld Christina Elmore Kathleen A. Feeney Deborah L. McNabb Geroge Jay Quist J. Joseph Rossi Paul J. Sullivan Mark A. Trusock Christopher P. Yates Daniel V. Zemaitis
18	Bay	Harry P. Gill Joseph K. Sheeran
19	Benzie Manistee	David A. Thompson
20	Ottawa	Kent D. Engle Jon H. Hulsing Karen Jongekrijg Miedema Jon A. Van Allsburg
21	Isabella	Mark H. Duthie Sara Spencer-Noggle
22	Washtenaw	Archie Cameron Brown Patrick J. Conlin Jr. Timothy Patrick Connors Carol Anne Kuhnke David S. Swartz
23	Alcona Arenac Iosco Oscoda	David C. Riffel
24	Sanilac	Donald A. Teeple
25	Marquette	Jennifer Mazzuchi
26	Alpena Montmorency	Michael G. Mack
27	Newaygo Oceana	Robert D. Springstead
28	Missaukee Wexford	William M. Fagerman
29	Clinton Gratiot	Michelle M. Rick Randy L. Tahvonen
30	Ingham	Rosemarie E. Aquilina Laura L. Baird Clinton Canady III Joyce A. Draganchuk James S. Jamo Janelle A. Lawless Wanda M. Stokes
31	St. Clair	Daniel J. Kelly Cynthia A. Lane Michael L. West
32	Gogebic Ontonagon	Michael K. Pope
33	Charlevoix	Roy C. Hayes III

Circuit	County	Judge
34	Ogemaw Roscommon	Robert W. Bennett
35	Shiawassee	Matthew J. Stewart
36	Van Buren	Kathleen M. Brickley Jeffrey J. Dufon
37	Calhoun	John A. Hallacy Tina Yost Johnson Brian K. Kirkham Sarah Soules Lincoln
38	Monroe	Mark S. Braunlich Michael A. Weipert Daniel White
39	Lenawee	Anna Marie Anzalone
40	Lapeer	Nick O. Holowka Byron J. Konschuh
41	Dickinson Iron Menominee	Mary Brouillette Barglind Christopher S. Ninomiya
42	Midland	Michael J. Beale Stephen P. Carras
43	Cass	Mark A. Herman
44	Livingston	L. Suzanne Geddis Michael P. Hatty David J. Reader
45	St. Joseph	Paul E. Stutesman
46	Crawford Kalkaska Otsego	Colin G. Hunter George J. Mertz
47	Delta	John B. Economopoulos
48	Allegan	Margaret Bakker Roberts Kengis
49	Mecosta Osceola	Kimberly L. Booher Scott P. Hill-Kennedy
50	Chippewa	Nicholas J. Lambros
51	Lake Mason	Susan K. Sniegowski
52	Huron	Gerald M. Prill
53	Cheboygan Presque Isle	Aaron J. Gauthier
54	Tuscola	Amy Grace Gierhart
55	Clare Gladwin	Thomas R. Evans Roy G. Mienk
56	Eaton	Janice K. Cunningham John Douglas Maurer
57	Emmet	Charles W. Johnson

MICHIGAN PROBATE COURTS
AND PROBATE COURT DISTRICTS

**Constitution of Michigan of 1963,
Article VI, Sec. 15**

"In each county organized for judicial
purposes there shall be a probate court.
The legislature may create or alter probate
court districts of more than one county
if approved in each affected county by
a majority of the electors voting on the
question . . ."

2019 Courts and Judgeships

LEGEND	TOTALS
⊕ - Probate Court Districts	103 - Judgeships
(#) - Number of Probate Court Judgeships	78 - Number of Probate Courts

JUDGES OF THE PROBATE COURT

County	Judge of Probate	County	Judge of Probate
Alcona	Laura A. Frawley	Lenawee	Catherine Ann Sala
Alger, Schoolcraft	Charles C. Nebel	Livingston	Miriam Cavanaugh
Allegan	Michael L. Buck	Luce, Mackinac	W. Clayton Graham
Alpena	Thomas J. LaCross	Macomb	Kathryn A. George
Antrim	Norman R. Hayes		Sandra A. Harrison
Arenac	Richard E. Vollbach Jr.	Manistee	Thomas N. Brunner
Baraga	Timothy S. Brennan	Marquette	Cheryl L. Hill
Barry	William M. Doherty	Mason	Jeffrey C. Nellis
Bay	Jan A. Miner	Mecosta, Osceola	Tyler O. Thompson
Benzie	John Mead	Menominee	Daniel E. Hass
Berrien	Brian Berger	Midland	Dorene S. Allen
	Mabel Johnson Mayfield	Missaukee	Melissa J. Ransom
Branch	Kirk A. Kashian	Monroe	Frank L. Arnold
Calhoun	Michael L. Jaconette		Cheryl Lohmeyer
Cass	Susan L. Dobrich	Montcalm	Charles W. Simon III
Charlevoix, Emmet	Valerie Snyder	Montmorency	Benjamin T. Bolser
Cheboygan	Daryl Patrick Vizina	Muskegon	Gregory Christopher Pittman
Chippewa	Eric Blubaugh		Brenda E. Sprader
Clare, Gladwin	Marcy A. Klaus	Newaygo	Melissa K. Dykman
Clinton	Lisa Sullivan	Oakland	Jennifer S. Callaghan
Crawford	Monte Burmeister		Linda S. Hallmark
Delta	Perry R. Lund		Daniel A. O'Brien
Dickinson	Thomas D. Slagle		Kathleen A. Ryan
Eaton	Thomas K. Byerley	Oceana	Bradley G. Lambrix
Emmet, Charlevoix	Valerie Snyder	Ogemaw	Shana A. Lambourn
Genesee	Jennie E. Barkey	Ontonagon	Janis M. Burgess
	F. Kay Behm	Osceola, Mecosta	Tyler O. Thompson
Gladwin, Clare	Marcy A. Klaus	Oscoda	Casandra L. Morse-Bills
Gogebic	Anna Rose Talaska	Otsego	Michael K. Cooper
Grand Traverse	Melanie Stanton	Ottawa	Mark A. Feyen
Gratiot	Kristin M. Bakker	Presque Isle	Erik J. Stone
Hillsdale	Michelle Snell Bianchi	Roscommon	Mark Jernigan
Houghton	Fraser T. Strome	Saginaw	Patrick J. McGraw
Huron	David L. Clabuesch		Barbara L. Meter
	David B. Herrington	St. Clair	Elwood L. Brown
Ingham	Shauna Dunnings		John Tomlinson
	Richard Joseph Garcia	St. Joseph	David C. Tomlinson
Ionia	Robert S. Sykes Jr.	Sanilac	Gregory S. Ross
Iosco	Christopher P. Martin	Schoolcraft, Alger	Charles C. Nebel
Iron	Donald S. Powell	Shiawassee	Thomas J. Dignan
Isabella	Stuart Black	Tuscola	Nancy Thane
Jackson	Diane M. Rappleye	Van Buren	David DiStefano
Kalamazoo	Tiffany Ankley	Washtenaw	Darlene A. O'Brien
	Curtis J. Bell		Julia B. Owdziej
	G. Scott Pierangeli	Wayne	David Braxton
Kalkaska	Lynne Marie Buday		Freddie G. Burton Jr.
Kent	Terence Ackert		Judy A. Hartsfield
	Patricia D. Gardner		Terrance A. Keith
	G. Patrick Hillary		Lisa Marie Neilson
	David M. Murkowski		Lawrence Paolucci
Keweenaw	Keith Warren DeForge		David Perkins
Lake	Mark S. Wickens		Frank S. Szymanski
Lapeer	Justus C. Scott	Wexford	Edward Van Alst
Leelanau	Marian F. Kromkowski		

DISTRICT COURT — JUDICIAL DISTRICTS

Act 236 of 1961, Sec. 8101(1)

"A district court is established in the state. The district court is a court of record. The state is divided into judicial districts of the district court each of which is an administrative unit subject to the superintending control of the supreme court."

Unnumbered counties are
shown in detail on the following pages.

2019 Courts and Judgeships

LEGEND	TOTALS
# - District Court	235 - Judgeships
(#) - Number of District Court Judgeships*	103 - Number of District Courts

*In a few counties, the probate judge also serves as the district court judge. Those district courts are listed as having no judges.

JUDGES OF THE DISTRICT COURT

District	Geographical Area	Judge
1	Monroe County	Michael C. Brown William Paul Nichols Jack Vitale
2A	Lenawee County	Jonathan L. Poer Laura S. Schaedler
2B	Hillsdale County	Sara S. Lisznyai
3A	Branch County	Brent R. Weigle
3B	St. Joseph County	Jeffrey C. Middleton Robert Pattison
4	Cass County	Stacey A. Rentfrow
5	Berrien County	Gary J. Bruce Arthur J. Cotter Gordan Gary Hosbein Sterling R. Schrock Dennis M. Wiley
7	Van Buren County	Arthur H. Clarke III Michael T. McKay
8	Kalamazoo County	Anne E. Blatchford Christopher Haenicke Kathleen P. Hemingway Julie K. Phillips Richard A. Santoni Vincent C. Westra
10	Calhoun County & the City of Battle Creek	Paul K. Beardslee Jason C. Bomia Franklin K. Line Jr. Tracie L. Tomak
12	Jackson County	Joseph S. Filip Daniel A. Goostrey Michael J. Klaeren R. Darryl Mazur
14A	Washtenaw County, except City of Ann Arbor & Township of Ypsilanti	Richard E. Conlin J. Cedric Simpson Kirk W. Tabbey
14B	Township of Ypsilanti	Charles Pope
15	City of Ann Arbor	Joseph F. Burke Elizabeth Pollard Hines Karen Q. Valvo
16	City of Livonia	Sean P. Kavanagh Kathleen J. McCann
17	Township of Redford	Karen Khalil Krista Licata Haroutunian
18	City of Westland	Sandra A. Cicirelli Mark A. McConnell
19	City of Dearborn	L. Eugene Hunt Jr. Sam A. Salamey Mark W. Somers
20	City of Dearborn Heights	Mark J. Plawecki David Turfe
21	City of Garden City	Richard L. Hammer Jr.
22	City of Inkster	Sabrina L. Johnson
23	City of Taylor	Geno Salomone Joseph D. Slaven
24	Cities of Allen Park & Melvindale	John T. Courtright Richard A. Page
25	Cities of Lincoln Park & Ecorse	Gregory A. Clifton David J. Zelenak

District	Geographical Area	Judge
27	Cities of Wyandotte & Riverview	Elizabeth L. DiSanto
28	City of Southgate	James A. Kandrevas
29	City of Wayne	Laura Redmond Mack
30	City of Highland Park	Brigette R. Officer-Hill
31	City of Hamtramck	Alexis G. Krot
32A	City of Harper Woods	Daniel S. Palmer
33	Cities of Trenton, Gibraltar, Woodhaven, Rockwood & Flat Rock; Townships of Brownstown & Grosse Ile	Jennifer Coleman Hesson James Kurt Kersten Michael K. McNally
34	Cities of Romulus and Belleville; Townships of Sumpter, Van Buren & Huron	Tina Brooks Green Brian A. Oakley David M. Parrott
35	Cities of Northville & Plymouth; Townships of Northville, Plymouth & Canton	Michael J. Gerou Ronald W. Lowe James A. Plakas
36	City of Detroit	Lydia Nance Adams Roberta C. Archer Christopher Michael Blount Nancy McCaughan Blount Demetria Brue Esther L. Bryant-Weekes Donald Coleman Kahlilia Yvette Davis Deborah Geraldine Ford Austin William Garrett Ruth Ann Garrett Ronald Giles Adrienne Hinnant-Johnson Shannon A. Holmes Patricia L. Jefferson Kenyetta Stanford Jones Alicia A. Jones-Coleman Kenneth J. King Deborah L. Langston William McConico Donna Robinson Milhouse B. Pennie Millender Kevin F. Robbins David S. Robinson Jr. Aliyah Sabree Michael E. Wagner Larry D. Williams Jr.
37	Cities of Center Line & Warren	John M. Chmura Michael Chupa Suzanne Faunce Matthew P. Sabaugh
38	City of Eastpointe	Carl F. Gerds III
39	Cities of Roseville & Fraser	Joseph F. Boedeker Kathleen E. Tocco Catherine B. Steenland
40	City of St. Clair Shores	Mark A. Fratarcangeli Joseph Craigen Oster
41A	Cities of Utica & Sterling Heights; Townships of Shelby & Macomb	Annemarie M. Lepore Douglas P. Shepherd Stephen S. Sierawski Kimberley Anne Wiegand

JUDGES OF THE DISTRICT COURT *(Cont.)*

District	Geographical Area	Judge
41B	City of Mt. Clemens; Townships of Clinton & Harrison . . .	Linda Davis Carrie Lynn Fuca Sebastian Lucido
42, Div. 1	Cities of Memphis & Richmond; Townships of Bruce, Washington, Armada, Ray & Richmond	Denis R. LeDuc
Div. 2	City of New Baltimore; Townships of Lenox & Chesterfield.	William H. Hackel III
43	Cities of Madison Heights, Ferndale & Hazel Park	Charles G. Goedert Keith P. Hunt Joseph Longo
44	Cities of Royal Oak & Berkley	Derek W. Meinecke James L. Wittenberg
45	Cities of Huntington Woods, Oak Park & Pleasant Ridge; Township of Royal Oak	Michelle Friedman Appel David M. Gubow
46	Cities of Southfield & Lathrup Village; Township of Southfield	Cynthia Arvant Shelia R. Johnson Debra Nance
47	Cities of Farmington & Farmington Hills.	James Brady Marla E. Parker
48	Cities of Birmingham, Bloomfield Hills, Sylvan Lake, Keego Harbor & Orchard Lake Village; Townships of Bloomfield & West Bloomfield	Marc Barron Diane D'Agostini Kimberly Small
50	City of Pontiac	Ronda Fowlkes Gross Michael C. Martinez Preston G. Thomas Cynthia Thomas Walker
51	Township of Waterford	Todd A. Fox Richard D. Kuhn Jr.
52, Div. 1	Cities of Novi, South Lyon, Wixom & Walled Lake; Townships of Milford, Highland, Commerce, Lyon & Novi.	Robert Bondy Thomas David Law Travis Reeds
Div. 2	City of Clarkston; Townships of Springfield, Independence, Holly, Groveland, Rose, White Lake & Brandon	Joseph G. Fabrizio Kelley Renae Kostin
Div. 3	Cities of Rochester, Auburn Hills, Rochester Hills & Lake Angelus; Townships of Oxford, Addison, Orion & Oakland	Lisa L. Asadoorian Nancy Towlin Carniak Julie A. Nicholson
Div. 4	Cities of Clawson & Troy.	Kirsten Nielsen Hartig Maureen M. McGinnis
53	Livingston County	Daniel B. Bain Shauna Murphy
54A	City of Lansing	Louise Alderson Stacia J. Buchanan Kristen D. Simmons Cynthia M. Ward
54B	City of East Lansing.	Richard D. Ball Andrea Andrews Larkin
55	Ingham County, except Cities of Lansing & East Lansing. .	Donald L. Allen Thomas P. Boyd
56A	Eaton County	Julie O'Neill Julie H. Reincke
56B	Barry County	Michael Lee Schipper
57	Allegan County.	William A. Baillargeon Joseph S. Skocelas

District	Geographical Area	Judge
58	Ottawa County	Craig E. Bunce Susan A. Jonas Bradley S. Knoll Judith K. Mulder
59	Cities of Grandville & Walker	Peter P. Versluis
60	Muskegon County	Harold F. Closz III Maria Ladas Hoopes Raymond J. Kostrzewa Geoffrey Thomas Nolan
61	City of Grand Rapids	Nicholas S. Ayoub David J. Buter Michael J. Distel Jennifer Faber Jeanine Nemesi LaVille Kimberly A. Schaefer
62A	City of Wyoming	Pablo Cortes Steven M. Timmers
62B	City of Kentwood	William G. Kelly
63, Div. 1	Cities of Cedar Springs & Rockford; Townships of Tyrone, Solon, Nelson, Spencer, Sparta, Algoma, Courtland, Oakfield, Alpine, Plainfield, Cannon & Grattan	Jeffrey J. O'Hara
Div. 2	Cities of East Grand Rapids & Lowell; Townships of Grand Rapids, Ada, Vergennes, Cascade, Lowell, Byron, Gaines, Caledonia & Bowne	Sara J. Smolenski
64A	Ionia County	Raymond P. Voet
64B	Montcalm County	Donald R. Hemingsen
65A	Clinton County	Michael E. Clarizio
65B	Gratiot County	Stewart D. McDonald
66	Shiawassee County	Ward L. Clarkson Terrance P. Dignan
67, Div. 1	Cities of Flushing & Clio; Townships of Flushing, Flint, Montrose, Thetford & Vienna	David J. Goggins
Div. 2	Cities of Davison & Burton; Townships of Davison, Forest, Richfield & Atlas	Mark W. Latchana Jennifer J. Manley
Div. 3	City of Mt. Morris; Townships of Mt. Morris & Genesee	Vikki Bayeh Haley
Div. 4	Cities of Fenton, Grand Blanc & Swartz Creek; Townships of Fenton, Argentine, Grand Blanc, Mundy, Gaines & Clayton	Mark C. McCabe Christopher Odette
68	City of Flint	G. David Guinn William H. Crawford II Herman Marable Jr. Nathaniel C. Perry III
70, Div. 1	Cities of Saginaw & Zilwaukee; Townships of Zilwaukee, Buena Vista, Carrollton & Bridgeport	Terry L. Clark M. Randall Jurrens
Div. 2	Saginaw County, except Cities of Saginaw & Zilwaukee, Townships of Zilwaukee, Buena Vista, Carrollton & Bridgeport	Elian Fichtner Alfred T. Frank David D. Hoffman
71A	Lapeer County	Laura Cheger-Barnard
71B	Tuscola County	Jason E. Bitzer
72	St. Clair County	Michael L. Hulewicz John D. Monaghan Cynthia Siemen Platzer
73A*	Sanilac County	None
73B*	Huron County	None

District	Geographical Area	Judge
74	Bay County	Mark E. Janer Timothy J. Kelly Dawn A. Klida
75	Midland County	Michael Carpenter
76	Isabella County	Eric Janes
77	Mecosta & Osceola Counties	Peter Jaklevic
78	Oceana & Newaygo Counties	H. Kevin Drake
79	Mason & Lake Counties	Peter J. Wadel
80	Clare & Gladwin Counties	Joshua M. Farrell
81*	Alcona, Arenac, Iosco & Oscoda Counties	None
82	Ogemaw and Roscommon County	Richard E. Noble
84	Missaukee & Wexford Counties	Audrey D. Van Alst
85*	Benzie & Manistee Counties	None
86	Antrim, Grand Traverse & Leelanau Counties	Robert A. Cooney Michael Stepka
87A*	Otsego County	None
87B*	Kalkaska County	None
87C*	Crawford County	None
88*	Alpena & Montmorency Counties	None
89	Cheboygan & Presque Isle Counties	Maria I. Barton
90	Charlevoix & Emmet Counties	James N. Erhart
91*	Chippewa County	None
92	Luce & Mackinac Counties	Beth Gibson
93	Alger & Schoolcraft Counties	Mark E. Luoma
94	Delta County	Steve Parks
95A	Menominee County	Robert J. Jamo
95B	Dickinson & Iron Counties	Julie Ann LaCost
96	Marquette County	Roger W. Kangas Karl Weber
97	Baraga, Houghton & Keweenaw Counties	Mark A. Wisti
98*	Gogebic & Ontonagon Counties	None

* In a few counties, the probate judge also serves as the district court judge. Those district courts are listed as having no judges.

MUNICIPAL COURTS

Municipal courts are organized subject to Public Act 5 of 1956, although most were first organized under either Public Act 279 of 1909 or Public Act 269 of 1933. They have exclusive original jurisdiction over all ordinance violations, criminal jurisdiction equal to that of district court, and civil jurisdiction of claims limited to $6,000.

The District Court Act of 1968 abolished most of the municipal courts, but permitted some municipalities to retain their courts. Four such municipal courts remain: Grosse Pointe, Grosse Pointe Farms, Grosse Pointe Park, and Grosse Pointe Woods, all in Wayne County.

Municipal judges must be lawyers and residents and electors of their municipalities. They are paid by the municipalities and are elected for four-year terms.

In 2018, 29,343 cases were filed. Almost 30 percent of cases filed are traffic related.

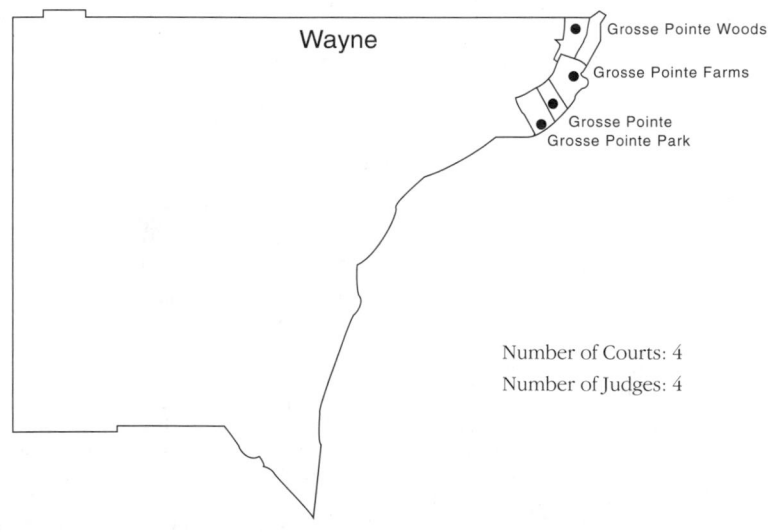

JUDICIAL BRANCH AGENCIES

State Appellate Defender Office

The Michigan Supreme Court established the State Appellate Defender Office (SADO) through a 1969 federal grant award, followed by Administrative Order 1970-1, charging it with providing high-quality and efficient legal representation to indigent criminal defendants in post-conviction matters. In 1979, legislation was enacted to formally establish and fund the office, with mandates to handle no less than 25 percent of statewide appellate assignments, and to provide legal resources to the criminal defense bar. Public Act 620 of 1978 (MCL 780.711 et seq.) created a 7-member Appellate Defender Commission, charged with developing and supervising a coordinated system for providing counsel for all indigent criminal appeals in Michigan.

SADO has offices in Detroit and Lansing providing appellate representation to indigent criminal appellants in all state and appropriate federal courts. Its attorneys routinely obtain corrections to client sentences that produce cost savings for Michigan taxpayers, as well as new trials and exonerations in a smaller percentage of cases. SADO has a comprehensive training program for its staff, and trains law students through clinics or classes offered at all Michigan law schools. Special projects are funded through a variety of federal grants. In recent years, projects have included: (1) a Crime Lab Project providing advocacy for persons adversely affected by the closure of the Detroit Police Crime Lab, (2) a Fast Response for Wrongful Conviction Project that identifies and investigates forensic and evidentiary issues in sufficient time to allow for their development on appeal, and (3) a Social Worker Sentencing Project that uses a social worker/attorney team to seek non-prison and shorter sentences for clients posing little risk to public safety. Community outreach and holistic client support are provided through a variety of special events and materials developed by SADO staff.

SADO's Criminal Defense Resource Center (CDRC) provides support services and training to Michigan's criminal defense community using its portal site, www.sado.org. Services include online databases (pleadings, expert testimony, and more), court opinion summaries, four practice manuals (the Defender Books), technology and sentencing training events throughout the state, an online discussion group, and direct research support for attorneys practicing in Michigan's busiest criminal court, Wayne Circuit Court. The CDRC administers approximately $300,000 in training funds awarded to SADO annually, partnering with the Criminal Defense Attorneys of Michigan, Criminal Advocacy Program of Wayne Circuit Court, and others. Dawn Van Hoek, Director.

Michigan Appellate Assigned Counsel System

Assigned private counsel handle 75 percent of all indigent felony appeals in Michigan. Until the advent of Michigan Appellate Assigned Counsel System (MAACS), there existed no uniform statewide method of qualifying and selecting those attorneys. Each jurisdiction had its own method of appointing appellate counsel and of paying them from county funds. The result was wide disparity in the quality of representation provided.

Public Act 620 of 1978 requires the Appellate Defender Commission to compile and keep current a statewide roster of attorneys eligible for, and willing to accept, appointment as criminal appellate defense counsel and to provide continuing legal education for those attorneys. MAACS is the administrative office that screens the qualifications of attorneys seeking to join the statewide roster, compiles local lists of roster attorneys willing to accept appointments in circuit court, provides training programs and resource materials to roster attorneys, and monitors compliance with the Minimum Standards for Indigent Criminal Appellate Defense Services.

Pursuant to its statutory mandate to develop a comprehensive service delivery system, the Appellate Defender Commission has adopted regulations designed to insure that appellate assignments are fairly distributed among qualified lawyers and that assigned private counsel remain professionally independent. MAACS monitors the process by which appellate counsel are selected in each jurisdiction, the distribution of cases among private counsel, and the allocation of cases between private counsel and SADO. MAACS also provides training programs and other reference materials to the attorneys on its roster. MAACS is located at 200 N. Washington, Suite 250, Lansing, MI 48933. Dawn Van Hoek, Director.

Attorney Discipline Board

The Michigan Attorney Discipline Board was created by the Michigan Supreme Court, effective October 1, 1978, as the adjudicative arm of the Supreme Court for the discharge of the court's constitutional responsibility to supervise and discipline Michigan attorneys.

The Attorney Discipline Board consists of nine members who serve without compensation and who are appointed by the Supreme Court as follows: six lawyers and three public members (nonlawyers), each of whom may serve no more than two 3-year terms.

The role of the board in disciplinary proceedings begins after a grievance has been investigated by the grievance administrator and approved by the Attorney Grievance Commission for the filing of a formal complaint with the board. Grievances against attorneys are confidential during the investigation stage; however, the formal complaint, pleadings, hearing transcript, and orders are a matter of public record. All hearings conducted by the Attorney Discipline Board and its hearing panels are open to the public.

As appointees of the Attorney Discipline Board, approximately 425 Michigan attorneys serve as volunteers on the 3-member panels, which act as the trial level of the board's proceedings. The board may also refer a matter for examination by a special master when a complaint involves specialized questions of fact or is of such complexity or volume that it requires prolonged hearing time or expedited attention.

Proceedings before a hearing panel are governed by the Michigan Court Rules applicable to a civil matter tried without a jury and by the Michigan Rules of Evidence. Special procedural rules apply in cases based upon an attorney's conviction of a crime or an adjudication of professional misconduct in another jurisdiction. In all other disciplinary proceedings, professional misconduct must be established by a preponderance of the evidence. If misconduct is established, the hearing panel must conduct a separate hearing to determine the appropriate level of discipline. A hearing panel may enter orders of probation, reprimand, suspension for a stated period of time (minimum — 30 days), or disbarment. A hearing panel is empowered to order restitution to the attorney's client(s) and must order reimbursement to the State Bar of Michigan of the expenses of the hearing. A separate court rule governs proceedings before a hearing panel based upon a complaint by the grievance administrator to place an attorney on inactive status because of mental or physical incapacity.

A hearing panel's order to dismiss a complaint or to impose discipline becomes a final order unless appealed to the Attorney Discipline Board. Appeals from hearing panel decisions are heard by the full board as a matter of right and are based upon the record before the panel. Appeals from a decision by the board may be pursued only by leave of the Michigan Supreme Court. Appeals may be filed by the grievance administrator, the respondent/attorney, or the original complainant(s).

Attorneys who are found to be physically or mentally unable to continue in the practice of law may be placed on inactive status for an indefinite period; disciplinary complaints against such individuals are held in abeyance during the period of incapacity.

Attorneys suspended for 179 days or less may be automatically reinstated upon the filing of an affidavit of compliance with the order of discipline. In cases of suspension for 180 days or more, the attorney must file a petition for reinstatement, which is followed by a new investigation and establishment by the respondent/attorney of his or her fitness to reenter the practice of law. Attorneys suspended for three years or more must, in addition to reinstatement proceedings, undergo examination and recertification by the State Board of Law Examiners. In Michigan, an attorney who has been disbarred may petition for reinstatement after five years. The office of the board is located in Suite 1410, 211 W. Fort St., Detroit, MI 48226. Mark Armitage, Executive Director.

Further information about the board, including board orders and opinions, notices of discipline and the most recent annual reports may be obtained at www.adbmich.org.

Attorney Grievance Commission

The Michigan Attorney Grievance Commission was created by the Michigan Supreme Court, effective October 1, 1978. Along with the simultaneously created Attorney Discipline Board, the commission succeeded the former State Bar Grievance Board. Pursuant to MCR 9.108(A), the commission is the prosecutorial arm of the supreme court for the discharge of its constitutional responsibility to supervise and discipline Michigan attorneys.

The Attorney Grievance Commission has nine members. Three members are lay persons and six are attorneys, appointed by the Supreme Court.

Pursuant to MCR 9.108(E)(1), the commission has the power and duty to recommend attorneys to the Supreme Court for appointment as grievance administrator and deputy grievance administrator. The grievance administrator serves as executive director and chief prosecutor.

Sub-chapter 9.100 of the Michigan Court Rules governs attorney disciplinary proceedings.

Grievances filed against attorneys are denominated "requests for investigation." Any person may file a request for investigation with the grievance administrator and the grievance administrator may also file a request.

Following the filing of a request for investigation, the grievance administrator must determine whether a prima facie allegation of professional misconduct, i.e., a violation of Michigan Court Rule 9.104, exists. The grievance administrator may reject the request for investigation on its face or after a preliminary investigation, or he or she may conduct a full investigation. If the grievance administrator does not reject the request for investigation, he or she will, upon conclusion of the investigation, recommend to the commission that (1) the matter be closed as there is not evidence of professional misconduct sufficient to sustain the burden of proof at a disciplinary proceeding, or (2) the commission admonish the respondent attorney pursuant to MCR 9.106(6) (this does not constitute discipline), or (3) authorization be granted for the issuance of a formal complaint.

Upon being authorized to file a formal complaint by the commission, the grievance administrator causes a complaint to be prepared and filed with the Attorney Discipline Board. The only exception to this is in the case of criminal convictions, where an order is issued by the board commanding the respondent to show cause why discipline should not be imposed.

Public hearings on charges of misconduct are held before 3-lawyer hearing panels of the Attorney Discipline Board. In the case of a formal complaint, the grievance administrator is required to prove his or her case by a preponderance of the evidence. Upon conclusion of the hearing, if the panel finds that the grievance administrator has failed to prove misconduct alleged in the formal complaint by a preponderance of the evidence, the charge against the respondent must be dismissed. If the panel concludes that misconduct has been proven by a preponderance of the evidence, the panel must enter an order of discipline, which may consist of a reprimand, probation, suspension, or disbarment. Restitution to an aggrieved party may also be required.

Any party may appeal an order of a hearing panel, as a matter of right, to the Attorney Discipline Board, and may seek leave to appeal to the Michigan Supreme Court from an order of the Attorney Discipline Board. The office of the commission is located in Suite 1700, 535 Griswold St., Detroit, MI 48226. Alan Gershel, Grievance Administrator.

Judicial Tenure Commission

Michigan's Judicial Tenure Commission was established in 1968 when voters approved H.J.R. PP, which added Sec. 30 to Article VI of the Michigan Constitution of 1963. The commission serves to promote the integrity of the judicial process and preserve public confidence in the courts by holding judges accountable for their misconduct without jeopardizing or compromising the essential independence of the judiciary. The basis for commission action is a violation of the Code of Judicial Conduct or the Rules of Professional Responsibility. The code is published with the Michigan Court Rules.

On recommendation of the Judicial Tenure Commission, the Michigan Supreme Court may censure, suspend with or without salary, retire, or remove a judge for conviction of a felony, physical or mental disability that prevents the performance of judicial duties, misconduct in office, persistent failure to perform duties, habitual intemperance, or conduct that is clearly prejudicial to the administration of justice. The office is located at Cadillac Place, 3034 W. Grand Blvd., Detroit, MI 48202. Lynn Helland, Executive Director. For more information, see www.jtc.courts.mi.gov.

State Board of Law Examiners

The State Board of Law Examiners, constituted by Public Act 236 of 1961, consists of five active members of the bar, each of whom holds office for five years and one of whom is appointed by the governor on nomination by the Supreme Court on the first day of July each year.

The board has charge of the investigation and examination of all persons who initially apply for admission to the bar of this state. The board offices are located at 4th Floor, Hall of Justice, P.O. Box 30052, Lansing, MI 48909. Maribeth Preston, Executive Director. For more information, see courts.mi.gov/courts/MichiganSupremeCourt/BLE.

STATE COURT ADMINISTRATIVE OFFICE

According to the Michigan Constitution of 1963, Article VI, Section 3, ". . . the supreme court shall appoint an administrator of the courts and other assistants of the supreme court as may be necessary to aid in the administration of the courts of this state. The administrator shall perform administrative duties assigned by the court." Under the general direction of the Supreme Court, the State Court Administrative Office (SCAO) is responsible for assisting in the administration of justice in Michigan's trial courts. The state court administrator is also responsible for advising the Supreme Court, as well as the executive and legislative branches, on matters relating to the management of Michigan's One Court of Justice. For more information on SCAO, go to www.courts.michigan.gov/scao.

The **State Court Administrative Office** (SCAO) provides management assistance and oversight to chief judges and judges of 244 trial courts and their trial court staff on matters relating to trial court management. SCAO collects, analyzes, and publishes management information regarding operations of trial courts. This information is used by the Supreme Court and state court administrator in evaluating the performance of Michigan courts and making decisions regarding their operations. The office provides analyses of legislative and executive branch policy initiatives in terms of their administrative impact on the judiciary. SCAO also assists in the evaluation of court rules and legislation affecting administration of courts, proposes changes to rules and statutes where appropriate, and advises the Supreme Court on administrative matters.

SCAO is comprised of seven divisions: Trial Court Services, Child Welfare Services, Friend of the Court Bureau, Office of Dispute Resolution, Judicial Information Systems, Michigan Judicial Institute, and Regional Administration. Each division has a director responsible for oversight, coordination, improvement efforts, and overall management of each of their respective divisions. Each division director reports directly to the state court administrator.

Trial Court Services is responsible for providing management assistance to courts: administering, participating in, and providing support to a variety of court improvement projects; developing and implementing polices and procedures; conducting legislative and policy analyses; providing standards for trial court operations; serving as liaison to court management organizations and executive and legislative branch agencies; and producing various publications, procedural manuals, and standard court forms are used in everyday operations within the courts. Trial Court Services' Friend of the Court Bureau offers policy and operational support to family division judges and friend of the court offices, including recommending procedures and guidelines for child support, custody, and parenting time cases. Trial Court Services also provides staff support to the Court Reporting and Recording Board of Review, which establishes criteria and administers tests for certification of court reporters and recorders. Special projects include the Drug Treatment Court Grant Program and Trial Court Collections.

Child Welfare Services (CWS) provides assistance to circuit court family divisions on child welfare matters, including child protective proceedings, foster care, adoption, coordination with Indian tribes, termination of parental rights, permanency outcomes, and data collection and analysis. CWS administers the Michigan Court Improvement Program (CIP) and the Foster Care Review Board Program (FCRB) and provides 25 to 30 multi-disciplinary trainings each year on a variety of child welfare issues. The CIP is part of a nationwide effort to improve how courts handle child abuse and neglect cases. The program is funded by federal grants that are guided by and operate through a statewide, cross-disciplinary task force aimed at improving the three key elements of child protective proceedings: safety, permanency, and well-being for children. The CIP allows Michigan to implement necessary reforms, track its progress toward meeting state and federal laws, national standards, and program improvement plans to improve child protective court proceedings. The FCRB provides independent, periodic review of cases in the state foster care system. A statewide advisory committee, including leaders from the child welfare community, ensures that the program fulfills its statutory mandates and provides maximum benefit to improving the foster care system.

The ***Friend of the Court Bureau*** (FOCB) offers policy and operational support to family division judges and friend of the court offices. The FOCB analyzes statistics, reviews laws, regulations, and court rules; and reviews grievances and responses to provide custody, parenting time and child support guidelines for FOCB operations. The division assists courts and FOCB offices in developing and implementing special projects to improve family court services. The FOCB also cooperates with the Michigan Department of Health and Human Service's Office of Child Support to coordinate FOCB offices in providing services under Title IV-D of the Social Security Act and is responsible for developing and revising the Michigan Child Support Formula.

The ***Office of Dispute Resolution*** is responsible for developing dispute resolution practices and protocols for the trial courts, providing technical assistance to the trial courts, implementing dispute resolution practices mandated or permitted by court rule or statute, evaluating dispute resolution systems, and providing recommendations to the state court administrator for improving dispute resolution services for Michigan citizens.

The office also provides project administration, oversight, and evaluation of the Community Dispute Resolution Program. Created by Public Act 260 of 1988, this program also provides financial support to nonprofit organizations that in turn provide free or low-cost mediation in a wide variety of disputes as an alternative to the traditional adversarial court process.

The office serves as liaison to dispute resolution service providers, academic programs, associations, courts, and other agencies and organizations having special focus on dispute resolution research, services, and evaluation.

The *Judicial Information Systems* (JIS) *Division*, with offices in Lansing and Detroit, is responsible for developing and maintaining office automation applications for the Michigan Supreme Court and to subscribers of its trial court applications. JIS currently provides support and training to more than 247 judicial branch employees and to 249 of 319 trial court locations that use its Circuit, District and Probate Courts case management system. Sixty-four locations use the Jury management system. JIS advises and assists trial courts in the selection, acquisition, installation, programming, and operation of automated data processing systems. The division coordinates with other state agencies in the development, support, accumulation, and submission of court-related data to state repositories. JIS also participates in other Supreme Court initiatives where technological advances contribute to improved service, performance, and access to the judiciary. These initiatives include trial court connectivity, improving electronic submission of data to state agencies, web-enabled applications for court payments and e-filing, data warehousing, and the next generation of case management software for the state's trial courts.

The *Michigan Judicial Institute* (MJI) was developed by the Michigan Supreme Court in 1977 to provide judges and court personnel with opportunities to develop and enhance professional skills. Continuing judicial branch education is provided in many formats, including live seminars; publications; distance learning opportunities; web-based training; a resource library that includes materials from the State Justice Institute, American Bar Association, American Judicature Society, National Association of State Judicial Educators, and National Association for Court Management; and MJI-sponsored programs. MJI is also responsible for the Supreme Court Learning Center, located in the Hall of Justice, and designed to educate the public on the Michigan court system. Electronic versions of MJI training materials can be accessed at www.courts.mi.gov/mji. The Supreme Court Learning Center information is available at www.courts.mi.gov/education/mji.

Regional Administration is comprised of six regional offices that provide direct services to the courts and serve as links between the Supreme Court and the local trial courts. Each regional office provides management assistance to trial court chief judges and staff in the administration of judicial business. They implement Supreme Court judicial administration policy, monitor workload and caseflow, and serve as a primary contact for local funding units and other local justice system stakeholders regarding judicial operations. Regional administrators and their staff visit courts in their respective regions and meet with judges, court staff, county commissioners, other local officials, attorneys, and litigants. In addition, the regional offices issue judicial assignments authorizing judges to serve in courts outside of their jurisdiction when necessary.

The *Region I State Court Administrative Office* is located in Detroit and serves the trial courts in Wayne county. The *Region II State Court Administrative Office* is located in Lansing and serves the trial courts in Clinton, Eaton, Genesee, Gratiot, Hillsdale, Ingham, Jackson, Lenawee, Livingston, Monroe, Shiawassee, and Washtenaw counties. The *Region III State Court Administrative Office* is located in Mt. Pleasant and serves the trial courts in Alcona, Arenac, Bay, Benzie, Clare, Gladwin, Huron, Ionia, Iosco, Isabella, Lake, Manistee, Mason, Mecosta, Midland, Montcalm, Newaygo, Oceana, Ogemaw, Osceola, Oscoda, Roscommon, Saginaw, Sanilac, and Tuscola counties. The *Region IV State Court Administrative Office* is located in Gaylord and serves the trial courts in Alger, Alpena, Antrim, Baraga, Charlevoix, Cheboygan, Chippewa, Crawford, Delta, Dickinson, Emmet, Gogebic, Grand Traverse, Houghton, Iron, Kalkaska, Keweenaw, Leelanau, Luce, Mackinac, Marquette, Menominee, Missaukee, Montmorency, Ontonagon, Otsego, Presque Isle, Schoolcraft, and Wexford counties. The *Region V State Court Administrative Office* is located in Lansing and serves the trial courts in Allegan, Barry, Berrien, Branch, Calhoun, Cass, Kalamazoo, Kent, Muskegon, Ottawa, St. Joseph, and Van Buren counties. The *Region VI State Court Administrative Office* is located in Detroit and serves the trial courts in Lapeer, Macomb, Oakland, and St. Clair counties.

Chapter VI

MICHIGAN'S
CONGRESSIONAL DELEGATION

2019–2020

INTRODUCTION

The United States Congress is the lawmaking branch of the federal government. It is a bicameral (two-house) legislature, consisting of the 100-member senate and the 435-member house of representatives. Each state has two senators who are elected statewide and serve 6-year terms. A senator must be at least 30 years of age, a citizen of the United States for at least nine years, and a resident of the state from which he or she is elected.

The number of members a state has in the house of representatives is determined according to population. A house member, who serves a 2-year term, must be at least 25 years of age, a citizen of the United States for at least seven years, and a resident of the state from which he or she is elected. The house of representatives is reapportioned after each decennial census to accommodate shifts in population.

Michigan's 16-member congressional delegation consists of two senators, both of whom are elected on a statewide basis, and 14 members of the house of representatives who are elected from congressional districts last apportioned by Public Act 128 of 2011, enacted on August 24, 2011. The average population of these house districts is 705,974. After reaching a peak representation of 19 members in the house during the 1960s, the state's delegation lost one house seat after the 1980 census, two more house seats after the 1990 census, and one more house seat after both the 2000 and 2010 census, reducing the number of Michigan seats in the house of representatives to 14.

MICHIGAN'S CONGRESSIONAL DELEGATION
THE 116TH U.S. CONGRESS

U.S. SENATORS

GARY C. PETERS (D–Bloomfield Township)
(Term Expires January 3, 2021)

DEBBIE STABENOW (D–Lansing)
(Term Expires January 3, 2025)

U.S. REPRESENTATIVES
(Terms Expire January 3, 2021)

JUSTIN AMASH (I–Cascade Charter Township) . . . District 3
JACK BERGMAN (R–Watersmeet) . . . . District 1
DEBBIE DINGELL (D–Dearborn) . . . . District 12
BILL HUIZENGA (R–Zeeland) . . . . District 2
DANIEL T. KILDEE (D–Flint Township) . . . . District 5
BRENDA L. LAWRENCE (D–Southfield) . . . . District 14
ANDY LEVIN (D–Bloomfield Township) . . . . District 9
PAUL MITCHELL (R–Dryden Township) . . . . District 10
JOHN MOOLENAAR (R–Midland) . . . . District 4
ELISSA SLOTKIN (D–Holly) . . . . District 8
HALEY STEVENS (D–Rochester Hills) . . . . District 11
RASHIDA TLAIB (D–Detroit) . . . . District 13
FRED S. UPTON (R–St. Joseph) . . . . District 6
TIM WALBERG (R–Tipton) . . . . District 7

SENATOR
GARY C. PETERS

Office: 724 Hart Senate Office Building, Washington, D.C. 20510. Phone: (202) 224-6221

Biography: Democrat, of Bloomfield Township; born December 1, 1958, in Pontiac; fifth generation Oakland County resident; married to Colleen Ochoa; father of three children, Gary Jr., Madeleine, and Alana; graduate, Rochester High School; B.A., Alma College; M.B.A., finance, University of Detroit; J.D., Wayne State University Law School; master's degree, philosophy, Michigan State University; Lieutenant Commander, United States Naval Reserve; more than 20 years of experience in financial sector as an investment advisor; professor, Oakland University; former professor, Central Michigan University; former Michigan Lottery Commissioner; former member, Rochester Hills City Council, 1991 to 1992; elected to the Michigan Senate, 1995 to 2002; elected to the U.S. House of Representatives, 2008, 2010, 2012; member, House Financial Services Committee; elected to the U.S. Senate, November 2014; currently serves on the Joint Economic Committee and the Senate Committees on Armed Services; Commerce, Science, and Transportation; and Homeland Security and Governmental Affairs.

SENATOR

DEBBIE STABENOW

Office: 731 Hart Senate Office Building, Washington, D.C. 20510-2204, (202) 224-4822, www.stabenow.senate.gov

Biography: Democrat, of Lansing; born April 29, 1950, in Gladwin, raised in Clare; two children, Todd and Michelle; a daughter-in-law, Sara; a son-in-law, Scott; four grandchildren; B.A., Michigan State University, 1972; M.S.W., Michigan State University, 1975; served in Michigan House of Representatives, 1979 to 1990, and Michigan Senate, 1991 to 1994; chair, Ingham County Board of Commissioners, 1975 to 1978; co-founder of the Michigan Leadership Institute, which specializes in leadership development and team building training for organizations and individuals; member, United Methodist Church. The Senator has been recognized nationally with over 200 awards by families, small businesses, and organizations for leadership and public service including Michiganian of the Year, 1982, *The Detroit News*; Outstanding Young American, 1986, U.S. Jaycees; Legislator of the Year, 1989, Child Welfare League of America; 1990 ATHENA Award; Congressional Leadership Award, 2005, National Urban League; Great Lakes Legislator of the Year, 2005, Great Lakes Maritime Task Force; Legislator of the Year, 2005, Michigan Association of Firefighters; Health Care Champion Award, 2012, American Hospital Association; Nathan Davis Award for Outstanding Government Service, 2012, American Medical Association; Champion of Agriculture, 2013, Michigan Agri-Business Association; elected to U.S. House of Representatives, November 1996, served two terms; elected to U.S. Senate, November 2000, 2006, 2012, and 2018; currently serving on the Senate Committees on Agriculture, Nutrition, and Forestry; Budget; Energy and Natural Resources; and Finance.

U.S. Representative
JUSTIN AMASH
I–3rd Congressional District

District: Counties of Barry, Calhoun, Ionia, Kent (part), and Montcalm (part)

Office: 114 Cannon House Office Building, Washington, D.C. 20515, (202) 225-3831

Biography: Independent, of Cascade Charter Township; born April 18, 1980, in Grand Rapids; wife, Kara; children, Alexander, Anwen and Evelyn; A.B., economics, University of Michigan; J.D., University of Michigan Law School; business lawyer and small business owner; member, St. Nicholas Antiochian Orthodox Christian Church, State Bar of Michigan, Grand Rapids Bar Association, Right to Life of Michigan, National Rifle Association, The Economic Club of Grand Rapids, Alumni Association of the University of Michigan, American Legislative Exchange Council Civil Justice Task Force; commissioner, Uniform Law Commission; chair, Liberty Caucus; elected Republican precinct delegate, 2008; elected to the Michigan House of Representatives, 2008; elected to 112th Congress, November 2010, reelected in 2012 and each succeeding Congress.

U.S. Representative
JACK BERGMAN
R–1st Congressional District

District: Counties of Alcona, Alger, Alpena, Antrim, Baraga, Benzie, Charlevoix, Cheboygan, Chippewa, Crawford, Delta, Dickinson, Emmet, Gogebic, Grand Traverse, Houghton, Iron, Kalkaska, Keweenaw, Leelenau, Luce, Mackinac, Manistee, Marquette, Mason (part), Menominee, Montmorency, Ontonagon, Oscoda, Otsego, Presque Isle, and Schoolcraft

Office: 414 Cannon House Office Building, Washington, D.C. 20515, (202) 225-4735, Website: www.bergman.house.gov

Biography: Republican, of Watersmeet; born February 2, 1947 in Shakopee, Minnesota; spouse, Cindy; bachelor's degree in business; Gustavus Adolphus College; retired three-star general, United States Marine Corps; former pilot, Northwest airlines; president, WINGS Medical Technologies; elected to Congress, 2016 and 2018; currently serves on the House Armed Services Committee and the House Veterans Affairs Committee.

U.S. Representative
DEBBIE DINGELL
D–12th Congressional District

District: Counties of Washtenaw (part) and Wayne (part)

Office: 116 Cannon House Office Building, Washington, D.C. 20515, (202) 225-4071

Biography: Democrat, of Dearborn; born in Detroit; widow of former U.S. Congressman John Dingell, Jr.; extensive extended family of stepchildren, godchildren, grandchildren and nieces and nephews; bachelor's degree in foreign service from Georgetown University and master's degree in liberal studies from Georgetown University; president of the GM Foundation and a senior executive responsible for public affairs; member, former Wayne State University Board of Governors, 8 years; founding chair, National Women's Health Resource Center and Children's Inn at the National Institutes of Health; member, Michigan Women's Foundation, Michigan Women's Economic Club, Susan B. Komen Foundation, and Barbara Karmanos Cancer Center; co-founder, Race for the Cures in Michigan and Washington, D.C.; former chair, Michigan Infant Mortality Task Force – Baby your Baby public education campaign; board member, Michigan's Children; served on the Early Childhood Investment Corporation and the Cherry Commission on Higher Education and Economic Growth; chair, Metropolitan Affairs Coalition; past chair and member of the Parade Company board of directors; co-hosted "Am I Right" on Detroit Public Television; member, Democratic National Committee; elected to the U.S. House of Representatives, 2014 and 2016; Senior Whip. The Congresswoman is currently a member of the House Committee on Energy and Commerce.

U.S. Representative
BILL HUIZENGA
R–2nd Congressional District

District: Counties of Allegan (part), Kent (part), Lake, Mason (part), Muskegon, Newaygo, Oceana, and Ottawa

Office: 2232 Rayburn House Office Building, Washington, D.C. 20515, (202) 225-4401, Website: huizenga.house.gov

Biography: Republican, of Zeeland; born January 31, 1969; graduated from Holland Christian High School; bachelor's degree, political science, Calvin College; wife, Natalie; five children; realtor, co-owner, Huizenga Gravel; former director of public policy, Congressman Pete Hoekstra; member, National Federation of Independent Business, local chamber of commerce; president, College Republican Club at Calvin College; Michigan Rural Health Association and Right to Life of Michigan representative; elected to the Michigan House of Representatives, 2002, 2004, 2006; elected to the 112th Congress, November 2010, reelected 2012 and each succeeding Congress; serves on the Committee on Financial Services.

U.S. Representative
DANIEL T. KILDEE
D–5th Congressional District

District: Counties of Arenac, Bay, Genesee, Iosco and parts of Saginaw and Tuscola

Office: 203 Cannon House Office Building, Washington, D.C. 20515, (202) 225-3611, Website: www.dankildee.house.gov

Biography: Democrat, of Flint Township; born August 11, 1958, in Flint; married to Jennifer; three children, Ryan, Kenneth, and Katy; B.A., Central Michigan University; completed a fellowship at the Kennedy School at Harvard University in 2005; co-creator, Genesee County Land Bank; president/co-founder, Center for Community Progress; former treasurer, Genesee County; former commissioner and chair of the board of commissioners, Genesee County; former member Flint Board of Education; elected to Congress in 2012 and each succeeding Congress; member, House Ways and Means Committee; currently serves as Chief Deputy Whip.

U.S. Representative
BRENDA L. LAWRENCE
D–14th Congressional District

District: Counties of Oakland (part) and Wayne (part)

Office: 2463 Rayburn House Office Building, Washington, D.C. 20515, (202) 225-5802

Biography: Democrat, of Southfield; born in Detroit; married to McArthur; two children and one granddaughter; bachelor's degree in Public Administration from Central Michigan University; employed 30 years with the U.S. Postal Service; member, the Miracle League and Girl Scouts of America; member, U.S. Conference of Mayors and the Democratic National Committee; served on the Southfield School Board as president, vice-president, and secretary; served on the Southfield City Council, 11 years as mayor of Southfield; elected to the U.S. House of Representatives in 2014, reelected in 2016 and 2018. Serves as a member of the House Appropriations Committee and the House Oversight and Reform Committee.

U.S. Representative
ANDY LEVIN
D–9th Congressional District

District: Counties of Macomb (part), Oakland (part)

Office: 228 Cannon House Office Building, Washington, D.C. 20515; Phone: (202) 225-4961

Biography: Democrat, of Bloomfield Township; born in Detroit; Jewish; spouse, Mary Freeman; four children; graduate Williams College and Harvard Law School, master's degree, University of Michigan; employed as a staff attorney to the presidential commission on the Future of Worker-Management Relations, worked in the U.S. Department of Labor secretary's office, served as assistant director of organizing at the national AFL-CIO; created Michigan's No Worker Left Behind initiative and the Michigan Academy for Green Mobility Alliance and co-creator of the Michigan's Green Jobs Initiative and Green Jobs Report; founder, Levin Energy Partners, LLC; elected to Congress in 2018; serving on the House Education and Labor Committee and the House Foreign Affairs Committee.

U.S. Representative
PAUL MITCHELL
R–10th Congressional District

District: Counties of Huron, Lapeer, Macomb (part), St. Clair, Sanilac, and Tuscola (part)

Office: 211 Cannon House Office Building, Washington, D.C. 20515, (202) 225-2106, Website: www.mitchell.house.gov

Biography: Republican, of Dryden Township; born November 14, 1956 in Boston; spouse, Sherry; six children; non-denominational Christian; bachelor's degree, James Madison College, Michigan State University; former CEO and co-owner, Ross Education; member, St. Clair City Council; finance chair, Michigan Republican Party; former chair, Faith and Freedom Coalition of Michigan; formed the Coalition Against Higher Taxes and Special Interest Deals to fight a proposed sales and gas tax increase in Michigan; volunteer with the St. Clair County Foundation; youth hockey coach; selected Freshman Representative to GOP House leadership; elected to the U.S. House of Representatives, November 2016 and reelected in 2018; serves on the House Transportation and Infrastructure Committee, the House Armed Services Committee, and the House Oversight and Government Reform Committee.

U.S. Representative
JOHN MOOLENAAR
R–4th Congressional District

District: Counties of Clare, Clinton, Gladwin, Gratiot, Isabella, Mecosta, Midland, Missaukee, Montcalm (part), Ogemaw, Osceola, Roscommon, Saginaw (part), Shiawassee, and Wexford

Office: 117 Cannon House Office Building, Washington, D.C. 20515, (202) 225-3561

Biography: Republican, of Midland; born May 8, 1961; married with six children; attended Hope College, bachelor's degree, chemistry; Harvard University, master's degree, public administration; administrator, Midland Academy of Advanced and Creative Studies; former member, Midland city council; director of business development, MITECH+; elected to the House of Representatives, 2002, 2004, and 2006; elected to the State Senate, 2010; elected to the U.S. House of Representatives, 2014, 2016, and 2018; currently serves on the House Committee on Appropriations; co-founder and co-chair of the bipartisan Chemistry Caucus.

U.S. Representative
ELISSA SLOTKIN
D–8th Congressional District

District: Counties of Ingham, Livingston, Oakland (part)

Office: 1531 Longworth House Office Building, Washington, D.C. 20515; Phone (202) 225-4872

Biography: Democrat, of Holly; spouse, Dave; attended Cornell University for her bachelor's degree and received a master's degree from Columbia University; Middle East analyst, Central Intelligence Agency, three tours in Iraq as a militia expert; worked under both President Bush and President Obama in the White House in the Office of the Director of National Intelligence, and the Pentagon; elected to the House of Representatives 2018; currently serving on the House Armed Services Committee and the House Homeland Security Committee.

U.S. Representative
HALEY STEVENS
D–11th Congressional District

District: Counties of Oakland (part), Wayne (part)

Office: 227 Cannon House Office Building, Washington, D.C. 20515; Phone: (202) 225-8171

Biography: Democrat, Rochester Hills; born June 24, 1983 in Rochester Hills; bachelor's degree in political science and philosophy and a master's degree in philosophy and social policy from the American University; director, workforce development and manufacturing engagement at UI Labs; special advisor to the Economic Development Administration at the U.S. Department of Commerce; chief of staff, President's Auto Task Force and President's Manufacturing Policy Team at the U.S Department of Treasury; elected to the House of Representatives, 2018; serves on the House committee on Education and Labor and the House committee on Science, Space and Technology.

U.S. Representative
RASHIDA TLAIB
D–13th Congressional District

District: County of Wayne (part)

Office: 1628 Longworth House Office Building, Washington, D.C. 20515; Phone: (202) 225-5126

Biography: Democrat, of Detroit; born July 24, 1976 in Detroit; Juris Doctorate, Thomas Cooley Law School; senior policy analyst, House Floor Leader Steve Tobocman; Arab American Community Center for Economic and Social Services, and International Institute of Metro Detroit; elected to the Michigan House of Representatives, 2008, 2010, and 2012; elected to the U.S. House of Representatives, 2018; serves on the House Financial Services Committee.

U.S. Representative
FRED S. UPTON
R–6th Congressional District

District: Counties of Allegan, Berrien, Cass, Kalamazoo, St. Joseph, and Van Buren

Office: 2183 Rayburn House Office Building, Washington, D.C. 20515, (202) 225-3761, Website: www.upton.house.gov

Biography: Republican, of St. Joseph; born April 23, 1953; B.A., journalism, University of Michigan, 1975; married Amey Rulon-Miller, 1983; children, Meg and Stephen; community liaison, U.S. Representative David Stockman, 1975 to 1980; legislative assistant, Office of Management and Budget, 1981 to 1983; Deputy Assistant Director for Legislative Affairs – OMB, 1983 to 1984; Director of Congressional Affairs – OMB, 1984 to 1985; elected to the 100th Congress, November 1986, and each succeeding Congress; chair 2011 to 2016 and current member, Energy and Commerce Committee.

U.S. Representative
TIM WALBERG
R–7th Congressional District

District: Counties of Branch, Eaton, Hillsdale, Jackson, Lenawee, Monroe, and Washtenaw (part)

Office: 2266 Rayburn House Office Building, Washington, D.C. 20515, (202) 225-6276

Biography: Republican, of Tipton; born in Chicago; married to Sue; children, Matthew, Heidi, and Caleb; studied at Western Illinois University, Moody Bible Institute, Taylor University in Fort Wayne, Indiana (formerly Fort Wayne Bible College) and Wheaton College Graduate School, earning his B.S. and M.A. degrees; served as pastor for nearly 10 years; served as member of the Michigan House of Representatives, 1983 to 1998; former president of the Warren Reuther Center for Education and Community Impact; former division manager for the Moody Bible Institute of Chicago; elected to the 110th Congress, November 2006 and to each succeeding Congress; member, House Committee on Energy and Commerce and House Committee on Education and Labor.

U.S. HOUSE OF REPRESENTATIVES DISTRICT POPULATIONS

District	2010 Population
1	705,974
2	705,970
3	705,943
4	706,010
5	705,993
6	705,974
7	705,981
8	705,975
9	705,931
10	705,956
11	706,198
12	706,110
13	705,831
14	705,794

MEMBERS OF THE U.S. CONGRESS
FROM MICHIGAN, SERVING 1837-2019

U.S. SENATORS

Lucius Lyon (D)[1]	1836-1840	Julius C. Burrows (R)	1895-1911
John Norvell[1]	1836-1841	Russell A. Alger (R)[9]	1902-1907
Augustus S. Porter[2]	1840-1845	William Alden Smith (R)	1907-1919
William Woodbridge (W)	1841-1847	Charles E. Townsend (R)[10]	1911-1923
Lewis Cass (D)[3]	1845-1848	Truman H. Newberry (R)[11]	1919-1922
Alpheus Felch (D)	1847-1853	James Couzens (R)[12]	1922-1936
Thomas Fitzgerald (D)	1848-1849	Woodbridge N. Ferris (D)[13]	1923-1928
Lewis Cass (D)	1849-1857	Arthur H. Vandenberg (R)[14]	1928-1951
Charles E. Stuart (D)	1853-1859	Prentiss M. Brown (D)	1936-1943
Zachariah Chandler (R)	1857-1875	Homer Ferguson (R)	1943-1954
Kinsley S. Bingham (R)[4]	1859-1861	Blair Moody (D)	1951-1953
Jacob M. Howard (R)	1862-1871	Charles E. Potter (R)	1953-1959
Thomas W. Ferry (R)	1871-1883	Patrick V. McNamara (D)[15]	1955-1966
Isaac P. Christiancy (R)[5]	1875-1879	Philip A. Hart (D)[16]	1959-1976
Zachariah Chandler (R)[6]	1879	Robert P. Griffin (R)	1966-1979
Henry P. Baldwin (R)	1879-1881	Donald W. Riegle Jr. (D)	1976-1994
Omar D. Conger (R)	1881-1887	Carl Levin (D)	1979-2014
Thomas W. Palmer (R)	1883-1889	Spencer Abraham (R)	1995-2000
Francis B. Stockbridge (R)[7]	1887-1894	Debbie Stabenow (D)	2001-
James McMillan (R)[8]	1889-1902	Gary C. Peters (D)	2015-
John Patton Jr. (R)	1894-1895		

Political Party Designations

D — Democrat
R — Republican
W — Whig

Information on party affiliation was not always available; therefore, some individuals may be listed without this data.

---

[1] First elected U.S. senator from Michigan, elected November 10, 1835, following adoption of the Constitution of 1835. However, due to Michigan's dispute with the U.S. Congress over the Toledo Strip and the state's admission to the Union, Congress refused to accept their credentials until it admitted Michigan as a state January 26, 1837. See U.S. Const, art I, § 3, cl 1, 2; art I, § 4, cl 1; art I, § 5, cl 1; legislative resolution approved November 10, 1835.

[2] Elected January 20, 1840, for a 6-year term beginning March 4, 1839. On February 13, 1839, the legislature in joint convention failed, after six votes, to elect a successor to Lucius Lyon. A vote was not taken again until January 20, 1840. See Revised Statutes of 1838, title II, chapter 10.

[3] Resigned May 29, 1848; Thomas Fitzgerald appointed to fill vacancy June 8, 1848. Cass became the 1848 Democratic nominee for U.S. president, but lost to Zachary Taylor; he was elected to fill the remainder of his own vacancy January 20, 1849. See Revised Statutes of 1846, title II, chapter 11.

[4] Died October 5, 1861; Jacob M. Howard elected to fill vacancy January 4, 1862. See Act 175 of the Extra Session of 1851, Laws of Michigan.

[5] Resigned February 10, 1879; Zachariah Chandler elected to fill vacancy February 19, 1879. See Act 1 of 1869, Laws of Michigan.

[6] Died November 1, 1879; Henry P. Baldwin appointed November 17, 1879, and elected to fill remainder of Christiancy's unexpired term January 19, 1881.

[7] Died April 30, 1894; John Patton Jr. appointed to fill vacancy May 5, 1894; Julius C. Burrows elected to fill remainder of unexpired term January 16, 1895.

[8] Died August 10, 1902; Russell A. Alger appointed to fill vacancy September 17, 1902, and elected to fill remainder of unexpired term January 21, 1903.

[9] Died January 24, 1907; William Alden Smith elected to fill remainder of unexpired term February 6, 1907.

[10] First senator nominated for office through the direct primary system, September 1910, and first senator elected by direct vote of the people, November 1916. See Act 281 of 1909; U.S. Const, art XVII; Act 24 of 1915; Act 156 of 1915.

[11] Resigned November 19, 1922; James Couzens appointed to fill vacancy November 29, 1922, and elected to fill remainder of unexpired term November 4, 1924. See Act 156 of 1915; Act 199 of 1923.

[12] Died October 22, 1936; Prentiss M. Brown appointed to fill vacancy November 16, 1936.

[13] Died March 23, 1928; Arthur H. Vandenberg appointed to fill vacancy March 31, 1928, and elected to remainder of unexpired term November 6, 1928.

[14] Died April 18, 1951; Blair Moody appointed to fill vacancy April 23, 1951, and Charles E. Potter elected to fill remainder of unexpired term November 4, 1952.

[15] Died April 30, 1966; Robert P. Griffin appointed to fill vacancy May 11, 1966. See Act 116 of 1954.

[16] Died December 26, 1976; Donald W. Riegle Jr., appointed to fill vacancy December 30, 1976.

U.S. REPRESENTATIVES

Congress	Session Years	Representative	District[1]
24	1835-1836	Isaac E. Crary (D)[2]	
25	1837-1838	Isaac E. Crary (D)	
26	1839-1840	Isaac E. Crary (D)	
27	1841-1842	Jacob M. Howard (W)	
28[3]	1843-1844	James B. Hunt (D)	3
		Lucius Lyon (D)	2
		Robert McClelland (D)	1
29	1845-1846	John S. Chipman (D)	2
		James B. Hunt (D)	3
		Robert McClelland (D)	1
30	1847-1848	Kinsley S. Bingham (D)	3
		Edward Bradley (D)[4]	2
		Robert McClelland (D)	1
		Charles E. Stuart (D)	2
31	1849-1850	Kinsley S. Bingham (D)	3
		Alexander W. Buel (D)	1
		William Sprague (FS)	2
32	1851-1852	James L. Conger	3
		Ebenezer J. Penniman (W)	1
		Charles E. Stuart (D)	2
33[5]	1853-1854	Samuel Clark	3
		David A. Noble (D)	2
		Hestor L. Stevens (D)	4
		David Stuart (D)	1
34	1855-1856	William A. Howard (R)	1
		George W. Peck (D)	4
		David S. Walbridge (R)	3
		Henry Waldron (R)	2
35	1857-1858	William A. Howard (R)	1
		DeWitt C. Leach (R)	4
		David S. Walbridge (R)	3
		Henry Waldron (R)	2
36	1859-1860	George B. Cooper (D)[6]	1
		William A. Howard (R)[6]	1
		Francis W. Kellogg (R)	3
		DeWitt C. Leach (R)	4
		Henry Waldron (R)	2
37	1861-1862	Fernando C. Beaman (R)	2
		Bradley F. Granger (R)	1
		Francis W. Kellogg (R)	3
		Rowland E. Trowbridge (R)	4
38[7]	1863-1864	Augustus C. Baldwin (D)	5
		Fernando C. Beaman (R)	1
		John F. Driggs (R)	6
		Francis W. Kellogg (R)	4
		John W. Longyear (R)	3
		Charles Upson (R)	2
39	1865-1866	Fernando C. Beaman (R)	1
		John F. Driggs (R)	6
		Thomas W. Ferry (R)	4
		John W. Longyear (R)	3
		Rowland E. Trowbridge (R)	5
		Charles Upson (R)	2
40	1867-1868	Fernando C. Beaman (R)	1
		Austin Blair (R)	3
		John F. Driggs (R)	6
		Thomas W. Ferry (R)	4
		Rowland E. Trowbridge (R)	5
		Charles Upson (R)	2

Congress	Session Years	Representative	District
41	1869-1870	Fernando C. Beaman (R)	1
		Austin Blair (R)	3
		Omar D. Conger (R)	5
		Thomas W. Ferry (R)	4
		William L. Stoughton (R)	2
		Randolph Strickland (R)	6
42	1871-1872	Austin Blair (R)	3
		Omar D. Conger (R)	5
		Thomas W. Ferry (R)[8]	4
		Wilder D. Foster (R)	4
		William L. Stoughton (R)	2
		Jabez G. Sutherland (D)	6
		Henry Waldron (R)	1
43[9]	1873-1874	Josiah Williams Begole (R)	6
		Nathan B. Bradley (R)	8
		Julius C. Burrows (R)	4
		Omar D. Conger (R)	7
		Moses W. Field (R)	1
		Wilder D. Foster (R)[10]	5
		Jay A. Hubbell (R)	9
		Henry Waldron (R)	2
		George Willard (R)	3
		William B. Williams (R)	5
44	1875-1876	Nathan B. Bradley (R)	8
		Omar D. Conger (R)	7
		George H. Durand (D)	6
		Jay A. Hubbell (R)	9
		Allen Potter (Ind)	4
		Henry Waldron (R)	2
		George Willard (R)	3
		Alpheus S. Williams (D)	1
		William B. Williams (R)	5
45	1877-1878	Mark S. Brewer (R)	6
		Omar D. Conger (R)	7
		Charles C. Ellsworth (R)	8
		Jay A. Hubbell (R)	9
		Edwin W. Keightley (R)	4
		Jonas H. McGowan (R)	3
		John W. Stone (R)	5
		Alpheus S. Williams (D)[11]	1
		Edwin Willits (R)	2
46	1879-1880	Mark S. Brewer (R)	6
		Julius C. Burrows (R)	4
		Omar D. Conger (R)	7
		Roswell G. Horr (R)	8
		Jay A. Hubbell (R)	9
		Jonas H. McGowan (R)	3
		John S. Newberry (R)	1
		John W. Stone (R)	5
		Edwin Willits (R)	2
47	1881-1882	Julius C. Burrows (R)	4
		Omar D. Conger (R)[12]	7
		Roswell G. Horr (R)	8
		Jay A. Hubbell (R)	9
		Edward S. Lacey (R)	3
		Henry W. Lord (R)	1
		John T. Rich (R)	7
		Oliver L. Spaulding (R)	6
		George W. Webber (R)	5
		Edwin Willits (R)	2
48[13]	1883-1884	Edward Breitung (R)	11
		Ezra C. Carleton (Fus)	7
		Byron M. Cutcheon (R)	9
		Nathaniel B. Eldredge (D)	2
		Herschel H. Hatch (R)	10
		Roswell G. Horr (R)	8

U.S. REPRESENTATIVES *(Cont.)*

Congress	Session Years	Representative	District
48 *(Cont.)*		Julius Houseman (Fus).............	5
		Edward S. Lacey (R)...............	3
		William C. Maybury (Fus)..........	1
		Edwin B. Winans (Fus)	6
		George L. Yaple (Fus)	4
49	1885-1886	Julius C. Burrows (R).............	4
		Ezra C. Carleton (Fus)	7
		Charles C. Comstock (D)	5
		Byron M. Cutcheon (R)	9
		Nathaniel B. Eldredge (D&U).......	2
		Spencer O. Fisher (D)	10
		William C. Maybury (Fus)..........	1
		Seth C. Moffatt (R)...............	11
		James O'Donnell (R)	3
		Timothy E. Tarsney (Fus)..........	8
		Edwin B. Winans (Fus)	6
50	1887-1888	Edward P. Allen (R)	2
		Mark S. Brewer (R)	6
		Julius C. Burrows (R).............	4
		J. Logan Chipman (D)	1
		Byron M. Cutcheon (R)	9
		Spencer O. Fisher (D)	10
		Melbourne H. Ford (D)	5
		Seth C. Moffatt (R)[14]...........	11
		James O'Donnell (R)	3
		Henry W. Seymour (R)..............	11
		Timothy E. Tarsney (Fus)..........	8
		Justin R. Whiting (Fus)...........	7
51	1889-1890	Edward P. Allen (R)...............	2
		Charles E. Belknap (R)............	5
		Aaron T. Bliss (R)	8
		Mark S. Brewer (R)	6
		Julius C. Burrows (R).............	4
		J. Logan Chipman (D)	1
		Byron M. Cutcheon (R)	9
		James O'Donnell (R)	3
		Samuel M. Stephenson (R)..........	11
		Frank W. Wheeler (R)	10
		Justin R. Whiting (Fus)...........	7
52	1891-1892	Charles E. Belknap (R)............	5
		Julius C. Burrows (R).............	4
		J. Logan Chipman (D)	1
		Melbourne H. Ford (D)[15].........	5
		James S. Gorman (D)...............	2
		James O'Donnell (R)	3
		Samuel M. Stephenson (R)..........	11
		Byron G. Stout (D&U)	6
		Thomas A. E. Weadock (D)	10
		Harrison H. Wheeler (R)	9
		Justin R. Whiting (Fus)...........	7
		Henry M. Youmans (D)	8
53[16]	1893-1894	David D. Aitken (R)...............	6
		John Avery (R)....................	11
		Julius C. Burrows (R).............	3
		J. Logan Chipman (D)[17]	1
		James S. Gorman (D)...............	2
		Levi T. Griffin (D)	1
		William S. Linton (R)	8
		John W. Moon (R)	9
		George F. Richardson (D)[18]......	5
		Samuel M. Stephenson (R)..........	12
		Henry Franklin Thomas (R)	4
		Thomas A. E. Weadock (D)	10
		Justin R. Whiting (D)	7
54	1895-1896	David D. Aitken (R)...............	6
		John Avery (R)....................	11
		Roswell P. Bishop (R)	9

Congress	Session Years	Representative	District
54 *(Cont.)*		Julius C. Burrows (R)[19]	3
		John B. Corliss (R)	1
		Rousseau O. Crump (R)	10
		William S. Linton (R)	8
		Alfred Milnes (R)	3
		William Alden Smith (R)	5
		Horace G. Snover (R)	7
		George Spalding (R)	2
		Samuel M. Stephenson (R)	12
		Henry Franklin Thomas (R)	4
55	1897-1898	Roswell P. Bishop (R)	9
		Ferdinand Brucker (DPUS)	8
		John B. Corliss (R)	1
		Rousseau O. Crump (R)	10
		Edward L. Hamilton (R)	4
		William S. Mesick (R)	11
		Carlos D. Shelden (R)	12
		Samuel W. Smith (R)	6
		William Alden Smith (R)	5
		Horace G. Snover (R)	7
		George Spalding (R)	2
		Albert M. Todd (DPUS)	3
56	1899-1900	Roswell P. Bishop (R)	9
		John B. Corliss (R)	1
		Rousseau O. Crump (R)	10
		Joseph W. Fordney (R)	8
		Washington Gardner (R)	3
		Edward L. Hamilton (R)	4
		William S. Mesick (R)	11
		Carlos D. Shelden (R)	12
		Henry C. Smith (R)	2
		Samuel W. Smith (R)	6
		William Alden Smith (R)	5
		Edgar Weeks (R)	7
57	1901-1902	Henry H. Aplin (R)	10
		Roswell P. Bishop (R)	9
		John B. Corliss (R)	1
		Rousseau O. Crump (R)[20]	10
		Archibald B. Darragh (R)	11
		Joseph W. Fordney (R)	8
		Washington Gardner (R)	3
		Edward L. Hamilton (R)	4
		Carlos D. Shelden (R)	12
		Henry C. Smith (R)	2
		Samuel W. Smith (R)	6
		William Alden Smith (R)	5
		Edgar Weeks (R)	7
58	1903-1904	Roswell P. Bishop (R)	9
		Archibald B. Darragh (R)	11
		Joseph W. Fordney (R)	8
		Washington Gardner (R)	3
		Edward L. Hamilton (R)	4
		George A. Loud (R)	10
		Alfred Lucking (D)	1
		Henry McMorran (R)	7
		Samuel W. Smith (R)	6
		William Alden Smith (R)	5
		Charles E. Townsend (R)	2
		H. Olin Young (R)	12
59	1905-1906	Roswell P. Bishop (R)	9
		Archibald B. Darragh (R)	11
		Edwin Denby (R)	1
		Joseph W. Fordney (R)	8
		Washington Gardner (R)	3
		Edward L. Hamilton (R)	4
		George A. Loud (R)	10
		Henry McMorran (R)	7

Congress	Session Years	Representative	District
59 *(Cont.)*		Samuel W. Smith (R)	6
		William Alden Smith (R).	5
		Charles E. Townsend (R)	2
		H. Olin Young (R)	12
60	1907-1908	Archibald B. Darragh (R)	11
		Edwin Denby (R).	1
		Gerrit J. Diekema (R).	5
		Joseph W. Fordney (R).	8
		Washington Gardner (R)	3
		Edward L. Hamilton (R)	4
		George A. Loud (R)	10
		James C. McLaughlin (R)	9
		Henry McMorran (R)	7
		Samuel W. Smith (R)	6
		William Alden Smith (R)[21].	5
		Charles E. Townsend (R)	2
		H. Olin Young (R)	12
61	1909-1910	Edwin Denby (R).	1
		Gerrit J. Diekema (R).	5
		Francis H. Dodds (R)	11
		Joseph W. Fordney (R).	8
		Washington Gardner (R)	3
		Edward L. Hamilton (R)	4
		George A. Loud (R)	10
		James C. McLaughlin (R)	9
		Henry McMorran (R)	7
		Samuel W. Smith (R)	6
		Charles E. Townsend (R)	2
		H. Olin Young (R)	12
62	1911-1912	Francis H. Dodds (R)	11
		Frank E. Doremus (D)	1
		Joseph W. Fordney (R).	8
		Edward L. Hamilton (R)	4
		George A. Loud (R)	10
		James C. McLaughlin (R)	9
		Henry McMorran (R)	7
		John M. C. Smith (R)	3
		Samuel W. Smith (R)	6
		Edwin F. Sweet (D)	5
		William W. Wedemeyer (R)	2
		H. Olin Young (R)	12
63[22]	1913-1914	Samuel W. Beakes (D).	2
		Louis C. Cramton (R)	7
		Frank E. Doremus (D)	1
		Joseph W. Fordney (R).	8
		Edward L. Hamilton (R)	4
		Patrick H. Kelley (R)[23]	
		Francis O. Lindquist (R)	11
		William J. MacDonald (Prog)[24]	12
		Carl E. Mapes (R).	5
		James C. McLaughlin (R)	9
		John M. C. Smith (R)	3
		Samuel W. Smith (R)	6
		Roy O. Woodruff (Prog).	10
		H. Olin Young (R)[24]	12
64	1915-1916	Samuel W. Beakes (D).	2
		Louis C. Cramton (R)	7
		Frank E. Doremus (D)	1
		Joseph W. Fordney (R).	8
		Edward L. Hamilton (R)	4
		W. Frank James (R)	12
		Patrick H. Kelley (R)	6
		George A. Loud (R)	10
		Carl E. Mapes (R).	5
		James C. McLaughlin (R)	9
		Charles A. Nichols (R)	13
		Frank D. Scott (R)	11
		John M. C. Smith (R)	3

Congress	Session Years	Representative	District
65	1917-1918	Mark R. Bacon (R)[25]	2
		Samuel W. Beakes (D)[25]	2
		Louis C. Cramton (R)	7
		Gilbert Archibald Currie (R)	10
		Frank E. Doremus (D)	1
		Joseph W. Fordney (R)	8
		Edward L. Hamilton (R)	4
		W. Frank James (R)	12
		Patrick H. Kelley (R)	6
		Carl E. Mapes (R)	5
		James C. McLaughlin (R)	9
		Charles A. Nichols (R)	13
		Frank D. Scott (R)	11
		John M. C. Smith (R)	3
66	1919-1920	Louis C. Cramton (R)	7
		Gilbert Archibald Currie (R)	10
		Frank E. Doremus (D)	1
		Joseph W. Fordney (R)	8
		Edward L. Hamilton (R)	4
		W. Frank James (R)	12
		Patrick H. Kelley (R)	6
		Carl E. Mapes (R)	5
		James C. McLaughlin (R)	9
		Clarence J. McLeod (R)	13
		Earl C. Michener (R)	2
		Charles A. Nichols (R)[26]	13
		Frank D. Scott (R)	11
		John M. C. Smith (R)	3
67	1921-1922	Vincent M. Brennan (R)	13
		George P. Codd (R)	1
		Louis C. Cramton (R)	7
		Joseph W. Fordney (R)	8
		William H. Frankhauser (R)[27]	3
		W. Frank James (R)	12
		Patrick H. Kelley (R)	6
		John C. Ketcham (R)	4
		Carl E. Mapes (R)	5
		James C. McLaughlin (R)	9
		Earl C. Michener (R)	2
		Frank D. Scott (R)	11
		John M. C. Smith (R)	3
		Roy O. Woodruff (R)	10
68	1923-1924	Robert H. Clancy (D)	1
		Louis C. Cramton (R)	7
		Grant M. Hudson (R)	6
		W. Frank James (R)	12
		John C. Ketcham (R)	4
		Carl E. Mapes (R)	5
		James C. McLaughlin (R)	9
		Clarence J. McLeod (R)	13
		Earl C. Michener (R)	2
		Frank D. Scott (R)	11
		John M. C. Smith (R)[28]	3
		Bird J. Vincent (R)	8
		Arthur B. Williams (R)	3
		Roy O. Woodruff (R)	10
69	1925-1926	Louis C. Cramton (R)	7
		Joseph L. Hooper (R)	3
		Grant M. Hudson (R)	6
		W. Frank James (R)	12
		John C. Ketcham (R)	4
		Carl E. Mapes (R)	5
		James C. McLaughlin (R)	9
		Clarence J. McLeod (R)	13
		Earl C. Michener (R)	2
		Frank D. Scott (R)	11
		John B. Sosnowski (R)	1

Congress	Session Years	Representative	District
69 *(Cont.)*		Bird J. Vincent (R)	8
		Arthur B. Williams (R)[29]	3
		Roy O. Woodruff (R)	10
70	1927-1928	Frank P. Bohn (R)	11
		Robert H. Clancy (R)	1
		Louis C. Cramton (R)	7
		Joseph L. Hooper (R)	3
		Grant M. Hudson (R)	6
		W. Frank James (R)	12
		John C. Ketcham (R)	4
		Carl E. Mapes (R)	5
		James C. McLaughlin (R)	9
		Clarence J. McLeod (R)	13
		Earl C. Michener (R)	2
		Bird J. Vincent (R)	8
		Roy O. Woodruff (R)	10
71	1929-1930	Frank P. Bohn (R)	11
		Robert H. Clancy (R)	1
		Louis C. Cramton (R)	7
		Joseph L. Hooper (R)	3
		Grant M. Hudson (R)	6
		W. Frank James (R)	12
		John C. Ketcham (R)	4
		Carl E. Mapes (R)	5
		James C. McLaughlin (R)	9
		Clarence J. McLeod (R)	13
		Earl C. Michener (R)	2
		Bird J. Vincent (R)	8
		Roy O. Woodruff (R)	10
72	1931-1932	Frank P. Bohn (R)	11
		Robert H. Clancy (R)	1
		Michael J. Hart (D)	8
		Joseph L. Hooper (R)	3
		W. Frank James (R)	12
		John C. Ketcham (R)	4
		Carl E. Mapes (R)	5
		James C. McLaughlin (R)[30]	9
		Clarence J. McLeod (R)	13
		Earl C. Michener (R)	2
		Seymour H. Person (R)	6
		Bird J. Vincent (R)[31]	8
		Jesse P. Wolcott (R)	7
		Roy O. Woodruff (R)	10
73[32]	1933-1934	Prentiss M. Brown (D)	11
		Claude E. Cady (D)	6
		John D. Dingell Sr. (D)	15
		George A. Dondero (R)	17
		George Foulkes (D)	4
		Michael J. Hart (D)	8
		Joseph L. Hooper (R)[33]	3
		W. Frank James (R)	12
		John C. Lehr (D)	2
		John Lesinski Sr. (D)	16
		Carl E. Mapes (R)	5
		Clarence J. McLeod (R)	13
		Harry W. Musselwhite (D)	9
		George G. Sadowski (D)	1
		Carl M. Weideman (D)	14
		Jesse P. Wolcott (R)	7
		Roy O. Woodruff (R)	10
74	1935-1936	William W. Blackney (R)	6
		Prentiss M. Brown (D)	11
		Fred L. Crawford (R)	8
		John D. Dingell Sr. (D)	15
		George A. Dondero (R)	17
		Albert J. Engel (R)	9
		Clare E. Hoffman (R)	4

Congress	Session Years	Representative	District
74 *(Cont.)*		Frank E. Hook (D)	12
		Henry M. Kimball (R)[34]	3
		John Lesinski Sr. (D)	16
		Verner W. Main (R)	3
		Carl E. Mapes (R)	5
		Clarence J. McLeod (R)	13
		Earl C. Michener (R)	2
		Louis C. Rabaut (D)	14
		George G. Sadowski (D)	1
		Jesse P. Wolcott (R)	7
		Roy O. Woodruff (R)	10
75	1937-1938	Fred L. Crawford (R)	8
		John D. Dingell Sr. (D)	15
		George A. Dondero (R)	17
		Albert J. Engel (R)	9
		Clare E. Hoffman (R)	4
		Frank E. Hook (D)	12
		John Lesinski Sr. (D)	16
		John Frederick Luecke (D)	11
		Carl E. Mapes (R)	5
		Earl C. Michener (R)	2
		George D. O'Brien (D)	13
		Louis C. Rabaut (D)	14
		George G. Sadowski (D)	1
		Paul W. Shafer (R)	3
		Andrew J. Transue (D)	6
		Jesse P. Wolcott (R)	7
		Roy O. Woodruff (R)	10
76	1939-1940	William W. Blackney (R)	6
		Fred Bradley (R)	11
		Fred L. Crawford (R)	8
		John D. Dingell Sr. (D)	15
		George A. Dondero (R)	17
		Albert J. Engel (R)	9
		Clare E. Hoffman (R)	4
		Frank E. Hook (D)	12
		Bartel J. Jonkman (R)	5
		John Lesinski Sr. (D)	16
		Carl E. Mapes (R)[35]	5
		Clarence J. McLeod (R)	13
		Earl C. Michener (R)	2
		Louis C. Rabaut (D)	14
		Paul W. Shafer (R)	3
		Rudolph G. Tenerowicz (D)	1
		Jesse P. Wolcott (R)	7
		Roy O. Woodruff (R)	10
77	1941-1942	William W. Blackney (R)	6
		Fred Bradley (R)	11
		Fred L. Crawford (R)	8
		John D. Dingell Sr. (D)	15
		George A. Dondero (R)	17
		Albert J. Engel (R)	9
		Clare E. Hoffman (R)	4
		Frank E. Hook (D)	12
		Bartel J. Jonkman (R)	5
		John Lesinski Sr. (D)	16
		Earl C. Michener (R)	2
		George D. O'Brien (D)	13
		Louis C. Rabaut (D)	14
		Paul W. Shafer (R)	3
		Rudolph G. Tenerowicz (D)	1
		Jesse P. Wolcott (R)	7
		Roy O. Woodruff (R)	10
78	1943-1944	John B. Bennett (R)	12
		William W. Blackney (R)	6
		Fred Bradley (R)	11
		Fred L. Crawford (R)	8

Congress	Session Years	Representative	District
78 *(Cont.)*		John D. Dingell Sr. (D)	15
		George A. Dondero (R)	17
		Albert J. Engel (R)	9
		Clare E. Hoffman (R)	4
		Bartel J. Jonkman (R)	5
		John Lesinski Sr. (D)	16
		Earl C. Michener (R)	2
		George D. O'Brien (D)	13
		Louis C. Rabaut (D)	14
		George G. Sadowski (D)	1
		Paul W. Shafer (R)	3
		Jesse P. Wolcott (R)	7
		Roy O. Woodruff (R)	10
79	1945-1946	William W. Blackney (R)	6
		Fred Bradley (R)	11
		Fred L. Crawford (R)	8
		John D. Dingell Sr. (D)	15
		George A. Dondero (R)	17
		Albert J. Engel (R)	9
		Clare E. Hoffman (R)	4
		Frank E. Hook (D)	12
		Bartel J. Jonkman (R)	5
		John Lesinski Sr. (D)	16
		Earl C. Michener (R)	2
		George D. O'Brien (D)	13
		Louis C. Rabaut (D)	14
		George G. Sadowski (D)	1
		Paul W. Shafer (R)	3
		Jesse P. Wolcott (R)	7
		Roy O. Woodruff (R)	10
80	1947-1948	John B. Bennett (R)	12
		William W. Blackney (R)	6
		Fred Bradley (R)[36]	11
		Howard A. Coffin (R)	13
		Fred L. Crawford (R)	8
		John D. Dingell Sr. (D)	15
		George A. Dondero (R)	17
		Albert J. Engel (R)	9
		Clare E. Hoffman (R)	4
		Bartel J. Jonkman (R)	5
		John Lesinski Sr. (D)	16
		Earl C. Michener (R)	2
		Charles E. Potter (R)	11
		George G. Sadowski (D)	1
		Paul W. Shafer (R)	3
		Jesse P. Wolcott (R)	7
		Roy O. Woodruff (R)	10
		Harold F. Youngblood (R)	14
81	1949-1950	John B. Bennett (R)	12
		William W. Blackney (R)	6
		Fred L. Crawford (R)	8
		John D. Dingell Sr. (D)	15
		George A. Dondero (R)	17
		Albert J. Engel (R)	9
		Gerald R. Ford Jr. (R)	5
		Clare E. Hoffman (R)	4
		John Lesinski Sr. (D)	16
		Earl C. Michener (R)	2
		George D. O'Brien (D)	13
		Charles E. Potter (R)	11
		Louis C. Rabaut (D)	14
		George G. Sadowski (D)	1
		Paul W. Shafer (R)	3
		Jesse P. Wolcott (R)	7
		Roy O. Woodruff (R)	10
82	1951-1952	John B. Bennett (R)	12
		William W. Blackney (R)	6
		Fred L. Crawford (R)	8

Congress	Session Years	Representative	District
82 *(Cont.)*		John D. Dingell Sr. (D)	15
		George A. Dondero (R)	17
		Gerald R. Ford Jr. (R)	5
		Clare E. Hoffman (R)	4
		John Lesinski Jr. (D)	16
		Thaddeus M. Machrowicz (D)	1
		George Meader (R)	2
		George D. O'Brien (D)	13
		Charles E. Potter (R)	11
		Louis C. Rabaut (D)	14
		Paul W. Shafer (R)	3
		Ruth Thompson (R)	9
		Jesse P. Wolcott (R)	7
		Roy O. Woodruff (R)	10
83[37]	1953-1954	John B. Bennett (R)	12
		Alvin M. Bentley (R)	8
		Elford A. Cederberg (R)	10
		Kit Clardy (R)	6
		John D. Dingell Sr. (D)	15
		George A. Dondero (R)	18
		Gerald R. Ford Jr. (R)	5
		Clare E. Hoffman (R)	4
		Victor A. Knox (R)	11
		John Lesinski Jr. (D)	16
		Thaddeus M. Machrowicz (D)	1
		George Meader (R)	2
		Charles G. Oakman (R)	17
		George D. O'Brien (D)	13
		Louis C. Rabaut (D)	14
		Paul W. Shafer (R)	3
		Ruth Thompson (R)	9
		Jesse P. Wolcott (R)	7
84	1955-1956	John B. Bennett (R)	12
		Alvin M. Bentley (R)	8
		Elford A. Cederberg (R)	10
		Charles C. Diggs Jr. (D)	13
		John D. Dingell Sr. (D)[38]	15
		John D. Dingell Jr. (D)	15
		George A. Dondero (R)	18
		Gerald R. Ford Jr. (R)	5
		Martha Wright Griffiths (D)	17
		Donald Hayworth (D)	6
		Clare E. Hoffman (R)	4
		August E. Johansen (R)	3
		Victor A. Knox (R)	11
		John Lesinski Jr. (D)	16
		Thaddeus M. Machrowicz (D)	1
		George Meader (R)	2
		Louis C. Rabaut (D)	14
		Ruth Thompson (R)	9
		Jesse P. Wolcott (R)	7
85	1957-1958	John B. Bennett (R)	12
		Alvin M. Bentley (R)	8
		William S. Broomfield (R)	18
		Elford A. Cederberg (R)	10
		Charles E. Chamberlain (R)	6
		Charles C. Diggs Jr. (D)	13
		John D. Dingell Jr. (D)	15
		Gerald R. Ford Jr. (R)	5
		Robert P. Griffin (R)	9
		Martha Wright Griffiths (D)	17
		Clare E. Hoffman (R)	4
		August E. Johansen (R)	3
		Victor A. Knox (R)	11
		John Lesinski Jr. (D)	16
		Thaddeus M. Machrowicz (D)	1
		Robert J. McIntosh (R)	7
		George Meader (R)	2
		Louis C. Rabaut (D)	14

Congress	Session Years	Representative	District
86	1959-1960	John B. Bennett (R)	12
		Alvin M. Bentley (R)	8
		William S. Broomfield (R)	18
		Elford A. Cederberg (R)	10
		Charles E. Chamberlain (R)	6
		Charles C. Diggs Jr. (D)	13
		John D. Dingell Jr. (D)	15
		Gerald R. Ford Jr. (R)	5
		Robert P. Griffin (R)	9
		Martha Wright Griffiths (D)	17
		Clare E. Hoffman (R)	4
		August E. Johansen (R)	3
		Victor A. Knox (R)	11
		John Lesinski Jr. (D)	16
		Thaddeus M. Machrowicz (D)	1
		George Meader (R)	2
		James G. O'Hara (D)	7
		Louis C. Rabaut (D)	14
87	1961-1962	John B. Bennett (R)	12
		William S. Broomfield (R)	18
		Elford A. Cederberg (R)	10
		Charles E. Chamberlain (R)	6
		Charles C. Diggs Jr. (D)	13
		John D. Dingell Jr. (D)	15
		Gerald R. Ford Jr. (R)	5
		Robert P. Griffin (R)	9
		Martha Wright Griffiths (D)	17
		James Harvey (R)	8
		Clare E. Hoffman (R)	4
		August E. Johansen (R)	3
		Victor A. Knox (R)	11
		John Lesinski Jr. (D)	16
		Thaddeus M. Machrowicz (D)[39]	1
		George Meader (R)	2
		Lucien N. Nedzi (D)	1
		James G. O'Hara (D)	7
		Louis C. Rabaut (D)[40]	14
		Harold M. Ryan (D)	14
88[41]	1963-1964	John B. Bennett (R)	12
		William S. Broomfield (R)	18
		Elford A. Cederberg (R)	10
		Charles E. Chamberlain (R)	6
		Charles C. Diggs Jr. (D)	13
		John D. Dingell Jr. (D)	15
		Gerald R. Ford Jr. (R)	5
		Robert P. Griffin (R)	9
		Martha Wright Griffiths (D)	17
		James Harvey (R)	8
		Edward Hutchinson (R)	4
		August E. Johansen (R)	3
		Victor A. Knox (R)	11
		John Lesinski Jr. (D)	16
		George Meader (R)	2
		Lucien N. Nedzi (D)	1
		James G. O'Hara (D)	7
		Harold M. Ryan (D)	14
		Neil Staebler (D)[42]	
89[43]	1965-1966	William S. Broomfield (R)	18
		Elford A. Cederberg (R)	10
		Charles E. Chamberlain (R)	6
		Raymond F. Clevenger (D)	11
		John Conyers Jr. (D)	1
		Charles C. Diggs Jr. (D)	13
		John D. Dingell Jr. (D)	16
		Billie S. Farnum (D)	19
		Gerald R. Ford Jr. (R)	5
		William D. Ford (D)	15
		Robert P. Griffin (R)[44]	9

Congress	Session Years	Representative	District
89 *(Cont.)*		Martha Wright Griffiths (D)...............	17
		James Harvey (R).......................	8
		Edward Hutchinson (R)..................	4
		John C. Mackie (D)....................	7
		Lucien N. Nedzi (D)....................	14
		James G. O'Hara (D)....................	12
		Paul H. Todd Jr. (D)...................	3
		Guy Vander Jagt (R)....................	9
		Weston E. Vivian (D)...................	2
90	1967-1968	William S. Broomfield (R)...............	18
		Garry E. Brown (R)....................	3
		Elford A. Cederberg (R)................	10
		Charles E. Chamberlain (R)..............	6
		John Conyers Jr. (D)....................	1
		Charles C. Diggs Jr. (D).................	13
		John D. Dingell Jr. (D).................	16
		Marvin L. Esch (R)....................	2
		Gerald R. Ford Jr. (R)..................	5
		William D. Ford (D)...................	15
		Martha Wright Griffiths (D).............	17
		James Harvey (R)......................	8
		Edward Hutchinson (R)..................	4
		Jack H. McDonald (R)..................	19
		Lucien N. Nedzi (D)....................	14
		James G. O'Hara (D)....................	12
		Donald W. Riegle Jr. (R)................	7
		Philip E. Ruppe (R)...................	11
		Guy Vander Jagt (R)...................	9
91	1969-1970	William S. Broomfield (R)...............	18
		Garry E. Brown (R)....................	3
		Elford A. Cederberg (R)................	10
		Charles E. Chamberlain (R)..............	6
		John Conyers Jr. (D)....................	1
		Charles C. Diggs Jr. (D).................	13
		John D. Dingell Jr. (D).................	16
		Marvin L. Esch (R)....................	2
		Gerald R. Ford Jr. (R)..................	5
		William D. Ford (D)...................	15
		Martha Wright Griffiths (D).............	17
		James Harvey (R)......................	8
		Edward Hutchinson (R)..................	4
		Jack H. McDonald (R)..................	19
		Lucien N. Nedzi (D)....................	14
		James G. O'Hara (D)....................	12
		Donald W. Riegle Jr. (R)................	7
		Philip E. Ruppe (R)...................	11
		Guy Vander Jagt (R)...................	9
92	1971-1972	William S. Broomfield (R)...............	18
		Garry E. Brown (R)....................	3
		Elford A. Cederberg (R)................	10
		Charles E. Chamberlain (R)..............	6
		John Conyers Jr. (D)....................	1
		Charles C. Diggs Jr. (D).................	13
		John D. Dingell Jr. (D).................	16
		Marvin L. Esch (R)....................	2
		Gerald R. Ford Jr. (R)..................	5
		William D. Ford (D)...................	15
		Martha Wright Griffiths (D).............	17
		James Harvey (R)......................	8
		Edward Hutchinson (R)..................	4
		Jack H. McDonald (R)..................	19
		Lucien N. Nedzi (D)....................	14
		James G. O'Hara (D)....................	12
		Donald W. Riegle Jr. (R)................	7
		Philip E. Ruppe (R)...................	11
		Guy Vander Jagt (R)...................	9
93[45]	1973-1974	William S. Broomfield (R)...............	19
		Garry E. Brown (R)....................	3

Congress	Session Years	Representative	District
93 *(Cont.)*		Elford A. Cederberg (R)	10
		Charles E. Chamberlain (R)	6
		John Conyers Jr. (D)	1
		Charles C. Diggs Jr. (D)	13
		John D. Dingell Jr. (D).	16
		Marvin L. Esch (R)	2
		Gerald R. Ford Jr. (R)[46].	5
		William D. Ford (D).	15
		Martha Wright Griffiths (D).	17
		James Harvey (R)[47].	8
		Robert J. Huber (R)	18
		Edward Hutchinson (R)	4
		Lucien N. Nedzi (D).	14
		James G. O'Hara (D)	12
		Donald W. Riegle Jr. (D)	7
		Philip E. Ruppe (R)	11
		Bob Traxler (D).	8
		Guy Vander Jagt (R)	9
		Richard F. VanderVeen (D)	5
94	1975-1976	James J. Blanchard (D).	18
		William M. Brodhead (D).	17
		William S. Broomfield (R).	19
		Garry E. Brown (R)	3
		M. Robert Carr (D).	6
		Elford A. Cederberg (R)	10
		John Conyers Jr. (D)	1
		Charles C. Diggs Jr. (D)	13
		John D. Dingell Jr. (D).	16
		Marvin L. Esch (R)	2
		William D. Ford (D).	15
		Edward Hutchinson (R)	4
		Lucien N. Nedzi (D).	14
		James G. O'Hara (D)	12
		Donald W. Riegle Jr. (D)	7
		Philip E. Ruppe (R)	11
		Bob Traxler (D).	8
		Guy Vander Jagt (R).	9
		Richard F. VanderVeen (D)	5
95	1977-1978	James J. Blanchard (D).	18
		David E. Bonior (D).	12
		William M. Brodhead (D).	17
		William S. Broomfield (R).	19
		Garry E. Brown (R)	3
		M. Robert Carr (D).	6
		Elford A. Cederberg (R)	10
		John Conyers Jr. (D)	1
		Charles C. Diggs Jr. (D)	13
		John D. Dingell Jr. (D).	16
		William D. Ford (D).	15
		Dale E. Kildee (D).	7
		Lucien N. Nedzi (D).	14
		Carl D. Pursell (R)	2
		Philip E. Ruppe (R)	11
		Harold S. Sawyer (R)	5
		David A. Stockman (R).	4
		Bob Traxler (D).	8
		Guy Vander Jagt (R).	9
96	1979-1980	Donald J. Albosta (D)	10
		James J. Blanchard (D).	18
		David E. Bonior (D).	12
		William M. Brodhead (D).	17
		William S. Broomfield (R).	19
		M. Robert Carr (D).	6
		John Conyers Jr. (D)	1
		George W. Crockett Jr. (D).	13
		Robert William Davis (R)	11
		Charles C. Diggs Jr. (D)[48]	13
		John D. Dingell Jr. (D).	16

Congress	Session Years	Representative	District
96 *(Cont.)*		William D. Ford (D)	15
		Dale E. Kildee (D)	7
		Lucien N. Nedzi (D)	14
		Carl D. Pursell (R)	2
		Harold S. Sawyer (R)	5
		David A. Stockman (R)	4
		Bob Traxler (D)	8
		Guy Vander Jagt (R)	9
		Howard E. Wolpe (D)	3
97	1981-1982	Donald J. Albosta (D)	10
		James J. Blanchard (D)	18
		David E. Bonior (D)	12
		William M. Brodhead (D)	17
		William S. Broomfield (R)	19
		John Conyers Jr. (D)	1
		George W. Crockett Jr. (D)	13
		Robert William Davis (R)	11
		John D. Dingell Jr. (D)	16
		James Dunn (R)	6
		William D. Ford (D)	15
		Dennis M. Hertel (D)	14
		Dale E. Kildee (D)	7
		Carl D. Pursell (R)	2
		Harold S. Sawyer (R)	5
		Mark D. Siljander (R)	4
		David A. Stockman (R)[49]	4
		Bob Traxler (D)	8
		Guy Vander Jagt (R)	9
		Howard E. Wolpe (D)	3
98[50]	1983-1984	Donald J. Albosta (D)	10
		David E. Bonior (D)	12
		William S. Broomfield (R)	18
		M. Robert Carr (D)	6
		John Conyers Jr. (D)	1
		George W. Crockett Jr. (D)	13
		Robert William Davis (R)	11
		John D. Dingell Jr. (D)	16
		William D. Ford (D)	15
		Dennis M. Hertel (D)	14
		Dale E. Kildee (D)	7
		Sander M. Levin (D)	17
		Carl D. Pursell (R)	2
		Harold S. Sawyer (R)	5
		Mark D. Siljander (R)	4
		Bob Traxler (D)	8
		Guy Vander Jagt (R)	9
		Howard E. Wolpe (D)	3
99	1985-1986	David E. Bonior (D)	12
		William S. Broomfield (R)	18
		M. Robert Carr (D)	6
		John Conyers Jr. (D)	1
		George W. Crockett Jr. (D)	13
		Robert William Davis (R)	11
		John D. Dingell Jr. (D)	16
		William D. Ford (D)	15
		Paul B. Henry (R)	5
		Dennis M. Hertel (D)	14
		Dale E. Kildee (D)	7
		Sander M. Levin (D)	17
		Carl D. Pursell (R)	2
		Bill Schuette (R)	10
		Mark D. Siljander (R)	4
		Bob Traxler (D)	8
		Guy Vander Jagt (R)	9
		Howard E. Wolpe (D)	3
100	1987-1988	David E. Bonior (D)	12
		William S. Broomfield (R)	18

Congress	Session Years	Representative	District
100 *(Cont.)*		M. Robert Carr (D)	6
		John Conyers Jr. (D)	1
		George W. Crockett Jr. (D)	13
		Robert William Davis (R)	11
		John D. Dingell Jr. (D)	16
		William D. Ford (D)	15
		Paul B. Henry (R)	5
		Dennis M. Hertel (D)	14
		Dale E. Kildee (D)	7
		Sander M. Levin (D)	17
		Carl D. Pursell (R)	2
		Bill Schuette (R)	10
		Bob Traxler (D)	8
		Fred S. Upton (R)	4
		Guy Vander Jagt (R)	9
		Howard E. Wolpe (D)	3
101	1989-1990	David E. Bonior (D)	12
		William S. Broomfield (R)	18
		M. Robert Carr (D)	6
		John Conyers Jr. (D)	1
		George W. Crockett Jr. (D)	13
		Robert William Davis (R)	11
		John D. Dingell Jr. (D)	16
		William D. Ford (D)	15
		Paul B. Henry (R)	5
		Dennis M. Hertel (D)	14
		Dale E. Kildee (D)	7
		Sander M. Levin (D)	17
		Carl D. Pursell (R)	2
		Bill Schuette (R)	10
		Bob Traxler (D)	8
		Fred S. Upton (R)	4
		Guy Vander Jagt (R)	9
		Howard E. Wolpe (D)	3
102	1991-1992	David E. Bonior (D)	12
		William S. Broomfield (R)	18
		David Camp (R)	10
		M. Robert Carr (D)	6
		Barbara-Rose Collins (D)	13
		John Conyers Jr. (D)	1
		Robert William Davis (R)	11
		John D. Dingell Jr. (D)	16
		William D. Ford (D)	15
		Paul B. Henry (R)	5
		Dennis M. Hertel (D)	14
		Dale E. Kildee (D)	7
		Sander M. Levin (D)	17
		Carl D. Pursell (R)	2
		Bob Traxler (D)	8
		Fred S. Upton (R)	4
		Guy Vander Jagt (R)	9
		Howard E. Wolpe (D)	3
103[51]	1993-1994	James A. Barcia (D)	5
		David E. Bonior (D)	10
		David Camp (R)	4
		M. Robert Carr (D)	8
		Barbara-Rose Collins (D)	15
		John Conyers Jr. (D)	14
		John D. Dingell Jr. (D)	16
		William D. Ford (D)	13
		Paul B. Henry (R)[52]	3
		Peter Hoekstra (R)	2
		Dale E. Kildee (D)	9
		Joe Knollenberg (R)	11
		Sander M. Levin (D)	12
		Nick H. Smith (R)	7
		Bart Stupak (D)	1
		Fred S. Upton (R)	6

Congress	Session Years	Representative	District
104	1995-1996	James A. Barcia (D)	5
		David E. Bonior (D)	10
		David Camp (R)	4
		Dick Chrysler (R)	8
		Barbara-Rose Collins (D)	15
		John Conyers Jr. (D)	14
		John D. Dingell Jr. (D)	16
		Vernon J. Ehlers (R)	3
		Peter Hoekstra (R)	2
		Dale E. Kildee (D)	9
		Joe Knollenberg (R)	11
		Sander M. Levin (D)	12
		Lynn Rivers (D)	13
		Nick H. Smith (R)	7
		Bart Stupak (D)	1
		Fred S. Upton (R)	6
105	1997-1998	James A. Barcia (D)	5
		David E. Bonior (D)	10
		David Camp (R)	4
		John Conyers Jr. (D)	14
		John D. Dingell Jr. (D)	16
		Vernon J. Ehlers (R)	3
		Peter Hoekstra (R)	2
		Dale E. Kildee (D)	9
		Carolyn Cheeks Kilpatrick (D)	15
		Joe Knollenberg (R)	11
		Sander M. Levin (D)	12
		Lynn Rivers (D)	13
		Nick H. Smith (R)	7
		Debbie Stabenow (D)	8
		Bart Stupak (D)	1
		Fred S. Upton (R)	6
106	1999-2000	James A. Barcia (D)	5
		David E. Bonior (D)	10
		David Camp (R)	4
		John Conyers Jr. (D)	14
		John D. Dingell Jr. (D)	16
		Vernon J. Ehlers (R)	3
		Peter Hoekstra (R)	2
		Dale E. Kildee (D)	9
		Carolyn Cheeks Kilpatrick (D)	15
		Joe Knollenberg (R)	11
		Sander M. Levin (D)	12
		Lynn Rivers (D)	13
		Nick H. Smith (R)	7
		Debbie Stabenow (D)	8
		Bart Stupak (D)	1
		Fred S. Upton (R)	6
107	2001-2002	James A. Barcia (D)	5
		David E. Bonior (D)	10
		David Camp (R)	4
		John Conyers Jr. (D)	14
		John D. Dingell Jr. (D)	16
		Vernon J. Ehlers (R)	3
		Peter Hoekstra (R)	2
		Dale E. Kildee (D)	9
		Carolyn Cheeks Kilpatrick (D)	15
		Joe Knollenberg (R)	11
		Sander M. Levin (D)	12
		Lynn Rivers (D)	13
		Mike Rogers (R)	8
		Nick H. Smith (R)	7
		Bart Stupak (D)	1
		Fred S. Upton (R)	6
108[53]	2003-2004	David Camp (R)	4
		John Conyers Jr. (D)	14
		John D. Dingell Jr. (D)	15
		Vernon J. Ehlers (R)	3

U.S. REPRESENTATIVES *(Cont.)*

Congress	Session Years	Representative	District
108 *(Cont.)*		Peter Hoekstra (R)	2
		Dale E. Kildee (D)	5
		Carolyn Cheeks Kilpatrick (D)	13
		Joe Knollenberg (R)	9
		Sander M. Levin (D)	12
		Thaddeus G. McCotter (R)	11
		Candice S. Miller (R)	10
		Mike Rogers (R)	8
		Nick H. Smith (R)	7
		Bart Stupak (D)	1
		Fred S. Upton (R)	6
109	2005-2006	David Camp (R)	4
		John Conyers Jr. (D)	14
		John D. Dingell Jr. (D)	15
		Vernon J. Ehlers (R)	3
		Peter Hoekstra (R)	2
		Dale E. Kildee (D)	5
		Carolyn Cheeks Kilpatrick (D)	13
		Joe Knollenberg (R)	9
		Sander M. Levin (D)	12
		Thaddeus G. McCotter (R)	11
		Candice S. Miller (R)	10
		Mike Rogers (R)	8
		John J. H. Schwarz (R)	7
		Bart Stupak (D)	1
		Fred S. Upton (R)	6
110	2007-2008	David Camp (R)	4
		John Conyers Jr. (D)	14
		John D. Dingell Jr. (D)	15
		Vernon J. Ehlers (R)	3
		Peter Hoekstra (R)	2
		Dale E. Kildee (D)	5
		Carolyn Cheeks Kilpatrick (D)	13
		Joe Knollenberg (R)	9
		Sander M. Levin (D)	12
		Thaddeus G. McCotter (R)	11
		Candice S. Miller (R)	10
		Mike Rogers (R)	8
		Bart Stupak (D)	1
		Fred S. Upton (R)	6
		Tim Walberg (R)	7
111	2009-2010	David Camp (R)	4
		John Conyers Jr. (D)	14
		John D. Dingell Jr. (D)	15
		Vernon J. Ehlers (R)	3
		Peter Hoekstra (R)	2
		Dale E. Kildee (D)	5
		Carolyn Cheeks Kilpatrick (D)	13
		Sander M. Levin (D)	12
		Thaddeus G. McCotter (R)	11
		Candice S. Miller (R)	10
		Gary C. Peters (D)	9
		Mike Rogers (R)	8
		Mark Schauer (D)	7
		Bart Stupak (D)	1
		Fred S. Upton (R)	6
112	2011-2012	Justin Amash (R)	3
		Dan Benishek (R)	1
		David Camp (R)	4
		Hansen Clarke (D)	13
		John Conyers Jr. (D)	14
		John D. Dingell Jr. (D)	15
		Bill Huizenga (R)	2
		Dale E. Kildee (D)	5
		Sander M. Levin (D)	12
		Thaddeus G. McCotter (R)	11
		Candice S. Miller (R)	10
		Gary C. Peters (D)	9

112 *(Cont.)*		Mike Rogers (R)............................	8
		Fred S. Upton (R)	6
		Tim Walberg (R)	7
113	2013-2014	Justin Amash (R)	3
		Dan Benishek (R)	1
		Kerry Bentivolio (R).......................	11
		David Camp (R)...........................	4
		John Conyers Jr. (D)	13
		John D. Dingell Jr. (D).....................	12
		Bill Huizenga (R)..........................	2
		Daniel T. Kildee (D)	5
		Sander M. Levin (D).......................	9
		Candice S. Miller (R)	10
		Gary C. Peters (D)........................	14
		Mike Rogers (R)...........................	8
		Fred S. Upton (R)	6
		Tim Walberg (R)	7
114	2015-2016	Justin Amash (R)	3
		Dan Benishek (R)	1
		Michael D. Bishop (R)	8
		John Conyers Jr. (D)	13
		Debbie Dingell (D)	12
		Bill Huizenga (R)..........................	2
		Daniel T. Kildee (D)	5
		Brenda L. Lawrence (D).....................	14
		Sander M. Levin (D).......................	9
		Candice S. Miller (R)	10
		John Moolenaar (R)	4
		David A. Trott (R)	11
		Fred S. Upton (R)	6
		Tim Walberg (R)	7
115	2017-2018	Justin Amash (R)	3
		Jack Bergman (R)	1
		Michael D. Bishop (R)	8
		John Conyers Jr. (D)	13
		Debbie Dingell (D)	12
		Bill Huizenga (R)..........................	2
		Daniel T. Kildee (D)	5
		Brenda L. Lawrence (D).....................	14
		Sander M. Levin (D).......................	9
		Paul Mitchell (R)	10
		John Moolenaar (R)	4
		David A. Trott (R)	11
		Fred S. Upton (R)	6
		Tim Walberg (R)	7
116	2019-2020	Justin Amash (Ind)[54].....................	3
		Jack Bergman (R)	1
		Debbie Dingell (D)	12
		Bill Huizenga (R)..........................	2
		Daniel T. Kildee (D)	5
		Brenda L. Lawrence (D).....................	14
		Andy Levin (D)	9
		Paul Mitchell (R)	10
		John Moolenaar (R)	4
		Elissa Slotkin (D).........................	8
		Haley Stevens (D)	11
		Rashida Tlaib (D)..........................	13
		Fred S. Upton (R)	6
		Tim Walberg (R)	7

Political Party Designations

D — Democrat	Ind — Independent	DPUS — Democratic Peoples Union Silver
R — Republican	Fus — Fusionist	Prog — Progressive
W — Whig	D&U — Democratic and Union	FS — Free Soil

Information on party affiliation was not always available; therefore, some individuals may be listed without this data.

---

[1] As Michigan's admission to the Union occurred between the 1830 and 1840 decennial censuses, it was entitled to one representative until the U.S. Congress enacted a new apportionment act following the 1840 census. See U.S. Constitution, article I, section 2, clause 3.

[2] The first elected U.S. representative from the state of Michigan, elected October 5 and 6, 1835. However, due to Michigan's dispute with the U.S. Congress over the Toledo Strip and the state's admission to the Union, Congress refused to accept his credentials until it admitted Michigan to the Union as a state January 26, 1837. See U.S. Const, art I, § 2, cl 1; art I, § 4, cl 1; art I, § 5, cl 1; An act in addition to an act to amend the several acts now in force, regulating the election of a delegate to the Congress of the United States, and the election of members of the legislative council of this Territory, and for other purposes, Laws of the Territory of Michigan.

[3] See Act 33 of 1843, Laws of Michigan.

[4] Elected November 3, 1846, but died before taking seat; Charles E. Stuart elected November 2, 1847, to fill vacancy.

[5] See Act 164 of the Extra Session of 1851, Laws of Michigan.

[6] George B. Cooper won the election of November 2, 1858, and was seated by the U.S. House of Representatives. William A. Howard contested the results in the U.S. House, alleging voting irregularities in several wards. Following its investigation, the Committee on Elections of the U.S. House of Representatives reported that the sitting member, Cooper, was not entitled to his seat and that the contestant Howard was. The House passed resolutions to that effect May 15, 1860, at which time Howard took the oath of office. See U.S. Const, art I, § 5, cl 1; Cong Globe, 36th Cong, 1st Sess (1859); Hinds' Precedents of the House of Representatives of the United States, Vol I, §§ 837-838.

[7] See Act 181 of 1861, Laws of Michigan.

[8] Elected to U.S. Senate January 18, 1871; Wilder D. Foster elected to fill vacancy April 4, 1871.

[9] See U.S. Const, art I, § 2, cl 3; art XIV, § 2; Act 44 of the Extra Session of 1872, Laws of Michigan.

[10] Died September 20, 1873; William B. Williams elected November 4, 1873, to fill vacancy.

[11] Died December 28, 1878; vacancy not filled.

[12] Elected to U.S. Senate January 18, 1881; John T. Rich elected April 4, 1881, to fill vacancy.

[13] See Act 21 of the Extra Session of 1882.

[14] Died December 22, 1887; Henry W. Seymour elected to fill vacancy February 14, 1888.

[15] Died April 20, 1891; Charles E. Belknap elected November 3, 1891, to fill vacancy.

[16] See Act 168 of 1891.

[17] Died August 17, 1893; Levi T. Griffin elected November 7, 1893, to fill vacancy.

[18] George F. Richardson won the November 8, 1892, election by a plurality of 10 votes, receiving a certificate of election from the board of state canvassers. The defeated candidate, Charles E. Belknap, applied for a Michigan Supreme Court order (writ of mandamus) to order the Ionia County Board of Canvassers to recount that vote, alleging irregularities in the vote tabulation. The Supreme Court issued that order February 3, 1893; the subsequent recount resulted in a plurality of 19 votes for Belknap. The new board of state canvassers then issued a certificate of election to Belknap. The contest was brought to the floor of the U.S. House of Representatives August 8, 1893. Following debate on the validity of the contestants' credentials, the House voted to seat Richardson, referring the matter to the Committee on Elections. Following further examination, the committee issued a report upholding Richardson's claim to the seat. See U.S. Const, art I, § 5, cl 1; *Belknap v The Board of Canvassers of Ionia County,* 94 Mich. 516 (1893); *Belknap v The Board of State Canvassers,* 95 Mich. 155 (1893); Cong Rec, 53rd Cong, 1st Sess (1893); Hinds' Precedents of the House of Representatives of the United States, Vol II, §1042.

[19] Elected to U.S. Senate January 16, 1895; Alfred Milnes elected April 18, 1895, to fill vacancy.

[20] Died May 1, 1901; Henry H. Aplin elected October 15, 1901, to fill vacancy.

[21] Elected to U.S. Senate February 6, 1907; Gerrit J. Diekema elected April 27, 1907, to fill vacancy.

[22] See An act for the apportionment of Representatives in Congress among the several States under the Thirteenth Census, PL 62-5, 37 Stat 13 (1911).

[23] Elected congressman at-large. On August 8, 1911, the U.S. Congress enacted the apportionment of representatives required by the U.S. Constitution, following the 1910 federal decennial census. That law increased Michigan's congressional delegation by 1 from 12 to 13 representatives. Michigan, however, did not redraw its congressional districts until 1913. See U.S. Const, art I, § 2, cl 3; Act 337 of 1913.

[24] Unofficial returns of the November 5, 1912, election indicated that William J. MacDonald, the Progressive candidate for the U.S. House of Representatives, won the seat by a plurality of 243 votes. The state board of canvassers, however, did not count 458 votes cast in Ontonagon County for Sheldon William J. MacDonald toward William J. MacDonald's vote total. It issued a certificate of election to H. Olin Young, based on a plurality of 215 votes; Young was seated by the U.S. House of Representatives based on those credentials. The election contest was brought to the floor of the U.S. House, where it was referred to the Committee on Elections. Following examination, the committee, citing honest mistake in the way MacDonald's name had been printed on the Ontonagon County ballot, unanimously reported a resolution awarding the 12th District seat to MacDonald. MacDonald took the oath of office August 26, 1913. See U.S. Const, art I, § 5, cl 1; Cong Rec, 63rd Cong, 1st Sess (1913).

[25] Official returns of the November 7, 1916, election showed that Mark R. Bacon had been elected by a majority of 49 votes over Samuel W. Beakes. Following the election, several of the election inspectors in Jackson County concluded that a mistake had been made in the vote count. Although state law at that time did not provide for a recount of ballots in the election of federal officials, attorneys for both Bacon and Beakes agreed to unofficially have the ballots cast for Congress examined. This examination occurred during an official recount of votes for county coroner; the examination showed that Beakes was, in fact, entitled to 87 more votes than the official returns had given him. Beakes contended that since the returns were conceded to be erroneous, they should be set aside and a recount of the vote made. Bacon, citing state law, insisted that as the ballot box had not been sealed and kept in safe custody, a recount would be invalid. Both the board of state canvassers and the Michigan Supreme Court refused an application for a recount. The Committee on Elections in the U.S. House of Representatives, after reviewing the circumstances and issues involved, elected to retabulate the official returns which they deemed to be unimpeached and added to those original votes from the district which had been rejected. The revised vote gave Beakes a majority of 132 votes. The committee unanimously reported resolutions stating that Bacon had not been elected to the seat and was not entitled to it, and that, in fact, Beakes was the elected representative of the district. The House seated Beakes on December 13, 1917. See U.S. Const, art I, § 5, cl 1; Act 320 of 1913; Cong Rec, 65th Cong, 1st and 2nd Sess (1917); Hinds' Precedents of the House of Representatives of the United States, Vol VI, § 144.

[26] Died April 26, 1920; Clarence J. McLeod elected to fill vacancy.

[27] Died May 9, 1921; John M. C. Smith elected June 28, 1921, to fill vacancy.

[28] Died March 23, 1923; Arthur B. Williams elected June 19, 1923, to fill vacancy.

[29] Died May 1, 1925; Joseph L. Hooper elected August 18, 1925, to fill vacancy.

[30] Died November 29, 1932; vacancy not filled.

[31] Died July 18, 1931; Michael J. Hart elected November 3, 1931, to fill vacancy.

[32] See Act 20 of 1931.

[33] Died February 22, 1934; vacancy not filled.

[34] Died October 19, 1935; Verner W. Main elected December 17, 1935, to fill vacancy.

[35] Died December 12, 1939; Bartel J. Jonkman elected February 19, 1940, to fill vacancy.

[36] Died May 24, 1947; Charles E. Potter elected August 26, 1947, to fill vacancy.

[37] See Act 64 of 1951.

[38] Died September 19, 1955; John D. Dingell Jr. elected December 13, 1955, to fill vacancy.

[39] Resigned September 18, 1961; Lucien N. Nedzi elected November 7, 1961, to fill vacancy.

[40] Died November 12, 1961; Harold M. Ryan elected February 13, 1962, to fill vacancy.

[41] See 2 PL 70-13, 46 Stat 26, 2 USC 2a; PL 77-291, 55 Stat 762, 2 USC 2b.

[42] Elected congressman at-large. Based on population figures compiled under the 1960 decennial census, Michigan's congressional delegation increased by 1 member, from 18 to 19. The state legislature, however, failed to reapportion the state's congressional districts in time for the 1962 election schedule. See U.S. Const, art I, § 2, cl 3; art XIV, 2 USC 2a-2b.

[43] The Michigan Legislature enacted Act 249 of 1963 to apportion the state's congressional districts as required by federal law. Subsequently, the apportionment was challenged in the U.S. District Court on the basis that it violated the "one man, one vote" rule. On March 26, 1964, the U.S. District Court ruled that Act 249 of 1963 violated the U.S. Constitution and was therefore void and invalid in its application. The court enjoined the secretary of state from enforcing or applying the statute in subsequent congressional elections; it also prohibited the election of Michigan's congressional delegation by districts until the legislature passed an apportionment act which met U.S. constitutional requirements. As a result, the legislature enacted Act 282 of 1964 to comply with the court order; it also enacted legislation, Act 280 of 1964, to change the election schedule for 1964 only due to the delay in the apportionment process. See U.S. Const, art I, § 2, cl 3; 2 USC 2a-2b; Act 249 of 1963; Act 282 of 1964; *Calkins* v *Hare*, 228 F. Supp. 824 (E.D. Mich. 1964).

[44] Resigned May 11, 1966; appointed to U.S. Senate; Guy Vander Jagt elected November 8, 1966, to fill vacancy.

[45] Based on population figures compiled under the 1970 decennial census, federal law required Michigan's legislature to reapportion the state's congressional districts to reflect population shifts among the districts. Having failed to do so as 1971 ended, suit was filed in the U.S. District Court challenging the constitutionality of Act 282 of 1964 because its districts did not reflect population changes and shifts among the districts since 1964, and seeking judicial relief in the event that the Michigan Legislature did not appropriately redistrict the state's congressional districts. The parties to the suit agreed that if the legislature did not act by February 29, 1972, any of them could petition the court for a hearing, at which time the court could request that each of the parties present their own apportionment plans for the court's consideration.

The legislature did not enact legislation and the court requested that the parties submit their own plans. Four such plans were submitted by the plaintiffs and intervening plaintiffs. On May 31, 1972, the court ordered adoption of the plan submitted by the intervening plaintiffs, with the modifications submitted in regard to certain districts. In its order, the court stated that the plan that it was ordering to be adopted met the criteria set forth in other court cases on congressional apportionment: (1) population variances among the districts were minimal, thereby preserving the "one man, one vote" standard; (2) the districts were contiguous; (3) the districts were reasonably compact, and (4) political subdivisions in the districts were maintained intact insofar as possible. See U.S. Const, art I, § 2, cl 3; PL 70-13, 46 Stat 26, 2 USC 2a; PL 90-196, 81 Stat 581, 2 USC 2c; *Dunnell* v *Austin*, 344 F. Supp. 210 (E.D. Mich. 1972).

[46] Resigned December 6, 1973, to be sworn in as vice president of the United States; Richard F. VanderVeen elected February 18, 1974, to fill vacancy.

[47] Resigned January 31, 1974; Bob Traxler elected April 16, 1974, to fill vacancy.

[48] Resigned June 3, 1980; George W. Crockett Jr., elected November 4, 1980, to fill vacancy.

[49] Resigned January 27, 1981, to become the director of the Office of Management and Budget; Mark D. Siljander elected April 21, 1981, to fill vacancy.

[50] Having not enacted apportionment legislation to reflect the population changes reported in the 1980 decennial census (which resulted in a reduction, from 19 to 18 members, in Michigan's congressional delegation), suit was filed on December 12, 1981, in the U.S. District Court. The plaintiffs, alleging that the current districts were unconstitutional in view of the 1980 census data, sought to enjoin future elections in the existing districts until reapportionment occurred; to have the court set a deadline for legislative action to establish new districts, and to require the court to assume jurisdiction and develop the reapportionment plan if the legislature did not act in timely fashion. Subsequently, intervening defendants filed a motion for judgment on the pleadings. The district court, on February 24, 1982, denied the motion, reasoning that sufficient time remained for the legislature to act; it also declined to set a deadline for legislative action. The court, however, did acknowledge that the congressional elections would be seriously jeopardized if action did not occur until after the third week in April.

On April 9, 1982, the court issued an order directing the parties to the suit to be prepared to submit reapportionment plans on twenty-four-hour notice. The order also stated that should the legislature fail to act by May 4, 1982, the court would invoke its jurisdiction under federal law and order the parties to submit reapportionment plans. The state legislature did pass House Bill 4020, which was vetoed by Governor William G. Milliken on April 27, 1982, as being unfair. Subsequently, the district court ordered the parties to submit redistricting plans on May 5, 1982, and to be prepared to argue the merits of the plans on May 7, 1982.

On May 24, 1982, the court issued its opinion, choosing what it called Democratic Plan A as the more balanced consideration of all factors in the apportionment process. The court, however, did make modifications to Districts 5 and 9, using a revision submitted by the Republican Party. In its decision, the court offered the following facts to support its decision: (1) Plan A as modified satisfied the U.S. Const, art 1, § 2, as being consistent with the "one person, one vote" rule; (2) Plan A as modified represented the will of the legislature, and (3) the proposed districts of Plan A as modified were relatively regular, compact, and contiguous. See U.S. Const, art I, § 2, cl 3; 2 USC 2a, 2c; veto message of William G. Milliken, April 27, 1982, regarding Enrolled House Bill 4020, Public and Local Acts of the Legislature of the State of Michigan, passed at the regular session of 1982; *Agerstrand* v *Austin*, Civ. No. 81-40256, May 24, 1982.

[51] In an order entered on March 23, 1992, the U.S. District Court for the Eastern and Western Districts of Michigan held in *Good* v *Austin*, No. 91-CV-74754DT that Michigan's current congressional districts violated art I, sec 2 of the United States Constitution and that the court was obligated to adopt a new congressional district plan for the State of Michigan. The court further held that it would not adopt any of the proposed districting plans submitted by the parties but would adopt a plan of its own design. The court's plan was attached to the order, and the parties were directed to show cause, in writing, not later than 5:00 p.m., Wednesday, April 1, 1992, why the court's redistricting plan should not be adopted by the court and incorporated in a final judgment.

The April 1st deadline passed, and none of the parties had filed written objections to the court's plan.

On April 6, 1992, the court ordered that:

1) The existing United States Congressional Districts of the State of Michigan, established by order of the United States District Court for the Eastern District of Michigan in *Agerstrand* v *Austin*, No. 31-40256 (E.D. Mich. May 20, 1982), are unconstitutional under art I, sec 2 of the United States Constitution because they contain substantially unequal population as reflected in the 1990 U.S. Decennial Census, and because it is necessary to reduce the number of congressional districts in Michigan from 18 to 16;

2) The defendant, Richard H. Austin, Secretary of State of Michigan, and, under applicable Michigan law, its chief election officer, and all election officials who are responsible for conducting congressional elections in Michigan are enjoined from conducting any primary, general, or special elections for the office of Representative to the United States Congress by use of the 1982 district plan described above;

3) The United States Congressional Districts created by the redistricting plan attached to this order, entitled "1992 Congressional Districts — U.S. House of Representatives" and including the erratum dated April 3, 1992, are adopted as the United States Congressional Districts for the State of Michigan;

4) The defendant, Richard H. Austin, Secretary of State of Michigan, and, under applicable Michigan law, its chief election officer, and all election officials who are responsible for conducting congressional elections in Michigan are directed to conduct all primary, general, and special elections for the office of Representative to the United States Congress from this day forward in accordance with this judgment and the congressional districts created by it; and

5) The opinion of the court in support of this judgment will be filed at a later date.

[52] Died July 31, 1993; Vernon J. Ehlers elected to fill the vacancy at a special election on December 7, 1993.

U.S. REPRESENTATIVES *(Cont.)*

[53] On September 11, 2001, apportionment legislation (2001 PA 115) was enacted to reflect the population changes reported in the 2000 decennial census (which resulted in a reduction, from 16 to 15 members, in Michigan's congressional delegation).

A group of registered Democrats brought an action in U.S. District Court, Eastern District of Michigan (Southern Division), challenging Michigan's 2001 congressional redistricting plan. Plaintiffs claimed that the challenged plan violated several provisions of the U.S. Const (Art 1, §§ 2 and 4 (as amended by § 2 of the Fourteenth Amendment), the Equal Protection Clause and the Privileges and Immunities Clause of the Fourteenth Amendment, the First Amendment, and the Fifteenth Amendment) and § 2 of the Voting Rights Act, 42 U.S.C. 1973. In addition, plaintiffs claimed that the plan's legitimacy was impaired by a number of procedural defects accompanying its enactment. (The Michigan Supreme Court resolved the plaintiffs' procedural claims against them in *LeRoux* v *Secretary of State*, 465 Mich. 594, 640 N.W.2d 849 (2002).) On May 24, 2002, the District Court dismissed plaintiffs' equal protection claim without prejudice and plaintiffs' remaining claims with prejudice. The Court's order further provided that if plaintiffs did not amend their complaint within 30 days, the matter would be closed and further challenges to the redistricting plan based on new evidence after subsequent elections would require a new filing. *O'Lear* v *Miller*, 222 F. Supp. 2d 850 (E.D. Mich. 2002).

The District Court's judgment was affirmed on appeal to the U.S. Supreme Court. *O'Lear* v *Miller*, 123 S.Ct. 512 (2002).

[54] Announced his withdrawal from the Republican Conference to become an Independent on July 4, 2019.

DATES OF CONGRESSIONAL ELECTIONS, 1835-2018

Congress	Date	Congress	Date	Congress	Date
24	Oct. 5, 6, 1835	55	Nov. 3, 1896	86	Nov. 4, 1958
25	Aug. 21, 22, 1837	56	Nov. 8, 1898	87	Nov. 8, 1960
26	Nov. 4, 5, 1839	57	Nov. 6, 1900	88	Nov. 6, 1962
27	Nov. 1, 2, 1841	58	Nov. 4, 1902	89	Nov. 3, 1964
28	Nov. 6, 7, 1843	59	Nov. 8, 1904	90	Nov. 8, 1966
29	Nov. 4, 5, 1844	60	Nov. 6, 1906	91	Nov. 5, 1968
30	Nov. 3, 1846	61	Nov. 3, 1908	92	Nov. 3, 1970
31	Nov. 7, 1848	62	Nov. 8, 1910	93	Nov. 7, 1972
32	Nov. 5, 1850	63	Nov. 5, 1912	94	Nov. 5, 1974
33	Nov. 2, 1852	64	Nov. 3, 1914	95	Nov. 2, 1976
34	Nov. 7, 1854	65	Nov. 7, 1916	96	Nov. 7, 1978
35	Nov. 4, 1856	66	Nov. 5, 1918	97	Nov. 4, 1980
36	Nov. 2, 1858	67	Nov. 2, 1920	98	Nov. 2, 1982
37	Nov. 6, 1860	68	Nov. 7, 1922	99	Nov. 6, 1984
38	Nov. 4, 1862	69	Nov. 4, 1924	100	Nov. 4, 1986
39	Nov. 8, 1864	70	Nov. 2, 1926	101	Nov. 8, 1988
40	Nov. 6, 1866	71	Nov. 6, 1928	102	Nov. 6, 1990
41	Nov. 3, 1868	72	Nov. 4, 1930	103	Nov. 3, 1992
42	Nov. 8, 1870	73	Nov. 8, 1932	104	Nov. 8, 1994
43	Nov. 5, 1872	74	Nov. 6, 1934	105	Nov. 5, 1996
44	Nov. 3, 1874	75	Nov. 3, 1936	106	Nov. 3, 1998
45	Nov. 7, 1876	76	Nov. 8, 1938	107	Nov. 7, 2000
46	Nov. 5, 1878	77	Nov. 5, 1940	108	Nov. 5, 2002
47	Nov. 2, 1880	78	Nov. 3, 1942	109	Nov. 2, 2004
48	Nov. 7, 1882	79	Nov. 7, 1944	110	Nov. 7, 2006
49	Nov. 4, 1884	80	Nov. 5, 1946	111	Nov. 4, 2008
50	Nov. 2, 1986	81	Nov. 2, 1948	112	Nov. 2, 2010
51	Nov. 6, 1888	82	Nov. 7, 1950	113	Nov. 6, 2012
52	Nov. 4, 1890	83	Nov. 4, 1952	114	Nov. 4, 2014
53	Nov. 8, 1892	84	Nov. 2, 1954	115	Nov. 8, 2016
54	Nov. 6, 1894	85	Nov. 5, 1956	116	Nov. 6, 2018

Chapter VII

INSTITUTIONS OF HIGHER EDUCATION

2019–2020

INTRODUCTION

PUBLIC UNIVERSITIES

Michigan has 15 public 4-year universities located throughout the state. These institutions range from those having large undergraduate, graduate, and professional student populations to one with a student population of just under 3,000. Michigan universities participate in complex academic and research activities, provide undergraduate programs in the liberal arts, and offer specialized areas of studies such as engineering and vocational-technical programs. Together these institutions of higher education offer comprehensive and diverse programs.

Higher education enjoys a relatively autonomous structure in Michigan. The Constitution of 1963, which created the current State Board of Education, authorizes the boards of control of the individual public universities to supervise their respective institutions and to control expenditure of institutional funds. Three of the public 4-year universities are supervised by individual boards of control elected by the voters of Michigan while each remaining public university is governed by a board of control appointed by the governor.

COMMUNITY COLLEGES

Michigan's 28 community colleges provide: 1) higher education opportunities to citizens for whom the cost, location of state universities and private colleges, or academic entrance requirements are barriers to attendance; 2) job training and retraining opportunities, including vocational, avocational, and nondegree courses and programs that may not be offered by other institutions; and 3) services that enhance the economic, cultural, intellectual, and social life of the community.

The Constitution of 1963 provides: "The legislature shall provide by law for the establishment and financial support of public community and junior colleges which shall be supervised and controlled by locally elected boards." This constitutional provision also established an eight-member State Board for Public Community Colleges to advise the State Board of Education in its general supervision and planning for community colleges. The creation and operation of community colleges are governed by Public Act 331 of 1966.

Michigan's public community colleges are located throughout the state. Two colleges are located in the Upper Peninsula, six in the northern Lower Peninsula, and the remaining 20 in southern Michigan. Over 80% of Michigan's 9.8 million citizens live in a community college district.

Although traditionally offering 2-year programs, the Legislature enacted Public Act 495 of 2012 to allow community colleges to grant baccalaureate degrees in cement technology, maritime technology, energy production technology, and the culinary arts.

INDEPENDENT COLLEGES AND UNIVERSITIES

Michigan's independent colleges provide a variety of specialized education opportunities and environments that complement public education offerings. They offer certificate and associate degree programs; church-affiliated programs; baccalaureate programs, including liberal arts and teacher education; and graduate/professional programs leading to postgraduate degrees in many disciplines. Independent colleges are required to offer programs leading to a degree or offer two or more years of courses for transfer to a degree-granting Michigan institution of higher education recognized by the state.

Independent colleges and universities are recognized by the State Board of Education when they have been incorporated under Public Act 327 of 1931. The State Board of Education ensures that the articles of incorporation clearly define the educational activity of the proposed corporation and that specific limits are defined. Any unincorporated nonpublic colleges are also brought under the authority of the State Board of Education to establish minimum requirements for degrees or awards.

CENTRAL MICHIGAN UNIVERSITY

Mt. Pleasant 48859

www.cmich.edu

BOARD OF TRUSTEES

Established in 1892, Central Michigan University is a major university with a strong sense of community, enrolling more than 21,700 students on its Mount Pleasant campus, online and at satellite locations across North America.

CMU is among the 5 percent of U.S. universities in the highest research classifications offering many nationally recognized programs within the university's eight academic colleges. With accomplished professors, opportunities for students to engage in applied research, and world-class facilities, CMU is committed to providing students with a superior learning environment and global perspective to compete in an increasingly complex world.

CMU offers academic programs at the undergraduate, master's, specialist, and doctoral levels, in entrepreneurship, journalism, music, audiology, teacher education, psychology, physician assistant, and health sciences. CMU also established a college of medicine in 2012, graduating its first class of medical doctors in May 2017.

The $95 million Biosciences Building opened for classes in January 2017, addressing growing student demand in the sciences and providing opportunities for undergraduate research using the latest technologies. In March 2018, construction began on the new 50,000-square-foot Center for Integrated Health Studies, which will allow CMU health care programs to expand. The center is scheduled to open in the fall of 2019.

CMU is accredited by the North Central Association of Colleges and Schools. CMU's impact and influence extend far beyond its main campus into the state, nation and world.

- CMU has been nationally recognized for its Sarah R. Opperman Leadership Institute and academic minor in leadership.

- The award-winning Honors Program administers the prestigious Centralis Scholarship Program and oversees approximately 200 faculty-mentored honors undergraduate capstone projects annually.

- Thousands of students work through the Mary Ellen Brandell Volunteer Center to help others locally, nationally and around the world with nearly 70 percent of students volunteering each year.

- Leadership Safari, a 5-day leadership experience for new students, celebrated its 23rd year in 2018. More than 2,000 students participate each year, led by nearly 300 student staff volunteers.

- CMU's economic impact on Michigan was $1.2 billion in fiscal year 2016, and CMU accounted for the creation of nearly 12,000 jobs throughout the state, according to an Anderson Economic Group study.

- CMU is a leader in the charter school movement, with 24 years of experience launching, supporting and overseeing charter public schools. CMU authorizes 58 schools educating more than 28,000 students in grades K-12.

- CMU's academic residential halls enhance learning and community in business, education and human services, health professions, science and engineering, music, honors, leadership, and public service.

- Fourteen new academic, athletic and residential buildings have been built on CMU's campus in the past 16 years, including the Biosciences Building, which opened September 2016, and the Center for Integrated Health Sciences, which is scheduled for completion in fall 2019.

- CMU is classified by the Carnegie Foundation for the Advancement of Teaching as a Doctoral Research University and currently provides more than 70 graduate programs at the master's, specialist and doctoral levels. CMU also provides ten accelerated master's degree programs, which allow undergraduate students at CMU to reduce the total number of credits required to complete their undergraduate and graduate degrees by applying up to 12 credit hours at the 500-600 level toward graduation requirements of both degree programs.

Cutting-edge Student Research

Students have conducted cutting-edge research in Parkinson's and Alzheimer's diseases, helped in the creation of biofuels and longer-lasting batteries, and developed improved methods of water purification. In addition, with the university's second $10 million Environmental Protection Agency grant in six years, CMU researchers lead the way in efforts to protect and restore coastal wetlands vital to the overall health of the Great Lakes through CMU's Institute for Great Lakes Research. CMU also has a MakerBot Innovation Center, a large-scale 3D printing installation. CMU's Biosciences Building is home to an electron microscope facility used for research in a variety of areas throughout the university.

Culture, Community, Resources

CMU is located in Mount Pleasant, Michigan, a classic college town at the heart of central lower Michigan. Mount Pleasant serves as the county seat for Isabella County and is home to 26,000 of the county's more than 70,000 people. Mount Pleasant offers a blend of natural features, family attractions and small-town life complemented by university culture. Friends, family members, siblings and visitors are always welcome to explore CMU's park-like campus or attend plays, concerts, speeches, athletic events, library exhibits, summer camps and much more. Features include:

Culture and Entertainment - University Theatre, University Events, the School of Music, and the student-run Program Board offer year-round world-class plays, entertainment, and other exciting activities. With more than 94,000 square feet of available space, the John G. Kulhavi Events Center serves the cultural and entertainment needs of the campus and community, hosting a wide variety of events, from commencement to concerts and speaking engagements to business expos.

Athletics - CMU competes in 18 men's and women's sports. CMU's NCAA Division I student-athletes are accomplished on the field and in the classroom. CMU has won more than 80 MAC championships in 16 different sports, and the football program has participated in a postseason bowl game in nine of the past 13 years. The CMU Chippewas won the league's top award, the Cartwright Award for overall excellence, in 2009 and 2015. CMU also earned its third consecutive MAC Institutional Sportsmanship award in 2017. CMU's student-athletes have averaged a GPA of 3.0 or higher for 40 consecutive semesters.

Fall Enrollment (fall head count)	*2016*	*2017*	*2018*
On-campus	19,280	18,430	16,975
Global Campus	5,165	4,905	4,730
TOTAL	24,445	23.335	21,705

STATEMENT OF OPERATING REVENUES AND EXPENDITURES

Total Revenues (all funds)	*2016-2017*	*2017-2018*
State Appropriation	$106,354,154	$88,417,969
Student Fees	$218,862,587	$215,802,403
Gifts, Grants and Federal Contracts	$51,115,392	$54,927,519
Other Income	$156,048,095	$128,980,407
TOTAL REVENUES	$532,380,228	$488,128,298

Total Expenditures (all funds)	*2016-2017*	*2017-2018*
Instruction and Research	$167,118,921	$163,567,194
Public Service	$17,324,809	$17,514,021
Student Services and Aid	$43,285,872	$42,744,934
Other Expenses	$249,023,206	$242,753,758
TOTAL EXPENDITURES	$476,752,808	$466,579,907

EASTERN MICHIGAN UNIVERSITY

Ypsilanti 48197

www.emich.edu

BOARD OF REGENTS

	Term expires
RICHARD L. BAIRD, Ann Arbor	Dec. 31, 2026
DENNIS BEAGEN, Northville	Dec. 31, 2022
MICHELLE CRUMM, Ann Arbor (Vice Chair)	Dec. 31, 2022
MICHAEL HAWKS, Okemos	Dec. 31, 2026
EUNICE JEFFRIES, Farmington Hills	Dec. 31, 2024
MARY TREDER LANG, Grosse Pointe Farms	Dec. 31, 2020
ALEXANDER SIMPSON, Southfield	Dec. 31, 2024
JAMES WEBB, Northville (Chair)	Dec. 31, 2020

JAMES M. SMITH, President

Eastern Michigan University is a doctoral-granting state university located in Ypsilanti. *The Princeton Review* has called Eastern "one of the best colleges in the Midwest, especially for being a great value." This is Eastern's 16th consecutive year receiving the honor. Founded in 1849 as Michigan State Normal School, the school was renamed Michigan State Normal College in 1899, Eastern Michigan College in 1956, and Eastern Michigan University in 1959. A constitutionally authorized, governor-appointed Board of Regents has governed Eastern Michigan University since January 1, 1963.

Mission

EMU enriches lives in a distinctly supportive, intellectually dynamic, and diverse community. Our dedicated faculty balance teaching and research to prepare students with relevant skills and real world awareness. We are an institution of opportunity, where students learn in and beyond the classroom to benefit the local and global communities. The University emphasizes student-centered learning, high quality academic programs, and community impact.

Our commitment extends to the wider community through numerous service initiatives and partnerships, such as VISION (Volunteers Incorporating Service Into Our Neighborhoods) and the Center for Entrepreneurship, which addresses local, national, and international opportunities and challenges; the LiveYpsi home loan program; the Hamilton Crossing Family Empowerment Program, and 21 Century Bright Futures Programs, which provide after school programming for more than 1,500 young people in some of southeast Michigan's low income communities. Based on such efforts, the Carnegie Foundation has cited Eastern for its exceptional community engagement.

Each spring, the University holds the Undergraduate Symposium, a crown jewel of the academic year, which showcases student research and creative work from a wide variety of disciplines, in which presenters work with faculty mentors on various projects and presentations. Eastern was recently reclassified as a R2 research university by Carnegie, placing it among the nation's top six percent in terms of funded research.

Colleges

The university is comprised of the following colleges: Arts and Sciences, Business, Education, Health and Human Services, and Technology.

Eastern Michigan also offers a graduate school, the Honors College, the Jean Noble Parsons Center for Art and Science, and the Eagle Crest Resort and Conference Center.

Undergraduate Programs

Eastern Michigan offers a wide variety of undergraduate programs through its colleges of Arts and Sciences, Business, Education, Health and Human Services, and Technology.

The **College of Arts and Sciences'** diverse departments and schools include the schools of art and design; communication, media, and theatre arts; and music and dance; and the departments of africology and African-American studies; computer science; economics; English language and literature; geography and geology; history and philosophy; mathematics; physics and astronomy; political science; psychology; sociology, anthropology and criminology; women's and gender studies; and world languages. Recently added degree programs include actuarial science and economics, data science and analytics, fermentation science, neuroscience, religious studies, and geospatial information science and technology.

The **College of Business** offers an innovative, cutting-edge curriculum that equips today's students for tomorrow's business environment. Many of the programs have an international component, reflective of our global economy.

Undergraduate programs include accounting, accounting information systems, computer information systems, economics, entrepreneurship, finance, general business, international business, management, marketing, supply chain management; and three combined bachelor's and master's degree programs that can be completed in 150 credit hours: a bachelor's in business administration (accounting) with a master of science (accounting), a bachelor's in business administration (accounting information systems) with a master of science (accounting), a bachelor's in business administration (accounting) with a master of science (taxation).

The **College of Education** is known for its long history of preparing educators and its exceptional public service. The college prepares educators in elementary education, special education, and in many diverse subject areas at the secondary and K-12 level. The educator preparation programs have a long history and ongoing commitment to excellence in education. EMU's educator preparation programs have been continuously accredited by the National Council for the Accreditation of Teacher Education since the organization's inception in 1954.

Teaching programs include elementary education (reading, mathematics, science, social studies, language arts, and early childhood), secondary education (mathematics, science, English language arts, social studies/history/geography/economics, communication and theaters arts, health and world languages), K-12 endorsements (music, visual arts, and physical education), and special education (cognitive impairment, emotional impairment, physical and other health impairments, speech and language impairment, learning disabilities, and autism). Recently added degree programs include Teaching English to Speakers of Other Languages and bilingual education.

The college also prepares educational leaders, counselors, and other school professionals to serve the needs of K-12 students, their families, and their communities.

The **College of Health and Human Services** seeks to partner with communities to prepare caring and competent professionals, generate knowledge, and advocate for social justice in order to enhance quality of life, health, and well-being. The college is noted for its comprehensive undergraduate programs, ranging from nursing, occupational therapy, and dietetics to exercise science. Faculty members are involved in such innovative programs as researching the latest in orthotics and prosthetics, improving services for mental health, the Healthy Asian American Project, which focuses on breast cancer awareness along with overall healthcare and dietary awareness and access among immigrants, and effective ways of helping children and youth cope with trauma and loss.

Majors include athletic training, dietetics, exercise science, health administration, medical laboratory science, occupational therapy, public health, physical education, sports management, therapeutic recreation, nursing (bachelor of science (BSN) and RN-BSN completion program), and social work. The University recently added a physician assistant program, housed in renovated facilities in the Rackham Building, that has a strong collaborative relationship with nearby St. Joseph Mercy Hospital. The college's recently added Clinical Research Administration program is rated among the nation's best.

The **College of Technology** prepares students for today's hottest careers, offering degrees that put students at the forefront of today's technological advances. Programs offer the combination of science, engineering, business, design, and other knowledge, along with technical hands-on skills. Programs include engineering technology; product design; mechanical engineering; information security; simulation, animation, and gaming; communication technology; computer engineering technology; management and technology; and military science. Recently added programs include mechanical engineering and computer and electrical engineering.

Specialty programs include apparel, textiles, and merchandising; aviation flight and management technology; computer engineering technology; hotel and restaurant management; information assurance and networking; interior design; mechanical engineering technology; mechanical engineering; paralegal; product design and development; simulation animation and gaming; and technology management. This college houses the Center for Regional and National Security and the Coatings and Research Institute.

Location

Eastern Michigan University is located in the lively and culturally active city of Ypsilanti, in southeastern Michigan. The campus comprises more than 800 scenic acres, and includes the College of Business (in downtown Ypsilanti), the Eagle Crest Resort and Conference Center (with an 18-hole championship golf course), the Kresge Environmental Education Center near Lapeer, and the Jean Noble Parsons Center for the Study of Art and Science near Traverse City and Interlochen.

Eastern opened an 181,000-square-foot student center in 2006 and completed a $42 million renovation of its Pray-Harrold classroom building, the largest classroom building on campus, in 2011. The new Science Complex addition and renovations, which were completed in 2011 and 2012 respectively, help meet the critical need for teachers in science, technology, engineering, and math. The $90 million renovation and expansion project was the largest single construction project in the university's history. Among its additions is a planetarium that is open to faculty, students, and the community. The final step in the Science Complex project is the $40 million renovation of Strong Hall, which houses numerous labs and various science programs. Strong Hall opened in January 2019, and capped the completion of the Science Complex. The University is now renovating Sill Hall, home of the College of Technology.

Housing

More than 3,400 students live in Eastern's residence halls and apartments. Residence halls also are used in the summer months to host conference guests and youth camps as well as students enrolled in the summer semester.

Extended Programs

Eastern Michigan University offers credit and noncredit courses at several sites throughout Michigan. The sites include the Kresge Environmental Center near Lapeer, and the Jean Noble Parsons Center for the Study of Art and Science near Traverse City.

	2016	2017	2018
Credit Enrollment (fall head count)	21,105	20,313	18,838

STATEMENT OF OPERATING REVENUES AND EXPENDITURES

Operating Revenues (all funds)	*2016-2017*	*2017-2018*
State Appropriations	$74,150,361	$75,836,240
Net Student Fees	$173,288,530	$171,643,078
Gifts, Grants, and Federal Contracts	$49,325,926	$51,037,886
Other Income	$66,234,158	$54,204,838
TOTAL REVENUES	$362,998,975	$352,722,042

Operating Expenditures (all funds)	*2016-2017*	*2017-2018*
Instruction and Research	$126,440,373	$124,653,96618
Public Service . . . .;. . .	$12,829,686	$11,342,91726
Student Services and Aid	$55,248,437	$53,169,2787
Other Expenses	$158,781,772	$156,693,541
TOTAL EXPENDITURES	$353,300,268	$345,859,702

FERRIS STATE UNIVERSITY

Big Rapids 49307

www.ferris.edu

BOARD OF TRUSTEES

	Term expires
AMNA P. SEIBOLD, East Grand Rapids (Chair)	Dec. 31, 2024
LORI A. GWIZDALA, Bay City	Dec. 31, 2020
ROBERT J. HEGBLOOM, Clarkston	Dec. 31, 2020
KURT A. HOFMAN, Grand Rapids	Dec. 31, 2026
ANA L. RAMIREZ-SAENZ, Caledonia	Dec. 31, 2022
KARI L. SEDERBURG, E. Lansing	Dec. 31, 2026
RUPESH K. SRIVASTAVA, Wixom	Dec. 31, 2022
LASHANDA R. THOMAS, Grosse Pointe	Dec. 31, 2024

DAVID L. EISLER, President

Ferris State University is a public university with a 941-acre main campus in Big Rapids. Ferris also has a statewide presence with 22 regional campuses throughout Michigan, concurrent classes offered at Michigan high schools, and online programs. Enrollment at Ferris State University for the fall 2018 semester was 13,250 students. Ferris attracts students from every county in Michigan, the majority of whom remain in the state after graduating.

Founded in 1884, Ferris is distinguished by its strong heritage of opportunity, commitment to diversity and inclusion, and focus on providing a professional education that links theory to practice. Ferris offers more than 190 programs, ranging from associate to doctoral degrees, through eight degree-granting academic colleges: Arts and Sciences, Business, Education and Human Services, Engineering Technology, Health Professions, Kendall College of Art and Design, Michigan College of Optometry, and Pharmacy.

Many of Ferris' offerings are tailored to prepare students for careers aligned with occupations experiencing a shortage of skilled professionals. A large number of these require expertise in science, technology, engineering and mathematics. For example, information security and intelligence, digital animation and game design, and heating, ventilation and air conditioning. Examples of strong programs at Ferris include construction management, criminal justice, finance, hospitality management, nursing, optometry, pharmacy, professional golf management, risk management, social work and welding.

More than 50 percent of Ferris classes have fewer than 20 students, giving students more direct contact with faculty, more opportunity for hands-on learning, and greater engagement. Full-time tenure-track faculty members with experience in their respective fields teach the majority of classes, providing real-world relevance. Ferris is committed to creating an environment in which learning and collaboration take place both inside and outside of the classroom.

Ferris partners with Michigan community colleges to create a regional campus network where students can earn their bachelor's degree on the community college campus near where they live. The University's online programs also offer students flexibility in completing their degrees, which can be especially helpful to adult learners who are currently employed and professionals looking to upgrade their skills. Ferris is a transfer school of choice for these students, facilitating expansion of their first two years of study at regional sites into four-year university degrees. Ferris' largest regional campus is at the Grand Rapids Community College Applied Technology Center.

Ferris State University is home to the state-of-the-art Michigan College of Optometry, the completely renovated University Center, and the nationally renowned Jim Crowe Museum, in Big Rapids. A facility on Grand Rapids' Medical Mile hosts third and fourth-year Pharmacy students. In Grand Rapids, the University also has transformed the historically important Federal Building into the Woodbridge N. Ferris building, serving students in its Kendall College of Art and Design, which includes the Urban Institute for Contemporary Arts. A new 402-bed residence hall on the Big Rapids campus was completed in fall 2017, an expansion to the Swan Annex serving welding engineering technology, advanced manufacturing, and mechanical engineering technology programs was completed in August 2018, a major renovation to the University Recreation Center was also completed in August 2018, and the Ken Janke Sr., Golf Learning Center was completed in spring 2019. Other recently upgraded facilities include Ferris' popular Rock Café, the Ferris Library for Information, Technology and Education, additions to the West Campus Apartments, and the East Campus Suites.

Ferris is named after its founders, Woodbridge Nathan Ferris (two-term Michigan governor and United States senator) and Helen Gillespie Ferris. Founded as the privately owned Big Rapids Industrial School, Ferris became a state institution in 1950, undergoing several name changes before becoming Ferris State University in 1987. The Ferris' founding philosophy of a practical, hands-on approach to education, where theory meets practice, enables students to learn practical skills for new jobs in a changing world still resonates today.

Credit Enrollment (fall head count)	2016	2017	2018
On-campus	10,016	9,868	9,553
Regional campuses	1,977	1,854	1,742
Online	980	1,005	944

STATEMENT OF OPERATING REVENUES AND EXPENDITURES

Operating Revenues (all funds)	*2016-2017*	*2017-2018*
State Appropriations	$53,159,620	$54,797,535
Net Student Fees	$122,091,696	$119,303,790
Gifts, Grants, and Federal Contracts	$30,017,994	$33,983,446
Other Income	$49,262,118	$44,800,765
TOTAL REVENUES	$254,531,428	$252,885,536

Operating Expenditures (all funds)	*2016-2017*	*2017-2018*
Instruction and Research	$98,678,739	$101,037,360
Public Service	$5,050,060	$4,981,880
Student Services and Aid	$35,942,946	$38,603,271
Other Expenses	$104,535,087	$111,796,188
TOTAL EXPENDITURES	$244,206,832	$256,418,699

GRAND VALLEY STATE UNIVERSITY

Grand Rapids/Allendale 49401

www.gvsu.edu

BOARD OF TRUSTEES

Grand Valley State University was founded in 1960 to bring higher education to the state's second-largest metropolitan area — the diversified business and industrial region that includes Kent, Muskegon, and Ottawa counties. Fully accredited, it serves the region from its 1,322-acre main campus in Allendale, its comprehensive operations in downtown Grand Rapids and Holland, and its centers in Muskegon, Traverse City, and Detroit. Students come to Grand Valley from all of Michigan's 83 counties. While 95 percent of students come from Michigan, they also come to Grand Valley from 45 states and 79 foreign countries, including Africa, Asia, Australia, Central and South America, the Middle East, and Europe. Of recent graduates, 95 percent are employed or pursuing advanced degrees. Of the recent graduates who are employed, more than 86 percent are working in Michigan communities.

Grand Valley grew slowly until about 1988, when it saw the beginning of very rapid growth, both in its popularity and stature. Enrollment has doubled since 1988 and is now 24,677.

To be transparent to the public, the university produced, in 2007, the first of its annual accountability reports, which can be viewed at **www.gvsu.edu/accountability**. The accountability report provides a public review of the university's academic and economic performances, including the proper use of resources, and demonstrates the university's ability to educate successful students in the state of Michigan. A version of the accountability report is now used by the Michigan Legislature to measure performance of all 15 state-supported universities.

A **liberal arts emphasis** teaches students critical thinking and problem resolution; an emphasis on diversity, sustainability, and community teaches students a range of thoughtful perspectives necessary for open inquiry. As an institution committed to teaching excellence, Grand Valley emphasizes personalized instruction, bolstered by relatively small classes taught by faculty members rather than graduate teaching assistants. Grand Valley has 1,780 full- and part-time faculty members. GVSU students, faculty, and staff have easy access through **University Libraries** campus locations and website to Grand Valley's collections: nearly 527,588 physical books, 943,719 e-books, and 1,563,660 total library resources.

A focus on **international education** is reflected in foreign exchange and foreign study programs. More than 780 students took part in study abroad programs in 2017-18.

Approximately 8,200 GVSU students annually participate in experiential education programs (internships, practicums, clinicals, student teaching, and co-ops) in business, industry, government, schools, hospitals, and public agencies, blending theoretical knowledge with practical applications. The undergraduate Bachelor of Science in Engineering program includes a cooperative education component that provides for at least 12 months of on-the-job experience before the degree is granted, and the College of Education requires 18 credit hours of in-class experience combined with a degree in a subject matter content area.

Forty-one graduate programs include master's degrees in accounting, applied linguistics, audiology, athletic training, adult and higher education, biology, biomedical sciences, biomedical engineering, business administration, biostatistics, cell and molecular biology, clinical dietetics, communications, computer information systems, criminal justice, college student affairs leadership, data science and analytics, education, education specialist in leadership, educational leadership, educational technology, engineering, English, executive MBA, health administration, health informatics and bioinformatics, instruction and curriculum, literacy studies, medical dosimetry, nursing, occupational therapy (D.O.T. and M.S.), philanthropy and nonprofit leadership, physical therapy, physician assistant studies, professional science Master's, public administration, public health, school counseling, school psychology, social innovation, social work, special education, speech-language pathology, student-initiated combined degree, and taxation. Grand Valley also offers the Clinical Doctorate in Physical Therapy program, a Doctor of Nursing Practice degree, and an Educational Specialist degree. Other career and professional programs include accounting, advertising and public relations, engineering, communications, computer sciences, business, hospitality and tourism management, international business, international relations, medical imaging, athletic training, therapeutic recreation, natural resource management, legal studies, criminal justice, nursing, social work, geology, and education, including special education.

Grand Valley is a leading provider of health care professionals in West Michigan. The **College of Health Professions** and the **Kirkhof College of Nursing** have nationally recognized and accredited programs. There are currently 22 programs in health sciences.

Faculty and graduate interns in social sciences and education help area communities meet needs in public administration, education, criminal justice, and social services. Examples include in-service training for teacher groups and school administrators, urban planning research and development, a summer police academy, programs for gifted and talented students, an annual summer camp for learning-disabled children, stress management workshops, public opinion polls, market surveys, and programs for senior citizens.

Through its outreach centers and curricular engagement, the **Seidman College of Business**, in downtown Grand Rapids, is dedicated to building strong links between academic programs and economic development and job creation in the region. Seidman provides management and leadership education, and training, economic research and consultation resources, market analysis, and planning services for existing and potential area businesses. The Seidman College of Business is also home to the **Small Business Development Corporation's** state headquarters which offers no-cost counseling, low-cost training, market research, and advocacy for small businesses.

The **Muskegon Innovation Hub** is a 25,000-square-foot business innovation center located on the shores of Muskegon Lake. The Hub provides coaching, funding, networking, and a synergistic work environment to help businesses and entrepreneurs maximize their growth potential. To accomplish this, the Hub utilizes four key components: a business incubator, co-working space, access to funding, and training and event space.

The **Robert B. Annis Water Resources Institute** conducts basic and applied research into Michigan's water resources and related topics, and offers outreach and educational services from the waterfront Lake Michigan Center in Muskegon. The institute operates two research vessels, the *D.J. Angus* and the *W.G. Jackson*. It brings applied research together with business, industry, agriculture, and government to develop proactive approaches to water quality and related environmental issues. An education aquatic science outreach program is also offered for a variety of audiences, including K-12 students and teachers.

The **Hauenstein Center for Presidential Studies** has advanced discussion of the American presidency among scholars, government leaders, student leaders, and the public. Its Cook Leadership Academy has become a center of leadership excellence. Its Common Ground Initiative is unique in higher education today. The center's Wheelhouse Talks inspire leaders, and its American Conversations engage citizens.

The **Van Andel Global Trade Center's** mission is to strengthen the community through increased global business by providing international consulting, training, and resources. The center has impacted over 22,000 business professionals through its research, educational training, and consulting, supporting the expansion of more than 7,400 Michigan businesses in the global marketplace. The center works closely with the MEDC to help Michigan businesses throughout the state grow internationally.

The **Dorothy A. Johnson Center for Philanthropy** was established in 1992 and is an academic center within the College of Community and Public Service. The Johnson Center is a university-based center leading a systems-based, comprehensive approach to serving nonprofits, foundations, and others seeking to transform their communities for the public good. Through professional development services, courses and trainings, philanthropic tools, and more, the Center supports nonprofit capacity building, provides education to grantmaking organizations, conducts research design and analysis, and creates information and insights for the field of philanthropy. The Frey Chair for Family Philanthropy and the W.K. Kellogg Community Philanthropy Chair support original research in the field, such as the NextGen report on new donors. *The Foundation Review* is the first peer-reviewed journal of philanthropy and is published by the Johnson Center. The Johnson Center's Community Research Institute is a valued community resource, providing innovative applied research and data to assist communities in assessing needs and measuring the social impact of programs and services.

Grand Valley has a long-standing tradition and commitment to providing quality education for students. As part of this mission, the Grand Valley Board of Trustees seeks to impact public K-12 education through its leadership in Michigan's charter schools. Grand Valley chartered its first three schools in 1995, serving a total of 350 students. As it enters the 24th year as an authorizer, the GVSU Charter Schools Office now serves more than 36,000 students in 75 schools.

The **Regional Math and Science Center** housed in the College of Liberal Arts and Sciences, serves students, teachers, parents, school districts, business and industry, and other organizations interested and involved in mathematics and science education in West Michigan. Some of the centers signature programs include Michigan Science Olympiad, Super Science Saturdays, Fall Science Update, summer student activities such as Energizing Our World and sHaPe health professions camp, Discovering STEM kits, and the *InterChange* newsletter. The center's staff is available for consultation in support of the Michigan standards for science and mathematics including curriculum development, professional learning tailored to district needs, and resources for classroom instruction.

Grand Forum, an education outreach program serving senior citizens, provides an opportunity for individuals of diverse backgrounds to meet in an academic setting for intellectual stimulation and social exchange. Through lectures and discussions, Grand Forum allows its members to broaden their horizons while developing an appreciation for knowledge of new or familiar subjects.

The **Autism Education Center** provides training, resources, and coordination to ensure that individuals diagnosed with Autism Spectrum Disorder are able to fully participate in their local community. An emphasis is placed on working with school-based teams to provide students with evidence-based educational programming that increases independence, social opportunities, and academic growth.

The **Meijer Broadcast Center** is the home of Grand Valley's public television and radio stations. WGVU-TV 35 and WGVK-TV 52, affiliated with the Public Broadcasting Service, present a variety of informative and entertaining programs including children's shows, public affairs, cultural offerings, and sports. WGVU 88.5 FM and AM 1480 (Grand Rapids) and WGVS 95.3 FM and 850 AM (Muskegon) are National Public Radio member stations that broadcast news and information programs.

Accreditations

Grand Valley State University has continued accreditation by the Higher Learning Commission, **www.hlcommission.org**. All other college and program accreditations will be found in the link to the university website, **www.gvsu.edu**.

Credit Enrollment (fall head count)	2018
On-campus	24,677

STATEMENT OF OPERATING REVENUES AND EXPENDITURES

Operating Revenues (all funds)	2017	2018
State Appropriations	$68,228,000	$70,133,000
Net Student Fees	$315,700,000	$324,114,000
Gifts, Grants, and Federal Contracts	$52,700,000	$57,728,000
Other Income (auxiliary)	$72,517,000	$73,036,000
TOTAL REVENUES	$509,145,000	$525,011,000

Operating Expenditures (all funds)	2017	2018
Instruction and Research	$164,223,000	$170,635,000
Public Service	$26,324,000	$26,396,000
Student Services and Aid	$30,807,000	$31,371,000
Other Expenses	$266,000	$266,000
TOTAL EXPENDITURES	$445,612,000	$461,097,000

LAKE SUPERIOR
STATE UNIVERSITY

Sault Ste. Marie 49783

www.lssu.edu

BOARD OF TRUSTEES

Lake Superior State University, on the Canadian border in Michigan's Eastern Upper Peninsula, is the smallest of the state's 15 public universities. With a five-year average academic year enrollment of just more than 2,450 students, LSSU is considered under the Carnegie Classification to be a small four-year undergraduate institution with a focus on professions and a single graduate program. LSSU's admission process is moderately selective with an undergraduate mix for entering students of approximately 67% new freshman and 33% transfers. For new freshmen, the average high school GPA is 3.3 and the average ACT composite is 22. The university grants 111 baccalaureate degrees in such diverse fields as fire science, criminal justice, engineering, business, health sciences, environmental chemistry, fisheries and wildlife management, conservation leadership, exercise science, applied geographic information science, English literature, communication, psychology, and sociology. Additionally, the university offers a master's degree in curriculum and instruction. LSSU has branch regional centers in Petoskey and Escanaba.

LSSU's main campus overlooks the sister cities of Sault Ste. Marie, Michigan (population 14,000) and Ontario, Canada (population 75,000). Three counties comprise the Eastern U.P. with a total population of 56,254 spread over 3,486 square miles. The region offers year-round recreation with access to three Great Lakes within 50 miles, thousands of acres of public lands, and hundreds of miles of streams, rivers, and inland lakes. Students enjoy the opportunity to study in a unique international setting abundant in natural resources and historical significance.

The Sault Ste. Marie area has been inhabited for more than 2,000 years, and the city was founded as a European settlement in 1668 by Father Jacques Marquette, a French Jesuit missionary. It was the first permanent European settlement west of the Appalachian Mountains and is believed to be the oldest continually inhabited European settlement in the Midwest. It is home to the famous Soo Locks that enable ships to traverse an 18-foot drop between Lake Superior and the lower Great Lakes. These federal locks, dating back to 1855, and other attractions have turned the twin Saults into a busy tourist destination that draws tens of thousands of visitors each year.

Credit Enrollment (fall head count)	2017	2018
On-campus.	765	791
Off-campus.	1,367	1,360
TOTAL	2,132	2,151

STATEMENT OF OPERATING REVENUES AND EXPENDITURES

Operating Revenues (all funds)	2015-2016	2018
State Appropriations	$13,269,782	$13,755,539
Net Student Fees.	$14,444,282	$13,790,107
Gifts, Grants, and Federal Contracts.	$5,564,462	$8,692,854
Other Income	$13,854,053	$12,919,009
TOTAL REVENUES.	$47,132,579	$45,157,509

Operating Expenditures (all funds)	2015-2016	2018
Instruction and Research.	$14,687,682	$13,690,434
Public Service.	$1,669,704	$1,655,232
Student Services and Aid.	$4,734,735	$4,557,534
Other Expenses	$28,709,235	$28,846,211
TOTAL EXPENDITURES.	$49,801,356	$48,749,411

MICHIGAN STATE UNIVERSITY

East Lansing 48824

www.msu.edu

BOARD OF TRUSTEES

Michigan State University has been working to advance the common good with uncommon will for more than 160 years. Founded in 1855, MSU was a bold experiment that democratized higher education, offering an innovative curriculum with elements of traditional studies but focused on discovering cutting-edge knowledge and practical instruction. MSU became the prototype for the 69 land-grant institutions established under the federal Morrill Act of 1862 and was the nation's first institution of higher learning to teach scientific agriculture.

The original 677-acre campus in what became East Lansing has grown to nearly 5,200 acres today, with approximately 2,100 acres in existing or planned development and 566 buildings, including 110 with academic or instructional space. MSU also operates 19,600 acres throughout Michigan for agricultural, animal, and forestry research.

Michigan State operates one of the largest single-campus residential systems in the country, its 27 residence halls grouped into five neighborhoods offering an abundance of dining and living options and delivering on-site academic support and other services.

Academics

MSU is a diverse and inclusive academic community that enrolls more than 50,000 students from all 50 states and more than 140 countries, employs 5,722 faculty members and academic staff, and offers more than 200 programs of undergraduate, graduate, and pre-professional study in 17 degree-granting colleges.

MSU has three on-campus medical schools, graduating allopathic (MD) and osteopathic (DO) physicians, as well as veterinarians (DVM). Community campuses across the state help train MSU medical students, and new physicians train in partnership with hospitals across Michigan.

The College of Human Medicine is based on the Grand Rapids "Medical Mile," and the new MSU Grand Rapids Research Center nearby when fully occupied will house approximately 44 medical research teams.

The MSU College of Nursing provides leadership for the education of nurses at the undergraduate, master's, and doctoral levels. The college's Bott Building for Nursing Education and Research supports the college's growth as a research leader and helps the state address a nursing shortage. The college opened access to working registered nurses with an online RN-to-BSN program, and partners with community colleges to offer a BSN program to their associate degree students.

Michigan State is a leader in providing the means to economic and social mobility and committed to continually improving the value of an MSU degree. MSU's student success initiative is linked to its nationally recognized Neighborhoods program for residential undergraduate support services, as well as to the Hub for Innovation in Learning and Technology, which supports development and application of new methods of teaching and learning across campus.

An entrepreneurial mindset is encouraged across the curriculum, regardless of major, through an entrepreneurship minor option, dedicated spaces for business idea development and support, and entrepreneurship organizations and events.

Reflecting its focus on connection with the community and the world to promote knowledge discovery, service to society, and student success, the university's nationally recognized service-learning program recorded 32,241 registrations for community service in 2017-18.

MSU registers more than 900 student organizations offering recreational, social, and educational experiences related to academics, business, the environment, international relations, politics, racial and ethnic issues, religious groups, women's interests, sports and leisure, and more. A member of the Big Ten athletic conference, the university offers 25 varsity sports, plus adaptive sports and dozens of club and intramural teams.

Dedicated to international engagement since the 1950s, MSU has 1,400 faculty members involved in research and teaching in more than 175 other countries. More than a half-million graduates living around the world—half of them residing in Michigan—comprise a global Spartan alumni network.

Research

As a top research university, Michigan State pushes the boundaries of knowledge and discovery in communities from East Lansing to East Africa. MSU forges enduring partnerships to confront the biggest challenges of our time—food and water security, health care and education, energy, advanced physical sciences, and engineering—and works at the forefront of emerging opportunities in areas such as bioengineering, precision medicine and genomics, advanced mobility, and computation.

Research dollars and other grants for the university totaled $695 million in 2017-18. MSU's research excellence and impact were endorsed by the U.S. Department of Energy in 2009 when it selected MSU to establish the Facility for Rare Isotope Beams. This $730 million facility slated for completion in 2022 will advance understanding of rare nuclear isotopes to yield new understanding of matter and spur breakthrough applications to benefit society, as it provides research opportunities for top scientists and students from around the nation and the globe.

Michigan State—particularly through AgBioResearch (formerly the Michigan Agricultural Experiment Station, founded in 1888) and MSU Extension—plays a key role in the state's annual $100 billion-plus food and agriculture system through partnerships, research, and educational programs in all 83 counties.

MSU's AgBioResearch performs research in laboratories and farm research plots, encompassing the work of more than 300 scientists in seven colleges at MSU: Agriculture and Natural Resources, Arts and Letters, Communication Arts and Sciences, Engineering, Natural Science, Social Science, and Veterinary Medicine. These researchers, in on-campus laboratories and at 14 outlying research centers across the state, investigate pressing issues including agricultural production and environmental impact, food safety, biofuels, antibiotic resistance, animal health, invasive species, beneficial insects and pest management, food safety, water quality, and biotechnology. MSU's Kellogg Biological Station in Hickory Corners has served as a site for integrated and long-term research in agriculture, natural resource conservation, and ecology since the 1920s.

Collectively, AgBioResearch and MSU Extension have more than a billion-dollar impact on the state each year. Every dollar the state spends is leveraged with additional dollars in federal funds and external contracts, grants, and other revenues to serve the state's residents.

MSU Extension

MSU Extension has reached out across the state for more than a century to people in their homes, farms, businesses, and communities. Michigan State hired its first livestock field agent in 1907, five years before the Legislature authorized counties to raise revenue to support Extension work. In 1914, the U.S. Congress passed the Smith-Lever Act, which created the nationwide Cooperative Extension System and directed the nation's land grant universities, including MSU, to oversee its work.

Today, Extension agents still deliver practical advice and cutting-edge knowledge one-on-one, supported by a wide variety of information systems including websites and webinars, social media, and electronic newsletters. Extension also helps prepare more than 200,000 youth annually for life and careers through activities including 4-H.

Being long embedded in Michigan communities gives Extension the capacity to quickly ramp up targeted services, such as the health, nutrition, and educational services it is delivering to Flint children to help them deal with the long-term health effects of lead-contaminated municipal water. Community economic health is another area of Extension's focus. MSU's Center for Local Government Finance and Policy offers outreach, advises cities during fiscal hardship, and helps them develop fiscal tools. In addition, the center is committed to connecting legislators with experts in public policy and forging partnerships in the public and private sectors.

The MSU Product Center helps entrepreneurs and companies develop and commercialize high value, consumer-responsive products and businesses in the agriculture and natural resource sectors. The MSU Product Center has provided more than 51,000 one-on-one client counseling sessions and helped 634 ventures launch since its opening in 2004, and acts as the state's hub for information, resources, and guidance for Michigan agriculture, food, and natural resource entrepreneurs.

Engagement and Economic Impact

All told, Michigan State's economic impact on the state exceeds $5 billion annually, with $511 million alone spent with local businesses. MSU is a key player in the University Research Corridor (URC), a collaboration with the state's other two top-tier research universities, the University of Michigan and Wayne State University. Annual benchmarking studies confirm that the URC is competitive with the nation's top research and development clusters in generating patents, businesses, and graduates with high-demand, tech-related degrees.

Michigan State's Office of the Associate Provost for University Outreach and Engagement connects faculty to the community to address priority issues, with the most extensive academic support structure designed to advance engagement scholarship in the nation. In all of its work, MSU emphasizes university-community partnerships that are collaborative, participatory, empowering, systemic, transformative, and anchored in scholarship. MSU was an inaugural Carnegie Foundation Community Engagement institution, and a founding member of the Engagement Scholarship Consortium, an international organization dedicated to building strong university-community partnerships and designed to help build community capacity in the 21st century. MSU is a recipient of the U.S. President's Award for Higher Education Community Service and the Michigan Campus Compact's Engaged Campus of the Year.

Entrepreneurship extends beyond the university's curriculum to promote technology transfer to the private sector and nourish Michigan's knowledge economy. The MSU Innovation Center is built on a strong partnership with the MSU Foundation, faculty, students, and local and statewide economic development organizations. It supports innovation, technology commercialization, new company startup, and a portfolio of dedicated business and community partnerships to bring cutting-edge ideas to the marketplace. Composed of Business CONNECT, MSU Technologies, and Spartan Innovations, the Innovation Center advances faculty, student, and commercial partner ideas, bringing more than 150 discoveries annually into a pipeline of patents, products, and startup businesses. Together, these solutions help build a diversified economy and jobs for Michigan.

The MSU Foundation also fuels economic development initiatives through commercialization of cutting-edge technologies invented by MSU faculty, staff, and students. At its core is an extensive program that focuses on the support of research, invention, and entrepreneurship.

Culture, arts, and athletics are popular MSU contributions to the region. The Wharton Center for Performing Arts hosts more than 200 stage events with an estimated 200,000 people attending Wharton presentations annually. The MSU Federal Credit Union Institute for Arts and Creativity presents educational programs to more than 30,000 K-12 students at Wharton each year.

The stunning Eli and Edythe Broad Art Museum, designed by world-renowned architect Zaha Hadid and opened in 2012, supports the university's arts programs and welcomes more than 62,000 visitors a year with exhibitions and community programs. Spartan Stadium seats 75,000 and hosts concerts and other special events in addition to home football games. The Breslin Student Events Center, home of Spartan basketball, seats 15,000 and hosts more than 260 campus and community events a year.

Other campus/community assets include the MSU Libraries system, which houses more than 4.5 million volumes; public broadcasting affiliated WKAR-TV and the WKAR-AM and WKAR-FM public broadcasting radio stations; six public gardens, including the W.J. Beal Botanical Garden, the oldest continuously operated teaching garden on a college campus in the nation; the MSU Museum, one of the state's largest public museums of natural and cultural history; and Abrams Planetarium.

	2016	*2017*	*2018*
Enrollment (fall head count)	50,344	50,019	50,351

STATEMENT OF OPERATING REVENUES AND EXPENDITURES

Operating Revenues (all funds)	*2017*	*2018*
Net Student Tuition and Fees.	$859,117,000	$867,902,000
Grants and Contracts.	$445,041,000	$462,618,000
Other Revenue	$627,395,000	$656,353,000
Nonoperating Revenues (all funds)		
State Appropriations	$337,778,000	$344,405,000
Gifts, Capital Grants, and Additions to Permanent Endowments	$248,740,000	$1,976,411,000
Other Revenue	$398,987,000	$325,618,000
TOTAL REVENUES.	$2,917,058,000	$4,533,307,000
Operating Expenditures	*2017*	*2018*
Instruction and Departmental Research	$762,112,000	$798,736,000
Research.	$380,481,000	$400,594,000
Public Service	$286,991,000	$326,524,000
Student Services and Aid.	$126,000,000	$126,453,000
Other Expenses	$887,324,000	$1,447,291,000
TOTAL EXPENDITURES	$2,442,908,000	$3,099,598,000

MICHIGAN TECHNOLOGICAL UNIVERSITY

Houghton 49931

www.mtu.edu

BOARD OF TRUSTEES

Established by Act 70 of 1885, the Michigan Mining School first offered instruction to students on September 15, 1886. The name was changed to Michigan College of Mines in 1897 and to Michigan College of Mining and Technology in 1927. The most recent name change to Michigan Technological University in 1964 was made to reflect the broad spectrum of programs offered in the physical, biological, and social sciences; engineering; forestry; business; the liberal arts; and technology.

Undergraduate Programs

The Bachelor of Science degree is conferred in accounting, anthropology, applied ecology and environmental sciences, applied geophysics, applied physics, audio production and technology, biochemistry and molecular biology, bioinformatics, biological sciences, biomedical engineering, chemical engineering, cheminformatics, chemistry, civil engineering, computer engineering, computer network and system administration, computer science, construction management, economics, electrical engineering, electrical engineering technology, engineering, engineering management, environmental engineering, exercise science, finance, forestry, geological engineering, geology, management, management information systems, marketing, materials science and engineering, mathematics, mechanical engineering, mechanical engineering technology, medical laboratory science, natural resources management, pharmaceutical chemistry, physics, psychology, scientific and technical communication, social sciences, software engineering, sports and fitness management, statistics, surveying engineering, sustainability science and society, theatre and entertainment technology, and wildlife ecology and management.

A Bachelor of Arts degree is conferred in liberal arts; English; history; communication, culture and media; physics; scientific and technical communication; sound design; and theatre and electronic media performance.

Graduate Programs

A graduate certificate is offered in advanced electric power engineering, automotive systems and controls, data science, hybrid electric drive vehicle engineering, nanotechnology, post-secondary STEM education, sustainability, and sustainable water resources systems.

A Master of Science degree is offered in accounting; applied cognitive science and human factors; applied ecology; applied natural resources economics; applied physics; applied science education; applied statistics; biological sciences; biomedical engineering; chemical engineering; chemistry; civil engineering; computer engineering; computer science; cybersecurity; data science; electrical engineering; engineering mechanics; environmental engineering; environmental engineering science; environmental and energy policy; forest ecology and management; forest molecular genetics and biotechnology; forestry; geological engineering; geology; geophysics; industrial archaeology; integrated geospatial technology; kinesiology; materials science and engineering; mathematical sciences; mechanical engineering; medical informatics; mining engineering; physics; rhetoric, theory and culture; and statistics.

A Master of Engineering, a Master of Business Administration, a Master of Geographic Information Science, and a Master of Forestry also are offered.

A doctoral degree is offered in applied cognitive science and human factors; applied physics; atmospheric sciences; biochemistry and molecular biology; biological sciences; biomedical engineering; chemical engineering; chemistry; civil engineering; computational science and engineering; computer engineering; computer science; electrical engineering; environmental and energy policy; environmental engineering; forest molecular genetics and biotechnology; forest science; geological engineering; geology; geophysics; industrial heritage and archaeology; integrative physiology; materials science and engineering; mathematical sciences; mechanical engineering—engineering mechanics; mining engineering; physics; rhetoric, theory and culture; and statistics.

Research Agencies

Specialized research units include the Advanced Power Systems Research Center; Center for Agile and Interconnected Microgrids; Center for Leadership and Innovation for Transformation; Center for Technology & Training; Earth, Planetary and Space Sciences Institute; Ecosystem Science Center; Great Lakes Research Center; Institute of Computing and Cybersystems; Institute of Materials Processing; Keweenaw Research Center; Michigan Tech Aerospace Engineering Research

Center; Michigan Tech Research Institute; Michigan Tech Transportation Institute; Multi-Scale Technologies Institute; Pre-College Innovative Outreach Institute; Research and Innovation in STEM Education Institute; Sustainable Futures Institute; and The Elizabeth and Richard Henes Center for Quantum Phenomena.

Accreditations

The university is accredited by the Higher Learning Commission. Its curricula in the following fields of engineering are accredited by the Engineering Accreditation Commission of ABET, **www.abet.org**: biomedical engineering, chemical engineering, civil engineering, computer engineering, electrical engineering, engineering (interdisciplinary or special focus), environmental engineering, geological engineering, materials science and engineering, and mechanical engineering. The following programs in engineering technology are accredited by the Engineering Technology Accreditation Commission of ABET, electrical engineering technology and mechanical engineering technology. The construction management program is accredited by the American Council of Construction Education; the computer network and system administration program is accredited by the Computing Accreditation Commission of ABET, and the surveying engineering program is accredited by the Engineering Accreditation Commission of ABET.

The Bachelor of Science degrees in Chemistry, Pharmaceutical Chemistry, and Cheminformatics are certified by the American Chemical Society. In Biological Sciences, the fourth year instruction in the medical laboratory science 3+1 option is carried out in hospitals accredited by the National Accrediting Agency for the Clinical Laboratory Sciences.

The Intensive English as a Second Language program is accredited by the Commission on English Language Program Accreditation.

The Bachelor of Science in Forestry and Master of Forestry programs are accredited by the Society of American Foresters.

All School of Business and Economics undergraduate degrees (accounting, finance, engineering management, management, management information systems, and marketing), as well as the Tech MBA and Master of Science in Accounting, are accredited by the Association to Advance Collegiate Schools of Business International. Accounting students may qualify to sit for professional certification exams, including the CPA exam, by choosing appropriate coursework.

Credit Enrollment (fall head count)	2017	2018
Undergraduate	5,917	5,828
Graduate	1,402	1,375
TOTAL	7,319	7,203

STATEMENT OF OPERATING REVENUES AND EXPENDITURES

Operating Revenues (all funds)	2016-2017	2017-2018
State Appropriations	$48,586,922	$49,081,629
Net Student Fees	$95,869,984	$98,449,561
Gifts, Grants, and Federal Contracts	$59,523,382	$65,801,442
Other Income	$50,152,237	$50,012,029
TOTAL REVENUES	$254,132,525	$263,344,661

Operating Expenditures (all funds)	2016-2017	2017-2018
Compensation and Benefits	$173,186,978	$173,526,912
Student Services and Aid	$8,814,735	$9,941,784
Other Expenses	$74,020,825	$73,515,417
TOTAL EXPENDITURE	$256,022,538	$256,984,113

Northern Michigan University

Marquette 49855

www.nmu.edu

BOARD OF TRUSTEES

Northern Michigan University was founded in 1899 as a coeducational, state-supported institution. The university serves the state and, in particular, the Upper Peninsula of Michigan, through a three-dimensional program of instruction, research, and service. Northern offers 177 academic programs, ranging from the certificate to associate, bachelor's, master's, and doctorate degrees.

The academic program is organized into 28 departments that fall under four colleges: the College of Arts and Sciences; the College of Business; the College of Health Sciences and Professional Studies; and the College of Technology and Occupational Sciences. There is also an Office of Graduate Education and Research.

Less Than Bachelor's Programs

Certification programs are offered in the subject areas of American Indian education, French, German, Spanish and Teaching English to Speakers of Other Languages (TESOL). Certificate programs are offered in advanced law enforcement, assistant behavior analyst, automotive maintenance, automotive service, aviation maintenance technology, clinical assistant, computer numerical control (CNC) technician, cosmetology, cosmetology instructor, deaf studies, electrical line technician, esthetics, geographic information systems, heating/ventilation/air conditioning and refrigeration (HVACR), industrial maintenance, local corrections, manicure, manufacturing production technician, practical nursing, welding and post-baccalaureate paralegal. Associate degree programs are available in art and design, automotive service technology, aviation maintenance technology, building technology, climate control technology, clinical laboratory technology, computer numerical control technology, criminal justice, electrical technology, engineering design, general business, general university studies, health information processing, hospitality management, industrial maintenance technology, information systems, insurance, law enforcement, Native American community services, paralegal, radiography and surgical technology.

Bachelor's Degree Programs

Four-year programs leading to a bachelor's degree are offered in accounting, accounting/corporate finance, accounting/information systems, anthropology, applied workplace leadership, art and design education, art and design—bachelor of arts or bachelor of science, art and design—bachelor of fine arts, biochemistry, biology, biology with concentrations in botany, ecology, general biology, microbiology, physiology or zoology; chemistry (ACS certified), clinical health science (radiography, surgical technology and respiratory therapy, clinical laboratory science with concentrations in anatomic pathology, clinical systems analyst, diagnostic genetics, laboratory medicine, microbiology or science technologist; communication studies, community health education, computer science, construction management, criminal justice, earth science, economics, electrical engineering technology, elementary education—two minors elementary education integrated science, elementary education language arts, elementary education mathematics, elementary education social studies, elementary education special education, embedded systems, English graduate bound, English, English writing, entrepreneurship, environmental science, environmental studies and sustainability, finance and risk management, fisheries and wildlife management, forensic biochemistry, French, geomatics, German studies, history, hospitality and tourism management, individually created programs/individualized studies, industrial technologies, information assurance/cyber defense, information systems, integrated science—with biology minor, with chemistry minor, with earth science minor, or with physics minor; international studies, loss prevention management, management—bachelor of applied science, management—bachelor of science, management of health and fitness, marketing, mathematics, mechanical engineering technology, medicinal plant chemistry, mobile and web app development, multimedia journalism, multimedia production, music, Native American studies, neuroscience, nursing, outdoor recreation leadership and management, paralegal, philosophy, physical education—coaching, physics, political science, psychology, psychology—behavior analysis, public relations, RN to baccalaureate nursing, secondary education—biology, chemistry, earth science, English, French, geography, history, industrial technology, integrated science, mathematics, music, physical education, physics, political science, social studies, Spanish or special education; ski area business management, social work, sociology, Spanish, speech, language and hearing sciences, sports science, theatre and entertainment arts. NMU also offers the following pre-professional programs: pre-chiropractic, pre-clinical psychology, pre-dental, pre-engineering, pre-law, pre-medical, pre-optometry, pre-pharmacy, pre-physical therapy, pre-physician assistant, and pre-veterinary medicine.

Master's Degree Programs

The university offers the Master of Arts degree in Arts and Sciences, English and in higher education in student affairs. A Master of Arts in Education is offered for early childhood education, educational administration in administration and supervision or American Indian education administration and supervision, educational instruction, learning disabilities, reading K-8, or reading specialist K-12. An education specialist degree is also available in administration and supervision. The Master of Science degree is available in applied behavior analysis, arts and sciences, biology, clinical molecular genetics, exercise science, integrated biosciences, postsecondary biology education and psychological science. The Master of Fine Arts is offered in creative writing. Master's degrees in business administration and in public administration are also offered. A variety of approvals, endorsements, certifications, certificates, and licenses at the graduate level also exist.

Doctorate Degree Programs

The university offers a Doctor of Nursing Practice (DNP) consisting of two tracks: a post-baccalaureatae or post-master's.

Off-Campus Programs

Numerous online programs are offered through NMU's Global Campus to off- and on-campus students: an associate degree in criminal justice; bachelor's degrees in applied science in management, applied workplace leadership, clinical lab sciences/laboratory medicine (MLT-MLS), criminal justice, loss prevention management, psychology, RN to BSN and undeclared. A variety of minors are offered online as well. Master's degrees are offered in higher education and student affairs, early childhood education, educational administration: administration and supervision, educational administration: administration and supervision (American Indian education emphasis), instruction, learning disabilities, reading for K-8, reading specialist for K-12, public administration and clinical molecular genetics. An education specialist (Ed.S) is also offered. Educational endorsements are available in early childhood, learning disabilities and reading. A family nurse practitioner doctorate is also offered.

Accreditations

Northern Michigan University is accredited by the Commission on Institutions of Higher Education, the Higher Learning Commission, and Northern Central Association. All education programs are accredited by the Teacher Education Accreditation Council (TEAC). Other accreditations include the Accreditation Board for Engineering and Technology; American Alliance for Health, Physical Education, Recreation and Dance; American Chemical Society; American Society of Cytology; Commission on Accreditation of Allied Health Education Professionals (Surgical Technology); Committee on Accreditation for Respiratory Care of the Commission on Accreditation of Allied Health Education Programs; Council on Social Work Education; Department of Transportation Federal Aviation Administration Certification; International Association of Counseling Services, Inc.; Joint Review Committee on Education in Radiologic Technology; Michigan Department of Licensing and Regulation, State Board of Nursing; National Accrediting Agency for Clinical Laboratory Sciences; and the National Association of Schools of Music. In addition, the nursing programs (practical nursing, baccalaureate, and master's degrees) are fully approved by the Michigan Department of Licensing and Regulation, State Board of Nursing and the baccalaureate and master's degrees are fully accredited by the Commission on Collegiate Nursing Education (CCNE).

The baccalaureate degree programs of the College of Business are accredited by the Association to Advance Collegiate Schools of Business.

Credit Enrollment (fall head count)	2016	2017	2018
Enrollment	7,750	7,612	7,595

STATEMENT OF OPERATING REVENUES AND EXPENDITURES

Operating Revenues (all funds)	2016-2017	2017-1018
State Appropriations	$46,741,705	$47,603,952
Net Student Fees.	$60,310,217	$61,533,017
Gifts, Grants, and Federal Contracts	$17,472,247	$18,644,643
Other Income	$33,114,629	$32,575,068
TOTAL REVENUES.	$157,638,798	$160,356,680

Operating Expenditures (all funds)	2016-2017	2017-2018
Instruction and Research	$45,291,724	$46,987,901
Public Service	$8,360,513	$8,929,331
Student Services and Aid	$23,242,131	$26,508,632
Other Expenses	$74,935,281	$76,188,092
TOTAL EXPENDITURES	$151,829,649	$158,613,956

OAKLAND
UNIVERSITY

Rochester 48309

www.oakland.edu

BOARD OF TRUSTEES

Oakland University was established in 1957 when the late Alfred G. and Matilda R. Wilson donated $2 million and their Meadow Brook estate and surrounding farms to begin a new college in Oakland County, Michigan. From its beginnings, the university has provided an undergraduate education that prepares students with a portfolio of skills and values that lead to success in work and life.

Oakland University is a doctoral university with high research activity. It offers 142 undergraduate majors and 138 graduate degree and certificate programs, including master's and doctoral degrees. Oakland has seen remarkable student enrollment growth over the last two decades and today is home to more than 19,000 students. The university offers a unique, hands-on education for undergraduate and graduate students through the College of Arts and Sciences, the Schools of Business Administration, Engineering and Computer Science, Health Sciences, Education and Human Services, Nursing, the Honors College, and the Oakland University William Beaumont School of Medicine. According to the Anderson Economic Group, its regional economic footprint in 2013 was estimated at more than $700 million annually.

Of the university's 614 full-time faculty members, approximately 88 percent hold doctoral degrees in specialized fields of study from many of the nation's finest research institutions. This ratio rises to 94 percent when accounting for full-time faculty members with terminal degrees in their fields. These renowned faculty members teach in Oakland University's classrooms. In fact, graduate assistants teach less than one percent of all OU courses. Small classes mean students receive hands-on, high-quality attention from inspirational and innovative faculty members.

Oakland University continues to move toward its goal of creating an even more distinctive undergraduate education by 2020. Oakland is expanding on its core strengths to become known for its cross-disciplinary approach to education, unique opportunities for undergraduate research, personalized attention, and its tradition of producing liberally educated leaders.

Credit Enrollment (fall head count)	2016	2017	2018
On-campus	20,012	19,333	19,309

STATEMENT OF OPERATING REVENUES AND EXPENDITURES

Operating Revenues (all funds)	2016-2017	2017-2018
State Appropriations	$50,082,867	$51,243,200
Net Student Fees	$207,391,734	$206,331,783
Gifts, Grants, and Federal Contracts	$37,768,326	$40,957,974
Other Income	$53,605,715	$51,253,758
TOTAL REVENUES	$348,848,642	$349,786,715

Operating Expenditures (all funds)	2016-2017	2017-2018
Instruction and Research	$127,963,215	$130,885,262
Public Service	$5,082,052	$4,879,635
Student Services and Aid	$44,418,715	$43,673,463
Other Expenses	$149,155,631	$151,494,179
TOTAL EXPENDITURES	$326,619,613	$330,932,539

SAGINAW VALLEY STATE UNIVERSITY

University Center 48710

www.svsu.edu

BOARD OF CONTROL

Term expires

JOHN D. CHERRY JR., Clio . . . . July 21, 2027
JOANN T. CRARY, Frankenmuth . . . . July 21, 2025
DENNIS DURCO, Pinckney. . . . . July 21, 2021
LINDSEY EGGERS, Linwood . . . . July 21, 2025
JOHN KUNITZER, Saginaw . . . . July 21, 2021
VICKI L. RUPP, Saginaw . . . . July 21, 2023
RAJ KUMARI WIENER, Williamston . . . . July 21, 2027

DONALD J. BACHAND, President

Saginaw Valley State University began operations in 1963 as a private institution and received a charter as a state college in 1965. The campus is located within the triangle formed by Bay City, Midland, and Saginaw. Facilities include academic and administration buildings, conference facilities, residence halls and apartments, and an athletic complex.

The undergraduate curriculum is comprehensive and constantly expanding to suit the needs of our students. Academic tracks are available for pre-health professions, pre-agriculture and pre-law. Programs requiring pre-admission status where students must complete pre-requisites before entering their program of study include: athletic training, occupational therapy and social work. The College of Science, Engineering and Technology offers a degree program in engineering technology management to individuals with associate's degrees. General majors offered include: Accounting, applied mathematics, art, biochemistry, biology, business chemistry, chemical physics, chemistry, communications, computer information systems, computer science, creative writing, criminal justice, early childhood education, economics, electrical engineering, elementary education, elementary teaching for international students, English, exercise science, family business management, finance, fine arts, French, general business, general studies, geography, graphic design, health sciences, history, international business, international studies, kinesiology, literature, management, marketing, mathematics, mechanical engineering, medical laboratory science, middle/secondary teaching for international students, modern foreign languages, music, neuroscience, nursing, optical physics, physical education, physics, political science, professional and technical writing, professional sales, psychology, public administration, public health, rehabilitation medicine, secondary education, sociology, Spanish, special education, supply chain management and theatre.

Minors in most of these disciplines are also offered as well as specific minors offered in agricultural studies, alternative energy, Asian studies, athletic coaching, Black studies, cybersecurity, emergency management, engineering and technology, entrepreneurship, gender studies, geospatial techniques, gerontology, Japanese, leadership and service, legal philosophy, legal studies, musical theatre, philosophy, public history, religious studies, Spanish for health professions, and youth services.

Many major and minor programs are available for teacher certification as well as an early childhood endorsement.

At the master's degree level, the College of Education offers Master of Arts degrees in teaching, instructional technology, and teaching Chinese as a Foreign Language (in collaboration with Ming Chuan University, Taiwan) and offers concentrations in early childhood, reading, special education, principalship, and instructional technology/e-learning. The College of Education also offers a postbaccalaureate accelerated teacher certification and residency. A Master of Business Administration degree is conferred by the College of Business and Management. The College of Arts and Behavioral Sciences awards a Master of Arts degree in Public Administration and a Master of Arts degree in Communication and Multimedia Administration. The Crystal M. Lange College of Nursing and Health Sciences offers a Master of Science in Nursing, a Master of Science in Social Work, a Master of Science in Public Health, a Master of Science in Occupational Therapy, and a Master of Science in health administration and leadership. The College of Science, Engineering and Technology offers a Master of Science in Energy and Materials.

At the doctoral degree level, The Crystal M. Lange College of Nursing and Health Sciences offers the Doctor of Nursing Practice.

Saginaw Valley State University is accredited by the Higher Learning Commission — North Central Association of Colleges and Schools, the American Assembly of Collegiate Schools of Business — International, the Accreditation Board for Engineering and Technology, the National Council for Accreditation of Teacher Education, the American Society of Clinical Pathologists and the American Medical Association (Medical Technology), the National Association of Schools of Music, the Council of Social Work Education (Social Work), the National League for Nursing (Nursing), and the Accreditation Council for Occupational Therapy Education.

Credit Enrollment (fall head count)	2014	2016	2018
On-campus.	9,135	8,396	8,195
Off-campus.	694	769	340

STATEMENT OF OPERATING REVENUES AND EXPENDITURES

Operating Revenues (all funds)	*2016-2017*	*2017-2018*
State Appropriations	$29,197,274	$29,779,000
Net Student Fees.	$69,871,057	$68,416,895
Gifts, Grants, and Federal Contracts	$21,029,333	$20,723,966
Other Income	$28,450,197	$30,370,355
TOTAL REVENUES.	$148,547,861	$149,290,216

Operating Expenditures (all funds)	*2016-2017*	*2017-2018*
Instruction and Research	$43,972,742	$44,422,255
Public Service	$4,131,839	$3,943,067
Student Services and Aid	$16,720,384	$16,377,059
Other Expenses	$76,076,353	$75,470,767
TOTAL EXPENDITURES	$140,901,318	$140,213,148

UNIVERSITY OF MICHIGAN

Ann Arbor 48109

www.umich.edu

BOARD OF REGENTS

Term expires

JORDAN B. ACKER, Ann Arbor	Jan. 1, 2027
MICHAEL J. BEHM, Grand Blanc	Jan. 1, 2023
MARK J. BERNSTEIN, Ann Arbor	Jan. 1, 2021
PAUL W. BROWN, Ann Arbor	Jan. 1, 2027
SHAUNA RYDER DIGGS, Grosse Pointe	Jan. 1, 2021
DENISE ILITCH, Bingham Farms	Jan. 1, 2025
RON WEISER, Ann Arbor	Jan. 1, 2025
KATHERINE E. WHITE, Ann Arbor	Jan. 1, 2023

MARK S. SCHLISSEL, President and Ex Officio

Section 5 of Article VIII of the Constitution of 1963 provides for the Regents of the University of Michigan. The board consists of eight members elected for eight-year terms. The president of the university, who is elected by the board, is an ex officio member. The regents are a body corporate and have general supervision of the institution and the control and direction of all expenditures from the institution's funds.

The University of Michigan was founded in Detroit by an act of the territorial legislature in 1817. The territorial legislature planned "a university of Michigania" as a territory wide public educational system. The largest single gift to the early University was a land grant of 1,920 acres from the Ojibwe, Odawa, and Bodewadami Nations, ceded through the Treaty at the Foot of the Rapids, so that their children could be educated.

The university was moved to Ann Arbor in 1837 to take advantage of an offer of 40 acres of land at the edge of town. The acreage ceded by the three tribes was sold, and the proceeds remain part of the university's permanent endowment. The university earned the title "Mother of State Universities" when it became the first model of a complete state university in America. The original 40-acre Ann Arbor campus has expanded to more than 3,270 acres with 594 major buildings and 1,100 family housing units. The University of Michigan-Flint opened in 1956 with a gift from the Mott Foundation. The University of Michigan-Dearborn followed in 1959 on the land of the Henry Ford Estate, a gift from the Ford Motor Company.

Schools and Colleges, Students and Faculty

The schools and colleges located on the Ann Arbor campus are: A. Alfred Taubman College of Architecture and Urban Planning; Penny W. Stamps School of Art and Design; Stephen M. Ross School of Business; School of Dentistry; School of Education; College of Engineering; School for Environment and Sustainability; School of Information; School of Kinesiology; Law School; College of Literature, Science, and the Arts; Medical School; School of Music, Theatre and Dance; School of Nursing; College of Pharmacy; School of Public Health; Gerald R. Ford School of Public Policy; Horace H. Rackham School of Graduate Studies; and School of Social Work. The Dearborn campus has four schools and colleges: College of Arts, Sciences, and Letters; College of Business; College of Education, Health, and Human Services; and College of Engineering and Computer Science. The Flint campus has five schools and colleges: College of Arts and Sciences; School of Health Sciences; School of Education and Human Services; School of Management; and School of Nursing.

University of Michigan students, who hail from all 50 states and 128 countries, participate in more than 1,500+ student organizations; volunteer their time and talents in Ann Arbor, Detroit, and beyond; and broaden their horizons through the hundreds of concerts, lectures, and symposia Michigan hosts each year. Michigan's 611,000 living alumni continue to make substantial contributions to the world's intellectual, scientific, and cultural growth. Michigan's teaching faculty counts among its ranks distinguished world authorities, Pulitzer Prize winners, Nobel laureates, MacArthur grantees, and internationally acclaimed artists, composers, and performers who thrive in the university's open, diverse, and collaborative atmosphere. Regardless of their career level, UM faculty have numerous opportunities to develop as researchers and teachers.

Libraries and Museums

The Library System has more than 20 libraries with over 14.2 million volumes and nearly 222,000 serial titles including both hard copy and online journals and magazines. The university's libraries are national leaders in the development of digital library resources. The University of Michigan has 12 museums and four galleries including the Detroit Observatory, Kelsey Museum of Archaeology, Matthaei Botanical Gardens, Museum of Art, Museum of Natural History, Nichols Arboretum, Herbarium, Museum of Anthropology, Museum of Paleontology, Museum of Zoology, Sindecuse Museum of Dentistry, and the Stearns Collection of Musical Instruments, as well as the Robbins Gallery, Slusser Gallery, Work: Ann Arbor, and Work: Detroit.

Research

Research expenditures have risen dramatically over the last decade to $1.55 billion in fiscal year 2018, with about 55 percent of the total volume of research at UM being conducted under contract with the federal government. The growing investment in UM research is partly a measure of the confidence of university sponsors in the value faculty, staff, and students bring to society.

With 19 schools and colleges and more than 200 centers and institutes across campus, UM conducts research in virtually every major area of science, engineering, medicine, social sciences, management, education, and the humanities. Working together across disciplines is a hallmark of the UM research environment, as researchers join with colleagues in other fields to advance knowledge, solve challenging problems, and create marketable products. In recent years, the university has invested in several major research initiatives that address emerging challenges and opportunities in areas of broad potential impact, ranging in scope from data science, poverty and precision health to biosciences and the humanities.

In fiscal year 2018, UM researchers reported 484 new inventions, a 10 percent increase from the previous year. The number of startups launched at UM nearly doubled to 21 in fiscal year 2018, as UM inventors went to market with a broad array of discoveries.

The university further strengthens its research enterprise through relationships with industry. The Business Engagement Center has ongoing relationships with more than 1,200 companies in Michigan and beyond, helping connect industry broadly across UM at all schools, colleges, and campuses based on interest and opportunity.

Michigan Medicine: The University's Academic Medical Center

Michigan Medicine, the University of Michigan's academic medical center, comprises a broad range of clinical, research, and education activity. It includes the UM Medical School and its faculty group practice known as the UM Medical Group, and more than 3,700 clinical and research faculty. It also includes the three UM hospitals, a number of specialty centers, and more than 40 outpatient health centers, an extensive home care service, and affiliations and partnerships with other healthcare institutions including the Veterans Administration's Ann Arbor Healthcare System, Mid-Michigan Health and Metro Health in west Michigan.

The Health System serves patients from every county in Michigan as well as from other states and nations. Residency training at the UM Health System is highly regarded. The Health System's focus on high-quality care for even the most complex patients has earned numerous other awards and accreditations, and recognitions for patient safety.

Economic Impact of the University

The university, with campuses in Ann Arbor, Flint, and Dearborn, makes significant economic contributions to the state of Michigan. There are more than 242,500 UM alumni and 54,250 UM employees who live and work in Michigan. UM enrolls nearly 40,000 students from the state, and there are more than 2.8 million visits by state residents to UM hospitals and clinics. UM has nearly $1.5 billion in purchases of goods and services from about 40,400 Michigan companies.

UM is metro Detroit's fourth largest employer. Student retail spending is estimated at more than $300 million per year. Each home football game in Ann Arbor generates an estimated $12 million for the local economy, and cultural activities attract more than 350,000 attendees each year.

Gifts

In addition to receiving funds from the state of Michigan, the University of Michigan also relies on private gifts that support student financial aid, faculty research and teaching, facilities, and programs. Many buildings and facilities on campus owe their existence to the generosity of donors. In the fiscal year that ended on June 30, 2018, nearly 122,000 alumni and friends, corporations, foundations, and associations demonstrated their commitment to the future of the university by making gifts.

Credit Enrollment (fall head count)	2016	2017	2018
Ann Arbor campus only	44,718	46,002	46,716
Ann Arbor, Flint and Dearborn	61,893	63,177	63,716

STATEMENT OF OPERATING REVENUES AND EXPENSES

Operating Revenues	*2017*	*2018*
Net student tuition and fees	$1,240,584,000	$1,310,941,000
Federal grants and contracts	942,287,000	982,143,000
State and local grants and contracts	11,405,000	13,304,000
Nongovernmental sponsored programs	226,556,000	233,919,000
Sales and services of educational departments . . .	135,212,000	140,139,000
Auxiliary enterprises:		
Patient care revenues.	4,200,081,000	4,438,744,000
Student residence fees	112,478,000	117,866,000
Other revenues	208,628,000	227,288,000
Student loan interest income and fees	2,448,000	2,537,000
TOTAL OPERATING REVENUES	**7,079,679,000**	**7,466,881,000**

Operating Expenses	*2017*	*2018*
Instruction	$1,099,800,000	$1,153,200,000
Research.	803,500,000	823,600,000
Public service	187,800,000	211,500,000
Institutional and academic support	646,700,000	681,000,000
Auxiliary enterprises:		
Patient care	3,976,100,000	4,349,200,000
Other	198,100,000	264,600,000
Operations and maintenance of plant	316,400,000	350,900,000
Depreciation	537,700,000	568,700,000
Scholarships and fellowships	143,900,000	156,700,000
TOTAL OPERATING EXPENSES	**7,910,000,000**	**8,559,400,000**

WAYNE STATE UNIVERSITY

Detroit 48202

www.wayne.edu

BOARD OF GOVERNORS

	Term expires
BRYAN C. BARNHILL II, Detroit	Dec. 31, 2026
MICHAEL J. BUSUITO, Troy	Dec. 31, 2024
MARK GAFFNEY, Detroit	Dec. 31, 2024
MARILYN JEAN KELLY, Bloomfield Hills	Dec. 31, 2022
ANIL KUMAR, Bloomfield Hills	Dec. 31, 2026
SANDRA HUGHES O'BRIEN, Northville	Dec. 31, 2020
DANA THOMPSON, Detroit	Dec. 31, 2022
KIM TRENT, Detroit	Dec. 31, 2020

M. ROY WILSON, President

For more than 150 years, Wayne State University has been changing the world from the heart of Detroit. What started as a small medical college in 1868 is now one of the nation's premier research institutions.

Located in Detroit's Midtown neighborhood, Wayne State's 200-acre main campus comprises more than 100 buildings, including residence halls, laboratories, and theatres. Students learn in the center of a vibrant city, rich with culture and countless opportunities to take part in Detroit's dramatic rebirth. Wayne State's reach expands throughout Southeast Michigan, with five satellite campuses in Wayne, Oakland and Macomb counties.

Wayne State is home to more than 27,000 students from all walks of life, 90 percent of whom are Michigan residents. The university has a diverse student body, with students coming from around the nation and the world. More than 3,000 students live on campus in Wayne State's residence halls and apartments.

Academics

Wayne State offers more than 350 academic programs, ranging from undergraduate to doctoral programs, with several certificate options. Its 13 schools and colleges prepare students to thrive in a variety of fields, including medicine, law, business, the arts, social work, education, nursing, library sciences, and more. Faculty members are chosen for their expertise outside of the classroom and renowned for contributions they've made in their chosen fields. Students have the opportunity to study globally, with nearly 30 study abroad opportunities available on five continents.

The university's proximity to renowned hospitals, businesses, theatres and sports arenas provides students with internship opportunities and firsthand experiences in their fields of study. This, coupled with the unparalleled teaching they receive in the classroom, prepares them to thrive and lead after graduation. Wayne State is accredited by the North Central Association of Colleges and Secondary Schools and its academic programs are accredited by the appropriate agencies.

Research

Wayne State combines high research activity, a comprehensive doctoral program, a medical campus, and a large graduate and undergraduate population. Faculty members mentor students and provide hands-on experiences throughout the Detroit area, where Wayne State researchers make vital contributions to the environmental, health, and engineering fields, among others. Wayne State is also home to the $90 million Integrative Biosciences Center, a state-of-the-art research facility dedicated to addressing health disparities in Detroit and around the world.

The School of Medicine is affiliated with the hospitals of the Detroit Medical Center, which include Children's Hospital of Michigan, the Rehabilitation Institute of Michigan, Hutzel Women's Hospital, Detroit Receiving Hospital, Harper University Hospital, Sinai-Grace Hospital, Huron Valley-Sinai Hospital, and the Michigan Orthopedic Specialty Hospital. It maintains a research and education partnership with the Henry Ford Health System in Detroit and coordinates teaching experiences with 14 community hospitals through the Southeast Michigan Center for Medical Education. It is the home of the National Institutes of Health (NIH) Perinatology Research Branch, one of only a few branches located outside of the NIH's main campus in Maryland. The branch supports research related to pregnancy and maternal health, embryonic development, fetal growth, and infant well-being.

Economic impact

Wayne State is home to TechTown, a business incubator that accelerates economic growth in Detroit by growing strong businesses and driving regional collaboration. Since its inception, TechTown has assisted more than 600 companies, which have created more than 1,000 jobs. Wayne State is also part of Michigan's University Research Corridor (URC), along with Michigan State University and the University of Michigan. In 2017, the URC universities contributed $18.7 billion to Michigan's economy.

Wayne State has played a vital role in Detroit's recent resurgence. The university's police department has helped create a safe college campus, and its efforts have been recognized for helping to spur Midtown's renaissance. Events such as the annual Baroudeur bring visitors from across the nation to campus to experience Detroit. Wayne State's students, faculty and staff are involved in numerous community service and charity efforts, giving back to the city the university calls home.

Credit Enrollment (fall head count)   *2018*
On-campus and at extension centers 27,053

STATEMENT OF OPERATING REVENUES AND EXPENDITURES

Operating Revenues (all funds)	*2016-2017*	*2017-2018*
State Appropriations	$196,649,000	$199,170,000
Net Student Fees.	$278,606,000	$282,821,000
Gifts, Grants, and Federal Contracts	$207,299,000	$210,568,000
Other Income	$252,722,000	$200,089,000
TOTAL REVENUES.	$935,276,000	$892,648,000

Operating Expenditures (all funds)		
Instruction and Research	$432,901,000	$433,536,000
Public Service	$62,188,000	$62,021,000
Student Services and Aid	$66,806,000	$63,439,000
Other Expenses	$286,774,00	$296,786,000
TOTAL EXPENDITURES	$848,669,000	$855,782,000

WESTERN MICHIGAN UNIVERSITY

Kalamazoo 49008

www.wmich.edu

BOARD OF TRUSTEES

Western Michigan University is a national research institution with a small-college feel. Founded in 1903 as a teacher-preparation school, WMU has grown to become a major university known for preparing job-ready graduates. It builds intellectual inquiry, investigation, and discovery into its academic programs, yet remains focused on providing personal attention as well as preparing both undergraduate and graduate students for success in work and life.

Recognition: WMU is nationally recognized on several fronts including for its support of veterans pursuing higher education, commitment to diversity and inclusion, collegiate support for former foster-care youth, intensive English language program for international students, and constructing or renovating buildings with energy conservation and sustainability in mind.

Size and scope: WMU enrolls more than 22,500 students and is an NCAA Division I school in the Mid-American Conference (Football Bowl Subdivision) and National Collegiate Hockey Conference. Its campuses encompass more than 170 buildings as well as nearly 1,300 acres, and all University property—inside and out—is tobacco free. In addition, WMU has some of the finest instructional and performance spaces in the Midwest.

The main campus is located close to downtown Kalamazoo and includes a growing East Campus that features a mix of modern and historic buildings. This campus has become a hub for health and human services programs and direct-service clinics that play a critical role in the WMU Homer Stryker M.D. School of Medicine, a private medical school based in downtown Kalamazoo. The University's highly rated engineering college and thriving Business Technology and Research Park are based three miles away at the Parkview Campus, while its nationally known aviation college is based at the W.K. Kellogg Airport in Battle Creek, Michigan.

WMU has long met the state's regional needs for higher education and career development programs. It continues to serve thousands of Michigan residents annually through its Online and Lifelong Learning offices, as well as its regional locations in eight Michigan municipalities: Auburn Hills, Battle Creek, Benton Harbor, Clinton Township, Grand Rapids (downtown and the east side), Lansing, Muskegon, and Traverse City.

Academic programs: WMU continues to collaborate and innovate, offering new cutting-edge academic programs in response to emerging economic opportunities as well as state and national needs. New program examples from recent years include cybersecurity training and certification, the Bachelor of Science in sustainable brewing, Bachelor of Fine Arts in product design, and Doctor of Physical Therapy. These and many other innovative or high-demand programs attract private financial support and collaborations. They also serve as a base around which external partners can focus their research, development, and training needs or fast-track students into jobs.

WMU shapes its academic programs so its graduates are immediately ready to add value to their workplaces and communities. Within three months of graduation, 91 percent of alumni are employed, engaged in military service or full-time volunteer work, or continuing their education; 88 percent are satisfied with their jobs; and 85 percent have jobs related to their degree. While on campus, 93 percent of these graduates take advantage of an experiential learning offering to help them prepare for a lifetime of careers.

Degrees are granted through seven colleges: Arts and Sciences, Aviation, Haworth College of Business, Education and Human Development, Engineering and Applied Sciences, Fine Arts, and Health and Human Services. In addition, the Lee Honors College serves as an intimate home for more than 1,700 of the exceptionally talented undergraduates the University attracts, while the Graduate College assists nearly 5,000 students pursuing advanced degrees.

WMU offers the second largest number of undergraduate majors of any public university in Michigan. Students may choose from 265 programs — 152 at the bachelor's level, 78 at the master's level, one at the specialist level, and 34 at the doctoral level. Many of these offerings are nationally or internationally recognized, such as those in aviation, clinical psychology, creative writing, education, evaluation, geosciences, graph theory, integrated supply management, jazz studies, medieval studies, occupational therapy, public affairs, rehabilitation counseling, and sales and business marketing.

Faculty: The university's faculty is comprised of 871 full-time members, 559 part-time instructors, and 878 graduate assistants and associates. These scholars are dedicated to providing quality teaching at both the undergraduate and graduate levels, advancing the university's public service mission, and creating knowledge as well as putting it to work in daily life.

Despite its size and complexity, WMU has a 17-to-1 student-to-faculty ratio, and two-thirds of undergraduate classes have 30 or fewer students. In addition, full-time professors teach most undergraduate as well as graduate classes. Seventy-one percent of WMU's faculty is tenured.

Student support: WMU creates an environment for its students that is both challenging and supportive and one that provides wide-ranging opportunities. A variety of resources and services focus on the academic and career success of students, such as every first-year student being matched with a mentor and underclassmen being given room to pursue a professional passion and receive an additional marketable designation on their diploma. Plus, several offices are dedicated to meeting the special needs of such select groups as former foster-care youth, military veterans, transfer students, and students who are undecided about their majors.

Creating a home away from home, the university operates 21 residence halls, three apartment complexes, four dining facilities, and eight campus cafés. The residence halls provide a network of living-learning communities that engage students in their academic disciplines and personal development.

WMU recognizes that college is a time for students to have fun as well as further their individual skills and interests. Educational, social, and recreational opportunities abound through hundreds of student organizations, fraternities and sororities, professional groups, intramural and club sports, and fitness and wellness programs. In addition, the university has nationally recognized arts programs, a lively cultural calendar, and in 2018 launched an esports club as well as opened a cutting-edge esports arena.

International perspective and diversity: The University is home to a diverse student body that includes more than 1,800 international students from some 100 countries. International students comprise 8 percent of the student body, while minority students make up 23 percent and graduate students 21 percent. Eighty-two percent of all students are Michigan residents.

WMU infuses the campus-learning environment with a global perspective in and out of the classroom. Along with scores of international-related events and student groups, the University is home to several international study centers along with a world-renowned intensive English language program for international students. It also offers some 100 study abroad programs in more than 40 countries and access to overseas study opportunities in almost every other country through linkages with universities and organizations around the world.

Research: Faculty members advance knowledge across Michigan and around the world, and undergraduate as well as graduate students have ample opportunities to work closely with these outstanding researchers. A growing amount of their funded research is the product of partnerships with business, industry, and government in areas such as advanced engineering and manufacturing, homeland security, information technology, the life sciences, and nanotechnology.

The University's basic and applied collaborations not only enhance classroom instruction and career opportunities for students, they also foster economic development in Michigan while building the state's 21st-century knowledge base. In addition, the University has placed greater emphasis in recent years on bringing entrepreneurship into its research, academic, and collaborative initiatives. These efforts include the Starting Gate student business accelerator, which gives students rich and valuable resources to develop their own startup companies, providing a fast-track to business launch.

Economic impact: WMU's regional impact in 2016-17 was $1.6 billion. For every one of the $104 million the state invested in WMU that year, the University returned $15.40 in economic vitality to the Calhoun, Kalamazoo, and Van Buren county region. A 2018 study found that WMU annually supports nearly 17,000 direct, indirect, and induced jobs in the local area, while students individually spend $11,500 and collectively contribute 235,000 hours to volunteer service and other off-campus community engagement activities.

Among the University's many economic success stories is the Business Technology and Research Park (BTR), which is expanding with the help of a grant from the U.S. Department of Commerce's Economic Development Administration. The park's first phase has attracted more than $150 million in investment and generated more than 850 jobs as well as hundreds of internships for WMU students in 42 private companies located there. Now, with all BTR 1 property having been developed or under option for growth by companies in the park, the BTR 2 expansion is underway on a parcel located across the street.

Cost: WMU's relatively low cost makes it a great higher education value. WMU ranks eighth in tuition and fees among the state's 15 public universities.

WMU awards some $266 million annually in financial aid, offers merit-based scholarships, and regularly introduces initiatives to keep its costs low and offer opportunity to underrepresented populations. One such initiative is the Seita Scholars Program, which supports up to 150 young people who have aged out of foster care. The nationally acclaimed program is the nation's largest and most comprehensive collegiate strategy for foster care youth, providing full-tuition scholarships, a year-round place to live, and a coaching network to support both personal growth and academic success.

Credit Enrollment
(fall count; includes duplicates)	*2016*	*2017*	*2018*
On-campus	20,837	20,365	19,994
Regional sites and online education	6,536	6,745	7,120

STATEMENT OF OPERATING REVENUES AND EXPENDITURES

Operating Revenues (all funds)	*2016-2017*	*2017-2018*
State Appropriations	$107,764,905	$110,571,948
Net Student Fees........................	$239,409,677	$243,427,391
Gifts, Grants, and Federal Contracts	$96,629,012	$87,363,230
Other Income	$146,386,144	$147,306,591
TOTAL REVENUES...................	$590,189,738	$588,669,160

Operating Expenditures (all funds)	*2016-2017*	*2017-2018*
Instruction and Research..................	$255,029,893	$253,991,566
Public Service..........................	$9,797,946	$9,027,300
Student Services and Aid..................	$45,364,000	$41,235,789
Other Expenses	$266,792,407	$253,771,743
TOTAL EXPENDITURES................	$576,984,246	$558,026,398

COMMUNITY COLLEGES

Institution	Location	President
Alpena Community College	Alpena	Dr. Donald MacMaster
Bay College	Escanaba	Dr. Laura L. Coleman
Delta College	University Center	Dr. Jean Goodnow
Glen Oaks Community College	Centreville	Dr. David Devier
Gogebic Community College	Ironwood	Vacant
Grand Rapids Community College	Grand Rapids	Dr. Bill Pink
Henry Ford Community College	Dearborn	Mr. Russell A. Kavalhuna
Jackson Community College	Jackson	Dr. Daniel Phelan
Kalamazoo Valley Community College	Kalamazoo	Dr. L. Marshall Washington
Kellogg Community College	Battle Creek	Mr. Mark O'Connell
Kirtland Community College	Roscommon	Dr. Thomas Quinn
Lake Michigan College	Benton Harbor	Dr. Trevor Kubatzke
Lansing Community College	Lansing	Dr. Brent Knight
Macomb Community College	Warren	Dr. James Sawyer, IV
Mid Michigan Community College	Harrison	Dr. Christine Hammond
Monroe County Community College	Monroe	Dr. Kojo Quartey
Montcalm Community College	Sidney	Mr. Robert Ferrentino
Mott Community College	Flint	Dr. Beverly Walker-Griffea
Muskegon Community College	Muskegon	Dr. Dale K. Nesbary
North Central Michigan College	Petoskey	Dr. David R. Finley
Northwestern Michigan College	Traverse City	Mr. Timothy Nelson
Oakland Community College	Bloomfield Hills	Mr. Peter Provenzano, Jr.
St. Clair County Community College	Port Huron	Dr. Deborah Snyder
Schoolcraft College	Livonia	Dr. Conway A. Jeffress
Southwestern Michigan College	Dowagiac	Dr. David M. Mathews
Washtenaw Community College	Ann Arbor	Dr. Rose Bellanca
Wayne County Community College	Detroit	Dr. Curtis L. Ivery
West Shore Community College	Scottville	Mr. Scott Ward

Source: Directory of Michigan Public Community Colleges, Workforce Development Agency, State of Michigan, 2015. Updated, Legislative Service Bureau, 2019.

INDEPENDENT COLLEGES AND UNIVERSITIES

Institution	Location	President[1]
Adrian College	Adrian	Dr. Jeffrey R. Docking
Albion College	Albion	Dr. Mauri Ditzler
Alma College	Alma	Dr. Jeff Abernathy
Andrews University	Berrien Springs	Dr. Andrea Luxton
Aquinas College	Grand Rapids	Dr. Kevin Quinn
Baker College System	Multiple	Dr. Bart Daig
Calvin College	Grand Rapids	Dr. Michael LeRoy
Calvin Theological Seminary	Grand Rapids	Dr. Julius Medenblik
Cleary University – Livingston	Howell	Mr. Jayson Boyers
Cleary University – Washtenaw	Ann Arbor	Mr. Jayson Boyers
College for Creative Studies	Detroit	Mr. Richard Rogers
Concordia University	Ann Arbor	Rev. Dr. Patrick T. Ferry
Cornerstone University	Grand Rapids	Dr. Joseph Stowell
Cranbrook Academy of Art	Bloomfield Hills	Ms. Susan R. Ewing
Davenport University	Grand Rapids	Dr. Richard J. Pappas
DeVry University	Southfield	Mr. James Bartholomew
Ecumenical Theological Seminary	Detroit	Rev. Dr. Kenneth E. Harris
Finlandia University	Hancock	Rev. Dr. Phillip Johnson
Grace Christian University	Grand Rapids	Dr. Ken Kemper
Great Lakes Christian College	Lansing	Mr. Lawrence L. Carter
Hillsdale College	Hillsdale	Dr. Larry P. Arnn
Hope College	Holland	Rev. Dennis N. Voskuil
Kalamazoo College	Kalamazoo	Dr. Jorge G. Gonzalez
Kettering University	Flint	Dr. Robert K. McMahan, Jr.
Kuyper College	Grand Rapids	Dr. Patricia R. Harris
Lawrence Technological University	Southfield	Dr. Virinder Moudgil
Madonna University	Livonia	Dr. Michael Grandillo
Marygrove College	Detroit	Dr. Elizabeth A. Burns
Michigan School of Professional Psychology	Farmington Hills	Dr. Fran Brown
Moody Theological Seminary – Michigan	Plymouth	Dr. Mark Jobe
Northwood University	Midland	Mr. Keith A. Pretty
Olivet College	Olivet	Dr. Steven Corey
Rochester College	Rochester Hills	Dr. Brian Stogner
Sacred Heart Major Seminary	Detroit	Rev. Msgr. Todd J. Lajiness
SS Cyril and Methodius Seminary	Orchard Lake	Most Reverend Francis Reiss
Siena Heights University	Adrian	Sister Peg Albert, OP, Ph.D.
Spring Arbor University	Spring Arbor	Dr. Brent Ellis
University of Detroit Mercy	Detroit	Dr. Antoine M. Garibaldi
University of Phoenix – Southfield	Southfield	Mr. Peter Cohen
University of Phoenix – West Michigan Campus	Grand Rapids	Mr. Peter Cohen
Walsh College of Accountancy and Business	Troy	Ms. Marsha Kelliher
Western Michigan University Cooley Law School	Lansing	Mr. Jeffrey L. Martlew (Interim)
Western Theological Seminary	Holland	Mr. Felix Theonugraha
Yeshiva Gedolah of Greater Detroit	Oak Park	Rabbi L. Bakst

[1] This also includes chief executive officers with a variety of titles, including "dean," "director," etc.

Sources: National Association of Independent Colleges and Universities. Membership Directory. https://www.naicu.edu/membership/membership-directory?Alpha=&keyword=&AddressState=MI&Search=Search. (accessed March 18, 2019).

The Council of Independent Colleges. Member Listing. http://www.cic.edu/about/members/listing. (accessed March 18, 2019).

Updated, Legislative Service Bureau, March 2019.

FORMER MEMBERS OF
UNIVERSITY GOVERNING BOARDS
REGENTS OF THE UNIVERSITY OF MICHIGAN, 1837-2019[1]

Thomas Fitzgerald	1837	Henry Whiting	1858-1863
Robert McClelland	1837	Oliver L. Spaulding	1858-1863
Michael Hoffman	1837-1838	Luke Parsons	1858-1862
John F. Porter	1837-1838	Edward C. Walker	1864-1881
Lucius Lyon	1837-1839	George Willard	1864-1873
John Norvell	1837-1839	Thomas D. Gilbert	1864-1875
Seba Murphy	1837-1839	Thomas J. Joslin	1864-1867
John J. Adam	1837-1840	Henry C. Knight	1864-1867
Samuel Denton	1837-1840	Alvah Sweetzer	1864
Gideon O. Whittemore	1837-1840	James A. Sweezey	1864-1871
Henry R. Schoolcraft	1837-1841	Cyrus M. Stockwell	1865-1871
Isaac E. Crary	1837-1843	J. M. B. Sill	1867-1869
Ross Wilkins	1837-1842	Hiram A. Burt	1868-1875
Zina Pitcher	1837-1852	Joseph Estabrook	1870-1877
Gurdon C. Leech	1838-1840	Jonas H. McGowan	1870-1877
Jonathan Kearsley	1838-1852	Claudius B. Grant	1872-1879
Joseph W. Brown	1839-1840	Charles Rynd	1872-1879
Charles C. Trowbridge	1839-1842	Andrew Climie	1874-1881
George Duffield	1839-1848	Byron M. Cutcheon	1876-1883
Daniel Hudson	1840-1841	Samuel S. Walker	1876-1883
Samuel W. Dexter	1840-1841	Victory P. Collier	1877
Francis J. Higginson	1840-1841	George Duffield, Jr.	1877-1885
Michael A. Patterson	1840-1842	George L. Maltz	1878-1880
William Draper	1840-1844	Jacob J. Van Riper	1880-1885
Oliver C. Comstock	1841-1843	Ebenezer O. Grosvenor	1880-1887
George Goodman	1841-1843	James Shearer	1880-1887
John G. Owen	1841-1848	Austin Blair	1881-1889
Martin Kundig	1841-1845	James Frederic Joy	1882-1886
Randolph Manning	1842	Lyman D. Norris	1883
Andrew M. Fitch	1842-1846	Arthur M. Clark	1884-1891
Elisha Crane	1842-1846	Charles J. Willett	1884-1891
William A. Fletcher	1842-1846	Charles S. Draper	1886-1892
Lewis Cass	1843-1844	Moses W. Field	1886-1889
Dewitt C. Walker	1843-1844	Charles R. Whitman	1886-1893
Marvin Allen	1843-1852	Roger W. Butterfield	1888-1903
Robert R. Kellogg	1844-1845	Charles Hebard	1888-1895
Edward Mundy	1844-1848	Hermann Kiefer	1889-1901
Alexander H. Redfield	1844-1852	William J. Cocker[2]	1890-1901
Minot T. Lane	1845-1849	Peter N. Cook	1892-1899
Austin E. Wing	1845-1850	Henry Howard	1892-1894
Elon Farnsworth	1846-1857	Levi L. Barbour	1892-1897
Charles C. Taylor	1846-1850	Henry S. Dean	1894-1907
Elijah Pilcher	1846-1852	Frank W. Fletcher	1894-1909
John G. Atterbury	1848-1852	Charles H. Hackley	1896
Justus Goodwin	1848-1852	George A. Farr	1896-1903
Benjamin F. H. Witherell	1848-1852	Charles D. Lawton	1898-1905
Edwin M. Cust	1849	Eli R. Sutton[3]	1900-1902
Robert McClelland	1850-1852	Arthur Hill[4]	1901-1909
Gustavus L. Foster	1850-1852	Levi L. Barbour	1902-1907
Epaphroditus Ransom	1850-1852	Henry W. Carey	1902-1909
Andrew Parsons	1852-1853	Peter White[5]	1904-1908
Elisha Ely	1852-1854	Loyal E. Knappen[6]	1904-1911
James C. Kingsley	1852-1857	Walter H. Sawyer[7]	1906-1931
Edward S. Moore	1852-1857	Chase S. Osborn[8]	1908-1911
Charles H. Palmer	1852-1857	Frank B. Leland	1908-1923
Michael F. Patterson	1852-1857	Junius E. Beal	1908-1939
William Upjohn	1852-1857	John H. Grant[9]	1909-1913
Henry H. Northrop	1854-1857	George P. Codd[10]	1910-1911
George W. Pack	1858	William L. Clements	1910-1933
John Van Vleck	1858	Harry C. Bulkley	1911-1917
Benjamin L. Baxter	1858-1863	Benjamin S. Hanchett[11]	1911-1929
Levi Bishop	1858-1863	Lucius L. Hubbard[12]	1911-1933
George Bradley	1858-1863	William A. Comstock	1913
Ebenezer L. Brown	1858-1863	Victor M. Gore	1914-1929
William M. Ferry	1858-1863	James O. Murfin	1918-1937
J. Eastman Johnson	1858-1869	Ralph Stone	1924-1939
Donald McIntyre	1858-1863	Esther March Cram[13]	1929-1943

R. Perry Shorts[14]	1930-1934		Otis M. Smith	1967-1971
Richard R. Smith	1931-1937		Robert J. Brown[26]	1967-1975
Edmund C. Shields	1933-1935		Gertrude V. Huebner	1967-1975
Charles F. Hemans	1934-1941		Lawrence B. Lindemer[27]	1968-1975
Franklin M. Cook	1934-1941		Gerald R. Dunn	1969-1985
David H. Crowley	1936-1943		Robert E. Nederlander	1969-1985
John D. Lynch	1938-1945		Paul W. Brown	1971-1994
Edmund C. Shields	1938-1945		James L. Waters	1971-1994
Harry G. Kipke	1940-1947		Deane Baker	1973-1996
J. Joseph Herbert	1940-1955		Sarah Goddard Power[28]	1975-1987
Alfred B. Connable	1942-1957		Thomas A. Roach	1975-1991
Earl L. Burhans[15]	1942		David Laro	1975-1981
Franklin M. Cook[16]	1942-1943		Nellie M. Varner	1981-1996
Vera Burridge Baits	1943-1957		Neal D. Nielsen	1985-1993
R. Spencer Bishop[17]	1943-1946		Veronica Latta Smith	1985-1993
Ralph A. Hayward[18]	1944-1951		Philip H. Power	1987-1999
Roscoe O. Bonisteel, Sr.	1946-1959		Shirley M. McFee	1991-1999
Otto E. Eckert	1946-1961		Laurence B. Deitch	1993-2016
Charles S. Kennedy	1946-1961		Rebecca McGowan	1993-2009
Kenneth M. Stevens	1948-1955		Andrea Fischer Newman	1995-2018
Murray D. Van Wagoner	1951		Daniel D. Horning	1995-2003
Leland I. Doan	1952-1959		Olivia P. Maynard	1997-2012
Paul L. Adams[19]	1956-1957		S. Martin Taylor	1997-2012
Eugene B. Power[20]	1956-1966		David A. Brandon	1999-2006
Donald M. D. Thurber	1958-1963		Katherine E. White	1999-
Carl Brablec	1958-1967		Andrew C. Richner	2003-2018
Irene Ellis Murphy	1958-1967		Julia Donovan Darlow	2007-2014
William K. McInally[21]	1960-1964		Denise Ilitch	2009-
Frederick C. Matthaei[22]	1960-1967		Mark J. Bernstein	2013-
Paul G. Goebel	1962-1971		Shauna Ryder Diggs	2013-
Allan R. Sorenson[23]	1962-1967		Michael J. Behm	2015-
Robert P. Briggs[24]	1964-1968		Ron Weiser	2017-
William B. Cudlip	1964-1973		Jordan B. Acker	2019-
Alvin M. Bentley[25]	1966-1969		Paul W. Brown	2019-
Frederick C. Matthaei, Jr.	1967-1969			

[1] Originally established as the Catholepistemiad or University of Michigania by an act of the territorial legislature in 1817, the first governing board of the institution consisted of the president and didactors or professors appointed by the governor. See An Act to establish the Catholepistemiad, or University of Michigania (1817), Laws of the Territory of Michigan.

In 1821, the territorial legislature established the university in Detroit as The University of Michigan. The governing board became a board of 21 trustees, to serve at the pleasure of the legislature and whose vacancies were to be filled by the legislature. The members of this first board were appointed in the act. See An Act for the establishment of An University (1821). An 1831 amendment changed the manner in which the trustees were chosen, making them appointments by the governor by and with the advice and consent of the legislative council. See An Act to amend the several acts to provide for the establishment of the University of Michigan (1831), Laws of the Territory of Michigan.

Act LV of 1837 reorganized the government of The University of Michigan by vesting responsibility in a 12-member board of regents to be appointed by the governor by and with the advice and consent of the senate. The first members appointed under the provisions of Act No. LV were divided into classes of three, each class serving terms of one, two, three, and four years. A subsequent amendment provided for the appointment of three members for four-year terms beginning January 1, 1838. See Revised Statutes of 1838, title XI, ch. 2.

With the implementation of the Constitution of 1850, the post of regent became an elective one, with one regent elected in each judicial circuit for a term to be the same as that of a circuit judge. Public Act 25 of 1851 called for the first election of regents on the first Monday in April of 1851 and every sixth year thereafter. During this period, the size of the board ranged from eight to ten members.

In 1862, voters approved Joint Resolution No. 17, which reduced board membership to eight members beginning in 1863. To be elected at the same time as justices of the supreme court, two members first elected under this constitutional amendment each served terms of two, four, six, and eight years. Subsequently, voters elected two regents at each regular election for terms of eight years. Vacancies which occurred were filled by appointment of the governor.

The Constitution of 1908 did not change the composition or terms of the board; it merely called for the election of regents to occur at the regular biennial spring election, independently of elections for other state posts.

Implementation of the Constitution of 1963 resulted in the extension of the terms of the sitting board (Brablec, Murphy, McInally, Matthaei, Goebel, Sorenson, Cudlip and E. Power) with the enactment of Act 23 of the 2nd Extra Session of 1963. The first election of regents under the provisions of the Constitution of 1963 occurred at the November 1966 general election. See Public Act 5 of the 2nd Extra Session of 1963.

[2] Deceased; succeeded by Arthur Hill June 10, 1901.

[3] Resigned; succeeded by Levi L. Barbour June 20, 1902.

[4] Deceased; succeeded by John H. Grant December 23, 1909.

[5] Deceased; succeeded by Chase S. Osborn July 3, 1908.

[6] Resigned; succeeded by Benjamin S. Hanchett April 3, 1911.

[7] Deceased; succeeded by Richard R. Smith May 11, 1931.

[8] Resigned; succeeded by Lucius L. Hubbard January 11, 1911.

[9] Deceased; succeeded by William A. Comstock February 14, 1913.

[10] Resigned; succeeded by Harry C. Bulkley April 7, 1911.

[11] Resigned; succeeded by Esther March Cram November 1, 1929.

[12] Resigned; succeeded by Edmund C. Shields January 11, 1933.

[13] Resigned; succeeded by R. Spencer Bishop January 28, 1943.

[14] Resigned; succeeded by James O. Murfin March 21, 1934.

REGENTS OF THE UNIVERSITY OF MICHIGAN *(Cont.)*

[15] Following the April 7, 1941, election at which voters elected Burhans to the Board of Regents, third-place finisher Franklin M. Cook sought to oust Burhans from the office, on the grounds that Burhans had no legal right to the seat. Burhans, who at the time of his election to the Board of Regents held the office of state senator from the 8th district, answered that the board office was his by right of a valid election. The secretary of state certified the election of Burhans and the other winning candidate, and Burhans had filed his oath as a regent and acted in that capacity. Cook asked the court to oust Burhans and to rule that he was the regent.

Citing the provisions of Const. 1908, art. V, §7, and a previous decision, the Michigan Supreme Court held that Burhans was not a regent of the University of Michigan because every vote cast for him was void. The constitutional provisions and case law the court cited prohibited a member of the legislature from receiving any civil or elected appointment during the term for which the member was elected. The court also dismissed Burhans' contention that the regents were not state officers, but only officers of a corporate body known as the board of regents of the university. In dismissing the claim, the court again cited its previous decisions establishing the Board of Regents as a department of the state, created by the constitution to perform state functions.

Stating, "Defendant is a usurper in the office of regent . . . this ouster creates a vacancy in the office of regent," the court ousted Burhans on December 23, 1942. The court did, however, disagree on the means of filling the vacancy. The governor resolved the issue by appointing Franklin M. Cook to succeed Burhans on December 24, 1942. See *Attorney General, ex rel Cook* v *Burhans*, 304 Mich. 108 (1941).

[16] Deceased; succeeded by Vera Burridge Baits May 21, 1943.

[17] Deceased; succeeded by Roscoe O. Bonisteel, Sr. November 2, 1946.

[18] Resigned; succeeded by Murray D. Van Wagoner January 24, 1951.

[19] Resigned to become Michigan attorney general; succeeded by Donald M. D. Thurber January 4, 1958.

[20] Resigned; succeeded by Alvin M. Bentley April 4, 1966.

[21] Deceased; succeeded by Robert P. Briggs November 10, 1964.

[22] Resigned; succeeded by Frederick C. Matthaei, Jr. June 12, 1967.

[23] Resigned; succeeded by Otis M. Smith March 7, 1967.

[24] Resigned; succeeded by Lawrence B. Lindemer May 15, 1968.

[25] Deceased; succeeded by Lawrence B. Lindemer April 23, 1969.

[26] First members elected under Constitution of 1963; Public Act 5 of the 2nd Extra Session of 1963; Public Act 23 of the 2nd Extra Session of 1963.

[27] Resigned; succeeded by David Laro June 3, 1975.

[28] Deceased; succeeded by Philip H. Power June 17, 1987.

Sources: Archives, *Michigan Department of State Record of Civil Officers, 1835-1962*; Bentley Historical Library, University of Michigan; Bureau of Elections, Michigan Department of State; *Constitutions of the State of Michigan*; Great Seal Office, *Michigan Department of State Record of Civil Officers, 1963 - present*; *Laws of Michigan*; *Laws of the Territory of Michigan*; *Michigan Reports, Volume 304*; *Public and Local Acts of Michigan*; and *Revised Statutes of 1846*.

BOARD OF TRUSTEES OF
MICHIGAN STATE UNIVERSITY, 1861-2019[1]

Philo Parsons	1861-1865
Charles Rich	1861-1867
Silas Yerkes	1861-1867
Justus Gage	1861-1869
David Carpenter	1861-1871
Hezekiah G. Wells	1861-1883
A. S. Welch	1863-1869
Abraham C. Prutzman	1867-1873
S. O. Knapp	1867-1873
Oramel Hosford	1869-1875
J. Webster Childs	1869-1887
George W. Phillips	1871-1883
A. Smith Dyckman	1873-1879
Franklin Wells[2]	1873-1903
Milton J. Gard	1875-1881
Henry G. Reynolds	1879-1885
Thomas D. Dewey	1881-1887
Elijah W. Rising	1883-1889
Henry Chamberlain	1883-1897
Cyrus G. Luce	1885-1891
William B. McCreery	1887-1890
Charles W. Garfield	1887-1899
Oscar Palmer	1889-1891
Asa C. Glidden	1889-1895
Edwin Phelps	1891-1895
Ira Butterfield	1893
Charles Freeman Moore	1893-1899
Charles J. Monroe	1895-1907
W. E. Boyden	1895-1897
Arthur C. Bird	1897-1899
Thomas Frank Marston[3]	1897-1909
Edward P. Allen	1899-1905
Hollister F. Marsh	1899-1905
L. Whitney Watkins	1899-1905
William H. Wallace[4]	1903-1921
Aaron P. Bliss	1903-1910
Charles Freeman Moore[5]	1903-1905
Henry F. Buskirk	1905-1907
William J. Oberdorffer	1905-1911
Robert D. Graham	1905-1919
Alfred J. Doherty	1907-1919
I. Roy Waterbury	1907-1921
William L. Carpenter	1909-1911
John W. Beaumont[6]	1912-1921
Jason Woodman	1912-1923
Dora H. Stockman	1920-1931
L. Whitney Watkins	1920-1931
John A. Doelle[7]	1921-1922
Clark L. Brody	1921-1959
Jay R. McColl	1922-1933
Melville B. McPherson	1922-1933
Herbert W. Gowdy	1924-1929
William H. Berkey	1930-1947
Matilda R. Wilson	1932-1937
Gilbert L. Daane	1932-1937
Benjamin H. Halstead	1934-1939
Charles E. Downing	1934-1939
Lavina Masselink	1938-1943
James J. Jakway	1938-1943
Melville B. McPherson[8]	1940-1945
Forest H. Akers	1940-1957
Winfred G. Armstrong[9]	1944-1954
Sarah Van Hoosen Jones	1944-1955
Frederick H. Mueller	1945-1957
Ellsworth B. More[10]	1948-1950
Connor D. Smith	1950-1953
Arthur K. Rouse	1954-1959
Connor D. Smith	1954-1969
William E. Baker[11]	1956-1957
C. Allen Harlan	1957-1969
Jan B. Vanderploeg	1958-1963
Don Stevens	1958-1979
Frank Merriman	1960-1975
Warren M. Huff	1960-1977
Paul D. Bagwell[12]	1964-1965
John S. Pingel[12]	1964-1965
Stephen S. Nisbet	1964-1971
Frank Hartman[13]	1965-1973
Clair A. White[13]	1965-1973
Kenneth W. Thompson	1967-1975
Blanche Martin	1969-1985
Patricia M. Carrigan	1971-1979
Aubrey Radcliffe	1973-1981
Jack M. Stack	1973-1981
John B. Bruff[14]	1975-1983
Raymond W. Krolikowski	1975-1983
Michael J. Smydra[15]	1977-1980
Carole Lick	1979-1987
Barbara J. Sawyer	1979-1994
Peter B. Fletcher	1980-1985
Elizabeth P. Howe[16]	1981-1983
Thomas Reed[17]	1981-1992
Bobby D. Crim[18]	1983-1984
Patrick J. Wilson	1983-1989
Malcolm G. Dade, Jr.	1983-1991
Lawrence D. Owen	1984-1991
Dean Pridgeon	1985-1993
Kathleen M. Wilbur[19]	1985-1991
Joel I. Ferguson	1987-1994
Robert E. Weiss[20]	1989-2002
Dolores Cook	1991-2006
John Shingleton	1991-1999
Melanie Reinhold	1991-1993
Russell Mawby[21]	1992-1996
Dorothy Gonzales	1993-2009
Bob Traxler[22]	1993-2000
Donald W. Nugent	1995-2011
Colleen M. McNamara	1995-2011
David Porteous	1996-1997
Joel I. Ferguson	1997-
David Porteous	1999-2006
Scott Romney	2000-2009
Randall Pittman	2002-2004
Melanie Foster	2005-2012
Faylene Owen	2007-2014
George Perles[23]	2007-2018
Dianne Byrum	2009-
Diann Woodard	2009-2016
Brian Breslin	2011-2018
Mitch Lyons	2011-2018
Brian Mosallam	2013-
Melanie Foster	2015-
Dan Kelly	2017-
Nancy Schlichting	2018-
Brianna T. Scott	2019-
Kelly Tebay	2019-

[1] Established as the Agricultural College of the State of Michigan by Public Act 130 of 1855, the Board of Instruction (professors and teachers) of the college acted as the first governing board of the institution. The act empowered the board to establish rules and regulations for the government of the college, subject to alteration or approval by the Board of Education.

Public Act 188 of 1861 reorganized the college, created a six-member state board of agriculture to govern it, defined the board's powers and duties, and named and appointed the first board (D. Carpenter, Gage, Parsons, Wells, Yerkes, and Rich), allowing those members to determine their terms of office by lot, two members each serving terms of two, four, and six years. Subsequent terms were six years in length. With the enactment of Public Act 308 of 1905, the membership of the board was increased to seven.

In the Constitution of 1908, new sections 7 and 8, relative to the state board of agriculture, had the effect of making the governing body a constitutional board elected by the people instead of a statutory board appointed by the governor. *Bauer* v *State Board of Agriculture*, 164 Mich. 415 (1911). The number of board members was reduced to six. The first elected board consisted of two members each elected to terms of two (W. Carpenter, Oberdorffer), four (Doherty, Graham), and six (Wallace, Waterbury) years. Subsequent vacancies were filled at the regular biennial spring election for terms of six years.

In 1959, the name of the governing board of what had become Michigan State University of Agriculture and Applied Science was changed to "board of trustees." On April 6, 1959, voters approved Joint Resolution 2 as an amendment to the Constitution of 1908.

Under the Constitution of 1963, the membership of the board of trustees was increased to eight and members' terms were lengthened to eight years. To facilitate the transition of board operations, Public Act 23 of the 2nd Extra Session of 1963 extended the terms of the sitting board (Smith, Harlan, Stevens, Merriman, Huff, Nisbet) by one year and provided for the governor's appointment of two additional members to serve one-year terms only. The election of the first board members under the provisions of the Constitution of 1963 occurred at the general election in November 1964. See Public Act 5 of the 2nd Extra Session of 1963.

[2] Deceased; succeeded by Charles Freeman Moore July 24, 1903.

[3] Resigned; succeeded by William L. Carpenter May 27, 1909.

[4] Resigned; succeeded by John A. Doelle September 17, 1921.

[5] Resigned; succeeded by Henry F. Buskirk January 6, 1905.

[6] Resigned; succeeded by Clark L. Brody October 8, 1921.

[7] Resigned; succeeded by Jay R. McColl April 5, 1922.

[8] Deceased; succeeded by Frederick H. Mueller August 2, 1945; Mueller reappointed February 20, 1946.

[9] Deceased; succeeded by Connor D. Smith December 9, 1954.

[10] Deceased; succeeded by Connor D. Smith May 24, 1950.

[11] Resigned; succeeded by C. Allen Harlan October 29, 1957.

[12] Appointed to one-year term January 10, 1964. See Public Act 23 of the 2nd Extra Session of 1963; Public Act 5 of the 2nd Extra Session of 1963.

[13] First members elected under Constitution of 1963, Public Act 5 of the 2nd Extra Session of 1963, and Public Act 23 of the 2nd Extra Session of 1963.

[14] Resigned; succeeded by Malcolm G. Dade, Jr., March 14, 1983.

[15] Resigned; succeeded by Peter B. Fletcher May 20, 1980.

[16] Resigned; succeeded by Patrick J. Wilson March 14, 1983.

[17] Resigned; succeeded by Russell Mawby January 1992.

[18] Resigned; succeeded by Lawrence D. Owen October 3, 1984.

[19] Resigned; succeeded by Melanie Reinhold January 18, 1991, who completed Wilbur's term ending January 1, 1993.

[20] Resigned; succeeded by Randall Pittman February 5, 2002.

[21] Resigned; succeeded by David Porteous June 19, 1996, who completed Mawby's term ending January 1, 1997.

[22] Resigned; succeeded by Scott Romney August 15, 2000, who completed Traxler's term ending January 1, 2001.

[23] Resigned; succeeded by Nancy Schlichting December 21, 2018, to complete Perles's term ending January 1, 2023.

Sources: Archives, *Michigan Department of State Record of Civil Officers, 1835-1962*; Bureau of Elections, Michigan Department of State; *Constitutions of the State of Michigan*; Great Seal Office, *Michigan Department of State Record of Civil Officers, 1963 - present*; *Laws of Michigan*; *Michigan Reports, Volume 164*; *Public and Local Acts of Michigan*; and Secretary of the Board of Trustees, Michigan State University.

BOARD OF GOVERNORS OF
WAYNE STATE UNIVERSITY, 1956-2019[1]

Betty S. Becker	1956-1959	Dauris Jackson (Mrs.)[13]	1977-1979
Gladys F. Canty	1956-1959	Richard C. VanDusen[14]	1979-1991
Warren B. Cooksey	1956-1959	George Romney	1979-1985
Louise C. Grace	1956-1959	Murray E. Jackson[15]	1981-2001
Leonard Kasle	1956-1959	C. Gary Artinian	1985-1993
William D. Merrifield	1956-1959	George N. Bashara	1985-1993
Remus G. Robinson	1956-1959	Robert H. Naftaly	1987-1994
Roscoe O. Bonisteel, Sr.	1956-1959	Elizabeth Hardy	1991-2006
Forest H. Akers[2]	1956-1957	Brenda M. Scott[16]	1991-1995
Charles G. Burns[3]	1956-1957	Michael Timmis[17]	1991-1997
Melvin E. Bleich	1956-1959	Denise J. Lewis	1993-2001
Connor D. Smith[4]	1957-1958	Edgar A. Scribner	1993-2001
Chris H. Magnusson	1957-1959	Diane Dunaskiss	1995-2018
Don Stevens	1958-1959	Vernice D. Anthony[18]	1995-1998
Clair A. White	1959-1961	Annetta Miller	1997-2012
DeWitt T. Burton	1959-1969	John Kelly[19]	1999-2002
Michael Ference, Jr.[5]	1959-1965	Paul E. Massaron	2001-2016
Leonard Woodcock[6]	1959-1970	Jacquelin E. Washington	2001-2009
Benjamin D. Burdick[7]	1959-1964	Paul Hillegonds	2002-2004
Jean McKee	1959-1967	Eugene Driker	2002-2014
Thomas B. Adams	1962-1969	Richard H. Bernstein	2003-2010
Alfred H. Whittaker	1964-1971	Tina Abbott	2005-2012
Charles H. Gershenson[8]	1964-1965	Debbie Dingell	2007-2014
Norman O. Stockmeyer, Sr.	1964-1975	Gary S. Pollard	2009-2016
William B. Hall[9]	1965-1967	Danialle Karmanos[20]	2011-2013
Benjamin M. Rose[10]	1965-1969	David A. Nicholson	2013-2018
Alfred H. Sokolowski	1967-1975	Sandra Hughes O'Brien	2013-
Wilber M. Brucker, Jr.[11]	1967-1979	Kim Trent	2013-
Augustus J. Calloway	1969-1977	Marilyn Jean Kelly	2015-
Kurt R. Keydel	1969-1981	Dana Thompson	2015-
George C. Edwards	1969-1985	Michael J. Busuito	2017-
Leon H. Atchison	1970-2003	Mark Gaffney	2017-
Max J. Pincus[12]	1971-1987	Bryan C. Barnhill, II	2019-
Michael Einheuser	1975-1991	Anil Kumar	2019-
Mildred Jeffrey	1975-1991		

[1] Public Act 183 of 1956, establishing Wayne State University as a state institution of higher learning, also fixed the membership and powers of its governing board. Section 2 of the act created a temporary board of governors to serve until a "permanent" board could be elected at the regular biennial spring election of 1959. This temporary board consisted of 11 members representing the following: Detroit Board of Education (seven members serving on the effective date of Public Act 183 of 1956) - Becker, Canty, Cooksey, Grace, Kasle, Merrifield, Robinson; University of Michigan Board of Regents (one member) - Bonisteel; State Board of Agriculture (one member) - Akers; State Board of Education (one member) - Burns; Governor's Office (one member) - Bleich. This original board served from June 14, 1956 to May 19, 1959.

Section 3 of Public Act 183 provided for the election of a permanent, six-member board, two members each to serve terms of two (Burton, White), four (Ference, Woodcock), and six (Burdick, McKee) years. Following the election of this first permanent board, two members were each elected for terms of six years, beginning with the spring election of 1961.

To facilitate the transition of board operations under the provisions of the Constitution of 1908 to those of the Constitution of 1963, Public Act 23 of the 2nd Extra Session of 1963 was enacted. The act extended by one year the terms of office of the six members of the sitting board (McKee, Burdick, Burton, Adams, Whittaker, Woodcock) and required the appointment by the governor of an additional two members to each serve a one-year term. These appointments increased board membership to eight, as required by the Constitution of 1963. The election of the first board members under the Constitution of 1963 occurred at the general election in November 1964. See Public Act 5 of the 2nd Extra Session of 1963.

[2] Resigned; succeeded by Connor D. Smith September 1957.

[3] Term of office on State Board of Education expired June 30, 1957; succeeded by Chris H. Magnusson August 1957.

[4] Resigned; succeeded by Don Stevens February 1958.

[5] Appointed to one-year term January 21, 1964. See Public Act 23 of the 2nd Extra Session of 1963; Public Act 5 of the 2nd Extra Session of 1963.

[6] Resigned; succeeded by Leon H. Atchison November 18, 1970.

[7] Resigned; succeeded by Norman O. Stockmeyer, Sr. January 21, 1964.

[8] Appointed to one-year term January 21, 1964. See Public Act 23 of the 2nd Extra Session of 1963; Public Act 5 of the 2nd Extra Session of 1963.

[9] One of first members elected under Constitution of 1963 and Public Act 5 of the 2nd Extra Session of 1963; resigned and succeeded by Wilber M. Brucker, Jr., September 19, 1967.

[10] One of first members elected under Constitution of 1963 and Public Act 5 of the 2nd Extra Session of 1963; deceased; succeeded by Kurt R. Keydel April 30, 1969.

[11] Resigned; succeeded by Richard C. VanDusen April 1, 1979.

[12] Deceased; succeeded by Robert H. Naftaly September 4, 1987.

[13] Deceased; succeeded by George Romney November 29, 1979.

[14] Deceased; succeeded by Michael Timmis September 24, 1991.

[15] Resigned November 12, 2001; succeeded by Paul Hillegonds January 30, 2002.

[16] Resigned October 25, 1995; succeeded by Michael Timmis following his resignation from the term he was completing, which was to expire on December 31, 1996.

BOARD OF GOVERNORS OF WAYNE STATE UNIVERSITY *(Cont.)*

[17] Appointed by Governor John Engler on September 24, 1991, to complete Richard VanDusen's term, which expired December 31, 1996; resigned on November 27, 1995, and reappointed on November 28, 1995, to complete Brenda Scott's term, which was to expire on December 31, 1998; resigned from second appointment effective December 31, 1996; Timmis succeeded by Vernice D. Anthony on November 28, 1995 (to complete VanDusen's original term expiring December 31, 1996) and on January 1, 1997 (to complete Scott's original term expiring December 31, 1998).

[18] Appointed by Governor John Engler on November 28, 1995, to fill vacancy created by resignation of Michael Timmis, who was completing Richard VanDusen's term expiring December 31, 1996; appointed to fill vacancy effective January 1, 1997, created by resignation of Michael Timmis, who was completing Brenda Scott's term expiring December 31, 1998.

[19] Resigned December 18, 2002; succeeded by Eugene Driker December 18, 2002.

[20] Resigned February 1, 2013; succeeded by David A. Nicholson February 4, 2013.

Sources: Archives, *Michigan Department of State Record of Civil Officers, 1835-1962*; Bureau of Elections, Michigan Department of State; *Constitutions of the State of Michigan*; Great Seal Office, *Michigan Department of State Record of Civil Officers, 1963 - present*; *Public and Local Acts of Michigan*; and Secretary of the Board of Governors, Wayne State University.

Chapter VIII

LOCAL GOVERNMENT

2019–2020

MICHIGAN'S SYSTEM OF LOCAL GOVERNMENT

Introduction

According to the 2017 Census of Governments, Michigan has 2,863 units of local government, including counties, cities, villages, townships, and school districts. The number of units of local government is considerably higher in Michigan than many other states.

The creation of local units of government is often the result of local initiative. Some local governments predate the formation of the state of Michigan itself. Several counties, townships, and a few cities were first organized on the authority of the Michigan territorial government and the **Northwest Ordinance**. However, most local units came into being after Michigan was admitted to the Union in 1837 on the basis of permissive legislation — that is, citizens petitioned Lansing for the right to organize under one statute or another.

There is no overall state plan as to how the system of local governments should be arranged. Rather than impose a preconceived structure, the state has chosen a flexible, incremental approach. In general, it permits people in local areas to decide what form of local government they want based on the concerns and needs of the area.

The Michigan Approach

The Michigan approach to creating local governments is based on the premises that the state requires a comprehensive system of governments through which it could extend its authority to all parts of the state and that rural areas would need less local government than urban areas.

A two-tiered network of government comprised of **counties** and **townships** turned out to meet both requirements of the state. The **county system** creates an overlay of governments through which the state can effectively manage its vast territory. Having a system of such outposts was essential during a time when transportation was laborious and communications slow.

The county system was imported from England, but modified by individual states to fit their needs and circumstances. Michigan borrowed and adapted the **New York model** in which the county board of commissioners included each township supervisor in the county. This model emerged as a way to stem clashes between township government advocates and county supporters. In 1968, the state legislature created the county commissioner system of county representation. Under this plan, commissioners are directly elected from districts within the county.

Townships were the result of an organizational plan conceived by Thomas Jefferson and incorporated in the Northwest Ordinance of 1785, adopted by Congress. Under the Northwest Ordinance, government lands that would comprise the future states of Ohio, Indiana, Illinois, Michigan, Wisconsin, and Minnesota were surveyed and divided into townships each comprised of 36 1-square-mile parcels. The local government in the territory was to be patterned after the town meeting system of New England. When settlers from the east came to Michigan, they began organizing township governments — governments for rural areas that would eventually blanket the entire state.

Through these two forms of local government, state officials had their counterpart officers at the county and township levels through which state laws could be enforced, birth and death records maintained, roads built, land records recorded, taxes collected, and the like.

However, these two governments were not adequate for more densely populated areas where certain municipal services, such as water, sewer, police, and fire, were desired. For these areas, the legislature provided for the establishment of city governments. Prior to 1909, petitions were submitted to the state seeking approval for an area to become a city, and the legislature chartered each city by passing a special act. Beginning in 1909, cities were granted home rule by the legislature, a grant of authority that permitted cities to draft and adopt their own charters by vote of the people.

Villages are an intermediate level of government. They have most of the special powers of cities but not the duties the state demands, and so villages remain part of the townships in which they are located. Village residents participate in township affairs and pay township taxes. Like cities, villages may have home rule status, which they were granted by legislative act in 1895. Previously, the state legislature enacted village charters by special act, similar to cities.

The Michigan approach to local government included two processes for adjusting boundaries to expanding settlements. Township territories can be annexed or joined to adjacent cities with voter approval in the involved units. Many cities, such as Detroit, Grand Rapids, Flint, and others, when first incorporated, included only one or two square miles of area. They expanded through the mechanism of **annexation**. Eventually, annexation would cause bitter relations between a city and its neighboring townships.

Consolidation is the second process and is intended to accommodate a governmental merger of units that have come together socially and economically, but not politically. This process has been used infrequently.

The Contemporary Reality

At the local level, cities, villages, and townships exercise the primary governing authority. The three units have similar, but not identical, service and regulatory powers. The major differences are that townships do not have full territorial integrity or control over the road system. They also have limited general taxing power and only limited flexibility in structuring the government. Villages differ from cities in that villages are not legally separated from the township and are not required to assess property for tax purposes or conduct state and national elections. Unlike cities, neither townships nor villages are empowered to levy a personal income tax.

County governments have undergone change from earlier days. The change, though, has been more in detail than in role. That is, county government, in many ways, still exists to extend the outreach of state government and serve state interests. Moreover, this role is perhaps being strengthened. For instance, counties are partners with the state in state programs such as public health, mental health, courts, vital records, land and property records, disaster preparedness, solid waste management, highway and road administration and maintenance, property tax administration, law enforcement, elections administration, and incarceration of convicts. In many areas the role of counties is being expanded.

Counties are also a local government in that they conduct some services that are local, rather than state, in orientation. Parks and recreation programs, senior citizen services, medical care facilities (nursing homes), hospital and ambulance services, county highway patrols, public transportation, libraries, drainage systems, and water and sewer facilities are some examples of programs in which counties are engaged for local reasons. In many instances, counties operate these programs in partnership with cities, villages, and townships.

Despite the many services provided by these four general purpose governments, other needs arise that fall outside their jurisdiction. To address some of these needs, local officials and citizens establish special districts or authorities. In some cases, a community government may establish a special district pursuant to general statutes; in other cases, the state legislature may adopt a law customized to fit a particular situation. Formation of a special district is then generally subject to voter approval. Special districts are often attractive for several reasons. One is that voters can be reasonably assured that a particular problem will be addressed, often financed by user fees rather than general property taxation. Another is that special districts provide a degree of flexibility in forming service jurisdictions that address areas of need or want for a particular service. Moreover, they provide a means of crossing municipal boundaries without threatening the integrity of the general purpose units.

State-Local Relations

State government now assumes a greater administrative role over the local governments than in times past. Examples include general statutes setting rules on open meetings; free access to records and documents; and uniform budgeting and accounting procedures including financial audits, annual financial reports, and assignment of emergency managers in units that face a financial crisis. The state court system may establish other rules in the areas of employment practices, discrimination, or zoning, among others.

In addition, various state agencies have partnership programs with local units. State agencies, like the departments of transportation and health and human services, exercise a significant supervisory role with respect to the planning, conduct, and reporting of particular programs.

State financial aid forms another cornerstone in the relationship between the state and local governments. Property taxes and fees for services constitute the main source of locally raised funds in most units, but state aid substantially supplements local financing. Some state aid, such as that from the sales tax, is mandated by the constitution or statute and deposited to the local units' general fund. Other assistance — such as that for schools, roads, mental health, public health, libraries, and cultural facilities — is restricted to the purpose for which it is granted.

Sources: Professor Ken VerBurg, Department of Resource Development, Michigan State University; VerBurg K., *Managing the Modern Michigan Township*, Michigan State University, Department of Resource Development, 2002; *Statistical Abstract of the United States*, 2001, U.S. Census Bureau; Center for Educational Performance and Information, State of Michigan; *Directory of Michigan Municipal Officials*, Michigan Municipal League, 2003; Vanderberg, Alan, *Michigan Local Government Structure, Services and Practices*, July, 2002. Updated by the Legislative Service Bureau, 2015 and 2019.

MICHIGAN COUNTIES

NOTE: Michigan has 83 counties. According to the 2010 federal decennial census, they range in population from 2,156 persons in Keweenaw County in the Upper Peninsula to Wayne County's 1,820,584 persons (approximately 40 percent of whom reside in the city of Detroit) in the southeastern part of the state.

SELECTED COUNTY OFFICERS

County	Officers
Alcona	*Board of Commissioners* – Adam Brege, Carolyn Brummund, Dan Gauthier, Craig Johnston, Gary Wnuk *Clerk* – Stephany Eller *Drain Commissioner* – Jesse Campbell *Prosecuting Attorney* – Thomas Jay Weichel *Register of Deeds* – Melissa A. Cordes *Road Commissioners* – Harry Harvey, Alfred Scully, Theodore Somers *Sheriff* – Douglas M. Atchison *Treasurer* – Cheryl Franks
Alger	*Board of Commissioners* – Jerry Doucette, Esley Mattson, Catherine Pullen, Mickey Rondeau, Joseph VanLandschoot *Clerk* – Mary Ann Froberg *Drain Commissioner* – Doug Miron *Prosecuting Attorney* – Karen Bahrman *Register of Deeds* – Mary Ann Froberg *Road Commissioners* – Doug Miron, John Hermann, Paul Heyrman *Sheriff* – Todd Brock *Treasurer* – Pamela Johnson
Allegan	*Board of Commissioners* – Rick Cain, Mark DeYoung, Gale Dugan, Tom Jessup, Dean Kapenga, Jim Storey, Max Thiele *Clerk* – Bob Genetski *Drain Commissioner* – Denise Medemar *Prosecuting Attorney* – Myrene K. Koch *Register of Deeds* – Bob Genetski *Road Commissioners* – Larry Brown, John Kleinheksel, James Rybicki *Sheriff* – Frank Baker *Surveyor* – Kevin Miedema *Treasurer* – Sally Brooks
Alpena	*Board of Commissioners* – Robert Adrian, Lynn Bunting, Brenda Fournier, Bonnie Friedrichs, Cameron Habermehl, John Kozlowski, Ronald McDonald, Brad McRoberts, Nick Modrzynski, Bill Peterson, Tammy Sumerix-Bates *Clerk* – Bonnie Friedrichs *Drain Commissioner* – Gerald Fournier *Prosecuting Attorney* – K. Edward Black *Register of Deeds* – Kathy Matash *Road Commissioners* – Thomas Heise, Gerald Lucas, Thomas Spaulding *Sheriff* – Steven Kieleszewski *Treasurer* – Kim Ludlow

County	Officers
Antrim	*Board of Commissioners* – Karen Bargy, Ed Boettcher, David Heeres, Jason Helwig, Dawn LaVanway, Christian Marcus, Brenda Ricksgers, Terry VanAlstine, Joshua Watrous *Clerk* – Sheryl Guy *Drain Commissioner* – Mark Stone *Prosecuting Attorney* – James Rossiter *Register of Deeds* – Patricia Niepoth *Road Commissioners* – Dieter Amos, Pete Hoogerhyde, Fred Hunt Jr. *Sheriff* – Daniel Bean *Treasurer* – Sherry Comben
Arenac	*Board of Commissioners* – Bobbe Burke, Adam Kroczaleski, Sally Mrozinski, Lisa Salgat, Harold Woolhiser *Clerk* – Ricky Rockwell *Drain Commissioner* – Jeff Trombley *Prosecuting Attorney* – Curtis Broughton *Register of Deeds* – Darlene Mikkola *Road Commissioners* – Ken Stawowy, Ron Schwab, Olen Swartz *Sheriff* – James Mosciski *Treasurer* – Dennis Stawowy
Baraga	*Board of Commissioners* – Gale Eilola, Mike Koskinen, William Menge, Dan Robillard, William Rolof *Clerk* – Wendy Goodreau *Drain Commissioner* – Douglas Mills *Mine Inspector* – Donald Carlson *Prosecuting Attorney* – Joseph O'Leary *Register of Deeds* – Wendy Goodreau *Road Commissioners* – Roy Koski, Nicholas Lindemann, Harold Miron *Sheriff* – Richard Johnson *Treasurer* – Anne Koski
Barry	*Board of Commissioners* – Vivian Conner, Ben Geiger, Howard Gibson, David Jackson, Dan Parker, Jon Smelker, Heather Lynn Wing *Clerk* – Pamela Palmer *Drain Commissioner* – Jim Dull *Prosecuting Attorney* – Julie Nakfoor Pratt *Register of Deeds* – Barbara Hurless *Road Commissioners* – D. David Dykstra, David Solmes, Jake Welch *Sheriff* – Dar Leaf *Treasurer* – Susan VandeCar
Bay	*Board of Commissioners* – Vaughn Begick, Kim Coonan, Michael Duranczyk, Thomas Herek, Ernie Krygier, Michael Lutz, Tom Ryder *Clerk* – Cynthia Luczak *Drain Commissioner* – Joseph L. Rivet *Prosecuting Attorney* – Nancy Borushko *Register of Deeds* – Brandon Krause *Road Commissioners* – Michael Rivard, Edward Rivet, William Schumacher *Sheriff* – Troy Cunningham *Treasurer* – Shawna Walraven

County	Officers
Benzie	**Board of Commissioners** – Coury Carland, Linda Farrell, Art Jeannot, Bob Roelofs, Gary Sauer, Sherry Taylor, Evan Warsecke
	Clerk – Dawn Olney
	Drain Commissioner – Edward Hoogterp
	Prosecuting Attorney – Sarah Swanson
	Register of Deeds – Amy Bissell
	Road Commissioners – Jim Bowers, Ted Mick, Robert Rosa
	Sheriff – Ted Schendel
	Surveyor – John Smendzuik
	Treasurer – Michelle Thompson
Berrien	**Board of Commissioners** – Bill Chickering, Jim Curran, Mac Elliott, Teri Sue Freehling, Bob Harrison, Jon Hinkelman, Chris Heugel, Michael Majerek, Don Meeks, Ezra Scott, David Vollrath, Mamie Yarbrough
	Clerk – Sharon Tyler
	Drain Commissioner – Christopher Quattrin
	Prosecuting Attorney – Michael Sepic
	Register of Deeds – Lora Freehling
	Road Commissioners – Bill Chickering, Jim Curran, Mac Elliott, Teri Sue Freehling, Bob Harrison, Jon Hinkelman, Chris Heugel, Michael Majerek, Don Meeks, Ezra Scott, David Vollrath, Mamie Yarbrough
	Sheriff – L. Paul Bailey
	Treasurer – Bret Witkowski
Branch	**Board of Commissioners** –Ted Gordon, Randall Hazelbaker Leonard Kolcz, Terri Norris, Donald Vrablic
	Clerk – Terry Ann Kubasiak
	Drain Commissioner – Michael Hard
	Prosecuting Attorney –
	Register of Deeds – Nancy Hutchins
	Road Commissioners – Gary Malcolm, Robert Mayer, Steve Weigt
	Sheriff – C. John Pollack
	Treasurer – Ann Vrablic
Calhoun	**Board of Commissioners** – Steven Frisbie, Rochelle Hatcher, Derek King, Tommy Miller, Jake W. Smith, Gary Tompkins, Kathy-Sue Vette
	Clerk – Anne Norlander
	Prosecuting Attorney – David Gilbert
	Register of Deeds – Anne Norlander
	Sheriff – Matthew Saxton
	Treasurer – Brian Wensauer
	Water Resources Commissioner – Fred Heaton
Cass	**Board of Commissioners** – Terry Ausra, Robert Benjamin, E. Clark Cobb, Skip Dyes, Dixie Ann File, Michael Grice, Roseann Marchetti,
	Clerk – Monica McMichael
	Drain Commissioner – Bruce Campbell
	Prosecuting Attorney – Victor Fitz
	Register of Deeds – Monica McMichael
	Road Commissioners – Kent Clark, Les McClelland, Sandra Seanor, Jamie Stafne, Bob Thompson
	Sheriff – Richard Behnke
	Treasurer – Hope Anderson

County	Officers
Charlevoix	*Board of Commissioners* – Chris Christensen, Robert Draves, Nancy Ferguson, George Lasater, Ronald Reinhardt, Shirley Roloff *Clerk* – Cheryl Potter Browe *Drain Commissioner* – Diane Gustin *Prosecuting Attorney* – Allen Telgenhof *Register of Deeds* – Shirley Coblentz *Road Commissioners* – Russell MaGee, Keith Ogden, Denny Way *Sheriff* – Charles Vondra *Treasurer* – Marilyn Cousineau
Cheboygan	*Board of Commissioners* – Cal Gouine, Roberta Matelski, Michael Newman, Richard Sangster, Mary Ellen Tryban, John Wallace, Steve Warfield *Clerk* – Karen Brewster *Drain Commissioner* – Cameron Cavitt *Prosecuting Attorney* – Melissa Goodrich *Register of Deeds* – Karen Brewster *Road Commissioners* – David Brandt, David Brown, Henry Ginop, Richard LaHaie, Kenneth Paquet *Sheriff* – Dale Clarmont *Treasurer* – Buffy Jo Weldon
Chippewa	*Board of Commissioners* – Conor Egan, Jim Martin, Don McLean, Robert Savoie, Scott Shackleton *Clerk* – Cathy Maleport *Drain Commissioner* – Anthony Stockpoole *Prosecuting Attorney* – Robert Stratton III *Register of Deeds* – Sharon Kennedy *Road Commissioners* – Jeremy Gagnon, Robert Laitinen, Bradley Ormsbee, Richard Timmer *Sheriff* – Mike Bitnar *Surveyor* – Sam Wenz *Treasurer* – Marjorie Hank
Clare	*Board of Commissioners* – Sandra Bristol, Jim Gelios, Jack Kleinhardt, Karen Lipovsky, Dale Majewski, Samantha Pitchford, Leonard Strouse *Clerk* – Lori Martin *Drain Commissioner* – Carl Parks *Prosecuting Attorney* – Michelle Ambrozaitis *Register of Deeds* – Lori Martin *Road Commissioners* – Richard Haynak, Tim Haskin, Karen Hulliberger *Sheriff* – John S. Wilson *Treasurer* – Jenny Beemer-Fritzinger
Clinton	*Board of Commissioners* – Bruce DeLong, Kenneth B. Mitchell, David Pohl, Robert Showers, Adam Stacey, Kam Washburn, Dr. Dwight Washington *Clerk* – Diane Zuker *Drain Commissioner* – Phil Hanses *Prosecuting Attorney* – Charles Sherman *Register of Deeds* – Diane Zuker *Road Commissioners* – Michael Frederick, Kevin Holt, Gail Watkins *Sheriff* – Lawrence Jerue *Treasurer* – Tina Ward

County	Officers
Crawford	*Board of Commissioners* – Laurie Jamison, Carey Jansen, Phil Lewis, Jamie McClain, Shelly Pinkelman, Sherry Powers, Sharon Priebe *Clerk* – Sandra Moore *Drain Commissioner* – Donald Babcock *Prosecuting Attorney* – Sierra Koch *Register of Deeds* – Sandra Moore *Road Commissioners* – Jim Burtch, Ryan Halstead, Gary Summers *Sheriff* – Shawn Kraycs *Treasurer* – Joseph Wakeley
Delta	*Board of Commissioners* – Patrick Johnson, David Moyle, Theresa Nelson, David Rivard, Gerard Tatrow *Clerk* – Nancy Kolich *Drain Commissioner* – George Maciejewski *Prosecuting Attorney* – Brett Gardner *Register of Deeds* – Nancy Kolich *Road Commissioners* – Bob Aschbacher, Randy Bjork, Mike Larrabee, John Malnar, Dennis Stanek *Sheriff* – Edward Oswald *Surveyor* – Mel Davis *Treasurer* – Sherry Godfrey
Dickinson	*Board of Commissioners* – John Degenaer Jr., Barbara Kramer, Joe Stevens, Kevin Pirlot, Henry Wender *Clerk* – Dolly Cook *Drain Commissioner* – Kevin Trevillian *Mine Inspector* – Steven Smith *Prosecuting Attorney* – Lisa Richards *Register of Deeds* – Dolly Cook *Road Commissioners* – Jim Carey, Allan Bilski, Dave Brisson, Ron Milbrath, Dale Johnson *Sheriff* – Scott Rutter *Treasurer* – Lorna Carey
Eaton	*Board of Commissioners* – Terrance Augustine, Matthew Bowen, Joseph Brehler, Brian Droscha, Glenn Freeman III, Brandon Haskell, Brian Lautzenheiser, Jim Mott, Blake Mulder, Rob Piercefield, Wayne Ridge, Jane Whitacre, Heather Wood, Jeanne Pearl-Wright, Barbara Rogers *Clerk* – Diana Bosworth *Drain Commissioner* – Richard Wagner *Prosecuting Attorney* – Douglas R. Lloyd *Register of Deeds* – Diana Bosworth *Road Commissioners* – Duane Eldred, Jerry Frazier, Timothy Lamoreaux, Benjamin Lyons, Dorothy Maxwell *Sheriff* – Tom Reich *Treasurer* – Bob Robinson

County	Officers
Emmet	*Board of Commissioners* – Neil Ahrens, Toni Drier, James Kargol, Izzy Lyman, Charlie Macinnis, Bill Shorter, David White *Clerk* – Juli Wallin *Drain Commissioner* – Arden Bawkey *Prosecuting Attorney* – James Linderman *Register of Deeds* – Karen Cosens *Road Commissioners* – Leroy Sumner, Larry Williams, Frank Zulski Jr. *Sheriff* – Peter Wallin *Treasurer* – Marilyn May
Genesee	*Board of Commissioners* – Brenda J. Clack, Kim Courts, Martin Cousineau, Ellen Ellenburg, Ted Henry, David Martin, Bryant Nolden, Shaun Shumaker, Mark Young *Clerk* – John J. Gleason *Drain Commissioner* – Jeff Wright *Prosecuting Attorney* – David Leyton *Register of Deeds* – John J. Gleason *Road Commissioners* – David Arceo, Cloyce Dickerson, Robert Johnson, Shirley Kautman-Jones, John Mandelaris *Sheriff* – Robert Pickell *Surveyor* – Kim Carlson *Treasurer* – Deborah L. Cherry
Gladwin	*Board of Commissioners* – Kyle Grove, Rick Grove, Sharron Smith, Ron Taylor, Joel Vernier *Clerk* – Laura Brandon-Maveal *Drain Commissioner* – Robert Evans *Prosecuting Attorney* – Aaron Miller *Register of Deeds* – Ann Manning-Clayton *Road Commissioners* – Ronald Brabon, Steve Cameron, Charles Hinman *Sheriff* – Michael Shea *Treasurer* – Christy VanTiem
Gogebic	*Board of Commissioners* – Joe Bonovetz, James Byrns, Tom Laabs, James Lorenson, Bob Orlich, George Peterson III, Dan Siirila *Clerk* – Gerry Pelissero *Drain Commissioner* – Dan Wood *Prosecuting Attorney* – Nicholas Jacobs *Register of Deeds* – Gerry Pelissero *Road Commissioners* – Roy D'Antonio, Kevin Haustein, John Matonich, Dan Peterson, Dennis Skinner *Sheriff* – Pete Matonich *Treasurer* – Lisa Hewitt
Grand Traverse	*Board of Commissioners* – Ron Clous, Betsy Coffia, Rob Hentschel, Bryce Hundley, Brad Jewett, Gordie LaPointe, Addison Wheelock Jr. *Clerk* – Bonnie Scheele *Drain Commissioner* – Steve Largent *Prosecuting Attorney* – Noelle Moeggenberg *Register of Deeds* – Peggie Haines *Road Commissioners* – Carl Brown, Jason Gillman, Andy Marek, Marc McKellar, William Mouser *Sheriff* – Thomas Bensley *Treasurer* – Heidi Scheppe

County	Officers
Gratiot	*Board of Commissioners* – George Bailey, Jan Bunting, Tim Lambrecht, Chuck Murphy, Samuel Smith *Clerk* – Angie Thompson *Drain Commissioner* – Bernard Barnes *Prosecuting Attorney* – Keith Kushion *Register of Deeds* – Mary Merchant *Road Commissioners* – Wesley Federspiel, Denis Netzley, John Wilson *Sheriff* – Michael Morris *Treasurer* – Michelle Thomas
Hillsdale	*Board of Commissioners* – Ruth Brown, Bruce Caswell, Julie Games, Tim Shaw, Mark Wiley *Clerk* – Marney Kast *Drain Commissioner* – Matt Word *Prosecuting Attorney* – Neal Brady *Register of Deeds* – Bambi Somerlott *Road Commissioners* – Bob Watkins, Bob Godfrey, Michael Parney *Sheriff* – Timothy Parker *Surveyor* – Michael Lodzinski *Treasurer* – Stephenie Kyser
Houghton	*Board of Commissioners* – Glenn Anderson, Roy Britz, Gretchen Janssen, Al Koskela, Tom Tikkanen *Clerk* – Jennifer Kelly *Drain Commissioner* – John Pekkala *Mine Inspector* – Murray Gillis *Prosecuting Attorney* – Michael Makinen *Register of Deeds* – Jennifer Kelly *Road Commissioners* – Gene Londo, Kenneth Rowe Sr., Bill Siler *Sheriff* – Brian McLean *Treasurer* – Lisa Mattila
Huron	*Auditors* – Roland Tkach *Board of Commissioners* – Mary Babcock, Michael Meissner, John Nugent, Todd Talaski, Steve Vaughan, Ron Wruble *Clerk* – Lori Neal *Drain Commissioner* – Gary Osminski, P.E. *Prosecuting Attorney* – Tim Rutkowski *Register of Deeds* – Sarah Durr *Road Commissioners* – John Hunt, Alan McTaggart, Michael Power *Sheriff* – Kelly Hanson *Treasurer* – Debra McCollum
Ingham	*Board of Commissioners* – Victor Celentino, Bryan Crenshaw, Mark Grebner, Carol Koenig, Randy Maiville, Thomas Morgan, Robin Naeyaert, Mark Polsdofer, Randy Schafer, Ryan Sebolt, Derrell Slaught, Emily Stivers, Todd Tennis *Clerk* – Barb Byrum *Drain Commissioner* – Pat Lindemann *Prosecuting Attorney* – Carol Siemon *Register of Deeds* – Derrick Quinney *Sheriff* – Scott Wriggelsworth *Treasurer* – Eric Schertzing

County	Officers
Ionia	*Board of Commissioners* – James Banks, Chris Bredice, David Hodges, Georgia Sharp, Jack Shattuck, Larry Tiejema, Scott Wirtz *Clerk* – Janae Cooper *Drain Commissioner* – Robert Rose *Prosecuting Attorney* – Kyle Butler *Register of Deeds* – Diane Adams *Road Commissioners* – Al Almy, Karen Bota, Robert Dunton, Ken Gasper, Chuck Minkley *Sheriff* – Charlie Noll *Treasurer* – Judith Clark
Iosco	*Board of Commissioners* – Terry Dutcher, Robert Huebel, Mark McKulsky, John Moehring, Donald O'Farrell *Clerk* – Nancy Huebel *Drain Commissioner* – Fred Strauer *Prosecuting Attorney* – Gary Rapp *Register of Deeds* – Ericka Earl *Road Commissioners* – Ben Brewer, Frank Leiva, Calvin McLaren *Sheriff* – Allan MacGregor *Treasurer* – Elite Shellenbarger
Iron	*Board of Commissioners* – Tim Aho, Raymond Coates, Sharon Leonoff, Patti Peretto, Mike Stafford *Clerk* – Joetta Greig *Drain Commissioner* – Thomas Clark *Mine Inspector* – Thomas Karvala *Prosecuting Attorney* – Melissa Powell *Register of Deeds* – Joetta Greig *Road Commissioners* – Chuck Battan, Sue Clisch, Ron Fralling, Dan Germic, Ernest Schmidt *Sheriff* – Mark Valesano *Treasurer* – Melanie Camps
Isabella	*Board of Commissioners* – Frank Engler, George Green, Tobin Hope, Jim Horton, Jerry Jaloszynski, James Moreno, Steve Swaney *Clerk* – Minde Lux *Drain Commissioner* – Robert Willoughby *Prosecuting Attorney* – David Barberi *Register of Deeds* – Karen Jackson *Road Commissioners* – Kelly Beltnick, Bob Curtiss, John Graham, David Livermore, Terry Turnwald *Sheriff* – Michael Main *Treasurer* – Steven Pickens
Jackson	*Board of Commissioners* – Tony Bair, David Elwell, Philip Duckham, Corey Kennedy, Daniel Mahoney, James Shotwell Jr., Allan Tompkins, Rodney Walz, Darius Williams *Clerk* – Amanda Kirkpatrick *Drain Commissioner* – Geoffrey Snyder *Prosecuting Attorney* – Jerard Jarzynka *Register of Deeds* – Amanda Kirkpatrick *Sheriff* – Steven P. Rand *Surveyor* – Dean Gutekunst *Treasurer* – Karen Coffman

County	Officers

Kalamazoo

Board of Commissioners – John Gisler, Paul Haag, Tracy Hall, Ron Kendall, Stephanie Moore, Christine Morse, Meredith Place, Mike Quinn, Julie Rogers, Michael Seals, Roger Tuinier
Clerk – Timothy Snow
Drain Commissioner – Patricia Crowley
Prosecuting Attorney – Jeffrey Getting
Register of Deeds – Timothy Snow
Road Commissioners – Deborah Buchholtz, Daniel Moyle, David Pawloski, Larry Stehouwer, David Worthams
Sheriff – Richard Fuller III
Surveyor – Gary Hahn
Treasurer – Mary Balkema

Kalkaska

Board of Commissioners – David Comai, Patty Cox, Craig Crambell, Kohn Fisher, Leigh Ngirarsaol, James Sweet, John West
Clerk – Deborah Hill
Drain Commissioner – Seth Phillips
Prosecuting Attorney – Michael Perreault
Register of Deeds – Jo Ann DeGraaf
Road Commissioners – Warren Allen, Denny Corrado, Mike Cox, David Gill, Louis Walter
Sheriff – Patrick Whiteford
Treasurer – Valerie Thornburg

Kent

Board of Commissioners – Tom Antor, Mandy Bolter, Emily Brieve, David Bulkowski, Carol Hennessy, Diane Jones, Matt Kallman, Betsy Melton, Roger Morgan, Stan Ponstein, Jim Saalfeld, Phil Skaggs, Monica Sparks, Stan Stek, Jim Talen, Ted Vonk, Harold Voorhees, Robert Womack, Stephen Wooden
Clerk – Lisa Posthumus Lyons
Drain Commissioner – Ken Yonker
Prosecuting Attorney – Christopher Becker
Register of Deeds – Lisa Posthumus Lyons
Road Commissioners – Cynthia Porter James, Patrick Malone, Dave Medema, David Morren, Mark Rambo, Rob VerHeulen
Sheriff – Michelle LaJoye-Young
Treasurer – Kenneth Parrish

Keweenaw

Board of Commissioners – Robert Demarois, Sandra Gayk, Don Piche, Del Rajala, James Vivian Jr.
Clerk – Julie Carlson
Drain Commissioner – Gregg M. Patrick
Mine Inspector – James Kaura
Prosecuting Attorney – Charles Miller
Register of Deeds – Julie Carlson
Road Commissioners – Richard Olson, Richard Schaefer, Joseph Waananen
Sheriff – William Luokkanen
Treasurer – Eric Hermanson

County	Officers
Lake	*Board of Commissioners* – Don Arquette, Christine Balulis, Betty Dermyer, Howard Lodholtz, Dawn Martin, Robert Sanders, Karl Walls *Clerk* – Patti Pacola *Drain Commissioner* – Richard Haslock *Prosecuting Attorney* – Craig Cooper *Register of Deeds* – Patti Pacola *Road Commissioners* – Richard Haslock, Richard Runnels, Gary Truxton *Sheriff* – Richard Martin *Treasurer* – Brenda Kutchinski
Lapeer	*Board of Commissioners* – Dyle Henning, Linda Jarvis, C. Ian Kempf, Brenden Miller, Gary Roy, Lenny Schneider, Rick Warren *Clerk* – Theresa Spencer *Drain Commissioner* – Joseph Suma *Prosecuting Attorney* – Michael Sharkey *Register of Deeds* – Lorie Gebhardt *Road Commissioners* – Dale Duckert, Les Nicols, James Novak *Sheriff* – Scott McKenna *Surveyor* – Richard Duthler *Treasurer* – Dana Miller
Leelanau	*Board of Commissioners* – Tony Ansorge, William Bunek, Melinda Lautner, Patricia Soutas-Little, Carolyn Rentenbach, Debra Rushton, Ty Wessell *Clerk* – Michelle Crocker *Drain Commissioner* – Steven Christensen *Prosecuting Attorney* – Joseph Hubbell *Register of Deeds* – Dorothy Miller *Road Commissioners* – Jim Calhoun, Tom Eckerle, Robert Joyce, Greg Mikowski, John Popa *Sheriff* – Michael Borkovich *Treasurer* – John Gallagher III
Lenawee	*Board of Commissioners* – Dawn Bales, Karol Bolton, Terry Collins, Nancy Jenkins-Arno, Bob Knoblauch, John Lapham, David Stimpson, Ralph Tillotson, Chris Wittenbach *Clerk* – Roxann Holloway *Drain Commissioner* – Jennifer Escott *Prosecuting Attorney* – R. Burke Castleberry Jr. *Register of Deeds* – Carolyn Bater *Road Commissioners* – Bob Emery, Michael Slusarski, Stan Wilson *Sheriff* – Troy Bevier *Treasurer* – Marilyn Woods

County	Officers
Livingston	*Board of Commissioners* – Robert Bezotte, Gary Childs, Dennis Dolan, Carol Griffith, William Green, Douglas Helzerman, Kate Lawrence, Wes Nakagiri, Donald Parker *Clerk* – Elizabeth Hundley *Drain Commissioner* – Brian Jonckheere *Prosecuting Attorney* – William Vailliencourt *Register of Deeds* – Brandon Denby *Road Commissioners* – Stephen Crane, John Dunleavy, David Peckens *Sheriff* – Michael Murphy *Treasurer* – Jennifer Nash
Luce	*Board of Commissioners* – Michelle Clark, Kevin Erickson, Phyllis French, Bill Henry, Nancy Morrison *Clerk* – Sharon Price *Drain Commissioner* – Stanley Ronquist *Prosecuting Attorney* – Josh Freed *Register of Deeds* – Sharon Price *Road Commissioners* – Michael Aho, Robert Ottenhoff, Peter Paramski *Sheriff* – John Cischke *Treasurer* – Darlene Kisro
Mackinac	*Board of Commissioners* – Jim Hill, Paul Krause, Daniel Litzner, Calvin McPhee, Mike Patrick *Clerk* – Lori Johnston *Drain Commissioner* – Lester Livermore *Prosecuting Attorney* – J. Stuart Spencer *Register of Deeds* – Deborah Holle *Road Commissioners* – Tom Doty, Lester Livermore Jr., William Wagner *Sheriff* – Scott Strait *Surveyor* – Jeff Davis *Treasurer* – Jennifer Goudreau
Macomb	*Board of Commissioners* – Don Brown, Jim Carabelli, Leon Drolet, Andrey Duzyj, Harold Haugh, Veronica Klinefelt, Phil Kraft, Robert Leonetti, Elizabeth Lucido, Rob Mijac, Joseph Romano, Marv Sauger, Bob Smith *Clerk* – Fred Miller *Drain Commissioner* – Candice S. Miller *Prosecuting Attorney* – Eric Smith *Register of Deeds* – Fred Miller *Sheriff* – Anthony Wickersham *Treasurer* – Larry Rocca
Manistee	*Board of Commissioners* – Margaret Batzer, Mark Bergstrom, Jeff Dontz, Karen Goodman, Pauline Jaquish, Richard Schmidt, Brook Shafer *Clerk* – Jill Nowak *Drain Commissioner* – Kenneth Hilliard *Prosecuting Attorney* – Jason Haag *Register of Deeds* – Marilyn Wrzesinski *Road Commissioners* – Richard Graham, Annie Hooghart, Sally Reckow, Robert Rishel, James Russell *Sheriff* – John O'Hagan *Surveyor* – Patrick Bentley *Treasurer* – Russell Pomeroy

County	Officers
Marquette	*Board of Commissioners* – Stephen Adamini, Karen Alholm, Gerald Corkin, Johnny DePetro, Joseph Derocha, Bill Nordeen *Clerk* – Linda Talsma *Drain Commissioner* – Mike Farrell *Mine Inspector* – John Carlson *Prosecuting Attorney* – Matt Wiese *Register of Deeds* – Carla L'huillier *Road Commissioners* – David Hall, William Luetzow, Raymond Roberts, Joseph Valente, Russell Williams *Sheriff* – Gregory Zyburt *Treasurer* – Anne Giroux
Mason	*Board of Commissioners* – Janet Andersen, Ron Bacon, Gary Castonia, Steven Hull, Charles Lange, Lewis Squires, Wally Taranko *Clerk* – Cheryl Kelly *Drain Commissioner* – Jim Riffle *Prosecuting Attorney* – Paul Spaniola *Register of Deeds* – Diane Engelbrecht *Road Commissioners* – Mike Ingison, Doug Robidoux, Bill Schwass *Sheriff* – Kim Cole *Surveyor* – Rex Pope P.S. *Treasurer* – Andrew Kmetz, IV
Mecosta	*Board of Commissioners* – Linda Howard, Wendy Nystrom, Tom O'Neil, William Routley, Raymond Steinke, Jerrilynn Strong, Marilynn Vargo *Clerk* – Marcee Purcell *Drain Commissioner* – Jackie Fitzgerald *Prosecuting Attorney* – Brian Thiede *Register of Deeds* – Karen Hahn *Road Commissioners* – John Currie, Van Johnson, Mike Wernette *Sheriff* – Todd Purcell *Treasurer* – Sherry Earnest
Menominee	*Board of Commissioners* – William Cech, Steven Gromala, Jan Hafeman, Larry Johnson Jr., Bernie Lang, Larry Phelps, Gerald Piche, David Prestin, Larry Schei *Clerk* – Marc Kleiman *Drain Commissioner* – Caleb Kleiman *Prosecuting Attorney* – William Merkel *Register of Deeds* – Marc Kleiman *Road Commissioners* – Kenneth Bower, Anthony Kakuk, Ken Kline *Sheriff* – Kenny Marks *Treasurer* – Diane Lesperance

County	Officers

Midland

Board of Commissioners – Mark Bone, Eric Dorrien, James Geisler, Steve Glaser, Scott Noesen, Jeanette Snyder, Gaye Terwillegar
Clerk – Anne Manary
Drain Commissioner – Doug Enos
Prosecuting Attorney – J. Dee Brooks
Register of Deeds – Julie Atkinson
Road Commissioners – Michael Atton, Alan Kloha, Donald Terwillegar
Sheriff – Scott Stephenson
Treasurer – Catherine Lunsford

Missaukee

Board of Commissioners – Lan Bridson, Star Hughston, Pamela Niebrzydowski, Roger Ouwinga, Dean Smallegan, Frank Vanderwal, Hubert Zuiderveen
Clerk – Jessica Nielsen
Drain Commissioner – Jack McGee
Prosecuting Attorney – David DenHouten
Register of Deeds – Jessica Nielsen
Road Commissioners – Lonny Lutke, Jack McGee, Larry Norman
Sheriff – Wilbur Yancer
Treasurer – Lori Cox

Monroe

Board of Commissioners – Dawn Asper, Mark Brant, David Hoffman, George Jondro, J. Henry Lievens, Greg Moore Jr., Jerry Oley, Jason Turner, Gary Wilmoth
Clerk – Sharon Lemasters
Drain Commissioner – David Thompson
Prosecuting Attorney – Michael G. Roehrig
Register of Deeds – Sharon Lemasters
Road Commissioners – Paul Iacoangeli, Charles Londo, Dan Minton, Greg Stewart, Jack Thayer, P.E.
Sheriff – Dale Malone
Treasurer – Kay Sisung

Montcalm

Board of Commissioners – Ron Baker, Patrick Carr, Chris Johnston, Betty Kellenberger, Phil Kohn, Brendan Mahar, Jeremy Miller, Adam Petersen, Tom Porter
Clerk – Kristen Millard
Drain Commissioner – Sandy Raines
Prosecuting Attorney – Andrea Krause
Register of Deeds – Lori Wilson
Road Commissioners – Robert Brundage, Dale Linton, S. Michael Scott
Sheriff – Michael Williams
Treasurer – JoAnne Vukin

Montmorency

Board of Commissioners – Don Edwards, Gary Girardin, Albert LaFleche, Daryl Peterson, Dave Wagner
Clerk – Cheryl Neilsen
Drain Commissioner – Todd Behring
Prosecuting Attorney – Vicki Kundinger
Register of Deeds – Teresa Walker
Road Commissioners – Charles Arbour, Ted Orm, Ken Werner
Sheriff – Chad Brown
Treasurer – Jean Klein

County	Officers

Muskegon

Board of Commissioners – Gary Foster, Marcia Hovey-Wright, Susie Hughes, Zach Lahring, Kenneth Mahoney, Charles Nash, Robert Scolnik, I. John Snider II, Rillastine Wilkins
Clerk – Nancy Waters
Drain Commissioner – Brenda Moore
Prosecuting Attorney – D.J. Hilson
Register of Deeds – Mark Fairchild
Road Commissioners – Melvin Black, Lewis Collins, John DeWolf, Jack Kennedy, Gerald Walter
Sheriff – Michael Poulin
Treasurer – Tony Moulatsiotis

Newaygo

Board of Commissioners – Brenda Bird, Burt Cooper, Ken DeLaat, Bryan Kolk, Mike Kruithoff, James Maike, Chuck Trapp
Clerk – Jason VanderStelt
Drain Commissioner – Dale Twing
Prosecuting Attorney – Worth Stay
Register of Deeds – Stewart Sanders
Road Commissioners – William Gonyon, Douglas Harmon, Louis Meeuwenberg
Sheriff – Bob Mendham
Treasurer – Holly Moon

Oakland

Board of Commissioners – Marcia Gershenson, Michael J. Gingell, Robert Hoffman, Janet Jackson, Adam L. Kochenderfer, Eileen T. Kowall, Thomas Kuhn, Christine Long, Penny Luebs, Gwen Markham, Gary R. McGillivray, Thomas Middleton, William Miller, Kristen Nelson, Angela Powell, Nancy L. Quarles, Michael Spisz, Shelley Goodman Taub, Philip J. Weipert, Dave Woodward, Helaine Zack
Clerk – Lisa Brown
Drain Commissioner – Jim Nash
Prosecuting Attorney – Jessica Cooper
Register of Deeds – Lisa Brown
Road Commissioners – Ron Fowkes, Gregory Jamian, Dennis Kolar, Andrea LaLonde, Gary Piotrowicz
Sheriff – Michael Bouchard
Treasurer – Andrew E. Meisner

Oceana

Board of Commissioners – James Brown, Larry Byl, Dean Gustafson, Martha Meyette, Denny Powers, Andrew Sebolt, Robert Walker
Clerk – Rebecca Griffin
Drain Commissioner – Michelle Martin
Prosecuting Attorney – Joseph Bizon
Register of Deeds – Richard Hodges
Road Commissioners – Allen Blohm, Bob Carr, Cathy Forbes, Lloyd Gowell, William Myers
Sheriff – Craig Mast
Treasurer – Mary Lou Phillips

County	Officers
Ogemaw	*Board of Commissioners* – Jenny David, Brad Neubecker, Bruce Reetz, Craig Scott, Ronald Vaughn *Clerk* – Gary Klacking *Drain Commissioner* – Michael DeMatio *Prosecuting Attorney* – LaDonna Schultz *Register of Deeds* – Denise Simmons *Road Commissioners* – Klint Marshall, Van Sheltrown, Dan Winter *Sheriff* – Howie Hanft *Treasurer* – Dwight McIntyre
Ontonagon	*Board of Commissioners* – Richard Bourdeau, Marlene Broemer, John Cane, Robert Nousiainen, Carl R. Nykanen *Clerk* – Stacy Preiss *Drain Commissioner* – Donald Bussiere *Mine Inspector* – William Turin *Prosecuting Attorney* – Michael Findlay *Register of Deeds* – Stacy Preiss *Road Commissioners* – Donald Bussiere, Walter Lannet, Ken Truscott *Sheriff* – Dale Rantala *Treasurer* – Jeanne Pollard
Osceola	*Board of Commissioners* – James Custer, Larry Emig, Roger Elkins, Mark Gregory, Jill Halladay, Timothy Michell, Jack Nehmer *Clerk* – Karen Bluhm *Drain Commissioner* – Jerry Powell *Prosecuting Attorney* – Anthony Badovinac *Register of Deeds* – Nancy Crawford *Road Commissioners* – Alan Gingrich, Alan Johnson, Douglas Kanouse, Gary Wemple, Donald Williams *Sheriff* – Justin Halladay *Surveyor* – William Sikkema *Treasurer* – Lori Leudeman
Oscoda	*Board of Commissioners* – Jackie Bondar, Libby Marsh, Tom McCauley, Chuck Varner, Kyle Yoder *Clerk* – Jeri Winton *Drain Commissioner* – Steve Defour *Prosecuting Attorney* – Kristy L. McGregor *Register of Deeds* – Jeri Winton *Road Commissioners* – James R. Houlton, Dennis P. Morse, Tom Siegler, Roger Weigand, David Yoder *Sheriff* – Kevin Grace *Treasurer* – William Kendall
Otsego	*Board of Commissioners* – Ken Borton, Bruce Brown, Kenneth Glasser, Doug Johnson, Paul Liss, Henry Mason, Rob Pallarito, Julie Powers, Duane Switalski *Clerk* – Susan DeFeyter *Drain Commissioner* – Jason Melancon *Prosecuting Attorney* – Brendan Curran *Register of Deeds* – Susan DeFeyter *Road Commissioners* – James Camiller, Michael Dipzinski, Kathy Heinz, William Holewinski Jr., Troy Huff *Sheriff* – Matthew Nowicki *Treasurer* – Diann Axford

County	Officers
Ottawa	*Board of Commissioners* – Joe Baumann, Roger A. Bergman, Allen Dannenberg, Greg J. DeJong, Matthew Fenske, Franciso C. Garcia, James Holtvluwer, Philip D. Kuyers, Randall Meppelink, Kyle Terpstra, Doug Zylstra *Clerk* – Justin Roebuck *Prosecuting Attorney* – Ronald Frantz *Register of Deeds* – Justin Roebuck *Road Commissioners* – Tom Bird, Tom Elhart, Betty Gajewski, Timothy Grifhorst, Jim Miedema *Sheriff* – Steve Kempker *Treasurer* – Amanda Price *Water Resources Commissioner* – Joe Bush
Presque Isle	*Board of Commissioners* – Carl L. Altman, John Chappa, Michael Darga, Lee Gapczynski, Stephen Lang, Nancy Shutes *Clerk* – Ann Marie Main *Drain Commissioner* – Mary Ann Heidemann *Prosecuting Attorney* – Kenneth Radzibon *Register of Deeds* – Vicky Kowalewsky *Road Commissioners* – Ronald Bischer, Thomas Catalano, Stephen Lang *Sheriff* – Joseph Brewbaker *Treasurer* – Bridget LaLonde
Roscommon	*Board of Commissioners* – Ken Melvin, Marc J. Milburn, Tim Muckenthaler, David Russo, Bob Schneider *Clerk* – Michelle Stevenson *Drain Commissioner* – Rex Wolfsen *Prosecuting Attorney* – Mary Beebe *Register of Deeds* – Michelle Stevenson *Road Commissioners* – Fred Chidester, John Earley, Jim Porath, Clint Stauffer, Brian Vaughn *Sheriff* – Ed Stern *Treasurer* – Rebecca Ragan
Saginaw	*Board of Commissioners* – Kathy Dwan, Cheryl M. Hadsall, Kyle R. Harris, Kirk W. Kilpatrick, Dennis H. Krafft, Amos O'Neal, Carl E. Ruth, Chuck Stack, James G. Theisen, Michael A. Webster *Clerk* – Michael Hanley *Drain Commissioner* – Brian Wendling *Prosecuting Attorney* – John McColgan Jr. *Register of Deeds* – Katie Kelly *Road Commissioners* – Dave Adams, Richard H. Crannell, Todd M. Hare, Deb Kestner, John D. Sangster *Sheriff* – William Federspiel *Treasurer* – Timothy Novak

County	Officers
Sanilac	*Board of Commissioners* – Bob Conely, Daniel Dean, Gary Heberling, Joe O'Mara, Joel Wyatt Jr. *Clerk* – Denise McGuire *Drain Commissioner* – Greg Alexander *Prosecuting Attorney* – James Young *Register of Deeds* – Michele VanNorman *Road Commissioners* – Ronald Gerstenberger, Randall Horst, Donald Rickett Jr. *Sheriff* – Garry Biniecki *Surveyor* – John A. Milletics *Treasurer* – Trudy Nicol-Bowers
Schoolcraft	*Board of Commissioners* – Daniel P. Hoholik, Larry Mersnick, Allan Ott, Christine Rantanen, Craig Reiter *Clerk* – Beth Edwards *Drain Commissioner* – Brad Stauffer *Prosecuting Attorney* – Timothy Noble *Register of Deeds* – Beth Edwards *Road Commissioners* – Dale DuFour, Thomas Klarich, Bernard J. Lund *Sheriff* – Paul Furman *Treasurer* – Julie Roscioli
Shiawassee	*Board of Commissioners* – Cindy Garber, Gary Holzhausen, John Horvath, Brandon Marks, John Plowman, Jeremy Root, Marlene Webster *Clerk* – Caroline Wilson *Drain Commissioner* – Tony Newman *Prosecuting Attorney* – Deana Finnegan *Register of Deeds* – Lori Kimble *Road Commissioners* – Mike Constine, Ric Crawford, John Michalec *Sheriff* – Brian BeGole *Surveyor* – William Wascher, P.S. *Treasurer* – Thomas Dwyer
St. Clair	*Board of Commissioners* – Jeffrey L. Bohm, Duke Dunn, Bill Gratopp, Howard Heidemann, Greg McConnell, David Rushing, Karl Tomion *Clerk* – Jay M. DeBoyer *Drain Commissioner* – Robert Wiley *Prosecuting Attorney* – Michael Wendling *Register of Deeds* – Jay M. DeBoyer *Road Commissioners* – William Blumerich, Timothy LaLonde, Timothy Ward *Sheriff* – Timothy Donnellon *Surveyor* – Charles Koob *Treasurer* – Kelly Roberts-Burnett

County	Officers

St. Joseph

Board of Commissioners – Dennis Allen, Allen J. Balog, Daniel R. Czajkowski, Ken Malone, Kathy Pangle
Clerk – Lindsay Oswald
Drain Commissioner – Jeffrey Wenzel
Register of Deeds – Lindsay Oswald
Prosecuting Attorney – John McDonough
Road Commissioners – Dave Allen, John Bippus, Rodney Chupp, Vinve Mifsud, Eric Shafer
Sheriff – Bradley Balk
Surveyor – David Mostrom
Treasurer – Judith Ratering

Tuscola

Board of Commissioners – Thomas Bardwell, Dan Grimshaw, Mark Jensen, Kim Vaughan, Tom Young
Clerk – Jodi Fetting
Drain Commissioner – Robert Mantey
Prosecuting Attorney – Mark Reene
Register of Deeds – John Bishop
Road Commissioners – David Kennard, Jack Laurie, Julie Matuszak, Gary Parsell, Duane Weber
Sheriff – Glen Skrent
Treasurer – Patricia Donovan-Gray

Van Buren

Board of Commissioners – Mike Chappell, Kurt Doroh, Gail Patterson-Gladney, Richard Godfrey, Donald Hanson, Randall Peat, Paul Schincariol
Clerk – Suzie Roehm
Drain Commissioner – Joe Parman
Prosecuting Attorney – Michael Bedford
Register of Deeds – Paul DeYoung
Road Commissioners – W.C. Askew, Reginald D. Boze, Doug Burleson, Gregory H. Kinney, Geoff Moffat
Sheriff – Daniel Abbott
Surveyor – Donald Gilchrist
Treasurer – Trisha Nesbitt

Washtenaw

Board of Commissioners – Shannon Beeman, Felicia Brabec, Ruth Ann Jamnick, Ricky Jefferson, Andy LaBarre, Jason Maciejewski, Jason Morgan, Katie Scott, Sue Shink
Clerk – Lawrence Kestenbaum
Prosecuting Attorney – Brian Mackie
Register of Deeds – Lawrence Kestenbaum
Road Commissioners – Barbara Fuller, Douglas Fuller, Roderick Green
Sheriff – Jerry Clayton
Treasurer – Catherine McClary
Water Resources Commissioner – Evan Pratt

County	Officers
Wayne	*Auditor* – Marcella Cora *Board of Commissioners* – Glenn S. Anderson, Raymond E. Basham, Sam Baydoun, Alisha Bell, Irma Clark-Coleman, Melissa Daub, Al Haidous, Timothy Killeen, Terry Marecki, Monique Baker McCormick, Joseph Palamara, Martha G. Scott, Ilona Varga, Jewel Ware, Diane Webb *Clerk* – Cathy Garrett *Drain Commissioner* – Elmeka N. Steele *Prosecuting Attorney* – Kim Worthy *Register of Deeds* – Bernard Youngblood *Sheriff* – Benny Napoleon *Treasurer* – Eric Sabree
Wexford	*Board of Commissioners* – Mike Bengelink, Michael Bush, Joseph Hurlburt, Michael Musta, Judy Nichols, Brian Potter, Gary Taylor, Julie Theobald, Ben Townsend *Clerk* – Elaine Richardson *Drain Commissioner* – Michael Solomon *Prosecuting Attorney* – Jason Elmore *Register of Deeds* – Lorie Sorensen *Road Commissioners* – Harold Falan, Lorne Haase, Harry Hagstrom, Dean Jurik, Jim Leggett *Sheriff* – Trent Taylor *Surveyor* – Craig Pullen *Treasurer* – Jayne Stanton

Sources: Various county websites, accessed between May 13 and May 16, 2019.

Area Name	Population	Area Name	Population
Alcona County	**10,942**	**Antrim County**	**23,580**
Alcona township	968	Ellsworth village	349
Caledonia township	1,161	Balance of Banks township	1,260
Curtis township	1,236	Central Lake village	952
Greenbush township	1,409	Balance of Central Lake township	1,246
Lincoln village (part)	148	Chestonia township	511
Balance of Gustin township	647	Custer township	1,136
Harrisville city	493	Echo township	877
Harrisville township	1,348	Elk Rapids village	1,642
Lincoln village (part)	189	Balance of Elk Rapids township	989
Balance of Hawes township	918	Bellaire village (part)	481
Haynes township	722	Balance of Forest Home township	1,239
Mikado township	947	Helena township	1,001
Millen township	404	Jordan township	992
Mitchell township	352	Bellaire village (part)	605
Alger County	**9,601**	Balance of Kearney township	1,160
Au Train township	1,138	Mancelona village	1,390
Burt township	522	Balance of Mancelona township	3,010
Grand Island township	47	Milton township	2,204
Limestone township	438	Star township	926
Mathias township	554	Torch Lake township	1,194
Munising city	2,355	Warner township	416
Munising township	2,983	**Arenac County**	**15,899**
Onota township	352	Adams township	563
Chatham village	220	Arenac township	903
Balance of Rock River township	992	Au Gres city	889
Allegan County	**111,408**	Au Gres township	953
Allegan city	4,998	Clayton township	1,097
Allegan township	4,406	Sterling village	530
Casco township	2,823	Balance of Deep River township	1,619
Cheshire township	2,199	Lincoln township	942
Clyde township	2,084	Twining village (part)	103
Dorr township	7,439	Balance of Mason township	748
Douglas city	1,232	Moffatt township	1,184
Fennville city	1,398	Omer city	313
Fillmore township	2,681	Sims township	1,095
Ganges township	2,530	Standish city	1,509
Gunplain township	5,895	Standish township	1,900
Heath township	3,317	Turner village	114
Holland city (part)	7,016	Twining village (part)	78
Hopkins village	610	Balance of Turner township	358
Balance of Hopkins township	1,991	Whitney township	1,001
Laketown township	5,505	**Baraga County**	**8,860**
Lee township	4,015	Arvon township	450
Leighton township	4,934	Baraga village (part)	2,053
Manlius township	3,017	Balance of Baraga township	1,762
Martin village	410	Covington township	476
Balance of Martin township	2,219	L'Anse village	2,011
Monterey township	2,356	Balance of L'Anse township	1,832
Otsego city	3,956	Spurr township	276
Otsego township	5,594	**Barry County**	**59,173**
Overisel township	2,911	Assyria township	1,986
Plainwell city	3,804	Baltimore township	1,861
Salem township	4,446	Barry township	3,378
Saugatuck city	925	Freeport village (part)	47
Saugatuck township	2,944	Balance of Carlton township	2,344
South Haven city (part)	3	Nashville village (part)	1,556
Trowbridge township	2,502	Balance of Castleton township	1,915
Valley township	2,018	Hastings city	7,350
Watson township	2,063	Hastings charter township	2,948
Wayland city	4,079	Hope township	3,239
Wayland township	3,088	Freeport village (part)	436
Alpena County	**29,598**	Balance of Irving township	2,814
Alpena city	10,483	Johnstown township	3,008
Alpena township	9,060	Nashville village (part)	72
Hillman village (part)	4	Balance of Maple Grove township	1,521
Balance of Green township	1,224	Orangeville township	3,311
Long Rapids township	1,010	Prairieville township	3,404
Maple Ridge township	1,690	Rutland charter township	3,987
Ossineke township	1,675	Middleville village	3,319
Sanborn township	2,116		
Wellington township	307		
Wilson township	2,029		

Area Name	Population	Area Name	Population
Barry County *(Cont.)*		**Berrien County** *(Cont.)*	
Balance of Thornapple township	4,565	Michiana village	182
Woodland village	425	Balance of New Buffalo township	1,932
Balance of Woodland township	1,622	Niles city (part)	11,599
Yankee Springs township	4,065	Niles township	14,164
		Berrien Springs village	1,796
Bay County	**107,771**	Balance of Oronoko charter township	7,397
Auburn city	2,087	Eau Claire village (part)	189
Bangor charter township	14,641	Balance of Pipestone township	2,123
Bay City city	34,932	Royalton township	4,766
Beaver township	2,885	St. Joseph city	8,365
Essexville city	3,478	Shoreham village	862
Frankenlust township	3,562	Balance of St. Joseph charter township	9,166
Fraser township	3,192	Sodus township	1,932
Garfield township	1,743	Three Oaks village	1,622
Gibson township	1,210	Balance of Three Oaks township	952
Hampton charter township	9,652	Watervliet city	1,735
Kawkawlin township	4,848	Watervliet township	3,102
Merritt township	1,441	Weesaw township	1,936
Midland city (part)	157		
Monitor charter township	10,735	**Branch County**	**45,248**
Mount Forest township	1,392	Algansee township	1,974
Pinconning city	1,307	Batavia township	1,339
Pinconning township	2,431	Bethel township	1,434
Portsmouth charter township	3,306	Bronson city	2,349
Williams charter township	4,772	Bronson township	1,349
		Butler township	1,467
Benzie County	**17,525**	California township	1,040
Lake Ann village	268	Coldwater city	10,945
Balance of Almira township	3,377	Coldwater township	6,102
Benzonia village	497	Gilead township	661
Beulah village	342	Girard township	1,780
Balance of Benzonia township	1,888	Kinderhook township	1,497
Blaine township	551	Matteson township	1,218
Thompsonville village (part)	154	Noble township	520
Balance of Colfax township	503	Ovid township	2,326
Crystal Lake township	957	Quincy village	1,652
Frankfort city	1,286	Balance of Quincy township	2,633
Elberta village	372	Sherwood village	309
Balance of Gilmore township	449	Balance of Sherwood township	1,785
Honor village	328	Union City village (part)	1,559
Balance of Homestead township	2,029	Balance of Union township	1,309
Inland township	2,070		
Joyfield township	799	**Calhoun County**	**136,146**
Lake township	759	Albion city	8,616
Platte township	354	Albion township	1,123
Thompsonville village (part)	287	Athens village	1,024
Balance of Weldon township	255	Balance of Athens township	1,530
		Battle Creek city	52,347
Berrien County	**156,813**	Bedford charter township	9,357
Bainbridge township	2,850	Burlington village	261
Baroda village	873	Union City village (part)	40
Balance of Baroda township	1,928	Balance of Burlington township	1,640
Benton charter township	14,749	Clarence township	1,985
Benton Harbor city	10,038	Clarendon township	1,139
Berrien Springs village (part)	4	Convis township	1,636
Eau Claire village (part)	436	Eckford township	1,303
Balance of Berrien township	4,644	Emmett charter township	11,770
Bertrand township	2,657	Fredonia township	1,626
Bridgman city	2,291	Homer village	1,668
Buchanan city	4,456	Balance of Homer township	1,347
Buchanan township	3,523	Lee township	1,213
Chikaming township	3,100	Leroy township	3,712
Coloma city	1,483	Marengo township	2,213
Coloma charter township	5,020	Marshall city	7,088
Galien village	549	Marshall township	3,115
Balance of Galien township	903	Newton township	2,551
Hagar township	3,671	Pennfield charter township	9,001
Lake charter township	2,972	Sheridan township	1,936
Stevensville village	1,142	Springfield city	5,260
Balance of Lincoln charter township	13,549	Tekonsha village	717
New Buffalo city	1,883	Balance of Tekonsha township	928
Grand Beach village	272		

Area Name	Population	Area Name	Population
Cass County	**52,293**	**Chippewa County** *(Cont.)*	
Calvin township	2,037	De Tour Village village	325
Dowagiac city	5,879	Balance of Detour township	482
Howard township	6,207	Drummond township	1,058
Jefferson township	2,541	Hulbert township	168
Cassopolis village	1,774	Kinross charter township	7,561
Balance of La Grange township	1,726	Pickford township	1,595
Marcellus village	1,198	Raber township	647
Balance of Marcellus township	1,341	Rudyard township	1,370
Mason township	2,945	Sault Ste. Marie city	14,144
Milton township	3,878	Soo township	3,141
Newberg township	1,632	Sugar Island township	652
Niles city (part)	1	Superior township	1,337
Edwardsburg village	1,259	Trout Lake township	384
Balance of Ontwa township	5,290	Whitefish township	575
Vandalia village	301	**Clare County**	**30,926**
Balance of Penn township	1,473	Arthur township	647
Pokagon township	2,029	Clare city (part)	3,071
Porter township	3,798	Franklin township	825
Silver Creek township	3,218	Freeman township	1,157
Volinia township	1,112	Frost township	1,047
Wayne township	2,654	Garfield township	1,882
Charlevoix County	**25,949**	Grant township	3,259
Bay township	1,122	Greenwood township	1,041
Boyne City city	3,735	Hamilton township	1,829
Boyne Falls village	294	Harrison city	2,114
Balance of Boyne Valley township	901	Hatton township	933
Chandler township	248	Hayes township	4,675
Charlevoix city	2,513	Lincoln township	1,824
Charlevoix township	1,645	Redding township	526
East Jordan city	2,351	Sheridan township	1,575
Evangeline township	712	Summerfield township	456
Eveline township	1,484	Farwell village	871
Hayes township	1,919	Balance of Surrey township	2,735
Hudson township	691	Winterfield township	459
Marion township	1,714	**Clinton County**	**75,382**
Melrose township	1,403	Bath township	11,598
Norwood township	723	Bengal township	1,188
Peaine township	292	Bingham township	2,859
St. James township	365	Fowler village	1,208
South Arm township	1,873	Balance of Dallas township	1,161
Wilson township	1,964	DeWitt city	4,507
Cheboygan County	**26,152**	DeWitt charter township	14,321
Aloha township	949	Elsie village	966
Beaugrand township	1,168	Balance of Duplain township	1,397
Benton township	3,206	Eagle village	123
Burt township	680	Balance of Eagle township	2,548
Cheboygan city	4,867	East Lansing city (part)	1,969
Ellis township	596	Maple Rapids village	672
Forest township	1,045	Balance of Essex township	1,238
Grant township	846	Grand Ledge city (part)	2
Hebron township	269	Greenbush township	2,199
Inverness township	2,261	Hubbardston village (part)	44
Koehler township	1,283	Balance of Lebanon township	561
Mackinaw City village (part)	300	Olive township	2,476
Balance of Mackinaw township	239	Ovid village (part)	1,597
Mentor township	818	Balance of Ovid township	2,198
Mullett township	1,312	Riley township	2,024
Munro township	571	St. Johns city	7,865
Wolverine village (part)	182	Victor township	3,460
Balance of Nunda township	860	Watertown township	4,836
Tuscarora township	3,038	Westphalia village	923
Walker township	327	Balance of Westphalia township	1,442
Waverly township	457	**Crawford County**	**14,074**
Wolverine village (part)	62	Beaver Creek township	1,736
Balance of Wilmot township	816	Frederic township	1,341
Chippewa County	**38,520**	Grayling city	1,884
Bay Mills township	1,477	Grayling township	5,827
Bruce township	2,128	Lovells township	626
Chippewa township	213	Maple Forest township	653
Dafter township	1,263	South Branch township	2,007

Area Name	Population	Area Name	Population
Delta County	**37,069**	**Emmet County** *(Cont.)*	
Baldwin township	759	Balance of Maple River township	1,149
Bark River township	1,578	Petoskey city	5,670
Bay de Noc township	305	Pleasant View township	823
Brampton township	1,050	Readmond township	581
Cornell township	593	Resort township	2,697
Ensign township	748	Springvale township	2,141
Escanaba city	12,616	Mackinaw City village (part)	506
Escanaba township	3,482	Balance of Wawatam township	155
Fairbanks township	281	West Traverse township	1,606
Ford River township	2,054		
Garden village	221	**Genesee County**	**425,790**
Balance of Garden township	529	Argentine township	6,913
Gladstone city	4,973	Goodrich village	1,860
Maple Ridge township	766	Balance of Atlas township	6,133
Masonville township	1,734	Burton city	29,999
Nahma township	495	Lennon village (part)	82
Wells township	4,885	Balance of Clayton charter township	7,499
		Clio city	2,646
Dickinson County	**26,168**	Davison city	5,173
Breen township	499	Davison township	19,575
Breitung charter township	5,853	Fenton city	11,746
Felch township	752	Fenton charter township	15,552
Iron Mountain city	7,624	Flint city	102,434
Kingsford city	5,133	Flint charter township	31,929
Norway city	2,845	Flushing city	8,389
Norway township	1,489	Flushing charter township	10,640
Sagola township	1,106	Otisville village	864
Waucedah township	804	Otter Lake village (part)	69
West Branch township	63	Balance of Forest township	3,769
		Gaines village	380
Eaton County	**107,759**	Balance of Gaines township	6,440
Bellevue village	1,282	Genesee township	21,581
Balance of Bellevue township	1,868	Grand Blanc city	8,276
Benton township	2,796	Grand Blanc charter township	37,508
Brookfield township	1,537	Linden city	3,991
Carmel township	2,855	Montrose city	1,657
Charlotte city	9,074	Montrose charter township	6,224
Chester township	1,747	Mt. Morris city	3,086
Delta charter township	32,408	Mt. Morris township	21,501
Eaton township	4,073	Mundy township	15,082
Eaton Rapids city	5,214	Richfield township	8,730
Eaton Rapids township	4,113	Swartz Creek city	5,758
Grand Ledge city (part)	7,784	Thetford township	7,049
Hamlin township	3,343	Vienna township	13,255
Kalamo township	1,842		
Lansing city (part)	4,734	**Gladwin County**	**25,692**
Olivet city	1,605	Beaverton city	1,071
Oneida charter township	3,865	Beaverton township	1,964
Potterville city	2,617	Bentley township	844
Mulliken village	553	Billings township	2,416
Balance of Roxand township	1,295	Bourret township	461
Sunfield village	578	Buckeye township	1,308
Balance of Sunfield township	1,419	Butman township	1,999
Vermontville village	759	Clement township	901
Balance of Vermontville township	1,294	Gladwin city	2,933
Walton township	2,266	Gladwin township	1,116
Dimondale village	1,234	Grim township	136
Balance of Windsor charter township	5,604	Grout township	1,964
		Hay township	1,362
Emmet County	**32,694**	Sage township	2,457
Bear Creek township	6,201	Secord township	1,151
Bliss township	620	Sherman township	1,043
Carp Lake township	759	Tobacco township	2,566
Center township	568		
Cross Village township	281	**Gogebic County**	**16,427**
Friendship township	889	Bessemer city	1,905
Harbor Springs city	1,194	Bessemer township	1,176
Alanson village	738	Erwin township	326
Balance of Littlefield township	2,240	Ironwood city	5,387
Little Traverse township	2,380	Ironwood township	2,333
Pellston village (part)	623	Marenisco township	1,727
Balance of McKinley township	674	Wakefield city	1,851
Pellston village (part)	199	Wakefield township	305
		Watersmeet township	1,417

Area Name	Population	Area Name	Population
Grand Traverse County..............	**86,986**	**Houghton County**.................	**36,628**
Acme township	4,375	South Range village	758
Blair township	8,209	Balance of Adams township	1,815
East Bay township	10,663	Calumet village.................	726
Fife Lake village................	443	Copper City village..............	190
Balance of Fife Lake township.........	2,348	Laurium village.................	1,977
Garfield township.................	16,256	Balance of Calumet township	3,596
Grant township.................	1,066	Chassell township...............	1,812
Green Lake township	5,784	Duncan township................	236
Long Lake township	8,662	Elm River township..............	177
Mayfield township	1,550	Franklin township...............	1,466
Kingsley village	1,480	Hancock city	4,634
Balance of Paradise township	3,233	Hancock township...............	461
Peninsula township.................	5,433	Houghton city	7,708
Traverse City city (part)...........	14,482	Laird township	555
Union township.................	405	Osceola township................	1,888
Whitewater township	2,597	Portage township................	3,221
		Quincy township	270
Gratiot County.................	**42,476**	Lake Linden village..............	1,005
Alma city	9,383	Balance of Schoolcraft township	834
Arcada township.................	1,681	Stanton township	1,419
Bethany township.................	1,407	Lake Linden village (part)...........	2
Ashley village...................	563	Balance of Torch Lake township	1,878
Balance of Elba township	833		
Emerson township	952	**Huron County**..................	**33,118**
Perrinton village.................	406	Bad Axe city....................	3,129
Balance of Fulton township..........	2,115	Ubly village	858
Hamilton township.................	465	Balance of Bingham township.......	851
Ithaca city	2,910	Bloomfield township..............	455
Lafayette township	591	Owendale village	241
Newark township.................	1,093	Balance of Brookfield township	519
New Haven township	1,004	Caseville village	777
North Shade township	665	Balance of Caseville township.......	1,793
North Star township	888	Chandler township	472
Pine River township	2,279	Colfax township	1,884
St. Louis city....................	7,482	Kinde village (part)...............	306
Seville township..................	2,173	Balance of Dwight township........	452
Sumner township	1,930	Fairhaven township	1,107
Washington township	870	Gore township	144
Breckenridge village...............	1,328	Grant township.................	913
Balance of Wheeler township	1,458	Harbor Beach city...............	1,703
		Hume township	749
Hillsdale County	**46,688**	Huron township.................	437
North Adams village	477	Lake township..................	855
Balance of Adams township	2,016	Kinde village (part)...............	142
Allen village....................	191	Balance of Lincoln township.......	665
Balance of Allen township	1,466	McKinley township..............	445
Amboy township	1,173	Balance of Meade township	720
Cambria township.................	2,533	Elkton village	808
Camden village..................	512	Balance of Oliver township.........	675
Montgomery village	342	Paris township..................	481
Balance of Camden township	1,193	Pointe Aux Barques township	10
Jonesville village.................	2,258	Port Austin village...............	664
Balance of Fayette township	1,068	Balance of Port Austin township	760
Hillsdale city	8,305	Port Hope village	267
Hillsdale township...............	2,033	Balance of Rubicon township	465
Jefferson township	3,063	Sand Beach township.............	1,221
Litchfield city	1,369	Sebewaing village................	1,759
Litchfield township...............	1,003	Balance of Sebewaing township	965
Moscow township.................	1,470	Sheridan township	712
Pittsford township................	1,603	Sherman township	1,083
Ransom township.................	932	Sigel township	465
Reading city	1,078	Verona township.................	1,259
Reading township................	1,765	Pigeon village..................	1,208
Scipio township	1,884	Balance of Winsor township	699
Somerset township	4,623		
Wheatland township...............	1,351	**Ingham County**	**280,895**
Woodbridge township..............	1,325	Alaiedon township	2,894
Waldron village..................	538	Aurelius township................	3,525
Balance of Wright township	1,117	Bunker Hill township	2,119
		Delhi charter township	25,877
		East Lansing city (part)	46,610

Area Name	Population	Area Name	Population
Ingham County *(Cont.)*		**Iron County** *(Cont.)*	
Dansville village	563	Hematite township	338
Balance of Ingham township	1,889	Iron River city	3,029
Lansing city (part)	109,563	Iron River township	1,027
Lansing charter township	8,126	Mansfield township	241
Webberville village	1,272	Alpha village	145
Balance of Leroy township	2,258	Balance of Mastodon township	511
Leslie city	1,851	Stambaugh township	1,140
Leslie township	2,389		
Locke township	1,791	**Isabella County**	**70,311**
Mason city	8,252	Lake Isabella village (part)	509
Meridian charter township	39,688	Balance of Broomfield township	1,340
Onondaga township	3,158	Chippewa township	4,654
Stockbridge village	1,218	Clare city (part)	47
Balance of Stockbridge township	2,678	Shepherd village	1,515
Vevay township	3,537	Balance of Coe township	1,564
Wheatfield township	1,632	Coldwater township	777
White Oak township	1,173	Deerfield township	3,188
Williamston city	3,854	Denver township	1,148
Williamstown township	4,978	Fremont township	1,455
		Gilmore township	1,459
Ionia County	**63,905**	Rosebush village	368
Belding city	5,757	Balance of Isabella township	1,885
Berlin township	2,116	Lincoln township	2,115
Saranac village	1,325	Mount Pleasant city	26,016
Balance of Boston township	4,384	Nottawa township	2,282
Clarksville village	394	Rolland township	1,305
Balance of Campbell township	1,994	Lake Isabella village (part)	1,172
Danby township	2,988	Balance of Sherman township	1,819
Easton township	3,082	Union charter township	12,927
Ionia city	11,394	Vernon township	1,369
Lyons village (part)	53	Wise township	1,397
Balance of Ionia township	3,726		
Keene township	1,831	**Jackson County**	**160,248**
Lyons village (part)	736	Blackman township	24,051
Muir village	604	Brooklyn village	1,206
Pewamo village	469	Cement City village (part)	33
Balance of Lyons township	1,656	Balance of Columbia township	6,181
Hubbardston village (part)	351	Concord village	1,050
Balance of North Plains township	928	Balance of Concord township	1,673
Lake Odessa village	2,018	Grass Lake village	1,173
Balance of Odessa township	1,760	Balance of Grass Lake charter township	4,511
Orange township	987	Hanover village	441
Orleans township	2,743	Balance of Hanover township	3,254
Otisco township	2,282	Henrietta township	4,705
Portland city	3,883	Jackson city	33,534
Portland township	3,404	Leoni township	13,807
Ronald township	1,869	Liberty township	2,961
Sebewa township	1,171	Napoleon township	6,776
		Norvell township	2,963
Iosco County	**25,887**	Parma village (part)	222
Alabaster township	487	Balance of Parma township	2,504
Au Sable charter township	2,047	Pulaski township	2,075
Baldwin township	1,694	Rives township	4,683
Burleigh township	787	Parma village (part)	547
East Tawas city	2,808	Balance of Sandstone township	3,437
Grant township	1,546	Spring Arbor township	8,267
Oscoda township	6,997	Springport village	800
Plainfield township	3,799	Balance of Springport township	1,359
Reno township	590	Summit township	22,508
Sherman township	448	Tompkins township	2,671
Tawas township	1,744	Waterloo township	2,856
Tawas City city	1,827		
Whittemore city	384	**Kalamazoo County**	**250,331**
Wilber township	729	Alamo township	3,762
		Vicksburg village (part)	635
Iron County	**11,817**	Balance of Brady township	3,613
Bates township	921	Augusta village (part)	33
Caspian city	906	Balance of Charleston township	1,942
Crystal Falls city	1,469	Climax village	767
Crystal Falls township	1,743	Balance of Climax township	1,696
Gaastra city	347	Comstock charter township	14,854

Area Name	Population	Area Name	Population
Kalamazoo County *(Cont.)*		**Keweenaw County**	**2,156**
Cooper charter township	10,111	Ahmeek village	146
Galesburg city	2,009	Balance of Allouez township	1,425
Kalamazoo city	74,262	Eagle Harbor township	217
Kalamazoo charter township	21,918	Grant township	219
Oshtemo charter township	21,705	Houghton township	82
Parchment city	1,804	Sherman township	67
Pavilion township	6,222		
Portage city	46,292	**Lake County**	**11,539**
Prairie Ronde township	2,250	Chase township	1,137
Richland village	751	Cherry Valley township	396
Balance of Richland township	6,829	Dover township	395
Augusta village (part)	852	Eden township	487
Balance of Ross township	3,812	Elk township	985
Schoolcraft village	1,525	Luther village (part)	120
Vicksburg village (part)	2,271	Balance of Ellsworth township	697
Balance of Schoolcraft township	4,418	Lake township	862
Texas township	14,697	Luther village (part)	198
Wakeshma township	1,301	Balance of Newkirk township	434
		Peacock township	492
Kalkaska County	**17,153**	Pinora township	717
Bear Lake township	667	Baldwin village (part)	560
Blue Lake township	387	Balance of Pleasant Plains township	1,021
Boardman township	1,530	Sauble township	333
Clearwater township	2,444	Sweetwater township	245
Cold Springs township	1,464	Baldwin village (part)	648
Excelsior township	953	Balance of Webber township	1,051
Garfield township	804	Yates township	761
Kalkaska village	2,020		
Balance of Kalkaska township	2,702	**Lapeer County**	**88,319**
Oliver township	281	Almont village	2,674
Orange township	1,233	Balance of Almont township	3,909
Rapid River township	1,145	Arcadia township	3,113
Springfield township	1,523	Attica township	4,755
		Brown City city (part)	9
Kent County	**602,622**	Clifford village	324
Ada township	13,142	Balance of Burlington township	1,154
Algoma township	9,932	Burnside township	1,864
Alpine township	13,336	Deerfield township	5,695
Bowne township	3,084	Dryden village	951
Byron township	20,317	Balance of Dryden township	3,817
Caledonia village	1,511	Elba township	5,250
Balance of Caledonia township	10,821	Goodland township	1,828
Cannon township	13,336	Hadley township	4,528
Cascade charter township	17,134	Imlay township	3,128
Cedar Springs city	3,509	Imlay City city	3,597
Courtland township	7,678	Lapeer city	8,841
East Grand Rapids city	10,694	Lapeer township	5,056
Gaines township	25,146	Columbiaville village	787
Grand Rapids city	188,040	Otter Lake village (part)	320
Grand Rapids charter township	16,661	Balance of Marathon township	3,461
Grandville city	15,378	Mayfield township	7,955
Grattan township	3,621	Metamora village	565
Kentwood city	48,707	Balance of Metamora township	3,684
Lowell city	3,783	North Branch village	1,033
Lowell charter township	5,949	Balance of North Branch township	2,612
Sand Lake village	500	Balance of Oregon township	5,786
Balance of Nelson township	4,264	Rich township	1,623
Oakfield township	5,782		
Plainfield township	30,952	**Leelanau County**	**21,708**
Rockford city	5,719	Bingham township	2,497
Solon township	5,974	Centerville township	1,274
Sparta village	4,140	Cleveland township	1,031
Balance of Sparta township	4,970	Elmwood charter township	4,503
Spencer township	3,960	Empire village	375
Casnovia village (part)	176	Balance of Empire township	807
Kent City village	1,057	Glen Arbor township	859
Balance of Tyrone township	3,498	Kasson township	1,609
Vergennes township	4,189	Northport village	526
Walker city	23,537	Balance of Leelanau township	1,501
Wyoming city	72,125	Leland township	2,043
		Solon township	1,509

Area Name	Population	Area Name	Population
Leelanau County *(Cont.)*		**Mackinac County**	**11,113**
Suttons Bay village	618	Bois Blanc township	95
Balance of Suttons Bay township	2,364	Brevort township	594
Traverse City city (part)	192	Clark township	2,056
		Garfield township	1,146
Lenawee County	**99,892**	Hendricks township	153
Adrian city	21,133	Hudson township	181
Adrian township	6,035	Mackinac Island city	492
Blissfield village (part)	3,332	Marquette township	603
Balance of Blissfield township	641	Moran township	994
Onsted village	917	Newton township	427
Balance of Cambridge township	4,816	Portage township	981
Clinton village	2,336	St. Ignace city	2,452
Balance of Clinton township	1,268	St. Ignace township	939
Deerfield village	898		
Balance of Deerfield township	670	**Macomb County**	**840,978**
Clayton village (part)	171	Armada village	1,730
Balance of Dover township	1,663	Balance of Armada township	3,649
Fairfield township	1,764	Romeo village (part)	1,753
Franklin township	3,174	Balance of Bruce township	6,947
Hudson city	2,307	Center Line city	8,257
Clayton village (part)	173	Chesterfield township	43,381
Balance of Hudson township	1,324	Clinton township	96,796
Macon township	1,486	Eastpointe city	32,442
Madison charter township	8,621	Fraser city	14,480
Medina township	1,090	Harrison township	24,587
Morenci city	2,220	Village of Grosse Pointe Shores city (part)	79
Ogden township	973	New Haven village	4,642
Blissfield village (part)	8	Balance of Lenox township	5,828
Balance of Palmyra township	2,076	Macomb township	79,580
Raisin township	7,559	Memphis city (part)	823
Britton village	586	Mount Clemens city	16,314
Balance of Ridgeway township	956	New Baltimore city	12,084
Balance of Riga township	1,406	Ray township	3,739
Addison village (part)	430	Richmond city (part)	5,733
Balance of Rollin township	2,840	Richmond township	3,665
Rome township	1,791	Roseville city	47,299
Seneca township	1,230	St. Clair Shores city	59,715
Tecumseh city	8,521	Shelby charter township	73,804
Tecumseh township	1,972	Sterling Heights city	129,699
Addison village (part)	175	Utica city	4,757
Cement City village (part)	405	Warren city	134,056
Balance of Woodstock township	2,925	Romeo village (part)	1,843
		Balance of Washington township	23,296
Livingston County	**180,967**		
Brighton city	7,444	**Manistee County**	**24,733**
Brighton township	17,791	Arcadia township	639
Cohoctah township	3,317	Bear Lake village	286
Conway township	3,546	Balance of Bear Lake township	1,465
Deerfield township	4,170	Brown township	747
Fenton city (part)	10	Copemish village	194
Genoa township	19,821	Balance of Cleon township	763
Green Oak township	17,476	Dickson township	993
Hamburg township	21,165	Filer charter township	2,325
Fowlerville village	2,886	Manistee city	6,226
Balance of Handy township	5,120	Eastlake village	512
Hartland township	14,663	Balance of Manistee township	3,572
Howell city	9,489	Kaleva village	470
Howell township	6,702	Balance of Maple Grove township	846
Iosco township	3,801	Marilla township	393
Marion township	9,996	Norman township	1,553
Oceola township	11,936	Onekama village	411
Pinckney village	2,427	Balance of Onekama township	918
Balance of Putnam township	5,821	Pleasanton township	818
Tyrone township	10,020	Springdale township	781
Unadilla township	3,366	Stronach township	821
Luce County	**6,631**	**Marquette County**	**67,077**
Columbus township	204	Champion township	297
Lakefield township	1,061	Chocolay township	5,903
Newberry village	1,519	Ely township	1,952
Balance of McMillan township	1,173	Ewing township	160
Pentland township	2,674	Forsyth township	6,164

Area Name	Population	Area Name	Population
Marquette County *(Cont.)*		**Menominee County** *(Cont.)*	
Humboldt township	464	Ingallston township	935
Ishpeming city	6,470	Lake township	556
Ishpeming township	3,513	Mellen township	1,150
Marquette city	21,355	Menominee city	8,599
Marquette township	3,905	Menominee township	3,488
Michigamme township	349	Meyer township	1,001
Negaunee city	4,568	Carney village	192
Negaunee township	3,088	Balance of Nadeau township	969
Powell township	816	Powers village	422
Republic township	1,060	Balance of Spalding township	1,252
Richmond township	882	Stephenson city	862
Sands township	2,285	Stephenson township	670
Skandia township	826	**Midland County**	**83,629**
Tilden township	1,013	Coleman city	1,243
Turin township	153	Edenville township	2,551
Wells township	231	Geneva township	1,056
West Branch township	1,623	Greendale township	1,751
		Homer township	4,009
Mason County	**28,705**	Hope township	1,361
Amber township	2,535	Ingersoll township	2,751
Branch township	1,328	Jasper township	1,180
Custer village	284	Sanford village	859
Balance of Custer township	970	Balance of Jerome township	3,937
Eden township	582	Larkin township	5,136
Free Soil village	144	Lee township	4,315
Balance of Free Soil township	678	Lincoln township	2,474
Grant township	909	Midland city (part)	41,706
Hamlin township	3,408	Midland township	2,287
Logan township	312	Mills township	1,939
Ludington city	8,076	Mt. Haley township	1,678
Meade township	181	Porter township	1,277
Pere Marquette charter township	2,366	Warren township	2,119
Riverton township	1,153	**Missaukee County**	**14,849**
Scottville city	1,214	Aetna township	413
Sheridan township	1,072	Bloomfield township	531
Fountain village	193	Butterfield township	489
Balance of Sherman township	993	Caldwell township	1,317
Summit township	924	Clam Union township	882
Victory township	1,383	Enterprise township	194
		Forest township	1,157
Mecosta County	**42,798**	Holland township	248
Morley village (part)	306	Lake township	2,800
Balance of Aetna township	1,993	Lake City city	836
Austin township	1,561	McBain city	656
Big Rapids city	10,601	Norwich township	611
Big Rapids charter township	4,208	Pioneer township	451
Chippewa township	1,212	Reeder township	1,128
Colfax township	1,933	Richland township	1,491
Morley village (part)	187	Riverside township	1,179
Balance of Deerfield township	1,629	West Branch township	466
Barryton village	355		
Balance of Fork township	1,249	**Monroe County**	**152,021**
Grant township	686	Carleton village	2,345
Green charter township	3,292	Balance of Ash township	5,438
Hinton township	1,126	Bedford township	31,085
Martiny township	1,625	Estral Beach village	418
Stanwood village	211	South Rockwood village	1,675
Balance of Mecosta township	2,404	Balance of Berlin charter township	7,206
Millbrook township	1,113	Dundee village	3,957
Mecosta village	457	Balance of Dundee township	2,802
Balance of Morton township	3,854	Erie township	4,517
Sheridan township	1,393	Maybee village	562
Wheatland township	1,403	Balance of Exeter township	3,406
		Frenchtown township	20,428
Menominee County	**24,029**	Ida township	4,964
Cedarville township	253	La Salle township	4,894
Daggett village	258	London township	3,048
Balance of Daggett township	456	Luna Pier city	1,436
Faithorn township	243	Milan township	1,601
Gourley township	420	Milan city (part)	2,066
Harris township	1,968		
Holmes township	335		

Area Name	Population	Area Name	Population
Monroe County (*Cont.*)		**Muskegon County** (*Cont.*)	
Monroe city	20,733	Norton Shores city	23,994
Monroe township	14,568	Ravenna village	1,219
Petersburg city	1,146	Balance of Ravenna township	1,686
Raisinville township	5,816	Roosevelt Park city	3,831
Summerfield township	3,308	Sullivan township	2,441
Whiteford township	4,602	Whitehall city	2,706
		Whitehall township	1,739
Montcalm County	**63,342**	White River township	1,335
Belvidere township	2,209		
Bloomer township	3,904	**Newaygo County**	**48,460**
Sheridan village (part)	25	Ashland township	2,773
Balance of Bushnell township	1,579	Barton township	717
Carson City city	1,093	Beaver township	509
Lakeview village	1,007	Big Prairie township	2,573
Balance of Cato township	1,728	Bridgeton township	2,141
Crystal township	2,689	Brooks township	3,510
McBride village	205	Croton township	3,228
Balance of Day township	967	Dayton township	1,949
Douglass township	2,180	Hesperia village (part)	339
Eureka township	3,959	Balance of Denver township	1,589
Sheridan village (part)	458	Ensley township	2,635
Balance of Evergreen township	2,400	Everett township	1,862
Sheridan village (part)	3	Fremont city	4,081
Balance of Fairplain township	1,833	Garfield township	2,537
Ferris township	1,422	Goodwell township	547
Greenville city	8,481	Grant city	894
Edmore village	1,201	Grant township	3,294
Balance of Home township	1,341	Home township	232
Maple Valley township	1,944	Lilley township	797
Montcalm township	3,350	Lincoln township	1,275
Pierson village	172	Merrill township	667
Balance of Pierson township	3,044	Monroe township	320
Pine township	1,834	Newaygo city	1,976
Howard City village	1,808	Norwich township	607
Balance of Reynolds township	3,502	Sheridan charter township	2,510
Richland township	2,778	Sherman township	2,109
Sheridan village (part)	163	Troy township	283
Balance of Sidney township	2,411	White Cloud city	1,408
Stanton city	1,417	Wilcox township	1,098
Winfield township	2,235		
		Oakland County	**1,202,362**
Montmorency County	**9,765**	Leonard village	403
Albert township	2,526	Balance of Addison township	5,948
Avery township	646	Auburn Hills city	21,412
Briley township	1,860	Berkley city	14,970
Hillman village	697	Birmingham city	20,103
Balance of Hillman township	1,478	Bloomfield charter township	41,070
Loud township	293	Bloomfield Hills city	3,869
Montmorency township	1,117	Ortonville village	1,442
Rust township	561	Balance of Brandon charter township	13,733
Vienna township	587	Clawson city	11,825
		Wolverine Lake village	4,312
Muskegon County	**172,188**	Balance of Commerce charter township	35,874
Blue Lake township	2,399	Farmington city	10,372
Casnovia village (part)	143	Farmington Hills city	79,740
Balance of Casnovia township	2,662	Ferndale city	19,900
Cedar Creek township	3,186	Groveland township	5,476
Lakewood Club village	1,291	Hazel Park city	16,422
Balance of Dalton township	8,009	Highland charter township	19,202
Egelston township	9,909	Holly village	6,086
Fruitland township	5,543	Balance of Holly township	5,276
Fruitport township	1,093	Huntington Woods city	6,238
Balance of Fruitport charter township	12,505	Independence charter township	34,681
Holton township	2,515	Keego Harbor city	2,970
Laketon township	7,563	Lake Angelus city	290
Montague city	2,361	Lathrup Village city	4,075
Montague township	1,600	Lyon charter township	14,545
Moorland township	1,575	Madison Heights city	29,694
Muskegon city	38,401	Milford village	6,175
Muskegon township	17,840	Balance of Milford charter township	9,561
Muskegon Heights city	10,856		
North Muskegon city	3,786		

Area Name	Population	Area Name	Population
Oakland County *(Cont.)*		**Ogemaw County** *(Cont.)*	
Northville city (part)	3,231	Rose township	1,368
Novi city	55,224	Rose City city	653
Novi township	150	West Branch city	2,139
Oakland charter township	16,779	West Branch township	2,593
Oak Park city	29,319		
Orchard Lake Village city	2,375	**Ontonagon County**	**6,780**
Lake Orion village	2,973	Bergland township	467
Balance of Orion charter township	32,421	Bohemia township	82
Oxford village	3,436	Carp Lake township	722
Balance of Oxford charter township	17,090	Greenland township	792
Pleasant Ridge city	2,526	Haight township	212
Pontiac city	59,515	Interior township	336
Rochester city	12,711	McMillan township	478
Rochester Hills city	70,995	Matchwood township	94
Rose township	6,250	Ontonagon village	1,494
Royal Oak city	57,236	Balance of Ontonagon township	1,085
Royal Oak charter township	2,419	Rockland township	228
Southfield city	71,739	Stannard township	790
Beverly Hills village	10,267		
Bingham Farms village	1,111	**Osceola County**	**23,528**
Franklin village	3,150	Tustin village	230
Balance of Southfield township	19	Balance of Burdell township	1,101
South Lyon city	11,327	Cedar township	455
Springfield charter township	13,940	Evart city	1,903
Sylvan Lake city	1,720	Evart township	1,483
Troy city	80,980	Hartwick township	567
Village of Clarkston city	882	Hersey village	350
Walled Lake city	6,999	Balance of Hersey township	1,600
Waterford charter township	71,707	Highland township	1,250
West Bloomfield charter township	64,690	Le Roy village	256
White Lake charter township	30,019	Balance of Le Roy township	956
Wixom city	13,498	Lincoln township	1,500
		Marion village	872
Oceana County	**26,570**	Balance of Marion township	820
Benona township	1,437	Middle Branch township	843
Claybanks township	777	Orient township	773
Colfax township	462	Osceola township	1,076
Crystal township	838	Reed City city	2,425
Elbridge township	971	Richmond township	1,554
Ferry township	1,292	Rose Lake township	1,373
Golden township	1,742	Sherman township	1,042
New Era village (part)	58	Sylvan township	1,099
Rothbury village	432		
Balance of Grant township	2,486	**Oscoda County**	**8,640**
Greenwood township	1,184	Big Creek township	2,827
Hart city	2,126	Clinton township	441
Hart township	1,853	Comins township	1,970
Walkerville village	247	Elmer township	1,138
Balance of Leavitt township	644	Greenwood township	1,121
Hesperia village (part)	615	Mentor township	1,143
Balance of Newfield township	1,786		
Otto township	826	**Otsego County**	**24,164**
Pentwater village	857	Bagley township	5,886
Balance of Pentwater township	658	Charlton township	1,354
New Era village (part)	393	Chester township	1,292
Shelby village	2,065	Vanderbilt village	562
Balance of Shelby township	1,611	Balance of Corwith township	1,186
Weare township	1,210	Dover township	561
		Elmira township	1,687
Ogemaw County	**21,699**	Gaylord city	3,645
Churchill township	1,713	Hayes township	2,619
Cumming township	698	Livingston township	2,525
Edwards township	1,413	Otsego Lake township	2,847
Foster township	843		
Goodar township	398	**Ottawa County**	**263,801**
Hill township	1,361	Allendale township	20,708
Horton township	927	Blendon township	5,772
Klacking township	614	Chester township	2,017
Logan township	551	Coopersville city	4,275
Mills township	4,291	Crockery township	3,960
Ogemaw township	1,223	Ferrysburg city	2,892
Prescott village	266	Georgetown township	46,985
Balance of Richland township	648	Grand Haven city	10,412

Area Name	Population	Area Name	Population
Ottawa County *(Cont.)*		**Saginaw County** *(Cont.)*	
Grand Haven charter township	15,178	Balance of Jonesfield township	889
Holland city (part)	26,035	Kochville township	5,078
Holland township	35,636	Lakefield township	1,029
Hudsonville city	7,116	Maple Grove township	2,668
Jamestown township	7,034	Marion township	923
Olive township	4,735	Richland township	4,144
Park township	17,802	Saginaw city	51,508
Polkton township	2,423	Saginaw charter township	40,840
Port Sheldon township	4,240	St. Charles village (part)	1,885
Robinson township	6,084	Balance of St. Charles township	1,445
Spring Lake village	2,323	Spaulding township	2,153
Balance of Spring Lake township	11,977	St. Charles village (part)	146
Tallmadge township	7,575	Balance of Swan Creek township	2,310
Wright township	3,147	Taymouth township	4,520
Zeeland city	5,504	Thomas township	11,985
Zeeland township	9,971	Tittabawassee township	9,726
		Zilwaukee city	1,658
Presque Isle County	**13,376**	Zilwaukee township	67
Allis township	948		
Bearinger township	369	**St. Clair County**	**163,040**
Belknap township	751	Algonac city	4,110
Bismarck township	386	Berlin township	3,285
Millersburg village	206	Brockway township	2,022
Balance of Case township	697	Burtchville township	4,008
Krakow township	705	Casco township	4,105
Metz township	302	China township	3,551
Moltke township	296	Clay township	9,066
North Allis township	521	Clyde township	5,579
Ocqueoc township	655	Columbus township	4,070
Onaway city	880	Cottrellville township	3,559
Posen village	234	East China township	3,788
Balance of Posen township	616	Emmett village	269
Presque Isle township	1,656	Balance of Emmett township	2,385
Pulawski township	343	Fort Gratiot charter township	11,108
Rogers township	984	Grant township	1,891
Rogers City city	2,827	Greenwood township	1,538
		Ira township	5,178
Roscommon County	**24,449**	Kenockee township	2,470
Au Sable township	255	Kimball township	9,358
Backus township	330	Lynn township	1,229
Denton township	5,557	Marine City city	4,248
Gerrish township	2,993	Marysville city	9,959
Roscommon village	1,075	Memphis city (part)	360
Balance of Higgins township	857	Capac village	1,890
Lake township	1,215	Balance of Mussey township	2,316
Lyon township	1,370	Port Huron city	30,184
Markey township	2,360	Port Huron charter township	10,654
Nester township	295	Richmond city (part)	2
Richfield township	3,731	Riley township	3,353
Roscommon township	4,411	St. Clair city	5,485
		St. Clair township	6,817
Saginaw County	**200,169**	Wales township	3,248
Albee township	2,160	Yale city	1,955
Birch Run village	1,555		
Balance of Birch Run township	4,478	**St. Joseph County**	**61,295**
Reese village (part)	6	Burr Oak village	828
Balance of Blumfield township	1,954	Balance of Burr Oak township	1,783
Oakley village	290	Colon village	1,173
Balance of Brady township	1,928	Balance of Colon township	2,156
St. Charles village (part)	23	Constantine village	2,076
Balance of Brant township	1,989	Balance of Constantine township	2,141
Bridgeport charter township	10,514	Fabius township	3,248
Buena Vista charter township	8,676	Fawn River township	1,477
Carrollton township	6,103	Florence township	1,242
Chapin township	1,060	Flowerfield township	1,562
Chesaning village	2,394	Leonidas township	1,185
Balance of Chesaning township	2,265	Centreville village (part)	69
Frankenmuth city	4,944	Balance of Lockport township	3,718
Frankenmuth township	1,959	Mendon village	870
Fremont township	2,096	Balance of Mendon township	1,849
James township	2,023	Mottville township	1,436
Merrill village	778	Centreville village (part)	1,356
		Balance of Nottawa township	2,502
		Park township	2,600

Area Name	Population	Area Name	Population
St. Joseph County *(Cont.)*		**Shiawassee County** *(Cont.)*	
Sherman township	3,205	Ovid village (part)	6
Sturgis city	10,994	Balance of Middlebury township	1,504
Sturgis township	2,261	New Haven township	1,329
Three Rivers city	7,811	Owosso city	15,194
White Pigeon village	1,522	Owosso township	4,821
Balance of White Pigeon township	2,231	Perry city	2,188
		Morrice village	927
Sanilac County	**43,114**	Balance of Perry township	3,400
Argyle township	759	Rush township	1,291
Austin township	665	Sciota township	1,833
Carsonville village (part)	166	Bancroft village	545
Balance of Bridgehampton township	688	Balance of Shiawassee township	2,295
Brown City city (part)	1,316	Lennon village (part)	429
Buel township	1,265	Balance of Venice township	2,149
Croswell city	2,447	Vernon village	783
Custer township	1,006	Balance of Vernon township	3,831
Forestville village	136	Woodhull township	3,810
Balance of Delaware township	720		
Peck village	632	**Tuscola County**	**55,729**
Balance of Elk township	894	Akron village (part)	252
Elmer township	806	Balance of Akron township	1,251
Evergreen township	924	Caro village	4,229
Flynn township	1,050	Balance of Almer township	2,115
Forester township	1,011	Arbela township	3,070
Fremont township	1,051	Unionville village	508
Greenleaf township	781	Balance of Columbia township	776
Lamotte township	919	Balance of Dayton township	1,848
Lexington village	1,178	Reese village (part)	1,448
Balance of Lexington township	2,480	Balance of Denmark township	1,620
Maple Valley township	1,221	Cass City village (part)	2,428
Deckerville village	830	Balance of Elkland township	1,100
Balance of Marion township	829	Ellington township	1,332
Marlette city	1,875	Gagetown village	388
Marlette township	1,763	Balance of Elmwood township	819
Minden City village	197	Akron village (part)	150
Balance of Minden township	348	Fairgrove village	563
Moore township	1,203	Balance of Fairgrove township	866
Sandusky city	2,679	Mayville village	950
Port Sanilac village	623	Balance of Fremont township	2,362
Balance of Sanilac township	1,808	Gilford township	741
Melvin village	180	Balance of Indianfields township	2,805
Balance of Speaker township	1,303	Juniata township	1,567
Applegate village	248	Kingston village (part)	385
Carsonville village (part)	361	Balance of Kingston township	1,189
Balance of Washington township	1,050	Kingston village (part)	55
Watertown township	1,320	Balance of Koylton township	1,530
Wheatland township	488	Millington village	1,072
Worth township	3,894	Balance of Millington township	3,282
		Balance of Novesta township	1,491
Schoolcraft County	**8,485**	Tuscola township	2,082
Doyle township	624	Vassar city	2,697
Germfask township	486	Vassar township	4,093
Hiawatha township	1,302	Watertown township	2,202
Inwood township	733	Wells township	1,773
Manistique city	3,097	Wisner township	690
Manistique township	1,095		
Mueller township	234	**Van Buren County**	**76,258**
Seney township	119	Almena township	4,992
Thompson township	795	Lawton village	1,900
		Mattawan village	1,997
Shiawassee County	**70,648**	Paw Paw village (part)	87
Antrim township	2,161	Balance of Antwerp township	8,198
Bennington township	3,168	Arlington township	2,073
Byron village	581	Bangor city	1,885
Balance of Burns township	2,876	Bangor township	2,147
Caledonia township	4,475	Bloomingdale village	454
Corunna city	3,497	Balance of Bloomingdale township	2,649
Durand city	3,446	Breedsville village	199
Fairfield township	755	Balance of Columbia township	2,389
New Lothrop village	581	Covert township	2,888
Balance of Hazelton township	1,490	Decatur village	1,819
Laingsburg city	1,283		

Area Name	Population	Area Name	Population
Van Buren County *(Cont.)*		**Wayne County** *(Cont.)*	
Balance of Decatur township	1,907	Garden City city	27,692
Geneva township	3,573	Gibraltar city	4,656
Gobles city	829	Grosse Ile township	10,371
Hamilton township	1,489	Grosse Pointe city	5,421
Hartford city	2,688	Grosse Pointe Shores village (part)	2,929
Hartford township	3,274	Grosse Pointe Farms city	9,479
Keeler township	2,169	Grosse Pointe Park city	11,555
Lawrence village	996	Grosse Pointe Woods city	16,135
Balance of Lawrence township	2,263	Hamtramck city	22,423
Paw Paw village (part)	3,447	Harper Woods city	14,236
Balance of Paw Paw township	3,594	Highland Park city	11,776
Pine Grove township	2,949	Huron charter township	15,879
Porter township	2,466	Inkster city	25,369
South Haven city (part)	4,400	Lincoln Park city	38,144
South Haven township	3,983	Livonia city	96,942
Waverly township	2,554	Melvindale city	10,715
		Northville city (part)	2,739
Washtenaw County	**344,791**	Northville township	28,497
Ann Arbor city	113,934	Plymouth city	9,132
Barton Hills village	294	Plymouth township	27,524
Balance of Ann Arbor township	4,067	Redford township	48,362
Augusta township	6,745	River Rouge city	7,903
Bridgewater township	1,674	Riverview city	12,486
Chelsea city	4,944	Rockwood city	3,289
Dexter township	6,042	Romulus city	23,989
Freedom township	1,428	Southgate city	30,047
Lima township	3,307	Sumpter township	9,549
Lodi township	6,058	Taylor city	63,131
Lyndon township	2,720	Trenton city	18,853
Manchester village	2,091	Van Buren charter township	28,821
Balance of Manchester township	2,478	Wayne city	17,593
Milan city (part)	3,770	Westland city	84,094
Northfield township	8,245	Woodhaven city	12,875
Pittsfield charter township	34,663	Wyandotte city	25,883
Salem township	5,627		
Saline city	8,810	**Wexford County**	**32,735**
Saline township	1,896	Balance of Antioch township	815
Dexter village (part)	3,611	Harrietta village (part)	130
Balance of Scio township	16,470	Balance of Boon township	557
Sharon township	1,737	Cadillac city	10,355
Superior township	13,058	Cedar Creek township	1,757
Sylvan township	2,833	Cherry Grove township	2,377
Dexter village (part)	456	Clam Lake township	2,467
Balance of Webster township	6,328	Colfax township	840
York township	8,708	Greenwood township	587
Ypsilanti city	19,435	Buckley village	697
Ypsilanti charter township	53,362	Balance of Hanover township	863
		Haring township	3,173
Wayne County	**1,820,584**	Henderson township	163
Allen Park city	28,210	Liberty township	861
Belleville city	3,991	Manton city	1,287
Brownstown charter township	30,627	Selma township	2,093
Canton charter township	90,173	Harrietta village (part)	13
Dearborn city	98,153	Balance of Slagle township	490
Dearborn Heights city	57,774	South Branch township	383
Detroit city	713,777	Mesick village (part)	394
Ecorse city	9,512	Balance of Springville township	1,361
Flat Rock city (part)	9,878	Wexford township	1,072

NOTES: Cities that cross county lines are split between the pertinent counties, and each part of the city is followed by the designation "(part) ".

Villages with population in two or more townships are split between the pertinent townships and each part of the village is followed by the designation "(part) ".

Villages are part of the township(s) in which they are located. The total population of a township which contains villages is obtained by adding the population of its villages to the "balance" of the township.

Source: Michigan Department of Technology, Management, and Budget, Office of Shared Solutions. 2010 Census Data for Michigan. *Population of Michigan Cities and Townships: 2000 and 2010.* www.michigan.gov/cgi/0,4548,7-158-54534-252541--,00.html.

POPULATION OF INDIAN RESERVATIONS AND
TRUST LANDS IN MICHIGAN, 2010

Area Name		Population
Bay Mills Reservation and Off-Reservation Trust Land		**1,014**
Bay Mills township (part)	Chippewa County	499
Sugar Island township (part)	Chippewa County	26
Superior township (part)	Chippewa County	156
Bay Mills township (part)	*Chippewa County*	*329*
Dafter township (part)	*Chippewa County*	*0*
Superior township (part)	*Chippewa County*	*4*
Grand Traverse Reservation and Off-Reservation Trust Land		**608**
Suttons Bay township (part)	Leelanau County	2
Helena township (part)	*Antrim County*	*0*
Milton township (part)	*Antrim County*	*23*
Benzonia township (part)	Benzie County	92
Eveline township (part)	*Charlevoix County*	*35*
Acme township (part)	*Grand Traverse County*	*0*
Whitewater township (part)	*Grand Traverse County*	*0*
Suttons Bay township (part)	Leelanau County	456
Hannahville Indian Community and Off-Reservation Trust Land		**523**
Gourley township (part)	Menominee County	5
Harris township (part)	Menominee County	259
Bark River township (part)	*Delta County*	*8*
Harris township (part)	*Menominee County*	*251*
Huron Potawatomi Reservation and Off-Reservation Trust Land		**52**
Athens township (part)	Calhoun County	51
Emmet charter township (part)	*Calhoun County*	*1*
Isabella Reservation		**26,274**
Standish township (part)	Arenac County	11
Chippewa township (part)	Isabella County	3,326
Deerfield township	Isabella County	3,188
Denver township	Isabella County	1,148
Isabella township	Isabella County	2,253
Mount Pleasant city (part)	Isabella County	8,480
Nottawa township	Isabella County	2,282
Union charter township (part)	Isabella County	4,189
Wise township	Isabella County	1,397
Lac Vieux Desert Reservation		**137**
Watersmeet township (part)	Gogebic County	137
L'Anse Reservation and Off-Reservation Trust Land		**3,703**
Arvon township (part)	Baraga County	48
Baraga village (part)	Baraga County	1,719
L'Anse township (part)	Baraga County	1,799
L'Anse township (part)	*Baraga County*	*22*
Chocolay charter township (part)	*Marquette County*	*115*
Little River Reservation and Off-Reservation Trust Land		**57**
Manistee township (part)	Manistee County	1
Brown township (part)	*Manistee County*	*0*
Manistee township (part)	*Manistee County*	*56*
Custer township (part)	*Mason County*	*0*
Little Traverse Bay Reservation and Off-Reservation Trust Land		**51**
Hayes township (part)	Charlevoix County	2
St. James township (part)	Charlevoix County	0
Bear Creek township (part)	Emmet County	0
Bliss township (part)	Emmet County	0
Center township (part)	Emmet County	0
Little Traverse township (part)	Emmet County	4
Petoskey city (part)	Emmet County	0
Readmond township (part)	Emmet County	0
Resort township (part)	Emmet County	0
Wawatam township (part)	Emmet County	0
West Traverse township (part)	Emmet County	45
Hayes township (part)	*Charlevoix County*	*0*
Bear Creek township (part)	*Emmet County*	*0*
McKinley township (part)	*Emmet County*	*0*
Match-e-be-nash-she-wish Band of Pottawatomi Reservation		**0**
Wayland township (part)	Allegan County	0

POPULATION OF INDIAN RESERVATIONS AND
TRUST LANDS IN MICHIGAN, 2010 *(Cont.)*

Area Name		Population
Ontonagon Reservation		**0**
Ontonagon township (part).	Ontonagon County	0
Pokagon Reservation and Off-Reservation Trust Land		**29**
New Buffalo township (part	Berrien County	4
Pokagon township (part).	*Cass County*	*8*
Silver Creek township (part)	*Cass County*	*0*
Wayne township	*Cass County*	*3*
Bangor township (part).	*Van Buren County*	*9*
Hartford township (part).	*Van Buren County*	*5*
Sault Ste. Marie Reservation and Off-Reservation Trust Land		**1,747**
Sault Ste. Marie city (part).	Chippewa County	332
Sugar Island township (part).	Chippewa County	6
Au Train township (part)	*Alger County*	*2*
Munising township (part)	*Alger County*	*48*
Kinross charter township (part)	*Chippewa County*	*887*
Sault Ste. Marie city (part)	*Chippewa County*	*27*
Escanaba city (part)	*Delta County*	*71*
Pentland township (part)	*Luce County*	*53*
Clark township (part)	*Mackinac County*	*59*
St. Ignace township (part).	*Mackinac County*	*161*
Marquette city (part).	*Marquette County*	*0*
Manistique township (part).	*Schoolcraft County*	*101*
Total on Reservations.		**31,369**
Total in Off-Reservation Trust Lands		*1,490*
GRAND TOTAL.		**34,195**

NOTE: Components of reservations and tribal-designated statistical areas (TDSAs) are shown in regular type; components of trust lands are shown in italic. Some reservation lands are uninhabited or under development.

TDSAs are areas that contain a concentration of people who identify with a tribe and in which there are organized and structured tribal activities, but they do not include a federally recognized land base.

Source: U.S. Census Bureau, 2010 Census, Summary File 1.

PUBLIC SCHOOL SYSTEM IN MICHIGAN
TABLE 1
HISTORICAL DATA, 1836-1968

Year	Number of School Days[1]	Public School Academies (PSAs)	Local Educational Authorities (LEAs)	Teachers	Number of Children[2]	Total Salaries for Instruction
1836	70		55	98	2,377	$ 3,540
1840	90		1,560	1,870	48,817	42,310
1850	102		3,097	4,087	132,234	140,889
1860	124		4,087	7,921	246,802	468,988
1870	138		5,108	11,014	384,554	1,393,228
1880	150		6,352	13,949	506,221	1,917,983
1890	154		7,168	15,990	654,502	3,323,881
1894	156		7,160	16,190	696,234	3,895,264
1895	158		7,159	16,013	699,828	3,968,600
1896	172		7,167	15,896	700,069	4,083,309
1897	161		7,151	15,601	701,244	4,050,832
1898	162		7,157	15,673	703,730	4,152,878
1899	163		7,161	15,564	713,690	4,312,245
1900	164		7,163	15,924	721,698	4,501,508
1901	164		7,171	16,054	730,101	4,735,192
1902	166		7,204	16,252	738,182	5,002,605
1903	167		7,229	16,664	744,603	5,308,373
1904	166		7,255	16,765	745,010	5,688,103
1905	174		7,267	16,823	743,184	6,007,652
1906	170		7,294	16,924	747,887	6,357,221
1907	170		7,302	17,286	743,030	7,091,866
1908	178		7,310	17,407	747,276	7,700,993
1909	178		7,330	17,763	755,935	8,271,923
1910	171		7,333	17,987	771,471	8,771,896
1911	170		7,361	18,207	783,770	9,327,930
1912	172		7,362	18,824	795,423	9,952,326
1913	172		7,327	19,500	815,840	10,539,963
1914	172		7,335	19,734	826,400	10,795,281
1915	172		7,337	20,161	845,754	11,932,392
1916	173		7,339	20,979	866,570	12,702,856
1917	175		7,333	21,992	892,787	13,837,995
1918	166		7,329	23,051	919,666	15,452,303
1919	161		7,312	23,388	937,330	18,824,799
1920	176		7,273	24,302	978,412	23,391,537
1921	175		7,189	24,938	1,020,699	32,627,184
1922	170		6,984	25,755	1,038,897	35,302,485
1923	174		6,953	27,008	1,075,890	37,033,098
1924	178		6,925	27,918	1,124,551	39,395,203
1925	170		6,890	29,390	1,160,435	42,293,488
1926	170		6,863	30,327	1,199,260	45,991,575
1927	170		6,873	31,184	1,247,932	48,783,937
1928	175		6,878	33,119	1,274,478	50,061,837
1929	176		6,842	33,724	1,337,018	53,622,280
1930	174		6,822	34,552	1,365,007	56,033,919
1931	176		6,779	34,806	1,373,585	57,798,090
1932	174		6,746	34,049	1,383,124	55,132,527
1933	170		6,709	32,007	1,389,417	39,638,378
1934	174		6,710	31,830	1,392,822	36,505,650
1935	174		6,692	31,340	1,398,348	40,739,466
1936	175		6,642	32,583	1,397,679	44,523,700
1937	174		6,604	31,816	1,402,672	46,185,263
1938	176		6,558	32,583	1,399,769	49,664,658
1939	175		6,466	32,702	1,389,347	50,516,474
1940	175		6,386	32,447	1,385,576	52,287,755
1941	175		6,318	32,017	1,382,979	53,178,877
1942	180		6,274	32,119	1,384,446	55,163,582
1943	180		6,239	32,567	1,400,170	57,829,978
1944	180		6,152	31,569	1,410,623	63,658,796
1945	180		6,029	31,966	1,403,493	67,514,467
1946	180		5,823	32,508	1,398,112	74,666,168
1947	180		5,434	32,574	1,414,196	84,998,948
1948	180		5,186	33,811	1,439,750	100,892,520

TABLE 1
HISTORICAL DATA, 1836-1968 *(Cont.)*

Year	Number of School Days[1]	Public School Academies (PSAs)	Local Educational Authorities (LEAs)	Teachers	Number of Children[2]	Total Salaries for Instruction
1949	180		5,031	35,200	1,466,972	$ 113,085,113
1950	180		4,918	37,157	1,489,351	123,881,270
1951	180		4,841	38,688	1,518,759	136,814,060
1952	180		4,736	40,460	1,589,923	150,555,706
1953	180		4,532	45,528	1,664,726	166,669,837
1954	180		4,246	43,957	1,746,789	183,412,303
1955	180		3,855	47,040	1,823,080	206,032,556
1956	180		3,495	49,663	1,910,552	241,620,490
1957	180		2,854	53,171	1,988,293	269,407,840
1958	180		2,499	55,794	2,058,028	297,950,653
1959	180		2,301	58,251	2,124,139	320,621,419
1960	180		2,149	60,394	2,199,545	344,193,814
1961	180		1,989	63,271	2,272,279	373,200,341
1962	180		1,794	66,024	2,339,079	402,153,331
1963	180		1,580	68,099	2,415,696	428,844,667
1964	180		1,436	69,380	2,466,676	449,173,953
1965	180		1,227	72,935	2,539,032	569,152,686
1966	180		993	76,047	2,620,663	643,666,205
1967	180		866	80,637	3,448,802	754,691,245
1968	180		712	85,346	3,434,754	881,028,258

TABLE 2
HISTORICAL DATA, 1969-2019

Year	Number of School Days[1]	Public School Academies (PSAs)	Local Educational Authorities (LEAs)	Teachers[3]	Pupil Count[4]	Total Salaries for Instruction
1969	180		648	87,487	2,122,915	$ 1,004,226,891
1970	180		638	88,959	2,164,386	1,133,674,901
1971	180		624	90,672	2,178,745	1,274,476,441
1972	180		608	91,190	2,212,505	1,369,280,071
1973	180		602	93,852	2,193,270	1,464,596,394
1974	180		597	94,221	2,159,966	1,573,636,026
1975	180		590	93,580	2,139,720	1,721,180,426
1976	180		587	92,677	2,127,917	1,835,639,963
1977	180		581	90,780	2,081,936	1,888,170,123
1978	180		579	90,312	2,023,944	2,017,898,474
1979	180		576	88,652	1,965,685	1,777,508,874
1980	180		575	87,487	1,910,385	1,919,577,320
1981	180		574	84,041	1,859,934	2,049,304,264
1982	180		574	78,447	1,792,331	2,114,391,081
1983	180		573	74,814	1,742,831	2,138,297,412
1984	180		570	74,312	1,712,103	2,245,977,550
1985	180		567	75,193	1,678,458	2,383,994,751
1986	180		566	76,166	1,666,281	2,560,133,526
1987	180		564	76,791	1,657,423	2,704,312,116
1988	180		563	77,779	1,657,844	2,898,679,091
1989	180		562	77,861	1,640,294	3,044,945,212
1990	180		562	77,737	1,637,592	3,245,914,951
1991	180		561	79,660	1,651,502	3,484,278,059
1992	180		559	81,079	1,673,020	3,723,930,094
1993	180		559	66,247	1,675,465	3,915,816,062
1994	180	1	557	81,024	1,602,622	4,138,560,056
1995	180	14	557	85,349	1,653,949	4,233,280,674
1996	180	44	555	86,446	1,673,879	4,423,924,668
1997	180	78	555	89,667	1,680,693	4,588,225,573
1998	180	108	555	91,823	1,694,320	4,740,083,034
1999	180	138	555	75,564	1,710,365	4,955,604,025
2000	180	171	555	77,720	1,714,815	5,215,769,144
2001	180	184	554	76,970	1,720,335	5,397,501,298
2002	180	189	554	77,818	1,731,092	5,548,528,908

TABLE 2
HISTORICAL DATA, 1969-2019 *(Cont.)*

Year	Number of School Days[1]	Public School Academies (PSAs)	Local Educational Authorities (LEAs)	Teachers[3]	Pupil Count[4]	Total Salaries for Instruction
2003	*	188	553	78,734	1,750,631	$ 5,674,487,104
2004	*	199	553	78,148	1,734,019	5,755,361,150
2005	*	216	552	76,319	1,723,087	5,741,440,589
2006	*	225	552	74,544	1,712,133	5,691,371,878
2007	*	229	552	74,256	1,693,436	5,740,806,784
2008	*	230	552	72,961	1,661,461	5,736,428,686
2009	*	232	551	72,021	1,628,628	5,792,111,684
2010	165	240	551	69,996	1,605,951	5,746,574,681
2011	165	247	551	67,950	1,577,606	5,425,572,103
2012	170	256	549	61,775	1,550,550	5,370,155,338
2013	170	277	549	60,580	1,542,691	5,233,354,463
2014	175	298	545	59,957	1,530,457	5,118,224,280
2015	175	302	541	59,237	1,520,074	5,037,549,823
2016	180	302	540	58,233	1,507,743	4,950,937,414
2017	180	301	538	58,038	1,486,733	4,969,381,625
2018	180	295	537	58,738	1,479,329	5,016,498,830

[1] Number of school days initially reflects an average number of school days and later, statute-mandated time of instruction. Years 1836 to 1928 list average number of school days; 1929 to 1971, statute mandated at least nine months of instruction; 1972 to 2002, statute mandated a minimum number of days of instruction; 2003 to 2009, statute mandated a minimum of 1,098 hours of instruction. Public Act 121 of 2009 requires a minimum number of days of pupil instruction, in which a minimum of 1,098 hours of instruction will be given, beginning in 2010 to the present.

[2] Number of school aged children (whether in public school or not) based on the annual school census.

[3] Teacher counts for 1999 and later reflect total FTE basic program teachers.

[4] Number of enrolled students in public schools based on the public school full-time equivalent (FTE) membership count.

* Minimum hours rather than days prescribed by statute.

Sources: Michigan Department of Education, Center for Educational Performance and Information, Bulletin 1011 and Table.

Number of Public School Districts in Michigan, www.michigan.gov/documents/numbsch_26940_7.pdf.

Legislative Service Bureau Research, 2019.

NUMBER OF SCHOOL DISTRICTS

Number of Students	2015-2016	2016-2017	2017-2018
10,000 and over	17	16	16
5,000 - 9,999	48	49	47
4,000 - 4,999	21	21	21
3,000 - 3,999	50	42	48
2,000 - 2,999	77	85	75
1,000 - 1,999	154	148	153
500 - 999	200	201	205
below 500	272	268	260
TOTAL	**839**	**830**	**825**

REVENUE, ALL FUNDS

Source	2015-2016	2016-2017	2017-2018
From local sources	$ 4,699,218,154	$ 4,657,623,159	$ 4,790,613,566
State school aid	11,107,987,016	11,343,292,849	11,707,353,698
Federal aid	1,247,561,222	1,196,520,685	1,192,350,964
Other sources	14,534,183	13,816,672	18,625,768
TOTAL	**17,069,300,575**	**17,211,253,365**	**17,708,943,996**

Sources: Bulletin 1011, <u>Analysis of Michigan Public School Districts, Revenues and Expenditures</u>, Michigan Department of Education, 2015-2016 published February 2017, 2016-2017 published February 2018, 2017-2018 published February 2019.

INTERMEDIATE SCHOOL DISTRICTS

---

[1] Educational Service District.
[2] Regional Educational Service District.
[3] Regional Educational Service Agency.
[4] Educational Service Agency.

Source: michigan.gov/som/0,4669,7-192-78943_78944_78955-406941--,00.html. Accessed July 9, 2019.

Chapter IX

ELECTIONS

2019–2020

HOW AN ISSUE BECOMES A BALLOT PROPOSAL

Background

Historically, the phenomenon of "direct democracy" — voters casting ballots to amend statutes or the state constitution — has its roots in the populist movement of the turn of the twentieth century. Since 1898, when South Dakota adopted a statewide initiative and referendum capability, many states have incorporated mechanisms for direct citizen participation in lawmaking. Michigan provides more access to the ballot for its citizens than most states. Only 15 states, including Michigan, provide for all three of the tools for citizens to place proposals on the ballot: the initiative to propose changes to the state constitution, the initiative to propose legislation, and the power of citizens to invoke the referendum on laws passed by the legislature.

The mechanisms of the referendum and initiative, through which many proposals reach the ballot, have been part of Michigan law for many years. The Michigan Constitution of 1908 contained the right of initiative and the right of referendum (as a result of a 1913 amendment). The referendum used by the legislature to submit any bill to a vote of the people and the right of the people to propose amendments to the constitution are also found in the 1908 constitution. The right of initiative is defined in the Constitution of the State of Michigan of 1963, as amended, as ". . . the power to propose laws and to enact and reject laws . . .", and the people's right of referendum is defined as ". . . the power to approve or reject laws enacted by the legislature . . .".

An issue can become a statewide ballot proposal as a result of any of the following actions:

- A citizen petition invoking the **initiative** relative to Michigan's statutes.
- A citizen petition invoking the **referendum** relative to recently enacted laws.
- A citizen petition seeking to **amend Michigan's constitution**.
- Legislation enacted by the legislature which includes a provision that says the legislation cannot become law unless approved by a majority of voters.
- A measure adopted by the legislature seeking to amend the constitution.
- A constitutionally mandated provision which automatically places on the ballot each sixteenth year the question of a general revision of the constitution. This question appeared on the ballot in 1978, 1994, and 2010.

With the exception of the constitutionally mandated provision that automatically places the question of a general revision of the constitution before the electorate every 16 years, every ballot proposal is the result of either citizen or legislative action.

Initiative

In order to exercise the right to initiate legislation, a citizen or group must secure, on petitions, the signatures of registered electors in an amount not less than eight percent of the total vote cast for all candidates for governor at the last gubernatorial election.

The Michigan Election Law, 1954 PA 116, as amended, establishes requirements and provisions that must be followed in order for a proposed piece of legislation to reach the ballot. These requirements include page and print size specifications, the full text of the proposed law to be printed on the petitions, and the manner in which they are to be circulated. Before they are circulated for signatures, all petitions to initiate legislation or amend the constitution must be filed with the Secretary of State to be made available to the public. Completed petitions to initiate legislation are filed with the Secretary of State and the Board of State Canvassers, which then must check validity and sufficiency of the signatures and make an official declaration of approval or disapproval at least two months before the election. The Elections Bureau of the Secretary of State recommends that petitions be filed at least 160 days prior to the general election to assure placement on the ballot, if required. The legislature has 40 days from the time it receives the petition to enact or reject the proposed law or to propose a different measure on the same question. If not enacted, the original initiative proposal and any different measure passed by the legislature must go before the voters as ballot proposals. A substitute passed by the legislature would be a separate proposal. Regarding situations where legislative and citizen-originated measures, or any proposals, are approved and conflict, the constitution provides:

> If two or more measures approved by the electors at the same election conflict, that receiving the highest affirmative vote shall prevail.

If an initiated proposal is passed by a majority of those voting, the new law takes effect ten days after the date of the official declaration of the vote. A new initiated law thus passed cannot be vetoed by the governor. It can only be amended or repealed by a subsequent vote of the electors or by a three-fourths vote of the members in each chamber of the legislature. (Article 2, Section 9, Constitution of the State of Michigan of 1963, as amended.)

The method of initiative used in Michigan is sometimes called the indirect initiative because the measure is first submitted to the legislature rather than directly to the voters.

Referendum

A referendum is also exercised through the gathering of signatures. The number of registered voters needed to invoke the referendum is five percent of the total vote cast for all candidates for governor at the last gubernatorial election. A referendum cannot be proposed to approve or reject a law that appropriates money for state institutions or to meet deficiencies in state funds. A referendum petition must be filed within 90 days of the final adjournment of the legislative session during which the law in question was enacted. As with the initiative, these petitions are filed with the Secretary of State and the Board of State Canvassers is responsible for ascertaining the validity and sufficiency of the signatures.

After the referendum is properly invoked, the law in question must be suspended until the next general election, at which time the law will appear before voters as a ballot proposal. A law approved through the referendum by a majority of the voters takes effect ten days after the date of the official declaration of the vote. Unlike laws approved as a result of the initiative, which require a three-fourths majority of each legislative chamber to be amended, a law approved under referendum may be amended using the normal legislative process. If the law is rejected, it does not go into effect. (Article 2, Section 9, Constitution of the State of Michigan of 1963, as amended.)

Constitutional Amendments

Citizen action, through the petition, can also be used to amend the constitution. In the case of proposed constitutional amendments, signatures of registered voters must equal at least 10 percent of the number of votes cast for all candidates in the last gubernatorial election in order for the matter to go before the electorate. As in the case of initiative and referendum, petitions seeking amendments to the state's constitution are filed with the Secretary of State, and the Board of State Canvassers is responsible for ascertaining the validity and sufficiency of the signatures. Petitions must be filed at least 120 days prior to the election. After the correct number of valid signatures are ascertained, the proposed amendment to the constitution is placed on the ballot at least 60 days prior to the election. Any proposal that is approved by a majority of those voting becomes part of the constitution and takes effect 45 days after the date of the election at which it was approved. (Article 12, Section 2, Constitution of the State of Michigan of 1963, as amended.)

Legislative Action

Ballot proposals placed before the electorate as the result of legislative action are of three types: proposed amendments to the constitution (traditionally proposed as joint resolutions of the two legislative chambers), bills passed by the legislature and approved by the governor that stipulate that voter approval is necessary for the bill to become law, and questions pertaining to the state borrowing money for specific purposes.

Nothing in the constitution may be altered without the approval of the voters. Thus, any measure by the legislature to amend the constitution must be placed on the ballot. An amendment proposed by the legislature in the form of a joint resolution can be introduced into either the Senate or the House of Representatives. In order to become a ballot proposal, such a measure must be agreed to by a two-thirds majority of the members in each chamber. If passed by the legislature at least 60 days before the election, the measure is placed on the ballot at the next general or special election. If approved by a majority of those voting on the ballot proposal, the measure becomes part of the constitution 45 days after the date of the election at which it was approved. (Article 12, Section 1, Constitution of the State of Michigan of 1963, as amended.)

The legislature may, in effect, ask for voter approval of a bill. This may be done for any bill that has passed the legislature and has been approved by the governor, except one appropriating money. In order for a ballot proposal to go before the voters in this manner, the bill must contain a provision that the bill cannot become law unless it receives approval from a majority of those voting. (Article 4, Section 34, Constitution of the State of Michigan of 1963, as amended.)

Another manner in which a proposal goes before the people involves the state borrowing money for specific purposes. Through an act (or acts) by the legislature which is adopted by a two-thirds majority of the members in each chamber, the question of borrowing money may go before the electorate. The proposal must state the amount to be borrowed, the specific purpose to which the funds are to be devoted, and the method of repayment. (Article 9, Section 15, Constitution of the State of Michigan of 1963, as amended.)

Ballot Proposal Language

A great deal of attention, and occasional controversy, is often focused on the actual ballot language of proposals. The language that is printed on the ballots as "Proposal 17-1," "Proposal 17-2," etc. is often different than the wording of the actual amendment or law that is being considered. The length of some measures and the technical language used to gain legal clarity prevent an entire measure from being reproduced on the ballot. The important task of approving the summary of each proposal into a yes or no question in less than 100 words (excluding the title) is the responsibility of the Board of State Canvassers. The wording that is finalized as the ballot proposal is often the result of many hours of discussion and may involve public input.

Recent Ballot Proposals

Since the ratification by Michigan voters of the current constitution in 1963, there have been many significant changes in our state that have come about because of ballot proposals. Many elements of our everyday lives have been impacted by this method of direct citizen participation. Things such as daylight savings time, the legal drinking age, the removal of sales tax on food and prescription drugs, the prohibition of nonreturnable beverage containers, the Vietnam era veterans bonus, tax limitations, school financing, and setting term limits for state elected officials.

In all, there have been 80 proposed amendments to the Michigan Constitution of 1963. Thirty-three of these have resulted from initiatory petitions, while 44 have been placed on the ballot by the legislature. Also included are three questions of calling a constitutional convention: in 1978, 1994, and 2010, which were all defeated. Of the 80 total proposed amendments to the constitution, 34 have been approved by the voters of Michigan.

There have been 14 occasions in which the initiative has brought a proposed law before the people for a vote under our present state constitution. Eight of these proposals have been passed by the voters. There have been nine instances of the legislature approving initiatives proposed by the citizens, which eliminated the need for the measures to go before voters.

Twenty-four instances of the referendum (citizen and legislative) bringing legislation to the electorate for approval or rejection have occurred since the Michigan Constitution of 1963 became effective on January 1, 1964. Eleven of these referenda were approved by the voters.

LAWS PROPOSED BY INITIATIVE PETITION AND SUBMITTED TO THE PEOPLE, 1964-2018

Subject of Petition	Date of Election	Action	Vote For	Against
New legislation to allow licensed physicians to perform abortions upon demand if period of gestation has not exceeded 20 weeks.	Nov. 1972	Rejected	1,270,416	1,958,265
Repeal Act 6 of 1967, to permit the establishment of daylight saving time in Michigan.	Nov. 1972	Adopted	1,754,887	1,460,724
New legislation to prohibit use of nonreturnable beverage containers; to require refundable cash deposits for returnable containers; and to provide penalties for violation of the law.	Nov. 1976	Adopted[1]	2,160,398	1,227,254
Amend section 33 of, and add section 33a to, Act 232 of 1953, to revise standards for grant of parole and to prohibit grant of parole for certain defined crimes until court-imposed minimum sentence is served.	Nov. 1978	Adopted[2]	2,075,599	711,262
Amend sections 3105, 3140, and 3204 of Act 236 of 1961, to prohibit a lender from using a "due on sale" clause in foreclosure proceedings on a mortgage or land contract unless security is impaired.	Nov. 1982	Rejected	1,344,463	1,445,897
Amend title and sections 6a and 6b of Act 3 of 1939, to prohibit utility increases without full notice or hearing and to amend rate adjustment provisions.	Nov. 1982	Adopted[3]	1,472,442	1,431,884
New legislation calling for mutual, verifiable nuclear weapons freeze between the United States and the Union of Soviet Socialist Republics and requiring transmission of communication to United States government officials.	Nov. 1982	Adopted[4]	1,585,809	1,216,172
Amendments to auto insurance statutes.	Nov. 1992	Rejected	1,482,577	2,480,032
Amend the Natural Resources and Environmental Protection Act to limit bear hunting season and prohibit the use of bait and dogs to hunt bear. . . .	Nov. 1996	Rejected	1,379,340	2,225,675
New legislation to permit casino gaming in qualified cities.	Nov. 1996	Adopted[5]	1,878,542	1,768,156
Amendatory legislation to legalize the prescription of a legal dose of medication to terminally ill, competent, informed adults in order to commit suicide.	Nov. 1998	Rejected	859,381	2,116,154
Amend School Aid Act to set mandatory funding levels.	Nov. 2006	Rejected	1,366,355	2,259,247
New legislation, the Medical Marihuana Act.	Nov. 2008	Adopted[6]	3,006,820	1,790,889
Authorize and legalize possession, use and cultivation of marijuana products by individuals who are at least 21 years of age and older, and commercial sales of marijuana through state-licensed retailers	Nov. 2018	Approved	2,356,422	1,859,675

[1] Compiled as §445.571 et seq. of the Michigan Compiled Laws.

[2] Compiled as §§791.233 and 791.233b of the Michigan Compiled Laws.

[3] Following the enactment of Public Act 212 of 1982, which amended Public Act 3 of 1939 and was made subject to referendum, the legislature received an initiative petition to amend the 1939 statute, upon which it failed to act. Under the provisions of Const 1963, art II, §9, the petition was placed on the ballot as Proposal D. Public Act 212 was placed on the ballot as Proposal H, following a court challenge to its submission to the voters (*Michigan State Chamber of Commerce* v *Secretary of State*, Court of Appeals No 65841 (1982)).

At the November 1982 general election, both Proposals D and H were approved, with Proposal H receiving 1,670,381 votes to Proposal D's 1,472,442 votes. Subsequently, an action was commenced in Ingham County Circuit Court seeking a declaratory judgment as to which of the two conflicting proposals would become effective. At the request of the governor, the Michigan Supreme Court asked the lower court to certify the controlling questions directly to the supreme court. Addressing the issue of whether Proposal H was validly enacted, the supreme court ruled that the legislature had enacted Proposal H subject to voter approval consistent with its power to approve legislation subject to referendum under Const 1963, art IV, §34. The court rejected the argument that the legislature was bound to act on the initiative under Const 1963, art II, §9, pointing out that when the legislature enacted Proposal H, it had not yet received the certified initiative petition which later became Proposal D. *In re Proposals D and H, Michigan State Chamber of Commerce* v *State of Michigan,* 417 Mich 409, 398 NW2d 848 (1983).

To determine which proposal would become effective, the court "borrowed" the provision of Const 1963, art II, §9, which states that if 2 or more measures approved by voters conflict, that receiving the highest affirmative vote shall prevail. The court held that Proposal H would become the effective statute based on its higher affirmative vote in the election. *In re Proposals D and H, supra.*

[4] Compiled as §3.851 et seq. of the Michigan Compiled Laws.

[5] Compiled as §432.201 et seq. of the Michigan Compiled Laws.

[6] Compiled as §333.26421 et seq. of the Michigan Compiled Laws.

REFERENDA ON LEGISLATION ENACTED
BY THE LEGISLATURE, 1964-2018

Subject of Referendum	Date of Election	Action	Vote	
			For	Against
Act 240 of 1964, to amend sections 685, 696, 706, 737, 775, 782, 786, 803, and 804 of Act 116 of 1954, to institute use of Massachusetts ballot in Michigan to prevent straight party ticket voting.[1] *(Referendum Petition)*	Nov. 1964	Rejected	795,546	1,515,875
Act 6 of 1967, to permit establishment of daylight saving time in Michigan.[1] *(Referendum Petition)*	Nov. 1968	Rejected	1,402,562	1,403,052
Act 76 of 1968, to authorize issuance of bonds for planning, acquisition, and construction of facilities for prevention and abatement of water pollution and for loans and grants to municipalities.[2] *(Legislative Action)*	Nov. 1968	Adopted[3]	1,906,385	796,079
Act 257 of 1968, to authorize issuance of bonds to provide funding for public recreational facilities and programs and for loans and grants to municipalities.[2] *(Legislative Action)*	Nov. 1968	Adopted[4]	1,384,254	1,235,681
Act 304 of 1969, to authorize issuance of bonds for urban redevelopment to increase the supply of low-income housing and for loans and grants to municipalities and redevelopment corporations.[2] *(Legislative Action)*	Nov. 1970	Rejected	921,482	1,388,737
Act 231 of 1972, to authorize issuance of bonds to provide funding for bonus payments and educational benefits to Vietnam and other veterans.[2] *(Legislative Action)*	Nov. 1972	Rejected	1,490,968	1,603,203
Act 106 of 1974, to authorize issuance of bonds to provide funding for bonus payments to Vietnam and other veterans.[2] *(Legislative Action)*	Nov. 1974	Adopted[5]	1,668,641	700,041
Act 245 of 1974, to authorize issuance of bonds to provide funding to plan, acquire, construct, and equip transportation systems and to make loans and grants for that purpose.[2] *(Legislative Action)*	Nov. 1974	Rejected	963,576	1,319,586
Act 250 of 1980, to amend sections 51 and 475 of Act 281 of 1976, to increase the state income tax 0.1% for 5 years to fund the construction of regional correctional facilities, the demolition of the Michigan Reformatory, and other state and local correctional projects.[6] *(Legislative Action)*	Nov. 1980	Rejected	1,288,999	2,202,042
Act 212 of 1982, to amend sections 6a and 6b of Act 3 of 1939, to prohibit certain utility rate adjustment clauses, utility rate increases without notice and hearing, and acceptance of employment with any utility for 2 years by member of 81st Legislature.[6] *(Legislative Action)*	Nov. 1982	Adopted[7]	1,670,381	1,131,990
Act 59 of 1987, to prohibit use of public funds for the abortion of a recipient of welfare benefits unless the abortion is necessary to save the life of the mother.[1] *(Referendum Petition)*	Nov. 1988	Adopted[8]	1,959,727	1,486,371
Act 326 of 1988, to authorize issuance of bonds to finance environmental protection programs that would clean up environmental contamination sites and address related problems.[2] *(Legislative Action)*	Nov. 1988	Adopted[9]	2,528,109	774,451
Act 327 of 1988 to authorize issuance of bonds to finance state and local public recreation projects.[2] *(Legislative Action)*	Nov. 1988	Adopted[10]	2,055,290	1,206,465
Act 143 of 1993, to reduce auto insurance rates; place limits on personal injury benefits, fees paid to health care providers, and right to sue; and allow rate reduction for accident-free driving. *(Referendum Petition)*	Nov. 1994	Rejected	1,165,732	1,812,526
Act 118 of 1994, to amend certain sections of Michigan Bingo Act. *(Referendum Petition)*	Nov. 1996	Rejected	1,511,063	1,936,198

REFERENDA ON LEGISLATION ENACTED
BY THE LEGISLATURE, 1964-2018 *(Cont.)*

Subject of Referendum	Date of Election	Action	Vote For	Vote Against
Act 377 of 1996, an amendment regarding the management of Michigan's wildlife populations. *(Legislative Action)*	Nov. 1996	Adopted[11]	2,413,730	1,099,262
Act 284 of 1998, to authorize bonds for environmental and natural resources protection programs. *(Legislative Action)*	Nov. 1998	Adopted[12]	1,821,006	1,081,988
Act 269 of 2001, to amend certain sections of Michigan election law. *(Referendum Petition)*	Nov. 2002	Rejected	1,199,236	1,775,043
Act 396 of 2002, to authorize bonds for sewage treatment works projects, storm water projects and water pollution projects.[2] *(Legislative Action)*	Nov. 2002	Adopted[13]	1,774,053	1,172,612
Act 160 of 2004, to allow hunting season for mourning doves.	Nov. 2006	Rejected	1,137,379	2,534,680
Act 4 of 2011, to authorize the governor to appoint an emergency manager to act in place of local government officials.	Nov. 2012	Rejected	2,130,354	2,370,601
Act 80 of 2014, to allocate use tax revenue for various local purposes.	Aug. 2014	Adopted[14]	863,459	382,770
Act 520 of 2012, to designate wolf as game for hunting purposes and authorize the first wolf hunting season.	Nov. 2014	Rejected	1,318,080	1,606,328
Act 21 of 2013, to allow the Natural Resources Commission to designate certain animals as game for hunting purposes and establish the first hunting season for game animals without legislative action. ..	Nov. 2014	Rejected	1,051,426	1,856,603

[1] Referendum invoked by petition pursuant to Const 1963, art II, §9.

[2] Referendum required to borrow money for specific purposes pursuant to Const 1963, art IX, §15.

[3] Compiled as §323.371 et seq. of the Michigan Compiled Laws.

[4] Compiled as §318.351 et seq. of the Michigan Compiled Laws.

[5] Compiled as §35.1001 et seq. of the Michigan Compiled Laws.

[6] Referendum invoked by statute pursuant to Const 1963, art IV, §34.

[7] Following the enactment of Public Act 212 of 1982, which amended Public Act 3 of 1939 and was made subject to referendum, the legislature received an initiative petition to amend the 1939 statute, upon which it failed to act. Under the provisions of Const 1963, art II, §9, the petition was placed on the ballot as Proposal D. Public Act 212 was placed on the ballot as Proposal H, following a court challenge to its submission to the voters (*Michigan State Chamber of Commerce* v *Secretary of State*, Court of Appeals No 65841 (1982)).

    At the November 1982 general election, both Proposals D and H were approved, with Proposal H receiving 1,670,381 votes to Proposal D's 1,472,442 votes. Subsequently, an action was commenced in Ingham County Circuit Court seeking a declaratory judgment as to which of the two conflicting proposals would become effective. At the request of the governor, the Michigan Supreme Court asked the lower court to certify the controlling questions directly to the supreme court. Addressing the issue of whether Proposal H was validly enacted, the supreme court ruled that the legislature had enacted Proposal H subject to voter approval consistent with its power to approve legislation subject to referendum under Const 1963, art IV, §34. The court rejected the argument that the legislature was bound to act on the initiative under Const 1963, art II, §9, pointing out that when the legislature enacted Proposal H, it had not yet received the certified initiative petition which later became Proposal D. *In re Proposals D and H, Michigan State Chamber of Commerce* v *State of Michigan*, 417 Mich 409, 398 NW2d 848 (1983).

    To determine which proposal would become effective, the court "borrowed" the provision of Const 1963, art II, §9, which states that if 2 or more measures approved by voters conflict, that receiving the highest affirmative vote shall prevail. The court held that Proposal H would become the effective statute based on its higher affirmative vote in the election. *In re Proposals D and H, supra.*

    Compiled as §§460.6a and 460.6b of the Michigan Compiled Laws.

[8] This added section was proposed by initiative petition pursuant to Const 1963, art II, §9. On June 17, 1987, the initiative petition was approved by an affirmative vote of the majority of the senators-elect and filed with the secretary of state. On June 23, 1987, the initiative petition was approved by an affirmative vote of the majority of the members-elect of the house of representatives and filed with the secretary of state. The legislature did not vote pursuant to Const 1963, art IV, §27 to give immediate effect to this enactment.

    In affirming the decision of the court of appeals in *Frey* v *Director, Department of Social Services*, the Michigan Supreme Court held that when a law is proposed by initiative and enacted by the legislature without change or amendment within forty days as required by Const 1963, art II, §9, it takes effect ninety days after the end of the session in which it was passed unless two-thirds of the members of each house of the legislature, as provided by Const 1963, art IV, §27, vote to give the law immediate effect. Public Act 59 of 1987, not having received votes in favor of immediate effect by two-thirds of the elected members of each house, may not take effect until ninety days after the end of the session in which it was enacted. *Frey* v *Director, Department of Social Services*, 429 Mich 315; 414 NW2d 873 (1987).

    On March 1, 1988, petitions to invoke the power of referendum with regard to Public Act 59 of 1987 were filed with the secretary of state. On April 13, 1988, the board of state canvassers certified the validity of a sufficient number of petition signatures to invoke the referendum.

REFERENDA ON LEGISLATION ENACTED
BY THE LEGISLATURE, 1964-2018 *(Cont.)*

In a letter opinion to C. Patrick Babcock, Director, Department of Social Services, dated March 28, 1988, the attorney general addressed the following question: "[I]f the filing of petitions, which include, if they are valid, a sufficient number of signatures to properly invoke a referendum, stays the effective date of Public Act 59 of 1987, which will otherwise become effective on March 30, 1988?" The attorney general concluded that "when a petition seeking referendum, which on its face meets legal requirements, is filed the signatures appearing on that petition are presumed valid and the statute at issue is stayed or suspended until either the petitions are found to be invalid or a vote of the people occurs."

Public Act 59 of 1987, as enacted by the legislature, was submitted to the people by referendum petition and approved by a majority of the votes cast at the general election held November 8, 1988. The board of state canvassers officially declared the vote to be 1,959,727 (for) and 1,486,371 (against) on December 2, 1988.

[9] Compiled as §299.651 et seq. of the Michigan Compiled Laws.

[10] Compiled as §318.551 et seq. of the Michigan Compiled Laws.

[11] Compiled as §324.40113a of the Michigan Compiled Laws.

[12] Compiled as §324.95101 et seq. of the Michigan Compiled Laws.

[13] Compiled as §324.95201 et seq. of the Michigan Compiled Laws.

[14] Compiled as §205.91 et seq. of the Michigan Compiled Laws.

Please see page 98 for proposed consitutional amendments placed on the ballot.

Official Canvass
of Votes

———⟫•⟪———

Special Primary Election
August 8, 2017

Special Primary Election
August 7, 2018

Primary Election
August 7, 2018

Special General Election
November 7, 2017

Special General Election
November 6, 2018

General Election
November 6, 2018

SPECIAL PRIMARY ELECTIONS

AUGUST 8, 2017

———◆———

STATE REPRESENTATIVE

1st State Representative District   *Partial Term Ending January 1, 2019[1]*

County	Total by County	Mark Corcoran (Rep.)	William Phillips (Rep.)	Sandra Bucciero (Dem.)	Ronald D. Diebel (Dem.)	John William Donahue (Dem.)	Burgess Dwight Foster (Dem.)	Kirkland W. Garey (Dem.)
Wayne........	7,884	819	282	956	36	76	78	107
Totals	7,884	819	282	956	36	76	78	107

Keith D. Hollowell (Dem.)	Justin Johnson (Dem.)	Gowana Mancill, Jr. (Dem.)	Pamela M. Sossi (Dem.)	Tenisha Yancey (Dem.)	Washington Youson (Dem.)	Gregory Creswell (Lib.)
150	615	45	2,017	2,215	415	73
150	615	45	2,017	2,215	415	73

109th State Representative District   *Partial Term Ending January 1, 2019[2]*

County	Total by County	Rich Rossway (Rep.)	Sara Cambensy (Dem.)	Tom Curry (Dem.)	Joseph Derocha (Dem.)	Jeremy Hosking (Dem.)
Alger.........	1,154	284	407	170	134	159
Luce	275	130	62	7	14	62
Marquette	9,330	1,111	2,882	186	2,172	2,979
Schoolcraft	554	146	126	23	115	144
Total......	11,313	1,671	3,477	386	2,435	3,344

---

[1] To fill a remaining term ending January 1, 2019 after Representative Brian Banks resigned effective February 6, 2017.
[2] To fill a remaining term ending January 1, 2019 after the death of Representative John Kivela on May 9, 2017.

SPECIAL PRIMARY ELECTIONS

AUGUST 7, 2018

───≫─◦─≪───

U.S. CONGRESS

13th Congressional District *Partial Term Ending 01/03/2019[1]*

County	Total by County	David Dudenhoefer (Rep.) Write-in	Ian Conyers (Dem.)	Brenda Jones (Dem.)	Rashida Tlaib (Dem.)	Bill Wild (Dem.)	Royce Kinniebrew (Dem.) Write-in	Clyde Darnell Lynch (Dem.) Write-in
Wayne........	87,092	277	9,749	32,769	31,121	13,174	0	2
Total......	87,092	277	9,749	32,769	31,121	13,174	0	2

───≫─◦─≪───

STATE REPRESENTATIVE

68th State Representative District *Partial Term Ending 1/1/2019[2]*

County	Total by County	Rosalinda Hernandez (Rep.)	Sarah Anthony (Dem.)	Grant Bradley (Dem.)	Kelly Collison (Dem.)	Paul DeWeese (Dem.)	Eric Nelson (Dem.)
Ingham.......	16,531	2,909	7,986	477	3,236	1,477	446
Total......	16,531	2,909	7,986	477	3,236	1,477	446

───≫─◦─≪───

STATE SENATE

2nd State Senate District[3]

County	Total by County	Abraham Aiyash (Dem.)	Brian Banks (Dem.)	George Cushingberry, Jr. (Dem.)	Adam Hollier (Dem.)	LaMar Lemmons (Dem.)	John Olumba (Dem.)	Joe Ricci (Dem.)
Wayne........	26,971	6,462	5,055	1,355	7,084	3,086	1,967	1,957
Total......	26,971	6,462	5,055	1,355	7,084	3,086	1,967	1,957

William Phillips (Dem.) Write-in	Regina Williams (Dem.) Write-in
0	5
0	5

---

[1] To fill a remaining term ending January 3, 2019 after Congressman John Conyers, Jr. resigned effective December 5, 2017.
[2] To fill a remaining term ending January 1, 2019 after Representative Andy Schor resigned to take a position in local government.
[3] To fill a remaining term ending January 1, 2019 after Senator Bert Johnson resigned effective March 2, 2018.

GOVERNOR
4-YEAR TERM

County	Total by County	Brian N. Calley (Rep.)	Patrick Colbeck (Rep.)	Jim Hines (Rep.)	Bill Schuette (Rep.)	Evan Space (Rep.)	William Cobbs (Dem.)	Abdul El-Sayed (Dem.)	Shri Thanedar (Dem.)	Gretchen Whitmer (Dem.)	Bill Gelineau (Lib.)	John J. Tater (Lib.)
Alcona	3,170	371	373	317	1,102	0	0	132	187	677	7	4
Alger	2127	253	112	179	486	0	0	249	320	525	2	1
Allegan	26,225	4,397	1,827	2,173	8,434	0	0	2,721	1,601	4,948	80	44
Alpena	6,419	681	450	584	1,995	0	0	394	439	1,855	16	5
Antrim	6,470	1,158	737	424	1,775	0	0	664	272	1,428	9	3
Arenac	3,510	465	166	320	1,282	0	0	226	297	740	9	5
Baraga	1434	121	67	164	463	0	0	104	178	336	0	1
Barry	14,568	4,369	925	838	3,790	0	0	1,162	887	2,529	37	31
Bay	23,338	2,365	741	1,617	6,097	0	0	2,727	3,051	6,685	35	20
Benzie	5,222	780	282	292	1,384	0	0	726	302	1,446	7	3
Berrien	28,105	3,181	2957	2178	9,060	0	0	3,407	1,323	5,890	61	48
Branch	7,917	1,105	598	707	2,890	0	0	573	602	1,416	20	6
Calhoun	22,874	3,136	1,458	1,563	6,822	0	0	2,498	2,186	5,126	46	39
Cass	7,282	691	906	644	2,519	0	0	688	323	1,490	11	10
Charlevoix	6,572	1,264	344	443	1,830	0	1	604	351	1,719	6	10
Cheboygan	6,265	1,114	842	449	1,642	0	0	340	400	1,459	12	7
Chippewa	6,538	1,036	315	514	1,886	0	0	518	513	1,729	18	9
Clare	5,516	780	234	462	2,003	0	2	341	391	1,289	7	7
Clinton	17,748	3,768	1,208	997	3,614	0	0	1,429	1,147	5,520	32	33
Crawford	3,163	610	121	257	1,073	0	0	181	204	698	12	6
Delta	7,093	546	182	647	2,498	0	0	410	988	1,809	7	6
Dickinson	5,122	390	212	649	2,003	0	0	332	608	919	2	7
Eaton	25,564	4,099	1,946	1,707	5,009	0	1	2,001	2,453	8,249	55	44
Emmet	8,840	1,590	669	490	2,421	0	0	983	411	2,249	17	10
Genesee	81,446	6,582	3,147	4,551	16,849	0	15	11,492	11,826	26,766	117	101
Gladwin	5,869	674	295	525	2,227	0	0	317	475	1,342	6	8
Gogebic	3,159	274	122	239	710	0	0	264	378	1,165	4	3
Grand Traverse	26,760	4,222	1,238	1,454	6,765	1	7	5,231	1,191	6,566	54	31
Gratiot	6,741	966	270	447	2,320	0	0	719	479	1,519	5	16

GOVERNOR (Cont.)

County	Total by County	Brian N. Calley (Rep.)	Patrick Colbeck (Rep.)	Jim Hines (Rep.)	Bill Schuette (Rep.)	Evan Space (Rep.)	William Cobbs (Dem.)	Abdul El-Sayed (Dem.)	Shri Thanedar (Dem.)	Gretchen Whitmer (Dem.)	Bill Gelineau (Lib.)	John J. Tater (Lib.)
Hillsdale	7,711	1,105	849	890	2,595	0	1	395	654	1,191	16	15
Houghton	6,418	431	612	440	1,683	0	0	902	649	1,675	16	10
Huron	7,650	1,488	337	744	3,205	0	0	369	431	1,070	2	4
Ingham	61,600	6,168	2,431	2,441	7,476	0	0	9,490	6,210	27,142	150	92
Ionia	11,405	4,156	593	540	2,337	0	1	866	645	2,228	21	19
Iosco	5,878	682	330	582	1,868	0	0	368	533	1,494	13	7
Iron	2333	230	147	315	552	0	0	159	421	503	4	2
Isabella	12,075	1,780	447	635	3,380	0	0	1,823	798	3,175	21	16
Jackson	31,837	4,317	2,531	3,228	8,537	0	0	2,561	3,562	6,913	87	101
Kalamazoo	54,760	6,412	1,802	2,720	11,472	1	0	11,825	4,898	15,404	144	82
Kalkaska	3,980	691	353	341	1,299	0	0	272	233	775	8	8
Kent	133,450	20,258	8,355	7,149	32,672	1	1	26,653	9,278	28,544	358	181
Keweenaw	765	65	65	61	225	0	0	81	73	193	1	1
Lake	2515	408	105	200	789	0	0	116	260	633	3	1
Lapeer	21,132	3,033	1,557	1,559	7,719	0	0	1,605	1,111	4,467	43	38
Leelanau	8,523	1,268	336	390	2,088	1	0	1,577	390	2,463	4	7
Lenawee	16,230	1,768	2,021	1,094	4,350	0	0	2,103	717	4,112	36	29
Livingston	48,456	6,520	7,768	2,349	13,238	0	3	5,362	1,834	11,204	123	55
Luce	1,209	238	45	103	404	0	0	50	75	286	3	5
Mackinaw	3,100	562	174	246	915	0	0	187	177	832	3	4
Macomb	177,101	19,537	9,870	7,774	49,835	0	7	24,323	14,319	50,841	317	278
Manistee	6,031	926	339	434	1,905	0	0	476	446	1,491	9	5
Marquette	13,709	1,003	369	958	2,579	0	1	2,765	1,829	4,159	25	21
Mason	7,497	1,055	850	460	2,326	0	0	512	452	1,808	16	18
Mecosta	7,633	1,306	333	579	2,680	0	2	614	395	1,696	14	14
Menominee	2,979	312	169	201	1,013	0	1	228	175	865	12	3
Midland	19,623	1,983	580	1,076	8,226	0	0	2,165	1,120	4,406	40	27
Missaukee	3,644	704	188	421	1,539	0	0	116	151	518	4	3
Monroe	26,966	2,806	1,712	1,768	8,293	28	11	2,901	1,938	7,398	58	53
Montcalm	11,787	2,577	748	852	3,609	0	0	883	844	2,219	26	29
Montmorency	2541	470	243	220	825	0	0	82	173	519	5	4
Muskegon	32,655	3,130	2,077	1,701	7,957	0	4	4,426	4,375	8,887	69	29
Newaygo	10,617	1,490	1,419	727	3,793	0	0	704	688	1,754	23	19
Oakland	315,581	37,388	17,007	9,728	67,253	0	39	59,491	24,619	99,111	552	393
Oceana	5,794	772	579	366	2,012	0	0	443	402	1,199	14	7
Ogemaw	5,576	730	273	712	1,976	0	0	313	449	1,112	7	4
Ontonagon	1532	107	167	230	342	0	0	83	194	400	7	2
Osceola	4,717	881	306	510	1,856	0	0	221	182	744	11	6

GOVERNOR (Cont.)

County	Total by County	Brian N. Calley (Rep.)	Patrick Colbeck (Rep.)	Jim Hines (Rep.)	Bill Schuette (Rep.)	Evan Space (Rep.)	William Cobbs (Dem.)	Abdul El-Sayed (Dem.)	Shri Thanedar (Dem.)	Gretchen Whitmer (Dem.)	Bill Gelineau (Lib.)	John J. Tater (Lib.)
Oscoda	2069	347	182	255	719	0	0	82	120	358	3	3
Otsego	6,148	1,294	427	541	1,970	0	0	379	304	1,210	15	5
Ottawa	61,416	11,282	5,947	4,892	19,649	0	1	7,494	2,593	9,318	149	91
Presque Isle	3,647	724	208	301	1,139	0	0	167	269	826	5	8
Roscommon	6,905	1,060	245	674	2,519	0	0	301	450	1,639	8	9
Saginaw	42,698	4,188	1,197	4,410	12,029	0	4	4,606	5,117	11,014	76	57
St. Clair	33,884	4,174	2,143	2,489	11,089	1	0	3,473	2,203	8,179	74	59
St. Joseph	8,559	1,116	443	778	2,958	0	0	849	707	1,679	17	12
Sanilac	8,696	1,370	517	822	3,453	0	0	544	444	1,508	18	20
Schoolcraft	1766	149	91	135	524	0	0	84	243	522	0	0
Shiawassee	14,480	1,852	925	1,014	4,336	16	6	1,279	1,104	3,889	34	25
Tuscola	11,867	1,786	491	1,287	4,256	0	0	740	897	2,381	15	14
Van Buren	14,544	2,178	595	960	4,411	0	0	1,736	1,231	3,365	38	30
Washtenaw	94,979	5,172	6,205	1,700	9,049	0	9	33,193	6,073	33,317	163	98
Wayne	336,579	21,118	18,835	7,103	45,261	3	70	77,828	59,065	106,457	450	389
Wexford	7,715	1,630	364	799	2,825	0	0	481	342	1,254	10	10
Totals	2,127,998	249,185	129,646	108,735	501,959	51	187	342,179	200,645	588,436	4,034	2,941

PRIMARY ELECTION

AUGUST 7, 2018

U.S. SENATE
6-YEAR TERM

County	Total by County	John James (Rep.)	Sandy Pensler (Rep.)	William F. White (Rep. Write-in)	Debbie Stabenow (Dem.)	Tim Yow (Lib. Write-in)
Alcona	2,993	1,221	835	1	936	0
Alger.	2,039	630	349	0	1,060	0
Allegan	24,882	9,150	7,133	0	8,599	0
Alpena	6,099	2,080	1,491	0	2,527	1
Antrim.	6,154	1,815	2,114	0	2,225	0
Arenac	3,310	1,022	1,137	0	1,151	0
Baraga.	1,354	492	269	0	593	0
Barry.	13,595	4,803	4,583	0	4,209	0
Bay.	21,934	4,653	5,724	0	11,557	0
Benzie.	4,934	1,139	1,473	0	2,322	0
Berrien	26,729	10,324	6,258	0	10,147	0
Branch	7,448	2,582	2,526	0	2,340	0
Calhoun	21,738	6,480	6,074	0	9,183	1
Cass	7,019	3,164	1,480	0	2,375	0
Charlevoix.	6,245	1,661	2,066	0	2,517	1
Cheboygan	5,961	1,688	2,199	0	2,071	3
Chippewa	6,159	1,560	2,029	0	2,570	0
Clare.	5,262	1,523	1,861	0	1,878	0
Clinton	16,360	5,500	3,469	0	7,387	4
Crawford.	2,945	810	1,164	0	971	0
Delta.	6,726	2,246	1,429	0	3,051	0
Dickinson	4,857	1,923	1,171	0	1,763	0
Eaton	23,819	7,014	4,959	0	11,844	2
Emmet	8,374	2,368	2,576	0	3,430	0
Genesee	76,424	15,656	14,261	1	46,505	1
Gladwin	5,486	1,612	1,894	0	1,980	0
Gogebic	3,061	892	406	0	1,763	0
Grand Traverse. .	25,250	5,911	7,150	7	12,182	0
Gratiot.	6,306	2,011	1,819	0	2,476	0
Hillsdale	7,156	3,168	1,997	1	1,990	0
Houghton	6,077	1,882	1,091	0	3,104	0
Huron	7,214	2,258	3,204	0	1,752	0
Ingham	57,752	10,298	7,137	0	40,317	0
Ionia	10,404	3,802	3,245	0	3,357	0
Iosco.	5,554	1,612	1,705	0	2,237	0
Iron.	2,236	843	383	0	1,010	0
Isabella	11,242	3,005	2,859	0	5,378	0
Jackson	29,339	9,873	7,705	0	11,761	0
Kalamazoo	51,450	11,130	10,325	0	29,992	3
Kalkaska	3,768	1,073	1,515	0	1,180	0
Kent	126,297	36,006	30,060	3	60,224	4
Keweenaw	719	233	158	0	328	0
Lake	2,369	586	844	0	939	0
Lapeer.	19,885	7,470	5,773	0	6,642	0
Leelanau	8,056	1,885	2,017	0	4,153	1
Lenawee	15,321	6,096	2,762	0	6,463	0
Livingston	45,574	17,476	11,207	0	16,885	6
Luce	1,146	330	433	0	383	0
Mackinac.	2,923	739	1,082	0	1,102	0
Macomb	167,542	43,823	40,254	1	83,459	5
Manistee	5,712	1,509	1,937	0	2,266	0
Marquette	13,047	2,979	1,684	0	8,384	0
Mason.	7,098	2,242	2,232	0	2,624	0

County	Total by County	John James (Rep.)	Sandy Pensler (Rep.)	William F. White (Rep. Write-in)	Debbie Stabenow (Dem.)	Tim Yow (Lib Write-in)
Mecosta.	7,277	2,122	2,632	0	2,523	0
Menominee	2,884	1,135	517	0	1,232	0
Midland.	18,167	5,705	5,362	0	7,100	0
Missauke	3,479	1,289	1,464	0	726	0
Monroe	25,394	8,372	5,652	25	11,320	25
Montcalm	10,983	3,727	3,703	0	3,553	0
Montmorency . .	2,400	731	963	0	706	0
Muskegon	30,450	7,058	7,311	0	16,080	1
Newaygo.	10,012	3,456	3,683	0	2,873	0
Oakland	295,976	75,529	50,653	0	169,774	20
Oceana	5,387	1,830	1,711	0	1,846	0
Ogemaw	5,208	1,594	1,893	0	1,721	0
Ontonagon	1,450	525	277	0	648	0
Osceola.	4,484	1,418	2,015	0	1,051	0
Oscoda	1,927	674	752	0	501	0
Otsego	5,756	1,838	2,176	0	1,742	0
Ottawa	58,218	22,505	17,800	0	17,908	5
Presque Isle. . . .	3,399	897	1,321	0	1,181	0
Roscommon . . .	6,482	1,666	2,630	0	2,186	0
Saginaw	39,626	9,464	11,103	1	19,057	1
St. Clair	31,895	10,877	8,305	0	12,713	0
St. Joseph	8,064	2,779	2,376	0	2,908	1
Sanilac	8,303	3,554	2,423	0	2,326	0
Schoolcraft	1,651	476	366	0	809	0
Shiawassee	13,603	4,256	3,514	14	5,765	54
Tuscola	11,185	3,469	3,982	0	3,734	0
Van Buren	13,590	3,993	3,783	0	5,814	0
Washtenaw	88,686	13,376	7,760	0	67,547	3
Wayne.	309,463	49,446	39,372	3	220,632	10
Wexford	7,365	2,555	2,878	0	1,932	0
Total.	1,994,108	518,564	429,885	57	1,045,450	152

PRIMARY ELECTION

AUGUST 7, 2018

U.S. HOUSE OF REPRESENTATIVES
2-YEAR TERM

1st Congressional District

County	Total by County	Jack Bergman (Rep.)	Matthew Morgan (Dem.)
Alcona	2,042	1,914	128
Alger	1,415	952	463
Alpena	3,965	3,391	574
Antrim	4,594	3,626	968
Baraga	997	755	242
Benzie	3,651	2,437	1,214
Charlevoix	4,487	3,471	1,016
Cheboygan	4,056	3,526	530
Chippewa	4,072	3,408	664
Crawford	2,019	1,788	231
Delta	4,868	3,593	1,275
Dickinson	3,611	3,014	597
Emmet	6,343	4,624	1,719
Gogebic	1,850	1,265	585
Grand Traverse . .	19,199	12,046	7,153
Houghton	4,298	2,901	1,397
Iron	1,180	1,180	0
Kalkaska	2,816	2,404	412
Keweenaw	497	374	123
Leelanau	6,224	3,554	2,670
Luce	845	708	137
Mackinac	2,006	1,685	321
Manistee	3,834	3,140	694
Marquette	8,910	4,522	4,388
Mason	1,258	1,161	97
Menominee	1,953	1,567	386
Montmorency . .	1,627	1,547	80
Ontonagon	1,070	795	275
Oscoda	1,360	1,300	60
Otsego	4,161	3,712	449
Presque Isle	2,287	2,085	202
Schoolcraft	1,070	827	243
Total	112,565	83,272	29,293

2nd Congressional District

County	Total by County	Bill Huizenga (Rep.)	Rob Davidson (Dem.)
Allegan	419	262	157
Kent	26,667	14,219	12,448
Lake	2,170	1,306	864
Mason	4,949	3,054	1,895
Muskegon	28,231	13,188	15,043
Newaygo	9,367	6,684	2,683
Oceana	5,037	3,302	1,735
Ottawa	55,001	37,605	17,396
Total	131,841	79,620	52,221

3rd Congressional District

County	Total by County	Justin Amash (Rep.)	Joe Farrington (Rep.)	Cathy Albro (Dem.)	Fred Wooden (Dem.)
Barry.........	12,313	8,221	0	2,903	1,189
Calhoun	19,422	10,544	8	6,034	2,836
Ionia.........	9,334	6,039	34	2,330	931
Kent.........	90,529	44,552	10	31,101	14,866
Montcalm	793	461	0	251	81
Total......	132,391	69,817	52	42,619	19,903

4th Congressional District

County	Total By County	John Moolenaar (Rep.)	Jerry Hilliard (Dem.)	Zigmond Kozicki (Dem.)
Clare.........	4,884	3,080	1,302	502
Clinton	14,448	7,855	4,377	2,216
Gladwin	5,090	3,282	1,284	524
Gratiot.......	5,926	3,632	1,607	687
Isabella	10,281	5,407	3,220	1,654
Mecosta.......	6,752	4,364	1,573	815
Midland.......	17,165	10,435	3,608	3,122
Missaukee.....	3,264	2,585	484	195
Montcalm	8,917	5,988	2,148	781
Ogemaw......	4,672	3,098	1,122	452
Osceola.......	4,118	3,144	671	303
Roscommon ...	5,897	3,852	1,454	591
Saginaw	18,525	11,781	4,553	2,191
Shiawassee	12,311	6,991	3,716	1,604
Wexford	6,564	4,796	1,144	624
Total......	128,814	80,290	32,263	16,261

5th Congressional District

County	Total County by County	Travis Wines (Rep.)	Daniel Kildee (Dem.)
Arenac	2,833	1,699	1,134
Bay..........	19,598	8,142	11,456
Genesee	70,414	23,676	46,738
Iosco.........	4,906	2,683	2,223
Saginaw	17,448	6,235	11,213
Tuscola.......	3,202	1,970	1,232
Total......	118,401	44,405	73,996

6th Congressional District

County	Total by County	Fred Upton (Rep.)	David Benac (Dem.)	Rich Eichholz (Dem.)	George Franklin (Dem.)	Matt Longjohn (Dem.)
Allegan	22,665	14,340	1,595	1,146	2,514	3,070
Berrien	25,428	15,124	2,401	1,920	2,533	3,450
Cass	6,552	4,143	486	416	736	771
Kalamazoo	49,839	19,395	6,675	3,011	9,046	11,712
St. Joseph	7,597	4,552	657	510	796	1,082
Van Buren.....	12,922	6,958	1,053	716	1,868	2,327
Total......	125,003	64,512	12,867	7,719	17,493	22,412

7th Congressional District

County	Total by County	Tim Walberg (Rep.)	Gretchen Driskell (Dem.)	Steven Friday (Dem.)
Branch	7,183	4,812	1,929	442
Eaton	22,829	10,923	10,371	1,535
Hillsdale	6,837	4,822	1,705	310
Jackson	27,981	16,354	9,464	2,163
Lenawee	15,134	8,457	5,506	1,171
Monroe	24,773	13,214	10,038	1,521
Washtenaw	26,024	10,666	13,417	1,941
Total	130,761	69,248	52,430	9,083

8th Congressional District

County	Total by County	Mike Bishop (Rep.)	Lokesh Kumar (Rep.)	Elissa Slotkin (Dem.)	Chris Smith (Dem.)	Brian Ellison (Lib.)
Ingham	57,949	15,570	2,270	26,302	13,590	217
Livingston	45,939	27,011	1,887	11,699	5,203	139
Oakland	60,106	32,822	2,097	19,818	5,203	166
Total	163,994	75,403	6,254	57,819	23,996	522

9th Congressional District

County	Total by County	Candius Stearns (Rep.)	Martin Brook (Dem.)	Andy Levin (Dem.)	Ellen Cogen Lipton (Dem.)
Macomb	87,725	32,400	2,926	31,148	21,251
Oakland	54,336	15,010	1,939	18,464	18,923
Total	142,061	47,410	4,865	49,612	40,174

10th Congressional District

County	Total by County	Paul Mitchell (Rep.)	Frank Accavitti, Jr. (Dem.)	Kimberly Bizon (Dem.)	Michael McCarthy (Dem.)
Huron	6,466	4,779	310	839	538
Lapeer	18,321	12,015	1,301	3230	1,775
Macomb	65,451	37,716	10,301	11,371	6,063
St. Clair	30,189	17,249	4,022	4,384	4,534
Sanilac	7,919	5,589	661	964	705
Tuscola	6,865	4,519	452	1,156	738
Total	135,211	81,867	17,047	21,944	14,353

11th Congressional District

County	Total by County	Kerry Bentivolio (Rep.)	Lena Epstein (Rep.)	Klint Kesto (Rep.)	Mike Kowall (Rep.)	Rocky Raczkowski (Rep.)	Tim Greimel (Dem.)	Suneel Gupta (Dem.)
Oakland	109,544	5,304	16,509	9,098	12,120	13,157	13,131	11,073
Wayne.	68,326	4,527	10,416	3,115	3,891	9,059	6,542	8,177
Total.	177,870	9,831	26,925	12,213	16,011	22,216	19,673	19,250

Fayrouz Saad (Dem.)	Nancy Skinner (Dem.)	Haley Stevens (Dem.)	Leonard Schwartz (Lib.)
9,009	5,615	14,213	315
8,490	3,792	10,096	221
17,499	9,407	24,309	536

12th Congressional District

County	Total by County	Jeff Jones (Rep.)	Debbie Dingell (Dem.)
Washtenaw	59,734	7,380	52,354
Wayne.	77,383	26,459	50,924
Total.	137,117	33,839	103,278

13th Congressional District

County	Total by County	David Dudenhoefer (Rep.) Write-in	Ian Conyers (Dem.)	Shanelle Jackson (Dem.)	Brenda Jones (Dem.)	Rashida Tlaib (Dem.)	Bill Wild (Dem.)	Coleman Young, II (Dem.)
Wayne.	89,740	419	5,866	4,853	26,941	27,841	12,613	11,172
Total.	89,740	419	5,866	4,853	26,941	27,841	12,613	11,172

Royce Kinniebrew (Dem.) Write-in	Kimberly Knott (Dem.) Write-in
2	33
2	33

14th Congressional District

County	Total by County	Marc Herschfus (Rep.)	Brenda L. Lawrence (Dem.)
Oakland	67,020	12,000	55,020
Wayne.	57,990	6,546	51,444
Total.	125,010	18,546	106,464

PRIMARY ELECTION
AUGUST 7, 2018

STATE SENATE
4-YEAR TERM

1st State Senate District

County	Total by County	Pauline Montie (Rep.)	Stephanie Chang (Dem.)	James Cole, Jr. (Dem.)	Nicholas Rivera (Dem.)	Stephanie Roehm (Dem.)	Bettie Cook Scott (Dem.)	Alberta Talabi (Dem.)
Wayne.........	41,383	8,426	16,427	1,717	941	1,464	3,698	8,710
Total......	41,383	8,426	16,427	1,717	941	1,464	3,698	8,710

2nd State Senate District

County	Total by County	John Hauler (Rep.)	Lisa Papas (Rep.)	Abraham Aiyash (Dem.)	Brian Banks (Dem.)	Tommy Campbell (Dem.)	George Cushingberry, Jr. (Dem.)	Lawrence Gannan (Dem.)
Wayne.........	34,654	3,289	3,879	5,766	4,725	265	1,121	555
Total......	34,654	3,289	3,879	5,766	4,725	265	1,121	555

Adam Hollier (Dem.)	LaMar Lemmons (Dem.)	Anam Miah (Dem.)	John Olumba (Dem.)	William Phillips (Dem.)	Regina Williams (Dem.)
6,938	2,512	931	1,747	328	2,598
6,938	2,512	931	1,747	328	2,598

3rd State Senate District

County	Total by County	Kathy Stecker (Rep.)	Anita Belle (Dem.)	Terry Burrell (Dem.)	Sylvia Santana (Dem.)	Gary Woronchak (Dem.)
Wayne.........	34,699	4,233	4,367	1,668	12,646	11,785
Total......	34,699	4,233	4,367	1,668	12,646	11,785

4th State Senate District

County	Total by County	Angela Savino (Rep.)	Marshall Bullock II (Dem.)	Fred Durhal III (Dem.)	Carron Pinkins (Dem.)
Wayne.........	33,320	5,345	12,384	10,706	4,885
Total......	33,320	5,345	12,384	10,706	4,885

5th State Senate District

County	Total by County	DeShawn Wilkins (Rep.)	Betty Jean Alexander (Dem.)	David Knezek (Dem.)
Wayne.	39,675	4,944	18,928	15,803
Total.	39,675	4,944	18,928	15,803

6th State Senate District

County	Total by County	Brenda Jones (Rep.)	Erika Geiss (Dem.)	Robert Kosowski (Dem.)
Wayne.	41,968	12,013	19,596	10,359
Total.	41,968	12,013	19,596	10,359

7th State Senate District

County	Total by County	Laura Cox (Rep.)	Dayna Polehanki (Dem.)	Ghulam Qadir (Dem.)	Joseph LeBlanc (Lib.)
Wayne.	67,170	29,094	27,826	10,016	234
Total.	67,170	29,094	27,826	10,016	234

8th State Senate District

County	Total by County	Ken Goike (Rep.)	Pete Lucido (Rep.)	Patrick Biange (Dem.)	Raymond Filipek (Dem.)	Paul Francis (Dem.)
Wayne.	55,540	9,565	24,261	6,612	4,989	10,113
Total.	55,540	9,565	24,261	6,612	4,989	10,113

9th State Senate District

County	Total by County	Jeff Bonnell (Rep.)	Fred Kuplicki (Rep.)	Kristina Lodovisi (Dem.)	Paul J. Wojno (Dem.)
Macomb	44,040	7,861	7,003	10,688	18,488
Total.	44,040	7,861	7,003	10,688	18,488

10th State Senate District

County	Total by County	Joseph Bogdan (Rep.)	Mike MacDonald (Rep.)	Michael Shallal (Rep.)	Henry Yanez (Dem.)	Mike Saliba (Lib.)
Macomb	49,091	3,568	15,073	6,704	23,610	136
Total.	49,091	3,568	15,073	6,704	23,610	136

11th State Senate District

County	Total by County	Boris Tuman (Rep.)	Crystal Bailey (Dem.)	Jeremy Moss (Dem.)	Vanessa Moss (Dem.)	James Turner (Dem.)	James Young (Lib.)
Oakland	62,359	11,090	10,839	26,447	9,446	4,375	162
Total.	62,359	11,090	10,839	26,447	9,446	4,375	162

12th State Senate District

County	Total by County	Michael McCready (Rep.)	Vernon Molnar (Rep.)	Jim Tedder (Rep.)	Terry Whitney (Rep.)	Rosemary Bayer (Dem.)	Jeff Pittel (Lib.)
Oakland	55,499	12,524	770	12,239	2,073	27,744	149
Total.	55,499	12,524	770	12,239	2,073	27,744	149

13th State Senate District

County	Total by County	Marty Knollenberg (Rep.)	Mallory McMorrow (Dem.)
Oakland	62,693	27,329	35,364
Total.	62,693	27,329	35,364

14th State Senate District

County	Total by County	Katherine Houston (Rep.)	Ruth Johnson (Rep.)	Cris Rariden (Dem.)	Jason Waisanen (Dem.)	Renee Watson (Dem.)
Genesee	20,535	2,871	6,684	2,367	1,128	7,485
Oakland	30,067	3,527	14,274	1,902	1,280	9,084
Total.	50,602	6,398	20,958	4,269	2,408	16,569

15th State Senate District

County	Total by County	Jim Runestad (Rep.)	Mike Saari (Rep.)	Julia Pulver (Dem.)
Oakland	58,170	25,757	3,013	29,400
Total.	58,170	25,757	3,013	29,400

16th State Senate District

County	Total by County	Matt Dame (Rep.)	Mike Shirkey (Rep.)	Val Toops (Dem.)	Ronald Muszynski (Lib.)
Branch	7,261	2,109	3,015	2,116	21
Hillsdale	7,091	2,351	2,962	1,754	24
Jackson	28,608	5,929	12,128	10,385	166
Total.	42,960	10,389	18,105	14,255	211

17th State Senate District

County	Total by County	Dale Zorn (Rep.)	Bill LaVoy (Dem.)	Chad McNamara (Lib.)
Lenawee	14,541	8,421	6,072	48
Monroe	24,236	13,208	10,931	97
Total	38,777	21,629	17,003	145

18th State Senate District

County	Total by County	Martin Church (Rep.)	Michelle Deatrick (Dem.)	Jeff Irwin (Dem.)	Matthew Miller (Dem.)	Anuja Rajendra (Dem.)
Washtenaw	65,549	9,770	19,634	19,875	1,597	14,673
Total	65,549	9,770	19,634	19,875	1,597	14,673

19th State Senate District

County	Total by County	John Bizon (Rep.)	Mike Callton (Rep.)	Jason Nobel (Dem.)	Joseph Gillotte (Lib.)
Barry	13,461	4,429	5,049	3,922	61
Calhoun	21,323	9,894	2,871	8,487	71
Ionia	9,958	2,840	4,040	3,049	29
Total	44,742	17,163	11,960	15,458	161

20th State Senate District

County	Total by County	Margaret O'Brien (Rep.)	Sean McCann (Dem.)	Lorence R. Wenke (Lib.)
Kalamazoo	49,237	20,009	29,026	202
Total	49,237	20,009	29,026	202

21st State Senate District

County	Total by County	Kim LaSata (Rep.)	Dave Pagel (Rep.)	Ian Haight (Dem.)
Berrien	27,787	9,821	8,321	9,645
Cass	7,138	2,655	2,206	2,277
St. Joseph	7,809	2,868	2,234	2,707
Total	42,734	15,344	12,761	14,629

22nd State Senate District

County	Total by County	Joseph Marinaro (Rep.)	Lana Theis (Rep.)	Adam Dreher (Dem.)
Livingston	42,355	6,135	21,089	15,131
Washtenaw	19,419	2,597	4,868	11,954
Total	61,774	8,732	25,957	27,085

23rd State Senate District

County	Total by County	Nancy Denny (Rep.)	Andrea Pollack (Rep.)	Curtis Hertel, Jr. (Dem.)
Ingham	48,619	5,833	6,811	35,975
Total.	48,619	5,833	6,811	35,975

24th State Senate District

County	Total by County	Tom Barrett (Rep.)	Brett Roberts (Rep.)	Kelly Rossman-McKinney (Dem.)	Katie Nepton (Lib.)
Clinton	15,905	6,578	2,500	6,778	49
Eaton	23,758	9,314	3,322	11,042	80
Ingham	4,166	1,609	552	1,986	19
Shiawassee	12,956	4,626	2,915	5,384	31
Total.	56,785	22,127	9,289	25,190	179

25th State Senate District

County	Total by County	Dan Lauwers (Rep.)	Debbie Bourgois (Dem.)
Huron	6,187	4,559	1,628
Macomb	4,888	2,903	1,985
St. Clair	28,930	17,171	11,759
Sanilac	7,578	5,406	2,172
Total.	47,583	30,039	17,544

26th State Senate District

County	Total by County	Bob Genetski (Rep.)	Aric Nesbitt (Rep.)	Don Wickstra (Rep.)	Garnet Lewis (Dem.)	Erwin Haas (Lib.)
Allegan	24,640	6,256	5,962	4,294	8,017	111
Kent	13,903	2,331	4,041	1,379	6,103	49
Van Buren	13,570	790	6,526	770	5,426	58
Total.	52,113	9,377	16,529	6,443	19,546	218

27th State Senate District

County	Total by County	Donna Kekesis (Rep.)	Jim Ananich (Dem.)
Genesee	34,649	8,512	26,137
Total.	34,649	8,512	26,137

28th State Senate District

County	Total by County	Peter MacGregor (Rep.)	Craig Beach (Dem.)	Gidget Groendyk (Dem.)	Ryan Jeanette (Dem.)	Nathan Hewer (Lib.)
Kent	49,258	30,475	7,689	6,444	4,426	224
Total.	49,258	30,475	7,689	6,444	4,426	224

29th State Senate District

County	Total by County	Chris Afendoulis (Rep.)	Daniel Oesch (Rep.)	Winnie Brinks (Dem.)	Robert VanNoller (Lib.)
Kent	56,873	19,374	4,445	32,882	172
Total	56,873	19,374	4,445	32,882	172

30th State Senate District

County	Total by County	Rett DeBoer (Rep.)	Daniela Garcia (Rep.)	Joe Haveman (Rep.)	Roger Victory (Rep.)	Jeanette Schipper (Dem.)	Mary Buzuma (Lib.)
Ottawa	57,833	2,399	10,647	10,585	16,895	17,119	188
Total	57,833	2,399	10,647	10,585	16,895	17,119	188

31st State Senate District

County	Total by County	Kevin Daley (Rep.)	Gary Glenn (Rep.)	Joni Batterbee (Dem.)	Bill Jordan (Dem.)	Cynthia Luczak (Dem.)	Chuck Stadler (Dem.)
Bay	22,078	5,517	4,821	982	2,196	7,806	756
Lapeer	19,872	9,017	4,745	1,218	1,024	2,677	1,191
Tuscola	11,168	4,014	3,588	589	1,070	1,028	879
Total	53,118	18,548	13,154	2,789	4,290	11,511	2,826

32nd State Senate District

County	Total by County	Ken Horn (Rep.)	Henry Gaudreau (Dem.)	Phil Phelps (Dem.)
Genesee	13,683	6,968	1,987	4,728
Saginaw	36,613	19,238	7,951	9,424
Total	50,296	23,966	9,938	14,152

33rd State Senate District

County	Total by County	Greg Alexander (Rep.)	Rick Outman (Rep.)	Mark Bignell (Dem.)	John Hoppough (Dem.)
Clare	4,632	1,092	1,816	1,132	592
Gratiot	5,829	910	2,690	1,293	936
Isabella	9,669	1,653	3,384	2,941	1,691
Mecosta	6,500	1,327	2,847	1,417	909
Montcalm	10,923	1,572	5,944	1,510	1,897
Total	37,553	1,092	1,816	1,132	592

34th State Senate District

County	Total by County	Jon Bumstead (Rep.)	Holly Hughes (Rep.)	Collene Lamonte (Dem.)	Poppy Sias-Hernandez (Dem.)	Max Riekse (Lib.)
Muskegon	31,971	6,137	8,647	7,865	9,242	80
Newaygo.	10,292	4,644	2,734	1,428	1,450	36
Oceana	5,630	2,598	1,113	791	1,111	17
Total.	47,893	13,379	12,494	10,084	11,803	133

35th State Senate District

County	Total by County	Ray Franz (Rep.)	Bruce Rendon (Rep.)	Cary Urka (Rep.)	Curtis S. VanderWall (Rep.)	Mike Taillard (Dem.)	Timothy Coon (Lib.)
Benzie.	4,762	1,049	120	88	1,425	2,071	9
Crawford.	2,814	320	851	58	712	856	17
Kalkaska	3,610	520	965	87	952	1,072	14
Lake	2,288	306	133	91	907	846	5
Leelanau	7,651	1,464	196	84	2,221	3,676	10
Manistee	5,605	1,683	134	172	1,633	1,972	11
Mason.	7,263	1,086	131	145	3,401	2,468	32
Missaukee	3,488	258	1,197	42	1,331	653	7
Ogemaw	5,013	514	2,063	107	799	1,518	12
Osceola.	4,338	517	635	115	2,111	943	17
Roscommon . . .	6,261	437	2,395	127	1,318	1,968	16
Wexford	7,118	1,270	1,012	191	2,903	1,725	17
Total.	60,211	9,424	9,832	1,307	19,713	19,768	167

36th State Senate District

County	Total by County	Jim Stamas (Rep.)	Joe Weir (Dem.)
Alcona	2,763	1,934	829
Alpena	5,655	3,396	2,259
Arenac	2,879	1,823	1,056
Gladwin	5,027	3,256	1,771
Iosco.	5,034	2,975	2,059
Midland.	17,021	10,449	6,572
Montmorency . .	2,161	1,548	613
Oscoda	1,706	1,259	447
Otsego	5,287	3,685	1,602
Presque Isle. . . .	3,060	2,055	1,005
Total.	50,593	32,380	18,213

37th State Senate District

County	Total by County	Jim Gurr (Rep.)	Wayne Schmidt (Rep.)	Jim Page (Dem.)
Antrim.	5,819	1,063	2,763	1,993
Charlevoix.	5,855	582	2,980	2,293
Cheboygan	5,484	739	2,863	1,882
Chippewa	5,770	508	2,963	2,299
Emmet	7,747	930	3,749	3,068
Grand Traverse. .	24,333	2,714	10,305	11,314
Luce	1,072	103	626	343
Mackinac.	2,646	285	1,444	917
Total.	58,726	6,924	27,693	24,109

38th State Senate District

County	Total by County	Mike Carey (Rep.)	Ed McBroom (Rep.)	Scott Dianda (Dem.)
Alger.	1,970	375	617	978
Baraga.	1,424	257	559	608
Delta.	6,861	561	3,399	2,901
Dickinson	5,158	943	2,538	1,677
Gogebic	3,056	670	611	1,775
Houghton	6,209	1,110	1,921	3,178
Iron.	2,309	549	726	1,034
Keweenaw	755	175	230	350
Marquette	12,826	1,620	3,157	8,049
Menominee	2,973	416	1,399	1,158
Ontonagon	1,485	302	523	660
Schoolcraft	1,614	245	635	734
Total.	46,640	7,223	16,315	23,102

STATE HOUSE OF REPRESENTATIVES
2-YEAR TERM

1st State Representative District

County	Total by County	Mark Corcoran (Rep.)	Shaun Maloy (Dem.)	Tenisha Yancey (Dem.)	Gregory Creswell (Lib.)
Wayne........	12,451	2,927	1,919	7,580	25
Total......	12,451	2,927	1,919	7,580	25

2nd State Representative District

County	Total by County	John Palffy (Rep.)	Kinda Anderson (Dem.)	Carol Banks (Dem.)	Willie Bell (Dem.)	Latisha Johnson (Dem.)	E. Regina Jones (Dem.)	Joseph Tate (Dem.)
Wayne........	12,941	2,543	367	1,575	1,199	1,748	463	2,951
Total......	12,941	2,543	367	1,575	1,199	1,748	463	2,951

Carla Tinsley-Smith (Dem.)
2,095
2,095

3rd State Representative District

County	Total by County	Dolores Brodersen (Rep.)	Wendell Byrd (Dem.)	China Cochran (Dem.)	John Cromer (Dem.)	Christopher Owens (Dem.)	Omar Proctor (Dem.)	.
Wayne........	10,125	194	5,435	1,697	1,275	656	868	
Total......	10,125	194	5,435	1,697	1,275	656	868	

4th State Representative District

County	Total by County	Howard Weathington (Rep.)	Md Alam (Dem.)	Saad Almasmari (Dem.)	Derek Boston (Dem.)	Christopher Collins (Dem.)	Matt Friedrichs (Dem.)	Justin Jessop (Dem.)
Wayne........	11,486	269	162	1,765	71	297	324	68
Total......	11,486	269	162	1,765	71	297	324	68

Myya Jones (Dem.)	Ernest Little (Dem.)	Diane McMillan (Dem.)	Jeffrey Nolish (Dem.)	Michele Oberholtzer (Dem.)	Rico Razo (Dem.)	Syed Rob (Dem.)
877	236	657	560	1,750	1,115	953
877	236	657	560	1,750	1,115	953

4th State Representative District (cont'd.)

	Isaac Robinson (Dem.)	Andre Godwin (Dem.) (W)
	2,381	1
	2,381	1

5th State Representative District

County	Total by County	Dorothy Patterson (Rep.)	Cynthia Johnson (Dem.)	Mark Murphy, Jr. (Dem.)	Mark Payne, Jr. (Dem.)	Rita Ross (Dem.)	Jermaine Tobey (Dem.)	Cliff Woodards, II (Dem.)
Wayne........	5,968	161	2,149	319	723	2,140	153	323
Total......	12,941	2,543	367	1,575	1,199	1,748	463	2,951

6th State Representative District

County	Total by County	Linda Sawyer (Rep.)	Willie Burton (Dem.)	Tyrone Carter (Dem.)	Tom Choske (Dem.)	Terra DeFoe (Dem.)	Aghogho Edevbie (Dem.)	Paula Humphries (Dem.)
Wayne........	11,802	456	976	2,398	532	1,492	1,247	552
Total......	11,802	456	976	2,398	532	1,492	1,247	552

	Samantha Magdaleno (Dem.)	David Sanchez (Dem.)	Ricardo White (Dem.)	Charlesetta Wilson (Dem.)
	541	696	780	2,132
	541	696	780	2,132

7th State Representative District

County	Total by County	Marcelis Turner (Rep.)	Ronald Cole (Dem.)	LaTanya Garrett (Dem.)	Najanava Harvey-Quinn (Dem.)	Jeff Jones (Dem.)	Elene Robinson (Dem.)
Wayne........	12,156	73	66	9,680	633	832	872
Total......	12,156	73	66	9,680	633	832	872

8th State Representative District

County	Total by County	Valerie Parker (Rep.)	LaSonya Beaver (Dem.)	George Etheridge (Dem.)	Sherry Gay-Dagnogo (Dem.)	Jasmine Henry (Dem.)	Seydi Sarr (Dem.)
Wayne........	12,858	228	1,026	1,333	7,892	1,624	755
Total......	12,858	228	1,026	1,333	7,892	1,624	755

9th State Representative District

County	Total by County	James Stephens (Rep.)	Gary S. Pollard (Dem.)	Donald Stuckey, II (Dem.)	Karen Whitsett (Dem.)
Wayne........	9,117	257	3,069	791	5,000
Total......	9,117	257	3,069	791	5,000

10th State Representative District

County	Total by County	Articia Bomer (Rep.)	William Brang (Rep.)	Rhonda Barley (Dem.)	James Brenner (Dem.)	Tyson Kelley (Dem.)	Leslie Love (Dem.)	Jeremy Morgan (Lib.)
Wayne........	14,942	277	1,617	1,844	1,347	556	9,273	28
Total......	14,942	277	1,617	1,844	1,347	556	9,273	28

11th State Representative District

County	Total by County	James Townsend (Rep.)	Jewell Jones (Dem.)	Randy Walker (Dem.)
Wayne........	13,237	3,246	6,210	3,781
Total......	13,237	3,246	6,210	3,781

12th State Representative District

County	Total by County	Michelle Bailey (Rep.)	Tomeka Boles (Dem.)	Alex Garza (Dem.)	Lauretha Shelton (Dem.)	Alexandria Taylor (Dem.)
Wayne........	12,709	3,459	1,031	4,311	550	3,358
Total......	12,709	3,459	1,031	4,311	550	3,358

13th State Representative District

County	Total by County	Annie Spencer (Rep.)	Asmaa Alhasani (Dem.)	Frank Liberati (Dem.)
Wayne........	13,523	4,605	2,060	6,858
Total......	13,523	4,605	2,060	6,858

14th State Representative District

County	Total by County	Darrell Stasik (Rep.)	Cara Clemente (Dem.)	Mark Kremer (Dem.)
Wayne........	11,622	3,843	6,469	1,310
Total......	11,622	3,843	6,469	1,310

15th State Representative District

County	Total by County	Doug Mitchell (Rep.)	Abdullah Hammoud (Dem.)
Wayne........	15,049	3,310	11,739
Total......	15,049	3,310	11,739

16th State Representative District

County	Total by County	Jody Rice-White (Rep.)	Kevin Coleman (Dem.)	Bill Johnson (Dem.)	Jacob Johnson (Dem.)	Mike McDermott (Dem.)
Wayne........	13,522	3,143	4,093	2,603	397	3,286
Total......	13,522	3,143	4,093	2,603	397	3,286

17th State Representative District

County	Total by County	Joe Bellino, Jr. (Rep.)	Michelle LaVoy (Dem.)
Monroe.......	10,341	5,335	5,006
Wayne........	3,416	1,423	1,993
Total......	13,757	6,758	6,999

18th State Representative District

County	Total by County	Kyle McKee (Rep.)	Kevin Hertel (Dem.)
Macomb	17,681	6,552	11,129
Total......	17,681	6,552	11,129

19th State Representative District

County	Total by County	Brian Meakin (Rep.)	Dan Centers (Dem.)	Laurie Pohutsky (Dem.)
Wayne........	20,917	9,541	5,152	6,224
Total......	20,917	9,541	5,152	6,224

20th State Representative District

County	Total by County	Jeff Noble (Rep.)	Matt Koleszar (Dem.)
Wayne........	21,606	10,063	11,543
Total......	21,606	10,063	11,543

21st State Representative District

County	Total by County	Darian Moore (Rep.)	Kristy Pagan (Dem.)
Wayne........	19,864	7,153	12,711
Total......	19,864	7,153	12,711

22nd State Representative District

County	Total by County	Arthur Blundell (Rep.)	John Chirkun (Dem.)	Matt Kuehnel (Dem.)
Macomb	12,257	4,252	7,958	47
Total......	12,257	4,252	7,958	47

23rd State Representative District

County	Total by County	Michael Frazier (Rep.)	Darrin Camilleri (Dem.)
Wayne........	17,559	7,394	10,165
Total......	17,559	7,394	10,165

24th State Representative District

County	Total by County	Steve Marino (Rep.)	Laura Winn (Dem.)
Macomb	16,848	8,760	8,088
Total......	16,848	8,760	8,088

25th State Representative District

County	Total by County	Jazmine Early (Rep.)	Nate Shannon (Dem.)
Macomb	14,544	6,288	8,256
Total......	14,544	6,288	8,256

26th State Representative District

County	Total by County	Al Gui (Rep.)	Jim Ellison (Rep.)
Oakland	17,702	4,924	12,778
Total......	17,702	4,924	12,778

27th State Representative District

County	Total by County	Janet Flessland (Rep.)	Michelangelo Fortuna, III (Dem.)	Robert Wittenberg (Dem.)	Benjamin Carr (Lib.)
Oakland	21,769	3,283	3,024	15,379	83
Total.	21,769	3,283	3,024	15,379	83

28th State Representative District

County	Total by County	Aaron Delikta (Rep.)	Patrick Green (Dem.)	Lori Stone (Dem.)	Ryan Manier (Lib.)
Macomb	12,690	3,941	4,110	4,584	55
Total.	12,690	3,941	4,110	4,584	55

29th State Representative District

County	Total by County	Timothy Carrier (Rep.)	Kone Bowman (Dem.)	Brenda Carter (Dem.)	Mike Demand (Dem.)	Chris Jackson (Dem.)	Keyon Payton (Dem.)	Kermit Williams (Dem.)
Oakland	12,713	2,682	1,555	3,075	319	1,636	969	2,477
Total.	12,713	2,682	1,555	3,075	319	1,636	969	2,477

30th State Representative District

County	Total by County	Diana Farrington (Rep.)	Wisam Naoum (Dem.)	John Spica (Dem.)
Macomb	13,426	7,115	2,922	3,389
Total.	13,426	7,115	2,922	3,389

31st State Representative District

County	Total by County	Catherine Dinka (Rep.)	Lisa Valerio-Nowc (Rep.)	Michelle Robertson (Dem.)	Bill Sowerby (Dem.)
Macomb	15,694	2,947	3,002	4,271	5,474
Total.	15,694	2,947	3,002	4,271	5,474

32nd State Representative District

County	Total by County	Pamela Hornberger (Rep.)	Paul Manley (Dem.)
Macomb	9,343	5,092	4,251
St. Clair	5,203	3,362	1,841
Total.	14,546	8,454	6,092

33rd State Representative District

County	Total by County	Jeff Yaroch (Rep.)	Andrea Geralds (Dem.)
Macomb	15,758	9,306	6,452
Total.	15,758	9,306	6,452

34th State Representative District

County	Total by County	Henry Swift (Rep.)	Steven Greene (Dem.)	Sheldon Neeley (Dem.)	Syrron Williams (Dem.)
Genesee	9,526	654	636	7,808	428
Total.	9,526	654	636	7,808	428

35th State Representative District

County	Total by County	Theodore Alfonsetti, III (Rep.)	Kyra Bolden (Dem.)	Lisa Cece (Dem.)	Vincent Gregory (Dem.)	Alex Meyers (Dem.)	Michael Poole (Dem.)	Katie Reiter (Dem.)
Oakland	25,033	2,846	10,061	547	4,980	577	819	5,203
Total.	25,033	2,846	10,061	547	4,980	577	819	5,203

36th State Representative District

County	Total by County	Scott Czasak (Rep.)	Frank Lams (Rep.)	Karen Potchynok-Lund (Rep.)	Tom Stanis (Rep.)	Douglas Wozniak (Rep.)	Robert Murphy (Dem.)	Kristopher Pratt (Dem.)
Macomb	17,939	1,874	226	3,936	654	5,594	3,298	2,306
Total.	17,939	1,874	226	3,936	654	5,594	3,298	2,306

	Benjamin Dryke (Lib.)
	51
	51

37th State Representative District

County	Total by County	Dylan Gomula (Rep.)	Mitch Swoboda (Rep.)	Christine Greig (Dem.)
Oakland	19,857	1,502	4,651	13,704
Total.	19,857	1,502	4,651	13,704

38th State Representative District

County	Total by County	Kathy Crawford (Rep.)	Chase Turner (Rep.)	Aditi Bagchi (Dem.)	Kelly Breen (Dem.)	Joe Petrillo (Dem.)	Brian Wright (Lib.)
Oakland	21,060	5,492	4,779	3,670	5,238	1,822	59
Total.	21,060	5,492	4,779	3,670	5,238	1,822	59

39th State Representative District

County	Total by County	Ryan Berman (Rep.)	Phillip Hoyt (Rep.)	Marsha Kosmatka (Rep.)	Kevin Tatulyan (Rep.)	Jennifer Suidan (Dem.)	Anthony Croff (Lib.)
Oakland	20,058	4,172	672	3,817	1,418	9,932	47
Total.	20,058	4,172	672	3,817	1,418	9,932	47

40th State Representative District

County	Total by County	Mike Banerian (Rep.)	Malissa Bossardet (Rep.)	Paul Secrest (Rep.)	Paul Taros (Rep.)	David Wolkinson (Rep.)	Joe Zane (Rep.)	Nicole Bedi (Dem.)
Oakland	28,510	1,878	1,828	1,112	1,179	3,368	2,348	7,883
Total.	28,510	1,878	1,828	1,112	1,179	3,368	2,348	7,883

Mari Manoogian (Dem.)
8,914
8,914

41st State Representative District

County	Total by County	Ethan Baker (Rep.)	Ronald Dwyer (Rep.)	Doug Tietz (Rep.)	Padma Kuppa (Dem.)
Oakland	20,871	4,581	854	4,952	10,484
Total.	20,871	4,581	854	4,952	10,484

42nd State Representative District

County	Total by County	Ann Bollin (Rep.)	Mona Shand (Dem.)
Livingston	21,955	12,840	9,115
Total.	21,955	12,840	9,115

43rd State Representative District

County	Total by County	Jose Aliaga (Rep.)	Anthony Bartolotta (Rep.)	Andrea K. Schroeder (Rep.)	Nicole Breadon (Dem.)
Oakland	20,935	3,526	3,358	5,572	8,479
Total.	20,935	3,526	3,358	5,572	8,479

44th State Representative District

County	Total by County	April Guiles (Rep.)	Matt Maddock (Rep.)	Michael Mamut (Rep.)	Matt Marko (Rep.)	Lynn O'Brien (Rep.)	Laura Dodd (Dem.)	Steven White, Jr. (Dem.)
Oakland	22,179	486	8,561	192	1,816	2,525	7,688	911
Total.	22,179	486	8,561	192	1,816	2,525	7,688	911

45th State Representative District

County	Total by County	Michael Webber (Rep.)	Kyle Cooper (Dem.)	Ted Golden (Dem.)
Oakland	19,164	9,871	5,256	4,037
Total......	19,164	9,871	5,256	4,037

46th State Representative District

County	Total by County	John Reilly (Rep.)	Mindy Denninger (Dem.)	Tom Watson (Dem.)
Oakland	19,209	11,110	6,392	1,707
Total......	19,209	11,110	6,392	1,707

47th State Representative District

County	Total by County	Hank Vaupel (Rep.)	Colleen Turk (Dem.)
Livingston	17,905	11,638	6,267
Total......	17,905	11,638	6,267

48th State Representative District

County	Total by County	Sherri Cross (Rep.)	Al Hardwick (Rep.)	Eric Gunnels (Dem.)	Sheryl Kennedy (Dem.)	Jordan Tiffany (Dem.)
Genesee	16,135	2,712	3,812	1,702	7,042	867
Total......	16,135	2,712	3,812	1,702	7,042	867

49th State Representative District

County	Total by County	Patrick Duvendeck (Rep.)	John Cherry (Dem.)	LaShaya Darisaw (Dem.)	Justin Dickerson (Dem.)	Jacky King (Dem.)	Dayne Walling (Dem.)	Don Wright (Dem.)
Genesee	14,730	3,487	5,266	979	198	1,016	3,484	300
Total......	14,730	3,487	5,266	979	198	1,016	3,484	300

50th State Representative District

County	Total by County	Trace Fisher (Rep.)	Tim Sneller (Dem.)
Genesee	15,769	6,172	9,597
Total......	15,769	6,172	9,597

51st State Representative District

County	Total by County	Matthew Anderton (Rep.)	Mike Mueller (Rep.)	Drew Shapior (Rep.)	Ian Shetron (Rep.)	David Lossing (Dem.)
Genesee	15,625	584	5,995	1,590	946	6,510
Oakland	4,485	190	1,746	544	316	1,689
Total	20,110	774	7,741	2,134	1262	8,199

52nd State Representative District

County	Total by County	Teri Aiuto (Rep.)	Donna Lasinski (Dem.)
Washtenaw	23,122	8,273	14,849
Total	23,122	8,273	14,849

53rd State Representative District

County	Total by County	Jean Holland (Rep.)	Yousef Rabhi (Dem.)
Washtenaw	19,811	1,227	18,584
Total	19,811	1,227	18,584

54th State Representative District

County	Total by County	Colton Campbell (Rep.)	Ora Wright (Rep.)	Roderick Casey (Dem.)	Isaac London, II (Dem.)	Ronnie Peterson (Dem.)	William Riney (Dem.)
Washtenaw	17,589	2,174	958	3,012	1,312	8,345	1,788
Total	17,589	2,174	958	3,012	1,312	8,345	1,788

55th State Representative District

County	Total by County	Bob Baird (Rep.)	Bill Boring (Rep.)	Miha Todd (Rep.)	Shauna McNally (Dem.)	Rebekah Warren (Dem.)
Washtenaw	20,807	1,898	1,022	922	3,919	13,046
Total	20,807	1,898	1,022	922	3,919	13,046

56th State Representative District

County	Total by County	Jason Sheppard (Rep.)	Ernie Whiteside (Dem.)
Monroe	13,411	7,846	5,565
Total	13,411	7,846	5,565

57th State Representative District

County	Total by County	Bronna Kahle (Rep.)	Amber Pedersen (Dem.)
Lenawee	13,555	7,895	5,660
Total	13,555	7,895	5,660

58th State Representative District

County	Total by County	Eric Leutheuser (Rep.)	Tamara Barnes (Dem.)
Branch	6,982	4,817	2,165
Hillsdale	6,675	4,920	1,755
Total	13,657	9,737	3,920

59th State Representative District

County	Total by County	Aaron Miller (Rep.)	Dennis Smith (Dem.)
Cass	4,199	2,665	1,534
St. Joseph	7,731	4,968	2,763
Total	11,930	7,633	4,297

60th State Representative District

County	Total by County	William Baker (Rep.)	Jon Hoadley (Dem.)
Kalamazoo	14,813	3,037	11,776
Total	14,813	3,037	11,776

61st State Representative District

County	Total by County	Brandt Iden (Rep.)	Alberta Griffin (Dem.)	Corey Kendal (Dem.)	Thomas Whitener (Dem.)
Kalamazoo	19,435	8,808	6,149	1,323	3,155
Total	19,435	8,808	6,149	1,323	3,155

62nd State Representative District

County	Total by County	Dave Morgan (Rep.)	Jim Haadsma (Dem.)
Calhoun	12,255	6,162	6,093
Total	12,255	6,162	6,093

63rd State Representative District

County	Total by County	Paul Foust (Rep.)	Matt Hall (Rep.)	David Maturen (Rep.)	Jennifer Aniano (Dem.)	Ronald Hawkins (Lib.)
Calhoun	8,084	282	3,124	2,082	2,564	32
Kalamazoo	10,375	369	3,484	2,174	4,300	48
Total	18,459	651	6,608	4,256	6,864	80

64th State Representative District

County	Total by County	Julie Alexander (Rep.)	Brock Bachelder (Dem.)	Sheila Troxel (Dem.)	Norman Peterson (Lib.)
Jackson	14,294	8,168	1,235	4,802	89
Total	14,294	8,168	1,235	4,802	89

65th State Representative District

County	Total by County	Todd Brittain (Rep.)	Matt Eyer (Rep.)	Sarah Lightner (Rep.)	Carl Rice, Jr. (Rep.)	Terri McKinnon (Dem.)	Jason Rees (Lib.)
Eaton	2,596	328	96	1,101	82	975	14
Jackson	14,020	2,506	705	4,270	1,464	4,996	79
Lenawee	1072	152	57	359	98	398	8
Total	17,688	2,986	858	5,730	1,644	6,369	101

66th State Representative District

County	Total by County	Beth Griffin (Rep.)	Dan Seibert (Dem.)
Kalamazoo	3,352	1,780	1,572
Van Buren	12,566	7,180	5,386
Total	15,918	8,960	6,958

67th State Representative District

County	Total by County	Leon Clark (Rep.)	Clyde Thomas (Rep.)	Brent Domann (Dem.)	Max Donovan (Dem.)	Alec Findlay (Dem.)	Kara Hope (Dem.)	Derek Stephens (Dem.)
Ingham	18,361	4,967	2,640	521	941	870	7,615	707
Total	18,361	4,967	2,640	521	941	870	7,615	707

Zachary Moreau (Lib.)
100
100

68th State Representative District

County	Total by County	Rosalinda Hernandez (Rep.)	Sarah Anthony (Dem.)	Grant Bradley (Dem.)	Kelly Collison (Dem.)	Paul DeWeese (Dem.)	Benjamin Guins (Dem.)	Eric Nelson (Dem.)
Ingham	16,676	2,985	7,910	344	2,941	1,430	131	346
Total	16,676	2,985	7,910	344	2,941	1,430	131	346

	Farhan Sheikh-Omar (Dem.)
	589
	589

69th State Representative District

County	Total by County	George Nastas (Rep.)	Teri Banas (Dem.)	Julie Brixie (Dem.)	Penelope Tsernoglou (Dem.)
Ingham	20,044	4,393	2,487	7,432	5,732
Total	20,044	4,393	2,487	7,432	5,732

70th State Representative District

County	Total by County	James Lower (Rep.)	Kresta Train (Dem.)
Gratiot	2,772	1,521	1,251
Montcalm	9,548	6,487	3,061
Total	12,320	8,008	4,312

71st State Representative District

County	Total by County	Christine Barnes (Rep.)	Chuck Cascarilla (Rep.)	Chris Steward (Rep.)	Claris Trevino (Rep.)	Beth Bowen (Dem.)	Dominic Natoli (Dem.)	Angela Witwer (Dem.)
Eaton	20,688	4,247	3,154	2,215	481	3,463	764	6,364
Total	20,688	4,247	3,154	2,215	481	3,463	764	6,364

72nd State Representative District

County	Total by County	Jennifer Antel (Rep.)	Steve Johnson (Rep.)	Ron Draayer (Dem.)	Jamie Lewis (Lib.)
Allegan	4,910	979	2,782	1,127	22
Kent	13,897	1,806	5,971	6,068	52
Total	18,807	2,785	8,753	7,195	74

73rd State Representative District

County	Total by County	Lynn Afendoulis (Rep.)	Ken Fortier (Rep.)	Robert Regan (Rep.)	David Spencer (Rep.)	Bill Saxton (Dem.)
Kent	24,044	7,166	2,119	3,503	1,840	9,416
Total	24,044	7,166	2,119	3,503	1,840	9,416

74th State Representative District

County	Total by County	Mark Huizenga (Rep.)	Meagan Carr (Dem.)
Kent	17,055	10,417	6,638
Total	17,055	10,417	6,638

75th State Representative District

County	Total by County	Daniel Schutte (Rep.)	David LaGrand (Dem.)
Kent	12,324	2,211	10,113
Total	12,324	2,211	10,113

76th State Representative District

County	Total by County	Amanda Brand (Rep.)	Rachel Hood (Dem.)
Kent	20,327	7,430	12,897
Total	20,327	7,430	12,897

77th State Representative District

County	Totaly by County	Tommy Brann (Rep.)	Jordan Oesch (Rep.)	Dana Knight (Dem.)	Robert Van Kirk (Dem.)	Patty Malowney (Lib.)
Kent	15,802	8,974	814	3,943	1,997	74
Total	15,802	8,974	814	3,943	1,997	74

78th State Representative District

County	Total by County	Steve Bury (Rep.)	Dana Daniels (Rep.)	Daniel Hinkl (Rep.)	David Mann (Rep.)	Brad Paquette (Rep.)	Kelly Priede (Rep.)	Dean Hill (Dem.)
Berrien	10,765	142	390	585	1,328	3,373	1,033	3,914
Cass	2,626	34	118	157	380	899	276	762
Total.	13,391	176	508	742	1,708	4,272	1,309	4,676

79th State Representative District

County	Total by County	JoAnn DeMeulenaere (Rep.)	Bruce Gorenflo (Rep.)	Maria Moen (Rep.)	Troy Rolling (Rep.)	Pauline Wendzel (Rep.)	Joey Andrews (Dem.)	Marletta Seats (Dem.)
Berrien	17,024	400	1,236	2,406	1,828	5,041	3,485	2,628
Total	17,024	400	1,236	2,406	1,828	5,041	3,485	2,628

80th State Representative District

County	Total by County	Mary Whiteford (Rep.)	Erik Almquist (Dem.)	Mark Ludwig (Dem.)
Allegan	18,157	11,557	1,884	4,716
Total	18,157	11,557	1,884	4,716

81st State Representative District

County	Total by County	Gary Eisen (Rep.)	John Mahaney (Rep.)	Keneth Nicholl (Rep.)	Michael Pratt (Rep.)	Eric Stocker (Rep.)	Dan Tollis (Rep.)	Dan Turke (Rep.)
St. Clair	16,919	2,659	335	2,637	853	2,499	201	999
Total	16,919	2,659	335	2,637	853	2,499	201	999

Joel Williams (Rep.)	Joshua Rivard (Dem.)
745	5,991
745	5,991

82nd State Representative District

County	Total by County	Gary Howell (Rep.)	Christopher Giles (Dem.)
Lapeer.	17,992	12,293	5,699
Total	17,992	12,293	5,699

83rd State Representative District

County	Total by County	Shane Hernandez (Rep.)	Stefanie Brown (Dem.)
St. Clair	7,211	3,429	3,782
Sanilac	7,828	5,678	2,150
Total	15,039	9,107	5,932

84th State Representative District

County	Total by County	Matthew Bierlein (Rep.)	Phil Green (Rep.)	Dean Smith (Rep.)	William Shoop (Dem.)
Huron	7,266	1,448	2,052	2,174	1,592
Tuscola	10,892	3,545	3,109	947	3,291
Total.	18,158	4,993	5,161	3,121	4,883

85th State Representative District

County	Total by County	Ben Frederick (Rep.)	Eric Sabin (Dem.)
Saginaw	4,249	2,762	1,487
Shiawassee	12,293	7,030	5,263
Total.	16,542	9,792	6,750

86th State Representative District

County	Total by County	Thomas Albert (Rep.)	Lauren Taylor (Dem.)
Ionia	2,988	1,891	1,097
Kent	15,294	9,484	5,810
Total.	18,282	11,375	6,907

87th State Representative District

County	Total by County	Julie Calley (Rep.)	Shawn Winters (Dem.)
Barry.	12,408	8,498	3,910
Ionia	6,312	4,367	1,945
Total.	18,720	12,865	5,855

88th State Representative District

County	Total by County	Michael Bosch (Rep.)	Brent Huddleston (Rep.)	Luke Meerman (Rep.)	Jason Minier (Rep.)	Heidi Zuniga (Dem.)
Ottawa	18,403	2,862	404	8,709	1,849	4,579
Total.	18,403	2,862	404	8,709	1,849	4,579

89th State Representative District

County	Total by County	Jim Lilly (Rep.)	Beverly Zimmerman (Rep.)	Jerry Sias (Dem.)
Ottawa	20,328	10,287	2,704	7,337
Total.	20,328	10,287	2,704	7,337

90th State Representative District

County	Total by County	Orlando Estrada (Rep.)	Bradley Slagh (Rep.)	Christopher Banks (Dem.)
Ottawa	16,784	1,872	9,943	4,969
Total.	16,784	1,872	9,943	4,969

91st State Representative District

County	Total by County	Alan Jager (Rep.)	Greg VanWoerkom (Rep.)	Tanya Cabala (Dem.)	Andy O'Riley (Dem.)
Muskegon	17,694	2,144	7,054	5,118	3,378
Total.	17,694	2,144	7,054	5,118	3,378

92nd State Representative District

County	Total by County	Gail Eichorst (Rep.)	Terry Sabo (Dem.)
Muskegon	11,772	3,928	7,844
Total.	11,772	3,928	7,844

93rd State Representative District

County	Total by County	Madhu Anderson (Rep.)	Graham Filler (Rep.)	Anne Hill (Rep.)	Dawn Levey (Dem.)	Tyler Palmer (Lib.)
Clinton	15,557	1,078	5,153	2,631	6,641	54
Gratiot.	3,061	230	1,122	745	955	9
Total.	18,618	1,308	6,275	3,376	7,596	63

94th State Representative District

County	Total by County	Steven Gerhardt (Rep.)	Rick Riebschleger (Rep.)	Rodney Wakeman (Rep.)	Dave Adams (Dem.)
Saginaw	21,431	5,742	1,322	5,772	8,595
Total.	21,431	5,742	1,322	5,772	8,595

95th State Representative District

County	Total by County	Dorothy Tanner (Rep.)	Vanessa Guerra (Dem.)
Saginaw	10,998	3,200	7,798
Total.	10,998	3,200	7,798

96th State Representative District

County	Total by County	Susan Kowalski (Rep.)	Brian Elder (Dem.)
Bay..........	15,635	6,307	9,328
Total......	15,635	6,307	9,328

97th State Representative District

County	Total by County	Jason Wentworth (Rep.)	Bob Townsend (Dem.)	Celia Young-Wenkel (Dem.)
Arenac	2,921	1,811	504	606
Clare.........	4,941	3,112	963	866
Gladwin	5,079	3,237	958	884
Osceola.......	2,035	1,522	217	296
Total......	14,976	9,682	2,642	2,652

98th State Representative District

County	Total by County	Annette Glenn (Rep.)	Carl Hamann (Rep.)	Sarah Schulz (Dem.)
Bay..........	3,996	1,223	1,079	1,694
Midland.......	13,816	4,778	3,449	5,589
Total......	17,812	6,001	4,528	7,283

99th State Representative District

County	Total by County	Roger Hauck (Rep.)	Kristen Brown (Dem.)	Randall Doyle (Dem.)	Allison Quast-Lents (Dem.)
Isabella	11,243	5,702	3,085	380	2,076
Midland.......	3,607	2,298	749	215	345
Total......	14,850	8,000	3,834	595	2,421

100th State Representative District

County	Total by County	Scott VanSingel (Rep.)	Sandy Clarke (Dem.)
Lake	2,208	1,287	921
Newaygo......	9,342	6,648	2,694
Oceana	4,958	3,225	1,733
Total......	16,508	11,160	5,348

101st State Representative District

County	Total by County	Carolyn Cater (Rep.)	Jack O'Malley (Rep.)	Edward Hoogterp (Dem.)	Kathy Wiejaczka (Dem.)
Benzie.	5,034	305	2,373	359	1,997
Leelanau	8,047	510	3,395	323	3,819
Manistee	5,762	469	3,019	248	2,026
Mason.	7,162	928	3,609	295	2,330
Total.	26,005	2,212	12,396	1,225	10,172

102nd State Representative District

County	Total by County	William Barnett (Rep.)	Michele Hoitenga (Rep.)	Dion Adams (Dem.)	Bruce Reges (Dem.)
Mecosta.	7,031	1,424	3,287	1,354	966
Osceola.	2,199	621	1,118	250	210
Wexford	7,349	2,051	3,612	886	800
Total.	16,579	4,096	8,017	2,490	1,976

103rd State Representative District

County	Total by County	Daire Rendon (Rep.)	Steve Loomis (Dem.)	Tim Schaiberger (Dem.)
Crawford.	2,562	1,641	460	461
Kalkaska	3,212	2,172	569	471
Missaukee	3,094	2,436	391	267
Ogemaw.	4,638	2,903	600	1,135
Roscommon . . .	5,626	3,649	1,094	883
Total.	19,132	12,801	3,114	3,217

104th State Representative District

County	Total by County	Larry Inman (Rep.)	Dan O'Neil (Dem.)
Grand Traverse. .	23,447	11,769	11,678
Total.	23,447	11,769	11,678

105th State Representative District

County	Total by County	Triston Cole (Rep.)	Melissa Fruge (Dem.)
Antrim.	5,656	3,639	2,017
Charlevoix.	5,803	3,448	2,355
Montmorency . .	2,164	1,554	610
Oscoda	1,691	1,261	430
Otsego	5,298	3,702	1,596
Total.	20,612	13,604	7,008

106th State Representative District

County	Total by County	Sue Allor (Rep.)	Lora Greene (Dem.)	John Norton, III (Dem.)
Alcona	2,854	1,967	759	128
Alpena	6,001	3,404	2,337	260
Cheboygan	3,167	2,077	911	179
Iosco.	5,052	2,950	1,739	363
Presque Isle. . . .	3,256	2,127	989	140
Total.	20,330	12,525	6,735	1,070

107th State Representative District

County	Total by County	Lee Chatfield (Rep.)	Bruce Newville, Jr. (Rep.)	Joanne Galloway (Dem.)	Kurt Perron (Dem.)
Cheboygan	2,493	1,376	283	730	104
Chippewa	6,269	3,206	471	1,881	711
Emmet	8,429	4,143	947	3,058	281
Mackinac.	2,896	1,559	260	955	122
Total.	20,087	10,284	1,961	6,624	1,218

108th State Representative District

County	Total by County	Beau LaFave (Rep.)	Bob Romps (Dem.)
Delta.	6,556	3,668	2,888
Dickinson	4,719	3,077	1,642
Menominee	2,738	1,597	1,141
Total.	14,013	8,342	5,671

109th State Representative District

County	Total by County	Melody Wagner (Rep.)	Sara Cambensy (Dem.)
Alger.	1,899	852	1,047
Luce	1,014	648	366
Marquette	11,524	3,733	7,791
Schoolcraft	1,511	728	783
Total.	15,948	5,961	9,987

110th State Representative District

County	Total by County	Keith LaCosse (Rep.)	Greg Markkanen (Rep.)	Kirk Schott (Rep.)	Brady Tervo (Rep.)	Ken Summers (Dem.)
Baraga.	1350	105	255	196	187	607
Gogebic	2,804	208	377	364	199	1,656
Houghton	5,926	396	983	459	1,129	2,959
Iron.	2064	301	241	414	139	969
Keweenaw	700	55	166	38	130	311
Marquette	793	130	50	55	48	510
Ontonago	1459	57	106	628	52	616
Total.	15,096	1,252	2,178	2,154	1,884	7,628

SPECIAL GENERAL ELECTIONS

NOVEMBER 7, 2017

STATE REPRESENTATIVE

1st State Representative District *Partial Term Ending January 1, 2019[1]*

County	Total by County	Mark Corcoran (Rep.)	Tenisha Yancey (Dem.)	William Phillips (Dem.) Write-in	Gregory Creswell (Lib.)
Wayne........	10,152	2,551	7,266	1	334
Total......	10,152	2,551	7,266	1	334

109th State Representative District *Partial Term Ending January 1, 2019[2]*

County	Total by County	Rich Rossway (Rep.)	Sara Cambensy (Dem.)	Wade Roberts (Grn.)
Alger.........	2,533	1,228	1,257	48
Luce	920	592	316	12
Marquette	15,265	5,821	9,255	189
Schoolcraft	1,969	1,049	893	27
Total......	20,687	8,690	11,721	276

---

[1] To fill a remaining term ending January 1, 2019 after Representative Brian Banks resigned effective February 6, 2017.
[2] To fill a remaining term ending January 1, 2019 after the death of Representative John Kivela on May 9, 2017.

SPECIAL GENERAL ELECTIONS

NOVEMBER 6, 2018

U.S. CONGRESS

13th Congressional District *Partial Term Ending 01/03/2019[1]*

County	Total by County	Brenda Jones (Dem.)	Marc Joseph Sosnowski (UST)	D. Etta Wilcoxon (Grn.)	David Anthony Dudenhoefer (Write-in)	Royce Kinniebrew (Write-in)	Clyde Darnell Lynch (Write-in)	Jonathan Lee Pommerville (Write-in)
Wayne.	194,993	169,330	17,302	8,319	36	0	0	5
Total.	194,993	169,330	17,302	8,319	36	0	0	5

DaNetta L. Simpson (Write-in)
1
1

STATE REPRESENTATIVE

68th State Representative District *Partial Term Ending 1/1/2019[2]*

County	Total by County	Rosalinda Hernandez (Rep.)	Sarah Anthony (Dem.)
Ingham	35,291	8,400	26,891
Total.	35,291	8,400	26,891

STATE SENATE

2nd State Senate District *Partial Term Ending 1/1/2019[3]*

County	Total by County	Adam Hollier (Dem.)
Wayne.	55,827	55,827
Total.	55,827	55,827

---

[1] To fill a remaining term ending January 3, 2019 after Congressman John Conyers, Jr. resigned effective December 5, 2017.
[2] To fill a remaining term ending January 1, 2019 after Representative Andy Schor resigned to take a position in local government.
[3] To fill a remaining term ending January 1, 2019 after Senator Bert Johnson resigned effective March 2, 2018.

GENERAL ELECTION

NOVEMBER 6, 2018

GOVERNOR
4-YEAR TERM

County	Total by County[1]	Bill Schuette (Rep.)	Gretchen Whitmer (Dem.)	Bill Gelineau (Lib.)	Todd Schleiger (UST)	Jennifer V. Kurland (Grn.)	Keith Butkovich (NL)
Alcona	5,534	3,408	1,982	40	42	41	21
Alger	4,159	2,097	1,950	42	29	33	8
Allegan	49,853	28,648	19,497	839	366	367	136
Alpena	13,072	7,031	5,595	161	112	127	46
Antrim	12,900	7,480	5,025	163	91	93	48
Arenac	6,758	3,881	2,631	99	65	53	28
Baraga	3,237	1,789	1,356	37	25	21	9
Barry	26,858	15,573	10,272	495	237	199	81
Bay	46,531	21,847	23,159	661	373	359	132
Benzie	9,793	4,963	4,551	131	61	62	25
Berrien	62,036	32,161	27,861	901	433	491	189
Branch	15,212	9,381	5,324	198	121	130	58
Calhoun	50,044	24,711	23,484	828	423	432	166
Cass	19,457	11,538	7,255	246	172	151	95
Charlevoix	13,677	7,556	5,720	191	76	102	32
Cheboygan	12,555	7,249	4,838	218	118	80	52
Chippewa	13,978	7,381	6,187	174	98	91	47
Clare	11,836	6,955	4,424	189	112	91	57
Clinton	37,157	17,649	18,495	566	201	178	68
Crawford	6,259	3,613	2,367	119	58	60	42
Delta	16,430	9,061	6,991	153	101	90	34
Dickinson	11,333	6,914	4,119	107	74	84	33
Eaton	51,106	22,438	27,003	840	373	332	120
Emmet	17,882	9,539	7,788	257	108	144	45
Genesee	168,545	63,537	100,073	2,182	1,198	1,217	337
Gladwin	11,005	6,512	4,155	129	114	66	28
Gogebic	6,507	3,003	3,312	65	46	49	32
Grand Traverse . .	48,801	24,031	23,220	802	253	357	138
Gratiot	14,353	7,690	6,170	211	136	100	46
Hillsdale	16,821	11,088	5,166	226	151	129	61
Houghton	14,311	7,372	6,539	191	49	93	67
Huron	13,732	8,519	4,828	120	125	98	42
Ingham	119,230	35,579	80,292	1,648	605	871	235
Ionia	23,830	13,007	9,929	443	208	165	78
Iosco	11,690	6,534	4,772	140	99	107	38
Iron	5,403	2,970	2,269	49	44	49	22
Isabella	22,485	10,097	11,656	330	146	177	79
Jackson	60,852	32,021	26,704	1,017	473	482	155
Kalamazoo	114,862	44,183	67,023	1,912	596	896	249
Kalkaska	8,357	5,190	2,782	152	90	85	58
Kent	280,291	129,988	141,629	4,773	1,357	2,014	527
Keweenaw	1,316	707	571	15	9	13	1
Lake	4,700	2,602	1,904	68	47	52	27
Lapeer	39,372	23,209	14,798	571	374	290	130
Leelanau	14,202	6,630	7,264	165	45	79	19
Lenawee	40,052	21,225	17,624	529	280	272	122
Livingston	97,578	55,842	39,187	1,333	483	571	161
Luce	2,420	1,469	851	31	27	13	29
Mackinaw	5,716	3,229	2,345	47	38	21	36
Macomb	360,226	169,073	181,603	4,276	2,028	2,377	869
Manistee	11,717	5,928	5,420	149	83	100	37
Marquette	30,002	11,963	17,173	416	128	260	62
Mason	13,710	7,420	5,823	198	110	104	55

County	Total by County	Bill Schuette (Rep.)	Gretchen Whitmer (Dem.)	Bill Gelineau (Lib.)	Todd Schleiger (UST)	Jennifer V. Kurland (Grn.)	Keith Butkovich (NL)
Mecosta.	15,654	8,686	6,408	248	140	118	54
Menominee	8,784	5,030	3,528	74	61	64	27
Midland.	38,505	21,215	16,238	532	238	206	76
Missaukee	6,566	4,641	1,759	68	52	27	19
Monroe	61,539	32,336	27,413	843	429	372	146
Montcalm	23,357	13,408	9,003	411	258	181	96
Montmorency . .	4,625	2,976	1,508	57	52	21	11
Muskegon	73,660	29,655	37,029	1,115	5,140	516	205
Newaygo.	20,327	12,621	6,944	336	175	179	72
Oakland	605,267	244,417	347,080	7,467	2,241	3,197	862
Oceana	10,757	6,151	4,260	147	97	70	32
Ogemaw	9,134	5,471	3,335	109	117	71	31
Ontonagon	3,140	1,741	1,293	27	26	30	23
Osceola.	9,391	6,098	2,901	181	78	91	42
Oscoda	3,732	2,379	1,226	41	51	22	13
Otsego	11,356	6,903	4,064	166	94	90	39
Ottawa	128,588	77,691	47,380	1,994	565	735	222
Presque Isle. . . .	6,677	3,751	2,704	83	62	52	25
Roscommon . . .	11,800	6,859	4,561	158	103	70	49
Saginaw	80,998	36,306	42,693	925	426	465	183
St. Clair	67,434	36,840	28,089	1,016	644	587	258
St. Joseph	20,438	11,962	7,611	329	241	220	75
Sanilac	16,402	10,443	5,383	218	171	131	56
Schoolcraft	3,743	2,094	1,533	35	31	17	33
Shiawassee	29,790	14,943	13,834	439	253	234	87
Tuscola	22,291	13,286	8,272	285	209	182	57
Van Buren.	29,544	14,824	13,580	493	270	251	126
Washtenaw	173,508	44,850	124,910	2,032	526	962	227
Wayne.	659,859	180,057	463,703	6,691	3,115	4,611	1,677
Wexford	13,976	8,419	4,995	243	143	109	67
Total	4,250,585	1,859,534	2,266,193	56,606	29,219	28,799	10,202

[1] Additional candidates receiving votes include Patrick O'Neal Burney (1), William Cobbs (3), Lance Herman (4), Henry Joseph Lester (1), Clyde Darnell Lynch (1), Chaneika Ranell Penny (1), Francis L. Rowley (11), Robin Lee Sanders (2), and Evan Space (8). The total votes cast per county include the votes received by the candidates listed here.

GENERAL ELECTION
NOVEMBER 6, 2018

U.S. SENATE
6-YEAR TERM

County	Total by County[1]	John James (Rep.)	Debbie Stabenow (Dem.)	George E. Huffman III (UST)	Marcia Squier (Grn.)	John Howard Wilhelm (NL)
Alcona	5,555	3,541	1,915	47	44	8
Alger.........	4,162	2,162	1,911	34	36	19
Allegan	49,762	29,834	18,890	340	478	220
Alpena	13,083	7,380	5,412	96	126	68
Antrim........	12,866	7,629	4,953	108	117	59
Arenac	6,735	3,995	2,582	57	65	36
Baraga........	3,250	1,825	1,344	31	33	17
Barry.........	26,737	16,260	9,857	216	273	131
Bay..........	46,333	22,752	22,502	400	461	218
Benzie........	9,773	5,080	4,484	60	105	44
Berrien	61,986	33,229	27,345	535	587	289
Branch	15,199	9,666	5,144	146	161	82
Calhoun	50,045	25,950	22,739	488	583	285
Cass	19,445	11,811	7,079	226	221	108
Charlevoix.....	13,662	7,783	5,596	88	144	51
Cheboygan	12,525	7,384	4,825	129	109	74
Chippewa	13,978	7,767	5,901	107	132	71
Clare.........	11,851	7,048	4,513	120	91	79
Clinton	37,074	18,946	17,564	187	285	92
Crawford......	6,253	3,751	2,306	68	79	49
Delta.........	16,416	9,197	6,932	116	121	50
Dickinson	11,363	6,982	4,162	69	97	53
Eaton	50,952	23,771	26,147	367	454	213
Emmet	17,891	9,875	7,620	121	197	78
Genesee	168,278	68,648	95,903	1,284	1,799	644
Gladwin	11,005	6,604	4,160	101	79	61
Gogebic	6,527	3,078	3,311	35	64	39
Grand Traverse..	48,728	24,903	22,757	257	592	219
Gratiot........	14,299	8,180	5,764	141	133	81
Hillsdale	16,800	11,310	5,079	126	196	89
Houghton	14,321	7,503	6,533	70	163	52
Huron........	13,673	8,312	5,087	104	97	73
Ingham	119,163	38,870	78,012	610	1,270	399
Ionia.........	23,730	13,834	9,259	262	252	123
Iosco.........	11,699	6,694	4,752	91	111	51
Iron..........	5,410	3,000	2,259	56	60	35
Isabella	22,418	10,536	11,304	164	305	109
Jackson	60,782	33,490	25,858	499	659	276
Kalamazoo	114,648	46,243	65,686	793	1,478	448
Kalkaska	8,328	5,340	2,737	82	114	55
Kent	279,474	136,227	137,089	1,699	3,364	1,095
Keweenaw	1,323	704	598	4	14	3
Lake	4,708	2,633	1,936	53	45	41
Lapeer........	39,420	24,206	14,396	296	345	177
Leelanau	14,192	6,775	7,216	50	127	24
Lenawee	39,960	21,981	17,084	308	404	183
Livingston	96,982	58,020	37,450	429	839	242
Luce	2,402	1,524	811	25	23	19
Mackinac......	5,713	3,298	2,325	30	31	29
Macomb	359,469	173,369	179,975	2,076	2,899	1,146
Manistee	11,712	6,183	5,242	95	129	63
Marquette	29,985	12,348	16,977	176	366	118
Mason........	13,677	7,625	5,708	125	145	74

County	Total by County	John James (Rep.)	Debbie Stabenow (Dem.)	George E. Huffman III (UST)	Marcia Squier (Grn.)	John Howard Wilhelm (NL)
Mecosta.	15,594	8,857	6,317	164	162	94
Menominee	8,809	4,982	3,653	69	65	40
Midland.	38,344	21,696	15,959	251	282	156
Missauke	6,555	4,650	1,783	49	34	39
Monroe	61,423	33,607	26,651	413	485	267
Montcalm	23,317	13,878	8,758	289	243	149
Montmorency . .	4,610	2,978	1,537	36	28	31
Muskegon	68,765	30,831	35,957	686	874	417
Newaygo.	20,259	12,870	6,858	209	196	126
Oakland	603,819	256,017	338,986	2,468	4,833	1,511
Oceana	10,757	6,263	4,213	117	100	64
Ogemaw	9,109	5,592	3,280	100	77	60
Ontonagon	3,129	1,752	1,313	23	24	17
Osceola.	9,392	6,186	2,934	93	111	68
Oscoda	3,717	2,410	1,221	37	30	19
Otsego	11,334	7,092	3,969	85	127	61
Ottawa	128,198	80,318	45,696	650	1,159	375
Presque Isle. . . .	6,686	3,788	2,760	50	48	40
Roscommon . . .	11,807	6,864	4,643	120	96	84
Saginaw	80,814	37,809	41,472	542	667	324
St. Clair	67,505	38,329	27,540	555	681	400
St. Joseph	20,403	12,489	7,278	233	275	128
Sanilac	16,443	10,657	5,418	144	123	101
Schoolcraft	3,737	2,099	1,547	44	22	25
Shiawassee	29,720	15,865	13,043	301	314	197
Tuscola	22,260	13,495	8,197	214	225	129
Van Buren	29,443	15,379	13,191	319	360	194
Washtenaw	173,226	47,380	123,305	556	1,582	403
Wayne.	658,391	190,884	455,176	4,083	5,731	2,517
Wexford	13,983	8,745	4,832	154	148	104
Total.	4,237,271	1,938,818	2,214,478	27,251	40,204	16,502

---

[1] Individuals receiving votes as write-in candidates include Tom Bagwell (10), Valerie L. Willis (5), and Tim Yow (3). The total votes cast per county include the votes received by the candidates listed here.

U.S. HOUSE OF REPRESENTATIVES
2-YEAR TERM

1st Congressional District

County	Total by County	Jack Bergman (Rep.)	Matthew Morgan (Dem.)
Alcona	5,448	3,721	1,727
Alger.	4,126	2,211	1,915
Alpena	12,871	7,638	5,233
Antrim.	12,767	7,792	4,975
Baraga.	3,225	1,916	1,309
Benzie.	9,678	5,127	4,551
Charlevoix.	13,525	7,901	5,624
Cheboygan	12,399	7,739	4,660
Chippewa	13,886	8,311	5,575
Crawford.	6,180	3,912	2,268
Delta.	16,323	9,351	6,972
Dickinson	11,315	7,124	4,191
Emmet	17,774	10,018	7,756
Gogebic	6,480	3,309	3,171
Grand Traverse. .	48,503	24,855	23,648
Houghton	14,236	7,759	6,477
Iron.	5,370	3,106	2,264
Kalkaska	8,258	5,406	2,852
Keweenaw	1,306	726	580
Leelanau	14,111	6,816	7,295
Luce	2,369	1,554	815
Mackinac.	5,661	3,476	2,185
Manistee	11,591	6,334	5,257
Marquette	29,731	12,753	16,978
Mason.	3,693	2,301	1,392
Menominee	8,714	5,243	3,471
Montmorency . .	4,565	3,094	1,471
Ontonagon	3,124	1,786	1,338
Oscoda	3,668	2,513	1,155
Otsego	11,253	7,301	3,952
Presque Isle. . . .	6,639	3,980	2,659
Schoolcraft	3,708	2,178	1,530
Total.	332,497	187,251	145,246

2nd Congressional District

County	Total by County	Bill Huizenga (Rep.)	Rob Davidson (Dem.)	Ronald E. Graeser (UST)
Allegan	945	506	426	13
Kent	65,089	32,182	31,822	1,085
Lake	4,620	2,730	1,767	123
Mason.	9,880	5,514	4,143	223
Muskegon	67,627	30,603	35,685	1,339
Newaygo.	20,126	12,763	6,798	565
Oceana	10,651	6,218	4,205	228
Ottawa	126,525	78,454	46,408	1,663
Total.	305,463	168,970	131,254	5,239

3rd Congressional District

County	Total by County	Justin Amash (Rep.)	Cathy Albro (Dem.)	Ted Gerrard (UST)	Joe Farrington (Write-in)
Barry.........	26,374	16,803	8,730	841	0
Calhoun	48,927	26,630	20,857	1,438	2
Ionia.........	23,155	14,517	7,805	833	0
Kent	210,526	110,084	96,156	4,285	1
Montcalm	1,758	1,073	637	48	0
Total......	310,740	169,107	134,185	7,445	3

4th Congressional District

County	Total by County	John Moolenaar (Rep.)	Jerry Hilliard (Dem.)
Clare.........	11,652	7,687	3,965
Clinton	35,383	19,876	15,507
Gladwin	10,810	7,311	3,499
Gratiot........	14,013	8,827	5,186
Isabella	21,897	11,445	10,452
Mecosta.......	15,277	9,543	5,734
Midland.......	37,897	23,469	14,428
Missaukee.....	6,464	4,943	1,521
Montcalm	20,504	13,330	7,174
Ogemaw......	8,804	5,977	2,827
Osceola.......	9,223	6,663	2,560
Roscommon ...	11,507	7,556	3,951
Saginaw	38,890	25,391	13,499
Shiawassee	29,062	17,222	11,840
Wexford	13,667	9,270	4,397
Total......	285,050	178,510	106,540

5th Congressional District

County	Total by County	Travis Wines (Rep.)	Daniel T. Kildee (Dem.)	Kathy Goodwin (WC)
Arenac	6,565	3,307	2,858	400
Bay..........	45,614	18,577	24,523	2,514
Genesee	165,167	55,850	102,509	6,808
Iosco.........	11,439	5,794	5,004	641
Saginaw	40,288	11,788	26,594	1,906
Tuscola.......	7,340	3,949	3014	377
Total......	276,413	99,265	164,502	12,646

6th Congressional District

County	Total by County	Fred S. Upton (Rep.)	Matt Longjohn (Dem.)	Stephen J. Young (UST)
Allegan	48,295	28,257	17,654	2,384
Berrien	61,981	33,033	26,679	2,269
Cass	19,454	11,824	6,756	874
Kalamazoo	114,103	47,312	63,215	3,576
St. Joseph	20,292	11,908	7,206	1,178
Van Buren.....	29,313	15,102	12,572	1,639
Total......	293,438	147,436	134,082	11,920

7th Congressional District

County	Total by County	Tim Walberg (Rep.)	Gretchen D. Driskell (Dem.)
Branch	15,034	9,937	5,097
Eaton	49,746	23,956	25,790
Hillsdale	16,609	11,470	5,139
Jackson.	60,183	33,653	26,530
Lenawee	39,794	21,908	17,886
Monroe	60,670	34,078	26,592
Washtenaw	53,024	23,728	29,296
Total.	295,060	158,730	136,330

8th Congressional District

County	Total by County	Michael D. Bishop (Rep.)	Elissa Slotkin (Dem.)	Brian Ellison (Lib.)	David J. Lillis (UST)
Ingham	118,614	35,085	80,785	1,937	807
Livingston	96,981	56,266	37,773	2,056	886
Oakland	125,998	68,431	54,322	2,309	936
Total.	341,593	159,782	172,880	6,302	2,629

9th Congressional District

County	Total by County	Candius Stearns (Rep.)	Andy Levin (Dem.)	John V. McDermott (Grn.)	Andrea Kirby (WC)
Macomb	195,753	75,888	112,192	2,545	5,128
Oakland	108,810	36,235	69,542	1,364	1,669
Total.	304,563	112,123	181,734	3,909	6,797

10th Congressional District

County	Total by County	Paul Mitchell (Rep.)	Kimberly Bizon (Dem.)	Harley Mikkelson (Grn.)	Jeremy Peruski (NPA)
Huron.	13,501	8,478	3,652	98	1,273
Lapeer.	38,606	24,697	12,442	455	1,012
Macomb	154,007	91,993	57,552	1,235	3,227
St. Clair	66,059	38,562	23,719	726	3,052
Sanilac	16,340	10,113	4,084	118	2,025
Tuscola	14,551	8,965	4,612	219	755
Total.	303,064	182,808	106,061	2,851	11,344

11th Congressional District

County	Total by County	Lena Epstein (Rep.)	Haley Stevens (Dem.)	Leonard Schwartz (Lib.)	Cooper Nye (NPA)
Oakland	219,602	102,206	110,307	3,796	3,293
Wayne.	131,299	56,257	71,605	2,003	1,434
Total.	350,901	158,463	181,912	5,799	4,727

12th Congressional District

County	Total by County	Jeff Jones (Rep.)	Debbie Dingell (Dem.)	Gary Walkowicz (WC)	Niles Niemuth (NPA)
Washtenaw	117,674	20,279	94,772	1,690	933
Wayne........	176,954	64,836	105,816	5,022	1,280
Total......	294,628	85,115	200,588	6,712	2,213

13th Congressional District

County	Total by County	Rashida Tlaib (Dem.)	D. Etta Wilcoxon (Grn.)	Sam Johnson (WC)	James S. Casha (Write-in)	John Conyers III (Write-in)	David Anthony Dudenhoefer (Write-in)	Douglas W. Gardner (Write-in)
Wayne........	196,299	165,355	7,980	22,186	1	2	75	0
Total......	196,299	165,355	7,980	22,186	1	2	75	0

Brenda Jones (Write-in)	Royce Kinniebrew (Write-in)	Kimberly Hill Knott (Write-in)	Jonathan Lee Pommerville (Write-in)	DaNetta L. Simpson (Write-in)
633	2	1	61	3
633	2	1	61	3

14th Congressional District

County	Total by County	Marc Herschfus (Rep.)	Brenda L. Lawrence (Dem.)	Philip Kolody (WC)
Oakland	137,395	29,251	105,696	2,448
Wayne........	127,599	16,648	108,638	2,313
Total......	264,994	45,899	214,334	4,761

WC = Working Class
NPA = No Party Affiliation
UST = US Taxpayers

GENERAL ELECTION

NOVEMBER 6, 2018

SECRETARY OF STATE

4-YEAR TERM

County	Total by County	Mary Treder Lang (Rep.)	Jocelyn Benson (Dem.)	Gregory Scott Stempfle (Lib.)	Robert Gale (UST)
Alcona	5,473	3,512	1,794	83	84
Alger	4,086	2,085	1,856	87	58
Allegan	49,295	28,816	18,763	1,075	641
Alpena	12,906	7,204	5,197	261	244
Antrim	12,741	7,592	4,688	255	206
Arenac	6,604	3,742	2,548	161	153
Baraga	3,162	1,787	1,254	72	49
Barry	26,587	15,730	9,804	638	415
Bay	45,531	21,176	22,621	960	774
Benzie	9,656	4,966	4,340	218	132
Berrien	61,528	32,677	26,712	1,366	773
Branch	15,002	9,421	5,005	305	271
Calhoun	49,432	24,539	23,046	1,088	759
Cass	19,303	11,605	6,960	414	324
Charlevoix	13,485	7,620	5,387	296	182
Cheboygan	12,318	7,300	4,414	323	281
Chippewa	13,674	7,457	5,702	277	238
Clare	11,610	6,827	4,196	295	292
Clinton	36,325	18,357	16,870	727	371
Crawford	6,110	3,676	2,139	166	129
Delta	16,066	8,862	6,680	294	230
Dickinson	11,114	6,837	3,899	210	168
Eaton	50,135	23,145	25,125	1,123	742
Emmet	17,614	9,677	7,270	424	243
Genesee	165,844	62,829	97,490	3,230	2,295
Gladwin	10,796	6,389	4,012	198	197
Gogebic	6,402	3,035	3,170	123	74
Grand Traverse . .	47,893	24,353	21,830	1,194	516
Gratiot	14,056	7,636	5,774	358	288
Hillsdale	16,571	11,083	4,862	325	301
Houghton	14,069	7,322	6,267	334	146
Huron	13,420	8,406	4,558	218	238
Ingham	117,844	37,387	76,814	2,497	1,146
Ionia	23,294	13,160	9,113	580	441
Iosco	11,544	6,522	4,567	224	231
Iron	5,317	2,965	2,170	93	89
Isabella	21,974	9,844	11,271	501	358
Jackson	60,090	32,485	25,449	1,296	860
Kalamazoo	113,613	43,444	66,341	2,676	1,152
Kalkaska	8,146	5,139	2,598	222	187
Kent	276,968	130,325	137,834	6,257	2,552
Keweenaw	1,284	688	558	21	17
Lake	4,627	2,551	1,845	107	124
Lapeer	38,851	23,003	14,293	905	650
Leelanau	14,001	6,805	6,864	239	93
Lenawee	39,519	21,385	16,708	812	614
Livingston	95,868	54,810	38,339	1,833	886
Luce	2,356	1,510	732	62	52
Mackinaw	5,595	3,259	2,142	84	110
Macomb	354,826	163,485	181,526	5,950	3,865
Manistee	11,516	6,033	5,020	267	196
Marquette	29,494	11,918	16,501	730	345
Mason	13,454	7,419	5,453	311	271

County	Total by County	Mary Treder Lang (Rep.)	Jocelyn Benson (Dem.)	Gregory Scott Stempfle (Lib.)	Robert Gale (UST)
Mecosta.	15,391	8,674	6,047	386	284
Menominee	8,693	4,972	3,450	154	117
Midland.	37,718	20,447	15,916	884	471
Missaukee	6,454	4,569	1,631	133	121
Monroe	60,486	31,782	26,628	1,271	805
Montcalm	22,863	13,236	8,513	569	545
Montmorency . .	4,536	2,963	1,394	82	97
Muskegon	67,763	28,619	36,416	1,614	1,114
Newaygo.	20,035	12,355	6,813	481	386
Oakland	595,905	239,348	342,103	10,405	4,049
Oceana	10,591	5,988	4,095	219	289
Ogemaw	8,816	5,252	3,181	182	201
Ontonagon	3,075	1,710	1,228	64	73
Osceola.	9,243	6,056	2,716	231	240
Oscoda	3,639	2,353	1,111	88	87
Otsego	11,181	7,043	3,687	271	180
Ottawa	126,577	77,459	45,452	2,613	1,053
Presque Isle. . . .	6,558	3,826	2,503	108	121
Roscommon . . .	11,560	6,793	4,265	258	244
Saginaw	79,469	35,658	41,388	1,438	985
St. Clair	66,573	36,474	27,543	1,440	1,116
St. Joseph	20,235	11,829	7,538	456	412
Sanilac	16,204	10,299	5,265	322	318
Schoolcraft	3,634	2,064	1,442	53	75
Shiawassee	29,337	15,016	13,088	646	587
Tuscola	21,939	13,081	7,954	446	458
Van Buren	29,127	14,665	13,181	727	554
Washtenaw	171,417	44,110	123,445	2,931	931
Wayne.	652,277	175,213	460,267	10,249	6,548
Wexford	13,741	8,464	4,612	363	302
Total	4,184,026	1,840,118	2,213,243	81,849	48,816

GENERAL ELECTION
NOVEMBER 6, 2018

>———◆◇◆———<

ATTORNEY GENERAL
4-YEAR TERM

County	Total by County	Tom Leonard (Rep.)	Dana Nessel (Dem.)	Lisa Lane Gioia (Lib.)	Gerald T. Van Sickle (UST)	Chris Graveline (NPA)
Alcona	5,440	3,545	1,661	89	73	72
Alger.	4,065	2,095	1,757	85	48	80
Allegan	48,834	29,650	16,650	1,224	526	784
Alpena	12,629	7,284	4,721	273	145	206
Antrim.	12,562	7,686	4,284	250	139	203
Arenac	6,561	3,947	2,201	147	131	135
Baraga.	3,152	1,810	1,187	71	30	54
Barry.	26,403	16,404	8,460	710	392	437
Bay.	45,488	22,524	19,600	933	582	1,849
Benzie.	9,564	5,101	4,027	206	74	156
Berrien	60,907	32,203	25,777	1,478	499	950
Branch	14,927	9,764	4,399	324	201	239
Calhoun	49,012	25,827	20,341	1,223	803	818
Cass	19,137	11,413	6,710	444	212	358
Charlevoix.	13,353	7,756	4,985	284	112	216
Cheboygan	12,170	7,446	3,982	286	172	284
Chippewa	13,554	7,798	5,035	298	171	252
Clare.	11,585	7,006	3,655	261	224	439
Clinton	36,338	20,081	14,935	630	236	456
Crawford.	6,065	3,755	1,897	154	116	143
Delta.	15,901	8,981	6,182	308	156	274
Dickinson	11,009	6,803	3,711	197	131	167
Eaton	49,346	23,641	23,264	1,054	561	826
Emmet	17,486	9,785	6,843	409	132	317
Genesee	165,063	68,768	87,945	3,590	1,705	3,055
Gladwin	10,806	6,054	3,236	178	149	1,189
Gogebic	6,339	3,020	3,050	121	60	88
Grand Traverse. .	47,880	24,857	20,597	1,238	339	849
Gratiot.	14,100	8,494	4,855	306	196	249
Hillsdale	16,372	11,046	4,534	329	217	246
Houghton	13,945	7,427	5,927	318	82	191
Huron	13,301	8,721	3,934	223	177	246
Ingham	117,232	38,918	72,973	2,510	910	1,921
Ionia	23,039	13,842	7,761	603	380	453
Iosco.	11,468	6,794	4,041	240	153	240
Iron.	5,249	3,008	1,993	106	62	80
Isabella	21,866	10,435	10,269	470	259	433
Jackson	59,601	32,939	23,611	1,376	725	950
Kalamazoo	112,738	46,801	60,271	2,910	841	1,915
Kalkaska	8,078	5,227	2,315	201	136	199
Kent	273,649	135,015	125,055	6,824	2,149	4,606
Keweenaw	1259	692	511	25	10	21
Lake	4,606	2,613	1,620	117	165	91
Lapeer.	38,502	23,931	12,583	801	515	672
Leelanau	13,902	6,909	6,530	235	57	171
Lenawee	39,175	21,351	15,776	782	699	567
Livingston	95,182	56,903	34,229	1,902	742	1,406
Luce	2,344	1,540	658	57	34	55
Mackinaw	5,549	3,376	1,927	90	52	104
Macomb	349,821	172,135	162,515	6,944	2,811	5,416
Manistee	11,423	6,241	4,462	291	211	218
Marquette	29,129	12,081	15,578	723	240	507
Mason	13,433	7,614	5,003	276	309	231

ATTORNEY GENERAL *(Cont.)*

County	Total by County	Tom Leonard (Rep.)	Dana Nessel (Dem.)	Lisa Lane Gioia (Lib.)	Gerald T. Van Sickle (UST)	Chris Graveline (NPA)
Mecosta.......	15,310	8,961	5,379	400	298	272
Menominee....	8,599	4,884	3,379	125	91	120
Midland.......	37,571	21,167	14,240	817	380	967
Missaukee.....	6,439	4,689	1,445	121	81	103
Monroe.......	59,750	32,770	24,209	1,267	564	940
Montcalm	22,711	13,968	7,170	573	571	429
Montmorency ..	4,481	3,000	1,217	97	85	82
Muskegon.....	66,919	30,623	32,524	1,585	949	1,238
Newaygo......	19,895	12,740	5,818	453	551	333
Oakland	588,799	249,115	316,050	10,991	2,818	9,825
Oceana	10,505	6,223	3,581	190	357	154
Ogemaw......	8,709	5,436	2,723	194	174	182
Ontonagon	3,039	1,724	1,171	56	39	49
Osceola.......	9,196	6,251	2,343	244	168	190
Oscoda	3,597	2,415	971	73	71	67
Otsego	11,099	7,161	3,356	221	135	226
Ottawa	125,088	79,493	40,316	2,699	860	1,720
Presque Isle....	6,503	4,019	2,188	112	76	108
Roscommon ...	11,476	7,066	3,779	210	197	224
Saginaw	78,841	37,747	37,222	1,571	832	1,469
St. Clair.......	65,885	38,019	24,309	1,471	898	1,188
St. Joseph	20,059	12,411	6,469	554	244	381
Sanilac	16,096	10,630	4,543	301	331	291
Schoolcraft	3,594	2,078	1,347	58	51	60
Shiawassee	29,200	16,162	11,332	710	433	563
Tuscola	21,816	13,798	6,741	452	377	448
Van Buren.....	28,802	15,413	11,651	751	405	582
Washtenaw	169,897	46,119	117,446	2,948	727	2,657
Wayne........	643,964	184,219	434,116	12,072	4,903	8,654
Wexford	13,665	8,759	4,059	367	197	283
Total......	4,142,044	1,916,117	2,031,117	86,807	38,114	69,889

GENERAL ELECTION

NOVEMBER 6, 2018

―――＞●＜―――

STATE SENATE
4-YEAR TERM

1st State Senate District

County	Total by County	Pauline Montie (Rep.)	Stephanie Chang (Dem.)	David Bullock (Grn.)
Wayne.	86,207	20,879	62,071	3,257
Total.	86,207	20,879	62,071	3,257

2nd State Senate District

County	Total by County	Lisa Papas (Rep.)	Adam Hollier (Dem.)	Yolanda James (Write-in)
Wayne.	71,209	17,288	53,920	1
Total.	71,209	17,288	53,920	1

3rd State Senate District

County	Total by County	Kathy Stecker (Rep.)	Sylvia Santana (Dem.)	Hali McEachern (WC)
Wayne.	71,428	10,928	58,405	2,095
Total.	71,428	10,928	58,405	2,095

4th State Senate District

County	Total by County	Angela Savino (Rep.)	Marshall Bullock II (Dem.)
Wayne.	74,222	16,115	58,107
Total.	74,222	16,115	58,107

5th State Senate District

County	Total by County	DeShawn Wilkins (Rep.)	Betty Jean Alexander (Dem.)	Larry Betts (WC)
Wayne.	90,433	16,479	70,010	3,944
Total.	90,433	16,479	70,010	3,944

6th State Senate District

County	Total by County	Brenda Jones (Rep.)	Erika Geiss (Dem.)
Wayne........	99,090	38,301	60,789
Total......	99,090	38,301	60,789

7th State Senate District

County	Total by County	Laura Cox (Rep.)	Dayna Polehanki (Dem.)	Joseph LeBlanc (Lib.)
Wayne........	137,327	65,001	69,434	2,892
Total......	137,327	65,001	69,434	2,892

8th State Senate District

County	Total by County	Pete Lucido (Rep.)	Paul Francis (Dem.)
Wayne........	123,326	76,172	47,154
Total......	123,326	76,172	47,154

9th State Senate District

County	Total by County	Jeff Bonnell (Rep.)	Paul J. Wojno (Dem.)
Macomb	99,749	34,013	65,736
Total......	99,749	34,013	65,736

10th State Senate District

County	Total by County	Mike MacDonald (Rep.)	Henry Yanez (Dem.)	Mike Saliba (Lib.)
Macomb	112,410	57,353	52,277	2,780
Total......	112,410	57,353	52,277	2,780

11th State Senate District

County	Total by County	Boris Tuman (Rep.)	Jeremy Moss (Dem.)	James Young (Lib.)
Oakland	130,253	27,157	99,916	3,180
Total......	130,253	27,157	99,916	3,180

12th State Senate District

County	Total by County	Michael McCready (Rep.)	Rosemary Bayer (Dem.)	Jeff Pittel (Lib.)	Eugene Sinta (Write-in)
Oakland	120,071	58,363	59,302	2,404	2
Total	120,071	58,363	59,302	2,404	2

13th State Senate District

County	Total by County	Marty Knollenberg (Rep.)	Mallory McMorrow (Dem.)
Oakland	140,944	67,798	73,146
Total	140,944	67,798	73,146

14th State Senate District

County	Total by County	Ruth Johnson (Rep.)	Renee Watson (Dem.)	Jessicia Smith (Grn.)
Genesee	48,789	24,152	23,648	989
Oakland	66,622	40,101	24,930	1,591
Total	115,411	64,253	48,578	2,580

15th State Senate District

County	Total by County	Jim Runestad (Rep.)	Julia Pulver (Dem.)
Oakland	130,288	67,352	62,936
Total	130,288	67,352	62,936

16th State Senate District

County	Total by County	Mike Shirkey (Rep.)	Val Toops (Dem.)	Ronald Muszynski (Lib.)
Branch	14,901	10,248	4,282	371
Hillsdale	16,544	11,899	4,213	432
Jackson	59,424	34,833	22,634	1,957
Total	90,869	56,980	31,129	2,760

17th State Senate District

County	Total by County	Dale Zorn (Rep.)	Bill LaVoy (Dem.)	Chad McNamara (Lib.)
Lenawee	39,311	22,860	15,239	1,212
Monroe	60,559	34,911	23,957	1,691
Total	99,870	57,771	39,196	2,903

18th State Senate District

County	Total by County	Martin Church (Rep.)	Jeff Irwin (Dem.)	Thomas Repasky (WC)
Washtenaw	126,465	26,620	96,891	2,954
Total	126,465	26,620	96,891	2,954

19th State Senate District

County	Total by County	John Bizon (Rep.)	Jason Nobel (Dem.)	Joseph Gillotte (Lib.)
Barry	26,043	16,036	9,016	991
Calhoun	48,877	27,510	20,108	1,259
Ionia	22,766	13,696	8,338	732
Total	97,686	57,242	37,462	2,982

20th State Senate District

County	Total by County	Margaret O'Brien (Rep.)	Sean McCann (Dem.)	Lorence R. Wenke (Lib.)
Kalamazoo	113,997	48,195	60,528	5,274
Total	113,997	48,195	60,528	5,274

21st State Senate District

County	Total by County	Kim LaSata (Rep.)	Ian Haight (Dem.)
Berrien	61,333	33,711	27,622
Cass	18,925	11,937	6,988
St. Joseph	19,803	12,516	7,287
Total	100,061	58,164	41,897

22nd State Senate District

County	Total by County	Lana Theis (Rep.)	Adam Dreher (Dem.)	Eric Borregard (Grn.)
Livingston	93,809	58,494	33,462	1,853
Washtenaw	42,060	17,549	23,705	806
Total	135,869	76,043	57,167	2,659

23rd State Senate District

County	Total by County	Andrea Pollack (Rep.)	Curtis Hertel, Jr. (Dem.)
Ingham	106,910	33,721	73,189
Total	106,910	33,721	73,189

24th State Senate District

County	Total by County	Tom Barrett (Rep.)	Kelly Rossman-McKinney (Dem.)	Katie Nepton (Lib.)	Matthew Shepard (UST)
Clinton	36,601	19,820	15,896	556	329
Eaton	50,619	26,492	22,811	809	507
Ingham	8,700	4,806	3,669	142	83
Shiawassee	29,176	15,851	11,976	557	792
Total	125,096	66,969	54,352	2,064	1,711

25th State Senate District

County	Total by County	Dan Lauwers (Rep.)	Debbie Bourgois (Dem.)
Huron	12,716	8,433	4,283
Macomb	11,953	7,569	4,384
St. Clair	64,164	39,823	24,341
Sanilac	15,808	11,101	4,707
Total	104,641	66,926	37,715

26th State Senate District

County	Total by County	Aric Nesbitt (Rep.)	Garnet Lewis (Dem.)	Erwin Haas (Lib.)	Robert M. Always (Grn.)
Allegan	48,533	29,375	17,465	1,163	530
Kent	30,904	15,191	14,783	635	295
Van Buren	29,095	16,943	11,247	577	328
Total	108,532	61,509	43,495	2,375	1,153

27th State Senate District

County	Total by County	Donna Kekesis (Rep.)	Jim Ananich (Dem.)
Genesee	83,050	23,942	59,108
Total	83,050	23,942	59,108

28th State Senate District

County	Total by County	Peter MacGregor (Rep.)	Craig Beach (Dem.)	Nathan Hewer (Lib.)
Kent	117,745	68,749	45,937	3,059
Total	117,745	68,749	45,937	3,059

29th State Senate District

County	Total by County	Chris Afendoulis (Rep.)	Winnie Brinks (Dem.)	Robert VanNoller (Lib.)	Louis Palus (WC)
Kent	124,225	50,225	70,715	1,840	1,445
Total	124,225	50,225	70,715	1,840	1,445

30th State Senate District

County	Total by County	Roger Victory (Rep.)	Jeanette Schipper (Dem.)	Mary Buzuma (Lib.)
Ottawa	125,416	79,323	42,904	3,189
Total.	125,416	79,323	42,904	3,189

31st State Senate District

County	Total by County	Kevin Daley (Rep.)	Cynthia Luczak (Dem.)
Bay.	45,622	22,702	22,920
Lapeer.	38,003	26,149	11,854
Tuscola	21,602	14,543	7,059
Total.	105,227	63,394	41,833

32nd State Senate District

County	Total by County	Ken Horn (Rep.)	Phil Phelps (Dem.)
Genesee	32,735	18,906	13,829
Saginaw	79,698	43,469	36,229
Total.	112,433	62,375	50,058

33rd State Senate District

County	Total by County	Rick Outman (Rep.)	Mark Bignell (Dem.)	Christopher Comden (UST)	Timothy Joe Prantle (Write-in)
Clare	11,448	6,956	4,153	339	0
Gratiot.	13,873	8,271	5,056	546	0
Isabella	21,474	10,381	10,496	597	0
Mecosta.	15,127	9,074	5,622	431	0
Montcalm	22,942	15,174	7,048	720	0
Total.	84,864	49,856	32,375	2,633	0

34th State Senate District

County	Total by County	Jon Bumstead (Rep.)	Poppy Sias-Hernandez (Dem.)	Max Riekse (Lib.)
Muskegon	68,411	30,692	35,759	1,960
Newaygo.	20,061	13,115	6,303	643
Oceana	10,678	6,506	3,879	293
Total.	99,150	50,313	45,941	2,896

35th State Senate District

County	Total by County	Curtis S. VanderWall (Rep.)	Mike Taillard (Dem.)	Timothy Coon (Lib.)
Benzie.........	9,614	5,388	3,990	236
Crawford......	6,012	3,808	2,025	179
Kalkaska......	8,072	5,338	2,455	279
Lake.........	4,590	2,809	1,677	104
Leelanau......	13,907	7,266	6,380	261
Manistee......	11,529	7,004	4,250	275
Mason........	13,591	8,931	4,385	275
Missaukee.....	6,452	4,928	1,384	140
Ogemaw.......	8,620	5,406	2,927	287
Osceola.......	9,172	6,504	2,413	255
Roscommon ...	11,407	7,101	4,000	306
Wexford......	13,676	9,205	4,037	434
Total......	116,642	73,688	39,923	3,031

36th State Senate District

County	Total by County	Jim Stamas (Rep.)	Joe Weir (Dem.)
Alcona	5,430	3,740	1,690
Alpena	12,887	8,044	4,843
Arenac	6,542	4,228	2,314
Gladwin	10,736	7,125	3,611
Iosco.........	11,347	7,340	4,007
Midland.......	37,710	22,996	14,714
Montmorency ..	4,532	3,215	1,317
Oscoda	3,615	2,547	1,068
Otsego	11,091	7,530	3,561
Presque Isle....	6,563	4,248	2,315
Total......	110,453	71,013	39,440

37th State Senate District

County	Total by County	Wayne Schmidt (Rep.)	Jim Page (Dem.)
Antrim........	12,546	7,996	4,550
Charlevoix.....	13,317	8,052	5,265
Cheboygan	12,143	7,677	4,466
Chippewa	13,622	8,162	5,460
Emmet	17,411	10,156	7,255
Grand Traverse..	47,480	26,183	21,297
Luce	2,342	1,633	709
Mackinac......	5,553	3,479	2,074
Total......	124,414	73,338	51,076

38th State Senate District

County	Total by County	Ed McBroom (Rep.)	Scott Dianda (Dem.)	Wade Paul Roberts (Grn.)
Alger.........	4,136	2,282	1,774	80
Baraga........	3,250	1,854	1,349	47
Delta.........	16,416	10,453	5,733	230
Dickinson	11,453	7,901	3,393	159
Gogebic	6,546	3,040	3,363	143
Houghton	14,360	6,991	7,128	241
Iron..........	5,452	3,183	2,164	105
Keweenaw	1,320	583	720	17
Marquette	29,842	13,516	15,691	635
Menominee....	8,869	5,356	3,320	193
Ontonagon	3,141	1,760	1,340	41
Schoolcraft	3,736	2,371	1,304	61
Total......	108,521	59,290	47,279	1,952

GENERAL ELECTION
NOVEMBER 6, 2018

STATE HOUSE OF REPRESENTATIVES
2-YEAR TERM

1st State Representative District

County	Total by County	Mark Corcoran (Rep.)	Tenisha Yancey (Dem.)	Gregory Creswell (Lib.)
Wayne........	29,887	7,466	21,790	631
Total......	29,887	7,466	21,790	631

2nd State Representative District

County	Total by County	John Palffy (Rep.)	Joseph Tate (Dem.)
Wayne........	30,014	7,954	22,060
Total......	30,014	7,954	22,060

3rd State Representative District

County	Total by County	Dolores Brodersen (Rep.)	Wendell Byrd (Dem.)
Wayne........	22,930	751	22,179
Total......	22,930	751	22,179

4th State Representative District

County	Total by County	Howard Weathington (Rep.)	Isaac Robinson (Dem.)	Md Rabbi Alam (Write-in)	Andre Dwan Godwin (Write-in)
Wayne........	21,368	1,159	20,209	0	0
Total......	21,368	1,159	20,209	0	0

5th State Representative District

County	Total by County	Dorothy Patterson (Rep.)	Cynthia Johnson (Dem.)	Rita Ross (Write-in)
Wayne........	13,874	765	12,839	270
Total......	13,874	765	12,839	270

6th State Representative District

County	Total by County	Linda Sawyer (Rep.)	Tyrone Carter (Dem.)
Wayne........	23,061	2,056	21,005
Total......	23,061	2,056	21,005

7th State Representative District

County	Total by County	Marcelis Turner (Rep.)	LaTanya Garrett (Dem.)
Wayne........	26,468	630	25,838
Total......	26,468	630	25,838

8th State Representative District

County	Total by County	Valerie Parker (Rep.)	Sherry Gay-Dagnogo (Dem.)
Wayne........	28,017	1,022	26,995
Total......	28,017	1,022	26,995

9th State Representative District

County	Total by County	James Stephens (Rep.)	Karen Whitsett (Dem.)
Wayne........	21,848	1,065	20,783
Total......	21,848	1,065	20,783

10th State Representative District

County	Total by County	William Brang (Rep.)	Leslie Love (Dem.)	Jeremy Morgan (Lib.)	Articia Bomer (Write-in)
Wayne........	34,180	4,837	28,713	630	0
Total......	34,180	4,837	28,713	630	0

11th State Representative District

County	Total by County	James Townsend (Rep.)	Jewell Jones (Dem.)
Wayne........	30,958	10,252	20,706
Total......	30,958	10,252	20,706

12th State Representative District

County	Total by County	Michelle Bailey (Rep.)	Alex Garza (Dem.)
Wayne........	31,671	10,567	21,104
Total......	31,671	10,567	21,104

13th State Representative District

County	Total by County	Annie Spencer (Rep.)	Frank Liberati (Dem.)
Wayne........	34,321	12,783	21,538
Total......	34,321	12,783	21,538

14th State Representative District

County	Total by County	Darrell Stasik (Rep.)	Cara Clemente (Dem.)
Wayne........	29,389	10,695	18,694
Total......	29,389	10,695	18,694

15th State Representative District

County	Total by County	Doug Mitchell (Rep.)	Abdullah Hammoud (Dem.)
Wayne........	30,079	9,445	20,634
Total......	30,079	9,445	20,634

16th State Representative District

County	Total by County	Jody Rice-White (Rep.)	Kevin Coleman (Dem.)
Wayne........	32,756	10,728	22,028
Total......	32,756	10,728	22,028

17th State Representative District

County	Total by County	Joe Bellino, Jr. (Rep.)	Michelle LaVoy (Dem.)
Monroe.......	24,473	14,101	10,372
Wayne........	8,790	4,412	4,378
Total......	33,263	18,513	14,750

18th State Representative District

County	Total by County	Kyle McKee (Rep.)	Kevin Hertel (Dem.)
Macomb	41,214	15,394	25,820
Total	41,214	15,394	25,820

19th State Representative District

County	Total by County	Brian Meakin (Rep.)	Laurie Pohutsky (Dem.)
Wayne	46,684	23,230	23,454
Total	46,684	23,230	23,454

20th State Representative District

County	Total by County	Jeff Noble (Rep.)	Matt Koleszar (Dem.)
Wayne	48,227	23,430	24,797
Total	48,227	23,430	24,797

21st State Representative District

County	Total by County	Darian Moore (Rep.)	Kristy Pagan (Dem.)
Wayne	44,390	16,946	27,444
Total	44,390	16,946	27,444

22nd State Representative District

County	Total by County	Arthur Blundell (Rep.)	John Chirkun (Dem.)	Matt Kuehnel (Lib.)
Macomb	30,214	10,374	18,841	999
Total	30,214	10,374	18,841	999

23rd State Representative District

County	Total by County	Michael Frazier (Rep.)	Darrin Camilleri (Dem.)
Wayne	42,528	18,603	23,925
Total	42,528	18,603	23,925

24th State Representative District

County	Total by County	Steve Marino (Rep.)	Laura Winn (Dem.)
Macomb	38,516	21,391	17,125
Total.	38,516	21,391	17,125

25th State Representative District

County	Total by County	Jazmine Early (Rep.)	Nate Shannon (Dem.)
Macomb	35,309	16,228	19,081
Total.	35,309	16,228	19,081

26th State Representative District

County	Total by County	Al Gui (Rep.)	Jim Ellison (Dem.)
Oakland	40,815	12,853	27,962
Total.	40,815	12,853	27,962

27th State Representative District

County	Total by County	Janet Flessland (Rep.)	Robert Wittenberg (Dem.)	Benjamin Carr (Lib.)
Oakland	44,652	8,270	35,054	1,328
Total.	44,652	8,270	35,054	1,328

28th State Representative District

County	Total by County	Aaron Delikta (Rep.)	Lori Stone (Dem.)	Ryan Manier (Lib.)
Macomb	29,399	10,115	18,513	771
Total.	29,399	10,115	18,513	771

29th State Representative District

County	Total by County	Timothy Carrier (Rep.)	Brenda Carter (Dem.)
Oakland	26,938	6,974	19,964
Total.	26,938	6,974	19,964

30th State Representative District

County	Total by County	Diana Farrington (Rep.)	John Spica (Dem.)
Macomb	30,795	17,511	13,284
Total.	30,795	17,511	13,284

31st State Representative District

County	Total by County	Lisa Valerio-Nowc (Rep.)	Bill Sowerby (Dem.)
Macomb	34,716	13,925	20,791
Total.	34,716	13,925	20,791

32nd State Representative District

County	Total by County	Pamela Hornberger (Rep.)	Paul Manley (Dem.)
Macomb	23,253	13,656	9,597
St. Clair	12,679	8,436	4,243
Total.	35,932	22,092	13,840

33rd State Representative District

County	Total by County	Jeff Yaroch (Rep.)	Andrea Geralds (Dem.)
Macomb	39,794	25,929	13,865
Total.	39,794	25,929	13,865

34th State Representative District

County	Total by County	Henry Swift (Rep.)	Sheldon Neeley (Dem.)
Genesee	20,988	2,102	18,886
Total.	20,988	2,102	18,886

35th State Representative District

County	Total by County	Theodore Alfonsetti, III (Rep.)	Kyra Harris Bolden (Dem.)
Oakland	47,518	6,912	40,606
Total.	47,518	6,912	40,606

36th State Representative District

County	Total by County	Douglas Wozniak (Rep.)	Robert Murphy (Dem.)	Benjamin Dryke (Lib.)
Macomb	40,675	26,974	12,894	807
Total	40,675	26,974	12,894	807

37th State Representative District

County	Total by County	Mitch Swoboda (Rep.)	Christine Greig (Dem.)
Oakland	42,809	14,032	28,777
Total	42,809	14,032	28,777

38th State Representative District

County	Total by County	Kathy Crawford (Rep.)	Kelly Breen (Dem.)	Brian Wright (Lib.)
Oakland	45,460	22,474	21,886	1,100
Total	45,460	22,474	21,886	1,100

39th State Representative District

County	Total by County	Ryan Berman (Rep.)	Jennifer Suidan (Dem.)	Anthony Croff (Lib.)
Oakland	42,797	23,173	18,093	1,531
Total	42,797	23,173	18,093	1,531

40th State Representative District

County	Total by County	David Wolkinson (Rep.)	Mari Manoogian (Dem.)
Oakland	53,444	23,222	30,222
Total	53,444	23,222	30,222

41st State Representative District

County	Total by County	Doug Tietz (Rep.)	Padma Kuppa (Dem.)
Oakland	43,490	21,170	22,320
Total	43,490	21,170	22,320

42nd State Representative District

County	Total by County	Ann Bollin (Rep.)	Mona Shand (Dem.)
Livingston	49,837	29,897	19,940
Total	49,837	29,897	19,940

43rd State Representative District

County	Total by County	Andrea K. Schroeder (Rep.)	Nicole Breadon (Dem.)
Oakland	42,570	24,061	18,509
Total	42,570	24,061	18,509

44th State Representative District

County	Total by County	Matt Maddock (Rep.)	Laura Dodd (Dem.)
Oakland	45,515	26,186	19,329
Total	45,515	26,186	19,329

45th State Representative District

County	Total by County	Michael Webber (Rep.)	Kyle Cooper (Dem.)
Oakland	42,863	23,628	19,235
Total	42,863	23,628	19,235

46th State Representative District

County	Total by County	John Reilly (Rep.)	Mindy Denninger (Dem.)
Oakland	44,684	26,786	17,898
Total	44,684	26,786	17,898

47th State Representative District

County	Total by County	Hank Vaupel (Rep.)	Colleen Turk (Dem.)
Livingston	43,586	28,948	14,638
Total	43,586	28,948	14,638

48th State Representative District

County	Total by County	Al Hardwick (Rep.)	Sheryl Kennedy (Dem.)
Genesee	36,472	16,474	19,998
Total.	36,472	16,474	19,998

49th State Representative District

County	Total by County	Patrick Duvendeck (Rep.)	John Cherry (Dem.)
Genesee	31,464	8,695	22,769
Total.	31,464	8,695	22,769

50th State Representative District

County	Total by County	Trace Fisher (Rep.)	Tim Sneller (Dem.)
Genesee	38,572	16,515	22,057
Total.	38,572	16,515	22,057

51st State Representative District

County	Total by County	Mike Mueller (Rep.)	David Lossing (Dem.)
Genesee	34,226	20,155	14,071
Oakland	10,656	6,715	3,941
Total.	44,882	26,870	18,012

52nd State Representative District

County	Total by County	Teri Aiuto (Rep.)	Donna Lasinski (Dem.)	Teresa Spiegelberg (Write-in)
Washtenaw	49,713	19,589	30,089	35
Total.	49,713	19,589	30,089	35

53rd State Representative District

County	Total by County	Jean Holland (Rep.)	Yousef Rabhi (Dem.)
Washtenaw	38,796	5,095	33,701
Total.	38,796	5,095	33,701

54th State Representative District

County	Total by County	Colton Campbell (Rep.)	Ronnie Peterson (Dem.)
Washtenaw	36,237	7,737	28,500
Total	36,237	7,737	28,500

55th State Representative District

County	Total by County	Bob Baird (Rep.)	Rebekah Warren (Dem.)
Washtenaw	40,814	10,629	30,185
Total	40,814	10,629	30,185

56th State Representative District

County	Total by County	Jason Sheppard (Rep.)	Ernie Whiteside (Dem.)
Monroe	35,268	21,979	13,289
Total	35,268	21,979	13,289

57th State Representative District

County	Total by County	Bronna Kahle (Rep.)	Amber Pedersen (Dem.)
Lenawee	36,428	22,936	13,492
Total	36,428	22,936	13,492

58th State Representative District

County	Total by County	Eric Leutheuser (Rep.)	Tamara Barnes (Dem.)
Branch	14,786	9,955	4,831
Hillsdale	16,257	12,115	4,142
Total	31,043	22,070	8,973

59th State Representative District

County	Total by County	Aaron Miller (Rep.)	Dennis Smith (Dem.)
Cass	11,479	7,174	4,305
St. Joseph	20,099	13,748	6,351
Total	31,578	20,922	10,656

60th State Representative District

County	Total by County	William Baker (Rep.)	Jon Hoadley (Dem.)
Kalamazoo	34,953	8,181	26,772
Total......	34,953	8,181	26,772

61st State Representative District

County	Total by County	Brandt Iden (Rep.)	Alberta Griffin (Dem.)
Kalamazoo	46,721	24,002	22,719
Total......	46,721	24,002	22,719

62nd State Representative District

County	Total by County	Dave Morgan (Rep.)	Jim Haadsma (Dem.)
Calhoun	30,737	14,800	15,937
Total......	30,737	14,800	15,937

63rd State Representative District

County	Total by County	Matt Hall (Rep.)	Jennifer Aniano (Dem.)	Ronald Hawkins (Lib.)	John Anthony La Pietra (Grn.)
Calhoun	17,816	10,869	6,127	504	316
Kalamazoo	22,320	11,842	9,682	555	241
Total......	40,136	22,711	15,809	1,059	557

64th State Representative District

County	Total by County	Julie Alexander (Rep.)	Sheila Troxel (Dem.)	Norman Peterson (Lib.)
Jackson.......	31,256	18,050	12,470	736
Total......	31,256	18,050	12,470	736

65th State Representative District

County	Total by County	Sarah Lightner (Rep.)	Terri McKinnon (Dem.)	Jason Rees (Lib.)
Eaton	5,978	3,477	2,333	168
Jackson.......	27,980	16,636	10,573	771
Lenawee	2,784	1,661	1,036	87
Total......	36,742	21,774	13,942	1,026

66th State Representative District

County	Total by County	Beth Griffin (Rep.)	Dan Seibert (Dem.)
Kalamazoo	7,530	4,205	3,325
Van Buren	28,684	16,372	12,312
Total	36,214	20,577	15,637

67th State Representative District

County	Total by County	Leon Clark (Rep.)	Kara Hope (Dem.)	Zachary Moreau (Lib.)
Ingham	42,013	18,454	22,565	994
Total	42,013	18,454	22,565	994

68th State Representative District

County	Total by County	Rosalinda Hernandez (Rep.)	Sarah Anthony (Dem.)	Robin Lea Laurain (Grn.)
Ingham	35,598	8,210	26,664	724
Total	35,598	8,210	26,664	724

69th State Representative District

County	Total by County	George Nastas (Rep.)	Julie Brixie (Dem.)
Ingham	38,200	10,847	27,353
Total	38,200	10,847	27,353

70th State Representative District

County	Total by County	James Lower (Rep.)	Kresta Train (Dem.)
Gratiot	6,725	3,816	2,909
Montcalm	22,275	14,054	8,221
Total	29,000	17,870	11,130

71st State Representative District

County	Total by County	Christine Barnes (Rep.)	Angela Witwer (Dem.)
Eaton	43,289	21,299	21,990
Total	43,289	21,299	21,990

72nd State Representative District

County	Total by County	Steve Johnson (Rep.)	Ron Draayer (Dem.)	Jamie Lewis (Lib.)
Allegan	9,057	6,256	2,512	289
Kent	30,775	15,118	14,761	896
Total.	39,832	21,374	17,273	1185

73rd State Representative District

County	Total by County	Lynn Afendoulis (Rep.)	Bill Saxton (Dem.)
Kent	51,213	30,783	20,430
Total.	51,213	30,783	20,430

74th State Representative District

County	Total by County	Mark Huizenga (Rep.)	Meagan Carr (Dem.)
Kent	40,409	24,445	15,964
Total.	40,409	24,445	15,964

75th State Representative District

County	Total by County	Daniel Schutte (Rep.)	David LaGrand (Dem.)	Jacob Straley (Grn.)
Kent	30,502	5,841	23,709	952
Total.	30,502	5,841	23,709	952

76th State Representative District

County	Total by County	Amanda Brand (Rep.)	Rachel Hood (Dem.)
Kent	44,375	17,366	27,009
Total.	44,375	17,366	27,009

77th State Representative District

County	Total by County	Tommy Brann (Rep.)	Dana Knight (Dem.)	Patty Malowney (Lib.)	Brandon Hoezee (UST)
Kent	37,597	22,514	13,819	866	398
Total.	37,597	22,514	13,819	866	398

78th State Representative District

County	Total by County	Brad Paquette (Rep.)	Dean Hill (Dem.)
Berrien	26,022	15,534	10,488
Cass	7,552	5,062	2,490
Total	33,574	20,596	12,978

79th State Representative District

County	Total by County	Pauline Wendzel (Rep.)	Joey Andrews (Dem.)
Berrien	34,862	19,411	15,451
Total	34,862	19,411	15,451

80th State Representative District

County	Total by County	Mary Whiteford (Rep.)	Mark Ludwig (Dem.)
Allegan	39,275	25,000	14,275
Total	39,275	25,000	14,275

81st State Representative District

County	Total by County	Gary Eisen (Rep.)	Joshua Rivard (Dem.)
St. Clair	35,941	22,811	13,130
Total	35,941	22,811	13,130

82nd State Representative District

County	Total by County	Gary Howell (Rep.)	Christopher Giles (Dem.)
Lapeer	38,132	26,616	11,516
Total	38,132	26,616	11,516

83rd State Representative District

County	Total by County	Shane Hernandez (Rep.)	Stefanie Brown (Dem.)
St. Clair	15,691	8,434	7,257
Sanilac	15,712	11,751	3,961
Total	31,403	20,185	11,218

84th State Representative District

County	Total by County	Phil Green (Rep.)	William Shoop (Dem.)
Huron	13,063	9,067	3,996
Tuscola	21,571	14,150	7,421
Total.	34,634	23,217	11,417

85th State Representative District

County	Total by County	Ben Frederick (Rep.)	Eric Sabin (Dem.)
Saginaw	9,438	6,080	3,358
Shiawassee	28,906	17,612	11,294
Total.	38,344	23,692	14,652

86th State Representative District

County	Total by County	Thomas Albert (Rep.)	Lauren Taylor (Dem.)	Sue Norman (NPA)
Ionia	7,914	4,487	3,079	348
Kent	35,713	21,689	12,947	1,077
Total.	43,627	26,176	16,026	1,425

87th State Representative District

County	Total by County	Julie Calley (Rep.)	Shawn Winters (Dem.)
Barry.	25,951	17,369	8,582
Ionia	14,777	10,146	4,631
Total.	40,728	27,515	13,213

88th State Representative District

County	Total by County	Luke Meerman (Rep.)	Heidi Zuniga (Dem.)
Ottawa	40,260	28,593	11,667
Total.	40,260	28,593	11,667

89th State Representative District

County	Total by County	Jim Lilly (Rep.)	Jerry Sias (Dem.)
Ottawa	44,978	27,917	17,061
Total.	44,978	27,917	17,061

90th State Representative District

County	Total by County	Bradley Slagh (Rep.)	Chritopher Banks (Dem.)
Ottawa	37,175	24,421	12,754
Total	37,175	24,421	12,754

91st State Representative District

County	Total by County	Greg VanWoerkom (Rep.)	Tanya Cabala (Dem.)
Muskegon	37,530	20,914	16,616
Total	37,530	20,914	16,616

92nd State Representative District

County	Total by County	Gail Eichorst (Rep.)	Terry Sabo (Dem.)
Muskegon	28,531	8,917	19,614
Total	28,531	8,917	19,614

93rd State Representative District

County	Total by County	Graham Filler (Rep.)	Dawn Levey (Dem.)	Tyler Palmer (Lib.)
Clinton	35,483	18,154	16,286	1,043
Gratiot.	6,963	4,111	2,627	225
Total	42,446	22,265	18,913	1,268

94th State Representative District

County	Total by County	Rodney Wakeman (Rep.)	Dave Adams (Dem.)
Saginaw	42,105	23,366	18,739
Total	42,105	23,366	18,739

95th State Representative District

County	Total by County	Dorothy Tanner (Rep.)	Vanessa Guerra (Dem.)
Saginaw	26,570	7,149	19,421
Total	26,570	7,149	19,421

96th State Representative District

County	Total by County	Susan Kowalski (Rep.)	Brian Elder (Dem.)
Bay	35,702	15,527	20,175
Total	35,702	15,527	20,175

97th State Representative District

County	Total by County	Jason Wentworth (Rep.)	Celia Young-Wenkel (Dem.)
Arenac	6,415	4,063	2,352
Clare	11,325	7,816	3,509
Gladwin	10,593	7,148	3,445
Osceola	4,795	3,449	1,346
Total	33,128	22,476	10,652

98th State Representative District

County	Total by County	Annette Glenn (Rep.)	Carl Hamann (Rep.)
Bay	9,114	5,062	4,052
Midland	29,724	15,147	14,577
Total	38,838	6,001	4,528

99th State Representative District

County	Total by County	Roger Hauck (Rep.)	Kristen Brown (Dem.)
Isabella	22,255	11,084	11,171
Midland	7,934	5,043	2,891
Total	30,189	16,127	14,062

100th State Representative District

County	Total by County	Scott VanSingel (Rep.)	Sandy Clarke (Dem.)
Lake	4,548	2,662	1,886
Newaygo	19,695	13,701	5,994
Oceana	10,370	6,526	3,844
Total	34,613	22,889	11,724

101st State Representative District

County	Total by County	Jack O'Malley (Rep.)	Kathy Wiejaczka (Dem.)
Benzie	9,678	5,596	4,082
Leelanau	14,058	7,257	6,801
Manistee	11,621	7,069	4,552
Mason	13,607	8,327	5,280
Total	48,964	28,249	20,715

102nd State Representative District

County	Total by County	Michele Hoitenga (Rep.)	Dion Adams (Dem.)
Mecosta.	15,027	9,571	5,456
Osceola.	4,243	3,090	1,153
Wexford	13,615	9,625	3,990
Total	32,885	22,286	10,599

103rd State Representative District

County	Total by County	Daire Rendon (Rep.)	Tim Schaiberger (Dem.)
Crawford.	5,913	3,722	2,191
Kalkaska	7,828	5,241	2,587
Missaukee	6,300	4,703	1,597
Ogemaw	8,715	5,188	3,527
Roscommon . . .	11,371	7,112	4,259
Total	40,127	25,966	14,161

104th State Representative District

County	Total by County	Larry Inman (Rep.)	Dan O'Neil (Dem.)
Grand Traverse. .	47,793	24,071	23,722
Total	47,793	24,071	23,722

105th State Representative District

County	Total by County	Triston Cole (Rep.)	Melissa Fruge (Dem.)
Antrim.	12,637	8,126	4,511
Charlevoix.	13,377	7,936	5,441
Montmorency . .	4,472	3,164	1,308
Oscoda	3,557	2,464	1,093
Otsego	11,068	7,422	3,646
Total	45,111	29,112	15,999

106th State Representative District

County	Total by County	Sue Allor (Rep.)	Lora Greene (Dem.)
Alcona	5,444	3,560	1,884
Alpena	12,946	7,265	5,681
Cheboygan	7,075	4,707	2,368
Iosco.	11,372	6,921	4,451
Presque Isle. . . .	6,596	4,045	2,551
Total	43,433	26,498	16,935

107th State Representative District

County	Total by County	Lee Chatfield (Rep.)	Joanne Galloway (Dem.)
Cheboygan	5,216	3,236	1,980
Chippewa	13,759	8,178	5,581
Emmet	17,700	9,982	7,718
Mackinac.	5,607	3,438	2,169
Total.	42,282	24,834	17,448

108th State Representative District

County	Total by County	Beau LaFave (Rep.)	Bob Romps (Dem.)
Delta.	16,311	9,561	6,750
Dickinson	11,351	7,599	3,752
Menominee	8,727	5,271	3,456
Total.	36,389	22,431	13,958

109th State Representative District

County	Total by County	Melody Wagner (Rep.)	Sara Cambensy (Dem.)
Alger.	4,072	2,013	2,059
Luce	2,348	1,519	829
Marquette	27,264	10,072	17,192
Schoolcraft	3,616	2,027	1,589
Total.	37,300	15,631	21,669

110th State Representative District

County	Total by County	Greg Markkanen (Rep.)	Ken Summers (Dem.)
Baraga.	3,211	1,631	1,580
Gogebic	6,380	2,895	3,485
Houghton	14,090	7,291	6,799
Iron.	5,284	2,873	2,411
Keweenaw	1,281	672	609
Marquette	2,093	943	1,150
Ontonago	3,042	1,675	1,367
Total.	35,381	17,980	17,401

GENERAL ELECTION

NOVEMBER 6, 2018

JUSTICE OF THE SUPREME COURT

8-YEAR TERM (2)

County	Total by County	Samuel Bagenstos	Megan Kathleen Cavanagh	Elizabeth T. Clement	Doug Dern	Kerry Lee Morgan	Kurtis T. Wilder
Alcona	7,850	550	1,702	2,492	320	544	2,242
Alger.	5,966	584	1,405	1,932	264	439	1,342
Allegan	75,158	5,842	15,001	25,665	2,945	4,258	21,447
Alpena	19,547	1,484	4,319	6,167	738	1,515	5,324
Antrim.	19,552	2,001	4,157	6,120	623	1,305	5,346
Arenac	9,864	717	2,568	2,942	448	631	2,558
Baraga.	4,646	448	1,217	1,478	187	304	1,012
Barry.	40,925	2,846	7,954	13,837	1,611	2,572	12,105
Bay.	68,302	5,819	18,901	20,522	2,452	3,941	16,667
Benzie.	14,682	2,036	3,695	4,328	431	837	3,355
Berrien	93,230	8,820	20,547	29,906	3,551	5,728	24,678
Branch	22,552	1,444	4,627	8,170	998	1,192	6,121
Calhoun	74,475	5,568	16,162	24,259	2,898	5,778	19,810
Cass	28,905	2,125	5,857	9,632	1,420	2,040	7,831
Charlevoix.	20,486	1,943	4,493	6,591	748	1,256	5,455
Cheboygan	18,554	1,635	3,899	5,969	712	1,230	5,109
Chippewa	20,836	1,780	4,347	6,905	656	1,551	5,597
Clare.	17,317	1,254	3,765	5,289	837	1,265	4,907
Clinton	54,809	5,281	12,754	18,720	1,891	2,617	13,546
Crawford.	8,850	670	1,815	2,829	386	646	2,504
Delta.	23,356	2,208	5,222	7,451	826	1,636	6,013
Dickinson	16,553	1,203	3,522	5,457	793	1,188	4,390
Eaton	76,883	7,741	18,078	25,311	2,840	4,329	18,584
Emmet	26,961	2,752	5,871	8,708	892	1,598	7,140
Genesee	251,624	28,428	69,150	72,582	8,986	15,998	56,480
Gladwin	15,995	1,017	3,987	4,949	739	1,121	4,182
Gogebic	9,198	968	2,379	2,790	362	647	2,052
Grand Traverse. .	72,255	10,302	18,216	22,587	1,906	3,546	15,698
Gratiot.	21,491	1,684	5,355	6,591	890	1,534	5,437
Hillsdale	24,200	1,551	4,403	8,531	1,026	1,442	7,247
Houghton	20,591	2,446	5,083	6,229	685	1,323	4,825
Huron	20,286	1,387	5,057	6,534	769	1,060	5,479
Ingham	188,354	27,470	51,831	55,636	5,206	10,349	37,862
Ionia	34,761	2,575	7,050	11,603	1,588	2,120	9,825
Iosco.	17,158	1,272	4,342	5,342	644	1,092	4,466
Iron.	7,759	531	1,779	2,600	395	595	1,859
Isabella	33,253	3,335	8,879	10,118	1,263	2,209	7,449
Jackson	91,394	7,618	20,810	30,290	3,665	5,465	23,546
Kalamazoo	174,546	22,691	41,827	54,338	5,225	9,607	40,858
Kalkaska	11,785	810	2,409	3,751	571	924	3,320
Kent	428,963	45,006	94,579	139,932	12,392	23,942	113,112
Keweenaw	1,856	197	461	606	61	119	412
Lake	6,841	471	1,414	2,139	337	552	1,928
Lapeer.	57,420	4,015	13,074	18,117	2,393	3,402	16,419
Leelanau	21,847	3,108	5,541	6,459	531	1,131	5,077
Lenawee	59,067	5,116	13,733	18,413	2,533	3,837	15,435
Livingston	141,210	13,721	34,166	43,028	5,288	6,843	38,164
Luce	3,387	224	653	1,180	207	229	894
Mackinac.	8,187	617	1,778	2,743	270	645	2,134
Macomb	529,248	50,801	138,485	162,336	18,401	28,837	130,388
Manistee	17,563	1,598	3,850	5,683	734	1,241	4,457
Marquette	44,275	5,641	11,493	13,418	1,372	2,894	9,457
Mason.	21,250	1,757	4,501	6,799	868	1,624	5,701
Mecosta.	23,244	1,973	4,942	7,579	1,054	1,490	6,206

County	Total by County	Samuel Bagenstos	Megan Kathleen Cavanagh	Elizabeth T. Clement	Doug Dern	Kerry Lee Morgan	Kurtis T. Wilder
Menominee	12,232	1,063	2,873	3,679	609	1,029	2,979
Midland.	55,915	4,957	13,269	18,146	1,940	3,046	14,557
Missaukee	9,790	499	1,623	3,305	392	724	3,247
Monroe	87,308	7,784	21,667	26,051	4,010	5,203	22,593
Montcalm	33,560	2,354	6,757	10,781	1,669	2,191	9,808
Montmorency . .	6,602	477	1,310	2,190	315	424	1,886
Muskegon	100,716	9,844	23,968	31,658	3,998	6,416	24,832
Newaygo.	29,838	1,904	5,595	10,056	1,280	1,803	9,200
Oakland	869,214	121,845	237,589	247,017	24,926	43,759	194,078
Oceana	15,792	1,261	3,275	5,139	647	923	4,547
Ogemaw	12,920	769	3,202	3,927	602	968	3,452
Ontonagon	4,388	369	974	1,281	246	401	1,117
Osceola.	14,007	850	2,663	4,528	736	1,101	4,129
Oscoda	5,195	363	1,052	1,647	232	371	1,530
Otsego	16,526	1,249	3,297	5,651	549	992	4,788
Ottawa	193,191	14,874	34,642	69,133	6,237	8,886	59,419
Presque Isle. . . .	9,872	734	2,045	3,090	363	818	2,822
Roscommon . . .	16,857	1,169	3,521	5,498	822	1,142	4,705
Saginaw	117,488	10,136	30,923	35,614	4,134	7,136	29,545
St. Clair	98,294	7,705	24,592	29,783	4,208	6,127	25,879
St. Joseph	30,951	2,073	6,211	10,260	1,320	2,161	8,926
Sanilac	24,496	1,385	5,608	7,927	1,117	1,494	6,965
Schoolcraft	5,091	369	1,227	1,635	191	374	1,295
Shiawassee	45,046	3,465	11,284	14,058	1,980	2,885	11,374
Tuscola	32,998	2,170	8,033	10,222	1,463	1,993	9,117
Van Buren	44,062	3,647	9,580	14,785	1,644	2,760	11,646
Washtenaw	277,176	66,353	90,366	60,017	5,548	10,193	44,699
Wayne.	942,962	130,839	270,156	243,992	27,194	59,967	210,814
Wexford	20,637	1,474	4,105	6,809	903	1,353	5,993
Total.	6,262,391	717,062	1,584,512	1,871,462	209,103	360,858	1,519,394

JUDGES OF THE CIRCUIT COURT

2nd Circuit Court *(1 incumbent position, 6-year term)*

County	Total by County	Angela M. Pasula
Berrien	45,380	45,380
Total	45,380	45,380

3rd Circuit Court *(16 incumbent positions, 6-year terms)*

County	Total by County	Annette J. Berry	Gregory D. Bill	Karen Y. Braxton	Jerome C. Cavanagh	Kevin J. Cox	Paul John Cusick
Wayne.	3,159,309	239,572	171,153	227,278	221,566	208,304	165,694
Total	3,159,309	239,572	171,153	227,278	221,566	208,304	165,694

Prentis Edwards, Jr.	Edward Ewell, Jr.	Adel A. Harb	Dana Margaret Hathaway	Charles S. Hegarty	Catherine L. Heise
175,133	167,159	168,962	248,761	156,625	187,777
175,133	167,159	168,962	248,761	156,625	187,777

Qiana Denise Lillard	Kathleen M. McCarthy	Leslie Kim Smith	Deborah A. Thomas
178,880	212,946	188,721	240,778
178,880	212,946	188,721	240,778

3rd Circuit Court *(3 non-incumbent positions, 6-year terms)*

County	Total by County	John C. Cahalan	Tracy E. Green	Bridget Mary Hathaway	Delicia Coleman	Suzette Samuels	Regina Daniels Thomas
Wayne.	1,094,344	188,366	209,638	231,521	103,501	139,597	221,721
Total	1,094,344	188,366	209,638	231,521	103,501	139,597	221,721

3rd Circuit Court *(2 positions to fill partial terms ending January 1, 2021)*

County	Total by County	Mariam Bazzi	Donald Knapp	Lynn Hawkins (Write-in)
Wayne.	634,201	320,710	313,478	13
Total	634,201	320,710	313,478	13

4th Circuit Court *(1 incumbent position, 6-year term)*

County	Total by County	Thomas D. Wilson
Jackson	45,185	45,185
Total	45,185	45,185

6th Circuit Court *(5 incumbent positions, 6-year terms)*

County	Total by County	Leo Bowman	Karen D. McDonald	Phyllis C. McMillen	Denise Langford Morris	Michael D. Warren Jr.
Oakland	1,301,143	261,649	279,690	256,287	263,504	240,013
Total	1,301,143	261,649	279,690	256,287	263,504	240,013

6th Circuit Court *(1 non-incumbent position, 6-year term)*

County	Total by County	Dan Christ	Jacob James Cunningham
Oakland	414,559	196,560	217,999
Total	414,559	196,560	217,999

6th Circuit Court *(1 new judgeship position, 6-year term)*

County	Total by County	Julie A. McDonald	Michael J. Blau	Maryann Bruder	Edward M. Nahhat	Corinne Shoop
Oakland	340,536	334,376	947	1,374	3,110	729
Total	340,536	334,376	947	1,374	3,110	729

7th Circuit Court *(1 incumbent position, 6-year term)*

County	Total by County	Celeste D. Bell	Tabitha M. Marsh
Genesee	132,206	78,825	53,381
Total	132,206	78,825	53,381

7th Circuit Court *(2 non-incumbent positions, 6-year terms)*

County	Total by County	Chris Christenson	Elizabeth Anne Kelly	Richard F. McNally	Brian S. Pickell
Genesee	239,659	60,759	71,963	35,274	71,663
Total	239,659	60,759	71,963	35,274	71,663

9th Circuit Court *(2 incumbent positions, 6-year terms)*

County	Total by County	Paul J. Bridenstine	Pamela L. Lightvoet
Kalamazoo	141,155	67,062	74,093
Total	141,155	67,062	74,093

10th Circuit Court *(2 incumbent positions, 6-year terms)*

County	Total by County	Janet M. Boes	Darnell Jackson
Saginaw	99,505	48,295	51,210
Total	99,505	48,295	51,210

10th Circuit Court *(1 position to fill partial term ending January 1, 2021)*

County	Total by County	Manvel Trice, III
Saginaw	57,617	57,617
Total	57,617	57,617

13th Circuit Court *(1 position to fill partial term ending January 1, 2021)*

County	Total by County	Kevin A. Elsenheimer
Antrim.	9,276	9,276
Grand Traverse. .	32,351	32,351
Leelanau	8,994	8,994
Total	50,621	50,621

14th Circuit Court *(1 incumbent position, 6-year term)*

County	Total by County	Annette R. Smedley
Muskegon	48,842	48,842
Total	48,842	48,842

16th Circuit Court *(5 incumbent positions, 6-year terms)*

County	Total by County	James M. Biernat Jr.	Jennifer Faunce	Edward A. Servitto, Jr.	Mark S. Switalski	Tracey A. Yokich
Macomb	855,301	165,543	180,425	176,791	170,826	161,716
Total	855,301	165,543	180,425	176,791	170,826	161,716

16th Circuit Court *(1 new judgeship position, 8-year term)*

County	Total by County	Julie Lynn Gatti	Elizabeth A. Pyden
Macomb	268,233	168,616	99,617
Total	268,233	168,616	99,617

17th Circuit Court *(2 incumbent positions, 6-year terms)*

County	Total by County	Mark A. Trusock	Christopher P. Yates
Kent	334,288	165,193	169,095
Total	334,288	165,193	169,095

17th Circuit Court *(2 non-incumbent positions, 6-year terms)*

County	Total by County	Curt A. Benson	Alida Bryant	Christina Elmore	Scott A. Noto
Kent	372,892	101,355	84,276	99,219	88,042
Total	372,892	101,355	84,276	99,219	88,042

20th Circuit Court *(1 incumbent position, 6-year term)*

County	Total by County	Jon A. Van Allsburg
Ottawa	88,405	88,405
Total	88,405	88,405

21st Circuit Court *(1 incumbent position, 6-year term)*

County	Total by County	Mark H. Duthie
Isabella	16,369	16,369
Total	16,369	16,369

22nd Circuit Court *(2 incumbent positions, 6-year terms)*

County	Total by County	Timothy Patrick Connors	Carol Anne Kuhnke
Washtenaw	202,652	97,463	105,189
Total	202,652	97,463	105,189

27th Circuit Court *(1 incumbent position, 6-year term)*

County	Total by County	Robert D. Springstead
Newaygo.	14,908	14,908
Oceana	7,658	7,658
Total	22,566	22,566

30th Circuit Court *(2 incumbent positions, 6-year terms)*

County	Total by County	Laura L. Baird	James S. Jamo
Ingham	147,342	82,227	65,115
Total	147,342	82,227	65,115

31st Circuit Court *(1 incumbent position, 6-year term)*

County	Total by County	Michael L. West
St. Clair	48,480	48,480
Total	48,480	48,480

36th Circuit Court *(1 incumbent position, 6-year term)*

County	Total by County	Kathleen M. Brickley
Van Buren	21,490	21,490
Total	21,490	21,490

37th Circuit Court *(1 incumbent position, 6-year term)*

County	Total by County	John Hallacy
Calhoun	38,580	38,580
Total	38,580	38,580

38th Circuit Court *(1 incumbent position, 6-year term)*

County	Total by County	Mark S. Braunlich
Monroe	43,280	43,280
Total	43,280	43,280

39th Circuit Court *(1 incumbent position, 6-year term)*

County	Total by County	Anna Marie Anzalone
Lenawee	28,801	28,801
Total	28,801	28,801

41st Circuit Court *(1 position to fill partial term ending January 1, 2021)*

County	Total by County	Christopher S. Ninomiya
Dickinson	9,421	9,421
Iron.	3,991	3,991
Menominee	5,977	5,977
Total	19,389	19,389

42nd Circuit Court *(1 incumbent position, 6-year term)*

County	Total by County	Stephen P. Carras
Midland.	26,994	26,994
Total	26,994	26,994

44th Circuit Court *(1 incumbent position, 6-year term)*

County	Total by County	Michael P. Hatty
Livingston	61,582	61,582
Total	61,582	61,582

44th Circuit Court *(1 new judgeship position, 8-year term)*

County	Total by County	Dennis L. Brewer	L. Suzanne Geddis
Livingston	76,025	37,223	38,802
Total	76,025	37,223	38,802

45th Circuit Court *(1 incumbent position, 6-year term)*

County	Total by County	Paul E. Stutesman
St. Joseph	15,683	15,683
Total	15,683	15,683

48th Circuit Court *(1 position to fill partial term ending January 1, 2021)*

County	Total by County	Roberts Kengis
Allegan	35,399	35,399
Total	35,399	35,399

49th Circuit Court *(1 incumbent position, 6-year term)*

County	Total by County	Scott P. Hill-Kennedy
Mecosta.	11,831	11,831
Osceola.	7,167	7,167
Total	18,998	18,998

50th Circuit Court *(1 incumbent position, 6-year term)*

County	Total by County	James P. Lambros
Chippewa	11,118	11,118
Total	11,118	11,118

54th Circuit Court *(1 incumbent position, 6-year term)*

County	Total by County	Amy Grace Gierhart
Tuscola	17,611	17,611
Total	17,611	17,611

55th Circuit Court *(1 incumbent position, 6-year term)*

County	Total by County	Roy G. Mienk
Clare	8,862	8,862
Gladwin	8,119	8,119
Total	16,981	16,981

56th Circuit Court *(1 incumbent position, 6-year term)*

County	Total by County	Janice K. Cunningham
Eaton	36,052	36,052
Total	36,052	36,052

56th Circuit Court *(1 position to fill partial term ending January 1, 2021)*

County	Total by County	John Douglas Maurer
Eaton	35,128	35,128
Total	35,128	35,128

57th Circuit Court *(1 incumbent position, 6-year term)*

County	Total by County	Charles W. Johnson
Emmet	12,780	12,780
Total	12,780	12,780

VOTER REGISTRATION AND ELECTION TURNOUT STATISTICS FOR MICHIGAN GENERAL ELECTIONS, 1948-2018

PRESIDENTIAL ELECTIONS

Year	Number Voting[1]	Number Registered[2]	Voting Age Population (VAP)[3]	Turnout (% of VAP)
1948	2,109,609	Not Available	4,041,000	52.2
1952	2,798,592	Not Available	4,193,000	66.7
1956	3,080,468	3,128,573	4,538,000	67.9
1960	3,318,097	3,454,804	4,564,000	72.7
1964	3,203,102	3,351,730	4,658,000	68.8
1968	3,306,250	4,022,378	4,953,000	66.8
1972	3,490,325	4,762,764[4]	5,874,000[5]	59.4
1976	3,722,384	5,202,379[6]	6,268,000	59.4
1980	3,978,647	5,725,713	6,510,000	61.1
1984	3,884,854	5,888,808	6,551,000	59.3
1988	3,745,751	5,952,513	6,774,000	55.3
1992	4,341,909	6,147,083	6,947,000	62.5
1996	3,912,261	6,677,079[7]	7,177,000	54.5
2000	4,279,299	6,859,332	7,358,000	58.2
2004	4,875,692	7,164,047	7,541,000	64.7
2008	5,039,080	7,470,764	7,613,000	66.2
2012	4,780,701	7,454,553	7,616,490	63.0
2016	4,874,619	7,514,055	7,737,250	63.0

GUBERNATORIAL ELECTIONS

Year	Number Voting[1]	Number Registered[2]	Voting Age Population (VAP)[3]	Turnout (% of VAP)
1950	1,879,382	Not Available	4,137,000	45.4
1954	2,187,027	Not Available	4,342,000	50.4
1958	2,312,184	3,489,626	4,623,000	50.0
1962	2,764,839	3,710,798	4,605,000	60.0
1966	2,461,909	3,613,463	4,718,000	52.2
1970	2,656,162	3,969,807	5,148,000	51.6
1974	2,657,017	4,785,689	6,037,000	44.0
1978	2,984,829	5,230,345	6,405,000	46.6
1982	3,135,978	5,624,573	6,554,000	47.8
1986	2,468,009	5,790,753	6,675,000	37.0
1990	2,641,649	5,892,001[8]	6,851,000	38.6
1994	3,177,740	6,207,662	6,983,000	45.5
1998	3,143,432	6,300,000[9]	7,227,000	43.5
2002	3,219,864	6,797,293	7,400,000	43.5
2006	3,852,008	7,180,778	7,597,000	50.7
2010	3,268,217	7,276,237	7,620,000	42.9
2014	3,188,956	7,446,280	7,660,000	41.6
2018	4,341,340	7,471,088	7,831,250	55.4

[1] As a "poll book total" was not kept prior to 1976, the turnout figures for elections held between 1948 and 1974 are based on the greatest number of votes cast for an office in the election.

[2] A registration figure for the state was not compiled for elections held prior to 1956.

[3] Voting age population figures obtained from U.S. Bureau of the Census, P-25 Series and *Source Book of American Presidential Campaign and Election Statistics, 1948-1968*, compiled and edited by John H. Runyon, Jennifer Verdini and Sally Runyon, c 1971 by Frederick Unger, New York.

[4] The large increase in the number of registered voters in the state from 1970 to 1972 was the result of a March 1972 Michigan Supreme Court ruling which declared that it was unconstitutional to purge the registration of a voter who had not voted over a period of two years as Michigan law then required. In effect, this compelled clerks to reinstate the registrations of "non-voters" who had been purged from the registration rolls since 1968. *Michigan State UAW Community Action Program Council* v *Secretary of State*, 387 Mich. 506, 198 NW2d 385 (1972).

[5] The large increase in the state's voting age population from 1970 to 1972 was the result of the 26th Amendment to the U.S. Constitution which lowered the minimum voting age from 21 to 18.

[6] Two events occurred in 1975 which affected the 1976 registration total: (1) the Secretary of State Branch Office Voter Registration program was put into effect in October and (2) provisions allowing for the creation of "inactive" voter registration files were put into effect. Registration totals listed for 1976 to 1984 reflect only those registrations held in 4-year "active" files.

[7] The National Voter Registration Act, effective January 1, 1995, eliminated the initiation of any voter registration cancellations for inactivity and introduced several new voter registration programs in the state, including mail-in registration.

[8] Public Act 142 of 1989 authorized city and township clerks to establish a 5-year voter registration file and eliminate their "inactive" files. Registration totals listed for 1990 to 1994 are based on the 5-year voter registration files maintained by the clerks.

[9] In 1998, approximately 600,000 duplicate voter registration records were purged from the state's registration rolls through the implementation of the Qualified Voter File — a statewide voter registration database mandated under Public Act 441 of 1994.

Source: Bureau of Elections, Department of State

SUMMARY OF VOTE FOR GOVERNOR, 1835-2018

Year	Name	Vote	Year	Name	Vote
1835	Mason, Democrat	7,558	1860	Blair, Republican	87,806
	Biddle, Whig	814		Barry, Democrat	67,221
	Scattering	94		Scattering	27
	Mason's majority	6,744		Blair's majority	20,585
1837	Mason, Democrat	15,314	1862	Blair, Republican	68,716
	Trowbridge, Whig	14,800		Stout, Union	62,102
	Scattering	544		Scattering	40
	Mason's majority	514		Blair's majority	6,614
1839	Woodbridge, Whig	18,195	1864[2]	Crapo, Republican	81,744
	Farnsworth, Democrat	17,037		Fenton, Democrat	71,301
	Scattering	55		Scattering	18
	Woodbridge's majority	1,158		Crapo's majority	10,443
1841	Barry, Democrat	20,993	1866	Crapo, Republican	96,746
	Fuller, Whig	15,439		Williams, Democrat	67,708
	Fitch, Liberty Party	1,223		Scattering	146
	Scattering	68		Crapo's majority	29,038
	Barry's plurality	5,554	1868	Baldwin, Republican	128,051
1843	Barry, Democrat	21,392		Moore, Democrat	97,290
	Pitcher, Whig	14,899		Scattering	705
	Birney, Liberty Party	2,776		Baldwin's majority	30,761
	Scattering	74	1870	Baldwin, Republican	100,176
	Barry's plurality	6,493		Comstock, Democrat	83,391
1845	Felch, Democrat	20,123		Fish, Prohibition	2,710
	Vickery, Whig	16,316		Scattering	230
	Birney, Liberty Party	3,023		Baldwin's plurality	16,785
	Scattering	127	1872	Bagley, Republican	137,602
	Felch's plurality	3,807		Blair, Liberal	80,958
1847	Ransom, Democrat	24,639		Ferry, Straight Democrat	2,720
	Edmunds, Whig	18,990		Fish, Prohibition	1,231
	Gurney, Liberty Party	2,585		Scattering	39
	Scattering	145		Bagley's plurality	56,644
	Ransom's plurality	5,649	1874	Bagley, Republican	111,519
1849	Barry, Democrat	27,837		Chamberlain, Democrat	105,550
	Littlejohn, Whig and Free Soil . .	23,540		Carpenter, Prohibition	3,937
	Scattering	192		Scattering	417
	Barry's majority	4,297		Bagley's plurality	5,969
1851[1]	McClelland, Democrat	23,827	1876	Croswell, Republican	165,926
	Gidley, Whig	16,901		Webber, Democrat	142,492
	Scattering	156		Sparks, Greenback	8,297
	McClelland's majority	6,926		Croswell's plurality	23,434
1852[1]	McClelland, Democrat	42,798	1878	Croswell, Republican	126,280
	Chandler, Whig	34,660		Barnes, Democrat	78,503
	Christiancy, Free Soil	5,850		Smith, Greenback	73,313
	Scattering	68		Snyder, Prohibition	3,469
	McClelland's plurality	8,138		Scattering	1,200
1854	Bingham, Republican	43,652		Croswell's plurality	47,777
	Barry, Democrat	38,675	1880	Jerome, Republican	178,944
	Scattering	39		Holloway, Democrat	137,671
	Bingham's majority	4,977		Woodman, Greenback	31,085
1856	Bingham, Republican	71,402		McKeever, Prohibition	1,114
	Felch, Democrat	54,085		Quick, Am. Labor	220
	Scattering	71		Scattering	134
	Bingham's majority	17,317		Jerome's plurality	41,273
1858	Wisner, Republican	65,202	1882	Begole, Fusionist	154,269
	Stuart, Democrat	56,067		Jerome, Republican	149,697
	Scattering	146		Sagendorph, Prohibition	5,854
	Wisner's majority	9,135		May, National	2,006
				Foote	343
				Begole's plurality	4,572

SUMMARY OF VOTE FOR GOVERNOR (Cont.)

Year	Name	Vote	Year	Name	Vote
1884	Alger, Republican	190,840	1902	Bliss, Republican	211,261
	Begole, Fusionist	186,887		Durand, Democrat	174,077
	Preston, Prohibition	22,207		Westerman, Prohibition.	11,326
	Miller, Butler Greenback	364		Walter, Socialist.	4,271
	Scattering.	50		Cowles, Socialist Labor	1,282
	Alger's plurality.	3,953		Scattering	9
				Bliss' plurality	37,184
1886	Luce, Republican	181,474			
	Yaple, Fusionist	174,042	1904	Warner, Republican.	283,799
	Dickie, Prohibition	25,179		Ferris, Democrat.	223,571
	Scattering.	190		Shackleton, Prohibition.	10,395
	Luce's plurality	7,432		Lamb, Socialist	6,170
				Meyer, Socialist Labor	782
1888	Luce, Republican	233,595		Scattering.	4
	Burt, Fusionist	216,450		Warner's plurality	60,228
	Cheney, Prohibition	20,342			
	Mills, Union Labor	4,388	1906	Warner, Republican.	227,567
	Scattering.	17		Kimmerle, Democrat.	130,018
	Luce's plurality	17,145		Reed, Prohibition	9,139
				Walker, Socialist	5,925
1890	Winans, Democrat	183,725		Richter, Socialist Labor	1,153
	Turner, Republican.	172,205		Scattering.	4
	Patridge, Prohibition.	28,681		Warner's plurality	97,549
	Belden, Industrial	13,198			
	Scattering.	47	1908	Warner, Republican.	262,141
	Winans' plurality.	11,520		Hemans, Democrat.	252,611
				Gray, Prohibition	16,092
1892	Rich, Republican.	221,228		Stirton, Socialist	9,447
	Morse, Democrat	205,138		McInnis, Socialist Labor.	845
	Ewing, People's	21,417		Nichols, Independence	612
	Russell, Prohibition.	20,777		Scattering.	19
	Scattering.	77		Warner's plurality	9,530
	Rich's plurality	16,090			
			1910	Osborn, Republican	202,803
1894	Rich, Republican.	237,215		Hemans, Democrat.	159,770
	Fisher, Democrat	130,823		Warnock, Socialist.	9,992
	Nichols, People's	30,012		Corbett, Prohibition	9,989
	Todd, Prohibition	18,788		Richter, Socialist Labor	1,204
	Scattering.	150		Scattering.	4
	Rich's plurality	106,392		Osborn's plurality	43,033
1896	Pingree, Republican	304,431	1912	Ferris, Democrat.	194,017
	Sligh, D.P.U.S.[3]	221,022		Musselman, Republican.	169,963
	Sprague, Democrat	9,738		Watkins, National Progressive . .	152,909
	Safford, Prohibition.	5,499		Hoogerhyde, Socialist	21,398
	Giberson, National	1,944		Leland, Prohibition	7,811
	Scattering.	5,168		Richter, Socialist Labor	359
	Pingree's plurality	83,409		Scattering.	2,464[4]
				Ferris' plurality	24,054
1898	Pingree, Republican	243,239			
	Whiting, D.P.U.S.	168,142	1914	Ferris, Democrat.	212,063
	Cheever, Prohibition	7,006		Osborn, Republican	176,254
	Cook, People's	1,656		Pattengill, Progressive	36,747
	Hasseler, Socialist	1,101		Hoogerhyde, Socialist	11,056
	Scattering	20		Eayrs, Prohibition	3,830
	Pingree's plurality	75,097		Richter, Socialist Labor	497
				Harris.	1
1900	Bliss, Republican	305,612		Ferris' plurality	35,809
	Maybury, Democrat	226,228			
	Goodrich, Prohibition	11,834	1916	Sleeper, Republican	363,724
	Ramsay, Social Democrat	2,709		Sweet, Democrat	264,440
	Ulbricht, Social Labor	958		Moore, Socialist	15,040
	Thompson, People's	871		Woodruff, Prohibition	7,255
	Pingree, Social Democrat	2		Murray, Socialist Labor	963
	Bliss' plurality	79,384		Pattengill, Progressive	95
				Durfee	1
				Sleeper's plurality	99,284

Year	Name	Vote	Year	Name	Vote
1918	Sleeper, Republican	266,738	1934	Fitzgerald, Republican.	659,743
	Bailey, Democrat	158,142		Lacy, Democrat.	577,044
	Moore, Socialist	7,068		Larsen, Socialist	12,002
	McColl, Prohibition	1,637		Anderson, Communist.	5,734
	Hinds, Socialist Labor	790		Alderdyce, Farmer-Labor	2,105
	Scattering	1		Fraser, Socialist Labor	1,040
	Sleeper's plurality	108,596		Buell, Commonwealth	800
				Pointer, People's Prog.	198
1920	Groesbeck, Republican	703,180		Meadow, National.	164
	Ferris, Democrat.	310,566		Lee, American	95
	Blumenberg, Socialist	23,542		Fitzgerald's plurality	82,699
	Jeffries, Farmer-Labor	11,817	1936	Murphy, Democrat	892,774
	Johnston, Prohibition	6,990		Fitzgerald, Republican.	843,855
	Markley, Socialist Labor	2,097		Monarch, Socialist.	6,631
	Scattering	347[5]		Martin, Farmer-Labor	3,289
	Groesbeck's plurality.	392,614		Raymond, Communist.	2,071
				O'Donohue, Socialist Labor.	524
1922	Groesbeck, Republican	356,933		Fuller, Commonwealth	433
	Cummins, Democrat.	218,252		Mann, American	170
	Blumenberg, Socialist	4,452		Scattering	22
	Hoyt, Prohibition	2,744		Murphy's plurality	48,919
	Markley, Socialist Labor	1,279	1938	Fitzgerald, Republican.	847,245
	Scattering	1		Murphy, Democrat	753,752
	Groesbeck's plurality.	138,681		Burnett, Socialist.	2,896
1924	Groesbeck, Republican	799,225		O'Donohue, Socialist Labor.	446
	Frensdorf, Democrat.	343,577		Hammond, American	257
	Johnston, Prohibition	11,118		Beshgetoor, Commonwealth	242
	Dinger, Socialist Labor	4,079		Holmes, Square Deal	205
	Krieghoff, Socialist	2,725		Gover, Protestants United	177
	Scattering	194		Scattering	21
	Groesbeck's plurality.	455,648		Fitzgerald's plurality	93,493
1926	Green, Republican	399,564	1940	VanWagoner, Democrat.	1,077,065
	Comstock, Democrat.	227,155		Dickinson, Republican	945,784
	Titus, Prohibition	2,507		Whitmore, Socialist.	4,124
	Reynolds, Workers	1,512		Raymond, Communist.	2,387
	Scattering	14		Naylor, Socialist Labor.	702
	Green's plurality	172,409		Scattering	7
				VanWagoner's plurality	131,281
1928	Green, Republican	961,179	1942	Kelly, Republican	645,335
	Comstock, Democrat.	404,546		VanWagoner, Democrat.	573,314
	Lockwood, Socialist	2,850		Goodrich, Prohibition	8,065
	Brooks, Prohibition.	2,575		Scattering	60
	Reynolds, Workers	2,537		Kelly's plurality	72,021
	Dinger, Socialist Labor	654	1944	Kelly, Republican	1,208,859
	Green's plurality	556,633		Fry, Democrat	989,307
				Davey, Prohibition	5,744
1930	Brucker, Republican	483,990		Odell, Socialist	2,851
	Comstock, Democrat.	357,664		Marion, America First Party	2,121
	Billups, Workers.	3,988		Grove, Socialist Labor	1,364
	Campbell, Socialist	3,903		Kelly's plurality	219,552
	McCone, Prohibition.	1,336	1946	Sigler, Republican.	1,003,878
	Scattering	11		VanWagoner, Democrat.	644,540
	Brucker's plurality.	126,326		Phillips, Prohibition	11,974
				Sim, Socialist Labor.	5,071
1932	Comstock, Democrat.	887,672		Scattering	12
	Brucker, Republican	696,935		Sigler's plurality.	359,338
	Panzner, Socialist	20,108	1948	Williams, Democrat.	1,128,664
	Reynolds, Communist	7,906		Sigler, Republican.	964,810
	Holmes, Prohibition	2,031		Phillips, Prohibition	15,249
	Fraser, Socialist Labor	1,107		Seidler, Socialist	2,115
	Renner, Proletarian	318		Chenoweth, Socialist Labor	1,405
	Bergman, Liberty	182		Lerner, Socialist Workers	870
	Scattering	3		Scattering	9
	Comstock's plurality	190,737		William's plurality	163,854

Year	Name	Vote	Year	Name	Vote
1950	Williams, Democrat.	935,152	1974	Milliken, Republican.	1,356,865
	Kelly, Republican	933,998		Levin, Democrat.	1,242,247
	Hayden, Prohibition	8,511		Ferency, Human Rights.	28,675
	Groves, Socialist Labor	1,077		Davidson, Am. Indepen.	20,278
	Lerner, Socialist Workers	636		Andrews, Conservative	4,117
	Scattering.	8		Maisel, Socialist Workers	1,505
	Williams' plurality	1,154		Horvath, Socialist Labor	1,296
1952	Williams, Democrat.	1,431,893		Dennis, Communist	1,119
	Alger, Republican	1,423,275		Signorelli, U.S. Labor	898
	Munn, Prohibition.	8,990		Milliken's plurality.	114,618
	Grove, Socialist Labor	1,192	1978	Milliken, Republican.	1,628,485
	Lerner, Socialist Workers	628		Fitzgerald, Democrat.	1,237,256
	Scattering.	2		Scattering.	1,471
	Williams' plurality	8,618		Milliken's plurality.	391,229
1954	Williams, Democrat.	1,216,308	1982	Blanchard, Democrat	1,561,291
	Leonard, Republican.	963,300		Headlee, Republican.	1,369,582
	Munn, Prohibition.	5,824		Tisch, Tisch Independent Citizens	80,288
	Grove, Socialist Labor	980		Jacobs, Libertarian	15,603
	Lovell, Socialist Workers	615		Phillips, Am. Indepen.	7,356
	Williams' plurality	253,008		Craine, Socialist Workers	3,682
1956	Williams, Democrat.	1,666,689		McLaughlin, Worker's League . .	1,980
	Cobo, Republican	1,376,376		Scattering.	226
	Halsted, Prohibition	6,538		Blanchard's plurality	191,709
	Scattering.	48	1986	Blanchard, Democrat	1,632,138
	Williams' plurality	290,313		Lucas, Republican.	753,647
1958	Williams, Democrat.	1,225,533		McLaughlin, Worker's League . .	9,477
	Bagwell, Republican	1,078,089		Write-In	1,302
	Muncy, Socialist Labor	3,983		Blanchard's plurality	878,491
	Severance, Prohibition	3,622	1990	Engler, Republican	1,276,134
	Lovell, Socialist Workers	957		Blanchard, Democrat	1,258,539
	Williams' plurality	147,444		Roundtree, Worker's World	28,091
1960	Swainson, Democrat.	1,643,634		Write-In	1,799
	Bagwell, Republican	1,602,022		Engler's plurality.	17,595
	Himmel, Socialist Workers.	3,387	1994	Engler, Republican	1,899,101
	Gibbons, Prohibition.	2,183		Wolpe, Democrat	1,188,438
	Toohey, Tax Cut.	1,899		Write-In	1,538
	Grove, Socialist Labor	1,479		Engler's plurality.	710,663
	Pursell, Independent Amer.	1,354	1998	Engler, Republican	1,883,005
	Scattering.	33		Fieger, Democrat	1,143,574
	Swainson's plurality.	41,612		Write-In	525
1962	Romney, Republican.	1,420,086		Engler's plurality.	739,431
	Swainson, Democrat.	1,339,513	2002	Granholm, Democrat	1,633,796
	Sim, Socialist Labor.	5,219		Posthumus, Republican.	1,506,104
	Scattering.	21		Campbell, Green	25,236
	Romney's plurality.	80,573		Pilchak, U.S. Taxpayers.	12,411
1964	Romney, Republican.	1,764,355		Write-In	18
	Staebler, Democrat	1,381,442		Granholm's plurality	127,692
	Lovell, Socialist Workers	5,649	2006	Granholm, Democrat	2,142,513
	Cleage, Freedom Now	4,767		DeVos, Republican	1,608,086
	Horvath, Socialist Labor	1,777		Cresswell, Libertarian	23,524
	Scattering.	112		Campbell, Green	20,009
	Romney's plurality.	382,913		Dashairya, U.S. Taxpayers.	7,087
1966	Romney, Republican[6]	1,490,430		Write-In	37
	Ferency, Democrat	963,383		Granholm's plurality	534,427
	Horvath, Socialist Labor	8,017	2010	Snyder, Republican.	1,874,834
	Scattering.	79		Bernero, Democrat.	1,287,320
	Romney's plurality.	527,047		Proctor, Libertarian	22,390
1970	Milliken, Republican.	1,339,047		Mathia, U.S. Taxpayers	20,818
	Levin, Democrat.	1,294,638		Mikkelson, Green	20,699
	McCormick, Am. Indepen.	18,006		Write-In	27
	Bouse, Socialist Workers	2,220		Snyder's plurality.	587,514
	Horvath, Socialist Labor	2,144			
	Scattering.	107			
	Milliken's plurality.	44,409			

Year	Name	Vote	Year	Name	Vote
2014	Snyder, Republican..........	1,607,399	2018	Whitmer, Democrat..........	2,266,193
	Schauer, Democrat..........	1,479,057		Schuette, Republican.........	1,859,534
	Buzuma, Libertarian.........	35,723		Gelineau, Libertarian.........	56,606
	McFarlin, U.S. Taxpayers......	19,368		Schleiger, U.S. Taxpayers	29,219
	Homeniuk, Green...........	14,934		Kurland, Green............	28,799
	Write-In	50		Butkovich, Natural Law.......	10,202
	Snyder's plurality..........	128,342		Write-In	32
				Whitmer's plurality	406,659

[1] See Constitution of 1850, art. V, sec. 3, and art. IV, sec. 34; Public Act 175 of the Extra Session of 1851, Laws of Michigan.

[2] Totals do not include soldiers' vote of 9,612 for Crapo and 2,992 for Fenton. See Constitution of 1850, art. VII, sec. 1, and Public Act 21 of the Extra Session of 1864, Laws of Michigan.

[3] Democratic People's Union Silver.

[4] Total includes 2,463 votes cast for L. Whitney Watkins.

[5] Total includes 206 votes cast for Benjamin J. Blumenberg.

[6] First governor elected to 4-year term. See Constitution of 1963, art. V, sec. 21, and sched. sec. 5.

Chapter X

GENERAL INFORMATION

2019–2020

REPORT OF THE STATE TREASURER'S COMMON CASH FUND, 2016-2017
CASH BALANCES AND TRANSACTIONS BY FUND, OCTOBER 1, 2016 THROUGH SEPTEMBER 30, 2017
(In Thousands of Dollars)

Fund	Cash Balances 10-1-16	Receipts(a)	Disbursements	Transfers In	Transfers Out	Cash Balances 9-30-17	Warrants Outstanding	Available Balances 9-30-17
GENERAL AND SCHOOL AID								
General	$2,193,285	$43,971,757	$43,860,309	$ 283,766	$ 416,360	$2,172,139	$106,268	$2,065,871
Budget Stabilization	612,359	101,334	3,698	-0-	-0-	709,996	-0-	709,996
School Aid	(1,387,493)	13,449,117	14,251,100	1,101,076	125,124	(1,213,524)	399	(1,213,923)
Total General and School Aid	$1,418,151	$57,522,209	$58,115,107	$1,384,842	$ 541,485	$1,668,610	$106,667	$1,561,944
SPECIAL REVENUE								
Game and Fish Protection	$ 15,040	$ 69,806	$ 85,954	$ 16,640	$ 891	$ 14,641	$ 77	$ 14,564
Michigan Employment Security Act - Administration	(19,916)	136,232	141,281	20,714	1,297	(5,548)	234	(5,781)
State Aeronautics	(5,065)	135,468	133,997	6,000	4,727	(2,321)	251	(2,571)
Michigan Veterans' Trust	2,943	21,863	21,966	-0-	9	2,830	11	2,819
State Trunkline	835,856	868,649	1,810,113	1,080,445	212,111	762,725	5,032	757,693
Michigan State Waterways	25,848	19,283	33,076	17,982	347	29,690	70	29,620
Blue Water Bridge	64,463	22,214	9,616	-0-	7,040	70,021	7	70,015
Michigan Transportation	93,432	2,624,488	1,377,811	1,436	1,305,367	36,178	5,404	30,774
Comprehensive Transportation	91,213	180,340	339,615	228,347	18,449	141,837	1,294	140,542
Game and Fish Protection Trust	(8,229)	131,239	103,995	-0-	16,640	2,375	-0-	2,375
State Park Improvement	31,801	69,011	57,844	-0-	1,872	41,097	64	41,033
Forest Development	21,594	46,196	39,261	-0-	443	28,086	16	28,070
Michigan Natural Resources Trust	35,483	289,144	295,853	-0-	14	28,760	-0-	28,760
Michigan State Parks Endowment	10,557	169,280	161,905	-0-	241	17,691	74	17,617
Safety Education and Training	7,606	11,380	9,831	-0-	135	9,021	22	8,999
Bottle Deposits	51,492	32,665	31,225	-0-	2,521	50,412	186	50,227
State Construction Code	8,288	10,002	8,736	-0-	106	9,447	7	9,440
Children's Trust	2,941	13,910	14,714	-0-	4	2,134	35	2,099
State Casino Gaming	14,931	36,734	29,639	4,511	12,070	14,467	4	14,463
Homeowner Construction Lien Recovery	242	19	-0-	-0-	-0-	260	-0-	260
Michigan Nongame Fish and Wildlife	2,714	1,958	3,228	-0-	4	1,440	1	1,439
21st Century Jobs Trust	285,516	75,000	150,232	93,900	-0-	304,184	-0-	304,184
Michigan Merit Award Trust	789	30,278	25,832	-0-	29	5,206	-0-	5,206
Outdoor Recreation Legacy	2,973	2,406	3,556	1,349	29	3,143	12	3,130
Off-Road Vehicle	10,325	8,252	7,207	-0-	62	11,308	13	11,295
Snowmobile	10,496	7,943	9,594	3,147	35	11,957	-0-	11,957
Community District Education Trust	-0-	72,000	66,642	-0-	-0-	5,358	-0-	5,358
Unemployment Obligation Trust	1,012	485,640	485,120	-0-	-0-	1,532	-0-	1,532
State Building Authority Advance Financing	(2,806)	36,333	35,356	-0-	-0-	(1,829)	-0-	(1,829)
Michigan Strategic	110,501	160,435	185,026	-0-	-0-	85,910	982	84,928

Funds	Cash Balances 10-1-16	Receipts[a]	Disbursements	Transfers In	Transfers Out	Cash Balances 9-30-17	Warrants Outstanding	Available Balances 9-30-17
SPECIAL REVENUE (Cont.)								
Land Bank Fast Track Authority	8,344	16,214	13,464	-0-	-0-	11,093	226	10,867
Jobs for Michigan Investment	186,162	181,319	180,182	-0-	-0-	187,299	248	187,052
Workforce Development Agency	-0-	-0-	-0-	-0-	-0-	-0-	-0-	-0-
Michigan Finance Authority - School Loan Revolving Fund	1,207,762	528,482	259,309	-0-	-0-	1,476,934	-0-	1,476,934
State Building Authority - Capital Project	63	(26)	(2)	-0-	-0-	40	-0-	40
Total Special Revenue	$3,104,370	$ 6,494,158	$ 6,131,176	$1,474,471	$1,584,444	$3,357,379	$ 14,268	$3,343,111
BOND AND DEBT SERVICE								
Clean Michigan Initiative Bond - Local Projects	$ 28	$ -0-	$ 27	-0-	$ 1	$ 1	$ -0-	$ 1
1994 State Trunkline Bond Proceeds	-0-	-0-	-0-	-0-	-0-	-0-	-0-	0
State Trunkline Bond Proceeds	43,841	118,567	1,507	-0-	43,732	117,169	-0-	117,169
Comprehensive Transportation Bond Proceeds	7,911	1,670	3,203	-0-	-0-	6,377	-0-	6,377
Combined State Trunkline Bond and Interest Redemption	5	1	213,029	213,023	-0-	-0-	-0-	-0-
Combined Comprehensive Transportation Bond and Interest Redemption	162	-0-	23,029	22,867	-0-	-0-	-0-	-0-
Recreation and Environmental Protection Bond Redemption	1,743	187	131,427	131,396	-0-	1,899	-0-	1,899
School Loan Bond Redemption	14	-0-	125,138	125,124	-0-	-0-	-0-	-0-
Total Bond and Debt Service	$ 53,703	$ 120,426	$ 497,360	$ 492,410	$ 43,732	$ 125,447	$ -0-	$ 125,447
ENTERPRISE								
Liquor Purchasing Revolving	$ 80,479	$ 1,127,517	$ 902,746	-0-	$ 221,579	$ 83,671	$ 704	$ 82,968
State Lottery	4,319	1,453,549	528,143	-0-	925,682	4,044	2,293	1,751
Michigan State Housing Development Authority	1,578	42,049	43,627	-0-	-0-	-0-	1	(1)
Michigan Finance Authority - State Water Revolving	66	164,942	124,916	-0-	-0-	40,092	-0-	40,092
Total Enterprise	$ 86,443	$ 2,788,056	$ 1,599,432	$ -0-	$1,147,261	$ 127,807	$ 2,998	$ 124,809
INTERNAL SERVICE								
Correctional Industries Revolving	$ (2,065)	$ 16,428	$ 15,012	-0-	$ 109	$ (757)	$ 39	$ (796)
Motor Transport	9,345	70,444	73,977	-0-	69	5,743	33	5,710
Office Services Revolving	15,227	169,709	164,117	-0-	208	20,611	262	20,348
Information Technology	222	888,324	908,163	-0-	3,375	(22,991)	2,820	(25,811)
Risk Management	12,971	28,505	27,710	-0-	31	13,735	17	13,718
State Sponsored Group Insurance	321,270	760,377	742,596	-0-	-0-	339,051	3	339,048
Total Internal Service	$ 356,971	$ 1,933,788	$ 1,931,574	$ -0-	$ 3,792	$ 355,392	$ 3,174	$ 352,219

REPORT OF THE STATE TREASURER'S COMMON CASH FUND, 2016-2017 (Cont.)

Fund	Cash Balances 10-1-16	Receipts(a)	Disbursements	Transfers In	Transfers Out	Cash Balances 9-30-17	Warrants Outstanding	Available Balances 9-30-17
RETIREMENT								
Legislative	$ 1,202	$ 53,508	$ 51,973	$ -0-	$ -0-	$ 2,738	$ 1	$ 2,736
State Police	10,824	588,218	585,983	-0-	2	13,057	3	13,054
State Employees'	73,842	5,894,138	5,829,910	-0-	35	138,035	116	137,919
Public School Employees'	155,650	19,265,038	19,272,590	-0-	202	147,896	717	147,179
Judges'	2,034	94,228	94,582	-0-	-0-	1,679	-0-	1,679
Military	3,718	10,789	14,605	-0-	-0-	(98)	-0-	(98)
Total Retirement	$ 247,271	$25,905,919	$25,849,643	$ -0-	$ 240	$ 303,307	$ 837	$ 302,469
TRUST AND AGENCY								
Michigan Employment Security Act Contingent	$ 159,917	$ 30,875	$ 22	$ -0-	$ 30,714	$ 160,056	$ -0-	$ 160,056
Military Family Relief	2,345	75	108	-0-	-0-	2,312	1	2,311
Intrastate Switched Toll Restructuring	3,007	18,850	17,042	-0-	9	4,806	196	4,610
Children's Institute Trust	103	1	-0-	-0-	-0-	104	-0-	104
Abandoned and Unclaimed Property (Escheats)	113,713	159,450	161,832	-0-	-0-	111,331	4,805	106,526
Gifts, Bequests and Deposits Investment	26,220	127,664	133,757	-0-	-0-	20,128	494	19,634
Silicosis, Dust Disease, and Logging Industry Compensation	1,277	1,919	1,381	-0-	5	1,809	34	1,775
Second Injury	11,105	9,621	10,649	-0-	22	10,055	98	9,957
Hospital Patients	128	633	606	-0-	-0-	155	15	140
Self-Insurers' Security	33,389	4,430	5,528	-0-	14	32,277	115	32,162
State Employees' Deferred Comp. I (457)	19	45,021	44,945	-0-	-0-	95	-0-	95
State Employees' Deferred Comp. II (401k)	292	46,756	46,961	-0-	-0-	87	-0-	87
State of Michigan MPSERS DC 457	2,427	121,427	120,275	-0-	-0-	3,580	-0-	3,580
State Employees' Defined Contribution Plan	257	322,305	322,302	-0-	-0-	259	-0-	259
Special Assessment Deferment	2,667	91	16	-0-	-0-	2,742	-0-	2,742
Environmental Quality Deposits	2,689	38	17	-0-	-0-	2,709	-0-	2,709
Insurance Carrier Deposits	3,194	48,400	49,352	-0-	-0-	2,242	-0-	2,242
Utility Consumer Representation	1,869	1,763	1,279	-0-	4	2,349	-0-	2,348
Transportation Related	(25,784)	301,568	321,420	-0-	-0-	(45,637)	109	(45,746)
State of Michigan MPSERS DC 401k	1,695	38	526	-0-	-0-	1,207	-0-	1,207
State of Michigan Personal Health Care	15	2,792	2,807	-0-	-0-	-0-	-0-	-0-
City Income Tax	8,790	156,775	156,986	-0-	-0-	8,580	607	7,973
Social Welfare	3,880	13,983	15,542	-0-	-0-	2,322	44	2,278
Total Trust and Agency	$ 353,215	$ 1,414,474	$ 1,413,351	$ -0-	$ 30,770	$ 323,568	$ 6,519	$ 317,049
GRAND TOTALS	$5,620,123	$96,179,030	$95,537,643	$3,351,723	$3,351,723	$6,261,510	$134,463	$6,127,047

(a) Totals may not foot due to rounding.

REPORT OF THE STATE TREASURER'S COMMON CASH FUND, 2017-2018
CASH BALANCES AND TRANSACTIONS BY FUND(a)(b), OCTOBER 1, 2017 THROUGH SEPTEMBER 30, 2018
(In Thousands of Dollars)

Fund	Cash Balances 10-1-17	Cash Balances 9-30-18	Warrants Outstanding	Available Balances 9-30-18
GENERAL AND SCHOOL AID				
General(a)	$2,882,135	$2,847,414	$ 79,764	$2,767,650
School Aid	(1,213,524)	(1,246,754)	263	(1,247,016)
Total General and School Aid	$1,668,610	$1,600,660	$ 80,027	$1,520,634
SPECIAL REVENUE				
Game and Fish Protection	$ 14,641	$ 15,117	$ 66	$ 15,051
Michigan Employment Security Act - Administration	(5,548)	(6,020)	54	(6,074)
State Aeronautics	(2,321)	2,216	41	2,176
Michigan Veterans' Trust	2,830	1,469	35	1,434
State Trunkline	762,725	764,916	7,316	757,600
Michigan State Waterways	29,690	34,909	164	34,746
Blue Water Bridge	70,021	74,305	8	74,297
Michigan Transportation	36,178	103,130	1,169	101,961
Comprehensive Transportation	141,837	204,898	260	204,638
Game and Fish Protection Trust	2,375	2,708	-0-	2,708
State Park Improvement	41,097	57,400	340	57,060
Forest Development	28,086	39,298	27	39,271
Michigan Natural Resources Trust	28,760	42,784	153	42,631
Michigan State Parks Endowment	17,691	13,308	110	13,198
Safety Education and Training	9,021	6,232	5	6,227
Bottle Deposits	50,412	54,332	121	54,211
State Construction Code	9,447	11,635	3	11,632
Children's Trust	2,134	1,988	3	1,985
State Casino Gaming	14,467	14,459	276	14,184
Homeowner Construction Lien Recovery	260	285	-0-	285
Michigan Nongame Fish and Wildlife	1,440	1,800	-0-	1,800
21st Century Jobs Trust	304,184	333,352	-0-	333,352
Michigan Merit Award Trust	5,206	16,094	118	15,975
Outdoor Recreation Legacy	3,143	4,493	12	4,481
Off-Road Vehicle	11,308	13,259	23	13,236
Snowmobile	11,957	15,660	-0-	15,660
Community District Education Trust	5,358	11,484	-0-	11,484
Unemployment Obligation Trust	1,532	1,554	-0-	1,554
State Building Authority Advance Financing	(1,829)	(8,313)	3,464	(11,777)
Michigan Strategic	85,910	101,897	690	101,208
Land Bank Fast Track Authority	11,093	13,833	-0-	13,833

REPORT OF THE STATE TREASURER'S COMMON CASH FUND, 2017-2018 *(Cont.)*

Fund	Cash Balances 10-1-17	Cash Balances 9-30-18	Warrants Outstanding	Available Balances 9-30-18
SPECIAL REVENUE *(Cont.)*				
Jobs for Michigan Investment	187,299	206,366	1,701	204,665
Michigan Finance Authority - School Loan Revolving	1,476,934	1,170,981	-0-	1,170,981
State Building Authority - Capital Projects	40	49	-0-	49
Total Special Revenue	$3,357,379	$3,321,897	$16,156	$3,305,723
BOND AND DEBT SERVICE				
Clean Michigan Initiative Bond - Local Projects	$ 1	$ -0-	$ -0-	$ -0-
1994 State Trunkline Bond Proceeds	-0-	27	-0-	27
State Trunkline Bond Proceeds	117,169	105,359	-0-	105,359
Comprehensive Transportation Bond Proceeds	6,377	4,556	-0-	4,556
Combined State Trunkline Bond and Interest Redemption	-0-	1	-0-	1
Combined Comprehensive Transportation Bond and Interest Redemption	-0-	0-	-0-	-0-
Recreation and Environmental Protection Bond Redemption	1,899	1,893	30	1,863
School Loan Bond Redemption	-0-	-0-	-0-	-0-
Total Bond and Debt Service	$ 125,447	$ 111,837	$ 30	$ 111,807
ENTERPRISE				
Liquor Purchasing Revolving	$ 83,671	$ 121,270	$ 2,409	$ 118,861
State Lottery	4,044	5,355	1,247	4,108
Michigan State Housing Development Authority	-0-	-0-	-0-	-0-
Michigan Finance Authority - State Water Revolving	40,092	45,030	-0-	45,030
Total Enterprise	$ 127,807	$ 171,655	$ 3,656	$ 167,999
INTERNAL SERVICE				
Correctional Industries Revolving	$ (757)	$ 610	$ 4	$ 606
Motor Transport	5,743	6,090	8	6,082
Office Services Revolving	20,611	22,635	49	22,586
Information Technology	(22,991)	58,247	3,002	55,245
Risk Management	13,735	13,515	15	13,500
State Sponsored Group Insurance	339,051	341,031	359	340,672
Total Internal Service	$ 355,392	$ 442,128	$ 3,437	$ 438,692
RETIREMENT				
Legislative	$ 2,738	$ 1,984	$ 3	$ 1,981
State Police	13,057	7,429	1,084	6,345
State Employees'	138,035	133,556	215	133,341

REPORT OF THE STATE TREASURER'S COMMON CASH FUND, 2017-2018 *(Cont.)*

Fund	Cash Balances 10-1-17	Cash Balances 9-30-18	Warrants Outstanding	Available Balances 9-30-18
RETIREMENT *(Cont.)*				
Public School Employees'	147,896	105,021	972	104,050
Judges'	1,679	864	-0-	864
Military	(98)	560	2	559
Total Retirement	$ 303,307	$ 249,414	$ 2,274	$ 247,139
TRUST AND AGENCY				
Michigan Employment Security Act Contingent	$ 160,056	$ 160,104	$ -0-	$160,104
Military Family Relief	2,312	2,396	-0-	2,396
Intrastate Switched Toll Restructuring	4,806	5,361	-0-	5,361
Children's Institute Trust	104	104	-0-	104
Abandoned and Unclaimed Property (Escheats)	111,331	111,316	10,666	100,650
Gifts, Bequests and Deposits Investment	20,128	23,088	319	22,770
Silicosis, Dust Disease, and Logging Industry Compensation	1,809	1,699	33	1,666
Second Injury	10,055	11,369	142	11,227
Hospital Patients	155	210	25	185
Self-Insurers' Security	32,277	32,042	152	31,890
State Employees' Deferred Comp. I (457)	95	348	-0-	348
State Employees' Deferred Comp. II (401k)	87	2,395	-0-	2,395
State of Michigan MPSERS DC 457	3,580	3,944	520	3,425
State Employees' Defined Contribution Plan	259	(2,197)	-0-	(2,197)
Special Assessment Deferment	2,742	2,716	-0-	2,716
Environmental Quality Deposits	2,709	2,682	-0-	2,682
Insurance Carrier Deposits	2,242	1,104	3	1,102
Utility Consumer Representation	2,349	2,579	-0-	2,579
Transportation Related	(45,637)	(36,077)	548	(36,625)
State of Michigan MPSERS DC 401k	1,207	1,454	-0-	1,454
State of Michigan Personal Health Care	-0-	-0-	-0-	-0-
City Income Tax	8,580	9,945	1,262	8,683
Social Welfare	2,322	2,211	129	2,082
EAA 457	-0-	18	-0-	18
EAA 401k	-0-	22	-0-	22
Total Trust and Agency	$ 323,568	$ 338,834	$ 13,797	$ 325,037
GRAND TOTALS	$6,261,510	$6,236,408	$119,377	$6,117,030

(a) In accordance with Governmental Accounting Standards Board (GASB) Statement No. 54 Fund Balance Reporting and Governmental Fund Type Definition, the Budget Stabilization Fund is a committed subfund of the General Fund.

(b) Due to changes in account reporting, the fund categories "Receipts," "Disbursements," "Transfers In" and "Transfers Out" are no longer included in Table 4.

2017 STATE EQUALIZED VALUATIONS BY STATE TAX COMMISSION

County	Agricultural	Commercial	Industrial	Residential	Timber Cutover	Developmental	Total Real Property	Total Personal Property
Alcona	$40,062,600	$27,711,200	$11,485,200	$685,340,600	$0	$0	$764,599,600	$36,607,300
Alger	8,815,100	37,361,677	10,196,700	405,692,428	0	0	462,065,905	18,391,060
Allegan	775,148,950	467,357,800	238,260,500	4,276,931,575	0	11,023,000	5,768,721,825	321,706,747
Alpena	87,631,400	114,683,700	35,140,000	732,622,600	0	0	970,077,700	71,666,280
Antrim	76,448,300	86,207,400	7,368,400	2,029,993,600	350,700	0	2,200,368,400	71,812,100
Arenac	104,564,910	44,918,800	8,013,700	475,876,100	0	0	633,373,510	42,691,950
Baraga	10,545,322	19,623,173	21,039,536	245,011,473	25,589,215	0	321,808,719	20,748,267
Barry	375,514,450	141,441,900	60,064,100	2,129,001,338	0	0	2,706,021,788	95,561,700
Bay	477,280,450	388,729,350	214,850,050	1,969,222,881	0	192,050	3,050,274,781	219,610,393
Benzie	24,145,700	90,849,369	4,578,800	1,519,372,467	2,231,958	0	1,641,178,294	40,269,200
Berrien	581,765,727	792,501,620	1,163,435,886	6,396,777,801	0	0	8,934,481,034	557,659,207
Branch	590,621,154	150,723,852	37,352,529	1,035,815,460	0	0	1,814,512,995	134,983,949
Calhoun	524,309,845	577,604,035	192,121,446	2,476,881,701	0	0	3,770,917,027	454,634,165
Cass	559,559,400	90,941,400	37,551,000	1,939,453,821	0	0	2,627,505,621	217,576,707
Charlevoix	52,705,100	166,444,656	44,469,300	2,271,990,799	0	3,535,000	2,535,609,855	84,574,877
Cheboygan	34,264,310	164,371,200	6,042,400	1,445,570,230	101,700	0	1,653,884,840	60,675,050
Chippewa	54,038,200	155,231,519	26,296,600	1,030,810,300	0	0	1,266,376,619	69,184,600
Clare	91,125,676	79,585,208	18,016,330	916,920,713	0	0	1,105,647,927	104,918,074
Clinton	759,930,929	403,209,583	56,315,067	2,146,109,160	0	11,380,000	3,376,944,739	140,158,590
Crawford	225,600	46,467,600	23,098,300	527,846,000	0	0	597,637,500	46,443,450
Delta	45,207,189	163,244,219	24,785,870	1,002,509,579	0	159,400	1,235,906,257	119,155,476
Dickinson	22,303,050	150,642,742	74,822,850	653,481,774	25,231,700	0	926,482,116	104,286,720
Eaton	508,573,940	652,909,238	183,754,728	2,511,869,176	0	9,008,500	3,866,115,582	264,485,433
Emmet	44,376,300	357,278,300	13,872,100	3,129,001,831	0	0	3,544,528,531	99,765,900
Genesee	193,997,600	2,072,265,800	271,068,300	7,655,357,447	0	0	10,192,689,147	628,382,344
Gladwin	94,054,800	50,283,050	10,237,800	902,786,738	0	0	1,057,362,388	44,582,854
Gogebic	1,237,081	56,283,546	12,752,637	500,782,745	26,115,230	0	597,171,239	67,858,513
Grand Traverse	147,924,856	987,731,000	84,171,700	4,610,492,699	0	0	5,830,320,235	246,857,341
Gratiot	878,146,243	119,236,500	31,946,300	585,111,263	0	0	1,614,440,306	378,632,200
Hillsdale	576,170,015	90,420,212	35,582,310	1,027,938,154	1,677,350	0	1,731,788,041	79,452,520
Houghton	17,343,669	169,840,768	12,789,901	910,424,720	0	2,288,437	1,134,882,569	64,078,777
Huron	1,750,319,639	118,515,767	40,374,600	1,055,248,053	22,195,074	0	2,964,458,059	691,992,863
Ingham	401,850,007	2,003,706,995	182,009,478	5,476,303,415	0	3,445,815	8,067,215,710	685,292,075
Ionia	637,591,794	147,904,123	42,594,017	1,242,668,364	0	0	2,070,758,298	111,467,100
Iosco	60,075,950	106,742,250	23,945,700	980,534,100	0	5,162,900	1,176,460,900	90,811,350
Iron	18,529,996	38,887,814	35,525,098	486,245,108	40,471,094	0	619,659,110	51,444,112
Isabella	402,791,681	483,859,766	32,398,300	1,192,624,329	0	0	2,111,674,076	121,099,536
Jackson	434,451,987	654,450,381	168,467,826	3,585,283,329	0	3,397,100	4,846,050,623	481,085,618
Kalamazoo	314,205,704	1,791,444,752	441,009,523	6,446,770,891	0	0	8,993,430,870	656,559,953
Kalkaska	22,755,100	51,102,200	8,969,500	719,241,900	0	0	802,068,700	145,437,600
Kent	359,750,646	5,105,513,010	1,210,706,400	17,638,777,919	0	0	24,314,747,975	1,599,633,700
Keweenaw	0	11,472,308	74,969	201,090,163	2,462,596	0	215,100,036	5,472,683
Lake	29,391,900	56,892,600	1,537,800	575,418,950	0	0	663,241,250	38,028,950

County	Agricultural	Commercial	Industrial	Residential	Timber Cutover	Developmental	Total Real Property	Total Personal Property
Lapeer	449,754,817	256,738,900	68,612,879	2,679,948,772	0	3,302,500	3,458,357,868	200,226,876
Leelanau	173,764,290	176,604,110	11,188,130	3,177,103,228	0	0	3,538,659,758	50,127,730
Lenawee	962,032,500	390,486,959	95,026,900	2,465,400,072	0	1,416,200	3,914,362,631	217,036,838
Livingston	260,703,229	1,006,855,056	268,925,528	8,393,949,673	0	4,939,200	9,935,372,686	517,866,706
Luce	5,304,400	17,488,700	3,089,500	204,195,690	666,100	0	230,744,390	10,763,407
Mackinac	14,536,236	211,568,990	18,818,115	835,441,079	3,996,507	0	1,084,360,927	154,559,924
Macomb	214,514,897	4,448,336,632	1,939,951,454	23,909,211,479	0	0	30,512,014,462	1,790,227,301
Manistee	38,986,700	100,404,300	53,043,400	1,100,710,195	0	0	1,293,144,595	96,733,800
Marquette	13,353,200	462,033,650	134,102,665	2,148,317,605	54,834,800	0	2,812,641,920	176,222,417
Mason	93,189,600	153,672,600	447,076,500	1,240,322,064	0	0	1,934,260,764	167,289,700
Mecosta	199,753,400	144,988,700	39,826,200	1,077,061,774	0	0	1,461,630,074	92,533,500
Menominee	101,432,753	72,425,754	38,063,025	732,230,543	0	0	944,152,075	72,831,362
Midland	167,398,638	480,088,900	262,265,685	2,242,180,651	0	0	3,151,933,874	531,101,140
Missaukee	166,925,100	44,481,900	7,491,000	522,027,450	0	0	740,925,450	73,077,700
Monroe	528,932,219	737,698,110	1,062,632,890	4,086,471,763	0	8,187,730	6,423,962,712	436,905,349
Montcalm	246,225,000	171,861,111	39,322,500	1,434,665,394	0	0	2,072,074,005	216,845,000
Montmorency	18,468,300	28,290,000	8,328,600	505,076,973	0	0	560,163,873	47,727,410
Muskegon	145,010,600	694,547,318	167,600,000	3,793,447,650	0	0	4,800,605,568	339,124,796
Newaygo	221,936,800	105,119,100	51,287,600	1,345,625,806	0	0	1,723,969,306	108,289,954
Oakland	70,329,430	10,486,445,800	1,954,501,320	53,043,295,649	0	0	65,554,572,199	3,453,780,010
Oceana	185,034,450	87,425,300	29,356,750	1,213,282,380	0	0	1,515,098,880	64,601,185
Ogemaw	92,777,400	108,593,200	8,249,500	757,595,781	0	0	967,215,881	60,675,086
Ontonagon	11,543,840	14,595,780	30,976,100	221,077,563	23,290,139	0	301,474,422	22,098,255
Osceola	131,658,100	38,802,800	26,695,350	579,803,800	0	0	776,960,050	85,359,200
Oscoda	11,357,100	25,110,800	8,406,700	363,499,420	0	0	408,374,020	43,991,100
Otsego	47,169,100	169,191,000	26,408,000	922,744,050	0	0	1,165,512,150	244,373,100
Ottawa	629,680,447	1,477,136,600	838,097,300	9,681,721,350	0	1,247,300	12,627,882,997	761,056,600
Presque Isle	80,112,200	24,449,800	27,283,000	646,498,188	84,000	14,500	778,441,688	30,008,270
Roscommon	4,903,100	101,861,600	1,837,000	1,347,973,013	16,400	0	1,456,574,713	43,708,042
Saginaw	639,018,224	1,012,462,315	132,676,200	3,348,783,833	0	0	5,132,956,972	428,251,150
Saint Clair	448,666,310	594,112,810	749,080,816	4,408,301,523	0	0	6,200,161,459	715,405,067
Saint Joseph	682,054,300	172,001,100	124,249,000	1,453,023,137	0	601,300	2,431,928,837	285,216,901
Sanilac	1,322,092,689	101,511,415	14,114,239	978,772,559	76,800	5,311,900	2,421,879,602	231,189,520
Schoolcraft	6,252,500	31,086,300	10,296,900	350,240,380	3,734,900	0	401,610,980	44,829,676
Shiawassee	526,550,895	181,974,190	29,270,220	1,370,324,543	0	0	2,108,119,848	104,076,600
Tuscola	1,049,895,623	91,761,900	33,642,357	1,031,884,701	0	0	2,207,184,581	411,113,795
Van Buren	470,865,500	262,907,200	80,654,200	2,663,226,298	0	0	3,477,653,198	703,542,800
Washtenaw	500,887,424	3,980,199,090	461,800,390	13,867,637,028	0	38,464,900	18,848,988,832	968,345,499
Wayne	25,528,800	8,662,983,686	2,986,980,086	30,875,493,532	0	11,747,100	42,562,733,204	4,108,348,869
Wexford	44,872,900	123,490,500	46,859,100	835,582,188	0	0	1,050,804,688	76,317,000
GRAND TOTAL	$23,373,256,261	$56,938,386,359	$17,497,180,650	$289,601,352,471	$231,448,913	$126,402,182	$387,768,026,836	$27,771,545,919

2018 STATE EQUALIZED VALUATIONS BY STATE TAX COMMISSION

County	Agricultural	Commercial	Industrial	Residential	Timber Cutover	Developmental	Total Real Property	Total Personal Property
Alcona	$39,270,800	$27,597,100	$11,561,500	$703,507,900	$0	$0	$781,937,300	$37,467,200
Alger	9,357,100	38,310,800	9,835,500	410,318,500	0	0	467,821,900	19,465,806
Allegan	796,042,600	480,590,113	242,578,450	4,481,135,361	0	5,565,200	6,005,911,724	313,184,975
Alpena	87,612,018	111,743,100	35,638,400	741,155,100	0	0	976,148,618	69,063,454
Antrim	78,147,800	90,098,500	8,367,100	2,079,127,700	0	0	2,255,741,100	79,514,800
Arenac	104,098,300	45,702,300	8,309,000	491,574,308	0	0	649,683,908	45,760,750
Baraga	10,838,938	19,980,769	21,140,637	246,953,789	24,058,410	0	322,972,543	18,835,193
Barry	383,893,650	147,750,100	64,976,800	2,192,641,283	0	0	2,789,261,833	103,818,600
Bay	500,741,302	399,121,100	205,124,100	1,994,687,915	0	192,050	3,099,866,467	215,701,365
Benzie	25,044,000	93,852,818	5,006,300	1,558,814,540	0	0	1,684,650,758	40,426,706
Berrien	550,714,530	777,985,289	1,224,380,100	6,460,592,681	0	0	9,013,672,600	525,058,814
Branch	610,473,969	161,621,290	38,337,771	1,068,318,661	0	0	1,878,751,691	145,389,286
Calhoun	542,392,093	583,466,484	202,147,623	2,539,567,602	0	0	3,867,573,802	468,274,379
Cass	548,739,900	103,035,200	40,261,400	2,006,192,006	0	0	2,698,228,506	224,567,688
Charlevoix	53,310,362	167,889,900	44,968,900	2,347,719,737	0	0	2,613,888,899	82,838,900
Cheboygan	33,684,500	165,795,254	6,079,100	1,478,216,195	100,900	3,713,800	1,687,589,749	64,024,550
Chippewa	50,829,900	159,866,800	26,512,600	1,034,520,200	0	0	1,271,729,500	75,508,600
Clare	95,133,063	78,839,668	18,814,880	927,456,331	0	0	1,120,243,942	110,427,198
Clinton	776,318,976	423,734,820	59,912,859	2,191,474,269	0	11,348,300	3,462,789,224	143,025,771
Crawford	226,300	48,049,500	42,849,200	535,209,675	0	0	626,334,675	62,799,050
Delta	45,669,464	169,170,950	26,137,538	1,019,208,937	0	88,300	1,260,275,189	121,692,462
Dickinson	22,525,045	149,341,539	50,826,600	662,871,913	25,231,700	0	910,794,797	104,390,126
Eaton	510,899,536	661,399,381	203,942,599	2,585,836,403	0	8,660,800	3,970,738,719	322,663,579
Emmet	45,390,400	371,284,750	13,897,100	3,175,592,000	0	0	3,606,164,250	105,025,300
Genesee	198,390,700	2,213,493,500	282,128,100	7,891,455,704	0	0	10,585,468,004	654,376,300
Gladwin	93,948,142	49,762,181	9,868,855	918,693,229	0	0	1,072,272,407	49,750,100
Gogebic	1,150,157	56,654,112	13,434,278	495,156,862	26,203,408	0	592,598,817	68,496,481
Grand Traverse	147,787,774	1,042,942,500	87,090,600	4,790,410,598	0	0	6,068,231,472	256,447,356
Gratiot	892,924,990	125,436,400	36,370,625	605,660,667	0	0	1,660,392,682	358,022,200
Hillsdale	572,046,989	90,192,712	40,505,350	1,051,950,502	0	1,709,510	1,756,405,063	85,000,209
Houghton	17,364,052	171,467,466	13,569,863	927,172,120	19,566,697	2,268,122	1,151,408,320	62,855,956
Huron	1,783,032,046	122,102,400	49,009,700	1,066,582,867	0	0	3,020,727,013	802,271,800
Ingham	403,958,200	2,118,791,829	198,365,290	5,627,095,246	0	3,291,600	8,351,502,165	678,075,893
Ionia	674,549,127	149,472,364	43,374,300	1,283,725,352	0	0	2,151,121,143	113,833,300
Iosco	61,716,854	106,545,200	24,169,300	989,988,700	0	4,689,000	1,187,109,054	87,664,500
Iron	18,617,317	38,840,655	39,499,188	490,390,490	38,953,950	0	626,301,600	51,274,734
Isabella	418,794,570	490,826,024	33,904,000	1,204,077,970	0	0	2,147,602,564	126,296,029
Jackson	442,244,397	686,423,832	178,063,272	3,679,173,147	0	3,156,900	4,989,061,548	477,419,162
Kalamazoo	333,502,116	1,912,116,583	434,847,395	6,636,198,436	0	0	9,316,664,530	640,101,811
Kalkaska	23,046,300	53,348,400	9,112,800	736,584,150	0	0	822,091,650	145,056,600
Kent	375,061,400	5,408,307,200	1,316,905,800	18,411,167,221	0	0	25,511,441,621	1,620,522,000
Keweenaw	0	11,035,882	75,044	203,919,716	2,439,277	0	217,469,919	5,376,518
Lake	29,430,500	57,158,600	1,525,600	587,676,100	0	0	675,790,800	38,379,850

County	Agricultural	Commercial	Industrial	Residential	Timber Cutover	Developmental	Total Real Property	Total Personal Property
Lapeer	448,253,998	254,529,004	69,240,513	2,758,586,965	0	2,820,900	3,533,431,380	227,289,311
Leelanau	170,956,280	180,923,320	11,267,680	3,256,892,255	0	0	3,620,039,535	53,495,613
Lenawee	972,176,681	410,977,400	98,720,100	2,539,766,451	0	1,294,100	4,022,934,732	237,719,293
Livingston	261,107,397	1,071,931,640	293,109,420	8,701,680,000	0	4,539,900	10,332,368,357	544,536,660
Luce	5,116,400	17,636,700	3,100,900	205,329,152	651,000		231,834,152	10,089,924
Mackinac	14,295,211	216,269,990	18,804,026	862,892,441	3,731,096		1,115,992,764	150,678,938
Macomb	203,820,000	4,677,140,870	2,111,823,420	24,748,408,455	0	0	31,741,192,745	1,736,247,837
Manistee	39,460,900	99,651,600	50,369,500	1,121,535,000	0	0	1,311,017,000	90,387,800
Marquette	13,555,000	487,899,965	115,748,700	2,169,884,020	54,413,458	0	2,841,501,143	171,541,447
Mason	94,361,000	153,190,200	495,469,000	1,253,609,300	0	0	1,996,629,500	162,690,400
Mecosta	194,606,600	149,074,800	55,041,500	1,106,308,990	0	0	1,505,031,890	97,701,200
Menominee	104,277,561	70,872,836	36,612,170	746,778,979	0	0	958,541,546	72,597,933
Midland	177,457,200	488,294,579	260,788,453	2,265,968,913	0	0	3,192,509,145	526,325,300
Missaukee	169,129,200	46,383,650	8,409,600	541,945,600	0	7,621,670	765,868,050	70,245,600
Monroe	541,586,160	753,419,656	1,069,733,380	4,190,892,771	0	0	6,563,253,637	460,838,206
Montcalm	436,953,662	175,270,350	39,517,300	1,482,365,800	0	0	2,134,107,112	211,302,000
Montmorency	18,783,700	26,901,548	8,380,800	506,098,677	0	0	560,164,725	45,928,717
Muskegon	148,560,553	701,863,500	170,198,000	3,924,469,500	0	0	4,945,091,553	332,824,200
Newaygo	227,417,400	111,692,050	52,075,400	1,382,505,024	0	0	1,773,689,874	114,385,921
Oakland	2,013,280	11,275,983,448	2,141,831,950	54,971,706,209	0	0	68,461,534,887	3,409,823,960
Oceana	196,367,704	93,289,500	35,701,800	1,246,136,228	0	0	1,571,495,232	58,734,700
Ogemaw	90,106,200	104,450,400	7,555,900	758,278,743	0	0	960,391,243	62,567,898
Ontonagon	11,234,220	14,946,554	30,857,628	224,401,665	22,772,568	0	304,212,635	19,720,511
Osceola	134,704,200	43,640,600	27,006,800	596,404,425	0	0	801,756,025	85,947,200
Oscoda	12,099,130	21,419,200	8,390,300	365,554,830	0	0	407,463,460	44,841,700
Otsego	47,765,300	169,734,708	26,268,300	948,648,000	0	0	1,192,416,308	245,152,200
Ottawa	645,419,700	1,598,488,900	636,799,300	10,147,195,838	84,000	155,900	13,028,059,638	857,435,300
Presque Isle	80,306,035	24,566,500	27,271,600	654,624,072	0	0	786,852,207	28,897,993
Roscommon	5,102,600	99,444,300	1,888,600	1,381,703,980	16,900	0	1,488,139,480	46,018,400
Saginaw	754,943,210	1,045,643,999	144,159,859	3,397,726,618	0	0	5,342,490,586	464,399,284
Saint Clair	457,459,860	632,776,798	787,646,500	4,563,302,894	0	0	6,441,186,052	751,715,432
Saint Joseph	712,860,887	177,399,500	124,398,800	1,501,071,912	0	0	2,515,731,099	279,550,679
Sanilac	1,333,403,553	104,689,101	17,384,035	995,543,616	93,900	5,066,800	2,456,181,005	229,729,756
Schoolcraft	5,890,100	30,133,000	11,789,700	350,310,500	1,488,500	0	399,611,800	46,146,574
Shiawassee	546,533,000	185,943,270	33,092,190	1,402,147,180	0	0	2,167,715,640	112,124,766
Tuscola	1,057,430,600	90,453,400	34,977,700	1,048,833,555	0	0	2,231,695,255	423,069,250
Van Buren	469,247,500	262,880,600	82,249,400	2,732,063,175	0	0	3,547,030,675	704,148,400
Washtenaw	520,389,750	4,331,687,680	497,293,645	14,314,537,485	0	37,317,400	19,701,225,960	1,032,328,754
Wayne	25,664,500	8,971,813,855	3,281,779	32,056,288,426	0	9,810,400	44,345,357,161	4,155,989,912
Wexford	45,415,500	132,087,600	49,011,100	853,532,146	0	0	1,080,046,346	72,943,163
GRAND TOTAL	$23,875,149,909	$59,886,541,936	$18,399,190,366	$298,806,291,873	$221,738,864	$113,310,652	$401,302,223,600	$28,268,257,483

NEWSPAPERS IN MICHIGAN

County Newspaper	Location
ALCONA	
Alcona County Review	Harrisville
ALGER	
Munising News	Munising
ALLEGAN	
The Allegan County News	Allegan
The Commercial Record	Saugatuck
The Union Enterprise	Plainwell
ALPENA	
Alpena News	Alpena
ANTRIM	
The Antrim Review	Bellaire
Elk Rapids News	Elk Rapids
BARAGA	
L'Anse Sentinel	L'Anse
BARRIEN	
Niles Daily Star	Niles
BARRY	
Hastings Banner	Hastings
The Sun and News	Hastings
BAY	
Bay City Times	Bay City
Pinconning Journal	Pinconning
BENZIE	
Benzie County Record Patriot	Frankfort
BERRIEN	
Berrien County Record	Buchanan
Harbor Country News	Michigan City, Indiana
Herald-Palladium	St. Joseph
The Journal Era	Berrien Springs
BRANCH	
Coldwater Daily Reporter	Coldwater
The Daily Reporter	Coldwater
Hometown Gazette	Union City
CALHOUN	
Ad-visor and Chronicle	Marshall
Battle Creek Enquirer	Battle Creek
Homer Index	Homer
The Recorder	Albion
CASS	
Cassopolis Vigilant	Niles
Dowagiac Daily News	Niles
Edwardsburg Argus	Edwardsburg
CHARLEVOIX	
Charlevoix Courier	Petoskey
The Boyne City Gazette	Boyne City
CHEBOYGAN	
Cheboygan Daily Tribune	Cheboygan
Straitsland Resorter	Indian River

County Newspaper	Location
CHIPPEWA	
Bay Mills News	Brimley
Drummond Island Digest	Drummond Island
The Evening News	Sault Ste. Marie
CLARE	
Clare County Review	Clare
CRAWFORD	
Crawford County Avalanche	Grayling
DELTA	
Daily Press	Escanaba
DICKINSON	
The Daily News	Iron Mountain
EATON	
The County Journal	Charlotte
EMMET	
Harbor Light	Harbor Springs
Petoskey News-Review	Petoskey
ESCANABA	
The Daily Press	Escanaba
GENESEE	
Burton View	Davison
Davison Index	Davison
Flint Journal	Flint
Flint Township View	Davison
Flushing View	Davison
Genesee County Legal News	Clio
Grand Blanc View	Davison
Mount Morris/Clio Herald	Mt. Morris
Swartz Creek View	Davison
Tri-County Times	Fenton
GLADWIN	
Gladwin County Record	Gladwin
GOGEBIC	
The Daily Globe	Ironwood
GRAND TRAVERSE	
The Northern Express	Traverse City
Traverse City Record-Eagle	Traverse City
GRATIOT	
Gratiot County Herald	Ithaca
Morning Sun	Alma
HILLSDALE	
Hillsdale Daily News	Hillsdale
HOUGHTON	
Daily Mining Gazette	Houghton
HURON	
Huron County View	Bad Axe
Huron Daily Tribune	Bad Axe
INGHAM	
Ingham County Legal News	Mason
Lansing City Pulse	Lansing
Lansing State Journal	Lansing

County Newspaper	Location

IONIA

Lakewood News	Hastings
Sentinel-Standard	Ionia

IOSCO

Iosco County News-Herald	East Tawas
Oscoda Press	Oscoda

IRON

Iron County Reporter	Iron River

JACKSON

County Press	Parma
Jackson Citizen Patriot	Jackson
Jackson County Legal News	Jackson
The Exponent	Brooklyn
The Grass Lake Times	Grass Lake

KALAMAZOO

Climax Crescent	Climax
Kalamazoo Gazette	Kalamazoo

KENT

Grand Rapids Business Journal	Grand Rapids
Grand Rapids Legal News	Grand Rapids
Grand Rapids Press	Grand Rapids
Grand Rapids Times	Grand Rapids
Lazo Cultural	Grand Rapids
Lowell Ledger	Lowell
MiBiz	Grand Rapids
The Rockford Squire	Rockford

LAKE

Lake County Star	Baldwin

LAPEER

Lapeer Area View	Lapeer
The County Press	Lapeer
Tri-City Times	Imlay City

LEELANAU

Leelanau Enterprise	Lake Leelanau

LENAWEE

Hudson Post-Gazette	Hudson
State Line Observer	Morenci
Tecumseh Herald	Tecumseh
The Advance	Blissfield
The Clinton Local	Clinton
The Daily Telegram	Adrian

LIVINGSTON

Fowlerville News and Views	Fowlerville
Livingston County Daily Press and Argus	Howell

LUCE

Newberry News	Newberry

MACKINAC

St. Ignace News	St. Ignace
Town Crier	Mackinac Island

MACOMB

Daily Tribune	Clinton Township
Farmington Press	Warren
Fraser-Clinton Township Chronicle	Warren
Macomb Chronicle	Warren

County Newspaper	Location
MACOMB *(Cont.)*	
Macomb County Legal News	Mt. Clemens
Roseville-Eastpointe Eastsider	Warren
Shelby Utica News	Warren
St. Clair Shores Sentinel	Warren
Sterling Heights Sentry	Warren
The Journal-News	Warren
The Macomb Daily	Clinton Township
The Source	Clinton Township
The Voice	Clinton Township
Warren Weekly	Warren
MANISTEE	
Manistee News-Advocate	Manistee
MARQUETTE	
The Mining Journal	Marquette
MASON	
Ludington Daily News	Ludington
MECOSTA	
The Pioneer	Big Rapids
MENOMINEE	
Menominee County Journal	Stephenson
MIDLAND	
Midland Daily News	Midland
MISSAUKEE	
The Missaukee Sentinel	Lake City
MONROE	
Bedford Now	Monroe
Monroe News	Monroe
The Independent	Dundee
MONTCALM	
Lakeview Area News	Lakeview
The Daily News/Carson City Gazette	Greenville
MONTMORENCY	
Montmorency County Tribune	Atlanta
MUSKEGON	
Muskegon Chronicle	Muskegon
Muskegon County Legal News	Muskegon
White Lake Beacon	Whitehall
NEWAYGO	
Times Indicator	Fremont
OAKLAND	
Between The Lines	Livonia
Birmingham-Bloomfield Eagle	Warren
Birmingham Eccentric	Novi
Clarkston News	Clarkston
Community Lifestyles	Rochester
Daily Tribune	Royal Oak
Detroit Jewish News	Southfield
Farmington Press	Warren
Madison-Park News	Warren
Michigan Lawyers Weekly	Rochester
Milford Times	Novi
Muslim Observer	Farmington
Novi News	Novi

NEWSPAPERS IN MICHIGAN *(Cont.)*

County Newspaper	Location
OAKLAND *(Cont.)*	
Oakland County Legal News	Troy
Oakland Press	Pontiac
Oxford Leader	Oxford
Rochester Post	Warren
Royal Oak Review	Warren
South Lyon Herald	Novi
Southfield Eccentric	Novi
Southfield Sun	Warren
Spinal Column Newsweekly	Highland
The Citizen	Ortonville
The Lake Orion Review	Lake Orion
Troy Times	Warren
West Bloomfield Beacon	Warren
Woodward Talk	Warren
OCEANA	
Oceana's Herald-Journal	Hart
OGEMAW	
Ogemaw County Herald	West Branch
ONTONAGON	
Ontonagon Herald	Ontonagon
OSCEOLA	
Herald-Review	Big Rapids
Marion Press	Marion
OSCODA	
Oscoda County Herald	Mio
OTSEGO	
Gaylord Herald Times	Gaylord
Our Home Town News	Vanderbilt
OTTAWA	
Grand Haven Tribune	Grand Haven
Holland Sentinel	Holland
PRESQUE ISLE	
Presque Isle County Advance & Onaway Outlook	Rogers City
ROSCOMMON	
Houghton Lake Resorter	Houghton Lake
SAGINAW	
Birch Run/Bridgeport Herald	Birch Run
Frankenmuth News	Frankenmuth
Saginaw News	Saginaw
The Township View	Saginaw
Tri-County Citizen	Chesaning
SANILAC	
Brown City Banner	Lapeer
Sanilac County News	Sandusky
Tribune-Recorder (Deckerville, Marlette, Sandusky)	Sandusky
SCHOOLCRAFT	
Pioneer-Tribune	Manistique
SHIAWASSEE	
Independent Newspapers	Owosso
The Argus-Press	Owosso
ST. CLAIR	
Thumb Print News	Algonac
Times Herald	Port Huron
Yale Expositor	Yale

County Newspaper	Location

ST. JOSEPH

Sturgis Journal	Sturgis
Three Rivers Commercial-News	Three Rivers

TUSCOLA

Cass City Chronicle	Cass City
Tuscola County Advertiser	Caro

VAN BUREN

South Haven Tribune	South Haven
The Courier-Leader	Paw Paw

WASHTENAW

LaPrensa	Saline
Michigan Korean Weekly	Ann Arbor
The Ann Arbor News	Ann Arbor
The Sun Times News	Chelsea
Washtenaw County Legal News	Ann Arbor

WAYNE

Belleville-Area Independent	Belleville
Between The Lines	Livonia
Canton Observer	Novi
Crain's Detroit Business	Detroit
Detroit Free Press	Detroit
Detroit Legal News	Detroit
Detroit News	Detroit
Farmington Observer	Farmington
Garden City Observer	Novi
Grosse Pointe News	Grosse Pointe Woods
Grosse Pointe Times	Warren
Hamtramck Review	Hamtramck
Livonia Observer	Novi
Metro Times	Detroit
Michigan Chronicle	Detroit
Northville Record	Novi
Plymouth Observer	Novi
Press & Guide	Southgate
The Eagle	Plymouth
The News-Herald	Southgate
Wayne-Westland Observer	Novi

WEXFORD

Cadillac News	Cadillac

Sources: Michigan Press Association, www.members.michiganpress.org. Accessed April 2019; USNPL. www.usnpl.com. Accessed April 2019; and Legislative Service Bureau, 2019.

ASSOCIATIONS IN MICHIGAN

Association	Address	Officers
County Road Association of Michigan	417 Seymour, Suite 1 Lansing 48933	President: Dave Pettersch Vice President: Richard Timmer Secretary/Treasurer: Burt Thompson
Michigan Association for Local Public Health	426 S. Walnut Street Lansing 48933	President: Steve Hall President-Elect: Angelique Joynes Secretary/Treasurer: Nick Derusha
Michigan Association of Counties	110 W. Michigan Avenue, Suite 200 Lansing 48933	President: Ken Borton First Vice President: Veronica Klinefelt Second Vice President: Phillip Kuyers Secretary-Treasurer: Stephan Currie
Michigan Association of County Clerks	120 N. Washington Square, Suite 110A Lansing 48933	President: Kristen Millard First Vice President: Laura Brandon-Maveal Second Vice President: Sharon Tyler Third Vice President: Marc Kleiman Treasurer: Cheryl Kelly Secretary: Jill Nowak
Michigan Association of County Drain Commissioners	120 N. Washington Square, Suite 110A Lansing 48933	President: Joe Bush First Vice President: Brian Wendling Second Vice President: Evan Pratt Secretary: Jennifer Escott Treasurer: Robert Mantey
Michigan Association of County Treasurers	401 W. Cedar Avenue Gladwin 48624	President: Christy Van Tiem First Vice President: Jenny Beemer-Fritzinger Second Vice President: Jennifer Nash Secretary: Bob Robinson Treasurer: Catherine Lunsford
Michigan Association of Intermediate School Administrators	1001 Centennial Way, Suite 300 Lansing 48917	President: Randy Liepa Past President: Stephen McNew
Michigan Association of Mayors	1675 Green Road Ann Arbor 48105	President: James Rynberg Vice President: Pauline Repp Secretary/Treasurer: Dan Gilmartin and Kelly Warren

ASSOCIATIONS IN MICHIGAN *(Cont.)*

Association	Address	Officers
Michigan Association of Municipal Clerks	120 N. Washington Square, Suite 110A Lansing 48933	President: Dan Kasunic First Vice President: Jennifer Venema Second Vice President: Jeremy Howard Third Vice President: Robert Crawford Secretary: JoAnne Kean Treasurer: Lanie McManus
Michigan Association of Register of Deeds	806 W. Houghton Avenue West Branch 48661 219 E. Paw Paw Street, Suite 102 Paw Paw 49079	President: Paul DeYoung First Vice President: Stewart Sanders Second Vice President: Michelle Stevenson Third Vice President: Brandon Denby Secretary: Ann Manning-Clayton Treasurer: Karen Jackson
Michigan Association of School Boards	1001 Centennial Way, Suite 400 Lansing 48917	President: Mark McKulsky President-Elect: Matthew Showalter Vice President: Jill Fennessy
Michigan Association of State Universities	101 S. Washington Square, Suite 600 Lansing 48933	Chair: M. Roy Wilson Vice Chair: Mark S. Schlissel Secretary/Treasurer: Fritz J. Erickson
Michigan Association of Township Supervisors	629 W. Hillsdale Street Lansing 48933	President: Robert Lewandowski Vice President: Adrienne Glover Treasurer: James Pitsch Secretary: Jim Koehn
Michigan Community College Association	222 North Chestnut Street Lansing 48933	Chairperson: Kojo Quartey Treasurer: Laura L. Coleman
Michigan District Judges Association	100 S. Marley Street, Room 55 St. Ignace 49781	President: Beth Gibson President-Elect: Timothy J. Kelly Vice President: Michelle Friedman Appel Secretary: Raymond P. Voet Treasurer: Kimberley Anne Wiegand
Michigan Judges Association	227 W. Michigan Avenue Kalamazoo 49007	President: Pamela L. Lightvoet President-Elect: Jon A. Van Allsburg Vice President: Martha Anderson Secretary: Christopher P. Yates Treasurer: Michelle M. Rick

ASSOCIATIONS IN MICHIGAN (Cont.)

Association	Address	Officers
Michigan Municipal League	1675 Green Road Ann Arbor 48105	President: Melanie Piana Vice President: Brenda Moore
Michigan Municipal Treasurers Association	P.O. Box 324 Tawas City 48764	President: Margaret Birch President-Elect: Rande Listerman Vice President: Tricia Wiggle-Bazzy Treasurer: Susan Daugherty Secretary: Rachel Piner
Michigan Probate Judges Association	200 W. Michigan Avenue Grayling 49738	President: Monte Burmeister President-Elect: Darlene A. O'Brien Vice President: Thomas D. Slagle Treasurer: John Tomlinson Secretary: William M. Doherty
Michigan Sheriffs' Association	620 S. Capitol Avenue, Suite 320A Lansing 48933	Board of Directors: Kim Cole, Patrick Whiteford, Michael Murphy, Peter Wallin, Mark Valesano, Mathew Saxton, Rick Behnke, L. Paul Bailey
Michigan Townships Association	512 Westshire Drive Lansing 48917	President: Jeffrey Sorenson First Vice President: Peter Kleiman Second Vice President: Bill Deater Treasurer: Pauline Bennett Secretary: Connie Cargill
Prosecuting Attorneys Association of Michigan	116 W. Ottawa Street, Suite 200 Lansing 48933	President: D.J. Hilson President-Elect: William Vailliencourt Vice President: Matt Wiese Secretary-Treasurer: Douglas R. Lloyd
State Bar of Michigan	306 Townsend Street Lansing 48933	President: Jennifer Grieco President-Elect: Dennis Barnes Vice President: Robert Buchanan Secretary: Dana Warnez Treasurer: James Heath

Source: Information collected from websites and personal contacts as of May 15, 2019.

POST OFFICES IN MICHIGAN

Post Office, County, ZIP Code	Post Office, County, ZIP Code
Acme, Grand Traverse, 49610	Bellevue, Eaton, 49021
Ada, Kent, 49301, 49355-49357	Belmont, Kent, 49306
Addison, Lenawee, 49220	Bentley, Bay, 48613
Adrian, Lenawee, 49221	Benton Harbor, Berrien, 49022, 49023
Afton, Cheboygan, 49705	Benzonia, Benzie, 49616
Ahmeek, Keweenaw, 49901	Bergland, Ontonagon, 49910
Akron, Tuscola, 48701	Berkley, Oakland, 48072
Alanson, Emmet, 49706	Berrien Center, Berrien, 49102
Alba, Antrim, 49611	Berrien Springs, Berrien, 49103, 49104
Albion, Calhoun, 49224	Bessemer, Gogebic, 49911
Alden, Antrim, 49612	Beulah, Benzie, 49617
Alger, Arenac, 48610	Big Bay, Marquette, 49808
Algonac, St. Clair, 48001	Big Rapids, Mecosta, 49307
Allegan, Allegan, 49010	Birch Run, Saginaw, 48415
Allen, Hillsdale, 49227	Birmingham, Oakland, 48009, 48012
Allendale, Ottawa, 49401	Bitely, Newaygo, 49309
Allen Park, Wayne, 48101	Black River, Alcona, 48721
Allenton, St. Clair, 48002	Blanchard, Isabella, 49310
Allouez, Keweenaw, 49805	Blissfield, Lenawee, 49228
Alma, Gratiot, 48801	Bloomfield Hills, Oakland, 48301-48304
Almont, Lapeer, 48003	Bloomingdale, Van Buren, 49026
Alpena, Alpena, 49707	Boon, Wexford, 49618
Alpha, Iron, 49902	Boyne City, Charlevoix, 49712
Alto, Kent, 49302	Boyne Falls, Charlevoix, 49713
Amasa, Iron, 49903	Bradley, Allegan, 49311
Anchorville, St. Clair, 48004	Branch, Mason, 49402
Ann Arbor, Washtenaw, 48103-48109, 48113	Brant, Saginaw, 48614
Applegate, Sanilac, 48401	Breckenridge, Gratiot, 48615
Arcadia, Manistee, 49613	Breedsville, Van Buren, 49027
Argyle, Sanillac, 48410	Brethren, Manistee, 49619
Armada, Macomb, 48005	Bridgeport, Saginaw, 48722
Arnold, Marquette, 49819	Bridgewater, Washtenaw, 48115
Ashley, Gratiot, 48806	Bridgman, Berrien, 49106
Athens, Calhoun, 49011	Brighton, Livingston, 48114, 48116
Atlanta, Montmorency, 49709	Brimley, Chippewa, 49715
Atlantic Mine, Houghton, 49905	Britton, Lenawee, 49229
Atlas, Genesee, 48411	Brohman, Newaygo, 49312
Attica, Lapeer, 48412	Bronson, Branch, 49028
Lum, 48452	Brooklyn, Jackson, 49230
Auburn, Bay, 48611	Brown City, Sanilac, 48416
Auburn Hills, Oakland, 48321, 48326	Bruce Crossing, Ontonagon, 49912
Au Gres, Arenac, 48703	Brutus, Emmet, 49716
Augusta, Kalamazoo, 49012	Buchanan, Berrien, 49107
Au Train, Alger, 49806	Buckley, Wexford, 49620
Avoca, St. Clair, 48006	Burlington, Calhoun, 49029
Azalia, Monroe, 48110	Burnips, Allegan, 49314
Bad Axe, Huron, 48413	Burr Oak, St. Joseph, 49030
Bailey, Muskegon, 49303	Burt, Saginaw, 48417
Baldwin, Lake, 49304	Burt Lake, Cheboygan, 49717
Bancroft, Shiawassee, 48414	Burton, Genesee, 48509, 48519, 48529
Bangor, Van Buren, 49013	Byron, Shiawassee, 48418
Bannister, Gratiot, 48807	Byron Center, Kent, 49315
Baraga, Baraga, 49908	Cadillac, Wexford, 49601
Barbeau, Chippewa, 49710	Caledonia, Kent, 49316
Bark River, Delta, 49807	Calumet, Houghton, 49913
Baroda, Berrien, 49101	Camden, Hillsdale, 49232
Barryton, Mecosta, 49305	Cannonsburg, Kent, 49317
Barton City, Alcona, 48705	Canton, Wayne 48187, 48188
Bath, Clinton, 48808	Capac, St. Clair, 48014
Battle Creek, Calhoun, 49014-49018, 49037	Carleton, Monroe, 48117
Bay City, Bay, 48706-48708, 48732	Carney, Menominee, 49812
Bay Port, Huron, 48720	Caro, Tuscola, 48723
Bay Shore, Charlevoix, 49711	Carp Lake, Emmet, 49718
Bear Lake, Manistee, 49614	Carrollton, Saginaw, 48724
Beaver Island, Charlevoix, 49782	Carson City, Montcalm, 48811
Beaverton, Gladwin, 48612	Carsonville, Sanilac, 48419
Bedford, Calhoun, 49020	Casco, St. Clair, 48064
Belding, Ionia, 48809	Caseville, Huron, 48725
Bellaire, Antrim, 49615	Casnovia, Muskegon, 49318
Belleville, Wayne, 48111, 48112	

Post Office, County, ZIP Code	Post Office, County, ZIP Code
Caspian, Iron, 49915	Dafter, Chippewa, 49724
Cass City, Tuscola, 48726	Daggett, Menominee, 49821
Cassopolis, Cass, 49031	Dansville, Ingham, 48819
Cedar, Leelanau, 49621	Davisburg, Oakland, 48350
Cedar Lake, Montcalm, 48812	Davison, Genesee, 48423
Cedar Springs, Kent, 49319	Dearborn, Wayne, 48120, 48121, 48123, 48126,
Cedarville, Mackinac, 49719	48128
Cement City, Lenawee, 49233	Dearborn Heights, Wayne, 48125, 48127
Center Line, Macomb, 48015	Decatur, Van Buren, 49045
Central Lake, Antrim, 49622	Decker, Sanilac, 48426
Centreville, St. Joseph, 49032	Deckerville, Sanilac, 48427
Ceresco, Calhoun, 49033	Deerfield, Lenawee, 49238
Champion, Marquette, 49814	Deerton, Alger, 49822
Channing, Dickinson, 49815	Deford, Tuscola, 48729
Charlevoix, Charlevoix, 49720	Delton, Barry, 49046
Charlotte, Eaton, 48813	De Tour Village, Chippewa, 49725
Chase, Lake, 49623	Detroit, Wayne, 48201-48202, 48204-48211,
Chassell, Houghton, 49916	48213-48217, 48219, 48221-48224,
Chatham, Alger, 49816	48226-48228, 48231-48235, 48238,
Limestone Twp.	48242-48288
Cheboygan, Cheboygan, 49721	DeWitt, Clinton, 48820
Chelsea, Washtenaw, 48118	Dexter, Washtenaw, 48130
Chesaning, Saginaw, 48616	Dimondale, Eaton, 48821
China, St. Clair, 48054	Dodgeville, Houghton, 49921
Chippewa Lake, Mecosta, 49320	Dollar Bay, Houghton, 49922
Clare, Clare, 48617	Dorr, Allegan, 49323
Clarklake, Jackson, 49234	Douglas, Allegan, 49406
Clarkston, Oakland, 48346-48348	Dowagiac, Cass, 49047
Clarksville, Ionia, 48815	Dowling, Barry, 49050
Clawson, Oakland, 48017	Drayton Plains, Oakland, 48330
Clayton, Lenawee, 49235	Drummond Island, Chippewa, 49726
Clifford, Lapeer, 48727	Dryden, Lapeer, 48428
Climax, Kalamazoo, 49034	Dundee, Monroe, 48131
Clinton, Lenawee, 49236	Durand, Shiawassee, 48429
Clinton Twp., Macomb, 48035, 48036, 48038	Eagle, Clinton, 48822
Clio, Genesee, 48420	East China, St. Clair, 48054
Cloverdale, Barry, 49035	East Grand Rapids, Kent, 49506, 49546
Cohoctah, Livingston, 48816	East Jordan, Charlevoix, 49727
Coldwater, Branch, 49036	Eastlake, Manistee, 49626
Coleman, Midland, 48618	East Lansing, Ingham, 48823-48826
Coloma, Berrien, 49038	East Leroy, Calhoun, 49051
Colon, St. Joseph, 49040	Eastpointe, Macomb, 48021
Columbiaville, Lapeer, 48421	Eastport, Antrim, 49627
Columbus, St. Clair, 48063	East Tawas, Iosco, 48730
Comins, Oscoda, 48619	Eaton Rapids, Eaton, 48827
Commerce Township, Oakland, 48382	Eau Claire, Berrien, 49111
Comstock, Kalamazoo, 49041	Eben Junction, Alger, 49825
Comstock Park, Kent, 49321	Eckerman, Chippewa, 49728
Concord, Jackson, 49237	Ecorse, Wayne, 48229
Conklin, Ottawa, 49403	Edenville, Midland, 48620
Constantine, St. Joseph, 49042	Edmore, Montcalm, 48829
Conway, Emmet, 49722	Edwardsburg, Cass, 49112
Cooks, Schoolcraft, 49817	Elberta, Benzie, 49628
Coopersville, Ottawa, 49404	Elk Rapids, Antrim, 49629
Copemish, Manistee, 49625	Elkton, Huron, 48731
Copper City, Houghton, 49917	Ellsworth, Antrim, 49729
Copper Harbor, Keweenaw, 49918	Elm Hall, Gratiot, 48830
Coral, Montcalm, 49322	Elmira, Otsego, 49730
Cornell, Delta, 49818	Elsie, Clinton, 48831
Corunna, Shiawassee, 48817	Elwell, Gratiot, 48832
Covert, Van Buren, 49043	Emmett, St. Clair, 48022
Covington, Baraga, 49919	Empire, Leelanau, 49630
Cross Village, Emmet, 49723	Engadine, Mackinac, 49827
Croswell, Sanilac, 48422	Erie, Monroe, 48133
Crystal, Montcalm, 48818	Escanaba, Delta, 49829
Crystal Falls, Iron, 49920	Essexville, Bay, 48732
Curran, Alcona, 48728	Eureka, Clinton, 48833
Curtis, Mackinac, 49820	Evart, Osceola, 49631
Custer, Mason, 49405	Ewen, Ontonagon, 49925

Post Office, County, ZIP Code	Post Office, County, ZIP Code
Fairgrove, Tuscola, 48733	Grant, Newaygo, 49327
Fair Haven, St. Clair, 48023	Grass Lake, Jackson, 49240
Fairview, Oscoda, 48621	Grawn, Grand Traverse, 49637
Falmouth, Missaukee, 49632	Grayling, Crawford, 49738, 49739
Farmington, Oakland, 48331-48336	Greenbush, Alcona, 48738
Farwell, Clare, 48622	Greenland, Ontonagon, 49929
Felch, Dickinson, 49831	Greenville, Montcalm, 48838
Fennville, Allegan, 49408	Gregory, Livingston, 48137
Fenton, Genesee, 48430	Grosse Ile, Wayne, 48138
Fenwick, Montcalm, 48834	Grosse Pointe, Wayne, 48230, 48236
Ferndale, Oakland, 48220	Gulliver, Schoolcraft, 49840
Ferrysburg, Ottawa, 49409	Gwinn, Marquette, 49841
Fife Lake, Grand Traverse, 49633	Hadley, Lapeer, 48440
Filer City, Manistee, 49634	Hager Shores, Berrien, 49039
Filion, Huron, 48432	Hale, Iosco, 48739
Flat Rock, Wayne, 48134	Hamburg, Livingston, 48139
Flint, Genesee, 48501-48507, 48531, 48532, 48550-48557	Hamilton, Allegan, 49419
	Hamtramck, Wayne, 48212
Flushing, Genesee, 48433	Hancock, Houghton, 49930
Forestville, Sanilac, 48434	Hanover, Jackson, 49241
Fort Gratiot, St. Clair, 48059	Harbert, Berrien, 49115
Foster City, Dickinson, 49834	Harbor Beach, Huron, 48441
Fostoria, Tuscola, 48435	Harbor Springs, Emmet, 49740
Fountain, Mason, 49410	Harper Woods, Wayne, 48225
Fowler, Clinton, 48835	Harrietta, Wexford, 49638
Fowlerville, Livingston, 48836	Harris, Menominee, 49845
Frankenmuth, Saginaw, 48734, 48787	Harrison, Clare, 48625
Frankfort, Benzie, 49635	Harrison Township, Macomb, 48045
Franklin, Oakland, 48025	Harrisville, Alcona, 48740
Fraser, Macomb, 48026	Harsens Island, St. Clair, 48028
Frederic, Crawford, 49733	Hart, Oceana, 49420
Freeland, Saginaw, 48623	Hartford, Van Buren, 49057
Freeport, Barry, 49325	Hartland, Livingston, 48353
Free Soil, Mason, 49411	Haslett, Ingham, 48840
Fremont, Newaygo, 49412, 49413	Hastings, Barry, 49058
Frontier, Hillsdale, 49239	Hawks, Presque Isle, 49743
Fruitport, Muskegon, 49415	Hazel Park, Oakland, 48030
Fulton, Kalamazoo, 49052	Hemlock, Saginaw, 48626
Gaastra, Iron, 49927	Henderson, Shiawassee, 48841
Gagetown, Tuscola, 48735	Hermansville, Menominee, 49847
Gaines, Genesee, 48436	Herron, Alpena, 49744
Galesburg, Kalamazoo, 49053	Hersey, Osceola, 49639
Galien, Berrien, 49113	Hesperia, Oceana, 49421
Garden, Delta, 49835	Hessel, Mackinac, 49745
Garden City, Wayne, 48135, 48136	Hickory Corners, Barry, 49060
Gaylord, Otsego, 49734, 49735	Higgins Lake, Roscommon, 48627
Genesee, Genesee, 48437	Highland, Oakland, 48356, 48357
Germfask, Schoolcraft, 49836	Highland Park, Wayne, 48203
Gladstone, Delta, 49837	Hillman, Montmorency, 49746
Gladwin, Gladwin, 48624	Hillsdale, Hillsdale, 49242
Glen Arbor, Leelanau, 49636	Holland, Ottawa, 49422-49424
Glenn, Allegan, 49416	Holly, Oakland, 48442
Glennie, Alcona, 48737	Holt, Ingham, 48842
Gobles, Van Buren, 49055	Holton, Muskegon, 49425
Goetzville, Chippewa, 49736	Homer, Calhoun, 49245
Goodells, St. Clair, 48027	Honor, Benzie, 49640
Good Hart, Emmet, 49737	Hope, Midland, 48628
Goodrich, Genesee, 48438	Hopkins, Allegan, 49328
Gould City, Mackinac, 49838	Horton, Jackson, 49246
Gowen, Montcalm, 49326	Houghton, Houghton, 49931
Grand Blanc, Genesee, 48439, 48480	Houghton Lake, Roscommon, 48629
Grand Haven, Ottawa, 49417	Houghton Lake Heights, Roscommon, 48630
Grand Junction, Van Buren, 49056	Howard City, Montcalm, 49329
Grand Ledge, Eaton, 48837	Howell, Livingston, 48843, 48844, 48855
Grand Marais, Alger, 49839	Hubbard Lake, Alpena, 49747
Grand Rapids, Kent, 49501-49508, 49510, 49512, 49514-49516, 49518, 49519, 49523, 49525, 49528, 49530, 49534, 49544, 49546, 49548, 49555, 49560, 49588, 49599	Hubbardston, Ionia, 48845
	Hubbell, Houghton, 49934
	Hudson, Lenawee, 49247
Grandville, Kent, 49418, 49468	Hudsonville, Ottawa, 49426

Post Office, County, ZIP Code	Post Office, County, ZIP Code
Hulbert, Chippewa, 49748	Lawton, Van Buren, 49065
Huntington Woods, Oakland, 48070	Leland, Leelanau, 49654
Ida, Monroe, 48140	Lennon, Genesee, 48449
Idlewild, Lake, 49642	Lenox, Macomb, 48048, 48050
Imlay City, Lapeer, 48444	Leonard, Oakland, 48367
Indian River, Cheboygan, 49749	Addison Twp.
Ingalls, Menominee, 49848	Leonidas, St. Joseph, 49066
Inkster, Wayne, 48141	Le Roy, Osceola, 49655
Interlochen, Grand Traverse, 49643	Leslie, Ingham, 49251
Ionia, Ionia, 48846	Levering, Emmet, 49755
Iron Mountain, Dickinson, 49801	Lewiston, Montmorency, 49756
Iron River, Iron, 49935	Lexington, Sanilac, 48450
Irons, Lake, 49644	Lincoln, Alcona, 48742
Ironwood, Gogebic, 49938	Lincoln Park, Wayne, 48146
Ishpeming, Marquette, 49849	Linden, Genesee, 48451
Ithaca, Gratiot, 48847	Linwood, Bay, 48634
Jackson, Jackson, 49201-49204	Litchfield, Hillsdale, 49252
Jamestown, Ottawa, 49427	Little Lake, Marquette, 49833
Jasper, Lenawee, 49248	Livonia, Wayne, 48150-48154
Jeddo, St. Clair, 48032	Long Lake, Iosco, 48743
Jenison, Ottawa, 49428, 49429	Loretto, Dickinson, 49852
Jerome, Hillsdale, 49249	Lowell, Kent, 49331
Johannesburg, Otsego, 49751	Ludington, Mason, 49431
Jones, Cass, 49061	Luna Pier, Monroe, 48157
Jonesville, Hillsdale, 49250	Lupton, Ogemaw, 48635
Kalamazoo, Kalamazoo, 49001, 49003-49009,	Luther, Lake, 49656
49019, 49048	Luzerne, Oscoda, 48636
Kaleva, Manistee, 49645	Lyons, Ionia, 48851
Kalkaska, Kalkaska, 49646	Macatawa, Ottawa, 49434
Kawkawlin, Bay, 48631	Mackinac Island, Mackinac, 49757
Kearsarge, Houghton, 49942	Mackinaw City, Cheboygan, 49701
Keego Harbor, Oakland, 48320	Macomb, Macomb, 48042, 48044
Kendall, Van Buren, 49062	Madison Heights, Oakland, 48071
Kent City, Kent, 49330	Mancelona, Antrim, 49659
Kewadin, Antrim, 49648	Manchester, Washtenaw, 48158
Kincheloe, Chippewa, 49784-49786, 49788	Manistee, Manistee, 49660
Kinde, Huron, 48445	Stronach
Kingsford, Dickinson, 49802	Manistique, Schoolcraft, 49854
Kingsley, Grand Traverse, 49649	Thompson
Kingston, Tuscola, 48741	Manitou Beach, Lenawee, 49253
Kinross, Chippewa, 49752	Manton, Wexford, 49663
Lachine, Alpena, 49753	Maple City, Leelanau, 49664
Lacota, Van Buren, 49063	Maple Rapids, Clinton, 48853
Laingsburg, Shiawassee, 48848	Marcellus, Cass, 49067
Lake, Clare, 48632	Marenisco, Gogebic, 49947
Lake Angelus, Oakland, 48326	Marine City, St. Clair, 48039
Lake Ann, Benzie, 49650	Marion, Osceola, 49665
Lake City, Missaukee, 49651	Marlette, Sanilac, 48453
Lake George, Clare, 48633	Marne, Ottawa, 49435
Lakeland, Livingston, 48143	Marquette, Marquette, 49855
Lake Leelanau, Leelanau 49653	Marshall, Calhoun, 49068
Lake Linden, Houghton, 49945	Martin, Allegan, 49070
Lake Odessa, Ionia, 48849	Marysville, St. Clair, 48040
Lake Orion, Oakland, 48359-48362	Mason, Ingham, 48854
Lakeport, St. Clair, 48059	Mass City, Ontonagon, 49948
Lakeside, Berrien, 49116	Mattawan, Van Buren, 49071
Lakeview, Montcalm, 48850	Maybee, Monroe, 48159
Lakeville, Oakland, 48366	Mayfield, Grand Traverse, 49666
Lambertville, Monroe, 48144	Mayville, Tuscola, 48744
Lamont, Ottawa, 49430	McBain, Missaukee, 49657
L'Anse, Baraga, 49946	McBrides, Montcalm, 48852
Lansing, Ingham, 48901, 48906, 48908-48913,	McMillan, Luce, 49853
48915-48919, 48922, 48924, 48929, 48930,	Mears, Oceana, 49436
48933, 48937, 48951, 48956, 48980	Mecosta, Mecosta, 49332
Lapeer, Lapeer, 48446	Melvin, Sanilac, 48454
La Salle, Monroe, 48145	Melvindale, Wayne, 48122
Lathrup Village, Oakland, 48076	Memphis, St. Clair, 48041
Laurium, Houghton, 49913	Riley
Lawrence, Van Buren, 49064	Mendon, St. Joseph, 49072

Post Office, County, ZIP Code	Post Office, County, ZIP Code
Menominee, Menominee, 49858	North Branch, Lapeer, 48461
Merrill, Saginaw, 48637	Northport, Leelanau, 49670
Merritt, Missaukee, 49667	North Star, Gratiot, 48862
Mesick, Wexford, 49668	North Street, St. Clair, 48049
Metamora, Lapeer, 48455	Clyde
Michigamme, Marquette, 49861	Ruby
Michigan Center, Jackson, 49254	Northville, Wayne, 48167, 48168
Middleton, Gratiot, 48856	Norvell, Jackson, 49263
Middleville, Barry, 49333	Norway, Dickinson, 49870
Midland, Midland, 48640-48642, 48667-48686	Nottawa, St. Joseph, 49075
Mikado, Alcona, 48745	Novi, Oakland, 48374-48377
Milan, Monroe, 48160	Nunica, Ottawa, 49448
Milford, Oakland, 48380, 48381	Oakland, Oakland, 48363
Millersburg, Presque Isle, 49759	Oakley, Saginaw, 48649
Millington, Tuscola, 48746	Oak Park, Oakland, 48237
Minden City, Sanilac, 48456	Oden, Emmet, 49764
Mio, Oscoda, 48647	Okemos, Ingham, 48805, 48864
Mohawk, Keweenaw, 49950	Old Mission, Grand Traverse, 49673
Eagle Harbor	Olivet, Eaton, 49076
Eagle River	Omena, Leelanau, 49674
Moline, Allegan, 49335	Omer, Arenac, 48749
Monroe, Monroe, 48161, 48162	Onaway, Presque Isle, 49765
Montague, Muskegon, 49437	Onekama, Manistee, 49675
Montgomery, Branch, 49255	Onondaga, Ingham, 49264
Montrose, Genesee, 48457	Onsted, Lenawee, 49265
Moran, Mackinac, 49760	Ontonagon, Ontonagon, 49953
Morenci, Lenawee, 49256	Orleans, Ionia, 48865
Morley, Mecosta, 49336	Ortonville, Oakland, 48462
Morrice, Shiawassee, 48857	Oscoda, Iosco, 48750
Moscow, Hillsdale, 49257	AuSable
Mosherville, Hillsdale, 49258	Oshtemo, Kalamazoo, 49077
Mount Clemens, Macomb, 48043, 48046	Osseo, Hillsdale, 49266
Mount Morris, Genesee, 48458	Ossineke, Alpena, 49766
Mount Pleasant, Isabella, 48804, 48858, 48859	Otisville, Genesee, 48463
Muir, Ionia, 48860	Otsego, Allegan, 49078
Mullett Lake, Cheboygan, 49761	Ottawa Lake, Monroe, 49267
Mulliken, Eaton, 48861	Otter Lake, Lapeer, 48464
Munger, Bay, 48747	Ovid, Clinton, 48866
Munising, Alger, 49862	Owendale, Huron, 48754
Christmas	Owosso, Shiawassee, 48867
Munith, Jackson, 49259	Oxford, Oakland, 48370-48371
Muskegon, Muskegon, 49440-49445	Painesdale, Houghton, 49955
Nadeau, Menominee, 49863	Palmer, Marquette, 49871
Nahma, Delta, 49864	Palms, Sanilac, 48465
Napoleon, Jackson, 49261	Palmyra, Lenawee, 49268
Nashville, Barry, 49073	Palo, Ionia, 48870
National City, Iosco, 48748	Paradise, Chippewa, 49768
National Mine, Marquette, 49865	Paris, Mecosta, 49338
Naubinway, Mackinac, 49762	Parma, Jackson, 49269
Nazareth, Kalamazoo, 49074	Paw Paw, Van Buren, 49079
Negaunee, Marquette, 49866	Peck, Sanilac, 48466
Newaygo, Newaygo, 49337	Pelkie, Houghton, 49958
New Baltimore, Macomb, 48047, 48051	Pellston, Emmet, 49769
Chesterfield	Pentwater, Oceana, 49449
Newberry, Luce, 49868	Perkins, Delta, 49872
New Boston, Wayne, 48164	Perrinton, Gratiot, 48871
New Buffalo, Berrien, 49117	Perronville, Menominee, 49873
Grand Beach	Perry, Shiawassee, 48872
Michiana	Petersburg, Monroe, 49270
New Era, Oceana, 49446	Petoskey, Emmet, 49770
New Haven, Macomb, 48048, 48050	Bay Harbor
Lenox	Bay View
New Hudson, Oakland, 48165	Pewamo, Ionia, 48873
New Lothrop, Shiawassee, 48460	Pickford, Chippewa, 49774
Newport, Monroe, 48166	Pierson, Montcalm, 49339
New Troy, Berrien, 49119	Pigeon, Huron, 48755
Niles, Berrien, 49120	Sand Point
Nisula, Houghton, 49952	Pinckney, Livingston, 48169
North Adams, Hillsdale, 49262	Pinconning, Bay, 48650

Post Office, County, ZIP Code	Post Office, County, ZIP Code
Pittsford, Hillsdale, 49271	Saginaw, Saginaw, 48601-48609, 48638, 48663
Prattville	Sagola, Dickinson, 49881
Plainwell, Allegan, 49080	Saint Charles, Saginaw, 48655
Pleasant Lake, Jackson, 49272	Saint Clair, St. Clair, 48079
Pleasant Ridge, Oakland, 48069	Saint Clair Shores, Macomb, 48080-48082
Plymouth, Wayne, 48170	Saint Helen, Roscommon, 48656
Pointe Aux Pins, Mackinac, 49775	Saint Ignace, Mackinac, 49781
Bois Blanc Island	Saint Johns, Clinton, 48879
Pompeii, Gratiot, 48874	Saint Joseph, Berrien, 49085
Pontiac, Oakland, 48340-48343	Saint Louis, Gratiot, 48880
Portage, Kalamazoo, 49002, 49024, 49081	Salem, Washtenaw, 48175
Port Austin, Huron, 48467	Saline, Washtenaw, 48176
Port Hope, Huron, 48468	Samaria, Monroe, 48177
Port Huron, St. Clair, 48060, 48061	Sand Creek, Lenawee, 49279
Portland, Ionia, 48875	Sand Lake, Kent, 49343
Port Sanilac, Sanilac, 48469	Sandusky, Sanilac, 48471
Posen, Presque Isle, 49776	Sanford, Midland, 48657
Potterville, Eaton, 48876	Saranac, Ionia, 48881
Powers, Menominee, 49874	Saugatuck, Allegan, 49453
Prescott, Ogemaw, 48756	Sault Ste. Marie, Chippewa, 49783
Presque Isle, Presque Isle, 49777	Sawyer, Berrien, 49125
Prudenville, Roscommon, 48651	Schoolcraft, Kalamazoo, 49087
Pullman, Allegan, 49450	Scotts, Kalamazoo, 49088
Quincy, Branch, 49082	Scottville, Mason, 49454
Quinnesec, Dickinson, 49876	Sears, Osceola, 49679
Ralph, Dickinson, 49877	Sebewaing, Huron, 48759
Ramsay, Gogebic, 49959	Seney, Schoolcraft, 49883
Rapid City, Kalkaska, 49676	Shaftsburg, Shiawassee, 48882
Rapid River, Delta, 49878	Shelby, Oceana, 49455
Ravenna, Muskegon, 49451	Shelby Township, Macomb, 48317
Ray, Macomb, 48096	Shelbyville, Allegan, 49344
Reading, Hillsdale, 49274	Shepherd, Isabella, 48883
Redford, Wayne, 48239-48240	Sheridan, Montcalm, 48884
Reed City, Osceola, 49677	Sherwood, Branch, 49089
Reese, Tuscola, 48757	Shingleton, Alger, 49884
Remus, Mecosta, 49340	Sidnaw, Houghton, 49961
Republic, Marquette, 49879	Sidney, Montcalm, 48885
Rhodes, Gladwin, 48652	Silverwood, Lapeer, 48760
Richland, Kalamazoo, 49083	Six Lakes, Montcalm, 48886
Richmond, Macomb, 48062	Skandia, Marquette, 49885
Richville, Tuscola, 48758	Skanee, Baraga, 49962
Riga, Lenawee, 49276	Smiths Creek, St. Clair, 48074
Riverdale, Gratiot, 48877	Kimball
River Rouge, Wayne, 48218	Smyrna, Ionia, 48887
Riverside, Berrien, 49084	Snover, Sanilac, 48472
Riverview, Wayne, 48192-48193	Sodus, Berrien, 49126
Rives Junction, Jackson, 49277	Somerset, Hillsdale, 49281
Rochester, Oakland, 48308	Somerset Center, Hillsdale, 49282
Rochester Hills, Oakland, 48306-48309	South Boardman, Kalkaska, 49680
Rock, Delta, 49880	South Branch, Ogemaw, 48761
Rockford, Kent, 49341, 49351	Southfield, Oakland, 48033, 48034, 48037,
Rockland, Ontonagon, 49960	48075, 48086
Rockwood, Wayne, 48173	Southgate, Wayne, 48195
Rodney, Mecosta, 49342	South Haven, Van Buren, 49090
Rogers City, Presque Isle, 49779	South Lyon, Oakland, 48178
Romeo, Macomb, 48065	South Range, Houghton, 49963
Bruce	South Rockwood, Monroe, 48179
Romulus, Wayne, 48174	Spalding, Menominee, 49886
Roscommon, Roscommon, 48653	Sparta, Kent, 49345
Rosebush, Isabella, 48878	Spring Arbor, Jackson, 49283
Rose City, Ogemaw, 48654	Spring Lake, Ottawa, 49456
Roseville, Macomb, 48066	Springport, Jackson, 49284
Rothbury, Oceana, 49452	Spruce, Alcona, 48762
Royal Oak, Oakland, 48067, 48068, 48073	Stambaugh, Iron, 49964
Rudyard, Chippewa, 49780	Standish, Arenac, 48658
Fibre	Stanton, Montcalm, 48888
Rumely, Alger, 49826	Stanwood, Mecosta, 49346
Ruth, Huron, 48470	Canadian Lakes
	Stephenson, Menominee, 49887

Post Office, County, ZIP Code	Post Office, County, ZIP Code
Sterling, Arenac, 48659	Wakefield, Gogebic, 49968
Sterling Heights, Macomb, 48310-48314	Waldron, Hillsdale, 49288
Stevensville, Berrien, 49127	Walhalla, Mason, 49458
Stockbridge, Ingham, 49285	Walker, Kent, 49534, 49544
Sturgis, St. Joseph, 49091	Walkerville, Oceana, 49459
Sumner, Gratiot, 48889	Wallace, Menominee, 49893
Sunfield, Eaton, 48890	Walled Lake, Oakland, 48390
Suttons Bay, Leelanau, 49682	Wolverine Lake
Peshawbestown	Walloon Lake, Charlevoix, 49796
Swartz Creek, Genesee, 48473	Warren, Macomb, 48088-48093, 48397
Sylvan Beach, Muskegon, 49463	Washington, Macomb, 48094, 48095
Tawas City, Iosco, 48763-48764	Waterford, Oakland, 48327-48329
Taylor, Wayne, 48180	Waters, Otsego, 49797
Tecumseh, Lenawee, 49286	Watersmeet, Gogebic, 49969
Tekonsha, Calhoun, 49092	Watervliet, Berrien, 49098
Temperance, Monroe, 48182	Watton, Baraga, 49970
Thompsonville, Benzie, 49683	Wayland, Allegan, 49348
Three Oaks, Berrien, 49128	Wayne, Wayne, 48184
Three Rivers, St. Joseph, 49093	Webberville, Ingham, 48892
Tipton, Lenawee, 49287	Weidman, Isabella, 48893
Toivola, Houghton, 49965	Wells, Delta, 49894
Topinabee, Cheboygan, 49791	Wellston, Manistee, 49689
Tower, Cheboygan, 49792	West Bloomfield, Oakland, 48322-48325
Traverse City, Grand Traverse, 49684-49686, 49696	West Branch, Ogemaw, 48661
	Westland, Wayne, 48185, 48186
Trenary, Alger, 49891	West Olive, Ottawa, 49460
Traunik	Weston, Lenawee, 49289
Trenton, Wayne, 48183	Westphalia, Clinton, 48894
Woodhaven	Wetmore, Alger, 49895
Trout Creek, Ontonagon, 49967	Wheeler, Gratiot, 48662
Trout Lake, Chippewa, 49793	White Cloud, Newaygo, 49349
Troy, Oakland, 48083-48085, 48098, 48099	Whitehall, Muskegon, 49461
Trufant, Montcalm, 49347	White Lake, Oakland, 48383, 48386
Turner, Arenac, 48765	White Pigeon, St. Joseph, 49099
Tustin, Osceola, 49688	White Pine, Ontonagon, 49971
Twining, Arenac, 48766	Whitmore Lake, Washtenaw, 48189
Twin Lake, Muskegon, 49457	Whittaker, Washtenaw, 48190
Ubly, Huron, 48475	Whittemore, Iosco, 48770
Union, Cass 49130	Williamsburg, Grand Traverse, 49690
Union City, Branch, 49094	Williamston, Ingham, 48895
Union Lake, Oakland, 48387	Willis, Washtenaw, 48191
Union Pier, Berrien, 49129	Wilson, Menominee, 49896
Unionville, Tuscola, 48767	Winn, Isabella, 48896
University Center, Bay 48710	Wixom, Oakland, 48393
Utica, Macomb, 48315-48318	Wolverine, Cheboygan, 49799
Shelby Twp.	Woodland, Barry, 48897
Vandalia, Cass, 49095	Wyandotte, Wayne, 48192
Vanderbilt, Otsego, 49795	Wyoming, Kent, 49509, 49519
Vassar, Tuscola, 48768	Yale, St. Clair, 48097
Vermontville, Eaton, 49096	Brockway
Vernon, Shiawassee, 48476	Lynn
Vestaburg, Montcalm, 48891	Ypsilanti, Washtenaw, 48197, 48198
Vicksburg, Kalamazoo, 49097	Zeeland, Ottawa, 49464
Vulcan, Dickinson, 49892	

Source: USPS.com. Look Up a Zip Code. tools.usps.com/go/ZipLookupResultsAction!input.action?resultMode=2&companyName=
&address1=&address2=&city=&state=Select&urbanCode=&postalCode=48235&zip= (Accessed May and July 2019).
www.zip-codes.com/state/mi.asp#zipcodes. Accessed June 2019.

PUBLIC HOLIDAYS IN MICHIGAN

New Year's Day . . . . January 1

Martin Luther King Jr. Day. . . . . .Third Monday in January

President's Day. . . . . .Third Monday in February

Memorial Day. . . . . Last Monday in May

Independence Day . . . . .July 4

Labor Day . . . . First Monday in September

General Election Day . . . . First Tuesday after November 1,
. . . . even numbered years

Veterans' Day . . . . November 11

Thanksgiving Day. . . . . .Fourth Thursday
    and the day after. . . . . and Friday in November

Christmas Eve and Christmas Day . . . . .December 24 and 25

New Year's Eve. . . . . December 31

Source: www.michigan.gov/som/0,4669,7-192-29938-90605--,00.html.

INDEXES

2019–2020

GENERAL INDEX

INDEX TO NAMES

State legislators who only appear in the manual on the list of all current and former legislators (pp. 261 to 349) are not included in this index. Legislators who appear on that list and appear in other sections of the manual are included in this index.

A

Abbott, Brian. 476
Abbott, Daniel. 653
Abbott, Robert. 357
Abbott, Tina 629
Abdallah, Dave 460
Abel, Gabriella 440
Abernathy, Jeff 623
Abood, Marcus 474
Abraham, Spencer 554
Accavitti, Frank, Jr. 261, 697
Acciavatti, Daniel J. 261, 467
Acharya, Chandragupta 431
Acker, Henry. 261, 353, 355
Acker, Jordan B. 611, 625
Acker, William H. 31
Ackerman, Greg 433
Ackerman, Ricky 462
Ackert, Terence. 526
Adair, Andrew 464
Adam, John J. . . . .
. . . . 21, 27, 261, 352, 357, 486, 624
Adam, Wales 28
Adamczyck, Gene 433
Adamini, Stephen 261, 647
Adams, Clark J. 261, 504
Adams, Dave. 651, 723, 764
Adams, Diane 643
Adams, Dion 725, 766
Adams, Edgar J. 31, 261, 353
Adams, Lydia Nance 529
Adams, Niki 447
Adams, Paul L. 485, 504, 625
Adams, Peter R. 28
Adams, Thomas. 430, 456
Adams, Thomas B. 629
Adams, William 21
Adcock, William 470
Adeyanju, Matthew 471
Adkins, Corbett 477
Adler, Ari. 455
Adler, Jessi 474
Adrian, Robert. 636
Afendoulis, Chris. 261, 704, 745
Afendoulis, Lynn . . . .
. . 168, 174-175, 178-179, 237, 261, 720, 761
Affolter-Caine, Britany L. 473
Agee, James 261, 434
Agnew, Valencia 467
Ahmad, Hassan 469
Aho, Michael. 646
Aho, Tim. 643
Ahrens, Kristin. 462
Ahrens, Neil 641
Aitken, David D. 557
Aiuto, Teri. 716, 757
Aiyash, Abraham 689, 699

Ajegba, Paul C. 421, 457, 473
Ajluni, Peter 434
Akers, Forest H. 627, 629
Alam, Md Rabbi. 707, 749
Alavi, Asim 431
Albert, Peg 623
Albert, Thomas A. 168,
174, 176, 178-179, 236-237, 261, 722, 763
Albosta, Donald J. 261, 567-568
Albro, Cathy 696, 734
Alden, Hiram. 355
Alderson, Louise 251, 530
Aldrich, Levi 29, 261
Alexander, Betty Jean. . . . .
. . . . 138, 142, 145-146, 240, 261, 700, 741
Alexander, Greg 652, 704
Alexander, James M. 523
Alexander, Julie. . . . .
168, 174-175, 178, 180, 236, 261, 718, 759
Alexander, Lorenzo P. 29, 261
Alexander, Lynn 450
Alfonsetti, Theodore, III. 713, 754
Alger, Fred M., Jr. 484
Alger, Russell A. 482, 554
Alhasani, Asmaa 709
Alholm, Karen. 647
Aliaga, Jose 714
Allen, Colleen 432, 443
Allen, Dave. 653
Allen, David J. 523
Allen, Dennis 653
Allen, Donald L. 530
Allen, Dorene S. 526
Allen, Edward P. 261, 355, 557, 627
Allen, Ethan 20
Allen, Glenn S., Jr. 33
Allen, James T. 255
Allen, John 468
Allen, Marvin. 624
Allen, Seneca. 254
Allen, Tonya 462, 606
Allen, Warren 644
Alles, Sheila A. 439, 445, 487
Allor, Sue 168, 174,
176, 178, 180, 235-236, 239, 262, 726, 766
Almasmari, Saad 707
Almquist, Erik 721
Almy, Al 643
Alpert, Gail S. 461
Altman, Carl L. 651
Alvord, Henry J. 28, 262
Alward, Dennis E. 352
Always, Robert M. 745
Alyea, Mark. 449
Amash, Justin . . . .
235-238, 262, 543, 546, 571-572, 696, 734
Ambler, William E. 350
Ambrozaitis, Michelle. 639

Bippus, John 653
Birch, Margaret 803
Bird, Arthur C. 627
Bird, Brenda 649
Bird, John E. 485, 503
Bird, Tom 651
Biris, Anne 429
Birkholz, Patricia L. 267, 351, 356
Birney, James 29, 267, 351, 483
Biro, Ladd 452
Bischer, Allen 433
Bischer, Ronald 651
Bishop, John 653
Bishop, Levi 624
Bishop, Michael D. . . 267, 350, 572, 697, 735
Bishop, Roswell P. 31-32, 267, 557-558
Bishop, R. Spencer 625
Bissell, Amy 638
Bitnar, Mike. 639
Bitzer, Jason E. 531
Bizon, John. 138,
    142-145, 148, 235-236, 247, 267, 702, 744
Bizon, Joseph 649
Bizon, Kimberly. 697, 735
Bjork, Randy 640
Black, Charles M. 31
Black, Eugene F. 485, 504
Black, Jessica. 455
Black, K. Edward. 636
Black, Lawrence 434
Black, Melvin 649
Black, Stuart 526
Black, William 434
Blackburn, Sharon 432
Blacker, Robert R. 484
Blackman, Samuel H. 29, 267
Blackmer, Terrence 447
Blackney, William W. 561-563
Blair, Austin. 267, 482, 555-556, 624
Blair, Charles A. 267, 485, 503
Blanchard, James J. 482, 567-568
Blanchard, Sheryl 429
Blandford, Robert H. 33
Blankenhorn, Anne 454
Blatchford, Anne E. 528
Blau, Michael J. 771
Bledsoe, Harold E. 33
Bleich, Melvin E. 629
Blessman, James 452
Bliss, Aaron P. 627
Bliss, Aaron T. 267, 482, 557
Bliss, Rosalynn 449
Blohm, Allen 649
Blomstrom, Brian. 447
Blount, Christopher Michael. 529
Blount, Nancy McCaughan. 529
Blubaugh, Eric. 526
Bluestein, Reginald 436
Bluhm, Karen 650
Blumerich, William 652
Blundell, Arthur. 711, 752
Bobier, Patrice. 461
Bocanegra, Juanita. 451
Bocks, Josh 476
Boe, Krista 432
Boedeker, Joseph F. 529

Boehm, Robert 457
Boes, Janet M. 523, 772
Boettcher, Ed. 637
Bogdan, Joseph 700
Bohm, Jeffrey L. 652
Bohn, Frank P. 268, 561
Boies, John K. 268, 350
Bolden, Kyra Harris. . . . .
    167, 174, 177-178, 182, 238, 268, 713, 754
Boles, Tomeka. 709
Bolger, James B. 478, 618
Bolger, Jase. 268, 354, 438
Bolger, Matt. 443
Bollin, Ann . . . .
    167, 174, 176, 178, 183, 237, 268, 714, 756
Bolser, Benjamin T. 526
Bolt, Andrew. 268, 355
Bolt, Christopher 475
Bolter, Mandy 644
Bolton, Karol. 645
Bomberg, Mark 471
Bomer, Articia 709, 750
Bomia, Jason C. 528
Bondar, Jackie. 650
Bondy, Robert. 530
Bone, Mark 648
Bonge, Barbara 456
Bonior, David E. 268, 567-570
Bonisteel, Roscoe O., Sr. 33, 625-626, 629
Bonnell, Jeff 700, 742
Bonovetz, Joe 641
Booher, Kimberly L. 524
Boone, Daniel. 4
Boonstra, Mark T. 509, 514
Boothby, Lee. 33
Borchard, James T. 438, 523
Bordine, Andrew. 477
Borenitsch, Robert. 432
Boring, Bill 716
Borkovich, Michael 645
Borregard, Eric 744
Borrello, André R. 523
Borrello, Stephen L. 509, 516
Borton, Ken 650, 801
Borushko, Nancy. 637
Bosch, Michael 463, 722
Boss, Michael 439
Bossardet, Malissa 714
Boston, Cynthia. 464
Boston, Derek 707
Bosworth, Diana 640
Bota, Karen 643
Bouchard, Michael. 268, 649
Bouchard-Wyant, Kathy 462
Boughton, Seleck C. 27
Bourdages, Brian 429
Bourdeau, Richard. 650
Bourgois, Debbie. 703, 745
Bourque, Thomas 461
Boutros, Henry 477
Bovin, Douglas R. 268
Bowen, Beth 719
Bowen, Matthew 640
Bowens, Robert. 33
Bower, Kenneth. 647
Bowers, Jim. 638

D'Ailleboust, Louis,
  Sieur de Coulonges. 480
Dale, Julia 477
Daley, Kevin 138, 142-143,
  145, 150, 235, 237, 239, 279, 704, 746
Dame, Matt. 701
Damman, James J. 279, 483
Damschroder, Tim 450
Damstra, Randall S. 449, 590
Danforth, Ephraim B. 28, 279
Danhof, Nancy 488
Danhof, Robert J. 33
Danielak, Timothy 466
Daniells, Nathaniel I. 29
Daniels, Dana 720
Daniels, Ebenezer 28, 279
Daniels, Rodney 442
Dannenberg, Allen. 651
D'Antonio, Roy 641
Darden, Julie. 473
Darga, Michael 651
Darin, Nick 467
Darisaw, LaShaya. 715
Darlow, Julia Donovan 625
Darr, Alexander 473
Darragh, Archibald B. 280, 558-559
D'Ascenzo, Anthony 439
Dashevskiy, Alicia 458
Datema, Douglas. 446
Datema, Richard 472
Daub, Melissa 654
Daugherty, Susan. 803
D'Avaugour, Baron Dubois. 480
David, Jenny 650
Davidson, Gretchen Gonzales 431
Davidson, Norman. 21
Davidson, Rob. 695, 733
Davies, Robert O. 580
Davis, Bryan 458
Davis, Charles J. 33, 35, 280
Davis, Glenn 439
Davis, J. D. 27
Davis, Jeff 646
Davis, Jefferson 10
Davis, Jonathan D. 280, 350
Davis, Joshua 431
Davis, Kahlilia Yvette. 529
Davis, Lara 465
Davis, Linda 530
Davis, Lori 433
Davis, Martin. 20
Davis, Mel. 640
Davis, Robert. 440
Davis, Robert William 280, 567-569
Davis, Rosevelt 27
Davis, Stanley J. 280, 356
Davis, Steven. 474
Davison, Norman 27
Dawley, Joanne. 479
Dawson, William 31
Day, Tony. 449
Deacon, Bradley 437
Dean, Daniel. 652
Dean, Henry S. 624
Dean, Kellie 445
Dean, Patrick. 469

Deater, Bill 803
Deatrick, Michelle 702
DeBano, Brian. 432
DeBoer, Rett 704
DeBoer, William 280, 438
DeBoyer, Jay M. 652
De Bras-de-Fer de Chateaufort,
  Marc Antoine 480
De Brisay, Jacques Rene,
  Marquis de Denonville 480
De Buade, Louis, Count de Frontenac . . 480
De Callieres, Louis Hector 480
De Champlain, Samuel. 480
De Chastes, Aymar, Sieur de Monts. 480
DeCock, Kenneth 429
De Conde, Prince 480
Deeb, Michael J. 488
DeFeyter, Susan. 650
DeFoe, Terra 708
DeForge, Keith Warren 526
Defour, Steve. 650
Degenaer, John, Jr. 640
DeGraaf, Jo Ann 644
DeGraw, David 439, 479
DeGrow, Dan L. 280, 350, 473
DeGrow, Katherine J. 488-489
Dehnke, Herman. 33
Deitch, Laurence B. 625
DeJong, Greg J. 651
DeLaat, Ken 649
De la Boische, Charles,
  Marquis de Beauharnois 480
DeLand, Charles J. 31, 280, 484
DeLand, Charles V. 281, 356
DeLano, Carl 281, 355
De La Salle, René Robert Cavelier. 3
De Lauson, Jean 480
De Lauson-Charny, Charles 480
Delikta, Aaron 712, 753
Dell, Clarence B. 33
DelliQuadri, Carmen L. 488
Dellisse, Peter 433
Deloney, Andy 457
DeLong, Bruce 639
DeLong, Eric 460
Delp, Johanna Marie 454
Demaio, Kirstin 438
Demand, Mike. 712
DeMarco, Nicole 479
Demarois, Robert. 644
DeMars-Johnson, Renee. 454
Demas, Lane 451
Demas, Lilian 431
Demashkieh, Rasha 437
DeMaso, Harry A. 281, 351
DeMatio, Michael. 650
DeMeulenaere, JoAnn 721
Deming-Burns, Trisha 456
De Montmagny, Charles Hualt 480
Dempsey, James 478
Denby, Brandon 445, 646, 802
Denby, Edwin 14, 281, 558-559
Denenfeld, Paul J. 524
DenHouten, David. 648
Denkins, Delbert 468
Denninger, Mindy 715, 756

E

Frantz, Ronald. 651
Franz, Ray. 288, 705
Fratarcangeli, Mark A. 529
Frawley, Laura A. 526
Frazier, Jerry 640
Frazier, Michael. 711, 752
Frederick, Ben. . . . .
    168, 174-175, 178, 193, 239, 288, 722, 763
Frederick, Michael. 639
Freed, Josh 646
Freehling, Lora 638
Freehling, Teri Sue. 638
Freeland, Allen M. 488
Freeman, Christopher 458
Freeman, Glenn, III 640
Freeman, Herbert L. 31
Freeman, Judy. 444
French, Neil 433
French, Phyllis. 646
Fresard, Patricia Susan. 523
Friday, Steven 697
Friedrichs, Bonnie. 636
Friedrichs, Matt 707
Frisbie, Steven. 437, 638
Fritz, Leslee. 446
Froberg, Mary Ann. 636
Fruge, Melissa 725, 766
Fry, Theodore I. 486
Fuca, Carrie Lynn 530
Fuehring, Dwight. 431
Fuller, Barbara. 653
Fuller, Douglas 653
Fuller, Oramel B. 288, 351, 355, 357
Fuller, Philo C. 288, 353, 355
Fuller, Richard, III 644
Furman, Paul. 652
Fyfe, Lawrence C. 31, 288

G

Gadola, John A. 523
Gadola, Michael F. 509, 516
Gadola, Paul V., Sr. 33
Gadola, Preeti 474
Gaffney, Mark 469, 615, 629
Gage, Justus 627
Gagnon, Jeremy 639
Gajewski, Betty. 651
Galbreath, David. 458
Gale, Elbridge 28, 289
Gale, Jon. 459
Gale, Robert 737-738
Gallagher, John, III 645
Gallant, Daryl 439
Galloway, Joanne 726, 767
Games, Julie 642
Gannan, Lawrence. 699
Gano, Charles 471
Gansser, Augustus H. 289, 351
Gapczynski, Lee 651
Garber, Cindy 652
Garcia, Daniela 289, 704
Garcia, Franciso C. 651
Garcia, Joseph. 434
Garcia, Richard Joseph. 526
Garcia-Rubio, Anthony. 451

Gard, Milton J. 627
Gardella, Robert C. 461
Gardiner, Earle P. 28
Gardner, Brett 640
Gardner, Dennis 472
Gardner, Douglas W. 736
Gardner, Lynn C. 289, 353
Gardner, Patricia D. 526
Gardner, Tressa 435
Gardner, Washington 484, 558-559
Garey, Kirkland W. 688
Garfield, Charles W. 289, 627
Garibaldi, Antoine M. 623
Garrett, Austin William. 529
Garrett, Cathy 654
Garrett, LaTanya 167,
    174, 177-178, 194, 240, 247, 289, 708, 750
Garrett, Mykale 438
Garrett, Ruth Ann 529
Garvin, Wynne C. 33
Garza, Alex. . . . .
    167, 174-175, 178, 194, 240, 289, 709, 751
Gasco-Bentley, Regina. 437
Gasper, Joseph M. 416, 433, 453
Gasper, Ken 643
Gass, Herschel R. 487
Gates, Parley W. C. 21
Gatti, Julie Lynn. 523, 772
Gaudreau, Henry. 704
Gaus, Jill 442
Gauthier, Aaron J. 524
Gauthier, Dan 636
Gay, Catherine 458
Gay-Dagnogo, Sherry. . . . .
    . . . . 167, 174, 178, 195, 240, 289, 708, 750
Gayk, Sandra. 644
Geake, R. Robert 246, 289
Gebhardt, Lorie. 645
Geddis, L. Suzanne 524, 775
Geiger, Ben. 637
Geisler, James 648
Geiss, Erika. . . . .
    . . . . 138, 142, 145, 151, 240, 289, 700, 742
Gelineau, Bill 690-692, 729-730
Gelios, Jim 639
Genetski, Bob 289, 636, 703
Genier, Rachel. 478
Gennety, Tiffany 458
Gentilozzi, Paul V. 473
George, Kathryn A. 526
Geralds, Andrea. 713, 754
Gerber, Liz 469
Gerds, Carl F., III 529
Gerhardt, Steven 723
Germic, Dan 643
Gerou, Michael J. 529
Gerrard, Ted 734
Gershel, Alan 536
Gershenson, Charles H. 629
Gershenson, Marcia 649
Gerstenberger, Ronald 652
Gerville-Reache, Gaetan. 461
Getting, Jeffrey 644
Ghafari, Yousif 434
Ghering, Cynthia 451
Gibson, Beth. 532, 802

Granger, Bradley F. 555
Granholm, Jennifer M. 19, 366, 482, 485
Grant, Beverly 439
Grant, Charles A. 21
Grant, Claudius B. 292, 355, 503, 624
Grant, James 434
Grant, John H. 624-625
Grant, Nanci J. 455, 523
Granzo, Cheryl 454
Gratopp, Bill 652
Grau, Jennifer 452
Graveline, Chris. 739
Graves, Benjamin F. 292, 503
Graves, William 484
Gray, Harvey. 21
Gray, Lisa 431
Gray, Myles F. 292, 356
Grebner, Mark 642
Green, Allison 292, 353, 357, 486
Green, Fred W. 482
Green, George. 643
Green, Jeffery 448
Green, Nelson 28, 292
Green, Patrick 292, 712
Green, Phil 168,
    174, 176, 178, 196, 236, 239, 292, 722, 763
Green, Roderick 653
Green, Sanford M. 292, 503
Green, Tina Brooks 529
Green, Tracy E. 523, 770
Green, William 292, 646
Greene, Jimmy 435
Greene, Lora 726, 766
Greene, Perry W. 292, 351
Greene, Steven 713
Greene, William O. 33
Greenhut, Marshall 471
Greenly, William L. 292, 350-351, 482-483
Greenwood, Karen 469
Gregory, John M. 487
Gregory, Mark 650
Gregory, Michael 455
Gregory, Robert. 430
Gregory, Vincent 292, 713
Gregory, William H. 292, 355
Greig, Christine . . . .
    167, 174, 178, 196, 238, 243, 292, 713, 755
Greig, Joetta 643
Greimel, Tim 292, 698
Greiner, Sarah 431
Greis, Walter F. 488
Grether, C. Heidi 466
Greydanus, Donald 461
Grice, Michael 638
Grieco, Jennifer 803
Griffin, Alberta 717, 759
Griffin, Beth . . . .
    168, 175, 178, 197, 237, 239, 293, 718, 760
Griffin, John 494
Griffin, Levi T. 557, 573
Griffin, Rebecca. 649
Griffin, Robert P. 504, 554, 564-565
Griffith, Carol 646
Griffiths, Martha Wright . . . .
    . . . . 17, 293, 483, 564-567
Grifhorst, Timothy 651

Grim, Denise. 437
Grimshaw, Dan 653
Griswold, Augustus D. 293, 355
Griswold, George R. 293, 350, 356, 483
Griswold, Stanley. 481
Groendyk, Gidget 703
Groesbeck, Alexander J. 365, 482, 485
Gromala, Steven 647
Groner, David Alan 523
Gross, Ronda Fowlkes 530
Grosvenor, Ebenezer O. . . . .
    . . . . 293, 483, 486, 624
Grove, Kyle. 641
Grove, Rick 641
Gruber, Frederick 436
Gruden, Beth 479
Grunewald, David 479
Guasco, Jesse 464
Gubow, David M. 293, 530
Guerra, Santino 448
Guerra, Vanessa. . . . .
    . . . . 168, 174, 178, 197, 239, 293, 723, 764
Guerrant, Kyle. 456
Gui, Al 711, 753
Guido-Allen, Debra 435
Guiles, April 714
Guinn, G. David 531
Guins, Benjamin 719
Gulick, Lia. 459
Gulick, Robert F. 29
Gundry, George T. 357
Gunnels, Eric. 715
Gupta, Suneel 698
Gurr, Jim 705
Gusmano, Philip 467
Gust, Rockwell T., Jr. 33
Gustafson, Dean 649
Gustafson, Scott. 430
Gustin, Diane 639
Gutekunst, Dean 643
Guthrie, Tiffany 469
Guy, Sheryl 637
Gwizdala, Lori A. 447, 587
Gyure, Dale. 451

H

Haadsma, Jim . . . .
    168, 174-175, 178, 198, 235, 293, 717, 759
Haag, Jason. 446, 646
Haag, Paul 644
Haarer, John W. 486
Haas, Erwin 703, 745
Haase, Lorne 654
Habermehl, Cameron. 636
Habermehl, Donald M. 33
Hackel, William H., III 530
Hackley, Charles H. 624
Haddad, Ronald. 460
Hadsall, Cheryl M. 651
Haenicke, Christopher 528
Hafeman, Jan 647
Haggerty, John S. 484
Hagstrom, Harry 654
Hahn, Gary 644
Hahn, Karen 473, 647
Haidous, Al 449, 654

Hathaway, Hiram. 28, 295
Hathaway, Thomas M.J. 523
Hatty, Michael P. 524, 774
Hauck, Roger . . . .
  168, 175, 178, 199, 236, 238, 296, 724, 765
Haugh, Harold. 296, 646
Hauler, John 699
Hauser, Matthew 464
Haustein, Kevin. 641
Haveman, James K. 462, 603
Haveman, Joseph 296, 453, 704
Hawkins, Lynn 770
Hawkins, Ronald. 718, 759
Hawkins, Victor. 31
Hawks, Gary D. 487
Hawks, Michael. 444, 583
Hawks, Orlene 405, 446
Hayes, Michael D. 296, 475
Hayes, Norman R. 526
Hayes, Roy C., III 524
Hayes, Walter J. 351
Haynak, Richard 639
Hayward, Ralph A. 625
Hayworth, Donald. 564
Hazelbaker, Randall. 638
Hazen, Ezra. 29, 296
Heacock, Steven R. 449
Heald, Henry T. 31, 296
Heartwell, George 475
Heath, James 803
Heaton, Anna E. 447
Heaton, Fred. 638
Hebard, Charles. 296, 624
Heberling, Gary. 652
Heck, Gerald. 479
Heck, Michael 479
Heckert, Benjamin Franklin 31, 296
Heeres, David 637
Hegarty, Charles S. 523, 770
Hegbloom, Robert J. 447, 587
Hegeman-Dingle, Rozelle. 450
Heideman, Bert M. 34
Heidemann, Howard 652
Heidemann, Mary Ann. 651
Heidkamp, Adolph F. 296, 351
Heinowski, Carol. 476
Heins, Richard. 456
Heinz, Kathy 650
Heise, Catherine L. 523, 770
Heise, Thomas. 636
Helland, Lynn 536
Helwig, Jason 637
Helzerman, Douglas 646
Hemans, Charles F. 625
Hemans, Lawton T. 31, 296
Hemenway, Eric 451
Hemingsen, Donald R. 531
Hemingway, Kathleen P. 528
Hemy, Sigal. 431
Henderson, Eden F. 29, 296
Henderson, William. 440
Hendges, Phil 439
Hendrian, Catherine. 479
Hendrix, Freman 450, 469
Henige, Brenda. 469
Henkel, Peter 29

Hennessy, Carol 644
Henning, Dyle. 645
Henry, Bill. 646
Henry, David. 477
Henry, Jasmine 708
Henry, Paul B. 297, 488, 568-569
Henry, Ted 641
Hentschel, Rob 641
Herbart, Paula 434
Herbert, J. Joseph 625
Herek, Thomas 637
Herford, Rita 446
Herman, Lance 730
Herman, Mark A. 524
Hermann, John 636
Hermanson, Eric 644
Hernandez, Jeremiah. 451
Hernandez, Rosalinda . . . 689, 719, 728, 760
Hernandez, Shane 168, 174,
  176-178, 200, 239, 243, 247, 297, 721, 762
Hernandez, Sonya 451
Herren, Larry. 471
Herrington, Caleb 27, 297
Herrington, David B. 526
Herrygers, Eric. 431
Herschfus, Marc. 698, 736
Hert, Richard. 447
Hertel, Curtis. 297, 354
Hertel, Curtis, Jr. 138,
  142-143, 145, 151, 236, 242, 297, 703, 744
Hertel, Dennis M. 297, 568-569
Hertel, Kevin. . . . .
  . . . . 167, 175, 178, 200, 237, 297, 710, 752
Hesson, Jennifer Coleman 529
Heugel, Chris 638
Hewer, Nathan 703, 745
Hewitt, Lisa. 641
Heydenburg, Shari. 470
Heyrman, Paul 636
Hicks, Timothy G. 523
Hicswa, Amy. 478
Higgins, Bob. 455
Higginson, Francis J. 624
Higgs, Milton E. 34
Hiipakka, Scott 439
Hildenbrand, Gerald 473
Hill, Anne 723
Hill, Arthur 624-625
Hill, Cheryl L. 526
Hill, Dean 720, 762
Hill, Deborah 644
Hill, Jim 646
Hill, John 477
Hillary, G. Patrick 526
Hillegonds, Paul 297, 354, 469, 629
Hiller, Michael 438
Hilliard, Jerry. 696, 734
Hilliard, Kenneth. 646
Hill-Kennedy, Scott P. 524, 775
Hills, David. 464
Hilson, D.J.. . . . . 251, 441, 649, 803
Hiltunen, Lindsay. 451
Hines, Elizabeth Pollard. 443, 528
Hines, Jim. 690-692
Hines, Stefani 432
Hinkelman, Jon. 638

K

Neilsen, Cheryl 648
Neilson, Lisa Marie 526
Neitzel, David 433
Nellis, Jeffrey C. 526
Nelson, Albert Taylor, Jr. 446
Nelson, Charles D. 318, 350
Nelson, Christine 471
Nelson, Eric 689, 719
Nelson, Kristen 649
Nelson, Mike 446
Nelson, Rodney 456, 594
Nelson, Theodore 487
Nelson, Theresa 640
Nelson, Timothy 622
Nepton, Katie 703, 745
Nesbary, Dale K. 622
Nesbitt, Aric 138, 142-143,
   145, 159, 235, 237, 239, 318, 351, 703, 745
Nesbitt, Trisha 653
Nessel, Dana 371, 375, 382, 485, 739-740
Netzley, Denis 642
Neubecker, Brad 650
Newberry, John S. 556
Newberry, Samuel 488
Newberry, Seneca 27-28, 318
Newberry, Truman H. 554
Newblatt, David J. 523
Newman, Andrea Fischer 625
Newman, Michael 639
Newman, Tony 652
Newman-Bale, Scott. 444
Newton, James 20, 27, 319
Newville, Bruce, Jr. 726
Ngirarsaol, Leigh 644
Nicholas, Christina 251
Nicholl, Keneth 721
Nichols, Charles A. 559-560
Nichols, Edwin C. 32
Nichols, Judy 654
Nichols, William Paul. 528
Nicholson, David A. 443, 629-630
Nicholson, James B. 455
Nicholson, Julie A. 530
Nickels, Dennis 478
Nickels, Frank 452
Nicol-Bowers, Trudy 652
Nicolet, Jean 3
Nicols, Les. 645
Niebrzydowski, Pamela 648
Nielsen, Jessica 648
Nielsen, Neal D. 625
Niemer, Laurie 470
Niemuth, Niles 736
Niepoth, Patricia 445, 637
Niergarth, Lisa 436
Ninde, Thomas 29
Ninomiya, Christopher S. 524, 774
Nisbet, Stephen S. 33-34, 488, 627-628
Nobel, Jason 702, 744
Nobis, Kenneth Paul 442
Noble, Charles 254
Noble, David A. 555
Noble, Elnathan 20
Noble, Jeff 710, 752
Noble, Nathaniel 21, 27
Noble, Richard E. 532

Noble, Timothy 652
Noel, Jeff. 444
Noesen, Scott 648
Noffsiner, Kevin. 433
Nolan, Geoffrey Thomas 531
Nolan, Michael E. 260
Nolden, Bryant 448, 641
Nolish, Jeffrey 707
Noll, Charlie 643
Nord, Melvin 34
Nordeen, Bill. 647
Norlander, Anne 638
Norman, Larry 648
Norman, Naomi. 460
Norman, Sue 763
Norris, Harold 34
Norris, Lyman D. 29, 319, 624
Norris, Terri. 638
North, Walter H. 503-504
Northrop, Henry H. 624
Norton, John, III 726
Norvell, John. 27, 255, 319, 554, 624
Noto, Scott A. 773
Nousiainen, Robert 650
Novak, Edwin L. 488
Novak, James 645
Novak, Timothy. 651
Nowak, Jill 646, 801
Nowicki, Leo J. 483
Nowicki, Matthew 650
Nowicki, Stacy. 456
Nowka, James 476
Noyes, Horace A. 20-21, 319
Nugent, Donald W. 627
Nugent, Howard 319, 353
Nugent, James 475
Nugent, John. 642
Nunn, Jon 475
Nyberg, Dave 461
Nyberg, Tracy 478
Nye, Cooper 735
Nykanen, Carl R. 650
Nystrom, Wendy 647

O

Oakley, Brian A. 529
Oakman, Charles G. 564
Obeid, Nabeel R. 460
Oberdorffer, William J. 32, 320, 627-628
Oberholtzer, Michele 707
O'Brien, Colleen A. 509, 513
O'Brien, Daniel A. 526
O'Brien, Daniel Patrick 523
O'Brien, Darlene A. 526, 803
O'Brien, George D. 562-564
O'Brien, Lynn 478, 714
O'Brien, Margaret E. . . . .
   . . . . 138, 241, 246, 320, 352, 435, 702, 744
O'Brien, Morgan 28
O'Brien, Patrick H. 320, 485
O'Brien, Sandra Hughes. 615, 629
Oca, Melisa 435
Ochalek, Mary. 446
O'Connell, Mark 622
O'Connor, Glenn 462

Odell, Samuel 320, 486
O'Dell, James 20, 27, 320
Odette, Christopher. 531
O'Donnell, James. 557
Oesch, Daniel 704
Oesch, Jordan 720
Oeschger, Dale 433
O'Farrell, Donald. 643
Officer-Hill, Brigette R. 529
Ogden, Keith. 639
Ognisanti, Louis. 479
Ognjan, Anthony 464
O'Grady, Patrick W. 523
Oh, David 463
O'Hagan, John. 646
O'Hara, James G. 565,-567
O'Hara, Jeffrey J. 531
O'Hara, John J. 357
O'Hara, Michael D. 504
O'Keefe, George A. 253, 320
Oldani, Thomas. 438
Oldham, Kelli 464
Olds, Ransom E. 11-12
O'Leary, Joseph. 637
Oley, Jerry. 648
Olney, Dawn. 638
Olsen, Dan 439
Olsen, Stephen 474
Olshove, Dennis 320, 457
Olson, Michael 477
Olson, Richard. 644
Olson, Rick 320
Olumba, John 320, 689, 699
O'Malley, Charles M. 320, 355
O'Malley, Jack 168, 174-175,
178, 217, 235, 237-238, 320, 725, 765
O'Mara, Joe. 652
O'Neal, Amos 651
O'Neil, Dan. 725, 766
O'Neil, James F. 488
O'Neil, Tom. 647
O'Neill, Judith 444
O'Neill, Julie 530
O'Neill, Steve 473
Oomen, Jared 435
Oomen, Kristin 463
Oomen, Nick. 431
Oomen, Ralph. 435
Oomen, Thomas John 431
Oppewall, Peter 488
Oren, Horace M. 485
O'Riley, Andy 723
Orlich, Bob 641
Orm, Ted 648
Ormsbee, Bradley 639
Orr, Joseph W. T. 28
Orzechowski, Tom, Jr. 443
Osborn, Chase S. 13, 482, 624-625
Osman, Amna 454
Osminski, Gary 642
Osmun, Gilbert R. 484
Osmun, William E. 32
Oster, Joseph Craigen 529
Ostrander, Russell C. 503
Ostrow, Samuel B. 34
Oswald, Edward 640

Oswald, Lindsay 653
Otis, Asa H. 27, 321
Ott, Allan 652
Ottenhoff, Robert. 646
Outman, Rick 138, 142-143,
145, 160, 235-236, 238, 321, 704, 746
Ouwinga, Roger 648
Ovink, Shelley. 471
Owczarski, Lester 439
Owdziej, Julia B. 251, 526
Owen, Faylene 627
Owen, Gary 353
Owen, John G. 321, 486, 624
Owen, Lawrence D. 627-628
Owen, Zachary 441
Owens, Christopher. 707
Owens, Jack 473
Owens, Richard. 475
Oza, Vaijanthi 442
Ozkan, Eric. 467

P

Pacis, Reginald 431
Pack, George W. 624
Packard, Benjamin H. 21
Pacola, Patti 645
Pagan, Kristy. . . . .
167, 174, 176, 178, 218, 240, 321, 711, 752
Page, G. Keyes 34
Page, Jim. 705, 747
Page, Joab. 21
Page, Richard A. 528
Pagel, Dave. 321, 702
Paine-McGovern, Carol 444
Palamara, Joseph 246, 321, 654
Palazzolo, William 465
Palffy, John 707, 749
Pallarito, Rob. 650
Pallone, Dominic. 460
Palmer, Charles H. 624
Palmer, Dale 434
Palmer, Daniel S. 529
Palmer, Milton R. 321, 355
Palmer, Oscar 321, 627
Palmer, Pamela 637
Palmer, Thomas W. 321, 554
Palmer, Tyler. 723, 764
Palmer, Valerie. 463
Palmer, William 321, 351
Palms, Andrew 449
Palus, Louis. 745
Pangle, Kathy 653
Paolucci, Lawrence 526
Papas, Lisa 699, 741
Papazian, Gerald 440
Pape, Cynthia 460
Pappas, Richard J. 623
Paquet, Kenneth 639
Paquette, Brad. . . . .
. . . . 168, 174, 178, 218, 235, 321, 720, 762
Paquette, James 455
Paramski, Peter 646
Parent, David 439
Parker, Ann. 456, 594
Parker, Dan. 637

Pierce, Nathan. 28
Pierce, Phillip 434
Piercefield, Rob 640
Pietryga, Timothy 447
Pigeon, Ed 476
Pilcher, Elijah. 624
Pillon, Jeffrey 466
Pinals, Debra. 459
Pincus, Max J. 629
Piner, Rachel 803
Pingatore, Randy 456, 594
Pingel, John S. 627
Pingree, Hazen S. 12, 482
Pink, Bill. 622
Pinkelman, Franklin C. 357
Pinkelman, Shelly 640
Pinkins, Carron 699
Pintar, Jennifer. 436
Pinter, Christopher. 432
Piotrowicz, Gary 649
Pirlot, Kevin 640
Pitcher, Zina 624
Pitchford, Samantha. 639
Pitsch, James 802
Pittel, Jeff 701, 743
Pittman, Gregory Christopher. 526
Pittman, Randall 627-628
Pittsenbarger, Sally. 440
Place, Meredith 644
Plakas, James A. 324, 529
Plank, Raymond A. 34
Platt, Frederick A. 488
Platt, James E. 352
Platt, Zephaniah 485
Platz, Timothy 467
Platzer, Cynthia Siemen 531
Plawecki, Edward J., Jr. 435, 580
Plawecki, Mark J. 528
Plowman, John 652
Poer, Jonathan L. 528
Poet, Jeffrey 479
Pohl, David 639
Pohutsky, Laurie . . . .
. . . . 167, 174, 178, 219, 240, 324, 710, 752
Polan, Nicki. 478
Poland, Cara 459
Polehanki, Dayna . . . .
. . . . 138, 142, 145, 160, 240, 324, 700, 742
Policicchio, Domenic, III 446
Pollack, Andrea 703, 744
Pollack, C. John. 638
Pollard, Gary S. 629, 709
Pollard, Jeanne 650
Polley, Ira 487
Pollock, Greg 439
Pollock, James K. 34
Polsdofer, Mark 642
Pomeroy, Russell. 646
Pommerville, Jonathan Lee. 728, 736
Pond, Ashley. 30
Ponstein, Stan 644
Pontiac, Chief 4
Pontti, Mark 466
Pontz, Vicki. 461
Poole, Michael. 713
Poole, Rachel 454

Popa, John 645
Pope, Charles 528
Pope, Michael K. 524
Pope, Rex 647
Popiel, Jerome. 466
Popke, Lita Masini 523
Porath, Jim 651
Porteous, David. 627-628
Porter, Augustus S. 554
Porter, George B. 7, 481
Porter, Henry. 27
Porter, James B. 484
Porter, John. 324
Porter, John F. 624
Porter, John W. 487
Porter, Solomon. 27
Porter, Tom 648
Posont, Larry 434
Post, Floyd L. 32, 324
Post, Maurice E. 324, 355
Posthumus, Richard 324, 350, 457, 483
Potchynok-Lund, Karen 713
Potter, Allen 324, 556
Potter, Brian 654
Potter, Charles E. 554, 563-564, 573
Potter, William W. 324, 485, 503-504
Poulin, Michael 474, 649
Powell, Angela 649
Powell, Donald S. 526
Powell, Herbert E. 32, 324
Powell, Jerry 650
Powell, Melissa 643
Powell, Stanley M. 34, 324
Power, Eugene B. 625
Power, Michael 642
Power, Philip H. 625-626
Power, Sarah Goddard. 625
Power, Thomas G. 324, 523
Powers, Carl 463
Powers, Denny 649
Powers, Julie. 650
Powers, Michael W. 448
Powers, Perry F. 357, 488
Powers, Sherry 640
Poyma, Michael. 469
Prantle, Timothy Joe 746
Pratt, Abner. 324, 503
Pratt, Daniel L. 29
Pratt, Evan. 653, 801
Pratt, Frank S. 32
Pratt, Julie Nakfoor 436
Pratt, Kristopher 713
Pratt, Michael 721
Pratt, William A. 325, 355
Pray, Esek 21, 325
Preiss, Stacy 650
Prescott, Charles T. 325, 351
Prescott, George A. 325, 484
Prestin, David 647
Preston, Brian 442
Preston, John L. 350
Preston, Maribeth 536
Preston, Shane. 477
Prettie, Kenneth G. 34
Pretty, Keith A. 450, 623
Prevost, F. J. 28

Roehm, Stephanie 699
Roehm, Suzie 653
Roehrig, Michael G. 648
Roelofs, Bob 638
Roels, Patricia 442
Rogers, Barbara 640
Rogers, Donald 457
Rogers, Frank F. 489
Rogers, James 459, 465
Rogers, Jeffrey 429
Rogers, Julie 644
Rogers, Matthew 477
Rogers, Mike 328, 570-572
Rogers, Paul D. 408, 453
Rogers, Richard 623
Rogers, Robert 4
Roling, Matthew 429
Rolling, Jason 474
Rolling, Troy 721
Rolof, William 637
Roloff, Shirley 639
Romano, Joseph 646
Romaya, Michael 460
Romney, George 17, 33-34, 482, 629
Romney, Scott 627-628
Romps, Bob 726, 767
Ronayne Krause, Amy 251, 509, 516-517
Rondeau, Mickey 636
Rondon, Ruth 452
Ronquist, Stanley 646
Rood, James R. 34
Roosevelt, Theodore 13, 18
Root, Jeremy 652
Root, Simeon P. . . . : 29
Rosa, Robert 638
Rosario, Ryan 431
Roscioli, Julie 652
Rose, Benjamin M. 629
Rose, Carol 479
Rose, Jean 434
Rose, Kelly 454
Rose, Robert 643
Rose, Ronald 443
Rose, Roy 469
Rospond, Laurie 465
Ross, Gregory S. 526
Ross, John Q. 483
Ross, Karol 458
Ross, Rita 708, 749
Rossi, J. Joseph 524
Rossiter, James 637
Rossmaessler, Tyler 431
Rossman-McKinney, Kelly 703, 745
Rossway, Rich 688, 727
Rothstein, Charles P. 473
Roth, Stephen J. 485
Rouse, Arthur K. 627
Routley, William 647
Rowe, George E. 32
Rowe, Kenneth, Sr. 642
Rowe, Natalie 469
Rowland, Thomas 484
Rowley, Francis L. 730
Roy, Edgar 479
Roy, Gary 645
Ruiz, Traci 459

Rulison, Stacie 432
Rumsey, Henry 254, 329
Runco, William J. 329, 439
Runestad, Jim . . . .
    138, 142-143, 145, 161, 238, 329, 701, 743
Runkel, Phillip E. 487
Runnels, Richard 645
Rupp, John 450
Rupp, Vicki L. 470, 608
Ruppe, Philip E. 566-567
Rush, Allen F. 34, 329
Rush, W. Omari 431
Rushing, David 652
Rushton, Debra 645
Rushton, Herbert J. 329, 485
Russell, Frederick J. 32
Russell, James 646
Russell, John G. 449, 590
Russo, David 651
Rustem, William R. 461
Rusthoven, Brad 449
Ruth, Carl E. 651
Rutkowski, Tim 642
Rutledge, David 329, 477
Rutter, Scott 640
Ryan, Brenda 460, 600
Ryan, Harold M. 329, 565, 574
Ryan, James L. 504-505
Ryan, Joseph 455
Ryan, Kathleen A. 526
Ryan, Thomas J. 455
Ryan, William A. 329, 353, 356
Rybicki, James 636
Ryder, Tom 637
Ryker, Don 452
Rynberg, James 801
Rynd, Charles 624
Ryzewski, Krystal 451

S

Saab, Manal 460
Saad, Bill 476
Saad, Fayrouz 698
Saalfeld, Jim 644
Saari, Mike 701
Sabaugh, Matthew P. 529
Sabin, Eric 722, 763
Sabin, Ron 448
Sablich, Joseph F. 34
Sabo, Terry J. . . . .
    168, 174, 176, 178, 222, 238, 329, 723, 764
Sabourin, Brian 469
Sabree, Aliyah 529
Sabree, Eric 654
Sachs, Tori 462
Sadowski, George G. 329, 561-563
Safford, Susan 451
Safiedine, Ali 465-466
Sahr, Matthew 468
Sahr, Michael 472
Sak, Michael G. 329, 356
Sakwa, Jeffrey 437
Sala, Catherine Ann 526
Salamey, Sam A. 528
Salas, Gumecindo 488

T

V

Vailliencourt, William 646, 803
Valbuena, Felix, Jr. 432
Valente, Joseph 647
Valentine, Victoria Ann 523
Valenzuela, Alma 251
Valerio-Nowc, Lisa 712, 754
Valesano, Mark 643, 803
Valvo, Karen Q. 528
Van Allsburg, Jon A. 524, 773, 802
Van Alst, Audrey D. 532
Van Alst, Edward 526
VanAlstine, Terry 637
Van Coppenolle, George 450
VanDam, Paul Kaiser 454
VandeCar, Susan 637
Vandenberg, Arthur H. 15, 554
Vandenberg, William C. 341, 483
Vander Jagt, Guy 341, 566-569, 574
Vander Kolk, Mary 462
VanderLaan, Robert 341, 350
VanderMey, Jim 450
Vanderploeg, Jan B. 341, 627
VanderStelt, Jason 649
VanderVeen, J. David 429
VanderVeen, Richard F. 567, 574
Vandervennet, Michael 446
Vanderwal, Frank 648
VanderWall, Curtis S. 138,
    142, 145, 164, 235, 237-240, 341, 705, 747
Vander Werp, Don 341, 351
Vandette, Edmund F. 488
VanDusen, Richard C. 35, 341, 629-630
Van Duser, Zachariah 20-21, 341
Van Dyke, Daniel 442
VanEvery, Peter 27
Van Hoek, Dawn 534
VanHouten, Margaret M. 523
Van Kirk, Robert 720
Van Kleeck, James 32, 341
VanLandschoot, Joseph 636
VanLangevelde, Aaron 472
VanNoller, Robert 704, 745
VanNorman, Michele 652
Van Peursem, George M. 341, 353
Van Raalte, A. C. 9
Van Riper, Jacob J. 29, 485, 624
Van Sickle, Gerald T. 739-740
VanSingel, Scott 168,
    174, 176, 178, 226, 237-238, 341, 724, 765
Van Tiem, Christy 641, 801
Van Valkenburg, Wade 341, 353
Van Valkenburgh, Jacob 28-29
Van Vleck, John 624
Van Wagoner, Murray D. . . 482, 489, 625-626
VanWoerkom, Greg . . . .
    168, 174, 176, 178, 227, 238, 341, 723, 764
Van Wormer, Sara 467
Varga, Ilona 341, 654
Vargo, Marilynn 647
Varner, Chuck 650
Varner, Daniel 488
Varner, Nellie M. 625
Vaughan, Coleman C. 341, 484
Vaughan, Kim 653

Vaughan, Steve 642
Vaughn, Brian 651
Vaughn, Jackie, III 341, 351
Vaughn, Mary Jo 463
Vaughn, Ronald 650
Vaupel, Henry . . . .
    167, 174-175, 178, 227, 237, 341, 715, 756
Veenstra, Henry 450
Velasquez, Christian A. 461
Vendittelli, Deborah 462
Venegas, Jesse 451
Venema, Jennifer 802
Verheek, Andrew 251, 441
VerHeulen, Rob 341, 644
Verna, Xavier 431
Vernier, Joel 641
Versluis, Peter P. 531
Vette, Kathy-Sue 638
Victor, Mary Ann 464
Victory, Roger . . . .
    138, 142-143, 145, 165, 239, 341, 704, 746
Vilmont, Brian 477
Vincent, Bird J. 560-561
Vitale, Jack 528
Vitale, John 446
Vitto, Perry 433
Viventi, Carol Morey 352
Vivian, James, Jr. 644
Vivian, Weston E. 566
Viviano, David F. 494, 501, 504-505
Viviano, Kathryn A. 523
Viviano, Vincent Philip 476
Vizina, Daryl Patrick 526
Voelker, John D. 504
Voelker, Paul F. 487
Voelker, Ross 433
Voet, Raymond P. 251, 531, 802
Vogel, Glenn 435
Vogelsang, Kathleen 479
Volkema, Harold J. 341
Vollbach, Richard E., Jr. 526
Vollrath, David 638
Vondra, Charles 639
Vonk, Ted 644
Vono, Jonathan 470
Voorhees, Harold 644
Voorheis, Isaac I. 27, 342
Voorhies, Paul W. 485
Voskuil, Dennis N. 623
Voss, Bradley 437
Voss, Joe 447
Vrablic, Ann 638
Vrablic, Donald 638
Vukin, JoAnne 648
Vyskocil, Frank 479

W

Waananen, Joseph 644
Wachtel, Philip B. 342, 353
Wadel, Peter J. 532
Wadhams, Ralph 21, 27, 342
Wagar, Martin 468
Wagenaar, Larry 451
Wagner, Brent 479
Wagner, Dave 648

Woodruff, Henry H. 32
Woodruff, Roy O. 559-564
Woods, Marilyn 645
Woodward, Augustus B. 494
Woodward, Dave. 649
Woodward, Lysander 30, 348
Woolfenden, Henry L. 35
Woolhiser, Harold 637
Woons, Lisa. 479
Wooster, William 474
Word, Matt 642
Worm, Jeremy 476
Woronchak, Gary. 348, 699
Worthams, David. 468, 644
Worthy, Kim 654
Wozniak, Douglas . . . .
    167, 174, 177-178, 233, 237, 348, 713, 755
Wresinski, Francine Marie 440
Wriggelsworth, Scott 642
Wright, Benjamin. 21
Wright, Brian. 713, 755
Wright, Don 715
Wright, Harvey 29
Wright, Jeff 641
Wright, Katie. 472
Wright, Luther L. 487-488
Wright, Ora 716
Wruble, Ron 642
Wrzesinski, Marilyn 646
Wunsch, Isaiah 436
Wyatt, George, III 439
Wyatt, Joel, Jr. 652
Wyett, Todd 475
Wykes, Roger I.. . . . . 32, 485
Wyse, Ned. 440

Y

Yachcik, Larry 477
Yancer, Wilbur. 648
Yancey, Tenisha 167, 174-175,
    178, 234, 240, 250, 348, 688, 707, 727, 749
Yanez, Henry. 348, 700, 742
Yankowski, Michael. 437
Yaple, George L. 557
Yaple, Roy. 454
Yarbrough, Mamie. 638
Yaroch, Jeff . . . .
    167, 174, 176, 178, 234, 237, 348, 713, 754
Yates, Christopher P. 524, 772, 802
Yatooma, Chris 475
Yaw, Natalie 446
Yeager, Weldon O. 35, 348
Yehia, Hassan 442
Yeomans, Sanford A.. . . . . 29, 348
Yeomans, Tammy 443
Yerkes, Silas 627
Yoder, David. 650
Yoder, Jonathan. 467

Yoder, Kyle 650
Yokich, Tracey A. 349, 523, 772
Yonker, Ken 349, 644
Youmans, Henry M.. . . . . .349, 557
Young, Coleman Alexander 35, 349
Young, Coleman, II 349, 698
Young, H. Olin 349, 558-559, 573
Young, James 652, 701, 742
Young, Maria. 464
Young, Mark 448, 641
Young, Robert P., Jr. 504-505
Young, Stephen E.. . . . . .462, 603
Young, Stephen J. 734
Young, Tom 653
Youngblood, Bernard 654
Youngblood, Charles N., Jr. 35, 349
Youngblood, Harold F. 563
Younger, Andy 465
Youngquist, Mark 430
Young-Wenkel, Celia 724, 765
Youson, Washington 688
Yow, Tim 693-694, 732
Yuille, Richard B. 523

Z

Zaagman, Milton 349-351
Zack, Helaine 649
Zahn, Dale 435
Zahra, Brian K. 494, 502, 504
Zaidan, Jonathan. 429
Zalewski, Matthew. 470
Zamora, Kristie 471
Zane, Joe 714
Zaroukian, Michael 450
Zatkoff, Justin 465
Zeerip, Helen 475
Zeile, Richard 488
Zelenak, David J. 528
Zemaitis, Daniel V. 524
Zemke, Adam F. 461
Zieger, Jennifer 475
Ziegler, Charles M. 489
Zimmerman, Beverly 722
Zimmerman, Gregory 463
Zorn, Dale W.. 138,
    142-143, 145, 166, 237-238, 349, 702, 743
Zuiderveen, Hubert 648
Zuker, Diane 639
Zulski, Frank, Jr. 641
Zuniga, Heidi 722, 763
Zupko, Ronald 469
Zurbrick, Matt 439
Zwolan, Teresa 432
Zyble, David 436
Zyburt, Gregory. 456, 647
Zyler, Brian. 434
Zylstra, Doug 651

MICHIGAN MANUAL
ERRATA SHEET

The following errors have been noted in the 2017/2018 printed edition of the *Michigan Manual*. These errors have been corrected in the online version.

1. Page 165, Ed Canfield, District 84, should be listed with an "R", not a "D."
2. Page 256, the number of public acts enacted in 2016 should be 563, not 280.

The following errors have been noted in the 2015/2016 printed edition of the *Michigan Manual*. These errors have been corrected in the online version.

1. Page 166, Ed Canfield, District 84, should be listed with an "R", not a "D."
2. Page 254, the number of session days in 2013 should be 103 for the Senate and 107 for the House. The number of session days for 2014 should be 86 for the Senate and 88 for the House.
3. Page 410, under "District" should read "Counties of Barry, Calhoun, Ionia, Kent (part), and Montcalm (part)."
4. Page 225, Rep. Tedder is Vice Chair of the Workforce and Talent Development Committee.

The following errors have been noted in the 2013/2014 printed edition of the *Michigan Manual*. These errors have been corrected in the online version.

1. Page 102, Senate Joint Resolution V to ban felons from public office/positions amended Article 11, not Article 7.
2. Page 196, State Representative Martin Howrylak should be noted as an R-41st Representative District, not a D-41st Representative District.
3. Page 394, under "District" should read "Counties of Barry, Calhoun, Ionia, Kent (part), and Montcalm (part)."

The following error has been noted in the 2011/2012 printed edition of the *Michigan Manual*. This error has been corrected in the online version.

1. Page 100, Senate Joint Resolution V to ban felons from public office/positions amended Article 11, not Article 7.